Name and Type of Organization Used in Main Illustration of Each Chapter

Chapter Title	Organization Used in Main Illustration	Organization Logo	Type of Organization
11. Flexible Budgeting and Overhead Cost Control	Sousa Division		Manufacturer of brass musical instruments
12. Responsibility Accounting and Total Quality Management	Aloha Hotels and Resorts; Handico		Hotel chain and manufacturer of cordless telephones, respectively
13. Investment Centers and Transfer Pricing	Suncoast Food Centers		Retail grocery chain
14. Decision Making: Relevant Costs and Benefits	Worldwide Airways		Airline company
15. Cost Analysis and Pricing Decisions	Sydney Sailing Supplies		Manufacturer of sailboats in Sydney, Australia
16. Capital Expenditure Decisions: An Introduction	City of Mountainview		City government
17. Further Aspects of Capital Expenditure Decisions	High Country Department Stores		Retail department store chain
18. Cost Allocation: A Closer Look	Riverside Clinic; International Chocolate Company		Health care institution and food products company, respectively
19. Variable and Absorption Costing	Orion Company		Manufacturer of hand-held electronic calculators

(For a listing of Web sites for companies and organizations cited in the text, see the inside back cover.)

Managerial Accounting

Fourth Edition

4

Managerial Accounting

Ronald W. Hilton
Cornell University

Irwin
McGraw-Hill

Boston   Burr Ridge, IL   Dubuque, IA   Madison, WI
New York   San Francisco   St. Louis
Bangkok   Bogotá   Caracas   Lisbon   London
Madrid   Mexico City   Milan   New Delhi   Seoul

Irwin/McGraw-Hill

A Division of The **McGraw·Hill** *Companies*

MANAGERIAL ACCOUNTING

This book is printed on acid-free paper.

international 1 2 3 4 5 6 7 8 9 0 VNH/VNH 9 3 2 1 0 9 8
domestic   1 2 3 4 5 6 7 8 9 0 VNH/VNH 9 3 2 1 0 9 8

ISBN 0-07-059339-6 (student's edition)
ISBN 0-07-290291-4 (annotated instructor's edition)
ISBN 0-07-031356-3 (*Business Week* edition)

Vice president and editorial director: *Michael W. Junior*
Publisher: *Jeffrey J. Shelstad*
Sponsoring editor: *George Werthman*
Editorial assistant: *Irene Baki*
Senior marketing manager: *Rhonda Seelinger and Michelle Hudson*
Senior project manager: *Susan Trentacosti*
Senior photo research coordinator: *Keri Johnson*
Photo research: *Charlotte Goldman*
Senior production supervisor: *Melonie Salvati*
Designer: *Michael Warrell*
Development: *Burrston House*
Supplement coordinator: *Cathy L. Tepper*
Compositor: *Shepard Poorman Communications*
Typeface: *10/12 Times Roman*
Printer: *Von Hoffmann Press, Inc.*

Material from the Uniform CPA Examination, Questions and Unofficial Answers, Copyright © 1978, 1979, 1980,
1981, 1982, 1983, 1984, 1987, 1988, 1989, 1990, 1991 by the American Institute of Certified Public Accountants,
Inc. is adapted with permission.

Material from the Certificate in Management Accounting Examinations, Copyright © 1977, 1978, 1979, 1980,
1981, 1982, 1983, 1984, 1987, 1989, 1990, 1991, 1992, 1993, 1994, 1995, 1996, 1997, 1998 by the Institute of
Management Accountants is adapted with permission.

Logos from Wal-Mart Stores, Inc. and Southwest Airlines Co. appear in this text with permission from those
companies.

Library of Congress Cataloging-in-Publication Data

Hilton, Ronald W.
    Managerial accounting/Ronald W. Hilton.—4th ed.
       p.   cm.
    Includes index.
    ISBN 0-07-059339-6
    1. Managerial accounting.   I. Title.
HF5657.4.H55   1999
   658.15'11—dc21   98-23851

INTERNATIONAL EDITION

When ordering the title, use ISBN 0-07-115729-8

http://www.mhhe.com

To my wife, Meg, and our sons, Tim and Brad.

About the Author

Photo by Jon Reis/PHOTOLINK

Ronald W. Hilton is a Professor of Accounting at Cornell University. With bachelor's and master's degrees in accounting from The Pennsylvania State University, he received his Ph.D. from The Ohio State University.

A Cornell faculty member since 1977, Professor Hilton also has taught accounting at Ohio State and the University of Florida, where he held the position of Walter J. Matherly Professor of Accounting. Prior to pursuing his doctoral studies, Hilton worked for Peat, Marwick, Mitchell and Company and served as an officer in the United States Air Force.

Professor Hilton is a member of the Institute of Management Accountants and has been active in the American Accounting Association. He has served as associate editor of *The Accounting Review* and as a member of its editorial board. Hilton also has served on the editorial board of the *Journal of Management Accounting Research*. He has been a member of the resident faculties of both the Doctoral Consortium and the New Faculty Consortium sponsored by the American Accounting Association.

With wide-ranging research interests, Hilton has published articles in many journals, including the *Journal of Accounting Research, The Accounting Review, Management Science, Decision Sciences, The Journal of Economic Behavior and Organization,* and *Contemporary Accounting Research.* He also has published a monograph in the AAA *Studies in Accounting Research* series, is a co-author of *Budgeting: Profit Planning and Control,* and is a co-author of *Cost Accounting: Concepts and Managerial Applications.* Professor Hilton's current research interests focus on contemporary cost management systems and international issues in managerial accounting. In recent years, he has toured manufacturing facilities and consulted with practicing managerial accountants in North America, Europe, Asia, and Australia.

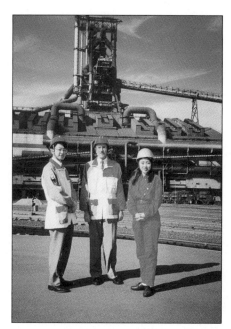

Guided by former students, Professor Hilton tours one of the world's largest steel mills, which is located near Tokyo. In recent years, Professor Hilton has consulted with practicing managerial accountants throughout the world.

Preface

Managers in all types of organizations rely heavily on managerial accounting information for decision making, planning, and control. The goal of this text is to acquaint students of management with the fundamentals of managerial accounting. The emphasis throughout the book is on *using* accounting information in managing an organization. *Managerial Accounting* is intended to be used by students after they have completed a basic course in financial accounting. Most of the material in the text can be covered in one semester or one and one-half quarters. The book includes enough material, however, to allow an instructor some choice of topics when designing the course.

In preparing the fourth edition of *Managerial Accounting*, many features of the first three editions were retained. However, the fourth edition of *Managerial Accounting* has benefited from the most extensive review process ever in the history of this text. Several improvements and changes have been made based on the comments of the reviewers, instructors, and students who have used the text. This preface provides a summary of the text's key features and the changes in the fourth edition.

Key Features of This Textbook

Each chapter is built around one major illustration, in which all aspects of the chapter's coverage are addressed. The illustration is used consistently throughout the chapter, allowing students to gain a deeper understanding of all dimensions of the topic. Each illustration has a management case flavor, with enough descriptive background to involve students in the scenario. These illustrations are built around realistic situations with plausible decisions and believable people. The types of illustrations vary widely across chapters. Although these major chapter illustrations are set in fictitious organizations, they are generally based on real-world companies and situations. As a result the illustrations, though not real, are extremely realistic.

> Conveying the importance of managerial accounting and stimulating students' interest

The text includes frequent descriptions of the actual managerial-accounting practices of real-world organizations. These illustrations from *management accounting practice* are highlighted to catch the students' attention and are dispersed throughout the book. Among the many organizations represented in these real-world scenarios are Aetna Casualty and Life; American Can; American Express; Arnot Ogden Memorial Hospital; Blue Shield; British Airways; B. F. Goodrich; Caterpillar; Chrysler; Compaq; Cornell University; Corning Glass Works; Cummins Engine, Daihatsu; Deere & Company; Dow Chemical; Dutch Pantry; Federal Express; Firestone Tire & Rubber; General Electric; Harley-Davidson; Hewlett-Packard; Honeywell; H. J. Heinz; ITT; Ingersoll-Rand; J. C. Penney; Leonard Morse Hospital; McDonald's; Motorola; Rockwell International; Southwest Airlines; Toyota; United Parcel Service; Xerox; and Wal-Mart.

A large percentage of the students pursuing studies in management will choose careers in nonmanufacturing environments. It is important that students realize the applicability of managerial accounting to a variety of organizations. Some managerial accounting topics are integrally related to the manufacturing sector; others are just as applicable in nonmanufacturing settings. The major illustrations, around which the chapters in this text are built, are drawn from a wide variety of enterprises. As the chapter outline on the front endpaper shows, nine of the illustrations are set in the manufacturing sector, six illustrations involve service-industry firms, three illustrations are built around retail companies, and three illustrations involve nonprofit or governmental settings.

> Balanced coverage of managerial accounting topics in manufacturing, retail, nonprofit, and service-industry settings

Flexible sequence of chapters written in modular style

Since managerial accounting instructors often have differing views on the optimal chapter sequence, flexibility in usage was a paramount objective in writing the text. Each chapter is a module, which can be assigned out of sequence if the instructor desires. For example, some instructors might prefer to cover cost behavior and estimation (Chapter 7) and cost-volume-profit analysis (Chapter 8) before delving into cost-accumulation issues. Other instructors may wish to cover these two topics in the section of the course on decision making. In this text, Chapter 7 and 8 can be assigned as early as immediately after Chapter 2, or as late as just prior to Chapter 14. The decision-oriented chapters (14, 15, 16, and 17) can be moved up to an earlier point in the course if the instructor prefers. These four chapters could be assigned any time after the students have completed Chapters 1, 2, 7, and 8. Chapter 18 covers the details of cost allocation for service departments and joint products. These two modules in Chapter 18 could be covered along with the cost accumulation chapters (3, 4, and 5) if the instructor prefers. Chapters 12 and 13, which cover a variety of issues pertaining to responsibility accounting and decentralization, can be assigned later in the course if desired.

Instructors' preferences vary widely with respect to the best place in the course for the topic of variable versus absorption costing. Some instructors prefer to cover the topic immediately after cost-volume-profit analysis (covered in Chapter 8). Others prefer to cover the topic after standard costing and overhead variances, so that the effect of the fixed-overhead volume variance can be included in the discussion. To satisfy both approaches, variable and absorption costing is covered in Chapter 19. However, the main body of Chapter 19, excluding the appendix, can be covered immediately after Chapter 8 (CVP) by instructors who want to emphasize the connection between CVP relationships and variable costing. Alternatively, instructors who wish to cover the fixed-overhead volume variance (in Chapter 11) first, can assign Chapter 19 after Chapter 11 has been completed. The effect of the volume variance on the variable versus absorption costing issue is examined in the Appendix to Chapter 19. Or, the main body of Chapter 19 can be assigned immediately after Chapter 8, and the Appendix to Chapter 19 can be covered after Chapter 11.

In short, the instructor has a great deal of flexibility in course design and topical sequence when using *Managerial Accounting*.

Blend of traditional material and up-to-date coverage of emerging topics in managerial accounting

There is no doubt that managerial accounting is undergoing a revolution in thought and practice. Much of this change is due to recent changes in manufacturing technology and philosophy. Such innovations as just-in-time inventory systems, flexible manufacturing, and computer-integrated manufacturing systems are dramatically changing the manufacturing environment. As a result, managerial accounting systems are changing as well. New concepts and procedures have been devised, and many traditional approaches have been challenged.

Managerial Accounting provides thorough coverage of these contemporary issues. Two complementary approaches are taken. First, these emerging issues are thoroughly integrated throughout the text. Virtually every chapter includes major coverage of some aspect of contemporary cost management systems and the new manufacturing environment. This provides for continual reinforcement of these topics throughout the course, and also allows students to study the issues in a variety of organizational contexts.

Second, Chapters 5 and 6 are devoted entirely to contemporary cost management systems. Issues such as cost drivers, activity-based costing, activity-based management, non-value-added costs, target costing, and kaizen costing are covered in these chapters. By covering many of these topics together, in the context of a particular company, students are better able to understand how these diverse issues are interrelated.

This textbook is thoroughly comprehensive in that it includes all topics of relevance for an introductory managerial accounting course. Moreover, the book provides enough depth to give students an appreciation for the relationship of each topic to the management process. When appropriate, the behavioral implications of managerial accounting information and procedures are explored. For a thorough understanding of managerial accounting, students should not only be able to produce accounting information, but also understand how managers are likely to use and react to the information.

> **Breadth and depth of coverage**

To help students learn managerial accounting and gain an appreciation for its importance, *Managerial Accounting* includes a wide range of pedagogical features.

> **Pedagogical features designed to enhance the learning process**

- *Learning objectives.* Each chapter begins with a list of learning objectives to help students identify the most important issues in the chapter. The learning objectives are repeated in the margin throughout the chapter to direct students' attention to material related to each learning objective. Moreover, the learning objectives covered in each exercise, problem, and case are indicated in the end-of-chapter material.
- *Comprehensive illustrations with a real-world flavor.* As noted previously, each chapter is built around a major illustration that progresses throughout the chapter. These diverse illustrations include enough background to add realism to the presentation and stimulate the students' interest in the topic. To engage student interest, each chapter begins with a simulated news article highlighting the organization featured in the chapter.
- *Photos.* A photograph at the beginning of each chapter and a logo for each organization add to the realism of the presentation. In addition, numerous photos from practice are included throughout each chapter. These photos are intended to enhance the students' interest and emphasize key points.
- *Clarity and step-by-step presentation.* Great care was taken to write this text in a clear, readable, and lively style. Extensive review by managerial accounting instructors coupled with extensive classroom use have helped in achieving this goal. The text contains numerous exhibits, graphs, tables, and step-by-step instructions to help students master the material.
- *Management accounting practice.* As noted previously, the managerial accounting practices of well-known, real-world organizations are highlighted in these numerous illustrations. They are intended to stimulate student interest and provide a springboard for classroom discussion.
- *Review problems.* Most chapters include a review problem along with its solution to provide students with a vehicle for testing their understanding of the material.
- *Key terms.* Each chapter includes a list of key terms with page references. A complete glossary is included at the end of the text. The key terms, along with their definitions, are also repeated in the margin throughout each chapter for ease of reference.
- *Review questions, exercises, problems, and cases.* Each chapter includes a wide selection of assignment material. This end-of-chapter material, which has been classroom tested, is comprehensive in covering the points in the chapter. The assignment material exhibits a wide range of difficulty, and the *Instructor's Guide* provides guidance for the instructor on the difficulty level and time required for each problem. Numerous adapted CMA and CPA problems are included in the text. In many cases, these problems were very heavily adapted to preserve the essence of the problems while ensuring that they were pitched at a level appropriate for the text.
- *Current Issues in Managerial Accounting.* A new end-of-chapter element has been added in the fourth edition. This assignment material is drawn from the business news media, such as *The Wall Street Journal* and *Business Week*. It highlights current events of relevance to the practice of managerial accounting.

Changes in the Fourth Edition

The key features of the first three editions have been retained. However, several changes have been made to improve on those strengths. Some of the more significant changes are described here.

Expanded Pedagogical Material

In responding to the comments of adopters and reviewers of the third edition, new pedagogical material has been added where indicated. For example, at the suggestion of a reviewer, graphical presentations have been added to the coverage of total quality management, now covered in Chapter 12. The learning objectives are repeated in the margins throughout each chapter to help students identify the coverage of each learning objective. The relevant learning objectives are also shown with each exercise, problem, and case in the end-of-chapter assignment material. The key terms are repeated, along with their definitions, in the margins throughout each chapter for easy student reference.

Significant Revision of Introductory Chapter

Students are introduced to managerial accounting in Chapter 1, and this chapter has been heavily revised to reflect the ongoing changes in the field. The definition of managerial accounting has been revised, and the role of the managerial accountant has been revised and updated. The goal of the revision is to emphasize to students that managerial accounting is an integral part of the management process and managerial accountants are important strategic partners in an organization's management team. The management team seeks to create value for the organization by managing resources, activities, and people to achieve the organization's goals effectively. *Added* to the objectives of managerial accounting activity is "assessing the organization's competitive position, and working with other managers in ensuring the organization's long-run competitiveness in its industry." Particular emphasis is given to the *proactive* participation of managerial accountants as part of the management team in the decision making and planning processes.

The revision of Chapter 1 also expands and updates the coverage of many other important topics. The goal here is to acquaint students with some of the important issues in the ever-changing contemporary business environment. The coverage of global competition is expanded to include a brief discussion of multinationals and exchange rate issues. The importance of having a customer focus is discussed, as is the prevalence of cross-functional teams in managing an enterprise. The discussion of total quality management has been updated and expanded. The topic of time-based competition is explored, with its emphasis on time-to-market issues.

The traditional discussion of computer information systems has been replaced with a contemporary treatment of information and communication technology. Explored here are the effects of networked personal computers, spreadsheet programs, the Internet, and integrated business software systems, such as *SAP* and *PeopleSoft*.

Chapter 1's overview of many other topics has been retained from the third edition. Among the topics discussed are cost management systems, activity-based costing, activity-based management, strategic cost management, and the value chain. The coverage of the ethical standards for management accountants has been updated to incorporate the recent modifications made by the Institute of Management Accountants.

Reorganization of Process-Costing Coverage

Chapter 4, which covers process costing, has been reorganized as follows:

- *Main part of Chapter 4:* Covers general concepts of process costing, such as equivalent units, and the *weighted-average* process-costing method in a *single production department.*
- *Appendix to Chapter 4:* Covers process costing in *sequential production departments* using the weighted-average method.

These changes in the process-costing coverage were made to provide instructors with the maximum flexibility in course design. Based on the recommendations of an overwhelming majority of reviewers, the FIFO method is no longer covered in Chapter 4. This change is consistent with practice, since the weighted-average method is virtually always used in practice. However, for any instructor who still desires to cover FIFO process costing, this material will be made available by the publisher on a custom-publishing basis. (Free upon adoption.)

Coverage of Total Quality Management

The discussion of total quality management has been revised, expanded and updated. In the fourth edition, this material appears in Chapter 12, "Responsibility Accounting and Total Quality Management." Included in the coverage are measuring and reporting quality costs, product grade, quality of design, quality of conformance, observable versus hidden quality costs, and the changing view of experts on the optimal level of product quality. The discussion is augmented by graphical analyses of optimal product quality. Cause and effect diagrams and Pareto diagrams are explored as means of identifying quality-control problems. The concept of total quality management (or TQM) is discussed, as are the ISO 9000 standards, which are used internationally for assessing the effectiveness of a company's quality control system.

Coverage of Financial Statement Analysis and the Statement of Cash Flows

These primarily financial accounting topics, covered in Chapters 19 and 20 in the third edition, have not been included in the fourth edition. This decision was based on consistent reviewer comments that the chapters were not widely used. However, these chapters are available from the publisher on a custom-publishing basis. (Free upon adoption.)

Further Integration of Material on Cost Management Systems and Today's Manufacturing Environment

In the fourth edition, virtually every chapter includes significant coverage of various emerging topics in managerial accounting and the contemporary business environment. Some of the topics covered in various chapters are as follows:

Chapter 1. Managerial accounting as an integral part of the management process; the proactive role of the managerial accountant as part of the management team; global competition; focus on the customer; cross-functional teams; time-based competition; information and communication technology; just-in-time production and inventory management; total quality management; cost management systems; strategic cost management and the value chain.

Chapter 2. Cost drivers; volume-based versus operations-based cost drivers.

Chapter 3. Discussion and exhibits covering two-stage cost allocation and departmental overhead rates.

Also in Chapter 3 is an introduction to activity-based costing. The main part of the chapter includes a conceptual introduction to ABC, without getting into the details. Then the Appendix to Chapter 3 provides follow-up material with a straightforward numerical illustration. The appendix briefly shows the effects on product costs of the following three alternative approaches to product costing: plantwide overhead rate, departmental overhead rates, and activity-based costing.

The ABC coverage in Chapter 3 is intended for those instructors who prefer to introduce activity-based costing early in the course, without getting into a lot of details about ABC systems. A much more in-depth treatment of ABC is given in Chapter 5.

Chapter 4. Hybrid product-costing systems and operation costing.

Chapter 5. This chapter provides an in-depth treatment of activity-based costing and cost management systems. The fourth edition includes many pedagogical devices to help students understand how an activity-based costing system works, and how ABC reduces product cost distortion. To make room for the expanded pedagogical material, several topics have been moved to other chapters. This has increased the integration of the material on contemporary cost management systems throughout the text.

Chapter 6. This chapter covers activity-based management and the new manufacturing environment. Topical coverage includes the implications of advanced manufacturing technology for managerial accounting, just-in-time inventory and production management systems, two-dimensional activity-based costing, activity-based management, elimination of non-value-added costs, target costing, kaizen costing, continuous improvement, and the keys to successful implementation of ABC and ABM.

The Aerotech Corporation illustration runs throughout Chapters 5 and 6. Chapter 5 focuses on activity-based *costing*. Chapter 6 is devoted more to activity-based *management*. In general, Chapter 5 is more quantitative while Chapter 6 is more qualitative. In the fourth edition, the two chapters follow the natural evolution of a new cost management system from focusing primarily on cost assignment to impacting management of the organization's activities.

Chapters 5 and 6 make up a module on cost management systems. In general, Chapters 5 and 6 should be covered consecutively. However, the two-chapter module can be shifted around in the design of a course; they could be covered at either the beginning or end of the course.

Chapter 7. Shifting cost structure in the new manufacturing environment; volume-based versus operations-based cost drivers.

Chapter 8. The implications of activity-based costing for CVP analysis; impact on CVP relationships of labor intensive production systems versus advanced manufacturing systems; and the implications of JIT and flexible manufacturing systems.

Chapter 9. Budgeting product life-cycle costs; and JIT versus EOQ views of inventory planning (appendix).

In addition, this chapter includes a considerable amount of pedagogical material to help students understand the linkage between production and purchasing, and how cash receipts and cash disbursements are budgeted.

Chapter 10. Performance measurement in today's manufacturing environment; limitations of standard costing; and relationships between ABC and standard costing.

Chapter 11. Implications of activity-based costing and contemporary cost management systems for flexible budgeting.

Chapter 12. Activity-based responsibility accounting; total quality management.

Chapter 13. International and ethical issues in cost management systems.

Chapter 14. Implications of activity-based costing for relevant cost analysis.

Chapter 15. Pricing based on target costing; pricing implications of activity-based costing; and impact of distorted product costs on cost-based prices.

Chapter 16. Justification of investments in advanced manufacturing systems.

Chapter 17. Real-world capital-budgeting practices, including an international discussion.

Chapter 18. Relationships between service department cost allocation, two-stage allocation, and ABC systems.

Chapter 19. Implications of a JIT manufacturing environment for variable and absorption costing issues.

Revision of End-of-Chapter Assignment Material

Many new exercises, problems, and cases have been added in the fourth edition. In addition to the new assignment items, most of the exercises, problems, and cases in the third edition have been revised. The result is that roughly three-quarters of the items in the fourth edition are new or revised.

Every chapter in the text includes one or more problems and cases dealing with ethical issues. Moreover, there is an increase in the number of problems and cases that include international issues, critical thinking skills, and written communications requirements. Icons have been placed in the margins to identify exercises, problems, and cases involving ethics or international issues. Another icon identifies each assignment item which explicitly requires an oral or written response by the student or which lends itself well to such an assignment by the instructor. An additional icon appears in the Current Issues in Managerial Accounting section to identify where students will be asked to work in groups.

Ethics   Oral/Written   International   Group Work

The assignment material also includes many missing-data problems. These problems help students think through the conceptual linkages in a technique by requiring them to "work backwards" from the information given to reconstruct the missing data. Also, several integrative cases are included, for example, in the budgeting and standard costing chapters.

Many exercises and problems can be solved using the spreadsheet software (SPATS). Icons have also been placed in the margins next to these exercises and problems for easy identification.

Supplements for the Instructor

Solutions Manual (ISBN 0-07-561979-2), prepared by Ronald W. Hilton, Cornell University. Contains complete solutions to all of the text's end-of-chapter review questions, exercises, problems, cases, and current issues in managerial accounting.

Key Figures (ISBN 0-07-228423-4) prepared by Ronald W. Hilton, Cornell University. Provided for end-of-chapter exercises, problems, and cases in the text. Available in class quantities.

Annotated Instructor's Edition (ISBN 0-07-290291-4). Annotations were created by Al Chen of North Carolina State University. The fourth edition is made more instructor-friendly with the new annotated edition. Useful teaching tips, additional service examples, and related press articles are located in the margin of the annotated edition.

Instructor's Resource Manual (ISBN 0-07-059341-8), authored by Lanny Solomon of the University of Texas at Arlington. A comprehensive guide for instructors. In addition to chapter outlines and topical summaries, this supplement topically cross-references all the key supplements including the Study Guide, Test Bank, Managerial Accounting Video Series, and PowerPoint slides. Instructors no longer have to waste valuable time trying to coordinate their lecture with videos, PowerPoint, and assignment material. It has been done for them in the Instructor's Resource Manual.

Test Bank (ISBN 0-07-059342-6), authored by Lanny Solomon of the University of Texas at Arlington. The test bank contains true/false questions, matching exercises, and short problems. Each test item is coded for length of time and level of difficulty.

Computerized Test Bank (ISBN 0-07-290292-2). The computerized version of the test bank (available in Windows version).

Teletest allows instructors to call a toll-free number, specify the content of desired exams, and have a laser-printed copy of the exam mailed to them.

Solutions Transparencies (ISBN 0-07-290294-9). Solutions to all the end-of-chapter exercises, problems, and cases in the text.

Ready Shows (ISBN 0-07-561978-4) and **Ready Slides** (ISBN 0-07-228424-2) are teaching enhancement packages prepared by Jon A. Booker, Charles W. Caldwell, Susan C. Galbreath, and Richard S. Rand, all of Tennessee Technological University. *Ready Shows* are PowerPoint slides that illustrate key chapter topics. *Ready Slides* are four-color teaching transparencies of selected PowerPoint slides.

Irwin/McGraw-Hill Managerial/Cost Accounting Video Series. These short, action-oriented videos provide the impetus for lively classroom discussion and illustrate managerial accounting issues in manufacturing, service, retail, and governmental/nonprofit enterprises.

Presentation Manager (ISBN 0-07-290293-0). This integrated CD-ROM allows instructors to customize their own classroom presentations. It contains key instructor supplements such as PowerPoint, Test Bank, Instructor's Resource Manual, Solutions Manual, and Videos. The Presentation Manager makes it easy for instructors to create multimedia presentations.

SPATS-Instructor (ISBN 0-07-290296-5). Spreadsheet Application Template Software allows students to solve selected end-of-chapter assignments using Excel templates.

Interactive Managerial Accounting Lab, created by Diane Pattison (University of San Diego), Patrick McKenzie (Arizona State University), and Rick Birney (Arizona State University). This Windows-based program gives students a hands-on, highly interactive environment in which to learn managerial accounting. It is available in a network version (0-07-561333-2), as well as a take-home version (0-07-561332-8).

Web Page. Located at *www.mhhe.com/business/accounting/hilton*, this homepage provides additional resources for the instructor and student. Check it out.

Supplements for the Student

Study Guide (ISBN 0-07-059343-4), created by Jeannie Folk (College of DuPage). Developed to help students study more effectively, the study guide incorporates many of the accounting survival skills essential to student success. Each chapter contains the following sections: *Chapter Focus Suggestions; Read and Recall Questions; Self-Test Questions and Exercises; Solutions to the Self-Test Questions and Exercises;* and *Ideas for Your Study Group.* In addition to reinforcing and applying the key concepts in the text, the study guide teaches students how to study, individually and in groups.

SPATS-Student (ISBN 0-07-228422-6). Spreadsheet Application Template Software includes Excel templates for selected exercises and problems from the text.

Tutorial Software (ISBN 0-07-290297-3). Fill-in-the-blank, multiple-choice, true/false, journal entry, and glossary review questions can be randomly accessed by students. This software reinforces the key concepts of the text and provides the student with explanations for correct and incorrect answers.

Ramblewood Manufacturing, Inc. (ISBN 0-256-17807-0). This computerized practice set was created by Leland Mansuetti and Keith Weidkamp (both of Sierra College). This software simulates the operation of a company that manufactures customized fencing. It can be used to illustrate Job-order costing systems with JIT inventory in a realistic setting. The entire simulation requires 10 to 14 hours to complete.

The Phish Corporation, A Practice Case in Managerial Accounting, prepared by Mark Zmijewski, University of Chicago; Sanford Gunn, State University of New York, Buffalo; Ronald Huefner, State University of New York, Buffalo; and Robert Derstine, Villanova University. This comprehensive application brings together all of the elements of managerial accounting in a realistic on-the-job environment. Thirteen modules cover such topics as cost classification, product costing, budgeting, standard costs, cost-volume-profit analysis, and special decisions. All assignments are drawn from a common database for a manufacturing company.

Interactive Managerial Accounting Lab (ISBN 0-07-561520-4), prepared by Diane Pattison, University of San Diego; Patrick McKenzie, Arizona State University; and Rick Birney, Arizona State University. A Windows-based program giving students a hands-on, highly interactive environment in which to learn managerial accounting. This software includes exercises, activities, and problems on content covered throughout the course.

Web Page. Located at *www.mhhe.com/business/accounting/hilton*, this homepage provides additional resources for the instructor and student. Check it out.

Acknowledgments

I would like to express my appreciation to several people who have provided assistance in the development of this textbook. First, my gratitude goes to the thousands of managerial accounting students I have had the privilege to teach over many years. Their enthusiasm, comments, and questions have challenged me to clarify my thinking about many topics in managerial accounting. Second, I express my sincere thanks to the following professors who provided extensive reviews for the fourth edition: Tarek S. Amer, *Northern Arizona University*; Bruce M. Bradford, *Fairfield University*; Thomas G. Calderon, *University of Akron*; Thomas M. Carment, *Northeastern State University*; Al Chen, *North Carolina State University*; Maureen Crane, *California State University, Fresno*; Carleton Donchess, *Bridgewater State College*; Jim Emig, *Villanova University*; Hubert W. Gill, *University of North Florida*; Steven C. Hall, *Widener University*; John L. Haverty, *Saint Joseph's University*; Leslie Kren, *University of Wisconsin, Milwaukee*; Lisa Martin, *Western Michigan University*; Kathy Otero, *University of Texas at El Paso*; Edwin Pinto, *San Jose State University*; Antonio L. Que, *Clarion University*; Mary S. Rolfes, *Mankato State University*; Gordon Smith, *Florida State University*; William E. Smith, *Xavier University*; and Nancy Thorbahn, *University of Wisconsin—Madison*.

Third, I want to thank James M. Emig, *Villanova University*, and Carleton Donchess, *Bridgewater State College*, for their thorough checking of the text and solutions manual for accuracy and completeness.

I acknowledge the Institute of Management Accountants for allowing the use of excerpts from *Management Accounting* and for permission to use problems from Certified Management Accountant (CMA) examinations. I also acknowledge the American Institute of Certified Public Accountants for permission to use problems from the Uniform CPA Examinations, Questions, and Unofficial Answers. I am indebted to Professors Roland Minch and David Solomons for allowing the use of their case materials in the text. The source for the actual company information in Chapter 2 regarding H. J. Heinz, Wal-Mart, and Southwest Airlines was the companies' published annual reports.

Finally, I wish to express my gratitude to the fine people at Irwin/McGraw-Hill who so professionally guided this book through the publication process. In particular, I wish to acknowledge George Werthman, Susan Trentacosti, Michael Warrell, Irene Baki, Rhonda Seelinger, Michelle Hudson, Keri Johnson, Melonie Salvati, and Cathy Tepper. A special acknowledgment goes to Kalista Johnston-Nash for her superb proofreading of the text.

Ronald W. Hilton

Contents in Brief

Contents

● Red dots denote contemporary topics.

Chapter **6**

Activity-Based Management and the New Manufacturing Environment   204

Part Three **Planning and Control Systems**

Chapter **7**

Activity Analysis, Cost Behavior, and Cost Estimation   242

Chapter

Cost-Volume-Profit Analysis 288

Illustration of Cost-Volume-Profit Analysis 290

Chapter 9

Budgeting: Profit Planning and Control Systems   334

Chapter 10

Standard Costing and Performance Measures for Today's Manufacturing Environment   392

Chapter **11**

Flexible Budgeting and Overhead Cost Control   440

Part Four # Using Accounting Information in Decision Making

Chapter # 14   Decision Making: Relevant Costs and Benefits   562

Chapter # 15   Cost Analysis and Pricing Decisions   618

xxxii   Contents

Chapter

19 Variable and Absorption Costing   768

Managerial Accounting

1 Chapter One

Managerial Accounting: An Overview

After completing this chapter, you should be able to:

1 Explain four fundamental management processes that help organizations attain their goals.

2 List and describe five objectives of managerial accounting activity.

3 Explain the major differences between managerial and financial accounting.

4 Describe the roles of an organization's controller, treasurer, and internal auditor.

5 Briefly describe some of the major contemporary themes in managerial accounting.

6 Discuss the professional organizations, certification process, and ethical standards in the field of managerial accounting.

OLYMPIA
Regional Hospital

NEW CLINIC COMES TO THE RESCUE

Cincinnati—What started as one of those lazy, hazy, crazy days of summer ended in a close brush with death for a westside boy yesterday. Seven-year old Shaun Mason was treated at the new Olympia Outreach Clinic for a severe allergic reaction to the bee stings he had received minutes before in a pick-up baseball game at Riverside Park. Dr. Marguerite Overhoff, chief of pediatrics at Olympia Regional Hospital, which operates the new outreach clinic, credited Mason's friends with saving his life. "Apparently Shaun disturbed a yellow jacket nest when he scooped up a ground ball in the outfield," Overhoff said. "He was stung numerous times and suffered a severe allergic reaction. Within minutes, Shaun was struggling to breathe, and the other kids knew he was in trouble." Several of the stricken boy's friends carried him the half mile to Olympia Outreach

Clinic, which had first opened its doors one year ago to the day. "We might have called 911 if there'd been a phone handy," explained nine-year old Jennifer Wilson, "but there wasn't, so we took turns carrying Shaun to the clinic." After initial emergency care at the clinic, the boy was transported by ambulance to Olympia Regional Hospital, where today he is listed in stable condition. "A few minutes can make all the difference in the world in a case like this," according to Dr. Overhoff. "Those kids really knew what to do."

The bee sting case is just the latest in a series of startling successes for Olympia's new outreach clinic. The facility was established to bring better medical care into an economically depressed area of the community. "People in that section of the city tended to use the emergency room at Olympia Regional Hospital as their family doctor," explained Dr. Overhoff. "They

would often let a condition go too long before seeking treatment. Our purpose in opening the outreach clinic was to bring preventive and therapeutic medical care into the community, and educate people at the same time. We also wanted to ease the financial pressures on the hospital. Acute care in the ER is an expensive alternative to preventive medicine."

Asked if the clinic's goal of putting Olympia Regional Hospital on sounder financial footing was being met, Overhoff had this to say: "Yes, the hospital's in much better shape now, and the clinic is financially sound, too. We had a very good management team plan the clinic, and the financial analysis was superb. But, you know, that's not really the most important issue after all." Then Dr. Overhoff looked me right in the eye and asked, "What value would you place on that boy's life?"

Many different kinds of organizations affect our daily lives. Manufacturers, retailers, service industry firms, agribusiness companies, nonprofit organizations, and government agencies provide us with a vast array of goods and services. All of these organizations have two things in common. First, every organization has a set of *goals* or objectives. An airline's goals might be profitability and customer service. A city police department's goals would include public safety and security coupled with cost minimization. Second, in pursuing an organization's goals, managers need *information*. The information needs of management range across financial, production, marketing, legal, and environmental issues. Generally, the larger the organization is, the greater is management's need for information.

Managerial accounting
is the process of
identifying, measuring,
analyzing, interpreting,
and communicating
information in pursuit of
an organization's goals.

Managerial accounting is the process of identifying, measuring, analyzing, interpreting, and communicating information in pursuit of an organization's goals. Managerial accounting is an integral part of the management process, and managerial accountants are important strategic partners in an organization's management team. The management team seeks to create value for the organization by managing resources, activities, and people to achieve the organization's goals effectively.

In this chapter, we will explore the role of managerial accounting within the overall management process. In the remaining chapters, we will expand our study by exploring the many concepts and tools used in managerial accounting.

MANAGING RESOURCES, ACTIVITIES, AND PEOPLE

LO 1   Explain four fundamental management processes that help organizations attain their goals.

The owners, directors, or trustees of an organization set its goals, often with the help of management. For example, IBM's goals are set by its board of directors, who are elected by the company's stockholders. Olympia Regional Hospital's trustees have established the hospital's overall goal as providing preventive and therapeutic medical care to all segments of the community.

In pursuing its goals, an organization acquires *resources*, hires *people*, and then engages in an organized set of *activities*. It is up to the management team to make the best use of the organization's resources, activities, and people in achieving the organization's goals. The day-to-day work of the management team comprises four activities:

- Decision making.
- Planning.
- Directing operational activities.
- Controlling.

Decision Making

Several years ago Olympia Regional Hospital's board of trustees chose, as one of the hospital's goals, to establish comprehensive health care in a nearby economically depressed neighborhood.* What was the best way to accomplish that goal? Should an outpatient clinic be built in the neighborhood? Or would several mobile health units serve the purpose more effectively? Perhaps a community outreach program should be established, in which physicians speak in schools and civic organizations. How would each of these alternatives mesh with the hospital's other goals, which include financial self-sufficiency? The hospital's management team had to *make a decision* regarding the best way to bring health care into the neighborhood, which entailed *choosing among the available alternatives*.

Planning

As the chapter's opening story indicated, Olympia Regional Hospital's trustees decided to build an outpatient clinic. How would the clinic be organized and operated? How

---

*The focus organizations around which the chapters are built are not real organizations. They are, however, realistic settings in which to discuss business and managerial accounting issues. In most cases they are based on real organizations. Similarly, the news articles in the chapter openers (such as on the preceding page) are not real newspaper articles, but most of them are based on real events. These realistic illustrations and scenarios are intended to help students connect the business and managerial accounting issues discussed in this book to everyday life.

many physicians, nurses, medical technicians, and support personnel would be needed? How many examination and treatment rooms would be required, and how should they be equipped? How much would it cost to operate the clinic for a year, and how much money would be saved at the hospital? Finally, how should the clinic's services be priced, keeping in mind its economically depressed location? The hospital's management team had to *plan* for running the clinic, which meant *developing a detailed financial and operational description of anticipated operations.*

Directing Operational Activities

Now the clinic has been built, equipped, and staffed. How many physicians should be on duty on Saturday morning? How much penicillin should be kept on hand? Should sports physicals be done at the clinic or in the school? How much cash will be needed to meet the payroll, pay the utility bills, and buy medical supplies next month? All of these questions fall under the general heading of *directing operational activities*, which means *running the organization on a day-to-day basis.*

Controlling

The clinic has operated for a year now. Is the clinic's goal being accomplished? More specifically, have the clinic's operations adhered to the plans developed by management for achieving the goal? In seeking to answer these questions, management is engaged in *control*, which means *ensuring that the organization operates in the intended manner and achieves its goals.*

Role of Managerial Accounting

For all of the managerial activities described in the preceding section, managers need information. That information comes from a variety of sources, including economists, financial experts, marketing and production personnel, and the organization's managerial accounting system.

Objectives of Managerial Accounting Activity

Managerial accounting activity has five major objectives, which may be characterized as follows:

LO 2 List and describe five objectives of managerial accounting activity.

- Providing information for decision making and planning, and proactively participating as part of the management team in the decision-making and planning processes.
- Assisting managers in directing and controlling operational activities.
- Motivating managers and other employees toward the organization's goals.
- Measuring the performance of activities, subunits, managers, and other employees within the organization.
- Assessing the organization's competitive position, and working with other managers to ensure the organization's long-run competitiveness in its industry.

Nowadays managerial accounting analysis is considered so crucial in managing an enterprise that in most cases managerial accountants are integral members of the management team. Far from playing a passive role as information providers, managerial accountants take a proactive role in both the strategic and day-to-day decisions that confront an enterprise.

Although much of the information provided by the managerial accounting system is financial, there is a strong trend toward the presentation of substantial nonfinancial data as well. Managerial accountants supply all kinds of information to management and act as strategic business partners in support of management's role in decision making and managing the organization's activities. As we will see in subsequent chapters, contemporary managerial accounting systems are focusing more and more on the activities that occur on all levels of the organization. Measuring, managing, and continuously improving operational activities are critical to an organization's success.

To illustrate the objectives of managerial accounting activity, let us continue with the example of Olympia Regional Hospital.

Providing Information for Decision Making and Planning and Proactively Participating as Part of the Management Team in the Decision-Making and Planning Processes   For virtually all major decisions, the hospital's management team would rely largely on managerial accounting information. For example, the *decision* to establish the new clinic would be influenced heavily by estimates of the costs of building the clinic and maintaining it throughout its life. The hospital's managers also would rely on managerial accounting data in formulating plans for the clinic's operations. Prominent in those *plans* would be a budget detailing the projected revenues and costs of providing health care.

While the trustees contemplated their decision about the clinic, the hospital's managerial accountant could not simply gather information and then sit on the sidelines. The managerial accountant was a key participant in the management team as decisions were made and plans formulated for the clinic's operations.

Assisting Managers in Directing and Controlling Operational Activities   Directing and controlling day-to-day operations requires a variety of data about the process of providing health care services. For example, in *directing* operational activities, the management team would need data about the cost of providing medical services in order to set service fees and seek reimbursement from insurance companies. Finally, in *controlling* operations, management would compare actual costs incurred with those specified in the budget.

The **attention-directing function** of managerial accounting information directs managers' attention to issues that need their attention.

Managerial accounting information often assists management through its **attention-directing function.** Managerial accounting reports rarely solve a decision problem. However, managerial accounting information often directs managers' attention to an issue that requires their skills. To illustrate, suppose Olympia Regional Hospital's clinic incurred electricity costs that significantly exceeded the budget. This fact does not explain why the budget was exceeded, nor does it tell management what action to take, but it does direct management's attention to the situation. Suppose that upon further investigation, the accounting records reveal that the local electric rates have increased substantially. This information will help management in framing the decision problem. Should steps be taken to conserve electricity? Should the clinic's hours be curtailed? Perhaps management should consider switching to natural gas for heating.

Motivating Managers and Other Employees toward the Organization's Goals   Organizations have goals. However, organizations are comprised of people who have goals of their own. The goals of individuals are diverse, and they do not always match those of the organization. A key purpose of managerial accounting is to motivate managers and other employees to direct their efforts toward achieving the organization's goals. One means of achieving this purpose is through budgeting. In establishing a budget for Olympia Regional Hospital's outpatient clinic, top management indicates how resources are to be allocated and what activities are to be emphasized. When actual operations do not conform to the budget, the clinic's managers will be asked to explain the reasons for the deviation.

Empowerment is the concept of encouraging and authorizing workers to take initiative to improve operations, reduce costs, and improve product quality and customer service.

One way in which employees can be motivated toward the organization's goals is through *empowerment*. Employee **empowerment** is the concept of encouraging and authorizing workers to take the initiative to improve operations, reduce costs, and improve product quality and customer service. At the Olympia Outreach Clinic, for example, medical reception personnel were authorized to design some aspects of the patient reception process. The result was less paperwork, a streamlined reception process, and more satisfied patients.

Measuring the Performance of Activities, Subunits, Managers, and Other Employees within the Organization   One means of motivating people toward the organization's goals is to measure their performance in achieving those goals. Such measurements then can be used as the basis for rewarding performance through positive feedback, promotions, and pay raises. For example, most large corporations compensate their executives, in part, on the basis of the profit achieved by the subunits they manage. For Olympia Regional Hospital's outpatient clinic, performance measures might focus on the success of the clinic in promoting prenatal care and other forms of preventive medicine in the neighborhood. Achieving such goals would also support the main hospital's goal of reducing crowding in its emergency room.

In addition to measuring the performance of people, the managerial accounting system measures the performance of an organization's subunits, such as divisions, product lines, geographical territories, and departments. These measurements help the subunits' managers obtain the highest possible performance level in their units. Such measurements also help top management decide whether a particular subunit is a viable economic investment. For example, it may turn out that Olympia Regional Hospital's new clinic will prove to be too costly an activity to continue, despite the efforts of a skilled management team.

Assessing the Organization's Competitive Position and Working with Other Managers to Ensure the Organization's Long-Run Competitiveness in Its Industry   Nowadays the business environment is changing very rapidly. These changes are reflected in global competition, rapidly advancing technology, and improved communication systems, such as the Internet. The activities that make an enterprise successful today may no longer be sufficient next year. A crucial role of managerial accounting is to continually assess how an organization stacks up against the competition, with an eye toward continuously improving. Among the questions asked in assessing an organization's competitive position are the following:

- How well is the organization doing in its internal operations and business processes?
- How well is the organization doing in the eyes of its customers? Are their needs being served as well as possible?
- How well is the organization doing from the standpoint of innovation, learning, and continuously improving operations? Is the organization a trendsetter that embraces new products, new services, and new technology? Or is it falling behind?
- How well is the organization doing financially? Is the enterprise viable as a continuing entity?[1]

The managers of any enterprise need to continually ask these questions if the organization is to remain viable in a changing and ever more competitive business environment. Olympia Regional Hospital is no exception. The hospital's management team must be concerned with the cost effectiveness of its business processes as well as its medical procedures. Management must continually monitor the needs of its patients and assess their level of satisfaction with the services provided. The hospital's overall financial strength also must be prominent in management's thinking. Finally, is Olympia "keeping up with the times" in medical practices and technology? Is the hospital's staff innovative, or does it tend to follow advances made by others?

Managerial versus Financial Accounting

Take another look at the major objectives of managerial accounting activity. Notice that the focus in each of these objectives is on *managers*. Thus, the focus of **managerial accounting** is on the needs of managers *within* the organization, rather than interested parties outside the organization.

> **LO 3**   Explain the major differences between managerial and financial accounting.

---

[1]These questions paraphrase those raised by Robert S. Kaplan and David D. Norton in "The Balanced Scorecard: Measures That Drive Performance," *Harvard Business Review* 70, no. 1, pp. 71–79.

Financial accounting is the use of accounting information for reporting to parties outside the organization.

Financial accounting is the use of accounting information for reporting to parties outside the organization. The annual report distributed by McDonald's Corporation to its stockholders is an example of the output from a financial accounting system. Users of financial accounting information include current and prospective stockholders, lenders, investment analysts, unions, consumer groups, and government agencies.

There are many similarities between managerial accounting information and financial accounting information because they both draw upon data from an organization's basic *accounting system.* This is the system of procedures, personnel, and computers used to accumulate and store financial data in the organization. One part of the overall accounting system is the **cost accounting system,** which accumulates cost data for use in both managerial and financial accounting. For example, production cost data typically are used in helping managers set prices, which is a managerial accounting use. However, production cost data also are used to value inventory on a manufacturer's balance sheet, which is a financial accounting use.

Exhibit 1–1 depicts the relationships among an organization's basic accounting system, cost accounting system, managerial accounting, and financial accounting. Although similarities exist between managerial and financial accounting, the differences are even greater. Exhibit 1–2 lists the most important differences.

The **cost accounting system** is a part of the basic accounting system that accumulates cost data for use in both managerial and financial accounting.

Managerial Accounting in Different Types of Organizations

All organizations need information, whether they are profit-seeking or nonprofit enterprises and regardless of the activities they pursue. As a result, managerial accounting information is vital in all organizations. Chrysler, Sears, American Airlines, Marriott Hotels, Prudential Insurance, American Express, Cornell University, The United Way, Mayo Clinic, the City of Los Angeles, and the Department of Defense all have managerial accountants who provide information to management. Moreover, the five basic purposes of managerial accounting activity are relevant in each of these organizations.

Role of the Managerial Accountant

To understand the managerial accountant's role in an organization, we must know how organizations are structured. To focus our discussion, we will rely on the organization chart for Olympia Regional Hospital presented in Exhibit 1–3 (page 12). Olympia is a public hospital, partially supported by funds from the state and local governments. The hospital's governing body is the board of trustees, and its chief executive officer is the administrator. Also included in top management is the deputy administrator.

Line and Staff Positions

Line positions are held by managers who are directly involved in the provision of goods and services or in the operation of the facilities.

Staff positions are held by managers who are only indirectly involved in operations.

The other positions shown in the organization chart are of two types: line positions and staff positions. Managers in **line positions** are *directly* involved in the provision of medical care or in the operation of the facilities. Olympia Regional Hospital's line positions include the various chiefs of the hospital's professional medical personnel, the director of admissions and patient records, and the director of purchasing, housekeeping, and facilities. All of these people are involved directly in serving patients or in operating the physical facilities.

Managers in **staff positions** supervise activities that support the hospital's mission, but they are *indirectly* involved in the hospital's operation. The counsel is the hospital's lawyer, and the human resources director hires the hospital's employees and maintains all employment records. The controller and treasurer are Olympia Regional Hospital's chief accountants. The existence of two staff-level accounting positions reflects a division of responsibilities, as portrayed in Exhibit 1–4 (page 13).

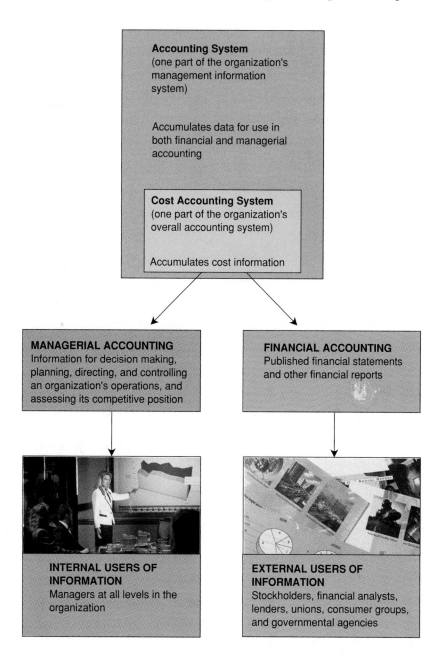

Exhibit 1–1

Managerial Accounting, Financial Accounting, and Cost Accounting

Controller   In most organizations, the **controller** (sometimes called the **comptroller**) is the chief managerial and financial accountant. The controller usually is responsible for supervising the personnel in the accounting department and for preparing the information and reports used in both managerial and financial accounting. As the organization's chief managerial accountant, the controller often interprets accounting information for line managers and participates as an integral member of the management team. Most controllers are involved in planning and decision making at all levels and across all functional areas of the enterprise. This broad role has enabled many managerial accountants to rise to the top of their organizations. In recent years, former accountants have served as top executives in such companies as General Motors, Singer, General Electric, and Fruehauf.

Treasurer   The **treasurer** typically is responsible for raising capital and safeguarding the organization's assets. Olympia Regional Hospital's treasurer oversees the relationships between the hospital and its donors, lenders, investors, and the governmental

LO 4   Describe the roles of an organization's controller, treasurer, and internal auditor.

The **controller** is the top managerial and financial accountant in an organization.

The **treasurer** is responsible for raising capital and safeguarding the organization's assets.

	Managerial Accounting	**Financial Accounting**
Users of Information	Managers, *within the organization.*	Interested parties, *outside the organization.*
Regulation	*Not required* and *unregulated,* since it is intended only for management.	*Required* and must conform to generally accepted accounting principles. *Regulated* by the Financial Accounting Standards Board, and, to a lesser degree, the Securities and Exchange Commission.
Source of Data	The organization's *basic accounting system, plus various other sources,* such as rates of defective products manufactured, physical quantities of material and labor used in production, occupancy rates in hotels and hospitals, and average take-off delays in airlines.	Almost exclusively drawn from the organization's *basic accounting system,* which accumulates financial information.
Nature of Reports and Procedures	*Reports often focus on subunits* within the organization, such as departments, divisions, geographical regions, or product lines. Based on a combination of historical data, estimates, and projections of future events.	*Reports focus on the enterprise in its entirety.* Based almost exclusively on historical transaction data.

An organization's
internal auditor is
responsible for reviewing
the accounting
procedures, records, and
reports in both the
controller's and the
treasurer's areas of
responsibility.

agencies that supply partial funding. In addition, the treasurer is responsible for the hospital's assets, the management of its investments, its credit policy, and its insurance coverage.

Internal Auditor Olympia Regional Hospital does not have an internal auditor, but most large corporations and many governmental agencies do. An organization's **internal auditor** is responsible for reviewing the accounting procedures, records, and reports in both the controller's and the treasurer's areas of responsibility. The auditor then expresses an opinion to top management regarding the effectiveness of the organization's accounting system. In some organizations, the internal auditor also makes a broad performance evaluation of middle and lower management.

Major Themes in Managerial Accounting

LO 5 Briefly describe some of the major contemporary themes in managerial accounting.

Several major themes influence virtually all aspects of managerial accounting. We will briefly introduce these themes now, and they will be apparent throughout the text.

Information and Incentives

The need for information is the driving force behind managerial accounting. However, managerial accounting information often serves two functions: a *decision-facilitating* function and a *decision-influencing* function. Information usually is supplied to a decision maker to assist that manager in choosing an alternative. Often, that information is also intended to influence the manager's decision.

To illustrate, let us consider Olympia Regional Hospital's annual budget. Although the budget is prepared under the direction of the controller, it must be approved by the hospital's administrator and, ultimately, by the board of trustees. As part of the budget approval process, the administrator and the trustees will make important decisions that determine how the hospital's resources will be allocated. Throughout the year, the decisions of management will be facilitated by the information contained in the budget. Management decisions also will be influenced by the budget, since at year-end actual expenditures will be compared with the budgeted amounts. Explanations will then be requested for any significant deviations.

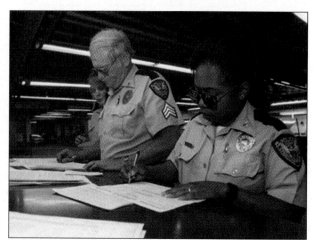

Managerial accounting information is vital in all types of organizations. Managerial accountants act as strategic business partners in support of management's roles in decision making and directing operational activities. Pictured here are a manufacturer, a service-industry firm, a retailer, and a governmental unit. How would managerial accounting be important in each of these organizations?

Behavioral Issues

The reactions of both individuals and groups to managerial accounting information will significantly affect the course of events in an organization. How will Olympia Regional Hospital's chief of surgery react to a budget? How will data regarding the cost of providing radiological services affect the way the supervisor of radiology prices those services? How much detail should be included in the quarterly accounting reports to the administrator? If too much detail is provided, will the administrator be overloaded with information and distracted from the main points?

All of these questions involve the behavioral tendencies of people and their cognitive limitations in using information. The better a managerial accountant's understanding of human behavior is, the more effective he or she will be as a provider of information.

Costs and Benefits

Information is a commodity, much like wheat or corn. Like other goods, information can be produced, purchased, and consumed. It can be of high or low quality, timely or late, appropriate for its intended use or utterly irrelevant. As is true of all goods and services, information entails both costs and benefits. The costs of providing managerial accounting information to the managers in Olympia Regional Hospital include the cost

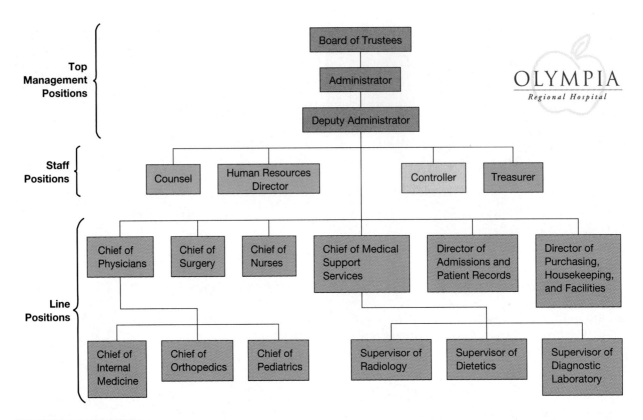

Exhibit 1–3

Organization Chart for
Olympia Regional Hospital

of compensation for the controller and Accounting Department personnel, the cost of purchasing and operating computers, and the cost of the time spent by the information users to read, understand, and utilize the information. The benefits include improved decisions, more effective planning, greater efficiency of operations at lower costs, and better direction and control of operations.

Thus, there are both costs and benefits associated with managerial accounting information. The desirability of any particular managerial accounting technique or information must be determined in light of its costs and benefits. We will reinforce this cost-benefit trade-off throughout the text by pointing out areas where managerial accounting information could be improved, but only at too great a cost.

Evolution and Adaptation in Managerial Accounting

LO 5   Briefly describe some of the major contemporary themes in managerial accounting.

Compared to financial accounting, managerial accounting is a young discipline. As a result, managerial accounting concepts and tools are still evolving as new ways are found to provide information that assists management. Moreover, the business environment is changing rapidly. For managerial accounting to be as useful a tool in the future as it has been in the recent past, managerial accounting information must be adapted to reflect those changes. Several changes in the business environment that are especially pertinent to managerial accounting are discussed briefly here. The effect of these changes on various topics in managerial accounting will be explored in subsequent chapters.

Service versus Manufacturing Firms   The service sector occupies a growing role in the United States economy. Moreover, several key service industries have been deregulated by the government. The telecommunications, financial services, and airline industries are among them. As more and more companies provide financial, medical, communi-

Controller	**Treasurer**
1. Supervises the accounting department.	1. Manages relationships with donors, creditors, investors, and government agencies that provide financial support
2. Prepares all reports for external parties (financial accounting)	2. Maintains custody of cash and other assets
3. Prepares all reports and information for internal users (managerial accounting)	3. Manages investments
4. Assists line managers throughout the hospital in interpreting and using managerial accounting information. Participates actively as a member of the management team.	4. Responsible for credit policy and collection of accounts
5. Prepares reports required for taxation and governmental reporting; advises management on tax-related issues	5. Manages the hospital's insurance coverage

Exhibit 1–4

Controller versus Treasurer at Olympia Regional Hospital

OLYMPIA
Regional Hospital

cation, transportation, consulting, and hospitality services, managerial accounting techniques must be adapted to meet the needs of managers in those industries. The key difference between service and manufacturing firms is that most services are consumed as they are produced. Most services cannot be inventoried like manufactured goods. Service organizations also tend to be more labor-intensive than manufacturing firms. Many of the techniques developed for measuring costs and performance in manufacturing companies have been adapted successfully to service industry firms. Throughout the text, you will notice that roughly two-thirds of the illustrations of managerial accounting techniques involve service industry firms and nonprofit organizations.

Emergence of New Industries Scientific discoveries are opening up whole new industries that were not even contemplated a short time ago. Such discoveries as genetic engineering, superconductivity, and artificial hearts have spawned business activities in which managers face new challenges. Managerial accountants also face new challenges as they seek to provide relevant information in these new high-tech industries.

Global Competition "It's a small world!" Although this cliché has been around a long time, it concisely sums up today's business environment. Nowadays the marketplace is truly a global one. A firm is just as likely to be in competition with a company from Japan, Germany, or Korea as its crosstown rival. Intense international competition is forcing companies to strive for excellence in product quality and service more than ever before.

Moreover, new economic arrangements and potential trade agreements are constantly in the news, as national economies become more and more intertwined. Organizations such as the European Union (EU) and the World Trade Organization (WTO), as well as international agreements like the North American Free Trade Agreement (NAFTA), all have the potential to dramatically change international commerce.

A *multinational* company is an organization that has operational subunits, such as manufacturing plants or sales facilities, in two or more countries. Multinational firms face several challenges that do not confront domestic companies. Political systems, accounting rules for external reporting, legal systems, and cultural norms vary widely among countries. Managers of multinationals must be aware of these differences to successfully carry out operations across international boundaries. Income tax systems differ among countries also. In planning international operations, managers of multinationals must take into account the different tax laws and rates in the countries where they do business.

Monetary systems also differ among countries, and multinationals must continually monitor the fluctuating values of foreign currencies. The price at which one

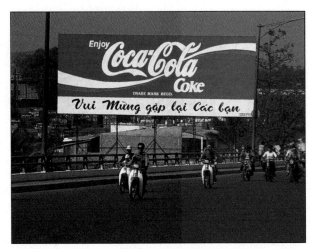

Today's marketplace is a global one. Many U.S. firms have operations worldwide, and a vast array of international goods are available in most countries. Pictured here are Nintendo products on sale in New Jersey and a Coca-Cola billboard in Vietnam.

country's currency can be converted into that of another country is called an *exchange rate*. For example, on the day this paragraph is being written, it takes $1.60 in U.S. dollars to buy one British pound. Yesterday, however, the U.S.-British exchange rate was $1.58. Thus, the exchange rate can fluctuate daily as various forces shape the world economy. An American planning a vacation in Great Britain would be sensible to time the trip to take advantage of a more favorable U.S.-British exchange rate. Managers of multinationals face the same kinds of challenges on a much larger scale as they sign contracts, buy and sell goods, and conduct business operations in many countries.

Focus on the Customer   "The customer is always right," a traditional saying in the retail industry, has never been more pertinent. To succeed in this era, businesses of all types must continually focus on their customers. Managers are increasingly aware of their product's value to the customer, which is the customer's perceived difference between the benefits the customer receives and the sacrifice the customer incurs to receive the product. The value of a product or service to the customer is affected by such diverse attributes as product price, quality, functionality, user-friendliness, customer service, warranty, and maintenance costs. In response to this heightened customer focus, managerial accounting systems now often measure various attributes of customer value.

Cross-Functional Teams   In years past, managers tended to stick to their own turf. Production managers focused on how best to manufacture a product or produce a service. Marketing managers concentrated on selling the product or service. Design engineers often emphasized engineering elegance rather than designing a product for manufacturability. Managerial accountants provided information for decision making, planning, control, and performance evaluation.

Today a cross-functional approach has replaced this narrow managerial perspective. Cross-functional managerial teams bring together production and operations managers, marketing managers, purchasing and material-handling specialists, design engineers, quality management personnel, and managerial accountants to focus their varied expertise and experience on virtually all management issues. If products are to be designed and manufactured with the customers' needs in mind, a cross-functional approach is crucial. Marketing managers have the best feel for customer needs, and production managers are up on the latest in manufacturing technology. Design engineers know how to build the functionality into a product that customers demand, and purchasing managers can acquire the materials, parts, and services necessary to get the job done. Managerial accounting information is the glue that holds the cross-functional team together. The managerial accountant designs an information system and provides data ranging across all aspects of the organization's internal operations and external environment. Then the managerial accountant works as an integral member of the cross-functional team, interpreting information and analyzing the implications of decision alternatives. Working together, the cross-functional team creates value for the organization by meeting the customer's needs in the most effective manner possible.

Computer-Integrated Manufacturing   Over a long period of time, manufacturing processes have evolved from labor-intensive methods to more automated processes, in which most of the work is accomplished by machines. This trend continues today, as *computer-integrated-manufacturing* (or *CIM*) systems become more common. A CIM process is fully automated, with computers controlling the entire production process. In CIM systems, the types of costs incurred by the manufacturer are quite different from those in traditional manufacturing environments.

Product Life Cycles and Diversity   One impact of highly automated manufacturing systems has been to enable manufacturers to produce an ever-more diverse set of products. Moreover, the rate at which technology is changing means that the life cycles of most products are becoming shorter. In the computer industry, for example, product models are used only a few years before they are replaced by more powerful versions. To be competitive, manufacturers must keep up with the rapidly changing marketplace. Managers must have timely information about production costs and other product characteristics in order to respond quickly and effectively to the competition.

Time-Based Competition   *Response time, lead time, on time,* and *downtime* are among the many time-based phrases that dot the conversations of today's managers. Why are managers so concerned with time? In the global competitive environment, time has become a crucial element in many companies' strategies for success. By reducing the time it takes to develop a new product and getting the product on the market more quickly, a company can gain an important advantage over its competitors. Thus, the *time to market* becomes a critical objective for many companies. Reducing the time elapsed from the new product concept stage to having the product in Wal-Mart requires

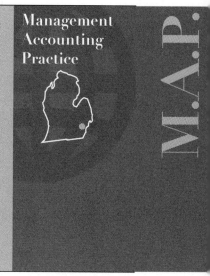

Chrysler Corporation

Chrysler Corporation successfully applied the concepts of time-based competition to reorganize its design and development process. Before the reorganization, the firm required five years to develop a new line of automobiles and get the new cars to market. Chrysler's style, engineering design, procurement, and manufacturing departments operated independently in the development process. For example, when the style department finished its design work, it passed the job on to the engineering department, whose task was to design the parts for the new line of cars. Chrysler managers referred to this process as "throwing the job over the wall." If style-related problems came to light in the engineering phase, the engineers would "throw the job back over the wall" to the style department. This insular approach to new vehicle design added significantly to the overall time to market. Chrysler then reorganized its development process to take a team approach, where the team included representatives from the style, engineering, procurement, and manufacturing departments. By working together closely in the early design stages, the team was able to identify and solve problems early, saving time in the overall development process. Chrysler built a new technology center laid out to facilitate the development team working together. The result was that Chrysler reduced the time to market for a new car line from five years to three and a half years. Many experts credit this successful application of time-based competition with saving the company from bankruptcy.[2]

Management Accounting Practice

---

[2]The source of this illustration was information presented by George Stalk, Jr., and Thomas M. Hout in a management video entitled *Time-Based Competition: Behind the Scenes* (Boston: President and Fellows of Harvard College), 1995.

careful time management at each stage of a product's development. The product must be designed with the customer's needs in mind and with a view toward manufacturability. Delays between product development stages must be reduced or eliminated. The production process must be efficient and product quality must be high. A cross-functional approach to management is crucial in managing the time to market. Once again managerial accounting information is critical for the cross-functional management team. Information about the trade-offs between time and cost in all phases of a product's development is particularly important. For example, how much more would it cost to get a new product to market six months earlier? Can these cost increases be reflected in the product's price? How much higher would sales be if our company beats the competition by six more months? The answers to these and similar questions are increasingly important to managers as they are ever more likely to find themselves competing against time.

Information and Communication Technology   We are all confronted with the breakneck pace of technological change. Just as we learn how to get the most out of our personal computers or to program our VCRs, they are replaced by new and better models. It would be hard to underestimate the impact of technological innovation on the business environment. Although large mainframe computers still perform certain kinds of tasks, businesses now make heavy use of personal computers. In most offices, virtually every employee has a personal computer for such tasks as word processing, data analysis, report generation, presentation preparation, and communication. These PCs are usually linked together in a network that enables employees to electronically transfer files and reports, share data, and communicate via e-mail. Often called an *intranet,* these networked PCs are invaluable tools in the era of cross-functional management teams. Moreover, these intranets are not confined to the walls of a building, as the World Wide Web or *Internet* allows computer-to-computer interface anywhere in the world.

Managerial accounting analyses that in years past would have to be scheduled on a mainframe computer are now done on PCs using a variety of software products. Spreadsheet programs, such as EXCEL® or LOTUS® 1-2-3®, are in wide use for data analysis.[3] Software packages specifically designed for accounting applications are also widely available. Many businesses are adopting integrated business software packages that handle a broad range of computing needs, such as customer and supplier databases, personnel and payroll functions, production scheduling and management, inventory records, and financial and managerial accounting functions. Among the integrated software packages in wide use are SAP, which stands for Systems Applications and Products in Data Processing, and PeopleSoft. Managerial accountants often play significant roles in selecting software for their organizations or designing in-house software to meet the organization's unique needs.

Other innovations have also served to speed communications and link business parties around the world. Global cellular phone technology now enables voice communications from the most remote locations. The global positioning satellite system (GPS) now enables trucking, railroad, shipping, and rental car companies to more easily track vehicles. This virtual explosion in data availability has enabled managerial accounting systems to provide information that would have been impossible to supply only a few years ago.

Just-in-Time Inventory Management   In traditional manufacturing settings, inventories of raw materials and parts, partially completed components, and finished goods were kept as a buffer against the possibility of running out of a needed item. However, large buffer inventories consume valuable resources and generate hidden costs. Consequently, many companies have completely changed their approach to production and inventory management. These manufacturers have adopted a strategy for controlling the flow of

---

[3]EXCEL® is a registered trademark of Microsoft Corporation; LOTUS® 1-2-3® is a registered trademark of Lotus Development Corporation.

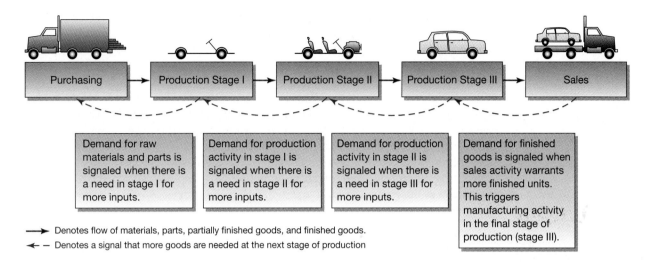

| Demand for raw materials and parts is signaled when there is a need in stage I for more inputs. | Demand for production activity in stage I is signaled when there is a need in stage II for more inputs. | Demand for production activity in stage II is signaled when there is a need in stage III for more inputs. | Demand for finished goods is signaled when sales activity warrants more finished units. This triggers manufacturing activity in the final stage of production (stage III). |

⟶ Denotes flow of materials, parts, partially finished goods, and finished goods.
◄ ─ Denotes a signal that more goods are needed at the next stage of production

Exhibit 1–5

Just-in-Time (JIT) Production and Inventory Management System

manufacturing in a multistage production process. In a **just-in-time** (or **JIT**) **production system,** raw materials and parts are purchased or produced just in time to be used at each stage of the production process. This approach to inventory and production management brings considerable cost savings from reduced inventory levels.

The key to the JIT system is the "pull" approach to controlling manufacturing. To visualize this approach, look at Exhibit 1–5, which displays a simple diagram of a multistage production process. The flow of manufacturing activity is depicted by the solid arrows running across the page from one stage of production to the next. However, the signal that triggers more production activity in each stage comes from the *next* stage of production. These signals, depicted by the dashed-line arrows, run from right to left. We begin with sales at the right-hand side of the exhibit. When sales activity warrants more production of finished goods, the goods are "pulled" from production stage III by sending a signal that more goods are needed. Similarly, when production employees in stage III need more inputs, they send a signal back to stage II. This triggers production activity in stage II. Working our way back to the beginning of the process, purchases of raw materials and parts are triggered by a signal that they are needed in stage I. This pull system of production management, which characterizes the JIT approach, results in a smooth flow of production and significantly reduced inventory levels. The result is considerable cost savings for the manufacturer.

Further details of the JIT production system and other changes in the manufacturing environment will be covered in subsequent chapters. The impact of these changes will be a recurrent theme throughout the book.

Total Quality Management   One implication of a just-in-time inventory philosophy is the need to emphasize product quality. If a component is to be produced just in time for the next production stage, it must be "just right" for its intended purpose. One flawed component can shut down the entire production line, entailing considerable cost. Therefore, managerial accountants have become involved increasingly in monitoring product quality and measuring the costs of maintaining quality. This information helps companies maintain programs of **total quality management,** or **TQM.** This refers to the broad set of management and control processes designed to focus the entire organization and all of its employees on providing products or services that do the best possible job of satisfying the customer.

Continuous Improvement   Global competition is forcing companies to continuously improve their operations. **Continuous improvement** is the constant effort to eliminate waste, reduce response time, simplify the design of both products and processes, and improve quality and customer service. Managerial accountants are contributing to the

In a **just-in-time (JIT) production system,** raw materials and parts are purchased or produced just in time to be used at each stage of the production process.

Total quality management (TQM) refers to the broad set of management and control processes designed to focus the entire organization and all of its employees on providing products or services that do the best possible job of satisfying the customer.

Continuous improvement is the constant effort to eliminate waste, reduce response time, simplify the design of both products and processes, and improve quality and customer service.

continuous improvement programs of many organizations through the development of cost management systems, which are discussed next.

Cost Management Systems

A **cost management system** measures the cost of significant activities, identifies non-value-added costs, and identifies activities that will improve organizational performance.

The explosion in technology we are experiencing, coupled with increasing worldwide competition, is forcing managers to produce high-quality goods and services, provide outstanding customer service, and do so at the lowest possible cost. These demands are placing ever-greater requirements on the information provided by managerial accounting systems. Many companies have moved away from a historical cost accounting perspective and toward a proactive *cost management* perspective. A **cost management system** is a management planning and control system with the following objectives.[4]

- To measure the cost of the resources consumed in performing the organization's significant *activities*.

Non-value-added costs are costs of activities that can be eliminated without deterioration of product quality, performance, or perceived value.

- To identify and eliminate **non-value-added costs.** These are the costs of *activities* that can be eliminated with no deterioration of product quality, performance, or perceived value.

- To determine the efficiency and effectiveness of all major *activities* performed in the enterprise.

- To identify and evaluate new *activities* that can improve the future performance of the organization.

Activity accounting is the emphasis of a cost management system on the organization's activities.

Notice the emphasis of a cost management system on the organization's activities. This emphasis, sometimes called **activity accounting,** is crucial to the goal of producing quality goods and services at the lowest possible cost. In keeping with the focus on activities, managerial accountants have developed a system for determining the cost of producing goods or services called **activity-based costing (ABC).** In an ABC system, the costs of the organization's significant activities are accumulated and then assigned to goods or services in accordance with how the activities are used in the production of those goods and services. An ABC system helps management to understand the causal linkages between activities and costs.

Activity-based costing (ABC) is a system that managerial accountants have developed for determining the cost of producing goods or services.

Activity-based management (ABM) uses an activity-based costing system to improve the operations of an organization.

Using an activity-based costing system to improve the operations of an organization is called **activity-based management** or **ABM.** We will have considerably more to say about activity-based costing, activity-based management, and the role of cost management systems throughout the text.

Strategic Cost Management and the Value Chain

LO 5   Briefly describe some of the major contemporary themes in managerial accounting.

The **value chain** is an organization's set of linked, value-creating activities, ranging from securing basic raw materials and energy to the ultimate delivery of products and services.

How are the goods and services that we all consume created?[5] Usually many activities are involved in securing basic raw materials and turning them into valuable products or services. The set of linked, value-creating activities, ranging from securing basic raw materials and energy to the ultimate delivery of products and services, is called the **value chain.** Although there may be only one organization involved in a particular value chain, usually there are many. For example, Olympia Regional Hospital's value chain would include not only the hospital but also the suppliers of pharmaceutical products and medical supplies, the

---

[4]This section draws upon Callie Berliner and James A. Brimson, eds., *Cost Management for Today's Advanced Manufacturing* (Boston: Harvard Business School Press, 1988), pp. 3, 10, 13–15.

[5]This section draws upon the following sources: John Shank and Vijay Govindarajan, "Strategic Cost Management and the Value Chain," *Journal of Cost Management* 5, no. 4, pp. 5–21; John Shank and Vijay Govindarajan, "Strategic Cost Management: The Value Chain Perspective," *Journal of Cost Management* 6, no. 3, pp. 179–97; and Michael E. Porter, *Competitive Advantage: Creating and Sustaining Superior Performance* (New York: The Free Press, 1985).

| Securing raw materials, energy, and other resources | Research and development | Product design | Production |

| Marketing | Distribution | Customer service |

Exhibit 1–6

Manufacturer's Value Chain

Goodyear's value chain consists of a myriad of activities, from securing raw materials through distribution and customer service.

manufacturers of diagnostic equipment, the private-practice physicians whose patients use Olympia, and the ambulance services that transport patients to the hospital. The major steps in the value chain of a manufacturing firm are depicted in Exhibit 1–6.

In order for any organization to most effectively achieve its goals, it is important for its managers to understand the *entire* value chain in which their organization participates. This understanding can help managers ask, and answer, important questions about their organization's strategy. Should the company concentrate on only a narrow link in the value chain, such as manufacturing and assembly? Or should it expand its operational scope to include securing the raw materials or distributing the final product to end users? Are there opportunities to form beneficial linkages with suppliers, which come earlier in the value chain? Or with customers?

These questions involve fundamental, strategic issues about how an organization can best meet its goals. Although many factors affect such decisions, one important factor concerns the costs incurred in creating value in each link in the value chain. In order for a company to achieve a sustainable competitive advantage, it must either ① perform one or more activities in the value chain at the same quality level as its competitors, but at a lower cost, or ② perform its value chain activities at a higher quality level than its competitors, but at no greater cost. Understanding the value chain, and the factors that cause costs to be incurred in each activity in the value chain, is a crucial step in the development of a firm's strategy. These cost-causing factors are called **cost drivers,** and we will have much more to say about them throughout the text. The overall recognition of the importance of cost relationships among the activities in the value chain, and the process of managing those cost relationships to the firm's advantage, are called **strategic cost management.** Issues in strategic cost management will arise in a variety of contexts as we pursue our study of managerial accounting.

Theory of Constraints   Along with a value-chain analysis, managers should carefully examine the chain of linked activities with a view toward identifying the constraints that prevent their organization from reaching a higher level of achievement. Sometimes called the **theory of constraints,** this approach seeks to find the most cost-effective

A **cost driver** is a characteristic of an event or activity that results in the incurrence of costs by that event or activity.

Strategic cost management is a broad-based managerial accounting analysis that supports strategic management systems.

The **theory of constraints** is a management approach that focuses on identifying and releasing the constraints that limit an organization's ability to reach a higher level of goal attainment.

ways to alleviate an organization's most limiting constraints. When binding constraints are relaxed, the organization can reach a higher level of goal attainment.[6]

The importance of value-chain analysis and strategic cost management is apparent in the following real-world illustrations.

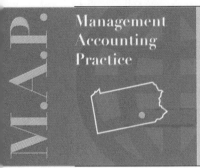

Management Accounting Practice

Chocolate Industry

Producers of bulk chocolate used to package their product in 10-pound, molded bars. The bars were shipped to candy manufacturers, which melted them down to make chocolate bars and other candies. Later it became apparent that cost savings could be enjoyed both by the bulk chocolate producers and the candy manufacturers by transporting the bulk chocolate as a liquid in tank cars. The bulk producers no longer needed to mold and package the bars, and the candy makers no longer needed to melt them down.

This change illustrates a beneficial linkage between suppliers and customers. It was facilitated by viewing the entire value chain, only one part of which is bulk chocolate production, and a strategic cost analysis of the activities in the value chain.[7]

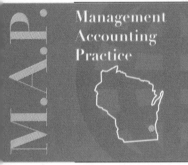

Management Accounting Practice

Beverage Container Industry

Another example of value-chain analysis is given by the container industry. Some container manufacturers have built production facilities near breweries, and they deliver the beer containers on conveyors directly to the customers, the breweries. The mutually beneficial supplier-customer linkage made possible by the strategic location of the container plants was apparent from a strategic cost analysis. The previous activity of transporting bulky and heavy empty containers was eliminated, with significant cost savings to both parties.[8]

Managerial Accounting as a Career

LO 6 Discuss the professional organizations, certification process, and ethical standards in the field of managerial accounting.

Managerial accountants serve a crucial function in virtually any enterprise. As the providers of information, they are often in touch with the heartbeat of the organization. In most businesses, managerial accountants interact frequently with sales personnel, finance specialists, production people, and managers at all levels. To perform their duties effectively, managerial accountants must be knowledgeable not only in accounting but in the other major business disciplines as well. Moreover, strong oral and written communication skills are becoming increasingly important for success as a managerial accountant.

Professional Organizations

To keep up with new developments in their field, managerial accountants often belong to one or more professional organizations. The largest of these is the Institute of Management Accountants (IMA). The IMA publishes a monthly journal entitled *Management Accounting*, and it also has published many research studies on mana-

---

[6]See E. Goldratt, *Theory of Constraints* (Croton-on-Hudson, NY: North River Press, 1990); and E. Goldratt and J. Cox, *The Goal* (Croton-on-Hudson, NY: North River Press, 1986).

[7]See John Shank and Vijay Govindarajan, "Strategic Cost Management and the Value Chain," pp. 8 and 9; and Michael E. Porter, p. 88.

[8]See John Shank and Vijay Govindarajan, "Strategic Cost Management and the Value Chain," p. 9; and M. Hergert and D. Morris, "Accounting Data for Value Chain Analysis," *Strategic Management Journal* 10, no. 5, pp. 175–88.

gerial accounting topics. Other professional organizations in which managerial accountants hold membership include the Financial Executives Institute, the American Institute of Certified Public Accountants, the Institute of Internal Auditors, and the American Accounting Association.

The primary professional association for managerial accountants in Canada is the Society of Management Accountants of Canada (La Société des Comptables en Management du Canada). Great Britain's main professional organization is the Institute of Chartered Management Accountants, and Australia's organization is the Institute of Chartered Accountants in Australia. In all, over 75 countries have professional organizations for their practicing accountants.

Professional Certification

In keeping with the importance of their role and the specialized knowledge they must have, managerial accountants can earn a professional certification. In the United States, the IMA administers the Certified Management Accountant (CMA) program. The requirements for becoming a **Certified Management Accountant** include meeting specified educational requirements and passing the CMA examination.[9] In Canada, a managerial accountant may be certified as a Registered Industrial Accountant (RIA) by the Society of Management Accountants of Canada. Great Britain and many other countries also have professional certification programs for their managerial accountants.

A **Certified Management Accountant** has earned professional certification in managerial accounting.

Professional Ethics

As professionals, managerial accountants have an obligation to themselves, their colleagues, and their organizations to adhere to high standards of ethical conduct. In recognition of this obligation, the IMA developed the following recently revised ethical standards for practitioners of managerial accounting and financial management.[10]

Competence Practitioners of managerial accounting and financial management have a responsibility to:

- Maintain an appropriate level of professional competence by ongoing development of their knowledge and skills.
- Perform their professional duties in accordance with relevant laws, regulations, and technical standards.
- Prepare complete and clear reports and recommendations after appropriate analyses of relevant and reliable information.

Confidentiality Practitioners of managerial accounting and financial management have a responsibility to:

- Refrain from disclosing confidential information acquired in the course of their work except when authorized, unless legally obligated to do so.
- Inform subordinates as appropriate regarding the confidentiality of information acquired in the course of their work and monitor their activities to assure the maintenance of that confidentiality.

---

[9]For information about the CMA program, write to the Institute of Management Accountants, 10 Paragon Drive, Montvale, NJ 07645-0405.

[10]In 1997, the Institute of Management Accountants (IMA) revised its statement of the standards of ethical conduct for practitioners of managerial accounting and financial management. See *Management Accounting* 79, no. 1, pp. 20, 21. The original statement of ethical standards was published in 1983 by the IMA's predecessor, the National Association of Accountants, in its *Statement on Management Accounting, Standards of Ethical Conduct for Management Accountants* (Montvale, NJ: National Association of Accountants, 1983). See also *Management Accounting* 71, no. 12, which is entirely devoted to ethics in managerial accounting.

- Refrain from using or appearing to use confidential information acquired in the course of their work for unethical or illegal advantage either personally or through third parties.

Integrity Practitioners of managerial accounting and financial management have a responsibility to:

- Avoid actual or apparent conflicts of interest and advise all appropriate parties of any potential conflict.
- Refrain from engaging in any activity that would prejudice their ability to carry out their duties ethically.
- Refuse any gift, favor, or hospitality that would influence or appear to influence their actions.
- Refrain from either actively or passively subverting the attainment of the organization's legitimate and ethical objectives.
- Recognize and communicate professional limitations or other constraints that would preclude responsible judgment or successful performance of an activity.
- Communicate unfavorable as well as favorable information and professional judgments or opinions.
- Refrain from engaging in or supporting any activity that would discredit the profession.

Objectivity Practitioners of managerial accounting and financial management have a responsibility to:

- Communicate information fairly and objectively.
- Disclose fully all relevant information that could reasonably be expected to influence an intended user's understanding of the reports, comments, and recommendations presented.

In resolving an ethical problem, the managerial accountant should discuss the situation with his or her immediate supervisor, assuming that individual is not involved in the problem. If the supervisor is involved in the ethical problem, the accountant should discuss the matter with the next higher level of management. Note: *Various problems and cases at the end of each chapter in this text include ethical issues to be resolved. In addressing those issues, readers will need to refer to these ethical standards.*

Chapter Summary

All organizations have goals, and their managers need information as they strive to attain those goals. Information is needed for the management functions of decision making, planning, directing operations, and controlling. Managerial accounting is the process of identifying, measuring, analyzing, interpreting, and communicating information in pursuit of an organization's goals. Managerial accounting is an integral part of the management process, and managerial accountants are important strategic partners in an organization's management team.

Managerial accounting is an important part of any organization's management information system. The five objectives of managerial accounting activity are: (1) providing information for decision making and planning, and proactively participating as part of the management team in the decision-making and planning processes; (2) assisting managers in directing and controlling operations; (3) motivating managers and other employees toward the organization's goals; (4) measuring the performance of activities, subunits, managers, and other employees within the organization; and (5) assessing the organization's competitive position, and working with other managers to ensure the organization's long-run competitiveness in its industry.

Managerial accounting differs from financial accounting in several ways. The users of managerial accounting information are managers inside the organization. Managerial accounting information is not mandatory, is unregulated, and draws on data from the basic accounting system as well as other data sources. The users of financial accounting information are interested parties outside the organization, such as investors and creditors. Financial accounting information is required for publicly held companies, is regulated by the Financial Accounting Standards Board, and is based almost entirely on historical transaction data.

Managerial accounting continually evolves and adapts as the business environment changes. The growth of international competition and dramatic changes in technology are placing ever-greater demands on the information provided by managerial accounting systems. Many organizations have moved away from a historical cost accounting perspective and toward a proactive cost management perspective. Under this approach, the managerial accountant is part of cross-functional management team that seeks to create value for the organization by managing resources, activities, and people to achieve the organization's goals.

Managerial accounting is a profession with a certification process and a code of ethical standards. Managerial accountants are highly trained professionals, who can contribute significantly to the success of any enterprise.

Key Terms

For each term's definition refer to the indicated page, or turn to the glossary at the end of the text.

activity accounting, pg. 18

activity-based costing (ABC), pg. 18

activity-based management (ABM), pg. 18

attention-directing function, pg. 6

Certified Management Accountant (CMA), pg. 21

continuous improvement, pg. 17

controller (or comptroller), pg. 9

cost-accounting system, pg. 8

cost driver, pg. 19

cost management system, pg. 18

empowerment, pg. 6

financial accounting, pg. 8

internal auditor, pg. 10

just-in-time (JIT) production system, pg. 17

line positions, pg. 8

managerial accounting, pg. 4

non-value-added costs, pg. 18

staff positions, pg. 8

strategic cost management, pg. 19

theory of constraints, pg. 19

total quality management (TQM), pg. 17

treasurer, pg. 9

value chain, pg. 18

Review Questions

1–1. List two plausible goals for each of these organizations: American Red Cross, General Motors, J. C. Penney, the City of Pittsburgh, and Hertz.

1–2. List and define the four basic management activities.

1–3. Give examples of each of the four primary management activities in the context of a national fast-food chain.

1–4. Give examples of how each of the objectives of managerial accounting activity would be important in an airline company.

1–5. List and describe four important differences between managerial and financial accounting.

1–6. Distinguish between cost accounting and managerial accounting.

1–7. Distinguish between line and staff positions. Give two examples of each in a university setting.

1–8. Distinguish between the following two accounting positions: controller and treasurer.

1–9. What is meant by the following statement? "Managerial accounting often serves an attention-directing role."

1–10. What is the chief difference between manufacturing and service industry firms?

1–11. Define the following terms: just-in-time, computer-integrated manufacturing, cost management system, empowerment, and total quality management.

1–12. Define and explain the significance of the term *CMA*.

1–13. Briefly explain what is meant by each of the following ethical standards for managerial accountants: competence, confidentiality, integrity, and objectivity.

1–14. What is meant by the term *non-value-added costs*?

1–15. Managerial accounting is an important part of any enterprise's management information system. Name two other information systems that supply information to management.

1–16. Can managerial accounting play an important role in a nonprofit organization? Explain your answer.

1–17. A large manufacturer of electronic machinery stated the following as one of its goals: "The company should become the low-cost producer in its industry." How can managerial accounting help the company achieve this goal?

1–18. What do you think it means to be a professional? In your view, are managerial accountants professionals?

1–19. Name several activities in the value chain of (*a*) a manufacturer of cotton shirts and (*b*) an airline.

1–20. Define the term *strategic cost management*.

Exercises

■ **Exercise 1-21**
Objectives of Managerial
Accounting Activity
(LO 2, LO 3)

For each of the following activities, explain which of the objectives of managerial accounting activity is involved. In some cases, several objectives may be involved.

1. Determining the cost of manufacturing a tennis racket.
2. Measuring the cost of the inventory of compact disk players on hand in a retail electronics store.
3. Developing a bonus reward system for the managers of the various offices run by a large travel agency.
4. Comparing the actual and planned cost of a consulting engagement completed by an engineering firm.
5. Estimating the annual operating cost of a newly proposed branch bank.
6. Measuring the following costs incurred during one month in a hotel owned by a national hospitality-industry firm.
   a. Wages of table-service personnel.
   b. Property taxes.
7. Comparing a hotel's room rate structure, occupancy rate, and restaurant patronage with industry averages.

■ **Exercise 1-22**
Managerial Accounting and
Decision Making
(LO 1, LO 2)

Give an example of managerial accounting information that could help a manager make each of the following decisions.

1. The manager of a discount department store is deciding how many security personnel to employ for the purpose of reducing shoplifting.
2. The county board of representatives is deciding whether to build an addition onto the county library.
3. The president of a rental car agency is deciding whether to add luxury cars to the rental car fleet.
4. The production manager in an automobile plant is deciding whether to have routine maintenance performed on a machine weekly or biweekly.

Problems

■ **Problem 1–23**
Role of the Divisional
Controller
(LO 3, LO 4)

A division manager is responsible for each of Coastal Products Corporation's divisions. Each division's controller, assigned by the corporate controller's office, manages the division's accounting system and provides analysis of financial information for the division manager. The division manager evaluates the performance of the division controller and makes recommendations for salary increases and promotions. However, the final responsibility for promotion evaluation and salary increases rests with the corporate controller.

Each of Coastal's divisions is responsible for product design, sales, pricing, operating expenses, and profit. However, corporate management exercises tight control over divisional financial operations. For example, all capital expenditure above a modest amount must be approved by corporate management. The method of financial reporting from the division to corporate headquarters provides further evidence of the degree of financial control. The division manager and the division controller submit to corporate headquarters separate and independent commentary on the financial results of the division. Corporate management states that the division controller is there to provide an independent view of the division's operations, not as a spy.

Required:

1. Discuss the arrangements for line and staff reporting in Coastal Products Corporation.
2. The division manager for Coastal Products Corporation has a "dual reporting" responsibility. The controller is responsible both to the division manager, who makes recommendations on salary and promotion, *and* to the corporate controller, who has the final say in such matters.
   a. Identify and discuss the factors that make the division controller's role difficult in this type of situation.
   b. Discuss the effect of the dual reporting relationship on the motivation of the divisional controller.

(CMA, adapted)

StereoTech Corporation manufactures printed circuits for stereo amplifiers. A common product defect is a "drift" caused by failure to maintain precise heat levels during the production process. Rejects from the 100 percent testing program can be reworked to acceptable levels if the defect is drift. However, in a recent analysis of customer complaints, Marie Allen, the assistant controller, and the quality control engineer determined that normal rework does not bring the circuits up to standard. Sampling showed that about half of the reworked circuits will fail after extended amplifier operation. The incidence of failure in the reworked circuits is projected to be about 10 percent over five years.

Unfortunately, there is no way to determine which reworked circuits will fail, because testing will not detect the problem. The rework process could be changed to correct the problem, but the cost-benefit analysis for the suggested change indicates that it is not economically feasible. StereoTech's marketing analyst has indicated that this problem will have a significant impact on the company's reputation and customer satisfaction. Consequently, the board of directors would interpret this problem as having serious negative implications for the company's profitability.

Allen included the circuit failure and rework problem in her report prepared for the upcoming quarterly meeting of the board of directors. Due to the potential adverse economic impact, Allen followed a long-standing practice of highlighting this information. After reviewing the reports to be presented, the plant manager and his staff complained to the controller that he should control his people better. "We can't upset the board with this kind of material. Tell Allen to tone that down. Maybe we can get it by the board in this meeting and have some time to work on it. People who buy those cheap systems and play them that loud shouldn't expect them to last forever."

The controller called Allen into his office and said, "Marie, you'll have to bury this one. The probable failure of reworks can be mentioned briefly in the oral presentation, but it should not be mentioned or highlighted in the advance material mailed to the board."

Allen feels strongly that the board will be misinformed on a potentially serious loss of income if she follows the controller's orders. Allen discussed the problem with the quality control engineer, who simply remarked, "That's your problem, Marie."

■ **Problem 1–24**
Quality Control; Ethical Behavior
(LO 4, LO 5, LO 6)

Required:

1. Discuss the ethical considerations that Marie Allen should recognize in deciding how to proceed.
2. Explain what ethical responsibilities should be accepted by: (*a*) the controller, (*b*) the quality control engineer, and (*c*) the plant manager.
3. What should Marie Allen do? Explain your answer.

(CMA, adapted)

The external auditors for Heart Health Procedures (HHP) are currently performing the annual audit of HHP's financial statements. As part of the audit, the external auditors have prepared a representation letter to be signed by HHP's Chief Executive Officer (CEO) and Chief Financial Officer (CFO). The letter provides, among other items, a representation that appropriate provisions have been made for the following:

■ Reductions of any excess or obsolete inventories to appropriate values.
■ Losses from any purchase commitments for inventory quantities in excess of requirements or at prices in excess of market.

■ **Problem 1–25**
Ethical Conduct; Obsolete Inventory; Bonus Plan
(LO 4, LO 6)

HHP began operations by developing a unique balloon process to open obstructed arteries to the heart. In the last several years, HHP's market share has grown significantly because its major competitor was forced to cease its balloon operations by the Food and Drug Administration (FDA). HHP purchases the balloon's primary and most expensive component from a sole supplier. Two years ago, HHP entered into a five-year contract with this supplier at the then current price with inflation adjustments built into each of the five years. The long-term contract was deemed necessary to assure adequate supplies and discourage new competition. However, during the past year, HHP's major competitor developed a technically superior product, which utilizes an innovative, less costly component. This new product was recently approved by the FDA and has been introduced to the medical community, receiving high acceptance. It is expected that HHP's market share will experience a large decline, and that the primary component used in the HHP balloon will decrease in price as a result of the competitor's use of its recently developed superior component. The new component has been licensed by the major competitor to several outside sources of supply to maintain available quantity and price competitiveness. At this time, HHP is investigating the purchase of this new component.

HHP's officers are on a bonus plan that is tied to overall corporate profits. Jim Honig, vice president of manufacturing, is responsible for both manufacturing and warehousing. During the course of the audit, he advised the CEO and CFO that he was neither aware of any obsolete inventory nor any inventory or purchase commitments where current, or expected, prices were significantly below acquisition or commitment prices. Honig took this position even though Marian Nevins, assistant controller, had apprised him of both the existing excess inventory attributable to the declining market share and the significant loss associated with the remaining years of the five-year purchase commitment.

Nevins has brought this situation to the attention of her superior, the controller, who also participates in the bonus plan and reports directly to the CFO. Nevins works closely with the external audit staff and subsequently ascertained that the external audit manager was unaware of the inventory and purchase commitment problems. Nevins is concerned about the situation and is not sure how to handle the matter.

Required:

1. Assuming that the controller did not apprise the CEO and CFO of the situation, explain the ethical considerations of the controller's apparent lack of action by discussing specific standards of ethical conduct for management accountants.

2. Assuming Nevins believes the controller has acted unethically and has not apprised the CEO and CFO of his findings, describe the steps that she should take to resolve the situation.

3. Describe actions that Heart Health Procedures can take to improve the ethical climate within the company.

(CMA, adapted)

Current Issues in Managerial Accounting

■ **Issue 1–26**
Accounting and
Computers

"How CMAs Use the Internet," *Management Accounting Internet/Intranet Supplement,* **1997, Lois Mahoney and Pamela B. Roush.**

Overview
This article summarizes and analyzes management accountants' responses to a survey regarding their computer use. The survey consists of questions involving desktop, e-mail, and Internet applications.

Suggested Discussion Questions
In groups, list 10 ways management accountants use the computer in their jobs. Next, rank the 10 uses from most frequent to least frequent. It is likely that one of the uses you have listed is e-mail. List five to ten ways that management accountants use e-mail. Discuss how the Internet is and should be used by management accountants to achieve their objectives.

■ **Issue 1–27**
Professional Ethics

"IMA Revises SMA 1C, Standards of Ethical Conduct," *Management Accounting,* **July 1997.**

Overview
Recently, the IMA revised its code of ethics. Changes range from recognition of its global applicability to management accounting and financial management to recommendations regarding legal issues.

Suggested Discussion Questions

Individually, list the categories of the IMA's Standards of Ethical Conduct. Write a one-paragraph case involving at least one of the standards. Exchange your case with another member of your class. Write a solution to the case you received by applying the new code's provisions. Present the cases and solutions in class.

"Business Services: Prognosis 1998," *Business Week,* **January 12, 1998.**

Overview

The prognosis for the business service sector in 1998 is very good. According to *Business Week,* there will be a growing number of jobs and opportunities. Accounting firms are consolidating so that they can extend their services globally.

Suggested Discussion Questions

According to the article, corporate restructuring has increased demand for services such as accounting and legal work. Explain why. The article also states that turbulence in Asia has increased demand for business services. Do you think this statement has validity? Why? Who are the winners and losers when the world's largest accounting firms combine?

"Say Good-Bye to the Computer Geek," *Business Week,* **June 23, 1997.**

Overview

Computer innovations such as the PC and the Internet provide tools for researchers that are very powerful, yet portable. The advances have created an environment that has spawned high-quality advanced research from a variety of disciplines.

Suggested Discussion Questions

As a group, list five to ten advancements in accounting that are the result of the PC and the Internet. List five or ten PC- and Internet-related advancements that assist or have assisted you in your education or employment. What is the future of computer-related accounting applications? Provide examples.

"Code May Force CPAs to Inform on Employers," *The Wall Street Journal,* **August 4, 1995, Lee Berton.**

Overview

Management accountants who are CPAs may be forced to become whistle-blowers. Under a proposed professional standard, corporate accountants who are aware that the firm's financial statements are misstated must report the misstatement to superiors, outside auditors, or the Securities and Exchange Commission. Failure to follow these guidelines could result in a loss of the CPA's license.

Suggested Discussion Questions

Role Play: In groups of two, select one member to be a managerial accountant with the other being his/her immediate supervisor. Assume the managerial accountant, a CMA but not a CPA, has discovered a material misstatement in the financial statements. Role play how the managerial accountant should report this information to his/her supervisor. Do the same thing assuming the accountant is a CMA and a CPA.

"Oil Leaks: Global Spy Networks Eavesdrop on Projects of Petroleum Firms," *The Wall Street Journal,* **January 6, 1994, William Carley.**

Overview

British police discovered global spy networks that sought management accounting information. The spies were offering substantial sums of money to Exxon employees in exchange for information regarding Exxon's budgets, potential suppliers, and contract bids.

Suggested Discussion Questions

What does the emergence of these spy networks say about the value of managerial accounting information? What is more valuable, financial or managerial accounting information? What would a managerial accountant's ethical obligation be in a situation in which someone seeking similar information confronts him/her?

■ Issue 1–28
Employment Opportunities in Managerial Accounting

■ Issue 1–29
Accounting and Computers

■ Issue 1–30
Professional Ethics

■ Issue 1–31
Strategic Cost Management and the Value Chain; International; Ethics

2 Chapter Two

Basic Cost Terms and Concepts

After completing this chapter, you should be able to:

1. Explain what is meant by "different costs for different purposes."

2. Describe the behavior of variable and fixed costs, both in total and on a per-unit basis.

3. Understand the concept of a cost driver and the importance of identifying an organization's cost drivers.

4. Distinguish between direct and indirect costs and controllable and uncontrollable costs.

5. Give examples of three types of manufacturing costs.

6. Distinguish between product costs, period costs, and expenses.

7. Describe the role of costs on the income statement and balance sheet of a merchandising company, a manufacturing company, and a service industry firm.

8. Prepare a schedule of cost of goods manufactured, a schedule of cost of goods sold, and an income statement for a manufacturer.

9. Define and give examples of an opportunity cost, an out-of-pocket cost, a sunk cost, a differential cost, a marginal cost, and an average cost.

10. Explain the behavioral tendencies many people show when they encounter opportunity costs and sunk costs.

A GREAT YEAR FOR SOUTHWEST AIRLINES

Dallas, TX—It was another great year for Southwest Airlines. The low-fare, short-haul airline has had a remarkable string of over 25 consecutive profitable years. In spite of very high fuel prices throughout the airline industry, Southwest has managed to continue its high-quality service while holding the line on fares. How does Southwest continue to be so successful in the brutally competitive airline industry? Airline management attributes South-west's amazing success to its employees, who they say have the "Southwest Spirit." But management also talks of its never-ending crusade to lower costs. According to Southwest Airlines sources, "We're a short-haul carrier. Our average aircraft trip is roughly 425 miles, or a little over an hour in duration. Ground transportation is our most significant competitor, and it always has been. We have to have low fares to compete with ground transportation regardless of what our airline competitors charge. Our low-cost leadership within the industry remains comfortably intact, despite our competitors' efforts to lower costs. We remain the low-cost producer in the industry." It is notable, however, that Southwest's cost leadership has not come at the expense of customer satisfaction. The airline has garnered a reputation for safe and reliable operations, on-time service, and the best overall value in the industry.

IT'S INFORMATION TECHNOLOGY FOR WAL-MART

Bentonville, AR—With over $100 billion in sales and income in excess of $3 billion, Wal-Mart continues to be the world's leading merchandiser. What is behind Wal-Mart's phenomenal success? A focus on the customer, a brilliant strategy of locating stores, and a never-ending effort to keep costs low have made Wal-Mart the industry leader. One major reason for the company's low costs is investment in infor-mation technology. With an annual technology and com-munication budget of over a half billion dollars, Wal-Mart leads the retail industry in information technology. A typi-cal Wal-Mart store carries over 70,000 standard items in stock, and every item must be ordered, inventoried, and re-plenished. According to a Wal-Mart senior vice president, "Our technology helps us buy the right merchandise at the right time, and have it in the right place at the right price." The senior vice president goes on to say, "With this tech-nology, we're getting better, quicker, and more accurate information to manage and control every aspect of our business. Wal-Mart has always been intensely conscious of holding down expenses, because that's another way we can have lower prices, better merchandise and service for our customers, and better returns for our investors."

The process of management involves planning, control, decision making, and directing operational activities. Managers can perform each of these functions more effectively with managerial accounting information. Much of this information focuses on the costs incurred in the organization. For example, in *planning* the routes and flight schedules of Southwest Airlines, managers must consider aircraft fuel costs, salaries of flight crews, and airport landing fees. *Controlling* the costs of manufacturing prepared foods requires that H. J. Heinz accountants carefully measure and keep track of production costs. In *making decisions* about locating a new store, Wal-Mart managers need information about the cost of building, maintaining, equipping, and staffing the store. Finally, to *direct operational activities,* managers in all three of these companies need information about the cost of salaries, utilities, security, and a host of other goods and services.

Each of these examples focuses on costs of one type or another. An important first step in studying managerial accounting is to gain an understanding of the various types of costs incurred by organizations. In this chapter, we will study the cost terms, concepts, and classifications routinely used by managerial accountants.

Cost Classifications: Different Costs for Different Purposes

LO 1   Explain what is meant by "different costs for different purposes."

Cost is the sacrifice made, usually measured by the resources given up, to achieve a particular purpose.

The articles at the beginning of this chapter highlight two highly successful companies. Each of these firms owes its success to a variety of factors, such as a focus on the customer and a skilled management team. A relentless effort to control costs, though, also figures prominently in each of these companies' success stories. The first step in controlling costs in any business is achieving a good understanding of the many types of costs incurred.

At the most basic level, a **cost** may be defined as the sacrifice made, usually measured by the resources given up, to achieve a particular purpose. If we look more carefully, though, we find that the word *cost* can have different meanings depending on the context in which it is used. Cost data that are classified and recorded in a particular way for one purpose may be inappropriate for another use. For example, the costs incurred in producing gasoline last year are important in measuring Exxon's income for the year. However, those costs may not be useful in planning the company's refinery operations for the next year if the cost of oil has changed significantly or if the methods of producing gasoline have improved. The important point is that different cost concepts and classifications are used for different purposes. Understanding these concepts and classifications enables the managerial accountant to provide appropriate cost data to the managers who need it.

Fixed and Variable Costs

LO 2   Describe the behavior of variable and fixed costs, both in total and on a per-unit basis.

Activity refers to a measure of an organization's output of goods or services

A variable cost changes in total in direct proportion to a change in the level of activity.

One of the most important cost classifications involves the way a cost changes in relation to changes in the activity of the organization. **Activity** refers to a measure of the organization's output of products or services. The number of automobiles manufactured by General Motors, the number of days of patient care provided by Massachusetts General Hospital, and the number of insurance claims settled by Allstate are all measures of activity. The activities that cause costs to be incurred are also called *cost drivers.*

Variable Costs   A **variable cost** changes in total in direct proportion to a change in the level of activity (or cost driver). If activity increases by 20 percent, total variable cost increases by 20 percent also. For example, the cost of sheet metal used by Chrysler will increase by approximately 5 percent if automobile production increases by 5 percent. The cost of napkins and other paper products used at a Pizza Hut will increase by roughly 10 percent if the restaurant's patronage increases by 10 percent.

A. Graph of Total Variable Cost

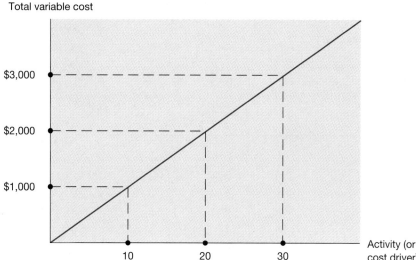

Exhibit 2–1

Variable Cost

B. Tabulation of Variable Cost

Activity (or cost driver)	Variable Cost per Unit	Total Variable Cost
1	$100	$ 100
4	100	400
18	100	1,800
30	100	3,000

Panel A of Exhibit 2–1 displays a graph of a variable cost. As this graph shows, *total* variable cost increases proportionately with activity. When activity doubles, from 10 to 20 units, total variable cost doubles, from $1,000 to $2,000. However, the variable cost *per unit* remains the same as activity changes. The variable cost associated with each unit of activity is $100, whether it is the first unit, the fourth, or the eighteenth. The table in panel B of Exhibit 2–1 illustrates this point.

To summarize, as activity changes, total variable cost increases or decreases proportionately with the activity change, but unit variable cost remains the same.

Fixed Costs   A **fixed cost** remains unchanged in total as the level of activity (or cost driver) varies. If activity increases or decreases by 20 percent, total fixed cost remains the same. Examples of fixed costs include depreciation of plant and equipment at a Texas Instruments factory, the cost of property taxes at a Ramada Inn, and the salary of a subway train operator employed by the New York Transit Authority.

A fixed cost is graphed in panel A of Exhibit 2–2.

From the graph in Exhibit 2–2, it is apparent that *total* fixed cost remains unchanged as activity changes. When activity triples, from 10 to 30 units, total fixed cost remains constant at $1,500. However, the fixed cost *per unit* does change as activity changes. If the activity level is only 1 unit, then the fixed cost per unit is $1,500 per unit ($1,500 ÷ 1). If the activity level is 10 units, then the fixed cost per unit declines to $150 per unit ($1,500 ÷ 10). The behavior of total fixed cost and unit fixed cost is illustrated by the table in panel B of Exhibit 2–2.

Another way of viewing the change in unit fixed cost as activity changes is in a graph, as shown in panel C of Exhibit 2–2. Unit fixed cost declines steadily as activity increases. Notice that the decreases in unit fixed cost when activity changes from 1 to 2 units is much larger than the decrease in unit fixed cost when activity changes from 10 to 11 units or from 20 to 21 units. Thus, the amount of the change in unit fixed cost declines as the activity level increases.

A **fixed cost** does not change in total as activity changes.

Exhibit 2–2

Fixed Cost

A. Graph of Total Fixed Cost

Total fixed cost

$1,500

Activity (or cost driver)

10   20   30

B. Tabulation of Fixed Cost

Activity (or cost driver)	Fixed Cost per Unit	Total Fixed Cost
1	$1,500.00	$1,500
2	750.00	1,500
5	300.00	1,500
10	150.00	1,500
11	136.36*	1,500
20	75.00	1,500
21	71.43*	1,500
30	50.00	1,500

*Rounded.

C. Graph of Unit Fixed Cost

Unit fixed cost

$1,500

$1,000

$ 500

Activity (or cost driver)

10   20   30

To summarize, as the activity level increases, total fixed cost remains constant but unit fixed cost declines. As you will see in subsequent chapters, it is vital in managerial accounting to thoroughly understand the behavior of both total fixed costs and unit fixed costs.

In tracking costs in the production of this Deere equipment, the company identifies a variety of cost drivers.

Cost Drivers at Deere and Company

Deere and Company is the leading manufacturer of heavy equipment for agriculture, forestry, and construction. Examples of cost drivers used in Deere's Harvester Works and Component Works are the following:[1]

Activity	Cost Driver
Machining operations	Machine hours
Setup	Setup hours
Production scheduling	Manufacturing orders
Inspection	Pieces inspected

Management Accounting Practice

Cost Drivers at Fisher Controls

Fisher Controls is the leading manufacturer of process control devices for the chemical, petroleum, and pulp and paper industries. Fisher Controls' cost drivers include these:[2]

Activity	Cost Driver
Purchasing	Purchase orders
Shop order handling	Shop orders
Valve assembly support	Customer requisitions
Inspection	Number of operations

Management Accounting Practice

---

[1] John B. MacArthur, "Activity-Based Costing: How Many Cost Drivers Do You Want?" *Journal of Cost Management* 6, no. 3, p. 38.

[2] Ibid., p. 40.

Identifying Cost Drivers

LO 3   Understand the concept of a cost driver and the importance of identifying an organization's cost drivers.

A **cost driver** is a characteristic of an activity or event that causes costs to be incurred by that activity or event.

An important first step in understanding the cost behavior in any organization is identifying the cost drivers upon which various types of costs depend. A **cost driver** is a characteristic of an activity or event that causes costs to be incurred by that activity or event. In most organizations different types of costs respond to widely differing cost drivers. For example, in a manufacturing firm the cost of assembly labor would be driven by the quantity of products manufactured as well as the number of parts in each product. In contrast, the cost of machine setup labor would be driven by the number of production runs. The cost of material-handling labor would be driven by material-related factors such as the quantity and cost of raw material used, the number of parts in various products, and the number of raw-material shipments received. Thus, it may be an oversimplification to lump all manufacturing labor costs together and say that they are driven by the quantity of products manufactured. In state-of-the-art cost management systems, accountants are careful to separate various types of costs into different cost pools and identify the most appropriate cost driver for each cost pool.

In identifying a cost driver, the managerial accountant should consider the extent to which a cost or pool of costs varies in accordance with the cost driver. The higher the correlation between the cost and the cost driver, the more accurate will be the resulting understanding of cost behavior. Another important consideration is the cost of measuring the cost driver. Thus, there is a cost-benefit trade-off in the identification of cost drivers. As the number of cost drivers used in explaining an organization's cost behavior increases, the accuracy of the resulting information will increase. However, the cost of the information will increase also. The concept of a cost driver will be an important aspect of many of the topics discussed in subsequent chapters. The examples on this and the previous page illustrate the identification of cost drivers in both the manufacturing and service sectors.

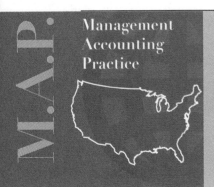

Management Accounting Practice

Cost Drivers in the Airline Industry

A recent study of the airline industry revealed that two distinct types of cost drivers have significant effects on an airline's costs.[3] *Volume-based cost drivers* include (1) aircraft capacity, including both passenger and cargo capacity, and (2) number of passengers. *Operations-based cost drivers* include the following characteristics of an airline's operations: (1) product-line diversity, as measured by route density—"by increasing the number of flights over its network, a carrier is offering a more diversified set of services"; (2) degree of hub concentration, which refers to the extent to which an airline structures its "route systems so that many flights arrive and depart hubs within a few hours of each other, with passengers and cargo exchanging planes in between"; and (3) hub domination, which is the extent to which an airline is able to monopolize, and thus control, the facilities and services at its hub airports.

Direct and Indirect Costs

LO 4   Distinguish between direct and indirect costs and controllable and uncontrollable costs.

A **direct cost** can be traced to a particular department

An important objective of managerial accounting is to assist managers in controlling costs. Sometimes cost control is facilitated by tracing costs to the department or work center in which the cost was incurred. Such tracing of costs to departments is known as *responsibility accounting*. A cost that can be traced to a particular department is called a **direct cost** of the department.

For example, the salary of an auto mechanic is a direct cost of the automotive service department in a Sears department store. The cost of paint used in the painting department of a Toyota plant is a direct cost of the painting department.

---

[3] This illustration is from R. Banker and H. Johnston, "An Empirical Study of Cost Drivers in the U.S. Airline Industry." *The Accounting Review* 68, no. 3, pp. 576–601.

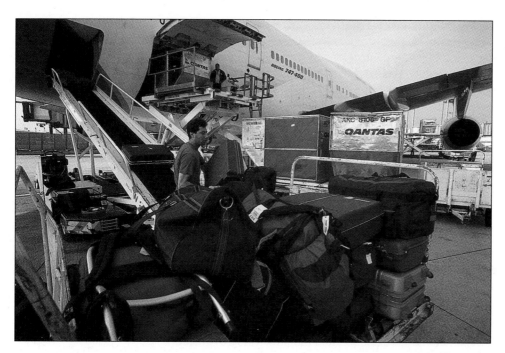

Cost drivers in the airline industry are complex. The capacity of an airplane and its passenger load drive costs, but so do a variety of other factors related to the airline's operations.

A cost that is not directly traceable to a particular department is called an **indirect cost** of the department. The costs of national advertising for Walt Disney World are indirect costs of each of the departments or subunits of the recreational complex, such as the Magic Kingdom and Epcot Center. The salary of a General Electric company plant manager is an indirect cost of each of the plant's production departments. The plant manager's duties are important to the smooth functioning of each of the plant's departments, but there is no way to trace a portion of the plant manager's salary cost to each department.

*An **indirect cost** cannot be traced to a particular department.*

Whether a cost is a direct cost or an indirect cost of a department often depends on which department is under consideration. A cost can be a direct cost of one department or subunit in the organization but an indirect cost of other departments. While the salary of the General Electric Company plant manager is an *indirect* cost of the plant's departments, the manager's salary is a *direct* cost of the plant.

The cost of the raw material used by a manufacturer such as Hewlett-Packard is largely controllable by the manufacturer.

An important objective of a *cost management system* is to trace as many costs as possible directly to the activities that cause them to be incurred. Sometimes called *activity accounting,* this process is vital to management's objective of eliminating *non-value-added costs.* These are costs of activities that can be eliminated without deterioration of product quality, performance, or perceived value.

Controllable and Uncontrollable Costs

Another cost classification that can be helpful in cost control involves the controllability of a cost item by a particular manager. If a manager can control or heavily influence the level of a cost, then that cost is classified as

LO 4   Distinguish between direct and indirect costs and controllable and uncontrollable costs.

> A **controllable cost** is subject to the control or substantial influence of a particular individual.

a **controllable cost** of that manager. Costs that a manager cannot influence significantly are classified as *uncontrollable costs* of that manager. Many costs are not completely under the control of any individual. In classifying costs as controllable or uncontrollable, managerial accountants generally focus on a manager's ability to influence costs. The question is not, Who controls the cost? But, Who is in the best position to influence the level of a cost item? Exhibit 2–3 lists several cost items along with their typical classification as controllable or uncontrollable.

Some costs may be controllable in the long run but not in the short run. For example, the long-term costs associated with computing equipment leased by a hospital are controllable when the 10-year lease is negotiated. In the short run, however, after the lease is signed, the rental costs are uncontrollable until the lease period ends.

Manufacturing Costs

> **LO 5**   Give examples of three types of manufacturing costs.

To assist managers in planning and cost control, managerial accountants classify costs by the functional area of the organization to which costs relate. Some examples of functional areas are manufacturing, service production, merchandise, marketing, administration, and research and development.

Manufacturing costs are further classified into the following three categories: direct material, direct labor, and manufacturing overhead.

> **Direct material** is raw material that is physically incorporated into the finished product.
>
> **Direct-labor cost** is the cost of salaries, wages, and fringe benefits for personnel who work directly on the manufactured products.

Direct Material   Raw material that is consumed in the manufacturing process, is physically incorporated in the finished product, and can be traced to products conveniently is called **direct material**. Examples include the sheet metal in a General Electric refrigerator and the paper in a *Sports Illustrated* magazine.

Some students are confused by the seemingly interchangeable use of the terms *raw material* and *direct material*. However, there is a difference in the meaning of these terms. *Before* material is entered into the production process, it is called *raw* material. *After* it enters production, it becomes *direct* material. Thus, the cost of raw material *used* is equal to the direct-material cost.

Direct Labor   The cost of salaries, wages, and fringe benefits for personnel who work directly on the manufactured products is classified as **direct-labor cost.** Examples include the wages of personnel who assemble Compaq computers and who operate the equipment in a Standard Oil Company refinery.

The cost of fringe benefits for direct-labor personnel, such as employer-paid health-insurance premiums and the employer's pension contributions, should also be classified as direct-labor costs. Such costs are just as much a part of the employees' compensation as are their regular wages. Although conceptually correct, this treatment of fringe benefits is not always observed in practice. Many companies classify all fringe-benefit costs as overhead, which is defined next.

Exhibit 2–3 Controllable and Uncontrollable Costs	Cost Item	Manager	Classification
	Cost of raw material used to produce circuit boards in a Hewlett-Packard factory	Supervisor of the production department for circuit boards	Controllable (The production supervisor can exercise some control over the quantity of material used by ensuring that waste and defective units are minimized.)
	Cost of food used in a McDonald's restaurant	Restaurant manager	Controllable (The restaurant manager exercises some control over the quantity of food used by scheduling production to ensure that excess food is not produced and wasted.)
	Cost of national advertising for the Hertz car rental company	Manager of the Hertz rental agency at the Syracuse airport	Uncontrollable
	Cost of national accounting and data processing operations for JCPenney	Manager of a JCPenney store in Gainesville, Florida	Uncontrollable

Manufacturing Overhead   All other costs of manufacturing are classified as **manufacturing overhead,** which includes three types of costs: indirect material, indirect labor, and other manufacturing costs.

Indirect Material   The cost of materials that are required for the production process but do not become an integral part of the finished product are classified as **indirect material** costs. An example is the cost of drill bits used in a metal-fabrication shop. The drill bits wear out and are discarded, but they do not become part of the product. Materials that do become an integral part of the finished product but are insignificant in cost are also often classified as indirect material. Materials such as glue or paint may be so inexpensive that it is not worth tracing their costs to specific products as direct materials.

Indirect Labor   The costs of personnel who do not work directly on the product, but whose services are necessary for the manufacturing process, are classified as **indirect labor.** Such personnel include production department supervisors, custodial employees, and security guards.

Other Manufacturing Costs   All other manufacturing costs that are neither material nor labor costs are classified as manufacturing overhead. These costs include depreciation of plant and equipment, property taxes, insurance, and utilities such as electricity, as well as the costs of operating service departments. **Service departments** are those that do not work directly on manufacturing products but are necessary for the manufacturing process to occur. Examples include equipment-maintenance departments and computer-aided-design (CAD) departments. In some manufacturing firms, departments are referred to as *work centers.*

Other manufacturing overhead costs include overtime premiums and the cost of idle time. An **overtime premium** is the extra compensation paid to an employee who works beyond the time normally scheduled. Suppose an electronics technician who assembles radios earns $16.00 per hour. The technician works 48 hours during a week instead of the scheduled time of 40 hours. The overtime pay scale is time and a half, or 150 percent of the regular wage. The technician's compensation for the week is classified as follows:

Direct-labor cost ($16 × 48)	$768
Overhead (overtime premium: ½ × $16 × 8)	64
Total compensation paid	$832

Only the *extra* compensation of $8 per hour is classified as overtime premium. The regular wage of $16 per hour is treated as direct labor, even for the eight overtime hours.

Idle time is time that is not spent productively by an employee due to such events as equipment breakdowns or new setups of production runs. Such idle time is an unavoidable feature of most manufacturing processes. The cost of an employee's idle time is classified as overhead so that it may be spread across all production jobs, rather than being associated with a particular production job. Suppose that during one 40-hour shift, a machine breakdown resulted in idle time of 1½ hours and a power failure idled workers for an additional ½ hour. If an employee earns $14 per hour, the employee's wages for the week will be classified as follows:

Direct-labor cost ($14 × 38)	$532
Overhead (idle time: $14 × 2)	28
Total compensation paid	$560

Both overtime premiums and the cost of idle time should be classified as manufacturing overhead, rather than associated with a particular production job, because the particular job on which idle time or overtime may occur tends to be selected at random. Suppose several production jobs are scheduled during an eight-hour shift, and the last job remains unfinished at the end of the shift. The overtime to finish the last job is necessitated by all of the jobs scheduled during the shift, not just the last one. Similarly,

Manufacturing overhead is all manufacturing costs other than direct-material and direct-labor cost.

Indirect materials are required for the production process but do not become an integral part of the finished product; or are materials consumed in production but insignificant in cost.

Indirect labor is the cost of personnel who do not work directly on the product, but whose services are necessary for the manufacturing process.

Service departments are subunits that are not directly involved in producing the organization's output of goods and services.

Overtime premium is the extra compensation paid to an employee who works beyond the normal period of time.

Idle time is unproductive time spent by employees due to factors beyond their control, such as power outages and machine breakdowns.

Conversion costs are direct-labor costs plus manufacturing-overhead costs.

Prime costs are the costs of direct material and direct labor.

if a power failure occurs during one of several production jobs, the idle time that results is not due to the job that happens to be in process at the time. The power failure is a random event, and the resulting cost should be treated as a cost of all of the department's production.

To summarize, manufacturing costs include direct material, direct labor, and manufacturing overhead. Direct labor and overhead are often called **conversion costs,** since they are the costs of "converting" raw material into finished products. Direct material and direct labor are often referred to as **prime costs.**

Production Costs in Service Industry Firms and Nonprofit Organizations

Service industry firms and many nonprofit organizations are also engaged in production. What distinguishes these organizations from manufacturers is that a service is consumed as it is produced, whereas a manufactured product can be stored in inventory. Such businesses as hotels, banks, airlines, professional sports franchises, and automotive repair shops are in the business of producing services. Similarly, nonprofit organizations such as the American Red Cross or the Greater Miami Opera Association also are engaged in service production. While less commonly observed in service firms, the same cost classifications used in manufacturing companies can be applied. For example, an airline produces air transportation services. Direct material includes such costs as jet fuel, aircraft parts, and food and beverages. Direct labor includes the salaries of the flight crew and the wages of aircraft-maintenance personnel. Overhead costs include depreciation of baggage-handling equipment, insurance, and airport landing fees.

The process of recording and classifying costs is important in service industry firms and nonprofit organizations for the same reasons as in manufacturing firms. Cost analysis is used in pricing banking and insurance services, locating travel and car-rental agencies, setting enrollment targets in universities, and determining cost reimbursements in hospitals. As such organizations occupy an ever-growing role in our economy, applying managerial accounting to their activities will take on ever-greater importance.

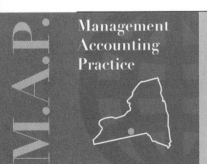

Management Accounting Practice

M.A.P.

Arnot Ogden Memorial Hospital

An article in *Business Week* reported that hospitals now track costs patient by patient, doctor by doctor, and disease by disease.[4] Hospitals employ computerized databases to help them organize and maintain the data they need to make cost-effective decisions in treating patients. For example, at Arnot Ogden Memorial Hospital in Elmira, New York, when a pharmacist fills a prescription, the data also are entered directly into the patient's computer file. Doctors also can place information on a patient's treatment directly into the patient's file. As a result, the hospital's accounting department can immediately determine the cost of a patient's treatment. Similarly, the hospital's accounting personnel can track treatment costs for each type of disease and each doctor who uses the hospital.

LO 6   Distinguish between product costs, period costs, and expenses.

An **expense** is the consumption of assets for generating revenue.

Product Costs, Period Costs, and Expenses

An important issue in both managerial and financial accounting is the timing with which the costs of acquiring assets or services are recognized as expenses. An **expense** is defined as the cost incurred when an asset is used up or sold for the purpose of generating revenue. The terms *product cost* and *period cost* are used to describe the timing with which various expenses are recognized.

---

[4] The Medicare Squeeze Pushes Hospitals into the Information Age," *Business Week,* no. 2847, pp. 87–90.

Hospitals track medical costs by patient, by doctor, and by disease.

A **product cost** is a cost assigned to goods that were either purchased or manufactured for resale. The product cost is used to value the inventory of manufactured goods or merchandise until the goods are sold. In the period of the sale, the product costs are recognized as an expense called **cost of goods sold.** The product cost of merchandise inventory acquired by a retailer or wholesaler for resale consists of the purchase cost of the inventory plus any shipping charges. The product cost of manufactured inventory consists of direct material, direct labor, and manufacturing overhead. For example, the labor cost of a production employee at Texas Instruments is included as a product cost of the calculators manufactured. Exhibit 2–4 illustrates the relationship between product costs and cost-of-goods-sold expense.

Another term for product cost is **inventoriable cost,** since a product cost is stored as the cost of inventory until the goods are sold. In addition to retailers, wholesalers, and manufacturers, the concept of product cost is relevant to other producers of inventoriable goods. Agricultural firms, lumber companies, and mining firms are examples of nonmanufacturers that produce inventoriable goods. Apples, timber, coal, and other such goods are inventoried at their product cost until the time period during which they are sold.

All costs that are not product costs are called **period costs.** These costs are identified with the period of time in which they are incurred rather than with units of purchased or produced goods. Period costs are recognized as expenses during the time period in which they are incurred. All research and development, selling, and administrative costs are treated as period costs. This is true in manufacturing, retail, and service industry firms.

Research and development costs include all costs of developing new products and services. The costs of running laboratories, building prototypes of new products, and testing new products are all classified as research and development (or R&D) costs. *Selling costs* include salaries, commissions and travel costs of sales personnel, and the costs of advertising and promotion. *Administrative costs* refer to all costs of running the organization as a whole. The salaries of top-management personnel and the costs of the accounting, legal, and public relations activities are examples of administrative costs.

Exhibit 2–5 illustrates the nature of period costs.

A **product cost** is a cost assigned to goods either purchased or manufactured for resale.

Cost of goods sold is the expense measured by the cost of the finished goods sold during a period of time.

An **inventoriable cost** is another name for a product cost, and it is stored as the cost of inventory until the goods are sold.

Period costs are expensed during the time period in which they are incurred.

Exhibit 2–4

Product Costs and Cost of
Goods Sold

At the end of Year 1, any
inventory on hand is an
asset, which is valued
at its **product cost.**

**Retailer
or
Wholesaler**

Merchandise is acquired:
product cost is equal
to the cost of purchase
plus transportation
cost.

Merchandise is sold:
expense called **cost of
goods sold** is equal to
the product cost
identified with the
merchandise sold.

Year 1   **Year 2**   **Time**

Manufacturer

Goods are manufactured:
product cost is equal
to manufacturing
costs of direct material,
direct labor, and
manufacturing overhead.

Goods are sold:
expense called **cost of
goods sold** is equal to
the product cost
identified with the
goods sold.

At the end of Year 1, any
inventory on hand is an
asset, which is valued
at its **product cost.**

Exhibit 2–5

Period Costs

Period costs, such
as selling and
administrative costs,
incurred in Year 1 are
recognized as **expenses**
in Year 1.

Period costs incurred in
Year 2 are recognized as
expenses in Year 2.

Year 1   **Year 2**   **Time**

Period costs are treated the
same way in all types of
companies: retailers and
wholesalers, manufacturers,
and service industry firms.

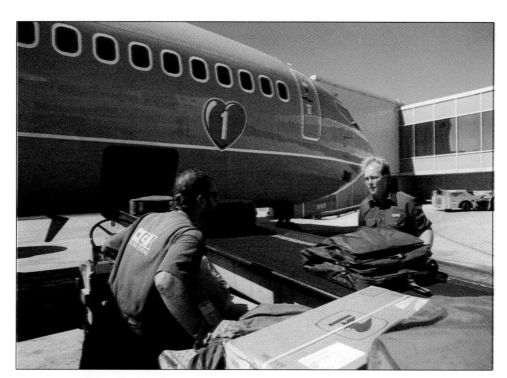

It is critical for a service company such as Southwest Airlines to keep track of its operating costs.

Costs on Financial Statements

The distinction between product costs and period costs is emphasized by examining financial statements from three different types of firms.

> **LO 7** Describe the role of costs on the income statement and balance sheet of a merchandising company, a manufacturing company, and a service industry firm.

Income Statement

Exhibit 2–6 displays recent income statements, in highly summarized form, from H. J. Heinz Company, Wal-Mart Stores, Inc. and Southwest Airlines Company. These companies are from three different industries. H. J. Heinz is a food processing company. Wal-Mart Stores is a large retail firm with merchandising operations throughout most of the nation. Representing the service industry is Southwest Airlines, a major airline serving the southwestern United States.

Selling and administrative costs are period costs on all three income statements shown in Exhibit 2–6. For example, H. J. Heinz lists $2,049,336,000 of selling and administrative expenses. Travel agency commissions, a selling expense on Southwest Airlines' income statement, amount to $140,940,000.

For H. J. Heinz, the costs of processed food inventory are product costs. Direct-material, direct-labor, and manufacturing-overhead costs are stored in inventory until the time period when the products are sold. Then the product costs of the inventory sold become cost of goods sold, an expense on the income statement.

Product costs for Wal-Mart include all costs of acquiring merchandise inventory for resale. These product costs are stored in inventory until the time period during which the merchandise is sold. Then these costs become cost of goods sold. (Wal-Mart uses the term "cost of sales.")

There are no inventoried product costs at Southwest Airlines. Although this firm does engage in the production of air transportation services, its service output is

Exhibit 2–6

Income Statements from Three Different Industries (all figures in thousands of dollars)

H. J. HEINZ COMPANY
Statement of Income for a Recent Year

Value measured by product costs →

Sales	$9,112,265
Cost of goods sold	5,775,357
Gross profit	$3,336,908
Less: Selling, general, and administrative expenses	2,049,336
Operating income	$1,287,572
Add: Interest income	44,824
Less: Interest expense	277,411
Less: Other expense, net	31,324
Income before income taxes	$1,023,661
Provision for income taxes	364,342
Net income	$ 659,319

WAL-MART STORES, INC.
Statement of Income for a Recent Year

Value measured by product costs →

Revenues:	
Net sales	$104,859,000
Other revenue (net)	1,287,000
Total	$106,146,000
Less expenses:	
Cost of sales	83,663,000
Operating, selling, and general and administrative expenses	16,788,000
Interest expense	845,000
Income before income taxes	$ 4,850,000
Provision for income taxes	1,794,000
Net income	$ 3,056,000

SOUTHWEST AIRLINES COMPANY
Statement of Income for a Recent Year

Operating revenue:	
Passenger	$3,269,238
Freight	80,005
Other	56,927
Total operating revenue	$3,406,170
Operating expenses:	
Salaries, wages, and benefits	$ 999,719
Fuel and oil	484,673
Maintenance materials and repairs	253,521
Agency commissions	140,940
Aircraft rentals	190,663
Landing fees and other rentals	187,600
Depreciation	183,470
Other operating expenses	614,749
Total operating expenses	$3,055,335
Operating income	$ 350,835
Other expenses (income):	
Interest expense	$ 59,269
Capitalized interest	(22,267)
Interest income	(25,797)
Nonoperating (gains) losses, net	(1,732)
Total other expenses	$ 9,473
Income before income taxes	$ 341,362
Provision for income taxes	134,025
Net income	$ 207,337

H. J. HEINZ COMPANY Partial Balance Sheet at the End of a Recent Year		
Current assets:		
Cash and cash equivalents		$ 90,064
Short-term investments		18,316
Accounts receivable (net)		1,207,874
Inventories:		
Finished goods and work in process		1,115,367
Raw material (packaging material and ingredients)		378,596
Prepaid expenses		221,669
Other current assets		14,806
Total current assets		$3,046,692

Value measured by product costs → (points to Heinz assets)

WAL-MART STORES, INC. Partial Balance Sheet at the End of a Recent Year		
Current assets:		
Cash and cash equivalents		$ 883,000
Receivables		845,000
Inventories		15,897,000
Prepaid expenses and other		368,000
Total current assets		$17,993,000

Value measured by product costs → (points to Wal-Mart assets)

Exhibit 2–7

Partial Balance Sheets for a Manufacturer and a Retailer (all figures in thousands of dollars)

consumed as soon as it is produced. Service industry firms, such as Southwest Airlines, Chase Manhattan Bank, Sheraton Hotels, Nationwide Insurance, and Burger King, generally refer to the costs of producing services as **operating expenses.** Operating expenses are treated as period costs and are expensed during the periods in which they are incurred. Southwest Airlines includes costs such as employee wages, aviation fuel, and aircraft maintenance in operating expenses for the period.

Operating expenses are costs incurred to produce services.

Balance Sheet

Since retailers, wholesalers, and manufacturers sell inventoriable products, their balance sheets are also affected by product costs. Exhibit 2–7 displays the current-assets section from recent balance sheets of H. J. Heinz and Wal-Mart. Included in the current-assets section of each of these balance sheets is inventory. Manufacturers, such as H. J. Heinz, have three types of inventory. **Raw-material** inventory includes all materials before they are placed into production. **Work-in-process** inventory refers to manufactured products that are only partially completed at the date when the balance sheet is prepared. **Finished-goods** inventory refers to manufactured goods that are complete and ready for sale. The values of the work-in-process and finished-goods inventories are measured by their product costs.

On the Wal-Mart balance sheet, the cost of acquiring merchandise is listed as the value of the merchandise inventories.

Raw material is material that will be entered into a manufacturing process.

Work in process is partially completed products not yet ready for sale.

Finished goods are completed products awaiting sale.

Cost Flows in a Manufacturing Company

Direct material, direct labor, and manufacturing overhead are the three types of production costs incurred by manufacturers. These costs are product costs because they are stored in inventory until the time period when the manufacturer's products are sold. Manufacturers have product-costing systems to keep track of the flow of these costs from the time production begins until finished products are sold. This flow of manufacturing costs is depicted in Exhibit 2–8. As direct material is consumed in production, its cost is added to work-in-process inventory. Similarly, the costs of direct labor and manufacturing overhead are accumulated in work in process. When products are finished, their costs are transferred from work-in-process inventory to finished-

Exhibit 2–8

Flow of Manufacturing Costs

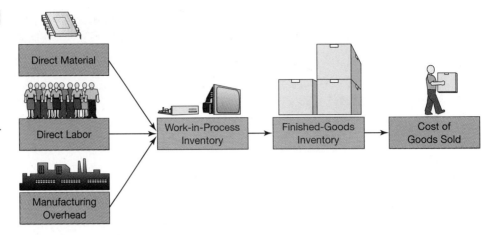

Product costs . . .   . . . are stored in inventory . . .   . . . until the products are sold.

The **schedule of cost of goods manufactured** is a detailed listing of the manufacturing costs incurred during an accounting period and showing the change in work-in-process inventory.

The **schedule of cost of goods sold** is a detailed schedule showing the costs of goods sold and change in finished-goods inventory during an accounting period.

goods inventory. The costs then are stored in finished goods until the time period when the products are sold. At that time, the product costs are transferred from finished goods to cost of goods sold, which is an expense of the period when the sale is made. Exhibit 2–8 concentrates on the conceptual basis of a product-costing system. The detailed procedures and ledger accounts used to keep track of product costs are covered in Chapters 3 and 4.

Manufacturers generally prepare a **schedule of cost of goods manufactured** and a **schedule of cost of goods sold** to summarize the flow of manufacturing costs during an accounting period. These schedules are intended for internal use by management and are generally not made available to the public. Exhibit 2–9 shows these two schedules along with an income statement for an illustrative manufacturer that we will call Ringo Percussion Instruments.

LO 8   Prepare a schedule of cost of goods manufactured, a schedule of cost of goods sold, and an income statement for a manufacturer

Economic Characteristics of Costs

LO 9   Define and give examples of an opportunity cost, an out-of-pocket cost, a sunk cost, a differential cost, a marginal cost, and an average cost.

In addition to accounting cost classifications, such as product costs and period costs, managerial accountants also employ economic concepts in classifying costs. Such concepts are often useful in helping accountants decide what cost information is relevant to the decisions faced by the organization's managers. Several of the most important economic cost concepts are discussed next.

Opportunity Costs

An **opportunity cost** is the potential benefit given up when the choice of one action precludes selection of a different action.

An **opportunity cost** is defined as the benefit that is sacrificed when the choice of one action precludes taking an alternative course of action. If beef and fish are the available choices for dinner, the opportunity cost of eating beef is the forgone pleasure associated with eating fish.

Opportunity costs arise in many business decisions. For example, suppose a baseball manufacturer receives a special order for softballs from the city of Boston. If the firm accepts the softball order, it will not have enough productive capacity (labor and machine time) to produce its usual output of baseballs for sale to a large chain of sporting-goods stores. The opportunity cost of accepting the softball order is the forgone benefit from the baseball production that cannot be achieved. This forgone benefit is measured by the potential revenue from the baseball sales minus the cost of manufacturing the baseballs.

Exhibit 2–9

Manufacturing Cost Schedules

RINGO PERCUSSION INSTRUMENTS
Schedule of Cost of Goods Manufactured
For the Year Ended December 31, 19x9

Direct material:		
Raw-material inventory, January 1	$ 10,000	
Add: Purchases of raw material	100,000	
Raw material available for use	$110,000	
Deduct: raw-material inventory, December 31	5,000	
Raw material used		$105,000
Direct labor		200,000
Manufacturing overhead:		
Indirect material	$ 8,000	
Indirect labor	17,000	
Depreciation on factory	50,000	
Depreciation on equipment	20,000	
Utilities	15,000	
Insurance	5,000	
Total manufacturing overhead		115,000
Total manufacturing costs		$420,000
Add: Work-in-process inventory, January 1		25,000
Subtotal		$445,000
Deduct: Work-in-process inventory, December 31		30,000
Cost of goods manufactured*		$415,000

*Notice the formula used to compute cost of goods manufactured:

Beginning inventory of work in process + Total manufacturing costs − Ending inventory of work in process = Cost of goods manufactured

RINGO PERCUSSION INSTRUMENTS
Schedule of Cost of Goods Sold
For the Year Ended December 31, 19x9

Finished-goods inventory, January 1	$ 80,000
Add: Cost of goods manufactured*	415,000
Cost of goods available for sale	$495,000
Finished-goods inventory, December 31	70,000
Cost of goods sold†	$425,000

*From the Schedule of Cost of Goods Manufactured.

†Notice the formula used to compute cost of goods sold:

Beginning inventory of finished goods + Cost of goods manufactured − Ending inventory of finished goods = Cost of goods sold

RINGO PERCUSSION INSTRUMENTS
Income Statement
For the Year Ended December 31, 19x9

Sales revenue	$700,000
Less: Cost of goods sold*	425,000
Gross margin	$275,000
Selling and administrative expenses	175,000
Income before taxes	$100,000
Income tax expense	40,000
Net income	$ 60,000

*From the Schedule of Cost of Goods Sold.

Opportunity costs also arise in personal decisions. The opportunity cost of a student's college education includes the salary that is forgone as a result of not taking a full-time job during the student's years in college.

From an economic perspective, a dollar of opportunity cost associated with an action should be treated as equivalent to a dollar of out-of-pocket cost. **Out-of-pocket costs** are those that require the payment of cash or other assets as a result of their incurrence. The out-of-pocket costs associated with the softball order consist of the manufacturing costs required to produce the softballs. In making the decision to accept or reject the softball order, the firm's management should consider *both* the out-of-pocket cost and the opportunity cost of the order.

> **Out-of-pocket costs** require the expenditure of cash or other assets.

Studies by behavioral scientists and economists have shown that many people have a tendency to ignore or downplay the importance of opportunity costs. For example, in one study people were asked if they would pay $500 for two 50-yard-line tickets to the Super Bowl. Most people responded that they would not. However, many of the same people said that they would not sell the Super Bowl tickets for $500 if they were given the tickets free of charge. These people refused to incur the $500 *out-of-pocket cost* of buying the Super Bowl tickets. However, they were willing to incur the $500 *opportunity cost* of going to the game rather than sell the tickets. In each case a couple that attends the game ends up $500 poorer than a couple that does not attend the game. (Try surveying your friends with this scenario.)

> **LO 10**   Explain the behavioral tendencies many people show when they encounter opportunity costs and sunk costs.

Behavior such as that illustrated in the Super Bowl example is economically inconsistent. Ignoring or downplaying the importance of opportunity costs can result in inconsistent and faulty business decisions.

Sunk Costs

Sunk costs are costs that have been incurred in the past. Consequently, they do not affect future costs and cannot be changed by any current or future action. Examples of such costs include the acquisition cost of equipment previously purchased and the manufacturing cost of inventory on hand. Regardless of the current usefulness of the equipment or the inventory, the costs of acquiring them cannot be changed by any prospective action. Hence these costs are irrelevant to all future decisions.

> **Sunk costs** have been incurred in the past and cannot be altered by any current or future decision.

Suppose, for example, that a university's traffic department purchased a minicomputer to assist in the vehicle registration process. A year has passed, the computer's warranty has expired, and the computer is not working well. An investigation reveals that this brand of computer is very sensitive to humidity and temperature changes. The traffic department is located in an old building with poor heating and no air-conditioning. As a result, the computer works only intermittently, repair bills have been high, and the office staff is fed up. The officer manager requests that the department director junk the computer and instruct the staff to return to the old manual registration system. The director responds by insisting, "We can't afford to junk the computer! We paid $3,400 for it."

This illustration is a typical example of the inappropriate attention paid to sunk costs. The $3,400 paid for the minicomputer is sunk. No future decision about the computer or the office's procedures can affect that cost. Future decisions should be based on future costs, such as the computer repair bills or the costs of upgrading the building's heating and air-conditioning systems.

Although it is incorrect, from an economic perspective, to allow sunk costs to affect future decisions, people often do so. It is human nature to attempt to justify past decisions. When there is a perceived need to demonstrate competence, either to themselves or to others, managers may seek to justify their decisions. The response of the traffic department director that "We can't afford to junk the computer!" may represent the director's need to justify the past decision to purchase the computer. It is important for managerial accountants to be

> **LO 10**   Explain the behavioral tendencies many people show when they encounter opportunity costs and sunk costs.

aware of such behavioral tendencies. Such an awareness enables the accountant to prepare the most relevant data for managers' decisions and, sometimes, to assist the managers in using the information.

Differential Costs

A **differential cost** is the amount by which the cost differs under two alternative actions. Suppose, for example, that a county government is considering two competing sites for a new landfill. If the northern site is chosen, the annual cost of transporting refuse to the site is projected at $85,000. If the southern site is selected, annual transportation charges are expected to be $70,000. The annual differential cost of transporting refuse is calculated as follows:

LO 9 Define and give examples of an opportunity cost, an out-of-pocket cost, a sunk cost, a differential cost, a marginal cost, and an average cost.

Annual cost of transporting refuse to northern site	$85,000
Annual cost of transporting refuse to southern site	70,000
Annual differential cost	$15,000

A differential cost is also known as an **incremental cost.** In the landfill example, the annual incremental cost of refuse transportation is $15,000 if the site is moved from the southern location to the northern location. Differential or incremental costs are found in a variety of economic decisions. The additional cost incurred by Gulliver's Travels, a travel agency, in locating a new office in the suburbs is the incremental cost of the new business location. The difference in the total cost incurred by the travel agency with or without the suburban location is the differential cost of the decision whether to establish the new office. Decisions about establishing new airline routes, adding additional shifts in a manufacturing firm, or increasing the nursing staff in a hospital all involve differential costs.

A **differential cost** is the difference in a cost item under two decision alternatives.

An **incremental cost** is the amount by which the cost of one action exceeds that of another.

Marginal Costs and Average Costs

A special case of the differential-cost concept is the **marginal cost,** which is the extra cost incurred when one additional unit is produced. The additional cost incurred by Executive Furniture, Inc. when one additional teak desk is made is the marginal cost of manufacturing the desk. The table in Exhibit 2–10 shows how marginal cost can change across different ranges of production quantities.

LO 9 Define and give examples of an opportunity cost, an out-of-pocket cost, a sunk cost, a differential cost, a marginal cost, and an average cost.

Marginal costs typically differ across different ranges of production quantities because the efficiency of the production process changes. At Executive Furniture, Inc. the marginal cost of producing a desk declines as output increases. It is much more efficient for the company to manufacture 101 desks than to make only one.

It is important to distinguish between *marginal costs* and *average costs*. In the Executive Furniture example, the marginal cost of the second desk is $1,900. However, the average cost per unit when two desks are manufactured is $3,900 divided by 2, or $1,950. Similarly, the marginal cost of the eleventh desk is $1,690, but the average cost per unit when 11 desks are produced is $1,790 (calculated by dividing $19,690 by 11). What is the marginal cost of the 101st desk? The average cost per unit when 101 desks are manufactured?[5]

To summarize, the marginal cost of production is the extra cost incurred when one more unit is produced. The **average cost per unit** is the total cost, for whatever quantity is manufactured, divided by the number of units manufactured. Marginal costs and average costs arise in a variety of economic situations. A Harvard University administrator might be interested in the marginal cost of educating one additional student, and a Toyota executive might want to know the marginal cost of producing

A **marginal cost** is the extra cost incurred in producing one additional unit of output.

The **average cost per unit** is the total cost of producing a particular quantity of product divided by the number of units produced.

---

[5] Marginal cost of 101st desk is $995 (from Exhibit 2–10). Average cost per unit when 101 desks are produced is $1,495 ($150,995 ÷ 101).

Exhibit 2–10

Marginal Cost of Producing
Teak Desks at Executive
Furniture, Inc.

Number of Teak Desks Produced	Total Cost of Producing Desks		Marginal Cost of Producing a Desk
1	$ 2,000		
		Difference is $1,900 ⟶	Marginal cost of 2nd desk is $1,900
2	3,900		
10	18,000		
		Difference is $1,690 ⟶	Marginal cost of 11th desk is $1,690
11	19,690		
100	150,000		
		Difference is $995 ⟶	Marginal cost of 101st desk is $995
101	150,995		

one more Toyota van. A bus tour company manager might be interested in the average cost per mile on the Pittsburgh to New York City route.

Costs and Benefits of Information

Many different cost concepts have been explored in this chapter. An important task of the managerial accountant is to determine which of these cost concepts is most appropriate in each situation. The accountant attempts to structure the organization's accounting information system to record data that will be useful for a variety of purposes. The benefits of measuring and classifying costs in a particular way are realized through the improvements in planning, control, and decision making that the information facilitates.

Another important task of the managerial accountant is to weigh the benefits of providing information against the costs of generating, communicating, and using that information. Some accountants, eager to show that they have not overlooked anything, tend to provide too much information. But when managers receive more data than they can utilize effectively, *information overload* occurs. Struggling to process large amounts of information, managers may be unable to recognize the most important facts. In deciding how much and what type of information to provide, managerial accountants should consider these human limitations. The following example is a case in point.

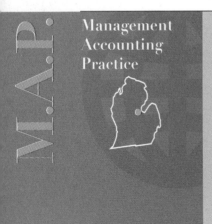

Management Accounting Practice

Dow Chemical Company

The controller for Dow Chemical Company suspected that too much internal accounting information was being provided for managers to use effectively. A complete set of monthly financial statements was provided to managers at all levels in the company. The controller realized that a lot of "time was being devoted to analysis of the data; but he questioned whether too much analysis was taking place. Were better decisions being made as a result of the faster information flow? Was the flow of information the most efficient?"

To follow up on his hunch, the controller and his staff interviewed managers throughout the company to determine what information was really needed. Managers were asked, "Who needs the information?" and "How is the information used?" The controller's survey revealed that too many reports were being provided, and managers were spending an excessive amount of time on analyzing the reports. As a result, the controller decided to switch to a quarterly internal-reporting cycle. Elimination of the monthly reports enabled the company to achieve large cost savings on information provision and managerial analysis. Yet the managers could do their jobs just as well with the quarterly reports.[6]

---

[6] Dennis Dankoski, "Dow Opts for Less—and Gains," *Management Accounting* 67, no. 12, pp. 56, 57.

Chapter Summary

The term *cost* is familiar to everyone. We all discuss the cost of a sweater, a movie ticket, or a semester's tuition. Yet, as we have seen in this chapter, the word *cost* can have a variety of meanings in different situations. Managerial accountants often find it useful to classify costs in different ways for different purposes. An understanding of cost terms, concepts, and classifications is fundamental in any study of managerial accounting.

Several cost terms are defined and illustrated in the chapter. A cost driver is any activity or event that causes costs to be incurred. Fixed and variable costs are defined by the behavior of total cost as the organization's activity level changes. Direct and indirect costs refer to the ability of the accountant to trace costs to various departments in the organization. The terms *controllable* and *uncontrollable* are used to describe the extent to which a manager can influence a cost. Costs are classified into such functional categories as manufacturing costs, selling costs, and administrative costs. Manufacturing costs are further subdivided into direct-material, direct-labor, and manufacturing-overhead costs. The terms *product cost* and *period cost* refer to the timing with which costs become expenses.

Economic concepts are also important in describing costs. An opportunity cost is the benefit forgone because the choice of one action precludes another action. Sunk costs are costs incurred in the past that cannot be altered by a current or future decision. The term *differential cost* or *incremental cost* refers to the difference in the costs incurred under two alternative actions. Marginal cost is defined as the cost of producing one additional unit. Finally, the average cost per unit is the total cost for whatever quantity is produced, divided by the number of units produced.

These cost terms are an integral part of the specialized language of business.

Review Problems on Cost Classifications

Problem 1

Several costs incurred by Myrtle Beach Golf Equipment, Inc. are listed below. For each cost, indicate which of the following classifications best describe the cost. More than one classification may apply to the same cost item. For example, a cost may be both a variable cost *and* a product cost.

Cost Classifications
a.   Variable
b.   Fixed
c.   Period
d.   Product
e.   Administrative
f.   Selling
g.   Manufacturing
h.   Research and development
i.   Direct material
j.   Direct labor
k.   Manufacturing overhead

Cost Items
1.   Metal used in golf clubs.   *i*
2.   Salary of plant manager.   *B*
3.   Cost of natural gas used to heat factory.   *R* *B* *K*
4.   Commissions paid to sales personnel.   *F*
5.   Wages paid to employees who assemble golf bags.   *J*
6.   Salary of engineer who is working on a prototype of a new solar-powered golf cart.   *D H*
7.   Depreciation on the word processing equipment used by the company president's secretary.   *B*

Problem 2

Listed below are several costs incurred in the loan department of Suwanee Bank and Trust Company. For each cost, indicate which of the following classifications best describe the cost. More than one classification may apply to the same cost item.

Cost Classifications

a. Controllable by the loan department manager
b. Uncontrollable by the loan department manager
c. Direct cost of the loan department
d. Indirect cost of the loan department
e. Differential cost
f. Marginal cost
g. Opportunity cost
h. Sunk cost
i. Out-of-pocket cost

Cost Items

1. The salary of the loan department manager.
2. Cost of office supplies used in the loan department.
3. Cost of the department's personal computers purchased by the loan department manager last year.
4. Cost of general advertising by the bank, which is allocated to the loan department.
5. The revenue that the loan department would have generated for the bank if a branch loan office had been located downtown instead of in the next county.
6. The difference in the cost incurred by the bank when one additional loan application is processed.

Solutions to Review Problems

Problem 1
1. a, d, g, i   **2.** b, d, g, k   **3.** a, d, g, k   **4.** a, c, f   **5.** a, d, g, j   **6.** b, c, h   **7.** b, c, e

Problem 2
1. b, c, i   **2.** a, c, i   **3.** a, c, h   **4.** b, d, i   **5.** g   **6.** e, f

Key Terms

For each term's definition refer to the indicated page, or turn to the glossary at the end of the text.

activity, pg. 30
average cost per unit, pg. 47
controllable cost, pg. 36
conversion costs, pg. 38
cost, pg. 30
cost drivers, pg. 34
cost of goods sold, pg. 39
differential cost, pg. 47
direct cost, pg. 34
direct-labor cost, pg. 36

direct material, pg. 36
expense, pg. 38
finished goods, pg. 43
fixed costs, pg. 31
idle time, pg. 37
incremental costs, pg. 47
indirect cost, pg. 35
indirect labor, pg. 37
indirect material, pg. 37
inventoriable cost, pg. 39

manufacturing
  overhead, pg. 37
marginal cost, pg. 47
operating expenses, pg. 43
opportunity cost, pg. 44
out-of-pocket costs, pg. 46
overtime premium, pg. 37
period costs, pg. 39
prime costs, pg. 38
product cost, pg. 39

raw material, pg. 43
schedule of cost of goods
  manufactured, pg. 44
schedule of cost of goods
  sold, pg. 44
service departments, pg. 37
sunk costs, pg. 46
variable cost, pg. 30
work in process, pg. 43

Review Questions

2–1. What is meant by the phrase "different costs for different purposes"?

2–2. Give examples to illustrate how the city of Tampa could use cost information in planning, controlling costs, and making decisions.

2–3. Distinguish between fixed costs and variable costs.

2–4. How does the fixed cost per unit change as the level of activity (or cost driver) increases? Why?

2–5. How does the variable cost per unit change as the level of activity (or cost driver) increases? Why?

2–6. Distinguish between volume-based and operations-based cost drivers in the airline industry.

2–7. Would each of the following characteristics be a volume-based or an operations-based cost driver in a college: (*a*) number of students, (*b*) number of disciplines offered for study, and (*c*) urban versus rural location?

2–8. List three direct costs of the food and beverage department in a hotel. List three indirect costs of the department.

2–9. List three costs that are likely to be controllable by a city's airport manager. List three costs that are likely to be uncontrollable by the manager.

2–10. Why is the cost of idle time treated as manufacturing overhead?

2–11. Explain why an overtime premium is included in manufacturing overhead.

2–12. Which of the following costs are likely to be controllable by the chief of nursing in a hospital?

  a. Cost of medication administered.

  b. Cost of overtime paid to nurses due to scheduling errors.

  c. Cost of depreciation of hospital beds.

2–13. Distinguish between product and period costs.

2–14. What is the most important difference between a manufacturing firm and a service industry firm, with regard to the classification of costs as product costs or period costs?

2–15. Why are product costs also called inventoriable costs?

2–16. Distinguish between out-of-pocket costs and opportunity costs.

2–17. Define the terms *sunk cost* and *differential cost.*

2–18. Distinguish between marginal and average costs.

2–19. Think about the process of registering for classes at your college or university. What additional information would you like to have before you register? How would it help you? What sort of information might create information overload for you?

2–20. Two years ago the manager of a large department store purchased new cash registers costing $48,000. A salesperson recently tried to sell the manager a new automated checkout system for the store. The new system would save the store a substantial amount of money each year. The recently purchased cash registers could be sold in the secondhand market for $20,000. The store manager refused to listen to the salesperson, saying, "I just bought those cash registers. I can't get rid of them until I get my money's worth out of them."

What type of cost is the cost of purchasing the old cash registers? What common behavioral tendency is the manager exhibiting?

2–21. Indicate whether each of the following costs is a direct cost or an indirect cost of the restaurant in a hotel.

  a. Cost of food served.

  b. Chef's salary and fringe benefits.

  c. Part of the cost of maintaining the grounds around the hotel, which is allocated to the restaurant.

  d. Part of the cost of advertising the hotel, which is allocated to the restaurant.

2–22. Refer to the chapter opening article about Southwest Airlines. What key part of the company's strategy was made possible by Southwest's success at remaining the low-cost producer in the industry?

Exercises

For each case below, find the missing amount.

■ **Exercise 2–23**
Cost of Goods Manufactured and Sold; Missing Data
(LO 7, LO 8)

	Case I	Case II	Case III
Beginning inventory of finished goods	$12,000	?	$ 7,000
Cost of goods manufactured during period	95,000	$419,000	?
Ending inventory of finished goods	8,000	98,000	21,000
Cost of goods sold	?	405,000	304,000

A hotel pays the phone company $100 per month plus $.25 for each call made. During January 6,000 calls were made. In February 5,000 calls were made.

■ **Exercise 2–24**
Fixed, Variable, Marginal, and Average Costs; Hotel
(LO 1, LO 2, LO 9)

Required:

1. Calculate the hotel's phone bills for January and February.

2. Calculate the cost per phone call in January and in February.

3. Separate the January phone bill into its fixed and variable components.

4. What is the marginal cost of one additional phone call in January?

5. What was the average cost of a phone call in January?

A foundry employee worked a normal 40-hour shift, but four hours were idle due to a small fire in the plant. The employee earns $18 per hour.

■ **Exercise 2–25**
Idle Time
(LO 5)

Required:

1. Calculate the employee's total compensation for the week.
2. How much of this compensation is a direct-labor cost? How much is overhead?

■ **Exercise 2–26**
Overtime Cost
(LO 5)

A loom operator in a textile factory earns $16.00 per hour. The employee earns $20.00 for overtime hours. The operator worked 45 hours during the first week of May, instead of the usual 40 hours.

Required:

1. Compute the loom operator's compensation for the week.
2. Calculate the employee's total overtime premium for the week.
3. How much of the employee's total compensation for the week is direct-labor cost? How much is overhead?

■ **Exercise 2–27**
Schedules of Cost of Goods
Manufactured and Sold;
Income Statement
(LO 7, LO 8)

Youngstown Aluminum Company, a manufacturer of recyclable soda cans, had the following inventory balances at the beginning and end of 19x9:

Inventory Classification	January 1, 19x9	December 31, 19x9
Raw material	$ 60,000	$ 70,000
Work in process	120,000	115,000
Finished goods	150,000	165,000

During 19x9, the company purchased $250,000 of raw material and spent $400,000 on direct labor. Manufacturing overhead costs were as follows:

Indirect material	$ 10,000
Indirect labor	25,000
Depreciation on plant and equipment	100,000
Utilities	25,000
Other	30,000

Sales revenue was $1,105,000 for the year. Selling and administrative expenses for the year amounted to $110,000. The firm's tax rate is 40 percent.

Required:

1. Prepare a schedule of cost of goods manufactured.
2. Prepare a schedule of cost of goods sold.
3. Prepare an income statement.

■ **Exercise 2–28**
Economic Characteristics of
Costs
(LO 1, LO 9, LO 10)

Martin Shrood purchased a vacant lot for $13,500, because he heard that a shopping mall was going to be built on the other side of the road. He figured that he could make a bundle by putting in a fast-food outlet on the site. As it turned out, the rumor was false. A sanitary landfill was located on the other side of the road, and Martin's land was worthless.

Required:

What type of cost is the $13,500 that Martin paid for the vacant lot?

■ **Exercise 2–29**
Differential Cost
(LO 1, LO 9, LO 10)

Satronics, Inc. manufactures communications satellites used in TV signal transmission. The firm currently purchases one component for its satellites from a European firm. A Satronics engineering team has found a way to use the company's own component, part number A200, instead of the European component. However, the Satronics component must be modified at a cost of $500 per part. The European component costs $8,900 per part. Satronics' part number A200 costs $5,100 before it is modified. Satronics currently uses 10 of the European components per year.

Required:

Calculate the annual differential cost between Satronics' two production alternatives.

The state Department of Education owns a computer system, which its employees use for word processing and keeping track of education statistics. The governor's office recently began using this computer also. As a result of the increased usage, the demands on the computer soon exceeded its capacity. The director of the Department of Education was soon forced to lease several personal computers to meet the computing needs of her employees. The annual cost of leasing the equipment is $14,000.

■ Exercise 2–30
Computing Costs;
Government Agency
(LO 1, LO 4, LO 9)

Required:

1. What type of cost is this $14,000?
2. Should this cost be associated with the governor's office or the Department of Education? Why?

Suppose you paid $60 for a ticket to see your university's football team compete in a bowl game. Someone offered to buy your ticket for $100, but you decided to go to the game.

■ Exercise 2–31
Economic Characteristics of
Costs
(LO 1, LO 9, LO 10)

Required:

1. What did it really cost you to see the game?
2. What type of cost is this?

List the costs that would likely be included in each of the following marginal-cost calculations.

■ Exercise 2–32
Marginal Costs
(LO 1, LO 9)

1. The marginal cost of serving one additional customer in a restaurant.
2. The marginal cost of one additional passenger on a jet flight.
3. The marginal cost of adding a flight from Honolulu to Seattle.
4. The marginal cost of keeping a travel agency open one additional hour on Saturdays.
5. The marginal cost of manufacturing one additional pair of water skis.

Mighty Muffler, Inc. operates an automobile service facility that specializes in replacing mufflers on compact cars. The following table shows the costs incurred during a month when 600 mufflers were replaced.

■ Exercise 2–33
Fixed and Variable Costs;
Automobile Service; Missing
Data
(LO 1, LO 2)

	Muffler Replacements		
	500	**600**	**700**
Total costs:			
Fixed costs	a	$42,000	b
Variable costs	c	30,000	d
Total costs	e	$72,000	f
Cost per muffler replacement:			
Fixed cost	g	h	i
Variable cost	j	k	l
Total cost per muffler replacement	m	n	o

Required:

Fill in the missing amounts, labeled (a) through (o), in the table.

Problems

The following cost data for the year just ended pertain to Heartstrings, Inc., a greeting card manufacturer:

■ Problem 2–34
Cost Terminology
(LO 1, LO 5, LO 6, LO 9)

Direct material	$2,100,000
Advertising expense	99,000
Depreciation on factory building	115,000
Direct labor: wages	485,000
Cost of finished goods inventory at year-end	115,000

Indirect labor: wages	140,000
Production supervisor's salary	45,000
Service department costs*	100,000
Direct labor: fringe benefits	95,000
Indirect labor: fringe benefits	30,000
Fringe benefits for production supervisor	9,000
Total overtime premiums paid	55,000
Cost of idle time: production employees	40,000
Administrative costs	150,000
Rental of office space for sales personnel†	15,000
Sales commissions	5,000
Product promotion costs	10,000

*All services are provided to manufacturing departments.

†The rental of sales space was made necessary when the sales offices were converted to storage space for raw material.

Required:

1. Compute each of the following costs for the year just ended: (a) total prime costs, (b) total manufacturing overhead costs, (c) total conversion costs, (d) total product costs, and (e) total period costs.

2. One of the costs listed above is an opportunity cost. Identify this cost, and explain why it is an opportunity cost.

3. One of the costs listed above is a sunk cost. Identify this cost, and explain why it is a sunk cost.

■ **Problem 2–35**
Variable Costs; Graphical and Tabular Analyses
(LO 1, LO 2, LO 3)

Carlson Sheet Metal, Inc. incurs a variable cost of $40 per pound for raw material to produce a special alloy used in manufacturing aircraft.

Required:

1. Draw a graph of the firm's raw material cost, showing the total cost at the following production levels: 10,000 pounds, 20,000 pounds, and 30,000 pounds.

2. Prepare a table that shows the unit cost and total cost of raw material at the following production levels: 1 pound, 10 pounds, and 1,000 pounds.

■ **Problem 2–36**
Fixed Costs; Graphical and Tabular Analyses
(LO 1, LO 2, LO 3)

Hightide Upholstery Company manufactures a special fabric used to upholster the seats in power boats. The company's annual fixed production cost is $100,000.

Required:

1. Draw a graph of the company's fixed production cost showing the total cost at the following production levels of upholstery fabric: 10,000 yards, 20,000 yards, 30,000 yards, and 40,000 yards.

2. Prepare a table that shows the unit cost and the total cost for the firm's fixed production costs at the following production levels: 1 yard, 10 yards, 10,000 yards, and 40,000 yards.

3. Prepare a graph that shows the unit cost for the company's fixed production cost at the following production levels: 10,000 yards, 20,000 yards, 30,000 yards, and 40,000 yards.

■ **Problem 2–37**
Direct, Indirect, Controllable, and Uncontrollable Costs
(LO 4, LO 7)

For each of the following costs, indicate whether the amount is a direct or indirect cost of the equipment maintenance department. Also indicate whether each cost is at least partially controllable by the department supervisor.

1. Depreciation on the building space occupied by the maintenance department.
2. Idle time of maintenance department employees.
3. Cost of plant manager's salary, which is allocated to the maintenance department.
4. Cost of property taxes allocated to the maintenance department.
5. Cost of electricity used in the maintenance department.

■ **Problem 2–38**
Product Costs and Period Costs
(LO 1, LO 6, LO 7)

Indicate for each of the following costs whether it is a product cost or a period cost.

1. Cost incurred by a department store chain to transport merchandise to its stores.
2. Cost of grapes purchased by a winery.

3. Depreciation on pizza ovens in a pizza restaurant.

4. Wages of aircraft mechanics employed by an airline.

5. Wages of drill-press operators in a manufacturing plant.

6. Cost of food in a TV dinner.

7. Cost of plant manager in a computer production facility.

8. Wages of security personnel in a department store.

9. Cost of utilities in a manufacturing facility.

Kaleidoscope Cutlery manufactures kitchen knives. One of the employees, whose job is to cut out wooden knife handles, worked 48 hours during a week in January. The employee earns $12 per hour for a 40-hour week. For additional hours the employee is paid an overtime rate of $16 per hour. The employee's time was spent as follows:

■ **Problem 2–39**
Direct and Indirect Labor
(LO 4, LO 5, LO 7)

Regular duties involving cutting out knife handles	38 hours
General shop cleanup duties	9 hours
Idle time due to power outage	1 hour

Required:

1. Calculate the total cost of the employee's wages during the week described above.

2. Determine the portion of this cost to be classified in each of the following categories:

   a. Direct labor

   b. Manufacturing overhead (idle time)

   c. Manufacturing overhead (overtime premium)

   d. Manufacturing overhead (indirect labor)

Refer to Exhibit 2–6, and answer the following questions.

Required:

1. List the major differences between the income statements shown for H. J. Heinz Company, Wal-Mart Stores, Inc., and Southwest Airlines Company.

2. Explain how cost-accounting data were used to prepare these income statements.

3. On the income statement for Southwest Airlines Company, where would the ticket agents' salaries be shown? Where would the costs of the computer equipment used to keep track of reservations be included on the statement?

4. On the income statement for Wal-Mart Stores, Inc., where would the cost of newspaper advertising be shown? How about the cost of merchandise?

5. Refer to the income statement for H. J. Heinz Company. Where would the salary of the brand manager who plans advertising for Heinz ketchup be shown? How about the salary of a production employee? Where would the cost of the ingredients in the company's products be included on the statement?

■ **Problem 2–40**
Interpretation of Accounting Reports
(LO 7)

Several costs incurred by Water's Edge Hotel and Restaurant are listed below. For each cost, indicate which of the following classifications best describe the cost. More than one classification may apply to the same cost item.

■ **Problem 2–41**
Cost Classifications; Hotel
(LO 1, LO 4, LO 7, LO 9)

Cost Classifications

a. Direct cost of the food and beverage department

b. Indirect cost of the food and beverage department

c. Controllable by the kitchen manager

d. Uncontrollable by the kitchen manager

e. Controllable by the hotel general manager

f. Uncontrollable by the hotel general manager

g. Differential cost

h. Marginal cost

i. Opportunity cost

j. Sunk cost

k. Out-of-pocket cost

Cost Items

(A) + (C) + (K) + (E)

(H) marginal

(B) + (D) + (K)

(E) + (I)

(E) + (I)

(A) + (K)

(G)

(E) + (J) + (K)

1. The cost of food used in the kitchen.

2. The difference in the total cost incurred by the hotel when one additional guest is registered.

3. The cost of general advertising by the hotel, which is allocated to the food and beverage department.

4. The cost of space (depreciation) occupied by the kitchen.

5. The cost of space (depreciation) occupied by a sauna next to the pool. The space could otherwise have been used for a magazine and bookshop.

6. The profit that would have been earned in a magazine and bookshop, if the hotel had one.

7. The discount on room rates given as a special offer for a "Labor Day Getaway Special."

8. The wages earned by table-service personnel.

9. The salary of the kitchen manager.

10. The cost of the refrigerator purchased 13 months ago. The unit was covered by a warranty for 12 months, during which time it worked perfectly. It conked out after 13 months, despite an original estimate that it would last five years.

11. The hotel has two options for obtaining fresh pies, cakes, and pastries. The goodies can be purchased from a local bakery for approximately $1,600 per month, or they can be made in the hotel's kitchen. To make the pastries on the premises, the hotel will have to hire a part-time pastry chef. This will cost $600 per month. The cost of ingredients will amount to roughly $700 per month. Thus, the savings from making the goods in the hotel's kitchen amount to $300 per month.

12. The cost of dishes broken by kitchen employees. *Made in hotel kitchen for $1,300*

13. The cost of leasing a computer used for reservations, payroll, and general hotel accounting.

14. The cost of a pool service that cleans and maintains the hotel's swimming pool.

15. The wages of the hotel's maintenance employees, who spent 11 hours (at $14 per hour) repairing the dishwasher in the kitchen.

■ **Problem 2–42**

Incomplete Data;
Manufacturing Costs
(LO 5, LO 6, LO 7, LO 8)

Determine the missing amounts in each of the following independent cases.

	Case A	Case B	Case C
Beginning inventory, raw material	$ 20,000	$ 15,000	?
Ending inventory, raw material	?	30,000	$ 90,000
Purchases of raw material	85,000	?	100,000
Direct material	95,000	?	70,000
Direct labor	100,000	125,000	?
Manufacturing overhead	?	160,000	250,000
Total manufacturing costs	345,000	340,000	520,000
Beginning inventory, work in process	20,000	?	35,000
Ending inventory, work in process	35,000	5,000	?
Cost of goods manufactured	?	350,000	525,000
Beginning inventory, finished goods	40,000	?	50,000
Cost of goods available for sale	?	370,000	?
Ending inventory, finished goods	?	25,000	?
Cost of goods sold	330,000	?	545,000
Sales	?	480,000	?
Gross margin	170,000	?	255,000
Selling and administrative expenses	75,000	?	?
Income before taxes	?	90,000	150,000
Income tax expense	45,000	?	40,000
Net income	?	55,000	?

Peter Marlas makes custom mooring covers for boats. Each mooring cover is hand sewn to fit a particular boat. If covers are made for two or more identical boats, each successive cover generally requires less time to make. Marlas has been approached by a local boat dealer to make mooring covers for all of the boats sold by the dealer. Marlas has developed the following cost schedule for mooring covers made to fit 17-foot outboard power boats.

■ **Problem 2–43**
Marginal Costs and Average Costs
(LO 1, LO 3, LO 9)

Mooring Covers Made	Total Cost of Covers
1	$ 450
2	850
3	1,210
4	1,540
5	1,850

Required:

Compute the following:

1. Marginal cost of second mooring cover.
2. Marginal cost of fourth mooring cover.
3. Marginal cost of fifth mooring cover.
4. Average cost if two mooring covers are made.
5. Average cost if four mooring covers are made.
6. Average cost if five mooring covers are made.

The Department of Natural Resources is responsible for maintaining the state's parks and forest lands, stocking the lakes and rivers with fish, and generally overseeing the protection of the environment. Several costs incurred by the agency are listed below. For each cost, indicate which of the following classifications best describe the cost. More than one classification may apply to the same cost item.

■ **Problem 2–44**
Cost Classifications; Government Agency
(LO 2, LO 4, LO 7, LO 9)

Cost Classifications

a. Variable
b. Fixed
c. Controllable by the department director
d. Uncontrollable by the department director
e. Differential cost
f. Marginal cost
g. Opportunity cost
h. Sunk cost
i. Out-of-pocket cost
j. Direct cost of the agency
k. Indirect cost of the agency
l. Direct cost of providing a particular service
m. Indirect cost of providing a particular service

Cost Items

1. Cost of the fish purchased from private hatcheries, which are used to stock the state's public waters.
2. Cost of live-trapping and moving beaver that were creating a nuisance in recreational lakes.
3. The department director's salary.
4. Cost of containing naturally caused forest fires, which are threatening private property.
5. Cost of the automobiles used by the department's rangers. These cars were purchased by the state, and they would otherwise have been used by the state police.
6. The difference between (a) the cost of purchasing fish from private hatcheries and (b) the cost of running a state hatchery.

7. Cost of producing literature that describes the department's role in environmental protection. This literature is mailed free, upon request, to schools, county governments, libraries, and private citizens.

8. Cost of sending the department's hydroengineers to inspect one additional dam for stability and safety.

9. Cost of operating the state's computer services department, a portion of which is allocated to the Department of Natural Resources.

10. Cost of administrative supplies used in the agency's head office.

11. Cost of providing an 800 number for the state's residents to report environmental problems.

12. The cost of replacing batteries in sophisticated monitoring equipment used to evaluate the effects of acid rain on the state's lakes.

13. Cost of a ranger's wages, when the ranger is giving a talk about environmental protection to elementary school children.

14. Cost of direct-mailing to 1 million state residents a brochure explaining the benefits of voluntarily recycling cans and bottles.

15. The cost of producing a TV show to be aired on public television. The purpose of the show is to educate people on how to spot and properly dispose of hazardous waste.

■ **Problem 2–45**
Overtime Premiums and
Fringe Benefit Costs; Airline
(LO 4, LO 5, LO 7)

Great Plains Airways operates commuter flights in three midwestern states. Due to a political convention held in Topeka, the airline added several extra flights during a two-week period. Additional cabin crews were hired on a temporary basis. However, rather than hiring additional flight attendants, the airline used its current attendants on overtime. Monica Gaines worked the following schedule on August 10. All of Gaines's flights on that day were extra flights that the airline would not normally fly.

| Regular time: | 2 round-trip flights between Topeka and St. Louis (8 hours) |
| Overtime: | 1 one-way flight from Topeka to Kansas City (3 hours) |

Gaines earns $12 per hour plus time and a half for overtime. Fringe benefits cost the airline $3 per hour for any hour worked, regardless of whether it is a regular or overtime hour.

Required:

1. Compute the direct cost of compensating Gaines for her services on the flight from Topeka to Kansas City.

2. Compute the cost of Gaines's services that is an indirect cost.

3. How should the cost computed in requirement (2) be treated for cost accounting purposes?

4. Gaines ended her workday on August 10 in Kansas City. However, her next scheduled flight departed Topeka at 11:00 a.m. on August 11. This required Gaines to "dead-head" back to Topeka on an early-morning flight. This means she traveled from Kansas City to Topeka as a passenger, rather than as a working flight attendant. Since the morning flight from Kansas City to Topeka was full, Gaines displaced a paying customer. The revenue lost by the airline was $82. What type of cost is the $82? To what flight, if any, is it chargeable? Why?

■ **Problem 2–46**
Fixed and Variable Costs;
Forecasting
(LO 2, LO 3)

Devoe Electronics Corporation incurred the following costs during 19x9. The company sold all of its products manufactured during the year.

Direct material	$3,000,000
Direct labor	2,200,000
Manufacturing overhead:	
Utilities (primarily electricity)	140,000
Depreciation on plant and equipment	230,000
Insurance	160,000
Supervisory salaries	300,000
Property taxes	210,000
Selling costs:	
Advertising	195,000
Sales commissions	90,000

Administrative costs:

Salaries of top management and staff	$ 372,000
Office supplies	40,000
Depreciation on building and equipment	80,000

During 19x9, the company operated at about half of its capacity, due to a slowdown in the economy. Prospects for 20x0 are slightly better, with the marketing manager forecasting a 20 percent growth in sales over the 19x9 level.

Required:

Categorize each of the costs listed above as to whether it is most likely variable or fixed. Forecast the 20x0 cost amount for each of the cost items listed above.

Outer Banks Shirt Shop manufactures T-shirts and decorates them with custom designs for retail sale on the premises. Several costs incurred by the company are listed below. For each cost, indicate which of the following classifications best describe the cost. More than one classification may apply to the same cost item.

■ **Problem 2–47**
Cost Classifications;
Manufacturer
(LO 2, LO 4, LO 5)

Cost Classifications

a. Variable
b. Fixed
c. Period
d. Product
e. Administrative
f. Selling
g. Manufacturing
h. Research and development
i. Direct material
j. Direct labor
k. Manufacturing overhead

Cost Items

1. Cost of fabric used in T-shirts.
2. Wages of shirtmakers.
3. Cost of new sign in front of retail T-shirt shop.
4. Wages of the employee who repairs the firm's sewing machines.
5. Cost of electricity used in the sewing department.
6. Wages of T-shirt designers and painters.
7. Wages of sales personnel.
8. Depreciation on sewing machines.
9. Rent on the building. Part of the building's first floor is used to make and paint T-shirts. Part of it is used for the retail sales shop. The second floor is used for administrative offices and storage of raw material and finished goods.
10. Cost of daily advertisements in local media.
11. Wages of designers who experiment with new fabrics, paints, and T-shirt designs.
12. Cost of hiring a pilot to fly along the beach pulling a banner advertising the shop.
13. Salary of the owner's secretary.
14. Cost of repairing the gas furnace.
15. Cost of insurance for the production employees.

The following terms are used to describe various economic characteristics of costs.

■ **Problem 2–48**
Economic Characteristics of
Costs
(LO 1, LO 9, LO 10)

Opportunity cost	Differential cost
Out-of-pocket cost	Marginal cost
Sunk cost	Average cost

Required:

Choose one of the terms listed above to characterize each of the amounts described below.

marginal — **1.** The cost of including one extra child in a day-care center.

sunk (D) — **2.** The cost of merchandise inventory purchased two years ago, which is now obsolete.

average — **3.** The cost of feeding 500 children in a public school cafeteria is $800 per day, or $1.60 per child per day. What economic term describes this $1.60 cost?

opportunity — **4.** The management of a high-rise office building uses 2,500 square feet of space in the building for its own management functions. This space could be rented for $250,000. What economic term describes this $250,000 in lost rental revenue?

differential — **5.** The cost of building an automated assembly line in a factory is $800,000. The cost of building a manually operated assembly line is $375,000. What economic term is used to describe the difference between these two amounts?

out-of-pocket — **6.** Referring to the preceding question, what economic term is used to describe the $800,000 cost of building the automated assembly line?

■ **Problem 2–49**
Variable and Fixed Costs;
Make or Buy a Component
(LO 1, LO 2, LO 9)

Vermont Industries currently manufactures 30,000 units of part MR24 each month for use in production of several of its products. The facilities now used to produce part MR24 have a fixed monthly cost of $150,000 and a capacity to produce 84,000 units per month. If the company were to buy part MR24 from an outside supplier, the facilities would be idle, but its fixed costs would continue at 40 percent of their present amount. The variable production costs of part MR24 are $11 per unit.

Required:

1. If Vermont Industries continues to use 30,000 units of part MR24 each month, it would realize a net benefit by purchasing part MR24 from an outside supplier only if the supplier's unit price is less than what amount?

2. If Vermont Industries is able to obtain part MR24 from an outside supplier at a unit purchase price of $12.875, what is the monthly usage at which it will be indifferent between purchasing and making part MR24?

(CMA, adapted)

■ **Problem 2–50**
Unit Costs; Profit-
Maximizing Output
(LO 1, LO 2, LO 3)

The controller for Oneida Vineyards, Inc. has predicted the following costs at various levels of wine output.

	Wine Output (.75 Liter Bottles)		
	10,000 Bottles	**15,000 Bottles**	**20,000 Bottles**
Variable production costs	$ 35,000	$ 52,500	$ 70,000
Fixed production costs	100,000	100,000	100,000
Variable selling and administrative costs	2,000	3,000	4,000
Fixed selling and administrative costs	40,000	40,000	40,000
Total	$177,000	$195,500	$214,000

The company's marketing manager has predicted the following prices for the firm's fine wines at various levels of sales.

	Wine Sales		
	10,000 Bottles	**15,000 Bottles**	**20,000 Bottles**
Sales price per .75-liter bottle	$18.00	$15.00	$12.00

Required:

1. Calculate the unit costs of wine production and sales at each level of output. At what level of output is the unit cost minimized?

2. Calculate the company's profit at each level of production. Assume that the company will sell all of its output. At what production level is profit maximized?

3. Which of the three output levels is best for the company?

4. Why does the unit cost of wine decrease as the output level increases? Why might the sales price per bottle decline as sales volume increases?

The following data refer to Fresno Fashions Company for the year 19x9:

Sales revenue	$950,000
Work-in-process inventory, December 31	30,000
Work-in-process inventory, January 1	40,000
Selling and administrative expenses	150,000
Income tax expense	90,000
Purchases of raw material	180,000
Raw-material inventory, December 31	25,000
Raw-material inventory, January 1	40,000
Direct labor	200,000
Utilities: plant	40,000
Depreciation: plant and equipment	60,000
Finished-goods inventory, December 31	50,000
Finished-goods inventory, January 1	20,000
Indirect material	10,000
Indirect labor	15,000
Other manufacturing overhead	80,000

Required:

1. Prepare Fresno Fashions' schedule of cost of goods manufactured for the year.
2. Prepare Fresno Fashions' schedule of cost of goods sold for the year.
3. Prepare Fresno Fashions' income statement for the year.

■ **Problem 2–51**
Schedules of Cost of Goods
Manufactured and Sold;
Income Statement
(LO 5, LO 7, LO 8)

Cases

Compucraft Company manufactures printers for use with home computing systems. The firm currently manufactures both the electronic components for its printers and the plastic cases in which the devices are enclosed. Jim Cassanitti, the production manager, recently received a proposal from Universal Plastics Corporation to manufacture the cases for Compucraft's printers. If the cases are purchased outside, Compucraft will be able to close down its Printer Case Department. To help decide whether to accept the bid from Universal Plastics Corporation, Cassanitti asked Compucraft's controller to prepare an analysis of the costs that would be saved if the Printer Case Department were closed. Included in the controller's list of annual cost savings were the following items:

■ **Case 2–52**
Economic Characteristics of
Costs; Closing a Department;
Ethics
(LO 1, LO 9, LO 10)

Building rental (The Printer Case Department occupies one-sixth of the factory building, which Compucraft rents for $177,000 per year.)	$29,500
Salary of the Printer Case Department supervisor	$50,000

In a lunchtime conversation with the controller, Cassanitti learned that Compucraft was currently renting space in a warehouse for $39,000. The space is used to store completed printers. If the Printer Case Department were discontinued, the entire storage operation could be moved into the factory building and occupy the space vacated by the closed department. Cassanitti also learned that the supervisor of the Printer Case Department would be retained by Compucraft even if the department were closed. The supervisor would be assigned the job of managing the assembly department, whose supervisor recently gave notice of his retirement. All of Compucraft's department supervisors earn the same salary.

Required:

1. You have been hired as a consultant by Cassanitti to advise him in his decision. Write a memo to Cassanitti commenting on the costs of space and supervisory salaries included in the controller's cost analysis. Explain in your memo about the "real" costs of the space occupied by the Printer Case Department and the supervisor's salary. What types of costs are these?
2. Independent of your response to requirement (1), suppose that Compucraft's controller had been approached by his friend Jack Westford, the assistant supervisor of the Printer Case Department. Westford is worried that he will be laid off if the Printer Case Department is closed down.

Westford has asked his friend to understate the cost savings from closing the department, in order to slant the production manager's decision toward keeping the department in operation. Comment on the controller's ethical responsibilities.

■ **Case 2–53**
Understanding Cost
Concepts
(LO 1, LO 2, LO 3, LO 9)

You just started a summer internship with the successful management consulting firm of Kirk, Spock, and McCoy. Your first day on the job was a busy one, as the following problems were presented to you.

Required:

Supply the requested comments in each of the following independent situations.

1. FastQ Company, a specialist in printing, has established 500 convenience copying centers throughout the country. In order to upgrade its services the company is considering three new models of laser copying machines for use in producing high-quality copies. These high-quality copies would be added to the growing list of products offered in the FastQ shops. The selling price to the customer for each laser copy would be the same, no matter which machine is installed in the shop. The three models of laser copying machines under consideration are: 1024S, a small-volume model; 1024M, a medium-volume model; and 1024G, a large-volume model. The annual rental costs and the operating costs vary with the size of each machine. The machine capacities and costs are as follows:

	Copier Model		
	1024S	**1024M**	**1024G**
Annual capacity (copies)	100,000	350,000	800,000
Costs:			
Annual machine rental	$8,000	$11,000	$20,000
Direct material and direct labor	.02	.02	.02
Variable overhead costs	.12	.07	.03

   a. Calculate the volume level in copies where FastQ Company would be indifferent to acquiring either the small-volume model laser copier, 1024S, or the medium-volume model laser copier, 1024M.

   b. The management of FastQ Company is able to estimate the number of copies to be sold at each establishment. Present a decision rule that would enable FastQ Company to select the most profitable machine without having to make a separate cost calculation for each establishment. (*Hint:* To specify a decision rule, determine the volume at which FastQ would be indifferent between the small and medium copiers. Then determine the volume at which FastQ would be indifferent between the medium and large copiers.)

2. Alderon Enterprises is evaluating a special order it has received for a ceramic fixture to be used in aircraft engines. Alderon has recently been operating at less than full capacity, so the firm's management will accept the order if the price offered exceeds the costs that will be incurred in producing it. You have been asked for advice on how to determine the cost of two raw materials that would be required to produce the order.

   a. The special order will require 800 gallons of endor, a highly perishable material that is purchased as needed. Alderon currently has 1,200 gallons of endor on hand, since the material is used in virtually all of the company's products. The last time endor was purchased, Alderon paid $5.00 per gallon. However, the average price paid for the endor in stock was only $4.75. The market price for endor is quite volatile, with the current price at $5.50. If the special order is accepted, Alderon will have to place a new order next week to replace the 800 gallons of endor used. By then the price is expected to reach $5.75 per gallon.

   Using the cost terminology introduced in Chapter 2, comment on each of the cost figures mentioned in the preceding discussion. What is the real cost of endor if the special order is produced?

   b. The special order would also require 1,500 kilograms of tatooine, a material not normally required in any of Alderon's regular products. The company does happen to have 2,000 kilograms of tatooine on hand, since it formerly manufactured a ceramic product that used the material. Alderon recently received an offer of $14,000 from Solo Industries for its entire supply of tatooine. However, Solo Industries is not interested in buying any quantity less than Alderon's entire 2,000-kilogram stock. Alderon's management is unenthusiastic about Solo's offer, since Alderon paid $20,000 for the tatooine. Moreover, if the tatooine were purchased at today's market price, it would cost $11.00 per kilogram. Due to the volatility of the tatooine,

Alderon will need to get rid of its entire supply one way or another. If the material is not used in production or sold, Alderon will have to pay $1,000 for each 500 kilograms that is transported away and disposed of in a hazardous waste disposal site.

Using the cost terminology introduced in Chapter 2, comment on each of the cost figures mentioned in the preceding discussion. What is the real cost of tatooine to be used in the special order?

3. A local PBS station has decided to produce a TV series on state-of-the-art manufacturing. The director of the TV series, Justin Tyme, is currently attempting to analyze some of the projected costs for the series. Tyme intends to take a TV production crew on location to shoot various manufacturing scenes as they occur. If the four-week series is shown in the 8:00–9:00 p.m. prime-time slot, the station will have to cancel a wildlife show that is currently scheduled. Management projects a 10 percent viewing audience for the wildlife show, and each 1 percent is expected to bring in donations of $10,000. In contrast, the manufacturing show is expected to be watched by 15 percent of the viewing audience. However, each 1 percent of the viewership will likely generate only $5,000 in donations. If the wildlife show is canceled, it can be sold to network television for $25,000.

Using the cost terminology introduced in Chapter 2, comment on each of the financial amounts mentioned in the preceding discussion. What are the relative merits of the two shows regarding the projected revenue to the station?

(CMA, adapted)

Current Issues in Managerial Accounting

"Behind Oxford's Billing Nightmare," *Business Week,* **November 17, 1997.**

Overview

Oxford Health Plans, a health care provider, installed a state-of-the-art computerized accounting and billing system that wound up costing the firm millions more than expected. Serious problems with software implementation resulted in cancelled policies, billing problems, and an increase in overdue accounts.

Suggested Discussion Questions

How do production costs for manufacturers and service providers differ? Explain the role cost estimation plays in a managed health care system. What if a firm's computer accounting system is consistently slow and inaccurate? What happened to Oxford Health Plans?

■ **Issue 2–54**
Differences in Accounting for Manufacturing and Service Organizations

"How to Be a Winner in the Profits Game," *The Wall Street Journal,* **April 3, 1997, Roger Lowenstein.**

Overview

A recent research study provides evidence that corporate managers may be manipulating accounting earnings. Evidence shows that the percentage of firms reporting earnings changes is greatest when there are small earnings increases.

Suggested Discussion Questions

How can managers manipulate costs so that a slight earnings increase is attained? If a firm is deferring costs, what happens in following periods? What if a firm accelerates costs? What incentives may be causing this behavior?

■ **Issue 2–55**
Cost on Financial Statements

"Southwest Airlines Begins to Upgrade Data Recorders at a Cost of $20 Million," *The Wall Street Journal,* **August 16, 1997, Scott McCartney.**

Overview

Southwest Airlines announced that it will spend $20 million on upgrading its flight data recorder systems. This action follows pressure imposed on airlines by the National Transportation Safety Board (NTSB) and Federal Aviation Administration (FAA) to upgrade the recorders.

Suggested Discussion Questions

Is the cost of the recorders volume-based or operations-based? Is the cost fixed or variable? Are these costs controllable or uncontrollable? Who ultimately bears the cost of the new recorders?

■ **Issue 2–56**
Cost Classifications: Different Costs for Different Purposes

3 Chapter Three

Product Costing and Job-Order Costing Systems

After completing this chapter, you should be able to:

1 Discuss the role of product and service costing in manufacturing and nonmanufacturing firms.

2 Diagram and explain the flow of costs through the manufacturing accounts used in product costing.

3 Distinguish between job-order costing and process costing.

4 Compute a predetermined overhead rate, and explain its use in job-order costing.

5 Prepare journal entries to record the costs of direct labor, direct material, and manufacturing overhead in a job-order costing system.

6 Prepare a schedule of cost of goods manufactured, a schedule of cost of goods sold, and an income statement for a manufacturer.

7 Discuss the cost-benefit issue of accuracy versus timeliness of information in accounting for overhead.

8 Describe the two-stage allocation process used to compute departmental overhead rates.

9 Diagram and describe the two-stage allocation process used in activity-based costing.

10 Describe the process of project costing used in service industry firms and nonprofit organizations.

MAKING CANOES IS AN ART FORM IN THIS ADIRONDACK COMMUNITY

Lake Placid, NY—As we skimmed across the lake, gliding almost effortlessly in our canoe, I was struck by the beauty of the Adirondack Mountains. "Many people don't realize it," said my host, "but New York's Adirondack Park is the largest state park in the nation. There are thousands of acres of unspoiled beauty." We made our way to shore and pulled our 16-foot canoe out of the water. My host was Meg Wilmore, founder of Adirondack Outfitters. Wilmore's company, which produces some of the finest canoes in the Northeast, is located several miles from Lake Placid. Scene of the 1960 and 1980 Winter Olympic Games, Lake Placid is known for its scenic beauty. Nestled in the hills outside this quaint community is Wilmore's highly successful business. "Making canoes is an art," said Wilmore. "I learned it from my grandfather, who made them as a hobby. My goal was to form a small company to make high-quality canoes and small boats in an environmentally friendly way. If you do things right—and we do—it's a non-polluting industry."

After testing an Adirondack Outfitters' canoe, I returned with Wilmore to her production facility. Giving me a brief tour, Wilmore explained that the company was currently working on two production jobs. "Our production is organized by production jobs," explained Wilmore. "Right now we're making deluxe wooden canoes and deluxe aluminum fishing boats. Both models are good sellers throughout the northeastern states and eastern Canada." Wilmore pointed out that a number of machines were used in the production process, but all were hand operated. In many cases, one employee was able to tend several machines simultaneously. "We strive for a balance between being competitive, requiring machine production, and keeping a hands-on feel to the process. Basically we're a small, traditional job shop. Each job is relatively small in terms of the number of units, and the differences between jobs are significant. There's not much similarity between a wooden canoe and an aluminum fishing boat." Asked what accounted for her company's success, Wilmore's answer was, "quality and price."

"In today's business environment, you have to be price competitive, whether you're into canoes or microchips. To give people a high-quality boat or canoe at the right price means that we have to know our costs inside and out. Since production jobs are so different, we track costs on a job-by-job basis. As in any manufacturing operation, you've got material, labor, and overhead. We accumulate these three costs for each production job. Dividing by the number of units in the job gives us our unit cost."

As we talked, it was clear that Wilmore relished her role as an entrepreneur. I ended the interview by asking her if there was anything she'd rather do than make canoes. "Yes," was her swift reply, "paddle them!"

Product and Service Costing

A **product-costing system** accumulates the costs incurred in a production process and assigns those costs to the organization's final products. Product costs are needed for a variety of purposes in both financial accounting and managerial accounting.

Use in Financial Accounting   In financial accounting, product costs are needed to value inventory on the balance sheet and to compute cost-of-goods-sold expense on the income statement. Under generally accepted accounting principles, inventory is valued at its cost until it is sold. Then the cost of the inventory becomes an expense of the period in which it is sold.

Use in Managerial Accounting   In managerial accounting, product costs are needed for planning, for cost control, and to provide managers with data for decision making. Decisions about product prices, the mix of products to be produced, and the quantity of output to be manufactured are among those for which product cost information is needed.

Use in Reporting to Interested Organizations   In addition to financial statement preparation and internal decision making, there is an ever-growing need for product cost information in relationships between firms and various outside organizations. Public utilities, such as electric and gas companies, record product costs to justify rate increases that must be approved by state regulatory agencies. Hospitals keep track of the costs of medical procedures that are reimbursed by insurance companies or by the federal government under the Medicare program. Manufacturing firms often sign cost-plus contracts with the government, where the contract price depends on the cost of manufacturing the product.

Product Costing in Nonmanufacturing Firms

The need for product costs is not limited to manufacturing firms. Merchandising companies include the costs of buying and transporting merchandise in their product costs. Producers of inventoriable goods, such as mining products, petroleum, and agricultural products, also record the costs of producing their goods. The role of product costs in these companies is identical to that in manufacturing firms. For example, the pineapples grown and sold by Dole are inventoried at their product cost until they are sold. Then the product cost becomes cost-of-goods-sold expense.

Service Firms and Nonprofit Organizations   The production output of service firms and nonprofit organizations consists of services that are consumed as they are produced. Since services cannot be stored and sold later like manufactured goods, there are no inventoriable costs in service industry firms and nonprofit organizations. However, such organizations need information about the costs of producing services. Banks, insurance companies, restaurants, airlines, law firms, hospitals, and city governments all record the costs of producing various services for the purposes of planning, cost control, and decision making. For example, in making a decision about adding a flight from Chicago to Los Angeles, United Airlines' management needs to know the cost of flying the proposed route. A manager can make a better decision as to whether a university or city government should begin a drug counseling program if the cost of providing similar, existing services is known.

Flow of Costs in Manufacturing Firms

Manufacturing costs consist of direct material, direct labor, and manufacturing overhead. The product-costing systems used by manufacturing firms employ several manufacturing accounts. As production takes place, all manufacturing costs are added to the *Work-in-Process Inventory* account. Work in process is partially completed inventory. A debit to the account increases

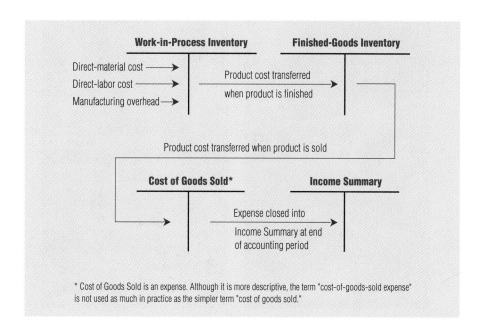

Exhibit 3–1

Flow of Costs through
Manufacturing Accounts

* Cost of Goods Sold is an expense. Although it is more descriptive, the term "cost-of-goods-sold expense"
is not used as much in practice as the simpler term "cost of goods sold."

the cost-based valuation of the asset represented by the unfinished products. As soon as
products are completed, their product costs are transferred from Work-in-Process
Inventory to *Finished-Goods Inventory.* This is accomplished with a credit to Work in
Process and a debit to Finished Goods. During the time period when products are sold,
the product cost of the inventory sold is removed from Finished Goods and added to
Cost of Goods Sold, which is an expense of the period in which the sale occurred. A
credit to Finished Goods and a debit to Cost of Goods Sold completes this step. Cost of
Goods Sold is closed into the Income Summary account at the end of the accounting
period, along with all other expenses and revenues of the period. Exhibit 3–1 depicts
the flow of costs through the manufacturing accounts.

Example of Manufacturing Cost Flows   Suppose that the Bradley Paper Company
incurred the following manufacturing costs during 19x9.

Direct material used	$30,000
Direct labor	20,000
Manufacturing overhead	40,000

During 19x9, products costing $60,000 were finished and products costing $25,000
were sold for $32,000. Exhibit 3–2 shows the flow of costs through the Bradley Paper
Company's manufacturing accounts and the effect of the firm's product costs on its
balance sheet and income statement.

Types of Product-Costing Systems

The detailed accounting procedures used in product-costing systems depend
on the type of industry involved. Two basic sets of procedures are used.

LO 3   Distinguish between job-order
costing and process costing.

Job-Order Costing Systems

Job-order costing is used by companies where goods are produced in distinct batches
and there are significant differences among the batches. Examples of firms that use job-
order costing are aircraft manufacturers, printers, custom furniture manufacturers, and
custom machining firms. In job-order costing, each distinct batch of production is called
a *job* or *job order.* The cost-accounting procedures are designed to assign costs to each
job. Then the costs assigned to each job are averaged over the units of production in the
job to obtain an average cost per unit. For example, suppose that AccuPrint worked on
two printing jobs during October, and the following costs were incurred.

Job-order costing is a
product-costing system in
which costs are assigned
to batches or job orders of
production.

The cost-accounting system keeps track of production costs as they flow from work-in-process inventory through finished-goods inventory and into cost of goods sold.

	Job A27 **(1,000 campaign posters)**	**Job B39** **(100 wedding invitations)**
Direct material	$100	$ 36
Direct labor	250	40
Manufacturing overhead	150	24
Total manufacturing cost	$500	$100

The cost per campaign poster is $.50 per poster ($500 divided by 1,000 posters), and the cost per wedding invitation is $1.00 ($100 divided by 100 invitations).

Procedures similar to those used in job-order costing are also used in many service industry firms, although these firms have no work-in-process or finished-goods inventories. In a public accounting firm, for example, costs are assigned to audit engagements in much the same way they are assigned to a batch of products by a furniture manufacturer. Similar procedures are used to assign costs to "cases" in health care facilities, to "programs" in government agencies, to research "projects" in universities, and to "contracts" in consulting and architectural firms.

Process-Costing Systems

Process costing is used by companies that produce large numbers of identical units. Firms that produce chemicals, microchips, gasoline, beer, fertilizer, textiles, processed food, and

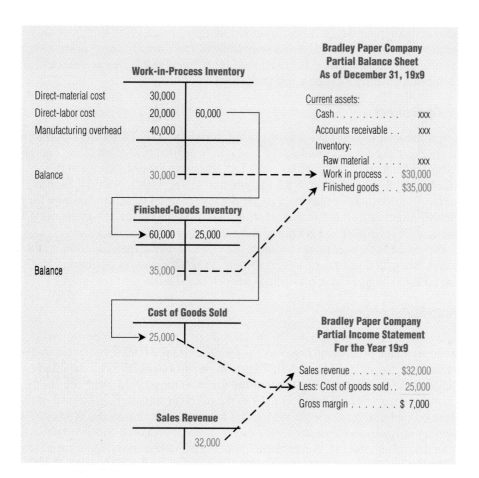

electricity are among those using process costing. In these kinds of firms, there is no need
to trace costs to specific batches of production, because the products in the different
batches are identical. A **process-costing system** accumulates all the production costs for
a large number of units of output, and then these costs are averaged over all of the units.
For example, suppose the Silicon Valley Company produced 40,000 microchips during
November. The following manufacturing costs were incurred in November.

A **process-costing system**
accumulates the costs of a
production process and
assigns them to the
products that comprise the
organization's output.

Direct material $1,000
Direct labor 2,000
Manufacturing overhead 3,000
Total manufacturing cost $6,000

The cost per microchip is $.15 (total manufacturing cost of $6,000 ÷ 40,000 units
produced).

Summary of Alternative Product-Costing Systems

The distinction between job-order and process costing hinges on the type of production
process involved. Job-order costing systems assign costs to distinct production jobs
that are significantly different. Then an average cost is computed for each unit of
product in each job. Process-costing systems average costs over a large number of
identical (or very similar) units of product.

The remainder of this chapter examines the details of job-order costing. The next
chapter covers process costing.

Accumulating Costs in a Job-Order Costing System

In a job-order costing system, costs of direct material, direct labor, and manufacturing
overhead are assigned to each production job. These costs comprise the *inputs* of the

A **job-cost sheet** records the costs of direct material, direct labor, and manufacturing overhead for a particular job or batch.

product-costing *system.* As costs are incurred, they are added to the Work-in-Process Inventory account in the ledger. To keep track of the manufacturing costs assigned to *each job,* a subsidiary ledger is maintained. The subsidiary ledger account assigned to each job is a document called a **job-cost sheet.**

Job-Cost Sheet

An example of a job-cost sheet is displayed in Exhibit 3–3. Three sections on the job-cost sheet are used to accumulate the costs of direct material, direct labor, and manufacturing overhead assigned to the job. The other two sections are used to record the total cost and average unit cost for the job, and to keep track of units shipped to customers. A job-cost sheet may be a paper document upon which the entries for direct material, direct labor, and manufacturing overhead are written. Increasingly, it is a computer file where entries are made using a computer terminal.

The procedures used to accumulate the costs of direct material, direct labor, and manufacturing overhead for a job constitute the *set of activities* performed by the job-order costing *system.* These procedures are discussed next.

Direct-Material Costs

A **material requisition form** is completed by the production department supervisor to request the release of raw materials for production.

A **source document** is used as the basis for an accounting entry.

As raw materials are needed for the production process, they are transferred from the warehouse to the production department. To authorize the release of materials, the production department supervisor completes a **material requisition form** and presents it to the warehouse supervisor. A copy of the material requisition form goes to the cost-accounting department. There it is used as the basis for transferring the cost of the requisitioned material from the Raw-Material Inventory account to the Work-in-Process Inventory account, and for entering the direct-material cost on the job-cost sheet for the production job in process. A document such as the material requisition form, which is used as the basis for an accounting entry, is called a **source document.** Exhibit 3–4 shows an example of a material requisition form.

In many factories, material requisitions are entered directly into a computer terminal by the production department supervisor. The requisition is automatically transmitted to terminals in the warehouse and in the cost-accounting department. Such automation reduces the flow of paperwork, minimizes clerical errors, and speeds up the product-costing process.

A **bill of materials** lists all the materials needed to manufacture a product or product component.

Material-Requirements Planning   For products and product components that are produced routinely, the required materials are known in advance. For these products and components, material requisitions are based on a **bill of materials** that lists all of the materials needed.

In complex manufacturing operations, in which production takes place in several stages, *material-requirements planning* (or *MRP*) may be used. MRP is an operations-management tool that assists managers in scheduling production in each stage of the manufacturing process. Such careful planning ensures that, at each stage in the production process, the required subassemblies, components, or partially processed materials will be ready for the next stage. MRP systems, which are generally computerized, include files that list all of the component parts and materials in inventory and all of the parts and materials needed in each stage of the production process.

Direct-Labor Costs

A **time ticket** records the amount of time an employee spends on each production job.

The assignment of direct-labor costs to jobs is based on time tickets filled out by employees. A **time ticket** is a form that records the amount of time an employee spends on each production job. The time ticket is the source document used in the cost-accounting department as the basis for adding direct-labor costs to Work-in-Process Inventory and to the job-cost sheets for the various jobs in process. In some factories, a computerized time-clock system may be used. Employees enter the time they begin

JOB-COST SHEET

Job Number _____   Description _____
Date Started _____   Date Completed _____
                                        Number of Units Completed _____

Direct Material				
Date	Requisition Number	Quantity	Unit Price	Cost

Direct Labor				
Date	Time Card Number	Hours	Rate	Cost

Manufacturing Overhead				
Date	Activity Base	Quantity	Application Rate	Cost

Cost Summary	
Cost Item	Amount
Total direct material Total direct labor Total manufacturing overhead	
Total cost	
Unit cost	

Shipping Summary		
Date	Number of Units Shipped	Cost Balance

Exhibit 3–3

Job-Cost Sheet

Material-Requisition Number ____352____   Date ____1/28/x9____
Job Number to Be Charged ____J621____   Department ____Painting____
Department Supervisor's Signature ____Timothy Williams____

Item	Quantity	Unit Cost	Amount
White enamel paint	8 gallons	$14.00	$112
Clear lacquer	2 gallons	11.00	22

Exhibit 3–4

Material Requisition Form

and stop work on each job into the time clock. The time clock is connected to a computer, which records the time spent on various jobs and transmits the information to the accounting department.

Exhibit 3–5 displays an example of a time ticket. As the example shows, most of the employee's time was spent working on two different production jobs. In the accounting department, the time spent on each job will be multiplied by the employee's wage rate, and the cost will be recorded in Work-in-Process Inventory and on the appropriate job-cost sheets. The employee also spent one-half hour on shop cleanup duties. This time will be classified by the accounting department as indirect labor, and its cost will be included in manufacturing overhead.

Manufacturing-Overhead Costs

It is relatively simple to trace direct-material and direct-labor costs to production jobs, but manufacturing overhead is not easily traced to jobs. By definition, manufacturing overhead is a heterogeneous pool of indirect production costs, such as indirect material, indirect labor, utility costs, and depreciation. These costs often bear no obvious relationship to individual jobs or units of product, but they must be incurred for production to take place. Therefore, it is necessary to assign manufacturing-overhead costs to jobs in order to have a complete picture of product costs. This process of assigning manufacturing-overhead costs to production jobs is called **overhead application** (or sometimes **overhead absorption**).

Overhead Application   For product-costing information to be useful, it must be provided to managers on a timely basis. Suppose the cost-accounting department waited until the end of an accounting period so that the *actual* costs of manufacturing overhead could be determined before applying overhead costs to the firm's products. The result would be very accurate overhead application. However, the information might be useless because it was not available to managers for planning, control, and decision making during the period.

Predetermined Overhead Rate   The solution to this problem is to apply overhead to products on the basis of estimates made at the beginning of the accounting period. The accounting department chooses some measure of productive activity to use as the basis for overhead application. In traditional product-costing systems, this measure is usually some **volume-based cost driver** (or **activity base**), such as direct-labor hours, direct-labor cost, or machine hours. An estimate is made of (1) the amount of manufacturing overhead that will be incurred during a specified period of time and (2) the amount of the cost driver (or activity base) that will be used or incurred during the same time period. Then a **predetermined overhead rate** is computed as follows:

$$\text{Predetermined overhead rate} = \frac{\text{Budgeted manufacturing-overhead cost}}{\text{Budgeted amount of cost driver (or activity base)}}$$

For example, suppose that AccuPrint has chosen machine hours as its cost driver (or activity base). For the next year, the firm estimates that overhead cost will amount to

Overhead application (or **absorption**) is the process of assigning manufacturing-overhead costs to production jobs.

LO 4   Compute a predetermined overhead rate, and explain its use in job-order costing.

A **volume-based cost driver** (or **activity base**) is closely associated with production volume, such as direct-labor hours or machine hours.

The **predetermined overhead rate** is used to apply manufacturing overhead to Work-in-Process Inventory.

Exhibit 3–5

Time Ticket

| Employee Name | W. B. McClelland | | Date | 1/22/x9 |
| Employee Number | 62 | | Department | Drilling |

Time Started	Time Stopped	Job Number
8:00	11:30	A267
11:30	12:00	Shop cleanup
1:00	5:00	J122

$90,000 and that total machine hours used will be 10,000 hours. The predetermined overhead rate is computed as follows:

$$\text{Predetermined overhead rate} = \frac{\$90{,}000}{10{,}000 \text{ hours}} = \$9.00 \text{ per machine hour}$$

In our discussion of the predetermined overhead rate, we have emphasized the term *cost driver,* because increasingly this term is replacing the more traditional term *activity base.* Furthermore, we have emphasized that *traditional* product-costing systems tend to rely on a *single, volume-based cost driver.* We will discuss more elaborate product-costing systems based on multiple cost drivers later in this chapter. The topic is examined in even greater detail in Chapter 5.

Applying Overhead Costs   The predetermined overhead rate is used to apply manufacturing overhead costs to production jobs. The quantity of the cost driver (or activity base) required by a particular job is multiplied by the predetermined overhead rate to determine the amount of overhead cost applied to the job. For example, suppose AccuPrint's job number C22, consisting of 1,000 brochures, requires three machine hours. The overhead applied to the job is computed as follows:

Predetermined overhead rate	$ 9
Machine hours required by job C22	× 3
Overhead applied to job C22	$27

The $27 of applied overhead will be added to Work-in-Process Inventory and recorded on the job-cost sheet for job C22. The accounting entries made to add manufacturing overhead to Work-in-Process Inventory may be made daily, weekly, or monthly, depending on the time required to process production jobs. Before the end of an accounting period, entries should be made to record all manufacturing costs incurred to date in Work-in-Process Inventory. This is necessary to properly value Work-in-Process Inventory on the balance sheet.

Summary of Event Sequence in Job-Order Costing

The flowchart in Exhibit 3–6 summarizes the sequence of activities performed by the job-order costing system. The role of the various documents used in job-order costing is also emphasized in the flowchart.

Illustration of Job-Order Costing

To illustrate the procedures used in job-order costing, we will examine the accounting entries made by Adirondack Outfitters, Inc. during November of 19x9. The company worked on two production jobs:

> **LO 5**   Prepare journal entries to record the costs of direct labor, direct material, and manufacturing overhead in a job-order costing system.

Job number C12, 80 deluxe wooden canoes

Job number F16, 80 deluxe aluminum fishing boats

The job numbers designate these as the twelfth canoe production job and the sixteenth fishing boat production job undertaken during the year. The events of November are described below along with the associated accounting entries.

ADIRONDACK
OUTFITTERS

Purchase of Material

Four thousand square feet of rolled aluminum sheet metal were purchased on account for $10,000. The purchase is recorded with the following journal entry.

(1)	Raw-Material Inventory	10,000	
	Accounts Payable		10,000

The postings of this and all subsequent journal entries to the ledger are shown in Exhibit 3–12, which appears on page 84.

Exhibit 3–6

Summary of Event Sequence
in a Job-Order Costing System

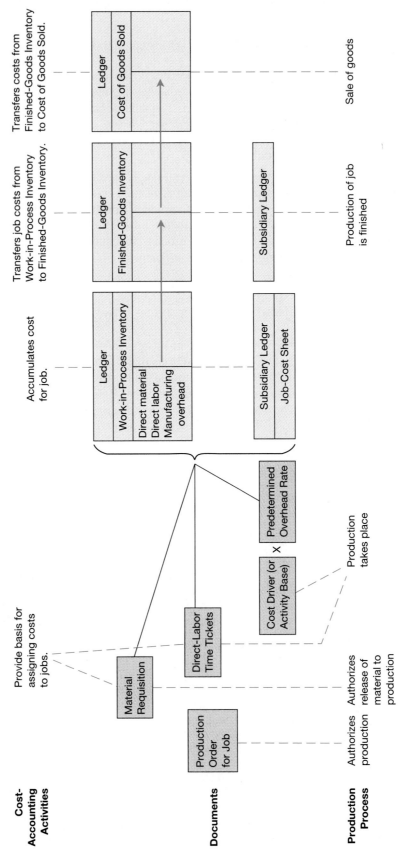

Use of Direct Material

On November 1, the following material requisitions were filed.

Requisition number 802: (for job number C12)	8,000 board feet of lumber, at $2 per board foot, for a total of $16,000
Requisition number 803: (for job number F16)	7,200 square feet of aluminum sheet metal, at $2.50 per square foot, for a total of $18,000.

The following journal entry records the release of these raw materials to production.

(2)	Work-in-Process Inventory	34,000	
	Raw-Material Inventory		34,000

The associated ledger posting is shown in Exhibit 3–12. These direct-material costs are also recorded on the job-cost sheet for each job. The job-cost sheet for job number F16 is displayed in Exhibit 3–7. Since the job-cost sheet for job number C12 is similar, it is not shown.

Use of Indirect Material

On November 15, the following material requisition was filed.

Requisition number 804:	5 gallons of bonding glue, at $10 per gallon, for a total cost of $50

Small amounts of bonding glue are used in the production of all classes of boats manufactured by Adirondack Outfitters. Since the cost incurred is small, no attempt is made to trace the cost of glue to specific jobs. Instead, glue is considered an indirect material, and its cost is included in manufacturing overhead. The company accumulates all manufacturing-overhead costs in the Manufacturing Overhead account. All actual overhead costs are recorded by debiting this account. The account is debited when indirect materials are requisitioned, when indirect-labor costs are incurred, when utility bills are paid, when depreciation is recorded on manufacturing equipment, and so forth. The journal entry made to record the usage of glue is as follows:

(3)	Manufacturing Overhead	50	
	Manufacturing Supplies Inventory		50

The posting of this journal entry to the ledger is shown in Exhibit 3–12. No entry is made on any job-cost sheet for the usage of glue, since its cost is not traced to individual production jobs.

This job shop records the cost of manufacturing canoes and other small boats. Direct material, direct labor, and manufacturing overhead costs are tracked.

Use of Direct Labor

At the end of November, the cost-accounting department uses the labor time tickets filed during the month to determine the following direct-labor costs of each job.

Direct labor: job number C12	$ 9,000
Direct labor: job number F16	12,000
Total direct labor	$21,000

The journal entry made to record these costs is as follows:

Exhibit 3–7

Job-Cost Sheet: Adirondack
Outfitters, Inc.

JOB-COST SHEET

Job Number ___F16___   **Description** ___80 deluxe aluminum fishing boats___

Date Started ___Nov. 1, 19x9___   **Date Completed** ___Nov. 22, 19x9___

Number of Units Completed ___80___

Direct Material

Date	Requisition Number	Quantity	Unit Price	Cost
11/1	803	7,200 sq ft	$2.50	$18,000

Direct Labor

Date	Time Card Number	Hours	Rate	Cost
Various dates	Various time cards	600	$20	$12,000

Manufacturing Overhead

Date	Activity Base	Quantity	Application Rate	Cost
11/30	Machine hours	2,000	$9.00	$18,000

Cost Summary

Cost Item	Amount
Total direct material	$18,000
Total direct labor	12,000
Total manufacturing overhead	18,000
Total cost	$48,000
Unit cost	$600

Shipping Summary

Date	Units Shipped	Units Remaining in Inventory	Cost Balance
11/30	60	20	$12,000

(4)	Work-in-Process Inventory		21,000	
	Wages Payable			21,000

The associated ledger posting is shown in Exhibit 3–12. These direct-labor costs are also recorded on the job-cost sheet for each job. The job-cost sheet for job number F16 is displayed in Exhibit 3–7. Only one direct-labor entry is shown on the job-cost sheet. In practice, there would be numerous entries made on different dates at a variety of wage rates for different employees.

Use of Indirect Labor

The analysis of labor time cards undertaken on November 30 also revealed the following use of indirect labor:

Indirect labor: not charged to any particular job, $14,000

This cost comprises the production supervisor's salary and the wages of various employees who spent some of their time on maintenance and general cleanup duties during November. The following journal entry is made to add indirect-labor costs to manufacturing overhead:

(5)	Manufacturing Overhead	14,000	
	Wages Payable		14,000

No entry is made on any job-cost sheet, since indirect-labor costs are not traceable to any particular job. In practice, journal entries (4) and (5) are usually combined into one compound entry as follows:

Work-in-Process Inventory	21,000	
Manufacturing Overhead	14,000	
Wages Payable		35,000

Incurrence of Manufacturing-Overhead Costs

The following manufacturing-overhead costs were incurred during November.

Manufacturing overhead:	
Rent on factory building	$ 3,000
Depreciation on equipment	5,000
Utilities (electricity and natural gas)	4,000
Property taxes	2,000
Insurance	1,000
Total	$15,000

The following compound journal entry is made on November 30 to record these costs.

(6)	Manufacturing Overhead	15,000	
	Prepaid Rent		3,000
	Accumulated Depreciation—Equipment		5,000
	Accounts Payable (utilities and property taxes)		6,000
	Prepaid Insurance		1,000

The entry is posted in Exhibit 3–12. No entry is made on any job-cost sheet, since manufacturing-overhead costs are not traceable to any particular job.

Application of Manufacturing Overhead

Various manufacturing-overhead costs were incurred during November, and these costs were accumulated by debiting the Manufacturing-Overhead account. However, no manufacturing-overhead costs have yet been added to Work-in-Process Inventory or recorded on the job-cost sheets. The application of overhead to the firm's products is based on a predetermined overhead rate. This rate was computed by the accounting department at the beginning of 19x9 as follows:

$$\text{Predetermined overhead rate} = \frac{\text{Budgeted total manufacturing overhead for 19x9}}{\text{Budgeted total machine hours for 19x9}}$$

$$= \frac{\$360,000}{40,000} = \$9.00 \text{ per machine hour}$$

Factory machine-usage records indicate the following usage of machine hours during November:

Machine hours used: job number C12 . . . . .1,200 hours
Machine hours used: job number F16 . . . . .2,000 hours
Total machine hours . . . . .3,200 hours

The total manufacturing overhead applied to Work-in-Process Inventory during November is calculated as follows:

	Machine Hours		Predetermined Overhead Rate		Manufacturing Overhead Applied
Job number C12:	1,200	×	$9.00	=	$10,800
Job number F16:	2,000	×	$9.00	=	18,000
Total manufacturing overhead applied					$28,800

Applied manufacturing overhead is the amount of manufacturing-overhead costs added to Work-in-Process Inventory during an accounting period.

The following journal entry is made to add **applied manufacturing overhead** to Work-in-Process Inventory.

| (7) Work-in-Process Inventory . . . . | 28,800 | |
| Manufacturing Overhead . . . . | | 28,800 |

The entry is posted in Exhibit 3–12, and the manufacturing overhead applied to job number F16 is entered on the job-cost sheet in Exhibit 3–7.

Summary of Overhead Accounting

As the following time line shows, three concepts are used in accounting for overhead. Overhead is *budgeted* at the *beginning* of the accounting period, it is *applied during* the period, and *actual* overhead is measured at the *end* of the period.

Actual manufacturing overhead is the actual costs incurred during an accounting period for manufacturing overhead.

Exhibit 3–8 summarizes the accounting procedures used for manufacturing overhead. The left side of the Manufacturing-Overhead account is used to accumulate **actual manufacturing-overhead** costs as they are incurred throughout the accounting period. The actual costs incurred for indirect material, indirect labor, factory rental, equipment depreciation, utilities, property taxes, and insurance are recorded as debits to the account.

The right side of the Manufacturing-Overhead account is used to record overhead *applied* to Work-in-Process Inventory.

While the left side of the Manufacturing-Overhead account accumulates *actual* overhead costs, the right side applies overhead costs using the predetermined overhead rate, based on *estimated* overhead costs. The estimates used to calculate the predetermined overhead rate will generally prove to be incorrect to some degree. Consequently, there will usually be a nonzero balance left in the Manufacturing-Overhead account at the end of the year. This balance is usually relatively small, and its disposition is covered later in this illustration.

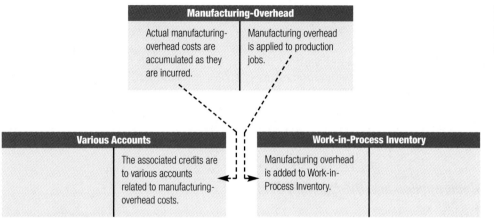

Exhibit 3–8

Manufacturing-Overhead Account

Selling and Administrative Costs

During November, Adirondack Outfitters incurred selling and administrative costs as follows:

Rental of sales and administrative offices	$ 1,500
Salaries of sales personnel	4,000
Salaries of management	8,000
Advertising	1,000
Office supplies used	300
Total	$14,800

Since these are not manufacturing costs, they are not added to Work-in-Process Inventory. Selling and administrative costs are period costs, not product costs. They are treated as expenses of the accounting period in which they are incurred. The following journal entry is made.

(8)	Selling and Administrative Expenses	14,800	
	Wages Payable		12,000
	Accounts Payable		1,000
	Prepaid Rent		1,500
	Office Supplies Inventory		300

The entry is posted in Exhibit 3–12.

Completion of a Production Job

Job number F16 was completed during November, whereas job number C12 remained in process. As the job-cost sheet in Exhibit 3–7 indicates, the total cost of job number F16 was $48,000. The following journal entry records the transfer of these job costs from Work-in-Process Inventory to Finished-Goods Inventory.

(9)	Finished-Goods Inventory	48,000	
	Work-in-Process Inventory		48,000

The entry is posted in Exhibit 3–12.

Sale of Goods

Sixty deluxe aluminum fishing boats manufactured in job number F16 were sold for $900 each during November. The cost of each unit sold was $600 as shown on the job-cost sheet in Exhibit 3–7. The following journal entries are made.

(10)	Accounts Receivable	54,000	
	Sales Revenue		54,000

| (11) Cost of Goods Sold .... | 36,000 | |
| Finished-Goods Inventory .... | | 36,000 |

These entries are posted in Exhibit 3–12.

The remainder of the manufacturing costs for job number F16 remain in Finished-Goods Inventory until some subsequent accounting period when the units are sold. Therefore, the cost balance for job number F16 remaining in inventory is $12,000 (20 units remaining times $600 per unit). This balance is shown on the job-cost sheet in Exhibit 3–7.

Underapplied and Overapplied Overhead

During November, Adirondack Outfitters incurred total *actual* manufacturing-overhead costs of $29,050, but only $28,800 of overhead was *applied* to Work-in-Process Inventory. The amount by which actual overhead exceeds applied overhead, called **underapplied overhead,** is calculated below.

Actual manufacturing overhead*	$29,050
Applied manufacturing overhead†	28,800
Underapplied overhead	$ 250

*Sum of debit entries in the Manufacturing-Overhead account: $50 + $14,000 + $15,000 = $29,050. See Exhibit 3–12.

†Applied overhead: $9.00 per machine hour × 3,200 machine hours.

> **Underapplied overhead** is the amount by which a period's actual manufacturing overhead exceeds applied manufacturing overhead.

If actual overhead had been less than applied overhead, the difference would have been called **overapplied overhead.** Underapplied or overapplied overhead is caused by errors in the estimates of overhead and activity used to compute the predetermined overhead rate. In this illustration, Adirondack Outfitters' predetermined rate was underestimated by a small amount.

> **Overapplied overhead** is the amount by which a period's applied manufacturing overhead exceeds actual manufacturing overhead.

Disposition of Underapplied or Overapplied Overhead   At the end of an accounting period, the managerial accountant has two alternatives for the disposition of underapplied or overapplied overhead. Under the most common alternative, the underapplied or overapplied overhead is closed into Cost of Goods Sold. This is the method used by Adirondack Outfitters, and the required journal entry is shown below.

| (12) Cost of Goods Sold .... | 250 | |
| Manufacturing Overhead .... | | 250 |

This entry, which is posted in Exhibit 3–12, brings the balance in the Manufacturing-Overhead account to zero. The account is then clear to accumulate manufacturing-overhead costs incurred in the next accounting period. Journal entry (12) has the effect of increasing cost-of-goods-sold expense. This reflects the fact that the cost of the units sold had been underestimated due to the slightly underestimated predetermined overhead rate. Most companies use this approach because it is simple and the amount of underapplied or overapplied overhead is usually small. Moreover, most firms wait until the end of the year to close underapplied or overapplied overhead into Cost of Goods Sold, rather than making the entry monthly as in this illustration.

Proration of Underapplied or Overapplied Overhead   Some companies use a more accurate procedure to dispose of underapplied or overapplied overhead. This approach recognizes that underestimation or overestimation of the predetermined overhead rate affects not only Cost of Goods Sold, but also Work-in-Process Inventory and Finished-Goods Inventory. As the following diagram shows, applied overhead passes through all three of these accounts. Therefore, all three accounts are affected by any inaccuracy in the predetermined overhead rate.

When underapplied or overapplied overhead is allocated among the three accounts shown above, the process is called **proration.** The amount of the current period's applied overhead remaining in each account is the basis for the proration procedure. In the Adirondack Outfitters illustration, the amounts of applied overhead remaining in the three accounts on November 30 are determined as follows:

Proration is the process of allocating underapplied or overapplied overhead to Work-in-Process Inventory, Finished-Goods Inventory, and Cost of Goods Sold.

Applied Overhead Remaining in Each Account on November 30

Account	Explanation	Amount	Percentage	Calculation of Percentages
Work in Process	Job C12 only	$10,800	37.5%	10,800 ÷ 28,800
Finished Goods	¼ of units in job F16	4,500	15.6%*	4,500 ÷ 28,800
Cost of Goods Sold	¾ of units in job F16	13,500	46.9%*	13,500 ÷ 28,800
Total overhead applied in November		$28,800	100.0%	

*Rounded

Using the percentages calculated above, the proration of Adirondack Outfitters' underapplied overhead is determined as follows:

Account	Underapplied Overhead	×	Percentage	=	Amount Added to Account
Work in Process	$250	×	37.5%	=	$ 93.75
Finished Goods	250	×	15.6%	=	39.00
Cost of Goods Sold	250	×	46.9%	=	117.25
Total underapplied overhead prorated					$250.00

If Adirondack Outfitters had chosen to prorate underapplied overhead, the following journal entry would have been made.

Work-in-Process Inventory	93.75	
Finished-Goods Inventory	39.00	
Cost of Goods Sold	117.25	
Manufacturing Overhead		250.00

Since this is *not* the method used by Adirondack Outfitters in our continuing illustration, this entry is *not* posted to the ledger in Exhibit 3–12.

Proration of underapplied and overapplied overhead is used by a small number of firms that are required to do so under the rules specified by the *Cost Accounting Standards Board (CASB)*. This federal agency was chartered by Congress in 1970 to

ADIRONDACK OUTFITTERS, INC.		
Schedule of Cost of Goods Manufactured		
For the Month of November, 19x9		
Direct material:		
Raw-material inventory, November 1	$30,000	
Add: November purchases of raw material	10,000	
Raw material available for use	$40,000	
Deduct: Raw-material inventory, November 30	6,000	
Raw material used		$34,000
Direct labor		21,000
Manufacturing overhead:		
Indirect material	$ 50	
Indirect labor	14,000	
Rent on factory building	3,000	
Depreciation on equipment	5,000	
Utilities	4,000	
Property taxes	2,000	
Insurance	1,000	
Total actual manufacturing overhead	$29,050	
Deduct: Underapplied overhead	250*	
Overhead applied to work in process		28,800
Total manufacturing costs		$83,800
Add: Work-in-process inventory, November 1		4,000
Subtotal		$87,800
Deduct: Work-in-process inventory, November 30		39,800
Cost of goods manufactured		$48,000

*The schedule of cost of goods manufactured lists the manufacturing costs *applied* to work in process. Therefore, the underapplied overhead, $250, must be deducted from total actual overhead to arrive at the amount of overhead *applied* to work in process during November. If there had been overapplied overhead, the balance would have been *added* to total actual manufacturing overhead.

The **schedule of cost of goods manufactured** details the manufacturing costs incurred during an accounting period and shows the change in Work-in-Process Inventory.

The **cost of goods manufactured** is the cost of direct labor, direct material, and manufacturing overhead transferred from Work-in-Process Inventory to Finished-Goods Inventory during an accounting period.

develop cost-accounting standards for large government contractors. The agency was discontinued by Congress in 1980, but it was recreated in 1990. The standards set forth by the agency apply to significant government contracts and have the force of federal law.

Schedule of Cost of Goods Manufactured

LO 6   Prepare a schedule of cost of goods manufactured, a schedule of cost of goods sold, and an income statement for a manufacturer.

Exhibit 3–9 displays the November **schedule of cost of goods manufactured** for Adirondack Outfitters. The schedule details the costs of direct material, direct labor, and manufacturing overhead *applied* to work in process during November and shows the change in Work-in-Process Inventory. The **cost of goods manufactured,** shown in the last line of the schedule, is $48,000. This is the amount transferred from Work-in-Process Inventory to Finished-Goods Inventory during November, as recorded in journal entry number (9).

Schedule of Cost of Goods Sold

The **schedule of cost of goods sold** shows the cost of goods sold and the change in finished-goods inventory during an accounting period.

A **schedule of cost of goods sold** for Adirondack Outfitters is displayed in Exhibit 3–10. This schedule shows the November cost of goods sold and details the changes in Finished-Goods Inventory during the month. Exhibit 3–11 displays the company's November income statement.

Posting Journal Entries to the Ledger

All of the journal entries in the Adirondack Outfitters illustration are posted to the ledger in Exhibit 3–12. An examination of these T-accounts provides a summary of the cost flows discussed throughout the illustration.

ADIRONDACK OUTFITTERS, INC. Schedule of Cost of Goods Sold For the Month of November, 19x9	
Finished-goods inventory, November 1	$12,000
Add: Cost of goods manufactured*	48,000
Cost of goods available for sale	$60,000
Deduct: Finished-goods inventory, November 30	24,000
Cost of goods sold	$36,000
Add: Underapplied overhead†	250
Cost of goods sold (adjusted for underapplied overhead)	$36,250

*The cost of goods manufactured is obtained from the schedule of cost of goods manufactured in Exhibit 3–9.

†The company closes underapplied or overapplied overhead into cost of goods sold. Hence the $250 balance in underapplied overhead is added to cost of goods sold for the month.

Exhibit 3–10

Schedule of Cost of Goods Sold

ADIRONDACK OUTFITTERS, INC. Income Statement For the Month of November, 19x9	
Sales revenue	$54,000
Less: Cost of goods sold*	36,250
Gross margin	$17,750
Selling and administrative expenses	14,800
Income before taxes	$ 2,950
Income tax expense	1,420
Net income	$ 1,530

*The cost of goods sold is obtained from the schedule of cost of goods sold in Exhibit 3–10.

Exhibit 3–11

Income Statement

Further Aspects of Overhead Application

Accuracy versus Timeliness of Information: A Cost-Benefit Issue

One of the themes of managerial accounting mentioned in Chapter 1 is the theme of costs and benefits. The issue of overhead application illustrates the importance of the cost-benefit theme. A product-costing system could be designed to use an **actual overhead rate** instead of a *predetermined overhead rate*. An actual overhead rate could be computed as follows:

LO 7   Discuss the cost-benefit issue of accuracy versus timeliness of information in accounting for overhead.

$$\text{Actual overhead rate} = \frac{\text{Actual overhead for the accounting period}}{\text{Actual amount of cost driver (or activity base)}}$$

An actual overhead rate can be computed only at the end of the accounting period. The result is more accurate, but rather untimely, product-costing information. A trade-off exists between accuracy and timeliness. Accurate information is useful when decisions are based on the information. Better pricing or cost-control decisions may result from more accurate product costs. However, late information entails a cost in terms of missed opportunities and late responses to events. Therefore, managers and managerial accountants must weigh the costs and benefits of the following choices.

The **actual overhead rate** is the rate at which overhead costs are actually incurred during an accounting period.

Actual Overhead Rate More accurate, but untimely information	**Predetermined Overhead Rate** Less accurate, but more timely information

Each entails costs and benefits
that must be considered.

Accounts Receivable		
Bal.	11,000	
(10)	54,000	

Accounts Payable		
	3,000	Bal.
	10,000	(1)
	6,000	(6)
	1,000	(8)

Prepaid Insurance		
Bal.	2,000	1,000	(6)

Wages Payable		
	10,000	Bal.
	21,000	(4)
	14,000	(5)
	12,000	(8)

Prepaid Rent		
Bal.	5,000	
		3,000	(6)
		1,500	(8)

Office Supplies Inventory		
Bal.	900	300	(8)

Manufacturing Supplies Inventory		
Bal.	750	50	(3)

Accumulated Depreciation: Equipment		
	105,000	Bal.
	5,000	(6)

Raw-Material Inventory		
Bal.	30,000	34,000	(2)
(1)	10,000		

Manufacturing Overhead		
(3)	50	28,800	(7)
(5)	14,000	250	(12)
(6)	15,000		

Work-in-Process Inventory		
Bal.	4,000	48,000	(9)
(2)	34,000		
(4)	21,000		
(7)	28,800		

Cost of Goods Sold		
(11)	36,000	
(12)	250	

Finished-Goods Inventory		
Bal.	12,000	36,000	(11)
(9)	48,000		

Selling and Administrative Expenses		
(8)	14,800	

Sales Revenue		
	54,000	(10)

*The numbers in parentheses relate T-account entries to the associated journal entries. The numbers in color are the November 1 account balances.

When designing product-costing systems, accountants generally recommend predetermined overhead rates.

It might be tempting to solve the overhead rate problem by using an actual rate and recomputing the rate frequently to provide more timely information. For example, the rate could be recomputed monthly. The problem with this approach is that some manufacturing-overhead costs are seasonal. For example, heating costs are higher in the winter, and air-conditioning costs are higher in the summer. Since overhead costs are incurred unevenly throughout the year, the monthly overhead rate would fluctuate widely. Moreover, the level of a volume-based cost driver, used as the denominator of the overhead rate, also may vary from period to period. Fluctuations in the number of workdays in a month and seasonal fluctuations in production volume can cause such variations. These activity variations can add to the fluctuations in the overhead rate.

Caterpillar uses normalized overhead rates in its production facilities, such as the one pictured here in Gosselies, Belgium.

The resulting inconsistency in product costs could give misleading signals for product pricing and other decisions that may depend on product cost information.

Accountants generally choose to smooth out fluctuations in the predetermined overhead rate by computing the rate over a long period of time. One-, two-, and three-year periods are common. A predetermined overhead rate computed in this fashion is called a **normalized overhead rate.** The use of a relatively long time period forces the accountant to face the trade-off between accuracy and timeliness that was discussed above. (Problem 3–56 illustrates the effects of using different time periods to compute overhead rates.) In the following illustration a manager from Caterpillar, Inc. stresses the importance of normalized product costs.

> A **normalized overhead rate** is a predetermined overhead rate calculated over a relatively long time period.

Caterpillar, Inc.
Normalizing smoothes the up-and-down effects that volume changes have on unit costs. We do not manage period costs to short-range volume swings, so if they aren't normalized, they could distort the inherent cost of products as volume increases or decreases. Normalizing is accomplished by spreading costs over long-term average volumes rather than current volume levels.[1]

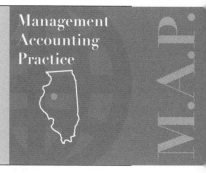

Management Accounting Practice

Actual and Normal Costing   Most firms use a predetermined overhead rate, based on overhead and activity estimates for a relatively long time period. When direct material and direct labor are added to Work-in-Process Inventory at their actual amounts, but overhead is applied to Work-in-Process Inventory using a *predetermined overhead rate,* the product-costing system is referred to as **normal costing.** This approach, which takes its name from the use of an overhead rate that is *normalized* over a fairly long period, is used in the Adirondack Outfitters illustration.

> **Normal costing** refers to a product-costing system where actual direct-material, actual direct-labor, and applied manufacturing-overhead costs are added to Work-in-Process Inventory.

---

[1]Excerpt from L. F. Jones, "Product Costing at Caterpillar," *Management Accounting* 72, no. 8, p. 38.

Actual costing refers to a product-costing system where actual direct-material, actual direct-labor, and actual manufacturing-overhead costs are added to Work-in-Process Inventory.

A few companies use **actual-costing,** a system in which direct material and direct labor are added to work in process at their actual amounts, and actual overhead is allocated to work in process using an *actual overhead rate* computed at the *end* of each accounting period. Note that even though an actual overhead rate is used, the amount of overhead assigned to each production job is still an allocated amount. Overhead costs, which are by definition indirect costs, cannot be traced easily to individual production jobs. Actual and normal costing may be summarized as follows:

ACTUAL COSTING Work-in-Process Inventory		NORMAL COSTING Work-in-Process Inventory	
Actual direct-material costs		Actual direct-material costs	
Actual direct-labor costs		Actual direct-labor costs	
Overhead allocated:		Overhead applied:	
Actual overhead rate (computed at *end* of period) ×	Actual amount of cost driver used (e.g., direct-labor hours)	*Predetermined* overhead rate (computed at *beginning* of period) ×	Actual amount of cost driver used (e.g., direct-labor hours)

Choosing the Cost Driver for Overhead Application

Manufacturing overhead includes various indirect manufacturing costs that vary greatly in their relationship to the production process. If a single, volume-based cost driver (or activity base) is used in calculating the predetermined overhead rate, it should be some productive input that is common across all of the firm's products. If, for example, all of the firm's products require direct labor, but only some products require machine time, direct-labor hours would be a preferable activity base. If machine time were used as the base, products not requiring machine time would not be assigned any overhead cost.

In selecting a volume-based cost driver (or activity base), the goal is to choose an input that varies in a pattern that is most similar to the pattern with which overhead costs vary. Products that indirectly cause large amounts of overhead costs should also require large amounts of the cost driver, and vice versa. During periods when the cost driver is at a low level, the overhead costs incurred should be low. Thus, there should be a correlation between the incurrence of overhead costs and use of the cost driver.

Throughput time (cycle time) is the average amount of time required to convert raw materials into finished goods ready to be shipped to customers.

Limitation of Direct Labor as a Cost Driver   In traditional product-costing systems, the most common volume-based cost drivers are direct-labor hours and direct-labor cost. However, there is a trend away from using direct labor as the overhead application base. Many production processes are becoming increasingly automated, through the use of robotics and computer-integrated manufacturing systems. Increased automation brings two results. First, manufacturing-overhead costs represent a larger proportion of total production costs. Second, direct labor decreases in importance as a factor of production. As direct labor declines in importance as a productive input, it becomes less appropriate as a cost driver. For this reason, some firms have switched to machine hours, process time, or throughput time as cost drivers that better reflect the pattern of overhead cost incurrence. **Throughput time** (or **cycle time**) is the average amount of time required to convert raw materials into finished goods ready to be shipped to customers. Throughput time includes the time required for material handling, production processing, inspection, and packaging.

As evidenced by these robotic welders, direct labor has declined in importance in many manufacturing processes.

Departmental Overhead Rates

In the Adirondack Outfitters illustration presented earlier in this chapter, all of the firm's manufacturing overhead was combined into a single cost pool. Then the overhead was applied to products using a single predetermined overhead rate based on machine hours. Since only one overhead rate is used in Adirondack Outfitters' entire factory, it is known as a **plantwide overhead rate.** In some production processes, the relationship between overhead costs and the firm's products differs substantially across production departments. In such cases, the firm may use **departmental overhead rates,** which differ across production departments. This usually results in a more accurate assignment of overhead costs to the firm's products.

A **plantwide overhead rate** is calculated by averaging manufacturing-overhead costs for the entire production facility.

A **departmental overhead rate** is calculated for a single production department.

Two-Stage Cost Allocation

LO 8   Describe the two-stage allocation process used to compute departmental overhead rates.

When a company uses departmental overhead rates, the assignment of manufacturing-overhead costs to production jobs is accomplished in two stages. In the first stage, all manufacturing-overhead costs are assigned to the production departments, such as machining and assembly. In the second stage, the overhead costs that have been assigned to each production department are applied to the production jobs that pass through the department. Let's examine this two-stage process in more detail.

Stage One   In the first stage all manufacturing-overhead costs are assigned to the firm's production departments. However, stage one often involves two different types of allocation processes. First, all manufacturing-overhead costs are assigned to **departmental overhead centers.** This step is called **cost distribution** (or sometimes **cost allocation**). For example, the costs of heating a factory with natural gas would be distributed among all of the departments in the factory, possibly in proportion to the cubic feet of space in each department. In the cost distribution step, manufacturing-overhead costs are assigned to *both* production departments and service departments. **Service departments,** such as equipment-maintenance and material-handling departments, are departments that do not work directly on the firm's products but are necessary for production to take place.

Departmental overhead centers are any departments to which overhead costs are assigned via overhead cost distribution.

Cost distribution (**cost allocation**) is the process of assigning manufacturing-overhead costs to all departmental overhead centers.

Service departments are not directly involved in producing the organization's output of goods and services.

Service department cost allocation is the process of assigning the manufacturing-overhead costs of a service department to the departments that use the services it provides.

Second, all service department costs are reassigned to the production departments through a process called **service department cost allocation.** In this step, an attempt is made to allocate service department costs on the basis of the relative proportion of each service department's output that is used by the various production departments. For example, production departments with more equipment would be allocated a larger share of the maintenance department's costs.

At the conclusion of stage one, all manufacturing-overhead costs have been assigned to the production departments.

Stage Two   In the second stage all of the manufacturing-overhead costs accumulated in each production department are assigned to the production jobs on which the department has worked. This process is called overhead application (or sometimes overhead absorption). In stage two, each production department has its own predetermined overhead rate. These rates often are based on different cost drivers.

The two-stage process of assigning overhead costs to production jobs is portrayed in Exhibit 3–13. Notice the roles of cost distribution, service department cost allocation, and overhead application in the exhibit. The techniques of overhead distribution and service department cost allocation will be covered later in the text. In this chapter we are focusing primarily on the process of overhead application.[2]

Exhibit 3–13

Developing Departmental
Overhead Rates Using
Two-Stage Allocation

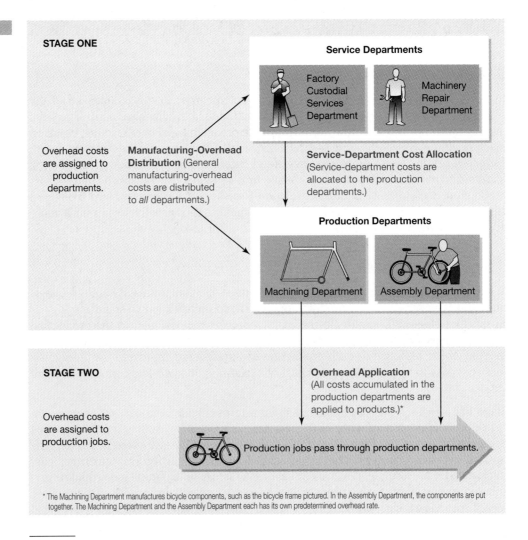

* The Machining Department manufactures bicycle components, such as the bicycle frame pictured. In the Assembly Department, the components are put together. The Machining Department and the Assembly Department each has its own predetermined overhead rate.

---

[2]One might legitimately ask why this is called two-stage cost allocation, when there are three types of allocation involved. The term *two-stage allocation* is entrenched in the literature and in practice. It stems from the fact that there are two *cost objects,* or entities to which costs are assigned: production *departments* in stage one and production *jobs* in stage two.

Activity-Based Costing: An Introduction

As manufacturing processes become more highly automated and the pressures of international competition increase, many manufacturers are introducing even more elaborate product-costing systems. Although departmental overhead rates provide more accurate product costs than a single plantwide rate, it is possible to achieve even greater accuracy by focusing on the many activities that comprise the production process. In an **activity-based costing** (or **ABC**) **system,** the two-stage cost allocation process is retained. However, instead of assigning overhead costs only to departments in stage one, overhead costs are assigned to a larger number of cost pools that represent the most significant *activities* comprising the production process. The activities identified vary across manufacturers, but such activities as engineering support, material handling, machine setup, production scheduling, inspection, receiving, shipping, and purchasing provide examples.

> **LO 9**   Diagram and describe the two-stage allocation process used in activity-based costing.

> An **activity-based costing (ABC) system** is a two-stage procedure for assigning overhead costs to products, which focuses on the major activities performed in the production process.

After assigning costs to the activity cost pools in stage one, cost drivers are identified that are appropriate for each cost pool. Then in stage two the overhead costs are allocated from each activity cost pool to each production job in proportion to the amount of activity consumed by the job. For example, the number of inspections might be the cost driver used to assign overhead costs from the inspection activity cost pool to the various production jobs. If job A required twice as many inspections as job B, it would be assigned twice as much overhead cost from the inspection activity cost pool.

Exhibit 3–14 portrays the two-stage allocation process used in activity-based costing systems. The increased product-costing accuracy in activity-based costing comes from (1) the identification of a large number of activity cost pools and (2) the specification of an appropriate cost driver for each activity. *The appendix at the end of this chapter provides a numerical example of activity-based costing.* The example in the appendix also compares the product costs obtained with a plantwide overhead rate, departmental overhead rates, and an ABC system.

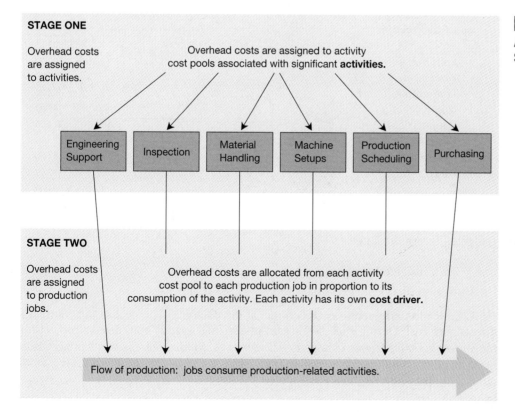

Exhibit 3–14

Activity-Based Costing System

STAGE ONE

Overhead costs are assigned to activities.

Overhead costs are assigned to activity cost pools associated with significant **activities.**

Engineering Support | Inspection | Material Handling | Machine Setups | Production Scheduling | Purchasing

STAGE TWO

Overhead costs are assigned to production jobs.

Overhead costs are allocated from each activity cost pool to each production job in proportion to its consumption of the activity. Each activity has its own **cost driver.**

Flow of production: jobs consume production-related activities.

Activity-based costing is a relatively new and very important topic in managerial accounting. It cannot be covered adequately in a few pages; we will examine activity-based costing in much greater detail in Chapter 5, along with other cost management techniques that are emerging in today's manufacturing environment.

Costs and Benefits   The theme of costs and benefits arises again with respect to using a single, plantwide overhead rate, departmental overhead rates, or an activity-based costing system. A product-costing system using multiple cost drivers and overhead rates is more complicated and more costly to use. However, the product-costing information that results is more accurate and more useful for decision making. Weighing these costs and benefits is part of the managerial accountant's job in designing a product-costing system.

The trend in today's highly automated manufacturing environments is toward greater use of multiple cost drivers for overhead application. Activity-based costing systems are coming into greater use as managers see the strategic importance of having highly accurate product cost information.

Project Costing: Job-Order Costing in Nonmanufacturing Organizations

LO 10   Describe the process of project costing used in service industry firms and nonprofit organizations.

Job-order costing also is used in nonmanufacturing organizations. However, rather than referring to production "jobs," such organizations use terminology that reflects their operations. Hospitals and law firms assigns costs to "cases," consulting firms and advertising agencies have "contracts," and governmental agencies often refer to "programs" or "missions." The need for cost accumulation exists in these and similar organizations for the same reasons found in manufacturing firms. For example, a NASA mission to launch a commercial satellite is assigned a cost for the purposes of planning, cost control, and pricing of the launch service.

To illustrate the cost-accumulation system used in a service industry firm, the following information is given for Midtown Advertising Agency, Inc.

Annual budgeted overhead:

Indirect labor (secretarial and custodial)	$120,000
Indirect materials	15,000
Photocopying	4,000
Computer leasing	17,000
Supplies	14,000
Utilities	21,000
Building rental	90,000
Insurance	8,000
Postage	11,000
Total	$300,000
Budgeted direct professional labor (salaries of advertising account executives)	$120,000

Budgeted Overhead Rate:

$$\frac{\text{Budgeted overhead}}{\text{Budgeted direct professional labor}} = \frac{\$300,000}{\$120,000} = 250\%$$

Overhead is assigned to each contract at the rate of 250 percent of the contract's direct-labor cost. During June, Midtown Advertising Agency completed a project for the Super Scoop Ice Cream Company. The contract required $800 in direct materials to build an advertising display to use in trade shows, and $4,000 in direct professional labor. The cost of the contract is computed as follows:

**Contract B628: Advertising Program
for Super Scoop Ice Cream Company**

Direct material	$ 800
Direct professional labor	4,000
Overhead (250% × $4,000)	10,000
Total contract cost	$14,800

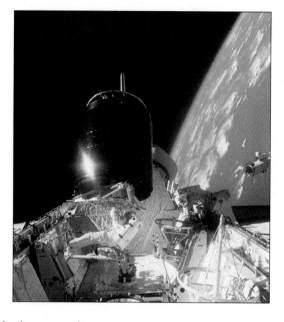

Project costing is used to measure the cost of launching a commercial satellite for the purposes of planning, cost control, and pricing of the launch service.

The contract cost of $14,800 includes actual direct-material and direct-labor costs, and applied overhead based on the predetermined overhead rate of 250 percent of direct-labor cost. The contract cost can be used by the firm in controlling costs, for planning cash flows and operations, and as one informational input in its contract-pricing decisions. In addition to the contract cost, the firm should also consider the demand for its advertising services and the prices charged by its competitors.

The discussion above provides only a brief overview of cost-accumulation procedures in service industry and nonprofit organizations. The main point is that job-order costing systems are used in a wide variety of organizations, and these systems provide important information to managers for planning, decision making, and control. The following illustration about Fireman's Fund insurance demonstrates the relevance of cost information in the insurance industry.

Fireman's Fund Insurance

Fireman's Fund is one of the top 20 U.S. providers of casualty and property insurance. As part of an effort to improve profitability, the company implemented a new cost reporting system that provides profit and loss information to local branch managers and product line managers. The system identifies revenue by product line (i.e., type of insurance policy), in addition to various cost components such as sales commissions, claim losses, and operating expenses. Managers at all levels are using this information in a variety of decisions, including office staffing, setting premiums, and office automation.[3]

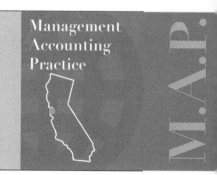

Management
Accounting
Practice

M.A.P.

Changing Technology in Manufacturing Operations

The technology of manufacturing is changing rapidly. These technological changes often affect the managerial accounting procedures used to collect data and transmit information to the intended users. Two such technological changes are electronic data interchange (or EDI) and the use of bar codes.

Electronic Data Interchange

Electronic data interchange (or *EDI*) is the direct exchange of data between organizations via a computer-to-computer interface. EDI is used to transmit such documents as purchase orders, shipping notices, receiving notices, invoices, and a host of other

---

[3]M. Crane and J. Meyer, "Focusing on the True Costs in a Service Organization," *Management Accounting* 75, no. 8, pp. 41–45.

production-related data. This eliminates the need for paperwork, speeding up the flow of information and substantially reducing errors. As the following examples show, EDI is now in widespread use.[4]

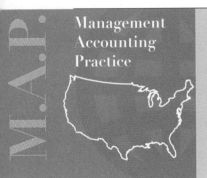

Management Accounting Practice

Electronic Data Interchange (EDI)

- *Wal-Mart and Kmart*   Wal-Mart Stores and Kmart Corporation gave deadlines to their suppliers for the installation of EDI capabilities. The suppliers had to comply or they would lose these giant retailers as customers.
- *Stride-Rite*   Stride-Rite Corporation responded to demands for faster delivery of shoes to retailers by implementing EDI for its ordering system. With EDI, Stride-Rite reduced its delivery time to a day and a half.
- *Greenwood Mills*   Greenwood Mills, a large textile manufacturer, installed EDI to let its customers know the exact width of the bolts of fabric to be shipped out. Greenwood's customers no longer had to measure bolts as they arrived, and they were able to program their automated cutting equipment to use almost every inch of fabric in each bolt.

Use of Bar Codes

We all have seen bar codes used to record inventory and sales information in retail stores. This efficient means of recording data is also becoming widely used in recording important events in manufacturing processes. Production employees can record the time they begin working on a particular job order by scanning the bar code on their employee ID badge and a bar code assigned to the production job order. When raw materials arrive at the production facility, their bar code is scanned and the event is recorded. Inventory records are updated automatically. Raw materials and partially completed components are assigned bar codes, and their movement throughout the production process is efficiently recorded. For example, raw materials may be requisitioned by a production employee simply by scanning the bar code assigned to the needed raw materials. When the materials are sent from the warehouse to the requisitioning production department, the bar code is scanned again. Inventory records are updated instantly. Bar codes represent one more instance where technology is changing both the production environment and the procedures used in accounting for production operations.

Many manufacturers use bar code technology to track orders through every stage of the production process, from requisitioning raw materials to shipping finished goods. Here a circuit board's progress is tracked by an employee of a computer manufacturer.

---

[4]F. Borthick and H. P. Roth, "EDI for Re-engineering Business Processes," *Management Accounting* 75, no. 4, pp. 32–37.

Chapter Summary

Product costing is the process of accumulating the costs of a production process and assigning them to the firm's products. Product costs are needed for three major purposes: (1) to value inventory and cost of goods sold in financial accounting; (2) to provide managerial accounting information to managers for planning, cost control, and decision making; and (3) to provide cost data to various organizations outside the firm, such as governmental agencies or insurance companies. Information about the costs of producing goods and services is needed in manufacturing companies, service industry firms, and nonprofit organizations.

Two types of product-costing systems are used, depending on the type of product manufactured. Process costing is used by companies that produce large numbers of nearly identical products, such as canned dog food and motor oil. Job-order costing, the topic of this chapter, is used by firms that produce relatively small numbers of dissimilar products, such as custom furniture and major kitchen appliances.

In a job-order costing system, the costs of direct material, direct labor, and manufacturing overhead are first entered into the Work-in-Process Inventory account. When goods are completed, the accumulated manufacturing costs are transferred from Work-in-Process Inventory to Finished-Goods Inventory. Finally, these product costs are transferred from Finished-Goods Inventory to Cost of Goods Sold when sales occur. Direct material and direct labor are traced easily to specific batches of production, called job orders. In contrast, manufacturing overhead is an indirect cost with respect to job orders or units of product. Therefore, overhead is applied to production jobs using a predetermined overhead rate, which is based on estimates of manufacturing overhead and the level of some cost driver (or activity base). The most commonly used volume-based cost drivers are direct-labor hours, direct-labor cost, and machine hours. Since these estimates will seldom be completely accurate, the amount of overhead applied during an accounting period to Work-in-Process Inventory will usually differ from the actual costs incurred for overhead items. The difference between actual overhead and applied overhead, called overapplied or underapplied overhead, may be closed out into Cost of Goods Sold or prorated among Work-in-Process Inventory, Finished-Goods Inventory, and Cost of Goods Sold.

The accuracy of product costs often can be increased by the use of departmental overhead rates instead of a single, plantwide overhead rate. Even greater accuracy can be achieved through the use of an activity-based costing system, which focuses on significant production-related activities and their cost drivers.

Job-order costing methods also are used in a variety of service industry firms and nonprofit organizations. Accumulating costs of projects, contracts, cases, programs, or missions provides important information to managers in such organizations as hospitals, law firms, and government agencies.

Key Terms

For each term's definition refer to the indicated page, or turn to the glossary at the end of the text.

activity base, pg. 72

activity-based costing (ABC) system, pg. 89

actual costing, pg. 86

actual manufacturing overhead, pg. 78

actual overhead rate, pg. 83

applied manufacturing overhead, pg. 78

bill of materials, pg. 70

cost distribution (sometimes called cost allocation), pg. 87

cost of goods manufactured, pg. 82

cycle time, pg. 86

departmental overhead centers, pg. 87

departmental overhead rate, pg. 87

job-cost sheet, pg. 70

job-order costing, pg. 67

material requisition form, pg. 70

normal costing, pg. 85

normalized overhead rate, pg. 85

overapplied overhead, pg. 80

overhead application (or absorption), pg. 72

plantwide overhead rate, pg. 87

predetermined overhead rate, pg. 72

process-costing system, pg. 69

product-costing system, pg. 66

proration, pg. 81

schedule of cost of goods manufactured, pg. 82

schedule of cost of goods sold, pg. 82

service departments, pg. 87

service department cost allocation, pg. 88

source document, pg. 70

throughput time, pg. 86

time ticket, pg. 70

two-stage cost allocation, pg. 87

underapplied overhead, pg. 80

volume-based cost driver, pg. 72

Appendix to Chapter 3

Different Overhead Rates under Plantwide, Departmental, and Activity-Based Costing Systems

LO 9   Diagram and describe the two-stage allocation process used in activity-based costing.

The accuracy of a product-costing system is affected by the number of cost drivers and overhead rates. A single, plantwide overhead rate based on only one volume-related cost driver generally is the least accurate. It is also the simplest system, however, and is the most commonly used method. A two-stage allocation process resulting in multiple departmental overhead rates typically will improve the accuracy of the product-costing system. This is particularly true when the production technology differs markedly among the departments. If, for example, one department relies chiefly on manual labor, while another department makes heavy use of machinery, departmental overhead rates with different cost drivers generally will increase product-costing accuracy. Even greater accuracy can be achieved with an activity-based costing system, with its multiple cost drivers and overhead rates.

Let's examine the effects of three alternative product-costing systems at Delta Controls Corporation, which manufactures two types of sophisticated control valves used in the food processing industry. Valve A has been Delta's main product for 15 years. It is used to control the flow of milk in various food processing operations, such as the production of cookies. Valve B, a more recently introduced product, is a specialty valve used to control the flow of thicker foods such as jelly and applesauce. The basic data for the illustration follow:

	Valve A	Valve B
Annual production and sales	30,000 units	5,000 units
Direct material	$140	$140
Direct labor:		
Machining Department	30 (1.5 hr. at $20)	30 (1.5 hr. at $20)
Assembly Department	30 (1.5 hr. at $20)	30 (1.5 hr. at $20)
Total prime costs	$200	$200
Machine time in Machining Department	1 hr.	3 hr.
Budgeted overhead costs:		
Machining Department	$630,000	
Assembly Department	$315,000	
Total	$945,000	

Now let's compute the applied overhead cost per valve under three alternative product-costing systems.

Plantwide Overhead Rate   Using a single, plantwide overhead rate based on direct-labor hours (DLH), each product is assigned $27 of overhead per unit.

	Valve A	Valve B
Applied overhead per unit*	$27 (3 DLH at $9 per DLH)	$27 (3 DLH at $9 per DLH)

*Total budgeted DLH = (30,000 units of A)(3 DLH per unit) + (5,000 units of B)(3 DLH per unit) = 105,000 DLH

$$\frac{\text{Predetermined}}{\text{overhead rate}} = \frac{\text{Total budgeted overhead}}{\text{Total budgeted DLH}} = \frac{\$945,000}{105,000} = \$9 \text{ per DLH}$$

Adding the $200 of prime costs for each valve, we have product costs of $227 per unit for each type of valve.

Departmental Overhead Rates

Now suppose we use departmental overhead rates. The Machining Department rate is based on machine hours (MH), whereas the Assembly Department rate is based on direct-labor hours (DLH). This approach yields assigned overhead costs of $23 per unit of valve A and $51 per unit of valve B.

	Valve A	Valve B
Applied overhead per unit:		
Machining Department*	$14 (1 MH at $14 per MH)	$42 (3 MH at $14 per MH)
Assembly Department†	9 (1.5 DLH at $6 per DLH)	9 (1.5 DLH at $6 per DLH)
Total	$23	$51

*Total budgeted MH = (30,000 units of A)(1 MH per unit) + (5,000 units of B)(3 MH per unit) = 45,000 MH

$$\text{Machining Department overhead rate} = \frac{\text{Machining Department overhead}}{\text{Budgeted MH}} = \frac{\$630,000}{45,000} = \$14 \text{ per MH}$$

†Total budgeted DLH in Assembly Department = (30,000 units of A)(1.5 DLH) + (5,000 units of B)(1.5 DLH) = 52,500 DLH

$$\text{Assembly Department overhead rate} = \frac{\text{Assembly Department overhead}}{\text{Budgeted DLH}} = \frac{\$315,000}{52,500} = \$6 \text{ per DLH}$$

Adding the $200 of prime costs for each valve, we have product costs of $223 for each unit of valve A and $251 for each unit of valve B. Valve A, which spends considerably less time in the more costly Machining Department than valve B, is now assigned a lower product cost than it was when a plantwide overhead rate was used. In contrast, valve B's assigned product cost has increased.

Activity-Based Costing (ABC)

Finally, let's see what happens to the assigned overhead costs under activity-based costing. Suppose Delta's accountants have established the following activity cost pools and cost drivers in stage one of the ABC method.

Activity	Activity Cost Pool	Quantity of Cost Driver	Cost per Unit of Cost Driver
Machine setups	$ 6,000	120 setups	$ 50 per setup
Engineering and design	210,000	7,000 engineering hrs.	$ 30 per engineering hr.
Material handling	22,000	220,000 lb. of material	$.10 per lb.
Quality control	32,000	800 inspections	$ 40 per inspection
Machinery-related costs	675,000	45,000 machine hrs.	$ 15 per machine hr.
Total	$945,000		

In stage two of the ABC method, Delta's accountants estimated how much of each cost driver is consumed by each *product line*. The ABC system then assigned overhead costs of $16.80 per unit of valve A and $88.20 per unit of valve B as follows:

	Valve A	Valve B
Applied overhead *per product line:*		
Setup ($50 per setup)	$ 1,000 (20 setups)	$ 5,000 (100 setups)
Engineering and design ($30 per hr.)	30,000 (1,000 hr.)	180,000 (6,000 hr.)
Material handling ($.10 per lb.)	17,000 (170,000 lb.)	5,000 (50,000 lb.)
Quality control ($40 per inspection)	6,000 (150 inspections)	26,000 (650 inspections)
Machinery-related costs ($15 per MH)	450,000 (30,000 MH)	225,000 (15,000 MH)
	$504,000*	$441,000*
Applied overhead per unit:	$16.80 $\left(\dfrac{\$504,000}{30,000 \text{ units}}\right)$	$88.20 $\left(\dfrac{\$441,000}{5,000 \text{ units}}\right)$

*Total applied overhead = $504,000 + $441,000 = $945,000

Adding the $200 of prime costs for each valve, we have product costs of $216.80 for each unit of valve A and $288.20 for each unit of valve B. Valve A, a high-volume and relatively simple product, is considerably less expensive to produce than valve B, a low-volume and relatively complex product.

Summary   The following table compares the total reported product costs of each product under the three alternative product-costing systems.

	Valve A	Valve B
Plantwide overhead rate	$227.00	$227.00
Departmental overhead rates	223.00	251.00
Activity-based costing	216.80	288.20

Activity-based costing yields the most accurate product cost for each valve. Notice that both the plantwide and departmental overhead costing systems significantly overcost the high-volume and relatively simple valve A, and undercost the low-volume and complex valve B.

Review Questions

3–1. List and explain three purposes of product costing.

3–2. How is the concept of product costing applied in service industry firms?

3–3. Explain the difference between job-order and process costing.

3–4. What are the purposes of the following documents: (*a*) material requisition form, (*b*) labor time ticket, and (*c*) job-cost sheet.

3–5. Why is manufacturing overhead applied to products when product costs are used in making pricing decisions?

3–6. Explain the benefits of using a predetermined overhead rate instead of an actual overhead rate.

3–7. Describe one advantage and one disadvantage of prorating overapplied or underapplied overhead.

3–8. Describe an important cost-benefit issue involving accuracy versus timeliness in accounting for overhead.

3–9. Explain the difference between actual and normal costing.

3–10. When a single, volume-based cost driver (or activity base) is used to apply manufacturing overhead, what is the managerial accountant's primary objective in selecting the cost driver?

3–11. Describe some costs and benefits of using multiple overhead rates instead of a plantwide overhead rate.

3–12. Describe the process of two-stage cost allocation in the development of departmental overhead rates.

3–13. Define each of the following terms, and explain the relationship between them: (*a*) overhead cost distribution, (*b*) service department cost allocation, and (*c*) overhead application.

3–14. Define *activity-based costing,* and explain how two-stage allocation is used in an ABC system.

3–15. Describe how job-order costing concepts are used in professional service firms, such as law practices and consulting firms.

3–16. What is meant by *material-requirements planning* or *MRP?*

3–17. What is meant by the term *cost driver?* What is a *volume-based cost driver?*

3–18. Describe the flow of costs through a product-costing system. What special accounts are involved, and how are they used?

3–19. Give an example of how a hospital might use job-order costing concepts.

3–20. Why are some manufacturing firms switching from direct-labor hours to machine hours or throughput time as the basis for overhead application?

3–21. What is the cause of overapplied or underapplied overhead?

3–22. Briefly describe two ways of closing out overapplied or underapplied overhead at the end of an accounting period.

3–23. Describe how a large retailer such as Home Depot could use EDI.

3–24. Explain how a Honeywell engineer might use bar code technology to record the time she spends on various activities.

Exercises

■ Exercise 3–25
Job-Order versus Process
Costing
(LO 1, LO 3)

For each of the following companies, indicate whether job-order or process costing is more appropriate.

1. Manufacturer of custom tool sheds.

2. Manufacturer of papers clips.

3. Engineering consulting firm.

4. Manufacturer of balloons.

5. Manufacturer of custom emergency rescue vehicles.

6. Manufacturer of swimming pool chemicals.

7. Manufacturer of custom hot tubs and spas.

8. Architectural firm.

9. Manufacturer of ceramic tile.

10. Producer of yogurt.

Alex Company manufactures finger splints for kids who get tendonitis from playing video games. The firm had the following inventories at the beginning and end of the month of January.

	January 1	January 31
Finished goods	$125,000	$117,000
Work in process	235,000	251,000
Raw material	134,000	124,000

■ **Exercise 3–26**
Job-Order Costing Basics
(LO 2, LO 6)

The following additional manufacturing data pertains to January operations.

Raw material purchased	$191,000
Direct labor	300,000
Actual manufacturing overhead	175,000

Alex Company applies manufacturing overhead at the rate of 60 percent of direct-labor cost. Any over-applied or underapplied manufacturing overhead is accumulated until the end of the year.

Required:

Compute the following amounts.

1. Alex Company's prime cost for January.
2. Alex Company's total manufacturing cost for January.
3. Alex Company's cost of goods manufactured for January.
4. Alex Company's cost of goods sold for January.
5. Alex Company's balance in the Manufacturing Overhead account on January 31. Debit or credit?

(CMA, adapted)

Crunchem Cereal Company incurred the following actual costs during 19x9.

Direct material used	$275,000 ✔
Direct labor	120,000 ✔
Manufacturing overhead	252,000 ✔

■ **Exercise 3–27**
Schedule of Cost of Goods
Manufactured
(LO 2, LO 6)

The firm's predetermined overhead rate is 210 percent of direct-labor cost. The January 1, 19x9 inventory balances were as follows:

Raw material	$30,000 ✔
Work in process	39,000 ✔
Finished goods	42,000 ✔

handwritten annotations:
10%   Dec 31/99 ✔
3,000   33,000 ✔
3,900   42,900 ✔
4,200   46,200

Each of these inventory balances was 10 percent higher at the end of the year.

Required:

1. Prepare a schedule of cost of goods manufactured for 19x9.
2. What was the cost of goods sold for the year?

Shawn Toy Company incurred the following costs to produce job number TB78, which consisted of 1,000 teddy bears that can walk, talk, and play cards.

■ **Exercise 3–28**
Job-Cost Sheet
(LO 2, LO 3, LO 4)

Direct Material

    4/1/x0 Requisition number 101: 400 yards of fabric at $.80 per yard

    4/5/x0 Requisition number 108: 500 cubic feet of stuffing at $.30 per cubic foot

Direct Labor

    4/15/x0 Time card number 72: 500 hours at $12 per hour

Manufacturing Overhead

    Applied on the basis of direct-labor hours at $2.00 per hour.

On April 30, 700 of the bears were shipped to a local toy store.

Required:

Prepare a job-cost sheet and record the information given above. (Use Exhibit 3–3 as a guide.)

■ **Exercise 3–29**
Cost Relationships; Normal
Costing System
(LO 2, LO 6)

Farber Company employs a normal costing system. The following information pertains to the year just ended.

■ Total manufacturing costs were $2,500,000.
■ Cost of goods manufactured was $2,425,000.
■ Applied manufacturing overhead was 30 percent of total manufacturing costs.
■ Manufacturing overhead was applied to production at a rate of 80 percent of direct-labor cost.
■ Work-in-process inventory on January 1 was 75 percent of work-in-process inventory on December 31.

Required:

1. Compute Farber Company's total direct-labor cost for the year.
2. Calculate the total cost of direct material used by Farber Company during the year.
3. Compute the value of Farber Company's work-in-process inventory on December 31.

(CMA, adapted)

■ **Exercise 3–30**
Manufacturing Cost Flows
(LO 2, LO 5, LO 6)

Jay Sports Equipment Company, Inc. incurred the following costs during 19x9.

Direct material used	$174,000
Direct labor	324,000
Manufacturing overhead applied	180,000

During 19x9, products costing $120,000 were finished, and products costing $132,000 were sold on account for $195,000. There were no purchases of raw material during the year. The beginning balances in the firm's inventory accounts are as follows:

Raw material	$227,000
Work in process	18,000
Finished goods	30,000

Required:

1. Prepare T-accounts to show the flow of costs through the company's manufacturing accounts during 19x9.
2. Prepare a partial balance sheet and a partial income statement to reflect the information given above. (Hint: See Exhibit 3–2.)

■ **Exercise 3–31**
Predetermined Overhead
Rate; Various Cost Drivers
(LO 4)

The following data pertain to the Borealis Restaurant Supply Company for the year just ended.

Actual manufacturing overhead	$340,000
Budgeted machine hours	10,000
Budgeted direct-labor hours	20,000
Budgeted direct-labor rate	$14
Budgeted manufacturing overhead	$364,000
Actual machine hours	11,000
Actual direct-labor hours	18,000
Actual direct-labor rate	$15

Required:

1. Compute the firm's predetermined overhead rate for the year using each of the following common cost drivers: (*a*) machine hours, (*b*) direct-labor hours, and (*c*) direct-labor dollars.
2. Calculate the overapplied or underapplied overhead for the year using each of the cost drivers listed above.

Refer to the data for the preceding exercise for Borealis Restaurant Supply Company. Prepare a journal entry to add to work-in-process inventory the total manufacturing overhead cost for the year, assuming:

1. The firm uses actual costing.
2. The firm uses normal costing, with a predetermined overhead rate based on machine hours.

■ **Exercise 3–32**
Actual versus Normal
Costing
(LO 4, LO 5)

Selected data concerning the past year's operations of the Fiberflex Manufacturing Company are as follows:

■ **Exercise 3–33**
Basic Manufacturing Cost
Flows
(LO 2, LO 6)

	Inventories	
	Beginning	**Ending**
Raw material	$71,000	$ 81,000
Work in process	80,000	30,000
Finished goods	90,000	110,000

Other data:

Direct materials used	$326,000
Total manufacturing costs charged to production during the year (includes direct material, direct labor, and manufacturing overhead applied at a rate of 60% of direct-labor cost)	686,000
Cost of goods available for sale	826,000
Selling and administrative expenses	31,500

Required:

1. What was the cost of raw materials purchased during the year?
2. What was the direct-labor cost charged to production during the year?
3. What was the cost of goods manufactured during the year?
4. What was the cost of goods sold during the year?

(CMA, adapted)

The following information pertains to Portsmouth Glass Works for the year just ended.

■ **Exercise 3–34**
Overapplied or Underapplied
Overhead
(LO 4, LO 5)

Budgeted direct-labor cost: 75,000 hours at $16 per hour	
Actual direct-labor cost: 80,000 hours at $17.50 per hour	
Budgeted manufacturing overhead: $997,500	

Actual manufacturing overhead:

Depreciation	$240,000
Property taxes	12,000
Indirect labor	82,000
Supervisory salaries	200,000
Utilities	59,000
Insurance	30,000
Rental of space	300,000
Indirect material (see data below)	79,000

Indirect material:

Beginning inventory, January 1	48,000
Purchases during the year	94,000
Ending inventory, December 31	63,000

Required:

1. Compute the firm's predetermined overhead rate, which is based on direct-labor hours.
2. Calculate the overapplied or underapplied overhead for the year.
3. Prepare a journal entry to close out the Manufacturing Overhead account into Cost of Goods Sold.

■ **Exercise 3–35**
Basic Journal Entries in Job-Order Costing
(LO 5)

Dewitt Educational Products started and finished job number B67 during June. The job required $4,600 of direct material and 40 hours of direct labor at $17 per hour. The predetermined overhead rate is $5 per direct-labor hour.

Required:

Prepare journal entries to record the incurrence of production costs and the completion of job number B67.

■ **Exercise 3–36**
Fixed and Variable Costs; Overhead Rate; Agribusiness
(LO 1, LO 4)

The controller for Tender Bird Poultry, Inc. estimates that the company's fixed overhead is $100,000 per year. She also has determined that the variable overhead is approximately $.10 per chicken raised and sold. Since the firm has a single product, overhead is applied on the basis of output units, chickens raised and sold.

Required:

1. Calculate the predetermined overhead rate under each of the following output predictions: 200,000 chickens, 300,000 chickens, and 400,000 chickens.
2. Does the predetermined overhead rate change in proportion to the change in predicted production? Why?

■ **Exercise 3–37**
Proration of Underapplied Overhead
(LO 5)

Heart's Content Confectionary incurred $157,000 of manufacturing overhead costs during the year just ended. However, only $141,000 of overhead was applied to production. At the conclusion of the year, the following amounts of the year's applied overhead remained in the various manufacturing accounts.

	Applied Overhead Remaining in Account on December 31
Work-in-Process Inventory	$35,250
Finished-Goods Inventory	49,350
Cost of Goods Sold	56,400

Required:

Prepare a journal entry to close out the balance in the Manufacturing Overhead account and prorate the balance to the three manufacturing accounts.

■ **Exercise 3–38**
Project Costing; Interior Decorating
(LO 1, LO 10)

Design Arts Associates is an interior decorating firm in St. Louis. The following costs were incurred in the firm's contract to redecorate the mayor's offices.

Direct material used	$3,500
Direct professional labor	6,000

The firm's budget for the year included the following estimates:

Budgeted overhead	$400,000
Budgeted direct professional labor	250,000

Overhead is applied to contracts using a predetermined overhead rate calculated annually. The rate is based on direct professional labor cost.

Required:

Calculate the total cost of the firm's contract to redecorate the mayor's offices.

■ **Exercise 3–39**
Choice of a Cost Driver for Overhead Application
(LO 1, LO 4)

Suppose you are the controller for a company that produces handmade glassware.

1. Choose a volume-based cost driver upon which to base the application of overhead. Write a memo to the company president explaining your choice.
2. Now you have changed jobs. You are the controller of a microchip manufacturer that uses a highly automated production process. Repeat the same requirements stated above.

■ **Exercise 3–40**
Cost Drivers; Different Production Methods
(LO 4, LO 5)

Hudson Bay Leatherworks, which manufactures saddles and other leather goods, has three departments. The Assembly Department manufactures various leather products, such as belts, purses, and saddlebags, using an automated production process. The Saddle Department produces handmade saddles and uses very little machinery. The Tanning Department produces leather. The tanning process requires little in the way of labor or machinery, but it does require space and process time. Due to the different production processes in the three departments, the company uses three different cost drivers for the application of manufacturing overhead. The cost drivers and overhead rates are as follows:

	Cost Driver	Predetermined Overhead Rate
Tanning Department	Square feet of leather	$3 per square foot
Assembly Department	Machine time	$9 per machine hour
Saddle Department	Direct-labor time	$4 per direct-labor hour

The company's deluxe saddle and accessory set consists of a handmade saddle, two saddlebags, a belt, and a vest, all coordinated to match. The entire set uses 100 square feet of leather from the Tanning Department, 3 machine hours in the Assembly Department, and 40 direct-labor hours in the Saddle Department.

Required:

Job number DS-20 consisted of 20 deluxe saddle and accessory sets. Prepare journal entries to record applied manufacturing overhead in the Work-in-Process Inventory account for each department.

Refer to Exhibit 3–13, which portrays the three types of allocation procedures used in two-stage allocation. Give an example of each of these allocation procedures in a hospital setting. The ultimate cost object is a patient-day of hospital care. This is one day of care for one patient. (Hint: First think about the various departments in a hospital. Which departments deal directly with patients; which ones are service departments and do not deal directly with patients? What kinds of costs does a hospital incur that should be distributed among all of the hospital's departments? Correct hospital terminology is not important here. Focus on the *concepts* of cost allocation portrayed in Exhibit 3–13.)

■ **Exercise 3–41**
Two-Stage Allocation
(LO 1, LO 8)

Service industry firms can make effective use of ABC systems as well as manufacturers. For each of the following businesses, list five key activities that are important in the provision of the firm's service. For each activity cost pool, suggest an appropriate cost driver to use in assigning costs from the activity cost pool to the services provided to customers.

■ **Exercise 3–42**
Activity-Based Costing
(LO 1, LO 9)

1. Airline
2. Restaurant
3. Fitness club

4. Bank
5. Hotel
6. Hospital

Problems

Hale Industries, a manufacturer of cable for the heavy construction industry, closes its books and prepares financial statements at the end of each month. The schedule of cost of goods sold for the month of April follows.

■ **Problem 3–43**
Schedule of Cost of Goods Manufactured
(LO 6)

HALE INDUSTRIES
Schedule of Cost of Goods Sold
For the Month of April
(in thousands)

Inventory of finished goods, March 31	$ 50
Add: Cost of goods manufactured	790
Cost of goods available for sale	$840
Deduct: Inventory of finished goods, April 30	247
Unadjusted cost of goods sold	$593
Add: Underapplied manufacturing overhead	25
Cost of goods sold (adjusted for underapplied overhead)	$618

Hale uses a first-in, first-out inventory flow system. The actual cost of direct materials and direct labor is used to value the inventories. However, manufacturing overhead is applied to production and carried to the inventories at a predetermined rate of $40 per ton of cable manufactured.

The preclosing trial balance as of May 31 is as follows:

HALE INDUSTRIES
Preclosing Trial Balance
As of May 31
(in thousands)

Account	Debit	Credit
Cash and marketable securities	$ 54	
Accounts and notes receivable	210	
Raw-material inventory, April 30	28	
Work-in-process inventory, April 30	150	
Finished-goods inventory, April 30	247	
Property, plant, and equipment (net)	1,140	
Accounts, notes, and taxes payable		$ 70
Bonds payable		600
Common stock		100
Retained earnings		930
Sales		1,488
Sales discounts	20	
Interest revenue		2
Purchases of raw material	525	
Direct labor	260	
Indirect labor	90	
Office salaries	122	
Sales salaries	66	
Utilities	135	
Rent	9	
Property taxes	60	
Insurance	20	
Depreciation	54	
Total	$3,190	$3,190

Additional Information:

- 80 percent of the utilities is related to the manufacture of cable; the remaining 20 percent is related to the sales and administrative functions in the office building.
- All of the rent is for the office building.
- The property taxes are assessed on the manufacturing plant.
- 60 percent of the insurance is related to the manufacture of cable; the remaining 40 percent is related to the sales and administrative functions.
- Depreciation expense includes the following:

Manufacturing plant	$20,000
Manufacturing equipment	30,000
Office equipment	4,000
Total	$54,000

- Hale manufactured 7,825 tons of cable during May.
- The inventory balances on May 31 are as follows:

Raw material	$ 23,000
Work in process	220,000
Finished goods	175,000

Required:

1. Prepare a schedule of cost of goods manufactured for Hale Industries for the month of May. Hale Industries closes all underapplied or overapplied manufacturing overhead to Cost of Goods Sold.

2. Describe an alternate treatment for closing underapplied or overapplied manufacturing overhead.

(CMA, adapted)

Devanshire Clock Works manufactures fine, handcrafted clocks. The firm uses a job-order costing system, and manufacturing overhead is applied on the basis of direct-labor hours. Estimated manufacturing overhead for the year is $240,000. The firm employs 10 master clockmakers, who constitute the direct-labor force. Each of these employees is expected to work 2,000 hours during the year. The following events occurred during October.

■ **Problem 3–44**
Basic Job-Order Costing;
Journal Entries
(LO 4, LO 5)

a. The firm purchased 3,000 board feet of mahogany veneer at $11 per board foot.

b. Twenty brass counterweights were requisitioned for production. Each weight cost $23.

c. Five gallons of glue were requisitioned for production. The glue cost $20 per gallon. Glue is treated as an indirect material.

d. Depreciation on the clockworks building for October was $8,000.

e. A $400 utility bill was paid in cash.

f. Time cards showed the following usage of labor:
    Job number G60: 12 grandfather's clocks, 1,000 hours of direct labor
    Job number C81: 20 cuckoo clocks, 700 hours of direct labor

    The master clockmakers (direct-labor personnel) earn $20 per hour.

g. The October property tax bill for $910 was received but not yet paid in cash.

h. The firm employs laborers who perform various tasks such as material handling and shop cleanup. Their wages for October amounted to $2,500.

i. Job number G60, which was started in July, was finished in October. The total cost of the job was $14,400.

j. Nine of the grandfather's clocks from job number G60 were sold in October for $1,500 each.

Required:

1. Calculate the firm's predetermined overhead rate for the year.

2. Prepare journal entries to record the events described above.

Perfecto Pizza Company produces microwavable pizzas. The following accounts appeared in Perfecto's ledger as of December 31.

■ **Problem 3–45**
Manufacturing Cost Flows;
Analysis of T-Accounts
(LO 2, LO 5)

Raw-Material Inventory		
Bal. 1/1	21,000	
	?	?
Bal. 12/31	36,000	

Accounts Payable		
		2,500	Bal. 1/1
136,500	?	
	1,000	Bal. 12/31

Work-in-Process Inventory		
Bal. 1/1	17,000	
Direct material	?	?
Direct labor	?	
Manufacturing overhead	?	
Bal. 12/31	19,000	

Finished-Goods Inventory		
Bal. 1/1	12,000	
	?	?
Bal. 12/31	20,000	

Manufacturing Overhead	
?	?

Cost of Goods Sold	
710,000	

Wages Payable		
	2,000	Bal. 1/1
147,000	?	
	5,000	Bal. 12/31

Sales Revenue	
	?

Accounts Receivable		
Bal. 1/1	11,000	
	?	806,000
Bal. 12/31	15,000	

Additional Information:

a. Accounts payable is used only for direct material purchases.

b. Underapplied overhead of $2,500 for the year has not yet been closed into cost of goods sold.

Required:

Complete the T-accounts by computing the amounts indicated by a question mark.

■ **Problem 3–46**
Schedules of Cost of Goods
Manufactured and Sold;
Income Statement
(LO 6)

The following data refer to Joliet Donut Company for the year 19x9.

Work-in-process inventory, 12/31/x8	$ 8,100
Selling and administrative salaries	13,800
Insurance on factory and equipment	3,600
Work-in-process inventory, 12/31/x9	8,300
Finished-goods inventory, 12/31/x8	14,000
Indirect material used	4,900
Depreciation on factory equipment	2,100
Raw-material inventory, 12/31/x8	10,100
Property taxes on factory	2,400
Finished-goods inventory, 12/31/x9	15,400
Purchases of raw material in 19x9	39,000
Utilities for factory	6,000
Utilities for sales and administrative offices	2,500
Other selling and administrative expenses	4,000
Indirect-labor cost incurred	29,000
Depreciation on factory building	3,800
Depreciation on cars used by sales personnel	1,200
Direct-labor cost incurred	79,000
Raw-material inventory, 12/31/x9	11,000
Rental for warehouse space to store raw material	3,100
Rental of space for company president's office	1,700
Applied manufacturing overhead	58,000
Sales revenue	205,800
Income tax expense	5,100

Required:

1. Prepare Joliet Donut Company's schedule of cost of goods manufactured for 19x9.

2. Prepare the company's schedule of cost of goods sold for 19x9. The company closes overapplied or underapplied overhead into Cost of Goods Sold.

3. Prepare the company's income statement for 19x9.

■ **Problem 3-47**
Journal Entries in Job-Order
Costing
(LO 4, LO 5)

Sea Voyager Corporation manufactures outboard motors and an assortment of other marine equipment. The company uses a job-order costing system. Normal costing is used, and manufacturing overhead is applied on the basis of machine hours. Estimated manufacturing overhead for the year is $1,464,000, and management expects that 73,200 machine hours will be used.

Required:

1. Calculate the company's predetermined overhead rate for the year.

2. Prepare journal entries to record the following events, which occurred during April.

   a. The firm purchased marine propellers from Martin Marine Corporation for $7,850 on account.

   b. A requisition was filed by the Gauge Department supervisor for 300 pounds of clear plastic. The material cost $.60 per pound when it was purchased.

   c. The Motor Testing Department supervisor requisitioned 300 feet of electrical wire, which is considered an indirect material. The wire cost $.10 per foot when it was purchased.

   d. An electric utility bill of $800 was paid in cash.

   e. Direct-labor costs incurred in April were $75,000.

f. April's insurance cost was $1,800 for insurance on the cars driven by sales personnel. The policy had been prepaid in March.

g. Metal tubing costing $3,000 was purchased on account.

h. A cash payment of $1,700 was made on outstanding accounts payable.

i. Indirect-labor costs of $21,000 were incurred during April.

j. Depreciation on equipment for April amounted to $7,000.

k. Job number G22, consisting of 50 tachometers, was finished during April. The total cost of the job was $1,100.

l. During April, 7,000 machine hours were used.

m. Sales on account for April amounted to $176,000. The cost of goods sold in April was $139,000.

The following data refers to Franconia Corporation for the year 19x9.

Sales revenue	$2,105,000
Raw-material inventory, 12/31/x8	89,000
Purchases of raw material in 19x9	731,000
Raw-material inventory, 12/31/x9	59,000
Direct-labor cost incurred	474,000
Selling and administrative expenses	269,000
Indirect labor cost incurred	150,000
Property taxes on factory	90,000
Depreciation on factory building	125,000
Income tax expense	25,000
Indirect material used	45,000
Depreciation on factory equipment	60,000
Insurance on factory and equipment	40,000
Utilities for factory	70,000
Work-in-process inventory, 12/31/x8	-0-
Work-in-process inventory, 12/31/x9	40,000
Finished-goods inventory, 12/31/x8	35,000
Finished-goods inventory, 12/31/x9	40,000
Applied manufacturing overhead	577,500

■ Problem 3-48
Schedules of Cost of Goods Manufactured and Sold; Income Statement
(LO 6)

Required:

1. Prepare Franconia's schedule of cost of goods manufactured for 19x9.

2. Prepare Franconia's schedule of cost of goods sold for 19x9. The company closes overapplied or underapplied overhead into Cost of Goods Sold.

3. Prepare Franconia's income statement for 19x9.

Refer to the schedule of cost of goods manufactured prepared for Franconia Corporation in the preceding problem.

■ Problem 3-49
Interpreting the Schedule of Cost of Goods Manufactured
(LO 2, LO 6)

Required:

1. How much of the manufacturing costs incurred during 19x9 remained associated with work-in-process inventory on December 31, 19x9?

2. Suppose the company had increased its production in 19x9 by 20 percent. Would the direct-material cost shown on the schedule have been larger or the same? Why?

3. Answer the same question as in requirement (2) for depreciation on the factory building.

4. Suppose only half of the $60,000 in depreciation on equipment had been related to factory machinery, and the other half was related to selling and administrative equipment. How would this have changed the schedule of cost of goods manufactured?

■ Problem 3-50
Cost of Goods Manufactured; Prime and Conversion Costs
(LO 2, LO 6)

Magellan Map Company's cost of goods sold for March was $345,000. March 31 work-in-process inventory was 90 percent of March 1 work-in-process inventory. Manufacturing overhead applied was

50 percent of direct-labor cost. Other information pertaining to the company's inventories and production for the month of March is as follows:

Beginning inventories, March 1:

Raw material	$ 17,000
Work in process	40,000
Finished goods	102,000
Purchases of raw material during March	113,000

Ending inventories, March 31:

Raw material	26,000
Work in process	?
Finished goods	105,000

Required:

1. Prepare a schedule of cost of goods manufactured for the month of March.
2. Prepare a schedule to compute the prime costs (direct material and direct labor) incurred during March.
3. Prepare a schedule to compute the conversion costs (direct labor and manufacturing overhread) charged to work in process during March.

(CPA, adapted)

■ Problem 3-51
Overhead Application Using a Predetermined Overhead Rate
(LO 2, LO 4, LO 6)

Tina Jeffrey, the controller for Lafayette Furniture Company, is in the process of analyzing the overhead costs for the month of November. She has gathered the following data for the month.

Labor

Direct-labor hours:

Job 77	3,500 ✓
Job 78	3,000
Job 79	2,000

8500

Labor costs:

Direct-labor wages	$ 51,000 ✓
Indirect-labor wages (4,000 hours)	15,000
Supervisory salaries	6,000

Material

Inventories, November 1:

Raw material and supplies	$ 10,500
Work in process (job 77)	54,000
Finished goods	112,500

Purchases of raw material and supplies:

Raw material	$135,000
Supplies (indirect material)	15,000

Direct material and supplies requisitioned for production:

Job 77	$ 45,000
Job 78	37,500
Job 79	25,500
Supplies (indirect material)	12,000
Total	$120,000

Other

Building occupancy costs (heat, light, depreciation, etc.)

Factory facilities	$ 6,400
Sales offices	1,600
Administrative offices	1,000
Total	$ 9,000

Production equipment costs:

Power	$ 4,100
Repairs and maintenance	1,500
Depreciation	1,500
Other	1,000
Total	$ 8,100

The firm's job-order costing system uses direct-labor hours as the cost driver for overhead application. In December of the preceding year, Jeffrey had prepared the following budget for direct-labor and manufacturing-overhead costs for the current year. The plant is capable of operating at 150,000 direct-labor hours per year. However, Jeffrey estimates that the normal usage is 120,000 hours in a typical year. ✓

Direct-Labor Hours	Manufacturing Overhead	
	Variable	Fixed
100,000	$325,000	$216,000
✗120,000	390,000 +	216,000 = 606,000.
140,000	455,000	216,000

During November the following jobs were completed:

Job 77	Side chairs
Job 78	End tables

Required:

Assist Jeffrey by making the following calculations.

1. Calculate the predetermined overhead rate for the current year.
2. Calculate the total cost of job 77.
3. Compute the amount of manufacturing overhead applied to job 79 during November.
4. What was the total amount of manufacturing overhead applied during November?
5. Compute the actual manufacturing overhead incurred during November.
6. Calculate the overapplied or underapplied overhead for November.

(CMA, adapted)

Cedar Rapids Jewelry Company uses normal costing, and manufacturing overhead is applied to work-in-process on the basis of machine hours. On January 1 of the current year there were no balances in work-in-process or finished-goods inventories. The following estimates were included in the current year's budget.

Total budgeted manufacturing overhead	$235,000
Total budgeted machine hours	47,000

■ **Problem 3-52**
Proration of Overapplied or Underapplied Overhead
(LO 2, LO 4, LO 5, LO 6)

During January, the firm began the following production jobs:

A79:	1,000 machine hours
N08:	2,500 machine hours
P82:	500 machine hours

During January, job numbers A79 and N08 were completed, and job number A79 was sold. The actual manufacturing overhead incurred during January was $26,000.

Required:

1. Compute the company's predetermined overhead rate for the current year.
2. How much manufacturing overhead was applied to production during January?
3. Calculate the overapplied or underapplied overhead for January.
4. Prepare a journal entry to close the balance calculated in requirement (3) into Cost of Goods Sold.
5. Prepare a journal entry to prorate the balance calculated in requirement (3) among the Work-in-Process Inventory, Finished-Goods Inventory, and Cost of Goods Sold accounts.

Conundrum Corporation manufactures furniture. Due to a fire in the administrative offices, the accounting records for November of the current year were partially destroyed. You have been able to piece together the following information from the ledger.

■ **Problem 3-53**
Flow of Manufacturing Costs; Incomplete Data
(LO 2, LO 4, LO 5)

Raw-Material Inventory		Accounts Payable	
			12,000	Bal. 10/31
	40,000		
Bal. 11/30 45,000			

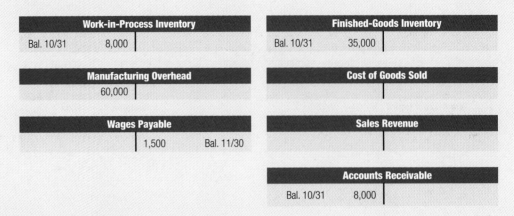

Upon examining various source documents and interviewing several employees, you were able to gather the following additional information.

a. Collections of accounts receivable during November amounted to $205,000.

b. Sales revenue in November was 120 percent of cost of goods sold. All sales are on account.

c. Overhead is applied using an annual predetermined overhead rate based on direct-labor hours.

d. The budgeted overhead for the current year is $720,000.

e. Budgeted direct-labor cost for the current year is $960,000. The direct-labor rate is $20 per hour.

f. The accounts payable balance on November 30 was $1,000. Only purchases of raw material are credited to accounts payable. A payment of $81,000 was made on November 15.

g. November's cost of goods sold amounted to $180,000.

h. The November 30 balance in finished-goods inventory was $5,000.

i. Payments of $79,500 were made to direct-labor employees during November. The October 31 balance in the Wages Payable account was $1,000.

j. The *actual* manufacturing overhead for November was $60,000.

k. An analysis of the furniture still in process on November 30 revealed that so far these items have required 500 hours of direct labor and $20,500 of direct material.

Required:

Calculate the following amounts. Then complete the T-accounts given in the problem.

1. Sales revenue for November. 216,000.
2. November 30 balance in accounts receivable. 19,000
3. Cost of raw material purchased during November.
4. November 30 balance in work-in-process inventory.
5. Direct labor added to work in process during November.
6. Applied overhead for November.
7. Cost of goods completed during November.
8. Raw material used during November.
9. October 31 balance in raw-material inventory.
10. Overapplied or underapplied overhead for November.

■ **Problem 3-54**
Comprehensive Job-Order
Costing Problem
(LO 2, LO 4, LO 5, LO 6)

Bandway Corporation manufactures brass musical instruments for use by high school students. The company uses a normal costing system, in which manufacturing overhead is applied on the basis of direct-labor hours. The company's budget for the current year included the following predictions.

Budgeted total manufacturing overhead	$411,600
Budgeted total direct-labor hours	19,600

During March, the firm worked on the following two production jobs:

Job number T81, consisting of 76 trombones

Job number C40, consisting of 110 cornets

The events of March are described as follows:

a. One thousand square feet of rolled brass sheet metal was purchased for $5,000 on account.

b. Four hundred pounds of brass tubing was purchased on account for $4,000.

c. The following requisitions were filed on March 5.

Requisition number 112: 250 square feet of brass sheet metal at $5 per square foot
  (for job number T81)

Requisition number 113: 1,000 pounds of brass tubing, at $10 per pound
  (for job number C40)

Requisition number 114: 10 gallons of valve lubricant, at $10 per gallon

All brass used in production is treated as direct material. Valve lubricant is an indirect material.

d. An analysis of labor time cards revealed the following labor usage for March.

Direct labor: Job number T81, 800 hours at $20 per hour

Direct labor: Job number C40, 900 hours at $20 per hour

Indirect labor: General factory cleanup, $4,000

Indirect labor: Factory supervisory salaries, $9,000

e. Depreciation of the factory building and equipment during March amounted to $12,000.

f. Rent paid in cash for warehouse space used during March was $1,200.

g. Utility costs incurred during March amounted to $2,100. The invoices for these costs were received, but the bills were not paid in March.

h. March property taxes on the factory were paid in cash, $2,400.

i. The insurance cost covering factory operations for the month of March was $3,100. The insurance policy had been prepaid.

j. The costs of salaries and fringe benefits for sales and administrative personnel paid in cash during March amounted to $8,000.

k. Depreciation on administrative office equipment and space amounted to $4,000.

l. Other selling and administrative expenses paid in cash during March amounted to $1,000.

m. Job number T81 was completed during March.

n. Half of the trombones in job number T81 were sold on account during March for $700 each.

The March 1 balances in selected accounts are as follows:

Cash	$ 10,000
Accounts Receivable	21,000
Prepaid Insurance	5,000
Raw-Material Inventory	149,000
Manufacturing Supplies Inventory	500
Work-in-Process Inventory	91,000
Finished-Goods Inventory	220,000
Accumulated Depreciation: Buildings and Equipment	102,000
Accounts Payable	13,000
Wages Payable	8,000

Required:

1. Calculate the company's predetermined overhead rate for the year.
2. Prepare journal entries to record the events of March.
3. Set up T-accounts, and post the journal entries made in requirement (2).
4. Calculate the overapplied or underapplied overhead for March. Prepare a journal entry to close this balance into Cost of Goods Sold.
5. Prepare a schedule of cost of goods manufactured for March.
6. Prepare a schedule of cost of goods sold for March.
7. Prepare an income statement for March.

■ **Problem 3-55**
Job-Cost Sheet;
Continuation of Preceding
Problem
(LO 2, LO 4, LO 6)

Refer to the preceding problem regarding Bandway Corporation. Complete the following job-cost sheet for job number T81.

JOB-COST SHEET

Job Number _____T81_____   Description _____
Date Started _____   Date Completed _____
                                  Number of Units Completed _____

Direct Material				
Date	Requisition Number	Quantity	Unit Price	Cost

Direct Labor				
Date	Time Card Number	Hours	Rate	Cost
3/8 to 3/12	308 to 312			

Manufacturing Overhead				
Date	Activity Base	Quantity	Application Rate	Cost
3/8 to 3/12				

Cost Summary	
Cost Item	Amount
Total direct material	
Total direct labor	
Total manufacturing overhead	
Total cost	
Unit cost	

Shipping Summary			
Date	Units Shipped	Units Remaining in Inventory	Cost Balance

■ **Problem 3-56**
Predetermined Overhead
Rate; Different Time Periods;
Pricing
(LO 4, LO 7)

Utica Electronics Company calculates its predetermined overhead rate on a quarterly basis. The following estimates were made for the current year.

	Estimated Manufacturing Overhead	Estimated Direct-Labor Hours	Quarterly Predetermined Overhead Rate (per direct-labor hour)
First quarter	$100,000	25,000	?
Second quarter	80,000	16,000	?
Third quarter	50,000	12,500	?
Fourth quarter	70,000	14,000	?
Total	$300,000	67,500	

The firm's main product, part number A200, requires $100 of direct material and 20 hours of direct labor per unit. The labor rate is $15 per hour.

Required:

1. Calculate the firm's *quarterly* predetermined overhead rate for each quarter.
2. Determine the cost of one unit of part number A200 if it is manufactured in January versus April.
3. Suppose the company's pricing policy calls for a 10 percent markup over cost. Calculate the price to be charged for a unit of part number A200 if it is produced in January versus April.
4. Calculate the company's predetermined overhead rate for the year if the rate is calculated *annually.*
5. Based on your answer to requirement (4), what is the cost of a unit of part number A200 if it is manufactured in January? In April?
6. What is the price of a unit of part number A200 if the predetermined overhead rate is calculated annually?

Jonah Blakesley has recently been hired as a cost accountant by Offset Press Company, a privately held company that produces a line of offset printing presses and lithograph machines. During his first few months on the job, Blakesley discovered that Offset has been underapplying factory overhead to the Work-in-Process Inventory account, while overstating expenses through the General and Administrative Expense account. This practice has been going on since the start of the company, which is in its sixth year of operation. The effect in each year has been favorable, having a material impact on the company's tax position. No internal audit function exists at Offset, and the external auditors have not yet discovered the underapplied factory overhead.

    Prior to the sixth-year audit, Blakesley had pointed out the practice and its effect to Mary Brown, the corporate controller, and had asked her to let him make the necessary adjustments. Brown directed him not to make the adjustments, but to wait until the external auditors had completed their work and see what they uncovered.

    The sixth-year audit has now been completed, and the external auditors have once again failed to discover the underapplication of factory overhead. Blakesley again asked Brown if he could make the required adjustments and was again told not to make them. Blakesley, however, believes that the adjustments should be made and that the external auditors should be informed of the situation.

    Since there are no established policies at Offset Press Company for resolving ethical conflicts, Blakesley is considering one of the following three alternative courses of action:

■ Follow Brown's directive and do nothing further.
■ Attempt to convince Brown to make the proper adjustments and to advise the external auditors of her actions.
■ Tell the Audit Committee of the Board of Directors about the problem and give them the appropriate accounting data.

Required:

1. For each of the three alternative courses of action that Blakesley is considering, explain whether or not the action is appropriate.
2. Independent of your answer to requirement (1), assume that Blakesley again approaches Brown to make the necessary adjustments and is unsuccessful. Describe the steps that Blakesley should take in proceeding to resolve this situation.

(CMA, adapted)

■ Problem 3-57
Ethical Issues;
Underapplication of
Manufacturing Overhead
(LO 1, LO 2, LO 4, LO 6)

Quality Pool Accessory Company manufactures a variety of accessory equipment for swimming pools. For many years the company has used a traditional product costing system with direct-labor hours as the only cost driver for overhead application. The firm is organized with five departments. The following list shows these departments and the key activities performed by each.

    Production Support Department (purchasing, receiving, inventory control, material handling, engineering, quality control, shipping).

■ Problem 3-58
Activity-Based Costing
Concepts; Two-Stage
Allocation; JIT; Robotics[5]
(LO 2, LO 8, LO 9)

---

[5]Additional problems covering activity-based costing are available in Chapter 5. In particular, the following problems could be assigned after completing the Appendix to Chapter 3: 5-23, 5-25, 5-28, 5-33, 5-35, and 5-36.

Machinery Department (equipment maintenance, equipment setup).

Cutting Department (cutting out metal and other parts to be used in various products).

Fabrication Department (forming and trimming operations on various parts and components).

Assembly Department (assembly of final products).

The pool accessory industry has recently experienced a significant increase in the level of competition, largely from overseas companies. As a result Quality Pool Accessory's profits have been squeezed. In response to the growing threat, the firm has moved to increase production efficiency through the introduction of a JIT production and inventory control system. Moreover, the level of automation in the Fabrication and Assembly Departments has been increased with the introduction of robotic equipment. Management's plans call for the eventual installation of a flexible manufacturing system. In addition to these changes in the production technology, Quality's management has altered its accounting system in order to get a more accurate picture of its product costs. Management hopes that this improved information will enable management to price products more competitively. The most significant change in the accounting system was the introduction of departmental overhead rates. The cost drivers used in the three production departments are the following: Cutting (machine hours), Fabrication (number of parts processed), Assembly (direct-labor hours).

So far the new accounting system seems to be effective. Management feels that the reported product costs are more in line with their intuition about what various products cost to manufacture. The controller, however, is considering a further improvement in the accounting system through the introduction of activity-based costing.

Required:

Draw three diagrams to depict the different product-costing systems discussed in the preceding description: (1) the firm's former system, (2) its current system, and (3) its contemplated ABC system. For the activity-based costing system, suggest cost drivers that could be used for each activity cost pool. Show the suggested cost drivers in your diagram. Make sure to show in your diagrams the roles of the predetermined overhead rate, departments, cost distribution, service department cost allocation, cost application, two-stage cost allocation, activity cost pools, cost drivers, and production jobs. (See Exhibits 3-13 and 3-14 for guidance.)

■ Problem 3-59
Plantwide versus
Departmental Overhead
Rates; Product Pricing
(LO 1, LO 8)

Aurora Telecommunications Corporation manufactures two different fax machines for the business market. Cost estimates for the two models for the current year are as follows:

	Basic System	Advanced System
Direct material	$ 400	$ 800
Direct labor (20 hours at $15 per hour)	300	300
Manufacturing overhead*	400	400
Total	$1,100	$1,500

* The predetermined overhead rate is $20 per direct-labor hour.

Each model of fax machine requires 20 hours of direct labor. The basic system requires 5 hours in department A and 15 hours in department B. The advanced system requires 15 hours in department A and 5 hours in department B. The overhead costs budgeted in these two production departments are as follows:

	Department A	Department B
Variable cost	$16 per direct-labor hour	$4 per direct-labor hour
Fixed cost	$200,000	$200,000

The firm's management expects to operate at a level of 20,000 direct-labor hours in each production department during the current year.

Required:

1. Show how the company's predetermined overhead rate was determined.
2. If the firm prices each model of fax machine at 10 percent over its cost, what will be the price of each model?
3. Suppose the company were to use departmental predetermined overhead rates. Calculate the rate for each of the two production departments.

4. Compute the product cost of each model using the departmental overhead rates calculated in requirement (3).

5. Compute the price to be charged for each model, assuming the company continues to price each product at 10 percent above cost. Use the revised product costs calculated in requirement (4).

6. Write a memo to the president of Aurora Telecommunications Corporation making a recommendation as to whether the firm should use a plantwide overhead rate or departmental rates. Consider the potential implications of the overhead rates and the firm's pricing policy. How might these considerations affect the firm's ability to compete in the marketplace?

Refer to the data given in the preceding problem for Aurora Telecommunications Corporation. The company has implemented an activity-based costing system with the following activity cost pools and cost drivers:

■ **Problem 3-60**
Activity-Based Costing Calculations; Continuation of Problem 3-59 (Appendix)
(LO 1, LO 8, LO 9)

| | | | Cost Drivers | |
| | | | Basic System | Advanced System |
Activity	Activity Cost	Total	Product Line	Product Line
Machine setup	$100,000	200 setups	50 setups	150 setups
Material receiving	60,000	80,000 lbs.	30,000 lbs.	50,000 lbs.
Inspection	80,000	1,600 inspections	700 inspections	900 inspections
Machinery-related	420,000	60,000 machine hrs.	20,000 machine hrs.	40,000 machine hrs.
Engineering	140,000	7,000 engineering hrs.	3,000 eng. hrs.	4,000 eng. hrs.
Total overhead	$800,000			

Aurora plans to produce 1,000 units of each model of fax machine.

Required:

1. Compute the cost rate per unit of each cost driver (e.g., the cost per setup).
2. Determine the total overhead to be assigned to each product line under activity-based costing.
3. Calculate the overhead assigned per unit of each type of fax machine under ABC.
4. Prepare a table comparing the total product cost assigned to each type of fax machine using a plantwide overhead rate, departmental overhead rates, and activity-based costing. (This requirement relies on the solution to the preceding problem.)

Cases

Constructo, Inc. is a manufacturer of furnishings for children. The company uses a job-order costing system. Constructo's work-in-process inventory on November 30 consisted of the following jobs:

■ **Case 3-61**
Interpreting Information from a Job-Order Costing System
(LO 1, LO 2, LO 3, LO 6)

Job No.	Description	Units	Accumulated Cost
CBS 102	Cribs	20,000	$ 900,000
PLP086	Playpens	15,000	420,000
DRS114	Dressers	25,000	250,000
Total			$1,570,000

The company's finished-goods inventory, which Constructo values using the FIFO (first-in, first-out) method, consisted of five items.

Item	Quantity and Unit Cost	Accumulated Cost
Cribs	7,500 units @ $64 each	$ 480,000
Strollers	13,000 units @ $23 each	299,000
Carriages	11,200 units @ $102 each	1,142,400
Dressers	21,000 units @ $55 each	1,155,000
Playpens	19,400 units @ $35 each	679,000
Total		$3,755,400

Constructo applies manufacturing overhead on the basis of direct-labor hours. The company's overhead budget for the year totals $4,500,000, and the company plans to use 600,000 direct-labor hours during this period. Through the first 11 months of the year, a total of 555,000 direct-labor hours were worked, and total overhead amounted to $4,273,500.

At the end of November, the balance in Constructo's Raw-Material Inventory account, which includes both raw material and purchased parts, was $668,000. Additions to inventory and requisitions from inventory during December included the following:

	Raw Material	Purchased Parts
Purchases	$242,000	$396,000
Requisitions:		
Job CBS102	51,000	104,000
Job PLP086	3,000	10,800
Job DRS114	124,000	87,000
Job STR077 (10,000 strollers)	62,000	81,000
Job CRG098 (5,000 carriages)	65,000	187,000

During December, Constructo's factory payroll consisted of the following:

CBS102	12,000 hrs.	$122,400
PLP086	4,400 hrs.	43,200
DRS114	19,500 hrs.	200,500
STR077	3,500 hrs.	30,000
CRG098	14,000 hrs.	138,000
Indirect labor	3,000 hrs.	29,400
Supervision		57,600
Total		$621,100

The following list shows the jobs that were completed and the unit sales for December.

	Production				Sales	
Job No.	Items	Quantity Completed		Items		Quantity Shipped
CBS102	Cribs	20,000		Cribs		17,500
PLP086	Playpens	15,000		Playpens		21,000
STR077	Strollers	10,000		Strollers		14,000
CRG098	Carriages	5,000		Dressers		18,000
				Carriages		6,000

Required:

1. Explain when it is appropriate for a company to use a job-order costing system.

2. Calculate the dollar balance in Constructo's Work-in-Process Inventory account as of December 31.

3. Calculate the dollar amount related to the playpens in Constructo's Finished-Goods Inventory account as of December 31.

(CMA, adapted)

■ Case 3-62
Cost Flows in a Job-Order
Costing System; Schedule
of Cost of Goods
Manufactured; Automation
(LO 2, LO 4, LO 6)

Valport Company, a manufacturer of fiber optic communications equipment, uses a job-order costing system. Since the production process is heavily automated, manufacturing overhead is applied on the basis of machine hours using a predetermined overhead rate. The current annual rate of $15 per machine hour is based on budgeted manufacturing overhead costs of $1,200,000 and a budgeted activity level of 80,000 machine hours. Operations for the year have been completed, and all of the accounting entries have been made for the year except the application of manufacturing overhead to the jobs worked on during December, the transfer of costs from Work in Process to Finished Goods for the jobs completed in December, and the transfer of costs from Finished Goods to Cost of Goods Sold for the jobs that have been sold during December. Summarized data as of November 30 and for the month of December are presented in the following table. Jobs T11-007, N11-013, and N11-015 were completed during December. All completed jobs except Job N11-013 had been turned over to customers by the close of business on December 31.

Work-in-Process		December Activity		
Job No.	Balance November 30	Direct Material	Direct Labor	Machine Hours
T11-007	$ 87,000	$ 1,500	$ 4,500	300
N11-013	55,000	4,000	12,000	1,000
N11-015	-0-	25,600	26,700	1,400
D12-002	-0-	37,900	20,000	2,500
D12-003	-0-	26,000	16,800	800
Total	$142,000	$95,000	$80,000	6,000

Operating Activity	Activity through November 30	December Activity
Actual manufacturing overhead incurred:		
Indirect material	$ 125,000	$ 9,000
Indirect labor	345,000	30,000
Utilities	245,000	22,000
Depreciation	385,000	35,000
Total overhead	$1,100,000	$96,000
Other data:		
Raw-material purchases*	$ 965,000	$98,000
Direct-labor costs	$ 845,000	$80,000
Machine hours	73,000	6,000

Account Balances at Beginning of Year	January 1
Raw-material inventory*	$105,000
Work-in-process inventory	60,000
Finished-goods inventory	125,000

* Raw-material purchases and raw-material inventory consist of both direct and indirect materials. The balance of the Raw-Material Inventory account as of December 31 of the year just completed is $85,000.

Required:

1. Explain why manufacturers use a predetermined overhead rate to apply manufacturing overhead to their jobs.

2. How much manufacturing overhead would Valport have applied to jobs through November 30 of the year just completed?

3. How much manufacturing overhead would have been applied to jobs by Valport during December of the year just completed?

4. Determine the amount by which manufacturing overhead is overapplied or underapplied as of December 31 of the year just completed.

5. Determine the balance in Valport Company's Finished-Goods Inventory account on December 31 of the year just completed.

6. Prepare a Schedule of Cost of Goods Manufactured for Valport Company for the year just completed. (Hint: In computing the cost of direct material used, remember that Valport includes both direct and indirect material in its Raw-Material Inventory account.)

(CMA, adapted)

Current Issues in Managerial Accounting

"Program of Pain: This German Software Is Complex, Expensive—and Wildly Popular," *The Wall Street Journal*, **March 14, 1997.**

Overview

SAP R/3 production, planning, and reporting software is in such high demand and use that it is becoming a global software standard. The software automates business processes such as sales, procurement, and production. Users include Microsoft, IBM, and Colgate-Palmolive.

■ **Issue 3–63**
Change of Technology in Manufacturing Operations

Suggested Discussion Questions

As a group, list advantages and disadvantages of a comprehensive business process software package. As the process becomes more complex, what effect would this have on a system like SAP R/3. Describe how a product like SAP R/3 would be implemented in a job shop. Would it be easier to implement in a job-order or process-costing accounting system?

■ **Issue 3–64**
Accounting and
Computers

"How SAP's R/3 Works," *Business Week,* **November 3, 1997.**

Overview

This article illustrates how SAP's R/3 system works by tracking a shoe order.

Suggested Discussion Questions

Form a software consulting team. Diagram how SAP's R/3 software could be used in a job-order environment (i.e., job shop). Include the processes listed below in your diagram.

1. Ordering.
2. Inventory management.
3. Production.
4. Human resources.
5. Purchasing.
6. Budgeting.
7. Reporting.

■ **Issue 3–65**
Strategic Cost
Management

"Iridium Is Looking a Little Star-Crossed," *Business Week,* **April 14, 1997.**

Overview

Iridium, LLC provides worldwide wireless phone services. Motorola formulated the Iridium low-orbit satellite concept and provided financial backing for the firm.

Suggested Discussion Questions

Iridium is experiencing increased competition. What effect would competition have on its internal cost accounting system? What overhead costs should be assigned to Iridium's phone services? What effect would increased competition have on Iridium's overhead application methods?

■ **Issue 3–66**
Types of Product
Costing Systems

"Boeing May Build Commuter Jet, Revamping McDonnell's MD-95," *The Wall Street Journal,* **September 17, 1997, Frederic M. Biddle.**

Overview

After paying $14 billion for McDonnell Douglas, Boeing is considering redesigning and selling McDonnell's commuter jet. The demand for the commuter jet is projected to be approximately 2,000 orders. Boeing has never sold commuter jets.

Suggested Discussion Questions

Would Boeing use a job-order or process-costing accounting system to account for the manufacturers of its commuter jets? If Boeing can capture one-half of the market for commuter jets in the next two years, should it change its accounting system? On average, how long does it take to manufacture one jet? Would this influence your choice of accounting system? How do unfinished aircraft appear on the financial statements?

■ **Issue 3–67**
Accumulating Costs in a
Film Studio

" 'Waterworld' Floats Atop Mixed Reviews and Takes in $21.6 Million on Opening," *The Wall Street Journal,* **July 31, 1995, Thomas R. King.**

Overview

Waterworld at the time of its release was the most expensive movie in the history of filmmaking. Some industry experts believed that it would not recover its costs and show a profit.

Suggested Discussion Questions

Would *Waterworld* be accounted for using job-order or process costing? Assume you are a management accountant charged with the responsibility of accounting for *Waterworld.* Write a memo to the president of MCA, Inc. explaining how you would allocate costs to the *Waterworld* project. Include in the memo a scenario illustrating how *Waterworld* could show a profit if it produces revenues of $100 million.

"CPA Group's Plan Would Standardize the Accounting for Software Expenses," *The Wall Street Journal,* **December 19, 1996.**

Overview

The American Institute of Certified Public Accountants (AICPA) proposed a rule that would require amortization of internally generated software costs as well as the cost of upgrading computer software. The rule would require firms to immediately expense software training costs.

Suggested Discussion Questions

As a group, prepare a chart that lists the group's reporting preference for internally generated software and software training costs. The following three reporting environments should be considered: managerial, financial, and tax.

■ **Issue 3–68**
Accounting for
Technology

Chapter Four

Process Costing and Hybrid Product-Costing Systems

After completing this chapter, you should be able to:

1. List and explain the similarities and important differences between job-order and process costing.

2. Prepare journal entries to record the flow of costs in a process-costing system with sequential production departments.

3. Prepare a table of equivalent units under weighted-average process costing.

4. Compute the cost per equivalent unit under the weighted-average method of process costing.

5. Analyze the total production costs for a department under the weighted-average method of process costing.

6. Prepare a departmental production report under weighted-average process costing.

7. Describe how an operation costing system accumulates and assigns the costs of direct-material and conversion activity in a batch manufacturing process.

8. After completing the appendix, prepare process-costing calculations for a sequential manufacturing process.

LOCAL SPORTS HERO CONTINUES WINNING WAYS IN BUSINESS

Milwaukee, WI—It was another outstanding season for local sports phenom Tim Bradley. But this time he wasn't on the pitcher's mound. Bradley's company, MVP Sports Equipment, just topped $10 million in annual revenue for the first time. Bradley, who starred in three sports at Central High and went on to play college and professional baseball, started MVP Sports Equipment Company eight years ago. Bradley's savings from a highly successful baseball career, along with the financial backing of two local banks, got MVP off and running. And there has been no looking back for Bradley.

I interviewed Bradley in his Milwaukee office yesterday. "I was disappointed when my shoulder injury ended my ball career early," Bradley said. "But I realized I had the skills and knowledge to do other things with my life besides throw a baseball."

Bradley feels his business degree prepared him well to take on the corporate world.

"It's amazing how much running a business is like playing a sport," he observed. "When I started MVP, I was a little nervous, just like I was before a big game in high school. But after awhile, you get a sense of the rhythm of the business environment you're in. I knew I wanted to get into manufacturing, and sports equipment was a natural thing to choose. We started out just making baseball gloves, but now we've expanded into other areas."

We left Bradley's office for a tour of the Milwaukee plant where MVP manufactures baseball gloves. I was impressed by how Bradley gave details about the manufacturing operation. "Producing baseball gloves is a two-step process," he explained. "Our operation is organized into two production departments. In the Cutting Department, we cut out the necessary pieces for the gloves from roll stock of imitation leather. Then in the Stitching Department, we sew the pieces together and stamp the label." Bradley's expla-

nation of manufacturing was interspersed with comments about running the business. "One thing I learned early on was the absolute necessity of keeping track of costs. Our aim is to manufacture a quality ball glove that kids and scholastic sports programs can afford. Affordability means keeping the price down, and that means cost awareness and control. Our process-costing system accumulates the production costs as the gloves move through each manufacturing department. As materials are used and labor and other costs are incurred, we accumulate the costs. This gives us good information on our unit costs. And that's the whole ball game . . . so to speak."

Smiling at the pun, and risking another one, I asked Tim Bradley if he had any final comments on the transition from the pitcher's mound to the board room, "Running a business is like mounting a successful pennant campaign," he said seriously. "They both take team work."

Food processing and paper production are among the industries using process costing.

We have seen that a product-costing system performs two primary functions:

1. Accumulating production costs.
2. Assigning those production costs to the firm's products.

Process-costing systems average production costs over a large number of product units.

A **repetitive production** environment is where large numbers of identical or very similar products are manufactured in a continuous flow.

Product costs are needed for the purposes of planning, cost control, decision making, and reporting to various outside organizations, such as governmental regulatory agencies.

Job-order costing was described in Chapter 3. This type of product-costing system is used when relatively small numbers of products are produced in distinct batches or job orders and these products differ significantly from each other. This chapter covers **process-costing systems**. Process costing is used in **repetitive production** environments, where large numbers of identical or very similar products are manufactured in a continuous flow. Industries using process costing include paper, petroleum, chemicals, textiles, food processing, lumber, and electronics.

Comparison of Job-Order Costing and Process Costing

LO 1   List and explain the similarities and important differences between job-order and process costing.

In many ways, job-order costing and process costing are similar. Both product-costing systems have the same ultimate purpose—assignment of production costs to units of output. Moreover, the flow of costs through the manufacturing accounts is the same in the two systems.

Flow of Costs   Exhibit 4–1 displays the flow of costs in two process-costing situations: one with a single production department and one with two production departments used in sequence. The same accounts are used in this process-costing illustration as were used in job-order costing in the preceding chapter. As the illustration shows, direct-material, direct-labor, and manufacturing-overhead costs are added to a Work-in-Process Inventory account. As goods are finished, costs are transferred to Finished-Goods Inventory. During the period when goods are sold, the product costs are transferred to Cost of Goods Sold. In the two-department case, when goods are finished in the first production department, costs accumulated in the Work-in-Process Inventory account for production department A are transferred to the Work-in-Process Inventory account for production department B.

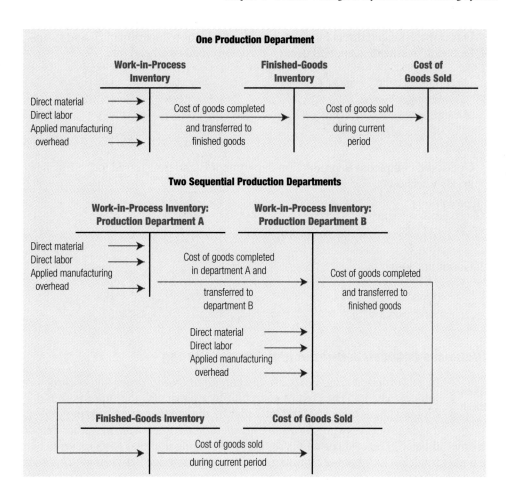

Exhibit 4–1

Flow of Costs in Process Costing Systems

The journal entries for the case of two sequential production departments, as illustrated in Exhibit 4–1, are as follows. (The numbers used in the journal entries are assumed for the purpose of showing the form of the entries.)

> **LO 2**   Prepare journal entries to record the flow of costs in a process-costing system with sequential production departments.

1. As direct material and direct labor are used in production department A, these costs are added to the Work-in-Process Inventory account for department A. Overhead is applied using a predetermined overhead rate. The predetermined overhead rate is computed in the same way in job-order and process costing.

Work-in-Process Inventory: Production Department A	100,000	
Raw-Material Inventory		50,000
Wages Payable		20,000
Manufacturing Overhead		30,000

2. When production department A completes its work on some units of product, these units are transferred to production department B. The costs assigned to these goods are transferred from the Work-in-Process Inventory account for department A to the Work-in-Process Inventory account for department B. In department B, the costs assigned to these partially completed products are called **transferred-in costs**.

> **Transferred-in costs** are assigned to partially completed products that are transferred into one production department from a prior department.

Work-in-Process Inventory: Production Department B	80,000	
Work-in-Process Inventory: Production Department A		80,000

3. Direct material and direct labor are used in production department B, and manufacturing overhead is applied using a predetermined overhead rate.

Work-in-Process Inventory: Production Department B	75,000	
Raw-Material Inventory		40,000
Wages Payable		15,000
Manufacturing Overhead		20,000

4. Goods are completed in production department B and transferred to the finished-goods warehouse.

Finished-Goods Inventory	130,000	
Work-in-Process Inventory: Production Department B ...		130,000

5. Goods are sold.

Cost of Goods Sold	125,000	
Finished-Goods Inventory		125,000

Differences between Job-Order and Process Costing

LO 1   List and explain the similarities and important differences between job-order and process costing.

In job-order costing, *costs are accumulated by job order* and recorded on job-cost sheets. The cost of each unit in a particular job order is found by dividing the total cost of the job order by the number of units in the job.

In process costing, *costs are accumulated by department*, rather than by job order or batch. The cost per unit is found by averaging the total costs incurred over the units produced. Exhibit 4–2 summarizes this key difference between job-order and process costing.

Equivalent Units: A Key Concept

LO 3   Prepare a table of equivalent units under weighted-average process costing.

Material, labor, and overhead costs often are incurred at different rates in a production process. Direct material is usually placed into production at one or more discrete points in the process. In contrast, direct labor and manufacturing overhead, called *conversion costs*, usually are incurred continuously throughout the process. When an accounting period ends, the partially completed goods that remain in process generally are at different stages of completion with respect to material and conversion activity. For example, the in-process units may be 75 percent complete with respect to conversion, but they may already include all of their direct materials. This situation is portrayed in Exhibit 4–3.

Equivalent Units   In the graphical illustration in Exhibit 4–3, suppose there are 1,000 physical units in process at the end of an accounting period. Each of the physical units is 75 percent complete with respect to conversion (direct labor and manufacturing overhead). How much conversion activity has been applied to these partially completed units? Conversion activity occurs uniformly throughout the production process. Therefore, the amount of conversion activity required to do 75 percent of the conversion on 1,000 units is *equivalent* to the amount of conversion activity required to do all of the conversion on 750 units. This number is computed as follows:

$$\text{1,000 partially completed physical units in process} \times \text{75\% complete with respect to conversion} = 750$$

Equivalent units refer to the amount of productive effort applied to a physical unit of production.

The term **equivalent units** is used in process costing to refer to the amount of manufacturing activity that has been applied to a batch of physical units. The *1,000 physical units* in process represent *750 equivalent units* of conversion activity.

A. Job-Order Costing: Accumulates Costs by Job Order

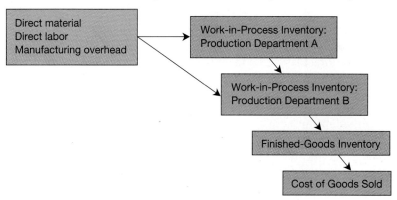

Exhibit 4–2

Comparison of Job-Order and
Process Costing

B. Process Costing: Accumulates Costs by Production Department

The term *equivalent units* is also used to measure the amount of direct materials represented by the partially completed goods. Since direct materials are incorporated at the beginning of the production process, the *1,000 physical units* represent *1,000 equivalent units of direct material* (1,000 physical units × 100% complete with respect to direct materials).

The most important feature of process costing is that the costs of direct material and conversion are assigned to equivalent units rather than to physical units. Refer again to Exhibit 4–3. For simplicity, suppose that the only production activity of the

Production Process (e.g., chemical refining process)

Conversion activity (direct labor and manufacturing overhead) applied uniformly throughout the process

Direct material is placed into production at the beginning of the production process.

When the accounting period ends, the partially completed goods are 75% complete with respect to conversion. The goods are 100% complete with respect to direct material.

Exhibit 4–3

Direct Material and
Conversion Activity in a
Typical Production Process

Process costing is used in the textile industry. First, raw material (in this case, raw cotton) is harvested and entered into production. The conversion costs are incurred in the production process. As shown here, at the end of the accounting period, partially completed units of fabric remain in process.

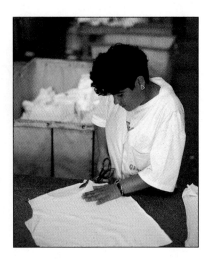

current accounting period was to start work on the 1,000 physical units and complete 75 percent of the required conversion activity. Assume that the costs incurred were $1,500 for conversion (direct labor and manufacturing overhead) and $5,000 for direct material. These costs would then be assigned as follows:

$$\frac{\$1,500 \text{ conversion cost}}{750 \text{ equivalent units of conversion}} = \begin{array}{c} \$2.00 \text{ per equivalent unit} \\ \text{for conversion} \end{array}$$

$$\frac{\$5,000 \text{ direct-material cost}}{1,000 \text{ equivalent units of direct material}} = \begin{array}{c} \$5.00 \text{ per equivalent unit} \\ \text{for direct material} \end{array}$$

This is a highly simplified example because there is no work-in-process inventory at the beginning of the accounting period and no goods were completed during the period. Nevertheless, it illustrates the important concept that under process costing, costs are assigned to equivalent units rather than physical units.

Illustration of Process Costing

The **departmental production report** is the key document in a process-costing system.

The key document in a typical process-costing system is the **departmental production report**, prepared for each production department at the end of every accounting period. This report replaces the job-cost sheet, which is used to accumulate costs by job in a job-order costing system. The departmental production report summarizes the flow of production quantities through the department, and it shows the amount of production cost transferred out of the department's Work-in-Process Inventory account during the period. The following four steps are used in preparing a departmental production report.

1. Analysis of physical flow of units.
2. Calculation of equivalent units (for direct material and conversion activity).
3. Computation of unit costs (i.e., the cost per equivalent unit for direct material and conversion).
4. Analysis of total costs (determine the cost to be removed from work in process and transferred either to the next production department or to finished goods).

The **weighted-average method** of process costing adds the cost assigned to beginning work-in-process inventory to the current-period production costs.

The method of process costing that we will focus on in this chapter is called the **weighted-average method**. *This method is almost always used in practice* by companies using process costing. There is another process-costing method called the *first-in, first-out, or FIFO, method.* This method is covered in some cost accounting courses, but it is rarely used in practice.

Basic Data for Illustration

The Wisconsin Division of MVP Sports Equipment Company manufactures baseball gloves in its Milwaukee plant. Two production departments are used in sequence: the Cutting Department and the Stitching Department. In the Cutting Department, direct material consisting of imitation leather is placed into production at the beginning of the process. Direct-labor and manufacturing overhead costs are incurred uniformly throughout the process. The material is rolled to make it softer and then cut into the pieces needed to produce baseball gloves. The predetermined overhead rate used in the Cutting Department is 125 percent of direct-labor *cost*.

Exhibit 4–4 presents a summary of the activity and costs in the Cutting Department during March. The direct-material and conversion costs listed in Exhibit 4–4 for the March 1 work in process consist of costs that were incurred during February. These costs were assigned to the units remaining in process at the end of February.

Based on the data in Exhibit 4–4, the Cutting Department's Work-in-Process Inventory account has the following balance on March 1:

Work-in-Process Inventory: Cutting Department	
March 1 balance 57,200	

The following journal entry is made during March to add the costs of direct material, direct labor, and manufacturing overhead to Work-in-Process Inventory.

Work-in-Process Inventory: Cutting Department	283,500	
Raw-Material Inventory		90,000
Wages Payable		86,000
Manufacturing Overhead		107,500

Exhibit 4–4

Basic Data for Illustration— Cutting Department

Work in process, March 1—20,000 units:	
Direct material: 100% complete, cost of	$ 50,000*
Conversion: 10% complete, cost of	7,200*
Balance in work in process, March 1	$ 57,200*
Units started during March	30,000 units
Units completed during March and transferred out of the Cutting Department	40,000 units
Work in process, March 31	10,000 units
Direct material: 100% complete	
Conversion: 50% complete	
Costs incurred during March:	
Direct material	$ 90,000
Conversion costs:	
Direct labor	$ 86,000
Applied manufacturing overhead	107,500†
Total conversion costs	$193,500

*These costs were incurred during the prior month, February.

$\dagger \left(\begin{smallmatrix} \text{Predetermined} \\ \text{overhead rate} \end{smallmatrix} \right) \times \left(\begin{smallmatrix} \text{Direct-} \\ \text{labor cost} \end{smallmatrix} \right) = 125\% \times \$86,000 = \$107,500$

Weighted-Average Method of Process Costing

We now present the four steps used to prepare a departmental production report using weighted-average process costing.

Step 1: Analysis of Physical Flow of Units   The first step is to prepare a table summarizing the physical flow of production units during March. The table is shown in Exhibit 4–5 and reflects the following inventory formula.

$$* \quad \begin{pmatrix} \text{Physical units} \\ \text{in beginning} \\ \text{work in process} \end{pmatrix} + \begin{pmatrix} \text{Physical} \\ \text{units} \\ \text{started} \end{pmatrix} - \begin{pmatrix} \text{Physical units} \\ \text{completed and} \\ \text{transferred out} \end{pmatrix} = \begin{pmatrix} \text{Physical units} \\ \text{in ending work} \\ \text{in process} \end{pmatrix}$$

LO 3   Prepare a table of equivalent units under weighted-average process costing.

Step 2: Calculation of Equivalent Units   The second step in the process-costing procedure is to calculate the equivalent units of direct material and conversion activity. A table of equivalent units, displayed in Exhibit 4–6, is based on the table of physical flows prepared in step 1 (Exhibit 4–5). The 40,000 physical units that were completed and transferred out of the Cutting Department were 100 percent complete. Thus, they represent 40,000 equivalent units for both direct material and conversion. The 10,000 units in the ending work-in-process inventory are complete with respect to direct material, and they represent 10,000 equivalent units of direct material. However, they are only 50 percent complete with respect to conversion. Therefore, the ending work-in-process inventory represents 5,000 equivalent units of conversion activity (10,000 physical units × 50% complete).

As Exhibit 4–6 indicates, the total number of equivalent units is calculated:

$$* \quad \begin{pmatrix} \text{Equivalent units of} \\ \text{activity in units completed} \\ \text{and transferred out} \end{pmatrix} + \begin{pmatrix} \text{Equivalent units of} \\ \text{activity in ending} \\ \text{work in process} \end{pmatrix} = \begin{pmatrix} \text{Total} \\ \text{equivalent units} \\ \text{of activity} \end{pmatrix}$$

Note that the total equivalent units of activity, for both direct material and conversion, exceeds the activity accomplished in the current period alone. Since only

Exhibit 4–5		**Physical Units**

Step 1: Analysis of Physical Flow of Units—Cutting Department

	Physical Units
Work in process, March 1	20,000
Units started during March	30,000
Total units to account for	50,000
Units completed and transferred out during March	40,000
Work in process, March 31	10,000
Total units accounted for	50,000

Exhibit 4–6

Step 2: Calculation of Equivalent Units—Cutting Department (weighted-average method)

	Physical Units	Percentage of Completion with Respect to Conversion	Equivalent Units Direct Material	Conversion
Work in process, March 1	20,000	10%		
Units started during March	30,000			
Total units to account for	50,000			
Units completed and transferred out during March	40,000	100%	40,000	40,000
Work in process, March 31	10,000	50%	10,000	5,000
Total units accounted for	50,000			
Total equivalent units			50,000	45,000

30,000 physical product units were started during March and direct material is added at the beginning of the process, only 30,000 equivalent units of direct material were actually placed into production during March. However, the total number of equivalent units of direct material used for weighted-average process costing is 50,000 (see Exhibit 4–6). The other 20,000 equivalent units of direct material were actually entered into production during the preceding month. *This is the key feature of the weighted-average method. The number of equivalent units of activity is calculated without making a distinction as to whether the activity occurred in the current accounting period or the preceding period.*

Step 3: Computation of Unit Costs   The third step in the process-costing procedure, calculating the cost per equivalent unit for both direct material and conversion activity, is presented in Exhibit 4–7. The cost per equivalent unit for direct material is computed by dividing the total direct-material cost, including the cost of the beginning work in process *and* the cost incurred during March, by the total equivalent units (from step 2, Exhibit 4–6). An analogous procedure is used for conversion costs.

> **LO 4** Compute the cost per equivalent unit under the weighted-average method of process costing.

Step 4: Analysis of Total Costs   Now we can complete the process-costing procedure by determining the total cost to be transferred out of the Cutting Department's Work-in-Process Inventory account and into the Stitching Department's Work-in-Process Inventory account. Exhibit 4–8 provides the required calculations. For convenience, the computations in step 3 are repeated in Exhibit 4–8. At the bottom of Exhibit 4–8, a check is made to be sure that the total costs of $340,700 have been fully accounted for in the cost of goods completed and transferred out and the balance remaining in work-in-process inventory.

> **LO 5** Analyze the total production costs for a department under the weighted-average method of process costing.

The calculations in Exhibit 4–8 are used as the basis for the following journal entry to transfer the cost of goods completed and transferred out to the Stitching Department.

Work-in-Process Inventory: Stitching Department	290,400	
Work-in-Process Inventory: Cutting Department		290,400

On March 31, the Cutting Department's Work-in-Process Inventory account appears as follows. The March 31 balance in the account agrees with that calculated in Exhibit 4–8.

Work-in-Process Inventory: Cutting Department			
March 1 balance	57,200		
March cost of direct material, direct labor, and applied manufacturing overhead	283,500	290,400	Cost of goods completed and transferred out of Cutting Department
March 31 balance	50,300		

	Direct Material	Conversion	Total
Work in process, March 1 (from Exhibit 4–4)	$ 50,000	$ 7,200	$ 57,200
Costs incurred during March (from Exhibit 4–4)	90,000	193,500	283,500
Total costs to account for	$140,000	$200,700	$340,700
Equivalent units (from step 2, Exhibit 4–6)	50,000	45,000	
Costs per equivalent unit	$ 2.80	$ 4.46	$ 7.26
	$\dfrac{\$140,000}{50,000}$	$\dfrac{\$200,700}{45,000}$	$2.80 + \$4.46

Exhibit 4–7

Step 3: Computation of Unit Costs—Cutting Department (weighted-average method)

Exhibit 4–8

Step 4: Analysis of Total
Costs—Cutting Department
(weighted-average method)

	Direct Material	Conversion	Total
Work in process, March 1 (from Exhibit 4–4)	$ 50,000	$ 7,200	$ 57,200
Costs incurred during March (from Exhibit 4–4)	90,000	193,500	283,500
Total costs to account for	$140,000	$200,700	$340,700
Equivalent units (from step 2, Exhibit 4–6)	50,000	45,000	
Costs per equivalent unit	$ 2.80	$ 4.46	$ 7.26

$$\frac{\$140,000}{50,000} \qquad \frac{\$200,700}{45,000} \qquad \$2.80 + \$4.46$$

Cost of goods completed and transferred out of the Cutting Department during March:

$$\left(\begin{array}{c}\text{Number of units}\\ \text{transferred out}\end{array}\right) \times \left(\begin{array}{c}\text{Total cost per}\\ \text{equivalent unit}\end{array}\right) \ldots \ldots \ldots \ldots \ldots \quad 40,000 \times \$7.26 \ldots \ldots \ldots \ldots \quad \underline{\$290,400}$$

Cost remaining in March 31 work-in-process inventory in the Cutting Department:

Direct material:

$$\left(\begin{array}{c}\text{Number of equivalent}\\ \text{units of direct material}\end{array}\right) \times \left(\begin{array}{c}\text{Cost per equivalent}\\ \text{unit of direct material}\end{array}\right) \ldots \ldots \quad 10,000 \times \$2.80 \ldots \ldots \ldots \ldots \quad \$ 28,000$$

Conversion:

$$\left(\begin{array}{c}\text{Number of equivalent}\\ \text{units of conversion}\end{array}\right) \times \left(\begin{array}{c}\text{Cost per equivalent}\\ \text{unit of conversion}\end{array}\right) \ldots \ldots \ldots \quad 5,000 \times \$4.46 \ldots \ldots \ldots \ldots \quad \underline{22,300}$$

Total cost of March 31 work in process . . . . $ 50,300

Check: Cost of goods completed and transferred out . . . . $ 290,400

        Cost of March 31 work-in-process inventory   50,300

        Total costs accounted for . . . . $ 340,700

LO 6   Prepare a departmental
production report under weighted-
average process costing.

Departmental Production Report   We have now completed all four steps necessary to prepare a production report for the Cutting Department. The report, which is displayed in Exhibit 4–9, simply combines the tables presented in Exhibits 4–6 and 4–8. The report provides a convenient summary of all of the process-costing calculations made under the weighted-average method.

Why is this process-costing method called the *weighted-average* method? Because the cost per equivalent unit for March, for both direct material and conversion activity, is computed as a weighted average of the costs incurred during two different accounting periods, February and March. To demonstrate this fact, we will focus on direct material. Since direct material is placed into production at the beginning of the process, the 20,000 physical units in the March 1 work in process already have their direct material. The direct-material cost per equivalent unit in the March 1 work in process is $2.50 ($50,000 ÷ 20,000, from Exhibit 4–4). This cost was actually incurred in *February.*

In March, 30,000 physical units were entered into work in process and received their direct material. The direct-material cost incurred in March was $90,000. Thus, the direct-material cost per equivalent unit experienced in *March* was $3.00 ($90,000 ÷ 30,000).

Under the weighted-average method of process costing, the cost per equivalent unit for direct material was calculated in Exhibit 4–7 to be $2.80. *This $2.80 unit-cost figure is a weighted average*, as the following calculation shows.

	Physical Units	Percentage of Completion with Respect to Conversion	Equivalent Units	
			Direct Material	Conversion
Work in process, March 1	20,000	10%		
Units started during March	30,000			
Total units to account for	50,000			
Units completed and transferred out during March	40,000	100%	40,000	40,000
Work in process, March 31	10,000	50%	10,000	5,000
Total units accounted for	50,000			
Total equivalent units			50,000	45,000

Exhibit 4–9

Production Report—Cutting Department (weighted-average method)

	Direct Material	Conversion	Total
Work in process, March 1 (from Exhibit 4–4)	$ 50,000	$ 7,200	$ 57,200
Costs incurred during March (from Exhibit 4–4)	90,000	193,500	283,500
Total costs to account for	$140,000	$200,700	$340,700
Equivalent units (from step 2, Exhibit 4–6)	50,000	45,000	
Costs per equivalent unit	$ 2.80	$ 4.46	$ 7.26

$$\frac{\$140,000}{50,000} \qquad \frac{\$200,700}{45,000} \qquad \$2.80 + \$4.46$$

Cost of goods completed and transferred out of the Cutting Department during March:

$$\left(\begin{array}{c} \text{Number of units} \\ \text{transferred out} \end{array} \right) \times \left(\begin{array}{c} \text{Total cost per} \\ \text{equivalent unit} \end{array} \right) \ldots\ldots\ldots\ldots\ldots \quad 40,000 \times \$7.26 \ldots\ldots\ldots\ldots \quad \underline{\$290,400}$$

Cost remaining in March 31 work-in-process inventory in the Cutting Department:

Direct material:

$$\left(\begin{array}{c} \text{Number of equivalent} \\ \text{units of direct material} \end{array} \right) \times \left(\begin{array}{c} \text{Cost per equivalent} \\ \text{unit of direct material} \end{array} \right) \ldots\ldots \quad 10,000 \times \$2.80 \ldots\ldots\ldots\ldots \quad \$ 28,000$$

Conversion:

$$\left(\begin{array}{c} \text{Number of equivalent} \\ \text{units of conversion} \end{array} \right) \times \left(\begin{array}{c} \text{Cost per equivalent} \\ \text{unit of conversion} \end{array} \right) \ldots\ldots \quad 5,000 \times \$4.46 \ldots\ldots\ldots\ldots \quad 22,300$$

Total cost of March 31 work in process	$ 50,300

Check: Cost of goods completed and transferred out	$ 290,400
Cost of March 31 work-in-process inventory	50,300
Total costs accounted for	$ 340,700

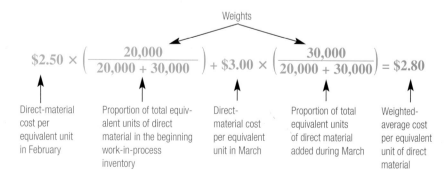

The point of this demonstration is that under weighted-average process costing, unit-cost figures are weighted averages of costs incurred over two or more accounting periods.

Other Issues in Process Costing

Several other issues related to process costing are worth discussion.

Actual versus Normal Costing   Our illustration of process costing assumed that *normal costing* was used. As explained in Chapter 3, in a normal costing system, direct material and direct labor are applied to Work-in-Process Inventory at their *actual* amounts, but manufacturing overhead is applied to Work-in-Process Inventory using a predetermined overhead rate. In contrast, under an *actual-costing* system, the actual costs of direct material, direct labor, *and manufacturing overhead* are entered into Work-in-Process Inventory.

Either actual or normal costing may be used in conjunction with a process-costing system. Our illustration used normal costing since a predetermined overhead rate was used to compute applied manufacturing overhead in Exhibit 4–4. This resulted in applied overhead for March of $107,500 (125% × $86,000). If actual costing had been used, the manufacturing overhead cost for March would have been the actual overhead cost incurred instead of the applied overhead amount given in Exhibit 4–4. In all other ways, the process-costing procedures used under actual and normal costing are identical.

When normal costing is used, there may be overapplied or underapplied overhead at the end of the period. This amount is either closed into Cost of Goods Sold or prorated, as explained in Chapter 3.

Other Cost Drivers for Overhead Application   Our illustration used a predetermined overhead rate based on direct-labor cost. Since the application of manufacturing overhead was based on direct-labor cost, direct labor and manufacturing overhead were combined into the single cost element *conversion costs*. This procedure is quite common in practice. If some cost driver (or activity base) other than direct labor had been used to apply manufacturing overhead, then overhead costs would be accounted for separately from direct-labor costs in the process-costing calculations.

Suppose, for example, that manufacturing overhead is applied on the basis of machine hours. A group of 100 physical units is 100 percent complete as to direct material, 60 percent complete as to direct labor, and 40 percent complete as to machine time. This situation could arise in a production process that is labor-intensive in its early stages but more automated in its later stages. In this case, the 100 physical units represent the following quantities of equivalent units:

	Equivalent Units		
Physical Units	**Direct Material**	**Direct Labor**	**Manufacturing Overhead**
100	100	60	40
	↑	↑	↑
	100 × 100%	100 × 60%	100 × 40%

Throughout the entire process-costing procedure, there will now be three cost elements (direct material, direct labor, and manufacturing overhead) instead of only two (direct material and conversion). In all other respects, the process-costing calculations will be identical to those illustrated earlier in the chapter.

Subsequent Production Departments   In our illustration, production requires two sequential production operations: cutting and stitching. Although the process-costing procedures for the second department are similar to those illustrated for the first, there is one additional complication. The cost of goods completed and transferred out of the Cutting Department must remain assigned to the partially completed product units as they undergo further processing in the Stitching Department. Process-costing procedures for subsequent production departments are covered in the appendix at the end of this chapter, which may be studied now.

Hybrid Product-Costing Systems

Job-order and process costing represent the polar extremes of product-costing systems. But some production processes exhibit characteristics of both job-order and process-costing environments. Examples of such production processes include some clothing and food processing operations. In these production processes, the conversion activities may be very similar or identical across all of the firm's product lines, even though the direct materials may differ significantly. Different clothing lines require significantly different direct materials, such as cotton, wool, or polyester. However, the conversion of these materials, involving direct labor and manufacturing overhead, may not differ much across product types. In the food industry, production of economy-grade or premium applesauce differs with regard to the quality and cost of the direct-material input, apples. However, the cooking, straining, and canning operations for these two product lines are similar.

Operation Costing for Batch Manufacturing Processes

The production processes described above often are referred to as **batch manufacturing** processes. Such processes are characterized by high-volume production of several product lines that differ in some important ways but are nearly identical in others. Since batch manufacturing operations have characteristics of both job-order costing and process-costing environments, a **hybrid product-costing system** is required. One common approach is called **operation costing**. This product-costing system is used when conversion activities are very similar across product lines, but the direct materials differ significantly. *Conversion costs* are accumulated by *department*, and process-costing methods are used to assign these costs to products. In contrast, *direct-material costs* are accumulated by *job order or batch*, and job-order costing is used to assign material costs to products.

> **LO 7** Describe how an operation costing system accumulates and assigns the costs of direct-material and conversion activity in a batch manufacturing process.

> **Batch manufacturing** is high-volume production of several product lines that differ in some important ways but are nearly identical in others.
>
> A **hybrid product-costing system** incorporates features from two or more alternative product-costing systems.
>
> **Operation costing** is a hybrid of job-order and process costing.

The main features of operation costing are illustrated in Exhibit 4–10. Notice in the exhibit that products pass sequentially through production departments A and B. Direct-material costs are traced directly to each batch of goods, but conversion costs are applied on a departmental basis. Direct labor and manufacturing overhead are combined in a single cost category called conversion costs, rather than separately identifying direct labor. Moreover, under operation costing, conversion costs are applied to products using a *predetermined application rate*. This predetermined rate is based on *budgeted conversion costs*, as follows:

$$\text{Predetermined application rate for conversion costs} = \frac{\text{Budgeted conversion costs (direct labor and manufacturing overhead)}}{\text{Budgeted cost driver (or activity base)}}$$

As an illustration of operation costing, we will focus on the Minnesota Division of MVP Sports Equipment Company. This division manufactures two different grades of basketballs: professional balls, which have genuine leather exteriors; and scholastic balls, which use imitation leather. The cutting and stitching operations for the two different products are identical. Scholastic balls are sold without special packaging, but professional balls are packaged in an attractive cardboard box.

During October two batches were entered into production and finished. There was no beginning or ending inventory of work in process for October. Cost and production data are given in Exhibit 4–11. Notice in Exhibit 4–11 that the direct-material costs are identified by *batch*. The conversion costs, however, are associated with the two production departments and the Packaging Department.

Exhibit 4–10

Operation Costing

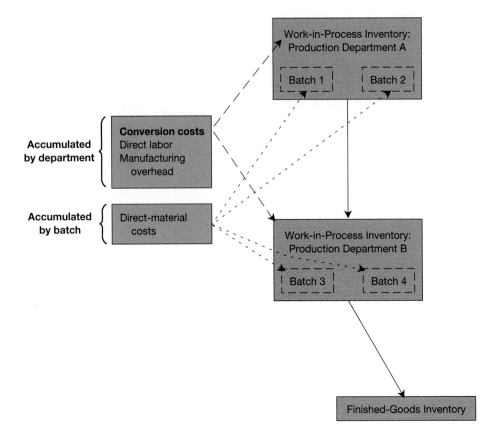

The product cost for each of the basketballs is computed as follows:

	Professional	**Scholastic**
Direct material:		
Batch P19 ($20,000 ÷ 1,000)	$20.00	
Batch S28 ($30,000 ÷ 3,000)		$10.00
Conversion: Preparation Department		
(conversion costs of $30,000 ÷ 4,000 units produced)*	7.50	7.50
Conversion: Finishing Department		
(conversion costs of $24,000 ÷ 4,000 units produced)*	6.00	6.00
Conversion: Packaging Department		
(conversion costs of $500 ÷ 1,000 units packaged)*	.50	–0–
Total product cost	$34.00	$23.50

*The two production departments each worked on a total of 4,000 balls, but the Packaging Department handled only the 1,000 professional balls.

Notice in the preceding display that each ball receives the same conversion costs in the Preparation Department and the Finishing Department, since these operations are identical for the two products. Direct-material costs and packaging costs, though, differ for the products. The total costs of $104,500 (Exhibit 4–11) are accounted for in the product costs, as shown below.

Professional balls: 1,000 × $34.00		$ 34,000
Scholastic balls: 3,000 × $23.50		70,500
Total		$104,500

The following journal entries are made to record the Minnesota Division's flow of costs. The first entry is made to record the requisition of raw material by the Preparation Department, when batch P19 is entered into production. (This amount excludes the $1,000 in packaging costs to be incurred subsequently for batch P19.)

Exhibit 4–11

Basic Data for Illustration of
Operation Costing

Direct-material costs:

Batch P19 (1,000 professional balls) . . . . $20,000   (includes $1,000 for
                                                                                                                                packaging material)

Batch S28 (3,000 scholastic balls)   30,000

Total direct-material costs $50,000

Conversion costs (budgeted):

Preparation Department . . . . $ 30,000

Finishing Department   24,000

Packaging Department   500

Total costs:

Direct material . . . . $ 50,000

Conversion: Preparation $30,000

Finishing   24,000

Packaging   500

Total conversion costs   54,500

Total $104,500

Predetermined application rates for conversion costs:*

Preparation Department

$$\frac{\text{Budgeted conversion costs}}{\text{Budgeted production}} = \frac{\$30,000}{4,000 \text{ units}} = \$7.50 \text{ per unit}$$

Finishing Department

$$\frac{\text{Budgeted conversion costs}}{\text{Budgeted production}} = \frac{\$24,000}{4,000 \text{ units}} = \$6.00 \text{ per unit}$$

Packaging Department

$$\frac{\text{Budgeted conversion costs}}{\text{Budgeted units packaged}} = \frac{\$500}{1,000 \text{ units}} = \$.50 \text{ per unit}$$

*The cost driver (or activity base) is the number of units processed.

Although the conversion activities are very similar for cashmere and acrylic sweaters, the materials differ significantly. Thus, operation costing is an appropriate product-costing system.

Work-in-Process Inventory: Preparation Department	19,000	
Raw-Material Inventory		19,000

The following entry is made to record the requisition of raw material by the Preparation Department, when batch S28 is entered into production.

Work-in-Process Inventory: Preparation Department	30,000	
Raw-Material Inventory		30,000

Conversion costs are applied in the Preparation Department with the following journal entry.

Work-in-Process Inventory: Preparation Department	30,000	
Applied Conversion Costs		30,000

The following entry records the transfer of the partially completed professional and scholastic basketballs to the Finishing Department.

Work-in-Process Inventory: Finishing Department	79,000	
Work-in-Process Inventory: Preparation Department		79,000

The conversion costs applied in the Finishing Department are recorded as follows:

Work-in-Process Inventory: Finishing Department	24,000	
Applied Conversion Costs		24,000

Next, the professional balls are transferred to the Packaging Department, and the scholastic balls are transferred to finished goods.

Work-in-Process Inventory: Packaging Department	32,500	
Finished-Goods Inventory	70,500	
Work-in-Process Inventory: Finishing Department		103,000

Raw-material (packaging) costs and conversion costs are recorded in the Packaging Department as follows:

Work-in-Process Inventory: Packaging Department	1,500	
Raw-Material Inventory		1,000
Applied Conversion Costs		500

Finally, the professional basketballs are transferred to finished goods.

Finished-Goods Inventory	34,000	
Work-in-Process Inventory: Packaging Department		34,000

Suppose that at the end of an accounting period, applied conversion costs differ from the actual conversion costs incurred. Then the difference, called overapplied or underapplied conversion costs, would be closed into Cost of Goods Sold. This accounting treatment is similar to that described in Chapter 3 for overapplied or underapplied overhead.

Adapting Product-Costing Systems to Technological Change

Managerial accountants should continually monitor the costs and benefits of the information they produce. In this age of rapidly changing production technologies and manufacturing practices, it is vital to reassess frequently the need for the data generated by traditional product-costing systems. As manufacturing processes are automated through the use of robots and other computer-controlled machinery, direct-labor costs decline in importance and manufacturing overhead increases. As JIT (just-in-time) production and inventory management systems are installed, the amount of work-in-process inventory declines substantially.[1] When these and other changes occur in the production environment, the product-costing system should be adapted to fit the new situation. Such adaptation is illustrated by the following description of circuitboard production.

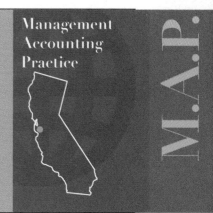

Hewlett-Packard Company

Hewlett-Packard Company introduced a JIT production and inventory management system in one of its divisions that manufactured circuit boards for use in personal computers. After the JIT system was implemented, the quantities of work-in-process and finished-goods inventories declined to very low levels. Moreover, automation in the production process resulted in direct-labor costs comprising only 3 to 5 percent of the total product cost. As a result, the company simplified its product-costing system. Direct labor was combined with manufacturing overhead in a single cost category. Much simpler methods were implemented to account for work-in-process inventories. An a result, thousands of journal entries per month were eliminated.

By adapting its product-costing system to its changing manufacturing environment, Hewlett-Packard realized considerable cost savings in information production while still providing the data needed by management. Hewlett-Packard subsequently has made similar cost-saving accounting changes in many of its other divisions.[2]

Management Accounting Practice

M.A.P.

Chapter Summary

Process costing is used in production processes where relatively large numbers of nearly identical products are manufactured. The purpose of a process-costing system is the same as that of a job-order costing system—to accumulate costs and assign these costs to units of product. Product costs are needed for planning, cost control, decision making, and reporting to various outside organizations.

The flow of costs in process-costing systems and job-order costing systems is the same. Costs of direct material, direct labor, and manufacturing overhead are added to a Work-in-Process Inventory account. Direct labor and manufacturing overhead are often combined into a single cost category termed *conversion costs*. When products are completed, the costs assigned to them are transferred either to Finished-Goods Inventory or to the next production department's Work-in-Process Inventory account. In sequential production processes, the cost of the goods transferred from one production department to another is called transferred-in cost.

There are some important differences between job-order and process-costing systems. Chief among these is that job-order costing systems accumulate production costs by job or batch, whereas process-costing systems accumulate costs by department. Another important difference is the focus on equivalent units in process costing. An equivalent unit is a measure of the amount of productive input that has been

---

[1]In a JIT production and inventory management system, inventories are kept to the bare minimum at all stages of production. Materials and components are ordered or manufactured "just in time" for their use in the production process. JIT systems minimize the costs of holding inventory.

[2]R. Hunt, L. Garrett, and C. M. Merz, "Direct-Labor Cost Not Always Relevant at HP," *Management Accounting* 66, no. 8, pp. 58–62.

applied to a fully or partially completed unit of product. In process costing, production costs per equivalent unit are calculated for direct-material and conversion costs.

The key document in a process-costing system is the departmental production report, rather than the job-cost sheet used in job-order costing. There are four steps in preparing a departmental production report: (1) analyze the physical flow of units, (2) calculate the equivalent units, (3) compute the cost per equivalent unit, and (4) analyze the total costs of the department.

In the weighted-average method of process costing, the cost per equivalent unit, for each cost category, is a weighted average of (1) the costs assigned to the beginning work-in-process inventory and (2) the costs incurred during the current period.

Job-order and process costing represent the polar extremes of product-costing systems. Operation costing is a hybrid of these two methods. It is designed for production processes in which the direct material differs significantly among product lines but the conversion activities are essentially the same. Direct-material costs are accumulated by batches of products using job-order costing methods. Conversion costs are accumulated by production departments and are assigned to product units by process-costing methods.

Key Terms

For each term's definition refer to the indicated page, or turn to the glossary at the end of the text.

batch manufacturing, pg. 131

departmental production report, pg. 124

equivalent units, pg. 122

hybrid product-costing system, pg. 131

operation costing, pg. 131

process-costing system, pg. 120

repetitive production, pg. 120

transferred-in costs, pg. 121

weighted-average method, pg. 124

Appendix to Chapter 4

Process Costing in Sequential Production Departments

In manufacturing operations with sequential production departments, the costs assigned to the units transferred out of one department remain assigned to those units as they enter the next department. In our illustration, the partially completed baseball gloves transferred out of the Cutting Department go next to the Stitching Department. There the cut-out pieces are stitched together. Since the cost of the thread used in the stitching is very small, it is treated as an indirect-material cost and included in manufacturing overhead. At the end of the process in the Stitching Department, rawhide lacing is woven through the fingers and along some edges of each baseball glove. The rawhide lacing is treated as a direct material.

The cost of goods completed and transferred out of the Cutting Department is transferred as shown below.

> **LO 8**   After completing the appendix, prepare process-costing calculations for a sequential manufacturing process.

As the T-accounts show, the Cutting Department has two cost elements: direct-material and conversion costs. However, the Stitching Department has three cost elements: direct-material, conversion, and *transferred-in costs*. Transferred-in costs are the costs assigned to the units transferred from the Cutting Department to the Stitching Department. Transferred-in costs are conceptually similar to direct-material costs. The only difference is that direct-material costs relate to raw materials, whereas transferred-in costs relate to partially completed products.

Exhibit 4–12 presents the basic data for our illustration of process costing in the Stitching Department. The March 1 work-in-process inventory in the department consists of 10,000 units that received some work in the Stitching Department during February but were not completed. The $61,000 of transferred-in costs in the March 1 work-in-process inventory are costs that were transferred into the Stitching Department's Work-in-Process Inventory account during February. Note that any partially completed baseball glove in the Stitching Department must have received all of its transferred-in input, or it would not have been transferred from the Cutting Department. The March 1 work-in-process inventory has not yet received any direct material in the Stitching Department, because the direct material (rawhide lacing) is not added until the end of the process.

As Exhibit 4–12 shows, 40,000 units were transferred into the Stitching Department during March. This agrees with Exhibit 4–4, which shows that 40,000 units were completed and transferred out of the Cutting Department during March. The Stitching Department completed 30,000 units during March and transferred them to finished-goods inventory. This left 20,000 units in the Stitching Department's March 31 work-in-process inventory.

Exhibit 4–12 shows that the costs incurred in the Stitching Department during March were $7,500 for direct material, $115,000 for direct labor, and $115,000 for *applied* manufacturing overhead. The predetermined overhead rate in the Stitching Department is 100 percent of direct-labor cost. Note that the predetermined overhead rates are different in the two production departments.

The March transferred-in cost in the Stitching Department is the cost of goods completed and transferred out of the Cutting Department. The amount shown in Exhibit 4–12, $290,400, comes from Exhibit 4–8.

Work in process, March 1—10,000 units:	
Transferred-in: 100% complete, cost of	$ 61,000*
Direct material: none	–0–
Conversion: 20% complete, cost of	7,600*
Balance in work in process, March 1	$ 68,600*
Units transferred in from Cutting Department during March	40,000 units
Units completed during March and transferred out to finished-goods inventory	30,000 units
Work in process, March 31	20,000 units
Transferred in: 100% complete	
Direct material: none	
Conversion: 90% complete	
Costs incurred during March:	
Transferred in from Cutting Department	
(assumes that weighted-average method was used for Cutting Department)	$290,400
Direct material	$ 7,500
Conversion costs:	
Direct labor	$115,000
Applied manufacturing overhead	115,000†
Total conversion costs	$230,000

*These costs were incurred during the prior month, February.

†(Predetermined overhead rate) × (Direct-labor cost) = 100% × $115,000 = $115,000

Exhibit 4–13 presents a completed production report for the Stitching Department using weighted-average process costing. Steps 1 through 4 are identified in the exhibit. The process-costing procedures used for the Stitching Department are identical to those used for the Cutting Department, except for one important difference. While there were only two cost elements (direct material and conversion) in the Cutting Department, there are three cost elements in the Stitching Department. In each of the four steps in Exhibit 4–13, transferred-in costs are listed along with direct material and conversion as a separate cost element.

The analysis of the physical flow of units (step 1 in Exhibit 4–13) is like the analysis for the Cutting Department. Now focus on step 2. In calculating equivalent units, we add a "transferred-in" column. Both the 30,000 units completed and transferred out of the Stitching Department and the March 31 work-in-process inventory are 100 percent complete as to transferred-in activity. Thus, the number of equivalent units is the same as the number of physical units. The calculation yields 50,000 total equivalent units of transferred-in activity for March. The equivalent units of direct material and conversion are determined as described earlier for the Cutting Department.

Costs per equivalent unit are computed in step 3. Since we are using the weighted-average method, the transferred-in costs in the March 1 work-in-process inventory are added to the March transferred-in costs before dividing by the equivalent units. Direct material and conversion costs are handled like those for the Cutting Department.

The analysis of total costs is done in step 4. The 30,000 units completed and transferred out of the Stitching Department are assigned a total weighted-average cost per unit of $12.228. This unit cost includes the transferred-in cost per equivalent unit of $7.028 calculated in step 3. The cost remaining in the work-in-process inventory on March 31 consists of two cost elements: transferred-in costs (20,000 equivalent units × $7.028 per equivalent unit) and conversion costs (18,000 equivalent units × $4.95 per equivalent unit). The March 31 work-in-process inventory has not yet received any direct material in the Stitching Department.

The following journal entry is made to transfer the cost of the units completed to the Finished-Goods Inventory account.

Finished-Goods Inventory	366,840	
Work-in-Process Inventory: Stitching Department		366,840
To transfer the cost of goods completed, as computed under the weighted-average method.		

	Step 1		Step 2		
			Equivalent Units		
	Physical Units	**Percentage of of Completion with Respect to Conversion**	**Transferred in**	**Direct Material**	**Conversion**
Work in process, March 1	10,000	20%			
Units transferred in during March	40,000				
Total units to account for	50,000				
Units completed and transferred out during March	30,000		30,000	30,000	30,000
Work in process, March 31	20,000	90%	20,000	–0–	18,000
Total units accounted for	50,000				
Total equivalent units			50,000	30,000	48,000

Step 3				
	Transferred in	**Direct Material**	**Conversion**	**Total**
Work in process, March 1 (from Exhibit 4–12)	$ 61,000	–0–	$ 7,600	$ 68,600
Costs incurred during March (from Exhibit 4–12)	290,400*	$ 7,500	230,000	527,900
Total costs to account for	$351,400	$ 7,500	$237,600	$596,500
Equivalent units	50,000	30,000	48,000	
Costs per equivalent unit	$ 7,028	$ .25	$ 4.95	$ 12.228
	↑	↑	↑	↑
	$351,400	$7,500	$237,600	$7.028
	50,000	30,000	48,000	+$.25
				+$4.95

Step 4

Cost of goods completed and transferred out of the Stitching Department during March:

$$\left(\begin{array}{c}\text{Number of units}\\ \text{transferred out}\end{array}\right) \times \left(\begin{array}{c}\text{Total cost per}\\ \text{equivalent unit}\end{array}\right) \dots\dots\dots\dots\dots \quad 30,000 \times \$12.228 \dots\dots\dots\dots \quad \underline{\$366,840}$$

Cost remaining in March 31 work-in-process inventory in the Stitching Department:

Transferred-in costs:

$$\left(\begin{array}{c}\text{Number of equivalent units}\\ \text{of transferred-in costs}\end{array}\right) \times \left(\begin{array}{c}\text{Cost per equivalent unit}\\ \text{of transferred-in cost}\end{array}\right) \dots\dots\dots\dots \quad 20,000 \times \$7.028 \dots\dots\dots \quad \$140,560$$

Direct material:

None

Conversion:

$$\left(\begin{array}{c}\text{Number of equivalent}\\ \text{units of conversion}\end{array}\right) \times \left(\begin{array}{c}\text{Cost per equivalent}\\ \text{unit of converison}\end{array}\right) \dots\dots\dots\dots\dots \quad 18,000 \times \$4.95 \dots\dots\dots\dots \quad \underline{89,100}$$

Total $229,660

*Cost of goods completed and transferred out of Cutting Department during March, under the *weighted-average* method (calculated in Exhibit 4–8).

Check:	Cost of goods completed and transferred out	$366,840
	Cost of March 31 work-in-process inventory	229,660
	Total costs accounted for	$596,500

Exhibit 4–13

Production Report—Stitching Department (weighted-average method)

Summary of Transferred-in Costs

When manufacturing is done in sequential production departments, the cost assigned to the units completed in each department is transferred to the next department's Work-in-Process Inventory account. This cost is termed *transferred-in cost,* and it is handled as a distinct cost element in the process-costing calculations. In this way, the final cost of the product is built up cumulatively as the product progresses through the production sequence.

Review Questions

4–1. List five types of manufacturing in which process costing would be an appropriate product-costing system. What is the key characteristic of these products that makes process costing a good choice?

4–2. List three nonmanufacturing businesses in which process costing could be used. For example, a public accounting firm could use process costing to accumulate the costs of processing clients' tax returns.

4–3. Explain the primary differences between job-order and process costing.

4–4. What are the purposes of a product-costing system?

4–5. Define the term *equivalent unit,* and explain how the concept is used in process costing.

4–6. List and briefly describe the purpose of each of the four process-costing steps.

4–7. Show how to prepare a journal entry to enter direct-material costs into the Work-in-Process Inventory account for the first department in a sequential production process. Show how to prepare the journal entry recording the transfer of goods from the first to the second department in the sequence.

4–8. What are *transferred-in costs*?

4–9. A food processing company has two sequential production departments: mixing and cooking. The cost of the January 1 work in process in the cooking department is detailed as follows:

Direct material	$ 80,000
Conversion	20,000
Transferred-in costs	175,000

During what time period and in what department were the $175,000 of costs listed above incurred? Explain your answer.

4–10. Explain the reasoning underlying the name of the weighted-average method.

4–11. How does process costing differ under normal or actual costing?

4–12. How would the process-costing computations differ from those illustrated in the chapter if overhead were applied on some activity base other than direct labor?

4–13. Explain the concept of *operation costing*. How does it differ from process or job-order costing? Why is operation costing well suited for batch manufacturing processes?

4–14. What is the purpose of a departmental production report prepared using process costing?

4–15. (Appendix) Referring to Exhibit 4–12, explain why the cost of direct material in the March 1 work in process is zero.

Exercises

■ **Exercise 4–16**
Physical Flow of Units
(LO 1, LO 3)

In each case below, fill in the missing amount.

1.	Work in process, February 1	13,000 kilograms
	Units started during February	1,500 kilograms
	Units completed during February	9,200 kilograms
	Work in process, February 28	5,300 ?
2.	Work in process, January 1	100,000 gallons
	Units started during the year	850,000 gallons
	Units completed during the year	750,000 ?
	Work in process, December 31	200,000 gallons
3.	Work in Process, September 1	9,000 units
	Units started during September	12,000 ?
	Units completed during September	19,000 units
	Work in process, September 30	2,000 units

Glass Creations, Inc. manufactures decorative glass products. The firm employs a process-costing system for its manufacturing operations. All direct materials are added at the beginning of the process, and conversion costs are incurred uniformly throughout the process. The company's production schedule for October follows.

	Units
Work in process on October 1 (60% complete as to conversion)	1,000
Units started during October	5,000
Total units to account for	6,000
Units from beginning work in process, which were completed and transferred out during October	1,000
Units started and completed during October	3,000
Work in process on October 31 (20% complete as to conversion)	2,000
Total units accounted for	6,000

■ **Exercise 4–17**
Equivalent Units; Weighted-Average
(LO 1, LO 3)

Required:

Calculate each of the following amounts using weighted-average process costing.

1. Equivalent units of direct material during October.
2. Equivalent units of conversion activity during October.

(CMA, adapted)

The Portsmouth plant of Healthy Foods Corporation produces low-fat salad dressing. The following data pertain to the year just ended.

■ **Exercise 4–18**
Physical Flow and Equivalent Units; Weighted-Average
(LO 1, LO 3)

		Percentage of Completion	
	Units	Direct Material	Conversion
Work in process, January 1	20,000 lb.	80%	60%
Work in process, December 31	15,000 lb.	70%	30%

During the year the company started 120,000 pounds of material in production.

Required:

Prepare a schedule analyzing the physical flow of units and computing the equivalent units of both direct material and conversion for the year. Use weighted-average process costing.

Energy Resources Company refines a variety of petrochemical products. The following data are from the firm's Amarillo plant.

■ **Exercise 4–19**
Equivalent Units; Weighted-Average
(LO 1, LO 3)

Work in process, November 1	2,000,000 gallons
Direct material	100% complete
Conversion	25% complete
Units started in process during November	950,000 gallons
Work in process, November 30	240,000 gallons
Direct material	100% complete
Conversion	80% complete

Required:

Compute the equivalent units of direct material and conversion for the month of November. Use the weighted-average method of process costing.

Montana Lumber Company grows, harvests, and processes timber for use in construction. The following data pertain to the firm's sawmill during November.

■ **Exercise 4–20**
Cost per Equivalent Unit; Weighted-Average
(LO 1, LO 3, LO 4)

Work in process, November 1:	
Direct material	$ 65,000
Conversion	180,000
Costs incurred during November:	
Direct material	$425,000
Conversion	690,000

The equivalent units of activity for November were as follows: 7,000 equivalent units of direct material, and 1,740 equivalent units of conversion activity.

Required:

Calculate the cost per equivalent unit, for both direct material and conversion, during November. Use weighted-average process costing.

■ **Exercise 4–21**
Cost per Equivalent Unit;
Weighted-Average
(LO 1, LO 3, LO 4)

Vancouver Glass Company manufactures window glass for automobiles. The following data pertain to the Plate Glass Department.

Work in process, June 1:	
Direct material	$ 37,000
Conversion	36,750
Costs incurred during June:	
Direct material	$150,000
Conversion	230,000

The equivalent units of activity for June were as follows: 17,000 equivalent units of direct material, and 48,500 equivalent units of conversion activity.

Required:

Calculate the cost per equivalent unit, for both direct material and conversion, during June. Use weighted-average process costing.

■ **Exercise 4–22**
Analysis of Total Costs;
Weighted-Average
(LO 5)

The following data pertain to Birmingham Paperboard Company, a manufacturer of cardboard boxes.

Work in process, February 1	10,000 units*
Direct material	$ 5,500
Conversion	17,000
Costs incurred during February	
Direct material	$110,000
Conversion	171,600

*Complete as to direct material; 40% complete as to conversion.

The equivalent units of activity for February were as follows:

Direct material (weighted-average method)	110,000
Conversion (weighted-average method)	92,000
Completed and transferred out	90,000

Required:

Compute the following amounts using weighted-average process costing.

1. Cost of goods completed and transferred out during February.
2. Cost of the February 28 work-in-process inventory.

■ **Exercise 4–23**
Analysis of Total Costs;
Weighted-Average
(LO 5)

Richmond Textiles Company manufactures a variety of natural fabrics for the clothing industry. The following data pertain to the Weaving Department for the month of September.

Equivalent units of direct material (weighted-average method)	60,000
Equivalent units of conversion (weighted-average method)	52,000
Units completed and transferred out during September	50,000

The cost data for September are as follows:

Work in process, September 1	
Direct material	$ 94,000
Conversion	44,400
Costs incurred during September	
Direct material	$164,000
Conversion	272,800

There were 20,000 units in process in the Weaving Department on September 1 (complete as to direct material, and 40% complete as to conversion).

Required:

Compute each of the following amounts using weighted-average process costing.

1. Cost of goods completed and transferred out of the Weaving Department.
2. Cost of the September 30 work-in-process inventory in the Weaving Department.

The November production of MVP's Minnesota Division consisted of batch P25 (2,000 professional basketballs) and batch S33 (4,000 scholastic basketballs). Each batch was started and finished during November, and there was no beginning or ending work in process. Costs incurred were as follows:

■ **Exercise 4–24**
Operation Costing
(LO 7)

Direct Material

> Batch P25, $42,000, including $2,500 for packaging material; batch S33, $45,000.

Conversion Costs

> Preparation Department, predetermined rate of $7.50 per unit; Finishing Department, predetermined rate of $6.00 per unit; Packaging Department, predetermined rate of $.50 per unit. (Only the professional balls are packaged.)

Required:

1. Draw a diagram depicting the division's batch manufacturing process. Refer to Exhibit 4–10 for guidance.
2. Compute the November product cost for each type of basketball.
3. Prepare journal entries to record the cost flows during November.

Pegasus Block Company produces cement blocks used in the foundations for buildings. The process takes place in two sequential departments. The following cost data pertain to the month of October.

■ **Exercise 4–25**
Cost Flows in Sequential
Production; Journal Entries
(Appendix)
(LO 2, LO 8)

	Pouring Department	Finishing Department
Direct material entered into production	$ 70,000	$ 25,000
Direct labor	340,000	280,000
Applied manufacturing overhead	680,000	420,000
Cost of goods completed and transferred out	900,000*	400,000†

*Cost of goods transferred to the Finishing Department.

†Cost of goods transferred to finished goods.

Required:

Prepare journal entries to record the following events.

1. Incurrence of costs for direct material and direct labor and application of manufacturing overhead in the Pouring Department.
2. Transfer of goods from Pouring to Finishing.
3. Incurrence of costs for direct material and direct labor and application of manufacturing overhead in the Finishing Department.
4. Transfer of goods from the Finishing Department to finished-goods inventory.

Problems

Pittsburgh Plastics Company manufactures a highly specialized plastic that is used extensively in the automobile industry. The following data have been compiled for the month of June. Conversion activity occurs uniformly throughout the production process.

■ **Problem 4–26**
Straightforward Weighted-
Average Process Costing,
Step-by-Step Approach
(LO 3, LO 4, LO 5)

Work in process, June 1—50,000 units:

Direct material: 100% complete, cost of	$120,000
Conversion: 40% complete, cost of	34,400
Balance in work in process, June 1	$154,400
Units started during June	200,000
Units completed during June and transferred out to finished-goods inventory	190,000

Work in process, June 30:

Direct material: 100% complete

Conversion: 60% complete

Costs incurred during June:

Direct material	$492,500

Conversion costs:

Direct labor	$ 87,450
Applied manufacturing overhead	262,350
Total conversion costs	$349,800

Required:

Prepare schedules to accomplish each of the following process-costing steps for the month of June. Use the weighted-average method of process costing.

190,000 × 4.15 = 788,500

1. Analysis of physical flow of units.
2. Calculation of equivalent units.
3. Computation of unit costs.
4. Analysis of total costs.

■ **Problem 4–27**
Step-by-Step Weighted-Average Process Costing
(LO 3, LO 4, LO 5)

Centura Corporation manufactures timing devices. During 19x9, 900,000 units were completed and transferred to finished-goods inventory. On December 31, 19x9 there were 300,000 units in work in process. These units were 50 percent complete as to conversion and 100 percent complete as to direct material. Finished-goods inventory consisted of 200,000 units. Materials are added to production at the beginning of the manufacturing process, and overhead is applied to each product at the rate of 60 percent of direct-labor costs. There was no finished-goods inventory on January 1, 19x9. A review of Centura's inventory cost records disclosed the following information:

		Costs	
	Units	Materials	Labor
Work in process, January 1, 19x9 (80% complete as to conversion)	200,000	$ 200,000	$ 315,000
Units started in production	1,000,000		
Direct material costs		$1,300,000	
Direct labor costs			$1,995,000

Required:

Prepare schedules as of December 31, 19x9 to compute the following:

1. Physical flow of units.
2. Equivalent units of production using the weighted-average method.
3. Costs per equivalent unit for material and conversion.
4. Cost of the December 31, 19x9 finished-goods inventory and work-in-process inventory.

(CPA, adapted)

■ **Problem 4–28**
Straightforward Weighted-Average Process Costing; Step-by-Step Approach
(LO 3, LO 4, LO 5)

Moravia Company processes and packages cream cheese. The following data have been compiled for the month of April. Conversion activity occurs uniformly throughout the production process.

Work in process, April 1—10,000 units:

Direct material: 100% complete, cost of	$ 22,000
Conversion: 20% complete, cost of	4,500
Balance in work in process, April 1	$ 26,500

Units started during April	100,000
Units completed during April and transferred out to finished-goods inventory	80,000

Work in process, April 30:

Direct material: 100% complete

Conversion: 33⅓% complete

Costs incurred during April:

Direct material	$198,000

Conversion costs:

Direct labor	$ 52,800
Applied manufacturing overhead	105,600
Total conversion costs	$158,400

Required:

Prepare schedules to accomplish each of the following process-costing steps for the month of April. Use the weighted-average method of process costing.

1. Analysis of physical flow of units.
2. Calculation of equivalent units.
3. Computation of unit costs.
4. Analysis of total costs.

Empire Company accumulates costs for its product using process costing. Direct material is added at the beginning of the production process, and conversion activity occurs uniformly throughout the process.

■ **Problem 4–29**
Partial Production Report;
Journal Entries; Weighted-
Average Method
(LO 2, LO 3, LO 4, LO 5)

Production Report
For August 19x9

	Physical Units	Percentage of Completion with Respect to Conversion	Equivalent Units Direct Material	Conversion
Work in process, August 1	40,000	80%		
Units started during August	80,000			
Total units to account for	120,000			
Units completed and transferred out during August	100,000		100,000	100,000
Work in process, August 31	20,000	30%	20,000	6,000
Total units accounted for	120,000			

	Direct Material	Conversion	Total
Work in process, August 1	$ 42,000	$ 305,280	$ 347,280
Costs incurred during August	96,000	784,400	880,400
Total costs to account for	$138,000	$1,089,680	$1,227,680

Required:

Use weighted-average process costing in completing the following requirements.

1. Prepare a schedule of equivalent units.
2. Compute the costs per equivalent unit.
3. Compute the cost of goods completed and transferred out during August.
4. Compute the cost remaining in the work-in-process inventory on August 31.
5. Prepare a journal entry to record the transfer of the cost of goods completed and transferred out during August.

■ **Problem 4–30**
Missing Data; Production
Report; Weighted-Average
(LO 4, LO 5, LO 6)

The following data pertain to the Hercules Tile Company for July.

Work in process, July 1 (in units)	20,000
Units started during July	?
Total units to account for	65,000
Units completed and transferred out during July	?
Work in process, July 31 (in units)	15,000
Total equivalent units: direct material	65,000
Total equivalent units: conversion	?
Work in process, July 1: direct material	$164,400
Work in process, July 1: conversion	?
Costs incurred during July: direct material	?
Costs incurred during July: conversion	659,400
Work in process, July 1: total cost	244,200
Total costs incurred during July	1,031,250
Total costs to account for	1,275,450
Cost per equivalent unit: direct material	8.25
Cost per equivalent unit: conversion	?
Total cost per equivalent unit	21.45
Cost of goods completed and transferred out during July	?
Cost remaining in ending work-in-process inventory: direct material	?
Cost remaining in ending work-in-process inventory: conversion	79,200
Total cost of July 31 work in process	202,950

Additional Information:

a. Direct material is added at the beginning of the production process, and conversion activity occurs uniformly throughout the process.

b. Hercules uses weighted-average process costing.

c. The July 1 work in process was 30 percent complete as to conversion.

d. The July 31 work in process was 40 percent complete as to conversion.

Required:

Compute the missing amounts, and prepare the firm's July production report.

✓■ **Problem 4–31**
Partial Production Report;
Journal Entries; Weighted-
Average Method
(LO 2, LO 3, LO 4, LO 5)

Neptune Corporation accumulates costs for its single product using process costing. Direct material is added at the beginning of the production process, and conversion activity occurs uniformly throughout the process. A partially completed production report for the month of May follows.

Production Report
For the Month of May

	Physical Units	Percentage of Completion with Respect to Conversion	Equivalent Units Direct Material	Conversion
Work in process, May 1	25,000	40%		
Units started during May	30,000			
Total units to account for	55,000			
Units completed and transferred out during May	35,000	100%	35,000	35,000
Work in process, May 31	20,000	80%	20,000	16,000
Total units accounted for	55,000		55000	51,000

	Direct Material	Conversion	Total
Work in process, May 1	$143,000	$ 474,700	$ 617,700
Costs incurred during May	165,000	2,009,000	2,174,000
Total costs to account for	$308,000	$2,483,700	$2,791,700
	55,000	51,000	
	5.60	48.70	= $54.30

Required:

1. Complete each of the following process-costing steps using the weighted-average method:

   a. Calculation of equivalent units.

   b. Computation of unit costs.

   c. Analysis of total costs.

2. Prepare a journal entry to record the transfer of the cost of goods completed and transferred out during May.

The following data pertain to the Guardian Tire and Rubber Company for the month of May.

■ **Problem 4–32** ✓
Missing Data; Production
Report; Weighted-Average
(LO 4, LO 5, LO 6)

Work in process, May 1 (in units)	15,000 ?
Units started during May	60,000
Total units to account for	75,000
Units completed and transferred out during May	65000 ?
Work in process, May 31 (in units)	10,000
Total equivalent units: direct material	75,000
Total equivalent units: conversion	?
Work in process, May 1: direct material	$135,000
Work in process, May 1: conversion	?
Costs incurred during May: direct material	?
Costs incurred during May: conversion	832,250
Work in process, May 1: total cost	172,500
Total costs incurred during May	1,402,250
Total costs to account for	1,574,750
Cost per equivalent unit: direct material	9.40
Cost per equivalent unit: conversion	?
Total cost per equivalent unit	21.65
Cost of goods completed and transferred out during May	?
Cost remaining in ending work-in-process inventory: direct material	?
Cost remaining in ending work-in-process inventory: conversion	73,500
Total cost of May 31 work in process	167,500

Additional Information:

a. Direct material is added at the beginning of the production process, and conversion activity occurs uniformly throughout the process.

b. Guardian uses weighted-average process costing.

c. The May 1 work in process was 20 percent complete as to conversion.

d. The May 31 work in process was 60 percent complete as to conversion.

Required:

Compute the missing amounts, and prepare the firm's May production report.

Beowulf and Grendel, a public accounting firm, is engaged in the preparation of income tax returns for individuals. The firm uses the weighted-average method of process costing for internal reporting. The following information pertains to February.

■ **Problem 4–33**
Process Costing in a Public
Accounting Firm
(LO 3, LO 4, LO 5)

Returns in process, February 1:	
(25% complete)	200
Returns started in February	825
Returns in process, February 28:	
(80% complete)	125
Returns in process, February 1:	
Labor	$ 6,000
Overhead	2,500
Labor, February (4,000 hours)	89,000
Overhead, February	45,000

Required:

1. Compute the following amounts for labor and for overhead:

   a. Equivalent units of activity.

  b. Cost per equivalent unit.

 2. Compute the cost of returns in process as of February 28.

(CMA, adapted)

■ **Problem 4–34**
Process Costing; Production
Report; Journal Entries;
Weighted-Average Method
(LO 2, LO 3, LO 4, LO 5,
LO 6)

HiGro Company manufactures a high-quality fertilizer, which is used primarily by commercial vegetable growers. Two departments are involved in the production process. In the Mixing Department, various chemicals are entered into production. After processing, the Mixing Department transfers a chemical called Chemgro to the Finishing Department. There the product is completed, packaged, and shipped under the brand name Vegegro.

  In the Mixing Department, the raw material is added at the beginning of the process. Labor and overhead are applied continuously throughout the process. All direct departmental overhead is traced to the departments, and plant overhead is allocated to the departments on the basis of direct-labor. The plant overhead rate for 19x9 is $.40 per direct-labor dollar.

  The following information relates to production during November 19x9 in the Mixing Department.

 a. Work in process, November 1 (4,000 pounds, 75% complete as to conversion):

Raw material	$22,800
Direct labor at $5.00 per hour	24,650
Departmental overhead	12,000
Allocated plant overhead	9,860

 b. Raw material:

Inventory, November 1, 2,000 pounds	10,000
Purchases, November 3, 10,000 pounds	51,000
Purchases, November 18, 10,000 pounds	51,500
Released to production during November, 16,000 pounds	

 c. Direct-labor cost at $5.00 per hour, $103,350

 d. Direct departmental overhead costs, $52,000

 e. Transferred to Finishing Department 15,000 pounds *15+1 = 16*

 f. Work in process, November 30, 5,000 pounds, 20% complete *4000 .*

  The company uses weighted-average process costing to accumulate product costs. However, for raw-material inventories the firm uses the FIFO inventory method.

Required:

 1. Prepare a production report for the Mixing Department for November 19x9. The report should show:

  a. Equivalent units of production by cost factor (i.e., direct material and conversion).

  b. Cost per equivalent unit for each cost factor. (Round your answers to the nearest cent.)

  c. Cost of Chemgro transferred to the Finishing Department.

  d. Cost of the work-in-process inventory on November 30, 19x9, in the Mixing Department.

 2. Prepare journal entries to record the following events:

  a. Release of direct material to production during November.

  b. Incurrence of direct-labor costs in November.

  c. Application of overhead costs for the Mixing Department (direct departmental and allocated plant overhead costs).

  d. Transfer of Chemgro out of the Mixing Department.

(CMA, adapted)

■ **Problem 4–35**
Operation Costing; Unit Costs
(LO 7)

(Contributed by Roland Minch.) Glass Glow Company manufactures a variety of glass windows in its Egalton plant. In department I clear glass sheets are produced, and some of these sheets are sold as finished goods. Other sheets made in department I have metallic oxides added in department II to form colored glass sheets. Some of these colored sheets are sold; others are moved to department III for etching and then are sold. The company uses operation costing.

Glass Glow Company's production costs applied to products in May are given in the following table. There was no beginning or ending inventory of work in process for May.

Cost Category	Dept. I	Dept. II	Dept. III
Direct material	$450,000	$72,000	–0–
Direct labor	38,000	22,000	$38,000
Manufacturing overhead	230,000	68,000	73,750

Products	Units	Dept. I Dir. Mat.	Dept. II Dir. Mat.
Clear glass, sold after dept. I	11,000	$247,500	–0–
Unetched colored glass, sold after dept. II	4,000	90,000	$32,000
Etched colored glass, sold after dept. III	5,000	112,500	40,000

Each sheet of glass requires the same steps within each operation.

Required:

Compute each of the following amounts.

1. The conversion cost per unit in department I.
2. The conversion cost per unit in department II.
3. The cost of a clear glass sheet.
4. The cost of an unetched colored glass sheet.
5. The cost of an etched colored glass sheet.

Atlantic Corporation manufactures a variety of plastic products including a series of molded chairs. The three models of molded chairs, which are all variations of the same design, are Standard (can be stacked). Deluxe (with arms), and Executive (with arms and padding). The company uses batch manufacturing and has an operation-costing system. The production process includes an extrusion operation and subsequent operations to form, trim, and finish the chairs. Plastic sheets are produced by the extrusion operation, some of which are sold directly to other manufacturers. During the forming operation, the remaining plastic sheets are molded into chair seats and the legs are added; the Standard model is sold after this operation. During the trim operation, the arms are added to the Deluxe and Executive models and the chair edges are smoothed. Only the Executive model enters the finish operation where the padding is added. All of the units produced receive the same steps within each operation. The May production run had a total manufacturing cost of $898,000. The units of production and direct-material costs incurred were as follows:

■ **Problem 4–36**
Operation Costing; Unit
Costs; Journal Entries
(LO 7)

	Units Produced	Extrusion Materials	Form Materials	Trim Materials	Finish Materials
Plastic sheets	5,000	$ 60,000			
Standard model	6,000	72,000	$24,000		
Deluxe model	3,000	36,000	12,000	$ 9,000	
Executive model	2,000	24,000	8,000	6,000	$12,000
Total	16,000	$192,000	$44,000	$15,000	$12,000

Manufacturing costs applied during the month of May were as follows:

	Extrusion Operation	Form Operation	Trim Operation	Finish Operation
Direct labor	$152,000	$60,000	$30,000	$18,000
Manufacturing overhead	240,000	72,000	39,000	24,000

Required:

1. For each product produced by Atlantic Corporation during the month of May, determine the (a) unit cost and (b) total cost. Be sure to account for all costs incurred during the month.
2. Prepare journal entries to record the flow of production costs during May.

(CMA, adapted)

Orbital Industries of Canada, Inc. manufactures a variety of materials and equipment for the aerospace industry. A team of R & D engineers in the firm's Winnipeg plant has developed a new material that will be useful for a variety of purposes in orbiting satellites and spacecraft. Tradenamed Ceralam, the material combines some of the best properties of both ceramics and laminated plastics. Ceralam is already being used for a variety of housings in satellites produced in three different countries. Ceralam

■ **Problem 4–37**
Operation Costing; Unit
Costs; Cost Flow; Journal
Entries
(LO 7)

sheets are produced in an operation called rolling, in which the various materials are rolled together to form a multilayer laminate. Orbital Industries sells many of these Ceralam sheets just after the rolling operation to aerospace firms worldwide. However, Orbital also processes many of the Ceralam sheets further in the Winnipeg plant. After rolling, the sheets are sent to the molding operation, where they are formed into various shapes used to house a variety of instruments. After molding, the sheets are sent to the punching operation, where holes are punched in the molded sheets to accommodate protruding instruments, electrical conduits and so forth. Some of the molded and punched sheets are then sold. The remaining units are sent to the dipping operation, in which the molded sheets are dipped in a special chemical mixture to give them a reflective surface.

During the month of March, the following products were manufactured at the Winnipeg plant. The direct-material costs are also shown.

	Units	Direct Materials Used in Ceralam Sheets	Direct Materials Used in Dipping
Ceralam sheets (sold after the rolling operation)	12,000	$480,000	
Nonreflective housings (sold after the punching operation)	5,000	200,000	
Reflective housings (sold after the dipping operation)	3,000	120,000	$30,000
Total	20,000	$800,000	$30,000

The costs incurred in producing the various Ceralam products in the Winnipeg plant during March are shown in the following table. Manufacturing overhead is applied on the basis of direct-labor dollars at the rate of 150 percent.

	Rolling	Molding	Punching	Dipping
Direct material	$ 800,000	–0–	–0–	$ 30,000
Direct labor	300,000	$112,000	$128,000	45,000
Manufacturing overhead	450,000	168,000	192,000	67,500
Total	$1,550,000	$280,000	$320,000	$142,500

Orbital Industries of Canada uses operation costing for its Ceralam operations in the Winnipeg plant.

Required:

1. Prepare a table that includes the following information *for each of the four operations*.
   - Total conversion costs.
   - Units manufactured.
   - Conversion cost per unit.
2. Prepare a second table that includes the following information *for each product* (i.e., rolled Ceralam sheets, nonreflective Ceralam housings, and reflective Ceralam housings).
   - Total manufacturing costs.
   - Units manufactured.
   - Total cost per unit.
3. Prepare journal entries to record the flow of all manufacturing costs through the Winnipeg plant's Ceralam operations during March. (Ignore the journal entries to record sales revenue.)

■ **Problem 4–38**
Transferred-in Costs;
Weighted-Average Method
(Appendix)
(LO 2, LO 4, LO 5, LO 8)

Erie Aluminum Company manufactures a variety of aluminum parts for the automotive industry. The company uses a weighted-average process-costing system. A unit of product passes through three departments—molding, assembly, and finishing—before it is completed.

The following activity took place in the Finishing Department during May.

	Units
Work-in-process inventory, May 1	1,400
Units transferred in from the Assembly Department	14,000
Units completed and transferred out to finished-goods inventory	11,900

Raw material is added at the beginning of processing in the Finishing Department. The work-in-process inventory was 70 percent complete as to conversion on May 1 and 40 percent complete as to conversion on May 31. The equivalent units and current period costs per equivalent unit of production for each cost factor are as follows for the Finishing Department.

	Equivalent Units	Current Period Costs per Equivalent Unit
Transferred-in costs	15,400	$5.00
Raw material	15,400	1.00
Conversion cost	13,300	3.00
Total		$9.00

Required:

1. Calculate the following amounts:

   a. Cost of units completed and transferred out to finished-goods inventory during May.

   b. Cost of the Finishing Department's work-in-process inventory on May 31.

2. The total costs of prior departments included in the work-in-process inventory of the Finishing Department on May 1 amounted to $6,750. Prepare the journal entry to record the transfer of goods from the Assembly Department to the Finishing Department during May.

(CMA, adapted)

Cases

Lawrence Leather Company manufactures high-quality leather goods. The company's profits have declined during the past nine months. In an attempt to isolate the causes of poor profit performance, management is investigating the manufacturing operations of each of its products.

One of the company's main products is fine leather belts. The belts are produced in a single, continuous process in the Sacramento Plant. During the process, leather strips are sewn, punched, and dyed. The belts then enter a final finishing stage to conclude the process. Labor and overhead are applied continuously during the manufacturing process. All materials, leather strips, and buckles are introduced at the beginning of the process. The firm uses the weighted-average method to calculate its unit costs.

The leather belts produced at the Sacramento Plant are sold wholesale for $9.95 each. Management wants to compare the current manufacturing costs per unit with the market prices for leather belts. Top management has asked the Sacramento Plant controller to submit data on the cost of manufacturing the leather belts for the month of October. These cost data will be used to determine whether modifications in the production process should be initiated or whether an increase in the selling price of the belts is justified. The cost per belt used for planning and control is $5.35.

The work-in-process inventory consisted of 400 partially completed units on October 1. The belts were 25 percent complete as to conversion. The costs included in the inventory on October 1 were as follows:

Leather strips	$ 990
Buckles	260
Conversion costs	300
Total	$1,550

During October 7,600 leather strips were placed into production. A total of 7,000 leather belts were completed. The work-in-process inventory on October 31 consisted of 1,000 belts, which were 50 percent complete as to conversion.

The costs charged to production during October were as follows:

Leather strips	$19,900
Buckles	5,250
Conversion costs	20,700
Total	$45,850

Required:

In order to provide cost data regarding the manufacture of leather belts in the Sacramento Plant to the top management of Lawrence Leather Company, compute the following amounts for the month of October.

1. The equivalent units for material and conversion.
2. The cost per equivalent unit of material and conversion.
3. The assignment of production costs to the October 31 work-in-process inventory and to goods transferred out.

■ **Case 4–39**
Weighted-Average Process Costing; Ethics
(LO 3, LO 4, LO 5, LO 6)

4. The weighted-average unit cost of leather belts completed and transferred to finished goods. Comment on the company's cost per belt used for planning and control.

5. Lawrence Leather Company's production manager, Jack Murray, has been under pressure from the company president to reduce the cost of conversion. In spite of several attempts to reduce conversion costs, they have remained more or less constant. Now Murray is faced with an upcoming meeting with the company president, at which he will have to explain why he has failed to reduce conversion costs. Murray has approached his friend, Jeff Daley, who is the corporate controller, with the following request: "Jeff, I'm under pressure to reduce costs in the production process. There is no way to reduce material cost, so I've got to get the conversion costs down. If I can show just a little progress in next week's meeting with the president, then I can buy a little time to try some other cost-cutting measures I've been considering. I want you to do me a favor. If we raise the estimate of the percentage of completion of October's inventory to 60 percent, that will increase the number of equivalent units. Then the unit conversion cost will be a little lower."

    By how much would Murray's suggested manipulation lower the unit conversion cost? What should Daley do? Discuss this situation, citing specific ethical standards for managerial accountants.

(CMA, adapted)

■ **Case 4–40**
Sequential Production
Departments; Weighted-
Average (Appendix)
(LO 3, LO 4, LO 5, LO 6)

Garden Life Company manufactures a plant nutrient known as Garden Pride. The manufacturing process begins in the Grading Department when raw materials are started in process. Upon completion of processing in the Grading Department, the output is transferred to the Saturating Department for the final phase of production. Here the product is saturated with water and then dried again. There is no weight gain in the process, and the water is virtually cost-free. The following information is available for the month of November.

Work-in-Process Inventories	Novermber 1 Quantity (pounds)	Cost	November 30 Quantity (pounds)
Grading Department	None	—	None
Saturating Department	1,600	$17,600*	2,000

*Includes $3,750 in Saturating Department conversion costs.

The work-in-process inventory in the Saturating Department is estimated to be 50 percent complete both at the beginning and end of November. Costs of production for November are as follows:

Costs of Production	Materials Used	Conversion
Grading Department	$265,680	$86,400
Saturating Department	—	85,920

The material used in the Grading Department weighed 36,000 pounds.

Required:

Use the weighted-average method to prepare production reports for both the Grading and Saturating Departments for the month of November. In calculating unit costs, round your answer to four decimal places. The answer should include:

1. Equivalent units of production (in pounds)
2. Total manufacturing costs
3. Cost per equivalent unit (pounds)
4. Cost of ending work-in-process inventory
5. Cost of goods completed and transferred out

(CPA, adapted)

Current Issues in Managerial Accounting

■ **Issue 4–41**
Just-in-Time (JIT)
Inventory Methods

"How JIT Staffing Can Add Value to Your Accounting Department," *Management Accounting,* **October 1996, Max Messmer.**

Overview
The author contends that just-in-time (JIT) manufacturing concepts should be applied to accounting department staffing. He argues that use of full-time and temporary employees can increase productivity and reduce costs.

Suggested Discussion Questions
Assume you are in a labor-intensive industry (e.g., accounting) that uses a process-costing system. What effect would JIT staffing have on process costing? Overall, what effect does JIT have on job-order or process cost accounting systems?

"Can Honda Build a World Car?" *Business Week,* **September 8, 1997.**

■ **Issue 4–42**
Costing Systems for Manufacturing Processes

Overview
Honda has reengineered its manufacturing process by moving away from a one-model-satisfies-all concept. Under the new process, Honda ships a uniform platform that is then customized in order to satisfy regional demand.

Suggested Discussion Questions
What type of manufacturing process is Honda implementing? What costing system should Honda use? How does this system differ from other costing systems?

"The Threat of Deflation," *Business Week,* **November 10, 1997.**

■ **Issue 4–43**
Strategic Cost Management

Overview
Global overcapacity in many industries could lead to a period of deflation. According to the article, deflation may cause consumers to buy more, even though it may also set off a series of personal and corporate bankruptcies.

Suggested Discussion Questions
Form three or four student teams. Assume the team works in the accounting division of a semiconductor manufacturer. Write a memo to your accounting manager explaining how deflation could affect your cost accounting system. Start by explaining causes for deflation and the probability that deflation will affect your firm. If your firm uses a process costing system, how will deflation impact your system?

"Bre-X Minerals Shares Soar as Investors Decipher Developments on Busang Field," *The Wall Street Journal,* **April 24, 1997, Mark Heinzl.**

■ **Issue 4–44**
Comparison of Job-Order Costing and Process Costing

Overview
Bre-X Minerals, Ltd. was a gold mining company whose shares' value dropped 83 percent in one day and increased 51 percent on another day as investors speculated as to the legitimacy of gold mining claims. Bre-X's claims regarding the greatest gold discovery ever were unfounded. The firm eventually went bankrupt.

Suggested Discussion Questions
Would a mining company similar to Bre-X account for the manufacture of minerals using a job-order or process cost accounting system? What costs should be allocated to the mineral inventory? How would valuation of mineral or commodity inventory differ from other types of inventory? What duties and obligations would a management accountant have in circumstances when the existence of inventory is uncertain?

"Power Struggle: Deregulation Sparks Marketing Battle," *The Wall Street Journal,* **May 13, 1996, Ross Kerber and Benjamin A. Holden.**

■ **Issue 4–45**
Other Issues in Process Costing

Overview
Deregulation of the electric utility industry has created an environment in which utilities compete for customers much like car companies and long-distance telephone providers compete. Several electric utilities have begun intensive ad campaigns to attract customers.

Suggested Discussion Questions
Write a one-page memo explaining the importance of the cost accounting system in both regulated and deregulated environments. In the memo, describe the type of system your company uses and how it allocates costs. How would this system allocate marketing costs?

"Despite Iffy Finances, Russian Oil Companies Draw Western Dollars," *The Wall Street Journal,* **March 29, 1996, Anne Reifenberg and Neela Banerjee.**

■ **Issue 4–46**
Other Issues in Process Costing; International Issues

Overview
Although Russian oil companies show promise, how much promise is a mystery. This article provides an example of the difficulty investors face when they assess the financial viability of Russian oil firms. When Lukoil issued convertible bonds, it did not provide a balance sheet, income statement, and statement of cash flows in its prospectus.

Suggested Discussion Questions
As a group, list the difficulties one could experience in assessing the financial condition of a foreign enterprise. Provide examples of how an oil company's cost accounting system could be manipulated to achieve management's goal of raising capital. What could a management accountant do to overcome these problems?

5 *Chapter Five*

Activity-Based Costing and Cost Management Systems

After completing this chapter, you should be able to:

1. Explain the key characteristics of a traditional manufacturing process and plant layout.

2. Compute product costs under a traditional, volume-based product-costing system and an activity-based costing system.

3. Explain how an activity-based costing system operates, including the use of a two-stage procedure for cost assignment, the identification of activity cost pools, and the selection of cost drivers.

4. Explain why traditional, volume-based costing systems tend to distort product costs.

5. Discuss several key issues in activity-based costing, including criteria for choosing cost drivers, transaction costing, storyboarding, and indicators that a new costing system is needed.

6. Describe the key features of a cost management system, including the elimination of non-value-added costs.

7. Briefly explain the concept of activity-based management.

AEROTECH ANNOUNCES NEW PRICING SCHEME—ACCOUNTANTS TO THE RESCUE?

Phoenix, AZ—Aerotech Corporation yesterday announced a major shake-up in its product pricing structure. The Phoenix-based company, which manufactures circuit boards used in aircraft radar and communications systems, has been facing stiff competition from both Asian and European firms. According to Kristin Scott, Aerotech's president, "For the past several years our competitors have been undercutting Aerotech's price on our Mode II circuit board. That's our highest-volume product, and we felt that our production process was as efficient as anyone's. We simply couldn't figure out how our competitors' costs could be any lower than ours. At the same time, we seemed to have captured a nice little niche all to ourselves for our Mode III board. The Mode III circuit board is our most complex product, and the demand is much lower than that for our Mode I or Mode II boards. The Mode III is a highly specialized product. Our competitors didn't seem to want to touch the Mode III market. Even though we had raised prices several times on the Mode IIIs, our customers didn't balk."

"We found the whole situation pretty puzzling," added John Stone, Aerotech's vice-president for manufacturing. "Puzzling and troubling both. How can you be producing a high-volume product as efficiently as possible, charging a mark-up that is modest for the industry, and still be undercut on the price? We were all getting concerned. The Mode II board is our bread and butter product."

So what happened, and what's behind Aerotech's radical price restructuring? "This is a genuine case of the accountants coming to the rescue," said Scott. "Our controller got wind of a new approach to product costing, which gives much more accurate results. It focuses on the activities that the company engages in to manufacture each of its products. It also measures the resources consumed by those activities. We did a pilot study using this method, called activity-based costing. We found that we had been overcosting our high-volume, relatively simple products. That would be the Mode I and Mode II boards. But we were drastically undercosting our Mode III circuit boards. The complexity and low volume of the Mode IIIs result in a disproportionate share of our support costs. Activities like engineering and material handling were much more costly than we realized for the Mode III boards."

Scott went on to explain that the new costing system showed Aerotech's management that they could easily afford to lower the price on the Mode II boards and be competitive with the Asians and Europeans. At the same time, though, a substantial price increase would be necessary on the Mode III boards in order to cover costs.

A revolution is transforming the manufacturing industry. Not since the mid-nineteenth century have we seen changes as sweeping and dramatic. The growth of international competition, the breakneck pace of technological innovation, and startling advances in computerized systems have created a new playing field for manufacturers around the globe. Some manufacturers have emerged as world-class producers, while others have fallen by the wayside.

What is behind these dramatic changes in the manufacturing industry? And what is the role of managerial accounting in this rapidly changing environment? These questions are the focus of this chapter and the next one. To explore these issues, we will review recent events in the life of Aerotech Corporation, an electronics manufacturer in the southwest.

Aerotech Corporation: A Tale of Two Cities

Aerotech Corporation manufactures complex printed circuit boards used in aircraft radar and communications equipment. The company has operated its Phoenix plant for 20 years. Within the past year, Aerotech opened a new production facility in Bakersfield, California. While the Phoenix plant utilizes a traditional plant layout and production process, the Bakersfield plant employs the latest in advanced manufacturing technology. In this chapter, we will begin by describing the production process used in the Phoenix facility. Then we will describe the adaptations Aerotech's controller has made in the managerial-accounting system used in the Phoenix plant.

In the next chapter, we will examine the production process and managerial-accounting system used in the Bakersfield plant. Then we will study several contemporary accounting and management techniques used by Aerotech to achieve success in its competitive environment.

Aerotech's Phoenix Plant: Traditional Production Process

LO 1   Explain the key characteristics of a traditional manufacturing process and plant layout.

Three complex printed circuit boards are manufactured in Aerotech's Phoenix plant. These products are referred to as Mode I, Mode II, and Mode III boards. Mode I is the simplest of the three circuit boards, and Aerotech sells 10,000 units of the product each year. The Mode II circuit board, which is only slightly more complex, has a high sales volume compared to the other two boards. Aerotech sells 20,000 Mode II boards each year. The Mode III circuit board, which is the most complicated, is a low-volume product with annual sales of 4,000 units.

Production Process

The production process for all three printed circuit boards involves the attachment of various electrical components to a raw circuit board. Aerotech purchases the raw boards and all of the electrical components from other electronics manufacturers. Most of the electrical devices are small axial-lead components, such as diodes and resistors. These components are attached to a circuit board by bending the two lead wires at 90-degree angles and inserting the leads into predrilled holes in the raw boards. A few of the electrical components are large or oddly shaped instruments that require special handling in the production process.

The sequence of production steps is the same for all three boards.[1]

1. *Sequencing.* The small axial-lead components are placed in the proper sequence for insertion into the board. Each type of axial-lead component is purchased in taped reels. The individual components can be peeled off the reel one at a time, just as a

---

[1]The circuit-board production process is based on the description given in James M. Patell, "Cost Accounting, Process Control, and Product Design: A Case Study of the Hewlett-Packard Personal Office Computer Division," *The Accounting Review* 62, no. 4, pp. 808–839.

piece of tape can be peeled off a roll. A sequencing machine is programmed to select the components from the proper reels in the sequence required for each type of circuit board.

2. *Auto-insertion.* The sequenced axial-lead components are fed into an auto-inserter machine, which bends the leads and inserts them into the predrilled holes in the raw boards.

3. *Hand-insertion.* Next, the large or oddly shaped components are manually attached to the boards.

4. *Wave soldering.* The boards pass through a wave-solder machine. Here a wave of molten solder passes under each board, and the components' leads are secured to the board.

5. *Wash/dry.* The wash/dry cycle is similar to the operation of a home dishwasher. The boards are washed to remove foreign particles; then they are dried with warm air.

6. *Hand-insertion.* The next step is to insert manually any components that could not withstand either the wave-solder or wash-dry operation.

7. *Bed of nails.* Each completed circuit board then is placed on a bed-of-nails tester. This machine consists of a set of vertical probes that make contact with the lead wires from each component on the circuit board. Each individual component then is tested independently. The bed-of-nails tester can be programmed so that its probes make contact with the different patterns of lead wires on the Mode I, Mode II, and Mode III circuit boards.

8. *Burn-in.* The final step is a burn-in test wherein electrical power is applied to each circuit board. This procedure takes three hours, and the entire board is tested for functionality. In other words, does the entire circuit board work properly? If problems are detected in a board, it is sent immediately to engineering for a full checkout procedure.

9. *Packaging.* After the burn-in test, the printed circuit boards are packaged and sent to finished-goods storage.

Plant Layout

The layout of Aerotech's Phoenix plant is shown in Exhibit 5–1. Colored arrows depict the flow of production from one operation to the next. Notice that each production operation is performed in a separate department. A storage area for work-in-process inventory is located next to each department. Here, partially completed circuit boards are stored until the next production department is ready for them.

This plant layout is referred to as a **process** (or **functional**) **layout,** since similar processes and functions are grouped together. For example, all auto-insertion activities are performed in one plant area (number 2 in Exhibit 5–1).

A **process** (or **functional**) **layout** organizes the elements of a production process so that similar processes and functions are grouped together.

Traditional, Volume-Based Product-Costing System

Until recently, Aerotech's Phoenix plant used a job-order product-costing system similar to the one described in Chapter 3 for Adirondack Outfitters. The cost of each product was the sum of its actual direct-material cost, actual direct-labor cost, and applied manufacturing

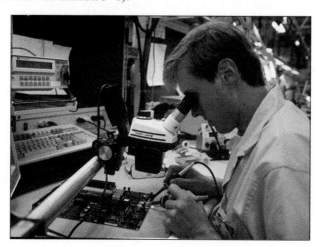

Traditional electronics manufacturing operations required considerable "touch labor," which refers to manual operations by production employees.

Exhibit 5–1

Aerotech Corporation's
Phoenix Plant

overhead. Overhead was applied using a predetermined overhead rate based on direct-labor hours. Exhibit 5–2 provides the basic data upon which the traditional costing system was based.

LO 2   Compute product costs under a traditional, volume-based product-costing system and an activity-based costing system.

Exhibit 5–3 shows the calculation of the product cost for each of the three circuit boards. Overhead is applied to the products at the rate of $33 per direct-labor hour. Notice that all of the Phoenix plant's budgeted manufacturing overhead costs are lumped together in a single cost pool. This total budgeted overhead amount ($3,894,000) then is divided by the plant's total budgeted direct-labor hours (118,000 hours).

Aerotech's labor-hour-based product-costing system is typical of many manufacturing companies. Labor hours are related closely to the volume of activity in the

	Mode I Boards	Mode II Boards	Mode III Boards
Production:			
Units	10,000	20,000	4,000
Runs	1 run of 10,000	4 runs of 5,000 each	10 runs of 400 each
Direct material	$50.00	$90.00	$20.00
(raw boards and components)			
Direct labor*	3 hours per board	4 hours per board	2 hours per board
(not including setup time)			
Setup time*	10 hours per run	10 hours per run	10 hours per run
Machine time	1 hour per board	1.25 hours per board	2 hours per board

*Direct labor and setup labor costs $20 per hour, including fringe benefits.

Exhibit 5–2

Basic Production and Cost Data: Aerotech Corporation's Phoenix Plant

	Mode I Boards	Mode II Boards	Mode III Boards
Direct material			
(raw boards and components) ..	$ 50.00	$ 90.00	$ 20.00
Direct labor			
(not including set-up time)	60.00 (3 hr. at $20)	80.00 (4 hr. at $20)	40.00 (2 hr. at $20)
Manufacturing overhead*	99.00 (3 hr. at $33)	132.00 (4 hr. at $33)	66.00 (2 hr. at $33)
Total	$209.00	$302.00	$126.00

Exhibit 5–3

Product Costs from Traditional, Volume-Based Product-Costing System: Aerotech Corporation's Phoenix Plant

*Calculation of predetermined-overhead rate:

Budgeted manufacturing overhead	$3,894,000
Direct labor, budgeted hours:	
Mode I: 10,000 units × 3 hours	30,000
Mode II: 20,000 units × 4 hours	80,000
Mode III: 4,000 units × 2 hours	8,000
Total	118,000

Predetermined overhead rate:

$$\frac{\text{Budgeted manufacturing overhead}}{\text{Budgeted direct-labor hours}} = \frac{\$3,894,000}{118,000} = \$33 \text{ per hour}$$

A **volume-based** (or **throughput-based**) **costing system** assigns costs to products on the basis of a single activity base related to volume.

factory, which sometimes is referred to as *throughput*. Consequently, these traditional product-costing systems often are said to be **volume-based** (or **throughput-based**) **costing systems.**[2]

Trouble in Phoenix

The profitability of Aerotech's Phoenix operation has been faltering in recent years. The company's pricing policy has been to set a target price for each circuit board equal to 125 percent of the full product cost. Thus, the target prices were determined as shown in Exhibit 5–4. Also shown are the actual prices that Aerotech has been obtaining for its products.

Mode I circuit boards were selling at their target price of $261.25. However, price competition from foreign companies had forced Aerotech to lower its price on Mode II boards to $328, well below the target price of $377.50. Even at this lower price, Aerotech was having difficulty getting orders for its planned volume of Mode II circuit-board production. Fortunately, the lower profitability of the Mode II boards was offset partially by greater-than-expected profits on the Mode III circuit boards. Aerotech's sales personnel had discovered that the company was swamped with orders for the Mode III boards when the target price of $157.50 was charged. Consequently,

[2]The illustration of the product-costing system in Aerotech's Phoenix plant is suggested by an example given by John Shank and Vijay Govindarajan, "The Perils of Cost Allocations Based on Production Volumes," *Accounting Horizons* 2, no. 4, pp. 71–79.

	Mode I Boards	Mode II Boards	Mode III Boards
Production cost under traditional, volume-based system (Exhibit 5–3)	$209.00	$302.00	$126.00
Target selling price (cost × 125%)	261.25	377.50	157.50
Actual selling price	261.25	328.00	250.00

Aerotech had raised the price on its Mode III boards several times, and eventually the product was selling at $250 per board. Even at this price, customers did not seem to hesitate to place orders. Moreover, Aerotech's competitors did not mount a challenge in the Mode III market. Aerotech's management was pleased to have a niche for the Mode III circuit boards, which appeared to be a highly profitable, low-volume specialty product. Nevertheless, concern continued to mount in Phoenix about the difficulty with the Mode II boards. After all, the Mode II board was the Phoenix plant's bread-and-butter product, with projected annual sales of 20,000 units.

Activity-Based Costing System

LO 2 Compute product costs under a traditional, volume-based product-costing system and an activity-based costing system.

Aerotech Corporation's controller, Chuck Dickens, had been thinking for some time about a refinement in the Phoenix plant's product-costing system. He wondered if the traditional, volume-based system was providing management with accurate data about product costs. Dickens had read about **activity-based costing (ABC) systems**, which follow a two-stage procedure to assign overhead costs to products. The first stage identifies significant activities and assigns overhead costs to each activity depending on the proportion of the organization's resources it uses. The overhead costs assigned to each activity comprise an **activity cost pool.**

An **activity-based costing (ABC) system** assigns overhead costs to products or services produced using a two-stage process that focuses on activities.

An **activity cost pool** is a grouping of overhead costs assigned to an activity identified in an activity-based costing system.

A **unit-level activity** must be done for each unit of production.

After assigning overhead costs to activity cost pools in stage one, cost drivers are identified that are appropriate for each cost pool. Then in stage two, the overhead costs are allocated from each activity cost pool to each product line in proportion to the amount of the cost driver consumed by the product line.

Dickens discussed activity-based costing with Anne Marley, the assistant controller. Together they met with all of Aerotech's production departments to discuss development of an ABC system. After initial discussion, an ABC proposal was made to Aerotech's top management. Approval was obtained, and an ABC project team was formed, which included Dickens, Marley, and representatives of various functional departments. Through several months of painstaking data collection and analysis, the project team was able to gather the data necessary to implement an ABC system.

LO 3 Explain how an activity-based costing system operates, including the use of a two-stage procedure for cost assignment, the identification of activity cost pools, and the selection of cost drivers.

Stage One Aerotech's ABC project team identified eight activity cost pools, which fall into four broad categories.[3] These are shown in Exhibit 5–5.

- *Unit level.* This type of activity must be done for each unit of production. Aerotech's machine-related activity cost pool represents a **unit-level activity** since every product unit requires machine time.

A **batch-level activity** must be accomplished for each batch of products rather than for each unit.

A **product-sustaining-level activity** supports an entire product line, but is not always performed every time a new unit or batch of products is produced.

- *Batch level.* These activities must be performed for each batch of products, rather than each unit. Aerotech's **batch-level activities** include the setup, receiving and inspection, material-handling, packaging and shipping, and quality-assurance activity cost pools.

- *Product-sustaining level.* This category includes activities that are needed to support an entire product line but are not always performed every time a new unit or batch of products is produced. Aerotech's project team identified engineering costs as a product-sustaining activity cost pool.

---

[3]These activity classifications are suggested by Robin Cooper, "Cost Classification in Unit-Based and Activity-Based Manufacturing Cost Systems," *Journal of Cost Management* 4, no. 3, pp. 4–14.

Exhibit 5–5

Stage One of Activity-Based
Costing: Identification of
Activity Cost Pools

■ *Facility (or general operations) level.* **Facility-level activities** are required in order for the entire production process to occur. Examples of such activity costs include plant management salaries, plant depreciation, property taxes, plant maintenance, and insurance.

> A **facility-** (or **general-operations**) **level activity** is required for an entire production process to occur.

Stage Two   In stage two of the activity-based costing project, Dickens and Marley identified cost drivers for each activity cost pool. Then they assigned the costs in each activity cost pool to Aerotech's three product lines according to the proportion of each cost driver consumed by each product line. In the following sections, we will discuss in detail how stage two of the ABC project was carried out for four of the activity cost pools identified in stage one. Then we will complete the ABC project by developing new product costs for each of Aerotech's three circuit boards.

> **LO 3**   Explain how an activity-based costing system operates, including the use of a two-stage procedure for cost assignment, the identification of activity cost pools, and the selection of cost drivers.

Machinery Cost Pool   The machinery cost pool, a unit-level activity, totals $1,212,600 and includes the costs of machine maintenance, depreciation, computer support, lubrication, electricity, and calibration. Dickens and Marley selected machine hours for the cost driver, since a product that uses more machine hours should bear a larger share of machine-related costs. Exhibit 5–6 shows how machinery costs are assigned to products in stage two of the ABC analysis. Budgeted machinery costs ($1,212,600) are divided by budgeted machine hours (43,000) to obtain a *pool rate* of $28.20 per machine hour. The **pool rate** is the cost per unit of the cost driver for a particular activity cost pool. Next, the pool rate of $28.20 per machine hour is multiplied by the number of machine hours required per unit of each product. For example, each Mode

> The **pool rate** is the cost per unit of the cost driver for a particular activity cost pool.

This technician is setting up a robot used in manufacturing the circuit boards used in high-definition TVs. Machine setup is a batch-level activity.

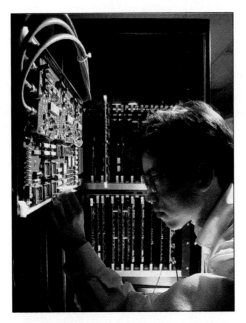

II circuit board is assigned a cost of $35.25 ($28.20 per machine hour × 1.25 machine hours per circuit board).

Setup Cost Pool   Setting up production runs is an example of a batch-level activity. The ABC calculations for the setup cost pool are displayed in Exhibit 5–7. In stage one the total setup cost is determined to be $3,000. The cost driver used to assign setup costs to the three product lines in stage two is the number of production runs. The pool rate is determined to be $200 per production run. Finally, the setup cost per circuit board is computed for each product line by dividing the setup cost per production run by the number of units in a run.[4]

Engineering Cost Pool   Engineering is classified as a product-sustaining level activity. Although engineering activities are crucial in supporting each product line, they typically are not carried out for each unit or batch of products. Exhibit 5–8 displays the ABC calculations for the engineering cost pool. In stage one, the total engineering cost is determined to be $700,000.

This engineer is using a computer-aided design (CAD) system for engineering design. This is an example of a product-sustaining-level cost.

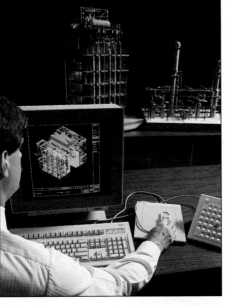

The cost driver selected in stage two is the number of engineering transactions, such as design specifications and change orders, relating to each product line. The calculations are slightly different here from those used in stage two for the machinery and setup cost pools. Instead of computing the engineering cost per transaction, the ABC project team estimated the percentage of engineering activity related to each product line. For example, since 25 percent of all engineering activity is related to the Mode I circuit boards, 25 percent of the engineering cost pool is assigned to the Mode I

A **transaction-based costing system** identifies multiple cost drivers and assigns costs of activities to products on the basis of the number of transactions they generate for the various cost drivers.

product line. Finally, the engineering cost per unit is computed by dividing the engineering cost assigned to each product line by the number of units produced in that line.

This approach to activity-based costing is sometimes called **transaction-based costing.** Under this method, costs are assigned from an activity cost pool to various product lines based on the relative proportion of the activity consumed by each product line, as measured by transactions. Here the term *transaction* is used in a general sense to mean a unit of activity that concludes in some well-defined result, such as a design spec or change order. In most cases, these transactions result in documents of some type, either in hard copy or computer form.

Facility Cost Pool   The facility-level (or general-operations-level) activity cost pool includes such costs as plant depreciation, plant management salaries, plant maintenance,

---

[4]Aerotech's setup cost pool, $3,000, is relatively small compared to the other cost pools. Often such a small cost pool is combined with another larger pool. However, the setup cost pool is identified separately in our example for two reasons. First, a setup cost pool is common in the ABC systems observed in practice. Second, it is worthwhile to see how the ABC calculations are done for the setup cost pool.

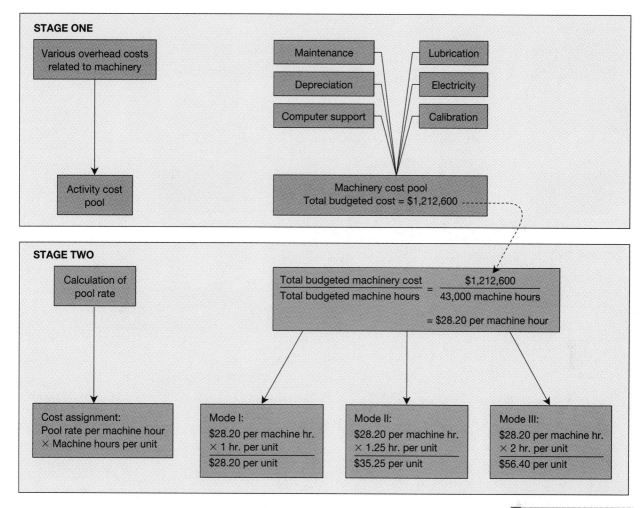

Exhibit 5–6

Activity-Based Costing:
Machinery Cost Pool

property taxes, and insurance. The ABC calculations are displayed in Exhibit 5–9. The total cost, determined in stage one, is $507,400. The cost driver selected in stage two is direct-labor hours. The pool rate is $4.30 per direct-labor hour. Finally, facilities costs are assigned to products by multiplying the pool rate by the number of direct-labor hours required by each circuit board.

Product Costs under Activity-Based Costing   The ABC calculations for the four remaining cost pools—receiving and inspection, material handling, quality assurance, and packaging and shipping—follow the approach for the engineering cost pool. A transaction-based costing approach is used, assigning each activity's costs to the three product lines on the basis of the relative proportion of the activity consumed by each product line. Exhibit 5–10, on p. 167, completes the calculation of the ABC product costs by totaling the costs assigned from each activity cost pool to each product line.

Examine Exhibit 5–10 carefully, as it details all the results of the activity-based costing system. Notice that the costs of direct material and direct labor remain the same as those in the traditional, volume-based costing system (Exhibit 5–3). However, there are big differences in the assignment of overhead costs to the three product lines under the ABC system.

LO 3 Explain how an activity-based costing system operates, including the use of a two-stage procedure for cost assignment, the identification of activity cost pools, and the selection of cost drivers.

Interpreting the ABC Product Costs

Chuck Dickens was amazed to see the product costs reported under the activity-based costing system. Both the Mode I and Mode II circuit boards exhibited much lower product costs under the ABC system than under the traditional system. This could explain the price competition Aerotech faced on its Mode II circuit boards. Aerotech's competitors could sell their Mode II boards at a lower price because they realized it cost less to produce a Mode II board than Aerotech's traditional costing system had indicated. However, as Dickens scanned the new product costs shown in Exhibit 5–10 he was alarmed by the substantial increase in the reported cost of a Mode III circuit board. The cost of a Mode III board had skyrocketed to over three times the company's original estimate. The complexity of the Mode III boards, and its impact on costs, was hidden completely by the traditional, volume-based costing system. To compare the results of the two alternative costing systems, Dickens prepared Exhibit 5–11 (p. 168).

The Mode I boards emerged as an extremely profitable product, selling for over 142 percent of their reported cost under the activity-based costing system ($261.25 ÷ $183.44). The Mode II boards were selling at approximately 125 percent of their new reported product cost ($328 ÷ $261.81). "No wonder we couldn't sell the Mode II boards at $377.50," said Dickens to Marley, as they looked over the data. "Our competitors probably knew the Mode II boards cost around $262, and they priced them accordingly." When he got to the Mode III column, Dickens was appalled. "We thought those Mode III's were a winner," lamented Dickens, "but we've been selling them at a loss of over $140 per board!" After looking over the data, Dickens almost ran to the president's office. "We've got to get this operation straightened out," he thought.

The Punch Line

What has happened at Aerotech's Phoenix plant? The essence of the problem is that the traditional, volume-based costing system was overcosting the high-volume product lines (Mode I and Mode II) and undercosting the complex, low-volume product line

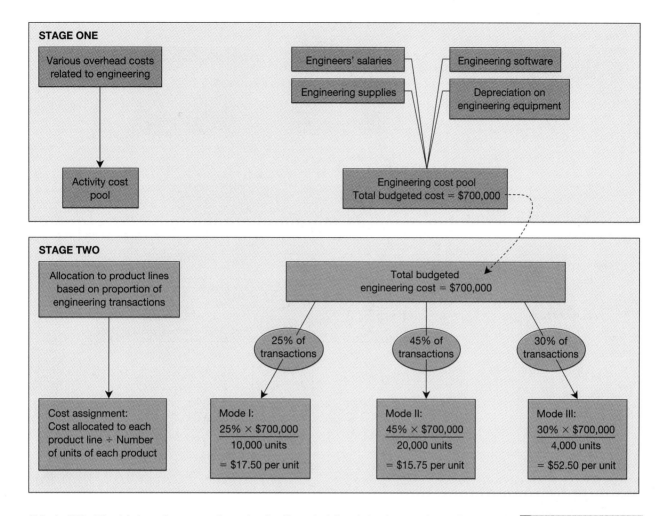

STAGE ONE

Various overhead costs related to engineering

Engineers' salaries

Engineering software

Engineering supplies

Depreciation on engineering equipment

Activity cost pool

Engineering cost pool
Total budgeted cost = $700,000

STAGE TWO

Allocation to product lines based on proportion of engineering transactions

Total budgeted engineering cost = $700,000

25% of transactions

45% of transactions

30% of transactions

Cost assignment: Cost allocated to each product line ÷ Number of units of each product

Mode I:
$$\frac{25\% \times \$700,000}{10,000 \text{ units}}$$
= $17.50 per unit

Mode II:
$$\frac{45\% \times \$700,000}{20,000 \text{ units}}$$
= $15.75 per unit

Mode III:
$$\frac{30\% \times \$700,000}{4,000 \text{ units}}$$
= $52.50 per unit

(Mode III). The high-volume products basically subsidized the low-volume line. The activity-based costing system revealed this problem by more accurately assigning overhead costs to the three product lines.

Exhibit 5–12 (p. 169) summarizes the effects of the cost distortion under the traditional product-costing system. Aerotech's traditional system *overcosted* each Mode I circuit board by $25.56, for a total of $255,600 for the Mode I product line on a volume of 10,000 units. Each Mode II board was *overcosted* by $40.19, for a total of $803,800 on a volume of 20,000 units for the Mode II product line. These excess costs had to come from somewhere, and that place was the Mode III product line. Each Mode III board was *undercosted* by $264.85, for a total of $1,059,400 for the Mode III product line on a volume of 4,000 units. Notice that the *total* amount by which the Mode I and II boards were overcosted equals the *total* amount by which the Mode III boards were undercosted.

Why Traditional, Volume-Based Systems Distort Product Costs

Why did Aerotech's traditional product-costing system distort its product costs? The answer lies in the use of a single, volume-based cost driver. Aerotech's old costing system assigned overhead to products on the basis of their relative usage of direct labor. Since the Mode I and Mode II circuit boards use more direct labor than the Mode III boards, the traditional system assigned them more overhead costs. A review of Exhibit 5–3 confirms this conclusion. Notice, for example, that each Mode II board is assigned twice as much overhead cost as a Mode III board, because each Mode II board requires twice as much direct labor as a Mode III board.

Exhibit 5–8

Activity-Based Costing: Engineering Cost Pool

LO 4 Explain why traditional, volume-based costing systems tend to distort product costs.

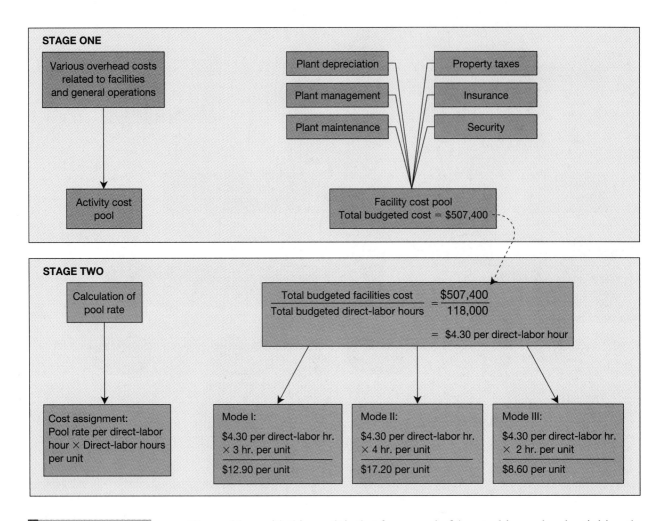

Activity-Based Costing:
Facility Cost Pool

The problem with this result is that for several of Aerotech's overhead activities, the proportion of the activity actually consumed by the Mode III boards is greater than that consumed by the Mode I or II boards. Examine the ABC calculations in Exhibit 5–10. Notice that for many of the overhead activities, the Mode III boards consume the largest share of the activity. The heavy consumption of overhead activities by the Mode III product line is due to its greater complexity and small production runs. We must conclude, therefore, that direct labor is not a suitable cost driver for Aerotech's overhead costs. Usage of direct labor does not drive most overhead costs in this company.

There are actually two factors working against Aerotech's old product-costing system.[5] First, many of the activities that result in Aerotech's overhead costs are *not unit-level activities*. Second, Aerotech manufactures a *diverse set of products*.

Nonunit-Level Overhead Costs   When Aerotech's ABC project team designed the activity-based costing system, only the machine-related overhead cost pool was classified as a unit-level activity. All of the other activities were classified as batch-level, product-sustaining level, or facility-level activities. This means that many of Aerotech's overhead

---

[5]This and the following sections are based on these sources: Robin Cooper, "The Rise of Activity-Based Costing—Part One: What Is an Activity-Based Costing System?" *Journal of Cost Management* 2, no. 2, pp. 45–54; Robin Cooper, "The Rise of Activity-Based Costing—Part Two: When Do I Need an Activity-Based Costing System?" *Journal of Cost Management* 2, no. 3, pp. 41–48; Robin Cooper, "The Rise of Activity-Based Costing—Part Three: How Many Cost Drivers Do You Need, and How Do You Select Them?" *Journal of Cost Management* 3, no. 4, pp. 34–46; Peter B. B. Turney, *Common Cents: The ABC Performance Breakthrough* (Hillsboro, OR: Cost Technology, 1991).

	Mode I Boards	Mode II Boards	Mode III Boards
Direct material (raw boards and components) ...	$50.00	$90.00	$20.00
Direct labor (not including setup time)	60.00 (3 hr. at $20)	80.00 (4 hr. at $20)	40.00 (2 hr. at $20)
Machinery[a]	28.20	35.25	56.40
Setup[b]	.02	.04	.50
Engineering[c]	17.50	15.75	52.50
Facility[d]	12.90	17.20	8.60
Receiving and inspection[e]	1.20	2.40	35.00
Material handling[f]	4.20	9.00	94.50
Quality assurance[g]	8.42	8.42	42.10
Packaging and shipping[h]	1.00	3.75	41.25
Total	$183.44	$261.81	$390.85

Exhibit 5–10

Product Costs from Activity-Based Costing System: Aerotech Corporation's Phoenix Plant

[a] Machinery Cost Pool (details in Exhibit 5–6):

   Mode I: ($1,212,600 ÷ 43,000 machine hr.) × 1   machine hr. = $28.20

   Mode II: ($1,212,600 ÷ 43,000 machine hr.) × 1.25 machine hr. = $35.25

   Mode III: ($1,212,600 ÷ 43,000 machine hr.) × 2   machine hr. = $56.40

[b] Setup Cost Pool (details in Exhibit 5–7):

   Mode I: ($3,000 ÷ 15 runs) ÷ 10,000 units per run = $.02

   Mode II: ($3,000 ÷ 15 runs) ÷ 5,000 units per run = $.04

   Mode III: ($3,000 ÷ 15 runs) ÷ 400 units per run = $.50

[c] Engineering Cost Pool (details in Exhibit 5–8):

   Mode I: ($700,000 × 25%) ÷ 10,000 units = $17.50

   Mode II: ($700,000 × 45%) ÷ 20,000 units = $15.75

   Mode III: ($700,000 × 30%) ÷ 4,000 units = $52.50

[d] Facility Cost Pool (details in Exhibit 5–9):

   Mode I: ($507,400 ÷ 118,000 direct-labor hr.) × 3 direct-labor hr. = $12.90

   Mode II: ($507,400 ÷ 118,000 direct-labor hr.) × 4 direct-labor hr. = $17.20

   Mode III: ($507,400 ÷ 118,000 direct-labor hr.) × 2 direct-labor hr. = $ 8.60

[e] Receiving and Inspection Cost Pool :

   Mode I: ($200,000 × 6%) ÷ 10,000 units = $ 1.20

   Mode II: ($200,000 × 24%) ÷ 20,000 units = $ 2.40

   Mode III: ($200,000 × 70%) ÷ 4,000 units = $35.00

[f] Material-Handling Cost Pool:

   Mode I: ($600,000 × 7%) ÷ 10,000 units = $ 4.20

   Mode II: ($600,000 × 30%) ÷ 20,000 units = $ 9.00

   Mode III: ($600,000 × 63%) ÷ 4,000 units = $94.50

[g] Quality-Assurance Cost Pool:

   Mode I: ($421,000 × 20%) ÷ 10,000 units = $ 8.42

   Mode II: ($421,000 × 40%) ÷ 20,000 units = $ 8.42

   Mode III: ($421,000 × 40%) ÷ 4,000 units = $42.10

[h] Packaging and Shipping Cost Pool:

   Mode I: ($250,000 × 4%) ÷ 10,000 units = $ 1.00

   Mode II: ($250,000 × 30%) ÷ 20,000 units = $ 3.75

   Mode III: ($250,000 × 66%) ÷ 4,000 units = $41.25

The percentages in these calculations are the proportions of each activity consumed by each product line, as estimated by the ABC project team.

costs are not incurred every time a unit is produced. Instead, many of these overhead costs are related to starting new production batches, supporting an entire product line, or running the entire operation. Since direct labor is a unit-level cost driver, it fails to capture the forces that drive these other types of costs. In Aerotech's new ABC system, cost drivers were chosen that were appropriate for each activity cost pool. For example, since setting up machinery for a new production run is a batch-level activity, the number of production runs is an appropriate batch-level cost driver.

Comparison of Product Costs
from Alternative Product-
Costing Systems: Aerotech
Corporation's Phoenix Plant

	Mode I Boards	Mode II Boards	Mode III Boards
Reported product costs:			
Traditional, volume-based			
costing system (from Exhibit 5–3)	$209.00	$302.00	$126.00
Activity-based costing system (from Exhibit 5–10)	183.44	261.81	390.85
Sales price data:			
Original target price (based on traditional,			
volume-based costing system; Exhibit 5–4)	261.25	377.50	157.50
New target price (based on activity-based			
costing system: 125% of reported ABC			
product costs)	229.30	327.26	488.56
Actual selling price (Exhibit 5–4)	261.25	328.00	250.00

In the manufacture of diverse product lines, a single cost driver cannot capture the widely differing usage of production-related activities by the different product lines.

Product Diversity   Aerotech manufactures three different products. Although all three are circuit boards used in aircraft radar and communications equipment, the three boards are quite different. The Mode I and II boards are high-volume, relatively simple boards. The Mode III board is a highly complex, low-volume product. As a result of this *product diversity,* Aerotech's three products consume overhead activities in different proportions. For example, compare the consumption ratios for the engineering and material-handling cost pools shown below. The **consumption ratio** is the proportion of an activity consumed by a particular product.

The **consumption ratio** is the proportion of an activity consumed by a particular product.

	Consumption Ratios*		
Activity Cost Pool	**Mode I**	**Mode II**	**Mode III**
Engineering	25%	45%	30%
Material handling	7%	30%	63%

*From the ABC calculations in Exhibit 5–10.

These widely varying consumption ratios result from Aerotech's product diversity. A single cost driver will not capture the widely differing usage of these activities by the

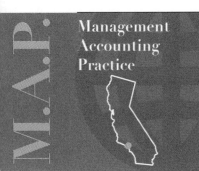

Cost Distortion at Rockwell International

When managers at Rockwell International noticed erratic sales in one of the company's lines of truck axles, they investigated. One of the company's best axle products was losing market share. A special cost study revealed that the firm's costing system, which applied costs to products in proportion to direct-labor costs, had resulted in major distortions. The reported product costs for high-volume axles were approximately 20 percent too high, and the low-volume axles were being undercosted by roughly 40 percent. The firm's practice of basing prices on reported product costs resulted in the overpricing of the high-volume axles. As a consequence, Rockwell's competitors entered the market for the high-volume axle business.[6]

[6]Ford S. Worthy, "Accounting Bores You? Wake Up," *Fortune* 116, no. 8, pp. 43–53.

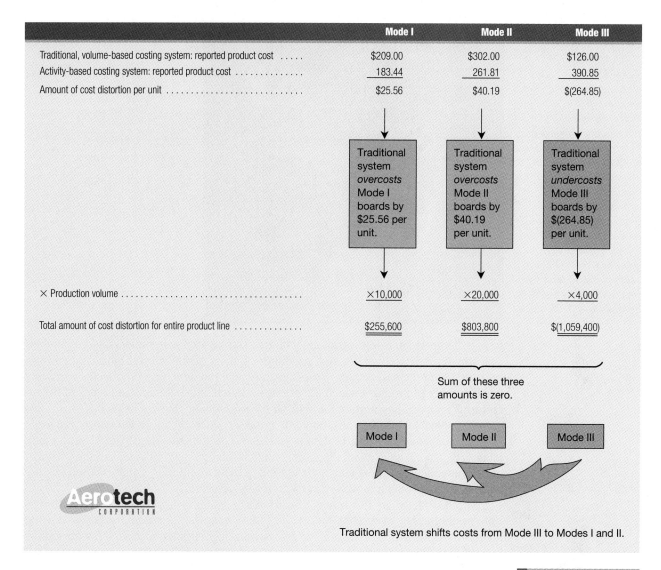

	Mode I	Mode II	Mode III
Traditional, volume-based costing system: reported product cost	$209.00	$302.00	$126.00
Activity-based costing system: reported product cost	183.44	261.81	390.85
Amount of cost distortion per unit	$25.56	$40.19	$(264.85)

Traditional system *overcosts* Mode I boards by $25.56 per unit.

Traditional system *overcosts* Mode II boards by $40.19 per unit.

Traditional system *undercosts* Mode III boards by $(264.85) per unit.

	Mode I	Mode II	Mode III
× Production volume	×10,000	×20,000	×4,000
Total amount of cost distortion for entire product line	$255,600	$803,800	$(1,059,400)

Sum of these three amounts is zero.

Mode I   Mode II   Mode III

Traditional system shifts costs from Mode III to Modes I and II.

three products. The activity-based costing system uses two different cost drivers to assign these costs to Aerotech's diverse products.

Exhibit 5–12

Cost Distortion under Aerotech's Traditional Product-Costing System

Two Key Points   To summarize, each of the following characteristics will undermine the ability of a volume-based product-costing system to assign overhead costs accurately.

- *A large proportion of nonunit-level activities.* A unit-level cost driver, such as direct labor, machine hours, or throughput, will not be able to assign the costs of nonunit-level activities accurately.
- *Product diversity.* When the consumption ratios differ widely between activities, no single cost driver will accurately assign the resulting overhead costs.

When either of these characteristics is present, a volume-based product-costing system is likely to distort product costs.

Does the sort of product-cost distortion experienced by Aerotech occur in other companies? The answer is yes, as illustrated by the examples from Rockwell International (preceding page) and Compaq (next page).

Activity-Based Costing: Some Key Issues

Aerotech Corporation's movement toward activity-based costing is typical of changes currently underway in many companies. Added domestic and

LO 5   Discuss several key issues in activity-based costing, including criteria for choosing cost drivers, transaction costing, storyboarding, and indicators that a new costing system is needed.

Compaq executives were convinced that they were more efficient in producing computers than other companies, but they were mystified as to how their competitors could sell similar equipment at lower prices and still be profitable. However, an ABC analysis revealed that Compaq's cost-accounting system was overcosting high-volume products, while low-volume products were being undercosted. Low-volume accessories also were being undercosted by a substantial amount.[7]

foreign competition is forcing manufacturers to strive for a better understanding of their cost structures. Moreover, the cost structures of many manufacturers have changed significantly over the past decade. Years ago, a typical manufacturer produced a relatively small number of products which did not differ much in the amount and types of manufacturing support they required. Labor was the dominant element in such a firm's cost structure. Nowadays, it's a different ball game. Products are more numerous, are more complicated, and vary more in their production requirements. Perhaps most important, labor is becoming an ever-smaller component of total production costs. All these factors mean manufacturers must take a close look at their traditional, volume-based costing systems and consider a move toward activity-based costing.

Another factor in the move toward ABC systems is related to the information requirements of such systems. The data required for activity-based costing are more readily available than in the past. Increasing automation, coupled with sophisticated real-time information systems, provides the kind of data necessary to implement highly accurate product-costing systems. Some key issues related to activity- based costing systems are discussed in the following sections.[8]

Cost Drivers

A **cost driver** is a characteristic of an activity or event that results in the incurrence of costs by that activity or event.

A **cost driver** is a characteristic of an event or activity that results in the incurrence of costs. In activity-based costing systems, the most significant cost drivers are identified. Then a database is created, which shows how these cost drivers are distributed across products. Three factors are important in selecting appropriate cost drivers.

1. *Degree of correlation.* The central concept of an activity-based costing system is to assign the costs of each activity to product lines on the basis of how each

---

[7]S. L. Mintz, "Compaq's Secret Weapon," *CFO* 10, no. 10, pp. 93–97.

[8]Many of the concepts in this and the remaining sections of the chapter are derived from the following sources: Callie Berliner and James A. Brimson, eds., *Cost Management for Today's Advanced Manufacturing* (Boston: Harvard Business School Press, 1988); Robin Cooper and Robert Kaplan, "How Cost Accounting Systematically Distorts Product Costs," in *Accounting and Management: Field Study Perspectives,* William J. Bruns, Jr., and Robert S. Kaplan, eds. (Boston: Harvard Business School Press, 1987), pp. 204–28; Robert D. McIlhattan, "How Cost Management Systems Can Support the JIT Philosophy," *Management Accounting* 69, no. 3, pp. 20–26; Robert A. Howell and Stephen R. Soucy, "Operating Controls in the New Manufacturing Environment," *Management Accounting* 69, no. 4, pp. 25–31; H. Thomas Johnson and Robert S. Kaplan, *Relevance Lost: The Rise and Fall of Management Accounting* (Boston: Harvard Business School Press, 1987); and Peter B. B. Turney, "Activity-Based Management," *Management Accounting* 73, no. 7, pp. 20–25.

product line consumes the cost driver identified for that activity. The idea is to *infer* how each product line consumes the activity by *observing* how each product line consumes the cost driver. Therefore, the accuracy of the resulting cost assignments depends on the *degree of correlation* between consumption of the activity and consumption of the cost driver.

Say that inspection cost is selected as an activity cost pool. The objective of the ABC system is to assign inspection costs to product lines on the basis of their consumption of the inspection activity. Two potential cost drivers come to mind: number of inspections and hours of inspection time. If every inspection requires the same amount of time for all products, then the number of inspections on a product line will be highly correlated with the consumption of inspection activity by that product line. On the other hand, if inspections vary significantly in the time required, then simply recording the number of inspections will not adequately portray the consumption of inspection activity. In this case, hours of inspection time would be more highly correlated with the actual consumption of the inspection activity.

2. *Cost of measurement.* Designing any information system entails cost-benefit trade-offs. The more activity cost pools there are in an activity-based costing system, the greater will be the accuracy of the cost assignments. However, more activity cost pools also entail more cost drivers, which results in greater costs of implementing and maintaining the system.

Similarly, the higher the correlation between a cost driver and the actual consumption of the associated activity, the greater the accuracy of the cost assignments. However, it may also be more costly to measure the more highly correlated cost driver. Returning to our example of the inspection activity, it may be that inspection hours make a more accurate cost driver than the number of inspections. It is likely, however, that inspection hours also will be more costly to measure and track over time.

3. *Behavioral effects.* Information systems have the potential not only to facilitate decisions but also to influence the behavior of decision makers. This can be good or bad, depending on the behavioral effects. In identifying cost drivers, an ABC analyst should consider the possible behavioral consequences. For example, in a JIT production environment a key goal is to reduce inventories and material-handling activities to the absolute minimum level possible. The number of material moves may be the most accurate measure of the consumption of the material-handling activity for cost assignment purposes. It may also have a desirable behavioral effect of inducing managers to reduce the number of times materials are moved, thereby reducing material-handling costs.

Dysfunctional behavioral effects are also possible. For example, the number of vendor contacts may be a cost driver for the purchasing activity of vendor selection. This could induce purchasing managers to contact fewer vendors, which could result in the failure to identify the lowest-cost or highest-quality vendor.

Some examples of cost drivers are given in the illustration from Hewlett-Packard on the next page.

Homogeneous Activity Cost Pools

In deciding how many activity cost pools (and their associated cost drivers) are needed, the ABC analyst should look carefully at the *homogeneity* of each potential cost pool. A **homogeneous cost pool** is a grouping of overhead costs in which each cost component is consumed in roughly the same proportion by each product line. A homogeneous cost pool can be allocated using a single cost driver. To illustrate, suppose Aerotech's receiving and inspection cost pool has the following characteristics.

> A **homogeneous cost pool** is a grouping of overhead costs in which each cost component is consumed in roughly the same proportion by each product line.

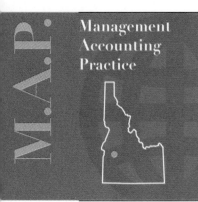

Cost Drivers at Hewlett-Packard

HP manufactures many different electronic circuit boards at its Boise Surface Mount Center. These boards then are used in the personal computers produced in other HP divisions. Some of the cost drivers used by HP in its circuit-board production are listed below.[9]

- Number of components placed on a board's surface.
- Number of components inserted through holes in the board.
- Minutes required to place any components that are hand-loaded rather than automatically placed.
- Number of unique parts in the board.
- Number of production scheduling hours.
- Number of minutes of setup time.
- Number of minutes of test and rework time.

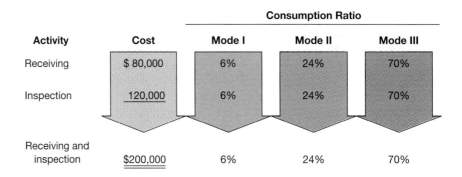

		Consumption Ratio		
Activity	Cost	Mode I	Mode II	Mode III
Receiving	$ 80,000	6%	24%	70%
Inspection	120,000	6%	24%	70%
Receiving and inspection	$200,000	6%	24%	70%

The combined receiving and inspection cost pool is homogeneous because the consumption ratios are the same for its components. As a result, Aerotech's ABC project team combined receiving and inspection costs into a single cost pool. Slight deviations from homogeneity can be tolerated without significant effects on cost assignment accuracy. However, the greater the deviations become, the greater is the chance of distorted product costs.

Transaction Costing

The output of an organization's various departments consists of the activities performed by personnel or machines in those departments. Activities usually result in paperwork or the generation of computer documents. For example, engineering departments typically deal with documents such as specification sheets and engineering change orders. Purchasing departments handle requisitions and orders, which may be either hard-copy or computer documents. The point is that transactions provide a readily measurable gauge of the activity in a department. In an ABC system, transaction costing can be used to assign the costs of activities to product lines on the basis of the number of transactions generated by each product.

Interviews and Paper Trails   The transaction information used in Aerotech's ABC system came initially from extensive interviews with key employees in each of the organization's support departments and a careful review of each department's records. In Aerotech's engineering area, for example, ABC project team members interviewed each engineer to determine the breakdown of time spent on each of the three products. They also examined every engineering change order completed in the past two years. The team concluded that engineering costs were driven largely by change orders and design specs, and that the breakdown was 25 percent for Mode I, 45 percent for Mode II, and 30 percent for Mode III.

---

[9]C. M. Merz and A. Hardy, "ABC Puts Accountants on Design Team at HP," *Management Accounting* 75, no. 3, pp. 22–27.

Storyboarding

As Aerotech's project team delved further into the ABC analysis, they made considerable use of another technique for collecting activity data. **Storyboarding** is a procedure used to develop a detailed process flowchart, which visually represents activities and the relationships among the activities. A storyboarding session involves all or most of the employees who participate in the activities oriented toward achieving a specific objective. A facilitator helps the employees identify the key activities involved in their jobs. These activities are written on small cards and placed on a large board in the order they are accomplished. Relationships among the activities are shown by the order and proximity of the cards. Other information about the activities is recorded on the cards, such as the amount of time and other resources that are expended on each activity and the events that trigger the activity. After several storyboarding sessions, a completed storyboard emerges, recording key activity information vital to the ABC project. Historically, storyboards have been used by Walt Disney and other film producers in the development of plots for animated films. More recently, storyboarding has been used by advertising agencies in developing event sequences for TV commercials.

Storyboarding provides a powerful tool for collecting and organizing the data needed in an ABC project. Aerotech's ABC project team used storyboarding very effectively to study each of the firm's activity cost pools. The team concluded that receiving and inspection costs were driven by the number of shipments received and inspected. Material-handling costs were driven by the number of times materials and partially completed units were moved, and by the length of time they remained in storage between production operations. Quality-assurance costs were driven by the number of production lots

> **Storyboarding** is a procedure used to develop a detailed process flowchart, which visually represents activities and the relationships among the activities.

Interviews with department personnel and storyboarding sessions are often used by activity-based costing project teams to accumulate the data needed for an ABC study. In the interview sessions, an ABC project team member asks departmental employees to detail their activities, as well as the time and other resources consumed by the activities. Storyboards, like the one depicted here, visually show the relationships between the activities performed in an organization.

to be tested and the complexity of the product being tested. Packaging and shipping costs were driven by the number of production runs to be packed and the number of shipments made, in addition to the total number of circuit boards being shipped.

In summary, the ABC project team conducted painstaking and lengthy analysis involving many employee interviews, the examination of hundreds of documents, and storyboarding sessions. The final result was the data used in the ABC calculations displayed in Exhibit 5–10.

Multidisciplinary ABC Project Teams

In order to gather information from all facets of an organization's operations, it is essential to involve personnel from a variety of functional areas. A typical ABC project team includes accounting and finance people as well as engineers, marketing personnel, production and operations managers, and so forth. A multidisciplinary project team not only designs a better ABC system but also helps in gaining credibility for the new system throughout the organization.

Direct versus Indirect Costs

In traditional, volume-based costing systems, only direct material and direct labor are considered direct costs. All other production costs are lumped together in one (or a few) overhead cost pools and applied to products on the basis of a volume-related measure such as direct labor. Thus, all of these costs are treated as indirect costs with respect to the firm's products. In contrast, under an activity-based costing system, an effort is made to account for as many costs as possible as direct costs of production. Any cost that can possibly be traced to a particular product line is treated as a direct cost of that product. A good example is setup time in Aerotech's Phoenix plant. Under the traditional costing system, the cost of setup time is included in manufacturing overhead and applied to products on the basis of direct-labor hours. Under the activity-based costing system, setup time is measured for each product line, and setup costs are assigned as *direct costs* to each type of circuit board.

When Is a New Product-Costing System Needed?

The redesign of a firm's product-costing system is a significant decision that requires the approval of top management and involves a major effort to accomplish. For this reason, many organizations shy away from such a major change. Yet most organizations that have implemented activity-based costing have found the benefits to be well worth the costs. Nevertheless, it bears emphasizing that designing an optimal information system involves trade-offs between the costs and benefits of increased accuracy. Exhibit 5–13 depicts this trade-off graphically. The optimal information system minimizes the total cost of designing, implementing, and maintaining the system, along with the costs of inferior decisions caused by faulty information.[10]

Indicators for ABC   When should management consider incurring the considerable cost of designing and implementing an activity-based costing system? Some indicators can signal the need for a new costing system.[11]

- Line managers do not believe the product costs reported by the accounting department.

---

[10]See Robin Cooper, "The Rise of Activity-Based Costing—Part Two: When Do I Need an Activity-Based Costing System?" *Journal of Cost Management* 2, no. 3, pp. 41–48.

[11]Robin Cooper, "Does Your Company Need a New Cost System?" *Journal of Cost Management* 1, no. 1, pp. 45–49, and Robin Cooper, "You Need a New Costing System When…," *Harvard Business Review* 67, no. 1, pp. 77–82. See also Peter B. B. Turney, *Common Cents: The ABC Performance Breakthrough.*

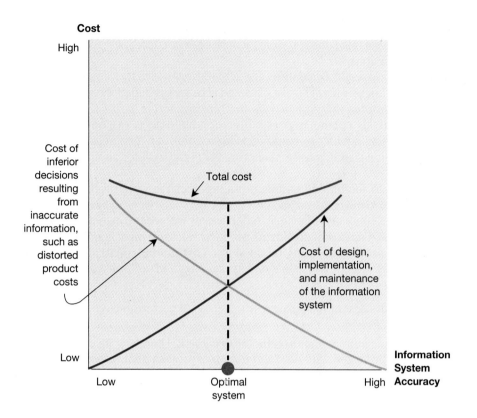

Exhibit 5–13

The Optimal Product-Costing System: A Cost-Benefit Trade-Off

- Marketing personnel are unwilling to use reported product costs in making pricing decisions.
- Complex products that are difficult to manufacture are reported to be very profitable, although they are not priced at a premium.
- Product-line profit margins are difficult to explain.
- Sales are increasing, but profits are declining.
- Line managers suggest that apparently profitable products be dropped.
- Marketing or production managers are using "bootleg costing systems," which are informal systems they designed, often on a personal computer.
- Some products that have reported high profit margins are not sold by competitors.
- The firm seems to have captured a highly profitable product niche all for itself.
- Overhead rates are very high, and increasing over time.
- Product lines are diverse.
- Direct labor is a small percentage of total costs.
- The results of bids are difficult to explain.
- Competitors' high-volume products seem to be priced unrealistically low.
- The accounting department spends significant amounts of time on special costing projects to support bids or pricing decisions.

Cost Management Systems

When Aerotech Corporation moved to an activity-based costing system in its Phoenix plant, the company was in a better position to price its products competitively. The firm's management was able to see why Aerotech was being forced to lower the price on its high-volume Mode II circuit boards. Moreover, the high cost of the complex, low-volume Mode III boards became apparent. The type of analysis undertaken by Aerotech's controller in the Phoenix plant

LO 6 Describe the key features of a cost management system, including the elimination of non-value-added costs.

Strategic cost analysis is a broad-based managerial-accounting analysis that supports strategic management decisions.

sometimes is called **strategic cost analysis.** This is a broad-based, managerial-accounting analysis that supports strategic management decisions, such as pricing and product-mix decisions.

A strategic cost analysis identifies the activities by which the organization creates a valuable product or service. This set of linked activities is called the value chain. Then the analysis identifies the cost drivers that determine the costs of these activities. Finally, the analysis examines possibilities for building a sustainable competitive advantage. Such an advantage could be achieved through a combination of strategic pricing, controlling cost drivers, and altering the organization's significant production activities.[12]

In addition to facilitating strategic pricing decisions, Aerotech's new product-costing system served as the catalyst for a new perspective on the role of managerial accounting in the company. Management no longer viewed the managerial-accounting system merely as a means of costing its products. Instead, management came to view the firm's managerial-accounting function as a **cost management system (CMS).** A cost management system is a management planning and control system with the following objectives.[13]

A **cost management system (CMS)** measures the cost of significant activities, identifies non-value-added costs, and identifies activities that will improve organizational performance.

Non-value-added costs can be eliminated without deterioration of product quality, performance, or perceived value.

- To measure the cost of the resources consumed in performing the organization's significant *activities*.
- To identify and eliminate **non-value-added costs.** These are the costs of *activities* that can be eliminated with no deterioration of product quality, performance, or perceived value.
- To determine the efficiency and effectiveness of all major *activities* performed in the enterprise.
- To identify and evaluate new *activities* that can improve the future performance of the organization.

A cost management system takes a more comprehensive role in an organization than a traditional cost-accounting system. "While cost accounting takes an historical perspective and focuses on reporting costs, cost management takes a proactive role in planning, managing and reducing costs."[14]

Non-Value-Added Costs

The emphasis of a cost management system on activities can help management to identify non-value-added costs and eliminate the activities that cause them. To see how this might occur, let's return to our illustration of Aerotech Corporation's Phoenix plant. How is the time spent in Aerotech's production process from the moment raw material arrives at the Phoenix plant until a finished circuit board is shipped to a customer? As in most manufacturing operations, the time is spent in the following five ways.[15]

- *Process time:* The time during which a product is undergoing conversion activity
- *Inspection time:* The amount of time spent assuring that the product is of high quality
- *Move time:* The time spent moving raw materials, work in process, or finished goods between operations

---

[12]Vijay Govindarajan and John K. Shank, "Strategic Cost Analysis: The Crown Cork and Seal Case," *Journal of Cost Management* 2, no. 4, p. 6.

[13]Berliner and Brimson, *Cost Management for Today's Advanced Manufacturing,* pp. 3, 10, 13–15.

[14]Ibid., p. 3.

[15]McIlhattan, "How Cost Management Systems Can Support the JIT Philosophy."

- *Waiting time:* The amount of time that raw materials or work in process spend waiting for the next operation
- *Storage time:* The time during which materials, partially completed products, or finished goods are held in stock before further processing or shipment to customers

Keep these five types of activities in mind as you reexamine the layout of Aerotech's Phoenix plant (Exhibit 5–1). **Process time** is the amount of time the circuit boards actually are being worked on in one of the production operations (departments 1 through 6) or the packaging operation (department 7). **Inspection time** is the time spent on the bed-of-nails or burn-in testing procedures (departments 7 and 8). **Move time** includes the following activities: receiving raw materials and moving them into storage; moving raw materials and components to the axial-lead sequencing operation (department 1) or the two hand-insertion operations (departments 3 and 6); moving partially completed products from one department to the next; and moving packaged circuit boards to finished-goods storage. **Waiting time** includes the time that partially completed circuit boards spend in the holding areas located next to each department waiting for the next production operation. **Storage time** includes the time spent by raw materials and parts in storage, and the time spent by packaged circuit boards in finished-goods storage.

Identifying Non-Value-Added Costs in the Phoenix Plant

Can you identify any activities in Exhibit 5–1 that potentially could result in non-value-added costs? The identification of non-value-added activities will vary from company to company, but each of the five types of activities mentioned above has at least some potential for causing non-value-added costs.

Storage Time   Perhaps the most obvious is storage time. Manufacturers traditionally have stored large inventories of materials, parts, and finished goods in order to avoid running out. In recent years, however, that philosophy has been challenged. More and more manufacturers are adopting a *just-in-time* approach, where nothing is purchased or produced until it is needed. In Aerotech's Phoenix operation, the large amounts of space devoted to storage activities are indicative of potentially large non-value-added costs of storage.

Waiting Time   Refer again to Exhibit 5-1. Notice the large amount of space devoted in the factory to partially completed circuit boards waiting for the next operation. This is again indicative of potentially large non-value-added costs. The firm's working capital is tied up in work in process, and space is unnecessarily wasted on numerous production queues.

Move Time   Think about the amount of time Aerotech's Phoenix employees must spend just moving materials and products around in the plant. Every product must be moved 17 times between the axial-lead sequencing operation (department 1) and finished-goods storage. In addition, raw materials and parts must be moved to three different production operations (departments 1, 3, and 6). Once again, we find the potential for significant non-value-added costs associated with the Phoenix plant's material-handling operations.

Inspection Time   Aerotech employs three inspection operations. As Exhibit 5–1 indicates, raw materials and components are inspected upon arrival. Later, the circuit boards are tested in the bed-of-nails procedure (department 7) and the burn-in test (department 8). It is difficult to say whether inspection procedures result in non-value-added costs without detailed knowledge of the production technology and inspection procedures. Certainly some type of inspection is necessary to assure product quality. However, many manufacturers are striving to reduce the costs of maintaining product quality and virtually eliminate the costs of reworking defective products.

Process time is the amount of time during which a product is undergoing conversion activity.

Inspection time is the time spent on quality inspections of raw materials, partially completed products, or finished goods.

Move time is the time spent moving raw materials, subassemblies, or finished products from one production operation to another.

Waiting time is the time during which partially completed products wait for the next phase of production.

Storage time is the time during which raw materials or finished products are stored in stock.

Process Time   The actual production process that transforms raw material into finished products is certainly a value-added activity *overall*. However, this does not preclude the possibility that some non-value-added activities exist within the overall production process. The goal of the cost management system is to evaluate the efficiency of every part of the production process. Is each step necessary? Is each operation being accomplished in the most efficient way? Should some production operations be outsourced?

Conclusion   Aerotech's management concluded that substantial non-value-added costs were being incurred in the Phoenix operation. The following activities were identified in a memo from Aerotech's president to key management personnel.

- *Storage:* A considerable reduction in storage space and time is both possible and essential.
- *Waiting:* Circuit boards should be processed through each operation only as they are required in the subsequent operation. Thus, the amount of time products spend waiting for the next operation should be virtually eliminated.
- *Moving:* The time devoted to moving raw material and work in process is excessive. Ways must be found to reduce the costs of these material-handling activities.
- *Inspection:* The bed-of-nails and burn-in tests appear to be necessary and efficiently conducted. Nevertheless, management should continually reassess the need for these inspection operations.
- *Processing:* The manual insertion of components in departments 3 and 6 can be performed by industrial robots. The desirability of this change should be explored.

We will study the elimination of non-value-added costs further in the next chapter.

Activity-Based Management

LO 7   Briefly explain the concept of activity-based management.

Activity-based management (ABM) uses an activity-based costing system to improve the operations of an organization.

Using an activity-based costing system to improve the operations of an organization is called **activity-based management (ABM).** Costs are incurred in organizations because of *activities*. A sales order triggers a series of activities, from the purchase of materials, through various production phases, ending with shipping the product. A key feature of activity-based costing systems is that they measure and track the costs of significant activities over time. In addition to using the activity *cost* information collected in an ABC system, activity-based management involves the collection of financial or operational *performance* information about significant activities in the enterprise. The motivation for this process is twofold. First, the costing system attempts to assign the costs of significant activities to the products that cause those costs to be incurred. Second, by identifying the cost of activities, managers can attempt the reduction or elimination of unnecessary costs. ABC and ABM tend to strike a familiar chord with a variety of managers and employees throughout an enterprise. Activities are expressed in terms of events that are familiar to such diverse people as sales personnel, engineers, purchasing managers, inspectors, material handlers, production employees, and shipping personnel.

We will study activity-based management in much greater depth in the next chapter.

Activity-Based Costing and Management in the Service Industry

We conclude this chapter with the important point that activity-based costing and activity-based management have found widespread usage in the service industry as well as in manufacturing. There have been many ABC success stories in such diverse organizations as airlines, insurance companies, banks, hospitals, financial services firms, hotels, and railroads. The overall objectives of ABC and ABM in service firms are no different than they are in manufacturing companies. Managers want more accurate information about the cost of producing the services they are selling. Moreover, they want to use this information to improve operations and to better meet the needs of their customers in a more cost-effective manner. The general approach of identifying activities, activity cost pools, and cost drivers may be used in the service industry as well as in manufacturing. The classification of activities into unit-level, batch-level, product-sustaining level, and facility-level activities also applies in service industry settings. For example Pennsylvania Blue Shield used these activity classifications in its ABC system.[16] Examples from the Blue Shield system are as follows:

- *Unit level:* Entering initial claim data into the computer (for each claim received).
- *Batch level:* Moving a batch of claims from one processing step to the next.
- *Product-sustaining level:* Maintenance of the medical-services provider network (i.e., maintaining relationships with physicians and hospitals providing medical care to claimants).
- *Facility (general operations) level:* General administration of the claims business unit.

Several examples of service industry applications of ABC and ABM follow.

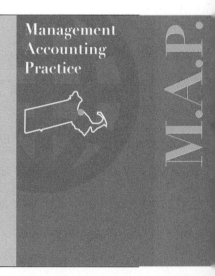

Braintree Hospital

Braintree Hospital is a private rehabilitation hospital in Boston.[17] An activity-based costing system has enabled the hospital's management to measure and track the cost of providing nursing care to each individual patient. "There is a wide variation in the amount of nursing services consumed by patients, just as there is a wide variety of patient ailments that require differing degrees of nursing attention. The health care industry has recognized this phenomenon, and third-party payers (e.g., insurance companies) are pushing very hard to pay only for services used by the patient and at the lowest price."[18] The ABC project team, which included both nurses and administrators, developed a nursing service classification data form. Nurses used the form to record the amount and type of nursing care provided to each patient. The forms were collected daily, and the data were entered into a computerized database. "The nursing staff openly accepted the study and, with few exceptions, completed the form accurately and in a timely manner."[19] The result was much more accurate tracking of such nursing tasks as checking vital signs, administering medication, turning patients, and so forth. The ABC success at Boston's Braintree Hospital was communicated to 32 other rehab facilities operated by Braintree's parent company. The hospital's administration believes the system has provided valuable information for managing the delivery of nursing services and for meeting the changing requirements of health care reimbursement procedures.

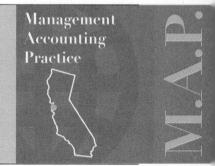

American Express

American Express implemented ABC in its Integrated Payment System (IPS), which manages American Express Money Orders.[20] The ABC analysis began in IPS's customer services department. Management wanted a better understanding of the fixed versus variable costs for each product line. In order to achieve more accurate costing of its services, as well as provide better quality service, management needed to answer difficult questions about how and where employees were spending their time. The ABC approach has helped management to better plan and manage the organization's costs.

[16]Angela Norkiewicz, "Nine Steps to Implementing ABC," *Management Accounting* 75, no. 10, pp. 28–33.

[17]Lawrence P. Carr, "Unbundling the Cost of Hospitalization," *Management Accounting* 75, no. 5, pp. 43–48.

[18]Ibid., p. 44.

[19]Ibid., p. 45.

[20]David Carlson and S. Mark Young, "Activity-Based Total Quality Management at American Express," *Journal of Cost Management* 7, no. 1, pp. 48–58.

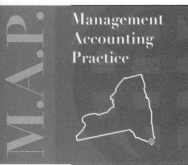

Chapter Summary

Sweeping changes are revolutionizing the manufacturing industry. Global competition coupled with rapid technological innovation are changing manufacturing in a dramatic way. Along with manufacturing systems, the role of managerial accounting is changing also. Many firms are moving from a traditional cost-accounting approach toward a more proactive cost management system perspective. A cost management system (CMS) measures the cost of significant activities, identifies non-value-added costs, and identifies activities that will improve organizational performance. The CMS emphasis on activities helps a company gain a competitive edge by facilitating production of a high-quality product at the lowest cost possible.

As the manufacturing environment has changed, many managers have come to believe that traditional, volume-based product-costing systems do not accurately reflect product costs. Product-costing systems structured on single, volume-based cost drivers, such as direct labor or machine hours, often tend to overcost high-volume products and undercost low-volume or complex products. These cost distortions can have serious effects on pricing and other decisions. To alleviate these problems, more and more firms are adopting an activity-based costing system based on multiple cost drivers. Such costing systems provide better information for strategic management decisions and help in the identification of non-value-added costs.

Activity-based costing has also found widespread successful implementation in the service industry.

Review Problem on Cost Drivers and Product-Cost Distortion

Edgeworth Box Corporation manufactures a variety of special packaging boxes used in the pharmaceutical industry. The company's Dallas plant is semiautomated, but the special nature of the boxes requires some manual labor. The controller has chosen the following activity cost pools, cost drivers, and pool rates for the Dallas plant's product-costing system.

Activity Cost Pool	Overhead Cost	Cost Driver	Budgeted Level for Cost Driver	Pool Rate
Purchasing, storage, and material handling	$200,000	Raw-material costs	$1,000,000	20% of material cost
Engineering and product design	100,000	Hours in design department	5,000 hr.	$20 per hour
Machine setup costs	70,000	Production runs	1,000 runs	$70 per run
Machine depreciation and maintenance	300,000	Machine hours	100,000 hr.	$3 per hour
Factory depreciation, taxes, insurance, and utilities	200,000	Machine hours	100,000 hr.	$2 per hour
Other manufacturing-overhead costs	150,000	Machine hours	100,000 hr.	$1.50 per hour
Total	$1,020,000			

[21]Terrence Hobdy, Jeff Thompson, and Paul Sharman, "Activity-Based Management at AT&T," *Management Accounting* 75, no. 11, pp. 35–39.

[22]Ibid., p. 39.

Two recent production orders had the following requirements.

	20,000 Units of Box C52	10,000 Units of Box W29
Direct-labor hours	42 hr.	21 hr.
Raw-material cost	$40,000	$35,000
Hours in design department	10	25
Production runs	2	4
Machine hours	24	20

Required

1. Compute the total overhead that should be assigned to each of the two production orders, C52 and W29.

2. Compute the overhead cost per box in each order.

3. Suppose the Dallas plant were to use a single predetermined overhead rate based on direct-labor hours. The direct-labor budget calls for 4,000 hours.

 a. Compute the predetermined overhead rate per direct-labor hour.

 b. Compute the total overhead cost that would be assigned to the order for box C52 and the order for box W29.

 c. Compute the overhead cost per box in each order.

4. Why do the two product-costing systems yield such widely differing overhead costs per box?

Solution to Review Problem

1.

	Box C52	Box W29
Purchasing, storage, and material handling	$8,000 (20% × $40,000)	$7,000 (20% × $35,000)
Engineering and product design	200 (10 × $20/hr.)	500 (25 × $20/hr.)
Machine setup costs	140 (2 × $70/run)	280 (4 × $70/run)
Machine depreciation and maintenance	72 (24 × $3/hr.)	60 (20 × $3/hr.)
Factory depreciation, taxes, insurance, and utilities	48 (24 × $2/hr.)	40 (20 × $2/hr.)
Other manufacturing overhead costs	36 (24 × $1.50/hr.)	30 (20 × $1.50/hr.)
Total overhead assigned to production order	$8,496	$7,910

2. Overhead cost per box $.4248 per box $\left(\dfrac{\$8,496}{20,000}\right)$ $.791 per box $\left(\dfrac{\$7,910}{10,000}\right)$

3. Computations based on single predetermined overhead rate based on direct-labor hours:

 a. $\dfrac{\text{Total budgeted overhead}}{\text{Total budgeted direct-labor hours}} = \dfrac{\$1,020,000}{4,000} = \$255/\text{hr.}$

 b. Total overhead assigned to each order:

   Box C52 order: 42 direct-labor hours × $255/hr. = $10,710

   Box W29 order: 21 direct-labor hours × $255/hr. = $5,355

 c. Overhead cost per box:

   Box C52: $10,710 ÷ 20,000 = $.5355 per box

   Box W29: $5,355 ÷ 10,000 = $.5355 per box

4. The widely differing overhead costs are assigned as a result of the inherent inaccuracy of the single, volume-based overhead rate. The relative usage of direct labor by the two production orders does not reflect their relative usage of other manufacturing support services.

Key Terms

For each term's definition refer to the indicated page, or turn to the glossary at the end of the text.

homogeneous cost pool, pg. 171	pool rate, pg. 161	storage time, pg. 177	unit-level activity, pg. 160
inspection time, pg. 177	process (or functional) plant layout, pg. 157	storyboarding, pg. 173	volume-based (or throughput-based) costing system, pg. 159
move time, pg. 177	process time, pg. 177	strategic cost analysis, pg. 176	waiting time, pg. 177
non-value-added costs, pg. 176	product-sustaining-level activity, pg. 160	transaction-based costing, pg. 162	

Review Questions

5–1. Briefly explain how a traditional, volume-based product-costing system operates.

5–2. Why was Aerotech Corporation's management being misled by the traditional product-costing system? What mistakes were being made?

5–3. Explain how an activity-based costing system operates.

5–4. What are cost drivers? What is their role in an activity-based costing system?

5–5. List and briefly describe the four broad categories of activities identified in stage one of an activity-based costing project.

5–6. How can an activity-based costing system alleviate the problems Aerotech was having under its traditional, volume-based product-costing system?

5–7. Why do product-costing systems based on a single, volume-based cost driver tend to overcost high-volume products? What undesirable strategic effects can such distortion of product costs have?

5–8. How is the distinction between direct and indirect costs handled differently under volume-based versus activity-based costing systems?

5–9. List four objectives of a cost management system.

5–10. What is meant by the term *non-value-added costs?* Give four examples.

5–11. List and define the five ways that time is spent in a manufacturing process. Which of these types of activities are likely candidates for non-value-added activities? Why?

5–12. Briefly explain two factors that tend to result in product cost distortion under traditional, volume-based product-costing systems.

5–13. Define the term *activity-based management.*

5–14. List three factors that are important in selecting cost drivers for an ABC system.

5–15. What is meant by a *homogeneous cost pool?*

5–16. Explain briefly why multidisciplinary ABC project teams are used.

5–17. List eight indicators that suggest management should consider implementing a new product-costing system.

5–18. Explain why a new product-costing system may be needed when line managers suggest that an apparently profitable product be dropped.

5–19. Explain why a manufacturer with diverse product lines may benefit from an ABC system.

5–20. Are activity-based costing systems appropriate for the service industry? Explain.

5–21. Explain how the concept of product-line diversity relates to the usefulness of ABC in the Braintree Hospital example given in the chapter.

5–22. Explain why the maintenance of the medical-services provider network is treated as a product-sustaining level activity by Pennsylvania Blue Shield.

Exercises

■ **Exercise 5–23**
Activity-Based Costing;
Quality Control Costs
(LO 2, LO 3, LO 4)

New-Rage Cosmetics has used a traditional cost accounting system to apply quality-control costs uniformly to all products at a rate of 14.5 percent of direct-labor cost. Monthly direct-labor cost for Satin Sheen makeup is $27,500. In an attempt to more equitably distribute quality-control costs, New-Rage is considering activity-based costing. The monthly data shown in the following chart have been gathered for Satin Sheen makeup.

Activity Cost Pool	Cost Driver	Pool Rates	Quantity of Driver for Satin Sheen
Incoming material inspection	Type of material	$11.50 per type	12 types
In-process inspection	Number of units	.14 per unit	17,500 units
Product certification	Per order	77.00 per order	25 orders

Required:

1. Calculate the monthly quality-control cost to be assigned to the Satin Sheen product line under each of the following product-costing systems. (Round to the nearest dollar.)

   a. Traditional system which assigns overhead on the basis of direct-labor cost.

   b. Activity-based costing.

2. Does the traditional product-costing system overcost or undercost the Satin Sheen product line with respect to quality-control costs? By what amount?

(CMA, adapted)

United Technologies Corporation is using activity-based costing in two of its subsidiaries: Otis Elevator Company and Carrier Corporation. The following table shows 27 activities and eight accounts identified at Carrier, along with the classification determined by the ABC project team.[23]

■ **Exercise 5–24**
United Technologies;
Classification of Activities
(LO 3, LO 5)

Name of Activity or Account	Classification by Activity Level
Acquiring material	Batch
Inspecting incoming materials	Batch
Moving materials	Batch
Planning production	Batch
Processing special orders	Batch
Processing supplier invoices	Batch
Receiving material	Batch
Scheduling production	Batch
Inspecting production processes	Batch
Processing purchase orders	Batch
Building occupancy	Facility
Depreciation	Facility
General management	Facility
Maintaining facilities	Facility
Managing the environment	Facility
Assuring quality	Sustaining
Expediting	Sustaining
Maintaining tools and dies	Sustaining
Maintaining/improving production processes	Sustaining
Managing human resources	Sustaining
Managing waste disposal	Sustaining
Processing payroll	Sustaining
Processing production information	Sustaining
Providing product cost	Sustaining
Setting manufacturing methods	Sustaining
Supervising production	Sustaining
Sustaining accounting	Sustaining
Maintaining production equipment	Sustaining
Direct-labor allowances	Unit
Direct-labor fringes	Unit
Utilities (equipment)	Unit
Overtime (hourly)	Unit
Rework	Unit
Shift differential	Unit
Spoilage	Unit

Required:

Choose two activities or accounts from each of the four classifications, and explain why you agree or disagree with the ABC project team's classification.

[23]Robert Adams and Ray Carter, "United Technologies' Activity-Based Accounting Is a Catalyst for Success," *As Easy as ABC* 18, p. 4. United Technologies uses the term *"structural-*level activity," instead of *"facility-*level activity" as we have done in the chapter and in the table presented here.

■ Exercise 5–25
Volume-Based Cost Driver versus ABC
(LO 2, LO 3, LO 4)

Genesco Corporation manufactures sophisticated lenses and mirrors used in large optical telescopes. The company is now preparing its annual profit plan. As part of its analysis of the profitability of individual products, the controller estimates the amount of overhead that should be allocated to the individual product lines from the following information.

	Mirrors	Lenses
Units produced	25	25
Material moves per product line	5	15
Direct-labor hours per unit	200	200
Budgeted material-handling costs	$50,000	

Required:

1. Under a costing system that allocates overhead on the basis of direct-labor hours, the material-handling costs allocated to one mirror would be what amount?
2. Answer the same question as in requirement (1), but for lenses.
3. Under activity-based costing (ABC), the material-handling costs allocated to one mirror would be what amount?
4. Answer the same question as in requirement (3), but for lenses.

(CMA, adapted)

■ Exercise 5–26
Cost Drivers; Activity Cost Pools
(LO 3, LO 5)

Victoria Video Corporation manufactures VCRs in its Newark plant. The following costs are budgeted for January.

Raw materials and components	$295,000
Insurance, plant	60,000
Electricity, machinery	12,000
Electricity, light	6,000
Engineering design	61,000
Depreciation, plant	70,000
Depreciation, machinery	140,000
Custodial wages, plant	4,000
Equipment maintenance, wages	15,000
Equipment maintenance, parts	3,000
Setup wages	4,000
Inspection	3,000
Property taxes	12,000
Natural gas, heating	3,000

Required:

Divide these costs into activity cost pools, and identify a cost driver for assigning each pool of costs to products.

■ Exercise 5–27
Categorizing Activity Cost Pools
(LO 3)

Refer to the information given in the preceding exercise. For each of the activity cost pools identified, indicate whether it represents a unit-level, batch-level, product-sustaining level, or facility-level activity.

■ Exercise 5–28
Use of Multiple Cost Drivers by Hewlett-Packard Company
(LO 3, LO 4, LO 5)

Hewlett-Packard Company's Personal Office Computer Division uses two overhead application rates based on two different cost drivers. One rate is based on direct labor and assigns overhead costs associated with production. The second rate is based on material cost and assigns overhead costs associated with procurement. Overhead costs are initially categorized into three cost categories, called "buckets" in the company's terminology. Then the overhead costs associated with overall manufacturing support functions are allocated between the production cost bucket and the procurement cost bucket. This allocation is based on the number of employees and the estimated percentage of time spent on these two types of activities. The following diagram illustrates the system.[24]

---

[24]This description was provided by James M. Patell, "Cost Accounting, Process Control, and Product Design: A Case Study of the Hewlett-Packard Personal Office Computer Division," *The Accounting Review* 62, no. 4, pp. 808–39.

```
┌──────────────────────────────────────────────────┐
│            Support Manufacturing Overhead          │
│                                                    │
│  Includes costs that support the entire manufacturing process │
│  but cannot be associated directly with either production or  │
│  procurement (e.g., production engineering, quality assurance,│
│  and central electronic data processing).          │
└──────────────────────────────────────────────────┘
          ↙                              ↘
┌─────────────────────────┐   ┌─────────────────────────┐
│       Production         │   │       Procurement        │
│  Manufacturing Overhead  │   │  Manufacturing Overhead  │
│                          │   │                          │
│  Includes such costs as production │ │  Includes such costs as purchasing, │
│  supervision, indirect labor,      │ │  receiving, inspection of raw        │
│  depreciation, and operating costs │ │  materials, material handling,       │
│  associated with production,       │ │  production planning and control,    │
│  assembly, testing, and shipping.  │ │  and subcontracting.                 │
└─────────────────────────┘   └─────────────────────────┘

┌─────────────────────────┐   ┌─────────────────────────┐
│ Applied on the basis of  │   │ Applied on the basis of  │
│    *direct labor.*       │   │   *direct material.*     │
└─────────────────────────┘   └─────────────────────────┘
```

Required:

1. Explain why Hewlett-Packard Company uses two cost drivers to assign overhead costs instead of a single predetermined overhead rate.

2. What benefits does such an approach provide to management?

3. What costs would such a system entail?

Finger Lakes Winery is a small, family-run operation in upstate New York. The winery produces two varieties of wine: riesling and chardonnay. Among the activities engaged in by the winery are the following:

■ **Exercise 5–29**
Winery; Classification of Activities
(LO 3)

1. Trimming: At the end of a growing season, the vines are trimmed, which helps prepare them for the next harvest.

2. Tying: The vines are tied onto wires to help protect them from the cold. (This also occurs at the end of the season.)

3. Hilling: Dirt is piled up around the roots to help protect them from frost.

4. Conditioning: After the snow melts in the spring, dirt is leveled back from the roots.

5. Untying: The vines are untied from the wires to allow them freedom to grow during the spring and summer months.

6. Chemical spraying: The vines are sprayed in the spring to protect them from disease and insects.

7. Harvesting: All of the grapes of both varieties are picked by hand to minimize damage.

8. Stemming and crushing: Batches of grapes are hand-loaded into a machine, which gently removes the stems and mildly crushes them.

9. Pressing: After removal from the stemmer/crusher, the juice runs freely from the grapes.

10. Filtering: The grapes are crushed mechanically to render more juice from them.

11. Fermentation: The riesling grape juice is placed in stainless steel tanks for fermentation. The chardonnay grape juice undergoes a two-stage fermentation process in oak barrels.

12. Aging: The riesling wines are aged in the stainless steel tanks for approximately a year. The chardonnays are aged in the oak barrels for about two years.

13. Bottling: A machine bottles the wine and corks the bottles.

14. Labeling: Each bottle is manually labeled with the name of the vintner, vintage, and variety.

15. Packing: The bottles are manually packed in twelve-bottle cases.

16. Case labeling: The cases are hand-stamped with the same information that the bottles received.

17. Shipping: The wine is shipped to wine distributors and retailers, mainly in central New York. Generally, about 100 cases are shipped at a time.

18. Maintenance on buildings: This is done during the slow winter months.

19. Maintenance on equipment: This is done when needed, and on a routine basis for preventive maintenance.

Required:

Classify each of the activities listed as a unit, batch, product-sustaining, or facility-level activity.

■ Exercise 5–30
ABC; Selling Costs
(LO 3, LO 4)

Sequoia Company sells crafts kits and supplies to retail outlets and through its catalog. Some of the items are manufactured by Sequoia, while others are purchased for resale. For the products it manufactures, the company currently bases its selling prices on a product-costing system that accounts for direct material, direct labor, and the associated overhead costs. In addition to these product costs, Sequoia incurs substantial selling costs, and Roger Jackson, controller, has suggested that these selling costs should be included in the product pricing structure.

After studying the costs incurred over the past two years for one of its products, skeins of knitting yarn, Jackson has selected four categories of selling costs and chosen cost drivers for each of these costs. The selling costs actually incurred during the past year and the cost drivers are as follows:

Cost Category	Amount	Cost Driver
Sales commissions	$675,000	Boxes of yarn sold to retail stores
Catalogs	295,400	Catalogs distributed
Costs of catalog sales	105,000	Skeins sold through catalog
Credit and collection	60,000	Number of retail orders
Total selling costs	$1,135,400	

The knitting yarn is sold to retail outlets in boxes, each containing twelve skeins of yarn. The sale of partial boxes is not permitted. Commissions are paid on sales to retail outlets but not on catalog sales. The cost of catalog sales includes telephone costs and the wages of personnel who take the catalog orders. Jackson believes that the selling costs vary significantly with the size of the order. Order sizes are divided into three categories as follows:

Order Size	Catalog Sales	Retail Sales
Small	1–10 skeins	1–10 boxes
Medium	11–20 skeins	11–20 boxes
Large	Over 20 skeins	Over 20 boxes

An analysis of the previous year's records produced the following statistics.

	Order Size			
	Small	**Medium**	**Large**	**Total**
Retail sales in boxes (12 skeins per box)	2,000	45,000	178,000	225,000
Catalog sales in skeins	79,000	52,000	44,000	175,000
Number of retail orders	485	2,415	3,100	6,000
Catalogs distributed	254,300	211,300	125,200	590,800

Required:

1. Prepare a schedule showing Sequoia Company's total selling cost for each order size and the per skein selling cost within each order size.

2. Explain how the analysis of the selling costs for skeins of knitting yarn is likely to impact future pricing and product decisions at Sequoia Company.

(CMA, adapted)

Wheelco, Inc. manufactures automobile and truck wheels. The company produces four basic, high-volume wheels used by each of the large automobile and pickup truck manufacturers. Wheelco also has two specialty wheel lines. These are fancy, complicated wheels used in expensive sports cars.

Lately, Wheelco's profits have been declining. Foreign competitors have been undercutting Wheelco's prices in three of its bread-and-butter product lines, and Wheelco's sales volume and market share have declined. In contrast, Wheelco's specialty wheels have been selling steadily, although in relatively small numbers, in spite of three recent price increases. At a recent staff meeting, Wheelco's president made the following remarks: "Our profits are going down the tubes, folks. It costs us 29 dollars to manufacture our A22 wheel. That's our best seller, with a volume last year of 17,000 units. But our chief competitor is selling basically the same wheel for 27 bucks. I don't see how they can do it. I think it's just one more example of foreign dumping. I'm going to write my senator about it! Thank goodness for our specialty wheels. I think we've got to get our sales people to push those wheels more and more. Take the D52 model, for example. It's a complicated thing to make, and we don't sell many. But look at the profit margin. Those wheels cost us 49 dollars to make, and we're selling them for 105 bucks each."

■ **Exercise 5–31**
Distortion of Product Costs
(LO 4, LO 5)

Required:

What do you think is behind the problems faced by Wheelco? Comment on the president's remarks. Do you think his strategy is a good one? What do you recommend, and why?

Refer to the description given for Wheelco, Inc. in the preceding exercise. Suppose the firm's president has decided to implement an activity-based costing system.

■ **Exercise 5–32**
Key Features of Activity-Based Costing
(LO 3, LO 4, LO 5)

Required:

1. List and briefly describe the key features that Wheelco's new product-costing system should have.
2. What impact will the new system be likely to have on the company's situation?
3. What strategic.options would you expect to be suggested by the product-costing results from the new system?

Problems

Continental Manufacturing has just completed a major change in its quality control (QC) process. Previously, products had been reviewed by QC inspectors at the end of each major process, and the company's 10 QC inspectors were charged as direct labor to the operation or job. In an effort to improve efficiency and quality, a computerized video QC system was purchased for $250,000. The system consists of a minicomputer, 15 video cameras, other peripheral hardware, and software. The new system uses cameras stationed by QC engineers at key points in the production process. Each time an operation changes or there is a new operation, the cameras are moved, and a new master picture is loaded into the computer by a QC engineer. The camera takes pictures of the units in process, and the computer compares them to the picture of a "good" unit. Any differences are sent to a QC engineer who removes the bad units and discusses the flaws with the production supervisors. The new system has replaced the 10 QC inspectors with two QC engineers.

■ **Problem 5–33** ✓
Overhead Application; Activity-Based Costing
(LO 2, LO 3, LO 4, LO 5)

The operating costs of the new QC system, including the salaries of the QC engineers, have been included as factory overhead in calculating the company's plantwide manufacturing-overhead rate, which is based on direct-labor dollars. The company's president is confused. His vice president of production has told him how efficient the new system is. Yet there is a large increase in the overhead rate. The computation of the rate before and after automation is as follows:

	Before	After
Budgeted manufacturing overhead	$1,900,000	$2,100,000
Budgeted direct-labor cost	1,000,000	700,000
Budgeted overhead rate	190%	300%

"Three hundred percent," lamented the president. "How can we compete with such a high overhead rate?"

Required:

1. *a.* Define "manufacturing overhead," and cite three examples of typical costs that would be included in manufacturing overhead.

    b. Explain why companies develop predetermined overhead rates.

2. Explain why the increase in the overhead rate should not have a negative financial impact on Continental Manufacturing.

3. Explain how Continental Manufacturing could change its overhead application system to eliminate confusion over product costs.

4. Discuss how an activity-based costing system might benefit Continental Manufacturing.

(CMA, adapted)

■ **Problem 5–34**
Automation; Robotics;
Overhead Application;
Activity-Based Costing
(LO 2, LO 3, LO 4, LO 5)

Eileen Butler has recently been hired as controller of Traxton, Inc., a sheet metal manufacturer. Traxton has been in the sheet metal business for many years and is currently investigating ways to modernize its manufacturing process. At the first staff meeting Butler attended, Bob Kelley, chief engineer, presented a proposal for automating the Drilling Department. Kelley recommended that Traxton purchase two robots that would have the capability of replacing the eight direct-labor employees in the department. The cost savings outlined in Kelley's proposal include the elimination of direct-labor cost in the Drilling Department plus a reduction of manufacturing overhead cost in the department to zero, because Traxton charges manufacturing overhead on the basis of direct-labor dollars using a plantwide rate. The president of Traxton was puzzled by Kelley's explanation: "This just doesn't make any sense. How can a department's overhead rate drop to zero by adding expensive, high-tech manufacturing equipment? If anything, it seems like the rate ought to go up."

Kelley responded by saying "I'm an engineer, not an accountant. But if we're charging overhead on the basis of direct labor, and we eliminate the labor, then we eliminate the overhead."

Butler agreed with the president. She explained that as firms become more automated, they should rethink their product-costing systems. The president then asked Butler to look into the matter and prepare a report for the next staff meeting. Butler gathered the following data on the manufacturing-overhead rates experienced by Traxton over the years. Butler also wanted to have some departmental data to present at the meeting and, by using Traxton's accounting records, she was able to estimate the following annual averages for each manufacturing department over the past several decades.

Historical Plantwide Data

Decade	Average Annual Manufacturing-Overhead Cost	Average Annual Direct-Labor Cost	Average Manufacturing-Overhead Application Rate
1950s	$1,000,000	$1,000,000	100%
1960s	3,000,000	1,200,000	250
1970s	7,000,000	2,000,000	350
1980s	12,000,000	3,000,000	400
1990s	20,000,000	4,000,000	500

Annual Averages during Recent Years

	Cutting Department	Grinding Department	Drilling Department
Manufacturing overhead	$11,000,000	$7,000,000	$2,000,000
Direct labor	2,000,000	1,750,000	250,000

Required:

1. Disregarding the proposed use of robots in the Drilling Department, describe the shortcomings of the system for applying overhead that is currently used by Traxton, Inc.

2. Explain the misconceptions underlying Kelley's statement that the manufacturing-overhead cost in the Drilling Department would be reduced to zero if the automation proposal was implemented.

3. Recommend ways to improve Traxton Inc.'s method for applying overhead by describing how it should revise its product-costing system for each of the following departments:

a. In the Cutting and Grinding Departments.

b. To accommodate automation in the Drilling Department.

(CMA, adapted)

The controller for Anaheim Photographic Supply Company has established the following activity cost pools and cost drivers.

■ **Problem 5–35**
Activity Cost Pools; Cost Drivers; Pool Rates
(LO 2, LO 3, LO 4)

Activity Cost Pool	Budgeted Overhead Cost	Cost Driver	Budgeted Level for Cost Driver	Pool Rate
Machine setups	$250,000	Number of setups	125	$2,000 per setup
Material handling	75,000	Weight of raw material	37,500 lb.	$2 per pound
Hazardous waste control	25,000	Weight of hazardous chemicals used	5,000 lb.	$5 per pound
Quality control	75,000	Number of inspections	1,000	$75 per inspection
Other overhead costs	200,000	Machine hours	20,000	$10 per machine hour
Total	$625,000			

An order for 1,000 boxes of film development chemicals has the following production requirements.

Cost driver

Machine setups	5 setups
Raw material	10,000 pounds
Hazardous materials	2,000 pounds
Inspections	10 inspections
Machine hours	500 machine hours

Required:

1. Compute the total overhead that should be assigned to the development-chemical order.

2. What is the overhead cost per box of chemicals?

3. Suppose Anaheim Photographic Supply Company were to use a single predetermined overhead rate based on machine hours. Compute the rate per hour.

4. Under the approach in requirement (3), how much overhead would be assigned to the development-chemical order?

    a. In total.

    b. Per box of chemicals.

5. Explain why these two product-costing systems result in such widely differing costs. Which system do you recommend? Why?

Refer to the original data given in the preceding problem for Anaheim Photographic Supply Company.

■ **Problem 5–36**
Overhead Cost Drivers
(LO 2, LO 3, LO 4)

Required:

Calculate the unit cost of a production order for 100 specially coated plates used in film development. In addition to direct material costing $120 per plate and direct labor costing $40 per plate, the order requires:

Machine setups	3
Raw material	900 pounds
Hazardous materials	300 pounds
Inspections	3
Machine hours	50

Montreal Electronics Company manufactures two large-screen television models, the Nova which has been produced since 19x0 and sells for $900, and the Royal, a new model introduced in early 19x8, which sells for $1,140. Based on the following income statement for 19x9, a decision has been made to concentrate Montreal's marketing resources on the Royal model and to begin to phase out the Nova model.

■ **Problem 5–37**
Activity-Based Costing;
Activity-Based Management
(LO 2, LO 3, LO 4, LO 5, LO 7)

MONTREAL ELECTRONICS COMPANY
Income Statement
For the Year Ended December 31, 19x9

	Royal	Nova	Total
Sales	$4,560,000	$19,800,000	$24,360,000
Cost of goods sold	3,192,000	12,540,000	15,732,000
Gross margin	$1,368,000	$ 7,260,000	$ 8,628,000
Selling and administrative expense	978,000	5,830,000	6,808,000
Net income	$ 390,000	$ 1,430,000	$ 1,820,000
Units produced and sold	4,000	22,000	
Net income per unit sold	$97.50	$65.00	

The standard unit costs for the Royal and Nova models are as follows:

	Royal	Nova
Direct material	$584	$208
Direct labor:		
Royal (3.5 hr. × $12)	42	
Nova (1.5 hr. × $12)		18
Machine usage:		
Royal (4 hr. × $18)	72	
Nova (8 hr. × $18)		144
Manufacturing overhead*	100	200
Standard cost	$798	$570

*Manufacturing overhead was applied on the basis of machine hours at a predetermined rate of $25 per hour.

Montreal Electronics Company's controller is advocating the use of activity-based costing and activity-based management and has gathered the following information about the company's manufacturing-overhead costs for 19x9.

Activity Center (cost driver)	Traceable Costs	Number of Events		
		Royal	Nova	Total
Soldering (number of solder joints)	$ 942,000	385,000	1,185,000	1,570,000
Shipments (number of shipments)	860,000	3,800	16,200	20,000
Quality control (number of inspections)	1,240,000	21,300	56,200	77,500
Purchase orders (number of orders)	950,400	109,980	80,100	190,080
Machine power (machine hours)	57,600	16,000	176,000	192,000
Machine setups (number of setups)	750,000	14,000	16,000	30,000
Total traceable costs	$4,800,000			

Required:

1. Using activity-based costing, determine if Montreal Electronics should continue to emphasize the Royal model and phase out the Nova model.

2. Briefly, explain the concept of activity-based management.

(CMA, adapted)

■ **Problem 5–38**
Activity-Based Costing
(LO 3, LO 4, LO 5)

Bristol Corporation manufactures several different types of printed circuit boards; however, two of the boards account for the majority of the company's sales. The first of these boards, a television circuit board, has been a standard in the industry for several years. The market for this type of board is competitive and price-sensitive. Bristol plans to sell 65,000 of the TV boards in 19x9 at a price of $150 per unit. The second high-volume product, a personal computer circuit board, is a recent addition to Bristol's product line. Because the PC board incorporates the latest technology it can be sold at a premium price. The 19x9 plans include the sale of 40,000 PC boards at $300 per unit.

Bristol's management group is meeting to discuss how to spend the sales and promotion dollars for 19x9. The sales manager believes that the market share for the TV board could be expanded by concentrating Bristol's promotional efforts in this area. In response to this suggestion, the production manager said, "Why don't you go after a bigger market for the PC board? The cost sheets that I get show that the contribution from the PC board is more than double the contribution from the TV board. I know we get a premium price for the PC board. Selling it should help overall profitability."

Bristol's cost-accounting system shows that the following costs apply to the PC and TV boards.

	PC Board	TV Board
Direct material	$140	$80
Direct labor	4 hr.	1.5 hr.
Machine time	1.5 hr.	.5 hr.

Variable manufacturing overhead is applied on the basis of direct-labor hours. For 19x9, variable overhead is budgeted at $1,120,000, and direct-labor hours are estimated at 280,000. The hourly rates for machine time and direct labor are $10 and $14, respectively. Bristol applies a material-handling charge at 10 percent of material cost. This material-handling charge is not included in variable manufacturing overhead. Total 19x9 expenditures for direct material are budgeted at $10,600,000.

Andrew Fulton, Bristol's controller, believes that before the management group proceeds with the discussion about allocating sales and promotional dollars to individual products, it might be worthwhile to look at these products on the basis of the activities involved in their production. Welch has prepared the following schedule to help the management group understand this concept.

"Using this information," Fulton explained, "we can calculate an activity-based cost for each TV board and each PC board and then compare it to the standard cost we have been using. The only cost that remains the same for both cost methods is the cost of direct material. The cost drivers will replace the direct labor, machine time, and overhead costs in the old standard cost figures."

Budgeted Cost		Cost Driver	Budgeted Annual Activity for Cost Driver
Procurement	$ 400,000	Number of parts	4,000,000 parts
Production scheduling	220,000	Number of boards	110,000 boards
Packaging and shipping	440,000	Number of boards	110,000 boards
Total	$1,060,000		
Machine setup	$446,000	Number of setups	278,750 setups
Hazardous waste disposal	48,000	Pounds of waste	16,000 pounds
Quality control	560,000	Number of inspections	160,000 inspections
General supplies	66,000	Number of boards	110,000 boards
Total	$1,120,000		
Machine insertion	$1,200,000	Number of parts	3,000,000 parts
Manual insertion	4,000,000	Number of parts	1,000,000 parts
Wave-soldering	132,000	Number of boards	110,000 boards
Total	$5,332,000		

Required per Unit	PC Board	TV Board
Parts:	55	25
Machine insertions	35	24
Manual insertions	20	1
Machine setups	3	2
Hazardous waste disposal	.35 lb.	.02 lb.
Inspections	2	1

Required:

1. Identify at least four general advantages that are associated with activity-based costing.
2. On the basis of Bristol's unit cost data given in the problem, calculate the total contribution margin expected in 19x9 for the PC board and the TV board.

3. On the basis of an activity-based costing system, calculate the total contribution margin expected in 19x9 for the PC board and the TV board.

4. Explain how a comparison of the results of the two costing methods may impact the decisions made by Bristol Corporation's management group.

(CMA, adapted)

■ **Problem 5–39**
Activity-Based Costing
(LO 2, LO 3, LO 4, LO 5)

Best Blend Coffee Company (BBCC) is a distributor and processor of different blends of coffee. The company buys coffee beans from around the world and roasts, blends, and packages them for resale. BBCC currently has 15 different coffees that it offers to gourmet shops in one-pound bags. The major cost is raw materials; however, there is a substantial amount of manufacturing overhead in the predominantly automated roasting and packing process. The company uses relatively little direct labor.

Some of the coffees are very popular and sell in large volumes, while a few of the newer blends have very low volumes. BBCC prices its coffee at full product cost, including allocated overhead, plus a markup of 30 percent. If prices for certain coffees are significantly higher than market, adjustments are made. The company competes primarily on the quality of its products, but customers are price-conscious as well.

Data for the 19x9 budget include manufacturing overhead of $3,000,000, which has been allocated on the basis of each product's direct-labor cost. The budgeted direct-labor cost for 19x9 totals $600,000. Based on the sales budget and raw-material budget, purchases and use of raw materials (mostly coffee beans) will total $6,000,000.

The expected prime costs for one-pound bags of two of the company's products are as follows:

	Hawaiian	Kenyan
Direct material	$3.20	$4.20
Direct labor	.30	.30

BBCC's controller believes the traditional product-costing system may be providing misleading cost information. She has developed an analysis of the 19x9 budgeted manufacturing-overhead costs shown in the following chart.

Activity	Cost Driver	Budgeted Activity	Budgeted Cost
Purchasing	Purchase orders	1,158	$ 579,000
Material handling	Setups	1,800	720,000
Quality control	Batches	720	144,000
Roasting	Roasting hours	96,100	961,000
Blending	Blending hours	33,600	336,000
Packaging	Packaging hours	26,000	260,000
Total manufacturing-overhead cost			$3,000,000

Data regarding the 19x9 production of Hawaiian and Kenyan coffee are shown in the following table. There will be no raw-material inventory for either of these coffees at the beginning of the year.

	Hawaiian	Kenyan
Budgeted sales	2,000 lb.	100,000 lb.
Batch size	500 lb.	10,000 lb.
Setups	3 per batch	3 per batch
Purchase order size	500 lb.	25,000 lb.
Roasting time	1 hr. per 100 lb.	1 hr. per 100 lb.
Blending time	.5 hr. per 100 lb.	.5 hr. per 100 lb.
Packaging time	.1 hr. per 100 lb.	.1 hr. per 100 lb.

Required:

1. Using BBCC's current product-costing system:
   a. Determine the company's predetermined overhead rate using direct-labor cost as the single cost driver.
   b. Determine the full product costs and selling prices of one pound of Hawaiian coffee and one pound of Kenyan coffee.

2. Develop a new product cost, using an activity-based costing approach, for one pound of Hawaiian coffee and one pound of Kenyan coffee.

3. What are the implications of the activity-based costing system with respect to:

   a. The use of direct labor as a basis for applying overhead to products?

   b. The use of the existing product-costing system as the basis for pricing?

(CMA, adapted)

Knickknack, Inc. manufactures two products: odds and ends. The firm uses a single, plantwide overhead rate based on direct-labor hours. Production and product-costing data are as follows:

■ **Problem 5–40**
Activity-Based Costing;
Activity Cost Pools; Pool
Rates; Calculation of Product
Costs; Cost Distortion
(LO 2, LO 3, LO 4, LO 5)

	Odds	**Ends**
Production quantity	1,000 units	5,000 units
Direct material	$ 40	$ 60
Direct labor (not including setup time)	30 (2 hr. at $15)	45 (3 hr. at $15)
Manufacturing overhead*	96 (2 hr. at $48)	144 (3 hr. at $48)
Total cost per unit	$166	$249

*Calculation of predetermined overhead rate:

Manufacturing overhead budget:

Machine-related costs	$450,000
Setup and inspection	180,000
Engineering	90,000
Plant-related costs	96,000
Total	$816,000

Predetermined overhead rate:

$$\frac{\text{Budgeted manufacturing overhead}}{\text{Budgeted direct-labor hours}} = \frac{\$816,000}{(1,000)(2) + (5,000)(3)} = \$48 \text{ per direct-labor hour}$$

Knickknack, Inc. prices its products at 120 percent of cost, which yields target prices of $199.20 for odds and $298.80 for ends. Recently, however, Knickknack has been challenged in the market for ends by a European competitor, Bricabrac Corporation. A new entrant in this market, Bricabrac has been selling ends for $220 each. Knickknack's president is puzzled by Bricabrac's ability to sell ends at such a low cost. She has asked you (the controller) to look into the matter. You have decided that Knickknack's traditional, volume-based product-costing system may be causing cost distortion between the firm's two products. Ends are a high-volume, relatively simple product. Odds, on the other hand, are quite complex and exhibit a much lower volume. As a result, you have begun work on an activity-based costing system.

Required:

1. Let each of the overhead categories in the budget represent an activity cost pool. Categorize each in terms of the type of activity (e.g., unit-level activity).

2. The following cost drivers have been identified for the four activity cost pools.

Activity Cost Pool	Cost Driver	Budgeted Level of Cost Driver
Machine-related costs	Machine hours	9,000 hr.
Setup and inspection	Number of production runs	40 runs
Engineering	Engineering change orders	100 change orders
Plant-related costs	Square footage of space	1,920 sq. ft.

You have gathered the following additional information:

■ Each odd requires 4 machine hours, whereas each end requires 1 machine hour.

■ Odds are manufactured in production runs of 50 units each. Ends are manufactured in 250 unit batches.

■ Three quarters of the engineering activity, as measured in terms of change orders, is related to odds.

■ The plant has 1,920 square feet of space, 80 percent of which is used in the production of odds.

For each activity cost pool, compute a pool rate.

3. Determine the unit cost, for each activity cost pool, for odds and ends.

4. Compute the new product cost per unit for odds and ends, using the ABC system.

5. Using the same pricing policy as in the past, compute prices for odds and ends. Use the product costs determined by the ABC system.

6. Show that the ABC system fully assigns the total budgeted manufacturing overhead costs of $816,000.

7. Show how Knickknack's traditional, volume-based costing system distorted its product costs. (Use Exhibit 5–12 for guidance.)

■ **Problem 5–41**
Activity-Based Costing;
Forecasting; Ethics
(LO 2, LO 3, LO 4)

Puget Sound Industries (PSI) was founded 45 years ago by Mark Preston as a small machine shop producing machined parts for the aircraft industry, which is prominent in the Seattle/Tacoma area of Washington. By the end of its first decade PSI's annual sales had reached $15 million, almost exclusively under government contracts. The next 30 years brought slow but steady growth as cost-reimbursement government contracts continued to be the main source of revenue. Realizing that PSI could not depend on government contracts for long-term growth and stability, Drew Preston, son of the founder and now president of the company, began planning for diversified commercial growth. By the end of 19x5, PSI had succeeded in reducing the ratio of government contract sales to 50 percent of total sales.

Traditionally, the costs of the Material-Handling Department have been allocated to direct material as a percentage of direct-material dollar value. This was adequate when the majority of the manufacturing was homogeneous and related to government contracts. Recently, however, government auditors have rejected some proposals, stating that "the amount of Material-Handling Department costs allocated to these proposals is disproportionate to the total effort involved."

Kara Lindley, the newly hired cost-accounting manager, was asked by the manager of the Government Contracts Unit, Paul Anderson, to find a more equitable method of allocating Material-Handling Department costs to the user departments. Her review has revealed the following information.

■ The majority of the direct-material purchases for government contracts are high-dollar, low-volume purchases, while commercial materials represent low-dollar, high-volume purchases.

■ Administrative departments such as marketing, finance and administration, human resources, and maintenance also use the services of the Material-Handling Department on a limited basis but have never been charged in the past for material-handling costs.

■ One purchasing agent with a direct phone line is assigned exclusively to purchasing high-dollar, low-volume material for government contracts at an annual salary of $36,000. Employee benefits are estimated to be 20 percent of the annual salary. The annual dedicated phone line costs are $2,800.

The components of the Material-Handling Department's budget for 19x7, as proposed by Lindley's predecessor, are as follows:

Payroll	$ 180,000
Employee benefits	36,000
Telephone	38,000
Other utilities	22,000
Materials and supplies	6,000
Depreciation	6,000
Direct-material budget:	
Government contracts	2,006,000
Commercial products	874,000

Lindley has estimated the number of purchase orders to be processed in 19x7 to be as follows:

Government contracts*	80,000
Commercial products	156,000
Marketing	1,800
Finance and administration	2,700
Human resources	500
Maintenance	1,000
Total	242,000

*Exclusive of high-dollar, low-volume materials.

Lindley recommended to Anderson that material-handling costs be allocated on a per purchase order basis. Anderson realizes and accepts that the company has been allocating to government contracts more material-handling costs than can be justified. However, the implication of Lindley's analysis could be a decrease in his unit's earnings and, consequently, a cut in his annual bonus. Anderson told Lindley to "adjust" her numbers and modify her recommendation so that the results will be more favorable to the Government Contracts Unit.

Being new in her position, Lindley is not sure how to proceed. She feels ambivalent about Anderson's instructions and suspects his motivation. To complicate matters for Lindley, Preston has asked her to prepare a three-year forecast of the Government Contracts Unit's results, and she believes that the newly recommended allocation method would provide the most accurate data. However, this would put her in direct opposition to Anderson's directives.

Lindley has assembled the following data to project the material-handling costs.

- Total direct-material costs increase 2.5 percent per year.
- Material-handling costs remain the same percentage of direct-material costs.
- Direct government costs (payroll, employee benefits, and direct phone line) remain constant.
- The number of purchase orders increases 5 percent per year.
- The ratio of government purchase orders to total purchase orders remains at 33 percent.
- In addition, she has assumed that government material in the future will be 70 percent of total material.

Required:

1. Calculate the material-handling rate that would have been used by Kara Lindley's predecessor at Puget Sound Industries.
2. *a.* Calculate the revised material-handling costs at Puget Sound Industries to be allocated on a per purchase order basis.
   b. Discuss why purchase orders might be a more reliable cost driver than the dollar amount of direct material.
3. Calculate the difference due to the change to the new method of allocating material-handling costs to government contracts by Puget Sound Industries.
4. Prepare a forecast of the cumulative dollar impact over a three-year period from 19x7 through 19x9 of Kara Lindley's recommended change for allocating Material-Handling Department costs to the Government Contracts Unit. Round all calculations to the nearest whole number.
5. Referring to the standards of ethical conduct for management accountants:
   a. Discuss why Kara Lindley has an ethical conflict.
   b. Identify several steps that Lindley could take to resolve the ethical conflict.

(CMA, adapted)

Alyssa Manufacturing produces two items in its Trumbull Plant: Tuff Stuff and Ruff Stuff. Since inception, Alyssa has used only one manufacturing-overhead cost pool to accumulate costs. Overhead has been allocated to products based on direct-labor hours. Until recently, Alyssa was the sole producer of Ruff Stuff and was able to dictate the selling price. However, last year Marvella Products began marketing a comparable product at a price below the cost assigned by Alyssa. Market share has declined rapidly, and Alyssa must now decide whether to meet the competitive price or to discontinue the product line. Recognizing that discontinuing the product line would place an additional burden on its remaining product, Tuff Stuff, Alyssa is using activity-based costing to determine if it would show a different cost structure for the two products.

The two major indirect costs for manufacturing the products are power usage and setup costs. Most of the power usage is used in fabricating, while most of the setup costs are required in assembly. The setup costs are predominantly related to the Tuff Stuff product line.

A decision was made to separate the Manufacturing Department costs into two activity cost pools as follows:

Fabricating: machine hours will be the cost driver.

Assembly: number of setups will be the cost driver

Alyssa's controller has gathered the following information.

■ **Problem 5–42**
Activity-Based Costing;
Production and Pricing
Decisions
(LO 2, LO 3, LO 4, LO 5)

Manufacturing Department
Annual Budget before Separation of Overhead

	Total	Product Line	
		Tuff Stuff	**Ruff Stuff**
Number of units		20,000	20,000
Direct labor hours*		2 hours per unit	3 hours per unit
Total direct-labor cost	$800,000		
Direct material		$5.00 per unit	$3.00 per unit
Budgeted overhead:			
Indirect labor	24,000		
Fringe benefits	5,000		
Indirect material	31,000		
Power..................................	180,000		
Setup	75,000		
Quality assurance	10,000		
Other utilities	10,000		
Depreciation	15,000		

*Direct-labor hourly rate is the same in both departments.

Manufacturing Department
Cost Structure after Separation of Overhead into Activity Cost Pools

	Fabrication	Assembly
Direct labor cost	75%	25%
Direct material (no change)	100%	0%
Indirect labor	75%	25%
Fringe benefits	80%	20%
Indirect material	$20,000	$11,000
Power	$160,000	$20,000
Setup	$5,000	$70,000
Quality assurance	80%	20%
Other utilities	50%	50%
Depreciation	80%	20%

Cost driver:	Product Line	
	Tuff Stuff	**Ruff Stuff**
Machine-hours per unit	4.4	6.0
Setups	1,000	272

Required:

1. Assigning overhead based on direct-labor hours, calculate the following:
   a. Total budgeted cost of the Manufacturing Department.
   b. Unit cost of Tuff Stuff and Ruff Stuff.

2. After separation of overhead into activity cost pools, compute the total budgeted cost of each department: fabricating and assembly.

3. Using activity-based costing, calculate the unit costs for each product. (In computing the pool rates for the fabricating and assembly activity cost pools, round to the nearest cent. Then, in computing unit product costs, round to the nearest cent.)

4. Discuss how a decision by Alyssa Manufacturing regarding the production and pricing of Ruff Stuff will be affected by the results of your calculations in the preceding requirements.

(CMA, adapted)

Madison Electric Motor Corporation manufactures electric motors for commercial use. The company produces three models, designated as standard, deluxe, and heavy-duty. The company uses a job-order cost-accounting system with manufacturing overhead applied on the basis of direct-labor hours. The system has been in place with little change for 25 years. Product costs and annual sales data are as follows:

■ **Problem 5–43**
Traditional versus Activity-Based Costing Systems
(LO 2, LO 3, LO 4, LO 5)

	Standard Model	Deluxe Model	Heavy-Duty Model
Annual sales (units)	20,000	1,000	10,000
Product costs:			
Raw material	$ 10	$ 25	$ 42
Direct labor	10 (.5 hr. at $20)	20 (1 hr. at $20)	20 (1 hr. at $20)
Manufacturing overhead*	85	170	170
Total product cost	$105	$215	$232

*Calculation of predetermined overhead rate:

Manufacturing-overhead budget:

Depreciation, machinery	$1,480,000
Maintenance, machinery	120,000
Depreciation, taxes, and insurance for factory	300,000
Engineering	350,000
Purchasing, receiving and shipping	250,000
Inspection and repair of defects	375,000
Material handling	400,000
Miscellaneous manufacturing overhead costs	295,000
Total	$3,570,000

Direct-labor budget:

Standard model:	10,000 hours
Deluxe model:	1,000 hours
Heavy-duty model:	10,000 hours
Total	21,000 hours

$$\text{Predetermined overhead rate:} \quad \frac{\text{Budgeted overhead}}{\text{Budgeted direct-labor hours}} = \frac{\$3,570,000}{21,000 \text{ hours}} = \$170 \text{ per hour}$$

For the past 10 years Madison's pricing formula has been to set each product's target price at 110 percent of its full product cost. Recently, however, the standard-model motor has come under increasing price pressure from offshore competitors. The result was that the price on the standard model has been lowered to $110.

The company president recently asked the controller, "Erin, why can't we compete with these other companies? They're selling motors just like our standard model for 106 dollars. That's only a buck more than our production cost. Are we really that inefficient? What gives?"

The controller responded by saying, "I think this is due to an outmoded product-costing system. As you may remember, I raised a red flag about our system when I came on board last year. But the decision was to keep our current system in place. In my judgment, our product-costing system is distorting our product costs. Let me run a few numbers to demonstrate what I mean."

Getting the president's go-ahead, the controller compiled the basic data needed to implement an activity-based costing system. These data are displayed in the following table. The percentages are the proportion of each cost driver consumed by each product line.

		Product Lines		
Activity Cost Pool	**Cost Driver**	**Standard Model**	**Deluxe Model**	**Heavy-Duty Model**
I: Depreciation, machinery Maintenance, machinery	Machine time	40%	13%	47%
II: Engineering Inspection and repair of defects	Engineering hours	47%	6%	47%
III: Purchasing, receiving, and shipping Material handling	Number of material orders	47%	8%	45%
IV: Depreciation, taxes, and insurance for factory Miscellaneous manufacturing overhead	Factory space usage	42%	15%	43%

Required:

1. Compute the target prices for the three models, based on the traditional, volume-based product-costing system.

2. Compute new product costs for the three products, based on the new data collected by the controller. Round to the nearest cent. (You may find it helpful to refer to Exhibits 5–8 and 5–10 for guidance.)

3. Calculate a new target price for the three products, based on the activity-based costing system. Compare the new target price with the current actual selling price for the standard model electric motor.

4. Write a memo to the company president explaining what has been happening as a result of the firm's traditional volume-based product-costing system.

5. What strategic options does Madison Electric Motor Corporation have? What do you recommend, and why?

■ **Problem 5–44**
Cost Distortion; Continuation of Preceding Case
(LO 4)

Refer to the product costs developed in requirement (2) of the preceding problem. Prepare a table showing how Madison Electric Motor Corporation's traditional, volume-based product-costing system distorts the product costs of the standard, deluxe, and heavy-duty models. (You may wish to refer to Exhibit 5–12 for guidance. Because of rounding in the calculation of the product costs, there will be a small rounding error in this cost distortion analysis as well.)

■ **Problem 5–45**
Ethical Issues Related to Product-Cost Distortion; Activity-Based Costing; Continuation of Problem 5–43
(LO 3, LO 5)

Madison Electric Motor Corporation's controller, Erin Jackson, developed new product costs for the standard, deluxe, and heavy-duty models using activity-based costing. It was apparent that the firm's traditional product-costing system had been undercosting the deluxe model electric motor by a significant amount. This was due largely to the low volume of the deluxe model motor. Before she could report back to the president, Jackson received a phone call from her friend, Alan Tyler. He was the production manager for the deluxe model electric motor. Tyler was upset, and he let Jackson know it. "Erin, I've gotten wind of your new product cost analysis. There's no way the deluxe model costs anywhere near what your numbers say. For years and years this line has been highly profitable, and its reported product cost was low. Now you're telling us it costs more than twice what we thought. I just don't buy it."

Jackson briefly explained to her friend about the principles of activity-based costing and why it resulted in more accurate product costs. "Alan, the deluxe model is really losing money. It simply has too low a volume to be manufactured efficiently."

Tyler was even more upset now. "Erin, if you report these new product costs to the president, he's going to discontinue the deluxe model. My job's on the line, Erin! How about massaging those numbers a little bit. Who's going to know?"

"I'll know, Alan. And you'll know," responded Jackson. "Look, I'll go over my analysis again, just to make sure I haven't made an error."

Required:

Discuss the ethical issues involved in this scenario.

1. Is the controller, Erin Jackson, acting ethically?

2. Is the production manager, Alan Tyler, acting ethically?

3. What are Jackson's ethical obligations? To the president? To her friend?

Cases

Gigabyte, Inc. manufactures three products for the computer industry:

■ **Case 5–46**
Traditional versus Activity-Based Costing Systems
(LO 2, LO 3, LO 4, LO 5)

Gismos (product G): annual sales, 8,000 units

Thingamajigs (product T): annual sales, 15,000 units

Whatchamacallits (product W): annual sales, 4,000 units

The company uses a traditional, volume-based product-costing system with manufacturing overhead applied on the basis of direct-labor dollars. The product costs have been computed as follows:

	Product G	Product T	Product W
Raw material	$ 35.00	$ 52.50	$17.50
Direct labor	16.00 (.8 hr. at $20)	12.00 (.6 hr. at $20)	8.00 (.4 hr. at $20)
Manufacturing overhead*	140.00	105.00	70.00
Total product cost	$191.00	$169.50	$95.50

*Calculation of predetermined overhead rate:

Manufacturing overhead budget:

Machine setup	$ 5,250
Machinery	1,225,000
Inspection	525,000
Material handling	875,000
Engineering	344,750
Total	$2,975,000

Direct-labor budget (based on budgeted annual sales):

Product G:	8000 × $16.00	=	$128,000
Product T:	15,000 × $12.00	=	180,000
Product W:	4,000 × $8.00	=	32,000
Total			$340,000

$$\text{Predetermined overhead rate} = \frac{\text{Budgeted overhead}}{\text{Budgeted direct labor}} = 875\%$$

Gigabyte's pricing method has been to set a target price equal to 150 percent of full product cost. However, only the thingamajigs have been selling at their target price. The target and actual current prices for all three products are the following:

	Product G	Product T	Product W
Product cost	$191.00	$169.50	$ 95.50
Target price	286.50	254.25	143.25
Actual current selling price	213.00	254.25	200.00

Gigabyte has been forced to lower the price of gismos in order to get orders. In contrast, Gigabyte has raised the price of whatchamacallits several times, but there has been no apparent loss of sales. Gigabyte, Inc. has been under increasing pressure to reduce the price even further on gismos. In contrast, Gigabyte's competitors do not seem to be interested in the market for whatchamacallits. Gigabyte apparently has this market to itself.

Required:

1. Is product G the company's least profitable product?
2. Is product W a profitable product for Gigabyte, Inc.?
3. Comment on the reactions of Gigabyte's competitors to the firm's pricing strategy. What dangers does Gigabyte, Inc. face?
4. Gigabyte's controller, Nan O'Second, recently attended a conference at which activity-based costing systems were discussed. She became convinced that such a system would help Gigabyte's management to understand its product costs better. She got top management's approval to design an activity-based costing system, and an ABC project team was formed. In stage one of the ABC project, each of the overhead items listed in the overhead budget was placed into its own activity cost pool. Then a cost driver was identified for each activity cost pool. Finally, the ABC project

team compiled data showing the percentage of each cost driver that was consumed by each of Gigabyte's product lines. These data are summarized as follows:

Activity Cost Pool	Cost Driver	Product G	Product T	Product W
Machine setup	Number of setups	20%	30%	50%
Machinery	Machine hours	25%	50%	25%
Inspection	Number of inspections	15%	45%	40%
Material handling	Raw-material costs	25%	69%	6%
Engineering	Number of change orders	35%	10%	55%

Show how the controller determined the percentages given above for raw-material costs. (Round to the nearest whole percent.)

5. Develop product costs for the three products on the basis of an activity-based costing system. (Round to the nearest cent. For guidance, you may wish to refer to Exhibits 5–8 and 5–10.)

6. Calculate a target price for each product, using Gigabyte's pricing formula. Compare the new target prices with the current actual selling prices and previously reported product costs.

■ **Case 5–47**
Strategic Cost Analysis;
Continuation of Preceding
Case
(LO 4, LO 5, LO 6)

Refer to the new target prices for Gigabyte's three products, based on the new activity-based costing system.

Required:

Write a memo to the company president commenting on the situation Gigabyte, Inc. has been facing regarding the market for its products and the actions of its competitors. Discuss the strategic options available to management. What do you recommend, and why?

■ **Case 5–48**
Cost Distortion; Continuation
of Case 5–46
(LO 4)

Refer to the product costs developed in requirement 5 of Case 5–46. Prepare a table showing how Gigabyte's traditional, volume-based product-costing system distorts the product costs of gismos, thinga-majigs, and whatchamacallits. (You may wish to refer to Exhibit 5–12 for guidance. Because of rounding in the calculation of the product costs, there will be a small rounding error in this cost distortion analysis as well.)

■ **Case 5–49**
Activity-Based Costing;
Budgeted Operating Margin
(LO 2, LO 3, LO 5)

Plymouth Company produces two subassemblies, KS–26 and LF–16, used in manufacturing trucks. Plymouth is currently using an absorption costing system that applies overhead based on direct-labor hours. The budget for the current year ending December 31, 19x9 is as follows:

PLYMOUTH COMPANY
Budgeted Statement of Operating Margin for 19x9

	KS–26	LF–16	Total
Sales in units	5,000	5,000	10,000
Sales revenue	$1,700,000	$2,200,000	$3,900,000
Cost of goods manufactured and sold:			
Beginning finished-goods inventory	$ 240,000	$ 300,000	$ 540,000
Add: Direct material	1,000,000	1,750,000	2,750,000
Direct labor	185,185	92,593	277,778
Applied manufacturing overhead*	544,025	272,013	816,038
Cost of goods available for sale	$1,969,210	$2,414,606	$4,383,816
Less: Ending finished-goods inventory	240,000	300,000	540,000
Cost of goods sold	$1,729,210	$2,114,606	$3,843,816
Gross margin	$ (29,210)	$ 85,394	$ 56,184

*Applied on the basis of direct-labor hours:

Machining	$424,528
Assembly	216,981
Material handling	56,604
Inspection	117,925
Total	$816,038

Mark Ward, Plymouth's president, has been reading about a new type of costing method called activity-based costing. Ward is convinced that activity-based costing will cast a new light on future profits. As a result, Brian Walters, Plymouth's cost accountant, has accumulated cost pool information for this year shown on the following chart. This information is based on a product mix of 5,000 units of KS–26 and 5,000 units of LF–16.

Cost Pool Information for 19x9			
Cost Pool	Activity	KS–26	LF–16
Direct labor	Direct-labor hours	10,000	5,000
Machining	Machine hours	15,000	30,000
Assembly	Assembly hours	6,000	5,500
Material handling	Number of parts	5	10
Inspection	Inspection hours	5,000	7,500

In addition, the following information is projected for the next calendar year, 20x0.

	KS–26	LF–16
Beginning inventory, finished goods (in units)	800	600
Ending inventory, finished goods (in units)	700	700
Sales (in units)	5,100	4,900

On January 1, 20x0, Plymouth is planning to increase the prices of KS–26 to $355 and LF–16 to $455. Material costs are not expected to increase in 20x0, but direct labor will increase by 8 percent, and all manufacturing overhead costs will increase by 6 percent. Due to the nature of the manufacturing process, Plymouth does not have any beginning or ending work-in-process inventories.

Plymouth uses a just-in-time inventory system and has materials delivered to the production facility directly from the vendors. The raw-material inventory both at the beginning and the end of the month is immaterial and can be ignored for the purposes of a budgeted income statement. Plymouth uses the first-in, first-out (FIFO) inventory method.

Required:

1. Explain how activity-based costing differs from traditional product-costing methods.
2. Using activity-based costing, calculate the total cost for the following activity cost pools: machining, assembly, material handling, and inspection. (Round to the nearest dollar.) Then, calculate the pool rate per unit of the appropriate cost driver for each of the four activities.
3. Prepare a table showing for each product line the estimated 20x0 cost for each of the following cost elements: direct material, direct labor, machining, assembly, material handling, and inspection. (Round to the nearest dollar.)
4. Prepare a budgeted statement showing the operating margin for Plymouth Company for 20x0, using activity-based costing. The statement should show each product and a total for the company. Be sure to include detailed calculations for the cost of goods manufactured and sold. (Round each amount in the statement to the nearest dollar.)

(CMA, adapted)

Current Issues in Managerial Accounting

"I'm Not Gonna Pay a Lot for This Aptiva," *Business Week*, October 13, 1997.

Overview
IBM incorrectly assessed the nature of the PC market and is now rethinking its strategy for its overpriced Aptiva PC. Losses from IBM's PC division in 1997 could reach $400 million.

Suggested Discussion Questions
Form a consulting group. Assume IBM has asked your group to help reengineer Aptiva's production process. List 10 activities that are involved in the production of a PC. Next to each activity provide possible cost drivers. How could the cost of an Aptiva be reduced by 50 percent? Is this necessary?

"Using ABC to Determine the Cost of Servicing Customers," *Management Accounting*, December 1997.

Overview
This article describes how ABC is being used by a seven-person firm, Mahany Welding Supply. Mahany distributes welding supplies and compressed gas.

■ **Issue 5–50**
Activity-Based Costing:
Some Key Issues

■ **Issue 5–51**
Activity-Based Costing:
Some Key Issues;
Cost Drivers

Suggested Discussion Questions

Listed below are 15 activities that Mahany identified as causing costs. List potential cost drivers next to each activity.

Activity	Driver(s)	Activity	Driver(s)
1. Sales		**9.** AP/GL	
2. Purchasing		**10.** Advertising	
3. Collections		**11.** Telephone	
4. Auditing		**12.** Legal and Accounting	
5. Administration		**13.** Miscellaneous	
6. Warehousing		**14.** Insurance	
7. Order Pulling		**15.** Rent and Utilities	
8. Billing			

■ **Issue 5–52**
Activity-Based Costing:
Some Key Issues;
Cost Drivers

"Applying ABC to Healthcare," *Management Accounting*, **February 1997.**

Overview

This article explains three different methods of allocating indirect costs in the healthcare setting. The methods applied to two types of dialysis treatment are cost-to-charge, manufacturing-based ABC, and healthcare ABC.

Suggested Discussion Questions

List types of costs that can be found in a healthcare facility. For each cost category, discuss different types of cost drivers that could be used to allocate these costs. Also discuss the ethical/moral decisions a healthcare provider faces when using costs to make decisions.

■ **Issue 5–53**
Activity-Based Costing:
Some Key Issues;
Cost Drivers

"Look Who's Pushing Productivity," *Business Week*, **April 7, 1997.**

Overview

Instead of hiring a large consulting firm, Aluminum Co. of America asked the International Machinists union to help reengineer its manufacturing process. The labor-management team has already improved internal relations.

Suggested Discussion Questions

Discuss ways in which labor and management can work to improve a firm's production process. List some advantages that can be derived from union-led changes. Also, list some disadvantages.

■ **Issue 5–54**
Cost Management
Systems; Activity-Based
Management

"Blue Blood: IBM's Finance Chief, Ax in Hand, Scours Empire for Costs to Cut," *The Wall Street Journal,* **January 26, 1994, Laurie Hays.**

"York Leaves IBM for a Possible Shot at Chrysler," *The Wall Street Journal,* **September 6, 1995, Gabriella Stern.**

"IBM's Method of Accounting for Cutbacks Bucks Trend of Taking Repeated Charges," *The Wall Street Journal,* **March 6, 1996, Bart Ziegler.**

"IBM Revamps Global Units to Cut Costs," *The Wall Street Journal,* **December 13, 1996, Bart Ziegler.**

Overview

These articles describe IBM's recent cost-cutting programs.

Suggested Discussion Questions

After you have read these articles, provide an example of how an IBM manager might approach a cost-cutting scenario. Start with the initial analysis of activities and follow the cost-reduction program to the final presentation of the financial statements.

■ **Issue 5–55**
Activity-Based Costing
System; Cost
Management Systems

"ABC in a Virtual Corporation," *Management Accounting*, **October 1996.**

Overview

A virtual corporation minimizes investment in human resources, fixed assets, and working capital. The virtual corporation consists of a core unit that is supported by a network of outsourced activities. This article describes how ABC can be applied in a virtual corporation.

Suggested Discussion Questions

Form groups that will be the core management team for a virtual donut shop. Formulate a strategy and list what services will be performed in-house and which ones will be outsourced. Develop an ABC system that can be used to determine costs and evaluate performance.

"Can ABC Bring Mixed Results?" *Management Accounting*, **March 1997.**

Overview

This article describes Hewlett Packard's experiences with activity-based costing. The article explains things that went wrong with ABC and suggests methods for successful implementation.

Suggested Discussion Questions

Listed below are specific problems that Hewlett Packard experienced when it implemented its ABC system. In teams, describe ways in which these problems can be overcome.

Problem

Too many drivers

No proper administration

No follow-through

Too much emphasis on consensus

"Building an ABC Data Warehouse," *Management Accounting,* **March 1996, Bill Fahey.**

Overview

This article describes an ABC data warehouse that can be used to support ABM.

Suggested Discussion Questions

Form a team and diagram an ABC information system. Include in your diagram activities, software tools and systems, and labor.

■ **Issue 5–56**
Activity-Based Costing:
Some Key Issues

■ **Issue 5–57**
Activity-Based Costing
System; Cost
Management Systems

6

Chapter Six

Activity-Based Management and the New Manufacturing Environment

After completing this chapter, you should be able to:

1   Describe the key features of a production facility employing advanced manufacturing technology.

2   List and explain eight important features of just-in-time inventory and production management systems.

3   Explain the concept of activity-based management.

4   Explain the concept of two-dimensional activity-based costing.

5   List and explain the steps in using ABM to eliminate non-value-added costs.

6   Define and give an example of target costing.

7   Explain the concept of kaizen costing, and prepare a kaizen costing chart.

8   Briefly explain the concepts of total quality control, continuous improvement, benchmarking, re-engineering, and the theory of constraints.

9   List and briefly explain five keys to successfully implementing ABC, ABM, and other cost management systems.

AEROTECH TO BUILD NEW PLANT IN BAKERSFIELD

Bakersfield, CA—There's a new kid in the park. The industrial park, that is. The mayor announced this week that Aerotech Corporation, the Phoenix-based aerospace company, would build a new plant in Bakersfield's five-year-old industrial park. A simultaneous announcement by Aerotech's president, Kristin Scott, cited Bakersfield's location as a prime factor in the decision. "Bakersfield is much closer to both our suppliers and our customers than is Phoenix. We're looking forward to our new partnership with the people of the Bakersfield area. But I want to emphasize, however, that our Phoenix employees are loyal and talented. The vast majority of them will have the opportunity to come with the company to Bakersfield when we eventually close down our Phoenix operation."

Asked if the Bakersfield plant would be modeled after the Phoenix plant, Scott said,

"The Bakersfield plant will be completely different than the Phoenix facility. The Phoenix plant represents a very traditional plant layout, which emphasizes individual manufacturing functions and departments. In contrast, the Bakersfield plant will employ what is called a flexible manufacturing system or FMS. The FMS approach is highly automated, both in terms of production machinery and material-handling equipment. Much of the production process will be computer controlled."

Scott went on to explain that the Bakersfield plant will employ a JIT production and inventory management system. JIT, which stands for "just in time," is becoming more and more widely used globally as a highly efficient system for manufacturing high-quality products while stocking only minimal inventories of materials, parts, and finished products.

According to Scott, "JIT goes hand in hand with several other desirable traits of a production process. A multi-skilled workforce, flexible facilities, an atmosphere of teamwork, and high-quality output are among the hallmarks of a JIT system."

Scott also talked enthusiastically about the new cost management system that would be installed in the Bakersfield plant. "We've learned a lot in our Phoenix operation these past two years. We learned how to really focus on the activities in which we engage to produce our products. We learned how to ask which activities add value and which ones don't. How can our processes be improved by eliminating or combining activities? The bottom-line is getting the most out of every dollar we spend on resources to manufacture the very best product we can."

To achieve and maintain a competitive advantage in today's global marketplace, many companies are investing heavily in new technology. In addition, many organizations are implementing new cost management systems to better meet the needs of management. These new systems, coupled with efforts at continuous improvement, are helping some companies achieve success as world-class competitors. In this chapter, we continue our discussion of Aerotech Corporation to address these important issues.

Aerotech's Bakersfield Plant: Advanced Manufacturing Technology

After a careful study, Aerotech's board of directors decided to build a new production facility. The site chosen for the new plant was Bakersfield, California, which is much nearer to Aerotech's material suppliers and customers. Initially, the plants in both Phoenix and Bakersfield would manufacture Aerotech's three lines of circuit boards. Eventually, however, all of Aerotech's production would be moved to Bakersfield.

> **LO 1**   Describe the key features of a production facility employing advanced manufacturing technology.

The Bakersfield plant was designed to employ state-of-the-art manufacturing technology. When the new plant was designed, Aerotech's management insisted on a plant layout and production processes that would reduce or eliminate the non-value-added costs incurred in the Phoenix operation. The two key features of the Bakersfield operation are a *just-in-time (JIT)* inventory and production management system and a *flexible manufacturing system (FMS)*. These key features of the Bakersfield plant are discussed next.

Just-in-Time Inventory and Production Management

A **just-in-time (JIT) inventory and production management system** is a comprehensive inventory and manufacturing control system in which no materials are purchased and no products are manufactured until they are needed. Raw materials and parts are purchased only as they are needed in some phase of the production process. Component parts and subassemblies are not manufactured in any stage of production until they are required in the next stage. Finished goods are manufactured only as they are needed to fill customer orders. A primary goal of a JIT production system is to *reduce or eliminate inventories* at every stage of production, from raw materials to finished goods. The JIT philosophy, made famous by Toyota, has been credited with the

A **just-in-time (JIT) inventory and production management system** is a comprehensive inventory and manufacturing control system in which no materials are purchased and no products are manufactured until they are needed.

This forklift operator is unloading a delivery truck right on the factory floor as part of a JIT inventory and production management system.

success of many of the world's leading manufacturers. Tremendous cost savings have been realized by many companies that have adopted the JIT approach.[1]

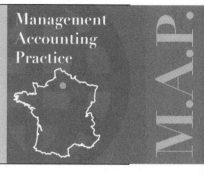

JIT Cost Savings: Ingersoll-Rand and Honeywell

In a large-scale installation of JIT systems by Ingersoll-Rand, the company saved $3,500,000. The installation of a JIT production system in only one of 10 production lines at Honeywell's Process Control Division netted cost savings of $26,000.

Management Accounting Practice

How does a JIT system achieve its vast reductions in inventory and associated cost savings? A production-systems expert lists the following key features of the JIT approach.[2]

LO 2 List and explain eight important features of just-in-time inventory and production management systems.

1. *A smooth, uniform production rate.* An important goal of a JIT system is to establish a smooth production flow, beginning with the arrival of materials from suppliers and ending with the delivery of goods to customers. Widely fluctuating production rates result in delays and excess work-in-process inventories. These non-value-added costs are to be eliminated.

2. *A pull method of coordinating steps in the production process.* Most manufacturing processes occur in multiple stages. Under the **pull method**, goods are produced in each manufacturing stage only as they are needed at the next stage. This approach reduces or eliminates work-in-process inventory between production steps. The result is a reduction in waiting time and its associated non-value-added cost.

   The pull method of production begins at the last stage of the manufacturing process.[3] When additional materials and parts are needed for final assembly, a message is sent to the immediately preceding work center to send the amount of materials and parts that will be needed over the next few hours. Often this message is in the form of a **withdrawal Kanban**, a card indicating the number and type of parts requested from the preceding work center. The receipt of the withdrawal Kanban in the preceding work center triggers the release of a **production Kanban**, which is another card specifying the number of parts to be manufactured in that work center. Thus, the parts are "pulled" from a particular work center by a need for parts in the subsequent work center. This *pull approach* to production is repeated all the way up the manufacturing sequence toward the beginning. Nothing is manufactured at any stage until its need is signaled from the subsequent process via a Kanban. As a result, no parts are produced until they are needed, no inventories build up, and the manufacturing process exhibits a smooth, uniform flow of production.[4]

> Under the **pull method,** goods are produced in each stage of manufacturing only as they are needed in the next stage.
>
> A **withdrawal Kanban** is a card sent to the preceding work center indicating the number and type of parts requested from that work center by the next work center.
>
> A **production Kanban** is a card specifying the number of parts to be manufactured in a particular work center.

---

[1]J. Swartley-Loush, "Just-in-Time: Is It Right for You?," *Production Engineering* 88, no. 6, pp. 61–64.

[2]James B. Dilworth, *Production and Operations Management*, 3d ed. (New York: Random House, 1986), pp. 354–61.

[3]You may find it helpful to review Exhibit 1–5 on page 17, which depicts the pull method of the JIT system.

[4]Toyota's ground-breaking JIT system originally was referred to as *Kanban*, a Japanese word meaning "signboard." See Takeo Tanaka, "Kaizen Budgeting: Toyota's Cost Control System under TQC," *Journal of Cost Management* 8, no. 3, p. 57.

3. *Purchase of materials and manufacture of subassemblies and products in small lot sizes.* This is an outgrowth of the pull method of production planning. Materials are purchased and goods are produced only as required, rather than for the sake of building up stocks. The result is a reduction in storage and waiting time, and the related non-value-added costs.

4. *Quick and inexpensive setups of production machinery.* In order to produce in small lot sizes, a manufacturer must be able to set up production runs quickly. Advanced manufacturing technology aids in this process, as more and more machines are computer-controlled.

5. *High quality levels for raw material and finished products.* If raw materials and parts are to arrive "just in time" for production, they must be "just right" for their intended purpose. Otherwise, the production line will be shut down and significant non-value-added costs of waiting will result. Moreover, if very small stocks of finished goods are to be maintained, then finished products must be of uniform high quality. For this reason, a **total quality control (TQC)** program often accompanies a just-in-time production environment.

6. *Effective preventive maintenance of equipment.* If goods are to be manufactured just in time to meet customer orders, a manufacturer cannot afford significant production delays. By strictly adhering to routine maintenance schedules, the firm can avoid costly down time from machine breakdowns.

7. *An atmosphere of teamwork to improve the production system.* A company can maintain a competitive edge in today's worldwide market only if it is constantly seeking ways to improve its product or service, achieve more efficient operations, and eliminate non-value-added costs. My favorite football coach often says that a team must improve from one week to the next. Otherwise the team will get worse, because it rarely will stay at the same level. So it goes in business as well. If a company's employees are not constantly seeking ways to improve the firm's performance, before long its competitors will pass it by. Many organizations encourage employees to make suggestions for improvement. Rewards are given when cost-saving suggestions are implemented.

8. *Multiskilled workers and flexible facilities.* To facilitate just-in-time production, manufacturing equipment must be flexible enough to produce a variety of components and products. Otherwise, if a particular production line can produce only one item, bottlenecks may result. A bottleneck can hold up production in subsequent manufacturing stages and result in the non-value-added costs associated with waiting time. As high-tech production equipment becomes more versatile, production employees must be capable of handling a variety of machines and operations. By grouping machines into *cells* that produce a variety of items requiring similar production technology, multiskilled workers are able to operate several machines. This approach is called *group technology*.

JIT Purchasing   In addition to a JIT production approach, Aerotech implemented *JIT purchasing* in its Bakersfield plant. Under this approach, materials and parts are purchased from outside vendors only as they are needed. This avoids the costly and wasteful buildup of raw-material inventories. The following are five key features of **JIT purchasing**.

1. *Only a few suppliers.* This results in less time spent on vendor relations. Only highly reliable vendors, who can invariably deliver high-quality goods on time, are used.

2. *Long-term contracts negotiated with suppliers.* This eliminates costly paperwork and negotiations with each individual transaction. The need for delivery can be communicated via a telephone call or computer message. The long-term contracts state the price, quality, and delivery terms of the goods.

Total quality control (TQC) is a product-quality program in which the objective is complete elimination of product defects.

JIT purchasing is an approach to purchasing management in which materials and parts are purchased only as they are needed.

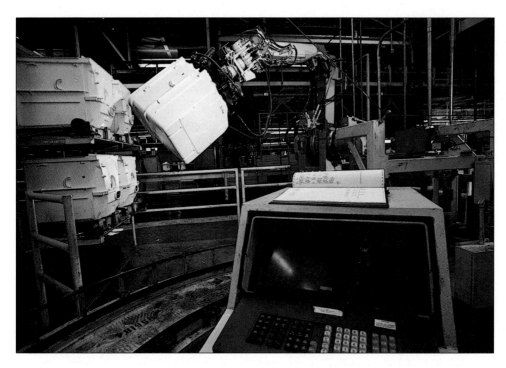

This General Electric facility is producing dishwashers using a state-of-the-art manufacturing process. Notice the computer-controlled process, robotic equipment, and absence of large amounts of inventory.

3. *Materials and parts delivered in small lot sizes immediately before they are needed.* This is the essence of the just-in-time philosophy. Costly inventories are avoided by having supplies arrive "just-in-time" to be placed into production.

4. *Only minimal inspection of delivered materials and parts.* The long-term contracts clearly state the quality of material required. Vendors are selected on the basis of their reliability in meeting these stringent standards and in delivering the correct amount of materials on time.

5. *Grouped payments to each vendor.* Instead of paying for each delivery, payments are made for batches of deliveries according to the terms of the contract. This reduces costly paperwork for both the vendor and the purchaser.

JIT purchasing is widely used in a variety of organizations. In manufacturing firms, it goes hand in hand with JIT production. In retail and service industry firms, JIT purchasing reduces costly warehouse inventories and streamlines the purchasing function.

Flexible Manufacturing System

To achieve the objectives of a just-in-time production environment listed in the preceding section, many manufacturers are moving toward more highly automated manufacturing systems. As you may know if you have recently shopped for a VCR, compact disk system, or personal computer, electronic and computer technology is changing at a breathtaking pace. Even as manufacturing facilities are built, engineering breakthroughs make even more efficient operations possible. As a result, a range of automation can be observed even among the most recent production facilities. Before describing Aerotech's Bakersfield plant, let's go over some of the terminology used to describe today's manufacturing environment.

> **LO 1** Describe the key features of a production facility employing advanced manufacturing technology.

Computer-numerically-controlled (CNC) machines. Stand-alone machines controlled by a computer via a numerical, machine-readable code. Each CNC machine is individually controlled by a single computer dedicated to that machine. An example of a CNC machine is the axial-lead sequencing machine

> **Computer-numerically-controlled (CNC) machines** are stand-alone machines controlled by a computer via a numerical, machine-readable code.

A **computer-aided manufacturing (CAM) system** is any production process in which computers are used to help control production.

A **computer-aided design (CAD) system** is computer software used by engineers in the design of a product.

An **automated material-handling system (AMHS)** is computer-controlled equipment that automatically moves materials, parts, and products from one production stage to another.

A **flexible manufacturing system (FMS)** is a series of manufacturing machines, controlled and integrated by a computer, which is designed to perform a series of manufacturing operations automatically.

An **FMS cell** is a group of machines and personnel within a flexible manufacturing system.

Cellular manufacturing organizes a production facility into FMS cells.

In a **computer-integrated manufacturing (CIM) system** virtually all parts of the production process are accomplished by computer-controlled machines and automated material-handling equipment.

used by Aerotech in its Phoenix plant. CNC machines represent one of the initial steps toward a computer-controlled manufacturing system.

Computer-aided manufacturing (CAM) system. Any production process in which computers are used to help control production equipment. Aerotech's Phoenix plant has a CAM system, since it utilizes some CNC machines.

Computer-aided design (CAD) system. Computer software used by engineers in the design of a product. CAD enables the engineer to visualize the contemplated design of a product on a video display terminal. Frequently, CAD/CAM systems are encountered that combine the features of both CAD and CAM.

Automated material-handling system (AMHS). Computer-controlled equipment that automatically moves materials, parts, and products from one production stage to another.

Flexible manufacturing system (FMS). An integrated system of computer-controlled machines and automated material-handling equipment, which is capable of producing a variety of technologically similar products.

FMS cell. A particular grouping of machines and personnel within a flexible manufacturing system.

Cellular manufacturing. The organization of a production facility into FMS cells.

Computer-integrated manufacturing (CIM) system. The most advanced level of automated manufacturing. Virtually all parts of the production process are accomplished by computer-controlled machines and automated material-handling equipment. Moreover, the entire production system is an integrated network centrally controlled via a computer.

Plant Layout at Aerotech's Bakersfield Facility

The layout of Aerotech's Bakersfield plant is shown in Exhibit 6–1. This facility is designed around the following advanced manufacturing features.

1. *Flexible manufacturing system.* The Bakersfield plant has three FMS cells. Each cell includes seven computer-controlled machines that are capable of performing almost all of the manufacturing operations on *any* of Aerotech's three circuit boards. With a minor setup operation, each of these FMS cells can be readied for a new production run. A close-up of one FMS cell is shown in Exhibit 6–2. Notice that the hand-insertion operations used in the Phoenix plant have been replaced by robots, which are programmed to insert odd-shaped or delicate electrical components.

2. *Automated material-handling system.* The Bakersfield plant uses an AMHS for two purposes: to move circuit boards between operations in each FMS cell, and to move completed circuit boards from each cell to the burn-in testing work center. The AMHS includes a conveyor that carries the boards while the burn-in testing procedure is completed on the way to the packaging work center. Bakersfield's AMHS has resulted in substantial reductions in the non-value-added costs of move time.

3. *Computer-aided design.* The Bakersfield plant utilizes a CAD system in its design department. Notice its location next to the computer department.

LO 1   Describe the key features of a production facility employing advanced manufacturing technology.

Observations on the Bakersfield Layout   Several features of the new plant's layout are noteworthy. Notice that the raw-material and parts storage area is located so that materials are easily accessible to each FMS cell. The space devoted to storage of raw materials and finished goods is much smaller in the Bakersfield plant than in the Phoenix facility. This reflects the JIT

Exhibit 6–1

Aerotech Corporation's
Bakersfield Plant

philosophy of little or no inventory and results in elimination of non-value-added storage costs. Notice that the holding areas next to the production departments in the Phoenix plant have been eliminated in Bakersfield. Now the circuit boards flow continuously through each FMS cell. This eliminates the non-value-added cost of waiting time. Orders that required days to complete in Phoenix, due to delays between operations, are completed in a few hours in Bakersfield.

The amount of space devoted to the computer department is greater in Bakersfield than in Phoenix. This reflects the significantly greater role of computer-aided manufacturing (CAM) in the Bakersfield operation. A large amount of space in Bakersfield also is devoted to design, engineering, and quality control. The JIT philosophy

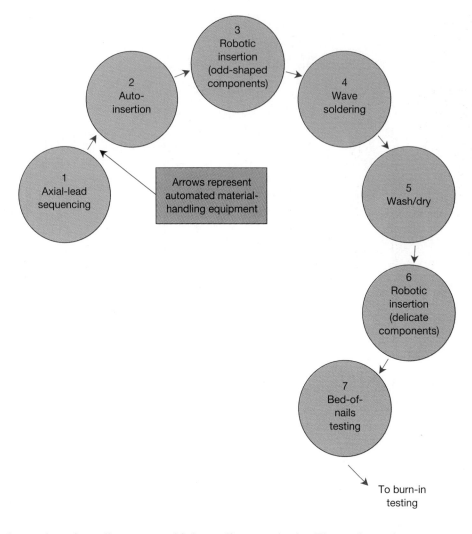

Off-line quality control refers to activities during the product design and engineering phases that will improve the manufacturability of the product, reduce production costs, and ensure high quality.

demands strict adherence to high quality standards. These three departments are located near each other to implement **off-line quality control**. This refers to activities during the product design and engineering phases that will improve the manufacturability of the product, reduce production costs, and ensure high quality.

Cost Management System in Bakersfield

The cost management system developed for the Bakersfield operation is an integral part of Aerotech's effort to regain a competitive edge in the market for its products. Several features of the CMS are discussed in this section.

Elimination of Non-Value-Added Costs We have discussed the features of the Bakersfield production system that enabled Aerotech to reduce or eliminate non-value-added costs. Chief among these is the elimination of storage and waiting time and the significant reduction in move time. The AMHS has virtually eliminated material-handling costs. Added to these cost reductions is a significant decrease in indirect-labor costs. Many manufacturing support jobs that were considered indirect labor (and thus overhead) in the Phoenix plant are performed by direct-labor personnel in the Bakersfield facility. In the new plant, direct-labor employees now operate each FMS cell. These workers are trained in the setup, operation, and routine maintenance of several machines. When a machine broke down in Phoenix, an entire production department could be shut down while maintenance department personnel were called in to do repairs. In the meantime, the direct-labor personnel in the department were

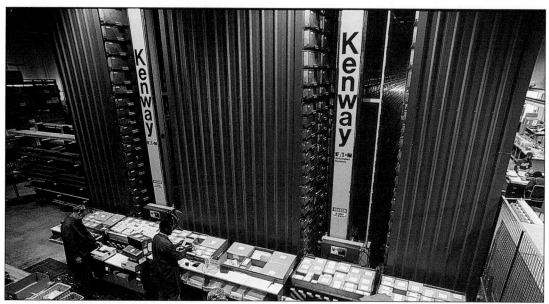

This automated material handling system has fully automated storage and retrieval capability. These technicians are responsible for programming the computer that controls the system.

idled. In contrast, the FMS cell operators in Bakersfield are trained to perform routine maintenance and repairs and spot other, more serious machinery problems before they get out of hand. The result of this multiskilled labor force is the reduction of manufacturing support costs in Bakersfield.

A crucial step in bringing about the significant reduction in non-value-added costs in the *Bakersfield plant* was the institution of *activity-based costing in the Phoenix plant*. It was this system of identifying costs with the key activities in the production process that first alerted Aerotech's management to the possibilities for cost reduction. Management's attitude is one of never being complacent about the existence of non-value-added costs. There is a continuing effort to identify and eliminate these barriers to maintaining the firm's competitive edge.

Cost Drivers and Activity-Based Costing   The ABC system developed for the Phoenix operation has been instituted in the Bakersfield plant. Cost drivers have been identified for each significant product cost.

Direct versus Indirect Costs   In the Bakersfield plant almost all production costs are traced directly to an FMS cell. Very few costs are considered to be general factory overhead as in more traditional cost-accounting systems. Direct-material costs are traced directly to products. Direct-labor costs have been reduced substantially, due to the advanced level of automation in the Bakersfield plant. In fact, direct labor has been reduced to the point where it is combined with other conversion costs traceable to each FMS cell. Depreciation on the computers and machinery in an FMS cell is traceable directly to the cell. The salaries of computer programmers and maintenance personnel also are traceable to each FMS cell. Conversion costs that have been traced directly to an FMS cell then are assigned to the products that are produced in the cell.

Shift in the Cost Structure   Aerotech's Bakersfield plant is **capital-intensive**, which means that the production process is accomplished largely by machinery rather than by manual labor. In contrast, the Phoenix plant is only *semiautomated*, with all the material handling and several significant production steps performed manually. Thus, the Phoenix plant is more **labor-intensive** than the Bakersfield facility.

A capital-intensive plant, such as the one in Bakersfield, generally has a *cost structure* with a much larger proportion of fixed costs than would be observed in a

In a **capital intensive** production process, manufacturing is accomplished largely by machinery.

In a **labor-intensive** production process, manufacturing is accomplished largely by manual labor.

Exhibit 6–3

Basic Production and Cost
Data: Aerotech Corporation's
Bakersfield Plant

	Mode I Boards	Mode II Boards	Mode III Boards
Production:			
Units	10,000	20,000	4,000
Runs	10	20	10
Direct material (raw boards and components)	$50.00	$90.00	$20.00
Machine time per board	1 hour per board	1.25 hours per board	2 hours per board
Conversion cost budget:			
Labor	$ 598,400 (including setup time)		
Machinery and facilities	3,397,000		
Engineering	600,000		
Receiving and inspection	50,000		
Material handling	100,000		
Quality assurance	350,000		
Packaging and shipping	250,000		
Total conversion costs	$5,345,400		

labor-intensive plant. Direct-labor costs, often a variable cost, are much lower. Depreciation on plant and equipment generally is much higher.

Reduced Product Costs in Bakersfield   The result of all Aerotech's efforts has been a significant reduction in the cost of producing its three circuit-board lines. Exhibit 6–3 displays the budgeted costs for the production of 10,000 Mode I boards, 20,000 Mode II boards, and 4,000 Mode III boards in Bakersfield. Labor is included along with other conversion costs in the budget. The costs of labor, receiving and inspection, and material handling are substantially lower in Bakersfield than in Phoenix.

Exhibit 6–4 shows the calculation of product costs for the product lines using Bakersfield's activity-based costing system. Direct-material costs are traced directly to each product line. Labor costs are assigned to products on a unit basis ($17.60 = budgeted labor cost of $598,400 ÷ 34,000 budgeted units of production).

Since the Bakersfield plant is heavily automated, facilities costs are assigned on the basis of machine hours instead of labor hours, as in Phoenix. Machinery costs are also assigned on the basis of machine hours. Since both the machinery and the facilities activity cost pools are assigned using the same cost driver (i.e., machine hours), these costs are combined into a single cost pool in the Bakersfield ABC system.

The other conversion costs are also assigned to products using the activity-based costing system. Since the Bakersfield plant opened only recently, the percentages used in the supporting calculations of Exhibit 6–4 are the same as those derived in the Phoenix plant. Eventually, as Aerotech gains more experience with the Bakersfield operation, these percentages are likely to change.

Exhibit 6–5 compares the product costs achieved in Bakersfield with those incurred in Phoenix. Each circuit board is produced at a significantly lower cost in the new plant.

Aerotech's Strategic Options   Examination of Exhibit 6-5 reveals that Mode I and Mode II boards are currently selling at a price well above the target price necessary to achieve a 25 percent markup. Aerotech has two strategic options for these two products. The prices can be kept at their current levels, since they are not out of line with competitors' prices. This strategy would allow Aerotech to earn large profits on these two products. Alternatively, Aerotech could lower the prices on these products with the aim of gaining a larger market share. Either way, Aerotech's new manufacturing facility, coupled with a first-rate cost management system, have given the firm a potential advantage over its competitors.

	Mode I Boards	Mode II Boards	Mode III Boards
Direct material (raw boards and components)	$ 50.00	$ 90.00	$ 20.00
Conversion costs:			
Labor (including setup time)	17.60	17.60	17.60
Engineering[a]	15.00	13.50	45.00
Receiving and inspection[b]	.30	.60	8.75
Material handling[c]	.70	1.50	15.75
Quality assurance[d]	7.00	7.00	35.00
Packaging and shipping[e]	1.00	3.75	41.25
Machinery and facilities[f]	79.00	98.75	158.00
Total product cost per unit	$170.60	$232.70	$341.35

The percentages in this column are the same as those used in the Phoenix plant (from the preceding chapter).

↓

[a]Engineering:
Mode I: ($600,000 × 25%) ÷ 10,000 units = $15.00
Mode II: ($600,000 × 45%) ÷ 20,000 units = $13.50
Mode III: ($600,000 × 30%) ÷ 4,000 units = $45.00

[b]Receiving and inspection:
Mode I: ($50,000 × 6%) ÷ 10,000 units = $ .30
Mode II: ($50,000 × 24%) ÷ 20,000 units = $ .60
Mode III: ($50,000 × 70%) ÷ 4,000 units = $ 8.75

[c]Material handling:
Mode I: ($100,000 × 7%) ÷ 10,000 units = $ .70
Mode II: ($100,000 × 30%) ÷ 20,000 units = $ 1.50
Mode III: ($100,000 × 63%) ÷ 4,000 units = $15.75

[d]Quality assurance:
Mode I: ($350,000 × 20%) ÷ 10,000 units = $ 7.00
Mode II: ($350,000 × 40%) ÷ 20,000 units = $ 7.00
Mode III: ($350,000 × 40%) ÷ 4,000 units = $35.00

[e]Packaging and shipping:
Mode I: ($250,000 × 4%) ÷ 10,000 units = $ 1.00
Mode II: ($250,000 × 30%) ÷ 20,000 units = $ 3.75
Mode III: ($250,000 × 66%) ÷ 4,000 units = $41.25

[f]Machinery and facilities:
  Calculation of machinery and facilities cost per hour:

From Exhibit 6–3: $\dfrac{\text{Total budgeted machinery and facilities costs}}{\text{Total budgeted machine hours}} = \dfrac{\$3,397,000}{43,000 \text{ hr.}} = \$79 \text{ per hour}$

  Machinery and facilities costs for each product:
    Mode I: 1 machine hr. × $79 = $ 79.00 per unit
    Mode II: 1.25 machine hr. × $79 = $ 98.75 per unit
    Mode III: 2 machine hr. × $79 = $158.00 per unit

Exhibit 6–4

Product Costs from Activity-Based Costing System: Aerotech Corporation's Bakersfield Plant

What about the Mode III circuit boards? Even with the lower costs in Bakersfield, an accurate product-costing system shows that these circuit boards cost $341.35 to manufacture. The current actual selling price is only $250. Aerotech could raise the price of these highly complex boards or redesign the boards to reduce their cost. Under a strategy called *target costing*, the market price for a product is taken as a given. Then an attempt is made to design the product so that it can be sold at the market price. We will explore target costing in more depth later in this chapter. Yet another option may

	Mode I Boards	Mode II Boards	Mode III Boards
Phoenix product costs (activity-based costing system)	$183.44	$261.81	$390.85
Bakersfield product costs (activity-based costing system)	$170.60	$232.70	$341.35
Percentage by which Phoenix product costs have been reduced	7.0%	11.1%	12.7%
$\left(\dfrac{\text{Phoenix cost} - \text{Bakersfield cost}}{\text{Phoenix cost}}\right)$			
New target price for products manufactured in Bakersfield (125% of full product cost)	$213.25	$290.88	$426.69
Actual current selling price	$261.25	$328.00	$250.00

Exhibit 6–5

Comparison of Product Costs in Phoenix and Bakersfield Plants

be to discontinue the product line, although this may not be feasible if Aerotech's Mode I and Mode II customers demand a supplier with a full product line. In any case, Aerotech's cost management system has directed management's attention to its strategic options.

Two-Dimensional ABC and Activity-Based Management

LO 3 Explain the concept of activity-based management.

LO 4 Explain the concept of two-dimensional activity-based costing.

Activity-based management (ABM) uses an activity-based costing system to improve the operations of an organization.

A **two-dimensional activity-based costing model** is a combination of the cost assignment view and the process analysis and evaluation role of ABC.

Activity analysis is the detailed identification and description of the activities conducted in an enterprise.

Using activity-based costing information to improve operations and eliminate non-value-added costs is called **activity-based management (ABM)**. We have already caught a glimpse of Aerotech's utilization of ABM in its use of the ABC information from both Phoenix and Bakersfield to improve operations and reduce costs. One way of picturing the relationship between ABC and ABM is in terms of the **two-dimensional activity-based costing model** depicted in Exhibit 6–6.[5] The vertical dimension of the model depicts the cost assignment view of an ABC system. From the *cost assignment viewpoint*, the ABC system uses two-stage cost allocation to *assign* the costs of resources to the firm's cost objects. These cost objects could be products manufactured (such as Aerotech's Mode I, II, and III circuit boards), services produced, or customers served.

Now focus on the horizontal dimension of the model. Depicted here is the *process view* of an ABC system. The emphasis now is on the activities themselves, the various processes by which work is accomplished in the organization. The left-hand side of Exhibit 6–6 depicts **activity analysis**, which is the detailed identification and description of the activities conducted in the enterprise. Activity analysis entails identification not only of the activities but also of their *root causes*, the events that *trigger* activities, and the *linkages* among activities. The right-hand side of Exhibit 6–6 depicts the evaluation of activities through performance measures. It is these processes of *activity analysis and evaluation* that comprise activity-based management. Notice that the *activities*, which appear in the center of both dimensions in Exhibit 6–6, are the focal point of ABC and ABM.

Using ABM to Eliminate Non-Value-Added Activities and Costs

LO 5 List and explain the steps in using ABM to eliminate non-value-added costs.

An important goal of activity-based management is to identify and eliminate non-value-added activities and costs. **Non-value-added activities** are operations that are either (1) unnecessary and dispensable or (2) necessary, but

[5]This section draws on Lewis J. Soloway, "Using Activity-Based Management in Aerospace and Defense Companies," *Journal of Cost Management* 6, no. 4, pp. 56–66, and Peter B. B. Turney, "What an Activity-Based Cost Model Looks Like," *Journal of Cost Management* 5, no. 4, pp. 54–60.

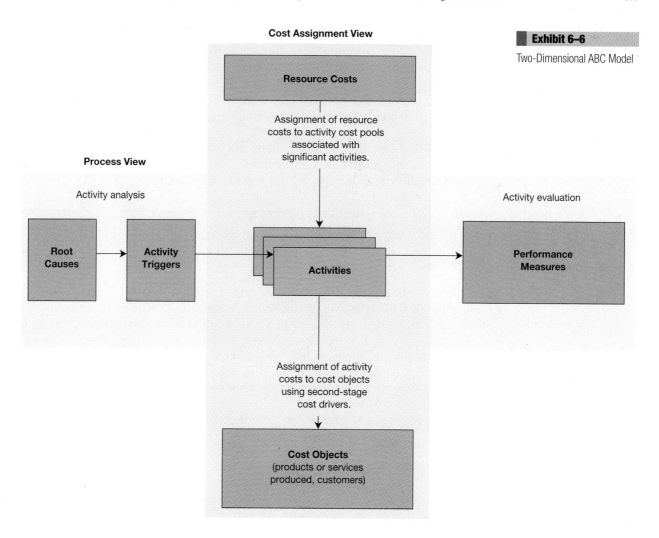

Cost Assignment View

Exhibit 6–6

Two-Dimensional ABC Model

inefficient and improvable.[6] **Non-value-added costs,** which result from such activities, are the costs of activities that can be eliminated without deterioration of product quality, performance, or perceived value. The following five steps provide a strategy for eliminating non-value-added costs in both manufacturing and service industry firms.

Identifying Activities   The first step is activity analysis, which identifies all of the organization's significant activities. The resulting activity list should be broken down to the most fundamental level practical. For example, rather than listing purchasing as an activity, the list should break down the purchasing operation into its component activities, such as obtaining part specifications, compiling vendor lists, vendor selection, negotiation, ordering, and expediting.

Identifying Non-Value-Added Activities   Three criteria for determining whether an activity adds value are as follows:

■ *Is the activity necessary?* If it's a duplicate or nonessential operation, it is non-value-added.

Non-value-added activities are operations that are either unnecessary and dispensable or necessary but inefficient and improvable.

Non-value-added costs can be eliminated without deterioration of product quality, performance, or perceived value.

---

[6]This definition, as well as other material in this section, is drawn from James A. Brimson, "Improvement and Elimination of Non-Value-Added Costs," *Journal of Cost Management* 2, no. 2, pp. 62–65.

■ *Is the activity efficiently performed?* In answering this question, it is helpful to compare the actual performance of the activity to a value-added baseline established using budgets, targets, or external benchmarks.

■ *Is an activity sometimes value-added and sometimes non-value-added?* For example, it may be necessary to move work-in-process units between production operations, but unnecessary to move raw materials around while in storage.

Understanding Activity Linkages, Root Causes, and Triggers   In identifying non-value-added activities, it is critical to understand the ways in which activities are linked together. The following chain of activities provides an example:

The rework of defective units is a non-value-added activity. The rework is *triggered* by the identification of defective products during inspection. The *root cause* of the rework, however, could lie in any one of a number of preceding activities. Perhaps the part specifications were in error. Or was an unreliable vendor selected? Were the wrong parts received? Or is the production activity to blame?

A set of linked activities (such as that depicted above) is called a **process**. Sometimes activity analysis is referred to as **process value analysis (PVA)**.

A **process** is a set of linked activities.

A **process value analysis (PVA)** is the detailed identification and description of the activities conducted in an enterprise.

Establishing Performance Measures   By continually measuring the performance of all activities, and comparing performance with benchmarks, management's attention may be directed to unnecessary or inefficient activities. We will explore performance measurement extensively in Chapters 10 and 11.

Reporting Non-Value-Added Costs   Non-value-added costs should be highlighted in activity center cost reports. By identifying non-value-added activities, and reporting their costs, management can strive toward the ongoing goals of process improvement and elimination of non-value-added costs.

Achieving Cost Reduction

LO 5   List and explain the steps in using ABM to eliminate non-value-added costs.

Once non-value-added activities have been identified, four techniques may be used to reduce the resulting non-value-added costs.[7]

■ *Activity reduction.* This technique simply scales back the activity, by reducing the time or other resources devoted to it.

■ *Activity elimination.* This approach assumes the activity is utterly unnecessary.

■ *Activity selection.* Under this strategy, the most efficient activity is selected from a set of alternatives.

■ *Activity sharing.* This technique finds ways to get more mileage out of an existing activity by combining functions in a more efficient manner. An example is the use of common parts in several related products, rather than designing each product to use unique parts.

---

[7]Peter B. B. Turney, "How Activity-Based Costing Helps Reduce Cost," *Journal of Cost Management* 4, no. 4, pp. 29–35.

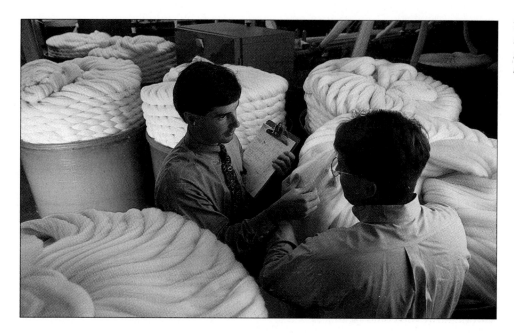

These quality-control inspectors are examining the cotton produced in this textile mill.

Target Costing, Kaizen Costing, and Continuous Improvement

To remain competitive in today's global market, businesses must continually improve. Moreover, this continuous improvement needs to apply across the spectrum of business activity: from product design and quality, through production operations and cost management, to customer service. **Continuous improvement** may be defined as the constant effort to eliminate waste, reduce response time, simplify the design of both products and processes, and improve quality and customer service.[8] One compelling reason for the need for continuous improvement is the *price down/cost down concept.* This refers to the tendency of prices to fall over the life cycle of a newly introduced product. Think, for example, about the prices of hand-held calculators, VCRs, personal listening devices, and CD players. When each of these products was first introduced, prices were quite high. However, as manufacturers gained experience in producing them, prices fell and the products became accessible to a much wider customer pool. However, if prices are to fall over time, manufacturers must continually reduce costs as well.[9]

> **Continuous improvement** is the constant effort to eliminate waste, reduce response time, simplify the design of both products and processes, and improve quality and customer service.

Two approaches to continuous improvement (i.e., reduction) in production costs were pioneered by Japanese manufacturers and are now in widespread use. These techniques are called *target costing* and *kaizen costing*.

Target Costing

Target costing refers to the design of a product, and the processes used to produce it, so that ultimately the product can be manufactured at a cost that will enable the firm to make a profit when the product is sold at an estimated market-driven price.[10] This estimated price is called the *target price,* the desired profit margin is called the *target profit,* and the cost at which the product must be manufactured is called the *target cost.*

> **LO 6**   Define and give an example of target costing.

> **Target costing** is the design of a product, and the processes used to produce it, so ultimately the product can be manufactured at a cost that will enable a firm to make a profit when the product is sold at an estimated market-driven price.

---

[8]Barry J. Brinker, ed., *Emerging Practices in Cost Management* (Boston: Warren, Gorham, Lamont, 1993), p. G2.

[9]See Robert A. Howell and Michiharu Sakurai, "Management Accounting (and Other) Lessons from the Japanese," *Management Accounting* 74, no. 6, pp. 28–34.

[10]Barry J. Brinker, *Emerging Practices,* p. G6.

To illustrate, suppose Aerotech's engineers have developed a new airborne device for detecting wind shear, which is a sudden change in wind direction and speed. Aerotech's management estimates that after a few years on the market, assuming the firm's competitors come out with comparable devices, its Shearsensor will sell for a *target price* of approximately $5,500. Moreover, management desires a *target profit* on its Shearsensor of $500. The *target cost,* then, for the manufacture of a Shearsensor is $5,000 ($5,500 − $500). The task faced by Aerotech's engineers now is to refine the Shearsensor's product design, and the processes that will be used to manufacture it, so that ultimately it will cost no more than $5,000 to produce.

One of the techniques Aerotech's engineers will use in achieving a product design that meets the target cost is *value engineering.* **Value engineering** (or **value analysis**) is a cost-reduction and process-improvement technique that utilizes information collected about a product's design and production process, and then examines various attributes of the design and process to identify candidates for improvement efforts. The attributes examined include such characteristics as part diversity and process complexity. Examples of value engineering in the area of direct materials include changing the quality or grade of materials, reducing the number of bolts in a part, using a component common to other products instead of a unique or specialized component, and changing the method of painting.[11] In the case of Aerotech's Shearsensor, engineers might be able to reduce the projected cost by several hundred dollars just by changing one component from a unique part to one used in Aerotech's other products.

> **Value engineering** (or **value analysis**) is a cost-reduction and process improvement technique that utilizes information collected about a product's design and production processes and then examines various attributes of the design and processes to identify candidates for improvement efforts.

Kaizen Costing

> **LO 7**   Explain the concept of Kaizen costing, and prepare a Kaizen costing chart.

> **Kaizen costing** is the process of cost reduction, brought about by continual and gradual improvement through small betterment activities.

Target costing applies to the *design* of a new product or model and the *design* of its production process. In contrast, **kaizen costing** is the process of cost reduction during the manufacturing phase of an existing product.[12] The Japanese word *kaizen* refers to continual and gradual improvement through small betterment activities, rather than large or radical improvement made through innovation or large investments in technology. The idea is simple. Improvement is the goal and responsibility of every worker, from the CEO to the manual laborers, in every activity, every day, all the time! Through the small but continual efforts of everyone, significant reductions in costs can be attained over time.

To help achieve the continuous cost reduction implied by the kaizen costing concept, an annual (or monthly) *kaizen cost goal* is established. Then, actual costs are tracked over time and compared to the kaizen goal. A kaizen costing chart used by Daihatsu (a Japanese auto manufacturer owned in part by Toyota) is shown in Exhibit 6–7.[13] Notice that the cost base or reference point is the actual cost performance at the end of the prior year. A kaizen goal is established for the cost-reduction rate and amount during the current year. Actual cost performance throughout the year is compared with the kaizen goal. At the end of the current year, the current actual cost becomes the cost base or reference point for the next year. Then, a new (lower) kaizen goal is established, and the cost-reduction effort continues.

How are kaizen costing goals met? The continual and relentless reduction of non-value-added activities and costs, the elimination of waste, and improvements in manufacturing cycle time all contribute to the effort. In addition, the improvement suggestions and kaizen efforts of all employees are taken seriously and implemented when appropriate. The result is a continually more efficient and cost-effective production process.

---

[11]Yasuhiro Monden and Kazuki Hamada, "Target Costing and Kaizen Costing in Japanese Automobile Companies," *Journal of Management Accounting Research* 3, p. 18.

[12]Ibid., p. 17.

[13]Yasuhiro Monden and John Lee, "How a Japanese Auto Maker Reduces Costs," *Management Accounting* 75, no. 2, p. 24.

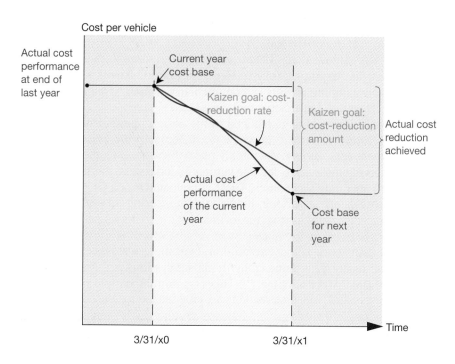

■ **Exhibit 6–7**

Kaizen Costing Chart Used by Daihatsu Motor Company (Osaka, Japan)

A good example of the successful use of both target costing and kaizen costing in bringing about continuous improvement is provided by Toyota, as the next section illustrates.

Toyota: Target Costing and Kaizen Costing in Action

Toyota Motor Corporation, Japan's largest automaker, is second in size only to General Motors on a worldwide basis. Toyota uses both target costing and kaizen costing to maintain its strong competitive position. "Cost planning at Toyota is mainly an effort to reduce cost at the design stage. Toyota sets goals for cost reduction, and then seeks to achieve those goals through design changes. To correctly assess the gains made, the exact amount of cost reduction through redesign is measured. Setting goals and

This Toyota factory shows the company's state-of-the-art manufacturing process. In addition to its advanced manufacturing system, Toyota uses target costing and kaizen costing to maintain its strong competitive position.

assessing the results based on cost differences between old and new models constitute the essence of cost control at Toyota."[14]

Toyota also has achieved significant cost reduction through the redesign of production processes. For example, "over a five-year period, Toyota reduced the setup time for its 800-ton stamping presses from more than one hour to under 12 minutes."[15] Time savings such as this significantly reduce costs.

In addition to the cost savings realized in the design phase, Toyota aggressively pursues kaizen costing to reduce costs in the manufacturing phase. "In July and January, plant managers submit six-month plans for attaining their kaizen goals. Methods for achieving these goals include cutting material costs per unit and improvements in standard operating procedures. These are pursued based on employee suggestions. For improvements involving industrial engineering or value engineering, employees often receive support from the technical staff. To draw up a kaizen plan after kaizen goals have been set by top management, employees look for ways to contribute to kaizen in their daily work. About two million suggestions were received from Toyota employees in one recent year alone (roughly 35 suggestions per employee). Ninety-seven percent of them were adopted."[16] This is a prime example of the concept of employee **empowerment**, in which workers are encouraged to take their own initiative to improve operations, reduce costs, and improve product quality and customer service.

Empowerment is the concept of encouraging and authorizing workers to take the initiative to improve operations, reduce costs, and improve product quality and customer service.

Benchmarking

Benchmarking is the continual search for the most effective method of accomplishing a task, by comparing existing methods and performance levels with those of other organizations or with other subunits within the same organization. The most effective methods of accomplishing various tasks in a particular industry, often discovered through benchmarking, are referred to as **best practices**. Xerox Corporation often is credited with originating the benchmarking concept, but now it is widely used by organizations throughout the world. Benchmarking (also called *competitive benchmarking*) provides one more tool for companies to use in identifying non-value-added activities and pursuing continuous improvement.

LO 8   Briefly explain the concepts of total quality control, continuous improvement, benchmarking, re-engineering, and the theory of constraints.

Benchmarking is the continual search for the most effective method of accomplishing a task by comparing existing methods and performance levels with those of other organizations or with other subunits within the same organization.

Best practices are the most effective methods of accomplishing various tasks in a particular industry, often discovered through benchmarking.

Re-engineering is the complete redesign of a process, with an emphasis on finding creative new ways to accomplish an objective.

Re-engineering

In contrast to the concept of kaizen, which involves small, incremental steps toward gradual improvement, re-engineering involves a giant leap. **Re-engineering** is the complete redesign of a process, with an emphasis on finding creative new ways to accomplish an objective. Re-engineering has sometimes been described as taking a blank piece of paper and starting from scratch to redesign a business process. Rather than searching continually for minute improvements, re-engineering involves a radical shift in thinking about how an objective should be met. In the words of one re-engineering consultant: "Re-engineering has captured the attention of U.S. business. Re-engineering prescribes radical, quick and significant change. Admittedly, this can entail high risks, but it can also bring big rewards. These benefits are most dramatic when new models are discovered for conducting business."[17]

As the following anecdotes illustrate, many organizations have recently implemented successful benchmarking and re-engineering projects.

---

[14]Takao Tanaka, "Target Costing at Toyota," *Journal of Cost Management* 7, no. 1, p. 4.

[15]Peter B. B. Turney and James M. Reeve, "The Impact of Continuous Improvement on the Design of Activity-Based Cost Systems," *Journal of Cost Management* 4, no. 2, p. 44.

[16]Takao Tanaka, "Kaizen Budgeting: Toyota's Cost Control System under TQC," *Journal of Cost Management* 8, no. 3, p. 62.

[17]C. Kevin Cherry, "Re-engineering: Harnessing Creativity and Innovation," *Journal of Cost Management* 8, no. 2, p. 49.

Florida Power & Light

In a recent benchmarking study, Florida Power & Light found that it ranked quite high in customer service, but that its costs were also high for the industry. As a result, the utility initiated several steps to cut costs without impairing customer service.[18]

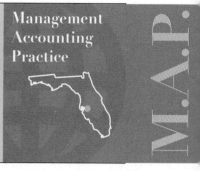

Cummins Engine

Cummins Engine has re-engineered virtually all of its business processes, including new product development, manufacturing, pricing, and distribution. "The result was a remarkable 40 percent reduction in engine costs and prices and significantly improved product quality.[19]

AMP

AMP, a manufacturer of electronic connectors, implemented a *benchmarking* study of the *best practices* of Federal Express, Frito-Lay, and American Airlines. Then AMP re-engineered its supplier management practices, with the following results:[20]

- Cut the supplier base by one-third.
- Reduced cycle time by 50 percent.
- Increased quality from 92 to 98 percent.
- Decreased late shipments from 30 percent to 10 percent.

Motorola

Motorola re-engineered its accounting functions, with the result being a reduction in the time required to close the books from 14 days to 4 days.[21]

---

[18]Robert W. Rutledge, "Life after the Deming Prize for Florida Power and Light Company," *Journal of Cost Management* 8, no. 2, pp. 18–25.

[19]Ibid., p. 60.

[20]Ibid.

[21]Ibid.

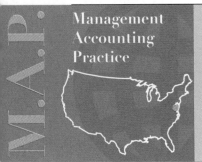

U.S. Department of Defense (DOD)

The DOD is in the midst of a re-engineering project, which is based heavily on activity-based costing methods. By analyzing DOD's business processes, identifying cost drivers, and eliminating non-value-added activities, DOD officials have set a goal of $35 billion over a seven-year period.[22]

Theory of Constraints

The **theory of constraints** focuses on identifying and relaxing the constraints that limit an organization's ability to reach a higher level of goal attainment.

The theory of constraints (or TOC) is another contemporary management tool that supports continuous improvement and cost management programs. The **theory of constraints** is a management approach that seeks to maximize long-run profit through proper management of organizational bottlenecks or constrained resources.[23] The key idea in TOC is to identify the constraints in a system that are preventing the organization from achieving a higher level of success, then to seek to relieve or relax those constraints. Moreover, TOC recommends subordinating all other management goals to the objective of solving the constraint problems. For example, if limited capacity in a particular machining operation is increasing cycle time, reducing throughput, and reducing profits, then management would concentrate much of its efforts on expanding the capacity of that bottleneck operation.

Keys to Successfully Implementing ABC and ABM

LO 9   List and briefly explain five keys to successfully implementing ABC, ABM, and other cost management systems.

In Chapters 5 and 6, we have discussed several contemporary management tools that can help an organization achieve and maintain a competitive position in the global market. Activity-based costing, activity-based management, continuous improvement programs, target costing, and kaizen costing are among the most important approaches we have addressed. All these techniques have the potential to significantly improve the operations and effectiveness of an organization. Yet, introducing significant change in an organization is never easy. People, by their very nature, often tend to resist change. Change can be threatening for a variety of reasons. An employee may worry, for example, that his or her job will be identified as a non-value-added activity and eliminated. None of the cost management tools we have studied constitute a panacea for success. Moreover, some organizations will inevitably benefit more from any of these tools than other organizations will. Nevertheless, there are several key factors that can increase the likelihood of successful implementation of ABC, ABM, and other cost management techniques.[24]

Organizational culture is the mindset of employees, including their shared beliefs, values, and goals.

Organizational Culture   The term **organizational culture** refers to the mindset of employees, including their shared beliefs, values, and goals.[25] A strong functional culture is characterized by clearly articulated beliefs, values, and goals. Such an orga-

---

[22]Robert D. Morevec and Michael S. Yoemans, "Using ABC to Support Business Re-engineering in the Department of Defense," *Journal of Cost Management* 6, no. 2, pp. 32–41.

[23]John B. MacArthur, "Theory of Constraints and Activity-Based Costing: Friends or Foes?" *Journal of Cost Management* 7, no. 2, p. 51.

[24]This section draws on Michael D. Shields and S. Mark Young, "A Behavioral Model for Implementing Cost Management Systems," *Journal of Cost Management* 2, no. 4, pp. 17–27; and Chris Argyris and Robert S. Kaplan, "Implementing New Knowledge: The Case of Activity-Based Costing," *Accounting Horizons* 8, no. 3, pp. 83–105.

[25]Shields and Young, "A Behavioral Model," p. 18.

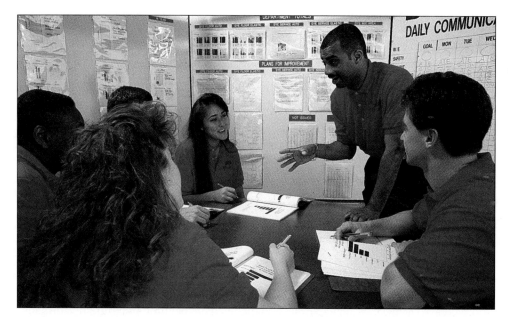

Continuing education and employee retraining are important keys to successfully initiating and managing change in an organization.

nizational culture usually exhibits high employee involvement and participation, long-term employment, and a sense of teamwork. Research in organizational behavior suggests that a strong functional culture is, in the long run, the most conducive to successful implementation of programs oriented toward continuous improvement.

Top-Management Support and Commitment   Cost management systems such as ABC and ABM require significant time and resources to implement. The support of top management, both in spirit and in terms of resources, is crucial to successful implementation.

Change Champion   The general support of top management, while necessary, is often not sufficient to successfully implement a new cost management technique. "Almost all successful innovations are initiated and implemented by a zealous, voluntary champion."[26] A **change champion** is an individual who recognizes the need for change and seeks to bring it about through his or her own efforts. A successful change champion is usually at a high level in the organizational hierarchy, has strong entrepreneurial skills, demonstrates political savvy within the organization, and has the ability to persuade and motivate others.

A **change champion** is an individual who recognizes the need for change and seeks to bring it about through his or her own efforts.

Change Process   Meaningful change is more likely to occur if there is a well-defined process established for change. A timetable for certain activities, a set of well-articulated goals, and follow-up are all important elements of such a process.

Continuing Education   Successful implementation of any of the cost management programs we have discussed requires involvement by virtually all of the employees in an organization. Moreover, each employee in the organization should be made aware of the goals of the program, the process by which the program will be implemented and evaluated, and the employee's role in making the program a success. Moreover, it is important to offer employees a continual opportunity to retrain and adapt their skills to the rapidly changing work environment. If employees recognize a commitment by their organization to ensure that their skills are current and useful, they will in turn be more likely to commit to the organization's process of continuous improvement.

---

[26]Ibid., p. 21.

Other Cost Management Issues in Today's Manufacturing Environment

The pressures of international competition, coupled with the advent of advanced manufacturing systems, are causing fundamental changes in the managerial-accounting systems used in manufacturing firms. We will briefly mention several of these changes here and then return to them in subsequent chapters.

Product life-cycle costing is the accumulation of costs for activities that occur over the entire life cycle of a product.

Product Life-Cycle Costs   A new area of reporting in cost management systems is **product life-cycle costing**, which is the accumulation of costs for activities that occur over the entire life cycle of a product.[27] A product's life cycle begins with its inception and continues through the following five stages: (1) product planning and concept design, (2) preliminary design, (3) detailed design and testing, (4) production, and (5) distribution and customer service. We will explore the techniques for managing product life-cycle costs in Chapter 9.

Performance Measurement   The appropriateness of using traditional criteria to measure manufacturing performance in today's manufacturing environment has been challenged. As a result, new operational performance measures have been suggested and implemented. Moreover, managerial accountants have begun to measure performance in whole new areas of operations previously considered beyond the domain of the accounting system. We will explore these measures in Chapters 10 and 11.

Justifying Investments in Advanced Manufacturing Systems   How do the managers of a company like Aerotech make a decision to invest in a new manufacturing system? Flexible manufacturing systems can cost $50 million or more. Such a huge investment must be given very special analysis and thought. In Chapters 16 and 17 we will explore techniques used by managers to make decisions involving large outlays of money and cash flows that occur over many years. We will leave the details of these techniques until then. It should be noted, however, that any analysis of investment in advanced manufacturing systems must consider the costs and benefits of the equipment over its entire life. This is a tall order, since the complexity of the equipment coupled with the rapid pace of technological change make the costs and benefits difficult to predict.

Chapter Summary

To achieve and maintain a competitive advantage in today's global marketplace, many companies are investing heavily in new technology. To reduce cycle time, make operations more efficient, and eliminate non-value-added costs, many companies are adopting a just-in-time inventory and production management philosophy. Under this production system, no raw materials are purchased and no products are manufactured until they are needed. Along with JIT production systems, many companies are modernizing their production processes with computer-assisted manufacturing systems. Although these systems are extremely expensive, the cost savings and strategic benefits they facilitate often justify their acquisition.

In addition to new technology, many organizations are implementing new cost management systems to better meet the needs of management in an economy that continually grows more competitive. One such cost management system is activity-based management, which is the use of activity-based costing information to improve operations and eliminate non-value-added costs. One way of depicting ABM is the two-dimensional ABC model. This model combines the cost assignment role of ABC with the process and evaluation view of an ABC system.

In today's competitive environment, a company must continually improve in order to remain successful. A continuous improvement program is a constant effort to eliminate waste, reduce response time,

---

[27]Callie Berliner and James A. Brimson, eds., *Cost Management for Today's Advanced Manufacturing* (Boston: Harvard Business School Press, 1988), pp. 22, 32–33, and 140–41.

simplify the design of both products and processes, and improve quality and customer service. Consistent with continuous improvement are the concepts of target costing and kaizen costing. Both of these methods seek to improve a product and its production process and, in so doing, reduce costs. Target costing focuses on the design phase, while kaizen costing concentrates on the manufacturing phase. Other management tools that are consistent with continuous improvement efforts include value engineering, benchmarking, re-engineering, and the theory of constraints.

Efforts at continuous improvement and the introduction of new cost management systems will not automatically succeed. Keys to successful implementation include a strong functional organizational culture, top-management support and commitment, a change champion, a well-defined change process, and continuing education for all employees.

Key Terms

For each term's definition refer to the indicated page, or turn to the glossary at the end of the text.

activity analysis, pg. 216

activity-based management (ABM), pg. 216

automated material-handling system (AMHS), pg. 210

benchmarking (or competitive benchmarking), pg. 222

best practices, pg. 222

capital-intensive, pg. 213

cellular manufacturing, pg. 210

change champion, pg. 225

computer-aided design (CAD) system, pg. 210

computer-aided manufacturing (CAM) system, pg. 210

computer-integrated manufacturing (CIM) system, pg. 210

computer-numerically-controlled (CNC) machines, pg. 209

continuous improvement, pg. 219

empowerment, pg. 222

flexible manufacturing system (FMS), pg. 210

FMS cell, pg. 210

just-in-time (JIT) inventory and production management system, pg. 206

just-in-time (JIT) purchasing, pg. 208

kaizen costing, pg. 220

labor-intensive, pg. 213

non-value-added activities, pg. 217

non-value-added costs, pg. 217

off-line quality control, pg. 212

organizational culture, pg. 224

process, pg. 218

process value analysis (PVA), pg. 218

production Kanban, pg. 207

product life-cycle costing, pg. 226

pull method, pg. 207

re-engineering, pg. 222

target costing, pg. 219

theory of constraints, pg. 224

total quality control (TQC), pg. 208

two-dimensional ABC model, pg. 216

value engineering (or value analysis), pg. 220

withdrawal Kanban, pg. 207

Review Questions

6–1. Briefly describe the JIT approach to production and inventory management.

6–2. List eight key features of a just-in-time inventory and production management system.

6–3. What is a *production Kanban*?

6–4. What is meant by *TQC*? Explain the importance of TQC in a JIT system.

6–5. Explain in words and then draw a diagram depicting the pull method of coordinating steps in a JIT system. (Refer to the JIT discussion in Chapter 6 and to the JIT exhibit in Chapter 1.)

6–6. List five features of JIT purchasing.

6–7. Define the following terms: *CMS, JIT, CNC, CAM, CAD, AMHS, FMS,* and *CIM*.

6–8. Briefly describe the key differences in plant layout between Aerotech's Phoenix and Bakersfield facilities.

6–9. How is a firm's cost structure likely to change if an FMS is installed?

6–10. Explain what is meant by *off-line quality control*.

6–11. Explain what is meant by *cellular manufacturing*.

6–12. Define *activity-based management*.

6–13. Explain the concept of *two-dimensional ABC*. Support your explanation with a diagram.

6–14. What is meant by the term *activity analysis*?

6–15. Give three criteria for determining whether an activity adds value.

6–16. Distinguish between an activity's *trigger* and its *root cause*. Give an example of each.

6–17. List four techniques for reducing or eliminating non-value-added costs.

6–18. Give an example of activity sharing.

6–19. What is meant by the term *continuous improvement*?

6–20. Briefly explain the *price down/cost down* concept. Give an example.

6–21. Define the following terms: *target costing, target price, target cost,* and *target profit*.

6–22. Explain the technique of *value engineering*.

6–23. What is meant by the term *kaizen costing*?

6–24. Which of the following terms is most consistent with the old saying, "Slow and steady wins the race": flexible manufacturing, advanced manufacturing system, product innovation, target costing, kaizen costing, or investment in high technology? Explain.

6–25. What is meant by *employee empowerment*?

6–26. Define and give an example of *benchmarking*.

6–27. What is meant by the term *best practices*?

6–28. Briefly explain the concept of *re-engineering*.

6–29. Explain how the concepts of *continuous improvement* and the *theory of constraints* are related.

6–30. Elimination of production bottleneck activities is an example of what management concept?

6–31. List five keys to the successful implementation of ABC, ABM, and other cost management approaches.

6–32. Define the terms *organizational culture* and *change champion*.

6–33. What behavioral problems can you think of that a company such as Aerotech might encounter in modifying its managerial-accounting system to fit today's manufacturing environment?

Exercises

■ **Exercise 6–34**
Design Your Own Production Process Using Advanced Manufacturing Systems; Non-Value-Added Costs
(LO 1, LO 5)

Since you have always wanted to be an industrial baron, invent your own product and describe at least five steps used in its production.

Required:

Design a plant layout using the latest in advanced manufacturing technology to manufacture your product. Explain how your plant will eliminate non-value-added costs.

■ **Exercise 6–35**
Direct and Indirect Costs; Traditional versus JIT Manufacturing Environment
(LO 1, LO 2)

The following costs were incurred in each of two automobile-parts factories in June.

Raw materials	Depreciation, plant	Direct labor
Electricity, machines	Depreciation, equipment	Supervisory salaries
Electricity, lighting, and air-conditioning	Insurance	Property taxes
Engineering salaries	Machine repair, wages	Factory supplies
Custodial wages	Machine repair, parts	Inspection

Required:

For every cost listed above, indicate whether it is more likely to be treated as a direct cost or an indirect cost in each of the following. Explain your choice for each cost item in each manufacturing environment.

1. A traditional factory with a traditional cost-accounting system.
2. A JIT/FMS factory with an activity-based costing system.

■ **Exercise 6–36** ✓
Non-Value-Added Costs
(LO 5)

These costs occur in nonmanufacturing firms also.

Required:

Identify four potential non-value-added costs in (1) an airline, (2) a bank, and (3) a hotel.

■ **Exercise 6–37**
Activity Analysis; Non-Value-Added Activities
(LO 3, LO 5)

Visit a restaurant for a meal or think carefully about a recent visit to a restaurant. List as many activities as you can think of that would be performed by the restaurant's employees for its customers.

Required:

For each activity on your list, indicate the following:

1. Value-added or non-value-added.
2. The trigger of the activity.
3. The possible root cause of the activity.

■ **Exercise 6–38**
College Registration; Re-engineering
(LO 5, LO 8)

Think carefully about the various activities and steps involved in the course registration process at your college or university.

Required:

1. List the steps in the registration process in the sequence in which they occur.

2. Prepare an activity analysis of the registration process. Discuss the activity linkages, triggers, and root causes.

3. Re-engineer your institution's course registration process with these goals in mind:

   a. Improve the convenience and effectiveness of the process for the student registering.

   b. Improve the effectiveness and cost efficiency of the process from the standpoint of the institution.

List five activities performed by the employees of an airline *on the ground*. For each of these activities, suggest a performance measure that could be used in activity-based management.

■ **Exercise 6–39**
Performance Measures in
Two-Dimensional ABC; ABM
(LO 3, LO 4)

Suppose you have just started a business to manufacture your newest invention, the photon gismo. Let's say you believe that after a few years on the market, photon gismos will sell for about $125. This allows for the introduction of similar devices by your competitors. Furthermore, let's say you want to make a profit of $25 on each gismo sold.

■ **Exercise 6–40**
Target Costing
(LO 6)

Required:

1. What is the target cost for the photon gismo?

2. What is the target profit?

3. What is the target price?

4. Suppose your engineers and cost accountants conclude that your design of the photo gismo will result in a unit cost of $115. How can you use the concept of target costing to help achieve your objective?

5. How could value engineering help in this process? Suggest an example.

6. How could two-dimensional activity-based costing help? Suggest an example.

Better Bagels, Inc. manufactures a variety of bagels, which are frozen and sold in grocery stores. The production process consists of the following steps.

■ **Exercise 6–41**
Basic Elements of a
Production Process; Non-
Value-Added Costs
(LO 3, LO 5)

1. Ingredients, such as flour and raisins, are received and inspected. Then they are stored until needed.

2. Ingredients are carried on hand carts to the mixing room.

3. Dough is mixed in 40-pound batches in four heavy-duty mixers.

4. Dough is stored on large boards in the mixing room until a bagel machine is free.

5. A board of dough is carried into the bagel room. The board is tipped, and the dough slides into the hopper of a bagel machine. This machine pulls off a small piece of dough, rolls it into a cylindrical shape, and then squeezes it into a doughnut shape. The bagel machines can be adjusted in a setup procedure to accommodate different sizes and styles of bagels. Workers remove the uncooked bagels and place them on a tray, where they are kept until a boiling vat is free.

6. Next the trays of uncooked bagels are carried into an adjoining room, which houses three 50-gallon vats of boiling water. The bagels are boiled for approximately one minute.

7. Bagels are removed from the vats with a long-handled strainer and placed on a wooden board. The boards full of bagels are carried to the oven room, where they are kept until an oven rack is free. The two ovens contain eight racks which rotate but remain upright, much like the seats on a Ferris wheel. A rack full of bagels is finished baking after one complete revolution in the oven. When a rack full of bagels is removed from the oven, a fresh rack replaces it. The oven door is opened and closed as each rack completes a revolution in the oven.

8. After the bagels are removed from the oven, they are placed in baskets for cooling.

9. While the bagels are cooling, they are inspected. Misshapen bagels are removed and set aside. (Most are eaten by the staff.)

10. After the bagels are cool, the wire baskets are carried to the packaging department. Here the bagels are dumped into the hopper on a bagging machine. This machine packages a half-dozen bagels in each bag and seals the bag with a twist tie.

11. Then the packaged bagels are placed in cardboard boxes, each holding 24 bags. The boxes are placed on a forklift and are driven to the freezer, where the bagels are frozen and stored for shipment.

Required:

1. Identify the steps in the bagel-production process that fall into each of the following categories: process time, inspection time, move time, waiting time, storage time.

2. List the steps in the production process that could be candidates for non-value-added activities.

■ **Exercise 6–42**
Key Features of JIT
Production Systems
(LO 1, LO 2)

Refer to the information given in the preceding exercise for Better Bagels, Inc.

Required:

Redesign the bagel production process so that it adheres to the JIT philosophy. Explain how the eight key features of JIT systems would be present in the new production process. What new equipment would the company need to purchase in order to implement the JIT approach fully?

■ **Exercise 6–43**
Benchmarking
(LO 8)

The continual search for the most effective method of accomplishing a task through comparison of existing methods and performance levels with those of other organizations or with other subunits within the same organization is called benchmarking. Sometimes organizations benchmark their operations against similar organizations, including their competitors. In other cases, organizations benchmark against a completely different type of organization. For example, a telecommunications company benchmarked its customer service operations against a NASCAR pit crew. The idea was to see how the telecommunications company's customer service unit could improve its response time by learning from the NASCAR crew. The pit crew, of course, had honed its procedures meticulously to get the necessary service accomplished in the least time possible. This type of benchmarking study is sometimes referred to as benchmarking "outside the box."

Required:

1. How could your college or university benefit from benchmarking against a similar institution of higher education? What departments, operations, or procedures might be appropriate for the focus of such a benchmarking study?

2. How could your college or university benefit from benchmarking outside the box? What departments, operations, or procedures might benefit from such a study? What noneducational organizations might be chosen for the benchmarking study?

Problems

■ **Problem 6–44**
Plant Layouts; Traditional
and Flexible Manufacturing
System
(LO 1, LO 2)

Skybolt Corporation manufactures special heavy bolts used in spacecraft. The production process consists of the following operations: (1) metal rods are cut to the proper length in a cutting machine; (2) a heading machine flattens the end of the cut rod to form a head; (3) a slotting machine cuts a slot in the bolt's head; (4) the bolt is run through a threading machine, which cuts the bolt's threads; (5) the bolt is washed to remove metal shavings and other foreign particles; (6) the bolt is heat-treated for hardness in a salt bath; (7) the bolt is inspected; (8) the bolt is wrapped and packaged.

The salt bath is a very expensive operation because of the electricity requirements. Another expensive operation is the central oil-filtration system, which is used to provide oil to all of the cutting and threading machines. The oil acts as a lubricant and coolant. After passing through a cutting machine, the oil is pumped back to a central oil-filtration station, which filters foreign particles from the oil.

Required:

1. Draw a factory-layout diagram showing how a traditional layout of Skybolt's production process might appear. (Refer to Exhibit 5–1 for guidance.)

2. Repeat requirement (1), assuming that Skybolt has adopted a JIT production system and purchased an FMS and an AMHS. Assume that only one central salt bath will be used, and that the company will keep its centralized oil-filtration system. (Refer to Exhibit 6–1 for guidance.)

■ **Problem 6–45**
Non-Value-Added Costs
(LO 3, LO 5)

Refer to the information given in the preceding problem for Skybolt Corporation.

Required:

Identify the non-value-added costs that might be present in Skybolt's traditional plant layout and production process. Write a memo to the company president pointing these costs out and advocating an FMS.

Kelifo Electric Vehicle Company (KEVCO) manufactures electric golf carts, electric all-terrain vehicles, and electric senior-citizen mobility scooters. Each of the three products has two or three models; a total of eight models are produced. Because of the somewhat erratic product demand and the lead-time needed for the setup for a model changeover, KEVCO has been increasing its raw-material and finished-goods inventories. Work-in-process inventories are relatively low and have consistent costs from one month to the next.

During the last five years, KEVCO has experienced increased inventory costs, decreasing profit margins, and customer complaints concerning the long lead-time to fill sales orders. KEVCO's president, Lou Watts, has been concerned about these problems and has been discussing ways to change these deteriorating conditions with his production, marketing, and accounting staff.

For the past few months, this top management group has been looking at how a just-in-time (JIT) manufacturing system utilizing a "kanban" concept could be used in their company. The team has assembled data that indicates that KEVCO could change their production process from one of "production push" to "demand pull" by rearranging their production floor into manufacturing cells that would be dedicated to one of the three products produced. Slight modifications to the equipment in the cell would be needed for a changeover from one model to another. Cell production teams would be responsible for cell performance, maintenance on machines and equipment, solving their production problems, and training. The management team is aware of, and has visited, other equipment manufacturing companies that have been quite successful in utilizing "demand pull" and cell manufacturing techniques.

The management team has reached a point where it needs outside help and has hired Grant Withers, a consultant, to provide help. KEVCO wants Withers to explain to them the procedures and issues involved in changing from a "production push" to a "demand pull" production process.

Required:

1. Discuss the effects on KEVCO's planning and operating processes if KEVCO implements a "demand pull" production system.

2. Identify and describe at least five benefits to KEVCO that should result from the "demand pull" production operating approach.

3. Discuss the behavioral effects of the proposed change at KEVCO on team participation in planning and production.

(CMA, adapted)

■ **Problem 6–46**
Just-in-Time Production
(LO 2)

Hearth and Home Housewares Corporation (HHHC) manufactures a variety of housewares for the consumer market in the midwest. The company's three major product lines are cooking utensils, tableware, and flatware. HHHC implemented activity-based costing four years ago and now has a well-developed ABC system in place for determining product costs. Only recently, however, has the ABC system been systematically used for the purposes of activity-based management. As a pilot project, HHHC's controller asked the ABC project team to do a detailed activity analysis of the purchasing activity. The following specific activities were identified.

1. Receipt of parts specifications from the Design Engineering Department.
2. Follow-up with design engineers to answer any questions.
3. Vendor (supplier) identification.
4. Vendor consultations (by phone or in person).
5. Price negotiation.
6. Vendor selection.
7. Ordering (by phone or mail).
8. Order follow-up.
9. Expediting (attempting to speed up delivery).
10. Order receiving.
11. Inspection of parts.
12. Return of parts not meeting specifications.
13. Consultation with design engineers and production personnel if parts do not satisfy intended purpose.

■ **Problem 6–47**
Two-Dimensional Activity-Based Costing; Activity Analysis; ABM
(LO 3, LO 4, LO 5)

14. Further consultation and/or negotiation with vendor if necessary.

15. Ship parts back to vendor if necessary.

16. If satisfactory, move parts to storage.

Required:

1. Draw a diagram to depict HHHC's two-dimensional activity-based costing efforts. The diagram should include the following:

   a. The cost assignment role of ABC, with the cost pools, activities, and product lines represented.

   b. The process view of ABC, with the purchasing activities displayed. Also indicated here will be the linkages among the activities. (To save space, indicate the activities by their numbers.)

   c. The activity evaluation phase of two-dimensional ABC.

2. Identify the triggers for each of the following activities in HHHC's purchasing activity analysis:

   Follow-up with design engineers (activity 2)

   Expediting (activity 9)

   Inspection of parts (activity 11)

   Return of parts (activity 12)

   Consultation with design engineers and production personnel (activity 13)

3. For each of the activities listed in requirement (2), identify the possible root causes.

4. Choose four activities in HHHC's purchasing function, and suggest a performance measure for each of these activities.

■ **Problem 6–48**
Activity Analysis; Non-Value-Added Activities; Re-engineering
(LO 5, LO 8)

Go shopping for groceries; then visit your bank and complete a relatively routine transaction. (Or, if that is inconvenient, think carefully about the last time you performed these errands.)

Required:

For each of the errands mentioned above, list the activities you performed as you completed the errand.

1. On your list show the activity sequence and linkages.

2. Indicate whether each specific activity was value-added or non-value-added. Explain how the non-value-added activities could be eliminated (or at least improved).

3. How have banks and grocery stores re-engineered their processes in recent years to improve efficiency both for the employees and for the customers?

■ **Problem 6–49**
JIT Cost Savings
(LO 2)

Zodiac Corporation is an automotive supplier that uses automatic screw machines to manufacture precision parts from steel bars. Zodiac's inventory of raw steel averages $600,000 with a turnover rate of four times per year. John Mercedes, president of Zodiac, is concerned about the costs of carrying inventory. He is considering the adoption of just-in-time inventory procedures in order to eliminate the need to carry any raw steel inventory. Mercedes has asked Katrina Gorman, Zodiac's controller, to evaluate the feasibility of JIT for the corporation. Gorman has identified the following effects of adopting JIT.

■ Without scheduling any overtime, lost sales due to stockouts would increase by 35,000 units per year. However, by incurring overtime premiums of $40,000 per year, the increase in lost sales could be reduced to 20,000 units. This would be the maximum amount of overtime that would be feasible for Zodiac.

■ Two warehouses presently used for steel bar storage would no longer be needed. Zodiac rents one warehouse from another company at an annual cost of $60,000. The other warehouse is owned by Zodiac and contains 12,000 square feet. Three-fourths of the space in the owned warehouse could be rented out for $1.50 per square foot per year.

■ Insurance totaling $14,000 per year would be eliminated.

   Zodiac's projected operating results for 19x9 are as follows. Long-term capital investments by Zodiac are expected to produce a rate of return of 20 percent before taxes.

ZODIAC CORPORATION
Budgeted Income Statement
For the Year Ended December 31, 19x9
(in thousands)

Sales (900,000 units)		$10,800
Cost of goods sold:		
Variable	$4,050	
Fixed	1,450	5,500
Gross margin		$ 5,300
Selling and administrative expenses:		
Variable	$ 900	
Fixed	1,500	2,400
Income before interest and income taxes		$ 2,900
Interest expense		900
Income before taxes		$ 2,000

Required:

1. Calculate the estimated savings or loss for Zodiac Corporation that would result in 19x9 from the adoption of just-in-time inventory methods. Ignore income taxes. (*Hint*: Try to estimate the costs and benefits associated with the JIT decision. Begin by computing the forgone contribution margin on the lost sales. The contribution margin is the sales revenue minus the variable cost.)

2. Identify and explain the conditions that should exist in order for a company to successfully install JIT.

(CMA, adapted)

Pickwick Paper Company's Charlotte plant manufactures paperboard. Its production process involves the following operations.

1. Harvested trees arrive by rail in the wood yard and are stored outside.
2. Logs are moved by a flume into the plant where they pass through a debarker and are cut up into chips.
3. The chips are stored in large bins near the chipping machines.
4. The chips then are transported by small trucks to another building and are placed in a digester, a large pressure cooker where heat, steam, and chemicals convert the chips into moist fibers.
5. The fibers are stored near the digester.
6. In the next step, the fibers are loaded by workers onto a conveyor belt, which carries the fibers to a depressurized blow tank. This operation separates the fibers.
7. The separated fibers are placed on wooden pallets and stored next to the blow tank.
8. Forklifts are used to carry the separated fibers to the refining area, where the fibers are washed, refined, and treated with chemicals and caustic substances until they become pulp.
9. The wood pulp then enters the paper machines through a headbox, which distributes pulp evenly across a porous belt of forming fabric.
10. Water is removed from the pulp by passing it over a wire screen.
11. Additional water is removed from the pulp in a series of presses.
12. Dryers then remove any remaining water from the pulp.
13. The thin, dry sheets of pulp are then smoothed and polished by large rollers called calenders.
14. Then the paperboard is wound into large rolls, and workers place the rolls on wooden pallets.
15. Forklifts are used to move the rolls of paperboard to the labeling building.
16. There the rolls are labeled and stored for shipment.
17. The rolls of paperboard are shipped to customers from the loading dock in the labeling building.

The partially processed product sometimes is stored between production operations for two to three days. This delay can be caused either by a faster production rate in the earlier processes than in the later processes or by breakdowns in the production machinery. The Charlotte plant's average cycle time is about 15 days.

■ **Problem 6–50**
Non-Value-Added Costs;
Changeover to a JIT
Production System
(LO 2, LO 3, LO 5)

Required:

Your consulting firm has been hired to advise Pickwick Paper's management on how to improve its production process.

1. Diagram the current production process.
2. Point out areas that you believe to be candidates for non-value-added activities.
3. Prepare a plan for Pickwick to change its production process to a JIT process. Include a diagram of your suggested process. The company is not in a position to buy new production machinery, but management will consider purchasing an AMHS. The plant currently operates in three buildings, which are not far apart. Management is willing to consider minor construction to connect the buildings.

■ **Problem 6–51**
Cost Drivers; Direct and Indirect Costs; Non-Value-Added Costs; JIT and FMS
(LO 1, LO 2, LO 5)

Northern Lights Autoworks Company manufactures a variety of small parts for the automotive industry. The company's manufacturing overhead cost budget for the current year is as follows:

Supervision	$176,000
Machine maintenance—labor	91,000
Machine maintenance—materials	23,000
Electrical power	45,000
Natural gas (for heating)	35,000
Factory supplies	40,000
Setup labor	30,000
Lubricants	10,000
Property taxes	25,000
Insurance	35,000
Depreciation on manufacturing equipment	105,000
Depreciation on trucks and forklifts	70,000
Depreciation on material conveyors	15,000
Building depreciation	160,000
Grinding wheels	5,000
Drill bits	2,000
Purchasing	80,000
Waste collection	4,000
Custodial labor	40,000
Telephone service	7,000
Engineering design	68,000
Inspection of raw materials	20,000
Receiving	20,000
Inspection of finished goods	30,000
Packaging	62,000
Shipping	30,000
Wages of parts clerks (find parts for production departments)	60,000
Wages of material handlers	70,000
Fuel for trucks and forklifts	30,000
Depreciation on raw-material warehouse	50,000
Depreciation on finished-goods warehouse	58,000
Total budgeted manufacturing overhead	$1,496,000

The budgeted amount of direct-labor for the year is 20,000 hours.

Required:

1. Compute the predetermined overhead rate based on direct-labor hours.
2. Northern Lights' management has decided to implement an activity-based costing system. The cost drivers under consideration are the following:

Production (in units)

Raw-material cost

Factory space

Machine hours

Number of production runs

Number of shipments of finished goods

Number of shipments of raw materials

Number of different raw materials and parts used in a product

Engineering specifications and change orders

Divide Northern Lights Autoworks' manufacturing-overhead costs into separate cost pools, and identify a cost driver for each cost pool.

3. For each overhead cost, indicate which of the five types of production activity (time) is involved.

4. Which of the overhead costs are candidates for elimination as non-value-added costs?

5. How would activity accounting help Northern Lights' management reduce or eliminate some of the company's overhead costs? Be specific.

6. Suppose that the firm adopted a JIT production approach and purchased an FMS. Which overhead costs are likely to be treated as direct costs of an FMS cell?

7. For those costs that are not likely to be traceable to an FMS cell, how would you assign them to Northern Lights Autoworks' products?

8. Suppose inspection of raw materials and receiving were combined to form an activity cost pool with the number of shipments of raw materials identified as the cost driver. Compute a pool rate for this cost pool, assuming that 400 shipments are anticipated.

Michael McKenna, manager of FarmCo's Service Division, dialed the division controller's number on his phone: "Janice, this is Mike McKenna. How's that JIT program doing? Has it saved us any money? I've got to report to the president next week, and I'd like to know how our inventory efforts are coming along."

"Give me a day or two, Mike, and I'll have some figures for you," responded Janice Grady, the division controller.

FarmCo is a manufacturer of farm equipment sold by a network of distributors throughout North America. A majority of the distributors are also repair centers for FarmCo Service Division to provide timely support of spare parts. In an effort to reduce the inventory costs incurred by the Service Division, McKenna implemented a just-in-time inventory program on January 2, 19x9. JIT has now been in place for a year. Grady has been able to document the following results of JIT implementation.

■ **Problem 6–52**
JIT Implementation; Cost Savings
(LO 2, LO 8)

■ The Service Division's average inventory declined from $550,000 to $150,000.

■ Projected annual insurance costs of $80,000 declined by 60 percent due to the lower average inventory.

■ A leased, 8,000-square-foot warehouse, previously used for raw-material storage, was not used at all during the year. The division paid $11,200 annual rent for the warehouse and was able to sublet three-quarters of the building to several tenants at $2.50 per square foot. The balance of the space remained idle.

■ Two warehouse employees whose services were no longer needed were transferred on January 2, 19x9, to the Purchasing Department to assist in the coordination of the JIT program. The annual salary expense for these two employees totaled $38,000 and continued to be charged to the indirect-labor portion of fixed overhead.

■ Despite the use of overtime to manufacture 7,500 spare parts, lost sales due to stockouts totaled 3,800 spare parts. The overtime premium incurred amounted to $5.60 per part manufactured. The use of overtime to fill spare parts orders was immaterial prior to January 1, 19x9.

Prior to the decision to implement the JIT inventory program, FarmCo's Service Division had completed its 19x9 budget. The division's budgeted income statement, without any adjustments for just-in-time inventory, follows. FarmCo's incremental borrowing rate for inventory is 15 percent. (Ignore income taxes in this problem.)

FARMCO SERVICE DIVISION
Budgeted Income Statement
For the Year Ended December 31, 19x9
(in thousands)

Sales (280,000 spare parts)		$6,160
Cost of goods sold:		
Variable	$2,660	
Fixed	1,120	3,780
Gross margin		$2,380
Selling and administrative expenses:		
Variable	$ 700	
Fixed	555	1,255
Operating income		$1,125
Other income		75
Income before interest and income taxes		$1,200
Interest expense		150
Income before income taxes		$1,050

Required:

1. Calculate the cash savings (loss) for FarmCo's Service Division that resulted during 19x9 from the adoption of the JIT inventory program. (*Hint*: One of the costs associated with the JIT decision is the forgone contribution margin on lost sales. The contribution margin is the sales revenue minus the variable cost.)

2. Discuss any factors, other than financial, that should be considered before a company implements a JIT program.

(CMA, adapted)

■ **Problem 6–53**
Ethical Standards; Lack of
Quality Control; Disclosure of
Product Quality Information
(LO 8)

Reliable Electronics Corporation (REC) is an eight-year-old company that developed a process to produce highly reliable electronic components at a cost well below that of the established competition. In seeking to expand its overall components business, REC decided to enter the facsimile equipment business because there was a niche for lower-priced facsimile machines in a vigorously growing marketplace. The market REC pursued consisted of small regional businesses not yet approached by the larger vendors. REC sells its machines with a one-year warranty and has established a maintenance force to handle machine breakdowns.

As REC customers learned of the benefits of fax transmissions, some increased their usage significantly. After six months, larger volume users began experiencing breakdowns, and the field technicians' portable test equipment was not sophisticated enough to detect hairline breaks in the electronic circuitry caused by the heavier than expected usage. Consequently, field technicians were required to replace the damaged components and return the defective ones to the company for further testing.

This situation caused an increase in maintenance costs, which added to the cost of the product. Unfortunately, there was no way to determine how many of the businesses would become heavy users and be subject to breakdowns. Some of the heavier volume users began switching to the more expensive machines available from the larger competitors. Although new sales orders masked the loss of heavier volume customers, the increased maintenance costs had an unfavorable impact on earnings. Andrew Fulton, REC's assistant controller, summarized this situation and its anticipated effect on earnings in his report prepared for the quarterly meeting of the board of directors.

Jack March, vice president of manufacturing, was concerned that the report did not provide any solutions to the problem. He asked Marie Waters, the controller, to have the matter deferred so that his engineering staff could work on the problem. He believed that the electronic component could be redesigned. This redesigned model, while more costly, could be an appropriate solution for heavier volume users who should not expect a low-cost model to service their increased needs. March was concerned that the board could decide to discontinue the product line if no immediate solution became available and that the company could miss a potentially profitable opportunity. March further believed that the tone of the report placed his organization in an unfavorable light.

The controller called Fulton into her office and asked him to suppress the part of his formal report related to the component failures. Waters asked Fulton just to cover it orally at the meeting, noting that engineering was working with marketing on the situation to reach a satisfactory solution. Fulton felt strongly that the board would be misinformed about a potentially serious impact on earnings if he followed Waters's advice.

Required:

1. Referring to the specific ethical standards for management accountants of competence, confidentiality, integrity, and objectivity, explain why Marie Waters's request to Andrew Fulton is unethical. Cite not only the concept of each standard but also Waters's action or nonaction that results in an unethical situation.

2. How can Andrew Fulton resolve the situation? What are some of his alternatives?

(CMA, adapted)

■ **Problem 6–54**
Target Costing; Value
Engineering; ABC; JIT
(LO 2, LO 4, LO 5)

Eileen Kunselman, president of Phoenix Electronics (PE), is concerned about the prospects of one of its major products. The president has been reviewing a marketing report with Jeff Keller, marketing product manager, for their 10-disk car compact disk (CD) changer. The report indicates another price reduction is needed to meet anticipated competitors' reductions in sales prices. The current selling price for their 10-disk car CD changers is $350 per unit. It is expected that within three months PE's two major competitors will be selling their 10-disk car CD changers for $300 per unit. This concerns Kunselman because their current cost of producing the CD changers is $315, which yields a $35 profit on each unit sold.

The situation is especially disturbing because PE had implemented an activity-based costing (ABC) system about two years ago. The ABC system helped them better identify costs, cost pools, cost drivers, and cost reduction opportunities. Changes made when adopting ABC reduced costs on this product by approximately 15 percent during the last two years. Now it appears that costs will need to be reduced considerably more to remain competitive and to earn a profit on the 10-disk car CD changers. Total costs to produce, sell, and service the CD changer units are as follows:

10-Disk Car CD Changer

		Per Unit
Material	Purchased components	$110
	All other material	40
Labor	Manufacturing, direct	65
	Setups	9
	Material handling	18
	Inspection	23
Machining	Cutting, shaping, and drilling	21
	Bending and finishing	14
Other	Finished-goods warehousing	5
	Warranty	10
	Total unit cost	$315

Kunselman has decided to hire Donald Collins, a consultant, to help decide how to proceed. After two weeks of review, discussion, and value engineering analysis, Collins suggested that PE adopt a just-in-time (JIT) cell manufacturing process to help reduce costs. He also suggested that using target costing would help in meeting the new target price.

By changing to a JIT cell manufacturing system, PE expects that manufacturing direct labor will increase by $15 per finished unit. However, setup, material handling, inspection, and finished goods warehousing will all be eliminated. Machine costs will be reduced from $35 to $30 per unit, and warranty costs are expected to be reduced by 40 percent.

Required:

1. Define *target costing*.
2. Define *value engineering*.
3. Determine Phoenix Electronics' unit target cost at the $300 competitive sales price while maintaining the same percentage of profit on sales as is earned on the current $350 sales price.
4. If the just-in-time cell manufacturing process is implemented with the changes in costs noted, will Phoenix Electronics meet the unit target cost you determined in Requirement 3? Prepare a schedule detailing cost reductions and the unit cost under the proposed JIT cell manufacturing process.

(CMA, adapted)

■ **Problem 6–55**
Kaizen Costing Chart
(LO 7, LO 8)

Great Barrier Television Corporation manufactures TV sets in Australia, largely for the domestic market. The company has recently implemented a kaizen costing program, with the goal of reducing the manufacturing cost per television set by 10 percent during 19x9, the first year of the kaizen effort. The cost per TV set at the end of 19x8 was $500. The following table shows the average cost per television set estimated during each month of 19x9.

Month	Cost per Set	Month	Cost per Set
January	$500	July	$485
February	500	August	470
March	495	September	460
April	492	October	460
May	490	November	450
June	485	December	440

Required:

Prepare a kaizen costing chart for 19x9 to show the results of Great Barrier Television Corporation's first year of kaizen costing. In developing the chart, use the following steps.

1. Draw and label the axes of the kaizen costing chart.
2. Indicate the current year cost base and the kaizen goal (cost reduction rate) on the chart.
3. Label the horizontal axis with the months of 19x9. Label the vertical axis with dollar amounts in the appropriate range.
4. Plot the 12 monthly estimates of the average cost per TV set. Then draw a line connecting the cost points that were plotted.
5. Complete the chart with any further labeling necessary.
6. Briefly explain the purpose of kaizen costing. How could a continuous quality-improvement program, coupled with the kaizen costing effort implemented by Great Barrier Television Corporation, help the firm begin competing in the worldwide market?

Cases

■ **Case 6–56**
Using an Activity-Based
Costing System to Modify
Behavior[28]
(LO 3, LO 4, LO 8, LO 9)

The Medical Instruments Division of Lifeline Corporation manufactures a variety of electronic medical equipment. The principal product of the Medical Instruments Division is a sophisticated instrument for measuring and graphically displaying a variety of medical phenomena, such as heart and respiration rates. The culture throughout the division was primarily engineering-oriented. One result of this culture was that the company's design engineers generally designed new products from scratch, rather than relying on modification of a current design. While this approach usually resulted in an "elegant" design from an engineering standpoint, it often resulted in the use of new or unique parts that were not already being used in the company's other products. The strategy of the Medical Instruments Division's management was to position the division as a product differentiator and price leader, not as the industry's low-cost producer. This means that the division generally led the medical instruments market with new products that exhibited greater functionality than competing products and that the products were priced at a premium. The company's competitors then would emulate a new product, produce it at a lower cost, and undercut the Lifeline price. However, by then Lifeline had moved on to a new product with even greater functionality. This strategy had been quite successful until the Japanese entered the medical instruments market in a major way. Lifeline's new competitors were able to set product prices some 25 percent below those of Lifeline, while maintaining close to the same level of functionality. In order to compete, the Medical Instruments Division had to lower its prices below its reported product costs. This resulted in significant losses for the division.

To remedy the situation, the Medical Instruments Division's management began an extensive continuous improvement program. The division changed its production and inventory management system

---

[28]This case draws on a scenario described in the following sources: Peter B. B. Turney, *Common Cents: The ABC Performance Breakthrough* (Hillsboro, Oregon: Cost Technology, 1991), pp. 34, 106, 139, 150, 156, 164, 182, 213, 214, 217, and 220; and Peter B. B. Turney and Bruce Anderson, "Accounting for Continuous Improvement," *Sloan Management Review* 30, no. 2, pp. 37–48.

to a JIT system, ideas of total quality control were aggressively pursued, and management attempted to develop an empowered workforce. All of these efforts paid off dramatically. However, production costs were still relatively high for the industry, and cycle times were considered too long by management. The general feeling was that in order to remain competitive in the long run, the division would have to further lower its production costs and shorten its production cycle times. As management contemplated the high production costs, one problem that kept coming up was the division's part number proliferation. As the engineering-dominated company continued to introduce new products, the number of different parts and components that had to be stocked in inventory continued to increase. Some members of management felt that the division's cost-reduction goals could be achieved (at least partially) by solving the problem of part number proliferation.

As management was pondering the division's cost-reduction goal, the controller was contemplating the introduction of a new cost-accounting system. The controller was thinking about introducing activity-based costing and activity-based management in the Medical Instruments Division.

Required:

1. Explain why the problem of part number proliferation could increase the division's production costs.
2. Explain how long production cycle times could increase the division's production costs.
3. How could an ABC system be used to help reduce costs by attacking the problem of part number proliferation? Allow yourself to contemplate an entirely new role for ABC that is quite different from the objective of more accurate product costs. The following specific questions may help in completing this requirement.
   a. What is the division's strategy in the marketplace?
   b. How are prices currently being determined?
   c. Does management really need more accurate product costs, given its strategy and the reality of market-driven prices?
   d. What is the current goal of management?
   e. What is (at least partially) to blame for high production costs?
   f. Who is (at least partially) to blame for high production costs?
   g. How could an ABC system help solve the problem and reduce production costs?
4. Following up your answer to requirement (3), what cost drivers could be employed to help solve the problem of part number proliferation? Which cost driver would work best? Explain.
5. How could an ABC system help highlight and solve the problem of production cycle times that are too long?
6. As succinctly as you can, state how the fundamental role of the ABC system differs here from the role described in the Aerotech illustration used in Chapters 5 and 6.

A discussion of Toyota's target costing and kaizen costing efforts was included in the chapter. Toyota relies heavily on these cost management tools to maintain a competitive edge worldwide in the production and sale of automobiles. The diagram presented on the next page depicts the various steps in Toyota's typical schedule for automobile development and production.[29]

Toyota has two different categories of automobile design efforts: new models and redesign of existing models. This case focuses on the redesign of existing vehicle models. Typically, vehicle models undergo a full redesign approximately every four years. The headings on the left-hand side of the diagram categorize the types of activities involved in a model redesign (e.g., design and test model production). Notice that one of these major activities is *costing*. Moving to the right across the diagram from one of these major headings, we see displayed the various steps in that activity classification and when these steps occur. For example, the development of an *equipment investment plan* falls under the general heading of *production preparations*, and the investment plan is developed 30 months prior to the beginning of mass production on the new vehicle model. As the diagram shows, the entire process of vehicle model redesign begins a full three years before the start of mass production. The first step is the preparation of a *development proposal*. The proposal typically includes the following:

■ **Case 6–57**
Target Costing at Toyota
(LO 5, LO 6)

[29]Takeo Tanaka, "Target Costing at Toyota," *Journal of Cost Management* 7, no. 1, p. 5.

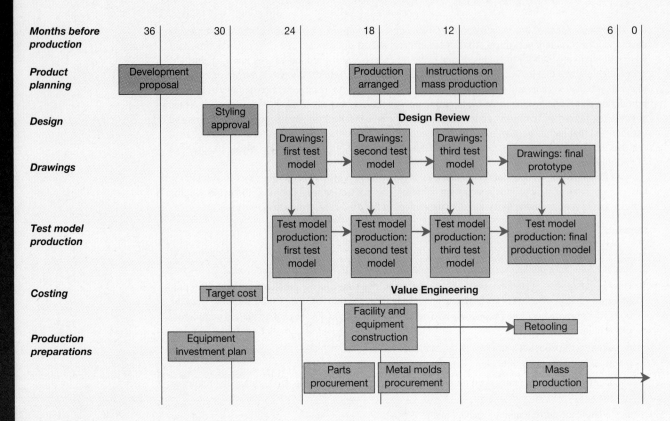

- Vehicle specifications, including overall dimensions, weight, engine type and size, transmission, chassis, and body components.
- A development budget.
- A development schedule.
- Target retail price and sales volume target.[30]

The establishment of the *target retail price* is the first formal step in the target costing process. "Retail prices and sales targets are usually proposed by the sales divisions. A principle used in setting the retail price is that the price remains the same if there is no change from the previous model in function or value to the driver. Ideally, therefore, prices change in accordance with changes in product value. Increases in retail price are decided by market recognition of additional value from new functions (e.g., when four-wheel steering and active suspension were introduced in the Celica model). In short, the price comes first."[31]

Required:

1. As the preceding quote suggests, *price comes first* in Toyota's target costing process. After the appropriate target retail price has been set in accordance with the new vehicle model's performance characteristics, what must be determined next from a target costing perspective?
2. What issues should be considered in determining the target profit on a new vehicle model?
3. After the target retail price and target profit have been determined, what happens next in the target costing process?
4. Referring to the diagram, discuss the role of value engineering in Toyota's target costing process. To which other steps depicted in the diagram would the value-engineering concept be related? Explain.
5. Suppose after giving it their best shot, the value-engineering team is unable to get the projected new vehicle model's cost down to the target cost. What can the company do now?

---

[30]Ibid., p. 5.

[31]Ibid., p. 6.

Current Issues in Managerial Accounting

"ABM," *Management Accounting,* **March 1997.**

Overview

This article describes how a regional bank holding company implemented an ABM program.

Suggested Discussion Questions

Discuss the differences between the use of ABC in manufacturing versus banking. List the activities, costs, and revenues associated with issuing a loan. What are the critical elements that determine profit? How could benchmarking be used in this setting?

"ABM at Lawson: Beyond the Technology," *Management Accounting,* **March 1997.**

Overview

This article outlines how ABC and ABM were implemented at a software company.

Suggested Discussion Questions

As a group, develop a plan for implementing an ABC/ABM system for a software company. Should ABC and ABM be used in this setting? What major problems does your team expect to encounter?

"O.K., He Cut Costs. Now Can He Sell Newspapers?" *Business Week,* **July 28, 1997.**

Overview

After CEO Mark Willes cut 10 percent of Time Mirror's (TM) workforce, TM's stock price more than doubled. Willes is currently focusing on sales growth, newsprint cost stabilization, and online service development.

Suggested Discussion Questions

As a group, write a memo to Times Mirror's board that explains how the firm should use activity-based management (ABM) to increase sales, control newspaper print costs, and provide online services. Include in your memo a discussion of how the 10 percent labor reduction could impact the firm's objectives.

"Going for Growth: Many Firms See Gains of Cost-Cutting Over, Push to Lift Revenues," *The Wall Street Journal,* **July 5, 1996.**

Overview

Cost-cutting, also known as reengineering, downsizing, dumbsizing, or rightsizing, may hinder revenue growth. Some companies that became lean through re-engineering programs are now learning how difficult it is to grow.

Suggested Discussion Questions

List five problems cost-cutting firms may face when they attempt to grow. Discuss how corporate culture must change in this period of growth. What is the effect of global competition on a firm's ability to grow?

"Behind the New Deal Mania," *Business Week,* **November 3, 1997.**

Overview

This article describes the following recent mergers: Starwood Lodging Trust and ITT, and Home Shopping Network and Seagram.

Suggested Discussion Questions

According to the article, firms are merging for growth, not to cut costs. In terms of activity-based management (ABM), how can consolidation facilitate growth? For each of the aforementioned mergers, discuss how the merger will alter internal business processes and facilitate growth.

"Next Big Thing: Re-Engineering Gurus Take Steps to Remodel Their Stalling Vehicles," *The Wall Street Journal,* **November 26, 1996.**

Overview

Firms that have re-engineered and cut costs are now facing a dilemma: they are experiencing difficulty growing.

Suggested Discussion Questions

Write a memo that describes the problems that might be encountered when streamlined cross-functional teams are asked to increase the firm's market share. Provide a proposal that would help solve these problems.

■ **Issue 6–58**
Two-Dimensional ABC and Activity-Based Management; Benchmarking

■ **Issue 6–59**
Keys to Successfully Implementing ABC and ABM

■ **Issue 6–60**
Two-Dimensional ABC and Activity-Based Management

■ **Issue 6–61**
Two-Dimensional ABC and Activity-Based Management

■ **Issue 6–62**
Two-Dimensional ABC and Activity-Based Management

■ **Issue 6–63**
Two-Dimensional ABC and Activity-Based Management

Chapter Seven

Activity Analysis, Cost Behavior, and Cost Estimation

After completing this chapter, you should be able to:

1. Explain the relationships between cost estimation, cost behavior, and cost prediction.

2. Define and describe the behavior of the following types of costs: variable, step-variable, fixed, step-fixed, semivariable (or mixed), and curvilinear.

3. Explain the importance of the relevant range in using a cost behavior pattern for cost prediction.

4. Define and give examples of engineered costs, committed costs, and discretionary costs.

5. Describe and use the following cost-estimation methods: account classification, visual fit, high-low, and least-squares regression.

6. Describe the multiple regression, engineering, work-measurement, and learning-curve approaches to cost estimation.

7. Describe some problems often encountered in collecting data for cost estimation.

TASTY DONUTS TAKES A BIG BITE OUT OF THE DONUT BUSINESS

Toronto, Ontario—Tasty Donuts, Inc. has announced that it will soon open two new donut shops. One shop will be located near the entrance to Ontario Place, a popular tourist attraction on Toronto's waterfront. The second shop will be located near the stadium. "We want to be in position to catch the crowds attending the Blue Jays games," said Will Andrews, company president. "These two new shops will be our 11th and 12th. I'm very pleased with the way the business is growing."

Andrews should be pleased. He started the company a short seven years ago after graduating from college with a degree in hospitality management. A native of Toronto, Andrews says he had his sights set on a restaurant chain from the beginning. "My parents were in the restaurant business, so I sort of grew up with it," said Andrews. "I knew the operational side pretty well from working in my parents' restaurant, so I concentrated on learning the financial and managerial aspects when I was in college." Andrews went on to explain that he started the business by getting what he termed "a hefty bank loan," and then buying two run-down donut shops in the suburbs.

"Now we have 10 restaurants, and we do all of the production of donuts and baked goods in our central bakery. We figured out early on that we could produce donuts centrally and transport them to the shops at a lower cost than we could produce goods in each shop. That was not obvious at first, though, and it took some careful cost analysis to reach that conclusion. We had to project how our costs would behave as we expanded the business over time. When you sell twice as many donuts, some costs, like ingredients for example, will pretty much double. But other costs, like property taxes and depreciation on the bakery building, stay more or less flat. It's tricky, projecting costs, but it's important to do it well if you're trying to stay profitable while growing your business."

Andrews sees a bright future for Tasty Donuts. "Toronto's a wonderful city, and the tourist trade is growing every year. We get a lot of people coming up from the states, as well as our own people from Ontario and Quebec. I'm hoping to have 20 restaurants and two bakeries within five more years. Then we're probably going to go after the pizza business."

Managers in almost any organization want to know how costs will be affected by changes in the organization's activity. The relationship between cost and activity, called **cost behavior**, is relevant to the management functions of planning, control, and decision making. In order to *plan* operations and prepare a budget, managers at Nabisco need to predict the costs that will be incurred at different levels of production and sales. To *control* the costs of providing commercial-loan services at Chase Manhattan Bank, executives need to have a feel for the costs that the bank should incur at various levels of commercial-loan activity. In *deciding* whether to add a new intensive care unit, a hospital's administrators need to predict the cost of operating the new unit at various levels of patient demand. In each of these situations, knowledge of *cost behavior* will help the manager to make the desired cost prediction. A **cost prediction** is a forecast of cost at a particular level of activity. In the first half of this chapter, we will study cost behavior patterns and their use in making cost predictions.

Cost behavior is the relationship between cost and activity.

A **cost prediction** is a forecast at a particular level of activity.

Cost estimation is the process of determining how a particular cost behaves.

LO 1   Explain the relationships between cost estimation, cost behavior, and cost prediction.

How does a managerial accountant determine the cost behavior pattern for a particular cost item? The determination of cost behavior, which is often called **cost estimation**, can be accomplished in a number of ways. One way is to analyze historical data concerning costs and activity levels. Cost estimation is covered in the second half of this chapter.

The following diagram summarizes the key points in the preceding discussion.

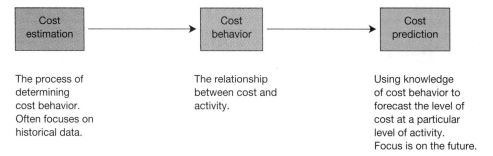

| Cost estimation | Cost behavior | Cost prediction |

The process of determining cost behavior. Often focuses on historical data.

The relationship between cost and activity.

Using knowledge of cost behavior to forecast the level of cost at a particular level of activity. Focus is on the future.

Cost Behavior Patterns

Our discussion of cost behavior patterns, also called *cost functions*, will be set in the context of a restaurant business. Tasty Donuts, Inc. operates a chain of 10 donut shops in the city of Toronto, Ontario. Each shop sells a variety of donuts, muffins, and sweet rolls as well as various beverages. Beverages, such as coffee and fruit juices, are prepared in each donut shop, but all of the company's donuts and baked products are made in a centrally located bakery. The company leases several small delivery trucks to transport the bakery items to its restaurants. Use of a central bakery is more cost-efficient. Moreover, this approach allows the firm to smooth out fluctuations in demand for each type of product. For example, the

Among the costs incurred to produce these donuts are the ingredients (direct material); the wages of the kitchen employees (direct labor); and the facilities, including the building, cooking equipment, and utilities (overhead).

demand for glazed donuts may change from day to day in each donut shop, but these fluctuations tend to cancel each other out when the total demand is aggregated across all 10 shops.

The corporate controller for Tasty Donuts has recently completed a study of the company's cost behavior to use in preparing the firm's budget for the coming year. The controller studied the following costs.

Direct material: ingredients for donuts, muffins, and sweet rolls; beverages; paper products, such as napkins and disposable cups

Direct labor: wages and fringe benefits of bakers, restaurant sales personnel, and delivery-truck drivers

Overhead:

Facilities costs: property taxes; depreciation on bakery building, donut shops, and equipment; salaries and fringe benefits of maintenance personnel

Indirect labor: salaries and fringe benefits of managers and assistant managers for bakery and restaurants

Delivery trucks: rental payments under lease contract; costs of gasoline, oil, tires, and maintenance

Utilities: electricity, telephone, and trash collection

In studying the behavior of each of these costs, the controller measured company *activity* in terms of *dozens of bakery items sold.* Thus, dozens of bakery items sold is the *cost driver* for each of the costs studied. A bakery item is one donut, muffin, or sweet roll. The costs to make each of these products are nearly identical. The number of bakery items sold each day is roughly the same as the number produced, since bakery goods are produced to keep pace with demand as reported by the company's restaurant managers.

Variable Costs

Variable costs were discussed briefly in Chapter 2. We will summarize that discussion here in the context of the Tasty Donuts illustration. A **variable cost** changes *in total* in direct proportion to a change in the activity level (or cost driver). Tasty Donuts' direct-material cost is a variable cost. As the company sells more donuts, muffins, and sweet rolls, the total cost of the ingredients for these goods increases in direct proportion to the number of items sold. Moreover, the quantities of beverages sold and paper products used by customers also increase in direct proportion to the number of bakery items sold. As a result, the costs of beverages and paper products are also variable costs.

> **LO 2**   Define and describe the behavior of the following types of costs: variable, step-variable, fixed, step-fixed, semi-variable (or mixed), and curvilinear.

> A **variable cost** changes in total in direct proportion to a change in an organization's activity.

Panel A of Exhibit 7–1 displays a graph of Tasty Donuts' direct-material cost. As the graph shows, *total* variable cost increases in proportion to the activity level (or cost driver). When activity triples, for example, from 50,000 dozen items to 150,000 dozen items, total direct-material costs triple, from $55,000 to $165,000. However, the variable cost *per unit* remains the same as activity changes. The total direct-material cost incurred *per dozen* items sold is constant at $1.10 per dozen. The table in panel B of Exhibit 7–1 illustrates this point. The variable cost per unit also is represented in the graph in panel A of Exhibit 7–1 as the slope of the cost line.

To summarize, as activity changes, total variable cost increases in direct proportion to the change in activity level, but the variable cost per unit remains constant.

Step-Variable Costs

Some costs are nearly variable, but they increase in small steps instead of continuously. Such costs, called **step-variable costs,** usually include inputs that are purchased and

> A **step-variable cost** is nearly variable, but increases in small steps instead of continuously.

Exhibit 7–1

Variable Cost: Direct-Material
Cost, Tasty Donuts, Inc.

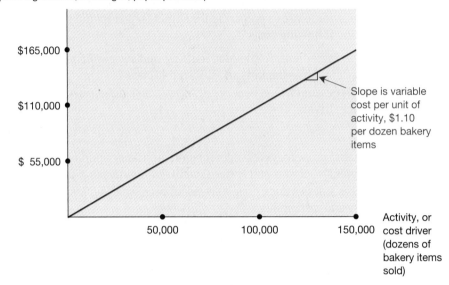

A. Graph of Total Direct-Material Cost

Total direct-material cost
(food ingredients, beverages, paper products)

$165,000

$110,000

$ 55,000

Slope is variable
cost per unit of
activity, $1.10
per dozen bakery
items

50,000   100,000   150,000

Activity, or
cost driver
(dozens of
bakery items
sold)

B. Tabulation of Direct-Material Cost

Activity (or cost driver)	Direct-Material Cost per Dozen Bakery Items Sold	Total Direct-Material Cost
50,000	$1.10	$ 55,000
100,000	1.10	110,000
150,000	1.10	165,000

used in relatively small increments. At Tasty Donuts, Inc. the direct-labor cost of bakers, restaurant counter-service personnel, and delivery-truck drivers is a step-variable cost. Many of these employees are part-time workers, called upon for relatively small increments of time, such as a few hours. On a typical day, for example, Tasty Donuts may have 35 employees at work in the bakery and the donut shops. If activity increases slightly, these employees can handle the extra work. However, if activity increases substantially, the bakery manager or various restaurant managers may call on additional help. Exhibit 7–2, a graph of Tasty Donuts' monthly direct-labor cost, shows that this cost remains constant within an activity range of about 5,000 dozen bakery items per month. When monthly activity increases beyond this narrow range, direct-labor costs increase.

Approximating a Step-Variable Cost   If the steps in a step-variable cost behavior pattern are small, the step-variable cost function may be approximated by a variable cost function without much loss in accuracy. Exhibit 7–3 shows such an approximation for Tasty Donuts' direct-labor cost.

Fixed Costs

A **fixed cost** does not change in total as activity changes.

Fixed costs were covered briefly in Chapter 2. We will summarize that discussion here, using the Tasty Donuts illustration. A **fixed cost** remains unchanged *in total* as the activity level (or cost driver) varies. Facilities costs, which include property taxes, depreciation on buildings and equipment, and the salaries of maintenance personnel, are fixed costs for Tasty Donuts, Inc. These fixed costs are graphed in panel A of Exhibit 7–4. This graph shows that the *total* monthly cost of property taxes, depreci-

Total direct-labor cost
(wages and fringe benefits of bakers, sales personnel,
and delivery-truck drivers)

Exhibit 7–2

Step-Variable Cost: Direct-
Labor Cost, Tasty Donuts, Inc.

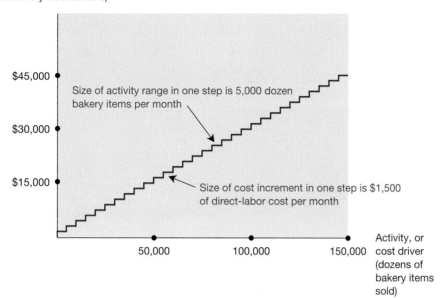

Total direct-labor cost
(wages and fringe benefits of bakers, sales personnel, and
delivery-truck drivers)

Exhibit 7–3

Approximating a Step-
Variable Cost, Tasty
Donuts, Inc.

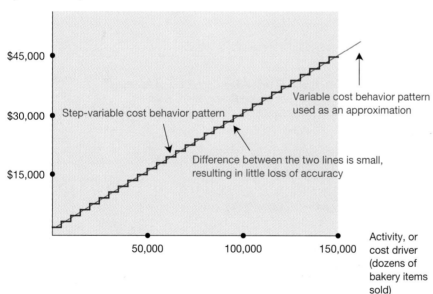

ation, and maintenance personnel is $200,000 regardless of how many dozen bakery items are produced and sold during the month.

The fixed cost *per unit* does change as activity varies. Exhibit 7–4 (panel B) shows that the company's facilities cost per dozen bakery items is $4.00 when 50,000 dozen items are produced and sold. However, this unit cost declines to $2.00 when 100,000 dozen items are produced and sold. If activity increases to 150,000 dozen items, unit fixed cost will decline further, to about $1.33.

A graph provides another way of viewing the change in unit fixed cost as activity changes. Panel C of Exhibit 7–4 displays a graph of Tasty Donuts' cost of property

Exhibit 7–4

Fixed Cost: Facilities Costs, Tasty Donuts, Inc.

A. Graph of Total Monthly Fixed Costs: Facilities Costs

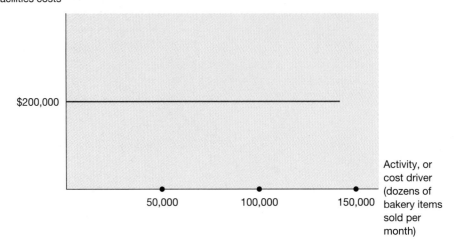

Total monthly fixed costs: facilities costs

$200,000

Activity, or cost driver (dozens of bakery items sold per month)

50,000　　100,000　　150,000

B. Tabulation of Monthly Fixed Costs: Facilities Costs

Activity (or cost driver)	Cost of Facilities per Dozen Bakery Items Sold	Total Monthly Cost of Facilities
50,000	$4.00	$200,000
100,000	2.00	200,000
150,000	1.33*	200,000

* Rounded.

C. Graph of Unit Fixed Cost: Cost of Facilities per Dozen Bakery Items Sold

Unit fixed cost: facilities costs

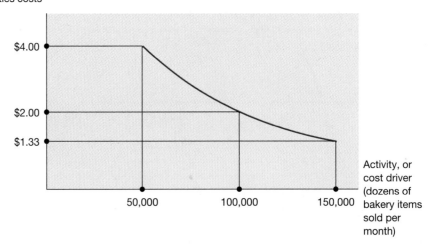

$4.00

$2.00

$1.33

Activity, or cost driver (dozens of bakery items sold per month)

50,000　　100,000　　150,000

taxes, depreciation, and maintenance personnel *per dozen bakery items*. As the graph shows, the fixed cost per dozen bakery items declines steadily as activity increases.

To summarize, as the activity level increases, total fixed cost does not change, but unit fixed cost declines. For this reason, it is preferable in any cost analysis to work with total fixed cost rather than fixed cost per unit.

Step-Fixed Costs

Some costs remain fixed over a wide range of activity but jump to a different amount for activity levels outside that range. Such costs are called **step-fixed costs**. Tasty Donuts' cost of indirect labor is a step-fixed cost. Indirect-labor cost consists of the salaries and fringe benefits for the managers and assistant managers of the company's bakery and restaurants. Tasty Donuts' monthly indirect-labor cost is graphed in Exhibit 7–5.

As Exhibit 7–5 shows, for activity in the range of 50,000 to 100,000 dozen bakery items per month, Tasty Donuts' monthly indirect-labor cost is $35,000. For this range of activity, the company employs a full-time manager and a full-time assistant manager in the bakery and in each restaurant. When monthly activity exceeds this range during the summer tourist season, the company employs additional part-time assistant managers in the bakery and in its busiest donut shops. The company hires college students who are majoring in restaurant administration for these summer positions. Their salaries boost the monthly indirect-labor cost to $45,000. Tasty Donuts has not experienced demand of less than 50,000 dozen bakery items per month. However, the controller anticipates that if such a decrease in demand were to occur, the company would reduce the daily operating hours for its donut shops. This would allow the firm to operate each restaurant with only a full-time manager and no assistant manager. As the graph in Exhibit 7–5 indicates, such a decrease in managerial personnel would reduce monthly indirect-labor cost to $25,000.

A **step-fixed cost** remains fixed over wide ranges of activity, but jumps to a different amount for activity levels outside that range.

Semivariable Cost

A **semivariable** (or **mixed**) **cost** has both a fixed and a variable component. The cost of operating delivery trucks is a semivariable cost for Tasty Donuts, Inc. These costs are graphed in Exhibit 7–6. As the graph shows, the company's delivery-truck costs have two components. The fixed-cost component is $3,000 per month, which is the monthly rental payment paid under the lease contract for the delivery trucks. The monthly rental payment is constant, regardless of the level of activity (or cost driver). The variable-cost component consists of the costs of gasoline, oil, routine maintenance, and tires. These costs vary with activity, since greater activity levels result in more deliveries. The distance between the fixed-cost line (dashed line) and the total-cost line in Exhibit 7–6 is the amount of variable cost. For example, at an activity level of 100,000 dozen bakery items, the total variable-cost component is $10,000.

The slope of the total-cost line is the variable cost per unit of activity. For Tasty Donuts, the variable cost of operating its delivery trucks is $.10 per dozen bakery items sold.

A **semivariable** (or **mixed**) **cost** has both a fixed and a variable component.

Curvilinear Cost

The graphs of all of the cost behavior patterns examined so far consist of either straight lines or several straight-line sections. A **curvilinear cost** behavior pattern has a curved graph. Tasty Donuts' utilities cost, depicted as the *solid curve* in Exhibit 7–7, is a curvilinear cost. For low levels of activity, this cost exhibits *decreasing marginal costs*. As the discussion in Chapter 2 indicated, a marginal cost is the cost of producing the next unit, in this case the next dozen bakery items. As the graph in Exhibit 7–7 shows, the marginal utilities cost of producing the next dozen bakery items declines as activity increases in the range zero to 100,000 dozen items per month. For activity greater than 100,000 dozen bakery items per month, the graph in Exhibit 7–7 exhibits *increasing marginal costs*.

Tasty Donuts' utilities cost includes electricity, telephone, and trash-collection costs. The utilities cost is curvilinear as a result of the company's pattern of electricity usage in the bakery. If the demand in a particular month is less than 100,000 dozen bakery items, the goods can be produced entirely in the modernized section of the

A **curvilinear cost** has a curved line for its graph.

Exhibit 7–5

Step-Fixed Cost: Indirect-
Labor Cost, Tasty Donuts, Inc.

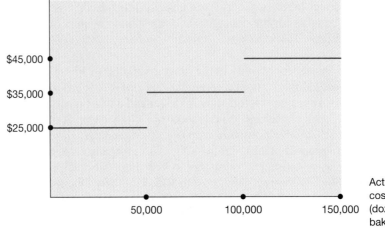

Total indirect-labor cost
(salaries and fringe benefits of bakery and restaurant
management personnel)

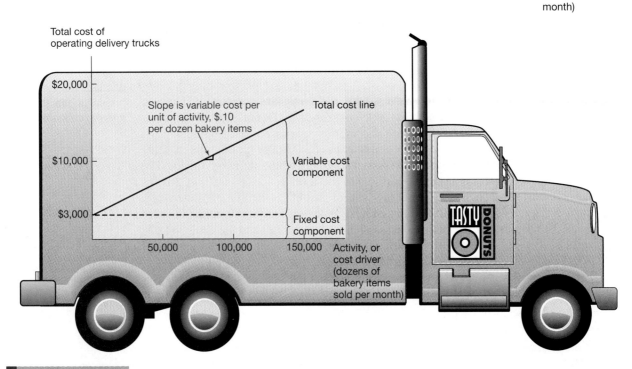

Exhibit 7–6

Semivariable Cost: Cost of
Operating Delivery Trucks,
Tasty Donuts, Inc.

bakery. This section uses recently purchased deep-fat fryers and ovens that are very energy-efficient. As long as the bakery operates only the modernized section, the utilities cost per dozen items declines as production increases.

During the summer tourist months, when Tasty Donuts' sales exceed 100,000 dozen items per month, the older section of the bakery also must be used. This section uses much older cooking equipment that is less energy-efficient. As a result, the marginal utilities cost per dozen bakery items rises as monthly activity increases in the range above 100,000 dozen items per month.

LO 3   Explain the importance of the relevant range in using a cost behavior pattern for cost prediction.

Relevant Range   The cost behavior graphed in Exhibit 7–7 is very different at low activity levels (below 50,000) than it is at high activity levels (above 125,000). However, management need not concern itself with these extreme

Total monthly cost of utilities

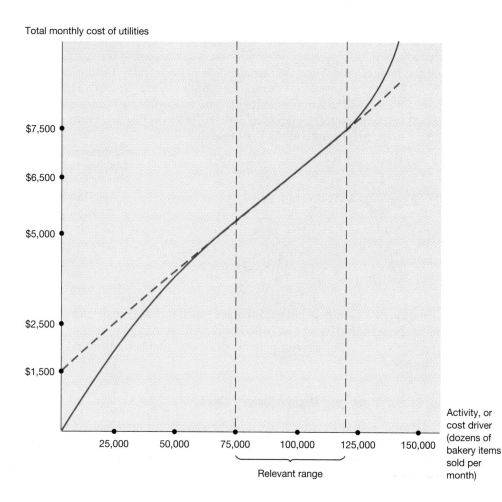

levels of activity if it is unlikely that Tasty Donuts, Inc. will operate at those activity levels. Management is interested in cost behavior within the company's **relevant range**, the range of activity within which management expects the company to operate. Tasty Donuts' management believes the firm's relevant range to be 75,000 to 120,000 dozen bakery items per month. Based on past experience and sales projections, management does not expect the firm to operate outside that range of monthly activity. Tasty Donuts' relevant range is shown in Exhibit 7–7 as the section of the graph between the dashed lines.

A **relevant range** is the range of activity within which management expects the organization to operate.

Approximating a Curvilinear Cost within the Relevant Range

The straight, dashed line in Exhibit 7–7 may be used to approximate Tasty Donuts' utilities cost. Notice that the approximation is quite accurate for activity levels within the relevant range. However, as the activity level gets further away from the boundary of the relevant range, the approximation declines in accuracy. For monthly activity levels of 25,000 or 150,000, for example, the approximation is very poor.

The straight, dashed line used to approximate Tasty Donuts' utilities cost *within the relevant range* represents a semivariable cost behavior pattern. This straight-line graph has a slope of $.05, which represents a unit variable-cost component of $.05 per dozen bakery items. The line intersects the vertical axis of the graph at $1,500, which represents a fixed-cost component of $1,500 per month. Managerial accountants often use a semivariable-cost behavior pattern to approximate a curvilinear cost. However, it is important to limit this approximation to the range of activity in which its accuracy is acceptable.

Using Cost Behavior Patterns to Predict Costs

How can Tasty Donuts' corporate controller use the cost behavior patterns identified in the cost study to help in the budgeting process? First, a sales forecast is made for each month during the budget year. Suppose management expects Tasty Donuts' activity level to be 110,000 dozen bakery items during the month of June. Second, a *cost prediction* is made for each of the firm's cost items. The following cost predictions are based on the cost behavior patterns discussed earlier. (Try to verify these cost predictions by referring to the graphs in Exhibits 7–1 through 7–7.)

Cost Item	Cost Prediction for June (110,000 dozen bakery items per month)
Direct material	$121,000
Direct labor	33,000
Overhead:	
Facilities costs	200,000
Indirect labor	45,000
Delivery trucks	14,000
Utilities	7,000

The preparation of a complete budget involves much more analysis and detailed planning than is shown here.[1] The point is that cost prediction is an important part of the planning process. The cost behavior patterns discussed in this chapter make those cost predictions possible.

Engineered, Committed, and Discretionary Costs

LO 4 Define and give examples of engineered costs, committed costs, and discretionary costs.

In the process of budgeting costs, it is often useful for management to make a distinction between engineered, committed, and discretionary costs. An **engineered cost** bears a definitive physical relationship to the activity measure. Tasty Donuts' direct-material cost is an engineered cost. It is impossible to produce more donuts without incurring greater material cost for food ingredients.

An **engineered cost** results from a definitive physical relationship with the activity measure.

A **committed cost** results from an organization's ownership or use of facilities and its basic organization structure.

A **discretionary cost** results from a discretionary management decision to spend a particular amount of money.

A **committed cost** results from an organization's ownership or use of facilities and its basic organization structure. Property taxes, depreciation on buildings and equipment, costs of renting facilities or equipment, and the salaries of management personnel are examples of committed fixed costs. Tasty Donuts' facilities cost is a committed fixed cost.

A **discretionary cost** arises as a result of a *management decision* to spend a particular amount of money for some purpose. Examples of discretionary costs include amounts spent on research and development, advertising and promotion, management development programs, and contributions to charitable organizations. For example, suppose Tasty Donuts' management has decided to spend $12,400 each month on promotion and advertising.

The distinction between committed and discretionary costs is an important one. Management can change committed costs only through relatively major decisions that have long-term implications. Decisions to build a new production facility, lease a fleet of vehicles, or add more management personnel to oversee a new division are examples of such decisions. These decisions will generally influence costs incurred over a long period of time. In contrast, discretionary costs can be changed in the short run much more easily. Management can be flexible about expenditures for advertising, promotion, employee training, or research and development. This does not imply that such programs are unimportant, but simply that management can alter them over time. For example, the management of a manufacturing firm may decide to spend $100,000

---

[1]The budgeting process is covered in Chapter 9.

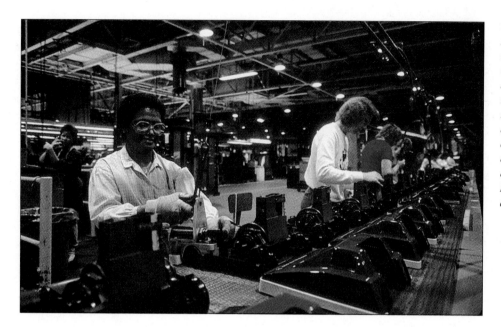

The raw material in these Hoover vacuum cleaners represents an engineered cost. In contrast, the depreciation and property taxes on this manufacturing facility are examples of committed costs. Expenditures on employee development or retraining for these Hoover assembly workers are discretionary costs.

on research and development in the current year, but cut back to $60,000 in the next year because of an anticipated economic downturn.

Whether a particular type of cost is committed or discretionary sometimes differs between organizations. For example, one company's board of directors may view the salaries of top management as a committed cost. Even in an economic downturn, it is important for a firm to keep its basic organization structure intact and retain its key executives. In contrast, the tradition in another firm might be to ask its top-management personnel to accept a salary cut during difficult economic times, in order to cut expenses and set an example for other employees.

Shifting Cost Structure in the New Manufacturing Environment

Fixed costs are becoming more prevalent in many industries. This is due to two factors. First, automation is replacing labor to an increasing extent. Second, labor unions have been increasingly successful in negotiating agreements that result in a relatively stable workforce. This makes management less flexible in adjusting a firm's workforce to the desired level of production.

In the advanced manufacturing environment that is emerging, many costs that once were largely variable have become fixed, most becoming *committed* fixed costs. Take the electronics industry, for example. Years ago, small electronic components were placed onto circuit boards, wired, and soldered by hand. Hundreds of employees performed these operations in "white rooms," which are sterile environments, in order to prevent the electronic units from being contaminated with dust or other foreign particles. Now much of the electronic industry is highly automated. Pick-and-place robots and auto-insertion machines place electronic components on circuit boards with incredible speed and precision. Wash and dry machines eliminate any contaminants, and wave-solder machines solder the connections. A large part of the manufacturing process is computerized. In the past, a major portion of the cost of electronics manufacturing was variable. The workforce could be adjusted as the economy grew rapidly or more slowly. In contrast, companies now spend hundreds of millions of dollars on computer-integrated manufacturing (CIM) systems and flexible manufacturing systems (FMS). Much of the manufacturing labor force consists of computer programmers and highly skilled operators of sophisticated production equipment. The depreciation, maintenance, and upgrades for the CIM systems constitute very large committed fixed costs. Moreover, the compensation costs for the highly skilled

In merchandising firms, the primary cost driver usually is sales revenue.

computer experts and equipment operators are largely committed fixed costs. Firms often cannot risk losing such highly trained personnel even during an economic downturn. Thus, the shifting cost structure we are observing in today's manufacturing environment has had a major impact on the nature of the cost behavior to be estimated in CIM and FMS settings.

Operations-Based versus Volume-Based Cost Drivers   Much of the discussion of cost behavior in this chapter focuses on production volume as the cost driver. As Chapter 5 pointed out, however, production costs are affected by operations-based cost drivers as well. Product complexity, the configuration of the manufacturing process, and the number of production runs are among the many operational cost drivers that have been identified. In today's highly competitive environment, it is crucial that managers thoroughly understand the effects of both operations-based and volume-based cost drivers on the costs incurred in their organizations. For example, it will cost more to produce 10,000 radios in 10 production runs of 1,000 units than in 4 runs of 2,500 units. Increasing the number of production runs will drive setup costs up, even though the other costs of producing each radio may not vary.

Cost Behavior in Other Industries

We have illustrated a variety of cost behavior patterns for Tasty Donuts' restaurant business. The same cost behavior patterns are used in other industries. The cost behavior pattern appropriate for a particular cost item depends on the organization and the activity base (or cost driver). In manufacturing firms, production quantity, direct-labor hours, and machine hours are common cost drivers. Direct-material and direct-labor costs are usually considered variable costs. Other variable costs include some manufacturing-overhead costs, such as indirect material and indirect labor. Fixed manufacturing costs are generally the costs of creating production capacity. Examples include depreciation on plant and equipment, property taxes, and the plant manager's salary. Such overhead costs as utilities and equipment maintenance are usually semivariable or curvilinear costs. A semivariable-cost behavior pattern is generally used to approximate a curvilinear cost within the relevant range. Supervisory salaries are usually step-fixed costs, since one person can supervise production over a range of activity. When activity increases beyond that range, such as when a new shift is added, an additional supervisor is added.

In merchandising firms, the activity base (or cost driver) is usually sales revenue. The cost of merchandise sold is a variable cost. Most labor costs are fixed or step-fixed costs, since a particular number of sales and stock personnel can generally handle sales activity over a fairly wide range of sales. Store facility costs, such as rent, depreciation on buildings and furnishings, and property taxes, are fixed costs.

In some industries, the choice of the cost driver is not obvious, and the cost behavior pattern can depend on the cost driver selected. In an airline, for instance, the cost driver could be air miles flown, passengers flown, or passenger miles flown. A passenger mile is the transportation of one passenger for one mile. Fuel costs are variable with respect to air miles traveled, but are not necessarily variable with respect to passenger miles flown. An airplane uses more fuel in flying from New York to San Francisco than from New York to Chicago. However, a plane does not require significantly more fuel to fly 200 people from one city to another than to fly 190 people the same distance. In contrast, an airport landing fee is a fixed cost for a particular number of aircraft arrivals, regardless of how far the planes have flown or how many people were transported. The point of this discussion is that both the organization and the cost driver are crucial determinants of the cost behavior for each cost item. Conclusions drawn about cost behavior in one industry are not necessarily transferable to another industry.

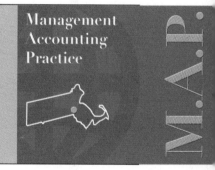

Cost Behavior in a Hospital

The Leonard Morse Hospital in Massachusetts has found that a variety of cost behavior patterns are represented in its labor costs. For example, the cost of compensating anesthesiologists is a step-fixed cost. One anesthesiologist is sufficient for up to 10 operations per day. For 11 or more daily operations, another anesthesiologist is required. In contrast, labor costs in the dietary department are fixed. The hospital has contracted with an outside firm to supply the services of dietitians for a fixed fee.[2]

Management Accounting Practice

Cost Estimation

As the preceding discussion indicates, different costs exhibit a variety of cost behavior patterns. **Cost estimation** is the process of determining how a particular cost behaves. Several methods are commonly used to estimate the relationship between cost and activity. Some of these methods are simple, while some are quite sophisticated. In some firms, managers use more than one method of cost estimation. The results of the different methods are then combined by the cost analyst on the basis of experience and judgment. We will examine five methods of cost estimation in the context of the Tasty Donuts illustration.

> **LO 5** Describe and use the following cost-estimation methods: account classification, visual fit, high-low, and least-squares regression.

> **Cost estimation** is the process of determining how a particular cost behaves.

Account-Classification Method

The **account-classification method** of cost estimation, also called **account analysis**, involves a careful examination of the organization's ledger accounts. The cost analyst classifies each cost item in the ledger as a variable, fixed, or semivariable cost. The classification is based on the analyst's knowledge of the organization's activities and experience with the organization's costs. For example, it may be obvious to the analyst

> The **account-classification method** (also called **account analysis**) involves a careful examination of the ledger accounts for the purpose of classifying each cost as variable, fixed, or semivariable.

[2]S. A. Larracey, "Hospital Planning for Cost Effectiveness," *Management Accounting* 64, no. 1, p. 47.

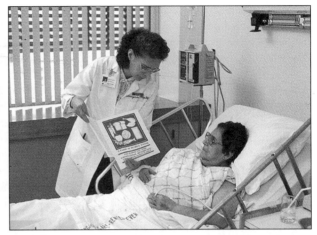

Different types of labor in the same organization can exhibit different cost behavior. The cost of anesthesiology in a hospital, for example, could be a step-fixed cost, while the cost of outsourcing the dietitian's work becomes a fixed cost.

going through the ledger that direct-material cost is variable, building depreciation is fixed, and utility costs are semivariable.

Once the costs have been classified, the cost analyst estimates cost amounts by examining job-cost sheets, paid bills, labor time cards, or other source documents. A property-tax bill, for example, will provide the cost analyst with the information needed to estimate this fixed cost. This examination of historical source documents is combined with other knowledge that may affect costs in the future. For example, the municipal government may have recently enacted a 10 percent property-tax increase, which takes effect the following year.

For some costs, particularly those classified as semivariable, the cost analyst may use one of several more systematic methods of incorporating historical data in the cost estimate. These methods are discussed next.

Visual-Fit Method

The **visual-fit method** of cost estimation draws a cost line through a scatter diagram according to the visual perception of the analyst.

A **scatter diagram** is a set of plotted cost observations at various activity levels.

When a cost has been classified as semivariable, or when the analyst has no clear idea about the behavior of a cost item, it is helpful to use the **visual-fit method** to plot recent observations of the cost at various activity levels. The resulting **scatter diagram** helps the analyst to visualize the relationship between cost and the level of activity (or cost driver). To illustrate, suppose Tasty Donuts' controller has compiled the following historical data for the company's utility costs.

Month	Utility Cost for Month	Activity or Cost Driver (dozens of bakery items sold per month)
January	$5,100	75,000
February	5,300	78,000
March	5,650	80,000
April	6,300	92,000
May	6,400	98,000
June	6,700	108,000
July	7,035	118,000
August	7,000	112,000
September	6,200	95,000
October	6,100	90,000
November	5,600	85,000
December	5,900	90,000

Utilities cost (for one month)

Exhibit 7–8

Scatter Diagram of Cost Data
with Visually Fit Cost Line,
Tasty Donuts, Inc.

The scatter diagram of these data is shown in Exhibit 7–8. The cost analyst can *visually fit a line* to these data by laying a ruler on the plotted points. The line is positioned so that a roughly equal number of plotted points lie above and below the line. Using this method, Tasty Donuts' controller visually fit the line shown in Exhibit 7–8.

Just a glance at the visually fit cost line reveals that Tasty Donuts' utilities cost is a semivariable cost *within the relevant range*. The scatter diagram provides little or no information about the cost relationship outside the relevant range. Recall from the discussion of Tasty Donuts' utilities cost (see Exhibit 7–7) that the controller believes the cost behavior pattern to be curvilinear over the *entire range* of activity. This judgment is based on the controller's knowledge of the firm's facilities and an understanding of electricity usage by the modern bakery equipment and the older bakery equipment. As Exhibit 7–7 shows, however, the curvilinear utilities cost can be approximated closely by a semivariable cost *within the relevant range*. The data plotted in the scatter diagram lie within the relevant range. Consequently, the data provide a sound basis for the semivariable approximation that the controller has chosen to use.

The visually fit cost line in Exhibit 7–8 intercepts the vertical axis at $1,500. Thus, $1,500 is the estimate of the fixed-cost component in the semi-variable-cost approximation. To determine the variable cost per unit, subtract the fixed cost from the total cost at any activity level. The remainder is the total variable cost for that activity level. For example, the total variable cost for an activity level of 50,000 dozen items is $2,500 (total cost of $4,000 minus fixed cost of $1,500). This yields a variable cost of $.05 per dozen bakery items ($.05 = $2,500 ÷ 50,000).

These variable and fixed cost estimates were used for the semivariable-cost approximation discussed earlier in the chapter (Exhibit 7–7). These estimates are valid only *within the relevant range*.

Evaluation of Visual-Fit Method   The scatter diagram and visually fit cost line provide a valuable first step in the analysis of any cost item suspected to be semivariable or curvilinear. The method is easy to use and to explain to others, and it provides a useful view of the overall cost behavior pattern.

The visual-fit method also enables an experienced cost analyst to spot *outliers* in the data. An **outlier** is a data point that falls far away from the other points in the scatter diagram and is not representative of the data. Suppose, for example, that the data point

An **outlier** is a data point that falls far away from the other points in a scatter diagram and is not representative of the data.

for January had been $6,000 for 75,000 units of activity. Exhibit 7–8 reveals that such a data point would be way out of line with the rest of the data. The cost analyst would follow up on such a cost observation to discover the reasons behind it. It could be that the data point is in error. Perhaps a utility bill was misread when the data were compiled, or possibly the billing itself was in error. Another possibility is that the cost observation is correct but due to unusual circumstances. Perhaps Toronto experienced a record cold wave during January that required the company's donut shops to use unusually high amounts of electric heat. Perhaps an oven in the bakery had a broken thermostat during January that caused the oven to overheat consistently until discovered and repaired. An outlier can result from many causes. If the outlier is due to an error or very unusual circumstances, the data point should be ignored in the cost analysis.

The primary drawback of the visual-fit method is its lack of objectivity. Two cost analysts may draw two different visually fit cost lines. This is not usually a serious problem, however, particularly if the visual-fit method is combined with other, more objective methods.

High-Low Method

The **high-low method** is a cost-estimation method in which a cost line is fit using exactly two data points—the high and low activity levels.

In the **high-low method** the semivariable-cost approximation is computed using exactly two data points. The high and low *activity levels* are chosen from the available data set. These activity levels, together with their associated cost levels, are used to compute the variable and fixed cost components as follows:

$$\text{Variable cost per dozen bakery items} = \frac{\text{Difference between the costs corresponding to the highest and lowest activity levels}}{\text{Difference between the highest and lowest activity levels}}$$

$$= \frac{\$7,035 - \$5,100}{118,000 - 75,000} = \frac{\$1,935}{43,000}$$

$$= \$.045 \text{ per dozen items}$$

Now we can compute the total variable cost at either the high or low activity level. At the low activity of 75,000 dozen items, the total variable cost is $3,375 ($.045 × 75,000). Subtracting the total variable cost from the total cost at the 75,000 dozen activity level, we obtain the fixed-cost estimate of $1,725 ($5,100 – $3,375). Notice that the high and low *activity* levels are used to choose the two data points. In general, these two points need not necessarily coincide with the high and low cost levels in the data set.

Exhibit 7–9 presents a graph of Tasty Donuts' utilities cost, which is based on the high-low method of cost estimation. As in any cost-estimation method, this estimate of the cost behavior pattern should be *restricted to the relevant range*.

Evaluation of High-Low Method   The high-low method is more objective than the visual-fit method, since it leaves no room for the cost analyst's judgment. However, the high-low method suffers from a major weakness. Only two data points are used to estimate the cost behavior pattern; the remainder of the data points are ignored. In this regard, the visual-fit method is superior to the high-low method, since the former approach uses all of the available data.

Least-Squares Regression Method

Statistical techniques may be used to estimate objectively a cost behavior pattern using all of the available data. The most common of these methods is called *least-squares*

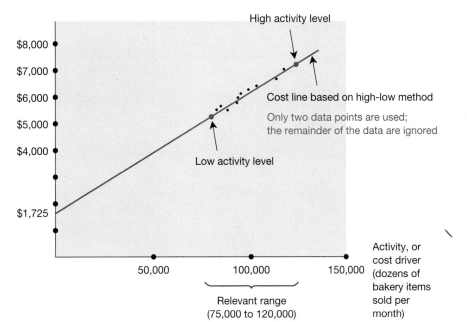

Utilities cost (for one month)

Exhibit 7–9

Graph of Utilities Cost Using High-Low Method, Tasty Donuts, Inc.

regression. To understand this method, examine Exhibit 7–10, which repeats the scatter diagram of Tasty Donuts' utilities cost data. The exhibit also includes a cost line that has been drawn through the plotted data points. Since the data points do not lie along a perfectly straight line, any cost line drawn through this scatter diagram will miss some or most of the data points. The objective is to draw the cost line so as to make the deviations between the cost line and the data points as small as possible.

In the **least-squares regression method**, the cost line is positioned so as to *minimize* the sum of the *squared deviations* between the cost line and the data points. The inset to Exhibit 7–10 depicts this technique graphically. Note that the deviations between the cost line and the data points are measured vertically on the graph rather than perpendicular to the line. The cost line fit to the data using least-squares regression is called a *least-squares regression line* (or simply a **regression line**).

Why is the regression method based on minimizing the *squares* of the deviations between the cost line and the data points? A complete answer to this question lies in the theory of statistics. In short, statistical theorists have proven that a least-squares regression line possesses some very desirable properties for making cost predictions and drawing inferences about the estimated relationship between cost and activity. As always, the least-squares regression estimate of the cost behavior pattern should be restricted to the relevant range.

Equation Form of Least-Squares Regression Line The least-squares regression line shown in Exhibit 7–10 may be represented by the equation of a straight line. In the following equation, X denotes Tasty Donuts' activity level for a month, and Y denotes the estimated utilities cost for that level of activity. The intercept of the line on the vertical axis is denoted by a, and the slope of the line is denoted by b. *Within the relevant range, a* is interpreted as an estimate of the fixed-cost component, and b is interpreted as an estimate of the variable cost per unit of activity.

$$Y = a + bX \tag{1}$$

In regression analysis, X is referred to as the **independent variable**, since it is the variable upon which the estimate is based. Y is called the **dependent variable**, since its estimate depends on the independent variable.

The **least-squares regression method** of cost estimation minimizes the sum of the squared deviations between the cost line and the data points.

The **regression line** is a line fit to a set of data points using least-squares regression.

The **independent variable** is the variable upon which the estimate is based in least-squares regression analysis.

The **dependent variable** is the variable whose value depends on the independent variable.

Utilities cost (for one month)

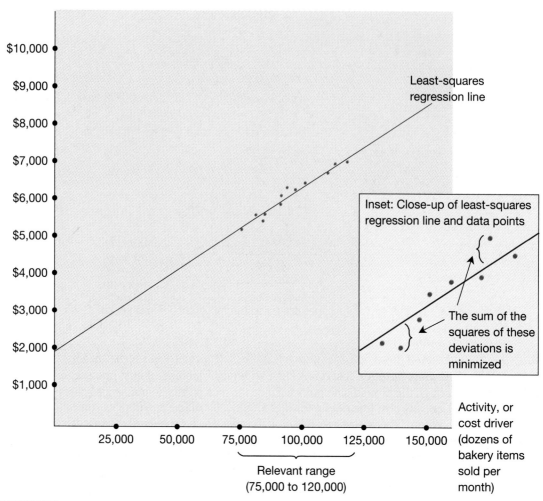

Least-squares
regression line

Inset: Close-up of least-squares
regression line and data points

The sum of the
squares of these
deviations is
minimized

Activity, or
cost driver
(dozens of
bakery items
sold per
month)

Relevant range
(75,000 to 120,000)

Exhibit 7–10

Graph of Utilities Cost Using
Least-Squares Regression
Method, Tasty Donuts, Inc.

   The least-squares regression line for Tasty Donuts' utilities cost is shown below in
equation form.

$$Y \ = \ 1,920 \ + \ .0448X$$

Estimated utilities
cost for one month

Activity level
for one month

Within the relevant range of activity, the regression estimate of the fixed-cost component is $1,920 per month, and the regression estimate of the variable-cost component
is $.0448 per dozen bakery items. These estimates are derived in the appendix at the
end of this chapter, which you may want to read now.

Evaluation of Least-Squares Regression Method   We have seen that least-squares
regression is an objective method of cost estimation that makes use of all available
data. Moreover, the regression line has desirable statistical properties for making cost
predictions and drawing inferences about the relationship between cost and activity.
The method does require considerably more computation than either the visual-fit or
high-low method. However, computer programs are readily available to perform least-
squares regression, even on small desktop computers.

Evaluating a Particular Least-Squares Regression Line   We have seen the benefits of least-squares regression *in general*. How does a cost analyst evaluate a *particular* regression line based on a specific set of data? A number of criteria may be used, including *economic plausibility* and *goodness of fit*.

The cost analyst should always evaluate a regression line from the perspective of *economic plausibility*. Does the regression line make economic sense? Is it intuitively plausible to the cost analyst? If not, the analyst should reconsider using the regression line to make cost predictions. It may be that the chosen independent variable is not a good predictor of the cost behavior being analyzed. Perhaps another independent variable should be considered. Alternatively, there may be errors in the data upon which the regression is based. Rechecking the data will resolve this issue. It could be that fundamental assumptions that underlie the regression method have been violated. In this case, the analyst may have to resort to some other method of cost estimation.

Another criterion commonly used to evaluate a particular regression line is to assess its **goodness of fit**. Statistical methods can be used to determine objectively how well a regression line fits the data upon which it is based. If a regression line fits the data well, a large proportion of the variation in the dependent variable will be explained by the variation in the independent variable. One frequently used measure of goodness of fit is described in the appendix at the end of this chapter.[3]

> **Goodness of fit** is the closeness with which a regression line fits the data upon which it is based.

Multiple Regression

In each of the cost-estimation methods discussed so far, we have based the estimate on a single independent variable. Moreover, all of Tasty Donuts' cost behavior patterns were specified with respect to a single activity (or cost driver), dozens of bakery items produced and sold. However, there may be two or more independent variables that are important predictors of cost behavior.

> **LO 6**   Describe the multiple regression, engineering, work-measurement, and learning-curve approaches to cost estimation.

To illustrate, we will continue our analysis of Tasty Donuts' utilities costs. The company uses electricity for two primary purposes: operating cooking equipment, such as deep-fat fryers and ovens, and heating the bakery and donut shops. The cost of electricity for food production is a function of the firm's activity, as measured in dozens of bakery items produced and sold. However, the cost of electricity for restaurant heating is related more closely to the number of customers than to the number of bakery items sold. A restaurant's heating costs go up each time the restaurant door is opened, resulting in loss of heat. Two customers purchasing half a dozen donuts each result in greater heating cost than one customer buying a dozen donuts.

Suppose Tasty Donuts' controller wants to estimate a cost behavior pattern for utilities cost that is based on both units of sales and number of customers. The method of *multiple regression* may be used for this purpose. **Multiple regression** is a statistical method that estimates a linear (straight-line) relationship between one dependent variable and two or more independent variables. In Tasty Donuts' case, the following regression equation would be estimated.

> **Multiple regression** estimates a linear (straight-line) relationship between a dependent variable and two or more independent variables.

$$Y = a + b_1 X_1 + b_2 X_2 \qquad (2)$$

where Y denotes the dependent variable, utilities cost
   X_1 denotes the first independent variable, dozens of bakery items sold
   X_2 denotes the second independent variable, number of customers served

---

[3]We have only scratched the surface of regression analysis as a tool for cost estimation. For an expanded discussion of the least-squares regression method, see any statistics text.

In regression equation (2), a denotes the regression estimate of the fixed-cost component, b_1 denotes the regression estimate of the variable utilities cost per dozen bakery items, and b_2 denotes the regression estimate of the variable utilities cost per customer served. The multiple-regression equation will likely enable Tasty Donuts' controller to make more accurate cost predictions than could be made with the *simple regression* discussed previously. A **simple regression** is based on a single independent variable. Multiple regression is covered more extensively in cost-accounting and statistics texts.

Simple regression analysis is based on a single independent variable.

Data Collection Problems

LO 7   Describe some problems often encountered in collecting data for cost estimation.

Regardless of the method used, the resulting cost estimation will be only as good as the data upon which it is based. The collection of data appropriate for cost estimation requires a skilled and experienced cost analyst. Six problems frequently complicate the process of data collection:

1. *Missing data.* Misplaced source documents or failure to record a transaction can result in missing data.
2. *Outliers.* We have discussed these extreme observations of cost-activity relationships. If outliers are determined to represent errors or highly unusual circumstances, they should be eliminated from the data set.
3. *Mismatched time periods.* The units of time for which the dependent and independent variables are measured may not match. For example, production activity may be recorded daily, but costs may be recorded monthly. A common solution is to aggregate the production data to get monthly totals.
4. *Trade-offs in choosing the time period.* In choosing the length of the time period for which data are collected, there are conflicting objectives. One objective is to obtain as many data points as possible, which implies a short time period. Another objective is to choose a long enough time period to ensure that the accounting system has accurately associated costs with time periods. If, for example, a cost that resulted from production activity in one period is recorded in a later period, the cost and activity data will not be matched properly. Longer time periods result in fewer recording lags in the data.
5. *Allocated and discretionary costs.* Fixed costs are often *allocated* on a per-unit-of-activity basis. For example, fixed manufacturing-overhead costs such as depreciation are allocated to units of production. As a result, such costs may appear to be variable in the cost records. *Discretionary* costs often are budgeted in a manner that makes them appear variable. A cost such as advertising, for example, may be fixed once management decides on the level of advertising. If management's policy is to budget advertising on the basis of sales dollars, however, the cost will appear to be variable to the cost analyst. An experienced analyst will be wary of such costs and take steps to learn how their amounts are determined.
6. *Inflation.* During periods of inflation, historical cost data may not reflect future cost behavior. One solution is to choose historical data from a period of low inflation and then factor in the current inflation rate. Other, more sophisticated approaches are also available, and they are covered in cost-accounting texts.

Engineering Method of Cost Estimation

LO 6   Describe the multiple regression, engineering, work-measurement , and learning-curve approaches to cost estimation.

All of the methods of cost estimation examined so far are based on historical data. Each method estimates the relationship between cost and activity by studying the relationship observed in the past. A completely differ-

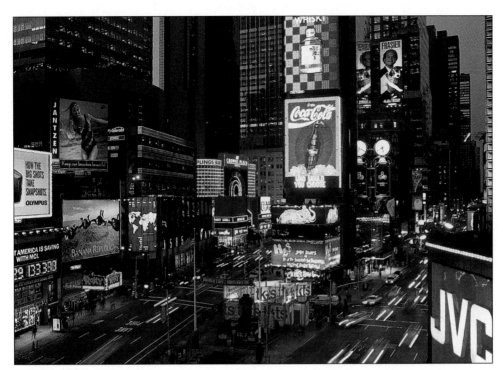

Advertising costs, which are so vividly depicted in this view of New York City's Times Square, often are discretionary fixed costs.

ent method of cost estimation is to study the process that results in cost incurrence. This approach is called the **engineering method** of cost estimation. In a manufacturing firm, for example, a detailed study is made of the production technology, materials, and labor used in the manufacturing process. Rather than asking the question, What was the cost of material last period?, the engineering approach is to ask, How much material should be needed and how much should it cost? Industrial engineers often perform *time and motion studies*, which determine the steps required for people to perform the manual tasks that are part of the production process. Cost behavior patterns for various types of costs are then estimated on the basis of the engineering analysis. Engineering cost studies are time-consuming and expensive, but they often provide highly accurate estimates of cost behavior. Moreover, in rapidly evolving, high-technology industries, there may not be any historical data on which to base cost estimates. Such industries as genetic engineering, superconductivity, and electronics are evolving so rapidly that historical data are often irrelevant in estimating costs.

> The **engineering method** of cost estimation makes a detailed study of the process that results in cost incurrence.

Effect of Learning on Cost Behavior

In many production processes, production efficiency increases with experience. As cumulative production output increases, the average labor time required per unit declines. A graphical expression of this phenomenon is called a **learning curve**. An example is shown in panel A of Exhibit 7–11. On this learning curve, when cumulative output doubles, the average labor time per unit declines by 20 percent. Panel B of Exhibit 7–11 displays the total labor time and average labor time per unit for various levels of cumulative output. As cumulative output doubles from 5 to 10 units, for example, the average labor time per unit declines by 20 percent, from 100 hours per unit to 80 hours per unit. As a manufacturer gains experience with a product, estimates of the cost of direct labor should be adjusted downward to take this learning effect into account.

> A **learning curve** is a graphical expression of the decline in the average labor time required per unit as cumulative output increases.

Exhibit 7–11

Learning Curve

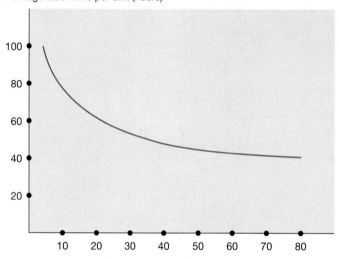

A. Graphical Presentation of Learning Curve

Average labor time per unit (hours)

Cumulative production output (units)

B. Tabular Presentation of Learning Curve

Cumulative Output (in units)	Average Labor Time per Unit (hours)	Total Labor Time (hours)
5	100.00	500.0
10	80.00	800.0
20	64.00	1,280.0
40	51.20	2,048.0
80	40.96	3,276.8

An **experience curve** is a graph (or other mathematical representation) that shows how a broad set of costs decline as cumulative production output increases.

Sometimes the learning-curve concept is applied to a broader set of costs than just labor costs. Then the phenomenon is referred to as an **experience curve**. Suppose, for example, that all labor and variable overhead costs are observed to decline by 20 percent every time cumulative output doubles. Then we would change the vertical axis of Exhibit 7–11 to *labor and variable overhead costs*. The graph would then be called an *experience curve*.

Learning curves have been used extensively in such industries as aircraft production, shipbuilding, and electronics to assist cost analysts in predicting labor costs. These cost predictions are then used in scheduling production, budgeting, setting product prices, and other managerial decisions. The following illustration demonstrates the importance of the learning-curve phenomenon.

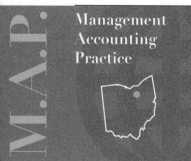

Management Accounting Practice

B. F. Goodrich Company

Fortune magazine reported that the learning curve for tire manufacturing helped B. F. Goodrich Company in formulating its business strategy. The learning curve showed the firm's management that it was not necessary to sell tires to automobile manufacturers at a minimal markup in order to obtain enough experience with a tire model to drive down costs. It was possible to move far enough out on the curve for efficient production simply by selling tires in the more lucrative market for replacements.[4]

---

[4]"The Decline of the Experience Curve," *Fortune* 104, no. 7.

Costs and Benefits of Information

We have discussed a variety of cost-estimation methods ranging from the simple visual-fit approach to sophisticated techniques involving regression or learning curves. Which of these methods is best? In general, the more sophisticated methods will yield more accurate cost estimates than the simpler methods. However, even a sophisticated method still yields only an imperfect estimate of an unknown cost behavior pattern.

All cost-estimation methods are based on simplifying assumptions. The two most important assumptions are as follows:

1. Except for the multiple-regression technique, all of the methods assume that cost behavior depends on *one activity variable*. Even multiple regression uses only a small number of independent variables. In reality, however, costs are affected by a host of factors including the weather, the mood of the employees, and the quality of the raw materials used.
2. Another simplifying assumption usually made in cost estimation is that cost behavior patterns are linear (straight lines) within the relevant range.

The cost analyst must consider on a case-by-case basis whether these assumptions are reasonable. The analyst also must decide when it is important to use a more sophisticated, and more costly, cost-estimation method and when it is acceptable to use a simpler approach. As in any choice among managerial-accounting methods, the costs and benefits of the various cost-estimation techniques must be weighed.

Work Measurement

LO 6 Describe the multiple regression, engineering, work-measurement, and learning-curve approaches to cost estimation.

Cost-estimation methods are used to determine the behavior of all kinds of costs in a wide variety of organizations. In organizations such as banks, insurance companies, and many government agencies, cost estimation is facilitated by a technique called *work measurement*. **Work measurement** is the systematic analysis of a task for the purpose of determining the inputs needed to perform the task. The analysis focuses on such factors as the steps required to perform the task, the time needed to complete each step, the number and type of employees required, and the materials or other inputs needed. Some examples of work-measurement applications are listed here.

Work measurement is the systematic analysis of a task for the purpose of determining the inputs needed to perform the task.

A **control factor unit** is a measure of work or activity used in work measurement.

Industry	Activity	Work Measure
Banking	Processing loan applications	Applications processed
U.S. Postal Service	Sorting mail	Pieces of mail sorted
Manufacturing	Billing customers	Invoices processed
Internal Revenue Service	Processing tax returns	Returns processed
Insurance	Settling claims	Claims settled
Airlines	Ticketing passengers	Passengers ticketed

The measure of work or activity is often called a **control factor unit**. In the loan department of a bank, for example, the control factor unit is loan applications processed. To apply work measurement to the loan department, experts would first determine the steps required to process a loan application, the most efficient order for those steps, and the average amount of time that should be needed for each step. The first steps in processing a car-loan application, for example, would be to (1) verify that the application is complete and filled out properly, and (2) verify the applicant's credit references, through phone calls or computer checks.

After the task has been analyzed in terms of its steps, time needed, and other inputs required, the cost of each of these steps is computed. For example, suppose it takes an average of 15 minutes to verify that a loan application is completed properly, and the loan-department employee's time costs $10.00 per hour (including fringe benefits). The cost of this loan-processing step is computed as follows:

$$\left(\begin{array}{c}\text{Time required to verify}\\\text{application is complete}\end{array}\right) \times \left(\begin{array}{c}\text{Cost of compensating employee for}\\\text{one hour, including fringe benefits}\end{array}\right)$$

$$(\text{¼ hour}) \times (\$10.00 \text{ per hour}) = \$2.50$$

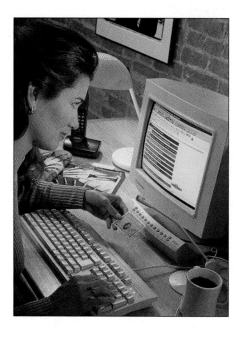

American Express successfully implemented a productivity-improvement program in its customer service department. This American Express customer is using her Amex card to make a purchase via the Internet.

The cost of each step in processing the loan application is determined in a similar manner. Other inputs, such as computer time and long-distance telephone calls, are also included in the cost of processing the loan application. When the average cost of processing a loan application has been determined, the cost behavior for this activity can be specified. Suppose that the variable cost of processing each car-loan application is determined to be $30. In addition, the car-loan department has fixed costs of $5,000 per month, which includes the department manager's salary, insurance, and depreciation on office space and computer equipment. Then the cost behavior of the car-loan-processing activity may be represented by the graph in Exhibit 7–12.

Exhibit 7–12

Cost Behavior Estimated through Work Measurement: Car-Loan Department of a Bank

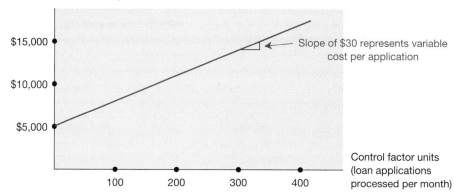

Total cost of car-loan department

Slope of $30 represents variable cost per application

$15,000

$10,000

$5,000

Control factor units (loan applications processed per month)

100   200   300   400

Work measurement has been successfully employed in a wide variety of organizations. The following case in point illustrates its use in the financial-services industry.

Management Accounting Practice

M.A.P.

American Express Company

American Express Company initiated a productivity-improvement program for its customer service department. Traditional industrial engineering methods were used to analyze various customer service tasks, such as replacing a lost American Express card. Each task was broken down into the steps required to perform the task, and the time required to complete each step was determined. *Business Week* reported that American Express executives feel the program has improved both department performance and customer satisfaction.[5]

[5]"Boosting Productivity at American Express," *Business Week*, no. 2708, pp. 66–68.

Chapter Summary

Understanding an organization's cost behavior enables managers to anticipate changes in cost when the organization's level of activity (or cost driver) changes. Cost predictions, which are based on cost behavior patterns, facilitate planning, control, and decision making throughout the organization. These cost predictions should be confined to the relevant range, which is the range of activity expected for the organization.

A variety of cost behavior patterns exist, ranging from simple variable and fixed costs to more complicated semivariable and curvilinear costs. Several cost-estimation methods are used to determine which cost behavior pattern is appropriate for a particular cost. The account-classification, visual-fit, high-low, and regression methods are all based on an analysis of historical cost data observed at a variety of activity levels. The engineering and work-measurement methods are based on a detailed analysis of the process in which the costs are incurred. These methods are frequently used in combination to provide a more accurate cost estimate.

As in selecting any managerial-accounting technique, the choice of a cost-estimation method involves a trade-off of costs and benefits. More accurate estimation methods provide the benefits of better information, but they are often more costly to apply.

Review Problems on Cost Behavior and Estimation

Problem 1

Erie Hardware, Inc. operates a chain of four retail stores. Data on the company's maintenance costs for its store buildings and furnishings are presented below.

Month	Maintenance Cost	Sales
January	$53,000	$600,000
February	55,000	700,000
March	47,000	550,000
April	51,000	650,000
May	45,000	500,000
June	49,000	610,000

Using the high-low method, estimate and graph the cost behavior for the firm's maintenance costs.

Problem 2

The *Keystone Sentinel* is a weekly newspaper sold throughout Pennsylvania. The following costs were incurred by its publisher during a week when circulation was 100,000 newspapers: total variable costs, $40,000; total fixed costs, $66,000. Fill in your predictions for the following cost amounts.

	Circulation	
	110,000 Newspapers	**120,000 Newspapers**
Total variable cost		
Variable cost per unit		
Total fixed cost		
Fixed cost per unit		

Solutions to Review Problems

Problem 1

	Sales	Cost
At high activity	$700,000	$55,000
At low activity	500,000	45,000
Difference	$200,000	$10,000

$$\text{Variable cost per sales dollar} = \frac{\$10,000}{200,000} = \$.05 \text{ per sales dollar}$$

Total cost at $700,000 of sales	$55,000
Total variable cost at $700,000 of sales (700,000 × $.05)	35,000
Difference is total fixed cost	$20,000

Problem 2

	Circulation	
	110,000 Newspapers	**120,000 Newspapers**
Total variable cost	$40,000 × $\left(\frac{110,000}{100,000}\right)$ = $44,000	$40,000 × $\left(\frac{120,000}{100,000}\right)$ = $48,000
Variable cost per unit	$44,000 ÷ 110,000 = $.40	$48,000 ÷ 120,000 = $.40
Total fixed cost	$66,000	$66,000
Fixed cost per unit	$66,000 ÷ 110,000 = $.60	$66,000 ÷ 120,000 = $.55

Key Terms

For each term's definition refer to the indicated page, or turn to the glossary at the end of the text.

account-classification
   method (also called
   account analysis), pg. 255
committed cost, pg. 252
control factor unit, pg. 265
cost behavior, pg. 244
cost estimation, pg. 244
cost prediction, pg. 244
curvilinear cost, pg. 249

dependent variable, pg. 259
discretionary cost, pg. 252
engineered cost, pg. 252
engineering method, pg. 263
experience curve, pg. 264
fixed cost, pg. 246
goodness of fit, pg. 261
high-low method, pg. 258

independent
   variable, pg. 259
learning curve, pg. 263
least-squares regression
   method, pg. 259
multiple regression, pg. 261
outlier, pg. 257
regression line, pg. 259
relevant range, pg. 251

scatter diagram, pg. 256
semivariable (or mixed)
   cost, pg. 249
simple regression, pg. 262
step-fixed costs, pg. 249
step-variable costs, pg. 245
variable cost, pg. 245
visual-fit method, pg. 256
work measurement, pg. 265

Appendix to Chapter 7

Finding the Least-Squares Regression Estimates

The least-squares regression line, which is shown below in equation form, includes two estimates. These estimates, which are called *parameters*, are denoted by a and b in the equation.

$$Y = a + bX \tag{3}$$

where X denotes the independent variable (activity level for one month)

          Y denotes the dependent variable (cost for one month)

Statistical theorists have shown that these parameters are defined by the following two equations, which are called **normal equations**.[6]

$$\Sigma XY = a\Sigma Y + b\Sigma X^2 \tag{4}$$
$$\Sigma Y = na + b\Sigma X \tag{5}$$

where n denotes the number of data points

          Σ denotes summation; for example, ΣY denotes the sum of the Y (cost) values in the data

> **Normal equations** are the equations used to solve for the parameters of a regression equation.

Equations (4) and (5) may be rearranged algebraically to solve for a and b, as shown below.

$$a = \frac{(\Sigma Y)(\Sigma X^2) - (\Sigma X)(\Sigma XY)}{n(\Sigma X^2) - (\Sigma X)(\Sigma X)} \tag{6}$$

$$b = \frac{n(\Sigma XY) - (\Sigma X)(\Sigma Y)}{n(\Sigma X^2) - (\Sigma X)(\Sigma X)} \tag{7}$$

Panel A of Exhibit 7–13 shows the numbers used to compute the regression parameters, a and b, for Tasty Donuts' utilities cost. Notice that the X values (activity levels) are expressed in thousands to make the numbers more convenient to handle. Substituting these numbers into equations (6) and (7) yields the following estimates for a and b.

$$a = \frac{(73,285)(106,759) - (1,121)(6,937,430)}{(12)(106,759) - (1,121)(1,121)} = 1,920^* \tag{8}$$

$$b = \frac{(12)(6,937,430) - (1,121)(73,285)}{(12)(106,759) - (1,121)(1,121)} = 44.82^* \tag{9}$$

*Rounded.

The intercept of the regression line on the vertical axis is $1,920. The slope of the line, as solved in equation (9) above, is $44.82. However, the X (activity) values were rescaled in Exhibit 7–13 to be expressed in thousands. Thus, the b value computed above represents a variable cost of $44.82 *per thousand* dozen bakery items. Dividing this number by 1,000 yields the variable cost per dozen bakery items, $.0448 (rounded to the nearest hundredth of a cent). This is the regression estimate of the variable cost per dozen bakery items reported earlier in the chapter.

Goodness of Fit   The goodness of fit for Tasty Donuts' regression line may be measured by the **coefficient of determination**, commonly denoted by R^2. This measure is defined as the percentage of the variability of the dependent variable about its mean that is explained by the variability of the independent variable about its mean. The higher the R^2, the better the regression line fits the data. The interpretation for a high R^2 is that the independent variable is a good predictor of the behavior of the dependent

> The **coefficient of determination** is a statistical measure of how closely a regression line fits the data on which it is based.

---

[6]The derivation of these equations, which requires calculus, is covered in any introductory statistics text.

Exhibit 7–13

Computation of Least-Squares Regression Estimates

Tasty Donuts, Inc.

(A) For computation of regression estimates, *a* and *b*

(B) For computation of R^2

Month of Preceding Year	Utility Cost for Month Y	Activity during Month (in thousands) X	X^2	XY	Predicted Cost Based on Regression Line* Y'	$(Y-Y')^2$	$(Y-\bar{Y})^2$
January	5,100	75	5,625	382,500	5,282	33,124	1,014,216
February ...	5,300	78	6,084	413,400	5,416	13,456	651,384
March	5,650	80	6,400	452,000	5,506	20,736	208,925
April	6,300	92	8,464	579,600	6,043	66,049	37,217
May	6,400	98	9,604	627,200	6,312	7,744	85,800
June	6,700	108	11,664	723,600	6,761	3,721	351,550
July	7,035	118	13,924	830,130	7,209	30,276	861,029
August	7,000	112	12,544	784,000	6,940	3,600	797,300
September ..	6,200	95	9,025	589,000	6,178	484	8,634
October	6,100	90	8,100	549,000	5,954	21,316	50
November ..	5,600	85	7,225	476,000	5,730	16,900	257,134
December ..	5,900	90	8,100	531,000	5,954	2,916	42,884
Total	73,285	1,121	106,759	6,937,430	73,285	220,322	4,316,123

*For example, at 75,000 units of activity, Y' is computed as follows: Y' = 1,920 + (44.82) (75) = 5,282

variable. In cost estimation, a high R^2 means that the cost analyst can be relatively confident in the cost predictions based on the estimated cost behavior pattern.

Statistical theorists have shown that R^2 can be computed using the following formula:

$$R^2 = 1 - \frac{\Sigma (Y - Y')^2}{\Sigma (Y - \bar{Y})^2} \tag{10}$$

where
Y denotes the observed value of the dependent variable (cost) at a particular activity level

Y' denotes the predicted value of the dependent variable (cost), based on the regression line, at a particular activity level

$\bar{Y}$ denotes the mean (average) observation of the dependent variable (cost)

The numbers needed for the R^2 formula are displayed in panel B of Exhibit 7–13 for the Tasty Donuts illustration. Substituting these numbers in equation (10) yields the following value for R^2:

$$R^2 = 1 - \frac{220,322}{4,316,123} = .949 \tag{11}$$

This is a high value for R^2, and Tasty Donuts' controller may be quite confident in the resulting cost predictions. As always, these predictions should be confined to the relevant range.

Key Terms: Appendix

For each term's definition refer to the indicated page, or turn to the glossary at the end of the text.

coefficient of determination, pg. 269

normal equations, pg. 269

Review Questions

7–1. Define the following terms, and explain the relationship between them: (*a*) cost estimation, (*b*) cost behavior, and (*c*) cost prediction.

7–2. Describe the importance of cost behavior patterns in planning, control, and decision making.

7–3. Suggest an appropriate activity base (or cost driver) for each of the following organizations: (*a*) hotel, (*b*) hospital, (*c*) computer manufacturer, (*d*) computer sales store, (*e*) computer repair service, and (*f*) public accounting firm.

7–4. Draw a simple graph of each of the following types of cost behavior patterns: (*a*) variable, (*b*) step-variable, (*c*) fixed, (*d*) step-fixed, (*e*) semivariable, and (*f*) curvilinear.

7–5. Explain the impact of an increase in the level of activity (or cost driver) on (*a*) total fixed cost and (*b*) fixed cost per unit of activity.

7–6. Explain why a manufacturer's cost of supervising production might be a step-fixed cost.

7–7. Explain the impact of an increase in the level of activity (or cost driver) on (*a*) total variable cost and (*b*) variable cost per unit.

7–8. Using graphs, show how a semivariable (or mixed) cost behavior pattern can be used to approximate (*a*) a step-variable cost and (*b*) a curvilinear cost.

7–9. Indicate which of the following descriptions is most likely to describe each cost listed below.

Description	Costs
Engineered cost	Annual cost of maintaining an interstate highway
Committed cost	Cost of ingredients in a breakfast cereal
Discretionary cost	Cost of advertising for a credit card company
	Depreciation on an insurance company's computer
	Cost of charitable donations that are budgeted as 1 percent of sales revenue
	Research and development costs, which have been budgeted at $45,000 per year

7–10. A cost analyst showed the company president a graph that portrayed the firm's utility cost as semivariable. The president criticized the graph by saying, "This fixed-cost component doesn't look right to me. If we shut down the plant for six months, we wouldn't incur half of these costs." How should the cost analyst respond?

7–11. What is meant by a *learning curve*? Explain its role in cost estimation.

7–12. How is work measurement used in cost estimation? Suggest an appropriate control factor unit for the following tasks.

   a. Handling materials at a loading dock.

   b. Registering vehicles at a county motor vehicle office.

   c. Picking oranges.

   d. Inspecting computer components in an electronics firm.

7–13. What is an *outlier*? List some possible causes of outliers. How should outliers be handled in cost estimation?

7–14. Explain the cost-estimation problem caused by allocated and discretionary costs.

7–15. Describe the visual-fit method of cost estimation. What are the main strengths and weaknesses of this method?

7–16. What is the chief drawback of the high-low method of cost estimation? What problem could an outlier cause if the high-low method were used?

7–17. Explain the meaning of the term *least squares* in the least-squares regression method of cost estimation.

7–18. Use an equation to express a least-squares regression line. Interpret each term in the equation.

7–19. Distinguish between *simple regression* and *multiple regression*.

7–20. What impact have advances in manufacturing technology had on the problem of cost estimation?

7–21. Briefly describe two methods that can be used to evaluate a particular least-squares regression line.

Exercises

Draw a graph of the cost behavior for each of the following costs incurred by the Fernando Valley Hospital. The hospital measures monthly activity in patient days. Label both axes and the cost line in each graph.

■ **Exercise 7–22**
Graphing Cost Behavior Patterns; Hospital
(LO 1, LO 2)

1. The cost of food varies in proportion to the number of patient days of activity. In January, the hospital provided 3,000 patient days of care, and food costs amounted to $24,000.

2. The cost of salaries and fringe benefits for the administrative staff totals $12,000 per month.

3. The hospital's laboratory costs include two components: (*a*) $40,000 per month for compensation of personnel and depreciation on equipment, and (*b*) $10 per patient day for chemicals and other materials used in performing the tests.

4. The cost of utilities depends on how many wards the hospital needs to use during a particular month. During months with activity under 2,000 patient days of care, two wards are used, resulting in utility costs of $10,000. During months with greater than 2,000 patient days of care, three wards are used, and utility costs total $15,000.

5. Many of the hospital's nurses are part-time employees. As a result, the hours of nursing care provided can be easily adjusted to the amount required at any particular time. The cost of wages and fringe benefits for nurses is approximately $2,500 for each block of 200 patient days of care provided during a month. For example, nursing costs total $2,500 for 1 to 200 patient days, $5,000 for 201 to 400 patient days, $7,500 for 401 to 600 patient days, and so forth.

■ **Exercise 7–23**
Behavior of Fixed and
Variable Costs; Television
Station
(LO 1, LO 2)

WMEJ is an independent television station run by a major state university. The station's broadcast hours vary during the year depending on whether the university is in session. The station's production-crew and supervisory costs are as follows for July and September.

Cost Item	Cost Behavior	Cost Amount	Broadcast Hours during Month
Production Crew	Variable		
July		$4,875	390
September		8,000	640
Supervisory employees	Fixed		
July		5,000	390
September		5,000	640

Required:

1. Compute the cost per broadcast hour during July and September for each of these cost items.
2. What will be the total amount incurred for each of these costs during December, when the station's activity will be 420 broadcast hours?
3. What will be the cost per broadcast hour in December for each of the cost items?

■ **Exercise 7–24**
Approximating a Curvilinear
Cost; Public School District
(LO 1, LO 2, LO 3)

The behavior of the annual maintenance and repair cost in the Bus Transportation Department of the Winterset Public School District is shown by the solid line in the following graph. The dashed line depicts a semivariable-cost approximation of the department's repair and maintenance cost.

Required:

1. What is the actual (curvilinear) and estimated (semivariable) cost shown by the graph for each of the following activity levels?

		Actual	Estimated
a.	20,000 miles		
b.	40,000 miles		
c.	60,000 miles		
d.	90,000 miles		

2. How good an approximation does the semivariable-cost pattern provide if the department's relevant range is 40,000 to 60,000 miles per month? What if the relevant range is 20,000 to 90,000 miles per month?

Chillicothe Meat Company produces one of the best sausage products in southern Ohio. The company's controller used the account-classification method to compile the following information.

a. Depreciation schedules revealed that monthly depreciation on buildings and equipment is $19,000.

b. Inspection of several invoices from meat packers indicated that meat costs the company $1.10 per pound of sausage produced.

c. Wage records showed that compensation for production employees costs $.70 per pound of sausage produced.

d. Payroll records showed that supervisory salaries total $10,000 per month.

e. Utility bills revealed that the company incurs utility costs of $4,000 per month plus $.20 per pound of sausage produced.

Required:

1. Classify each cost item as variable, fixed, or semivariable.

2. Write a cost formula to express the cost behavior of the firm's production costs. (Use the form $Y = a + bX$, where Y denotes production cost and X denotes quantity of sausage produced.)

■ **Exercise 7–25**
Account-Classification
Method; Food Processing
(LO 1, LO 2, LO 5)

The Kansas City Veterinary Laboratory performs a variety of diagnostic tests on commercial and domestic animals. The lab has incurred the following costs over the past year.

Month	Diagnostic Tests Completed	Cost
January	3,050	$61,000
February	4,500	74,500
March	7,100	99,000
April	6,200	95,600
May	4,700	74,800
June	5,900	89,000
July	6,000	91,000
August	6,100	90,000
September	5,300	87,000
October	4,900	76,200
November	4,800	78,100
December	5,050	80,700

■ **Exercise 7–26**
Visual-Fit Method; Veterinary
Laboratory
(LO 1, LO 2, LO 5)

Required:

1. Plot the data above in a scatter diagram. Assign cost to the vertical axis and the number of diagnostic tests to the horizontal axis. Visually fit a line to the plotted data.

2. Using the visually fit line, estimate the monthly fixed cost and the variable cost per diagnostic test.

Jonathan Macintosh is a highly successful Pennsylvania orchardman who has formed his own company to produce and package apple sauce. Apples can be stored for several months in cold storage, so apple sauce production is relatively uniform throughout the year. The recently hired controller for the firm is about to apply the high-low method in estimating the company's energy cost behavior. The following costs were incurred during the past 12 months:

■ **Exercise 7–27**
Estimating Cost Behavior;
High-Low Method
(LO 1, LO 2, LO 5)

Month	Pints of Apple Sauce Produced	Energy Cost
January	35,000	$23,400
February	21,000	22,100
March	22,000	22,000
April	24,000	22,450
May	30,000	22,900
June	32,000	23,350
July	40,000	28,000

Month	Pints of Apple Sauce Produced	Energy Cost
August	30,000	$22,800
September	30,000	23,000
October	28,000	22,700
November	41,000	24,100
December	39,000	24,950

Required:

1. Use the high-low method to estimate the company's energy cost behavior and express it in equation form.

2. Predict the energy cost for a month in which 26,000 pints of apple sauce are produced.

■ **Exercise 7–28**
Estimating Cost Behavior;
Visual-Fit Method
(LO 1, LO 2, LO 5)

Refer to the data in the preceding exercise.

Required:

1. Draw a scatter diagram and graph the company's energy cost behavior using the visual-fit method.
2. Predict the energy cost for a month in which 26,000 pints of apple sauce are produced.
3. What peculiarity is apparent from the scatter diagram? What should the cost analyst do?

■ **Exercise 7–29**
High-Low Method; Tour
Company
(LO 1, LO 2, LO 5)

Everglades Bus Tours has incurred the following bus maintenance costs during the recent tourist season.

Month	Miles Traveled by Tour Buses	Cost
November	8,500	$11,400
December	10,600	11,600
January	12,700	11,700
February	15,000	12,000
March	20,000	12,500
April	8,000	11,000

Required:

1. Use the high-low method to estimate the variable cost per tour mile traveled and the fixed cost per month.
2. Develop a formula to express the cost behavior exhibited by the company's maintenance cost.
3. Predict the level of maintenance cost that would be incurred during a month when 22,000 tour miles are driven.

■ **Exercise 7–30**
Work Measurement;
Government Agency
(LO 2, LO 6)

The State Department of Taxation processes and audits income-tax returns for state residents. The state tax commissioner has recently begun a program of work measurement to help in estimating the costs of running the department. The control factor unit used in the program is the number of returns processed. The analysis revealed that the following variable costs are incurred in auditing a typical tax return.

Time spent by clerical employees, 10 hours at $12 per hour

Time spent by tax professional, 20 hours at $25 per hour

Computer time, $50 per audit

Telephone charges, $10 per audit

Postage, $2 per audit

In addition, the department incurs $10,000 of fixed costs each month that are associated with the process of auditing returns.

Required: Draw a graph depicting the monthly costs of auditing state tax returns. Label the horizontal axis, "Control factor units; tax returns audited."

Weathereye, Inc. manufactures weather satellites. The final assembly and testing of the satellites is a largely manual operation involving dozens of highly trained electronics technicians. The following learning curve has been estimated for the firm's newest satellite model, which is about to enter production.

■ **Exercise 7–31**
Learning Curve; High Technology
(LO 1, LO 6)

Assembly and Testing

Required:

1. What will be the average labor time required to assemble and test each satellite when the company has produced four satellites? Eight satellites?

2. What will be the total labor time required to assemble and test all satellites produced if the firm manufactures only four satellites? Eight satellites?

3. How can the learning curve be used in the company's budgeting process? In setting cost standards?

Gator Beach Marts, a chain of convenience grocery stores in the Fort Lauderdale area, has store hours that fluctuate from month to month as the tourist trade in the community varies. The utility costs for one of the company's stores are listed below for the past six months.

■ **Exercise 7–32**
Estimating Cost Behavior by Multiple Methods (Appendix)
(LO 1, LO 2, LO 5)

Month	Total Hours of Operation	Total Utility Cost
January	550	$1,620
February	600	1,700
March	700	1,900
April	500	1,600
May	450	1,350
June	400	1,300

Required:

1. Use the high-low method to estimate the cost behavior for the store's utility costs. Express the cost behavior in formula form ($Y = a + bX$). What is the variable utility cost per hour of operation?

2. Draw a scatter diagram of the store's utility costs. Visually fit a cost line to the plotted data. Estimate the variable utility cost per hour of operation.

3. Use least-squares regression to estimate the cost behavior for the store's utility cost. Express the cost behavior in formula form. What is the variable utility cost per hour of operation?

4. During July, the store will be open 300 hours. Predict the store's total utility cost for July using each of the cost-estimation methods employed in requirements (1), (2), and (3).

Recent monthly costs of providing on-board flight service incurred by Lake Superior Airlines are shown in the following table.

■ **Exercise 7–33**
Airline; Least-Squares Regression (Appendix)
(LO 1, LO 2, LO 5)

Month	Thousands of Passengers	Cost of On-Board Flight Service (in thousands)
January	16	$18
February	17	18
March	16	19
April	18	20
May	15	18
June	17	19

Required:

1. Use least-squares regression to estimate the cost behavior of the airline's on-board flight service. Express the cost behavior in equation form. (*Hint:* When interpreting the regression, remember that the data are given in thousands.)
2. Calculate and interpret the R^2 value for the regression line.

Problems

■ **Problem 7–34**
Cost Behavior Patterns in a Variety of Settings; International Issues.
(LO 1, LO 2)

For each of the cost items described below, choose the graph on the next page that best represents it.

1. The salaries of the security personnel at a factory. The security guards are on duty around the clock.
2. The wages of table-service personnel in a restaurant. The employees are part-time workers, who can be called upon for as little as two hours at a time.
3. The salary costs of the shift supervisors at a truck depot. Each shift is eight hours. The depot operates with one, two, or three shifts at various times of the year.
4. The cost of electricity during peak-demand periods is based on the following schedule.

Up to 10,000 kilowatt-hours (kwh) ....$.09 per kwh
Above 10,000 kilowatt-hours ....$.14 per kwh

The price schedule is designed to discourage overuse of electricity during periods of peak demand.

5. The cost of sheet metal used to manufacture automobiles.
6. The cost of utilities at a university. For low student enrollments, utility costs increase with enrollment, but at a decreasing rate. For large student enrollments, utility costs increase at an increasing rate.
7. The cost of telephone service, which is based on the number of message units per month. The charge is $.95 per message unit, for up to 600 message units. Additional message units (above 600) are free.
8. The cost of the nursing staff in a hospital. The staff always has a minimum of nine nurses on duty. Additional nurses are used depending on the number of patients in the hospital. The hospital administrator estimates that this additional nursing staff costs approximately $195 per patient day.
9. The cost of chartering a private airplane. The cost is $410 per hour for the first three hours of a flight. Then the charge drops to $290 per hour.
10. Under a licensing agreement with a South American import/export company, your firm has begun shipping machine tools to several countries. The terms of the agreement call for an annual licensing fee of $100,000 to be paid to the South American import company if total exports are under $5,000,000. For sales in excess of $5,000,000, an additional licensing fee of 10 percent of sales is due.
11. Your winery exports wine to several Pacific Rim countries. In one nation, you must pay a tariff for every case of wine brought into the country. The tariff schedule is the following:

0 to 5,000 cases per year ....$11 per case
5,001 to 10,000 cases per year ....14 per case
Above 10,000 cases per year ....19 per case

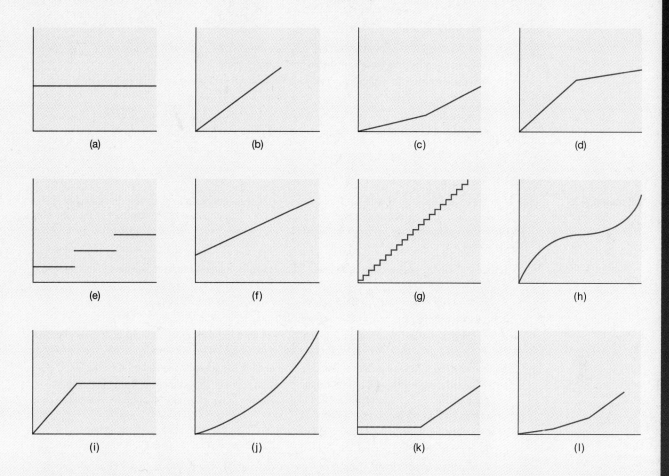

DC Health, Inc. operates a chain of fitness centers in the Washington, D.C., area. The firm's controller is accumulating data to be used in preparing its annual profit plan for the coming year. The cost behavior pattern of the firm's equipment maintenance costs must be determined. The accounting staff has suggested the use of an equation, in the form of $Y = a + bX$, for maintenance costs. Data regarding the maintenance hours and costs for last year are as follows:

■ **Problem 7–35**
High-Low Method; Fitness Centers
(LO 1, LO 2, LO 5)

Month	Hours of Maintenance Service	Maintenance Costs
January	520	$ 4,470
February	490	4,260
March	300	2,820
April	500	4,350
May	310	2,960
June	480	4,200
July	320	3,000
August	400	3,600
September	470	4,050
October	350	3,300
November	340	3,160
December	320	3,030
Total	4,800	$43,200
Average	400	$ 3,600

Required:

1. Using the high-low method of cost estimation, estimate the behavior of DC Health's maintenance costs. Express the cost behavior pattern in equation form.
2. Using your answer to requirement (1), what is the variable component of the maintenance cost?
3. Compute the predicted maintenance cost at 590 hours of activity.
4. Compute the variable cost per hour and the fixed cost per hour at 600 hours of activity. Explain why the fixed cost per hour could be misleading.

(CMA, adapted)

■ **Problem 7–36**
Account-Classification
Method; Private School
(LO 1, LO 2, LO 5)

The Potomac School of Music has hired you as a consultant to help in analyzing the behavior of the school's costs. Use the account-classification method of cost estimation to classify each of the following costs as variable, fixed, or semivariable. Before classifying the costs, choose an appropriate measure for the school's activity.

1. Cost of buying books, sheet music, and other academic materials that are supplied to the students by the school.
2. Salaries and fringe benefits of the school's full-time administrative staff.
3. Salaries and fringe benefits of the school's full-time teachers.
4. Repairs on musical instruments. The school employs a full-time repair technician. Repair jobs that are beyond the technician's capability are taken to a local musical-instrument dealer for repairs.
5. Fee charged by a local public accounting firm to audit the school's accounting records.
6. Wages of the school's part-time assistant recital instructors. These employees are hired on a temporary basis. For each student enrolled in the school's music programs, four hours of assistant instructor time are needed per week.
7. Depreciation on the school's musical instruments.
8. Rent for the building in which the school operates.
9. Electricity for the school. The school pays a fixed monthly charge plus $.10 per kilowatt-hour of electricity.

■ **Problem 7–37**
Approximating a Step-
Variable Cost; Visual-Fit
Method; Golf Course
(LO 1, LO 2, LO 5)

Redwood Golf Association is a nonprofit, private organization that operates three 18-hole golf courses north of San Francisco. The organization's financial director has just analyzed the course maintenance costs incurred by the golf association during recent summers. The courses are maintained by a full-time crew of four people, who are assisted by part-time employees. These employees are typically college students on their summer vacations. The course maintenance costs vary with the number of people using the course. Since a large part of the maintenance work is done by part-time employees, the maintenance crew size can easily be adjusted to reflect current needs. The financial director's analysis revealed that the course maintenance cost includes two components:

1. A fixed component of $12,000 per month (when the courses are open).
2. A step-variable cost component. For each additional 1 to 10 people teeing off in one day, $20 in costs are incurred. Thus if 101 to 110 people tee off, $220 of additional cost will be incurred. If 111 to 120 people tee off, $240 of additional cost will be incurred.

Required:

1. Draw a graph of Redwood Golf Association's course maintenance costs. Show on the graph the fixed-cost component and the step-variable cost component. Label each clearly.
2. Use a semivariable-cost behavior pattern to approximate the golf association's course maintenance cost behavior. Visually fit the semivariable cost line to your graph.
3. Using your graph, estimate the variable- and fixed-cost component included in your semivariable approximation. Express this approximate cost behavior pattern in equation form.
4. Fill in the following table of cost predictions.

	Predicted Course Maintenance Costs	
	Using Fixed Cost Coupled with Step-Variable Cost Behavior Pattern	**Using Semivariable Cost Approximation**
150 people tee off	?	?
158 people tee off	?	?

(*Note*: Instructors who wish to cover all three cost-estimation methods with the same data set may assign this problem in conjunction with the next one.) Nantucket Marine Supply is a wholesaler for a large variety of boating and fishing equipment. The company's controller, Mathew Knight, has recently completed a cost study of the firm's material-handling department in which he used work measurement to quantify the department's activity. The control factor unit used in the work-measurement study was hundreds of pounds of equipment unloaded or loaded at the company's loading dock. Knight compiled the following data.

■ Problem 7–38
Work Measurement; Cost Estimation with Different Methods; Wholesaler
(LO 1, LO 2, LO 5, LO 6)

Month	Control Factor Units of Activity	Material-Handling Department Costs
January	1,400	$11,350
February	1,200	11,350
March	1,100	11,050
April	2,600	12,120
May	1,800	11,400
June	2,000	12,000
July	2,400	12,550
August	2,200	11,100
September	1,000	10,200
October	1,300	11,250
November	1,600	11,300
December	1,800	11,700

Required:

1. Draw a scatter diagram of the cost data for the material-handling department.
2. Visually fit a cost line to the scatter diagram.
3. Estimate the variable and fixed components of the department's cost behavior pattern using the visually fit cost line.
4. Using your estimate from requirement (3), specify an equation to express the department's cost behavior.
5. Estimate the material-handling department's cost behavior using the high-low method. Use an equation to express the results of this estimation method.
6. Write a brief memo to the company's president explaining why the cost estimates developed in requirements (4) and (5) differ.
7. Predict the company's material-handling costs for a month when 2,300 control factor units of activity are recorded. Use each of your cost equations to make the prediction. Which prediction would you prefer to use? Why?

Refer to the data in the preceding problem for Nantucket Marine Supply.

■ Problem 7–39
Continuation of Preceding Problem; Computing Least-Squares Regression Estimates; Comparing Multiple Methods (Appendix)
(LO 1, LO 2, LO 5, LO 6)

Required:

1. Compute the least-squares regression estimate of the variable and fixed cost components in the company's material-handling department costs. Use the formulas given in the appendix to the chapter. (*Hint*: It is helpful to transform both columns of data to thousands. For example, the June observation will be 2 units of activity and $12 of costs. Be careful, however, how you interpret your results.)
2. Write the least-squares regression equation for the department's costs.

3. Predict the firm's material-handling department's costs for a month when 2,300 control factor units of activity are recorded.

4. Why do the three cost predictions computed in this and the preceding problem differ? Which method do you recommend? Why?

■ **Problem 7–40**
Comparing Regression and
High-Low Estimates;
Manufacturer
(LO 1, LO 2, LO 5)

The controller of Philadelphia Fiber Optics, Inc. believes that the identification of the variable and fixed components of the firm's costs will enable the firm to make better planning and control decisions. Among the costs the controller is concerned about is the behavior of indirect-materials cost. She believes there is a correlation between machine hours and the amount of indirect materials used.

A member of the controller's staff has suggested that least-squares regression be used to determine the cost behavior of indirect materials. The regression equation shown below was developed from 40 pairs of observations.

$$S = \$200 + \$4H$$

where S = Total monthly costs of indirect materials
              H = Machine hours per month

Required:

1. Explain the meaning of "200" and "4" in the regression equation $S = \$200 + \$4H$.

2. Calculate the estimated cost of indirect materials if 900 machine hours are to be used during a month.

3. To determine the validity of the cost estimate computed in requirement (2), what question would you ask the controller about the data used for the regression?

4. The high and low activity levels during the past four years, as measured by machine hours, occurred during April 19x9 and August 19x9, respectively. Data concerning machine hours and indirect-materials usage follow.

	April 19x9	August 19x9
Machine hours	1,100	800
Indirect supplies:		
Beginning inventory	$1,200	$ 950
Ending inventory	1,550	2,900
Purchases	6,000	6,100

Determine the cost of indirect materials used during April 19x9 and August 19x9.

5. Use the high-low method to estimate the behavior of the company's indirect-material cost. Express the cost behavior pattern in equation form.

6. Which cost estimate would you recommend to the controller, the regression estimate or the high-low estimate? Why?

(CMA, adapted)

■ **Problem 7–41**
Interpreting Least-Squares
Regression; Landscaping
Service; Activity-Based
Costing
(LO 1, LO 2, LO 5)

ProGro Corporation provides commercial landscaping services. Sasha Cairns, the firm's owner, wants to develop cost estimates that she can use to prepare bids on jobs. After analyzing the firm's costs, Cairns has developed the following preliminary cost estimates for each 1,000 square feet of landscaping.

Direct material	$400
Direct labor (5 direct-labor hours at $10 per hour)	50
Overhead (at $18 per direct-labor hour)	90
Total cost per 1,000 square feet	$540

Cairns is quite certain about the estimates for direct material and direct labor. However, she is not as comfortable with the overhead estimate. The estimate for overhead is based on the overhead costs that were incurred during the past 12 months as presented in the following schedule. The estimate of $18 per direct-labor hour was determined by dividing the total overhead costs for the 12-month period ($648,000) by the total direct-labor hours (36,000).

	Total Overhead	Regular Direct-Labor Hours	Overtime Direct-Labor Hours*	Total Direct-Labor Hours
January	$ 54,000	2,910	190	3,100
February	47,000	2,380	20	2,400
March	48,000	2,210	40	2,250
April	56,000	2,590	210	2,800
May	57,000	3,030	470	3,500
June	65,000	3,240	760	4,000
July	64,000	3,380	620	4,000
August	56,000	3,050	350	3,400
September	53,000	2,760	40	2,800
October	47,000	2,770	30	2,800
November	47,000	2,120	30	2,150
December	54,000	2,560	240	2,800
Total	$648,000	33,000	3,000	36,000

*The overtime premium is 50 percent of the direct-labor wage rate.

Cairns believes that overhead is affected by total monthly direct-labor hours. Cairns decided to perform a least-squares regression of overhead (OH) on total direct-labor hours (DLH). The following regression formula was obtained.

$$OH = 26,200 + 9.25DLH$$

Required:

1. The overhead rate developed from the least-squares regression is different from Cairns' preliminary estimate of $18 per direct-labor hour. Explain the difference in the two overhead rates.

2. Using the overhead formula that was derived from the least-squares regression, determine a total variable-cost estimate for each 1,000 square feet of landscaping.

3. Cairns has been asked to submit a bid on a landscaping project for the city government consisting of 60,000 square feet. Cairns estimates that 40 percent of the direct-labor hours required for the project will be on overtime. Calculate the incremental costs that should be included in any bid that Cairns would submit on this project. Use the overhead formula derived from the least-squares regression.

4. Should ProGro Corporation rely on the overhead formula derived from the least-squares regression as the basis for the variable overhead component of its cost estimate? Explain your answer.

5. After attending a seminar on activity-based costing, Cairns decided to further analyze ProGro's activities and costs. She discovered that a more accurate portrayal of the firm's cost behavior could be achieved by dividing overhead into three separate pools, each with its own cost driver. Separate regression equations were estimated for each of the cost pools, with the following results.

$$OH_1 = 10,000 + 4.10DLH,$$

where   DLH denotes direct-labor hours

$$OH_2 = 9,100 + 13.50SFS,$$

where   SFS denotes the number of square feet of turf seeded (in thousands)

$$OH_3 = 8,000 + 6.60PL,$$

where   PL denotes the number of individual plantings (e.g., trees and shrubs)

Assume that 5 direct-labor hours will be needed to landscape each 1,000 square feet, regardless of the specific planting material used.

a. Suppose the landscaping project for the city will involve seeding all 60,000 square feet of turf and planting 80 trees and shrubs. Calculate the incremental *variable overhead* cost that Cairns should include in the bid.

b. Recompute the incremental variable overhead cost for the city's landscaping project assuming half of the 60,000 square-foot landscaping area will be seeded and there will be 250 individual plantings. The plantings will cover the entire 60,000 square-foot area.

c. Briefly explain, using concepts from activity-based costing, why the incremental costs differ in requirements (*a*) and (*b*).

(CMA, adapted)

■ **Problem 7–42**
Missing Data; Multiple Cost Estimation Methods
(Appendix)
(LO 1, LO 2, LO 5)

You have been hired recently as a part-time cost analyst for your college's admissions office. Your first task is to estimate the relationship between the cost of operating the admissions office and the number of applications received. After painstakingly collecting six months worth of data, you analyzed the cost behavior using three different methods. You wrote up a brief report and headed for the admissions director's office. However, a gust of wind caught the papers in your hand and blew them out the window, where they were torn to bits by the hockey coach's dog. You and your roommate managed to piece together the following bits and pieces of information from your shredded report.

Month	Applications Received (in thousands) ?	Cost of Operating the Admissions Office (in thousands) ?	X^2	?
August	?	8.9	?	178.0
September	?	10.0	?	?
October	25	?	?	240.0
November	?	9.1	?	200.2
December	?	8.7	225	?
January	10	?	?	?
Total	?	?	2,734	?

a. Least-squares regression:

$$? = \frac{(54.3)(?) - (?)(1,128.7)}{(?)(?) - (?)(?)}$$

$$? = \frac{(6)(?) - (122)(?)}{(?)(?) - (?)(?)}$$

Total monthly admissions department costs = ? + ?X, where X denotes the ?.

b. High-low method:

$$\text{Variable cost per thousand applications} = \frac{? - ?}{30 - ?} = \frac{?}{?}$$

$$= \quad ? \quad \text{per thousand applications}$$

Total cost at ? thousand applications   ?

Total variable cost at ? thousand applications   ?

Fixed cost per month   ?

Total monthly admissions department costs   =   ? + ?X

c. Visual-fit method:

Total monthly admissions department costs = $7,100 + \$.095X$

Required:

Complete the cost analysis and report by finding the missing amounts.

Monroe County Airport handles several daily commuter flights and many private flights. The county budget officer has compiled the following data regarding airport costs and activity over the past year.

Month	Flights Originating at Monroe County Airport (in hundreds)	Airport Costs (in thousands)
January	11	$20
February	8	17
March	14	19
April	9	18
May	10	19
June	12	20
July	11	18
August	14	24
September	10	19
October	12	21
November	9	17
December	15	21

Required:

1. Draw a scatter diagram of the airport costs shown above.
2. Compute the least-squares regression estimates of the variable and fixed cost components in the airport's cost behavior pattern. Use the formulas given in the appendix to the chapter. (Use the data as they are presented in the problem: flights measured in hundreds and costs measured in thousands of dollars.)
3. Write the least-squares regression equation for the airport's costs.
4. Predict the airport's costs during a month when 1,600 flights originate at the airport.
5. Compute the coefficient of determination of (R^2) for the regression equation. Briefly interpret R^2.

Cases

Arena Sports Corporation manufactures athletic equipment such as soccer goals and basketball backboards in its four manufacturing departments. These four departments and one service department (Equipment Maintenance) are housed in one facility. Due to the distinctive characteristics of the costs and operations of the different manufacturing departments, departmental manufacturing-overhead rates are employed for each manufacturing department.

Arena has been reviewing its operations and plans to implement some changes in the budgeting and reporting for the manufacturing departments during the next year. The Fabrication Department is being reviewed first, and its cost and operating data for the last six months are presented in the following table.

FABRICATION DEPARTMENT
Actual Manufacturing Overhead Costs and Activity Measures

	July	August	September	October	November	December
Actual costs:						
Setup costs	$11,500	$15,250	$12,000	$14,000	$14,500	$22,750
Machine hour costs:						
Indirect labor ($5 per machine hr.)	57,500	67,500	62,500	42,500	47,500	50,000
Power ($.20 per kwh)	21,250	24,250	22,750	16,750	18,250	19,000
Material-handling costs ($1.40 per pound)	35,000	37,800	42,000	33,600	28,000	30,800
Equipment maintenance	15,000	18,000	12,000	19,000	16,000	35,000
Fixed costs	335,000	335,000	335,000	335,000	335,000	335,000
Total overhead	$475,250	$497,800	$486,250	$460,850	$459,250	$492,550

	July	August	September	October	November	December
Activity measures:						
Units produced	50,000	45,000	52,000	42,000	48,000	40,000
Machine setups	15	20	16	18	19	21
Pounds of material	25,000	27,000	30,000	24,000	20,000	22,000
Machine hours	11,500	13,500	12,500	8,500	9,500	10,000

This information has been accumulated to assist in developing the manufacturing-overhead budget for the coming year. All of these costs are traceable (direct) costs of the Fabrication Department except for a portion of the fixed costs and the equipment-maintenance costs. The fixed costs include the common building and operating costs, which are allocated to each of the manufacturing departments on the basis of square feet. The Equipment Maintenance Department costs are charged to the operating departments for services rendered. These costs represent the actual cost of parts and supplies ($150,000 for the current fiscal year) plus a charge of $50 per hour. The manager of the Equipment Maintenance Department determines the preventive maintenance schedule for each of the production departments. All other repairs are made on a "first come, first served" basis.

Management is comfortable with using the six-month data as the basis for the preliminary budget estimates, because most of the activity measures and costs appear to be representative. However, the following adjustments will have to be made for the coming year.

Cost Item	Cost Adjustment
Indirect labor	Cost increase of 8 percent
Equipment maintenance	Cost increase of 10 percent for parts, supplies, and the hourly charge
Fixed costs	$360,000 per month

In the past, the overhead cost driver in the Fabrication Department has been machine hours for all costs. However, management has used scatter diagrams to analyze the behavior of some costs and has concluded that there is more than one cost driver in this department. As shown in the following scatter diagram, which captures data for the 12-month period through December, the number of setups represents the behavior of the setup costs and is now the cost driver for these costs. Similarly, the cost driver that is most appropriate as an application base for material-handling costs is pounds of material processed. Machine hours will continue to be used as the cost driver for the remaining costs of the Fabrication Department.

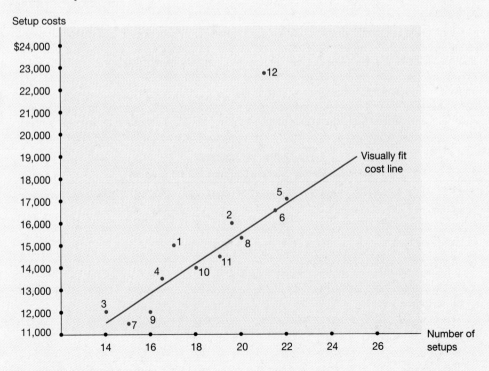

The numbers next to the points on the graph refer to the month of occurence (i.e., July = 7, etc.).

Sandy Mosman, vice president of manufacturing, has indicated that she wants to employ a responsibility reporting system where each manufacturing department will be held accountable for all costs included in its manufacturing-overhead budget. Actual monthly costs will be compared to the annual budget, and each department will be expected to come in at or below budgeted monthly costs.

Based on the production budgets, the activity measures for the Fabrication Department will be at the following levels for the coming year.

Activity Measure	Estimated Annual Amount
Units produced	520,000 units
Machine setups	200 setups
Pounds of material	280,000 pounds
Machine hours	135,000 hours
Power usage	2.5 kilowatt-hours per unit produced
Equipment maintenance	1,600 hours

Required:

1. Identify the benefits of using scatter diagrams in analyzing cost behavior.

2. *a.* Using the cost data presented for the six-month period of the current year, adjusted for the estimated changes expected to occur and the estimated activity measures for the coming year, develop a manufacturing-overhead budget for the Fabrication Department for the coming year. Use the high-low method to determine the fixed and variable components of the setup costs. (*Hint:* Does December look like a representative month?)

   b. Develop the overhead rate that should be employed in the Fabrication Department for the coming year for the costs that will still be applied on the basis of machine hours.

3. Sandy Mosman has recommended that a responsibility reporting system be employed in the manufacturing departments and that departmental managers be held responsible for all manufacturing-overhead costs included in the budget. Describe the likely behavior of the manufacturing departmental managers with respect to their accountability for equipment-maintenance costs.

(CMA, adapted)

(*Note:* Instructors who wish to cover all three cost-estimation methods with the same data set may assign this case in conjunction with the following case.) "I don't understand this cost report at all," exclaimed Jeff Mahoney, the newly appointed administrator of Lakeside General Hospital. "Our administrative costs in the new pediatrics clinic are all over the map. One month the report shows $8,300, and the next month it's $16,100. What's going on?"

Mahoney's question was posed to Megan McDonough, the hospital's controller. "The main problem is that the clinic has experienced some widely varying patient loads in its first year of operation. There seems to be some confusion in the public's mind about what services we offer in the clinic. When do they come to the clinic? When do they go to the emergency room? That sort of thing. As the patient load has varied, we've frequently changed our clinic administrative staffing."

Mahoney continued to puzzle over the report. "Could you pull some data together, Megan, so we can see how this cost behaves over a range of patient loads?"

"You'll have it this afternoon," McDonough responded. Later that morning, she gathered the following data:

■ **Case 7–45**
Approximating a Curvilinear Cost; Visual-Fit Method; Pediatrics Clinic
(LO 1, LO 2, LO 5)

Month	Patient Load	Administrative Cost
January	1,400	$13,900
February	500	7,000
March	400	6,000
April	1,000	10,000
May	1,300	11,900
June	900	9,200
July	1,100	10,200
August	300	4,100
September	700	9,400
October	1,200	11,100
November	600	8,300
December	1,500	16,100

McDonough does not believe the first year's widely fluctuating patient load will be experienced again in the future. She has estimated that the clinic's relevant range of monthly activity in the future will be 600 to 1,200 patients.

Required:

1. Draw a scatter diagram of the clinic's administrative costs during its first year of operation.

2. Visually fit a curvilinear cost line to the plotted data.

3. Mark the clinic's relevant range of activity on the scatter diagram by drawing vertical lines at each end of the relevant range.

4. Visually fit a semivariable-cost line to approximate the curvilinear cost behavior pattern within the clinic's relevant range.

5. Estimate the fixed and variable cost components of the visually fit semivariable-cost line.

6. Use an equation to express the semivariable-cost approximation of the clinic's administrative costs.

7. What is your prediction of the clinic's administrative cost during a month when 800 patients visit the clinic? When 300 patients visit? Which one of your visually fit cost lines did you use to make each of these predictions? Why?

■ **Case 7–46**
Comparing Multiple Cost
Estimation Methods; Ethics
(Appendix)
(LO 1, LO 2, LO 5)

Refer to the data and accompanying information in the preceding case.

Required:

1. Use the high-low method to estimate the cost behavior for the clinic's administrative costs. Express the cost behavior in formula form ($Y = a + bX$). What is the variable cost per patient?

2. Use least-squares regression to estimate the administrative cost behavior. Express the cost behavior in formula form. What is the variable cost per patient? (*Hint*: First, convert both columns of data to hundreds. For example, the January observation becomes a patient load of 14 and a cost of $139. Be careful how you interpret your analysis.)

3. Write a memo to the hospital administrator comparing the cost estimates using (*a*) least-squares regression, (*b*) the high-low method, and (*c*) the scatter diagram and visually fit semivariable-cost line from the preceding case (requirement 4). Make a recommendation as to which estimate should be used, and support your recommendation. Make any other suggestions you feel are appropriate.

4. After receiving the memo comparing the three cost estimates, Mahoney called McDonough to discuss the matter. The following exchange occurred.

    Mahoney: "As you know, Megan, I was never in favor of this clinic. It's going to be a drag on our administrative staff, and we'd have been far better off keeping the pediatrics operation here in the hospital."

    McDonough: "I was aware that you felt the clinic was a mistake. Of course, the board of trustees had other issues to consider. I believe the board felt the clinic should be built to make pediatric care more accessible to the economically depressed area on the other side of the city."

    Mahoney: "That's true, but the board doesn't realize how difficult it's going to make life for us here in the hospital. In any case, I called to tell you that when you and I report to the board next week, I'm going to recommend that the clinic be shut down. I want you to support my recommendation with one of your cost estimates showing that administrative costs will soar at high activity levels."

    McDonough: "But that estimate was based on the high-low method. It's not an appropriate method for this situation."

    Mahoney: It *is* an estimate, Megan, and it's based on a well-known estimation method. This is just the ammunition I need to make the board see things my way."

    McDonough: "I don't know, Jeff. I just don't think I can go along with that."

    Mahoney: "Be a team player, Megan. I've got a meeting now. Got to run."

    That night McDonough called to discuss the matter with her best friend, you. What would you advise her?

Current Issues in Managerial Accounting

"Can George Fisher Fix Kodak," *Business Week*, **October 20, 1997.**

Overview

Recently Kodak's stock price fell 33 percent. Chairman George Fisher formed a management team that will formulate strategies to change the firm's cost structure and marketing efforts.

Suggested Discussion Questions

In groups, list 10 ways Kodak can change its cost structure. Explain how the new manufacturing environment has changed the firm's cost structure. Present your list in class. What items appear most frequently? How has the global business environment affected the way Kodak does business?

■ **Issue 7–47**
Cost Behavior Patterns;
New Manufacturing
Environment

"AT&T Chief Halts Hiring, Shifts Budget," *The Wall Street Journal*, **December 19, 1997.**

Overview

AT&T announced that it has frozen hiring, redesigned compensation plans, and will attempt to cut more costs. AT&T's strategy is to invest the cost savings into projects that will provide revenue growth.

Suggested Discussion Questions

According to this article, AT&T's biggest expenses are access fees paid to local carriers; selling, general, and administrative expenses; network, computer, and billing systems; and depreciation. Are these expenses fixed, variable, or step-variable costs? Does the nature of these costs influence AT&T's method of reducing these costs? If so, how? Which costs would be the easiest to reduce? If the firm makes new investments, what costs would increase? What is the nature of these costs?

■ **Issue 7–48**
Cost Behavior Patterns

"The Axman Cometh," *Business Week*, **October 20, 1997.**

Overview

WorldCom, Inc.'s chairman, Bernard J. Ebbers, has a formula for success—he chooses a target, buys it, and cuts costs. He prefers not to spend money on items such as entertainment or advertising.

Suggested Discussion Questions

Listed below are costs that WorldCom's chairman attempts to reduce. Next to each cost, describe the nature of the cost (e.g., fixed or variable, engineered, committed, or discretionary).

1. Sales, general, and administrative costs.
2. Executive perks.
3. Entertainment.
4. Advertising.

■ **Issue 7–49**
Cost Behavior Patterns;
Engineered, Committed,
and Discretionary Costs

"How Ford Cut Costs on Its 1997 Taurus, Little by Little," *The Wall Street Journal*, **July 18, 1996.**

Overview

Ford engineers have redesigned the Taurus and saved $180 per car that could save the car company $73 million each year. Examples of changes include increased use of plastic.

Suggested Discussion Questions

Form teams to redesign the Taurus. Develop a five- to ten-step plan that could reduce the 1996 model's cost. Present the plan to your supervisor. Be sure to include in your analysis the nature of the costs you are eliminating.

■ **Issue 7–50**
Cost Behavior Patterns;
Engineered, Committed
and Discretionary Costs

"Investors Seek Firms That Offer Predictable Growth in Earnings," *The Wall Street Journal*, **May 5, 1997.**

Overview

Some investors prefer firms whose earnings are relatively predictable. However, other analysts and investors believe this sector is overvalued and that the real bargains exist in small stocks.

Suggested Discussion Questions

As a group, select one of the following industries: manufacturing, merchandising, or service. What effect does the nature of the cost structure in the new manufacturing environment have on a firm's ability to maintain steady growth? What effect does computer automation have on costs? Select one or more firms in your industry to illustrate your points. Present your ideas to a group of investors.

■ **Issue 7–51**
Shifting Cost Structure in
the New Manufacturing
Environment

Chapter Eight

Cost-Volume-Profit Analysis

After completing this chapter, you should be able to:

1   Compute a break-even point using the contribution-margin approach and the equation approach.

2   Compute the contribution-margin ratio, and use it to find the break-even point in sales dollars.

3   Prepare a cost-volume-profit graph, and explain how it is used.

4   Apply CVP analysis to determine the effect on profit of changes in fixed expenses, variable expenses, sales prices, and sales volume.

5   Compute the break-even point and prepare a profit-volume graph for a multiproduct enterprise.

6   List and discuss the key assumptions of CVP analysis.

7   Prepare and interpret a contribution income statement.

8   Explain the role of cost structure and operating leverage in CVP relationships.

9   Understand the implications of activity-based costing for CVP analysis.

10   Be aware of the effects of advanced manufacturing technology on CVP relationships.

SHAKESPEAREAN SPOOF LEADS OFF THE SEASON FOR SEATTLE CONTEMPORARY THEATER

Seattle, WA—Seattle Contemporary Theater has announced its schedule of productions for the coming year. According to Megan Joseph, the theater's managing director, the first play of the new season will be *The Compleat Works of Wllm Shkspr (Abridged)*. "People are going to love this play," said Joseph. "It's really hilarious. It has all the most famous one-liners from Shakespeare's best-loved plays. It's great fun to watch the players attempt to present 37 plays and 154 sonnets, all in just under two hours. All your favorites are in there. 'To be or not to be?' 'A horse! A horse! My kingdom for a horse!' 'Double, double, toil and trouble.'"

Joseph said she expects this to be the theater's best year yet, with around 8,000 tickets sold per month. "Keep in mind," she pointed out, "that a good year for us does not mean a large profit, because Seattle Contemporary Theater is a nonprofit organization. For us, a good year means lots of people seeing our plays, and

serving up the best contemporary theater art that we can."

For Joseph, the Seattle Contemporary Theater is a dream come true. "I studied fine arts in college," she said, "and I wanted to be an actress. I spent about 10 years doing off-Broadway stuff in the Big Apple and 2 more years getting an MFA in London. But I always knew that eventually I wanted to be a director. Seattle Contemporary Theater gives me everything I want. I manage this wonderful theater company in this grand old theater. I direct six plays a year, and I usually get to perform in one or two. That is, if I can make the cut in the auditions."

Joseph explained that the theater company got a big boost from the city of Seattle, when its council agreed to allow use of the historic downtown theater owned by the city. "The city gets a monthly rental charge plus a share of the price of each ticket sold. We try to keep the ticket prices quite reasonable because our goal is to bring theater into the lives of

as many people as possible. Financially, of course, our goal is to just break even each year. We don't want to make a profit, but we can't operate at a loss either. We still have to pay for royalties for use of the plays, salaries for our actors and other employees, insurance, utilities, and so forth. It's easy to get caught up in the sheer fun of being in theater, but it's an important part of my job to pay attention to the business side of things, too. Sometimes it's tricky to project where our break-even point will be. We have to project what our costs will be, decide on our ticket prices, and estimate how much we'll receive in charitable donations from our many friends and supporters. It's crucial that we keep our act together financially as well as artistically. We want to be bringing great theater to the people of Seattle for many years to come."

In the meantime, be sure to catch *The Compleat Works of Wllm Shkspr (Abridged)* which opens soon.

What effect on profit can United Airlines expect if it adds a flight on the Chicago to New York route? How will NBC's profit change if the ratings increase for its evening news program? How many patient days of care must Massachusetts General Hospital provide to break even for the year? What happens to this break-even patient load if the hospital leases a new computerized system for patient records?

Each of these questions concerns the effects on costs and revenues when the organization's activity changes. The analytical technique used by managerial accountants to address these questions is called **cost-volume-profit analysis**. Often called **CVP analysis** for short, this technique summarizes the effects of changes in an organization's *volume* of activity on its *costs*, revenue, and *profit*. Cost-volume-profit analysis can be extended to cover the effects on profit of changes in selling prices, service fees, costs, income-tax rates, and the organization's mix of products or services. What will happen to profit, for example, if the New York Yankees raise ticket prices for stadium seats? In short, CVP analysis provides management with a comprehensive overview of the effects on revenue and costs of all kinds of short-run financial changes.

Although the word *profit* appears in the term, cost-volume-profit analysis is not confined to profit-seeking enterprises. Managers in nonprofit organizations also routinely use CVP analysis to examine the effects of activity and other short-run changes on revenue and costs. For example, as the state of Florida gains nearly 1,000 people a day in population, the state's political leaders must analyze the effects of this change on sales-tax revenues and the cost of providing services, such as education, transportation, and police protection. Managers at such diverse nonprofit institutions as the New York Public Library, Harvard University, and the United Way all use CVP analysis as a routine operational tool.

> **Cost-volume-profit (CVP) analysis** is a study of the relationships between sales volume, expenses, revenue, and profit.

Illustration of Cost-Volume-Profit Analysis

To illustrate the various analytical techniques used in cost-volume-profit analysis, we will focus on a performing arts organization. The Seattle Contemporary Theater was recently formed as a nonprofit enterprise to bring contemporary drama to the Seattle area. The organization has a part-time, unpaid board of trustees comprised of local professional people who are avid theater fans. The board has hired the following full-time employees.

> *Managing director:* Responsibilities include overall management of the organization; direction of six plays per year.
>
> *Artistic director:* Responsibilities include hiring of actors and production crews for each play; direction of six plays per year.
>
> *Business manager and producer:* Responsibilities include managing the organization's business functions and ticket sales; direction of the production crews, who handle staging, lighting, costuming, and makeup.

The board of trustees has negotiated an agreement with the city of Seattle to hold performances in a historic theater owned by the city. The theater has not been used for 30 years, but the city has agreed to refurbish it and to provide lighting and sound equipment. In return, the city will receive a rental charge of $10,000 per month plus $8 for each theater ticket sold.

Projected Expenses and Revenue

The theater's business manager and producer, George Bernard, has made the following projections for the first few years of operation.

Fixed expenses per month:

Theater rental	$10,000
Employees' salaries and fringe benefits	8,000
Actors' wages	15,000
(to be supplemented with local volunteer talent)	
Production crew's wages	5,600
(to be supplemented with local volunteers)	
Playwrights' royalties for use of plays	5,000
Insurance	1,000
Utilities—fixed portion	1,400
Advertising and promotion	800
Administrative expenses	1,200
Total fixed expenses per month	$48,000

Variable expenses per ticket sold:

City's charge per ticket for use of theater	$ 8
Other miscellaneous expenses (for example, printing of playbills and tickets,	
variable portion of utilities)	2
Total variable cost per ticket sold	$10

Revenue:

Price per ticket	$16

Importance of Cost Behavior   Notice that the theater's expenses have been categorized according to their cost behavior; fixed or variable. Analyzing an organization's cost behavior, the topic of Chapter 7, is a necessary first step in any cost-volume-profit analysis. As we proceed through this chapter, the data pertaining to Seattle Contemporary Theater will be an important part of our cost-volume-profit analysis.

The Break-Even Point

As the first step in the CVP analysis for Seattle Contemporary Theater, we will find the **break-even point**. The break-even point is the volume of activity where the organization's revenues and expenses are equal. At this amount of sales, the organization has no profit or loss; it *breaks even*.

> **LO 1**   Compute a break-even point using the contribution-margin approach and the equation approach.

> The **break-even point** is the volume of activity at which an organization's revenues and expenses are equal.

Suppose Seattle Contemporary Theater sells 8,000 tickets during a play's one-month run. The following income statement shows that the profit for the month will be zero; thus, the theater will break even.

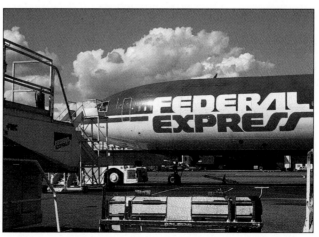

Whether running a small florist shop or a worldwide express delivery service, understanding cost-volume-profit relationships is crucial in managing a business.

Sales revenue (8,000 × $16)	$128,000
Less variable expenses (8,000 × $10)	80,000
Total contribution margin	$ 48,000
Less fixed expenses	48,000
Profit	$ 0

The **total contribution margin** is total sales revenue less total variable expenses.

Notice that this income statement highlights the distinction between variable and fixed expenses. The statement also shows the **total contribution margin**, which is defined as total sales revenue minus total variable expenses. This is the amount of revenue that is available to *contribute* to covering fixed expenses after all variable expenses have been covered. The contribution income statement will be covered in more depth later in the chapter. At this juncture, it provides a useful way to think about the meaning of breaking even.

How could we compute Seattle Contemporary Theater's break-even point if we did not already know it is 8,000 tickets per month? This is the question to which we turn our attention next.

Contribution-Margin Approach

Seattle Contemporary Theater will break even when the organization's revenue from ticket sales is equal to its expenses. How many tickets must be sold during one month (one play's run) for the organization to break even?

Each ticket sells for $16, but $10 of this is used to cover the variable expense per ticket. This leaves $6 per ticket to *contribute* to covering the fixed expenses of $48,000. When enough tickets have been sold in one month so that these $6 contributions per ticket add up to $48,000, the organization will break even for the month. Thus, we may compute the break-even volume of tickets as follows:

$$\frac{\text{Fixed expenses}}{\text{Contribution of each ticket toward covering fixed expenses}} = \frac{\$48,000}{\$6} = 8,000$$

Seattle Contemporary Theater must sell 8,000 tickets during a play's one-month run to break even for the month.

The **unit contribution margin** is the sales price minus the unit variable cost.

The $6 amount that remains of each ticket's price, after the variable expenses are covered, is called the **unit contribution margin**. The general formula for computing the break-even sales volume in units is given below.

$$\frac{\text{Fixed expenses}}{\text{Unit contribution margin}} = \text{Break-even point (in units)} \qquad (1)$$

LO 2   Compute the contribution-margin ratio, and use it to find the break-even point in sales dollars.

Contribution-Margin Ratio   Sometimes management prefers that the break-even point be expressed in sales *dollars* rather than *units*. Seattle Contemporary Theater's break-even point in sales dollars is computed as follows.

Break-even point in units (tickets)	8,000
Sales price per unit	× $16
Break-even point in sales dollars	$128,000

The following computation provides an alternative way to determine the break-even point in sales dollars.

$$\frac{\text{Fixed expenses}}{\dfrac{\text{Unit contribution margin}}{\text{Unit sales price}}} = \frac{\$48,000}{\dfrac{\$6}{\$16}} = \frac{\$48,000}{.375} = \$128,000$$

The unit contribution margin divided by the unit sales price is called the **contribution-margin ratio.** This ratio can also be expressed as a percentage, in which case it is called the *contribution-margin percentage.* Seattle Contemporary Theater's contribution-margin ratio is .375 (in percentage form, 37.5%). Thus, the organization's break-even point in sales dollars may be found by dividing its fixed expenses by its contribution-margin ratio. The logic behind this approach is that 37.5 percent of each sales dollar is available to make a contribution toward covering fixed expenses. The general formula is given below.

> The **contribution-margin ratio** is the unit contribution margin divided by the sales price per unit.

$$\frac{\text{Fixed expenses}}{\text{Contribution-margin ratio}} = \text{Break-even point in sales dollars} \quad (2)$$

Equation Approach

An alternative approach to finding the break-even point is based on the profit equation. Income (or profit) is equal to sales revenue minus expenses. If expenses are separated into variable and fixed expenses, the essence of the income (profit) statement is captured by the following equation.

> **LO 1** Compute a break-even point using the contribution-margin approach and the equation approach.

$$\text{Sales revenue} - \text{Variable expenses} - \text{Fixed expenses} = \text{Profit}$$

This equation can be restated as follows:

$$\left[\begin{pmatrix} \text{Unit} \\ \text{sales} \\ \text{price} \end{pmatrix} \times \begin{pmatrix} \text{Sales} \\ \text{volume} \\ \text{in units} \end{pmatrix} \right] - \left[\begin{pmatrix} \text{Unit} \\ \text{variable} \\ \text{expense} \end{pmatrix} \times \begin{pmatrix} \text{Sales} \\ \text{volume} \\ \text{in units} \end{pmatrix} \right] - \begin{pmatrix} \text{Fixed} \\ \text{expenses} \end{pmatrix}$$
$$= \text{Profit} \quad (3)$$

To find Seattle Contemporary Theater's break-even volume of ticket sales per month, we define profit in equation (3) to be zero.

$$(\$16 \times X) - (\$10 \times X) - \$48,000 = 0$$

$$\left[\begin{pmatrix} \text{Unit} \\ \text{sales} \\ \text{price} \end{pmatrix} \times \begin{pmatrix} \text{Sales} \\ \text{volume} \\ \text{in units} \end{pmatrix} \right] - \left[\begin{pmatrix} \text{Unit} \\ \text{variable} \\ \text{expense} \end{pmatrix} \times \begin{pmatrix} \text{Sales} \\ \text{volume} \\ \text{in units} \end{pmatrix} \right] - \begin{pmatrix} \text{Fixed} \\ \text{expenses} \end{pmatrix}$$
$$= \begin{pmatrix} \text{Break-even} \\ \text{profit (zero)} \end{pmatrix} \quad (4)$$

where

X denotes the number of sales units (tickets) required to break even.

Equation (4) can be solved for *X* as shown below.

$$\$16X - \$10X - \$48,000 = 0$$
$$\$6X = \$48,000$$
$$X = \frac{\$48,000}{\$6} = 8,000$$

Using the equation approach, we have arrived at the same general formula for computing the break-even sales volume (formula 1).

The contribution-margin and equation approaches are two equivalent techniques for finding the break-even point. Both methods reach the same conclusion, and so personal preference dictates which approach should be used. The following example illustrates the importance of the break-even point to a major U.S. auto maker.

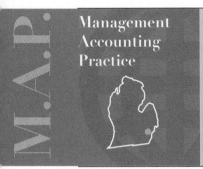

Chrysler Corporation

According to a Detroit Free Press report, for several years Chrysler Corporation operated at a loss. The company received loan guarantees from the United States government to enable it to survive until it became profitable again. Then the company initiated a cost-cutting program that reduced both variable and fixed costs drastically. Over a three-year period, these cost reductions enabled Chrysler's management to decrease the firm's break-even point from 2.2 million to 1.2 million automobiles. By reducing its break-even point, Chrysler was able to survive and to return to the ranks of profitable companies.

In May of 1998, after years of success and profitability, Chrysler announced that it would merge with Germany's Daimler-Benz to form one of the world's largest auto makers.

Graphing Cost-Volume-Profit Relationships

LO 3   Prepare a cost-volume-profit graph, and explain how it is used.

The **cost-volume-profit (CVP) graph** expresses the relationships between sales volume, expenses, revenue, and profit.

While the break-even point conveys useful information to management, it does not show how profit changes as activity changes. To capture the relationship between profit and volume of activity, a **cost-volume-profit (CVP) graph** is commonly used. The following steps are used to prepare a CVP graph for Seattle Contemporary Theater. The graph is displayed in Exhibit 8–1. Notice that the graph shows the *relevant range*, which is the range of activity within which management expects the theater to operate.

Step 1: Draw the axes of the graph. Label the vertical axis in dollars and the horizontal axis in units of sales (tickets).

Step 2: Draw the fixed-expense line. It is parallel to the horizontal axis, since fixed expenses do not change with activity.

Step 3: Compute *total* expense at any convenient volume. For example, select a volume of 6,000 tickets.

Variable expenses (6,000 × $10 per ticket)	$ 60,000
Fixed expenses	48,000
Total expenses (at 6,000 tickets)	$108,000

Plot this point ($108,000 at 6,000 tickets) on the graph. See point *A* on the graph in Exhibit 8–1.

Step 4: Draw the variable-expense line. This line passes through the point plotted in step 3 (point *A*) and the intercept of the fixed-expense line on the vertical axis ($48,000).

Step 5: Compute total sales revenue at any convenient volume. We will choose 6,000 tickets again. Total revenue is $96,000 (6,000 × $16 per ticket). Plot this point ($96,000 at 6,000 tickets) on the graph. See point *B* on the graph in Exhibit 8–1.

Step 6: Draw the total revenue line. This line passes through the point plotted in step 5 (point *B*) and the origin.

Step 7: Label the graph as shown in Exhibit 8–1.

Interpreting the CVP Graph

LO 3   Prepare a cost-volume-profit graph, and explain how it is used.

Several conclusions can be drawn from the CVP graph in Exhibit 8–1.

Break-Even Point   The break-even point is determined by the intersection of the total-revenue line and the total-expense line. Seattle Contemporary Theater breaks even for the month at 8,000 tickets, or $128,000 of ticket sales. This agrees with our calculations in the preceding section.

Profit and Loss Areas   The CVP graph discloses more information than the break-even calculation. From the graph, a manager can see the effects on profit of changes in volume. The vertical distance between the lines on the graph represents the profit or

$000 (per month)

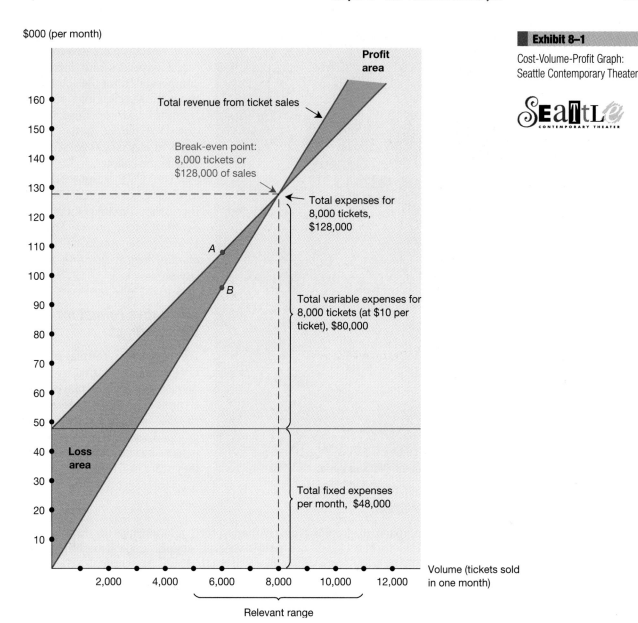

Profit area

Total revenue from ticket sales

Break-even point:
8,000 tickets or
$128,000 of sales

Total expenses for
8,000 tickets,
$128,000

A

B

Total variable expenses for
8,000 tickets (at $10 per
ticket), $80,000

Loss area

Total fixed expenses
per month, $48,000

Volume (tickets sold
in one month)

2,000   4,000   6,000   8,000   10,000   12,000

Relevant range

Exhibit 8–1

Cost-Volume-Profit Graph:
Seattle Contemporary Theater

loss at a particular sales volume. If Seattle Contemporary Theater sells fewer than 8,000 tickets in a month, the organization will suffer a loss. The magnitude of the loss increases as ticket sales decline. The theater organization will have a profit if sales exceed 8,000 tickets in a month.

Implications of the Break-Even Point   The position of the break-even point within an organization's relevant range of activity provides important information to management. The Seattle Contemporary Theater building seats 450 people. The agreement with the city of Seattle calls for 20 performances during each play's one-month run. Thus, the maximum number of tickets that can be sold each month is 9,000 (450 seats × 20 performances). The organization's break-even point is quite close to the maximum possible sales volume. This could be cause for concern in a nonprofit organization operating on limited resources.

What could management do to improve this situation? One possibility is to renegotiate with the city to schedule additional performances. However, this might not be feasible, because the actors need some rest each week. Also, additional performances

Shown here is Chrysler's St. Louis assembly plant. Automobile manufacturers such as Chrysler use break-even analysis and CVP relationships to help manage their businesses.

would likely entail additional costs, such as increased theater-rental expenses and increased compensation for the actors and production crew. Other possible solutions are to raise ticket prices or reduce costs. These kinds of issues will be explored later in the chapter.

The CVP graph will not resolve this potential problem for the management of Seattle Contemporary Theater. However, the graph will *direct management's attention* to the situation.

Alternative Format for the CVP Graph

An alternative format for the CVP graph, preferred by some managers, is displayed in Exhibit 8–2. The key difference is that fixed expenses are graphed above variable expenses, instead of the reverse as they were in Exhibit 8–1.

Profit-Volume Graph

The **profit-volume graph** expresses the relationship between profit and sales volume.

Yet another approach to graphing cost-volume-profit relationships is displayed in Exhibit 8–3. This format is called a **profit-volume graph**, since it highlights the amount of profit or loss. Notice that the graph intercepts the vertical axis at the amount equal to fixed expenses at the zero activity level. The graph crosses the horizontal axis at the break-even point. The vertical distance between the horizontal axis and the profit line, at a particular level of sales volume, is the profit or loss at that volume.

Target Net Profit

LO 4   Apply CVP analysis to determine the effect on profit of changes in fixed expenses, variable expenses, sales prices, and sales volume.

The board of trustees for Seattle Contemporary Theater would like to run free workshops and classes for young actors and aspiring playwrights. This program would cost $3,600 per month in fixed expenses, including teachers' salaries and rental of space at a local college. No variable expenses would be incurred. If Seattle Contemporary Theater could make a profit of $3,600 per month on its performances, the Seattle Drama Workshop could be opened. The board has asked George Bernard, the organization's business manager and producer, to determine how many theater tickets must be sold during each play's one-month run to make a profit of $3,600.

The **target net profit** (or **income**) is the profit level set as management's objective.

The desired profit level of $3,600 is called a **target net profit** (or **income**). The problem of computing the volume of sales required to earn a particular target net profit is very similar to the problem of finding the break-even point. After all, the break-even point is the number of units of sales required to earn a target net profit of zero.

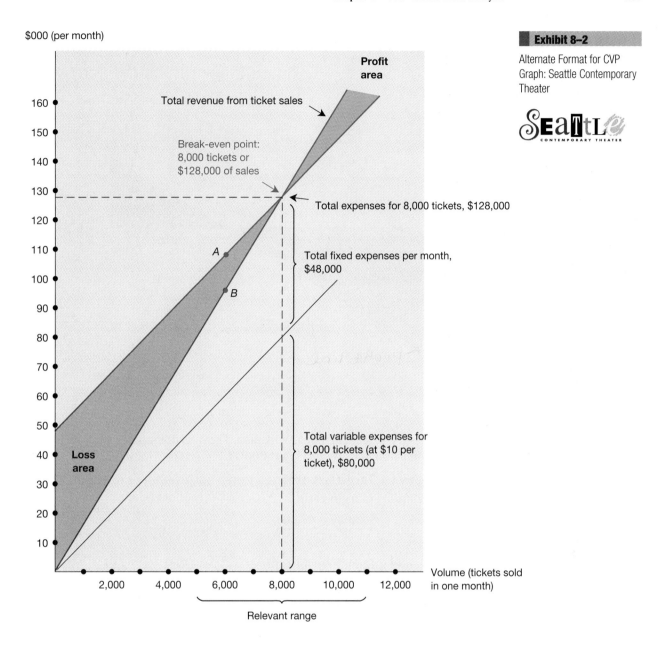

$000 (per month)

Exhibit 8–2

Alternate Format for CVP Graph: Seattle Contemporary Theater

Contribution-Margin Approach

Each ticket sold by Seattle Contemporary Theater has a unit contribution margin of $6 (sales price of $16 minus unit variable expense of $10). Eight thousand of these $6 contributions will contribute just enough to cover fixed expenses of $48,000. *Each additional ticket sold will contribute $6 toward profit*. Thus, we can modify formula (1) given earlier in the chapter as follows:

$$\frac{\text{Fixed expenses} + \text{Target net profit}}{\text{Unit contribution margin}} = \frac{\text{Number of sales units required}}{\text{to earn target net profit}} \quad (5)$$

$$\frac{\$48,000 + \$3,600}{\$6} = 8,600 \text{ tickets}$$

If Seattle Contemporary Theater sells 8,600 tickets during each play's one-month run, the organization will make a monthly profit of $3,600 on its performances. This profit

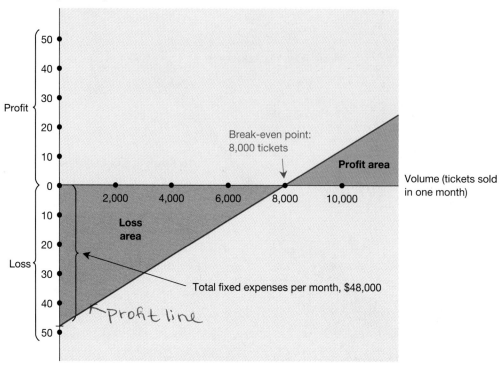

can be used to fund the Seattle Drama Workshop. The total dollar sales required to earn a target net profit is found by modifying formula (2) given previously.

$$\frac{\text{Fixed expenses + Target net profit}}{\text{Contribution-margin ratio}} = \begin{array}{c}\text{Dollar sales required to earn}\\\text{target net profit}\end{array} \qquad (6)$$

$$\frac{\$48,000 + \$3,600}{.375} = \$137,600$$

$$\text{where the contribution margin ratio} = \frac{\$6}{\$16} = .375$$

This dollar sales figure can also be found by multiplying the required sales of 8,600 tickets by the ticket price of $16 (8,600 × $16 = $137,600).

Equation Approach

The equation approach also can be used to find the units of sales required to earn a target net profit. We can modify the profit equation given previously as follows:

$$\left[\left(\begin{array}{c}\text{Unit}\\\text{sales}\\\text{price}\end{array}\right) \times \left(\begin{array}{c}\text{Sales volume}\\\text{required to}\\\text{earn target}\\\text{net profit}\end{array}\right)\right] - \left[\left(\begin{array}{c}\text{Unit}\\\text{variable}\\\text{expense}\end{array}\right) \times \left(\begin{array}{c}\text{Sales volume}\\\text{required to}\\\text{earn target}\\\text{net profit}\end{array}\right)\right]$$

$$- \left(\begin{array}{c}\text{Fixed}\\\text{expenses}\end{array}\right) = \text{Target net profit}$$

Filling in the values for Seattle Contemporary Theater, we have the following equation.

$$(\$16 \times X) - (\$10 \times X) - \$48,000 = \$3,600 \qquad (7)$$

where *X* denotes the sales volume required to earn the target net profit.

Equation (7) can be solved for X as follows:

$$\underline{\$16X - \$10X} - \$48,000 = \$\ 3,600$$
$$\$6X \qquad\qquad\qquad = \$51,600$$
$$X = \frac{\$51,600}{\$6} = 8,600$$

Graphical Approach

The profit-volume graph in Exhibit 8–3 can also be used to find the sales volume required to earn a target net profit. First, locate Seattle Contemporary Theater's target net profit of $3,600 on the vertical axis. Then move horizontally until the profit line is reached. Finally, move down from the profit line to the horizontal axis to determine the required sales volume.

Applying CVP Analysis

The cost-volume-profit relationships that underlie break-even calculations and CVP graphs have wide-ranging applications in management. We will look at several common applications illustrated by Seattle Contemporary Theater.

Safety Margin

The **safety margin** of an enterprise is the difference between the budgeted sales revenue and the break-even sales revenue. Suppose Seattle Contemporary Theater's business manager expects every performance of each play to be sold out. Then budgeted monthly sales revenue is $144,000 (450 seats × 20 performances of each play × $16 per ticket). Since break-even sales revenue is $128,000, the organization's safety margin is $16,000 ($144,000 − $128,000). The safety margin gives management a feel for how close projected operations are to the organization's break-even point. We will further discuss the safety margin concept later in the chapter.

> **LO 4**   Apply CVP analysis to determine the effect on profit of changes in fixed expenses, variable expenses, sales prices, and sales volume.

> The **safety margin** is the difference between budgeted sales revenue and break-even sales revenue.

Changes in Fixed Expenses

What would happen to Seattle Contemporary Theater's break-even point if fixed expenses change? Suppose the business manager is concerned that the estimate for fixed utilities expenses, $1,400 per month, is too low. What would happen to the break-even point if fixed utilities expenses prove to be $2,600 instead? The break-even calculations for both the original and the new estimate of fixed utilities expenses are as follows:

	Original Estimate	New Estimate
Fixed utilities expenses	$ 1,400	$ 2,600
Total fixed expenses	$48,000	$49,200
Break-even calculation	$\dfrac{\$48,000}{\$6}$	$\dfrac{\$49,200}{\$6}$
(Fixed expenses ÷ Unit contribution margin)		
Break-even point (units)	8,000 tickets	8,200 tickets
Break-even point (dollars)	$128,000	$131,200

The estimate of fixed expenses has increased by 2.5 percent, since $1,200 is 2.5 percent of $48,000. Notice that the break-even point also increased by 2.5 percent (200 tickets is 2.5 percent of 8,000 tickets). This relationship will always exist.

$$\frac{\text{Fixed expenses}}{\text{Unit contribution margin}} = \text{Break-even point (in units)}$$

$$\frac{\text{Fixed expenses} \times 1.025}{\text{Unit contribution margin}} = \text{(Break-even point in units)} \times 1.025$$

Donations to Offset Fixed Expenses   Nonprofit organizations often receive cash donations from people or organizations desiring to support a worthy cause. A donation is equivalent to a reduction in fixed expenses, and it reduces the organization's break-even point. In our original set of data, Seattle Contemporary Theater's monthly fixed expenses total $48,000. Suppose that various people pledge donations amounting to $6,000 per month. The new break-even point is computed as follows:

$$\frac{\text{Fixed expenses} - \text{Donations}}{\text{Unit contribution margin}} = \text{Break-even point (in units)}$$

$$\frac{\$48,000 - \$6,000}{\$6} = 7,000 \text{ tickets}$$

Changes in the Unit Contribution Margin

What would happen to Seattle Contemporary Theater's break-even point if miscellaneous variable expenses were $3 per ticket instead of $2? Alternatively, what would be the effect of raising the ticket price to $18?

Change in Unit Variable Expenses   If the theater organization's miscellaneous variable expenses increase from $2 to $3 per ticket, the unit contribution margin will fall from $6 to $5. The original and new break-even points are computed as follows:

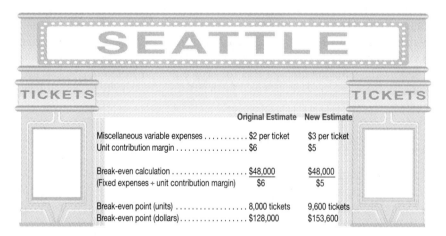

	Original Estimate	New Estimate
Miscellaneous variable expenses	$2 per ticket	$3 per ticket
Unit contribution margin	$6	$5
Break-even calculation	$48,000	$48,000
(Fixed expenses ÷ unit contribution margin)	$6	$5
Break-even point (units)	8,000 tickets	9,600 tickets
Break-even point (dollars)	$128,000	$153,600

If this change in unit variable expenses actually occurs, it will no longer be possible for the organization to break even. Only 9,000 tickets are available for each play's one-month run (450 seats × 20 performances), but 9,600 tickets would have to be sold to break even. Once again, CVP analysis will not solve this problem for management, but it will direct management's attention to potentially serious difficulties.

Change in Sales Price Changing the unit sales price will also alter the unit contribution margin. Suppose the ticket price is raised from $16 to $18. This change will raise the unit contribution margin from $6 to $8. The new break-even point will be 6,000 tickets ($48,000 × $8).

A $2 increase in the ticket price will lower the break-even point from 8,000 tickets to 6,000 tickets. Is this change desirable? A lower break-even point decreases the risk of operation with a loss if sales are sluggish. However, the organization may be more likely to at least break even with a $16 ticket price than with an $18 ticket price. The

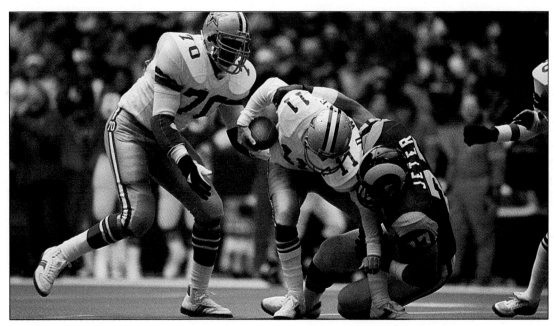

Cost-volume-profit analysis for a professional sports team must account for the huge impact of TV revenue, as well as ticket sales, players' salaries, and operating costs.

reason is that the lower ticket price encourages more people to attend the theater's performances. It could be that break-even sales of 8,000 tickets at $16 are more likely than break-even sales of 6,000 tickets at $18. Ultimately, the desirability of the ticket-price increase depends on management's assessment of the likely reaction by theater patrons.

Management's decision about the ticket price increase also will reflect the fundamental goals of Seattle Contemporary Theater. This nonprofit drama organization was formed to bring contemporary drama to the people of Seattle. The lower the ticket price, the more accessible the theater's productions to people of all income levels.

The point of this discussion is that CVP analysis provides valuable information, but it is only one of several elements that influence management's decisions.

Predicting Profit Given Expected Volume

So far, we have focused on finding the required sales volume to break even or achieve a particular target net profit. Thus, we have asked the following question.

Given:
$$\left\{ \begin{array}{l} \text{Fixed expenses} \\ \text{Unit contribution margin} \\ \text{Target net profit} \end{array} \right\}, \quad \text{Find: \{required sales volume\}}$$

We can also use CVP analysis to turn this question around and make the following query.

Given:
$$\left\{ \begin{array}{l} \text{Fixed expenses} \\ \text{Unit contribution margin} \\ \text{Expected sales volume} \end{array} \right\}, \quad \text{Find: \{expected profit\}}$$

Suppose the management of Seattle Contemporary Theater expects fixed monthly expenses of $48,000 and unit variable expenses of $10 per ticket. The organization's board of trustees is considering two different ticket prices, and the business manager has forecast monthly demand at each price.

Ticket Price		Forecast Monthly Demand
$16	....	9,000
$20	....	6,000

The total contribution margin is total sales revenue less total variable expenses.

Expected profit may be calculated at each price as shown below. In these profit calculations, the **total contribution margin** is the difference between *total* sales revenue and *total* variable expenses. This use of the term *contribution margin* is a "total" concept rather than the "per unit" concept used earlier in the chapter. The *total contribution margin* is the *total* amount left to contribute to covering fixed expenses after *total* variable expenses have been covered.

	Ticket Price	
	$16	**$20**
Sales revenue:		
9,000 × $16	$144,000	
6,000 × $20		$120,000
Less variable expenses:		
9,000 × $10	90,000	
6,000 × $10		60,000
Total contribution margin	$ 54,000	$ 60,000
Less fixed expenses	48,000	48,000
Profit	$ 6,000	$ 12,000

The difference in expected profit at the two ticket prices is due to two factors:

1. A different *unit* contribution margin, defined previously as *unit* sales price minus *unit* variable expenses
2. A different sales volume

Incremental Approach   Rather than presenting the entire income statement under each ticket price alternative, we can use a simpler incremental approach. This analysis focuses only on the difference in the total contribution margin under the two prices. Thus, the combined effect of the change in unit contribution margin and the change in sales volume is as follows:

Expected *total* contribution margin at $20 ticket price:	
6,000 × ($20 − $10)	$60,000
Expected *total* contribution margin at $16 ticket price:	
9,000 × ($16 − $10)	54,000
Difference in *total* contribution margin	$ 6,000

The $6,000 difference in expected profit, at the two ticket prices, is due to a $6,000 difference in the total contribution margin. The board of trustees will consider these projected profits as it decides which ticket price is best. Even though Seattle Contemporary Theater is a nonprofit organization, it may still have legitimate reasons for attempting to make a profit on its theater performances. For example, the board might use these profits to fund a free drama workshop, provide scholarships for local young people to study drama in college, or produce a free outdoor play for Seattle's residents.

Interdependent Changes in Key Variables

Sometimes a change in one key variable will cause a change in another key variable. Suppose the board of trustees is choosing between ticket prices of $16 and $20, and the business manager has projected demand as shown in the preceding section. A famous retired actress who lives in Seattle has offered to donate $10,000 per month to Seattle Contemporary Theater if the board will set the ticket price at $16. The actress is interested in making the theater's performances affordable by as many people as possible. The facts are now as follows:

Ticket Price	Unit Contribution Margin	Forecast Monthly Demand	Net Fixed Expenses (after subtracting donation)
$16	$ 6	9,000	$38,000 ($48,000 – $10,000)
20	10	6,000	48,000

The organization's expected profit at each price is computed as follows:

	Ticket Price	
	$16	**$20**
Sales revenue:		
9,000 × $16	$144,000	
6,000 × $20		$120,000
Less variable expenses:		
9,000 × $10	$ 90,000	
6,000 × $10		60,000
Total contribution margin	$ 54,000	$ 60,000
Less net fixed expenses	38,000	48,000
(net of donation)		
Profit	$ 16,000	$ 12,000

Now the difference in expected profit at the two ticket prices is due to three factors:

1. A different *unit* contribution margin.
2. A different sales volume.
3. A difference in the *net* fixed expenses, after deducting the donation.

Incremental Approach The combined effect of these factors is shown in the following analysis, which focuses on the effects of the price alternatives on the total contribution margin and the net fixed expenses.

Expected *total* contribution margin at $20 ticket price:	
6,000 × ($20 – $10)	$60,000
Expected *total* contribution margin at $16 ticket price:	
9,000 × ($16 – $10)	$54,000
Difference in *total* contribution margin	$ 6,000
(higher with $20 ticket price)	
Net fixed expenses at $20 ticket price	$48,000
Net fixed expenses at $16 ticket price	38,000
Difference in net fixed expenses (higher with $20 ticket price)	$10,000

The expected total contribution margin is $6,000 higher with the $20 ticket price, but net fixed expenses are $10,000 higher. Thus, Seattle Contemporary Theater will make $4,000 more in profit at the $16 price ($10,000 – $6,000).

CVP Information in Published Annual Reports

Cost-volume-profit relationships are so important to understanding an organization's operations that some companies disclose CVP information in their published annual reports. The following illustration is from the airline industry.

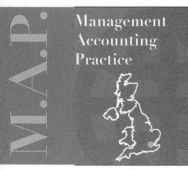

M.A.P.

Management
Accounting
Practice

British Airways

British Airways is a major airline with flight operations throughout the world. A recent annual report listed the company's *break-even passenger load factor* for each of the past five years. This factor is defined as the average percentage of seats that must be filled for the airline's operating revenues to equal its operating costs and interest expense. The break-even passenger load factor for the most recent year listed in the annual report was 64.5 percent.

Major airlines such as British Airways keep a close watch on the break-even passenger load factor.

CVP Analysis with Multiple Products

LO 5   Compute the break-even point and prepare a profit-volume graph for a multiproduct enterprise.

Our CVP illustration for Seattle Contemporary Theater has assumed that the organization has only one product, a theater seat at a dramatic performance. Most firms have more than one product, and this adds some complexity to their CVP analyses.

As we have seen, Seattle Contemporary Theater's monthly fixed expenses total $48,000, and the unit variable expense per ticket is $10. Now suppose that the city of Seattle has agreed to refurbish 10 theater boxes in the historic theater building. Each box has five seats, which are more comfortable and afford a better view of the stage than the theater's general seating. The board of trustees has decided to charge $16 per ticket for general seating and $20 per ticket for box seats. These facts are summarized as follows:

Seat Type	Ticket Price	Unit Variable Expense	Unit Contribution Margin	Seats in Theater	Seats Available per Month (20 performances)
Regular	$16	$10	$ 6	450	9,000
Box	20	10	10	50	1,000

Notice that 90 percent of the available seats are regular seats, and 10 percent are box seats. The business manager estimates that tickets for each type of seat will be sold in the same proportion as the number of seats available. If, for example, 5,000 tickets are sold during a month, sales will be as follows:

Regular seats:	90% × 5,000	4,500
Box seats:	10% × 5,000	500
Total		5,000

For any organization selling multiple products, the relative proportion of each type of product *sold* is called the **sales mix**. The business manager's estimate of Seattle Contemporary Theater's *sales mix* is 90 percent regular seats and 10 percent box seats.

The sales mix is an important assumption in multiproduct CVP analysis. The sales mix is used to compute a **weighted-average unit contribution margin**. This is the *average* of the several products' *unit contribution margins, weighted* by the relative sales proportion of each product. Seattle Contemporary Theater's weighted-average unit contribution margin is computed below.

$$\text{Weighted-average unit contribution margin} = (\$6 \times 90\%) + (\$10 \times 10\%) = \$6.40$$

The **sales mix** is the relative proportion of sales of each of an organization's multiple products.

The **weighted-average unit contribution margin** is the average of a firm's several products' unit contribution margins, weighted by the relative sales proportion of each product.

The organization's break-even point in units is computed using the following formula.

$$\text{Break-even point} = \frac{\text{Fixed expenses}}{\text{Weighted-average unit contribution margin}} \qquad (8)$$

$$= \frac{\$48,000}{\$6.40} = \textbf{7,500 tickets}$$

The break-even point of 7,500 tickets must be interpreted in light of the sales mix. Seattle Contemporary Theater will break even for the month if it sells 7,500 tickets as follows:

Break-even	Regular seats:	7,500 × 90%	6,750 tickets
sales in	Box seats:	7,500 × 10%	750 tickets
units	Total		7,500 tickets

The following income calculation verifies the break-even point.

Sales revenue:			
Regular seats:	6,750 × $16		$108,000
Box seats:	750 × $20		15,000
Total revenue:	7,500 seats in total		$123,000
Less variable expenses: 7,500 × $10			75,000
Total contribution margin			$ 48,000
Less fixed expenses			48,000
Profit			$ 0

The break-even point of 7,500 tickets per month is *valid only for the sales mix assumed* in computing the weighted-average unit contribution margin. If 7,500 tickets are sold in any other mix of regular and box seats, the organization will not break even.

Notice that break-even formula (8) is a modification of formula (1) given earlier in the chapter. The only difference is that formula (8) uses the *weighted-average* unit contribution margin.

Seattle Contemporary Theater's business manager has constructed the profit-volume graph in Exhibit 8–4. The PV graph shows the organization's profit at any level of total monthly sales, assuming the sales mix of 90 percent regular seats and 10 percent box seats. For example, if 9,000 tickets are sold in total, at the assumed sales mix, the PV graph indicates that profit will be $9,600.

With multiproduct CVP analysis, a managerial accountant can investigate the impact on profit of changes in sales volume, prices, variable costs, fixed costs, or the sales mix itself. For example, what would be the effect on Seattle Contemporary Theater's break-even point if the sales mix were 95 percent regular seats and 5 percent box seats? With this sales mix, the weighted-average unit contribution margin is computed as follows:

$$\text{Weighted-average unit contribution margin} = (\$6 \times 95\%) + (\$10 \times 5\%) = \$6.20$$

Exhibit 8–4

Profit-Volume Graph with
Multiple Products: Seattle
Contemporary Theater

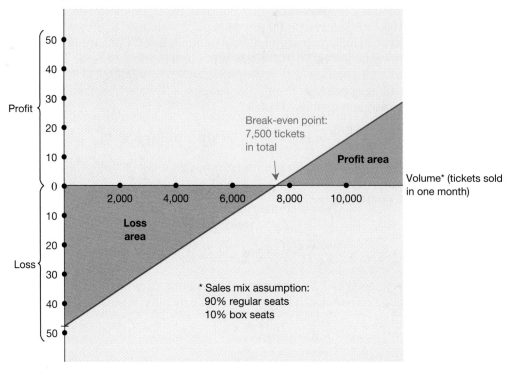

The break-even point increases from 7,500 tickets to approximately 7,742 tickets as a
result of the lower proportion of expensive seats in the sales mix.

$$\text{Break-even point} = \frac{\text{Fixed expenses}}{\text{Weighted-average unit contribution margin}}$$

$$= \frac{\$48,000}{\$6.20} = 7,742 \text{ tickets*}$$

*Rounded

Assumptions Underlying CVP Analysis

LO 6   List and discuss the key
assumptions of CVP analysis.

For any cost-volume-profit analysis to be valid, the following important
assumptions must be reasonably satisfied *within the relevant range.*

1. The behavior of total revenue is linear (straight-line). This implies that the price
   of the product or service will not change as sales volume varies within the relevant range.
2. The behavior of total expenses is linear (straight-line) over the relevant range.
   This implies the following more specific assumptions.
   a. Expenses can be categorized as fixed, variable, or semivariable. *Total* fixed
       expenses remain constant as activity changes, and the *unit* variable expense
       remains unchanged as activity varies.
   b. The efficiency and productivity of the production process and workers remain
       constant.
3. In multiproduct organizations, the sales mix remains constant over the relevant
   range.
4. In manufacturing firms, the inventory levels at the beginning and end of the
   period are the same. This implies that the number of units produced during the
   period equals the number of units sold.

Role of Computerized Planning Models and Electronic Spreadsheets

Cost-volume-profit analysis is based on the four general assumptions listed above as well as specific estimates of all the variables used in the analysis. Since these variables are rarely known with certainty, it is helpful to run a CVP analysis many times with different combinations of estimates. For example, Seattle Contemporary Theater's business manager might do the CVP analysis using different estimates for the ticket prices, sales mix for regular and box seats, unit variable expenses, and fixed expenses. This approach is called **sensitivity analysis**, since it provides the analyst with a feel for how sensitive the analysis is to the estimates upon which it is based. The widespread availability of personal computers and electronic spreadsheet software has made sensitivity analysis relatively easy to do.

> **Sensitivity analysis** is a technique for determining what would happen in a decision analysis if a key prediction or assumption proves to be wrong.

CVP Relationships and the Income Statement

The management functions of planning, control, and decision making all are facilitated by an understanding of cost-volume-profit relationships. These relationships are important enough to operating managers that some businesses prepare income statements in a way that highlights CVP issues. Before we examine this new income-statement format, we will review the more traditional income statement used in the preceding chapters.

Traditional Income Statement

An income statement for AccuTime Company, a manufacturer of digital clocks, is shown in Exhibit 8–5 (panel A). During 19x9 the firm manufactured and sold 20,000 clocks at a price of $25 each. This income statement is prepared in the traditional manner. *Cost of goods sold* includes both variable and fixed manufacturing costs, as measured by the firm's product-costing system. The *gross margin* is computed by subtracting cost of goods sold from sales. Selling and administrative expenses are then subtracted; each expense includes both variable and fixed costs. *The traditional income statement does not disclose the breakdown of each expense into its variable and fixed components.*

 AccuTime

Contribution Income Statement

Many operating managers find the traditional income-statement format difficult to use, because it does not separate variable and fixed expenses. Instead they prefer the **contribution income statement**. A contribution income statement for AccuTime is shown in Exhibit 8–5 (panel B). *The contribution format highlights the distinction between variable and fixed expenses.* The variable manufacturing cost of each clock is $14, and the total fixed manufacturing cost is $100,000. On the contribution income statement, all variable expenses are subtracted from sales to obtain the *contribution margin*. For AccuTime, $200,000 remains from total sales revenue, after all variable costs have been covered, to contribute to covering fixed costs and making a profit. All fixed costs are then subtracted from the contribution margin to obtain net income.

> **LO 7** Prepare and interpret a contribution income statement.

> The **contribution income statement** is an income statement on which fixed and variable expenses are separated.

Comparison of Traditional and Contribution Income Statements

Operating managers frequently prefer the contribution income statement, because its separation of fixed and variable expenses highlights cost-volume-profit relationships. It is readily apparent from the contribution-format statement how income will be affected when sales volume changes by a given percentage. Suppose management projects that sales volume in 20x0 will be 20 percent greater than in 19x9. No changes are anticipated in the sales price, variable cost per unit, or fixed costs.

A. Traditional Format

ACCUTIME COMPANY
Income Statement
For the Year Ended December 31, 19x9

Sales		$500,000
Less: Cost of goods sold		380,000
Gross margin		$120,000
Less: Operating expenses:		
Selling expenses	$35,000	
Administrative expenses	35,000	70,000
Net income		$ 50,000

B. Contribution Format

ACCUTIME COMPANY
Income Statement
For the Year Ended December 31, 19x9

Sales		$500,000
Less Variable expenses:		
Variable manufacturing	$280,000	
Variable selling	15,000	
Variable administrative	5,000	300,000
Contribution margin		$200,000
Less Fixed expenses:		
Fixed manufacturing	$100,000	
Fixed selling	20,000	
Fixed administrative	30,000	150,000
Net income		$ 50,000

Examination of the contribution income statement shows that if sales volume increases by 20 percent, the following changes will occur. (Our discussion ignores income taxes, which are covered in the appendix at the end of this chapter.)

Income Statement Item	19x9 Amount	Change	20x0 Amount
Sales	$500,000	$100,000 (20% × $500,000)	$600,000
Total variable expenses	$300,000	$ 60,000 (20% × $300,000)	$360,000
Contribution margin	$200,000	$40,000 (20% × $200,000)	$240,000
Total fixed expenses	$150,000	–0– (no change in fixed expenses when volume changes)	$150,000
Net income	$ 50,000	$ 40,000 (income changes by the amount of the contribution-margin change)	$ 90,000

Notice that net income increases by the same amount as the increase in the contribution margin. Moreover, the contribution margin changes in direct proportion to the change in sales volume. These two facts enable us to calculate the increase in net income using the following shortcut. Recall that the *contribution-margin ratio* is the percentage of contribution margin to sales.

$$\left(\begin{matrix}\text{Increase in}\\\text{sales revenue}\end{matrix}\right) \times \left(\begin{matrix}\text{Contribution-margin}\\\text{ratio}\end{matrix}\right) = \left(\begin{matrix}\text{Increase in}\\\text{net income}\end{matrix}\right)$$

$$\$100,000 \quad \times \quad .40 \quad = \quad \$40,000$$

$$\text{where} \quad \left(\begin{matrix}\text{Contribution-margin}\\\text{ratio}\end{matrix}\right) = \frac{\text{Contribution margin}}{\text{Sales revenue}}$$

$$.40 = \frac{\$200,000}{\$500,000}$$

The analysis above makes use of cost-volume-profit relationships that are disclosed in the contribution income statement. Such an analysis cannot be made with the information presented in the traditional income statement.

Cost Structure and Operating Leverage

The **cost structure** of an organization is the relative proportion of its fixed and variable costs. Cost structures differ widely among industries and among firms within an industry. A company using a computer-integrated manufacturing system has a large investment in plant and equipment, which results in a cost structure dominated by fixed costs. In contrast, a public accounting firm's cost structure has a much higher proportion of variable costs. The highly automated manufacturing firm is capital-intensive, whereas the accounting firm is labor-intensive.

An organization's cost structure has a significant effect on the sensitivity of its profit to changes in volume. A convenient way to portray a firm's cost structure is shown in Exhibit 8–6. The data for AccuTime Company (company A) comes from the firm's 19x9 contribution income statement in Exhibit 8–5. For comparison purposes, two other firms' cost structures are also shown. Although these three firms have the same sales revenue ($500,000) and net income ($50,000), they have very different cost structures. Company B's production process is largely manual, and its cost structure is dominated by variable costs. It has a low contribution-margin ratio of only 20 percent. In contrast, company C employs a highly automated production process, and its cost structure is dominated by fixed costs. The firm's contribution margin ratio is 90 percent. Company A falls between these two extremes with a contribution-margin ratio of 40 percent.

Suppose sales revenue increases by 10 percent, or $50,000, in each company. The resulting increase in each company's profit is calculated in Exhibit 8–7.

Notice that Company B, with its high variable expenses and low contribution-margin ratio, shows a relatively low *percentage* increase in profit. In contrast, the high fixed expenses and large contribution-margin ratio of company C result in a relatively high *percentage* increase in profit. Company A falls in between these two extremes.

LO 8   Explain the role of cost structure and operating leverage in CVP relationships.

Cost structure is the relative proportion of an organization's fixed and variable costs.

A   B

	Company A (AccuTime Company)		Company B (Manual System)		Company C (Automated System)	
	Amount	%	Amount	%	Amount	%
Sales	$500,000	100	$500,000	100	$500,000	100
Variable expenses	300,000	60	400,000	80	50,000	10
Contribution margin	$200,000	40	$100,000	20	$450,000	90
Fixed expenses	150,000	30	50,000	10	400,000	80
Net income	$ 50,000	10	$ 50,000	10	$ 50,000	10

Exhibit 8–6

Comparison of Cost Structures

	Increase in Sales Revenue	×	Contribution Margin Ratio	=	Increase in Net Income	Percentage Increase in Net Income
Company A (AccuTime)	$50,000	×	40%	=	$20,000	40% ($20,000 ÷ $50,000)
Company B (high variable expenses)	$50,000	×	20%	=	$10,000	20% ($10,000 ÷ $50,000)
Company C (high fixed expenses)	$50,000	×	90%	=	$45,000	90% ($45,000 ÷ $50,000)

The greater the proportion of fixed costs in a firm's cost structure, the greater the impact on profit from a given percentage change in sales revenue.

Operating Leverage

**Operating leverage is
the extent to which an
organization uses fixed
costs in its cost structure.**

The extent to which an organization uses fixed costs in its cost structure is called **operating leverage.** The operating leverage is greatest in firms with a large proportion of fixed costs, low proportion of variable costs, and the resulting high contribution-margin ratio. Exhibit 8–6 shows that company B has low operating leverage, company C has high operating leverage, and company A falls in between. To a physical scientist, *leverage* refers to the ability of a small force to move a heavy weight. To the managerial accountant, *operating leverage* refers to the ability of the firm to generate an increase in net income when sales revenue increases.

Measuring Operating Leverage   The managerial accountant can measure a firm's operating leverage, *at a particular sales volume,* using the **operating leverage factor:**

**The operating leverage
factor is computed by
dividing an organization's
total contribution margin
by its net income.**

$$\text{Operating leverage factor} = \frac{\text{Contribution margin}}{\text{Net income}}$$

Using the data in Exhibit 8–6, the operating leverage factors of companies A, B, and C, are computed as follows:

	Contribution Margin	÷	Net Income	=	Operating Leverage Factor
Company A (AccuTime)	$200,000	÷	$50,000	=	4
Company B (high variable expenses)	$100,000	÷	$50,000	=	2
Company C (high fixed expenses)	$450,000	÷	$50,000	=	9

The operating leverage factor is a measure, at a particular level of sales, of the *percentage* impact on net income of a given *percentage* change in sales revenue. Multiplying the *percentage* change in sales revenue by the operating leverage factor yields the *percentage* change in net income.

	Percentage Increase in Sales Revenue	×	Operating Leverage Factor	=	Percentage Change in Net Income
Company A (AccuTime)	10%	×	4	=	40%
Company B (high variable expenses)	10%	×	2	=	20%
Company C (high fixed expenses)	10%	×	9	=	90%

The percentage change in net income shown above for each company may be verified by re-examining Exhibit 8–7.

Break-Even Point and Safety Margin   A firm's operating leverage also affects its break-even point. Since a firm with relatively high operating leverage has proportionally high fixed expenses, the firm's break-even point will be relatively high. This fact is illustrated using the data from Exhibit 8–6.

	$\begin{pmatrix} \text{Fixed} \\ \text{Expenses} \end{pmatrix}$	÷	$\begin{pmatrix} \text{Contribution} \\ \text{Margin Ratio} \end{pmatrix}$	=	$\begin{pmatrix} \text{Break-Even} \\ \text{Sales Revenue} \end{pmatrix}$
Company A (AccuTime)	$150,000	÷	40%	=	$375,000
Company B (high variable expenses)	$ 50,000	÷	20%	=	$250,000
Company C (high fixed expenses)	$400,000	÷	90%	=	$444,444

*Rounded

The safety margin also is affected by a firm's operating leverage. Suppose the budgeted sales revenue for each of the three companies is $500,000. Then the safety margin, defined as budgeted sales revenue minus break-even sales revenue, is calculated as follows:

	Budgeted Sales Revenue	Break-Even Sales Revenue	Safety Margin
Company A (AccuTime)	$500,000	$375,000	$125,000
Company B (high variable expenses)	500,000	250,000	250,000
Company C (high fixed expenses)	500,000	444,444	55,556

To summarize, Company C's high fixed expenses result in a high break-even point and low safety margin. Company B displays the opposite characteristics, and Company A falls in between the two extremes.

Labor-Intensive Production Processes versus Advanced Manufacturing Systems   The effects of labor-intensive (manual) production processes and highly automated, advanced manufacturing systems illustrated by companies A, B, and C are typical. As Exhibit 8–8 shows, a movement toward an advanced manufacturing environment often results in a higher break-even point, lower safety margin, and higher operating

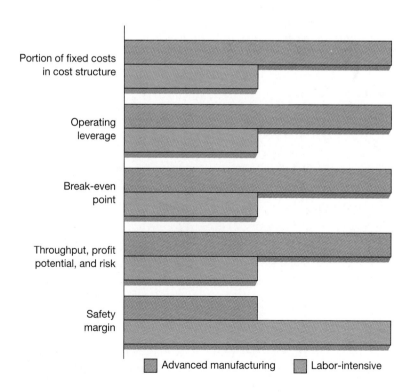

Exhibit 8–8

Labor-Intensive Production Processes Versus Advanced Manufacturing Systems leverage. However, high-technology manufacturing systems generally have greater throughput, thus allowing greater potential for profitability. Along with the increased potential for profitability comes increased risk. In an economic recession, for example, a highly automated company with high fixed costs will be less able to adapt to lower consumer demand than will a firm with a more labor-intensive production process.

Cost Structure and Operating Leverage: A Cost-Benefit Issue

An organization's cost structure plays an important role in determining its cost-volume-profit relationships. A firm with proportionately high fixed costs has relatively high operating leverage. The result of high operating leverage is that the firm can generate a large percentage increase in net income from a relatively small percentage increase in sales revenue. On the other hand, a firm with high operating leverage has a relatively high break-even point. This entails some risk to the firm.

The optimal cost structure for an organization involves a trade-off. Management must weigh the benefits of high operating leverage against the risks of large committed fixed costs and the associated high break-even point.

CVP Analysis, Activity-Based Costing, and Advanced Manufacturing Systems

LO 9 Understand the implications of activity-based costing for CVP analysis.

Traditional cost-volume-profit analysis focuses on the number of units sold as the only cost and revenue driver. Sales revenue is assumed to be linear in units sold. Moreover, costs are categorized as fixed or variable, with respect to the number of units sold, within the relevant range. This approach is consistent with traditional product-costing systems, in which cost assignment is based on a single, volume-related cost driver. In CVP analysis, as in product costing, the traditional approach can be misleading or provide less than adequate information for various management purposes. An activity-based costing system can provide a much more complete picture of cost-volume-profit relationships and thus provide better information to managers.

To illustrate the potential impact of activity-based costing on CVP analysis, we will continue our discussion of AccuTime Company. The basic data underlying the contribution income statement shown in Exhibit 8–5 are as follows:

Sales volume	20,000 units
Sales price	$25
Unit variable costs:	
Variable manufacturing	$14
Variable selling and administrative	1
Total unit variable cost	$15
Unit contribution margin	$10
Fixed costs:	
Fixed manufacturing	$100,000
Fixed selling and administrative	50,000
Total fixed costs	$150,000

These data are adequate for a traditional CVP analysis of various questions management may ask. For example, the break-even point is easily calculated as 15,000 units, as the following analysis shows:

$$\text{Break-even point} = \frac{\text{Fixed costs}}{\text{Unit contribution margin}} = \frac{\$150,000}{\$10} = 15,000 \text{ units}$$

Alternatively, management may determine how many clocks must be sold to earn a target net profit of $200,000, as the following calculation demonstrates:

$$\frac{\text{Sales volume required to earn}}{\text{target net profit of \$200,000}} = \frac{\text{Fixed costs + Target net profit}}{\text{Unit contribution margin}}$$

$$= \frac{\$150,000 + \$200,000}{\$10} = 35,000 \text{ units}$$

What do these questions have in common? They both focus on *sales volume* as the sole revenue and cost driver. The CVP analysis depends on a distinction between costs that are fixed and costs that are variable *with respect to sales volume*.

A Move Toward JIT and Flexible Manufacturing

Now let's examine another question AccuTime's management could face. Suppose management is considering the installation of a flexible manufacturing system and a move toward just-in-time (JIT) production. In the new production process, setups would be quicker and more frequent and production runs would be smaller. Fewer inspections would be required, due to the total quality control (TQC) philosophy that often accompanies JIT. Variable manufacturing costs would be lower, due to savings in direct labor. Finally, general factory overhead costs would increase, due to the greater depreciation charges on the new production equipment.

> **LO 10** Be aware of the effects of advanced manufacturing technology on CVP relationships.

Suppose management wants to answer the same two questions addressed previously, under the assumption that the production process changes are adopted. To properly address this issue, we need a much more detailed understanding of the impact of other, *non-volume-based cost drivers* on AccuTime's costs. This type of detail is the hallmark of an activity-based costing system. Suppose AccuTime's controller completes an ABC analysis of the company's 19x9 activity before the new equipment is installed. The results are shown in Exhibit 8–9.

There is a subtle but important point to realize about the cost behavior depicted in Exhibit 8–9. Setup, inspection, and material handling are listed as fixed costs. *They are fixed with respect to sales volume*. However, they are *not* fixed with respect to *other cost drivers*, such as the number of setups, inspections, and hours of material handling. This is the fundamental distinction between a traditional CVP analysis and an activity-based costing CVP analysis. The traditional CVP analysis recognizes a single, volume-based cost driver, namely, sales volume. The activity-based costing CVP analysis recognizes multiple cost drivers. As a result, some costs viewed as fixed under the

Exhibit 8–9

Activity-Based Costing Data
under Current Production
Process (19x9)

Sales price	$25
Unit variable costs:	
Variable manufacturing	$14
Variable selling and administrative	1
Total unit variable costs	$15
Unit contribution margin	$10
Fixed costs (fixed with respect to sales volume):	
General factory overhead (including depreciation on plant and equipment)	$ 60,000
Setup (52 setups at $100 per setup)*	5,200
Inspection [(52)(21) inspections at $20 per inspection]†	21,840
Material handling (1,080 hours at $12 per hour)	12,960
Total fixed manufacturing costs	$100,000
Fixed selling and administrative costs	50,000
Total fixed costs	$150,000

*One setup per week
†Three inspections per day, seven days a week (52 weeks per year).

Exhibit 8–10

Activity-Based Costing Data
under Proposed Production
Technology

Sales price	$25
Unit variable costs:	
Variable manufacturing	$ 9
Variable selling and administrative	1
Total unit variable costs	$10
Unit contribution margin	$15
Fixed costs (fixed with respect to sales volume):	
General factory overhead (including depreciation on plant and equipment)	$184,000
Setup (365 setups at $30 per setup)	10,950
Inspection (365 inspections at $10 per inspection)	3,650
Material handling (100 hours at $14 per hour)	1,400
Total fixed manufacturing costs	$200,000
Fixed selling and administrative costs	50,000
Total fixed costs	$250,000

traditional analysis are considered variable (with respect to the appropriate cost drivers) under the ABC approach.

Now let's return to management's decision regarding the installation of a flexible manufacturing system and the adoption of the JIT and TQC philosophies. The activity-based costing analysis of the proposed production technology is displayed in Exhibit 8–10. Due to the decreased use of direct labor, the unit variable manufacturing cost has declined from $14 to $9, thus bringing the total unit variable cost down to $10. This results in an increase in the unit contribution margin to $15. The installation of sophisticated new manufacturing equipment has more than tripled general factory overhead, from $60,000 to $184,000. Under the proposed JIT approach, setups will be daily instead of weekly; each setup will be quicker and less expensive. As a result of the emphasis on total quality control, only one inspection per day will be necessary, instead of three as before. Moreover, each inspection will be less expensive. Finally, the amount of material-handling activity will decline dramatically, although there will be a slight increase in the cost per hour. This is due to the higher skill grade of labor required to operate the new automated material-handling system.

Using the ABC data in Exhibit 8–10, we can answer the two CVP questions posed by management. If the new production technology is adopted, the following CVP computations will be appropriate.

$$\text{Break-even point} = \frac{\text{Fixed costs}}{\text{Unit contribution margin}} = \frac{\$250{,}000}{\$15} = \begin{array}{l}16{,}667 \text{ units}\\(\text{rounded})\end{array}$$

$$\begin{array}{l}\text{Sales volume required to earn}\\\text{target net profit of }\$200{,}000\end{array} = \frac{\text{Fixed costs} + \text{Target net profit}}{\text{Unit contribution margin}}$$

$$= \frac{\$250{,}000 + \$200{,}000}{\$15} = 30{,}000 \text{ units}$$

Notice that AccuTime's break-even point increased with the introduction of the advanced manufacturing system (from 15,000 to 16,667 units). However, the number of sales units required to earn a target net profit of $200,000 declined (from 35,000 to 30,000 units). These kinds of CVP changes are typical when firms install an advanced manufacturing system. Typically the cost structure of an advanced manufacturing environment is characterized by a lower proportion of variable costs and a larger proportion of costs that are fixed (with respect to sales volume).

ABC Provides a Richer Understanding of Cost Behavior and CVP Relationships. The important point in this section is that activity-based costing provides a richer description of a company's cost behavior. AccuTime's traditional costing system treated setup, inspection, and material handling as fixed costs. However, the ABC analysis showed that while these costs are largely fixed with respect to sales volume, they are not fixed with respect to other appropriate cost drivers. In analyzing the cost-volume-profit implications of the proposed changes in manufacturing technology, it was crucial to have an understanding of how these costs would change with respect to such cost drivers as the number of setups, number of inspections, and amount of material-handling activity.

Just as ABC can improve an organization's product-costing system, it also can facilitate a deeper understanding of cost behavior and CVP relationships.

Chapter Summary

An understanding of cost-volume-profit relationships is necessary for the successful management of any enterprise. CVP analysis provides a sweeping overview of the effects on profit of all kinds of changes in sales volume, expenses, product mix, and sales prices. Calculation of the sales volume required to break even or earn a target net profit provides an organization's management with valuable information for planning and decision making.

Cost-volume-profit relationships are important enough to operating managers that some firms prepare a contribution income statement. This income-statement format separates fixed and variable expenses, and helps managers discern the effects on profit from changes in volume. The contribution income statement also discloses an organization's cost structure, which is the relative proportion of its fixed and variable costs. An organization's cost structure has an important impact on its CVP relationships. The cost structure of an organization defines its operating leverage, which determines the impact on profit of changes in sales volume.

Activity-based costing can provide a richer description of an organization's cost behavior and CVP relationships than is provided by a traditional costing system. An ABC cost-volume-profit analysis recognizes that some costs that are fixed with respect to sales volume may not be fixed with respect to other important cost drivers. In many cases, management can benefit substantially from such an improved understanding of cost behavior and relationships.

Review Problem on Cost-Volume-Profit Analysis

Overlook Inn is a small bed-and-breakfast inn located in the Great Smoky Mountains of Tennessee. The charge is $50 per person for one night's lodging and a full breakfast in the morning. The retired couple who own and manage the inn estimate that the variable expense per person is $20. This includes such expenses as food, maid service, and utilities. The inn's fixed expenses total $42,000 per year. The inn can accommodate 10 guests each night.

Required:

Compute the following:

1. Contribution margin per unit of service. (A unit of service is one night's lodging for one guest.)
2. Contribution-margin ratio.
3. Annual break-even point in units of service and in dollars of service revenue.
4. The number of units of service required to earn a target net profit of $60,000 for the year. (Ignore income taxes.)

Solution to Review Problem

1. Contribution margin per unit of service = Nightly room charge − Variable expense per person

   $$\$30 \qquad = \qquad \$50 \qquad - \qquad \$20$$

2. Contribution margin ratio $= \dfrac{\text{Contribution margin per unit}}{\text{Nightly room charge}}$

   $$.60 \qquad = \dfrac{\$30}{\$50}$$

3. Break-even point in units of service $= \dfrac{\text{Fixed expenses}}{\text{Contribution margin per unit}}$

   $$1,400 \qquad = \dfrac{\$42,000}{\$30}$$

   Break-even point in dollars of revenue $= \dfrac{\text{Fixed expenses}}{\text{Contribution-margin ratio}}$

   $$\$70,000 \qquad = \dfrac{\$42,000}{.60}$$

4. Number of units of service required to earn target net profit $= \dfrac{\text{Fixed expenses} + \text{Target net profit}}{\text{Contribution margin per unit of service}}$

   $$3,400 \qquad = \dfrac{\$42,000 + \$60,000}{\$30}$$

Key Terms

For each term's definition refer to the indicated page, or turn to the glossary at the end of the text.

break-even point, pg. 291

contribution income
  statement, pg. 307

contribution-margin
  ratio, pg. 293

contribution-margin,
  total, pg. 292

cost structure, pg. 309

cost-volume-profit (CVP)
  analysis, pg. 290

cost-volume-profit graph,
  pg. 294

operating leverage, pg. 310

operating leverage factor,
  pg. 310

profit-volume graph, pg. 296

safety margin, pg. 299

sales mix, pg. 305

sensitivity analysis, pg. 307

target net profit
  (or income), pg. 296

total contribution
  margin, pg. 292

unit contribution
  margin, pg. 292

weighted-average unit
  contribution margin,
  pg. 305

Appendix to Chapter 8
Effect of Income Taxes

Profit-seeking enterprises must pay income taxes on their profits. A firm's **after-tax net income**, the amount of income remaining after subtracting the firm's income-tax expense, is less than its **before-tax income**. This fact is expressed in the following formula.

> (After-tax net income) = (Before-tax income) – t(Before-tax income)
>
> where t denotes the income-tax rate.

Rearranging this equation yields the following formula.

> (After-tax net income) = (Before-tax income) $(1 – t)$ (9)

After-tax net income is an organization's net income after its income-tax expense is subtracted.

Before-tax income is an organization's income before its income-tax expense is subtracted.

 AccuTime

To illustrate this formula, suppose AccuTime Company must pay income taxes of 40 percent of its before-tax income. The company's contribution income statement for 19x9 appears below.

Sales, 20,000 units at $25 each	$500,000
Variable expenses, 20,000 units at $15 each*	300,000
Contribution margin	$200,000
Fixed expenses	150,000
Income before taxes	$ 50,000
Income-tax expense, .40 × $50,000	20,000
Net income, $50,000 × (1 – .40)	$ 30,000

*Variable cost per unit is $15: variable manufacturing cost of $14 plus variable selling and administrative costs of $1.

The requirement that companies pay income taxes affects their cost-volume-profit relationships. To earn a particular after-tax net income will require greater before-tax income than if there were no tax. For example, if AccuTime's target after-tax net income were $30,000, the company would have to earn before-tax income of $50,000. AccuTime's income statement shows this relationship.

How much before-tax income must be earned in order to achieve a particular target after-tax net income? Rearranging equation (9) above yields the following formula.

$$\text{Target after-tax net income} = \left(\text{Target before-tax income}\right)(1 – t)$$

Divide both sides by $(1 – t)$

$$\frac{\text{Target after-tax net income}}{1 – t} = \left(\text{Target before-tax income}\right)\frac{1 – t}{1 – t}$$

$$\frac{\text{Target after-tax net income}}{1 – t} = \text{Target before-tax income}$$

If AccuTime Company's target after-tax net income is $30,000, its target before-tax income is calculated as follows:

$$\frac{\text{Target after-tax net income}}{1 – t} = \frac{\$30,000}{1 – .40} = \$50,000 = \text{Target before-tax income}$$

Now we are in a position to compute the number of digital clocks that AccuTime must sell in order to achieve a particular after-tax net income. We begin with the following before-tax income equation.

$$\text{Sales} - \text{Variable expenses} - \text{Fixed expenses} = \text{Before-tax income}$$

Now we use our formula for before-tax income.

$$\text{Sales} - \text{Variable expenses} - \text{Fixed expenses} = \frac{\text{After-tax net income}}{1 - t}$$

$$\begin{pmatrix} \text{Unit} \\ \text{sales} \\ \text{price} \end{pmatrix} \times \begin{pmatrix} \text{Sales} \\ \text{volume} \\ \text{in units} \end{pmatrix} - \begin{pmatrix} \text{Unit} \\ \text{variable} \\ \text{expense} \end{pmatrix} \times \begin{pmatrix} \text{Sales} \\ \text{volume} \\ \text{in units} \end{pmatrix} - \begin{pmatrix} \text{Fixed} \\ \text{expenses} \end{pmatrix} = \frac{\text{After-tax}}{1 - t}$$

Using the data for AccuTime Company, and assuming target after-tax net income of $30,000:

$$(\$25 \times X) - (\$15 \times X) - \$150,000 = \frac{\$30,000}{1 - .40}$$

where X denotes the number of units that must be sold to achieve the target after-tax net income.

Now we solve for X as follows:

$$\underline{(\$25 - \$15)} \times X = \$150,000 + \frac{\$30,000}{1 - .40}$$

$$\$10 \quad \times X = \$150,000 + \frac{\$30,000}{1 - .40}$$

$$X = \frac{\$150,000 + \dfrac{\$30,000}{1 - .40}}{\$10}$$

$$= 20,000 \text{ units}$$

In terms of sales revenue, AccuTime must achieve a sales volume of $500,000 (20,000 units × $25 sales price). We can verify these calculations by examining AccuTime's income statement given previously.

Notice in the calculations above that $10 is the unit contribution margin ($25 sales price minus $15 variable expense). Thus, the general formula illustrated above is the following:

$$\begin{array}{c} \text{Number of units of sales} \\ \text{required to earn target} \\ \text{after-tax net income} \end{array} = \frac{\text{Fixed expenses} + \dfrac{\text{Target after-tax net income}}{1 - t}}{\text{Unit contribution margin}}$$

where t denotes the income tax rate.

A cost-volume-profit graph for AccuTime Company is displayed in Exhibit 8–11. As the graph shows, 20,000 units must be sold to achieve $30,000 in after-tax net income. The company's break-even point is 15,000 units. The break-even point is not affected by income taxes, because at the break-even point, there is no income.

Notice that AccuTime Company must sell 5,000 units *beyond the break-even point* in order to achieve after-tax net income of $30,000. Each unit sold beyond the break-even point contributes $10 toward *before-tax* income. However, of that $10 contribution margin, $4 will have to be paid in income taxes. This leaves an *after-tax contribution* of $6 toward after-tax net income. Thus, selling 5,000 units beyond the break-even point results in after-tax net income of $30,000 (5,000 units × $6 after-tax contribution per unit).

Key Terms: Appendix

For each term's definition refer to the indicated page, or turn to the glossary at the end of the text.

after-tax net income, pg. 317   before-tax income, pg. 317

AccuTime Company

Exhibit 8–11

Cost-Volume-Profit Graph
(with income taxes)

$$^* \left(\text{Before-tax income} \right) \times (1 - \text{Tax rate}) = \text{After-tax income}$$

$$\$50,000 \times (1 - .40) = \$30,000$$

Review Questions

8–1. What is the meaning of the term unit contribution margin? Contribution to what?

8–2. Briefly explain each of the following methods of computing a break-even point in units: (*a*) contribution-margin approach, (*b*) equation approach, and (*c*) graphical approach.

8–3. What information is conveyed by a cost-volume-profit graph in addition to a company's break-even point?

8–4. What does the term *safety margin* mean?

8–5. Suppose the fixed expenses of a travel agency increase. What will happen to its break-even point, measured in number of clients served? Why?

8–6. Chesapeake Oyster Company has been able to decrease its variable expenses per pound of oysters harvested. How will this affect the firm's break-even sales volume?

8–7. In a strategy meeting, a manufacturing company's president said, "If we raise the price of our product, the company's break-even point will be lower." The financial

vice president responded by saying, "Then we should raise our price. The company will be less likely to incur a loss." Do you agree with the president? Why? Do you agree with the financial vice president? Why?

8–8. What will happen to a company's break-even point if the sales price and unit variable cost of its only product increase by the same dollar amount?

8–9. An art museum covers its operating expenses by charging a small admission fee. The objective of the nonprofit organization is to break even. A local arts enthusiast has just pledged an annual donation of $5,000 to the museum. How will the donation affect the museum's break-even attendance level?

8–10. How can a profit-volume graph be used to predict a company's profit for a particular sales volume?

8–11. List the most important assumptions of cost-volume-profit analysis.

8–12. Why do many operating managers prefer a contribution income statement instead of a traditional income statement?

8–13. What is the difference between a manufacturing company's *gross margin* and its total *contribution margin*?

8–14. East Company manufactures VCRs using a completely automated production process. West Company also manufactures VCRs, but its products are assembled manually. How will these two firms' cost structures differ? Which company will have a higher operating leverage factor?

8–15. When sales volume increases, which company will experience a larger percentage increase in profit: company X, which has mostly fixed expenses, or company Y, which has mostly variable expenses?

8–16. What does the term *sales mix* mean? How is a *weighted-average unit contribution margin* computed?

8–17. A car rental agency rents subcompact, compact, and full-size automobiles. What assumptions would be made about the agency's sales mix for the purpose of a cost-volume-profit analysis?

8–18. How can a hotel's management use cost-volume-profit analysis to help in deciding on room rates?

8–19. How could cost-volume-profit analysis be used in budgeting? In making a decision about advertising?

8–20. Two companies have identical fixed expenses, unit variable expenses, and profits. Yet one company has set a much lower price for its product. Explain how this can happen.

8–21. A company with an advanced manufacturing environment typically will have a higher break-even point, greater operating leverage, and larger safety margin than a labor-intensive firm. True or false? Explain.

8–22. Explain briefly how activity-based costing (ABC) affects cost-volume-profit analysis.

Exercises

■ **Exercise 8–23**
Sports Franchise; CVP Graph
(LO 3, LO 4)

The Houston Armadillos, a minor-league baseball team, play their weekly games in a small stadium just outside Houston. The stadium holds 10,000 people and tickets sell for $10 each. The franchise owner estimates that the team's annual fixed expenses are $180,000, and the variable expense per ticket sold is $1. (In the following requirements, ignore income taxes.)

Required:

1. Draw a cost-volume-profit graph for the sports franchise. Label the axes, break-even point, profit and loss areas, fixed expenses, variable expenses, total-expense line, and total-revenue line.
2. If the stadium is half full for each game, how many games must the team play to break even?

■ **Exercise 8–24**
Continuation of Preceding
Exercise; Profit-Volume
Graph; Safety Margin
(LO 3, LO 4)

Refer to the data given in the preceding exercise. (Ignore income taxes.)

Required:

1. Prepare a fully labeled profit-volume graph for the Houston Armadillos.
2. What is the safety margin for the baseball franchise if the team plays a 12-game season and the team owner expects the stadium to be 30 percent full for each game?
3. If the stadium is half full for each game, what ticket price would the team have to charge in order to break even?

■ **Exercise 8–25**
Pizza Delivery Business;
Basic CVP Analysis
(LO 1, LO 2, LO 4)

University Pizza delivers pizzas to the dormitories and apartments near a major state university. The company's annual fixed expenses are $40,000. The sales price of a pizza is $10, and it costs the company $5 to make and deliver each pizza. (In the following requirements, ignore income taxes.)

Required:

1. Using the contribution-margin approach, compute the company's break-even point in units (pizzas).
2. What is the contribution-margin ratio?
3. Compute the break-even sales revenue. Use the contribution-margin ratio in your calculation.
4. How many pizzas must the company sell to earn a target net profit of $65,000? Use the equation method.

■ **Exercise 8–26**
Manufacturing; Using
CVP Analysis
(LO 1, LO 4)

Air Safety Systems Company manufactures a component used in aircraft radar systems. The firm's fixed costs are $4,000,000 per year. The variable cost of each component is $2,000, and the components are sold for $3,000 each. The company sold 5,000 components during the prior year. (In the following requirements, ignore income taxes.)

Required: Answer requirements 1 through 4 independently.

1. Compute the break-even point in units.
2. What will the new break-even point be if fixed costs increase by 10 percent?
3. What was the company's net income for the prior year?
4. The sales manager believes that a reduction in the sales price to $2,500 will result in orders for 1,200 more components each year. What will the break-even point be if the price is changed?
5. Should the price change be made?

Fill in the missing data for each of the following independent cases. (Ignore income taxes.)

	Sales Revenue	Variable Expenses	Total Contribution Margin	Fixed Expenses	Net Income	Break-Even Sales Revenue
1.	$110,000	$22,000	?	?	$38,000	?
2.	?	40,000	?	$30,000	?	$40,000
3.	80,000	?	$15,000	?	?	80,000
4.	?	40,000	80,000	?	50,000	?

■ **Exercise 8–27**
Fill in Blanks; Basic CVP Relationships
(LO 1)

Tim's Bicycle Shop sells 21-speed bicycles. For purposes of a cost-volume-profit analysis, the shop owner has divided sales into two categories, as follows:

Product Type	Sales Price	Invoice Cost	Sales Commission
High-quality	$500	$275	$25
Medium-quality	300	135	15

Three-quarters of the shop's sales are medium-quality bikes. The shop's annual fixed expenses are $65,000. (In the following requirements, ignore income taxes.)

Required:

1. Compute the unit contribution margin for each product type.
2. What is the shop's sales mix?
3. Compute the weighted-average unit contribution margin, assuming a constant sales mix.
4. What is the shop's break-even sales volume in dollars? Assume a constant sales mix.
5. How many bicycles of each type must be sold to earn a target net income of $48,750? Assume a constant sales mix.

■ **Exercise 8–28**
Retail; CVP Analysis with Multiple Products
(LO 1, LO 5)

Pacifica Publications, Inc. specializes in reference books that keep abreast of the rapidly changing political and economic issues in the Pacific Rim. The results of the company's operations during the prior year are given in the following table. All units produced during the year were sold. (Ignore income taxes.)

■ **Exercise 8–29**
Publishing; Contribution Income Statement
(LO 7, LO 8)

Sales revenue	$2,000,000
Manufacturing costs:	
Fixed	500,000
Variable	1,000,000
Selling costs:	
Fixed	50,000
Variable	100,000
Administrative costs:	
Fixed	120,000
Variable	30,000

Required:

1. Prepare a traditional income statement and a contribution income statement for the company.
2. What is the firm's operating leverage for the sales volume generated during the prior year?
3. Suppose sales revenue increases by 10 percent. What will be the percentage increase in net income?
4. Which income statement would an operating manager use to answer requirement (3)? Why?

■ **Exercise 8–30**
Hotel and Restaurant; Cost
Structure and Operating
Leverage
(LO 8)

A contribution income statement for Mount Washington Lodge is shown below. (Ignore income taxes.)

Revenue	$500,000
Less: Variable expenses	300,000
Contribution margin	$200,000
Less: Fixed expenses	150,000
Net income	$ 50,000

Required:

1. Show the hotel's cost structure by indicating the percentage of the hotel's revenue represented by each item on the income statement.
2. Suppose the hotel's revenue declines by 15 percent. Use the contribution-margin percentage to calculate the resulting decrease in net income.
3. What is the hotel's operating leverage factor when revenue is $500,000?
4. Use the operating leverage factor to calculate the increase in net income resulting from a 20 percent increase in sales revenue.

■ **Exercise 8–31**
Continuation of Preceding
Exercise
(LO 7)

Refer to the income statement given in the preceding exercise. Prepare a new contribution income statement for Mount Washington Lodge in each of the following independent situations. (Ignore income taxes.)

1. The hotel's volume of activity increases by 20 percent, and fixed expenses increase by 40 percent.
2. The ratio of variable expenses to revenue doubles. There is no change in the hotel's volume of activity. Fixed expenses decline by $25,000.

■ **Exercise 8–32**
Consulting Firm; CVP
Analysis with Income Taxes
(Appendix)
(LO 1, LO 4)

Hydro Systems Engineering Associates, Inc. provides consulting services to city water authorities. The consulting firm's contribution-margin ratio is 20 percent, and its annual fixed expenses are $120,000. The firm's income-tax rate is 40 percent.

Required:

1. Calculate the firm's break-even volume of service revenue.
2. How much before-tax income must the firm earn to make an after-tax net income of $48,000?
3. What level of revenue for consulting services must the firm generate to earn an after-tax net income of $48,000?
4. Suppose the firm's income-tax rate rises to 45 percent. What will happen to the break-even level of consulting service revenue?

Problems

■ **Problem 8–33**
Basic CVP Computations
(LO 1, LO 2, LO 4)

DesignerPak Company produced and sold 60,000 backpacks during the year just ended at an average price of $20 per unit. Variable manufacturing costs were $8 per unit, and variable marketing costs were $4 per unit sold. Fixed costs amounted to $180,000 for manufacturing and $72,000 for marketing. There was no year-end work-in-process inventory. (Ignore income taxes.)

Required:

1. Compute DesignerPak's break-even point in sales dollars for the year.
2. Compute the number of sales units required to earn a net income of $180,000 during the year.
3. DesignerPak's variable manufacturing costs are expected to increase 10 percent in the coming year. Compute the firm's break-even point in sales dollars for the coming year.
4. If DesignerPak's variable manufacturing costs do increase 10 percent, compute the selling price that would yield the same contribution-margin ratio in the coming year.

(CMA, adapted)

The Sound Factory, Inc. manufactures and sells compact disks. Price and cost data are as follows:

Selling price per unit (package of two CDs)	$25.00
Variable costs per unit:	
Direct material	$10.50
Direct labor	5.00
Manufacturing overhead	3.00
Selling expenses	1.30
Total variable costs per unit	$19.80
Annual fixed costs:	
Manufacturing overhead	$ 192,000
Selling and administrative	276,000
Total fixed costs	$ 468,000
Forecasted annual sales volume (120,000 units)	$3,000,000

In the following requirements, ignore income taxes.

Required:

1. What is The Sound Factory's break-even point in units?
2. What is the company's break-even point in sales dollars?
3. How many units would The Sound Factory have to sell in order to earn $260,000?
4. What is the firm's margin of safety?
5. Management estimates that direct-labor costs will increase by 8 percent next year. How many units will the company have to sell next year to reach its break-even point?
6. If The Sound Factory's direct-labor costs do increase 8 percent, what selling price per unit of product must it charge to maintain the same contribution-margin ratio?

(CMA, adapted)

■ **Problem 8–34**
Basic CVP Relationships
(LO 1, LO 2, LO 4)

DisKing Company is a retailer for video disks. The projected net income for the current year is $200,000 based on a sales volume of 200,000 video disks. DisKing has been selling the disks for $16 each. The variable costs consist of the $10 unit purchase price of the disks and a handling cost of $2 per disk. DisKing's annual fixed costs are $600,000.

Management is planning for the coming year, when it expects that the unit purchase price of the video disks will increase 30 percent. (Ignore income taxes.)

Required:

1. Calculate DisKing Company's break-even point for the current year in number of video disks.
2. What will be the company's net income for the current year if there is a 10 percent increase in projected unit sales volume?
3. What volume of sales (in dollars) must DisKing Company achieve in the coming year to maintain the same net income as projected for the current year if the unit selling price remains at $16?
4. In order to cover a 30 percent increase in the disk's purchase price for the coming year and still maintain the current contribution-margin ratio, what selling price per disk must DisKing Company establish for the coming year?

(CMA, adapted)

■ **Problem 8–35**
Basic CVP Relationships;
Retailer
(LO 1, LO 2, LO 4)

Cross Country, Inc. manufactures warm-up suits. The company's projected income for the coming year, based on sales of 160,000 units, is as follows:

Sales		$8,000,000
Operating expenses:		
Variable expenses	$2,000,000	
Fixed expenses	3,000,000	
Total expenses		5,000,000
Net income		$3,000,000

■ **Problem 8–36**
CVP Graph; Cost Structure;
Operating Leverage
(LO 3, LO 4, LO 8)

Required: In completing the following requirements, ignore income taxes.

1. Prepare a CVP graph for Cross Country, Inc. for the coming year.
2. Calculate the firm's break-even point for the year in sales dollars.
3. What is the company's margin of safety for the year?
4. Compute Cross Country's operating leverage factor, based on the budgeted sales volume for the year.
5. Compute Cross Country's required sales in dollars in order to earn income of $4,500,000 in the coming year.
6. Describe the firm's cost structure. Calculate the percentage relationships between variable and fixed expenses and sales revenue.

(CMA, adapted)

■ **Problem 8–37**
Break-Even Point; Safety
Margin; Law Firm
(LO 1, LO 4)

Gary Arbo and two of his colleagues are considering opening a law office in a large metropolitan area that would make inexpensive legal services available to those who could not otherwise afford services. The intent is to provide easy access for their clients by having the office open 360 days per year, 16 hours each day from 7:00 A.M. to 11:00 P.M. The office would be staffed by a lawyer, paralegal, legal secretary, and clerk-receptionist for each of the two eight-hour shifts.

In order to determine the feasibility of the project, Arbo hired a marketing consultant to assist with market projections. The results of this study show that if the firm spends $490,000 on advertising the first year, the number of new clients expected each day will be 50. Arbo and his associates believe this number is reasonable and are prepared to spend the $490,000 on advertising. Other pertinent information about the operation of the office follows:

■ The only charge to each new client would be $30 for the initial consultation. All cases that warrant further legal work will be accepted on a contingency basis with the firm earning 30 percent of any favorable settlements or judgments. Arbo estimates that 20 percent of new client consultations will result in favorable settlements or judgments averaging $2,000 each. It is not expected that there will be repeat clients during the first year of operations.

■ The hourly wages of the staff are projected to be $25 for the lawyer, $20 for the paralegal, $15 for the legal secretary, and $10 for the clerk-receptionist. Fringe benefit expense will be 40 percent of the wages paid. A total of 400 hours of overtime is expected for the year; this will be divided equally between the legal secretary and the clerk-receptionist positions. Overtime will be paid at one and one-half times the regular wage, and the fringe benefit expense will apply to the full wage.

■ Arbo has located 6,000 square feet of suitable office space which rents for $28 per square foot annually. Associated expenses will be $27,000 for property insurance and $37,000 for utilities.

■ It will be necessary for the group to purchase malpractice insurance, which is expected to cost $180,000 annually.

■ The initial investment in the office equipment will be $60,000. This equipment has an estimated useful life of four years.

■ The cost of office supplies has been estimated to be $4 per expected new client consultation.

Required:

1. Determine how many new clients must visit the law office being considered by Gary Arbo and his colleagues in order for the venture to break even during its first year of operations.
2. Compute the law firm's safety margin.

(CMA, adapted)

■ **Problem 8–38**
Break-Even Point; After-Tax
Net Income; Profit-Volume
Graph; International Issues
(Appendix)
(LO 1, LO 3, LO4)

The European Division of Global Reference Corporation produces a pocket dictionary containing popular phrases in six European languages. Annual budget data for the coming year follow. Projected sales are 100,000 books.

	Fixed	Variable	
Sales			$1,000,000
Costs:			
Direct material	$ –0–	$300,000	
Direct labor	–0–	200,000	
Manufacturing overhead	100,000	150,000	
Selling and administrative	110,000	50,000	
Total costs	$210,000	$700,000	910,000
Budgeted operating income			$ 90,000

Required:

1. Calculate the break-even point in units and in sales dollars.

2. If the European Division is subject to an income-tax rate of 40 percent, compute the number of units the company would have to sell to earn an after-tax profit of $90,000.

3. If fixed costs increased $31,500 with no other cost or revenue factor changing, compute the firm's break-even sales in units.

4. Prepare a profit-volume graph for the European Division.

5. Due to an unstable political situation in the country in which the European Division is located, management believes the country may split into two independent nations. If this happens, the tax rate could rise to 50 percent. Assuming all other data as in the original problem, how many pocket dictionaries must be sold to earn $90,000 after taxes?

(CMA, adapted)

GameCo, Inc. manufactures pocket electronic games. Last year GameCo sold 25,000 games at $25 each. Total costs amounted to $525,000 of which $150,000 were considered fixed.

In an attempt to improve its product, the company is considering replacing a component part that has a cost of $2.50 with a new and better part costing $4.50 per unit in the coming year. A new machine would also be needed to increase plant capacity. The machine would cost $18,000 with a useful life of six years and no salvage value. The company uses straight-line depreciation on all plant assets. (Ignore income taxes.)

■ **Problem 8–39**
CVP Analysis of Changes in Sales Prices and Costs
(LO 1, LO 4)

Required:

1. What was GameCo's break-even point in number of units last year?

2. How many units of product would the company have had to sell in the last year to earn $140,000?

3. If GameCo holds the sales price constant and makes the suggested changes, how many units of product must be sold in the coming year to break even?

4. If the firm holds the sales price constant and makes the suggested changes, how many units of product will the company have to sell to make the same net income as last year?

5. If GameCo wishes to maintain the same contribution margin ratio, what selling price per unit of product must it charge next year to cover the increased direct-material cost?

(CMA, adapted)

Refer to the original data given for GameCo in the preceding problem. An activity-based costing study has revealed that GameCo's $150,000 of fixed costs include the following components:

■ **Problem 8–40**
Activity-Based Costing; Advanced Manufacturing Systems; Ethical Issues
(LO 4, LO 9, LO 10)

Setup (40 setups at $400 per setup)	$ 16,000
Engineering (500 hours at $25 per hour)	12,500
Inspection (1,000 inspections at $30 per inspection)	30,000
General factory overhead	61,500
Total	$120,000
Fixed selling and administrative costs	30,000
Total fixed costs	$150,000

Management is considering the installation of new, highly automated manufacturing equipment that would significantly alter the production process. In addition, management plans a move toward just-in-time inventory and production management. If the new equipment is installed, setups will be quicker and less expensive. Under the proposed JIT approach, there would be 300 setups per year at $50 per setup. Since a total quality control program would accompany the move toward JIT, only 100 inspections would be anticipated annually, at a cost of $45 each. After the installation of the new production system, 800 hours of engineering would be required at a cost of $28 per hour. General factory overhead would increase to $166,100. However, the automated equipment would allow GameCo to cut its unit variable cost by 20 percent. Moreover, the more consistent product quality anticipated would allow management to raise the price of electronic games to $26 per unit. (Ignore income taxes.)

Required:

1. Upon seeing the ABC analysis given in the problem, GameCo's vice president for manufacturing exclaimed to the controller, "I thought you told me this $150,000 cost was fixed. These don't look

like fixed costs at all. What you're telling me now is that setup costs us $400 every time we set up a production run. What gives?"

As GameCo's controller, write a short memo explaining to the vice president what is going on.

2. Compute GameCo's new break-even point if the proposed automated equipment is installed.

3. Determine how many units GameCo will have to sell to show a profit of $140,000, assuming the new technology is adopted.

4. If GameCo adopts the new manufacturing technology, will its break-even point be higher or lower? Will the number of sales units required to earn a profit of $140,000 be higher or lower? (Refer to your answers for the first two requirements of the preceding problem.) Are the results in this case consistent with what you would typically expect to find? Explain.

5. The decision as to whether to purchase the automated manufacturing equipment will be made by GameCo's board of directors. In order to support the proposed acquisition, the vice president for manufacturing asked the controller to prepare a report on the financial implications of the decision. As part of the report, the vice president asked the controller to compute the new break-even point, assuming the installation of the equipment. The controller complied, as in requirement (2) of this problem.

When the vice president for manufacturing saw that the break-even point would increase, he asked the controller to delete the break-even analysis from the report. What should the controller do? Which ethical standards for managerial accountants are involved here?

■ **Problem 8–41**
Break-Even Analysis; Profit-Volume Graph; Movie Theaters
(LO 1, LO 3, LO 4)

Galaxy Corporation owns and operates a nationwide chain of movie theaters. The 500 properties in the Galaxy chain vary from low-volume, small-town, single-screen theaters to high-volume, big-city, multi-screen theaters. The firm's management is considering installing popcorn machines, which would allow the theaters to sell freshly popped corn rather than prepopped corn. This new feature would be advertised to increase patronage at the company's theaters. The fresh popcorn will be sold for $1.75 per tub. The annual rental costs and the operating costs vary with the size of the popcorn machines. The machine capacities and costs are shown below. (Ignore income taxes.)

	Popper Model		
	Economy	**Regular**	**Super**
Annual capacity	45,000 tubs	90,000 tubs	140,000 tubs
Costs:			
Annual machine rental	$8,000	$11,000	$20,000
Popcorn cost per tub	.13	.13	.13
Other costs per tub	1.22	1.14	1.05
Cost of each tub	.08	.08	.08

Required:

1. Calculate each theater's break-even sales volume (measured in tubs of popcorn) for each model of popcorn popper.

2. Prepare a profit-volume graph for one theater, assuming that the Super Popper is purchased.

3. Calculate the volume (in tubs) at which the Economy Popper and the Regular Popper earn the same profit or loss in each movie theater.

(CMA, adapted)

■ **Problem 8–42**
Break-Even Analysis; Operating Leverage; New Manufacturing Environment
(LO 1, LO 8, LO 10)

Andromedea Company has decided to introduce a new product, which can be manufactured by either a computer-assisted manufacturing system or a labor-intensive production system. The manufacturing method will not affect the quality of the product. The estimated manufacturing costs by the two methods are as follows:

	Computer-Assisted Manufacturing System		Labor-Intensive Production System	
Direct material		$5.00		$5.60
Direct labor	.5DLH @ $12	6.00	.8DLH @ $9	7.20
Variable overhead	.5DLH @ $6	3.00	.8DLH @ $6	4.80
Fixed overhead*		$2,440,000		$1,320,000

*These costs are directly traceable to the new product line. They would not be incurred if the new product were not produced.

The company's marketing research department has recommended an introductory unit sales price of $30. Selling expenses are estimated to be $500,000 annually plus $2 for each unit sold. (Ignore income taxes.)

Required:

1. Calculate the estimated break-even point in annual unit sales of the new product if the company uses the (a) computer-assisted manufacturing system; (b) labor-intensive production system.

2. Determine the annual unit sales volume at which the firm would be indifferent between the two manufacturing methods.

3. Management must decide which manufacturing method to employ. One factor it should consider is operating leverage. Explain the concept of operating leverage. How is this concept related to Andromeda Company's decision?

4. Describe the circumstances under which the firm should employ each of the two manufacturing methods.

5. Identify some business factors other than operating leverage that management should consider before selecting the manufacturing method.

(CMA, adapted)

Kalifo Company manufactures a line of electric garden tools that are sold in general hardware stores. The company's controller, Will Fulton, has just received the sales forecast for the coming year for Kalifo's three products: hedge clippers, weeders, and leaf blowers. Kalifo has experienced considerable variations in sales volumes and variable costs over the past two years, and Fulton believes the forecast should be carefully evaluated from a cost-volume-profit viewpoint. The preliminary budget information for 19x9 follows:

■ **Problem 8–43**
CVP; Multiple Products;
Changes in Costs and Sales
Mix
(LO 4, LO 5)

	Weeders	Hedge Clippers	Leaf Blowers
Unit sales	50,000	50,000	100,000
Unit selling price	$28	$36	$48
Variable manufacturing cost per unit	13	12	25
Variable selling cost per unit	5	4	6

For 19x9, Kalifo's fixed manufacturing overhead is budgeted at $2,000,000, and the company's fixed selling and administrative expenses are forecasted to be $600,000. Kalifo has a tax rate of 40 percent.

Required:

1. Determine Kalifo Company's budgeted net income for 19x9.

2. Assuming the sales mix remains as budgeted, determine how many units of each product Kalifo Company must sell in order to break even in 19x9.

3. After preparing the original estimates, management determined that its variable manufacturing cost of leaf blowers would increase 20 percent, and the variable selling cost of hedge clippers could be expected to increase by $1.00 per unit. However, management has decided not to change the selling price of either product. In addition, management has learned that its leaf blower has been perceived as the best value on the market, and it can expect to sell three times as many leaf blowers as each of its other products. Under these circumstances, determine how many units of each product Kalifo Company would have to sell in order to break even in 19x9.

(CMA, adapted)

Condensed monthly income data for Grayden's Jewelry Stores are presented in the following table for November 19x8. (Ignore income taxes.)

■ **Problem 8–44**
CVP Relationships; Retail
Jewelry Business
(LO 1, LO 4)

	Mall Store	Downtown Store	Total
Sales	$80,000	$120,000	$200,000
Less: Variable expenses	32,000	84,000	116,000
Contribution margin	$48,000	$ 36,000	$ 84,000
Less: Fixed expenses	20,000	40,000	60,000
Operating income	$28,000	$ (4,000)	$ 24,000

Additional Information:

■ Management estimates that closing the downtown store would result in a 10 percent decrease in mall store sales, while closing the mall store would not affect downtown store sales.

- One-fourth of each store's fixed expenses would continue through December 31, 19x9 if either store were closed.
- The operating results for November 19x8 are representative of all months.

Required:

1. Calculate the increase or decrease in Grayden's monthly operating income during 19x9 if the downtown store is closed.

2. The management of Grayden's Jewelry Stores is considering a promotional campaign at the downtown store that would not affect the mall store. Annual promotional expenses at the downtown store would be increased by $60,000 in order to increase downtown store sales by 10 percent. What would be the effect of this promotional campaign on the company's monthly operating income during 19x9?

3. One-half of the downtown store's dollar sales are from items sold at their variable cost to attract customers to the store. Grayden's management is considering the deletion of these items, a move that would reduce the downtown store's direct fixed expenses by 15 percent and result in the loss of 20 percent of the remaining downtown store's sales volume. This change would not affect the mall store. What would be the effect on Grayden's monthly operating income if the items sold at their variable cost are eliminated?

(CMA, adapted)

■ **Problem 8–45**
CVP Relationships;
International Business;
Automation
(LO 1, LO 4, LO 10)

Pennsylvania Limestone Company produces thin limestone sheets used for cosmetic facing on buildings. The following income statement represents the operating results for the year just ended. The company had sales of 1,800 tons during the year. The manufacturing capacity of the firm's facilities is 3,000 tons per year. (Ignore income taxes.)

PENNSYLVANIA LIMESTONE COMPANY
Income Statement
For the Year Ended December 31, 19x8

Sales	$900,000
Variable costs:	
Manufacturing	$315,000
Selling costs	180,000
Total variable costs	$495,000
Contribution margin	$405,000
Fixed costs:	
Manufacturing	$100,000
Selling	107,500
Administrative	40,000
Total fixed costs	$247,500
Net income	$157,500

Required:

1. Calculate the company's break-even volume in tons for 19x8.

2. If the sales volume is estimated to be 2,100 tons in the next year, and if the prices and costs stay at the same levels and amounts, what is the net income that management can expect for 19x9?

3. Pennsylvania Limestone has been trying for years to get a foothold in the European market. The company has a potential German customer that has offered to buy 1,500 tons at $450 per ton. Assume that all of the firm's costs would be at the same levels and rates as in 19x8. What net income would the firm earn if it took this order and rejected some business from regular customers so as not to exceed capacity?

4. Pennsylvania Limestone plans to market its product in a new territory. Management estimates that an advertising and promotion program costing $61,500 annually would be needed for the next two or three years. In addition, a $25 per ton sales commission to the sales force in the new territory, over and above the current commission, would be required. How many tons would have to be sold in the new territory to maintain the firm's current net income? Assume that sales and costs will continue as in 19x8 in the firm's established territories.

5. Management is considering replacing its labor-intensive process with an automated production system. This would result in an increase of $58,500 annually in fixed manufacturing costs. The

variable manufacturing costs would decrease by $25 per ton. Compute the new break-even volume in tons and in sales dollars.

6. Ignore the facts presented in requirement (5). Assume that management estimates that the selling price per ton would decline by 10 percent next year. Variable costs would increase by $40 per ton, and fixed costs would not change. What sales volume in dollars would be required to earn a net income of $94,500 next year?

(CMA, adapted)

Great Northern Ski Company recently expanded its manufacturing capacity. The firm will now be able to produce up to 15,000 pairs of cross-country skis of either the mountaineering model or the touring model. The sales department assures management that it can sell between 9,000 and 13,000 units of either product this year. Because the models are very similar, the company will produce only one of the two models.

■ Problem 8–46
Cost-Volume-Profit Analysis
with Income Taxes and
Multiple Products (Appendix)
(LO 1, LO 2, LO 4, LO 5)

The following information was compiled by the accounting department.

	Model	
	Mountaineering	**Touring**
Selling price per unit	$88.00	$80.00
Variable costs per unit	52.80	52.80

Fixed costs will total $369,600 if the mountaineering model is produced but will be only $316,800 if the touring model is produced. Great Northern Ski Company is subject to a 40 percent income tax rate. (Round each answer to the nearest whole number.)

Required:

1. Compute the contribution-margin ratio for the touring model.
2. If Great Northern Ski Company desires an after-tax net income of $22,080, how many pairs of touring skis will the company have to sell?
3. How much would the variable cost per unit of the touring model have to change before it had the same break-even point in units as the mountaineering model?
4. Suppose the variable cost per unit of touring skis decreases by 10 percent, and the total fixed cost of touring skis increases by 10 percent. Compute the new break-even point.
5. Suppose management decided to produce both products. If the two models are sold in equal proportions, and total fixed costs amount to $343,200, what is the firm's break-even point in units?

(CMA, adapted)

Kitts Corporation manufactures telecommunications equipment. The company has always been production oriented and sells its products through agents. Agents are paid a commission of 15 percent of the selling price. Kitts Corporation's budgeted income statement for 19x9 follows:

■ Problem 8–47
CVP Analysis; Marketing
Decisions; Income Taxes
(Appendix)
(LO 1, LO 4)

KITTS CORPORATION
Budgeted Income Statement
For the Year Ended December 31, 19x9
(in thousands)

Sales		$16,000
Manufacturing costs:		
Variable	$7,200	
Fixed overhead	2,340	9,540
Gross margin		$ 6,460
Selling and administrative expenses:		
Commissions	$2,400	
Fixed marketing expenses	140	
Fixed administrative expenses	1,780	4,320
Net operating income		$ 2,140
Less fixed interest expense		540
Income before income taxes		$ 1,600
Less income taxes (30%)		480
Net income		$ 1,120

After the profit plan was completed for the coming year, Kitts' sales agents demanded that the commissions be increased to 22½ percent of the selling price. This demand was the latest in a series of actions that Vinnie McGraw, the company's president, believed had gone too far. He asked Maureen Elliott, the most sales-oriented officer in his production-oriented company, to estimate the cost to Kitts of employing its own sales force. Elliott's estimate of the additional annual cost of employing its own sales force, exclusive of commissions, follows. Sales personnel would receive a commission of 10 percent of the selling price in addition to their salary.

Estimated Annual Cost of Employing a Company Sales Force (in thousands)

Salaries:	
Sales manager	$100
Sales personnel	1,000
Travel and entertainment	400
Fixed marketing costs	900
Total	$2,400

Required:

1. Calculate Kitts Corporation's estimated break-even point in sales dollars for 19x9.
   a.   If the events that are represented in the budgeted income statement take place.
   b.   If Kitts employs its own sales force.
2. If Kitts continues to sell through agents and pays the increased commission of 22½ percent of the selling price, determine the estimated volume in sales dollars for 19x9 that would be required to generate the same net income as projected in the budgeted income statement.
3. Determine the estimated volume in sales dollars that would result in equal net income for 19x9 regardless of whether Kitts Corporation continues to sell through agents and pays a commission of 22½ percent of the selling price or employs its own sales force.

(CMA, adapted)

Cases

■ Case 8–48
Break-Even Analysis;
Hospital CVP Relationships
(LO 1, LO 4)

Susquehanna Medical Center operates a general hospital. The medical center also rents space and beds to separately owned entities rendering specialized services, such as Pediatrics and Psychiatric Care. Susquehanna charges each separate entity for common services, such as patients' meals and laundry, and for administrative services, such as billings and collections. Space and bed rentals are fixed charges for the year, based on bed capacity rented to each entity. Susquehanna Medical Center charged the following costs to Pediatrics for the year ended June 30, 19x8:

	Patient Days (variable)	Bed Capacity (fixed)
Dietary	$ 600,000	—
Janitorial	—	$ 70,000
Laundry	300,000	—
Laboratory	450,000	—
Pharmacy	350,000	—
Repairs and maintenance	—	30,000
General and administrative	—	1,300,000
Rent	—	1,500,000
Billings and collections	300,000	—
Total	$2,000,000	$2,900,000

During the year ended June 30, 19x8, Pediatrics charged each patient an average of $300 per day, had a capacity of 60 beds, and had revenue of $6 million for 365 days. In addition, Pediatrics directly employed personnel with the following annual salary costs per employee: supervising nurses, $25,000; nurses, $20,000; and aides, $9,000.

Susquehanna Medical Center has the following minimum departmental personnel requirements, based on total annual patient days:

Annual Patient Days	Aides	Nurses	Supervising Nurses
Up to 22,000	20	10	4
22,001 to 26,000	25	14	5
26,001 to 29,200	31	16	5

Pediatrics always employs only the minimum number of required personnel. Salaries of supervising nurses, nurses, and aides are therefore fixed within ranges of annual patient days.

Pediatrics operated at 100 percent capacity on 90 days during the year ended June 30, 19x8. Administrators estimate that on these 90 days, Pediatrics could have filled another 20 beds above capacity. Susquehanna Medical Center has an additional 20 beds available for rent for the year ending June 30, 19x9. Such additional rental would increase Pediatrics' fixed charges based on bed capacity. (In the following requirements, ignore income taxes.)

Required:

1. Calculate the minimum number of patient days required for Pediatrics to break even for the year ended June 30, 19x9, if the additional 20 beds are not rented. Patient demand is unknown, but assume that revenue per patient day, cost per patient day, cost per bed, and salary rates will remain the same as for the year ended June 30, 19x8.

2. Assume that patient demand, revenue per patient day, cost per patient day, cost per bed, and salary rates for the year ended June 30, 19x9 remain the same as for the year ended June 30, 19x8. Prepare a schedule of Pediatrics' increase in revenue and increase in costs for the year ended June 30, 19x9. Determine the net increase or decrease in Pediatrics' earnings from the additional 20 beds if Pediatrics rents this extra capacity from Susquehanna Medical Center.

(CPA, adapted)

Blue Ribbon Lawn Products, Inc. manufactures three product lines: Fertilawn (a balanced fertilizer), Weedout (a weed control spread), and Pestaway (a dry pest control product). The following income statement was prepared by product line. (Ignore income taxes.)

■ **Case 8–49**
Contribution-Margin Income Statement; CVP Analysis
(LO 5, LO 6, LO 7)

BLUE RIBBON LAWN PRODUCTS, INC.
Income Statement
For the Year Ended December 31, 19x9
(in thousands)

	Fertilawn	Weedout	Pestaway	Total
Sales (in pounds)	500	2,000	500	3,000
Sales revenue	$200	$1,000	$400	$1,600
Cost of goods sold:				
Direct material	$100	$ 330	$160	$ 590
Direct labor	20	90	40	150
Manufacturing overhead	24	108	48	180
Total cost of goods sold	$144	$ 528	$248	$ 920
Gross margin	$ 56	$ 472	$152	$ 680
Operating expenses:				
Selling expenses:				
Advertising	$ 20	$50	$ 30	$ 100
Commissions	20	50	40	110
Salaries and fringe benefits	10	30	20	60
Total selling expenses	$ 50	$ 130	$ 90	$ 270
General and administrative expenses:				
Licenses	$ 15	$ 50	$ 20	$85
Salaries and fringe benefits	15	60	25	100
Total general and administrative expenses	$ 30	$ 110	$ 45	$ 185
Total operating expenses	$ 80	$ 240	$135	$ 455
Operating income before taxes	$ (24)	$ 232	$ 17	$ 225

Other Data

■ *Cost of goods sold*. The company's inventories of raw materials and finished products do not vary significantly from year to year. The inventories on December 31, 19x9 were essentially identical to those on December 31, 19x8.

Manufacturing overhead was applied to products at 120 percent of direct-labor dollars. The manufacturing-overhead costs for 19x9 were as follows:

Indirect labor and supplies (variable)	$ 15,000
Employee benefits on indirect labor (variable)	30,000
Supervisory salaries and fringe benefits	35,000
Plant occupancy costs	100,000
Total	$180,000

There was no overapplied or underapplied overhead at year-end.

■ *Advertising*. The company has been unable to determine any direct causal relationship between the level of sales volume and the level of advertising expenditures. However, because management believes advertising is necessary, an annual advertising program is implemented for each product line. Each product line is advertised independently of the others.

■ *Commissions*. Sales commissions are paid to the sales force at the rates of 5 percent on Weedout and 10 percent on the other two products.

■ *Licenses*. Various licenses are required for each product line. These are renewed annually for each product line.

■ *Salaries and fringe benefits*. Sales and administrative personnel devote time and effort to all product lines. Their salaries and wages are allocated on the basis of management's estimates of time spent on each product line.

Required:

1. The controller of Blue Ribbon Lawn Products, Inc. has recommended that the company do a cost-volume-profit analysis of its operations. As a first step, the controller has requested that you prepare a revised income statement that employs a contribution-margin format, which will be useful in CVP analysis. The statement should show the contribution margin for each product line and the operating income before taxes for the company as a whole.

2. The controller is going to prepare a report to present to the other members of top management explaining cost-volume-profit analysis. Identify and explain the following points, which the controller should include in the report.

   a. The advantages that CVP analysis can provide to the company.

   b. The difficulties the company could experience in the calculations involved in CVP analysis.

   c. The dangers that management should be aware of in using the information derived from the CVP analysis.

(CMA, adapted)

■ **Case 8–50**
Sales Commissions in a
Wholesale Firm; Income
Taxes (Appendix)
(LO 1, LO 2, LO 4)

Ticonderoga Sporting Goods Company, a wholesale supply company, engages independent sales agents to market the company's products throughout New York and Ontario. These agents currently receive a commission of 20 percent of sales, but they are demanding an increase to 25 percent of sales made during the year ending December 31, 19x9. The controller already prepared the 19x9 budget before learning of the agents' demand for an increase in commissions. The budgeted 19x9 income statement is shown below. Assume that cost of goods sold is 100 percent variable cost.

TICONDEROGA SPORTING GOODS COMPANY
Budgeted Income Statement
For the Year Ended December 31, 19x9

Sales		$10,000,000
Cost of goods sold		6,000,000
Gross margin		$ 4,000,000
Selling and administrative expenses:		
Commissions	$2,000,000	
All other expenses (fixed)	100,000	2,100,000
Income before taxes		$ 1,900,000
Income tax (30%)		570,000
Net income		$ 1,330,000

Ticondreroga's management is considering the possibility of employing full-time sales personnel. Three individuals would be required, at an estimated annual salary of $30,000 each, plus commissions of 5 percent of sales. In addition, a sales manager would be employed at a fixed annual salary of $160,000. All other fixed costs, as well as the variable cost percentages, would remain the same as the estimates in the 19x9 budgeted income statement.

Required:

1. Compute Ticonderoga's estimated break-even point in sales dollars for the year ending December 31, 19x9, based on the budgeted income statement prepared by the controller.
2. Compute Ticonderoga's estimated break-even point in sales dollars for the year ending December 31, 19x9, if the company employs its own sales personnel.
3. Compute the estimated volume in sales dollars that would be required for the year ending December 31, 19x9, to yield the same net income as projected in the budgeted income statement, if Ticonderoga continues to use the independent sales agents and agrees to their demand for a 25 percent sales commission.
4. Compute the estimated volume in sales dollars that would generate an identical net income for the year ending December 31, 19x9, regardless of whether Ticonderoga Sporting Goods Company employs its own sales personnel or continues to use the independent sales agents and pays them a 25 percent commission.

(CPA, adapted)

Current Issues in Managerial Accounting

"Investors Set Sights Too High in Profit Season," *The Wall Street Journal*, October 20, 1997.

Overview

Investors began selling high-tech stocks despite firms reporting higher profits. One analyst attributed the sell-off to Intel's announced lower-than-expected third-quarter profit.

Suggested Discussion Questions

Using CVP analysis, discuss what factors could have led to Intel's profit decline. Repeat your analysis assuming volume remains constant. What factors could cause a temporary or seasonal change?

■ **Issue 8–51**
Applying CVP Analysis

"McDonald's: Now, It's Just Another Burger Joint," *Business Week*, March 17, 1997.

Overview

McDonald's $.55 Big Mac and McMuffin sandwich deals did not pay off. According to the article, the strategy may have damaged its brand image.

Suggested Discussion Questions

Apply CVP analysis to the $.55 Big Mac campaign. Use the analysis in the following scenarios: (1) assume no bundling with other products (e.g., french fries), and (2) assume the customer must buy a drink and fries to get the price break. Present your analysis in class.

■ **Issue 8–52**
CVP Analysis with Multiple Products

"At Home's IPO Sparks Buying Frenzy, Setting Market Value at $1.99 Billion," *The Wall Street Journal*, July 14, 1997.

Overview

Despite never showing a profit, the initial public offering (IPO) of At Home securities was extremely successful. At Home provides high-speed Internet connection service to about 7,000 customers. At the time of the offering, At Home had a greater market capitalization than Apple Computer.

Suggested Discussion Questions

As a group, prepare a CVP report that could have been used by At Home in its prospectus. Why didn't the firm show a profit? What are its costs? Do you think At Home disclosed CVP information? Is At Home's operating leverage high or low?

■ **Issue 8–53**
Applying CVP Analysis; CVP Information in Published Annual Reports; Cost Structure and Operating Leverage

"Profits Ease Off—From White-Hot to Simmering," *Business Week*, November 17, 1997.

Overview

In 1997, third quarter earnings for 900 companies in the Business Week Corporate Scoreboard were up 9 percent from the previous third quarter. Savings and loans' earnings increased the most.

Suggested Discussion Questions

Illustrate the impact low inflation and strong consumer spending would have on CVP analysis. What effect would low inflation and strong consumer spending have on profits? High inflation, weak spending?

■ **Issue 8–54**
Applying CVP Analysis; CVP Information in Published Annual Reports

9

Chapter Nine

Budgeting: Profit Planning and Control Systems

After completing this chapter, you should be able to:

1. List and explain five purposes of budgeting systems.

2. Describe the similarities and differences in the operational budgets prepared by manufacturers, service industry firms, merchandisers, and nonprofit organizations.

3. Prepare each of the following budgets: sales budget, production budget, direct-material budget, direct-labor budget, indirect-labor budget, overhead budget, selling and administrative expense budget, cash budget, budgeted income statement, and budgeted balance sheet.

4. Describe a typical organization's process of budget administration.

5. Discuss the role of assumptions and predictions in budgeting.

6. Understand the importance of budgeting product life-cycle costs.

7. Discuss the behavioral implications of budgetary slack and participative budgeting.

8. After completing the appendix, understand the differences between the economic-order-quantity and just-in-time approaches to inventory management.

HEALTHWORKS KEEPS LOCAL ATHLETES FIT

San Francisco, CA—The teenage boy was obviously working hard on the stationary bike, and he occasionally winced with pain from his swollen right knee. "I had a torn lateral meniscus cartilage," he told me. "I did it in a JV soccer game. I was the keeper, and I went down to make a save. I twisted my knee, and then I couldn't straighten it." Asked if he'd had an operation, the boy said he had arthroscopic surgery to repair the tear and reshape the meniscus. "Now I'm trying to get the knee back in shape," he said. "I'm hoping I can play keeper again next season." When I asked him if he made the save, his wincing reply was, "No, I missed it. But we still won the game."

My encounter with this young athlete was at Healthworks, a physical therapy practice near the Golden Gate Bridge. "Associates in Physical Therapy and Sports Medicine," reads the subhead on the firm's sign. Although Healthworks was established only two years ago, its clientele has

grown quickly. "Runners, joggers, cyclists, various other athletes, and surgical rehabilitation patients make up most of our clientele," said Mary Edwards, "and we also see lots of athletes from the local colleges." Edwards, one of the five founders of Healthworks, is herself a highly successful cyclist, having won the nationals in her age class.

"I started Healthworks with four friends from college," Edwards told me. "We all got degrees in physical therapy and sports medicine. We wanted to form a practice that would serve a variety of people, but have a specialty in sports medicine for amateur, college, and professional athletes. Things have gone well for us. We have as much business as we can handle, and we've been profitable. Fortunately, three of us had minors in business when we were in college. That training has been absolutely crucial to running the practice."

As I sat in Edwards' small office off the main exercise room, she was interrupted half

a dozen times to answer questions. One or two questions were consultations by other physical therapists about a client's rehabilitation regimen. But several were about Healthworks' budget. "This is a crazy time of year for me," Edwards said. "I've still got my normal client load, but we're also putting the finishing touches on next year's budget. We've found that we have to spend the time to get a good financial plan in place. We budget everything from projected office visits by clients, to salaries, to overhead items, to bad debts. In a small healthcare firm like ours, uncollectible billings can kill you if you don't plan for them in the budget. We employ a part-time business manager to do the groundwork on the budget, but my partners and I go over everything ourselves, too. We want to make sure that we have a financial plan in place for the coming year that is realistic and as accurate as possible. As they say in sports, it's important that we're all on the same page."

A **budget** is a detailed plan, expressed in quantitative terms, that specifies how resources will be acquired and used during a specified period of time.

Developing a budget is a critical step in planning any economic activity. This is true for businesses, for governmental agencies, and for individuals. We must all budget our money to meet day-to-day expenses and to plan for major expenditures, such as buying a car or paying for college tuition. Similarly, businesses of all types and governmental units at every level must make financial plans to carry out routine operations, to plan for major expenditures, and to help in making financial decisions.

Purposes of Budgeting Systems

LO 1   List and explain five purposes of budgeting systems.

A **budgeting system** is the set of procedures used to develop a budget.

A **budget** is a detailed plan, expressed in quantitative terms, that specifies how resources will be acquired and used during a specified period of time. The procedures used to develop a budget constitute a **budgeting system**. Budgeting systems have five primary purposes.

Planning   The most obvious purpose of a budget is to quantify a plan of action. The budgeting process forces the individuals who comprise an organization to plan ahead. The development of a quarterly budget for a Sheraton Hotel, for example, forces the hotel manager, the reservation manager, and the food and beverage manager to plan for the staffing and supplies needed to meet anticipated demand for the hotel's services.

Facilitating Communication and Coordination   For any organization to be effective, each manager throughout the organization must be aware of the plans made by other managers. In order to plan reservations and ticket sales effectively, the reservations manager for Delta Air Lines must know the flight schedules developed by the airline's route manager. The budgeting process pulls together the plans of each manager in an organization.

Allocating Resources   Generally, an organization's resources are limited, and budgets provide one means of allocating resources among competing uses. The city of Chicago, for example, must allocate its revenue among basic life services (such as police and fire protection), maintenance of property and equipment (such as city streets, parks, and vehicles), and other community services (such as child-care services and programs to prevent alcohol and drug abuse).

Controlling Profit and Operations   A budget is a plan, and plans are subject to change. Nevertheless, a budget serves as a useful benchmark with which actual results can be

Diverse organizations use budgets for a variety of reasons. The management of Carnival Cruise Lines uses budgets to plan for meeting the payroll and operating expenses, and to coordinate operations by matching staffing and equipment with projected cruise demand. Carnival also uses its budgeting process to allocate capital improvement funds to competing needs, such as expanding its fleet or improving its landside facilities.

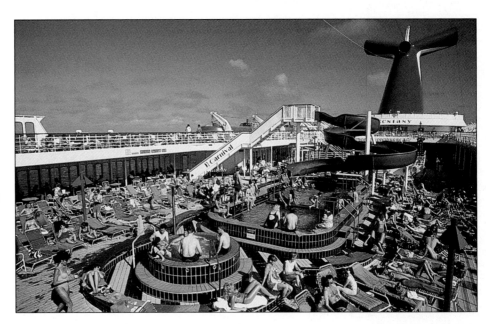

compared. For example, Prudential Insurance Company can compare its actual sales of insurance policies for a year against its budgeted sales. Such a comparison can help managers evaluate the firm's effectiveness in selling insurance. The next two chapters examine the control purpose of budgets in more depth.

Evaluating Performance and Providing Incentives Comparing actual results with budgeted results also helps managers to evaluate the performance of individuals, departments, divisions, or entire companies. Since budgets are used to evaluate performance, they can also be used to provide incentives for people to perform well. For example, General Motors Corporation, like many other companies, provides incentives for managers to improve profits by awarding bonuses to managers who meet or exceed their budgeted profit goals.

Types of Budgets

Different types of budgets serve different purposes. A **master budget**, or **profit plan**, is a comprehensive set of budgets covering all phases of an organization's operations for a specified period of time. We will examine a master budget in detail later in this chapter.

> A **master budget** (or **profit plan**) is a comprehensive set of budgets that covers all phases of an organization's operations for a specified period of time.

Budgeted financial statements, often called **pro forma financial statements**, show how the organization's financial statements will appear at a specified time if operations proceed according to plan. Budgeted financial statements include a *budgeted income statement*, a *budgeted balance sheet,* and a *budgeted statement of cash flows.*

> **Budgeted financial statements** (or **pro forma financial statements**) show what an organization's overall financial condition is expected to be at the end of the budget period if planned operations are carried out.

A **capital budget** is a plan for the acquisition of capital assets, such as buildings and equipment. Capital budgeting is covered in depth later in the text. A **financial budget** is a plan that shows how the organization will acquire its financial resources, such as through the issuance of stock or incurrence of debt.

> A **capital budget** shows planned acquisition and disposal of capital assets, such as land, buildings, and equipment.

Budgets are developed for specific time periods. *Short-range budgets* cover a year, a quarter, or a month, whereas *long-range budgets* cover periods longer than a year. **Rolling budgets** are continually updated by periodically adding a new incremental time period, such as a quarter, and dropping the period just completed. Rolling budgets are also called **revolving budgets** or **continuous budgets**.

> A **financial budget** outlines how an organization will acquire financial resources during the budget period.

The Master Budget: A Planning Tool

The master budget, the principal output of a budgeting system, is a comprehensive profit plan that ties together all phases of an organization's operations. The master budget is comprised of many separate budgets, or schedules, that are interdependent. Exhibit 9–1 portrays these interrelationships in a flowchart.

> A **rolling budget** (also **revolving** or **continuous budget**) is continually updated by adding another incremental time period and dropping the most recently completed period.

Sales of Services or Goods

The starting point for any master budget is a sales revenue budget based on forecast sales of services or goods. Airlines forecast the number of passengers on each of their routes. Banks forecast the number and dollar amount of consumer loans and home mortgages to be provided. Hotels forecast the number of rooms that will be occupied during various seasons. Manufacturing and merchandising companies forecast sales of their goods. Some companies sell both goods and services. For example, Penney's is a large merchandising company, but its automotive-service branch provides the firm with substantial service revenue.

> **Sales forecasting** is the process of predicting sales of services or goods.

Sales Forecasting All companies have two things in common when it comes to forecasting sales of services or goods. **Sales forecasting** is a critical step in the budgeting process, and it is very difficult to do accurately.

Sales Budget

Operational Budgets

Budgeted Financial Statements

Various procedures are used in sales forecasting and the final forecast usually combines information from many different sources. Many firms have a top-management-level market research staff whose job is to coordinate the company's sales forecasting efforts. Typically, everyone from key executives to the firm's sales personnel will be asked to contribute sales projections.

Major factors considered when forecasting sales include the following:

1. Past sales levels and trends:
   a. For the firm developing the forecast (for example, Exxon).
   b. For the entire industry (for example, the petroleum industry).
2. General economic trends. (Is the economy growing? How fast? Is a recession or economic slowdown expected?)
3. Economic trends in the company's industry. (In the petroleum industry, for example, is personal travel likely to increase, thereby implying increased demand for gasoline?)
4. Other factors expected to affect sales in the industry. (Is an unusually cold winter expected, which would result in increased demand for home heating oil in northern climates?)
5. Political and legal events. (For example, is any legislation pending in Congress that would affect the demand for petroleum, such as tax incentives to use alternative energy sources?)
6. The intended pricing policy of the company.
7. Planned advertising and product promotion.

8. Expected actions of competitors.
9. New products contemplated by the company or other firms. (For example, has an automobile firm announced the development of a new vehicle that runs on battery power, thereby reducing the demand for gasoline?)
10. Market research studies.

The starting point in the sales forecasting process is generally the sales level of the prior year. Then the market research staff considers the information discussed above along with input from key executives and sales personnel. In many firms, elaborate *econometric models* are built to incorporate all the available information systematically. (*Econometric* means economic measurement.) Statistical methods, such as regression analysis and probability distributions for sales, are often used. All in all, a great deal of effort generally goes into the sales forecast, since it is such a critical step in the budgeting process. Making a sales forecast is like shooting an arrow. If the archer's aim is off by only a fraction of an inch, the arrow will go further and further astray and miss the bull's-eye by a wide margin. Similarly, a slightly inaccurate sales forecast, coming at the very beginning of the budgeting process, will throw off all of the other schedules comprising the master budget.

Operational Budgets

Based on the sales budget, a company develops a set of **operational budgets** that specify how its operations will be carried out to meet the demand for its goods or services. The budgets comprising this operational portion of the master budget are depicted in the middle portion of Exhibit 9–1.

LO 2 Describe the similarities and differences in the operational budgets prepared by manufacturers, service industry firms, merchandisers, and non-profit organizations.

Manufacturing Firms   A manufacturing company develops a production budget, which shows the number of product units to be manufactured. Coupled with the production budget are ending-inventory budgets for both work in process and finished goods. Manufacturers plan to have some inventory on hand at all times to meet peak demand while keeping production at a stable level. From the production budget, a manufacturer develops budgets for the direct materials, direct labor, and overhead that will be required in the production process. A budget for selling and administrative expenses is also prepared.

Operational budgets specify how operations will be carried out to produce an organization's goods or services.

Merchandising Firms   The operational portion of the master budget is similar in a merchandising firm, but instead of a production budget for goods, a merchandiser develops a budget for merchandise purchases. A merchandising firm will not have a budget for direct material, because it does not engage in production. However, the merchandiser will develop budgets for labor (or personnel), overhead, and selling and administrative expenses.

Service Industry Firms   Based on the sales budget for its services, a service industry firm develops a set of budgets that show how the demand for those services will be met. An airline, for example, prepares the following operational budgets: a budget of planned air miles to be flown; material budgets for spare aircraft parts, aircraft fuel, and in-flight food; labor budgets for flight crews and maintenance personnel; and an overhead budget.

Cash Budget   Every business prepares a cash budget. This budget shows expected cash receipts, as a result of selling goods or services, and planned cash disbursements, to pay the bills incurred by the firm.

Summary of Operational Budgets   Operational budgets differ since they are adapted to the operations of individual companies in various industries. However, operational budgets are also similar in important ways. In each firm they encompass a detailed plan for using the basic factors of production—material, labor, and overhead—to produce a product or provide a service.

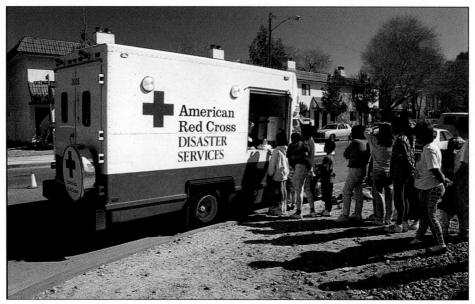

Nonprofit organizations must plan carefully in order to achieve their objectives. This disaster relief operation in Santa Clara, California, after a major earthquake would not have been possible without careful financial planning by the American Red Cross.

Budgeted Financial Statements

The final portion of the master budget, depicted in Exhibit 9–1, includes a budgeted income statement, a budgeted balance sheet, and a budgeted statement of cash flows. These budgeted financial statements show the overall financial results of the organization's planned operations for the budget period.

Nonprofit Organizations

The master budget for a nonprofit organization includes many of the components shown in Exhibit 9–1. However, there are some important differences. Many nonprofit organizations provide services free of charge. Hence, there is no sales budget as shown in Exhibit 9–1. However, such organizations do begin their budgeting process with a budget that shows the level of services to be provided. For example, the budget for the city of Houston would show the planned levels of various public services.

Nonprofit organizations also prepare budgets showing their anticipated funding. The city of Houston budgets for such revenue sources as city taxes, state and federal revenue sharing, and sale of municipal bonds.

In summary, all organizations begin the budgeting process with plans for (1) the goods or services to be provided and (2) the revenue to be available, whether from sales or from other funding sources.

An Illustration of the Master Budget

LO 3 Prepare each of the following budgets: sales budget, production budget, direct-material budget, direct-labor budget, indirect-labor budget, overhead budget, selling and administrative expense budget, cash budget, budgeted income statement, and budgeted balance sheet.

To illustrate the steps in developing a master budget, we will look at Healthworks, Inc., a physical therapy and sports medicine practice in San Francisco. The practice was established two years ago by five friends who had recently received degrees in physical therapy and sports medicine. Two of the firm's founders were collegiate track stars, and their local fame helped to publicize the practice. The firm's clientele has grown quickly. Most of the current clients are runners and joggers; the rest are various athletes, surgical rehabilitation patients, and victims of minor accidents.

Healthworks' clients require professional services such as muscle manipulation, supervised exercise, whirlpool treatment, and massage therapy. In addition, many of the firm's running clients need custom-made orthotic devices. An orthotic is an insert for a shoe, designed to compensate for imperfections in the alignment of the legs and spine. For many runners and joggers, an orthotic can help correct or prevent painful injuries to the knee and lower leg. Although generic orthotics are available, they are seldom as effective as custom-made devices.

Producing a custom-made orthotic requires the skill and knowledge of a trained physical therapist. In addition to shaping and constructing the orthotic device, the physical therapist must take detailed measurements of the alignment of the client's leg and foot. The increasing demand for orthotic devices among Healthworks' clientele requires careful planning by the firm's staff to ensure that the demand can be met. In 20x0, the sale of orthotics represented roughly 10 percent of Healthworks' revenues, and a slight increase is anticipated for 20x1.

The 20x1 master budget for Healthworks has just been completed. It contains the following schedules, which are displayed and explained in the following pages.

Schedule	Title of Schedule
1	Professional Services and Sales Budget
2	Production Budget: Construction of Orthotic Devices
3	Direct-Material Budget
4	Direct-Professional-Labor Budget
5	Indirect-Professional-Labor Budget
6	Overhead Budget
7	Selling and Administrative Expense Budget
8	Cash Receipts Budget
9	Cash Disbursements Budget
10	Summary Cash Budget
11	Budgeted Income Statement
12	Budgeted Balance Sheet

Professional Services and Sales Budget

The first step in developing Healthworks' master budget is to prepare the **professional services and sales budget**, which is displayed as schedule 1. This budget is divided into two parts, one for professional services and one for sales of orthotics. The professional services portion of the budget, which is shaded, shows the number of office visits forecast during each of the four quarters of 20x1. There is a slight seasonal pattern in demand for professional services. The greatest demand comes during the second quarter (April through June), when most high school and collegiate track programs are under way and enthusiasm for jogging peaks in the general population. Demand declines during the warm summer months and then increases slightly in the fall and winter. The budgeted revenue from professional services is computed by multiplying the projected number of visits by the appropriate fee.

The demand for orthotic devices follows the same seasonal pattern as office visits, but with greater swings in projected sales across the four quarters. The sales revenue from orthotics is determined by multiplying the number of units of expected sales by the sales price per orthotic.

The total budgeted revenue for each quarter and for the year, from both professional services and sales of orthotics, is shown in the last row of schedule 1. Roughly 13 percent of the year's revenue is expected to come from the sale of orthotics ($54,000 ÷ $405,000 = 13.333%).

A **professional services and sales budget** plans for revenue from the provision of professional services.

Schedule 1

HEALTHWORKS, INC.
Associates in Physical Therapy and Sports Medicine
Professional Services and Sales Budget
For the Year Ended December 31, 20x1

	Quarter				
	1st	2nd	3rd	4th	Year
Professional services:					
Office visits	1,940	2,000	1,920	1,940	7,800
Fee	× $45	× $45	× $45	× $45	× $45
Professional service revenue	$ 87,300	$ 90,000	$ 86,400	$ 87,300	$351,000
Sales of orthotic devices:					
Sales (in units)	150	180	120	150	600
Sales price	× $90	× $90	× $90	× $90	× $90
Sales revenue:	$ 13,500	$ 16,200	$ 10,800	$ 13,500	$ 54,000
Total revenue: professional services and sales	$100,800	$106,200	$ 97,200	$100,800	$405,000

Production Budget: Construction of Orthotic Devices

Although Healthworks is a service firm, it also engages in a related production activity. Constructing custom orthotics is time-consuming for the firm's licensed therapists, but the sale of orthotics represents an important source of revenue. As a result, it is important to plan carefully for the professional time and material required to make orthotics. The first step in such planning is to prepare a **production budget**. Healthworks' production budget is displayed as schedule 2. Notice that all of the orthotics are sold in the same quarter they are produced. Since orthotics are custom-made, Healthworks cannot store ready-made finished products in inventory. In contrast, manufacturers plan to have some finished goods in inventory at all times to meet peak sales demand.

> A **production budget** shows the number of units of services or goods that are to be produced during a budget period.

The demand for orthotics is greatest during the second quarter, but this is also the firm's busiest season for providing professional therapy services. As a result, the professional staff decided to do some preparatory work on orthotics during periods of slack demand. Each orthotic requires two hours of direct professional labor, as follows:

Step 1 (½ hr.):   Cut out the basic shape of the orthotic from a sheet of special material. Glue two layers of the material together. Heat-treat the resulting rough-cut orthotic to make the two layers adhere.

Step 2 (1 hr.):   Perform physical examination of client. Take detailed measurements of leg and spinal alignment.

Step 3 (½ hr.):   Mold a rough-cut orthotic to the shape of the client's foot. Adjust the thickness of the orthotic to correct the client's leg-alignment problems.

Step 1 can be done with no knowledge of a specific client's needs. Schedule 2 is based on the following formula.

Total units to be produced and sold	+	Desired ending inventory of rough-cut orthotics	=	Total units needed

Total units needed	−	Expected beginning inventory of rough-cut orthotics	=	Units to be started

Focus on the second-quarter column in schedule 2, which is shaded. Expected sales are 180 orthotics, and the staff plans to have 10 rough-cut orthotics in inventory at the end of the quarter. However, 50 rough-cut orthotics are expected to be in inventory at the beginning of the second quarter. Thus, only 140 new orthotics need to be started.

Schedule 2

HEALTHWORKS, INC.
Associates in Physical Therapy and Sports Medicine
Production Budget: Construction of Orthotic Devices
For the Year Ended December 31, 20x1

	Quarter				
	1st	2nd	3rd	4th	Year
Sales (total units to be produced and sold)	150	180	120	150	600
Add desired ending inventory of rough-cut orthotics	50	10	10	20	20
Total units needed	200	190	130	170	620
Less expected beginning inventory of rough-cut orthotics	20	50	10	10	20
Units to be started	180	140	120	160	600

Direct-Material Budget

The **direct-material budget**, displayed as schedule 3, shows the amount of material needed to construct orthotics during each quarter. Each orthotic requires 100 grams of raw material. Some of this material will be trimmed away in the molding and fitting process, leaving a finished orthotic of about 60 grams. The raw material needed for production in each quarter is equal to the number of orthotics to be started (from schedule 2) times 100 grams per orthotic. The shaded portion of schedule 3, which computes the amount of raw material to be purchased each quarter, is based on the following formula.

A **direct-material budget** shows the number of units and the cost of material to be purchased and used during a budget period.

Raw material needed for production	+	Desired ending raw material inventory	=	Total raw-material needs

Total raw-material needs	−	Expected beginning raw-material inventory	=	Raw material to be purchased

Schedule 3

HEALTHWORKS, INC.
Associates in Physical Therapy and Sports Medicine
Direct-Material Budget
For the Year Ended December 31, 20x1

	Quarter				
	1st	2nd	3rd	4th	Year
Units to be started (from schedule 2)	180	140	120	160	600
Raw material required per unit (grams)	× 100	× 100	× 100	× 100	× 100
Raw material needed for production	18,000	14,000	12,000	16,000	60,000
Add desired ending raw-material inventory	2,800	2,400	3,200	3,600	3,600
Total raw-material needs	20,800	16,400	15,200	19,600	63,600
Less expected beginning raw-material inventory	3,600	2,800	2,400	3,200	3,600
Raw material to be purchased	17,200	13,600	12,800	16,400	60,000
Price (per gram)	× $.10	× $.10	× $.10	× $.10	× $.10
Cost of raw-material purchases	$ 1,720	$ 1,360	$ 1,280	$ 1,640	$ 6,000

Production and Purchasing: An Important Link   Notice the important link between planned production and purchases of raw material. This link is apparent in schedule 3, and it is also emphasized in the formula preceding the schedule. Let's focus on the second quarter. Since 140 orthotics are to be started, 14,000 grams of material will be needed (140 units times 100 grams per unit). In addition, Healthworks' staff desires to have 2,400 grams of material in inventory at the end of the quarter. Thus, total needs are 16,400 grams. Does Healthworks need to purchase this much raw material? No, it does not, because 2,800 grams will be in inventory at the beginning of the quarter. Therefore, Healthworks needs to purchase only 13,600 grams of material during the quarter (16,400 grams less 2,800 grams in the beginning inventory).

This linkage between planned production and raw-material purchases is a particularly critical linkage in manufacturing firms. Thus, considerable effort is devoted to careful inventory planning and management.

Inventory Management   How did Healthworks' staff decide how much raw material to have in inventory at the end of each quarter? Examination of schedule 3 reveals that each quarter's desired ending inventory of raw material is 20 percent of the *material needed for production* in the next quarter. For example, 2,400 grams of raw material will be in inventory at the end of the second quarter, because 12,000 grams will be needed for production in the third quarter (2,400 = 20% × 12,000). The effect of this approach is to have a larger ending inventory when the next quarter's planned production is greater. Inventories are drawn down when the subsequent quarter's planned production is lower.

Planning how much inventory of raw materials and finished goods to keep on hand is an important decision in many businesses. Once inventory levels are established, they become an important input to the budgeting system. Inventory management is explored in the appendix at the end of this chapter.

A **direct-professional-labor budget** plans for meeting the salary expenses of the organization's professionals.

Direct-Professional-Labor Budget

Healthworks' **direct-professional-labor budget** is displayed as schedule 4. The shaded top portion shows the amount of time the firm's licensed physical therapists will spend in office visits with clients during each quarter. The lower part of schedule

4 computes the hours of direct professional labor needed to produce orthotic devices during each quarter. Focus on the column for the second quarter. The firm expects to sell 180 orthotics that will require 360 hours of direct professional labor. To this we must add the 5 hours needed to do the initial preparatory work on the 10 rough-cut orthotics that are to be in the ending inventory on June 30. Then we must subtract the 25 hours that have already been expended on the second-quarter beginning inventory of 50 rough-cut orthotics. Thus, 340 hours of direct professional labor will be needed to construct orthotics in the second quarter.

Schedule 4

HEALTHWORKS, INC.
Associates in Physical Therapy and Sports Medicine
Direct-Professional-Labor Budget
For the Year Ended December 31, 20x1

	Quarter				
	1st	2nd	3rd	4th	Year
Professional services:					
Office visits	1,940	2,000	1,920	1,940	7,800
Hours per visit	× 1	× 1	× 1	× 1	× 1
(a) Hours of direct professional service ...	1,940	2,000	1,920	1,940	7,800
Production of orthotic devices:					
Total units to be produced and sold	150	180	120	150	600
Direct labor required per unit	× 2	× 2	× 2	× 2	× 2
Subtotal	300	360	240	300	1,200
Add direct labor required to do initial work on ending inventory of rough-cut orthotics (units in ending inventory × .5 hour per unit):					
1st quarter: 50 × .5	25				
2nd quarter: 10 × .5		5			
3rd quarter: 10 × .5			5		
4th quarter: 20 × .5				10	10
Subtotal	325	365	245	310	1,210
Less direct labor already accomplished on the beginning inventory of rough-cut orthotics (units in beginning inventory × .5 hour per unit):					
1st quarter: 20 × .5	10				10
2nd quarter: 50 × .5		25			
3rd quarter: 10 × .5			5		
4th quarter: 10 × .5				5	
(b) Direct labor required for production ...	315	340	240	305	1,200
Total hours of direct professional labor [add rows (a) and (b)]	2,255	2,340	2,160	2,245	9,000
Cost of direct professional labor (hours of direct labor × $20 per hour)	$45,100	$46,800	$43,200	$44,900	$180,000

The final row of schedule 4 computes the cost to the firm of the total direct professional labor planned for each quarter. Each licensed physical therapist earns an annual salary of $40,000 for 2,000 hours of professional time. Thus, the cost to the firm is $20 per hour ($40,000 ÷ 2,000 hours).

Indirect-Professional-Labor Budget

As schedule 4 shows, Healthworks' staff expects to spend 9,000 hours during the year on direct professional services and the construction of orthotics. The remainder of the licensed physical therapists' time is designated as indirect professional labor. This time is needed for such activities as reading professional journals, attending educational seminars, and calibrating equipment. The cost of this indirect professional labor is computed in the top portion of the **indirect-professional-labor budget**, displayed as schedule 5. The schedule also shows the planned labor cost for two part-time student interns, who assist the licensed physical therapists in various ways.

An **indirect-professional-labor budget** plans for the wage expenses of indirect-labor employees.

Schedule 5

HEALTHWORKS, INC.
Associates in Physical Therapy and Sports Medicine
Indirect-Professional-Labor Budget
For the Year Ended December 31, 20x1

	Quarter				
	1st	**2nd**	**3rd**	**4th**	**Year**
Licensed physical therapists:					
Total hours of professional labor available	2,500	2,500	2,500	2,500	10,000
Less total hours of direct professional labor to be used (from schedule 4)	2,255	2,340	2,160	2,245	9,000
Total hours of indirect professional labor	245	160	340	255	1,000
Cost of indirect professional labor (hours of indirect labor × $20 per hour) ..	$4,900	$ 3,200	$6,800	$5,100	$20,000
Student interns:					
Cost of part-time student assistance	$3,000	$10,000	$3,000	$3,000	$19,000
Total cost of indirect professional labor: licensed physical therapists and student interns	$7,900	$13,200	$9,800	$8,100	$39,000

Overhead Budget

An **overhead budget** shows the cost of overhead expected to be incurred in the production of services or goods during a budget period.

Healthworks' **overhead budget**, displayed as schedule 6, lists the indirect-professional-labor cost (from schedule 5) along with all other costs incurred in the physical therapy and sports medicine practice. The receptionist/business manager spends half of her time on client reception and appointment scheduling. Therefore, as this portion of her work represents indirect labor, only half of her salary and fringe benefits are included on the overhead budget. The employee spends the other half of her time on billing and other business matters. Thus, the other half of her salary and fringe benefits are included on the selling and administrative expense budget.

Selling and Administrative Expense Budget

A **selling and administrative expense budget** shows the planned amounts of selling and administrative expenses during a budget period.

Healthworks' **selling and administrative expense budget** is displayed as schedule 7. This budget lists the expenses of administering the firm and advertising its services. Included here is uncollectible accounts expense, which is 5 percent of each quarter's revenue. This expense results from billings for services that prove to be uncollectible.

Schedule 6

HEALTHWORKS, INC.
Associates in Physical Therapy and Sports Medicine
Overhead Budget
For the Year Ended December 31, 20x1

	Quarter				
	1st	**2nd**	**3rd**	**4th**	**Year**
Indirect professional labor					
(from schedule 5)	$ 7,900	$13,200	$ 9,800	$ 8,100	$ 39,000
Salary: receptionist/business manager	2,125	2,125	2,125	2,125	8,500
Fringe benefits for manager	800	800	800	800	3,200
Linens, supplies, indirect material	1,100	1,400	1,100	1,100	4,700
Laundry service	900	1,100	900	900	3,800
Utilities (electricity, telephone)	2,000	2,200	2,000	2,000	8,200
Continuing education					
(seminars, publications,					
professional travel)	1,900	900	1,900	1,900	6,600
Building rent	7,550	7,550	7,550	7,550	30,200
Professional insurance	2,650	2,650	2,650	2,650	10,600
Equipment depreciation	1,000	1,000	1,000	1,000	4,000
Total overhead	$27,925	$32,925	$29,825	$28,125	$118,800

Schedule 7

HEALTHWORKS, INC.
Associates in Physical Therapy and Sports Medicine
Selling and Administrative Expense Budget
For the Year Ended December 31, 20x1

	Quarter				
	1st	**2nd**	**3rd**	**4th**	**Year**
Salary: receptionist/business manager . .	$ 2,125	$ 2,125	$ 2,125	$ 2,125	$ 8,500
Fringe benefits for manager	800	800	800	800	3,200
Utilities (electricity, telephone)	200	200	200	200	800
Postage	400	400	400	400	1,600
Advertising	250	250	250	250	1,000
Office supplies	180	140	120	160	600
Building rent	400	400	400	400	1,600
Interest	1,000	1,000	1,000	1,000	4,000
Uncollectible accounts expense	5,040	5,310	4,860	5,040	20,250
Equipment depreciation	200	200	200	200	800
Total selling and					
administrative expenses	$10,595	$10,825	$10,355	$10,575	$42,350

Cash Receipts Budget

The **cash receipts budget** for Healthworks is displayed as schedule 8. Healthworks collects 80 percent of its billings during the quarter in which the service is provided, and another 15 percent in the following quarter. Five percent of the billings are never collected, because they are rejected by the clients' insurance companies and then the clients are unable to pay.

The **cash receipts budget** details the expected cash collections during a budget period.

Schedule 8

HEALTHWORKS, INC.
Associates in Physical Therapy and Sports Medicine
Cash Receipts Budget
For the Year Ended December 31, 20x1

	Quarter				
	1st	2nd	3rd	4th	Year
Total revenue: professional services and sales (from schedule 1)	$100,800	$106,200	$97,200	$100,800	$405,000
Collections in quarter of service or sale (80% of billings)	$ 80,640	$ 84,960	$77,760	$ 80,640	$324,000
Collections in quarter following service or sale (15% of billings)	12,000 *	15,120	15,930	14,580	57,630
Total cash receipts	$ 92,640	$100,080	$93,690	$ 95,220	$381,630
Uncollectible billings (5% of total revenue)	$ 5,040	$ 5,310	$ 4,860	$ 5,040	$ 20,250

*15% of the billings during the fourth quarter of the previous year, 20x0.

How Cash Receipts Are Budgeted   To understand how the cash receipts budget is prepared, let's focus again on the second quarter column, which is shaded. The $106,200 of total revenue comes directly from schedule 1, which is the professional services and sales budget (second column, last row). Since Healthworks does not require its clients to pay in cash at the time of service, not all of the second quarter's revenue will be collected during the second quarter. The cash that Healthworks will collect during the second quarter comprises two components, as depicted in the following diagram.

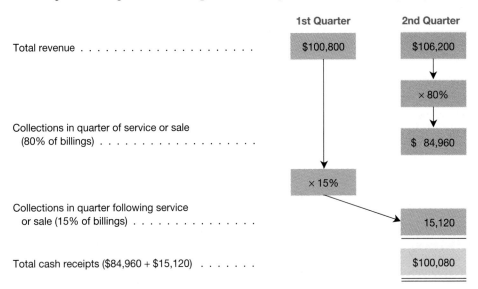

The second quarter's total cash receipts are the sum of $84,960 (which relates to second quarter billings) and $15,120 (which relates to first quarter billings).

One final point to notice is that 5 percent of each quarter's billings will never be collected. Thus, the $5,310 of second quarter uncollectible billings amounts to 5 percent of the second quarter's total revenue ($5,310 = 5\% \times \$106,200$).

The **cash disbursements budget** details the expected cash payments during a budget period.

Cash Disbursements Budget

Schedule 9 (on page 350) displays Healthworks' **cash disbursements budget**. The shaded top portion shows the schedule of cash payments for the materials and services

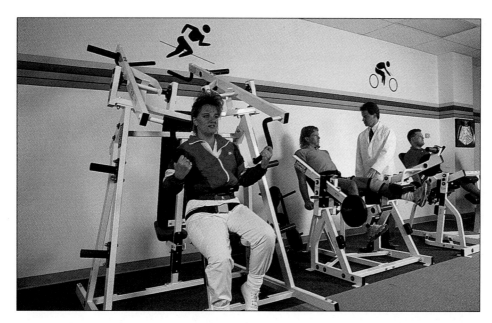

Careful budgeting is crucial in running businesses of all types. In this small physical therapy and sports medicine practice, budgeting cash flows is especially important.

the firm purchases on account. Healthworks pays for 80 percent of its purchases on account during the quarter in which the purchase was made. The remaining 20 percent of each quarter's purchases are paid for during the quarter following the purchase.

The lower portion of schedule 9 shows all of Healthworks' cash payments for services that are paid in advance or at the time of purchase.

How Cash Disbursements Are Budgeted   Healthworks purchases a variety of materials, supplies, services, and labor in order to run its physical therapy practice. Some of these purchases are made on account, which means payment is not made in cash at the time of the purchase. The shaded top portion of schedule 9 shows the items purchased on account. Let's focus on the second quarter column, which has a different color shading. The second quarter's various purchases on account are drawn from schedules 3, 6, and 7, which detail Healthworks' direct-material purchases, overhead expenses, and selling and administrative expenses, respectively. For example, the $1,360 for direct material comes from schedule 3 (second column, last row). The second quarter's purchases on account add up to $6,400.

Does Healthworks pay for all of the $6,400 of purchases on account during the same quarter? No, it does not. As the following diagram shows, the second quarter's actual cash payment for purchases made on account comprises two components.

	1st Quarter	**2nd Quarter**
Total purchases on account	$6,100	$6,400
		× 80%
Payments made during the same quarter as purchase (80% of purchases)		$5,120
	× 20%	
Payments made during the quarter following purchase (20% of purchases)		1,220
Total ($5,120 + $1,220)		$6,340

Schedule 9

HEALTHWORKS, INC.
Associates in Physical Therapy and Sports Medicine
Cash Disbursements Budget
For the Year Ended December 31, 20x1

	Quarter				
	1st	**2nd**	**3rd**	**4th**	**Year**
Purchases of materials and services on account (amounts from schedules 3, 6, and 7):					
Direct material	$ 1,720	$ 1,360	$ 1,280	$ 1,640	$ 6,000
Linens, supplies, indirect material	1,100	1,400	1,100	1,100	4,700
Laundry service	900	1,100	900	900	3,800
Utilities (overhead)	2,000	2,200	2,000	2,000	8,200
Utilities (selling and administrative)	200	200	200	200	800
Office supplies	180	140	120	160	600
Total purchases on account	$ 6,100	$ 6,400	$ 5,600	$ 6,000	$ 24,100
Cash disbursements:					
Cash payments made on account:					
Payments made during the same quarter as purchase (80% of purchases)	$ 4,880	$ 5,120	$ 4,480	$ 4,800	$ 19,280
Payments made during the quarter following purchase (20% of purchases)	1,100*	1,220	1,280	1,120	4,720
Total	$ 5,980	$ 6,340	$ 5,760	$ 5,920	$ 24,000
Other cash payments (amounts from schedules 6 and 7):					
Licensed physical therapists[†]	$50,000	$50,000	$50,000	$50,000	$200,000
Student interns	3,000	10,000	3,000	3,000	19,000
Salary: receptionist/ business manager[‡]	4,250	4,250	4,250	4,250	17,000
Fringe benefits for manager[‡]	1,600	1,600	1,600	1,600	6,400
Continuing education	1,900	900	1,900	1,900	6,600
Building rent: overhead	7,550	7,550	7,550	7,550	30,200
Building rent: selling and administrative	400	400	400	400	1,600
Professional insurance	2,650	2,650	2,650	2,650	10,600
Postage	400	400	400	400	1,600
Advertising	250	250	250	250	1,000
Interest on bank loan	1,000	1,000	1,000	1,000	4,000
Income taxes[§]	6,750	6,750	6,750	6,750	27,000
Total	$79,750	$85,750	$79,750	$79,750	$325,000
Total cash disbursements	$85,730	$92,090	$85,510	$85,670	$349,000

* 20% of the purchases on account during the fourth quarter of the previous year, 20x0.

† The total compensation for the licensed physical therapists is $50,000 each quarter. Part of this cost is designated direct professional labor (on schedule 4), and part is indirect professional labor (on schedule 5).

‡ Half of this employee's salary was allocated to overhead (schedule 6) and half to selling and administrative expense (schedule 7).

§ The income-tax amount comes from the budgeted income statement, discussed subsequently.

The second quarter's total cash payments *for purchases made on account* are the sum of $5,120 (which relates to second quarter purchases on account) and $1,220 (which relates to first quarter purchases on account).

We are not finished with the second quarter's cash disbursements yet, because *Healthworks also pays for some of its purchases in cash at the time of purchase*. These cash expenditures are detailed in the unshaded lower portion of schedule 9. The amounts are drawn from schedules 4, 5, 6, and 7, which detail expenditures for direct professional labor, indirect professional labor, overhead, and selling and administrative expenses, respectively. For example, schedule 4 lists $46,800 for direct professional labor cost in the second quarter (second column, last row), and schedule 5 lists $3,200 for indirect professional labor by Healthworks' licensed physical therapists (second column, third to last row).

Finally, the last row in the cash disbursements budget (schedule 9) shows the total cash disbursements during each quarter. Thus, the $92,090 total payment in the second quarter is the sum of $6,340 (for purchases on account) and $85,750 for purchases made in cash.

Summary Cash Budget

A **summary cash budget** is displayed as schedule 10. The shaded top portion pulls together the cash receipts and cash disbursements detailed in schedules 8 and 9. The lower portion of schedule 10 discloses Healthworks' plans to take out a short-term bank loan on January 2, 20x1 for the purpose of purchasing additional equipment. The loan will be repaid on December 31, 20x1. Most of the funds for this repayment will come from excess cash generated from operations during 20x1.

A **summary cash budget** combines the cash receipts and cash disbursements budgets.

Schedule 10

HEALTHWORKS, INC.
Associates in Physical Therapy and Sports Medicine
Summary Cash Budget
For the Year Ended December 31, 20x1

	Quarter				
	1st	2nd	3rd	4th	Year
Cash receipts (from schedule 8)	$92,640	$100,080	$93,690	$95,220	$381,630
Less cash disbursements (from schedule 9)	(85,730)	(92,090)	(85,510)	(85,670)	(349,000)
Change in cash balance during quarter due to operations	$ 6,910	$ 7,990	$ 8,180	$ 9,550	$ 32,630
Proceeds from bank loan (1/2/x1)	35,000				35,000
Less purchase of equipment (1/2/x1) . . .	(35,000)				(35,000)
Repayment of bank loan (12/31/x1)				(35,000)	(35,000)
Change in cash balance during 20x1 . . .					$ (2,370)
Cash balance, 1/1/x1					15,000
Cash balance, 12/31/x1					$ 12,630

Budgeted Income Statement

Healthworks' **budgeted income statement**, displayed as schedule 11, begins with the revenue anticipated from professional services and sales of orthotics. Then the cost of making orthotics is subtracted as cost of goods sold. Each of the 600 orthotics to be sold costs $50 ($10 for direct material and $40 for two hours of direct labor). No overhead is allocated as a product cost since it is judged to be negligible. From the gross margin are subtracted the firm's projected operating expenses. Included here are the following expenses: the cost of the time spent by the firm's licensed physical therapists on direct professional services; overhead expenses; and selling and administrative expenses. Finally, income taxes of $27,000 are anticipated.

A **budgeted income statement** shows the expected revenue and expenses for the budget period, assuming that planned operations are carried out.

Notice that the $156,000 expense for direct professional labor includes only the 7,800 hours of physical therapist time spent on office visits. (See the "Year" column in schedule 4, shaded top portion.) What about the other hours to be worked by the physical therapists? The construction of orthotic devices will require 1,200 hours (600 orthotics × 2 hours per unit, as shown in schedule 4.) The other 1,000 hours of physical therapist time will be spent on various activities designed as indirect professional labor (see schedule 5). Thus, we can account for the 10,000 hours of physical therapist time available during the year (5 licensed physical therapists × 2,000 hours per year).

Schedule 11

HEALTHWORKS, INC.
Associates in Physical Therapy and Sports Medicine
Budgeted Income Statement
For the Year Ended December 31, 20x1

Professional service and sales revenue (from schedule 1):		
Professional services		$351,000
Sales of orthotic devices		54,000
Total revenue		$405,000
Cost of goods sold (cost of direct material and direct labor)		30,000
Gross margin		$375,000
Operating expenses:		
Salaries: direct professional services		
(7,800 hours, from schedule 4, times $20 per hour)	$156,000	
Overhead expenses (see schedule 6 for details)	118,800	
Selling and administrative expenses (see schedule 7 for details)	42,350	
Total operating expenses		317,150
Income before taxes		$ 57,850
Income taxes		27,000
Net income		$ 30,850

Budgeted Balance Sheet

A budgeted balance sheet shows the expected end-of-period balances for the organization's assets, liabilities, and owners' equity, assuming that planned operations are carried out.

Healthworks' **budgeted balance sheet** for December 31, 20x1 is displayed as schedule 12, which appears on pages 354 and 355. To construct this budgeted balance sheet, we start with the firm's balance sheet projected for the *beginning* of the budget year (Exhibit 9–2) and adjust each account balance for the changes expected during 20x1.

Balance sheet December 31, 20x0 (Exhibit 9–2) → Expected changes in account balances during 20x1 → Balance sheet December 31, 20x1 (schedule 12)

Explanations for the account balances on the budgeted balance sheet for December 31, 20x1, are given in the second half of schedule 12. Examine these explanations carefully. Notice how the budgeted balance sheet pulls together information from most of the schedules comprising the master budget.

Using the Master Budget for Planning

Virtually all of the information contained in Healthworks' master budget is used in some way for planning purposes. For example, the revenue forecasts reflected in schedule 1 help the firm's staff plan for advertising. Healthworks plans only minimal advertising, since the firm's clientele has grown quickly without much advertising. The

HEALTHWORKS, INC. **Associates in Physical Therapy and Sports Medicine** **Balance Sheet** **December 31, 20x0**		
Assets		
Current assets:		
Cash		$15,000
Accounts receivable (net of allowance for uncollectible accounts)		12,000
Inventory:		
Raw material	$ 360	
Work in process (rough-cut orthotics)	400	
Professional supplies	1,940	
Office supplies	300	
Total inventory		3,000
Total current assets		$30,000
Long-lived assets:		
Equipment	$35,000	
Less accumulated depreciation	9,600	
Equipment, net of accumulated depreciation		25,400
Total assets		$55,400
Liabilities and Stockholders' Equity		
Current liabilities:		
Accounts payable		$ 1,100
Total current liabilities		$ 1,100
Long-term liabilities:		
Note payable (due on December 31, 20x4)		5,000
Total liabilities		$ 6,100
Stockholders' equity:		
Common stock	$41,000	
Retained earnings	8,300	
Total stockholders' equity		49,300
Total liabilities and stockholders' equity		$55,400

direct professional labor budget (schedule 4) helps the staff plan when to make rough-cut orthotics, when to schedule travel for seminars, and when to take personal vacations. The summary cash budget (schedule 10) helps the staff in planning to purchase equipment and pay off the bank loan due on December 31, 20x1.

Budget Administration

In small organizations, the procedures used to gather information and construct a master budget are usually informal. At Healthworks, for example, the budgeting process is coordinated by the business manager in consultation with the firm's founders. In contrast, larger organizations use a formal

LO 4   Describe a typical organization's process of budget administration.

Schedule 12

HEALTHWORKS, INC.
Associates in Physical Therapy and Sports Medicine
Budgeted Balance Sheet
December 31, 20x1

Assets

Current assets:			
Cash			$ 12,630 (a)
Accounts receivable (net of allowance for uncollectible accounts)			15,120 (b)
Inventory:			
Raw material	$	360 (c)	
Work in process (rough-cut orthotics)		400 (d)	
Professional supplies		1,940 (e)	
Office supplies		300 (e)	
Total inventory			3,000
Total current assets			$ 30,750
Long-lived assets:			
Equipment	$70,000 (f)		
Less accumulated depreciation	14,400 (g)		
Equipment, net of accumulated depreciation			55,600
Total assets			$ 86,350

Liabilities and Stockholders' Equity

Current liabilities:			
Accounts payable			$ 1,200 (h)
Total current liabilities			$ 1,200 (i)
Long-term liabilities:			
Note payable (due on December 31, 20x4)			5,000 (j)
Total liabilities			$ 6,200
Stockholders' equity:			
Common stock	$41,000 (k)		
Retained earnings	39,150 (l)		
Total stockholders' equity			80,150
Total liabilities and stockholders' equity			$ 86,350

(a)	Cash balance on 12/31/x0 balance sheet		$ 15,000
	Less decrease in cash during 20x1 (schedule 10)		(2,370)
	Cash balance (12/31/x1)		$ 12,630
(b)	Accounts receivable (net) on 12/31/x0 balance sheet		$ 12,000
	Add sales on account during 20x1 (schedule 1)		405,000
	Less collection of accounts receivable during 20x1 (schedule 8)		(381,630)
	Less expected uncollectible accounts from 20x1 sales (schedule 8)		(20,250)
	Accounts receivable (net), 12/31/x1		$ 15,120
(c)	From schedule 3: 3,600 grams at $.10 per gram.		
(d)	Planned number of rough-cut orthotics (schedule 2)		20
	× Cost per rough-cut orthotic ($10 material; ½ hour direct labor at $20 per hour)		× $20
	Planned balance for rough-cut orthotics, 12/31/x1		$ 400
(e)	All supplies purchased during 20x1 are expected to be used. Therefore, 12/31/x1 inventory balances are the same as balances on 12/31/x0.		
(f)	$35,000 from 12/31/x0 balance sheet, plus $35,000 equipment purchase.		
(g)	Accumulated depreciation, 12/31/x0		$ 9,600
	Add total depreciation expense for 20x1 (schedules 6 and 7)		4,800
	Accumulated depreciation, 12/31/x1		$ 14,400

(h)	Accounts payable on 12/31/x0 balance sheet	$ 1,100
	Add purchases on account during 20x1 (schedule 9)	24,100
	Less payments of accounts payable during 20x1 (schedule 9)	(24,000)
	Accounts payable, 12/31/x1	$ 1,200
(i)	Note that the $35,000 bank loan will be paid off, so it is not shown on the 12/31/x1 balance sheet.	
(j)	From 12/31/x0 balance sheet.	
(k)	From 12/31/x0 balance sheet.	
(l)	Retained earnings on 12/31/x0 balance sheet	$ 8,300
	Add net income for 20x1 (schedule 11)	30,850
	Retained earnings, 12/31/x1	$ 39,150

process to collect data and prepare the master budget. Such organizations usually designate a **budget director** or **chief budget officer**. This is often the organization's controller. The budget director specifies the process by which budget data will be gathered, collects the information, and prepares the master budget. To communicate budget procedures and deadlines to employees throughout the organization, the budget director often develops and disseminates a **budget manual**. The budget manual says who is responsible for providing various types of information, when the information is required, and what form the information is to take. For example, the budget manual for a manufacturing firm might specify that each regional sales director is to send an estimate of the following year's sales, by product line, to the budget director by September 1. The budget manual also states who should receive each schedule when the master budget is complete.

A **budget committee**, consisting of key senior executives, is often appointed to advise the budget director during the preparation of the budget. The authority to give final approval to the master budget usually belongs to the board of directors, or a board of trustees in many nonprofit organizations. Usually the board has a subcommittee whose task is to examine the proposed budget carefully and recommend approval or any changes deemed necessary. By exercising its authority to make changes in the budget and grant final approval, the board of directors, or trustees, can wield considerable influence on the overall direction the organization takes.

Budgeting is a major activity in every large organization. The master budget at ITT, a large, international conglomerate, consists of bound volumes that occupy 21 feet of shelf space.[1]

The **budget director** (or **chief budget officer**) is in charge of preparing an organization's budget.

The **budget manual** is a set of written instructions that specifies who will provide budgetary data, when and in what form the data will be provided, how the master budget will be prepared and approved, and who should receive the various schedules comprising the budget.

A **budget committee** is a group of top-management personnel who advise the budget director during the preparation of the budget.

Budget Administration at Cornell University

Cornell's annual budget covers the period from July 1 through the following June 30. The budgeting process begins in October, when the deans and senior vice presidents have meetings to discuss the programs the university will conduct during the following budget year. The university's priorities in educational, research, and public service programs are established during these meetings. In early January, the university's budget director, together with other members of the Operating Plans Committee, settles on a set of assumptions to be used during the remainder of the budgeting process. These assumptions include such key forecasts as the next year's inflation rate, interest rates, and tuition levels. Based on these assumptions, the dean of each of Cornell's colleges or professional schools must develop a detailed budget for salaries and general expenses. These detailed budgets are prepared during January and February by the financial staff in each college or professional school. In March, the university president and provost review these budgets with the deans. After any needed revisions have been made, the budgets for the various colleges and professional schools are consolidated by the university controller's staff into a master budget. This budget is presented to the university's board of trustees in May for their final approval.

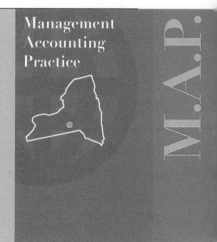

Management Accounting Practice

M.A.P.

---

[1]H. Geneen, "The Case for Managing by the Numbers," *Fortune* 110, no. 7, p. 80.

Assumptions and Predictions: The Underpinnings of the Master Budget

LO 5   Discuss the role of assumptions and predictions in budgeting.

A master budget is based on many assumptions and estimates of unknown parameters. What are some of the assumptions and estimates used in Healthworks' master budget? The professional services and sales budget (schedule 1) was built on an assumption about the seasonal nature of demand for professional services. The direct-material budget (schedule 3) uses an estimate of the direct-material price, $.10 per gram, and the quantity of material required per orthotic, 100 grams. An estimate of the direct labor required to make a custom orthotic was used in the direct professional labor budget (schedule 4).

In **zero-base budgeting**, the initial budget for each activity in an organization is set to zero.

These are only a few of the many assumptions and estimates used in Healthworks' master budget. Some of these estimates are much more likely to be accurate than others. For example, the amount of material required to construct an orthotic is not likely to differ from past experience unless the type of material or construction process is changed. In contrast, estimates such as the price of material, the cost of utilities, and the demand for professional services are much more difficult to predict.

Zero-Base Budgeting

In **base budgeting**, the initial budget for each of an organization's departments is set in accordance with a base package.

Zero-base budgeting is used in a wide variety of organizations, including Southern California Edison, Texas Instruments, and the state of Georgia. Under zero-base budgeting, the budget for virtually every activity in the organization is initially set to zero. To receive funding during the budgeting process, each activity must be justified in terms of its continued usefulness. The zero-base-budgeting approach forces management to rethink each phase of an organization's operations before allocating resources. The following example cites the use of zero-base budgeting in a public school district in suburban Rochester, New York.

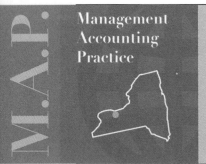

Management Accounting Practice

Zero-Base Budgeting in a Public School District

Zero-base budgeting is not a magic formula, but an attitude, woven into a structured analytical process. . . . The usual approach to budgeting is to begin with the present level of operation and spending and then justify the new programs or additional expenditures desired for next year. In zero-base budgeting there are no "givens." It starts with the basic premise that the budget for next year is zero—and that every expenditure, old or new, must be justified on the basis of its cost and benefit.[2]

A **base package** is an initial budget that includes the minimal resources needed for a subunit to exist at an absolute minimal level.

An **incremental package** is a budget that details the additional resources needed to add various activities to a base package.

Base Budgeting   Some organizations use a **base-budgeting** approach without going to the extreme of zero-base budgeting. Under this approach, the initial budget for each of the organization's departments is set in accordance with a **base package**, which includes the minimal resouces required for the subunit to exist at an absolute minimal level. Below this level of funding, the subunit would not be a viable entity. Any increases above the base package would result from a decision to fund an **incremental package**, which describes the resources needed to add various activities to the base package. The decision to approve such an incremental budget package would have to be justified on the basis of the costs and benefits of the activities included. Base budgeting has been effective in many organizations because it forces managers to take an evaluative, questioning attitude toward each of the organization's programs.

[2]Excerpt from A. F. Brueningsen, "SCAT—A Process of Alternatives," *Management Accounting* 58, no. 5, p. 56; reproduced with permission of the publisher.

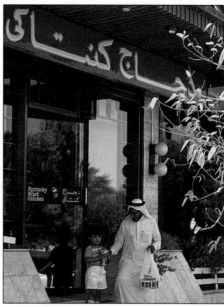

As these photos from Japan and Saudi Arabia show, Kentucky Fried Chicken operates restaurants throughout the world. Multinational companies like KFC face special challenges in preparing their budgets.

International Aspects of Budgeting

As the economies and cultures of countries throughout the world become intertwined, more and more companies are becoming multinational in their operations. Firms with international operations face a variety of additional challenges in preparing their budgets. First, a multinational firm's budget must reflect the translation of foreign currencies into U.S. dollars. Since almost all the world's currencies fluctuate in their values relative to the dollar, this makes budgeting for those translations difficult. Although multinationals have sophisticated financial ways of hedging against such currency fluctuations, the budgeting task is still more challenging. Second, it is difficult to prepare budgets when inflation is high or unpredictable. While the United States has experienced periods of high inflation, some foreign countries have experienced hyperinflation, sometimes with annual inflation rates well over 100 percent. Predicting such high inflation rates is difficult and further complicates a multinational's budgeting process. Finally, the economies of all countries fluctuate in terms of consumer demand, availability of skilled labor, laws affecting commerce, and so forth. Companies with off-shore operations face the task of anticipating such changing conditions in their budgeting processes.

Budgeting Product Life-Cycle Costs

A relatively recent focus of the budgeting process is to plan for all of the costs that will be incurred throughout a product's life cycle, before a commitment is made to the product.[3] Product life-cycle costs encompass the following five phases in a product's life cycle:

LO 6 Understand the importance of budgeting product life-cycle costs.

- Product planning and concept design.
- Preliminary design.

---

[3]This section draws on Callie Berliner and James A. Brimson, eds., *Cost Management for Today's Advanced Manufacturing* (Boston: Harvard Business School Press, 1988); and Norm Raffish, "How Much Does That Product Really Cost?" *Manufacturing Accounting* 72, no. 9, pp. 36–39.

■ Detailed design and testing.

■ Production.

■ Distribution and customer service.

In order to justify a product's introduction, the sales revenues it will generate over its life must be sufficient to cover all of these costs. Thus planning these life-cycle costs is a crucial step in making a decision about the introduction of a new product. This is particularly true for firms with very short product life cycles, such as some products in the computer and electronics industries. When product life cycles are as short as a year or two, the firm does not have time to adjust its pricing strategy or production methods to ensure that the product turns a profit. Management must be fairly certain before a commitment is made to the product that its life-cycle costs will be covered. As Exhibit 9–3 shows, most of a product's life-cycle costs are committed rather early in the product's life. By the time the planning, design, and testing phases are complete, roughly 85 percent of this product's life-cycle costs have been committed, while only about 5 percent actually have been incurred.

Given the early commitment that must be made to significant downstream costs in a product's life cycle, it is crucial to budget these costs as early as possible. Exhibit 9–4 displays a product life-cycle cost budget for an ancillary computer device with an anticipated five-year life cycle.

Behavioral Impact of Budgets

One of the underlying themes stressed in this text is the behavioral impact of managerial-accounting practices. There is no other area where the behavioral implications are more important than in the budgeting area. A budget affects virtually everyone in an organization: those who prepare the budget, those who use the budget to facilitate decision making, and those who are evaluated using the budget. The human reactions to the budgeting process can have considerable influence on an organization's overall effectiveness.

A great deal of study has been devoted to the behavioral effects of budgets. Here we will barely scratch the surface by briefly considering two issues: budgetary slack and participative budgeting.

Product life-cycle costing plans for the costs to be incurred throughout a product's life cycle. Pictured here are the design and production of fabric by a textile manufacturer.

Product life-cycle costs

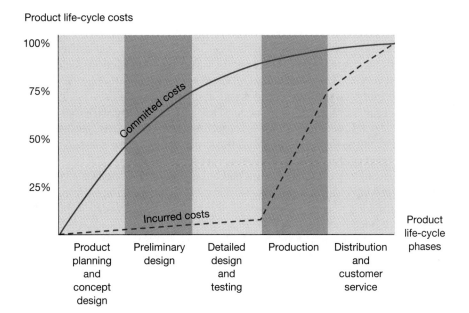

Exhibit 9–3

Product Life-Cycle Costs and
Cost Commitment for a
Typical Product

Exhibit 9–4

Product Life-Cycle Cost
Budget

Life-Cycle Phase	Year				
	20x0	20x1	20x2	20x3	20x4
Product planning and concept design	$300,000				
Preliminary design	100,000				
Detail design and testing		$600,000			
Production		300,000	$2,000,000	$2,700,000	$1,200,000
Distribution and customer service		50,000	750,000	1,000,000	1,000,000

Budgetary Slack: Padding the Budget

The information upon which a budget is based comes largely from people throughout
an organization. For example, the sales forecast relies on market research and analysis
by a market research staff but also incorporates the projections of sales personnel. If a
territorial sales manager's performance is evaluated on the basis of whether the sales
budget for the territory is exceeded, what is the incentive for the sales manager in projecting sales? The incentive is to give a conservative, or cautiously low sales estimate.
The sales manager's performance will look much better in the eyes of top management
when a conservative estimate is exceeded than when an ambitious estimate is not met.
At least that is the *perception* of many sales managers, and in the behavioral area per-
ceptions are what count most.

    When a supervisor provides a departmental cost projection for budgetary purposes,
there is an incentive to overestimate costs. When the actual cost incurred in the
department proves to be less than the inflated cost projection, the supervisor appears to
have managed in a cost-effective way.

    These illustrations are examples of **padding the budget**. Budget padding means
underestimating revenue or overestimating costs. The difference between the revenue
or cost projection that a person provides and a realistic estimate of the revenue or cost
is called **budgetary slack**. For example, if a plant manager believes the annual utilities
cost will be $18,000, but gives a budgetary projection of $20,000, the manager has
built $2,000 of slack into the budget.

Padding the budget is
the process of building
budgetary slack into a
budget by overestimating
expenses and
underestimating revenue.

Budgetary slack is the
difference between the
budgetary projection
provided by an individual
and his or her best
estimate of the item being
projected.

Why do people pad budgets with budgetary slack? There are three primary reasons. First, people often *perceive* that their performance will look better in their superiors' eyes if they can "beat the budget." Second, budgetary slack often is used to cope with uncertainty. A departmental supervisor may feel confident in the cost projections for 10 cost items. However, the supervisor also may feel that some unforeseen event during the budgetary period could result in unanticipated costs. For example, an unexpected machine breakdown could occur. One way of dealing with that unforeseen event is to pad the budget. If nothing goes wrong, the supervisor can beat the cost budget. If some negative event does occur, the supervisor can use the budgetary slack to absorb the impact of the event and still meet the cost budget.

The third reason why cost budgets are padded is that budgetary cost projections are often cut in the resource-allocation process. Thus, we have a vicious circle. Budgetary projections are padded because they will likely be cut, and they are cut because they are likely to have been padded.

How does an organization solve the problem of budgetary slack? First, it can avoid relying on the budget as a negative evaluation tool. If a departmental supervisor is harassed by the budget director or some other top manager every time a budgetary cost projection is exceeded, the likely behavioral response will be to pad the budget. In contrast, if the supervisor is allowed some managerial discretion to exceed the budget when necessary, there will be less tendency toward budgetary padding. Second, managers can be given incentives not only to achieve budgetary projections but also to *provide accurate projections*. This can be accomplished by asking managers to justify all or some of their projections and by rewarding managers who consistently provide accurate estimates.

Participative Budgeting

Participative budgeting is the process of involving people throughout an organization in the budgeting process.

Most people will perform better and make greater attempts to achieve a goal if they have been consulted in setting the goal. The idea of **participative budgeting** is to involve employees throughout an organization in the budgetary process. Such participation can give employees the feeling that "this is our budget," rather than the all-too-common feeling that "this is the budget you imposed on us." The effectiveness of budgetary participation is illustrated by the following description of budgeting at University Community Hospital in Tampa, Florida.

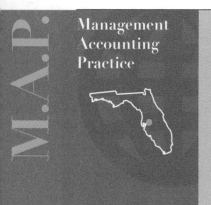

Management Accounting Practice

Participative Budgeting in a Hospital

Because the department directors, along with their first-line supervisors, vice presidents, the president, the finance committee, and the board of trustees, have been involved in the budgetary process, the budget is felt to be "owned" by all of them as a total document. This feeling of ownership is particularly true in the case of the individual department director with reference to his or her specific portion of the budget. This commitment is taken seriously.

The participative approach to budgeting has proven very successful at University Community Hospital. One supervisor commented, "Our budget projections have proven to be extremely accurate because of a combination of good forecasting and willingness to cooperate in taking corrective action to overcome adverse variances. In fact, our overall projections have generally been so close to our actual experience that our finance committee of the board has jokingly suggested the budget was prepared after the fact. It would be difficult to envision our budget effort being accomplished in an effective manner without the participative approach."[4]

---

[4]Excerpt from M. Feldbush, "Participative Budgeting in a Hospital Setting," *Management Accounting* 63, no. 3, pp. 43–46; reproduced with permission of the publisher.

While participative budgeting can be very effective, it can also have shortcomings. Too much participation and discussion can lead to vacillation and delay. Also, when those involved in the budgeting process disagree in significant and irreconcilable ways, the process of participation can accentuate those differences. Finally, the problem of budget padding can be severe unless incentives for accurate projections are provided.

Ethical Issues in Budgeting

A departmental or divisional budget often is used as the basis for evaluating a manager's performance. Actual results are compared with budgeted performance levels, and those who outperform the budget often are rewarded with promotions or salary increases. In many cases, bonuses are tied explicitly to performance relative to a budget. For example, the top-management personnel of a division may receive a bonus if divisional profit exceeds budgeted profit by a certain percentage.

Serious ethical issues can arise in situations where a budget is the basis for rewarding managers. For example, suppose a division's top-management personnel will split a bonus equal to 10 percent of the amount by which actual divisional profit exceeds the budget. This may create an incentive for the divisional budget officer, or other managers supplying data, to pad the divisional profit budget. Such padding would make the budget easier to achieve, thus increasing the chance of a bonus. Alternatively, there may be an incentive to manipulate the actual divisional results in order to maximize management's bonus. For example, year-end sales could be shifted between years to increase reported revenue in a particular year.

Budget personnel could have such incentives for either of two reasons: (1) they might share in the bonus, or (2) they might feel pressure from the managers who would share in the bonus. Padding the budget or manipulating reported results in order to maximize one's personal gain or that of others is a serious ethical violation. For a managerial accountant to engage in such behavior would violate several of the profession's stated ethical standards. (See Chapter 1 for a listing of these standards.)

Chapter Summary

The budget is a key tool for planning, control, and decision making in virtually every organization. Budgeting systems are used to force planning, to facilitate communication and coordination, to allocate resources, to control profit and operations, and to evaluate performance and provide incentives. Various types of budgets are used to accomplish these objectives.

The comprehensive set of budgets that covers all phases of an organization's operations is called a master budget. The first step in preparing a master budget is to forecast sales of the organization's services or goods. Based on the sales forecast, operational budgets are prepared to plan production of services or goods and to outline the acquisition and use of material, labor, and other resources. Finally, a set of budgeted financial statements is prepared to show what the organization's overall financial condition will be if planned operations are carried out.

Since budgets affect almost everyone in an organization, they can have significant behavioral implications and can raise difficult ethical issues. One common problem in budgeting is the tendency of people to pad budgets. The resulting budgetary slack makes the budget less useful because the padded budget does not present an accurate picture of expected revenue and expenses.

Participative budgeting is the process of allowing employees throughout the organization to have a significant role in developing the budget. Participative budgeting can result in greater commitment to meet the budget by those who participated in the process.

A relatively recent focus of the budgeting process is to plan for product life-cycle costs. A large portion of these costs often are committed early in a product's life cycle. It is important for management to be fairly certain that the revenue to be generated by a product will cover all of its life-cycle costs.[5]

---

[5]For an extensive treatment of budgeting issues, see Glenn Welsch, Ronald Hilton, and Paul Gordon, *Budgeting: Profit Planning and Control,* 5th ed. (Englewood Cliffs, NJ: Prentice-Hall, 1988).

Key Terms

For each term's definition refer to the indicated page, or turn to the glossary at the end of the text.

base budgeting, pg. 356

base package, pg. 356

budget, pg. 336

budget committee, pg. 355

budget director (or chief budget officer), pg. 355

budget manual, pg. 355

budgetary slack, pg. 359

budgeted balance sheet, pg. 352

budgeted financial statements (or pro forma financial statements), pg. 337

budgeted income statement, pg. 351

budgeting system, pg. 336

capital budget, pg. 337

cash disbursements budget, pg. 348

cash receipts budget, pg. 347

direct-material budget, pg. 343

direct-professional-labor budget, pg. 344

financial budget, pg. 337

incremental package, pg. 356

indirect-professional-labor budget, pg. 346

master budget (or profit plan), pg. 337

operational budgets, pg. 339

overhead budget, pg. 346

padding the budget, pg. 359

participative budgeting, pg. 360

production budget, pg. 342

professional services and sales budget, pg. 341

profit plan (or master budget), pg. 337

rolling budgets (also revolving or continuous budgets), pg. 337

sales forecasting, pg. 337

selling and administrative expense budget, pg. 346

summary cash budget, pg. 351

zero-base budgeting, pg. 356

Appendix to Chapter 9

Inventory Management

A key decision in manufacturing, retail, and some service industry firms is how much inventory to keep on hand. Once inventory levels are established, they become an important input to the budgeting system. Inventory decisions involve a delicate balance between three classes of costs: ordering costs, holding costs, and shortage costs. Examples of costs in each of these categories are given in Exhibit 9–5.

The following illustration emphasizes the benefits of a sound inventory policy.

LO 8 After completing the appendix, understand the differences between the economic-order-quantity and just-in-time approaches to inventory management.

Management Accounting Practice

Firestone Tire & Rubber Co.

According to an article in *The Wall Street Journal,* Firestone Tire & Rubber Co. had two firm policies: minimize the cost of producing quality tires, and avoid the loss of sales. While these are sound business practices, both policies tend to result in large inventories of raw materials and finished products. Realizing that large inventories were causing unacceptably high holding costs, Firestone's management hired a consulting firm to assist in overhauling its entire inventory-control system. The result was a massive inventory-cutting program and substantial cost savings.

Economic Order Quantity

Surfco manufactures fiberglass surfboards. One of the raw materials is a special resin used to bind the fiberglass in the molding phase of production. The production manager, Hi Wave, uses an **economic order quantity (EOQ)** decision model to determine the size and frequency with which resin is ordered. The EOQ model is a mathematical tool for determining the order quantity that minimizes the costs of ordering and holding inventory.

Resin is purchased in 50-gallon drums, and 9,600 drums are used each year. Each drum costs $400. The controller estimates that the cost of placing and receiving a typical resin order is $225. The controller's estimate of the annual cost of carrying resin in inventory is $3 per drum.

An **economic order quantity (EOQ)** is the order size that minimizes inventory ordering and holding costs.

Ordering Costs
>   Clerical costs of preparing purchase orders
>   Time spent finding suppliers and expediting orders
>   Transportation costs
>   Receiving costs (e.g., unloading and inspection)

Holding Costs
>   Costs of storage space (e.g., warehouse depreciation)
>   Security
>   Insurance
>   Forgone interest on working capital tied up in inventory
>   Deterioriation, theft, spoilage, or obsolescence

Shortage Costs
>   Disrupted production when raw materials are unavailable:
>>   Idle workers
>>   Extra machinery setups
>   Lost sales resulting in dissatisfied customers
>   Loss of quantity discounts on purchases

Exhibit 9–5

Inventory Ordering, Holding, and Shortage Costs

Tabular Approach   Suppose Wave orders 800 drums of resin in each order placed during the year. The total annual cost of ordering and holding resin in inventory is calculated as follows:

$$\frac{\text{Annual requirement}}{\text{Quantity per order}} = \frac{9{,}600}{800} = 12 = \text{Number of orders}$$

Annual ordering cost = 12 orders × $225 per order = $2,700

$$\text{Average quantity in inventory} = \frac{\text{Quantity per order}}{2} = \frac{800}{2} = 400 \text{ drums}$$

$$\text{Annual holding cost} = \binom{\text{Average quantity}}{\text{in inventory}} \times \binom{\text{Annual carrying}}{\text{cost per drum}}$$

$$= 400 \times \$3 = \$1{,}200$$

$$\text{Total annual cost of} \atop \text{inventory policy} = \text{Ordering} \atop \text{cost} + \text{Holding} \atop \text{cost} = \$2{,}700 + \$1{,}200 = \$3{,}900$$

Notice that the $3,900 cost does *not* include the purchase cost of the resin at $400 per drum. We are focusing only on the costs of *ordering* and *holding* resin inventory.

Can Wave do any better than $3,900 for the annual cost of his resin inventory policy? Exhibit 9–6, which tabulates the inventory costs for various order quantities, indicates that Wave can lower the costs of ordering and holding resin inventory. Of the five order quantities listed, the 1,200 drum order quantity yields the lowest total annual cost. Unfortunately, this tabular method for finding the least-cost order quantity is cumbersome. Moreover, it does not necessarily result in the optimal order quantity. It is possible that some order quantity other than those listed in Exhibit 9–6 is the least-cost order quantity.

Equation Approach   The total annual cost of ordering and holding inventory is given by the following equation.

$$\text{Total annual} \atop \text{cost} = \binom{\text{Annual requirement}}{\text{Order quantity}} \binom{\text{Cost per}}{\text{order}} + \binom{\text{Order quantity}}{2} \binom{\text{Annual}}{\text{holding} \atop \text{cost per} \atop \text{unit}}$$

The following formula for the least-cost order quantity, called the economic order quantity (or EOQ), has been developed using calculus.

Exhibit 9–6					
Tabulation of Inventory Ordering and Holding Costs					
Order size	800	960	1,200	1,600	2,400
Number of orders (9,600 ÷ Order size)	12	10	8	6	4
Ordering costs ($225 × Number of orders)	$2,700	$2,250	$1,800	$1,350	$ 900
Average inventory (Order size ÷ 2)	400	480	600	800	1,200
Holding costs ($3 × Average inventory)	$1,200	$1,440	$1,800	$2,400	$3,600
Total annual cost (Ordering cost + Holding cost)	$3,900	$3,690	$3,600	$3,750	$4,500
			↑ Minimum		

$$\text{Economic order quantity } = \sqrt{\frac{\text{(2) (Annual requirement)(Cost per order)}}{\text{(Annual holding cost per unit)}}}$$

Applying the EOQ formula in Surfco's problem yields the following EOQ for resin.

$$\text{EOQ} = \sqrt{\frac{\text{(2) (9,600) (225)}}{3}} = 1{,}200$$

Graphical Approach   Another method for solving the EOQ problem is the graphical method, which is presented in Exhibit 9–7. Notice that the ordering-cost line slants down to the right. This indicates a decline in these costs as the order size increases and the order frequency decreases. However, as the order size increases, so does the average inventory on hand. This results in an increase in holding costs, as indicated by the positive slope of the holding-cost line. The EOQ falls at 1,200 units, where the best balance is struck between these two costs. Total costs are minimized at $3,600.

Timing of Orders

The EOQ model helps management decide how much to order at a time. Another important decision is when to order. This decision depends on the **lead time**, which is the length of time it takes for the material to be received after an order is placed. Suppose the lead time for resin is one month. Since Surfco uses 9,600 drums of resin per year, and the production rate is constant throughout the year, this implies that 800 drums are used each month. Production manager Wave should order resin, in the economic order quantity of 1,200 drums, when the inventory falls to 800 drums. By the time the new order arrives, one month later, the 800 drums in inventory will have been used in production. Exhibit 9-8 depicts this pattern of ordering and using inventory. By placing an order early enough to avoid a stockout, management takes into account the potential costs of shortages.

Lead time is the time required to receive inventory after it has been ordered.

Total annual cost

Exhibit 9–7

Graphical Solution to Economic Order Quantity Decision

Exhibit 9–8

Ordering, Lead Time, and
Usage of Inventory

Safety Stock   Our example assumed that the usage of resin is constant at 800 drums per month. Suppose instead that monthly usage fluctuates between 600 and 1,000 drums. Although average monthly usage still is 800 drums, there is the potential for an excess usage of 200 drums in any particular month. In light of this uncertainty, management may wish to keep a **safety stock** of resin equal to the potential excess monthly usage of 200 drums. With a safety stock of 200 drums, the reorder point is 1,000 drums. Thus, Wave should order the EOQ of 1,200 drums whenever resin inventory falls to 1,000 drums. During the one-month lead time, another 600 to 1,000 drums of resin will be consumed in production. Although a safety stock will increase inventory holding costs, it will minimize the potential costs caused by shortages.

Safety stock is extra
inventory consumed
during periods of above-
average usage in a setting
with fluctuating demand.

JIT Inventory Management: Implications for EOQ

The EOQ model minimizes the total cost of ordering and holding purchased inventory. Thus, this inventory management approach seeks to balance the cost of ordering against the cost of storing inventory. Under the JIT philosophy, the goal is to keep *all* inventories as low as possible. *Any* inventory holding costs are seen as inefficient and wasteful. Moreover, under JIT purchasing, ordering costs are minimized by reducing the number of vendors, negotiating long-term supply agreements, making less frequent payments, and eliminating inspections. The implication of the JIT philosophy is that inventories should be minimized by more frequent deliveries in smaller quantities. This result can be demonstrated using the EOQ formula, as shown in Exhibit 9–9. As the cost of holding inventory increases, the EOQ decreases. Moreover, as the cost of placing an order declines, the EOQ decreases.

The economics underlying the EOQ model support the JIT viewpoint that inventory should be purchased or produced in small quantities, and inventories should be kept to the absolute minimum. However, the basic philosophies of JIT and EOQ are quite different. The EOQ approach takes the view that some inventory is necessary, and the goal is to optimize the order quantity in order to balance the cost of ordering against the cost of holding inventory. In contrast, the JIT philosophy argues that holding costs tend to be higher than may be apparent because of the inefficiency and waste of storing inventory. Thus, inventory should be minimized, or even eliminated completely if possible. Morever, under the JIT approach, orders typically will vary in size, depending on needs. The EOQ model, in contrast, results in a constant order quantity.

Key Terms: Appendix

For each term's definition refer to the indicated page, or turn to the glossary at the end of the text.

Holding Costs per Unit	Ordering Costs per Order				
	$225	**$150**	**$100**	**$50**	
$3	1,200*	980	800	566	EOQ declines
4	1,039	849	693	490	
5	930	759	620	438	
6	849	693	566	400	
	EOQ declines				

Exhibit 9–9

Economic Order Quantity with Different Ordering and Holding Costs

*The annual requirement is assumed to be 9,600 units for each case in this table. This was the annual requirement for drums of resin in the Surfco illustration. (Several of the EOQs in the table are rounded.)

Review Questions

9-1. Explain what a *master budget* is, and list five of its parts.

9-2. Explain how a budget facilitates communication and coordination.

9-3. Use an example to explain how a budget could be used to allocate resources in a university.

9-4. Draw a flowchart similar to the one in Exhibit 9–1 for a service station. The service station provides automotive maintenance services in addition to selling gasoline and related products.

9-5. Give an example of how general economic trends would affect sales forecasting in the airline industry.

9-6. What is meant by the term *operational budgets*? List three operational budgets that would be prepared by a hospital.

9-7. Give three examples of how New York City could use a budget for planning purposes.

9-8. Describe the role of a *budget director*.

9-9. What is the purpose of a *budget manual*?

9-10. How can a company's board of directors use the budget to influence the future direction of the firm?

9-11. Explain the concept of *zero-base budgeting*.

9-12. Discuss the importance of predictions and assumptions in the budgeting process.

9-13. Define the term *budgetary slack*, and briefly describe a problem it can cause.

9-14. How can an organization help to reduce the problems caused by budgetary slack?

9-15. Why is participative budgeting often an effective management tool?

9-16. Discuss this comment by a small-town bank president: "Budgeting is a waste of time. I've been running this business for forty years. I don't need to plan."

9-17. List the steps you would go through in developing a budget to meet your college expenses.

9-18. Briefly describe three issues that create special challenges for multinational firms in preparing their budgets.

9-19. List five phases in a product's *life cycle*, and explain why it is important to budget the costs in each of these phases.

9-20. (Appendix) Define and give examples of *inventory ordering*, *holding*, and *shortage costs*.

9-21. (Appendix) Explain the differences in the basic philosophies underlying the JIT and EOQ approaches to inventory management.

Exercises

Fill in the missing amounts in the following schedules.

	January	February	March
1. Sales*	$80,000	$60,000	$?
Cash receipts:			
From cash sales	$?	$?	$45,000
From sales on account†	?	34,000	?
Total cash receipts	$?	$?	$?

*Half of each month's sales are on account. December sales amounted to $60,000.

†60% of credit sales is collected in the month of sale; 40% is collected in the following month.

■ Exercise 9–22
Missing Amounts
(LO 2, LO 3)

2. Accounts receivable, 12/31/x0 .... $ 340,000
    Sales on account during 20x1 900,000
    Collections of accounts receivable during 20x1 780,000
    Accounts receivable, 12/31/x1 .... ?

3. Accounts payable, 12/31/x0 .... $ 300,000
    Purchase of goods and services on account during 20x1 1,200,000
    Payments of accounts payable during 20x1 .... ?
    Accounts payable, 12/31/x1 400,000

4. Accumulated depreciation, 12/31/x0 .... $ 810,000
    Depreciation expense during 20x1 150,000
    Accumulated depreciation, 12/31/x1 .... ?

5. Retained earnings, 12/31/x0 .... $2,050,000
    Net income for 20x1 400,000
    Dividends paid in 20x1 .... –0–
    Retained earnings, 12/31/x1 .... ?

■ **Exercise 9–23**
Cash Budgeting
(LO 2, LO 3)

The following information is from Montero Corporation's financial records.

Month	Sales	Purchases
April	$72,000	$42,000
May	66,000	48,000
June	60,000	36,000
July	78,000	54,000

Collections from customers are normally 70 percent in the month of sale, 20 percent in the month following the sale, and 9 percent in the second month following the sale. The balance is expected to be uncollectible. All purchases are on account. Montero takes full advantage of the 2 percent discount allowed on purchases paid for by the tenth of the following month. Purchases for August are budgeted at $60,000, and sales for August are forecasted at $66,000. Cash disbursements for expenses are expected to be $14,400 for the month of August. Montero's cash balance on August 1 was $22,000.

Required: Prepare the following schedules.

1. Expected cash collections during August.
2. Expected cash disbursements during August.
3. Expected cash balance on August 31.

(CPA, adapted)

■ **Exercise 9–24**
Budgeting Production and
Direct-Material Purchases
(LO 2, LO 3)

Adler Company budgets on an annual basis. The following beginning and ending inventory levels (in units) are planned for the year 19x9. Two units of raw material are required to produce each unit of finished product.

	January 1	December 31
Raw material	35,000	45,000
Work in process	12,000	12,000
Finished goods	80,000	50,000

Required:

1. If Adler Company plans to sell 480,000 units during the year, compute the number of units the firm would have to manufacture during the year.
2. If 500,000 finished units were to be manufactured by Adler Company during the year, determine the amount of raw material to be purchased.

(CMA, adapted)

FastGro Fertilizer Company plans to sell 200,000 units of finished product in July and anticipates a growth rate in sales of 5 percent per month. The desired monthly ending inventory in units of finished product is 80 percent of the next month's estimated sales. There are 160,000 finished units in inventory on June 30. Each unit of finished product requires four pounds of raw material at a cost of $1.15 per pound. There are 700,000 pounds of raw material in inventory on June 30.

■ Exercise 9–25
Budgeting Production and
Raw-Material Purchases
(LO 2, LO 3)

Required:

1. Compute FastGro's total required production in units of finished product for the entire three-month period ending September 30.
2. Independent of your answer to requirement (1), assume the company plans to produce 600,000 units of finished product in the three-month period ending September 30, and to have raw-material inventory on hand at the end of the three-month period equal to 25 percent of the use in that period. Compute the total estimated cost of raw-material purchases for the entire three-month period ending September 30.

(CMA, adapted)

Coyote Loco, Inc., a manufacturer of salsa, has the following historical collection pattern for its credit sales.

■ Exercise 9–26
Cash Collections
(LO 2, LO 3, LO 5)

> 70 percent collected in the month of sale.
>
> 15 percent collected in the first month after sale.
>
> 10 percent collected in the second month after sale.
>
> 4 percent collected in the third month after sale.
>
> 1 percent uncollectible.

The sales on account have been budgeted for the last seven months of 19x9 as follows:

June	$ 49,000
July	60,000
August	70,000
September	80,000
October	90,000
November	100,000
December	85,000

Required:

1. Compute the estimated total cash collections during October from credit sales during 19x9.
2. Compute the estimated total cash collections during the fourth quarter from sales made on account during the fourth quarter.

(CMA, adapted)

School Days, Inc. manufactures a variety of desks, chairs, tables, and shelf units which are sold to public school systems throughout the Midwest. The controller of the company's Desk Division is currently preparing a budget for the second quarter of the year. The following sales forecast has been made by the division's sales manager.

■ Exercise 9–27
Completion of Budget
Schedules
(LO 2, LO 3)

April	10,000 desk-and-chair sets
May	12,000 desk-and-chair sets
June	15,000 desk-and-chair sets

Each desk-and-chair set requires 10 board feet of pine planks and 1.5 hours of direct labor. Each set sells for $50. Pine planks cost $.50 per board foot, and the division ends each month with enough wood to cover 10 percent of the next month's production requirements. The division incurs a cost of $20.00 per hour for direct-labor wages and fringe benefits. The division ends each month with enough finished-goods inventory to cover 20 percent of the next month's sales.

Required:

Complete the following budget schedules.

1. Sales budget:	**April**	**May**	**June**
Sales (in sets)	10,000		
Sales price per set	x $50		
Sales revenue	$500,000		

2. Production budget (in sets):	**April**	**May**	**June**
Sales	10,000		
Add: Desired ending inventory	2,400		3,000
Total requirements	12,400		
Less: Projected beginning inventory	2,000		
Planned production	10,400		

3. Raw-material purchases:	**April**	**May**	**June**
Planned production (sets)	10,400		
Raw material required per set (board feet)	x 10		
Raw material required for production (board feet)	104,000		
Add: Desired ending inventory of raw material, in board feet (10% of next month's requirement)	12,600		16,000
Total requirements	116,600		
Less: Projected beginning inventory of raw material, in board feet (10% of current month's requirement) ..	10,400		
Planned purchases of raw material (board feet)	106,200		
Cost per board foot	x $.50		
Planned purchases of raw material (dollars)	$ 53,100		

4. Direct-labor budget:	**April**	**May**	**June**
Planned production (sets)	10,400		
Direct-labor hours per set	x 1.5		
Direct-labor hours required	15,600		
Cost per hour	x $20		
Planned direct-labor cost	$312,000		

■ **Exercise 9–28**
Professional Services
Budget; Dental Practice
(LO 2, LO 3)

San Francisco Dental Associates is a large dental practice in the Bay Area. The firm's controller is preparing the budget for the next year. The controller projects a total of 48,000 office visits, to be evenly distributed throughout the year. Eighty percent of the visits will be half-hour appointments, and the remainder will be one-hour visits. The average rates for professional dental services are $40 for half-hour appointments and $70 for one-hour office visits. Ninety percent of each month's professional service revenue is collected during the month when services are rendered, and the remainder is collected the month following service. Uncollectible billings are negligible. Metropolitan's dental associates earn $60 per hour.

Required:

Prepare the following budget schedules.

1. Direct-professional-labor budget for the month of June.
2. Cash collections during June for professional services rendered during May and June.

■ **Exercise 9–29**
Budgeted Financial
Statements; Retailer
(LO 2, LO 3)

Handy Hardware is a retail hardware store. Information about the store's operations follows.

■ November 19x9 sales amounted to $200,000.

■ Sales are budgeted at $220,000 for December 19x9 and $200,000 for January 20x0.

■ Collections are expected to be 60 percent in the month of sale and 38 percent in the month following the sale. Two percent of sales are expected to be uncollectible. Bad debts expense is recognized monthly.

■ The store's gross margin is 25 percent of its sales revenue.

■ A total of 80 percent of the merchandise for resale is purchased in the month prior to the month of sale, and 20 percent is purchased in the month of sale. Payment for merchandise is made in the month following the purchase.

■ Other monthly expenses paid in cash amount to $22,600.

■ Annual depreciation is $216,000.

The company's balance sheet as of November 30, 19x9 is as follows:

HANDY HARDWARE, INC.
Balance Sheet
November 30, 19x9
Assets

Cash	$ 22,000
Accounts receivable (net of $3,500 allowance for uncollectible accounts)	76,000
Inventory	140,000
Property, plant, and equipment (net of $590,000 accumulated depreciation)	862,000
Total assets	$1,100,000

Liabilities and Stockholders' Equity

Accounts payable	$ 162,000
Common stock	795,000
Retained earnings	143,000
Total liabilities and stockholders' equity	$1,100,000

Required: Compute the following amounts.

1. The budgeted cash collections for December 19x9.
2. The budgeted income (loss) before income taxes for December 19x9.
3. The projected balance in accounts payable on December 31, 19x9.

(CMA, adapted)

Laura Williams is the new accounts manager at West Bank of Mississippi. She has just been asked to project how many new bank accounts she will generate during 20x0. The economy of the county in which the bank operates has been growing, and the bank has experienced a 10 percent increase in its number of bank accounts over each of the past five years. In 19x9, the bank had 10,000 accounts.

The new accounts manager is paid a salary plus a bonus of $15 for every new account she generates above the budgeted amount. Thus, if the annual budget calls for 500 new accounts, and 540 new accounts are obtained, Williams's bonus will be $600 (40 × $15).

Williams believes the economy of the county will continue to grow at the same rate in 20x0 as it has in recent years. She has decided to submit a budgetary projection of 700 new accounts for 20x0. *low – should be 10% of 1,000.*

Required:

Your consulting firm has been hired by the bank president to make recommendations for improving its operations. Write a memorandum to the president defining and explaining the negative consequences of budgetary slack. Also discuss the bank's bonus system for the new accounts manager and how the bonus program tends to encourage budgetary slack.

■ **Exercise 9–30**
Budgetary Slack; Bank
(LO 7)

Sound Investments, Inc. is a large retailer of stereo equipment. The controller is about to prepare the budget for the first quarter of 19x9. Past experience has indicated that 75 percent of the store's sales are cash sales. The collection experience for the sales on account is as follows:

■ **Exercise 9–31**
Using Budgets for Financial Planning
(LO 1, LO 3, LO 5)

80 percent during month of sale

15 percent during month following sale

5 percent uncollectible

The total sales for December 19x8 are expected to be $190,000. The controller feels that sales in January 19x9 could range from $100,000 to $160,000.

Required:

1. Demonstrate how financial planning can be used to project cash receipts in January of 19x9 for three different levels of January sales. Use the following columnar format.

	Total Sales in January, 19x9		
	$100,000	$130,000	$160,000
Cash receipts in January 19x9:			
From December sales on account	$	$	$
From January cash sales			
From January sales on account			
Total cash receipts	$	$	$

2. How could the controller of Sound Investments, Inc. use this financial planning approach to help in planning operations for January?

■ **Exercise 9–32**
Economic Order Quantity
(Appendix)
(LO 8)

For each of the following independent cases, use the equation method to compute the economic order quantity.

	Case A	Case B	Case C
Annual requirement (in units)	1,681	560	13,230
Cost per order	$40	$10	$250
Annual holding cost per unit	20	7	6

■ **Exercise 9–33**
Lead Time and Safety Stock
(Appendix)
(LO 8)

Andrew and Fulton, Inc. uses 780 tons of a chemical bonding agent each year. Monthly demand fluctuates between 50 and 80 tons. The lead time for each order is one month, and the economic order quantity is 130 tons.

Required:

1. Determine the safety stock appropriate for the chemical bonding agent.

2. At what order point, in terms of tons remaining in inventory, should Andrew and Fulton, Inc. order the bonding agent?

Problems

■ **Problem 9–34**
Production, Materials, Labor,
and Overhead Budgets
(LO 2, LO 3)

The Wyoming Division of Reid Corporation produces an intricate component used in Reid's major product line. The division manager has been concerned recently by a lack of coordination between purchasing and production personnel and believes that a monthly budgeting system would be better than the present system

Wyoming's division manager has decided to develop budget information for the third quarter of the current year as an experiment before the budget system is implemented for an entire year. In response to the division manager's request, the divisional controller accumulated the following data.

Sales. Sales through June 30, the first six months of the current year, are 24,000 units. Actual sales in units for May and June and estimated unit sales for the next four months are detailed below.

May (actual)	4,000
June (actual)	4,000
July (estimated)	5,000
August (estimated)	6,000
September (estimated)	7,000
October (estimated)	7,000

Wyoming Division expects to sell 60,000 units during the current year.

Direct Material. Data regarding the materials used in the component are shown in the following schedule. The desired monthly ending inventory for all raw materials is an amount sufficient to produce the next month's estimated sales.

Raw Material	Units of Raw Material per Finished Component	Cost per Unit	Inventory Level June 30
No. 101	6	$2.40	35,000 units
No. 211	4	3.60	30,000 units
No. 242	2	1.20	14,000 units

Direct Labor. Each component must pass through three different processes to be completed. Data regarding direct labor follow.

Process	Direct-Labor Hours per Finished Component	Cost per Direct-Labor Hour
Forming	.40	$16.00
Assembly	1.00	11.00
Finishing	.125	12.00

Manufacturing Overhead. The division produced 27,000 components during the six-month period ending June 30. The actual variable overhead costs incurred during this six-month period are given in the following schedule. The divisional controller believes the variable overhead costs will be incurred at the same rate during the last six months of the current year.

Supplies	$ 59,400
Electricity	27,000
Indirect labor	54,000
Other	8,100
Total variable overhead	$148,500

The fixed overhead costs incurred during the first six months of the year amounted to $93,500. Fixed overhead costs are budgeted for the full year as follows:

Supervision	$ 60,000
Taxes	7,200
Depreciation	86,400
Other	32,400
Total fixed overhead	$186,000

Finished Goods. The desired monthly ending inventory of completed components is 80 percent of the next month's estimated sales. There are 5,000 finished units in inventory on June 30.

Required:

1. Prepare a production budget in units for the Wyoming Division for the third quarter of the current year, ending September 30.

2. Independent of your answer to requirement 1, assume the Wyoming Division plans to produce 18,000 units during the third quarter ending September 30, and 60,000 units for the entire year ending December 31.

   a. Prepare a raw material purchases budget, in units and dollars, for the third quarter ending September 30.

   b. Prepare a direct-labor budget, in hours and dollars, for the third quarter ending September 30.

   c. Prepare a manufacturing-overhead budget for the six-month period ending December 31 of the current year.

(CMA, adapted)

Spiffy Shades Corporation manufactures artistic frames for sunglasses. Talia Demarest, controller, is responsible for preparing the company's master budget. In compiling the budget data for 20x0, Demarest has learned that new automated production equipment will be installed on March 1. This will reduce the direct labor per frame from 1 hour to .75 hours.

■ **Problem 9–35**
Production and Direct-Labor Budgets; Automation
(LO 2, LO 3)

Labor-related costs include pension contributions of $.50 per hour, workers' compensation insurance of $.20 per hour, employee medical insurance of $.80 per hour, and employer contributions to Social Security equal to 7 percent of direct-labor wages. The cost of employee benefits paid by the company on its employees is treated as a direct-labor cost. Spiffy Shades Corporation has a labor contract that calls for a wage increase to $18.00 per hour on April 1, 20x0. Management expects to have 16,000 frames on hand at December 31, 19x9, and has a policy of carrying an end-of-month inventory of 100 percent of the following month's sales plus 50 percent of the second following month's sales.

These and other data compiled by Demarest are summarized in the following table.

	January	February	March	April	May
Direct-labor hours per unit	1.0	1.0	.75	.75	.75
Wage per direct-labor hour	$16.00	$16.00	$16.00	$18.00	$18.00
Estimated unit sales	10,000	12,000	8,000	9,000	9,000
Sales price per unit	$50.00	$47.50	$47.50	$47.50	$47.50

Required:

1. Prepare a production budget and a direct-labor budget for Spiffy Shades Corporation by month and for the first quarter of 20x0. Both budgets may be combined in one schedule. The direct-labor budget should include direct-labor hours and show the detail for each direct-labor cost category.

2. For each item used in the firm's production budget and direct-labor budget, identify the other components of the master budget that also would use these data.

(CMA, adapted)

■ **Problem 9–36**
Cash Budgeting in a
Hospital; Third-Party Billings
(LO 2, LO 3)

Lackawanna Medical Center provides a wide range of hospital services in northeastern Pennsylvania. The hospital's board of directors has recently authorized the following capital expenditures.

Neonatal Care equipment	$ 900,000
CT scanner	800,000
X-ray equipment	650,000
Laboratory equipment	1,450,000
Total	$3,800,000

The expenditures are planned for October 1, 19x9, and the board wishes to know the amount of borrowing, if any, necessary on that date. Marc Kelly, controller, has gathered the following information to be used in preparing an analysis of future cash flows.

■ Billings, made in the month of service, for the first six months of 19x9 are listed below.

Month	Actual Amount
January	$4,400,000
February	4,400,000
March	4,500,000
April	4,500,000
May	5,000,000
June	5,000,000

■ Ninety percent of the hospital's billings are made to third parties such as Blue Cross, federal or state governments, and private insurance companies. The remaining 10 percent of the billings are made directly to patients. Historical patterns of billing collections are presented below.

	Third-Party Billings	Direct Patient Billings
During month of service	20%	10%
During month following service	50%	40%
During second month following service	20%	40%
Uncollectible	10%	10%

■ Estimated billings for the last six months of 19x9 are detailed in the following schedule. The same billing and collection patterns that have been experienced during the first six months of 19x9 are expected to continue during the last six months of the year.

Month	Estimated Amount
July	$4,500,000
August	5,000,000
September	5,500,000
October	5,700,000
November	5,800,000
December	5,500,000

■ The purchases of the past three months and the planned purchases for the last six months of 19x9 are presented in the following schedule.

Month	Amount
April	$1,100,000
May	1,200,000
June	1,200,000
July	1,250,000
August	1,500,000
September	1,850,000
October	1,950,000
November	2,250,000
December	1,750,000

■ Additional information follows:

  a. Endowment fund income is expected to continue at the rate of $175,000 per month.

  b. The hospital has a cash balance of $300,000 on July 1, 19x9, and has a policy of maintaining a minimum end-of-month cash balance of 10 percent of the current month's purchases.

  c. All purchases are made on account, and accounts payable are paid in the month following the purchase.

  d. Salaries for each month during the remainder of 19x9 are expected to be $1,500,000 per month plus 20 percent of that month's billings. Salaries are paid in the month of service.

  e. The hospital's monthly depreciation charges are $125,000.

  f. The medical center incurs interest expense of $150,000 per month and makes interest payments of $450,000 on the last day of each quarter (i.e., March 31, June 30, September 30, and December 31).

Required:

1. Prepare a schedule of budgeted cash receipts by month for the third quarter of 19x9 (July through September).

2. Prepare a schedule of budgeted cash disbursements by month for the third quarter of 19x9.

3. Determine the amount of borrowing, if any, necessary on October 1, 19x9, to acquire the capital items totaling $3,800,000.

(CMA, adapted)

Horizon Electronics, Inc. manufactures two different types of coils used in electric motors. In the fall of the current year, Erica Becker, the controller, compiled the following data.

■ **Problem 9–37**
Sales, Production, and
Purchases Budgets
(LO 2, LO 3)

■ Sales forecast for 20x0:

Product	Units	Price
Light coil	60,000	$65
Heavy coil	40,000	95

■ Raw-material prices and inventory levels:

Raw Material	Expected Inventories January 1, 20x0	Desired Inventories, December 31, 20x0	Anticipated Purchase Price
Sheet metal	32,000 lb.	36,000 lb.	$8
Copper wire	29,000 lb.	32,000 lb.	5
Platform	6,000 units	7,000 units	3

■ Use of raw material:

	Amount Used per Unit	
Raw Material	**Light Coil**	**Heavy Coil**
Sheet metal	4 lb.	5 lb.
Copper wire	2 lb.	3 lb.
Platform		1 unit

■ Direct-labor requirements and rates:

Product	**Hours per unit**	**Rate per Hour**
Light coil	2	$15
Heavy coil	3	20

Overhead is applied at the rate of $2 per direct-labor hour.

■ Finished-goods inventories (in units):

Product	**Expected January 1, 20x0**	**Desired December 31, 20x0**
Light coil	20,000	25,000
Heavy coil	8,000	9,000

Required:

Prepare the following budgets for 19x8.

1. Sales budget (in dollars).
2. Production budget (in units).
3. Raw-material purchases budget (in quantities).
4. Raw-material purchases budget (in dollars).
5. Direct-labor budget (in dollars).
6. Budgeted finished-goods inventory on December 31, 20x0 (in dollars).

(CPA, adapted)

■ **Problem 9–38**
Revised Operating Budget;
Consulting Firm
(LO 1, LO 3)

Montreal Business Associates, a division of Maple Leaf Services Corporation, offers management and computer consulting services to clients throughout Canada and the northeastern United States. The division specializes in Web site development and other Internet applications. The corporate management at Maple Leaf Services is pleased with the performance of Montreal Business Associates for the first nine months of the current year and has recommended that the division manager, Richard Howell, submit a revised forecast for the remaining quarter, as the division has exceeded the annual plan year-to-date by 20 percent of operating income. An unexpected increase in billed hour volume over the original plan is the main reason for this increase in income. The original operating budget for the first three quarters for Montreal Business Associates follows.

MONTREAL BUSINESS ASSOCIATES
19x9 Operating Budget

	1st Quarter	2nd Quarter	3rd Quarter	Total for First Three Quarters
Revenue:				
Consulting fees:				
Computer system consulting	$421,875	$421,875	$421,875	$1,265,625
Management consulting	315,000	315,000	315,000	945,000
Total consulting fees	$736,875	$736,875	$736,875	$2,210,625
Other revenue	10,000	10,000	10,000	30,000
Total revenue	$746,875	$746,875	$746,875	$2,240,625
Expenses:				
Consultant salary expenses	$386,750	$386,750	$386,750	$1,160,250
Travel and related expenses	45,625	45,625	45,625	136,875
General and administrative expenses	100,000	100,000	100,000	300,000

	1st Quarter	2nd Quarter	3rd Quarter	Total for First Three Quarters
Depreciation expense	$ 40,000	$ 40,000	$ 40,000	$ 120,000
Corporate expense allocation	50,000	50,000	50,000	150,000
Total expenses	$622,375	$622,375	$622,375	$1,867,125
Operating income	$124,500	$124,500	$124,500	$ 373,500

Howell will reflect the following information in his revised forecast for the fourth quarter.

■ Montreal Business Associates currently has 25 consultants on staff, 10 for management consulting and 15 for computer systems consulting. Three additional management consultants have been hired to start work at the beginning of the fourth quarter in order to meet the increased client demand.

■ The hourly billing rate for consulting revenue will remain at $90 per hour for each management consultant and $75 per hour for each computer consultant. However, due to the favorable increase in billing hour volume when compared to the plan, the hours for each consultant will be increased by 50 hours per quarter.

■ The budgeted annual salaries and actual annual salaries, paid monthly, are the same: $50,000 for a management consultant and $46,000 for a computer consultant. Corporate management has approved a merit increase of 10 percent at the beginning of the fourth quarter for all 25 existing consultants, while the new consultants will be compensated at the planned rate.

■ The planned salary expense includes a provision for employee fringe benefits amounting to 30 percent of the annual salaries. However, the improvement of some corporatewide employee programs will increase the fringe benefits to 40 percent.

■ The original plan assumes a fixed hourly rate for travel and other related expenses for each billing hour of consulting. These are expenses that are not reimbursed by the client, and the previously determined hourly rate has proven to be adequate to cover these costs.

■ Other revenue is derived from temporary rentals and interest income and remains unchanged for the fourth quarter.

■ General and administrative expenses have been favorable at 7 percent below the plan; this 7 percent savings on fourth quarter expenses will be reflected in the revised plan.

■ Depreciation of office equipment and personal computers will stay constant at the projected straight-line rate.

■ Due to the favorable experience for the first three quarters and the division's increased ability to absorb costs, the corporate management at Maple Leaf Services has increased the corporate expense allocation by 50 percent.

Required:

1. Prepare a revised operating budget for the fourth quarter for Montreal Business Associates that Richard Howell will present to corporate management.

2. Discuss the reasons why an organization would prepare a revised operating budget.

(CMA, adapted)

Belco Industries produces and distributes industrial chemicals. Belco's earnings increased sharply in 19x9, and bonuses were paid to the management staff for the first time in several years. Bonuses are based in part on the amount by which reported income exceeds budgeted income.

Jim Kern, vice president of finance, was pleased with Belco's 19x9 earnings and thought that the pressure to show financial results would ease. However, Ellen North, Belco's president, told Kern that she saw no reason why the 20x0 bonuses should not be double those of 19x9. As a result, Kern felt pressure to increase reported income in order to exceed budgeted income by an even greater amount. This would assure increased bonuses.

Kern met with Bill Keller of Pristeel, Inc., a primary vendor of Belco's manufacturing supplies and equipment. Kern and Keller have been close business contacts for many years. Kern asked Keller to identify all of Belco's purchases of perishable supplies as equipment on Pristeel's sales invoices. The reason Kern gave for his request was that Belco's president had imposed stringent budget constraints on operating expenses but not on capital expenditures. Kern planned to capitalize the purchase of perishable supplies, and include them with the Equipment account on the balance sheet. In this way Kern could defer the expense recognition for these items to a later year. This procedure would increase reported earnings, leading to increased bonuses. Keller agreed to do as Kern had asked.

■ **Problem 9–39**
Ethics; Budgetary Pressure;
Management Bonuses;
Budgetary Constraints
(LO 4, LO 7)

While analyzing the second quarter financial statements, Gary Wood, Belco's controller, noticed a large decrease in supplies expense from one year ago. Wood reviewed the Supplies Expense account and noticed that only equipment and no supplies had been purchased from Pristeel, a major source for supplies. Wood, who reports to Kern, immediately brought this to Kern's attention.

Kern told Wood of North's high expectations and of the arrangement made with Keller of Pristeel. Wood told Kern that his action was an improper accounting treatment for the supplies purchased from Pristeel. Wood requested that he be allowed to correct the accounts and urged that the arrangement with Pristeel be discontinued. Kern refused the request and told Wood not to become involved in the arrangement with Pristeel.

After clarifying the situation in a confidential discussion with an objective and qualified peer within Belco, Wood arranged to meet with North, Belco's president. At the meeting, Wood disclosed the arrangement Kern had made with Pristeel.

Required:

1. Explain why the use of alternative accounting methods to manipulate reported earnings is unethical.

2. Is Gary Wood, Belco's controller, correct in saying that the supplies purchased from Priesteel Inc. were accounted for improperly? Explain your answer.

3. Assuming that Jim Kern's arrangement with Pristeel Inc. was in violation of the Standards of Ethical Conduct for Management Accountants, discuss whether the actions of Wood were appropriate or inappropriate. (The standards are given in Chapter 1.)

(CMA, adapted)

■ **Problem 9–40**
Interrelationships between Components of Master Budget
(LO 1, LO 2, LO 3, LO 4)

First Line Security Systems (FLSS) manufactures and sells security systems. The company started by installing photoelectric security systems in offices and has expanded into the private-home market. FLSS has a basic security system that has been developed into three standard products, each of which can be adapted to meet the specific needs of customers. The manufacturing operation is moderate in size, as the bulk of the component manufacturing is completed by independent contractors. The security systems are approximately 85 percent complete when received from contractors and require only final assembly in the FLSS plant. Each product passes through at least one of three assembly operations.

FLSS operates in a rapidly growing community. There is evidence that a great deal of new commercial construction will take place in the near future, and management has decided to pursue this new market. In order to be competitive, the firm will have to expand its operations.

In view of the expected increase in business, Sandra Feldman, the controller, believes that FLSS should implement a complete budgeting system. Feldman has decided to make a formal presentation to the company's president explaining the benefits of a budgeting system and outlining the budget schedules and reports that would be necessary.

Required:

1. Explain the benefits that FLSS would gain from implementing a budgeting system.
2. If Sandra Feldman develops a master budget:
   a. Identify, in order, the schedules that will have to be prepared.
   b. Identify the subsequent schedules that would be based on the schedules identified above.
   Use the following format for your answer.

   Schedule   Subsequent Schedule

(CMA, adapted)

■ **Problem 9–41**
Preparation of Master Budget
(LO 2, LO 3)

FreshPak Corporation manufactures two types of cardboard boxes used in shipping canned food, fruit, and vegetables. The canned food box (type C) and the perishable food box (type P) have the following material and labor requirements.

	Type of Box	
	C	**P**
Direct material required per 100 boxes:		
Paperboard ($.20 per pound)	30 pounds	70 pounds
Corrugating medium ($.10 per pound)	20 pounds	30 pounds
Direct labor required per 100 boxes ($12.00 per hour)	.25 hour	.50 hour

The following manufacturing-overhead costs are anticipated for the next year. The predetermined overhead rate is based on a production volume of 495,000 units for each type of box. Manufacturing overhead is applied on the basis of direct-labor hours.

Indirect material	$ 10,500
Indirect labor	50,000
Utilities	25,000
Property taxes	18,000
Insurance	16,000
Depreciation	29,000
Total	$148,500

The following selling and administrative expenses are anticipated for the next year.

Salaries and finge benefits of sales personnel	$ 75,000
Advertising	15,000
Management salaries and fringe benefits	90,000
Clerical wages and fringe benefits	26,000
Miscellaneous administrative expenses	4,000
Total	$210,000

The sales forecast for the next year is as follows:

	Sales Volume		Sales Price
Box type C	500,000 boxes		$ 90.00 per hundred boxes
Box type P	500,000 boxes		130.00 per hundred boxes

The following inventory information is available for the next year.

	Expected Inventory January 1		Desired Ending Inventory December 31
Finished goods:			
Box type C	10,000 boxes		5,000 boxes
Box type P	20,000 boxes		15,000 boxes
Raw material:			
Paperboard	15,000 pounds		5,000 pounds
Corrugating medium	5,000 pounds		10,000 pounds

Required:

Prepare a master budget for FreshPak Corporation for the next year. Assume an income tax rate of 40 percent. Include the following schedules.

1. Sales budget.
2. Production budget.
3. Direct-material budget.
4. Direct-labor budget.
5. Manufacturing-overhead budget.
6. Selling and administrative expense budget.
7. Budgeted income statement. (*Hint:* To determine cost of goods sold, first compute the manufacturing cost per unit for each type of box. Include *applied* manufacturing overhead in the cost.)

Micromodem Company was founded by Mark Dalid three years ago. The company produces a modem for use with microcomputers. Business has expanded rapidly since the company's inception. Bob Wells, the company's controller, recently prepared a budget for 20x0. The budget was based on the prior year's sales and production activity because Dalid believed that the sales growth experienced during the prior year would not continue at the same pace. The budgeted income statement and schedule of cost of goods manufactured and sold that were prepared as part of the budget process are as follows:

■ **Problem 9–42**
Budgeted Schedule of Cost of Goods Manufactured and Sold
(LO 2, LO 3)

MICROMODEM COMPANY
Budgeted Income Statement
For the Year Ending December 31, 20x0
(in thousands)

Sales revenue		$31,248
Less: Cost of goods sold		20,765
Gross margin		$10,483
Operating expenses:		
Marketing	$3,200	
General and administrative	2,200	5,400
Income from operations before income taxes		$ 5,083

MICROMODEM COMPANY
Budgeted Schedule of Cost of Goods Manufactured and Sold
For the Year Ending December 31, 20x0
(in thousands)

Direct material:		
Raw material inventory, 1/1/x0	$ 1,360	
Raw material purchased	14,476	
Raw material available for use	$15,836	
Raw material inventory, 12/31/x0	1,628	
Raw material consumed		$14,208
Direct labor		1,134
Manufacturing overhead:		
Indirect material	$ 1,421	
General overhead	3,240	4,661
Cost of goods manufactured*		$20,003
Finished-goods inventory, 1/1/x0		1,169
Cost of goods available for sale		$21,172
Finished-goods inventory, 12/31/x0		407
Cost of goods sold		$20,765

*There will be no beginning or ending work-in-process inventory.

On April 10, 20x0, Dalid and Wells met to discuss the first quarter operating results (i.e., results for the period January 1 through March 31, 20x0). Wells believed that several changes should be made to the original budget assumptions that had been used to prepare the budgeted statements. Wells prepared the following notes that summarized the changes that did not become known until the first quarter results had been compiled. The following data was submitted to Dalid.

■ The company has no work-in-process inventories.

■ The estimated production in units for the year should be revised upward from 162,000 units to 170,000 units with the balance of production being scheduled in equal segments over the last nine months of the year. Actual first quarter production was 35,000 units.

■ The planned ending inventory for finished goods of 3,300 units at the end of the year remains unchanged. The finished-goods inventory of 9,300 units as of January 1, 20x0 had dropped to 9,000 units by March 31, 20x0. The finished-goods inventory at the end of the year will be valued at the average manufacturing cost for the year.

■ The direct-labor rate will increase 8 percent as of October 1, 20x0, as a consequence of a new labor agreement that was signed during the first quarter. When the original budgeted statements were prepared, the expected effective date for this new labor agreement had been January 1, 20x1.

■ Raw material sufficient to produce 16,000 units was on hand at the beginning of the year. The plans for raw-material inventory to have the equivalent of 18,500 units of production at the end of the year remain unchanged. Raw-material inventory is valued on a first-in, first-out basis. Raw material equivalent to 37,500 units of output was purchased for $3,300,000 during the first quarter.

■ Micromodem's suppliers have informed the company that raw material prices will increase 5 percent on July 1, 20x0. Raw material needed for the rest of the year will be purchased evenly through the last nine months.

■ On the basis of historical data, indirect material cost is projected at 10 percent of the cost of direct material consumed.

■ Half of the general overhead and all of marketing and general and administrative expenses are considered fixed.

After an extended discussion, Dalid asked for new budgeted statements for the year ending December 31, 20x0.

Required:

1. Based on the revised data presented by Bob Wells, calculate Micromodem Company's projected sales for the year ending December 31, 20x0 in (*a*) units and (*b*) dollars.

2. Prepare the Budgeted Schedule of Cost of Goods Manufactured and Sold for the year, which Mark Dalid has requested.

(CMA, adapted)

"We really need to get this new material-handling equipment in operation just after the new year begins. I hope we can finance it largely with cash and marketable securities, but if necessary we can get a short-term loan down at MetroBank." This statement by Beth Davies-Lowry, president of Intercoastal Electronics Company, concluded a meeting she had called with the firm's top management. Intercoastal is a small, rapidly growing wholesaler of consumer electronic products. The firm's main product lines are small kitchen appliances and power tools. Marcia Wilcox, Intercoastal's General Manager of Marketing, has recently completed a sales forecast. She believes the company's sales during the first quarter of 20x1 will increase by 10 percent each month over the previous month's sales. Then Wilcox expects sales to remain constant for several months. Intercoastal's projected balance sheet as of December 31, 20x0 is as follows:

■ **Problem 9–43**
Comprehensive Master Budget; Borrowing; Acquisition of Automated Material-Handling System
(LO 2, LO 3)

Cash	$ 35,000
Accounts receivable	270,000
Marketable securities	15,000
Inventory	154,000
Buildings and equipment (net of accumulated depreciation)	626,000
Total assets	$1,100,000
Accounts payable	$ 176,400
Bond interest payable	12,500
Property taxes payable	3,600
Bonds payable (10%; due in 20x6)	300,000
Common stock	500,000
Retained earnings	107,500
Total liabilities and stockholders' equity	$1,100,000

Jack Hanson, the assistant controller, is now preparing a monthly budget for the first quarter of 20x1. In the process, the following information has been accumulated:

1. Projected sales for December of 20x0 are $400,000. Credit sales typically are 75 percent of total sales. Intercoastal's credit experience indicates that 10 percent of the credit sales are collected during the month of sale, and the remainder are collected during the following month.

2. Intercoastal's cost of goods sold generally runs at 70 percent of sales. Inventory is purchased on account, and 40 percent of each month's purchases are paid during the month of purchase. The remainder is paid during the following month. In order to have adequate stocks of inventory on hand, the firm attempts to have inventory at the end of each month equal to half of the next month's projected cost of goods sold.

3. Hanson has estimated that Intercoastal's other monthly expenses will be as follows:

Sales salaries	$21,000
Advertising and promotion	16,000
Administrative salaries	21,000
Depreciation	25,000
Interest on bonds	2,500
Property taxes	900

In addition, sales commissions run at the rate of 1 percent of sales.

4. Intercoastal's president, Davies-Lowry, has indicated that the firm should invest $125,000 in an automated inventory-handling system to control the movement of inventory in the firm's warehouse just after the new year begins. These equipment purchases will be financed primarily from the firm's cash and marketable securities. However, Davies-Lowry believes that Intercoastal needs to keep a minimum cash balance of $25,000. If necessary, the remainder of the equipment purchases will be financed using short-term credit from a local bank. The minimum period for such a loan is three months. Hanson believes short-term interest rates will be 10 percent per year at the time of the equipment purchases. If a loan is necessary, Davies-Lowry has decided it should be paid off by the end of the first quarter if possible.

5. Intercoastal's board of directors has indicated an intention to declare and pay dividends of $50,000 on the last day of each quarter.

6. The interest on any short-term borrowing will be paid when the loan is repaid. Interest on Intercoastal's bonds is paid semiannually on January 31 and July 31 for the preceding six-month period.

7. Property taxes are paid semiannually on February 28 and August 31 for the preceding six-month period.

Required:

Prepare Intercoastal Electronics Company's master budget for the first quarter of 20x1 by completing the following schedules and statements.

1. Sales budget:

	20x0	20x1			
	December	**January**	**February**	**March**	**1st Quarter**
Total sales					
Cash sales					
Sales on account					

2. Cash receipts budget:

	20x1			
	January	**February**	**March**	**1st Quarter**
Cash sales				
Cash collections from credit sales made during current month				
Cash collections from credit sales made during preceding month				
Total cash receipts				

3. Purchases budget:

	20x0	20x1			
	December	**January**	**February**	**March**	**1st Quarter**
Budgeted cost of goods sold					
Add: Desired ending inventory					
Total goods needed					
Less: Expected beginning inventory . .					
Purchases					

4. Cash disbursements budget:

	20x1			
	January	**February**	**March**	**1st Quarter**
Inventory purchases:				
Cash payments for purchases during the current month*				
Cash payments for purchases during the preceding month†				
Total cash payments for inventory purchases				
Other expenses:				
Sales salaries				
Advertising and promotion				
Administrative salaries				
Interest on bonds‡				
Property taxes‡				
Sales commissions				
Total cash payments for other expenses				
Total cash disbursements				

*40% of the current month's purchases (schedule 3).

†60% of the prior month's purchases (schedule 3).

‡Bond interest is paid every six months, on January 31 and July 31. Property taxes also are paid every six months, on February 28 and August 31.

5. Complete the first three lines of the summary cash budget. Then do the analysis of short-term financing needs in requirement (6). Then finish requirement (5).

Summary cash budget:

	20x1			
	January	**February**	**March**	**1st Quarter**
Cash receipts (from schedule 2)				
Less: Cash disbursements (from schedule 4)				
Change in cash balance during period due to operations				
Sale of marketable securities (1/2/x1)				
Proceeds from bank loan (1/2/x1)				
Purchase of equipment				
Repayment of bank loan (3/31/x1)				
Interest on bank loan				
Payment of dividends				
Change in cash balance during first quarter				
Cash balance, 1/1/x1				
Cash balance, 3/31/x1				

6. Analysis of short-term financing needs:

Projected cash balance as of December 31, 20x0	$
Less: Minimum cash balance	_____
Cash available for equipment purchases	$
Projected proceeds from sale of marketable securities	_____
Cash available	$
Less: Cost of investment in equipment	_____
Required short-term borrowing	$ _____

7. Prepare Intercoastal Electronics' budgeted income statement for the first quarter of 20x1. (Ignore income taxes.)

8. Prepare Intercoastal Electronics' budgeted statement of retained earnings for the first quarter of 20x1.

9. Prepare Intercoastal Electronics' budgeted balance sheet as of March 31, 20x1. (*Hint:* On March 31, 20x1, Bond Interest Payable is $5,000 and Property Taxes Payable is $900.)

■ Problem 9–44
Economic Order Quantity;
JIT Purchasing; International
(Appendix)
(LO 8)

Tucson Auto Glass is a regional distributor of automobile window glass. The windshields are manufactured in Mexico and shipped to Tucson. Management is expecting an annual demand of 10,800 windshields. The purchase price per windshield is $395. Other costs associated with ordering and maintaining an inventory of these windshields are as follows:

■ The historical ordering costs incurred in the Purchase Order Department for placing and processing orders are shown below.

Year	Orders Placed and Processed	Total Processing Costs
19x7	15	$11,900
19x8	50	12,075
19x9	95	12,300

Management expects the ordering costs to increase 16 percent over the amounts and rates experienced the last three years.

■ Each order is inspected by both Mexican and U.S. officials at the border. A $75 fee is charged.

■ A clerk in the Receiving Department receives, inspects, and secures the windshields as they arrive from the manufacturer. This activity requires eight hours per order received. This clerk has no other responsibilities and is paid at the rate of $9 per hour. Related variable overhead costs in this department are applied at the rate of $2.50 per hour.

■ Additional warehouse space will have to be rented to store the new windshields. Space can be rented as needed in a warehouse at an estimated cost of $2,500 per year plus $5.35 per windshield.

■ Breakage cost is estimated to average $3.00 per windshield.

■ Taxes and fire insurance on the inventory are $1.15 per windshield.

■ Other storage costs amount to $10.50 per windshield.

■ Tucson Auto Glass operates on a six-day work week for 50 weeks each year. The firm is closed two weeks each year.

  Six working days are required from the time the order is placed with the manufacturer until it is received.

Required:

Calculate the following values for Tucson Auto Glass Company.

1. The value of the ordering cost that should be used in the EOQ formula. (*Hint:* Use the high-low method to estimate the variable portion of the processing cost per order.)

2. The value of the storage cost that should be used in the EOQ formula.

3. The economic order quantity.

4. The minimum annual relevant cost of ordering and storage at the economic order quantity.

5. The reorder point in units.

6. Management has been able to negotiate a JIT purchasing agreement with the Mexican manufacturer, and the inspection fee has been renegotiated with the border officials. The purchasing manager has determined that JIT purchasing would enable the company to reduce the cost per order to $32.40. Moreover, she has analyzed the cost of storing windshields, taking care to include the cost of wasted space and inefficiency. She estimates that the real annual cost of holding inventory is $60 per windshield.

   a. Calculate the new EOQ, given the purchasing manager's new cost estimates.

   b. How many orders would now be placed each year?

   c. Compute the new minimum annual relevant cost of ordering and storage.

(CMA, adapted)

Glass Technology, Inc. manufactures glass fibers used in the communications industry. The company's materials and parts manager is currently revising the inventory policy for XL-20, one of the chemicals used in the production process. The chemical is purchased in 10-pound canisters for $95 each. The firm uses 4,800 canisters per year. The controller estimates that it costs $150 to place and receive a typical order of XL-20. The annual cost of storing XL-20 is $4 per canister.

Problem 9–45
Economic Order Quantity; Equation Approach; JIT Purchasing (Appendix)
(LO 8)

Required:

1. Write the formula for the total annual cost of ordering and storing XL-20.
2. Use the EOQ formula to determine the optimal order quantity.
3. What is the total annual cost of ordering and storing XL-20 at the economic order quantity?
4. How many orders will be placed per year?
5. Glass Technology's controller, Jay Turnbull, recently attended a seminar on JIT purchasing. Afterward he analyzed the cost of storing XL-20, including the costs of wasted space and inefficiency. He was shocked when he concluded that the real annual holding cost was $19.20 per canister. Turnbull then met with Doug Kaplan, Glass Technology's purchasing manager. Together they contacted Reno Industries, the supplier of XL-20, about a JIT purchasing arrangement. After some discussion and negotiation, Kaplan concluded that the cost of placing an order for XL-20 could be reduced to just $20. Using these new cost estimates, Turnbull computed the new EOQ for XL-20.
    a. Use the equation approach to compute the new EOQ.
    b. How many orders will be placed per year?

Refer to the *original* data given in the preceding problem for Glass Technology, Inc.

Problem 9–46
Economic Order Quantity; Tabular Approach (Appendix)
(LO 8)

Required:

1. Prepare a table showing the total annual cost of ordering and storing XL-20 for each of the following order quantities: 400, 600, and 800 canisters.
2. What are the weaknesses in the tabular approach?

Refer to the *original* data given in Problem 9–45 for Glass Technology, Inc.

Problem 9–47
Economic Order Quantity; Graphical Approach (Appendix)
(LO 8)

Required:

Prepare a graphical analysis of the economic order quantity decision for XL-20.

Refer to the *original* data given in Problem 9–45 for Glass Technology, Inc. The lead time required to receive an order of XL-20 is one month.

Problem 9–48
Economic Order Quantity; Lead Time and Safety Stock (Appendix)
(LO 8)

Required:

1. Assuming stable usage of XL-20 each month, determine the reorder point for XL-20.
2. Draw a graph showing the usage, lead time, and reorder point for XL-20.
3. Suppose that monthly usage of XL-20 fluctuates between 300 and 500 canisters, although annual demand remains constant at 4,800 canisters. What level of safety stock should the materials and parts manager keep on hand for XL-20? What is the new reorder point for the chemical?

Cases

Metro Court Club (MCC) offers racquetball and other physical fitness facilities to its members. There are four of these clubs in the metropolitan area. Each club has between 1,800 and 2,500 members. Revenue is derived from annual membership fees and hourly court fees. The annual membership fees are:

Case 9–49
Using Budgets to Evaluate Business Decisions
(LO 1, LO 2)

Individual	$40
Student	25
Family	95

The hourly court fees vary from $6 to $10 depending upon the season and the time of day (prime versus non-prime time).

The peak racquetball season is considered to run from September through April. During this period court usage averages 90 to 100 percent of capacity during prime time (5:00–9:00 P.M.) and 50 to 60 percent of capacity during the remaining hours. Daily court usage during the off-season (i.e., summer) averages only 20 to 40 percent of capacity.

Most of MCC's memberships have September expirations. A substantial amount of the cash receipts are collected during the early part of the racquetball season due to the renewal of the annual membership fees and heavy court usage. However, cash receipts are not as large in the spring and drop significantly in the summer months.

MCC is considering changing its membership and fee structure in an attempt to change its cash receipts. Under the new membership plan, only an annual membership fee would be charged, rather than a membership fee plus hourly court fees. There would be two classes of membership

Individual	$250
Family	400

The annual fee would be collected in advance at the time the membership application is completed. Members would be allowed to use the racquetball courts as often as they wish during the year under the new plan.

All future memberships would be sold under these new terms. Current memberships would be honored on the old basis until they expire. However, a special promotional campaign would be instituted to attract new members and to encourage current members to convert to the new membership plan immediately.

The annual fees for individual and family memberships would be reduced to $200 and $300, respectively, during the two-month promotional campaign. In addition, all memberships sold or renewed during this period would be for 15 months rather than the normal one-year period. Current members also would be given a credit toward the annual fee for the unexpired portion of their membership fee, and for all prepaid hourly court fees for league play which have not yet been used.

MCC's management estimates that 60 to 70 percent of the present membership would continue with the club. The most active members (45 percent of the present membership) would convert immediately to the new plan, while the remaining members who continue would wait until their current memberships expire. Those members who would not continue are not considered active (i.e., they play five or less times during the year). Management estimates that the loss of members would be offset fully by new members within six months of instituting the new plan. Furthermore, many of the new members would be individuals who would play during non-prime time. Management estimates that adequate court time will be available for all members under the new plan.

If the new membership plan is adopted, it would be instituted on February 1, well before the summer season. The special promotional campaign would be conducted during March and April. Once the plan is implemented, annual renewal of memberships and payment of fees would take place as each individual or family membership expires.

Required:

Your consulting firm has been hired to help MCC evaluate its new fee structure. Write a letter to the club's president answering the following questions.

1. Will Metro Court Club's new membership plan and fee structure improve its ability to plan its cash receipts? Explain your answer.

2. Metro Court Club should evaluate the new membership plan and fee structure completely before it decides to adopt or reject it.

   a. Identify the key factors that MCC should consider in its evaluation.

   b. Explain what type of financial analyses MCC should prepare in order to make a complete evaluation.

3. Explain how Metro Court Club's cash management would differ from the present if the new membership plan and fee structure were adopted.

(CMA, adapted)

Jeffrey Vaughn, president of Frame-It Company, was just concluding a budget meeting with his senior staff. It was November of 20x0, and the group was discussing preparation of the firm's master budget for 20x1. "I've decided to go ahead and purchase the industrial robot we've been talking about. We'll make the acquisition on January 2 of next year, and I expect it will take most of the year to train the personnel and reorganize the production process to take full advantage of the new equipment."

In response to a question about financing the acquisition, Vaughn replied as follows: "The robot will cost $1,000,000. We'll finance it with a one-year $1,000,000 loan from Shark Bank and Trust Company. I've negotiated a repayment schedule of four equal installments on the last day of each quarter. The interest rate will be 10 percent, and interest payments will be quarterly as well." With that the meeting broke up, and the budget process was on.

Frame-It Company is a manufacturer of metal picture frames. The firm's two product lines are designated as S (small frames; 5 × 7 inches) and L (large frames; 8 × 10 inches). The primary raw materials are flexible metal strips and 9-inch by 24-inch glass sheets. Each S frame requires a 2-foot metal strip; an L frame requires a 3-foot strip. Allowing for normal breakage and scrap glass, Frame-It can get either four S frames or two L frames out of a glass sheet. Other raw materials, such as cardboard backing, are insignificant in cost and are treated as indirect materials. Emily Jackson, Frame-It's controller, is in charge of preparing the master budget for 20x1. She has gathered the following information:

■ **Case 9–50**
Comprehensive Master
Budget; Short-Term
Financing; Acquisition of
Robotic Equipment
(LO 1, LO 2, LO 3)

1. Sales in the fourth quarter of 20x0 are expected to be 50,000 S frames and 40,000 L frames. The sales manager predicts that over the next two years, sales in each product line will grow by 5,000 units each quarter over the previous quarter. For example, S frame sales in the first quarter of 20x1 are expected to be 55,000 units.

2. Frame-It's sales history indicates that 60 percent of all sales are on credit, with the remainder of the sales in cash. The company's collection experience shows that 80 percent of the credit sales are collected during the quarter in which the sale is made, while the remaining 20 percent is collected in the following quarter. (For simplicity, assume the company is able to collect 100 percent of its accounts receivable.)

3. The S frame sells for $10, and the L frame sells for $15. These prices are expected to hold constant throughout 20x1.

4. Frame-It's production manager attempts to end each quarter with enough finished-goods inventory in each product line to cover 20 percent of the following quarter's sales. Moreover, an attempt is made to end each quarter with 20 percent of the glass sheets needed for the following quarter's production. Since metal strips are purchased locally, Frame-It buys them on a just-in-time basis; inventory is negligible.

5. All of Frame-It's direct-material purchases are made on account, and 80 percent of each quarter's purchases are paid in cash during the same quarter as the purchase. The other 20 percent is paid in the next quarter.

6. Indirect materials are purchased as needed and paid for in cash. Work-in-process inventory is negligible.

7. Projected manufacturing costs in 20x1 are as follows:

	S Frame	L Frame
Direct material:		
Metal strips:		
S: 2 ft. @ $1 per foot	$2	
L: 3 ft. @ $1 per foot		$ 3
Glass sheets:		
S: ¼ sheet @ $8 per sheet	2	
L: ½ sheet @ $8 per sheet		4
Direct labor:		
.1 hour @ $20	2	2
Manufacturing overhead:		
.1 direct-labor hour × $10 per hour	1	1
Total manufacturing cost per unit	$7	$10

8. The predetermined overhead rate is $10 per direct-labor hour. The following manufacturing overhead costs are budgeted for 20x1.

	1st Quarter	2nd Quarter	3rd Quarter	4th Quarter	Entire Year
Indirect material	$ 10,200	$ 11,200	$ 12,200	$ 13,200	$ 46,800
Indirect labor	40,800	44,800	48,800	52,800	187,200
Other overhead	31,000	36,000	41,000	46,000	154,000
Depreciation	20,000	20,000	20,000	20,000	80,000
Total overhead	$102,000	$112,000	$122,000	$132,000	$468,000

All of these costs will be paid in cash during the quarter incurred except for the depreciation charges.

9. Frame-It's quarterly selling and administrative expenses are $100,000, paid in cash.

10. Jackson anticipates that dividends of $50,000 will be declared and paid in cash each quarter.

11. Frame-It's projected balance sheet as of December 31, 20x0, follows:

Cash	$ 95,000
Accounts receivable	132,000
Inventory:	
Raw material	59,200
Finished goods	167,000
Plant and equipment (net of accumulated depreciation)	8,000,000
Total assets	$8,453,200
Accounts payable	$ 99,400
Common stock	5,000,000
Retained earnings	3,353,800
Total liabilities and stockholders' equity	$8,453,200

Required:

Prepare Frame-It Company's master budget for 20x1 by completing the following schedules and statements.

1. Sales budget:

	20x0	20x1				
	4th Quarter	1st Quarter	2nd Quarter	3rd Quarter	4th Quarter	Entire Year
S frame unit sales						
× S sales price						
S frame sales revenue						
L frame unit sales						
× L sales price						
L frame sales revenue						
Total sales revenue						
Cash sales*						
Sales on account†						

*40% of total sales.
†60% of total sales.

2. Cash receipts budget:

	20x1				
	1st Quarter	2nd Quarter	3rd Quarter	4th Quarter	Entire Year
Cash sales					
Cash collections from credit sales made during current quarter*					
Cash collections from credit sales made during previous quarter†					
Total cash receipts					

*80% of current quarter's credit sales.
†20% of previous quarter's credit sales.

3. Production budget:

	20x0	20x1				
	4th Quarter	1st Quarter	2nd Quarter	3rd Quarter	4th Quarter	Entire Year
S frames:						
Sales (in units)						
Add: Desired ending inventory						
Total units needed						
Less: Expected beginning inventory						
Units to be produced						
L frames:						
Sales (in units)						
Add: Desired ending inventory						
Total units needed						
Less: Expected beginning inventory						
Units to be produced						

4. Direct-material budget:

	20x0	20x1				
	4th Quarter	1st Quarter	2nd Quarter	3rd Quarter	4th Quarter	Entire Year
Metal strips:						
S frames to be produced						
× Metal quantity per unit (ft.)						
Needed for S frame production						
L frames to be produced						
× Metal quantity per unit (ft.)						
Needed for L frame production						
Total metal needed for production; to be purchased (ft.)						
× Price per foot						
Cost of metal strips to be purchased						
Glass sheets:						
S frames to be produced						
× Glass quantity per unit (sheets)						
Needed for S frame production						
L frames to be produced						
× Glass quantity per unit (sheets)						
Needed for L frame production						
Total glass needed for production (sheets)						
Add: Desired ending inventory						10,400	10,400
Total glass needs						
Less: Expected beginning inventory						
Glass to be purchased						
× Price per glass sheet						
Cost of glass to be purchased						
Total raw-material purchases (metal and glass)						

5. Cash disbursements budget:

	20x1				
	1st Quarter	2nd Quarter	3rd Quarter	4th Quarter	Entire Year
Raw-material purchases:					
Cash payments for purchases during the current quarter					
Cash payments for purchases during the preceding quarter					
Total cash payments for raw-material purchases					
Direct-labor:					
Frames produced (S and L)					
× Direct-labor hours per frame					
Direct-labor hours to be used					
× Rate per direct-labor hour					
Total cash payments for direct labor					
Manufacturing overhead:					
Indirect material					
Indirect labor					
Other					
Total cash payments for manufacturing overhead					
Cash payments for selling and administrative expenses					
Total cash disbursements					

6. Summary cash budget:

	20x1				
	1st Quarter	2nd Quarter	3rd Quarter	4th Quarter	Entire Year
Cash receipts (from schedule 2)					
Less: Cash disbursements (from schedule 5)					
Change in cash balance due to operations					
Payment of dividends					
Proceeds from bank loan (1/2/x1)					
Purchase of equipment					
Quarterly installment on loan principal					
Quarterly interest payment					
Change in cash balance during the period					
Cash balance, beginning of period					
Cash balance, end of period					

7. Prepare a budgeted schedule of cost of goods manufactured and sold for the year 20x1. (Refer to the format given in Exhibit 2–9 in Chapter 2. *Hint:* In the budget, actual and applied overhead will be equal.)

8. Prepare Frame-It's budgeted income statement for 20x1. (Ignore income taxes.)

9. Prepare Frame-It's budgeted statement of retained earnings for 20x1.

10. Prepare Frame-It's budgeted balance sheet as of December 31, 20x1.

Current Issues in Managerial Accounting

■ **Issue 9–51**
Budget Administration

"How to Set Up a Budgeting and Planning System," *Management Accounting,* **January 1997, Robert West and Amy Snyder.**

Overview
This article explains how to set up and operate a budgeting system.

Suggested Discussion Questions
In groups, prepare a plan that could be used to develop a budgeting system. Include the following items in your plan: (1) staffing, (2) information needs, (3) reporting classifications, (4) importance of existing

MIS system, (5) deliverables, and (6) timetable. Present your plan to the class as if they were the budget committee of the firm's board of directors.

"American Express Plans Layoffs of 3,300," *The Wall Street Journal,* January 28, 1997, Stephen Frank.

Overview

American Express announced its fourth layoff of the 1990s. According to a company spokesman, American Express will eliminate 3,300 jobs so it can pursue the firm's new growth strategies.

Suggested Discussion Questions

Discuss how a firm's plans to cut jobs can be used to facilitate growth. Trace how the cuts affect elements of the master budget. According to one analyst, American Express is not a very efficient company. Prepare abbreviated pro forma financial statements that illustrate how revenue growth may not be accompanied by an increase in profitability.

■ **Issue 9–52**
The Master Budget: A Planning Tool

"Before You Fly the Coup," *Business Week,* October 13, 1997.

Overview

This article explains some of the advantages of remaining at the same job. According to the article, before a job change an employee should compare salary, stock options, medical benefits, and retirement plans.

Suggested Discussion Questions

Diagram how the following items affect a firm's master budget. Be sure to include the item's effect on the cash budget and the budgeted financial statements.

1. Salary.
2. Stock options.
3. Medical benefits.
4. Retirement plans.

■ **Issue 9–53**
An Illustration of the Master Budget

"Budgeting: Keep Your Head Out of the Cockpit," *Management Accounting,* July 1995, Stephen Rehnberg.

Overview

This article shows how a budget should be developed with the organization's goals and strategies in mind.

Suggested Discussion Questions

As a group, develop a preliminary budget that contains the following elements: (1) a mission statement (i.e., the firm's goal), (2) at least two ways of achieving the goal, and (3) the resources needed to achieve the goal. Present the preliminary budget to the firm's board.

■ **Issue 9–54**
Behavioral Impact of Budgets

"Corporate Research: How Much Is It Worth?" *The Wall Street Journal,* May 22, 1995, Leslie Cauley.

Overview

Evidence shows that some of the largest U.S. multinationals cut research and development spending in the early 1990s. These firms are also changing the focus of their research efforts from basic to more applied research.

Suggested Discussion Questions

What procedures would a firm follow to change its research and development budget? Who decides what type of research the firm conducts? How would this decision impact the budgeting process?

■ **Issue 9–55**
Budget Administration

"Boeing Faced with Heavy Demand, Lost $696 Million as It Struggled to Speed Up Production," *Business Week,* November 17, 1997.

Overview

This title of the *Business Week* Corporate Scoreboard section should provoke an interesting discussion concerning how a firm can face heavy demand and report heavy losses.

Suggested Discussion Questions

Discuss how Boeing could report heavy losses when it faces great demand for its product. Analyze Boeing's inventory problem in terms of the costs listed below.

1. Ordering costs.
2. Holding costs.
3. Storage costs
4. Opportunity costs.

■ **Issue 9–56**
Inventory Management

Chapter Ten

Standard Costing and Performance Measures for Today's Manufacturing Environment

After completing this chapter, you should be able to:

1   Explain how standard costing is used to help control costs.

2   Describe two ways to set standards.

3   Distinguish between perfection and practical standards.

4   Compute and interpret the direct-material price and quantity variances and the direct-labor rate and efficiency variances.

5   Explain several methods for determining the significance of cost variances.

6   Describe some behavioral effects of standard costing.

7   Explain how standard costs are used in product costing.

8   Prepare journal entries to record and close out cost variances.

9   Summarize some advantages of standard costing.

10   Describe the changing role of standard-costing systems in today's manufacturing environment.

11   Describe the operational performance measures appropriate for today's manufacturing environment.

AMERICAN BRASS CELEBRATES 50TH

New Orleans, LA—Band after high school band marched past the reviewing stand and turned their heads in salute to the old gentleman. George Finney smiled broadly and waved, as if personally, to each band member. It was a day to be celebrated as its founder marked the 50th anniversary of American Brass Instrument Company, a venerable New Orleans manufacturer. Fifty years of producing musical instruments for middle-school and high-school musicians. Thousands upon thousands of trumpets, trombones, and tubas for the eager young band members from across the nation. George Finney was only 32 years old when he started American Brass here in New Orleans, but today at 82 he seems as fit as ever.

After the parade and anniversary celebration, I had the opportunity to interview Mr. Finney in his spacious office. We were in the main plant of the Sousa Division, as Finney's original New Orleans company is now called. Sousa Division also has a plant in St. Louis, and American Brass has other divisions in Memphis and Spokane.

"We make the best brass instruments in the country. Actually the best in the world. No two ways about it," boasted Finney. "I've always insisted on quality, and I get it. My employees are first-rate. And the company is consistently profitable. After a few rocky years at the beginning, we've been turning a profit every year. It's a closely held family business," he explained, "and the family's getting bigger all the time."

I asked Mr. Finney about the secrets of his success. "Quality control and cost control," was his terse reply. "We run a tight operation with very high product quality, an extremely low defect rate, and iron-clad cost control.

"Our business, like any other in this day and age, is highly competitive. We've got to have a high-quality product at a reasonable cost. We ensure quality by continually monitoring production to ensure that our very tight specs are being met on the factory floor. And we control costs with a highly developed standard costing system.

"We set standards for everything," said Finney.

"Material quantity and prices, labor efficiency and rates, and overhead. Our accountants produce frequent, detailed cost reports that show us if there are any deviations between the standard costs and the actual costs being incurred. If deviations crop up, we jump on the situation right away." Finney was quick to add, though, that the standard-costing system was not used punitively. "We never use it to beat people over the head. It's a diagnostic tool, that's all. It helps us keep tabs on the financial dimensions of our production process.

"We collect a lot of nonfinancial data as well," explained Finney. "We measure all kinds of things, like machine downtime, number of warranty claims, lead-time for raw material delivery, and a host of others. We're doing a lot with these nonfinancial, operational performance measures now."

Yes, George Finney is very much in touch with American Brass Instrument Company. He's gotten the company off to a good start for its second half century.

A budget provides a plan for managers to follow in making decisions and directing an organization's activities. At the end of a budget period, the budget serves another useful purpose. At that time, managers use the budget as a benchmark against which to compare the results of actual operations. Did the company make as much profit as anticipated in the budget? Were costs greater or less than expected? These questions involve issues of control. In this chapter, we will study the tools used by managerial accountants to assist managers in controlling an organization's operations and costs.

Controlling Costs

LO 1   Explain how standard costing is used to help control costs.

Any control system has three basic parts: a predetermined or *standard* performance level, a measure of *actual* performance, and a *comparison* between standard and actual performance. A thermostat is a control system with which we are all familiar. First, a thermostat has a predetermined or standard temperature, which can be set at any desired level. If you want the temperature in a room to be 68 degrees, you set the thermostat at the *standard* of 68 degrees. Second, the thermostat has a thermometer, which measures the *actual* temperature in the room. Third, the thermostat *compares* the preset or standard temperature with the actual room temperature. If the actual temperature falls below the preset or standard temperature, the thermostat activates a heating device. The three features of a control system are depicted in Exhibit 10–1.

A **standard cost** is a predetermined cost for the production of goods or services, which serves as a benchmark against which to compare the actual cost.

A managerial accountant's budgetary-control system works like a thermostat. First, a predetermined or **standard cost** is set. In essence, a standard cost is a budget for the production of one unit of product or service. It is the cost chosen by the managerial accountant to serve as the benchmark in the budgetary-control system. When the firm produces many units, the managerial accountant uses the standard unit cost to determine the total standard or budgeted cost of production. For example, suppose the standard direct-material cost for one unit of product is $5 and 100 units are manufactured. The total standard or budgeted direct-material cost, given an actual output of 100 units, is $500 ($5 × 100).

Second, the managerial accountant measures the actual cost incurred in the production process.

A **cost variance** is the difference between actual and standard cost.

Third, the managerial accountant compares the actual cost with the budgeted or standard cost. Any difference between the two is called a **cost variance**. Cost variances then are used in controlling costs.

Management by exception is a management technique in which only significant deviations from expected performance are investigated.

Management by Exception

Managers are busy people. They do not have time to look into the causes of every variance between actual and standard costs. However, they do take the time to investigate the causes of significant cost variances. This process of following up on only significant cost variances is called **management by exception**. When operations are going along as planned, actual costs and profit will typically be close to the budgeted

Exhibit 10–1

Control System: A Thermostat

1. **Predetermined or standard performance** (The thermostat is set to a standard temperature.)

2. **Measure of actual performance** (The thermometer measures the actual room temperature.)

3. **Comparison of actual and standard performance** (The thermostat compares the preset or standard temperature with the actual temperature.)

amounts. However, if there are significant departures from planned operations, such effects will show up as significant cost variances. Managers investigate these variances to determine their causes, if possible, and take corrective action when indicated.

What constitutes a significant variance? No precise answer can be given to this question, since it depends on the size and type of the organization and its production process. We will consider this issue later in the chapter when we discuss common methods for determining the significance of cost variances. First, however, we will turn our attention to the process of setting standards.

Setting Standards

Managerial accountants typically use two methods for setting cost standards: analysis of historical data and task analysis.

LO 2   Describe two ways to set standards.

Analysis of Historical Data   One indicator of future costs is historical cost data. In a mature production process, where the firm has a lot of production experience, historical costs can provide a good basis for predicting future costs. The methods for analyzing cost behavior that we studied in Chapter 7 are used in making cost predictions. The managerial accountant often will need to adjust these predictions to reflect movements in price levels or technological changes in the production process. For example, the amount of rubber required to manufacture a particular type of tire will likely be the same this year as last year, unless there has been a significant change in the process used to manufacture tires. However, the price of rubber is likely to be different this year than last, and this fact must be reflected in the new standard cost of a tire.

Despite the relevance of historical cost data in setting cost standards, managerial accountants must guard against relying on them excessively. Even a seemingly minor change in the way a product is manufactured may make historical data almost totally irrelevant. Moreover, new products also require new cost standards. For new products, such as genetically engineered medicines, there are no historical cost data upon which to base standards. In such cases, the managerial accountant must turn to another approach.

Task Analysis   Another way to set cost standards is to analyze the process of manufacturing a product to determine what it *should* cost. The emphasis shifts from what the product *did* cost in the past to what it *should* cost in the future. In using **task analysis**, the managerial accountant typically works with engineers who are intimately familiar with the production process. Together they conduct studies to determine exactly how much direct material should be required and how machinery should be used in the production process. Time and motion studies are conducted to determine how long each step performed by direct laborers should take.

Task analysis sets standards by analyzing the production process.

A Combined Approach   Managerial accountants often apply both historical cost analysis and task analysis in setting cost standards. It may be, for example, that the technology has changed for only one step in the production process. In such a case, the managerial accountant would work with engineers to set cost standards for the technologically changed part of the production process. However, the accountant would likely rely on the less expensive method of analyzing historical cost data to update the cost standards for the remainder of the production process.

Participation in Setting Standards

Standards should not be determined by the managerial accountant alone. People generally will be more committed to meeting standards if they are allowed to participate in setting them. For example, production supervisors should have a role in setting production cost standards, and sales managers should be involved in setting targets for sales prices and volume. In addition, knowledgeable staff personnel should participate in the standard-setting process. For example, task analysis should be carried out by a team consisting of production engineers, production supervisors, and managerial accountants.

Perfection versus Practical Standards: A Behavioral Issue

LO 3   Distinguish between perfection and practical standards.

How difficult should it be to attain standard costs? Should standards be set so that actual costs rarely exceed standard costs? Or should it be so hard to attain standards that actual costs frequently exceed them? The answers to these questions depend on the purpose for which standards will be used and how standards affect behavior.

A **perfection** (or **ideal**) **standard** is the cost expected under perfect or ideal operating conditions.

Perfection Standards   A **perfection** (or **ideal**) **standard** is one that can be attained only under nearly perfect operating conditions. Such standards assume peak efficiency, the lowest possible input prices, the best-quality materials obtainable, and no disruptions in production due to such causes as machine breakdowns or power failures. Some managers believe that perfection standards motivate employees to achieve the lowest cost possible. They claim that since the standard is theoretically attainable, employees will have an incentive to come as close as possible to achieving it.

Other managers and many behavioral scientists disagree. They feel that perfection standards discourage employees, since they are so unlikely to be attained. Moreover, setting unrealistically difficult standards may encourage employees to sacrifice product quality to achieve lower costs. By skimping on raw-material quality or the attention given manual production tasks, employees may be able to lower the production cost. However, this lower cost may come at the expense of a higher rate of defective units. Thus, the firm ultimately may incur higher costs than necessary as defective products are returned by customers or scrapped upon inspection.

A **practical** (or **attainable**) **standard** is the cost expected under normal operating conditions.

Practical Standards   Standards that are as tight as practical, but still are expected to be attained, are called **practical** (or **attainable**) **standards**. Such standards assume a production process that is as efficient as practical under normal operating conditions. Practical standards allow for such occurrences as occasional machine breakdowns and normal amounts of raw-material waste. Attaining a practical standard keeps employees on their toes, without demanding miracles. Most behavioral theorists believe that practical standards encourage more positive and productive employee attitudes than do perfection standards.

Use of Standards by Nonmanufacturing Organizations

Many service industry firms, nonprofit organizations, and governmental units make use of standard costs. For example, airlines set standards for fuel and maintenance costs. A county motor vehicle office may have a standard for the number of days required to process and return an application for vehicle registration. These and similar organizations use standards in budgeting and cost control in much the same way that manufacturers use standards. The following illustrations typify the use of standards in service industry firms.

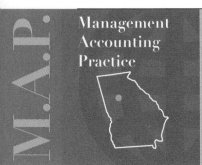

Management Accounting Practice

United Parcel Service

The Wall Street Journal reported on the use of standards by United Parcel Service (UPS). The firm's management used engineers to set performance standards for various delivery tasks. For example, UPS drivers were given a standard of three feet per second as the pace at which they should walk to a customer's door. Moreover, the drivers were instructed to knock on the door, rather than lose time looking for a doorbell.[1]

---

[1]"Up to Speed: United Parcel Service Gets Deliveries Done by Driving Its Workers," *The Wall Street Journal* 214, no. 81.

Service industry firms such as UPS use standards in controlling costs just as manufacturing companies do.

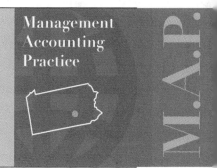

Dutch Pantry, Inc.

Dutch Pantry, Inc. operates over 50 restaurants throughout the eastern United States. Many of the food items served in the firm's restaurants are produced in a central plant. This facility produces over 150 different items, and a cost-accounting system is used to record the flow of costs through the various steps in food preparation. The cost-accounting system is based on standard costs established for a batch of each product. The firm's managerial accountants use the standards to monitor and control costs and to determine the cost of the food items produced.[2]

Management Accounting Practice

M.A.P.

Cost Variance Analysis

To illustrate the use of standards in controlling costs, we will focus on a manufacturer of musical instruments for use in schools. American Brass Instrument Company manufactures trumpets in its Sousa Division, located in New Orleans. The production process consists of several steps. First, brass tubing is packed with sand, heated, and bent into the shape of a trumpet. Then the valves are formed and attached to the trumpet, and all seams and joints are brazed. Finally, several coats of lacquer are applied, and the trumpet is manually inspected and tested.

LO 4   Compute and interpret the direct-material price and quantity variances and the direct-labor rate and efficiency variances.

     The divisional controller, John Phillips, has set standards for direct material and direct labor as follows.

Direct-Material Standards

Only the brass in a trumpet is considered direct material. The lacquer is inexpensive and is considered an indirect material, part of manufacturing overhead. The standard quantity and price of brass for the production of one trumpet are as follows:

---

[2]D. Boll, "How Dutch Pantry Accounts for Standard Costs," *Management Accounting* 64, no. 6, p. 32.

Standard quantity:	
Brass in finished product	9.5 pounds
Allowance for normal waste	.5 pound
Total standard quantity required per trumpet	10.0 pounds
Standard price:	
Purchase price per pound of brass (net of purchase discounts)	$6.50
Transportation cost per pound	.50
Total standard price per pound of brass	$7.00

The standard quantity of brass needed to manufacture one trumpet is 10 pounds, even though only 9.5 pounds actually remain in the finished product. Half a pound of brass is wasted as a normal result of the cutting and molding that is part of the production process. Therefore, the entire amount of brass needed to manufacture a trumpet is included in the standard quantity of material.

The standard price of brass reflects all of the costs incurred to acquire the material and transport it to the plant. Notice that the cost of transportation is added to the purchase price. Any purchase discounts would be subtracted out from the purchase price to obtain a net price.

To summarize, the **standard direct-material quantity** is the total amount of direct material normally required to produce a finished product, including allowances for normal waste or inefficiency. The **standard direct-material price** is the total delivered cost, after subtracting any purchase discounts.

The **standard direct-material quantity** is the total amount of material normally required to produce a finished product, including allowances for normal waste and inefficiency.

The **standard direct-material price** is the total delivered cost, after subtracting any purchase discounts taken.

Direct-Labor Standards

The standard quantity and rate for direct labor for the production of one trumpet are as follows:

Standard quantity:	
Direct labor required per trumpet	5 hours
Standard rate:	
Hourly wage rate	$16
Fringe benefits (25% of wages)	4
Total standard rate per hour	$20

The **standard direct-labor quantity** is the number of direct-labor hours normally needed to manufacture one unit of product. The **standard direct-labor rate** is the total hourly cost of compensation, including fringe benefits.

The **standard direct-labor quantity** is the number of labor hours normally needed to manufacture one unit of product.

The **standard direct-labor rate** is the total hourly cost of compensation, including fringe benefits.

Standard Costs Given Actual Output

During September the Sousa Division manufactured 2,000 trumpets. The total standard or budgeted costs for direct material and direct labor are computed as follows:

Direct material:	
Standard direct-material cost per trumpet (10 pounds × $7.00 per pound)	$ 70
Actual output	× 2,000
Total standard direct-material cost	$140,000
Direct labor:	
Direct labor cost per trumpet (5 hours × $20.00 per hour)	$ ˋ100
Actual output	× 2,000
Total standard direct-labor cost	$200,000

Notice that the total standard cost for the direct-material and direct-labor inputs is based on the Sousa Division's actual *output*. The division should incur costs of $340,000 for direct material and direct labor, *given that it produced 2,000 trumpets*. The total standard costs for direct material and direct labor serve as the managerial accountant's benchmarks against which to compare actual costs. This comparison then serves as the basis for controlling direct-material and direct-labor costs.

Analysis of Cost Variances

During September, the Sousa Division incurred the following actual costs for direct material and direct labor.

Direct material purchased: actual cost 25,000 pounds at $7.10 per pound $177,500

Direct material used: actual cost 20,500 pounds at $7.10 per pound $145,550

Direct labor: actual cost 9,800 hours at $21 per hour $205,800

Compare these actual expenditures with the total standard costs for the production of 2,000 trumpets. Sousa Division spent more than the budgeted amount for both direct material and direct labor. But why were these excess costs incurred? Is there any further analysis the managerial accountant can provide to help answer this question?

Direct-Material Variances

What caused the Sousa Division to spend more than the anticipated amount on direct material? First, the division purchased brass at a higher price ($7.10 per pound) than the standard price ($7.00 per pound). Second, the division used more brass than the standard amount. The amount actually used was 20,500 pounds instead of the standard amount of 20,000 pounds, which is based on actual output of 2,000 trumpets. The managerial accountant can show both of these deviations from standards by computing a **direct-material price variance** (or **purchase price variance**) and a **direct-material quantity variance**. The computation of these variances is depicted in Exhibit 10–2.

> The **direct-material price variance** (or **purchase price variance**) is the difference between actual and standard price multiplied by the actual quantity of material purchased.

The formula for the direct-material price variance is as follows:

$$\text{Direct-material price variance} = (PQ \times AP) - (PQ \times SP) = PQ(AP - SP)$$

where

PQ = Quantity purchased

AP = Actual price

SP = Standard price

Sousa Division's direct-material price variance for September is computed as follows:

$$
\begin{aligned}
\text{Direct-material price variance} &= PQ(AP - SP)\\
&= 25{,}000(\$7.10 - \$7.00)\\
&= \$2{,}500 \text{ Unfavorable}
\end{aligned}
$$

> The **direct-material quantity variance** is the difference between the actual and standard quantity multiplied by the standard price.

This variance is unfavorable, because the actual purchase price exceeded the standard price. Notice that the price variance is based on the quantity of material *purchased* (PQ), not the quantity actually used in production.

As Exhibit 10–2 shows, the following formula defines the direct-material quantity variance.

$$\text{Direct-material quantity variance} = (AQ \times SP) - (SQ \times SP) = SP(AQ - SQ)$$

where

AQ = Actual quantity used

SQ = Standard quantity allowed

Sousa Division's direct-material quantity variance for September is computed as follows:

$$
\begin{aligned}
\text{Direct-material quantity variance} &= SP(AQ - SQ)\\
&= \$7.00(20{,}500 - 20{,}000)\\
&= \$3{,}500 \text{ Unfavorable}
\end{aligned}
$$

This variance is unfavorable, because the actual quantity of direct material used in September exceeded the standard quantity allowed, *given actual September output* of 2,000 trumpets. The quantity variance is based on the quantity of material actually *used* in production (AQ).

Exhibit 10–2

Direct-Material Price and
Quantity Variances

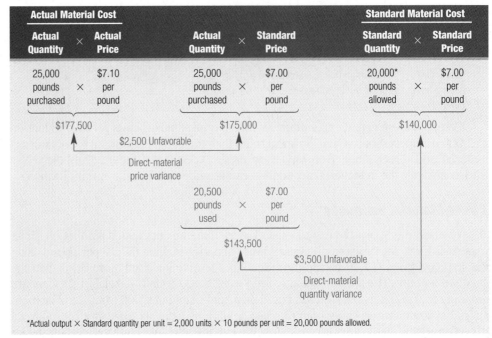

*Actual output × Standard quantity per unit = 2,000 units × 10 pounds per unit = 20,000 pounds allowed.

Quantity Purchased versus Quantity Used   As stated above, the direct-material price variance is based on the quantity purchased (PQ). This makes sense, because deviations between the actual and standard price, which are highlighted by the price variance, relate to the *purchasing* function in the firm. Timely action to follow up a significant price variance will be facilitated by calculating this variance as soon as possible after the material is *purchased*.

In contrast, the direct-material quantity variance is based on the amount of material *used* in production (AQ). The quantity variance highlights deviations between the quantity of material actually used (AQ) and the standard quantity allowed (SQ). Thus, it makes sense to compute this variance at the time the material is *used* in production.

Basing the Quantity Variance on Actual Output   Notice that the standard quantity of material must be based on the actual production output in order for the quantity variance to be meaningful. It would not make any sense to compare standard or budgeted material usage at one level of output (say, 1,000 trumpets) with the actual material usage at a *different* level of output (say, 2,000 trumpets). Everyone would expect more direct material to be used in the production of 2,000 trumpets than in the production of 1,000 trumpets. For the direct-material quantity variance to provide helpful information for management, the standard or budgeted quantity must be based on *actual output*. Then the quantity variance compares the following two quantities.

Direct-Labor Variances

Why did the Sousa Division spend more than the anticipated amount on direct labor during September? First, the division incurred a cost of $21 per hour for direct labor instead of the standard amount of $20 per hour. Second, the division used only 9,800 hours of direct labor, which is less than the standard quantity of 10,000 hours, given actual output of 2,000 trumpets. The managerial accountant analyzes direct-labor costs by computing a **direct-labor rate variance** and a **direct-labor efficiency variance**. Exhibit 10–3 depicts the computation of these variances.

The formula for the direct-labor rate variance is shown below.

$$\text{Direct-labor rate variance} = (AH \times AR) - (AH \times SR) = AH(AR - SR)$$

where

AH = Actual hours used

AR = Actual rate per hour

SR = Standard rate per hour

Sousa Division's direct-labor rate variance for September is computed as follows:

$$\text{Direct-labor rate variance} = AH(AR - SR)$$
$$= 9{,}800(\$21 - \$20) = \$9{,}800 \text{ Unfavorable}$$

This variance is unfavorable because the actual rate exceeded the standard rate during September.

As Exhibit 10–3 shows, the formula for the direct-labor efficiency variance is as follows:

$$\text{Direct-labor efficiency variance} = (AH \times SR) - (SH \times SR) = SR(AH - SH)$$

where

SH = Standard hours allowed

The Sousa Division's direct-labor efficiency variance for September is computed as follows:

$$\text{Direct-labor efficiency variance} = SR(AH - SH)$$
$$= \$20(9{,}800 - 10{,}000)$$
$$= \$4{,}000 \text{ Favorable}$$

This variance is favorable, because the actual direct-labor hours used in September were less than the standard hours allowed, *given actual September output* of 2,000 trumpets.

The **direct-labor rate variance** is the difference between actual and standard hourly labor rate multiplied by the actual hours of direct labor used.

The **direct-labor efficiency variance** is the difference between actual and standard hours of direct labor multiplied by the standard hourly labor rate.

Actual Labor Cost				Standard Labor Cost		
Actual Hours ×	**Actual Rate**	**Actual Hours** ×	**Standard Rate**	**Standard Hours** ×	**Standard Rate**	
9,800 hours used	×	$21 per hour	9,800 hours used	×	$20 per hour	10,000* hours allowed	×	$20 per hour

$205,800 $196,000 $200,000

← $9,800 Unfavorable →   ← $4,000 Favorable →
Direct-labor   Direct-labor
rate variance   efficiency variance

← $5,800 Unfavorable →
Direct-labor variance

*Actual output × Standard hours per unit = 2,000 units × 5 hours per unit = 10,000 hours allowed.

Exhibit 10–3

Direct-Labor Rate and Efficiency Variances

Sousa DIVISION

Notice that the direct-labor rate and efficiency variances add up to the total direct-labor variance. However, the rate and efficiency variances have opposite signs, since one variance is unfavorable and the other is favorable.

Direct-labor rate variance	$9,800 Unfavorable	Different signs of variances cancel just as plus
Direct-labor efficiency variance	4,000 Favorable	and minus signs cancel in arithmetic.
Direct-labor variance	$5,800 Unfavorable	

Basing the Efficiency Variance on Actual Output   The number of standard hours of direct labor allowed is based on the *actual* production output. It would not be meaningful to compare standard or budgeted labor usage at one level of output with the actual hours used at a different level of output.

Multiple Types of Direct Material or Direct Labor

Manufacturing processes usually involve several types of direct material. In such cases, direct-material price and quantity variances are computed for each type of material. Then these variances are added to obtain a total price variance and a total quantity variance, as follows:

	Price Variance	Quantity Variance
Direct material A	$1,000 F	$1,600 U
Direct material B	2,500 U	200 U
Direct material C	800 U	500 F
Total variance	$2,300 U	$1,300 U

Similarly, if a production process involves several types of direct labor, rate and efficiency variances are computed for each labor type. Then they are added to obtain a total rate variance and a total efficiency variance.

Allowing for Spoilage or Defects

In some manufacturing processes, a certain amount of spoilage or defective production is normal. This must be taken into account when the standard quantity of material is computed. To illustrate, suppose that 100 gallons of chemicals are normally required in a chemical process in order to obtain 80 gallons of good output. If total good output in January is 500 gallons, what is the standard allowed quantity of input?

$$\text{Good output quantity} = 80\% \times \text{Input quantity}$$

Dividing both sides of the equation by 80%

$$\frac{\text{Good output quantity}}{80\%} = \text{Input quantity allowed}$$

Using the numbers in the illustration

$$\frac{500 \text{ gallons of good output}}{80\%} = 625 \text{ gallons of input allowed}$$

The total standard allowed input is 625 gallons, given 500 gallons of good output.

Significance of Cost Variances

LO 5 Explain several methods for determining the significance of cost variances.

Managers do not have time to investigate the causes of every cost variance. Management by exception enables managers to look into the causes of only significant variances. But what constitutes an exception? How does the manager know when to follow up on a cost variance and when to ignore it?

These questions are difficult to answer, because to some extent the answers are part of the art of management. A manager applies judgment and experience in making guesses, pursuing hunches, and relying on intuition to determine when a variance should be investigated. Nevertheless, there are guidelines and rules of thumb that managers often apply.

	Amount		Percentage of Standard Cost
Direct material			
Standard cost, given actual output	$140,000		
Direct-material price variance	2,500	Unfavorable	1.79%
Direct-material quantity variance	3,500	Unfavorable	2.50%
Direct labor			
Standard cost, given actual output	$200,000		
Direct-labor rate variance	9,800	Unfavorable	4.9%
Direct-labor efficiency variance	4,000	Favorable	(2.0%)

Exhibit 10–4

Cost Variance Report for
September: Sousa Division

Size of Variances   The absolute size of a variance is one consideration. Managers are more likely to follow up on large variances than on small ones. The relative size of the variance is probably even more important. A manager is more likely to investigate a $20,000 material quantity variance that is 20 percent of the standard direct-material cost of $100,000, than a $50,000 labor efficiency variance that is only 2 percent of the standard direct-labor cost of $2,500,000. The *relative* magnitude of the $20,000 material quantity variance (20 percent) is greater than the *relative* magnitude of the $50,000 labor efficiency variance (2 percent). For this reason, managerial accountants often show the relative magnitude of variances in their cost-variance reports. For example, the September cost-variance report for the Sousa Division is shown in Exhibit 10–4.

Managers often apply a rule of thumb that takes into account both the absolute and the relative magnitude of a variance. An example of such a rule is the following: Investigate variances that are either greater than $10,000 or greater than 10 percent of standard cost.

Recurring Variances   Another consideration in deciding when to investigate a variance is whether the variance occurs repeatedly or only infrequently. Suppose a manager uses the rule of thumb stated above and the following direct-material quantity variances occur.

Month	Variance	Percentage of Standard Cost[†]
January	$3,000 F*	6.0%
February	3,200 F	6.4%
March	1,800 F	3.6%
April	3,100 F	6.2%

*F denotes a favorable variance.

[†]The standard direct-material cost is $50,000.

A strict adherence to the rule of thumb indicates no investigation, since none of the monthly variances is greater than $10,000 or 10 percent of standard cost. Nevertheless, the manager might investigate this variance in April, since it has *recurred* at a reasonably high level for several consecutive months. In this case, the consistency of the variance triggers an investigation, not its absolute or relative magnitude.

Trends   A trend in a variance may also call for investigation. Suppose a manager observes the following direct-labor efficiency variances.

Month	Variance	Percentage of Standard Cost[†]
January	$ 100 U*	.10%
February	550 U	.55%
March	3,000 U	3.00%
April	9,100 U	9.10%

*U denotes an unfavorable variance.

[†]The standard direct-labor cost is $100,000.

None of these variances is large enough to trigger an investigation if the manager uses the "$10,000 or 10 percent" rule of thumb. However, the four-month *trend* is worrisome. An alert manager will likely follow up on this unfavorable trend to determine its causes before costs get out of hand.

Controllability   Another important consideration in deciding when to look into the causes of a variance is the manager's view of the **controllability** of the cost item. A manager is more likely to investigate the variance for a cost that is controllable by someone in the organization than one that is not. For example, there may be little point to investigating a material price variance if the organization has no control over the price. This could happen, for example, if the firm has a long-term contract with a supplier of the material at a price determined on the international market. In contrast, the manager is likely to follow up on a variance that should be controllable, such as a direct-labor efficiency variance or a direct-material quantity variance.

Controllability is the extent to which managers are able to control or influence a cost or cost variance.

Favorable Variances   It is just as important to investigate significant favorable variances as significant unfavorable variances. For example, a favorable direct-labor efficiency variance may indicate that employees have developed a more efficient way of performing a production task. By investigating the variance, management can learn about the improved method. It may be possible to use a similar approach elsewhere in the organization.

Costs and Benefits of Investigation   The decision whether to investigate a cost variance is a cost-benefit decision. The costs of investigation include the time spent by the investigating manager and the employees in the department where the investigation occurs. Other potential costs include disruption of the production process as the investigation is conducted, and corrective actions taken to eliminate the cause of a variance. The benefits of a variance investigation include reduced future production costs if the cause of an unfavorable variance is eliminated. Another potential benefit is the cost saving associated with the lowering of cost standards when the cause of a favorable variance is discovered.

Weighing these considerations takes the judgment of skillful and experienced managers. Key to this judgment is an intimate understanding of the organization's production process and day-to-day contact with its operations.

A Statistical Approach

There are many reasons for cost variances. For example, a direct-labor efficiency variance could be caused by inexperienced employees, employee inefficiency, poor-quality raw materials, poorly maintained machinery, an intentional work slowdown due to employee grievances, or many other factors. In addition to these substantive reasons, there are purely random causes of variances. People are not robots, and they are not perfectly consistent in their work habits. Random fluctuations in direct-labor efficiency variances can be caused by such factors as employee illnesses, workers experimenting with different production methods, or simply random fatigue. Ideally, managers would be able to sort out the randomly caused variances from those with substantive and controllable underlying causes. It is impossible to accomplish this with 100 percent accuracy, but a **statistical control chart** can help.

A statistical control chart plots cost variances across time and compares them with a statistically determined *critical value* that triggers an investigation. This critical value is usually determined by assuming that cost variances have a normal probability distribution with a mean of zero. The critical value is set at some multiple of the distribution's standard deviation. Variances greater than the critical value are investigated.

A **statistical control chart** is a plot of cost variances across time, with a comparison to a statistically determined critical value.

Exhibit 10–5 shows a statistical control chart with a critical value of one standard deviation. The manager would investigate the variance observed in May, since it falls further than one standard deviation from the mean (zero). The variances for the remaining five months would not be investigated. The presumption is that these minor variances are due to random causes and are not worth investigating.[3]

Behavioral Impact of Standard Costing

Standard costs and variance analysis are useful in diagnosing organizational performance. These tools help managers discern "the story behind the story"—the details of operations that underlie reported cost and profit numbers. Standard costs, budgets, and variances are also used to evaluate the performance of individuals and departments. The performance of individuals, relative to standards or budgets, often is used to help determine salary increases, bonuses, and promotions. When standards and variances affect employee reward structures, they can profoundly influence behavior.

LO 6 Describe some behavioral effects of standard costing.

For example, suppose the manager of a hotel's Food and Beverage Department earns a bonus when food and beverage costs are below the budgeted amount, given actual sales. This reward structure will provide a concrete incentive for the manager to keep food and beverage costs under control. But such an incentive can have either positive or negative effects. The bonus may induce the manager to seek the most economical food suppliers and to watch more carefully for employee theft and waste. However, the bonus could also persuade the manager to buy cheaper but less tender steaks for the restaurant. This could ulti-

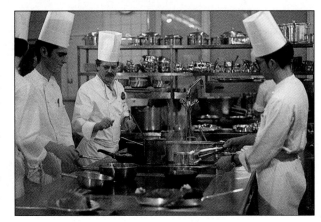

Incentive systems should be carefully designed so that employees try to carefully manage costs without allowing a deterioration in product or service quality. The head chef in this hotel's restaurant is evaluated both on his ability to control costs and on the satisfaction level of the restaurant's customers.

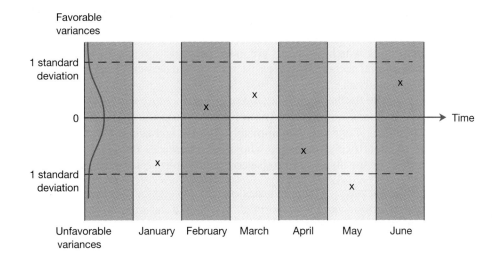

Exhibit 10–5

Statistical Control Chart

---

[3]For further discussion of statistical control charts, see Glenn Welsch, Ronald Hilton, and Paul Gordon, *Budgeting: Profit Planning and Control,* 5th ed. (Englewood Cliffs, NJ: Prentice Hall, 1988).

mately result in lost patronage for the restaurant and the hotel. One aspect of skillful management is knowing how to use standards, budgets, and variances to get the most out of an organization's employees. Unfortunately, there are no simple answers or formulas for success in this area.

Standards, budgets, and variances are used in the executive compensation schemes of many well-known companies, as this example suggests:

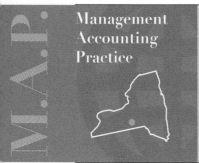

Management Accounting Practice

Corning Glass Works

A Harvard Business School management case reported on Corning Glass Works' system for determining managers' bonuses. In addition to individual performance factors, the bonus scheme gave considerable weight to the variance between actual and budgeted operating profit. In evaluating division managers, the performance review was broad enough to include all areas of the manager's performance. However, the key performance variable was divisional operating profit.[4]

The managers of this Corning division, which manufactures auto emission filters, are evaluated on a variety of factors. One key performance variable is divisional operating profit.

Controllability of Variances

Cost control is accomplished through the efforts of individual managers in an organization. By determining which managers are in the best position to influence each cost variance, the managerial accountant can assist managers in deriving the greatest benefit from cost variance analysis.

Who is responsible for the direct-material price and quantity variances? The direct-labor rate and efficiency variances? Answering these questions is often difficult, because it is rare that any one person completely controls any event. Nevertheless, it is often possible to identify the manager who is *most able to influence* a particular variance, even if he or she does not exercise complete control over the outcome.

Direct-Material Price Variance   The purchasing manager is generally in the best position to influence material price variances. Through skillful purchasing practices, an expert purchasing manager can get the best prices available for purchased goods and services.

---

[4]The source for this illustration is a Harvard Business School management case entitled "Corning Glass Works: Tom MacAvoy," prepared by Thomas N. Clough under the supervision of Richard F. Vancil, copyright by the President and Fellows of Harvard College.

To achieve this goal, the purchasing manager uses such practices as buying in quantity, negotiating purchase contracts, comparing prices among vendors, and global sourcing.

Despite these purchasing skills, the purchasing manager is not in complete control of prices. The need to purchase component parts with precise engineering specifications, the all-too-frequent rush requests from the production department, and worldwide shortages of critical materials all contribute to the challenges faced by the purchasing manager.

Direct-Material Quantity Variance The production supervisor is usually in the best position to influence material quantity variances. Skillful supervision and motivation of production employees, coupled with the careful use and handling of materials, contribute to minimal waste. Production engineers are also partially responsible for material quantity variances, since they determine the grade and technical specifications of materials and component parts. In some cases, using a low-grade material may result in greater waste than using a high-grade material.

Direct-Labor Rate Variance Direct-labor rate variances generally result from using a different mix of employees than that anticipated when the standards were set. Wage rates differ among employees due to their skill levels and their seniority with the organization. Using a higher proportion of more senior or more highly skilled employees than a task requires can result in unfavorable direct-labor rate variances. The production supervisor is generally in the best position to influence the work schedules of employees.

Direct-Labor Efficiency Variance Once again, the production supervisor is usually most responsible for the efficient use of employee time. Through motivation toward production goals and effective work schedules, the efficiency of employees can be maximized.

Interaction among Variances

Interactions among variances often occur, making it even more difficult to determine the responsibility for a particular variance. To illustrate, consider the following incident, which occurred in the Sousa Division of American Brass Instrument Company during May. The division's purchasing manager obtained a special price on brass alloy from a new supplier. When the material was placed into production, it turned out to be a lower grade of material than the production employees were used to. The alloy was of a slightly different composition, which made the material bend less easily during the formation of brass instruments. Sousa Division could have returned the material to the supplier, but that would have interrupted production and kept the division from filling its orders on time. Since using the off-standard material would not affect the quality of the company's finished products, the division manager decided to keep the material and make the best of the situation.

The ultimate result was that Sousa Division incurred four interrelated variances during May. The material was less expensive than normal, so the direct-material price variance was favorable. However, the employees had difficulty using the material, which resulted in more waste than expected. Hence, the division incurred an unfavorable direct-material quantity variance.

What were the labor implications of the off-standard material? Due to the difficulty in working with the metal alloy, the employees required more than the standard amount of time to form the instruments. This resulted in an unfavorable direct-labor efficiency variance. Finally, the production supervisor had to use his most senior employees to work with the off-standard material. Since these people earned relatively high wages, the direct-labor rate variance was also unfavorable.

To summarize, the purchase of off-standard material resulted in the following interrelated variances.

$$\text{Purchase of off-standard material} \Rightarrow \begin{cases} \textbf{Favorable direct-material price variance} \\ \textbf{Unfavorable direct-material quantity variance} \\ \textbf{Unfavorable direct-labor rate variance} \\ \textbf{Unfavorable direct-labor efficiency variance} \end{cases}$$

Such interactions of variances make it more difficult to assign responsibility for any particular variance.

Trade-offs among Variances   Does the incident described above mean that the decision to buy and use the off-standard material was a poor one? Not necessarily. Perhaps these variances were anticipated, and a conscious decision was made to buy the material anyway. How could this be a wise decision? Suppose the amounts of the variances were as follows:

$(8,500)	Favorable direct-material price variance
1,000	Unfavorable direct-material quantity variance
2,000	Unfavorable direct-labor rate variance
1,500	Unfavorable direct-labor efficiency variance
$(4,000)	Favorable net overall variance

The division saved money overall on the decision to use a different grade of brass alloy. Given that the quality of the final product was not affected, the division's management acted wisely.

Standard Costs and Product Costing

> **LO 7**   Explain how standard costs are used in product costing.

Our discussion of standard costing has focused on its use in controlling costs. But firms that use standard costs for control also use them for product costing. Recall from Chapter 3 that *product costing* is the process of accumulating the costs of a production process and assigning them to the completed products. Product costs are used for various purposes in both financial and managerial accounting.

As production takes place, product costs are added to the Work-in-Process Inventory account. The flow of product costs through a firm's manufacturing accounts is depicted in Exhibit 10–6.

> In a **standard-costing system**, cost variances are computed and production costs are entered into Work-in-Process Inventory at their standard amounts.

Different types of product-costing systems are distinguished by the type of costs that are entered into Work-in-Process Inventory. In Chapter 3, we studied *actual-* and *normal*-costing systems. In these product-costing systems, the *actual* costs of direct material and direct labor are charged to Work-in-Process Inventory. In a **standard-costing system** the *standard* costs of direct material and direct labor are entered into Work-in-Process Inventory.

Journal Entries under Standard Costing   To illustrate the use of standard costs in product costing, we will continue our illustration of the Sousa Division. During September the

> **Exhibit 10–6**
>
> Flow of Product Costs through Manufacturing Accounts

* Cost of Goods Sold is an expense. Although it is more descriptive, the term *cost-of-good-sold expense* is not used as much in practice as the simpler term *cost of goods sold*.

division purchased 25,000 pounds of direct material for $177,500. The actual quantity of material used in production was 20,500 pounds. However, the standard cost of direct material, given September's actual output of 2,000 trumpets, was only $140,000. The following journal entries record these facts and isolate the direct-material price and quantity variances.

LO 8   Prepare journal entries to record and close out cost variances.

Raw-Material Inventory	175,000	
Direct-Material Price Variance	2,500	
Accounts Payable		177,500
To record the purchase of raw material and the incurrence of an unfavorable price variance.		
Work-in-Process Inventory	140,000	
Direct-Material Quantity Variance	3,500	
Raw-Material Inventory		143,500
To record the use of direct material in production and the incurrence of an unfavorable quantity variance.		

Notice that the material purchase is recorded in the Raw-Material Inventory account at its standard price ($175,000 = 25,000 pounds purchased × $7.00 per pound). The $140,000 debit entry to Work-in-Process Inventory adds only the standard cost of the material to Work-in-Process Inventory as a product cost ($140,000 = 20,000 pounds allowed × $7.00 per pound). The two variances are isolated in their own variance accounts. Since they are both unfavorable, they are represented by debit entries.

The following journal entry records the actual September cost of direct labor, as an addition to Wages Payable. The entry also adds the standard cost of direct labor to Work-in-Process Inventory and isolates the direct-labor variances.

Work-in-Process Inventory	200,000	
Direct-Labor Rate Variance	9,800	
Direct-Labor Efficiency Variance		4,000
Wages Payable		205,800
To record the usage of direct labor and the direct-labor variances for September.		

Since the direct-labor efficiency variance is favorable, it is recorded as a credit entry.

Disposition of Variances   Variances are temporary accounts, like revenue and expense accounts, and they are closed out at the end of each accounting period. Most companies close their variance accounts directly into Cost of Goods Sold. The journal entry required to close out Sousa Division's September variance accounts is shown below.

Cost of Goods Sold	11,800	
Direct-Labor Efficiency Variance	4,000	
Direct-Labor Rate Variance		9,800
Direct-Material Price Variance		2,500
Direct-Material Quantity Variance		3,500

The increase of $11,800 in Cost of Goods Sold is explained as follows:

	Unfavorable Variances Increase Cost of Goods Sold	Favorable Variance Decreases Cost of Goods Sold	Net Increase in Cost of Goods Sold
Direct-labor efficiency variance		$4,000	
Direct-labor rate variance	$ 9,800		
Direct-material price variance	2,500		
Direct-material quantity variance	3,500		
Total	$15,800 –	$4,000 =	$11,800

The unfavorable variances represent costs of operating inefficiently, relative to the standards, and thus cause Cost of Goods Sold to be higher. The opposite is true for favorable variances.

An alternative method of variance disposition is to apportion all variances among Work-in-Process Inventory, Finished-Goods Inventory, and Cost of Goods Sold. This accounting treatment reflects the effects of unusual inefficiency or efficiency in all of the accounts through which the manufacturing costs flow. This method, called *variance proration,* is covered more fully in cost-accounting texts.

Cost Flow under Standard Costing   In a standard-costing system, since standard costs are entered into Work-in-Process Inventory, standard costs flow through all of the manufacturing accounts. Thus, in Exhibit 10–6, all of the product costs flowing through the accounts are standard costs. To illustrate, suppose the Sousa Division finished 2,000 trumpets in September and sold 1,500 of them. The journal entries to record the flow of standard direct-material and direct-labor costs are shown below.

Finished-Goods Inventory	340,000*	
Work-in-Process Inventory		340,000

*Total standard cost of direct material and direct labor: $340,000 = $140,000 + $200,000.

Cost of Goods Sold	255,000*	
Finished-Goods Inventory		255,000

*1,500 out of 2,000 trumpets sold; three-quarters of $340,000 is $255,000.

Our Sousa Division illustration is not really complete yet, because we have not discussed manufacturing-overhead costs. This topic is covered in the next chapter. The important point at this juncture is that in a standard-costing system, *standard costs flow through the manufacturing accounts rather than actual costs.*

Advantages of Standard Costing

LO 9 Summarize some advantages of standard costing.

Standard costing has been the predominant accounting system in manufacturing companies, for both cost control and product-costing purposes, for several decades. This remains true today, and the use of standard costing is spreading to nonmanufacturing firms as well. The widespread use of standard costing over such a long time period suggests that it has traditionally been perceived as offering several advantages. However, today's manufacturing environment is changing dramatically. Some managers are calling into question the usefulness of the traditional standard-costing approach. They argue that the role of standard-costing systems must change.

In this section, we will list some of the advantages traditionally attributed to standard-costing systems. In the next section, we will discuss some of the contemporary criticisms of the standard-costing approach, and suggest several ways in which the role of standard costing is beginning to change.

Some advantages traditionally attributed to standard costing include the following:

1. Standard costs provide a basis for *sensible cost comparisons.* As we discussed earlier, it would make no sense to compare budgeted costs at one (planned) activity level with actual costs incurred at a different (actual) activity level. Standard costs enable the managerial accountant to compute the standard allowed cost, given actual output, which then serves as a sensible benchmark to compare with the actual cost.

2. Computation of standard costs and cost variances enables managers to employ *management by exception.* This approach conserves valuable management time.

3. Variances provide a means of *performance evaluation* and rewards for employees.

4. Since the variances are used in performance evaluation, they provide *motivation* for employees to adhere to standards.

5. Use of standard costs in product costing results in *more stable product costs* than if actual production costs are used. Actual costs often fluctuate erratically, whereas standard costs are changed only periodically.

6. A standard-costing system is usually *less expensive* than an actual or normal product-costing system.

Like any tool, a standard-costing system can be misused. When employees are criticized for every cost variance, the positive motivational effects will quickly vanish. Moreover, if standards are not revised often enough, they will become outdated. Then the benefits of cost benchmarks and product costing will disappear.

Changing Role of Standard-Costing Systems in Today's Manufacturing Environment

The rise of global competition, the introduction of JIT production methods and flexible manufacturing systems, the goal of continuous process improvement, and the emphasis on product quality are dramatically changing the manufacturing environment. What are the implications of these changes for the role of standard-costing systems? We will begin by listing some contemporary criticisms of standard costing.

> **LO 10** Describe the changing role of standard-costing systems in today's manufacturing environment.

Criticisms of Standard Costing in Today's Manufacturing Environment

Listed below are several drawbacks attributed to standard costing in an advanced manufacturing setting.[5]

1. The variances calculated under standard costing are at too aggregate a level and come too late to be useful. Some managerial accountants argue that traditional standard costing is out of step with the philosophy of *cost management systems* and *activity-based management*. A production process comprises many activities. These activities result in costs. By focusing on the activities that cause costs to be incurred, by eliminating non-value-added activities, and by continually improving performance in value-added activities, costs will be minimized and profit maximized.[6] What is needed are performance measures that focus directly on performance in the activities that management wants to improve. For example, such activities could include product quality, processing time, and delivery performance. (We will explore such measures later in this chapter.)

2. Traditional cost variances are also too aggregate in the sense that they are not tied to specific product lines, production batches, or FMS cells. The aggregate nature of the variances makes it difficult for managers to determine their cause.

---

[5]The sources for this material are Robert S. Kaplan, "Limitations of Cost Accounting in Advanced Manufacturing Environments," in *Measures for Manufacturing Excellence,* Robert S. Kaplan, ed. (Boston: Harvard Business School Press, 1990), pp. 1–14; H. Thomas Johnson, "Performance Measurement for Competitive Excellence," in *Measures for Manufacturing Excellence,* Robert S. Kaplan, ed. (Boston: Harvard Business School Press, 1990), pp. 63–90; Robert A. Bonsack, "Does Activity-Based Costing Replace Standard Costing?" *Journal of Cost Management* 4, no. 4, pp. 46, 47; and Michiharu Sukurai, "The Influence of Factory Automation on Management Accounting Practices: A Study of Japanese Companies," in *Measures for Manufacturing Excellence,* Robert S. Kaplan, ed. (Boston: Harvard Business School Press, 1990), pp. 39–62.

[6]Cost management systems and activity-based management are covered in Chapters 5 and 6. Elimination of non-value-added costs is covered in Chapter 6.

3. Traditional standard-costing systems focus too much on the cost and efficiency of direct labor, which is rapidly becoming a relatively unimportant factor of production.

4. One of the most important conditions for the successful use of standard costing is a stable production process. Yet the introduction of flexible manufacturing systems has reduced this stability, with frequent switching among a variety of products on the same production line.

5. Shorter product life cycles mean that standards are relevant for only a short time. When new products are introduced, new standards must be developed.

6. Traditional standard costs are not defined broadly enough to capture various important aspects of performance. For example, the standard direct-material price does not capture all of the *costs of ownership*. In addition to the purchase price and transportation costs, the *cost of ownership* includes the costs of ordering, paying bills, scheduling delivery, receiving, inspecting, handling and storing, and any production-line disruptions resulting from untimely or incorrect delivery.[7]

7. Traditional standard-costing systems tend to focus too much on cost minimization, rather than increasing product quality or customer service. Indeed, standard-costing systems can cause dysfunctional behavior in a JIT/FMS environment. For example, buying the least expensive materials of a given quality, in order to avoid a material price variance, may result in using a vendor whose delivery capabilities are not consistent with JIT requirements.

8. Automated manufacturing processes tend to be more consistent in meeting production specifications. As a result, variances from standards tend to be very small or nonexistent.

Adapting Standard-Costing Systems

As a result of these criticisms, some highly automated manufacturers are deemphasizing standard costing in their control systems. Yet most manufacturing firms continue to use standard costing to some extent even after adopting advanced manufacturing methods.[8] However, such firms do make changes in their use of standard costing to reflect various features of the new manufacturing environment.

Reduced Importance of Labor Standards and Variances   As direct labor occupies a diminished role in the new manufacturing environment, the standards and variances used to control labor costs also decline in importance. The heavy emphasis of traditional standard-costing systems on labor efficiency variances must give way to variances that focus on the more critical inputs to the production process. Machine hours, material and overhead costs, product quality, and manufacturing cycle times take on greater importance as the objects of managerial control.

Emphasis on Material and Overhead Costs   As labor diminishes in importance, material and overhead costs take on greater significance. Controlling material costs and quality, and controlling overhead costs through cost-driver analysis, become key aspects of the cost management system (CMS).

Cost Drivers   Identification of the factors that drive production costs takes on greater importance in the CMS. Such cost drivers as machine hours, number of parts, engi-

---

[7]Some companies are developing cost of ownership reporting systems. Among them are Northrop Aircraft Division, McDonnell Douglas, Texas Instruments, and Black & Decker. See L. Carr and C. Ittner, "Measuring the Cost of Ownership," *Journal of Cost Management* 6, no. 3, pp. 42–51.

[8]For example, see James M. Patell, "Cost Accounting, Process Control, and Product Design: A Case Study of the Hewlett-Packard Personal Office Computer Division," *The Accounting Review* 62, no. 4, pp. 808–39; Jonathan B. Schiff, "ABC at Lederle," *Management Accounting* 75, no. 2, p. 58; and Robert A. Bonsack, "Does Activity-Based Costing Replace Standard Costing?" *Journal of Cost Management* 4, no. 4, pp. 46–47.

neering change orders, and production runs become the focus of the CMS and activity-based costing system.

Shifting Cost Structures   Advanced manufacturing systems require large outlays for production equipment, which entail a shift in the cost structure from variable costs toward fixed costs. Overhead cost control becomes especially critical. Chapter 11 explores the role of standard-costing systems in controlling overhead costs.

High Quality and Zero Defects   Total quality control (TQC) programs that typically accompany a JIT approach strive for very high quality levels for both raw materials and finished products. One result should be very low material price and quantity variances and low costs of rework.

Non-Value-Added Costs   A key objective of a CMS is the elimination of non-value-added costs. As these costs are reduced or eliminated, standards must be revised frequently to provide accurate benchmarks for cost control.

Shorter Product Life Cycles   As product life cycles shorten, standards must be developed and revised more frequently.

Real-Time Information Systems   A CIM system enables the managerial accountant to collect operating data as production takes place and to report relevant performance measures to management on a real-time basis. This enables managers to eliminate the causes of unfavorable variances more quickly.

Nonfinancial Measures for Operational Control   Managerial accountants traditionally have focused on financial measures of performance, such as deviations from budgeted costs. Financial measures are still very important, but to an ever-greater extent financial performance criteria are being augmented by nonfinancial measures. In the new manufacturing environment, operational measures are being developed to control key aspects of the production process. In the next section we will discuss some of these measures.

Benchmarking   One widely used method to control costs and improve operational efficiency is **benchmarking**. This is the continual search for the most effective method of accomplishing a task, by comparing existing methods and performance levels with those of other organizations, or with other subunits within the same organization. For example, hospitals routinely benchmark their costs of patient care by diagnostic-related groups (such as circulatory disorders), with the costs of other hospitals.

> **Benchmarking** is the continual search for the most effective method of accomplishing a task, by comparing existing methods and performance levels with those of other organizations or with other subunits within the same organization.

Operational Control Measures in Today's Manufacturing Environment

In today's advanced manufacturing environment, operational performance measures are taking on ever-greater importance.[9] Under the philosophy of *activity-based management,* the goal is to focus on continually improving each activity. As a result, the emerging operational control measures focus on the key *activities* in which the organization engages. To illustrate, Exhibit 10–7 lists some of the operational performance measures used by Sousa Division in its new St. Louis manufacturing facility. The new plant uses JIT methods and employs a flexible

> **LO 11**   Describe the operational performance measures appropriate for today's manufacturing environment.

---

[9]This section draws on Robert A. Howell and Stephen R. Soucy, "Operating Controls in the New Manufacturing Environment," *Management Accounting* 69, no. 4, pp. 25–31; George Foster and Charles T. Horngren, "Flexible Manufacturing Systems: Cost Management and Cost Accounting Implications," *Journal of Cost Management* 2, no. 3, pp. 16–24; Howard M. Armitage and Anthony A. Atkinson, "The Choice of Productivity Measures in Organizations," in Robert S. Kaplan, ed., *Measures for Manufacturing Excellence* (Boston: Harvard Business School Press, 1990), pp. 91–128; and Robert S. Kaplan and David P. Norton, "The Balanced Scorecard: Measures That Drive Performance," *Harvard Business Review* 70, no. 1, pp. 71–79.

Raw Material and Scrap

Number of vendors

Number of unique parts

Number of common parts

Raw material as a percentage of total cost

Lead time for material delivery

Percentage of orders received on time

Total raw-material cost

Deviations between actual and budgeted raw-material prices

Scrap as a percentage of raw-material cost

Cost of scrap

Quality of raw material

Inventory

Average value of inventory

Average amount of time various inventory items are held

Ratio of inventory value to sales revenue

Number of inventoried parts

Machinery

Hours of machine downtime

Percentage of machine downtime

Percentage of machine availability

Bottleneck machine downtime

Percentage of bottleneck machine downtime

Percentage of bottleneck machine availability

Detailed maintenance records

Percentage of on-time routine maintenance procedures

Setup time

Machine flexibility:

   Product switch-over times in an FMS cell

   Number of different products manufactured in an FMS cell

Product Quality

Customer acceptance measures:

   Number of customer complaints

   Number of warranty claims

   Number of products returned

   Cost of repairing returned products

In-process quality measures:

   Number of defects found

   Cost of rework

Quality costs

Production and Delivery

Manufacturing cycle time

Velocity

Manufacturing cycle efficiency

Percentage of on-time deliveries

Percentage of orders filled

Delivery cycle time

Productivity

Financial measures:

   Aggregate or total productivity (output in dollars ÷ total input in dollars)

   Partial or component productivity (output in dollars ÷ a particular input in dollars)

Operational (physical) measures:

   Partial or component productivity measures. These measures express relationships between inputs and outputs, in physical terms. For example:

      Musical instruments produced per day per employee

      Square feet of floor space required per instrument per day

      Electricity required per instrument produced

Innovation and Learning

New products:

   Percentage of sales from new products

   New products introduced by this firm versus introductions by competitors

Process improvements:

   Number of process improvements made

   Cost savings from process improvements

Exhibit 10–7

Operational Performance
Measures for an Advanced
Manufacturing Environment

manufacturing system. The measures listed in Exhibit 10–7 are representative, but not exhaustive, of those used in practice. In using these measures to control operations, Sousa's management emphasizes trends over time. The goal is to continually improve all aspects of the plant's operations.

Raw Material and Scrap   Raw material continues to be a significant cost element in any manufacturing process, whether labor-intensive or highly automated. Worldwide material sourcing and international competition have resulted in the purchasing function taking on greater importance in many firms. As a result, purchasing performance has become an important area of measurement; criteria include total raw-material cost, deviations between actual and budgeted material prices, the quality of raw materials, and the delivery performance of vendors.

The cost of scrap is highlighted as a separate item, rather than being included in the standard direct-material cost as a normal production cost. The objective is to reduce scrap to the absolute minimal level possible.

Inventory The essence of the just-in-time production environment is low inventories at every stage of production. Thus, inventory control is of paramount importance in achieving the benefits of the JIT philosophy. Inventory control measures include the average value of inventory, the average amount of time various inventory items are held, and other inventory turnover measures, such as the ratio of inventory value to sales revenue.

Machinery If inventories are to be kept low, as the JIT philosophy demands, then the production process must be capable of producing goods quickly. This goal requires that production machinery must work when it is needed, which means that routine maintenance schedules must be adhered to scrupulously. Performance controls in this area include measures of machine downtime and machine availability, and detailed maintenance records. Some manufacturers make a distinction between *bottleneck machinery* and nonbottleneck machinery. A bottleneck operation is one that limits the production capacity of the entire facility. It is vital that the machinery in bottleneck operations be available 100 percent of the time, excluding time for routine required maintenance. In an advanced manufacturing environment, based on JIT and FMS, the investment in machinery is extremely large. To obtain the anticipated return from this investment, through the benefits of JIT and FMS, the machinery has to be kept running. This emphasis on bottleneck operations is consistent with the management philosophy known as the *theory of constraints*. This approach stresses the importance of identifying and easing the organization's constraints, which are the phenomena that limit the organization's productive capacity.[10]

Setup time also is highlighted as a machinery performance measure, and the objective in a JIT/FMS setting is to minimize this non-value-added activity. Machine flexibility measures emphasize the value of producing many different products in the same FMS cell.

Product Quality A JIT philosophy demands adherence to strict quality standards for raw materials, manufactured components, and finished products. Various nonfinancial data are vital for assessing a manufacturer's effectiveness in maintaining product quality. **Customer-acceptance measures** focus on the extent to which a firm's customers perceive its product to be of high quality. Typical performance measures include the number of customer complaints, the number of warranty claims, the number of products returned, and the cost of repairing returned products. **In-process quality controls** refer to procedures designed to assess product quality before production is completed. For example, in a *quality audit program,* partially completed products are randomly inspected at various stages of production. Defect rates are measured, and corrective actions are suggested. A third area of quality measurement relates to *raw-material quality*. Suppliers are rated on the basis of the quality of their materials as well as customer service.

Some companies routinely prepare a *quality cost report,* which details the costs incurred in assuring product quality. We will discuss quality costs in Chapter 12.

Production and Delivery A company will achieve little success if it manufactures a great product but delivers it to the customer a week late. World-class manufacturers are striving toward a goal of filling 100 percent of their orders on time. Common measures of product delivery performance include the percentage of on-time deliveries and the percentage of orders filled. Another measure is **delivery cycle time,** the average time between the receipt of a customer order and delivery of the goods.

Delivering goods on time requires that they be produced on time. Various operational performance measures have been developed to assess the timeliness of the production process. **Manufacturing cycle time** is the total amount of production time (or throughput time) required per unit. It can be computed by dividing the total time

Customer-acceptance measures focus on the extent to which a firm's customers perceive its product to be of high quality.

In-process quality controls are procedures designed to assess product quality before production is completed.

Delivery cycle time is the average time between the receipt of a customer order and delivery of the goods.

Manufacturing cycle time is the total amount of production time (or throughput time) required per unit.

---

[10]Eliyahu M. Goldratt, *Theory of Constraints* (Croton-on-Hudson, New York: North River Press, 1990).

Velocity is the number of units produced in a given time period.

Manufacturing cycle efficiency (MCE) is the ratio of processing time to the sum of processing time, inspection time, waiting time, and move time.

required to produce a batch by the number of units in the batch. **Velocity** is defined as the number of units produced in a given time period. Perhaps an even more important operational measure is the **manufacturing cycle efficiency (MCE),** defined as follows:

$$\text{Manufacturing cycle efficiency} = \frac{\text{Processing time}}{\text{Processing time} + \text{Inspection time} + \text{Waiting time} + \text{Move time}}$$

The value of the MCE measure lies in its comparison between value-added time (processing) and non-value-added time (inspection, waiting, and moving). In many manufacturing companies, MCE is less than 10 percent.[11] Firms with advanced manufacturing systems strive for as high an MCE measure as possible.

Productivity   Global competitiveness has forced virtually all manufacturers to strive for greater productivity. One *financial* productivity measure is **aggregate (or total) productivity,** defined as total output divided by total input. A firm's total output is measured as the sum, across all of the goods and services produced, of those products and services times their sales prices. Total input is the sum of the direct-material, direct-labor, and overhead costs incurred in production. Another financial measure is a **partial (or component) productivity** measure, in which total output (in dollars) is divided by the cost of a particular input.

Aggregate (or total) productivity is total output divided by total input.

Partial (or component) productivity is total output (in dollars) divided by the cost of a particular input.

A preferable approach to productivity measurement is to record multiple physical measures that capture the most important determinants of a company's productivity. These *operational* (or *physical*) measures are also partial productivity measures, since each one focuses on a particular input. For example, a large automobile manufacturer routinely records the following data for one of its plants: the number of engines produced per day per employee, and the number of square feet of floor space required per engine produced in a day. A large chemical company keeps track of the amount of energy (in British thermal units, BTU) required to convert a kilogram of raw chemicals into a kilogram of finished product. Data such as these convey more information to management than a summary financial measure such as aggregate productivity.

Innovation and Learning   Global competition requires that companies continually improve and innovate. New products must be developed and introduced to replace those that become obsolete.

Although most large manufacturers continue to use standard-costing systems as aids to cost control and product costing, they are also placing greater emphasis on operational (nonfinancial) performance measures. A leader among such companies is Harley-Davidson.

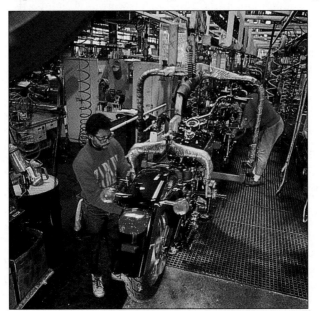

those that become obsolete. New processes must continually be developed to make production more efficient. In a world-class manufacturer or service firm, the one thing that is most constant is change.

To summarize, nonfinancial measures are being used increasingly to augment standard-costing systems. These operational performance measures assist management in its goal of continuous process improvement. To be most effective, operational controls should be tied to the strategic

---

[11]Callie Berliner and James A. Brimson, eds., *Cost Management for Today's Advanced Manufacturing* (Boston: Harvard Business School Press, 1988), p. 4.

objectives of the organization. Specific improvement targets can be set for various measures to provide motivation for improvement in the areas deemed most important by management.

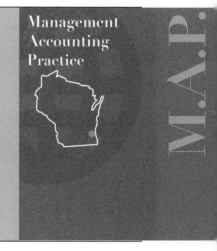

Harley-Davidson

Harley-Davidson, the well-known manufacturer of motorcycles, uses the following 10 criteria to measure its manufacturing effectiveness.

1. Attainment of production schedules.
2. Personnel requirements.
3. Conversion costs.
4. Overtime requirements.
5. Inventory levels.
6. Material-cost variance (difference between actual and budgeted cost).
7. Scrap and rework costs.
8. Manufacturing cycle time.
9. Product quality.
10. Productivity improvement.[12]

Management Accounting Practice

Gain-Sharing Plans

One widely used method of providing incentives to employees to improve their performance on various operational control measures is gain-sharing. A **gain-sharing plan** is an incentive system that specifies a formula by which cost or productivity gains achieved by a company are shared with the workers who helped accomplish the improvements. For example, suppose an electronics manufacturer reduced its defect rate in the Manual Insertion Department by 2 percent for a savings of $100,000. A gain-sharing formula might call for 25 percent of the savings to be shared with the employees in that department.

A **gain-sharing plan** is an incentive system that specifies a formula by which the cost savings from productivity gains achieved by a company are shared with the workers who helped accomplish the improvements.

The Balanced Scorecard

Managers of the most successful organizations do not rely on either financial or nonfinancial performance measures alone. They recognize that *financial performance measures* summarize the results of past actions. These measures are important to a firm's owners, creditors, employees, and so forth. Thus, they must be watched carefully by management as well. *Nonfinancial performance measures* concentrate on current activities, which will be the drivers of future financial performance. Thus, effective management requires a balanced perspective on performance measurement, a viewpoint that some call the *balanced scorecard* perspective. Exhibit 10–8 depicts the balanced scorecard, which integrates performance measures in four key areas: financial, internal operations, customer, and innovation and learning.[13]

---

[12] Robert D. McIlhattan, "How Cost Management Systems Can Support the JIT Philosophy," *Management Accounting 69*, no. 3, p. 25. For other examples, see Mark E. Beischel and K. Richard Smith, "Linking the Shop Floor to the Top Floor," *Management Accounting 73*, no. 4, pp. 25–29; and Michael R. Sellenheim, "Performance Measurement," *Management Accounting 73*, no. 3, pp. 50–53.

[13] Robert S. Kaplan and David D. Norton, "The Balanced Scorecard: Measures That Drive Performance," *Harvard Business Review 70*, no. 1, pp. 71–79. Also, see Lawrence S. Maisel, "Performance Measurement: The Balanced Scorecard Approach," *Journal of Cost Management 6*, no. 2, pp. 47–52.

Exhibit 10–8

The Balanced Scorecard

Chapter Summary

A standard-costing system serves two purposes: cost control and product costing. The managerial accountant works with others in the organization to set standard costs for direct material, direct labor, and manufacturing overhead through either historical cost analysis or task analysis. The accountant then uses the standard cost as a benchmark against which to compare actual costs incurred. Managers use management by exception to determine the causes of significant cost variances. This control purpose of the standard-costing system is accomplished by computing a direct-material price variance, a direct-material quantity variance, a direct-labor rate variance, and a direct-labor efficiency variance.

Managers determine the significance of cost variances through judgment and rules of thumb. The absolute and relative size of variances, recurrence of variances, variance trends, and controllability of variances are all considered in deciding whether variances warrant investigation. The managerial accountant achieves the product-costing purpose of the standard-costing system by entering the standard cost of production into Work-in-Process Inventory as a product cost. Standard-costing systems offer an organization many benefits. However, these benefits will be obtained only if the standard-costing system is used properly.

Today's manufacturing environment is rapidly changing, due to the influences of worldwide competition, JIT, FMS, and an emphasis on product quality and customer service. As a result, many manufacturers are adapting their standard-costing systems to reflect these aspects of the new manufacturing environment. Moreover, nonfinancial measures of operational performance are widely used to augment the control information provided by standard costing. These measures typically focus on raw material and scrap, inventory, machinery, product quality, production and delivery, productivity, and innovation and learning.

Rockwater is a global, undersea oil field construction company headquartered in Aberdeen, Scotland. Doing the undersea engineering and construction for drilling rigs such as the one pictured here requires diverse technical operations, both on- and offshore. Rockwater's management found the balanced scorecard to be an invaluable tool in clarifying the company's goals and communicating them to the employees. Among the measures in Rockwater's balanced scorecard are the following: cash flow and project profitability (financial); safety index and hours spent with customers on new work (internal); project pricing and customer satisfaction (customer); percentage of revenue from new services and number of employee suggestions (innovation and learning).[14]

Review Problems on Standard Costing and Operational Performance Measures

Problem 1

In November the Sousa Division produced 3,000 trumpets and incurred the following actual costs for direct material and direct labor.

Purchased 33,000 pounds of brass at $7.20 per pound.

Used 31,000 pounds of brass at $7.20 per pound.

Used 15,200 hours of direct labor at $22 per hour.

The standard costs for trumpet production were the same in November as those given earlier in the chapter for September.

Compute Sousa Division's direct-material and direct-labor variances for November using the format shown in Exhibits 10–2 and 10–3.

---

[14] Robert S. Kaplan and David P. Norton, "Putting the Balanced Scorecard to Work," *Harvard Business Review 71*, no. 5, pp. 134–47.

Solution to Review Problem 1

Direct-Material Price and Quantity Variances

Actual Material Cost				**Standard Material Cost**	
Actual Quantity $\times$	**Actual Price**	**Actual Quantity** $\times$	**Standard Price**	**Standard Quantity** $\times$	**Standard Price**
33,000 pounds purchased $\times$	$7.20 per pound	33,000 pounds purchased $\times$	$7.00 per pound	30,000 pounds allowed $\times$	$7.00 per pound
$237,600		$231,000		$210,000	

$6,600 Unfavorable

Direct-material price variance

		31,000 pounds used $\times$	$7.00 per pound		
		$217,000			

$7,000 Unfavorable

Direct-material quantity variance

Using Formulas

$$\text{Direct-material price variance} = PQ(AP - SP)$$
$$= 33{,}000(\$7.20 - \$7.00)$$
$$= \$6{,}600 \text{ Unfavorable}$$

$$\text{Direct-material quantity variance} = SP(AQ - SQ)$$
$$= \$7.00(31{,}000 - 30{,}000)$$
$$= \$7{,}000 \text{ Unfavorable}$$

Direct-Labor Rate and Efficiency Variances

Actual Labor Cost				**Standard Labor Cost**	
Actual Hours $\times$	**Actual Rate**	**Actual Hours** $\times$	**Standard Rate**	**Standard Hours** $\times$	**Standard Rate**
15,200 hours used $\times$	$22 per hour	15,200 hours used $\times$	$20 per hour	15,000 hours allowed $\times$	$20 per hour
$334,400		$304,000		$300,000	

$30,400 Unfavorable $4,000 Unfavorable

Direct-labor rate variance   Direct-labor efficiency variance

Using Formulas

$$\text{Direct-labor rate variance} = AH(AR - SR)$$
$$= 15{,}200(\$22 - \$20)$$
$$= \$30{,}400 \text{ Unfavorable}$$

$$\text{Direct-labor efficiency variance} = SR(AH - SH)$$
$$= \$20(15{,}200 - 15{,}000)$$
$$= \$4{,}000 \text{ Unfavorable}$$

Problem 2

Tuscarora Door Company manufactures high-quality wooden doors used in home construction. The following information pertains to operations during April.

Processing time (average per batch)	6 hours
Inspection time (average per batch)	1 hour
Waiting time (average per batch)	4 hours
Move time (average per batch)	5 hours
Units per batch	40 units

Compute the following operational measures: (1) average value-added time per batch; (2) average non-value-added time per batch; (3) manufacturing cycle efficiency; (4) manufacturing cycle time; (5) velocity.

Solution to Review Problem 2

1. Average value-added time per batch = Processing time = 6 hours
2. Average non-value-added time per batch = Inspection time + Waiting time + Move time
$$= 10 \text{ hours}$$

3. Manufacturing cycle efficiency $= \dfrac{\text{Processing time}}{\text{Processing time} + \text{Inspection time} + \text{Waiting time} + \text{Move time}}$

$$= \dfrac{6 \text{ hours}}{6 \text{ hours} + 1 \text{ hour} + 4 \text{ hours} + 5 \text{ hours}} = 37.5\%$$

4. Manufacturing cycle time $= \dfrac{\text{Total production time per batch}}{\text{Units per batch}}$

$$= \dfrac{16 \text{ hours}}{40 \text{ units per batch}} = .4 \text{ hours (or 24 minutes) per unit}$$

5. Velocity $= \dfrac{\text{Units per batch}}{\text{Total production time per batch}}$

$$= \dfrac{40 \text{ units}}{16 \text{ hours}} = 2.5 \text{ units per hour}$$

Key Terms

For each term's definition refer to the indicated page, or turn to the glossary at the end of the text.

aggregate (or total) productivity, pg. 416

benchmarking, pg. 413

controllability, pg. 404

cost variance, pg. 394

customer-acceptance measures, pg. 415

delivery cycle time, pg. 415

direct-labor efficiency variance, pg. 401

direct-labor rate variance, pg. 401

direct-material price variance (or purchase price variance), pg. 399

direct-material quantity variance, pg. 399

gain-sharing plan, pg. 417

in-process quality controls, pg. 415

management by exception, pg. 394

manufacturing cycle efficiency (MCE), pg. 416

manufacturing cycle time, pg. 415

partial (or component) productivity, pg. 416

perfection (or ideal) standard, pg. 396

practical (or attainable) standard, pg. 396

standard cost, pg. 394

standard-costing system, pg. 408

standard direct-labor quantity, pg. 398

standard direct-labor rate, pg. 398

standard direct-material price, pg. 398

standard direct-material quantity, pg. 398

statistical control chart, pg. 404

task analysis, pg. 395

velocity, pg. 416

Review Questions

10–1. List the three parts of a control system, and explain how such a system works.

10–2. What is meant by the phrase *management by exception?*

10–3. Describe two methods of setting standards.

10–4. Distinguish between *perfection* and *practical* standards. Which type of standard is likely to produce the best motivational effects?

10–5. Describe how a bank might use standards.

10–6. Explain how standard material prices and quantities are set.

10–7. What is the interpretation of the *direct-material price variance?*

10–8. What manager is usually in the best position to influence the direct-material price variance?

10–9. What is the interpretation of the *direct-material quantity variance?*

10–10. What manager is usually in the best position to influence the direct-material quantity variance?

10–11. Explain why the quantity purchased (PQ) is used in computing the direct-material price variance, but the actual quantity consumed (AQ) is used in computing the direct-material quantity variance.

10–12. What is the interpretation of the *direct-labor rate variance?* What are some possible causes?

10–13. What manager is generally in the best position to influence the direct-labor rate variance?

10–14. What is the interpretation of the *direct-labor efficiency variance?*

10–15. What manager is generally in the best position to influence the direct-labor efficiency variance?

10–16. Refer to Review Question 10–11. Why does an analogous question *not* arise in the context of the direct-labor variances?

10–17. Describe five factors that managers often consider when determining the significance of a variance.

10–18. Discuss several ways in which standard-costing systems should be adapted in today's manufacturing environment.

10–19. Describe how standard costs are used for product costing.

10–20. List six advantages of a standard-costing system.

10–21. List seven areas in which nonfinancial, operational performance measures are receiving increased emphasis in today's manufacturing environment.

10–22. Define the term *manufacturing cycle efficiency.*

10–23. List four examples of customer acceptance measures.

10–24. What is meant by *aggregate productivity,* and what are its limitations?

10–25. List eight criticisms of standard costing in an advanced manufacturing environment.

10–26. Suggest two performance measures in each of the four balanced scorecard categories for a service industry firm of your choosing.

10–27. Give an example of a gain-sharing plan that could be implemented by an airline.

Exercises

■ **Exercise 10–28**
Straightforward Calculation of Variances
(LO 1, LO 4)

During June, Spencer Company's material purchases amounted to 6,000 pounds at a price of $7.30 per pound. Actual costs incurred in the production of 2,000 units were as follows:

Direct labor:	$116,745 ($18.10 per hour)
Direct material:	$ 30,660 ($ 7.30 per pound)

The standards for one unit of Spencer Company's product are as follows:

Direct labor:	Direct material:
Quantity, 3 hours per unit	Quantity, 2 pounds per unit
Rate, $18 per hour	Price, $7 per pound

Required:

Compute the direct-material price and quantity variances and the direct-labor rate and efficiency variances. Indicate whether each variance is favorable or unfavorable.

■ **Exercise 10–29**
Diagramming Direct-Material and Direct-Labor Variances
(LO 4)

Refer to the data in the preceding exercise. Draw diagrams depicting the direct-material and direct-labor variances similar to the diagrams in Exhibits 10–2 and 10–3.

■ **Exercise 10–30**
Computing Standard Direct-Material Cost
(LO 2)

Cayuga Hardwoods produces handcrafted jewelry boxes. A standard-size box requires 8 board feet of hardwood in the finished product. In addition, 2 board feet of scrap lumber is normally left from the production of one box. Hardwood costs $4.00 per board foot, plus $1.50 in transportation charges per board foot.

Required:

Compute the standard direct-material cost of a jewelry box.

■ **Exercise 10–31**
Cost Variance Investigation
(LO 5)

The controller for Lane and Company uses a statistical control chart to help management determine when to investigate variances. The critical value is 1 standard deviation. The company incurred the following direct-labor efficiency variances during the first six months of the current year.

January	$250 F	April	$ 900 U
February	800 U	May	1,050 U
March	700 U	June	1,200 U

The standard direct-labor cost during each of these months was $19,000. The controller has estimated that the firm's monthly direct-labor variances have a standard deviation of $950.

Required:

1. Draw a statistical control chart and plot the variance data given above. Which variances will be investigated?
2. Suppose the controller's rule of thumb is to investigate all variances equal to or greater than 6 percent of standard cost. Then which variances will be investigated?
3. Would you investigate any of the variances listed above other than those indicated by the rules discussed in requirements (1) and (2)? Why?

Athena Can Company manufactures recyclable soft-drink cans. A unit of production is a case of 12 dozen cans. The following standards have been set by the production-engineering staff and the controller.

Direct labor:	Direct material:
Quantity, .25 hour	Quantity, 4 kilograms
Rate, $16 per hour	Price, $.80 per kilogram

Actual material purchases amounted to 240,000 kilograms at $.81 per kilogram. Actual costs incurred in the production of 50,000 units were as follows:

Direct labor:	$211,900 for 13,000 hours
Direct material:	$170,100 for 210,000 kilograms

Required:

Use the variance formulas to compute the direct-material price and quantity variances and the direct-labor rate and efficiency variances. Indicate whether each variance is favorable or unfavorable.

■ **Exercise 10–32**
Straightforward
Computation of Variances
(LO 1, LO 4)

Refer to the data in the preceding exercise. Use diagrams similar to those in Exhibits 10–2 and 10–3 to determine the direct-material and direct-labor variances. Indicate whether each variance is favorable or unfavorable.

■ **Exercise 10–33**
Determination of Variances
Using Diagrams
(LO 4)

Refer to the data in Exercise 10–32. Prepare journal entries to:

1. Record the purchase of direct material on account.
2. Add direct-material and direct-labor cost to Work-in-Process Inventory.
3. Record the direct-material and direct-labor variances.
4. Close these variances into Cost of Goods Sold.

■ **Exercise 10–34**
Journal Entries under
Standard Costing
(LO 7, LO 8)

Refer to your answer for Exercise 10–34. Set up T-accounts, and post the journal entries to the general ledger.

■ **Exercise 10–35**
Posting Journal Entries for
Variances
(LO 7, LO 8)

Due to evaporation during production, Portsmouth Plastics Company requires 8 pounds of material input for every 7 pounds of good plastic sheets manufactured. During May, the company produced 4,200 pounds of good sheets.

■ **Exercise 10–36**
Standard Allowed Input
(LO 2)

Required:

Compute the total standard allowed input quantity, given the good output produced.

Part of your company's accounting database was destroyed when Godzilla attacked the city. You have been able to gather the following data from your files. Reconstruct the remaining information using the available data. All of the raw material purchased during the period was used in production. (Hint: It is helpful to solve for the unknowns in the order indicated by the letters in the following table.)

■ **Exercise 10–37**
Reconstructing Standard-
Cost Information from
Partial Data
(LO 1, LO 4)

	Direct Labor	Direct Material
Standard price or rate per unit of input	e	$8 per pound
Standard quantity per unit of output	f	c
Actual quantity used per unit of output	3.5 hours	a
Actual price or rate per unit of input	$21 per hour	$7 per pound
Actual output	10,000 units	10,000 units
Direct-material price variance	—	$30,000 F
Direct-material quantity variance	—	b
Total of direct-material variances	—	$10,000 F
Direct-labor rate variance	d	—
Direct-labor efficiency variance	$100,000 F	—
Total of direct-labor variances	$ 65,000 F	—

■ **Exercise 10–38**
Operational Performance
Measures; JIT/FMS Setting
(LO 11)

Hiawatha Hydrant Company manufactures fire hydrants in Oswego, New York. The following information pertains to operations during May.

Processing time (average per batch)	8.5 hours
Inspection time (average per batch)	.5 hour
Waiting time (average per batch)	.5 hour
Move time (average per batch)	.5 hour
Units per batch	20 units

Required:

Compute the following operational measures: (1) manufacturing cycle efficiency; (2) manufacturing cycle time; (3) velocity.

■ **Exercise 10–39**
Productivity Measurement
(LO 11)

Managerial accounting procedures developed for the manufacturing industry often are applied in non-manufacturing settings also. Ontario Bank and Trust Company's total output of financial services during the year just ended was valued at $10 million. The total cost of the firm's inputs, primarily direct labor and overhead, was $8 million.

Required:

1. Compute Ontario's aggregate (or total) productivity for the year.
2. Do you believe this is a useful measure? Why? Suggest an alternative approach that Ontario Bank and Trust might use to measure productivity.

■ **Exercise 10–40**
Performance Measures for
Production and Delivery
(LO 11)

Data Screen Corporation is a highly automated manufacturing firm. The vice president of finance has decided that traditional standards are inappropriate for performance measures in an automated environment. Labor is insignificant in terms of the total cost of production and tends to be fixed, material quality is considered more important than minimizing material cost, and customer satisfaction is the number one priority. As a result, production and delivery performance measures have been chosen to evaluate performance. The following information is considered typical of the time involved to complete and ship orders.

Waiting time:	
From order being placed to start of production	8.0 days
From start of production to completion	7.0 days
Inspection time	1.5 days
Processing time	3.0 days
Move time	2.5 days

Required:

1. Calculate the manufacturing cycle efficiency.
2. Calculate the delivery cycle time.

(CMA, adapted)

Problems

Scorpio Corporation has established the following standards for the prime costs of one unit of its chief product, dartboards.

	Standard Quantity	Standard Price or Rate	Standard Cost
Direct material	8 pounds	$1.75 per pound	$14.00
Direct labor	.25 hour	$8.00 per hour	2.00
Total			$16.00

During May, Scorpio purchased 160,000 pounds of direct material at a total cost of $304,000. The total wages for May were $42,000, 90 percent of which were for direct labor. Scorpio manufactured 19,000 dartboards during May, using 142,500 pounds of direct material and 5,000 direct-labor hours.

Required:

Compute the following variances for May, and indicate whether each is favorable or unfavorable.

1. The direct-material price variance.
2. The direct-material quantity variance.
3. The direct-labor rate variance.
4. The direct-labor efficiency variance.

(CMA, adapted)

■ **Problem 10–41** ✔
Direct-Material and Direct-Labor Variances
(LO 1, LO 4)

During July Libra Fabrics Corporation manufactured 500 units of a special multilayer fabric with the trade name Stylex. The following information from the Stylex production department also pertains to July.

Direct material purchased: 18,000 yards at $1.38 per yard $24,840
Direct material used: 9,500 yards at $1.38 per yard 13,110
Direct labor: 2,100 hours at $9.15 per hour 19,215

The standard prime costs for one unit of Stylex are as follows:

Direct materials: 20 yards at $1.35 per yard $27
Direct labor: 4 hours at $9.00 per hour 36
Total standard prime cost per unit of output $63

Required:

Compute the following variances for the month of July, indicating whether each variance is favorable or unfavorable.

1. Direct-material price variance.
2. Direct-material quantity variance.
3. Direct-labor rate variance.
4. Direct-labor efficiency variance.

(CPA, adapted)

■ **Problem 10–42** ✔
Direct-Material and Direct-Labor Variances
(LO 1, LO 4)

Allegheny Chemical Company manufactures industrial chemicals. The company plans to introduce a new chemical solution and needs to develop a standard product cost. The new chemical solution is made by combining a chemical compound (nyclyn) and a solution (salex), heating the mixture, adding a second compound (protet), and bottling the resulting solution in 10-liter containers. The initial mix, which is 11 liters in volume, consists of 12 kilograms of nyclyn and 9.6 liters of salex. A 1-liter reduction in volume occurs during the boiling process. The solution is cooled slightly before 5 kilograms of protet are added. The addition of protet does not affect the total liquid volume.

The purchase price of the direct materials used in the manufacture of this new chemical solution are as follows:

■ **Problem 10–43**
Determining Standard Material Cost
(LO 2)

Nyclyn	$1.45 per kilogram
Salex	1.80 per liter
Protet	2.40 per kilogram

Required:

Determine the standard material cost of a 10-liter container of the new product.

(CMA, adapted)

■ **Problem 10–44**
Productivity; Standards;
Behavioral Implications
(LO 6, LO 11)

BankTech Corporation manufactures display screens used in automated teller machines (ATM). The company had been profitable until the last few years when foreign competition began to erode BankTech's market share. BankTech's management responded two years ago by implementing controls and systems to achieve lower production costs, improve quality, and shorten delivery times. The company's organizational and reporting structure has been instrumental in accomplishing these overall objectives. Bob Pleshman, manager of manufacturing, and Viola Walters, manager of quality control, report to Paul Bruckman, vice president of production. The production supervisors for each product line report to Pleshman.

These production supervisors have, in the past, received only a listing of the orders to be filled during the month and measured their performance by how many orders they were able to fill. High quality was always stressed, and they all worked together even if it meant some unfilled or reworked orders at the end of the month. Production data received from the floor were primarily used for accounting, financial reports, product pricing, and materials purchasing. Management reports went only to top management and the manager of quality control for scrap performance.

To improve its competitive edge, BankTech developed a new monthly productivity report for each product line that compares the company-established goals for the quantity of material used in production to the amount of actual scrap and the actual number of good units completed. This performance report is presented at a monthly meeting that includes Pleshman, Walters, the production supervisors, and a cost-accounting representative. Initially, the production supervisors were pleased with this system as it gave them an opportunity to participate and make suggestions. However, four months after the productivity measurement system and monthly meetings began, the following conversation occurred among three of the production supervisors.

Richards: I really dislike these monthly meetings. The accounting people present data on last month's production that we have never seen before, and Pleshman expects us to have immediate answers.

Green: It's like an ambush by the enemy. When the accounting people have finished with us, Walters hits us with her data.

Richards: Where do the standards for material usage come from anyway?

Green: I'm not sure. I think the bill of materials has something to do with it.

Richards: But the data they present are in dollars and the bill of materials is in units. And how does the scrap rate data Walters hits us with affect the accounting data? Let's talk to Pleshman about how all this information is assembled.

Green: Do you really want to talk to the boss right now after he just criticized us in the meeting?

Richards: But he criticizes us every month. All the departments are always at least 20 percent below the financial standards. In fact, I consider it a good month when my department performs at 75 percent of standard.

Green: Let's just forget it. At next month's meeting, we can look amazed at the results again, apologize, and say that we will do better next month. That's what we have been doing for the last four months.

Richards: I'm tired of looking bad at every monthly meeting. I'm going to find a way to look good at next month's meeting. Here comes Tilman. I wonder what he thinks.

Tilman: After the meeting, Pleshman gave me the production schedule requirements for my department for the rest of the month. I told him the schedule far exceeded the capability of my department. He told me that he was sure that I could find a way to meet the schedule. I told him that the product specifications had not yet been received from the Quality Control Department for many of the orders that the Sales Department had committed to ship before the end of the month. He just smiled and walked away.

Required:

1. Based upon the conversation among the three production supervisors of BankTech Corporation, discuss the likely motivation and behavior during the coming months of:

   a. The production supervisors.

   b. The employees who work for each of the production supervisors.

2. Based upon the conversation among the three production supervisors of BankTech Corporation, use the following format to:

    a. Identify and explain several weaknesses in BankTech Corporation's productivity measurement system and monthly meetings.

    b. Present a recommendation for correcting each identified weakness.

Identification and Explanation of Weakness	**Recommendation for Correcting Weakness**

(CMA, adapted)

Ohio Valve Company manufactured 7,800 units during January of a control valve used by milk processors in its Cleveland plant. Records indicated the following:

Direct labor	40,100 hr. at $14.60
Direct material purchased	25,000 lb. at $2.60
Direct material used	23,100 lb.

The control valve has the following standard prime costs.

Direct material:	3 lb. at $2.50 per lb.	$ 7.50
Direct labor:	5 hr. at $15.00 per hr.	75.00
Standard prime cost per unit		$82.50

■ **Problem 10–45** ✓
Direct-Material and Direct-Labor Variances
(LO 1, LO 4)

Required:

1. Prepare a schedule of standard production costs for January, based on actual production of 7,800 units.

2. For the month of January, compute the following variances, indicating whether each is favorable or unfavorable.

    a. Direct-material price variance.

    b. Direct-material quantity variance.

    c. Direct-labor rate variance.

    d. Direct-labor efficiency variance.

(CPA, adapted)

Associated Media Graphics (AMG) is a rapidly expanding company involved in the mass reproduction of instructional materials. Ralph Boston, owner and manager of AMG, has made a concentrated effort to provide a quality product at a fair price, with delivery on the promised date. Boston is finding it increasingly difficult to personally supervise the operations of AMG, and he is beginning to institute an organizational structure that would facilitate management control.

    One change recently made was the transfer of control over departmental operations from Boston to each departmental manager. However, the Quality Control Department still reports directly to Boston, as do the Finance and Accounting Departments. A materials manager was hired to purchase all raw materials and to oversee the material-handling (receiving, storage, etc.) and recordkeeping functions. The materials manager also is responsible for maintaining an adequate inventory based on planned production levels.

    The loss of personal control over the operations of AMG caused Boston to look for a method of efficiently evaluating performance. Dave Cress, a new managerial accountant, proposed the use of a standard-costing system. Variances for material and labor could then be calculated and reported directly to Boston.

■ **Problem 10–46**
Setting Standards;
Responsibility for Variances
(LO 2)

Required:

1. Assume that Associated Media Graphics is going to implement a standard-costing system and establish standards for materials and labor. Identify and discuss for each of these cost components:

    a. Who should be involved in setting the standards?

    b. What factors should be considered in establishing the standards?

2. Describe the basis for assignment of responsibility for variances under a standard-costing system.

(CMA, adapted)

■ Problem 10–47
Direct-Labor Variances
(LO 1, LO 4)

The controller for San Juan Instrument Corporation compares each month's actual results with a monthly plan. The standard direct-labor rates for the year just ended and the standard hours allowed, given the actual output in April, are shown in the following schedule.

	Standard Direct-Labor Rate per Hour		Standard Direct-Labor Hours Allowed, Given April Output
Labor class III	$16.00	....	500
Labor class II	14.00	....	500
Labor class I	10.00	....	500

A new union contract negotiated in March resulted in actual wage rates that differed from the standard rates. The actual direct-labor hours worked and the actual direct-labor rates per hour experienced for the month of April were as follows:

	Actual Direct-Labor Rate per Hour		Actual Direct-Labor Hours
Labor class III	$17.20	....	550
Labor class II	15.00	....	650
Labor class I	10.80	....	375

Required:

1. Compute the following variances for April. Indicate whether each is favorable or unfavorable.
   a. Direct-labor rate variance for *each* labor class.
   b. Direct-labor efficiency variance for *each* labor class.
2. Discuss the advantages and disadvantages of a standard-costing system in which the standard direct-labor rates are not changed during the year to reflect such events as a new labor contract.

(CMA, adapted)

■ Problem 10–48
Development of Standard Costs; Ethics
(LO 2, LO 6)

Ogwood Company's Johnstown Division is a small manufacturer of wooden household items. Al Rivkin, divisional controller, plans to implement a standard-costing system. Rivkin has collected information from several coworkers that will assist him in developing standards. One of the Johnstown Division's products is a wooden cutting board. Each cutting board requires 1.25 board feet of lumber and 12 minutes of direct-labor time to prepare and cut the lumber. The cutting boards are inspected after they are cut. Because the cutting boards are made of a natural material that has imperfections, one board is normally rejected for each five that are accepted. Four rubber foot pads are attached to each good cutting board. A total of 15 minutes of direct-labor time is required to attach all four foot pads and finish each cutting board. The lumber for the cutting boards cost $3.00 per board foot, and each foot pad costs $.05. Direct labor is paid at the rate of $8.00 per hour.

Required:

1. Develop the standard cost for direct material and direct labor of a cutting board.
2. Explain the role of each of the following people in developing standards.
   a. Purchasing manager.
   b. Industrial engineer.
   c. Managerial accountant.
3. Assume that Ogwood Company's standard-costing system has been in place for six months. Jack Smith, the purchasing manager, is about to place an order for wood to be used in Ogwood's cutting boards. Smith has found a supplier that will furnish the necessary wood at $2.00 per board foot, rather than the standard cost of $3.00. This is very appealing to Smith, since his annual bonus is influenced by any favorable price variances he is able to obtain. Smith is due to be transferred at the end of the year to Ogwood's Allentown Division, which manufactures metal kitchen utensils. The transfer is a promotion for Smith.

    After further discussions with the potential supplier, Smith realized that the wood being offered would not be well-suited for use in cutting boards. Although the wood would seem fine in the manufacturing process, and it would result in an attractive product, it would not hold up well over time. This particular type of wood, after repeated cycles of getting wet and then drying out, would tend to crack. Smith figured that it would take about a year for the cutting boards to deteriorate, and then Ogwood Company would be beset with customer complaints.

Smith mulled over the situation for awhile and then decided to accept the new supplier's offer. The $2.00 price would help him get a nice annual bonus, which he could use to help with the down payment on a new home. By the time the cutting boards cracked and customers started to complain, he would be long gone. Someone else could worry about the problem then, he reasoned. After all, he thought, people shouldn't expect a cutting board to last forever.

Several weeks later, when the invoice for the first shipment of wood came through, Rivkin noticed the large, favorable price variance. When he ran into Smith on the golf course, Rivkin congratulated Smith on the purchase. The following conversation resulted.

Rivkin: "That was quite a price break on that wood, Jack. How'd you swing it?"

Smith: "Hard-ball negotiating, Al. It's as simple as that."

Rivkin: "Is it good wood? And how about the supplier, Jack? Will they deliver on time?"

Smith: "This supplier is very timely in their deliveries. I made sure of that."

Rivkin: "How about the quality, Jack? Did you check into that?"

Smith: "Sure I did, Al. Hey, what is this? An interrogation? I thought we were here to play golf."

Rivkin was left feeling puzzled and disconcerted by Smith's evasiveness. The next day Rivkin talked to the production manager, Amy Wilcox, about his concerns. Later that day, Wilcox raised the issue with Smith. After a lengthy and sometimes heated exchange, the story came out.

Discuss the ethical issues involved in this scenario.

a. Did the purchasing manager, Jack Smith, act ethically?

b. Did the controller, Al Rivkin, act ethically when he asked Smith about the quality of the wood?

c. Did Rivkin act ethically when he went to the production manager with his concerns?

d. What should the controller do now?

(CMA, adapted)

Aquafloat Corporation manufactures rafts for use in swimming pools. The standard cost for material and labor is $89.20 per raft. This includes 8 kilograms of direct material at a standard cost of $5.00 per kilogram, and 6 hours of direct labor at $8.20 per hour. The following data pertain to November.

■ **Problem 10–49**
Variances; Journal Entries;
Missing Data
(LO 4, LO 7, LO 8)

- Work-in-process inventory on November 1: none.
- Work-in-process inventory on November 30: 800 units (75 percent complete as to labor; material is issued at the beginning of processing).
- Units completed: 5,600 units.
- Purchases of materials: 50,000 kilograms for $249,250.
- Total actual labor costs: $300,760.
- Actual hours of labor: 36,500 hours.
- Direct-material quantity variance: $1,500 unfavorable.

Required:

1. Compute the following amounts. Indicate whether each variance is favorable or unfavorable.
   a. Direct-labor rate variance for November.
   b. Direct-labor efficiency variance for November.
   c. Actual kilograms of material used in the production process during November.
   d. Actual price paid per kilogram of direct material in November.
   e. Total amounts of direct-material and direct-labor cost transferred to Finished-Goods Inventory during November.
   f. The total amount of direct-material and direct-labor cost in the ending balance of Work-in-Process Inventory at the end of November.

2. Prepare journal entries to record the following:
   - Purchase of raw material.
   - Adding direct material to Work-in-Process Inventory.
   - Adding direct labor to Work-in-Process Inventory.
   - Recording of variances.

(CMA, adapted)

■ **Problem 10–50**
Development of Standard
Costs; Causes of Variances;
Ethics
(LO 2, LO 6)

ColdKing Company is a small producer of fruit-flavored frozen desserts. For many years, ColdKing's products have had strong regional sales on the basis of brand recognition. However, other companies have begun marketing similar products in the area, and price competition has become increasingly important. John Wakefield, the company's controller, is planning to implement a standard costing system for ColdKing and has gathered considerable information on production and material requirements for ColdKing's products. Wakefield believes that the use of standard costing will allow ColdKing to improve cost control and make better pricing decisions.

ColdKing's most popular product is raspberry sherbet. The sherbet is produced in 10-gallon batches, and each batch requires six quarts of good raspberries. The fresh raspberries are sorted by hand before entering the production process. Because of imperfections in the raspberries and normal spoilage, one quart of berries is discarded for every four quarts of acceptable berries. Three minutes is the standard direct-labor time for sorting that is required to obtain one quart of acceptable raspberries. The acceptable raspberries are then blended with the other ingredients; blending requires 12 minutes of direct-labor time per batch. After blending, the sherbet is packaged in quart containers. Wakefield has gathered the following information from Teresa Adams, ColdKing's cost accountant.

- ColdKing purchases raspberries at a cost of $.80 per quart. All other ingredients cost a total of $.45 per gallon.
- Direct labor is paid at the rate of $9.00 per hour.
- The total cost of material and labor required to package the sherbet is $.38 per quart.

Adams has a friend who owns a berry farm that has been losing money in recent years. Because of good crops, there has been an oversupply of raspberries, and prices have dropped to $.50 per quart. Adams has arranged for ColdKing to purchase raspberries from her friend and hopes that $.80 per quart will help her friend's farm become profitable again.

Required:

1. Develop the standard cost of direct material, direct labor, and packaging for a 10-gallon batch of raspberry sherbet.
2. As part of the implementation of a standard-costing system at ColdKing, John Wakefield plans to train those responsible for maintaining the standards in the use of variance analysis. Wakefield is particularly concerned with the causes of unfavorable variances.
   a. Discuss the possible causes of unfavorable material price variances and identify the individual(s) who should be held responsible for these variances.
   b. Discuss the possible causes of unfavorable labor efficiency variances and identify the individual(s) who should be held responsible for these variances.
3. Citing the specific ethical standards of competence, confidentiality, integrity, and objectivity for management accountants, explain why Adams' behavior regarding the cost information provided to Wakefield is unethical.

(CMA, adapted)

■ **Problem 10–51**
Direct-Material Variances
(LO 1, LO 4)

Campco, Inc. has established the following direct-material standards for its two products.

	Standard Quantity	Standard Price
Standard camping tent	12 pounds	$6 per pound
Deluxe backpacking tent	6 pounds	$8 per pound

During March, the company purchased 2,100 pounds of tent fabric for its standard model at a cost of $13,440. The actual March production of the standard tent was 100 tents, and 1,250 pounds of fabric were used. Also during March, the company purchased 800 pounds of tent fabric for its deluxe backpacking tent at a cost of $6,320. The firm used 720 pounds of the fabric during March in the production of 120 deluxe tents.

Required:

1. Compute the direct-material price variance and quantity variance for March.
2. Prepare journal entries to record the purchase of material, use of material, and incurrence of variances in March.

McKeag and Sons, Inc. manufactures agricultural machinery. At a recent staff meeting, the following direct-labor variance report for the year just ended was presented by the controller.

■ **Problem 10–52**
Investigating Cost Variances
(LO 5)

McKEAG AND SONS, INC.
Direct-Labor Variance Report

	Direct-Labor Rate Variance			Direct-Labor Efficiency Variance	
	Amount	**Standard Cost, %**		**Amount**	**Standard Cost, %**
January	$ 800 F	.16%		$ 5,000 U	1.00%
February	4,900 F	.98%		7,500 U	1.50%
March	100 U	.02%		9,700 U	1.94%
April	2,000 U	.40%		12,800 U	2.56%
May	3,800 F	.76%		20,100 U	4.02%
June	3,900 F	.78%		17,000 U	3.40%
July	4,200 F	.84%		28,500 U	5.70%
August	5,100 F	1.02%		38,000 U	7.60%
September	4,800 F	.96%		37,000 U	7.40%
October	5,700 F	1.14%		42,000 U	8.40%
November	4,200 F	.84%		60,000 U	12.00%
December	4,300 F	.86%		52,000 U	10.40%

McKeag and Sons' controller uses the following rule of thumb: Investigate all variances equal to or greater than $30,000, which is 6 percent of standard cost.

Required:

1. Which variances would have been investigated during the year? (Indicate month and type of variance.)
2. What characteristics of the variance pattern shown in the report should draw the controller's attention, regardless of the usual investigation rule? Explain. Given these considerations, which variances would you have investigated? Why?
3. Is it important to follow up on favorable variances, such as those shown in the report? Why?
4. The controller believes that the firm's direct-labor rate variance has a normal probability distribution with a mean of zero and a standard deviation of $5,000. Prepare a statistical control chart, and plot the company's direct-labor rate variances for each month. The critical value is one standard deviation. Which variances would have been investigated under this approach?

Lakeview Pediatric Hospital in Chicago has adopted a standard-costing system for evaluation and control of nursing labor. Diagnosis Related Groups (DRGs), instituted by the U.S. government for health insurance reimbursement, are used as the output measure in the standard-cost system. A DRG is a patient classification scheme in which inpatient treatment procedures are related to the numbers and types of patient ailments treated. Lakeview Pediatric Hospital has developed standard nursing times for the treatment of each DRG classification, and nursing labor hours are assumed to vary with the number of DRGs treated within a time period.

■ **Problem 10–53**
Labor Variances; Hospital
(LO 1, LO 4)

The nursing unit on the third floor treats patients with four DRG classifications. The unit is staffed with registered nurses (RNs), licensed practical nurses (LPNs), and aides. The standard hourly rates are as follows: RN, $12.00; LPN, $8.00; and aide, $6.00. The standard nursing hours are shown in the following table.

Third Floor Nursing Unit: Standard Hours per Patient

DRG Classification	RN	LPN	Aide
1	6	4	5
2	26	16	10
3	10	5	4
4	12	7	10

For the month of June, the results of operations for the third-floor nursing unit are as follows:

Actual Number of Patients			RN	LPN	Aide
DRG 1	250	Actual hours	8,150	4,300	4,400
DRG 2	90	Actual salary	$100,245	$35,260	$25,300
DRG 3	240	Actual hourly rate	$12.30	$8.20	$5.75
DRG 4	140				
Total	720				

The accountant for Lakeview Pediatric Hospital calculated the following standard times for the third-floor nursing unit for June.

DRG Classification	Number of Patients	Standard Hours per Patient			Total Standard Hours		
		RN	LPN	Aide	RN	LPN	Aide
1	250	6	4	5	1,500	1,000	1,250
2	90	26	16	10	2,340	1,440	900
3	240	10	5	4	2,400	1,200	960
4	140	12	7	10	1,680	980	1,400
Total					7,920	4,620	4,510

The hospital calculates labor variances for each reporting period by labor classification (RN, LPN, Aide). The variances are used by nursing supervisors and hospital administrators to evaluate the performance of nursing labor.

The variances are calculated as follows:

■ A total nursing labor variance equal to the difference between the total actual nursing cost and the total standard nursing cost.

■ A nursing labor efficiency variance, computed as the sum of the efficiency variances across the three types of nursing labor.

■ A nursing labor rate variance, computed as the sum of the rate variances across the three types of nursing labor.

Required:

1. Calculate the hospital's nursing labor variances for June.

2. Comment on the interpretation of the nursing labor efficiency variance. Does this variance tell the whole story about nursing efficiency?

(CMA, adapted)

■ **Problem 10–54**
Production Efficiency Report;
Operational Performance
Measures
(LO 11)

Pittsburgh Plastics Corporation manufactures a range of molded plastic products, such as kitchen utensils and desk accessories. The production process in the North Hills plant is a JIT system, which operates in four FMS cells. An AMHS is used to transport products between production operations. Each month the controller prepares a production efficiency report, which is sent to corporate headquarters. The data compiled in these reports, for the first six months of the year are as follows:

PRODUCTION EFFICIENCY REPORT
Pittsburgh Plastics Corporation
North Hills Plant
January through June

	Jan.	Feb.	Mar.	Apr.	May	June	Average
Overtime hours	60	70	75	80	85	105	79.2
Total setup time	70	70	65	64	62	62	65.5
Cycle time (average in hours)	20	20	19	18	19	17	18.8
Manufacturing-cycle efficiency	95%	94%	96%	90%	89%	90%	92.3%
Percentage of orders filled	100%	100%	100%	100%	100%	100%	100%
Percentage of on-time deliveries	99%	98%	99%	100%	96%	94%	97.7%
Inventory value/sales revenue	5%	5%	5%	4%	5%	5%	4.8%
Number of defective units, finished goods	80	82	75	40	25	22	54

PRODUCTION EFFICIENCY REPORT
Pittsburgh Plastics Corporation
North Hills Plant
January through June

	Jan.	Feb.	Mar.	Apr.	May	June	Average
Number of defective units, in process	10	30	35	40	60	60	39.2
Number of raw-material shipments with defective materials	3	3	2	0	0	0	1.3
Number of products returned	0	0	0	0	0	0	0
Aggregate productivity	1.3	1.3	1.2	1.25	1.2	1.15	1.23
Power consumption (thousands of kilowatt-hours)	800	795	802	801	800	800	800
Machine downtime (hours)	30	25	25	20	20	10	21.7
Bottleneck machine downtime	0	0	2	0	15	2	3.2
Number of unscheduled machine maintenance calls	0	0	1	0	2	3	1

Required:

1. Write a memo to the company president evaluating the North Hills plant's performance. Structure your report by dividing it into the following parts: (*a*) production processing and productivity, (*b*) product quality and customer acceptance, (*c*) delivery performance, (*d*) raw material, scrap, and inventory, and (*e*) machine maintenance.

2. If you identify any areas of concern in your memo, indicate an appropriate action for management.

Springsteen Company manufactures guitars. The company uses a standard, job-order cost-accounting system in two production departments. In the Construction Department the wooden guitars are built by highly skilled craftsmen and coated with several layers of lacquer. Then the units are transferred to the Finishing Department, where the bridge of the guitar is attached and the strings are installed. The guitars also are tuned and inspected in the Finishing Department. The diagram below depicts the production process.

■ **Problem 10–55**
Comprehensive Problem on Variance Analysis
(LO 1, LO 4)

Each finished guitar contains seven pounds of veneered wood. In addition, one pound of wood is typically wasted in the production process. The veneered wood used in the guitars has a standard price of $12 per pound. The other parts needed to complete each guitar, such as the bridge and strings, cost $15 per guitar. The labor standards for Springsteen's two production departments are as follows:

Construction Department: 6 hours of direct labor at $20 per hour

Finishing Department: 3 hours of direct labor at $15 per hour

The following pertains to the month of July.

1. There were no beginning or ending work-in-process inventories in either production department.
2. There was no beginning finished-goods inventory.
3. Actual production was 500 guitars, and 300 guitars were sold on account for $400 each.
4. The company purchased 6,000 pounds of veneered wood at a price of $12.50 per pound.
5. Actual usage of veneered wood was 4,500 pounds.
6. Enough parts (bridges and strings) to finish 600 guitars were purchased at a cost of $9,000.
7. The Construction Department used 2,850 direct-labor hours. The total direct-labor cost in the Construction Department was $54,150.
8. The Finishing Department used 1,570 direct-labor hours. The total direct-labor cost in that department was $25,120.
9. There were no direct-material variances in the Finishing Department.

Required:

1. Prepare a schedule that computes the standard costs of direct material and direct labor in each production department.

2. Prepare three exhibits which compute the July direct-material and direct-labor variances in the Construction Department and the July direct-labor variances in the Finishing Department. (Refer to Exhibits 10–2 and 10–3 for guidance.)

3. Prepare a cost variance report for July similar to that shown in Exhibit 10–4.

■ **Problem 10–56**
Journal Entries under
Standard Costing;
Continuation of Preceding
Problem
(LO 7, LO 8)

Refer to the preceding problem.

Required:

1. Prepare journal entries to record all of the events listed for Springsteen Company during July. Specifically, these journal entries should reflect the following events.

   a. Purchase of direct material

   b. Use of direct material

   c. Incurrence of direct-labor costs

   d. Addition of production costs to the Work-in-Process Inventory account for each department

   e. Incurrence of all variances

   f. Completion of 500 guitars

   g. Sale of 300 guitars

   h. Closing of all variance accounts into Cost of Goods Sold

2. Draw T-accounts, and post the journal entries prepared in requirement (1). Assume the beginning balance in all accounts is zero.

■ **Problem 10–57**
Manufacturing Performance
Measurement
(LO 11)

Medical Systems Corporation manufactures diagnostic testing equipment used in hospitals. The company practices JIT production management and has a state-of-the-art manufacturing system, including an FMS and an AMHS. The following nonfinancial data were collected biweekly in the Harrisburg plant during the first quarter of the current year.

	Biweekly Measurement Period					
	1	2	3	4	5	6
Cycle time (days)	1.5	1.3	1.3	1.2	1.2	1.1
Number of defective finished products	4	4	3	4	3	3
Manufacturing-cycle efficiency	94%	94%	96%	96%	97%	96%
Customer complaints	6	7	6	5	7	8
Unresolved complaints	2	1	0	0	0	0
Products returned	3	3	2	2	1	1
Warranty claims	2	2	2	0	1	0
In-process products rejected	5	5	7	9	10	10
Aggregate productivity	1.5	1.5	1.5	1.5	1.4	1.5
Number of units produced per day per employee	410	405	412	415	415	420
Percentage of on-time deliveries	94%	95%	95%	97%	100%	100%
Percentage of orders filled	100%	100%	100%	98%	100%	100%
Inventory value/sales revenue	2%	2%	2%	1.5%	2%	1.5%
Machine downtime (minutes)	80	80	120	80	70	75
Bottleneck machine downtime (minutes)	25	20	15	0	60	10
Overtime (minutes) per employee	20	0	0	10	20	10
Average setup time (minutes)	120	120	115	112	108	101

Required:

1. For each nonfinancial performance measure, indicate which of the following areas of manufacturing performance is involved: (*a*) production processing, (*b*) product quality, (*c*) customer acceptance, (*d*) in-process quality control, (*e*) productivity, (*f*) delivery performance, (*g*) raw material and scrap, (*h*) inventory, (*i*) machine maintenance. Some measures may relate to more than one area.

2. Write a memo to management commenting on the performance data collected for the Harrisburg plant. Be sure to note any trends or other important results you see in the data. Evaluate the Harrisburg plant in each of the areas listed in requirement (1).

MedLine Equipment Corporation specializes in the manufacture of medical equipment, a field that has become increasingly competitive. Approximately two years ago, Ben Harrington, president of MedLine, became concerned that the company's bonus plan, which focused on division profitability, was not helping MedLine remain competitive. Harrington decided to implement a gain-sharing plan that would encourage employees to focus on operational areas that were important to customers and that added value without increasing cost. In addition to a profitability incentive, the revised plan also includes incentives for reduced rework costs, reduced sales returns, and on-time deliveries. Bonuses are calculated and awarded semiannually on the following basis. The bonuses are distributed among the relevant employees according to a formula developed by the division manager.

■ **Problem 10–58**
Gain-Sharing; Operational Performance Measures; Cost Reduction
(LO 6, LO 11)

- Profitability: Two percent of operating income.
- Rework: Costs in excess of 2 percent of operating income are deducted from the bonus amount.
- On-time delivery: $5,000 if over 98 percent of deliveries are on time, $2,000 if 96 to 98 percent of deliveries are on time, and no increment if on-time deliveries are below 96 percent.
- Sales returns: $3,000 if returns are less than 1.5 percent of sales. Fifty percent of any amount in excess of 1.5 percent of sales is deducted from the bonus amount.
- *Note:* If the calculation of the bonus results in a negative amount for a particular period, there is no bonus, and the negative amount is not carried forward to the next period.

The revised bonus plan was implemented on January 1, 20x0. Presented in the following table are the results for two of Medline's divisions, Charter and Mesa Divisions, for the first year under the new bonus plan. Both of these divisions had similar sales and operating income results for the prior year, when the old bonus plan was in effect. Based on the 19x9 results, the employees of the Charter Division earned a bonus of $27,060 while the employees of the Mesa Division earned $22,440.

	Charter Division		Mesa Division	
	January 20x0– June 20x0	July 20x0– December 20x0	January 20x0– June 20x0	July 20x0– December 20x0
Sales	$4,200,000	$4,400,000	$2,850,000	$2,900,000
Operating income	$462,000	$440,000	$342,000	$406,000
On-time delivery	95.4%	97.3%	98.2%	94.6%
Rework costs	$11,500	$11,000	$6,000	$8,000
Sales returns	$84,000	$70,000	$44,750	$42,500

Required:

1. For the Charter Division:
   a. Compute the semiannual installments and total bonus awarded for 20x0.
   b. Discuss the likely behavior of the Charter Division employees under the revised bonus plan.
2. For the Mesa Division:
   a. Compute the semiannual installments and total bonus awarded for 20x0.
   b. Discuss the likely behavior of the Mesa Division employees under the revised bonus plan.
3. Citing specific examples, evaluate whether or not Harrington's revisions to the bonus plan at MedLine Equipment Corporation have achieved the desired results, and recommend any changes that might improve the plan.

(CMA, adapted)

Cases

Trend Setter Fashions, Inc. manufactures women's blouses of one quality, which are produced in lots to fill each special order. Its customers are department stores in various cities. Trend Setter sews the particular stores' labels on the blouses. During November the company worked on three orders, for which the month's job-cost records disclose the following data.

■ **Case 10–59**
Direct-Material and Direct-Labor Variances; Job-Order Costing; Journal Entries
(LO 1, LO 4, LO 7, LO 8)

Lot Number		Boxes in Lot		Material Used (yards)		Hours Worked
22	....	1,000	....	24,100	....	2,980
23	....	1,700	....	40,440	....	5,130
24	....	1,200	....	28,825	....	2,890

The following additional information is available:

1. The firm purchased 95,000 yards of material during November at a cost of $106,400.

2. Direct labor during November amounted to $165,000. According to payroll records, production employees were paid $15.00 per hour.

3. There was no work in process on November 1. During November, lots 22 and 23 were completed. All material was issued for lot 24, which was 80 percent completed as to direct labor.

4. The standard costs for a box of six blouses are as follows:

Direct material .... 24 yards at $1.10	$ 26.40
Direct labor .... 3 hours at $14.70	44.10
Manufacturing overhead .... 3 hours at $12.00	36.00
Standard cost per box	$106.50

Required:

1. Prepare a schedule computing the standard cost of lots 22, 23, and 24 for November.

2. Prepare a schedule showing, for each lot produced during November:

   a. Direct-material price variance.

   b. Direct-material quantity variance.

   c. Direct-labor efficiency variance.

   d. Direct-labor rate variance.

   Indicate whether each variance is favorable or unfavorable.

3. Prepare journal entries to record each of the following events for Trend Setter Fashions.

   ■ Purchase of material.

   ■ Incurrence of direct-labor cost.

   ■ Addition of direct-material and direct-labor cost to Work-in-Process Inventory.

   ■ Recording of direct-material and direct-labor variances.

(CPA, adapted)

■ **Case 10–60**
Missing Data; Variances,
Ledger Accounts
(LO 1, LO 4)

MacGyver Corporation manufactures a product called Miracle Goo, which comes in handy for just about anything. The thick tarry substance is sold in six-gallon drums. Two raw materials are used; these are referred to by people in the business as A and B. Two types of labor are required also. These are mixers (labor class I) and packers (labor class II). You were recently hired by the company president, Pete Thorn, to be the controller. You soon learned that MacGyver uses a standard-costing system. Variances are computed and closed into Cost of Goods Sold monthly. After your first month on the job. you gathered the necessary data to compute the month's variances for direct material and direct labor. You finished everything up by 5:00 P.M. on the 31st, including the credit to Cost of Goods Sold for the sum of the variances. You decided to take all your notes home to review them prior to your formal presentation to Thorn first thing in the morning. As an afterthought, you grabbed a drum of Miracle Goo as well, thinking it could prove useful in some unanticipated way.

You spent the evening boning up on the data for your report and were ready to call it a night. As luck would have it though, you knocked over the Miracle Goo as you rose from the kitchen table. The stuff splattered everywhere, and, most unfortunately, obliterated most of your notes. All that remained legible is the following information.

Cost of Goods Sold	
143,000	
	1,510

Accounts Payable	
	1,500 Beg. Bal.
70,000	73,200
	4,700 End. bal

Other assorted data gleaned from your notes:

- The standards for each drum of Miracle Goo include 10 pounds of material A at a standard price of $5 per pound.
- The standard cost of material B is $15 for each drum of Miracle Goo.
- Purchases of material A were 12,000 pounds at $4.50 per pound.
- Given the actual output for the month, the standard allowed quantity of material A was 10,000 pounds. The standard allowed quantity of material B was 5,000 gallons.
- Although 6,000 gallons of B were purchased, only 4,800 gallons were used.
- The standard wage rate for mixers is $15 per hour. The standard labor cost per drum of product for mixers is $30 per drum.
- The standards allow 4 hours of direct labor II (packers) per drum of Miracle Goo. The standard labor cost per drum of product for packers is $48 per drum.
- Packers were paid $11.90 per hour during the month.

You happened to remember two additional facts. There were no beginning or ending inventories of either work in process or finished goods for the month. The increase in accounts payable relates to direct-material purchases only.

Required:

Now you've got a major problem. Somehow you've got to reconstruct all the missing data in order to be ready for your meeting with the president. You start by making the following list of the facts you want to use in your presentation. Before getting down to business, you need a brief walk to clear your head. Out to the trash you go, and toss the remaining Miracle Goo.

1. Actual output (in drums): _____

2. Direct material:

	A	B
a. Standard quantity per drum:	_____	_____
b. Standard price:	_____	_____
c. Standard cost per drum:	_____	_____
d. Standard quantity allowed, given actual output:	_____	_____
e. Actual quantity purchased:	_____	_____
f. Actual price:	_____	_____
g. Actual quantity used:	_____	_____
h. Price variance:	_____	_____
i. Quantity variance:	_____	_____

3. Direct labor:

	I (mixers)	II (packers)
a. Standard hours per drum:	_____	_____
b. Standard rate per hour:	_____	_____
c. Standard cost per drum:	_____	_____
d. Standard quantity allowed, given actual output:	_____	_____
e. Actual rate per hour:	_____	_____
f. Actual hours:	_____	_____
g. Rate variance:	_____	_____
h. Efficiency variance:	_____	_____

4. Total of all variances for the month: _____

Fill in the missing amounts in the list, using the available facts.

Current Issues in Managerial Accounting

■ **Issue 10–61**
Operational Control Measures in Today's Manufacturing Environment; The Balanced Scorecard

"JIT and the Balanced Scorecard: Linking Manufacturing Control to Management Control," *Management Accounting,* **September 1997, Douglas Clinton and Hsu Ko-Cheng.**

Overview

This article explains how just-in-time (JIT) processes and the balanced scorecard can be linked such that the overall effectiveness of both systems is enhanced.

Suggested Discussion Questions

Discuss how implementation of a balanced scorecard would be influenced by its environment. What factors should management consider when it implements a balanced scorecard in a JIT environment? Explain how standards and performance measures would be affected in this environment.

■ **Issue 10–62**
Controlling Costs; Setting Standards

"7-Eleven Operators Resist System to Monitor Managers," *The Wall Street Journal,* **June 16, 1997, Jon Shirouzu Bigness.**

Overview

A Japanese businessman who owns several 7-Eleven convenience stores in Japan has installed a point-of-sale (POS) computer system that allows him to track all stores' sales at the time of the sales. The system, which can be used to monitor many aspects of the stores' operations, may be installed in U.S. stores.

Suggested Discussion Questions

Discuss how the POS system could be used to control costs and analyze performance. How would you integrate it with a standard-costing system? How should standards be set? Which standards are the most important?

■ **Issue 10–63**
Use of Standards by Nonmanufacturing Organizations

"At UPS, Part-Time Work Is a Full-Time Issue," *Business Week,* **June 16, 1997.**

Overview

UPS is the most profitable firm in its industry. The firm minimizes labor costs by hiring part-time workers. However, part-time turnover rates are very high.

Suggested Discussion Questions

UPS has many different types of performance standards for its employees including expected walking rate. Should UPS use different standards for its part-time staff? According to the article, its annual turnover rate is 400 percent for its part-time staff. How would this influence the firm's standard-costing system?

■ **Issue 10–64**
The Balanced Scorecard

"Ask and It Shall Be Discounted," *Business Week,* **October 6, 1997.**

Overview

Buyers increasingly are being offered nonprice concessions to encourage purchases. Such concessions include delivery, quality, and upgrade guarantees.

Suggested Discussion Questions

How would a standard-costing system affect non-price-related purchase incentives, such as on-time delivery and quality guarantees? How could a balanced-scorecard measurement system be linked to these incentives?

■ **Issue 10–65**
Standard Costs and Product Costing

"Managing Complexity through Performance Measurement," *Management Accounting,* **August 1996, Frank Gonsalves and Robert Eiler.**

Overview

This article explains how complexity drives costs. It also provides suggestions concerning ways firms can monitor and manage processes so that complexity can be eliminated.

Suggested Discussion Questions

Form a change-management consulting group. As a group, list factors that drive complexity. Suggest ways that complexity and the cost of complexity can be measured. Design measures that can monitor and manage complexity. Compare your solution with that from another management consulting team. On what issues could you agree? Disagree?

"How Effective Is Your Performance Measrurement System," *Management Accounting,* **August 1995, Michael Vitale and Sarah Mavrinac.**

Overview

This article outlines seven warning signs that indicate a firm's performance measurement system needs to be updated.

Suggested Discussion Questions

Listed below are seven warning signs of a faulty performance measurement system. Next to each warning sign provide an explanation of why this outcome is observed. Also, provide a potential solution to the problem. Present your results to the class.

Warning Sign	Explanation	Solution
1. Performance is acceptable on all dimensions except profit.		
2. Customers don't buy even when prices are competitive.		
3. No one notices when performance reports aren't provided.		
4. Managers spend significant time debating the meaning of the performance measures.		
5. Share prices are lethargic despite solid financial performance.		
6. You haven't changed your measures in a long time.		
7. You've recently changed your corporate strategy.		

■ **Issue 10–66**
Significance of Cost Variances

"Efficient UPS Tries to Increase Efficiency," *The Wall Street Journal,* **May 24, 1995, Robert Frank.**

Overview

UPS announced that it plans to increase quality and cut costs despite having increasing revenues and profits.

Suggested Discussion Questions

Discuss what factors influenced UPS's decision to cut costs. The article contains charts showing steadily increasing revenues and profits. What other financial measures would you like to have seen reported? What are possible long-term effects of a continual cost-cutting program?

■ **Issue 10–67**
Use of Standards by Nonmanufacturing Organizations

Chapter Eleven

Flexible Budgeting and Overhead Cost Control

After completing this chapter, you should be able to:

1   Distinguish between static and flexible budgets, and explain the advantages of a flexible overhead budget.

2   Prepare a flexible overhead budget, using both a formula and a columnar format.

3   Explain how overhead is applied to Work-in-Process Inventory under standard costing.

4   Explain some important issues in choosing an activity measure for overhead budgeting and application.

5   Compute and interpret the variable-overhead spending and efficiency variances and the fixed-overhead budget and volume variances.

6   Prepare an overhead cost performance report.

7   Prepare journal entries to record manufacturing overhead under standard costing.

8   Explain how an activity-based flexible budget differs from a conventional flexible budget.

9   After studying the appendix, compute and interpret the sales-price and sales-volume variances.

Sousa
DIVISION

SOUSA DIVISION BRINGS HOME CONTRACT TO SUPPLY JAPAN

New Orleans, LA—American Brass Instrument Company announced today that it has signed a multimillion dollar contract to supply scholastic musical instruments to a consortium of high schools in Japan. The instruments are to be shipped over a five-year period. They will be manufactured by the company's Sousa Division in its New Orleans and St. Louis plants. The contract signing represents another major coup for American Brass. David G. Finney, company president and son of founder George Finney, held a press conference to make the announcement. According to Finney, "Most Japanese markets traditionally have been hard to break into for foreign companies, and the market for musical instruments was no exception. We have been trying for years to increase our exports, both to Europe and Asia, and our hard work finally is paying off. We signed major contracts in France and Italy last year, and the year before we started shipping to the Brits. I think our success in Europe paved the way for the Japanese contract to go through. And this is the most lucrative deal yet. We'll be ramping up our production both in New Orleans and in St. Louis. We'll definitely be doing some hiring in both places."

Finney was asked if the projected increase in production would strain capacity in either New Orleans or St. Louis. "We're looking closely at that now," said Finney. "I know we can get the product out the door in both places, but the question is what the increase in output will do to our costs. We employ a flexible budgeting system here at Sousa Division, and our controller is using it to project our overhead costs at various levels of activity. We express our activity in terms of machine hours. The controller can predict pretty accurately what our costs will be, at various levels of machine hours, for utilities, or engineering, or setup, or what have you. With this kind of planning, I'm sure we'll be able to meet our contracts and keep the lid on our costs, too."

Sousa Division will be making its first shipments to Japan in about six months.

How do manufacturing firms, such as Hewlett-Packard Company and Chrysler Corporation, control the many overhead costs incurred in their production processes? Unlike direct material and direct labor, manufacturing-overhead costs are not traceable to individual products. Moreover, manufacturing overhead is a pool of many different kinds of costs. Indirect material, indirect labor, and other indirect production costs often exhibit different relationships to productive activity. Some overhead costs are variable, and some are fixed. Moreover, different individuals in an organization are responsible for different types of overhead costs. Considering all of these issues together, controlling manufacturing overhead presents a challenge for managerial accountants. In this chapter, we will study an accounting system that is widely used to control overhead costs.

Overhead Budgets

LO 1 Distinguish between static and flexible budgets, and explain the advantages of a flexible overhead budget.

Since direct material and direct labor are traceable to products, it is straightforward to determine standard costs for these inputs. If a table requires 20 board feet of oak lumber at $4 per board foot, the standard direct-material cost for the table is $80. But how much electricity does it take to produce a table? How much supervisory time, equipment depreciation, or machinery repair services does the table require? Since all of these overhead costs are indirect costs of production, we cannot set overhead cost standards for the oak table. If standard costs do not provide the answer to controlling overhead, what does?

Flexible Budgets

The tool used by most companies to control overhead costs is called a **flexible budget**. A flexible budget resembles the budgets we studied in Chapter 9, with one important difference: *A flexible budget is not based on only one level of activity.* Instead, a flexible budget covers a range of activity within which the firm may operate. A *flexible overhead budget* is defined as a detailed plan for controlling overhead costs that is valid in the firm's *relevant range* of activity. In contrast, a **static budget** is based on a particular planned level of activity.

A **flexible budget** is valid for a range of activity.

A **static budget** is valid for only one planned activity level.

To illustrate, suppose the controller for Sousa Division's New Orleans plant determines that electricity is a variable cost, incurred at the rate of $.50 per machine hour. Two different budgets for electricity costs are shown in Exhibit 11–1. The static budget is based on management's predicted level of activity in the division for September, 7,500 machine hours. This estimate is based on planned production of 2,500 trumpets; each trumpet requires 3 machine hours. The flexible budget includes three different production activity levels within the relevant range: 6,000, 7,500, and 9,000 machine hours.

Exhibit 11–1

Static Budget versus Flexible Budget

	Static Budget	Flexible Budget		
Activity (machine hours)*	7,500	Activity (machine hours) 6,000	7,500	9,000
Budgeted electricity cost	$3,750	Budgeted electricity cost ... $3,000	$3,750	$4,500

Static budget:
based on only
one anticipated
activity level.

Flexible budget:
includes several
possible activity
levels.

*Based on planned September production of 2,500 trumpets, at 3 machine hours per trumpet.

Controlling overhead costs in this manufacturing operation is crucial if the company is to be profitable in its production of musical instruments. The flexible budget is an important tool in cost management.

Advantages of Flexible Budgets

Why is the distinction between static and flexible budgets so important? Suppose Sousa Division produced 2,000 trumpets during September, used 6,000 machine hours, and incurred electricity costs of $3,200. Does this constitute good control or poor control of electricity costs? Which budget in Exhibit 11–1 is more useful in answering this question?

A manager using the static budget makes the following comparison.

Actual Electricity Cost	Budgeted Electricity Cost (static budget)	Cost Variance
$3,200	$3,750	. . . . $550 Favorable

This comparison suggests that operating personnel maintained excellent control over electricity costs during September, generating a favorable variance of $550. Is this a valid analysis and conclusion?

The fault with this analysis is that the manager is comparing the electricity cost incurred at the *actual* activity level, 2,000 trumpets, with the budgeted electricity cost at the *planned* activity level, 2,500 trumpets. Since these activity levels are different, we should expect the electricity cost to be different.

A more sensible approach is to compare the actual electricity cost incurred with the cost that should be incurred when 2,000 trumpets are manufactured. At this production level, 6,000 machine hours should be used (3 per trumpet). The flexible budget in Exhibit 11–1 shows that the manager should expect $3,000 of electricity cost at the 6,000 machine-hour level of activity. Therefore, an analysis based on the flexible budget gives the following comparison.

Actual Electricity Cost	Budgeted Electricity Cost (flexible budget)	Cost Variance
$3,200	$3,000	. . . . $200 Unfavorable

Now the manager's conclusion is different; the revised analysis indicates an unfavorable variance. Electricity cost was greater than it should have been, given the actual level of output. The flexible budget provides the correct basis for comparison between actual and expected costs, given actual activity.

The Activity Measure

Notice that the flexible budget for electricity cost in Exhibit 11–1 is based on machine hours, which is an *input* in the production process. The machine-hour activity levels shown in the flexible budget are the standard allowed machine hours given various levels of output. If 2,000 trumpets are produced, and the standard allowance per trumpet is 3 machine hours, then the standard allowed number of machine hours is 6,000 hours.

Why are the activity levels in the flexible budget based on machine hours, an *input* measure, instead of the number of trumpets produced, an *output* measure? When only a single product is manufactured, it makes no difference whether the flexible budget is based on input or output. In our illustration, either of the flexible budgets shown in Exhibit 11–2 could be used.

Now suppose that during August, Sousa Division manufactured three different products: 1,000 trumpets, 1,500 trombones, and 600 tubas. The following standards have been assigned to these products.

Product	Standard Machine Hours per Unit
Trumpet	3
Trombone	5
Tuba	6

During August, the company's production output was 3,100 instruments. Is 3,100 instruments a meaningful output measure? Adding numbers of trumpets, trombones, and tubas, which require different amounts of productive inputs, is like adding apples and oranges. It would not make sense to base a flexible budget for electricity cost on units of output when the output consists of different products with different electricity requirements. In this case, the flexible budget must be based on an *input* measure. The standard allowed number of machine hours for the August production is computed as follows:

Product	Units Produced	Standard Machine Hours per Unit	Total Standard Allowed Machine Hours
Trumpets	1,000	 3	 3,000
Trombones	1,500	 5	 7,500
Tubas	600	 6	 3,600
Total			 14,100

Recall that the controller estimates electricity cost at $.50 per machine hour. Thus, the flexible-budget cost of electricity during August is computed as follows:

Standard allowed machine hours given August output	14,100
Electricity cost per machine hour	× $.50
Flexible budget for electricity cost	$ 7,050

The important point is that *units of output* usually is not a meaningful measure in a multiproduct firm, because it would require us to add numbers of unlike products. To

Exhibit 11–2

Flexible Budgets: Input versus Output

Flexible Budget (based on input)			
Activity: standard allowed machine hours	6,000	7,500	9,000
Budgeted electricity cost	$3,000	$3,750	$4,500

3 standard allowed machine hours per trumpet

Flexible Budget (based on output)			
Activity: trumpets manufactured	2,000	2,500	3,000
Budgeted electricity cost	$3,000	$3,750	$4,500

avoid this problem, output is measured in terms of the *standard allowed input, given actual output.* The flexible overhead budget is then based on this standard input measure.

Flexible Overhead Budget Illustrated

Sousa Division's monthly flexible overhead budget is shown in Exhibit 11–3. The overhead costs on the flexible budget are divided into variable and fixed costs. The total budgeted variable cost increases proportionately with increases in the activity. Thus, when the number of machine hours increases by 50 percent, from 6,000 hours to 9,000 hours, the total budgeted variable overhead cost also increases by 50 percent, from $30,000 to $45,000. In contrast, the

LO 2 Prepare a flexible overhead budget, using both a formula and a columnar format.

Exhibit 11–3

Flexible Overhead Budget

Monthly Flexible Overhead Budget SOUSA DIVISION			
	Machine Hours		
Budgeted cost	**6,000**	**7,500**	**9,000**
Variable costs:			
Indirect material:			
Lacquer..	$12,000	$15,000	$18,000
Valve lubricant	2,000	2,500	3,000
Plastic valve tops	2,000	2,500	3,000
Miscellaneous supplies	6,000	7,500	9,000
Indirect labor: maintenance	4,000	5,000	6,000
Utilities:			
Electricity	3,000	3,750	4,500
Natural gas	1,000	1,250	1,500
Total variable cost	$30,000	$37,500	$45,000
Fixed costs:			
Indirect labor:			
Inspection	$ 2,200	$ 2,200	$ 2,200
Production supervisors	6,000	6,000	6,000
Setup	3,000	3,000	3,000
Material handling	2,000	2,000	2,000
Depreciation: plant and equipment	500	500	500
Insurance and property taxes	100	100	100
Engineering	1,200	1,200	1,200
Total fixed cost.................................	$15,000	$15,000	$15,000
Total overhead cost	$45,000	$52,500	$60,000

total budgeted fixed overhead does not change with increases in activity; it remains constant at $15,000 per month.

Formula Flexible Budget   When overhead costs can be divided into variable and fixed categories, we can express the flexible overhead budget differently. The format used in Exhibit 11–3 is called a *columnar flexible budget*. The budgeted overhead cost for each overhead item is listed in a column under a particular activity level. Notice that the columnar format allows for only a limited number of activity levels. Sousa Division's flexible budget shows only three.

A more general format for expressing a flexible budget is called a *formula flexible budget*. In this format, the managerial accountant expresses the relationship between activity and total budgeted overhead cost by the following formula.

$$\text{Total budgeted monthly overhead cost} = \left(\begin{array}{c} \text{Budgeted variable-} \\ \text{overhead cost per} \\ \text{activity unit} \end{array} \times \begin{array}{c} \text{Total} \\ \text{activity} \\ \text{units} \end{array} \right) + \begin{array}{c} \text{Budgeted fixed-} \\ \text{overhead cost} \\ \text{per month} \end{array}$$

To use this formula for the Sousa Division, we first need to compute the budgeted variable-overhead cost per machine hour. Dividing total budgeted variable-overhead cost by the associated activity level yields a budgeted variable-overhead rate of $5 per machine hour. Notice that we can use any activity level in Exhibit 11–3 to compute this rate.

$$\frac{\$30,000}{6,000} = \frac{\$37,500}{7,500} = \frac{\$45,000}{9,000} = \$5 \text{ per machine hour}$$

Sousa Division's formula flexible overhead budget is shown below.

$$\text{Total budgeted monthly overhead cost} = (\$5 \times \text{Total machine hours}) + \$15,000$$

To check the accuracy of the formula, compute the total budgeted overhead cost at each of the activity levels shown in Exhibit 11–3.

Activity (machine hours)	Formula Flexible Overhead Budget	Budgeted Monthly Overhead Cost
6,000	$5 × 6,000 + $15,000 =	$45,000
7,500	$5 × 7,500 + $15,000 =	$52,500
9,000	$5 × 9,000 + $15,000 =	$60,000

The budgeted monthly overhead cost computed above is the same as that shown in Exhibit 11–3 for each activity level.

note { The formula flexible budget is more general than the columnar flexible budget, because the formula allows the managerial accountant to compute budgeted overhead costs at any activity level. Then the flexible-budgeted overhead cost can be used at the end of the period as a benchmark against which to compare the actual overhead costs incurred.

Overhead Application in a Standard-Costing System

LO 3   Explain how overhead is applied to Work-in-Process Inventory under standard costing.

Recall that *overhead application* refers to the addition of overhead cost to the Work-in-Process Inventory account as a product cost. In the normal-costing system, described in Chapter 3, overhead is applied as shown in the top panel of Exhibit 11–4. Overhead application is based on *actual* hours. In a standard-costing system, overhead application is based on standard hours allowed,

Normal Costing

Manufacturing Overhead		Work-in-Process Inventory	
Actual overhead	Applied overhead: **Actual hours** × Predetermined overhead rate	Applied overhead: **Actual hours** × Predetermined overhead rate	

Difference lies in the quantity of hours used.

Standard Costing

Manufacturing Overhead		Work-in-Process Inventory	
Actual overhead	Applied overhead: **Standard allowed hours** × Predetermined (or standard) rate	Applied overhead: **Standard allowed hours** × Predetermined (or standard) rate	

Exhibit 11–4

Overhead Application

given actual output. This system is depicted in the bottom panel of Exhibit 11–4. Notice that the difference between normal costing and standard costing, insofar as overhead is concerned, lies in the quantity of hours used.

Both normal- and standard-costing systems use a predetermined overhead rate. In a standard-costing system, the predetermined overhead rate also is referred to as the standard overhead rate. Sousa Division calculates its predetermined or standard overhead rate annually. The rate for the current year, computed in Exhibit 11–5, is based on *planned* activity of 7,500 machine hours per month. Notice that Sousa Division breaks its predetermined overhead rate into a variable rate and a fixed rate. We'll discuss further the use of standard costs for product costing later in this chapter.

Choice of Activity Measure

Sousa Division's flexible overhead budget is based on machine hours. A variety of activity measures are used in practice. Machine hours, direct-labor hours, direct-labor cost, total process time, and direct-material cost are among the most common measures. Choosing the appropriate activity measure for the flexible overhead budget is important, because the flexible budget is the chief tool for controlling overhead costs.

LO 4 Explain some important issues in choosing an activity measure for overhead budgeting and application.

	Budgeted Overhead	Planned Monthly Activity	Predetermined Overhead Rate
Variable	$37,500*	.... 7,500 machine hours	..... $5.00 per machine hour
Fixed	15,000*	.... 7,500 machine hours	..... $2.00 per machine hour
Total	$52,500	.... 7,500 machine hours	..... $7.00 per machine hour

*From the flexible budget (Exhibit 11–3) for planned monthly activity of 7,500 machine hours.

Exhibit 11–5

Predetermined Overhead Rate: Sousa Division

Sousa
DIVISION

Criteria for Choosing the Activity Measure

How should the managerial accountant select the activity measure for the flexible budget? The activity measure should be one that varies in a similar pattern to the way that variable overhead varies. As productive activity increases, both variable-overhead cost and the activity measure should increase in roughly the same proportion. As productive activity declines, both variable-overhead cost and the activity measure should decline in roughly the same proportion. In short, variable-overhead cost and the activity measure should *move together* as overall productive activity changes.

Changing Manufacturing Technology: Computer-Integrated Manufacturing   Direct-labor time has traditionally been the most popular activity measure in manufacturing firms. However, as automation increases, more and more firms are switching to such measures as machine hours or process time for their flexible overhead budgets. Machine hours and process time are linked more closely than direct-labor hours to the robotic technology and computer-integrated manufacturing (CIM) systems common in today's manufacturing environment.

Cost Drivers   As we discussed in Chapter 5, some companies have refined their cost management systems even further. *Cost drivers* are identified as the most significant factors affecting overhead costs. Then multiple overhead rates based on these cost drivers are used to compute product costs and control overhead expenditures. A relentless search for *non-value-added costs* is an integral part of such a cost management system. We will discuss the role of *activity-based costing* in flexible budgeting later in the chapter.

Beware of Dollar Measures   Dollar measures, such as direct-labor or raw-material costs, often are used as the basis for flexible overhead budgeting. However, such measures have significant drawbacks, and they should be avoided. Dollar measures are subject

As manufacturing has become increasingly automated, direct labor is becoming less appropriate as an activity measure in flexible budgeting. Moreover, computer-integrated manufacturing entails a shift in the cost structure away from direct-labor costs and toward greater overhead costs. Left, blowing glass is a labor-intensive process. Right, this robot is manufacturing compact discs.

to price-level changes and fluctuate more than physical measures. For example, the direct-labor *hours* required to manufacture a musical instrument will be relatively stable over time. However, the direct-labor *cost* will vary as wage levels and fringe-benefit costs change with inflation.

The choice of an activity measure upon which to base the flexible budget for variable overhead is really a cost-estimation problem, which we studied in Chapter 7.

Overhead Cost Variances

The flexible overhead budget is the managerial accountant's primary tool for the control of manufacturing-overhead costs. At the end of each accounting period, the managerial accountant uses the flexible overhead budget to determine the level of overhead cost that should have been incurred, given the actual level of activity. Then the accountant compares the overhead cost in the flexible budget with the actual overhead cost incurred. The managerial accountant then computes four separate overhead variances, each of which conveys information useful in controlling overhead costs.

> **LO 5** Compute and interpret the variable-overhead spending and efficiency variances and the fixed-overhead budget and volume variances.

To illustrate overhead variance analysis, we will continue our illustration of the Sousa Division.

Flexible Budget   Sousa's monthly flexible overhead budget, displayed in Exhibit 11–3, shows budgeted variable and fixed manufacturing-overhead costs at three levels of production activity. During September, Sousa Division manufactured 2,000 trumpets. Since production standards allow 3 machine hours per trumpet, the total standard allowed number of machine hours is 6,000 hours.

Actual production output	2,000	trumpets
Standard allowed machine hours per trumpet	× 3	
Total standard allowed machine hours	6,000	machine hours

From the 6,000 machine-hour column in Exhibit 11–3, the budgeted overhead cost for September is as follows:

	Budgeted Overhead Cost for September
Variable overhead	$30,000
Fixed overhead	15,000

From the cost-accounting records, the controller determined that the following overhead costs were actually incurred during September.

	Actual Cost for September
Variable overhead	$34,650
Fixed overhead	16,100
Total overhead	$50,750

The production supervisor's records indicate that actual machine usage in September was as follows:

Actual machine hours for September	6,300

Notice that the actual number of machine hours used (6,300) exceeds the standard allowed number of machine hours, given actual production output (6,000).

We now have assembled all of the information necessary to compute Sousa Division's overhead variances for September.

Variable Overhead

The **variable-overhead spending variance** is the difference between the actual variable-overhead cost and the product of the standard variable-overhead rate and actual hours of an activity base.

The **variable-overhead efficiency variance** is the difference between the actual and standard hours of an activity base multiplied by the standard variable-overhead rate.

Sousa Division's total variable-overhead variance for September is computed below.

Actual variable overhead	$34,650	
Budgeted variable overhead	30,000	
Total variable-overhead variance	$ 4,650	Unfavorable

What caused the company to spend $4,650 more than the budgeted amount on variable overhead? To discover the reasons behind this performance, the managerial accountant computes a **variable-overhead spending variance** and a **variable-overhead efficiency variance**. The computation of these variances is depicted in Exhibit 11–6.

Two equivalent formulas for the variable-overhead spending variance are shown below.

1. $\dfrac{\text{Variable-overhead}}{\text{spending variance}} = \text{Actual variable overhead} - (AH \times SVR)$, or

2. $\dfrac{\text{Variable-overhead}}{\text{spending variance}} = (AH \times AVR) - (AH \times SVR)$

where   AH denotes actual machine hours

AVR denotes actual variable-overhead rate
(actual variable overhead ÷ AH)

SVR denotes standard variable-overhead rate

These two formulas are equivalent because actual variable overhead is equal to actual hours times the actual variable overhead rate (AH × AVR). Formula 2 above can be simplified:

3.

$$\text{Variable-overhead spending variance} = AH(AVR - SVR)$$

Exhibit 11–6

Variable-Overhead Spending and Efficiency Variances

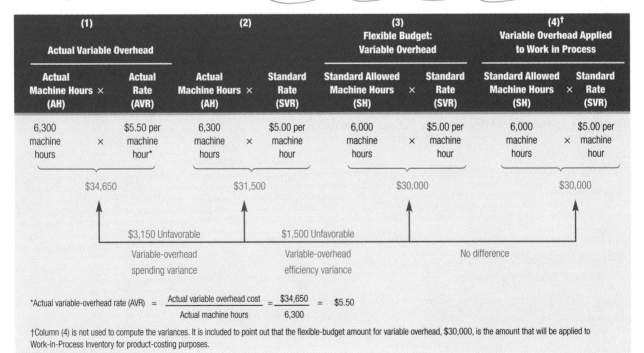

(1)		(2)		(3) Flexible Budget: Variable Overhead		(4)† Variable Overhead Applied to Work in Process	
Actual Variable Overhead							
Actual Machine Hours × (AH)	**Actual Rate (AVR)**	**Actual Machine Hours × (AH)**	**Standard Rate (SVR)**	**Standard Allowed Machine Hours × (SH)**	**Standard Rate (SVR)**	**Standard Allowed Machine Hours × (SH)**	**Standard Rate (SVR)**
6,300 machine hours	×	$5.50 per machine hour*	6,300 machine hours	×	$5.00 per machine hour	6,000 machine hours	×	$5.00 per machine hour	6,000 machine hours	×	$5.00 per machine hour
$34,650		$31,500		$30,000		$30,000	

$3,150 Unfavorable $1,500 Unfavorable   No difference

Variable-overhead   Variable-overhead
spending variance   efficiency variance

*Actual variable-overhead rate (AVR) $= \dfrac{\text{Actual variable overhead cost}}{\text{Actual machine hours}} = \dfrac{\$34,650}{6,300} = \$5.50$

†Column (4) is not used to compute the variances. It is included to point out that the flexible-budget amount for variable overhead, $30,000, is the amount that will be applied to Work-in-Process Inventory for product-costing purposes.

Sousa Division's variable-overhead spending variance for September is computed as follows (using formula 1):

$$\text{Variable-overhead spending variance} = \text{Actual variable overhead} - (\text{AH} \times \text{SVR})$$
$$= \$34,650 - (6,300 \times \$5.00)$$
$$= \$3,150 \text{ Unfavorable}$$

This variance is unfavorable because the actual variable-overhead cost exceeded the expected amount, after adjusting that expectation for the actual number of machine hours used.

As Exhibit 11–6 shows, the following formula defines the variable-overhead efficiency variance.

$$\text{Variable-overhead efficiency variance} = (\text{AH} \times \text{SVR}) - (\text{SH} \times \text{SVR})$$

where   **SH denotes standard machine hours**

Writing this formula more simply, we have the following expression.

$$\text{Variable-overhead efficiency variance} = \text{SVR}(\text{AH} - \text{SH})$$

Sousa Division's variable-overhead efficiency variance for September is computed as follows:

$$\text{Variable-overhead efficiency variance} = \text{SVR}(\text{AH} - \text{SH})$$
$$= \$5.00(6,300 - 6,000)$$
$$= \$1,500 \text{ Unfavorable}$$

This variance is unfavorable because actual machine hours exceeded standard allowed machine hours, given actual output.

Product Costing versus Control   Columns (1), (2), and (3) in Exhibit 11–6 are used to compute the variances for *cost-control purposes*. Column (4) in the exhibit shows the variable overhead applied to work in process for the *product-costing purpose*. Notice that the variable-overhead cost on the flexible budget, $30,000, is the same as the amount applied to work in process.

Graphing Variable-Overhead Variances   Exhibit 11–7 provides a graphical analysis of Sousa Division's variable-overhead variances for September. The graph shows the variable-overhead rate per machine hour on the vertical axis. The standard rate is $5.00 per machine hour, while the actual rate is $5.50 per machine hour (actual variable-overhead cost of $34,650 divided by actual machine hours of 6,300). Machine hours are shown on the horizontal axis.

The blue area on the graph represents the flexible-budget amount for variable overhead, given actual September output of 2,000 trumpets. The large area on the graph enclosed by colored lines on the top and right sides represents actual variable-overhead cost. The colored area in between, representing the total variable-overhead variance, is divided into the spending and efficiency variances.

Managerial Interpretation of Variable-Overhead Variances   What do the variable-overhead variances mean? What information do they convey to management? The formulas for computing the variable-overhead variances resemble those used to compute the direct-labor variances. To see this, compare Exhibit 11–6 (variable overhead) with Exhibit 10–3 (direct labor).

Despite the similar formulas, the interpretation of the variable-overhead variances is quite different from that applicable to the direct-labor variances.

Exhibit 11–7

Graphical Analysis of
Variable-Overhead Variances

Key:
Total variable-overhead variance: green areas
Variable-overhead spending variance: dark green area
Variable-overhead efficiency variance: light green area

Efficiency Variance Recall that an unfavorable direct-labor efficiency variance results when more direct labor is used than the standard allowed quantity. Thus, direct labor has been used inefficiently, relative to the standard. However, that is not the proper interpretation of an unfavorable variable-overhead efficiency variance. Sousa Division's variable-overhead efficiency variance did *not* result from using more of the variable-overhead items, such as electricity and indirect material, than the standard allowed amount. Instead, this variance resulted when the division used *more machine hours* than the standard quantity, given actual output. Recall that the divisional controller has found that variable-overhead cost varies in a pattern similar to that with which machine hours vary. Since 300 more machine hours were used than the standard quantity, the division's management should expect that variable-overhead costs will be greater. Thus, the variable-overhead efficiency variance has nothing to do with efficient or inefficient usage of electricity, indirect material, and other variable-overhead items. This variance simply reflects an adjustment in the managerial accountant's expectation about variable-overhead cost, because the division used more than the standard quantity of machine hours.

What is the important difference between direct labor and variable overhead that causes this different interpretation of the efficiency variance? Direct labor is a traceable cost and is budgeted on the basis of direct-labor hours. Variable overhead, on the other hand, is a pool of *indirect* costs that are budgeted on the basis of *machine hours*. The indirect nature of variable-overhead costs causes the different interpretation.

Spending Variance An unfavorable direct-labor rate variance is straightforward to interpret; the actual labor rate *per hour* exceeds the standard rate. Although the formula for computing the variable-overhead spending variance is similar to that for the direct-labor rate variance, its interpretation is quite different.

An unfavorable spending variance simply means that the total actual cost of variable overhead is greater than expected, after adjusting for the actual quantity of machine hours used. An unfavorable spending variance could result from paying a higher than expected price per unit for variable-overhead items. Or, the variance could result from using more of the variable-overhead items than expected.

Suppose, for example, that electricity were the only variable-overhead cost item. An unfavorable variable-overhead spending variance could result from paying a higher than expected price per kilowatt-hour for electricity, from using more than the expected amount of electricity, or from both.

Control of Variable Overhead   Since the variable-overhead efficiency variance says nothing about efficient or inefficient usage of variable overhead, the spending variance is the real control variance for variable overhead. Managers can use the spending variance to alert them if variable-overhead costs are out of line with expectations.

Fixed Overhead

To analyze performance with regard to fixed overhead, the managerial accountant calculates fixed-overhead variances.

Fixed-Overhead Budget Variance   The variance used by managers to control fixed overhead is called the **fixed-overhead budget variance**. It is defined as follows:

> The **fixed-overhead budget variance** is the difference between actual and budgeted fixed overhead.

$$\text{Fixed-overhead budget variance} = \text{Actual fixed overhead} - \text{Budgeted fixed overhead}$$

Sousa Division's fixed-overhead budget variance for September is as follows:

$$\text{Fixed-overhead budget variance} = \text{Actual fixed overhead} - \text{Budgeted fixed overhead}$$
$$= \$16{,}100 - \$15{,}000*$$
$$= \$1{,}100 \text{ Unfavorable}$$

*From the flexible budget (Exhibit 11–3).

The fixed-overhead budget variance is unfavorable, because the division spent more than the budgeted amount on fixed overhead. Notice that we need not specify an activity level to determine budgeted fixed overhead. All three columns in the flexible budget (Exhibit 11–3) specify $15,000 as budgeted fixed overhead.

Fixed-Overhead Volume Variance   The **fixed-overhead volume variance** is defined as follows:

> The **fixed-overhead volume variance** is the difference between budgeted and applied fixed overhead.

$$\text{Fixed-overhead volume variance} = \text{Budgeted fixed overhead} - \text{Applied fixed overhead}$$

Sousa Division's applied fixed overhead for September is $12,000:

$$\text{Applied fixed overhead} = \text{Predetermined fixed overhead rate} \times \text{Standard allowed hours}$$
$$= \$2.00 \text{ per machine hour} \times 6{,}000 \text{ machine hours}$$
$$= \$12{,}000$$

The $2.00 predetermined fixed-overhead rate was calculated in Exhibit 11–5. The 6,000 standard allowed machine hours is based on actual September production of 2,000 trumpets, each with a standard allowance of 3 machine hours.

Sousa Division's fixed-overhead volume variance is calculated below.

$$\text{Fixed-overhead volume variance} = \text{Budgeted fixed overhead} - \text{Applied fixed overhead}$$
$$= \$15{,}000 - \$12{,}000$$
$$= \$3{,}000$$

Exhibit 11–8

Fixed-Overhead Budget and
Volume Variances

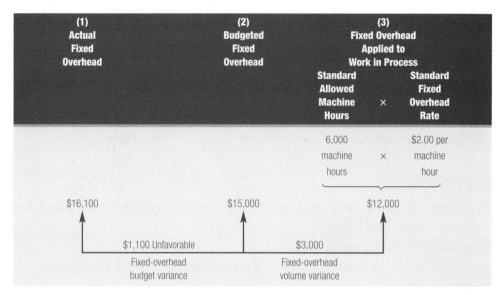

(1) Actual Fixed Overhead	(2) Budgeted Fixed Overhead	(3) Fixed Overhead Applied to Work in Process	
		Standard Allowed Machine Hours	×	Standard Fixed Overhead Rate
		6,000 machine hours	×	$2.00 per machine hour
$16,100	$15,000	$12,000	

$1,100 Unfavorable

Fixed-overhead
budget variance

$3,000

Fixed-overhead
volume variance

Managerial Interpretation of Fixed-Overhead Variances   Exhibit 11–8 shows Sousa Division's two fixed-overhead variances for September. The budget variance is the real control variance for fixed overhead, because it compares actual expenditures with budgeted fixed-overhead costs.

The volume variance provides a way of reconciling two different purposes of the cost-accounting system. For the *control purpose,* the cost-accounting system recognizes that fixed overhead does not change as production activity varies. Hence, budgeted fixed overhead is the same at all activity levels in the flexible budget. (Review Exhibit 11–3 to verify this.) Budgeted fixed overhead is the basis for controlling fixed overhead, because it provides the benchmark against which actual expenditures are compared.

For the *product-costing purpose* of the cost-accounting system, budgeted fixed overhead is divided by planned activity to obtain a predetermined (or standard) fixed-overhead rate. For Sousa Division, this rate is $2.00 per machine hour (budgeted fixed overhead of $15,000 divided by planned activity of 7,500 machine hours). This predetermined rate is then used to apply fixed overhead to Work-in-Process Inventory. During any period in which the standard allowed number of machine hours, given actual output, differs from the planned level of machine hours, the budgeted fixed overhead differs from applied fixed overhead.

Exhibit 11–9 illustrates this point graphically. Budgeted fixed overhead is constant at $15,000 for all levels of activity. However, applied fixed overhead increases with activity, since fixed overhead is applied to Work-in-Process Inventory at the rate of $2.00 per standard allowed machine hour. Notice that budgeted and applied fixed overhead are equal *only* if the number of standard allowed hours equals the planned activity level of 7,500 machine hours. When this happens, there is no fixed-overhead volume variance. Sousa Division has a $3,000 volume variance in September because the standard allowed hours and planned hours are different.

Capacity Utilization   A common, but faulty, interpretation of a positive volume variance is that it measures the cost of underutilizing productive capacity. Some firms even designate a positive volume variance as unfavorable. The reasoning behind this view is that the planned activity level used to compute the predetermined fixed-overhead rate is a measure of normal capacity utilization. Moreover, fixed-overhead costs, such as depreciation and property taxes, are costs incurred to create productive capacity. Therefore, the predetermined fixed-overhead rate measures the cost of providing an hour of productive capacity. If 7,500 machine hours are planned, but output is such that

Exhibit 11–9

Budgeted versus Applied
Fixed Overhead

only 6,000 standard machine hours are allowed, then capacity has been underutilized by 1,500 hours. Since each hour costs $2.00 (Sousa Division's predetermined fixed-overhead rate), the cost of underutilization is $3,000 (1,500 × $2.00), which is Sousa Division's volume variance.

The fault with this interpretation of the volume variance is that it ignores the real cost of underutilizing productive capacity. The real cost is due to the lost contribution margins of the products that are not produced when capacity is underutilized. Moreover, this interpretation fails to recognize that underutilizing capacity and reducing inventory may be a wise managerial response to slackening demand.

For this reason, we interpret the volume variance merely as a way of reconciling the two purposes of the cost-accounting system. Moreover, we choose not to designate the volume variance as either favorable or unfavorable.

Overhead Cost Performance Report

The variable-overhead spending and efficiency variances and the fixed-overhead budget variance can be computed for each overhead cost item in the flexible budget. When these itemized variances are presented along with actual and budgeted costs for each overhead item, the result is an **overhead cost performance report**. Sousa Division's performance report is displayed in Exhibit 11–10. This report would be used by management to exercise control over each of the division's overhead costs.

Notice that the performance report includes only spending and efficiency variances for the variable items, and only a budget variance for the fixed items. Upon receiving this report, a manager might investigate the relatively large variances for indirect maintenance labor, electricity, and production supervisory labor.

LO 6 Prepare an overhead cost performance report.

An **overhead cost performance report** shows the actual and flexible-budget cost levels for each overhead item, together with variable-overhead spending and efficiency variances and fixed-overhead budget variances.

Standard Costs and Product Costing

In a standard-costing system, the standard costs are used for product costing as well as for cost control. The costs of direct material, direct labor, and manufacturing overhead are all entered into Work-in-Process Inventory at their standard costs. (Review Exhibit 11–4.)

LO 7 Prepare journal entries to record manufacturing overhead under standard costing.

	(1) Flexible Budget (for 6,000 machine hr.)	(2) Standard Rate per Machine Hr. [variable costs only; col. (1) ÷ 6,000 machine hr.]	(3) 6,300 Actual Machine Hr. × Standard Rate	(4) Actual Cost	(5) Spending Variance [col. (4) − col. (3)]	(6) Efficiency Variance [col. (3) − col. (1)]	(7) Budget Variance [col. (4) − col. (1)]
Variable costs:							
Indirect material:							
Lacquer	$12,000	$2.00	$12,600	$12,700	$ 100 U	$ 600 U	
Valve lubricant	2,000	.33	2,079	2,090	11 U	79 U	
Plastic valve tops	2,000	.33	2,079	2,000	(79) F	79 U	
Miscellaneous supplies	6,000	1.00	6,300	6,500	200 U	300 U	
Indirect labor:							
Maintenance	4,000	.67	4,221	6,400	2,179 U	221 U	
Utilities:							
Electricity	3,000	.50	3,150	4,050	900 U	150 U	
Natural gas	1,000	.17	1,071	910	(161) F	71 U	
Total variable cost	$30,000	$5.00	$31,500	$34,650	$3,150 U	$1,500 U	
Fixed costs:							
Indirect labor:							
Inspection	$ 2,200			$ 2,210			$ 10 U
Production supervisors	6,000			7,000			1,000 U
Setup	3,000			3,000			−0−
Material handling	2,000			2,000			−0−
Depreciation:							
Plant and equipment	500			500			−0−
Insurance and property taxes	100			100			−0−
Engineering	1,200			1,290			90 U
Total fixed cost	$15,000			$16,100			$1,100 U
Total overhead cost	$45,000			$50,750			$1,100 U
Total variance between actual overhead cost and flexible budget		$5,750 U	Sum of spending, efficiency, and budget variances			$5,750 U	

Exhibit 11–10

Overhead Cost Performance Report: Sousa Division

Journal Entries under Standard Costing During September, Sousa Division incurred actual manufacturing-overhead costs of $50,750, which includes $34,650 of variable overhead and $16,100 of fixed overhead. A summary journal entry to record these actual expenditures follows.

Manufacturing Overhead	50,750	
Indirect-Material Inventory		23,290*
Wages Payable		20,610*
Utilities Payable		4,960
Accumulated Depreciation		500
Prepaid Insurance and Property Taxes		100
Engineering Salaries Payable		1,290

*The credit amounts can be verified in column (4) of Exhibit 11–10. For example, indirect-material costs amounted to $23,290 ($12,700 + $2,090 + $2,000 + $6,500). The credit to Wages Payable is for indirect-labor costs, which amounted to $20,610 ($6,400 + $2,210 + $7,000 + $3,000 + $2,000).

The application of manufacturing overhead to Work-in-Process Inventory is based on a predetermined overhead rate of $7.00 per machine hour (the total of the variable and the fixed rates) and 6,000 standard allowed machine hours, given an actual output of 2,000 trumpets. The summary journal entry is as follows:

Work-in-Process Inventory	42,000	
Manufacturing Overhead		42,000*

*Applied overhead = $7.00 × 6,000 = $42,000

Now the Manufacturing Overhead account appears as shown below.

Manufacturing Overhead			
Actual	$50,750	$42,000	Applied

The *underapplied overhead* for September is $8,750 ($50,750 − $42,000). This means that the overhead applied to Work-in-Process Inventory in September was $8,750 less than the actual overhead cost incurred. Notice that the underapplied overhead is equal to the sum of the four overhead variances for September. The total of the four overhead variances will always be equal to the overapplied or underapplied overhead for the accounting period.[1]

Disposition of Variances As explained in the preceding chapter, variances are temporary accounts, and most companies close them directly into Cost of Goods Sold at the end of each accounting period. The journal entry required to close out Sousa Division's underapplied overhead for September is shown below.

Cost of Goods Sold	8,750	
Manufacturing Overhead		8,750

The journal entry to close out underapplied or overapplied overhead typically is made only annually, rather than monthly.

An alternative accounting treatment is to prorate underapplied or overapplied overhead among Work-in-Process Inventory, Finished-Goods Inventory, and Cost of Goods Sold, as explained in Chapter 3.

Activity-Based Flexible Budget

The flexible budget shown in Exhibit 11–3, which underlies our variance analysis for Sousa Division, is based on a single cost driver. Overhead costs that vary with respect to *machine hours* are categorized as variable; all other overhead costs are treated as fixed. This approach is consistent with traditional, volume-based product-costing systems.

Under the more accurate product-costing method called activity-based costing, several cost drivers are identified.[2] Costs that may appear fixed with respect to a single volume-based cost driver, such as machine hours, may be variable with respect to some other cost driver. The activity-based costing approach can also be used as the basis for a flexible budget for planning and control purposes. Exhibit 11–11 displays an **activity-based flexible budget** for Sousa Division, using the same data as Exhibit 11–3.

Compare the conventional flexible budget (Exhibit 11–3) and the activity-based flexible budget (Exhibit 11–11). The key difference lies in the costs that were categorized as fixed on the conventional flexible budget. These costs *are* fixed with respect to

LO 8 Explain how an activity-based flexible budget differs from a conventional flexible budget.

An **activity-based flexible budget** is based on several cost drivers rather than on a single, volume-based cost driver.

---

[1]Overapplied and underapplied manufacturing overhead are discussed in Chapter 3.

[2]Activity-based costing, introduced conceptually in Chapter 3, is explored in detail in Chapter 5.

Exhibit 11–11

Activity-Based Flexible Budget

SOUSA DIVISION Monthly Flexible Overhead Budget			
Budgeted Cost		**Level of Activity**	
Cost Pool I (cost driver: machine hours)	**6,000**	**7,500**	**9,000**
Indirect material:			
Lacquer	$12,000	$15,000	$18,000
Valve lubricant	2,000	2,500	3,000
Plastic valve tops	2,000	2,500	3,000
Miscellaneous supplies	6,000	7,500	9,000
Indirect labor: maintenance	4,000	5,000	6,000
Utilities:			
Electricity	3,000	3,750	4,500
Natural gas	1,000	1,250	1,500
Total of cost pool I	$30,000	$37,500	$45,000
Cost Pool II (cost driver: production runs)	**8**	**12**	**16**
Indirect labor:			
Inspection	$ 2,200	$ 3,300	$ 4,400
Setup	3,000	4,500	6,000
Total of cost pool II	$ 5,200	$ 7,800	$10,400
Cost Pool III (cost driver: engineering change orders)	**20**	**30**	**40**
Engineering	$ 1,200	$ 1,800	$ 2,400
Total of cost pool III	$ 1,200	$ 1,800	$ 2,400
Cost Pool IV (cost driver: pounds of material handled)	**20,000**	**30,000**	**40,000**
Material handling	$ 2,000	$ 3,000	$ 4,000
Total of cost pool IV	$ 2,000	$ 3,000	$ 4,000
Cost Pool V (facility level costs)			
Indirect labor: production supervisors	$ 6,000	$ 6,000	$ 6,000
Depreciation: plant and equipment	500	500	500
Insurance and property taxes	100	100	100
Total of cost pool V	$ 6,600	$ 6,600	$ 6,600
Total overhead cost	**$45,000**	**$56,700**	**$68,400**

machine hours but are *not* fixed with respect to other more appropriate cost drivers. For example, cost pool II includes inspection and setup costs, which vary with respect to the number of production runs.

Effect on Performance Reporting The activity-based flexible budget provides a more accurate prediction (and benchmark) of overhead costs. For example, suppose that activity in December is as follows:

	Machine hours	6,000
December	Production runs	12
Activity	Engineering change orders	40
	Direct material handled (pounds)	30,000

An activity-based flexible budget is based on several cost drivers. For example, the cost driver for equipment maintenance costs might be machine hours, while the cost driver for inspection costs could be production runs. An appropriate cost driver for material handling often is the number of setups. Shown here is a technician inspecting the laminar flow in the production of circuit boards.

The following table compares the budgeted cost levels for several overhead items on the conventional and activity-based flexible budgets.

Overhead Cost Item	Conventional Flexible Budget	Activity-Based Flexible Budget
Electricity	$3,000	$3,000
Inspection	2,200	3,300
Setup	3,000	4,500
Engineering	1,200	2,400
Material handling	2,000	3,000
Insurance and property taxes	100	100

The budgeted electricity cost is the same on both budgets, because both use the same cost driver (machine hours). Insurance and property taxes are also the same, because both budgets recognize these as facility-level fixed costs. However, the other overhead costs are budgeted at different levels, because the conventional and activity-based flexible budgets use *different cost drivers* for these items. While the conventional budget treats inspection, setup, engineering, and material-handling costs as fixed, the activity-based flexible budget shows that they are all variable with respect to the appropriate cost driver.

These differences are important for performance reporting. The activity-based flexible budget provides a more accurate benchmark against which to compare actual costs. Suppose the actual inspection cost in December is $3,000. Using the conventional flexible budget would result in an unfavorable variance of $800 ($3,000 – $2,200). However, the activity-based flexible budget yields a favorable variance of $300 ($3,000 – $3,300).[3]

---

[3]For further reading on this topic, see Robert E. Malcolm, "Overhead Control Implications of Activity Costing," *Accounting Horizons 5*, no. 4, pp. 69–78; Y. T. Mak and Melvin L. Roush, "Flexible Budgeting and Variance Analysis in an Activity-Based Costing Environment," *Accounting Horizons 8*, no. 2, pp. 93–103; and Robert S. Kaplan, "Flexible Budgeting in an Activity-Based Costing Framework," *Accounting Horizons 8*, no. 2, pp. 104–9.

Chapter Summary

Overhead is a heterogeneous pool of indirect costs. Since overhead costs cannot be traced easily to products or services, a flexible budget is used to budget overhead costs at various levels of activity. A columnar flexible budget is based on several distinct activity levels, while a formula flexible budget is valid for a continuous range of activity. The flexible overhead budget is based on some activity measure that varies in a pattern similar to that of variable overhead. Machine hours, process time, and direct-labor hours are common activity bases.

In a standard-costing system, the flexible budget is used to control overhead costs. The managerial accountant uses the amount of overhead cost specified by the flexible budget as a benchmark against which to compare actual overhead costs. The accountant computes four overhead variances: the variable-overhead spending and efficiency variances and the fixed-overhead budget and volume variances. These variances help management to control overhead costs.

The managerial accountant also uses the standard or predetermined overhead rate as the basis for product costing in a standard-costing system. The amount of overhead cost entered into Work-in-Process Inventory is equal to the standard overhead rate multiplied by the standard allowed amount of the activity base, given actual output.

When an activity-based costing system is in use, an activity-based flexible budget may be developed. Such a flexible budget is more accurate than conventional budgets, because multiple cost drivers are identified to explain the behavior of overhead costs.

Review Problem on Overhead Variances

In November the Sousa Division produced 3,000 trumpets, used 9,100 machine hours, and incurred the following manufacturing-overhead costs.

Variable overhead	$45,955
Fixed overhead	$15,800

Sousa Division's monthly flexible overhead budget for November is the same as that given in Exhibit 11–3.

Compute Sousa Division's variable-overhead variances using the format shown in Exhibit 11–6. Compute the division's fixed-overhead variances using the format shown in Exhibit 11–8.

Exhibit 11–12

Variable-Overhead Spending and Efficiency Variances: Review Problem

Solution to Review Problem

The solution to the review problem is given in Exhibits 11–12 and 11–13.

(1)		(2)		(3) Flexible Budget: Variable Overhead		(4)† Variable Overhead Applied to Work in Process	
Actual Variable Overhead							
Actual Machine Hours × (AH)	Actual Rate (AVR)	Actual Machine Hours × (AH)	Standard Rate (SVR)	Standard Allowed Machine Hours × (SH)	Standard Rate (SVR)	Standard Allowed Machine Hours × (SH)	Standard Rate (SVR)
9,100 machine hours	×	$5.05 per machine hour*	9,100 machine hours	×	$5.00 per machine hour	9,000 machine hours	×	$5.00 per machine hour	9,000 machine hours	×	$5.00 per machine hour
$45,955		$45,500		$45,000		$45,000	

$455 Unfavorable

Variable-overhead spending variance

$500 Unfavorable

Variable-overhead efficiency variance

No difference

*Actual variable-overhead rate (AVR) = $\dfrac{\text{Actual variable-overhead cost}}{\text{Actual machine hours}} = \dfrac{\$45,955}{9,100} = \$5.05$

†Column (4) is not used to compute the variances. It is included to point out that the flexible-budget amount for variable overhead, $45,000, is the amount that will be applied to Work-in-Process Inventory for product-costing purposes.

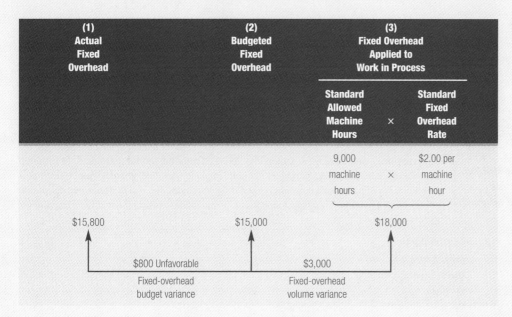

Exhibit 11–13

Fixed-Overhead Budget and
Volume Variances: Review
Problem

Key Terms

For each term's definition refer to the indicated page, or turn to the glossary at the end of the text.

activity-based flexible budget, pg. 457	**fixed-overhead volume variance, pg. 453**	**overhead cost performance report, pg. 455**	**variable-overhead efficiency variance, pg. 450**
fixed-overhead budget variance, pg. 453	**flexible budget, pg. 442**	**static budget, pg. 442**	**variable-overhead spending variance, pg. 450**

Appendix to Chapter 11
Sales Variances

The variances discussed in Chapters 10 and 11 focus on production costs. Managerial accountants also compute variances to help management analyze the firm's sales performance. To illustrate two commonly used sales variances, we will continue our discussion of the Sousa Division. The expected sales price and standard variable cost for a trumpet are as follows:

Expected sales price	$225
Standard variable costs:	
Direct material	$ 70
Direct labor	100
Variable overhead (3 machine hours at $5 per hour)	15
Total unit variable cost	$185

The **unit contribution margin** is the sales price minus the unit variable cost.

The **total contribution margin** is total sales revenue less total variable expenses.

The difference between the sales price and the unit variable cost is called the **unit contribution margin**. Sousa Division's unit contribution margin is $40 per trumpet ($225 – $185). This is the amount that the sale of one trumpet *contributes* toward covering the division's fixed costs and making a profit.

During October, Sousa Division's management expects to sell 1,500 trumpets. Based on this sales forecast, the controller computed the following budgeted **total contribution margin**.

Budgeted sales revenue (1,500 trumpets × $225)	$337,500
Budgeted variable costs (1,500 trumpets × $185)	277,500
Budgeted total contribution margin (1,500 trumpets × $40)	$ 60,000

The *actual* results for October were as follows:

Actual sales volume	1,600 trumpets
Actual sales price	$220
Actual unit variable cost	$185

Using these actual results, Sousa Division's actual total contribution margin for October is computed as follows:

Actual sales revenue (1,600 trumpets × $220)	$352,000
Actual variable costs (1,600 trumpets × $185)	296,000
Actual total contribution margin (1,600 trumpets × $35)	$ 56,000

Sousa Division's actual total contribution margin was $4,000 less in October than the budgeted amount. What caused this variance?

Two partially offsetting effects are present. First, the division sold more trumpets than expected. This will cause the total contribution margin to increase. Second, the sales price was lower than expected, and this will cause the total contribution margin to decline. The managerial accountant computes two sales variances to reflect these facts. These variances are defined and computed for Sousa Division as follows:

$$\text{Sales-price variance} = \begin{pmatrix} \text{Actual} \\ \text{sales} & - & \text{Expected} \\ \text{sales} \\ \text{price} & & \text{price} \end{pmatrix} \times \text{Actual sales volume}$$

$$= \quad (\$220 \quad - \quad \$225) \quad \times 1{,}600$$

$$= \$8{,}000 \text{ Unfavorable}$$

$$\text{Sales-volume variance} = \begin{pmatrix} \text{Actual} & \text{Budgeted} \\ \text{sales} & - & \text{sales} \\ \text{volume} & \text{volume} \end{pmatrix} \times \begin{array}{c} \text{Budgeted unit} \\ \text{contribution} \\ \text{margin} \end{array}$$

$$= (1{,}600 \ - \ 1{,}500) \quad \times \$40$$

$$= \$4{,}000 \text{ Favorable}$$

The **sales-price variance** is the difference between actual and expected unit sales price multiplied by the actual quantity of units sold.

Together, the **sales-price** and **sales-volume variances** explain the $4,000 variance between actual and budgeted total contribution margin.

Sales-price variance	$8,000	Unfavorable
Sales-volume variance	4,000	Favorable
Variance between actual and budgeted total contribution margin	$4,000	Unfavorable

The **sales-volume variance** is the difference between actual sales volume and budgeted sales volume multiplied by the budgeted unit contribution margin.

Key Terms: Appendix

For each term's definition refer to the indicated page, or turn to the glossary at the end of the text.

sales-price variance, pg. 463   sales-volume variance, pg. 463   total contribution margin, pg. 462   unit contribution margin, pg. 462

Review Questions

11–1. Distinguish between static and flexible budgets.

11–2. Explain the advantage of using a flexible budget.

11–3. Why are flexible overhead budgets based on an activity measure, such as machine hours or direct-labor hours?

11–4. Distinguish between a columnar and a formula flexible budget.

11–5. Show, using T-accounts, how manufacturing overhead is added to Work-in-Process Inventory when standard costing is used.

11–6. How has computer-integrated-manufacturing (CIM) technology affected overhead application?

11–7. What is the interpretation of the variable-overhead spending variance?

11–8. Jeffries Company's only variable-overhead cost is electricity. Does an unfavorable variable-overhead spending variance imply that the company paid more than the anticipated rate per kilowatt-hour?

11–9. What is the interpretation of the variable-overhead efficiency variance?

11–10. Distinguish between the interpretations of the direct-labor and variable-overhead efficiency variances.

11–11. What is the fixed-overhead budget variance?

11–12. What is the correct interpretation of the fixed-overhead volume variance?

11–13. Describe a common but misleading interpretation of the fixed-overhead volume variance. Why is this interpretation misleading?

11–14. Draw a graph showing budgeted and applied fixed overhead, and show a positive volume variance on the graph.

11–15. What types of organizations use flexible budgets?

11–16. What is the conceptual problem of applying fixed manufacturing overhead as a product cost?

11–17. Distinguish between the control purpose and the product-costing purpose of standard costing and flexible budgeting.

11–18. Why are fixed-overhead costs sometimes called capacity-producing costs?

11–19. Draw a graph showing both budgeted and applied variable overhead. Explain why the graph appears as it does.

11–20. Give one example of a plausible activity base to use in flexible budgeting for each of the following organizations: an insurance company, an express delivery service, a restaurant, and a state tax-collection agency.

11–21. Explain how an activity-based flexible budget differs from a conventional flexible budget.

Exercises

The following data are the actual results for Marvelous Marshmallow Company for October.

Actual output	9,000 cases
Actual variable overhead	$405,000
Actual fixed overhead	$122,000
Actual machine time	40,500 machine hours

■ **Exercise 11–22**
Straightforward Computation of Overhead Variances
(LO 5)

Standard cost and budget information for Marvelous Marshmallow Company follows:

Standard variable-overhead rate	$9.00 per machine hour
Standard quantity of machine hours	4 hours per case of marshmallows
Budgeted fixed overhead	$120,000 per month
Budgeted output	10,000 cases per month

Required:

Use any of the methods explained in the chapter to compute the following variances. Indicate whether each variance is favorable or unfavorable, where appropriate.

1. Variable-overhead spending variance.
2. Variable-overhead efficiency variance.
3. Fixed-overhead budget variance.
4. Fixed-overhead volume variance.

■ **Exercise 11–23**
Standard Hours Allowed;
Flexible Budgeting; Multiple
Products
(LO 1, LO 2)

Neptune Corporation produces binoculars of two quality levels: field and professional. The field model requires three direct-labor hours, while the professional binoculars require five hours. The firm uses direct-labor hours for flexible budgeting.

Required:

1. How many standard hours are allowed in May, when 200 field models and 300 professional binoculars are manufactured?
2. Suppose the company based its flexible overhead budget for May on the number of binoculars manufactured, which is 500. What difficulties would this approach cause?

■ **Exercise 11–24**
Construct a Flexible
Overhead Budget; Hospital
(LO 1, LO 2)

The controller for Rainbow Community Hospital estimates that the hospital uses 30 kilowatt-hours of electricity per patient-day, and that the electric rate will be $.10 per kilowatt-hour. The hospital also pays a fixed monthly charge of $1,000 to the electric utility to rent emergency backup electric generators.

Required:

Construct a flexible budget for the hospital's electricity costs using each of the following techniques.

1. Formula flexible budget.
2. Columnar flexible budget for 30,000, 40,000 and 50,000 patient-days of activity. List variable and fixed electricity costs separately.

■ **Exercise 11–25**
Straightforward
Computation of Overhead
Variances
(LO 5)

Andromeda Glassware Company has the following standards and flexible-budget data.

Standard variable-overhead rate	$6.00 per direct-labor hour
Standard quantity of direct labor	2 hours per unit of output
Budgeted fixed overhead	$100,000
Budgeted output	25,000 units

Actual results for April are as follows:

Actual output	20,000 units
Actual variable overhead	$320,000 ÷ 50,000 = 6.40
Actual fixed overhead	$97,000
Actual direct labor	50,000 hours

Required:

Use the variance formulas to compute the following variances. Indicate whether each variance is favorable or unfavorable, where appropriate.

1. Variable-overhead spending variance.
2. Variable-overhead efficiency variance.

3. Fixed-overhead budget variance.

4. Fixed-overhead volume variance.

Refer to the data in the preceding exercise. Use diagrams similar to those in Exhibits 11–6 and 11–8 to compute the variable-overhead spending and efficiency variances, and the fixed-overhead budget and volume variances.

■ **Exercise 11–26**
Diagram of Overhead Variances
(LO 5)

Refer to the data in Exercise 11–25 for Andromeda Glassware Company. Draw graphs similar to those in Exhibit 11–7 (variable overhead) and Exhibit 11–9 (fixed overhead) to depict the overhead variances.

■ **Exercise 11–27**
Graphing Overhead Variances
(LO 5)

Refer to the data in Exercise 11–25 for Andromeda Glassware Company. Prepare journal entries to:

- Record the incurrence of actual variable overhead and actual fixed overhead.

- Add variable and fixed overhead to Work-in-Process Inventory.

- Close underapplied or overapplied overhead into Cost of Goods Sold.

■ **Exercise 11–28**
Journal Entries for Overhead
(LO 7)

You recently received the following note from the production supervisor of the company where you serve as controller. "I don't understand these crazy variable-overhead efficiency variances. My employees are very careful in their use of electricity and manufacturing supplies, and we use very little indirect labor. What are we supposed to do?" Write a brief memo responding to the production supervisor's concern.

■ **Exercise 11–29**
Interpretation of Variable-Overhead Efficiency Variance
(LO 5)

You brought your work home one evening, and your nephew spilled his chocolate milk shake on the variance report you were preparing. Fortunately, you were able to reconstruct the obliterated information from the remaining data. Fill in the missing numbers below. (*Hint:* It is helpful to solve for the unknowns in the order indicated by the letters in the following table.)

■ **Exercise 11–30**
Reconstruct Missing Information from Partial Data
(LO 2, LO 5)

Standard machine hours per unit of output	4 hours
Standard variable-overhead rate per machine hour	$8.00
Actual variable-overhead rate per machine hour	b
Actual machine hours per unit of output	d
Budgeted fixed overhead	$50,000
Actual fixed overhead	a
Budgeted production in units	25,000
Actual production in units	c
Variable-overhead spending variance	$72,000 U
Variable-overhead efficiency variance	$192,000 F
Fixed-overhead budget variance	$15,000 U
Fixed-overhead volume variance	g
Total actual overhead	$713,000
Total budgeted overhead (flexible budget)	e
Total budgeted overhead (static budget)	f
Total applied overhead	$816,000

Refer to Sousa Division's activity-based flexible budget in Exhibit 11–12. Suppose that the New Orleans plant's activity in June is described as follows:

■ **Exercise 11–31**
Activity-Based Flexible Budget.
(LO 8)

Machine hours	7,500
Production runs	16
Engineering change orders	30
Direct material handled (pounds)	40,000

Required:

1. Determine the flexible budgeted cost for each of the following:
   - *a.* Indirect material
   - *b.* Utilities
   - *c.* Inspection
   - *d.* Engineering
   - *e.* Material handling
   - *f.* Total overhead cost

2. Compute the variance for setup cost during the month, assuming that the actual setup cost was $3,000:
   - *a.* Using the activity-based flexible budget.
   - *b.* Using Sousa Division's conventional flexible budget (Exhibit 11–3).

■ **Exercise 11–32**
Overhead Variances
(LO 5)

Able Control Company, which manufactures electrical switches, uses a standard-costing system. The standard manufacturing overhead costs per switch are based on direct-labor hours and are as follows:

Variable overhead (5 hours @ $8.00 per hour)	$ 40
Fixed overhead (5 hours @ $12.00 per hour)*	60
Total overhead	$100

* Based on capacity of 300,000 direct-labor hours per month.

The following information is available for the month of October.

- Variable overhead costs were $2,340,000.
- Fixed overhead costs were $3,750,000.
- 56,000 switches were produced, although 60,000 switches were scheduled to be produced.
- 275,000 direct-labor hours were worked at a total cost of $2,550,000.

Required:

Compute the variable-overhead spending and efficiency variances and the fixed-overhead budget and volume variances for October. Indicate whether a variance is favorable or unfavorable where appropriate.

(CMA, adapted)

■ **Exercise 11–33**
Sales Variances (Appendix)
(LO 9)

The following data pertain to Borealis Electronics for the month of February.

	Static Budget	Actual
Units sold	10,000	9,000
Sales revenue	$120,000	$103,500
Variable manufacturing cost	40,000	36,000
Fixed manufacturing cost	20,000	20,000
Variable selling and administrative cost	10,000	9,000
Fixed selling and administrative cost	10,000	10,000

Required:

Compute the sales-price and sales-volume variances for February.

Problems

■ **Problem 11–34**
Straightforward Overhead
Variances.
(LO 5)

Victoria Paper Company packages paper for photocopiers. The company has developed standard overhead rates based on a monthly capacity of 180,000 direct-labor hours as follows:

Standard costs per unit (one box of paper):

Variable overhead (2 hours @ $3)	$ 6
Fixed overhead (2 hours @ $5)	10
Total	$16

During April, 90,000 units were scheduled for production; however, only 80,000 units were actually produced. The following data relate to April.

1.   Actual direct-labor cost incurred was $1,567,500 for 165,000 actual hours of work.
2.   Actual overhead incurred totaled $1,371,500, of which $511,500 was variable and $860,000 was fixed.

Required:

Prepare two exhibits similar to Exhibits 11–6 and 11–8 in the chapter, which show the following variances. State whether each variance is favorable or unfavorable, where appropriate.

1.   Variable-overhead spending variance.
2.   Variable-overhead efficiency variance.
3.   Fixed-overhead budget variance.
4.   Fixed-overhead volume variance.

(CMA, adapted)

Countrytime Studios is a recording studio in Nashville. The studio budgets and applies overhead costs on the basis of production time. Countrytime's controller anticipates 10,000 hours of production time to be available during the year. The following overhead amounts have been budgeted for the year.

Variable overhead	$40,000
Fixed overhead	90,000

■ Problem 11–35
Graphing Budgeted and
Applied Overhead;
Recording Studio
(LO 1, LO 2, LO 3)

Required:

1.   Draw two graphs, one for variable overhead and one for fixed overhead. The variable on the horizontal axis of each graph should be production time, in hours, ranging from 5,000 to 15,000 hours. The variable on the vertical axis of each graph should be overhead cost (variable or fixed). Each graph should include two lines, one for the flexible-budget amount of overhead and one for applied overhead.
2.   Write a brief memo to Countrytime Studio's general manager, explaining the graphs so that she will understand the concepts of budgeted and applied overhead.

Galaxy Insurance Company uses a flexible overhead budget for its application-processing department. The firm offers five types of policies, with the following standard hours allowed for clerical processing.

Automobile	1 hour
Renter's	1 hour
Homeowner's	2 hours
Health	2 hours
Life	5 hours

■ Problem 11–36
Standard Hours Allowed;
Flexible Budget; Multiple
Products; Insurance
Company
(LO 1, LO 2, LO 4)

The following numbers of insurance applications were processed during July.

Automobile	250
Renter's	200
Homeowner's	100
Health	400
Life	200

The controller estimates that the variable-overhead rate in the application-processing department is $4.00 per hour, and that fixed-overhead costs will amount to $2,000 per month.

Required:

1.   How many standard clerical hours are allowed in July, given actual application activity?
2.   Why would it not be sensible to base the company's flexible budget on the number of applications processed instead of the number of clerical hours allowed?

3. Construct a formula flexible overhead budget for the company.

4. What is the flexible budget for total overhead cost in July?

■ **Problem 11–37**
Overhead Variances
(LO 5)

Panama Products Corporation developed its overhead application rate from the annual budget. The budget is based on an expected total output of 720,000 units requiring 3,600,000 machine hours. The company is able to schedule production uniformly throughout the year.

A total of 66,000 units requiring 315,000 machine hours were produced during May. Actual overhead costs for May amounted to $375,000. The actual costs, as compared to the annual budget and to one-twelfth of the annual budget, are as follows:

PANAMA PRODUCTS CORPORATION
Annual Budget

	Total Amount	Per Unit	Per Machine Hour	Monthly Budget	Actual Costs for May
Variable overhead:					
Indirect material	$1,224,000	$1.70	$ .34	$102,000	$111,000
Indirect labor	900,000	1.25	.25	75,000	75,000
Fixed overhead:					
Supervision	648,000	.90	.18	54,000	51,000
Utilities	540,000	.75	.15	45,000	54,000
Depreciation	1,008,000	1.40	.28	84,000	84,000
Total	$4,320,000	$6.00	$1.20	$360,000	$375,000

Required:

1. Prepare a schedule showing the following amounts for Panama Products for May.
   a. Applied overhead costs.
   b. Variable-overhead spending variance.
   c. Fixed-overhead budget variance.
   d. Variable-overhead efficiency variance.
   e. Fixed-overhead volume variance.
   Where appropriate, be sure to indicate whether each variance is favorable or unfavorable.

2. Draw a graph similar to Exhibit 11–7 to depict the variable-overhead variances.

3. Why does your graph differ from Exhibit 11–7, other than the fact that the numbers differ?

(CMA, adapted)

■ **Problem 11–38**
Overhead Variances; Journal
Entries
(LO 5, LO 7)

Winnipeg Apparel Company uses a standard-costing system. The firm estimates that it will operate its manufacturing facilities at 800,000 machine hours for the year. The estimate for total budgeted overhead is $2,000,000. The standard variable-overhead rate is estimated to be $2 per machine hour or $6 per unit. The actual data for the year are presented below.

Actual finished units	250,000
Actual machine hours	764,000
Actual variable overhead	$1,701,000
Actual fixed overhead	$ 392,000

Required:

1. Compute the following variances. Indicate whether each is favorable or unfavorable, where appropriate.
   a. Variable-overhead spending variance.
   b. Variable-overhead efficiency variance.
   c. Fixed-overhead budget variance.
   d. Fixed-overhead volume variance.

2. Prepare journal entries to:

- Record the incurrence of actual variable overhead and actual fixed overhead.
- Add variable and fixed overhead to Work-in-Process Inventory.
- Close underapplied or overapplied overhead into Cost of Goods Sold.

(CMA, adapted)

Smylan Company employs a standard-costing system using absorption costing. The standards for manufacturing overhead are established at the beginning of each year by estimating the total variable and fixed manufacturing overhead costs for the year and then dividing the costs by the estimated activity base. Smylan has an automated manufacturing operation, and the variable overhead closely follows machine-hour usage. Thus, machine hours are used to apply both variable and fixed manufacturing overhead.

The standard manufacturing overhead application rates were based on estimated manufacturing overhead for the coming year of $4,080,000, of which $1,440,000 is variable and $2,640,000 is fixed. These costs were expected to be incurred uniformly throughout the year. The total machine hours (MH) for the expected annual output, also expected to be uniform throughout the year, were estimated at 120,000 machine hours.

■ **Problem 11–39**
Calculation and
Interpretation of Overhead
Variances
(LO 1, LO 5)

Standard Manufacturing Overhead Application Rates

Variable	$12 per MH
Fixed	22 per MH
Total	$34 per MH

Smylan has reduced production in the past three months because orders have been down. In fact, manufacturing activity for the current month is 80 percent of what was expected. This reduced level of demand for Smylan's products is expected to continue for at least the next three months. Sara Edwards, assistant controller, has prepared some preliminary figures on manufacturing overhead for the current month at the request of Frank Paige, vice president for production. These amounts are as follows:

Preliminary Manufacturing Overhead Figures for the Month

Actual machine hours for the month		8,050 MH
Standard machine hours allowed, given actual output		8,000 MH
Total applied manufacturing overhead		$272,000
Actual manufacturing overhead:		
Variable	$ 95,800	
Fixed	211,200	307,000
Total manufacturing overhead variance		$ 35,000 U

Edwards and Paige had the following conversation about this analysis.

Paige: I just don't understand these numbers. I have tried to control my costs with the production cut back. I figured that my budget for one month should be about $340,000, which would give me a $33,000 favorable variance, yet you show that I have a $35,000 unfavorable variance.

Edwards: Well, you may have done a pretty good job in controlling your costs. You really cannot take one-twelfth of your annual estimated costs to get the monthly budget for comparison to your actual costs. A detailed variance analysis of manufacturing overhead would shed more light on your performance. The largest component may be your fixed manufacturing overhead volume variance.

Paige: Can you do that detailed variance analysis for me? What do I have to do to reduce or eliminate that fixed manufacturing overhead volume variance?

Edwards: Sure, we can do the detailed variance analysis. However, I'm not sure that you really can or want to reduce the volume variance under our present economic situation.

Required:

1. Sara Edwards indicated that Frank Paige should not take one-twelfth of the annual estimated costs to get a monthly budget figure for comparison to the actual costs for the month. Explain what Edwards meant by this comment.

2. Prepare a detailed variance analysis of the manufacturing overhead for Smylan Company for the current month by calculating the following variances: variable-overhead spending variance, variable-overhead efficiency variance, fixed-overhead budget variance, and fixed-overhead volume variance.

3. Sara Edwards also commented that Frank Paige might not be able to or want to reduce the fixed-overhead volume variance for the month.

    a. Explain the reason for the fixed-overhead volume variance.

    b. Explain how Paige could eliminate the fixed-overhead volume variance.

    c. Under the present economic conditions, would it be in Paige's best interest to eliminate the fixed-overhead volume variance? Explain your answer.

4. Discuss how Smylan Company could benefit by having Frank Paige participate more in the budgeting process.

(CMA, adapted)

■ **Problem 11–40**
Flexible Budget;
Performance Report
(LO 1, LO 6)

Mark Fletcher, president of SoftGro, Inc., was looking forward to seeing the performance reports for November because he knew the company's sales for the month had exceeded budget by a considerable margin. SoftGro, a distributor of educational software packages, had been growing steadily for approximately two years. Fletcher's biggest challenge at this point was to ensure that the company did not lose control of expenses during this growth period. When Fletcher received the November reports, he was dismayed to see the large unfavorable variance in the company's Monthly Selling Expense Report that follows.

SOFTGRO, INC.
Monthly Selling Expense Report
For the Month of November

	Annual Budget	November Budget	November Actual	November Variance
Unit sales	2,000,000	280,000	310,000	30,000
Dollar sales	$80,000,000	$11,200,000	$12,400,000	$1,200,000
Orders processed	54,000	6,500	5,800	(700)
Sales personnel per month	90	90	96	(6)
Advertising	$19,800,000	$ 1,650,000	$ 1,660,000	$ 10,000 U
Staff salaries	1,500,000	125,000	125,000	—
Sales salaries	1,296,000	108,000	115,400	7,400 U
Commissions	3,200,000	448,000	496,000	48,000 U
Per diem expense	1,782,000	148,500	162,600	14,100 U
Office expenses	4,080,000	340,000	358,400	18,400 U
Shipping expenses	6,750,000	902,500	976,500	74,000 U
Total expenses	$38,408,000	$ 3,722,000	$ 3,893,900	$ 171,900 U

Fletcher called in the company's new controller, Susan Porter, to discuss the implications of the variances reported for November and to plan a strategy for improving performance. Porter suggested that the company's reporting format might not be giving Fletcher a true picture of the company's operations. She proposed that SoftGro implement flexible budgeting. Porter offered to redo the Monthly Selling Expense Report for November using flexible budgeting so that Fletcher could compare the two reports and see the advantages of flexible budgeting.

Porter discovered the following information about the behavior of SoftGro's selling expenses.

■   The total compensation paid to the sales force consists of a monthly base salary and a commission; the commission varies with sales dollars.

■   Sales office expense is a semivariable cost with the variable portion related to the number of orders processed. The fixed portion of office expense is $3,000,000 annually and is incurred uniformly throughout the year.

■   Subsequent to the adoption of the annual budget for the current year, SoftGro decided to open a new sales territory. As a consequence, approval was given to hire six additional salespeople effective

November 1. Porter decided that these additional six people should be recognized in her revised report.

■ Per diem reimbursement to the sales force, while a fixed amount per day, is variable with the number of sales personnel and the number of days spent traveling. SoftGro's original budget was based on an average sales force of 90 people throughout the year with each salesperson traveling 15 days per month.

■ The company's shipping expense is a semivariable cost with the variable portion, $3.00 per unit, dependent on the number of units sold. The fixed portion is incurred uniformly throughout the year.

Required:

1. Citing the benefits of flexible budgeting, explain why Susan Porter would propose that SoftGro use flexible budgeting in this situation.

2. Prepare a revised Monthly Selling Expense Report for November that would permit Mark Fletcher to more clearly evaluate SoftGro's control over selling expenses. The report should have a line for each selling expense item showing the appropriate budgeted amount, the actual selling expense, and the monthly dollar variance.

(CMA, adapted)

Yard King Corporation manufactures power mowers that are sold throughout the United States and Canada. The company uses a comprehensive budgeting process and compares actual results to budgeted amounts on a monthly basis. Each month, Yard King's accounting department prepares a variance analysis and distributes the report to all responsible parties. Al Richmond, production manager, is upset about the results for May. Richmond, who is responsible for the cost of goods manufactured, has implemented several cost-cutting measures in the manufacturing area and is discouraged by the unfavorable variance in variable costs.

■ **Problem 11–41**
Flexible Budgeting; Variances; Impact on Behavior
(LO 1, LO 2, LO 5)

YARD KING CORPORATION
Operating Results
For the Month of May

	Master Budget	Actual	Variance
Units sold	5,000	4,800	200 U
Revenue	$1,200,000	$1,152,000	$48,000 U
Variable cost	760,000	780,000	20,000 U
Contribution margin	$ 440,000	$ 372,000	$68,000 U
Fixed overhead	180,000	180,000	—
Fixed general and administrative cost	120,000	115,000	5,000 F
Operating income	$ 140,000	$ 77,000	$63,000 U

When the master budget was prepared, Yard King's cost accountant, Joan Ballard, supplied the following unit costs: direct material, $60; direct labor, $44; variable overhead, $36; and variable selling, $12.

The total variable costs of $780,000 for May include $320,000 for direct material, $192,000 for direct labor, $176,000 for variable overhead, and $92,000 for variable selling expenses. Ballard believes that Yard King's monthly reports would be more meaningful to everyone if the company adopted flexible budgeting and prepared more detailed analyses.

Required:

1. Prepare a flexible budget for Yard King Corporation for the month of May that includes separate variable-cost budgets for each type of cost (direct material, etc.).

2. Determine the variance between the flexible budget and actual cost for each cost item.

3. Discuss how the revised budget and variance data are likely to impact the behavior of Al Richmond, the production manager.

(CMA, adapted)

■ **Problem 11–42**
Preparing and Using a
Columnar Flexible Budget;
Tour Company; Ethical
Issues
(LO 1, LO 2, LO 6)

Flaming Foliage Sky Tours is a small sightseeing tour company in New Hampshire. The firm specializes in aerial tours of the New England countryside during September and October, when the fall color is at its peak. Until recently, the company had not had an accounting department. Routine bookkeeping tasks, such as billing, had been handled by an individual who had little formal training in accounting. As the business began to grow, however, the owner recognized the need for more formal accounting procedures. Jacqueline Frost has recently been hired as the new controller, and she will have the authority to hire an assistant.

During her first week on the job, Frost was given the following performance report. The report was prepared by Red Leif, the company's manager of aircraft operations, who was planning to present it to the owner the next morning. "Look at these favorable variances for fuel and so forth," Leif pointed out, as he showed the report to Frost. "My operations people are really doing a great job." Later that day, Frost looked at the performance report more carefully. She immediately realized that it was improperly prepared and would be misleading to the company's owner.

FLAMING FOLIAGE SKY TOURS
Performance Report
For the Month of September

	Formula Flexible Budget (per air mile)	Actual (32,000 air miles)	Static Budget (35,000 air miles)	Variance
Passenger revenue	$3.50	$112,000	$122,500	$10,500 U
Less: Variable expenses:				
Fuel	.50	17,000	17,500	500 F
Aircraft maintenance	.75	23,500	26,250	2,750 F
Flight crew salaries	.40	13,100	14,000	900 F
Selling and administrative	.80	24,900	28,000	3,100 F
Total variable expenses	$2.45	$ 78,500	$ 85,750	$ 7,250 F
Contribution margin	$1.05	$ 33,500	$ 36,750	$ 3,250 U
	Per Month			
Less: Fixed expenses:				
Depreciation on aircraft	$ 2,900	$ 2,900	$ 2,900	$ 0
Landing fees	900	1,000	900	100 U
Supervisory salaries	9,000	8,600	9,000	400 F
Selling and administrative	11,000	12,400	11,000	1,400 U
Total fixed expenses	$23,800	$ 24,900	$ 23,800	$ 1,100 U
Net income		$ 8,600	$ 12,950	$ 4,350 U

Required:

1. Prepare a columnar flexible budget for Flaming Foliage Sky Tours' expenses, based on the following activity levels: 32,000 air miles, 35,000 air miles, and 38,000 air miles.

2. In spite of several favorable expense variances shown on the report above, the company's September net income was only about two-thirds of the expected level. Why?

3. Write a brief memo to the manager of aircraft operations explaining why the original variance report is misleading.

4. Prepare a revised expense variance report for September, which is based on the flexible budget prepared in requirement (1).

5. Jacqueline Frost presented the revised expense report to Leif along with the memo explaining why the original performance report was misleading. Leif did not take it well. He complained of Frost's "interference" and pointed out that the company had been doing just fine without her. "I'm taking my report to the owner tomorrow," Leif insisted. "Yours just makes us look bad." What are Frost's ethical obligations in this matter? What should she do?

For each of the following independent cases, fill in the missing information. The company budgets and applies manufacturing-overhead costs on the basis of direct-labor hours. (U denotes *unfavorable variance;* F denotes *favorable variance.*)

■ **Problem 11–43**
Finding Missing Data;
Overhead Accounting
(LO 1, LO 5)

		Case A	Case B
1.	Standard variable-overhead rate	? per hour	$2.50 per hour
2.	Standard fixed-overhead rate	? per hour	? per hour
3.	Total standard overhead rate	$13.00 per hour	? per hour
4.	Flexible budget for variable overhead	?	$90,000
5.	Flexible budget for fixed overhead	?	$210,000
6.	Actual variable overhead	?	?
7.	Actual fixed overhead	?	$207,000
8.	Variable-overhead spending variance	$2,000 U	$5,550 U
9.	Variable-overhead efficiency variance	$400 F	?
10.	Fixed-overhead budget variance	$1,080 U	?
11.	Fixed-overhead volume variance	$3,600 (positive sign)	?
12.	Under- (or over-) applied variable overhead	?	?
13.	Under- (or over-) applied fixed overhead	?	?
14.	Budgeted production (in units)	?	5,000 units
15.	Standard direct-labor hours per unit	2 hours per unit	6 hours per unit
16.	Actual production (in units)	?	?
17.	Standard direct-labor hours allowed, given actual production	1,600 hours	36,000 hours
18.	Actual direct-labor hours	1,500 hours	37,000 hours
19.	Applied variable overhead	?	?
20.	Applied fixed overhead	?	?

WoodCrafts, Inc. is a manufacturer of furniture for specialty shops throughout the Northeast and has an annual sales volume of $12 million. The company has four major product lines: bookcases, magazine racks, end tables, and bar stools. Each line is managed by a production manager. Since production is spread fairly evenly over the 12 months of operation, Sara McKinley, WoodCrafts controller, has prepared an annual budget divided into 12 periods for monthly reporting purposes.

WoodCrafts uses a standard-costing system and applies variable overhead on the basis of machine hours. Fixed production cost is allocated on the basis of square footage occupied using a predetermined plantwide rate; the size of the space occupied varies considerably among the product lines. All other costs are assigned on the basis of revenue dollars earned. At the monthly meeting to review November performance, Ken Ashley, manager of the bookcase line, receive the following report.

■ **Problem 11–44**
Flexible Budget; Improved
Performance Report;
Behavioral Issues
(LO 1, LO 6)

WOODCRAFTS INC.
Bookcase Production Performance Report
For the Month of November

	Actual	Budget	Variance
Units	3,000	2,500	500 F
Revenue	$161,000	$137,500	$23,500 F
Variable production costs:			
Direct material	$ 23,100	$ 20,000	$ 3,100 U
Direct labor	18,300	15,000	3,300 U
Machine time	19,200	16,250	2,950 U
Manufacturing overhead	41,000	35,000	6,000 U
Fixed production costs:			
Indirect labor	9,400	6,000	3,400 U
Depreciation	5,500	5,500	—
Property taxes	2,400	2,300	100 U
Insurance	4,500	4,500	—

	Actual	Budget	Variance
Administrative expenses	12,000	9,000	3,000 U
Marketing expenses	8,300	7,000	1,300 U
Research and development	6,000	4,500	1,500 U
Total expenses	$149,700	$125,050	$24,650 U
Operating income	$ 11,300	$ 12,450	$ 1,150 U

While distributing the monthly reports at the meeting, McKinley remarked to Ashley, "We need to talk about getting your division back on track. Be sure to see me after the meeting."

Ashley had been so convinced that his division did well in November that McKinley's remark was a real surprise. He spent the balance of the meeting avoiding the looks of his fellow managers and trying to figure out what could have gone wrong. The monthly performance report was no help.

Required:

1. *a.* Identify three weaknesses in WoodCrafts Inc.'s monthly Bookcase Production Performance Report.

   b. Discuss the behavioral implications of Sara McKinley's remarks to Ken Ashley during the meeting.

2. WoodCrafts Inc. could do a better job of reporting monthly performance to the production managers.

   a. Recommend how the report could be improved to eliminate weaknesses, and revise it accordingly.

   b. Discuss how the recommended changes in reporting are likely to affect Ken Ashley's behavior.

(CMA, adapted)

■ **Problem 11–45**
Interactions between
Variances; Flexible
Manufacturing System
(LO 5)

Clarke Auto Parts Company manufactures replacement parts for automobile repair. The company recently installed a flexible manufacturing system, which has significantly changed the production process. The installation of the new FMS was not anticipated when the current year's budget and cost structure were developed. The installation of the new equipment was hastened by several major break-downs in the company's old production machinery.

The new equipment was very expensive, but management expects it to cut the labor time required by a substantial amount. Management also expects the new equipment to allow a reduction in direct-material waste. On the negative side, the FMS requires a more highly skilled labor force to operate it than the company's old equipment.

The following cost variance report was prepared for the month of June, the first full month after the equipment was installed.

CLARKE AUTO PARTS COMPANY
Cost Variance Report
For the Month of June

Direct material:		
Standard cost	$602,450	
Actual cost	598,700	
Direct-material price variance	150	U*
Direct-material quantity variance	3,900	F
Direct labor:		
Standard cost	393,000	
Actual cost	383,800	
Direct-labor rate variance	4,800	U
Direct-labor efficiency variance	14,000	F
Manufacturing overhead:		
Applied to work in process	400,000	
Actual cost	408,000	
Variable-overhead spending variance	8,000	U
Variable-overhead efficiency variance	10,000	F
Fixed-overhead budget variance	30,000	U
Fixed-overhead volume variance	(20,000)†	

* F denotes favorable variance; U denotes unfavorable variance.

† The sign of the volume variance is negative, applied fixed overhead exceeded budgeted fixed overhead.

Required:

Comment on the possible interactions between the variances listed in the report. Which ones are likely to have been caused by the purchase of the new production equipment? The company budgets and applies manufacturing overhead on the basis of direct-labor hours. (You may find it helpful to review the discussion of variance interactions in Chapter 10.)

Chillco Corporation produces containers of frozen food. During April, Chillco produced 1,450 cases of food and incurred the following actual costs.

■ **Problem 11–46**
Complete Analysis of Cost Variances; Review of Chapters 10 and 11
(LO 5)

Variable overhead	$ 11,000
Fixed overhead	26,000
Actual labor cost (8,000 direct-labor hours)	151,200
Actual material cost (30,000 pounds purchased and used)	66,000

Standard cost and annual budget information are as follows:

Standard Costs per Case

Direct labor (5 hours at $18)	$ 90.00
Direct material (20 pounds at $2)	40.00
Variable overhead (5 hours at $1.50)	7.50
Fixed overhead (5 hours at $3)	15.00
Total	$152.50

Annual Budget Information

Variable overhead	$150,000
Fixed overhead	$300,000
Planned activity for year	100,000 direct-labor hours

Required:

Prepare as complete an analysis of cost variances as is possible from the available data.

Krein Gear Company has an automated production process, and production activity is quantified in terms of machine hours. A standard-costing system is used. The annual static budget for 19x9 called for 6,000 units to be produced, requiring 30,000 machine hours. The standard-overhead rate for the year was computed using this planned level of production. The 19x9 manufacturing cost report follows.

■ **Problem 11–47**
Using a Flexible Budget
(LO 1, LO 2, LO 5)

KREIN GEAR COMPANY
Manufacturing Cost Report
For 19x9
(in thousands of dollars)

	Static Budget	Flexible Budget		
Cost Item	**30,000 Machine Hours**	**31,000 Machine Hours**	**32,000 Machine Hours**	**Actual Cost**
Direct material:				
G27 aluminum	$ 252.0	$ 260.4	$ 268.8	$ 270.0
M14 steel alloy	78.0	80.6	83.2	83.0
Direct labor:				
Assembler	273.0	282.1	291.2	287.0
Grinder	234.0	241.8	249.6	250.0
Manufacturing overhead:				
Maintenance	24.0	24.8	25.6	25.0
Supplies	129.0	133.3	137.6	130.0
Supervision	80.0	82.0	84.0	81.0
Inspection	144.0	147.0	150.0	147.0
Insurance	50.0	50.0	50.0	50.0
Depreciation	200.0	200.0	200.0	200.0
Total cost	$1,464.0	$1,502.0	$1,540.0	$1,523.0

Krein develops flexible budgets for different levels of activity for use in evaluating performance. A total of 6,200 units was produced during 19x9, requiring 32,000 machine hours. The preceding manufacturing cost report compares the company's actual cost for the year with the static budget and the flexible budget for two different activity levels.

Required:

Compute the following amounts. For variances, indicate whether favorable or unfavorable where appropriate. Answers should be rounded to two decimal places when necessary.

1. The standard number of machine hours allowed to produce one unit of product.
2. The actual cost of direct material used in one unit of product.
3. The cost of material that should be processed per machine hour.
4. The standard direct-labor cost for each unit produced.
5. The variable-overhead rate per machine hour in a flexible-budget formula. (Hint: Use the high-low method to estimate cost behavior.)
6. The standard fixed-overhead rate per machine hour used for product costing.
7. The variable-overhead spending variance. (Assume management has determined that the actual fixed overhead cost in 19x9 amounted to $324,000.)
8. The variable-overhead efficiency variance.
9. The fixed-overhead budget variance.
10. The fixed-overhead volume variance. [Make the same assumption as in requirement (7).]
11. The total budgeted manufacturing cost (in thousands of dollars) for an output of 6,050 units. (Hint: Use the flexible-budget formula.)

(CMA, adapted)

■ **Problem 11–48**
Comprehensive Problem on
Overhead Accounting under
Standard Costing
(LO 2, LO 5, LO 7)

College Memories, Inc. publishes college yearbooks. A monthly flexible overhead budget for the firm follows.

COLLEGE MEMORIES, INC.
Monthly Flexible Overhead Budget

Budgeted Cost	Direct-Labor Hours		
	1,500	**1,750**	**2,000**
Variable costs:			
Indirect material:			
Glue	$ 750	$ 875	$ 1,000
Tape	300	350	400
Miscellaneous supplies	3,000	3,500	4,000
Indirect labor	7,500	8,750	10,000
Utilities:			
Electricity	1,500	1,750	2,000
Natural gas	450	525	600
Total variable cost	$13,500	$15,750	$18,000
Fixed costs:			
Supervisory labor	12,500	12,500	12,500
Depreciation	3,400	3,400	3,400
Property taxes and insurance	4,100	4,100	4,100
Total fixed cost	$20,000	$20,000	$20,000
Total overhead cost	$33,500	$35,750	$38,000

The planned monthly production is 6,400 yearbooks. The standard direct-labor allowance is .25 hours per book. During February, College Memories, Inc. produced 8,000 yearbooks and actually used 2,100 direct-labor hours. The actual overhead costs for the month were as follows:

Actual variable overhead	$19,530
Actual fixed overhead	37,600

Required:

1. Determine the formula flexible overhead budget for College Memories, Inc.

2. Prepare a display similar to Exhibit 11–6, which shows College Memories' variable-overhead variances for February. Indicate whether each variance is favorable or unfavorable.

3. Draw a graph similar to Exhibit 11–7, which shows College Memories' variable-overhead variances for February.

4. Explain how to interpret each of the variances computed in requirement (2).

5. Prepare a display similar to Exhibit 11–8, which shows College Memories' fixed-overhead variances for February.

6. Draw a graph similar to Exhibit 11–9, which depicts the company's applied and budgeted fixed overhead for February. Show the firm's February volume variance on the graph.

7. Explain the interpretation of the variances computed in requirement (5).

8. Prepare journal entries to record each of the following:

   ■ Incurrence of February's actual overhead cost.

   ■ Application of February's overhead cost to Work-in-Process Inventory.

   ■ Close underapplied or overapplied overhead into Cost of Goods Sold.

9. Draw T-accounts for all of the accounts used in the journal entries of requirement (8). Then post the journal entries to the T-accounts.

Lake Placid Sled Company manufactures children's snow sleds. The company's performance report for November is as follows.

■ **Problem 11–49**
Sales Variances (Appendix)
(LO 9)

	Actual	Budget
Sleds sold	5,000	6,000
Sales	$240,000	$300,000
Variable costs	145,000	180,000
Contribution margin	$ 95,000	$120,000
Fixed costs	84,000	80,000
Operating income	$ 11,000	$ 40,000

The company uses a flexible budget to analyze its performance and to measure the effect on operating income of the factors affecting the difference between budgeted and actual operating income.

Required:

Compute the following variances and indicate whether each is favorable or unfavorable.

1. November sales price variance.

2. November sales volume variance.

(CMA, adapted)

Pittsburgh Pen Company manufactures two lines of ballpoint pens. Actual and budgeted income statements for 19x9 are shown at the top of the next page.

■ **Problem 11–50**
Analyzing Sales
Performance; Variances
(Appendix)
(LO 1, LO 9)

Required:

1. Compute the percentage difference between the actual and budgeted break-even points in units.

2. The 19x9 budgeted total volume of 250,000 units was based on the company's achieving a market share of 10 percent. Actual industry volume reached 2,580,000 units. Calculate the portion of Pittsburgh Pen's increased volume due to improved market share.

3. Compute the variance of actual contribution margin from budgeted contribution margin attributable to the sales price. Indicate whether the variance is favorable or unfavorable. (Hint: Add the sales price variances computed for each product line.)

4. Compute the variance of actual contribution margin from budgeted contribution margin attributable to unit variable cost changes. Favorable or unfavorable?

(CMA, adapted)

PITTSBURGH PEN COMPANY
Actual and Budgeted Income Statements
For the Year Ended December 31, 19x9
(in thousands)

	Actual			Budget		
	Scholastic	Executive	Total	Scholastic	Executive	Total
Unit sales	130	130	260	150	100	250
Sales revenue	$780	$1,235	$2,015	$900	$1,000	$1,900
Variable expenses	390	975	1,365	450	750	1,200
Contribution margin	$390	$ 260	$ 650	$450	$ 250	$ 700
Fixed expenses:						
Manufacturing			$ 190			$ 200
Marketing			140			153
Administration			90			95
Total fixed expenses . . .			$ 420			$ 448
Income before taxes			$ 230			$ 252

Cases

■ **Case 11–51**
Integrative Case on Chapters
10 and 11; Drawing
Conclusions from Missing
Data
(LO 1, LO 3, LO 5)

Your next-door neighbor recently began a new job as assistant controller for Conundrum Corporation. As her first assignment, she prepared a performance report for January. She was scheduled to present the report to management the next morning, so she brought it home to review. As the two of you chatted in the backyard, she decided to show you the report she had prepared. Unfortunately, your dog thought the report was an object to be fetched. The pup made a flying leap and got a firm grip on the report. After chasing the dog around the block you managed to wrest the report from its teeth. Needless to say, it was torn to bits. Only certain data are legible on the report. This information follows:

CONUNDRUM CORPORATION
Performance Report For the Month of January

	Direct Material	Direct Labor	Variable Overhead	Fixed Overhead
Standard allowed cost given actual output	? (? kilograms at $12 per kilogram)	? (2 hours at $14 per hour)		
Flexible overhead budget			?	$40,000
Actual cost	$189,000 (14,000 kilograms at $13.50 per kilogram)	? (8,800 hours at ? per hour)	?	?
Direct-material price variance	?			
Direct-material quantity variance	$6,000 U			
Direct-labor rate variance		$8,800 U		
Direct-labor efficiency variance		2,800 F		
Variable-overhead spending variance			$2,640 U	
Variable-overhead efficiency variance			1,200 ?	
Fixed-overhead budget variance				$3,250 U
Fixed-overhead volume variance				?

In addition to the fragmentary data still legible on the performance report, your neighbor happened to remember the following facts.

- Planned production of Conundrum's sole product was 500 units more than the actual production.
- All of the direct material purchased in January was used in production.
- There were no beginning or ending inventories.
- Variable and fixed overhead are applied on the basis of direct-labor hours. The fixed overhead rate is $4.00 per hour.

Required:

Feeling guilty, you have agreed to help your neighbor reconstruct the following facts, which will be necessary for her presentation.

1. Planned production (in units).
2. Actual production (in units).
3. Actual fixed overhead.
4. Total standard allowed direct-labor hours.
5. Actual direct-labor rate.
6. Standard variable-overhead rate.
7. Actual variable-overhead rate.
8. Standard direct-material quantity per unit.
9. Direct-material price variance.
10. Applied fixed overhead.
11. Fixed-overhead volume variance.

Funtime Inc. manufactures video game machines. Market saturation and technological innovations have caused pricing pressures that have resulted in declining profits. To stem the slide in profits until new products can be introduced, top management has turned its attention to both manufacturing economies and increased production. To realize these objectives, an incentive program has been developed to reward production managers who contribute to an increase in the number of units produced and achieve cost reductions. In addition, a just-in-time purchasing program has been implemented, and raw materials are purchased on an as-needed basis.

The production managers have responded to the pressure to improve manufacturing performance in several ways that have resulted in an increased number of completed units over normal production levels. The video game machines put together by the Assembly Group require parts from both the Printed Circuit Boards (PCB) and the Reading Heads (RH) groups. To attain increased production levels, the PCB and RH groups started rejecting parts that previously would have been tested and modified to meet manufacturing standards. Preventive maintenance on machines used in the production of these parts has been postponed with only emergency repair work being performed to keep production lines moving. The Maintenance Department is concerned that there will be serious breakdowns and unsafe operating conditions.

The more aggressive Assembly Group production supervisors have pressured maintenance personnel to attend to their machines at the expense of other groups. This has resulted in machine downtime in the PCB and RH groups which, when coupled with demands for accelerated parts delivery by the Assembly Group, has led to more frequent parts rejections and increased friction among departments. Funtime operates under a standard-costing system. The standard costs are as follows:

■ Case 11–52
Comprehensive Review of Chapters 10 and 11; Variances; Behavioral Effects (Appendix)
(LO 5, LO 9)

	Standard Cost per Unit		
	Quantity	**Cost**	**Total**
Direct material:			
Housing unit	1 unit	$20	$20
Printed circuit boards	2 boards	15	30
Reading heads	4 heads	10	40

	Standard Cost per Unit		
	Quantity	**Cost**	**Total**
Direct labor:			
Assembly group	2.0 hours	$ 8	$ 16
PCB group	1.0 hour	9	9
RH group	1.5 hours	10	15
Total	4.5 hours		
Variable overhead*		2	9
Total standard cost per unit			$139

* Applied on the basis of direct labor: 4. 5 direct-labor hours at $2 per hour.

Funtime prepares monthly performance reports based on standard costs. The following table shows the contribution report for May, when production and sales both reached 2,200 units. The budgeted and actual unit sales price in May were the same at $200.

FUNTIME INC.
Contribution Report
For the Month of May

	Budgeted	**Actual**	**Variance**
Unit	2,000	2,200	200 F
Revenue	$400,000	$440,000	$40,000 F
Variable costs:			
Direct material	180,000	220,400	40,400 U
Direct labor	80,000	93,460	13,460 U
Variable overhead	18,000	18,800	800 U
Total variable costs	$278,000	$332,660	$54,660 U
Contribution margin	$122,000	$107,340	$14,660 U

Funtime's top management was surprised by the unfavorable contribution-margin variance in spite of the increased sales in May. Jack Rath, cost accountant, was assigned to identify and report on the reasons for the unfavorable contribution results as well as on the individuals or groups responsible. After a thorough review of the data, Rath prepared the following usage report.

FUNTIME INC.
Usage Report
For the Month of May

Cost Item	**Actual Quantity**	**Actual Cost**
Direct material:		
Housing units	2,200 units	$ 44,000
Printed circuit boards	4,700 boards	75,200
Reading heads	9,200 heads	101,200
Direct labor:		
Assembly	3,900 hours	31,200
Printed circuit boards	2,400 hours	23,760
Reading heads	3,500 hours	38,500
Total	9,800 hours	
Variable overhead		18,800
Total variable cost		$332,660

Rath reported that the PCB and RH groups supported the increased production levels but experienced abnormal machine downtime, causing idle personnel. This required the use of overtime to keep up with the accelerated demand for parts. The idle time was charged to direct labor. Rath also reported that the production managers of these two groups resorted to parts rejections, as opposed to testing and modification procedures formerly applied. Rath determined that the Assembly Group met management's objectives by increasing production while utilizing lower than standard hours.

Required:

1. Calculate the following variances, and prepare an explanation of the $14,660 unfavorable variance between the budgeted and actual contribution margin during May. Assume that all raw material purchased during May was placed into production.

    a. Direct-labor rate variance.

    b. Direct-labor efficiency variance.

    c. Direct-material price variance.

    d. Direct-material quantity variance.

    e. Variable-overhead spending variance.

    f. Variable-overhead efficiency variance.

    g. Sales-price variance.

    h. Sales-volume variance.

2. *a.* Identify and briefly explain the behavioral factors that may promote friction among the production managers and between the production managers and the maintenance manager.

    b. Evaluate Jack Rath's analysis of the unfavorable contribution results in terms of its completeness and its effect on the behavior of the production groups.

(CMA, adapted)

Current Issues in Managerial Accounting

"Forget the Huddled Masses: Send Nerds," *Business Week,* **July 21, 1997.**

Overview

The demand for computer programmers continues to grow. According to the article, 190,000 programming jobs in the United States cannot be filled.

Suggested Discussion Questions

As a group, illustrate how a firm's failure to satisfy its programming needs would impact its flexible overhead budget and cost variances. Provide reports, formulas, and calculations. Present your illustration to the class.

■ **Issue 11–53**
Flexible Overhead Budget Illustrated; Overhead Cost Variances

"The Satellite Biz Blasts Off," *Business Week,* **January 27, 1997.**

Overview

Communications satellite applications include wireless television and telephone systems. The technological innovations have created intense demand for satellite systems.

Suggested Discussion Questions

Firms such as Lockheed Martin and McDonnell-Douglas compete globally in the satellite launching market. The industry is plagued by high costs. List five to ten types of overhead costs incurred by satellite launch providers. What effect would launch volume have on prices?

■ **Issue 11–54**
Overhead Budgets

"Measuring the Costs of Quality," *Management Accounting,* **August 1995, Katheleen Rust.**

Overview

This article describes how Children's Hospital in San Diego reduced costs without sacrificing quality.

Suggested Discussion Questions

Discuss what problems/issues a hospital faces when it attempts to reduce costs. Why is the cost/quality trade-off uniquely important in this situation? In this setting, which activities can be changed or eliminated without sacrificing quality? How would a standard-costing system help a hospital achieve its goal of total quality management?

■ **Issue 11–55**
Trade-off between Cost and Quality

Chapter Twelve

12

Responsibility Accounting and Total Quality Management

After completing this chapter, you should be able to:

1   Explain the role of responsibility accounting in fostering goal congruence.

2   Define and give an example of a cost center, a revenue center, a profit center, and an investment center.

3   Prepare a performance report, and explain the relationships between the performance reports for various responsibility centers.

4   Use a cost allocation base to allocate costs.

5   Prepare a segmented income statement.

6   Prepare a quality cost report.

7   Discuss the traditional and contemporary views of the optimal level of product quality.

CONSTRUCTION BEGINS ON LUXURY TOWER AT WAIKIKI SANDS HOTEL

Honolulu, HI—Construction began today on the $50 million luxury tower at the Waikiki Sands Hotel. Located on world-famous Waikiki Beach, the hotel has undergone a major face-lift over the past two years since it was purchased by Aloha Hotels and Resorts. The new 20-story luxury tower will be the final step in the hotel chain's bid to make the Waikiki Sands the premier resort hotel on Oahu. According to a company officer, who wished to remain anonymous, the president of Aloha Hotels and Resorts made the final decision on the luxury tower. "It's lonely at the top, and the president felt she would have to take some big risks to separate the Waikiki Sands from the rest of the pack." And a big risk it was to give the go-ahead on the new tower. Aloha Hotels and Resorts will have to achieve a higher than average occupancy rate at the Waikiki Sands in order to make the kind of profit such a huge

investment will require. "That's what the president gets paid for," said our source. "She makes the call. And then she accepts the praise—or takes the heat—whichever way it goes."

Thomas Boudreau, vice president of Aloha's Oahu Division, was contacted for comment on the construction at the Waikiki Sands. "It was a gutsy move by our president," said Boudreau, "but I think she made the right decision. Tourism is still increasing by leaps and bounds in Hawaii. Just yesterday Japan Airlines announced two additional daily flights into Honolulu. I have no doubt the luxury tower will earn its keep. But keep in mind that's not all we're doing at the Waikiki Sands. Just yesterday, I approved construction of a new multilevel, free-form swimming pool at the hotel. And last year I approved a new fitness center for the Waikiki Sands."

Boudreau went on to explain that upon acquiring the

Waikiki Sands Hotel, Aloha had put in its own management team. "We have really experienced people at all management levels in the hotel," said Boudreau. "And we let them make significant decisions appropriate to their spheres of responsibility. For example, the hotel's general manager has authorized a lot of guest room redecorating without any divisional interference at all. We've got a great director of the Food and Beverage Department at the hotel, too. I've been told she's really changing the menu, entertainment, and special events schedule. We're really serious about making the Waikiki Sands the top hotel on the island."

Except for the new luxury tower, all of the projects contemplated for the Waikiki Sands Hotel are scheduled to be completed by October 31, in time for the high tourist season. The new tower is scheduled to be finished in 18 months.

LO 1   Explain the role of responsibility accounting in fostering goal congruence.

Goal congruence results when managers strive to achieve the goals set by top management.

Responsibility accounting refers to tools and concepts used to measure the performance of an organization's people and subunits.

Most organizations are divided into smaller units, each of which is assigned particular responsibilities. These units are called by various names, including divisions, segments, business units, and departments. Each department is comprised of individuals who are responsible for particular tasks or managerial functions. The managers of an organization should ensure that the people in each department are striving toward the same overall goals. **Goal congruence** results when the managers of subunits throughout an organization strive to achieve the goals set by top management.

How can an organization's managerial-accounting system promote goal congruence? **Responsibility accounting** refers to the various concepts and tools used by managerial accountants to measure the performance of people and departments in order to foster goal congruence.

Responsibility Centers

LO 2   Define and give an example of a cost center, a revenue center, a profit center, and an investment center.

A **responsibility center** manager is held accountable for specified financial results of its activities.

A **cost center** manager is accountable for its costs.

The basis of a responsibility-accounting system is the designation of each subunit in the organization as a particular type of *responsibility center*. A **responsibility center** is a subunit in an organization whose manager is held accountable for specified financial results of the subunit's activities. There are four common types of responsibility centers.

Cost Center   A **cost center** is an organizational subunit, such as a department or division, whose manager is held accountable for the costs incurred in the subunit. The Painting Department in an automobile plant is an example of a cost center.

Revenue Center   The manager of a **revenue center** is held accountable for the revenue attributed to the subunit. For example, the Reservations Department of an airline and the Sales Department of a manufacturer are revenue centers.

Profit Center   A **profit center** is an organizational subunit whose manager is held accountable for profit. Since profit is equal to revenue minus expense, profit-center

Exhibit 12–1

Organization Chart: Aloha Hotels and Resorts

managers are held accountable for both the revenue and expenses attributed to their subunits. An example of a profit center is a company-owned restaurant in a fast-food chain.

Investment Center   The manager of an **investment center** is held accountable for the subunit's profit *and the invested capital* used by the subunit to generate its profit. A division of a large corporation is typically designated as an investment center.[1]

Illustration of Responsibility Accounting

To illustrate the concepts used in responsibility accounting, we will focus on a hotel chain. Aloha Hotels and Resorts operates 10 luxury hotels in the state of Hawaii. The company is divided into the Maui Division, which operates seven hotels on the island of Maui, and the Oahu Division, with three properties on the island of Oahu. Exhibit 12–1 shows the company's organization chart, and Exhibit 12–2 depicts the responsibility-accounting system.

Corporate Level   The chief executive officer of Aloha Hotels and Resorts, Inc. is the company's president. The president, who is responsible to the company's stockholders, is accountable for corporate profit in relation to the capital (assets) invested in the company. Therefore, the entire company is an *investment center.* The president has the autonomy to make significant decisions that affect the company's profit and invested capital. For example, the final decision to add a new luxury tower to any of the company's resort properties would be made by the president.

---

[1]Although there is an important conceptual difference between profit centers and investment centers, the latter term is not always used in practice. Some managers use the term *profit center* to refer to both types of responsibility centers. Hence, when businesspeople use the term *profit center,* they may be referring to a true profit center (as defined in this chapter) or to an investment center.

A **revenue center** manager is accountable for its revenue.

A **profit center** manager is accountable for its profit.

An **investment center** manager is accountable for its profit and for the capital invested to generate that profit.

Exhibit 12–2

Responsibility Accounting System: Aloha Hotels and Resorts

This truck assembly department is a cost center. The telemarketing operation shown here is a revenue center. These fast-food restaurants in Kingston, New York, are profit centers. The Louisiana oil refinery pictured here is an investment center. What sort of responsibility center designation would be appropriate for your local car wash, hair salon, and laundromat?

Division Level   The vice president of the Oahu Division is accountable for the profit earned by the three resort hotels on Oahu in relation to the capital invested in those properties. Hence, the Oahu Division is also an *investment center.* The vice president has the authority to make major investment decisions regarding the properties on Oahu, up to a limit of $300,000. For example, the vice president could decide to install a new swimming pool at one of the Oahu resort hotels, but could not decide to add a new wing.

Hotel Level   The Waikiki Sands Hotel, in Honolulu, is one of the properties in the Oahu Division. The general manager of the Waikiki Sands Hotel is accountable for the profit earned by the hotel. The general manager does not have the authority to make major investment decisions, but is responsible for operational decisions. For example, the general manager hires all of the hotel's departmental managers, sets wage rates, determines procedures and standards for operations, approves decorating decisions, and generally oversees the hotel's operation. Since the hotel's general manager has no authority to make major investment decisions, she is held accountable only for the hotel's profit, not the capital invested in the property. Thus, the Waikiki Sands Hotel is a *profit center.*

Departmental Level   The Waikiki Sands Hotel has five departments, as shown in Exhibit 12–1. The Grounds and Maintenance Department includes landscaping, building and equipment maintenance, and hotel security. The Housekeeping and Custodial Services Department covers laundry and janitorial services. These two departments are called service departments, since they provide services to the hotel's other departments but do not deal directly with hotel guests. The Recreational Services Department operates the hotel's swimming pools, saunas, video arcade, and tennis courts. The Hospitality Department includes the hotel's reservations desk, rooms, bell staff, and shopping facilities. Finally, the Food and Beverage Department operates the resort's restaurants, coffee shop, lounges, poolside snack bar, banquet operations, and catering service.

The director of the Food and Beverage Department is accountable for the profit earned on all food and beverage operations. Therefore, this department is a *profit center.* The director has the authority to approve the menu, set food and beverage prices, hire the wait staff, schedule entertainers, and generally oversee all food and beverage operations.

Kitchen Level   The Food and Beverage Department is divided further into subunits responsible for Banquets and Catering, Restaurants, and the Kitchen.

The head chef manages the kitchen and is accountable for the costs incurred there. Thus, the Kitchen is a *cost center.* The head chef hires the kitchen staff, orders food supplies, and oversees all food preparation. The head chef is responsible for providing high-quality food at the lowest possible cost.

Performance Reports

The performance of each responsibility center is summarized periodically on a *performance report.* A **performance report** shows the budgeted and actual amounts of key financial results appropriate for the type of responsibility center involved. For example, a cost center's performance report concentrates on budgeted and actual amounts for various cost items attributable to the cost center. Performance reports also typically show the variance between budgeted and actual amounts for the financial results conveyed in the report. The data in a performance report help managers use *management by exception* to control an organization's operations effectively.

The performance report for the kitchen of the Waikiki Sands Hotel for February is shown in Exhibit 12–3.

As the organization chart in Exhibit 12–1 shows, Aloha Hotels and Resorts is a *hierarchy.* Each subunit manager reports to one higher-level manager, from the head chef all the way up to the president. In such an organization, there is also a hierarchy of performance reports, since the performance of each subunit constitutes part of the performance of the next higher-level subunit. For example, the cost performance in the kitchen of the Waikiki Sands Hotel constitutes part of the profit performance of the hotel's Food and Beverage Department.

> **LO 3**   Prepare a performance report, and explain the relationships between the performance reports for various responsibility centers.
>
> A **performance report** shows the budgeted and actual amounts of key financial results for a person or subunit.

	Flexible Budget		Actual Results		Variance*	
	February	**Year to Date**	**February**	**Year to Date**	**February**	**Year to Date**
Kitchen staff wages ..	$ 80,000	$ 168,000	$ 78,000	$ 169,000	$2,000 F	1,000 U
Food	675,000	1,420,000	678,000	1,421,000	3,000 U	1,000 U
Paper products	120,000	250,000	115,000	248,000	5,000 F	2,000 F
Variable overhead . . .	70,000	150,000	71,000	154,000	1,000 U	4,000 U
Fixed overhead	85,000	180,000	83,000	181,000	2,000 F	1,000 U
Total expense	$1,030,000	$2,168,000	$1,025,000	$2,173,000	$5,000 F	$5,000 U

*F denotes favorable variance; U denotes unfavorable variance.

Exhibit 12–3

Performance Report for February: Kitchen, Waikiki Sands Hotel

	Flexible Budget*		Actual Results*		Variance†	
	February	Year to Date	February	Year to Date	February	Year to Date
Company	$30,660	$64,567	$30,716	$64,570	$56 F	$ 3 F
Maui Division	$18,400	$38,620	$18,470	$38,630	$70 F	$10 F
Oahu Division	12,260	25,947	12,246	25,940	14 U	7 U
Total profit	$30,660	$64,567	$30,716	$64,570	$56 F	$ 3 F
Oahu Division						
Waimea Beach Resort	$ 6,050	$12,700	$ 6,060	$12,740	$10 F	$40 F
Diamond Head Lodge	2,100	4,500	2,050	4,430	50 U	70 U
Waikiki Sands Hotel	4,110	8,747	4,136	8,770	26 F	23 F
Total profit	$12,260	$25,947	$12,246	$25,940	$14 U	$ 7 U
Waikiki Sands Hotel						
Grounds and Maintenance	$ (45)	$ (90)	$ (44)	$ (90)	$ 1 F	—
Housekeeping and Custodial	(40)	(90)	(41)	(90)	1 U	—
Recreational Services	40	85	41	88	1 F	$ 3 F
Hospitality	2,800	6,000	2,840	6,030	40 F	30 F
Food and Beverage	1,355	2,842	1,340	2,832	15 U	10 U
Total profit	$ 4,110	$ 8,747	$ 4,136	$ 8,770	$26 F	$23 F
Food and Beverage Department						
Banquets and Catering	$ 600	$ 1,260	$ 605	$ 1,265	$ 5 F	$ 5 F
Restaurants	1,785	3,750	1,760	3,740	25 U	10 U
Kitchen	(1,030)	(2,168)	(1,025)	(2,173)	5 F	5 U
Total profit	$ 1,355	$ 2,842	$ 1,340	$ 2,832	$15 U	$10 U
Kitchen						
Kitchen staff wages	$ (80)	$ (168)	$ (78)	$ (169)	$ 2 F	$ 1 U
Food	(675)	(1,420)	(678)	(1,421)	3 U	1 U
Paper products	(120)	(250)	(115)	(248)	5 F	2 F
Variable overhead	(70)	(150)	(71)	(154)	1 U	4 U
Fixed overhead	(85)	(180)	(83)	(181)	2 F	1 U
Total expense	$ (1,030)	$ (2,168)	$ (1,025)	$ (2,173)	$ 5 F	$ 5 U

*Numbers without parentheses denote profit; numbers with parentheses denote expenses; numbers in thousands.

†F denotes favorable variance; U denotes unfavorable variance.

Exhibit 12–4

Performance Reports for February: Selected Subunits of Aloha Hotels and Resorts

Exhibit 12–4 shows the relationships between the February performance reports for several subunits of Aloha Hotels and Resorts. Notice that the numbers for the Grounds and Maintenance Department and the Kitchen are shown in parentheses. These two subunits are cost centers, so the numbers shown are expenses. All of the other subunits shown in Exhibit 12–4 are either profit centers or investment centers. The numbers shown for these subunits are profits, so they are not enclosed in parentheses. In addition to the profit figures shown, the performance reports for the investment centers should include data about invested capital. The Maui Division, the Oahu Division, and the company as a whole are investment centers. Performance evaluation in investment centers is covered in the next chapter.

Notice the relationships between the performance reports in Exhibit 12–4. The kitchen is the lowest-level subunit shown, and its performance report is the same as that displayed in Exhibit 12–3. The *total expense* line from the kitchen performance report is included as one line in the performance report for the Food and Beverage Department. Also included are the total profit figures for the department's other two subunits: Banquets and Catering, and Restaurants. How is the *total profit* line for the Food and Beverage Department used in the performance report for the Waikiki Sands Hotel? Follow the relationships emphasized with arrows in Exhibit 12–4.

The hierarchy of performance reports starts at the bottom and builds toward the top, just as the organization structure depicted in Exhibit 12–1 builds from the bottom upward. Each manager in the organization receives the performance report for his or her own subunit in addition to the performance reports for the major subunits in the next lower level. For example, the general manager of the Waikiki Sands Hotel receives the reports for the hotel, and each of its departments: Grounds and Maintenance, Recreational Services, Hospitality, and Food and Beverage. With these reports, the hotel's general manager can evaluate her subordinates as well as her own performance. This will help the general manager in improving the hotel's performance, motivating employees, and planning future operations.

Budgets, Variance Analysis, and Responsibility Accounting

Notice that the performance reports in Exhibit 12–4 make heavy use of budgets and variance analysis. Thus, the topics of budgeting, variance analysis, and responsibility accounting are closely interrelated. The flexible budget provides the benchmark against which actual revenues, expenses, and profits are compared. As you saw in Chapter 11, it is important to use a flexible budget so that appropriate comparisons can be made. It would make no sense, for example, to compare the actual costs incurred in the kitchen at Waikiki Sands Hotel with budgeted costs established for a different level of hotel occupancy.

The performance reports in Exhibit 12–4 also show variances between budgeted and actual performance. These variances often are broken down into smaller components to help management pinpoint responsibility and diagnose performance. Variance analysis, which was discussed in detail in Chapters 10 and 11, is an important tool in a responsibility-accounting system.

Cost Allocation

Many costs incurred by an organization are the joint result of several subunits' activities. For example, the property taxes and utility costs incurred by Aloha Hotels and Resorts for the Waikiki Sands Hotel are the joint result of all of the hotel's activities. One function of a responsibility-accounting system is to assign all of an organization's costs to the subunits that cause them to be incurred.

LO 4 Use a cost allocation base to allocate costs.

A collection of costs to be assigned is called a **cost pool.** At the Waikiki Sands Hotel, for example, all utility costs are combined into a *utility cost pool,* which includes the costs of electricity, water, sewer, trash collection, television cable, and telephone. The responsibility centers, products, or services to which costs are to be assigned are called **cost objects.** The Waikiki Sands' cost objects are its major departments. (See the organization chart in Exhibit 12–1.) The process of assigning the costs in the *cost pool* to the *cost objects* is called **cost allocation** or **cost distribution.**

A **cost pool** is a collection of costs to be assigned to a set of cost objects.

Cost objects are responsibility centers, products, or services to which costs are assigned.

Cost allocation (or distribution) is the process of assigning costs in a cost pool to the appropriate cost objects.

Cost Allocation Bases To distribute (or allocate) costs to responsibility centers, the managerial accountant chooses an *allocation base* for each cost pool. An **allocation base** is a measure of activity, physical characteristic, or economic characteristic that is associated with the responsibility centers, which are the cost objects in the allocation process. The allocation base chosen for a cost pool should reflect some characteristic of the various responsibility centers that is related to the incurrence of costs. An allocation base also may be referred to as a *cost driver.*

An **allocation base** is a measure of activity, physical characteristic, or economic characteristic that is associated with the responsibility centers which are the cost objects in an allocation process.

Exhibit 12–5 shows the Waikiki Sands Hotel's February cost distribution for selected cost pools. Each cost pool is distributed to each responsibility center in proportion to that center's relative amount of the allocation base. For example, the Food and Beverage Department receives 30 percent of the total administrative costs, $25,000, because that department's 36 employees constitute 30 percent of the hotel's employees. Notice that no marketing costs are allocated to either the Grounds and Maintenance Department or the Housekeeping and Custodial Department. Neither of these responsibility centers generates any sales revenue.

Allocation Bases Based on Budgets At the Waikiki Sands Hotel, administrative and marketing costs are distributed on the basis of *budgeted* amounts of the relevant allo-

Cost Pool	Responsibility Center	Allocation Base	Percentage of Total	Costs Distributed
Administration	Grounds and Maintenance	12 employees	10%	$ 2,500
	Housekeeping and Custodial	24 employees	20	5,000
	Recreational Services	12 employees	10	2,500
	Hospitality	36 employees	30	7,500
	Food and Beverage	36 employees	30	7,500
	Total	120 employees	100%	$25,000
Facilities	Grounds and Maintenance	2,000 sq. ft.	1.0%	$ 300
	Housekeeping and Custodial	2,000 sq. ft.	1.0	300
	Recreational Services	5,000 sq. ft.	2.5	750
	Hospitality	175,000 sq. ft.	87.5	26,250
	Food and Beverage	16,000 sq. ft.	8.0	2,400
	Total	200,000 sq. ft.	100.0%	$30,000
Marketing	Grounds and Maintenance	—	—	—
	Housekeeping and Custodial	—	—	—
	Recreational Services	$ 20,000 of sales	4%	$ 2,000
	Hospitality	400,000 of sales	80	40,000
	Food and Beverage	80,000 of sales	16	8,000
	Total	$500,000 of sales	100%	$50,000

Exhibit 12–5

Cost Distribution to
Responsibility Centers:
Waikiki Sands Hotel

cation bases, rather than *actual* amounts. The managerial accountant should design an allocation procedure so that the behavior of one responsibility center does not affect the costs allocated to other responsibility centers.

Suppose, for example, that the budgeted and actual February sales revenues for the hotel were as shown in Exhibit 12–6. Notice that the Hospitality Department's actual sales revenue is close to the budget. However, the actual sales of the Recreational Services Department and the Food and Beverage Department are substantially below the budget. If the distribution of marketing costs is based on actual sales, instead of budgeted sales, then the cost distributed to the Hospitality Department jumps from $40,000 to $45,000, an increase of 12.5 percent. Why does this happen? As a result of a sales performance substantially below the budget for the *other two departments*, the Hospitality Department is penalized with a hefty increase in its cost distribution. This is misleading and unfair to the Hospitality Department manager. A preferable cost distribution procedure is to use budgeted sales revenue as the allocation base, rather than actual sales revenue. Then the marketing costs distributed to each department do not depend on the performance in the other two departments.

Many organizations allocate the costs of centrally provided services on the basis of the amount of service provided, as the following example shows.

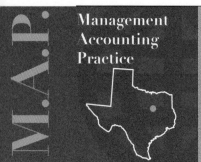

Management Accounting Practice

Cost Allocation Bases at JC Penney Co.

Business Week reported that JC Penney Co. has changed its cost allocation base for the corporate costs of auditing, legal, and personnel services. The new allocation base used to distribute these costs to the company's subsidiaries was the time spent providing these internally produced services to the subsidiaries. Formerly, JC Penney Co. based such allocations on the revenue earned by subsidiaries.[2]

---

[2]"Teamwork Pays Off at Penney's," *Business Week,* no. 2734, pp. 107, 108.

Responsibility Center	Budgeted Sales Revenue		Actual Sales Revenue		Marketing Cost Distribution	
					Based on Budget	Based on Actual
Recreational Services	$ 20,000	(4%)*	$ 4,500	(1%)*	$ 2,000	$ 500
Hospitality	400,000	(80%)	405,000	(90%)	40,000	45,000
Food and Beverage	80,000	(16%)	40,500	(9%)	8,000	4,500
Total	$500,000		$450,000		$50,000	$50,000

*Percentage of column total.

Exhibit 12–6

Cost Distribution: Budgeted versus Actual Allocation Bases

Aloha
HOTELS & RESORTS

Activity-Based Responsibility Accounting

Traditional responsibility-accounting systems tend to focus on the financial performance measures of cost, revenue, and profit for the *subunits* of an organization. Contemporary cost management systems, however, are beginning to focus more and more on *activities*. Costs are incurred in organizations and their subunits because of activities. *Activity-based costing (ABC)* systems associate costs with the activities that drive those costs. The database created by an ABC system, coupled with nonfinancial measures of operational performance for each activity, enables management to employ **activity-based responsibility accounting.**[3] Under this approach management's attention is directed not only to the cost incurred in an activity but also to the activity itself. Is the activity necessary? Does it add value to the organization's product or service? Can the activity be improved? By seeking answers to these questions, managers can eliminate non-value-added activities and increase the cost-effectiveness of the activities that do add value.[4]

Behavioral Effects of Responsibility Accounting

Responsibility-accounting systems can influence behavior significantly. Whether the behavioral effects are positive or negative, however, depends on how responsibility accounting is implemented.

Activity-based responsibility accounting measures the performance of an organization's people and subunits, focusing not only on the cost of performing activities but also on the activities themselves.

Information versus Blame

The proper focus of a responsibility-accounting system is *information*. The system should identify the individual in the organization who is in the best position to explain each particular event or financial result. The emphasis should be on providing that individual and higher-level managers with information to help them understand the reasons behind the organization's performance. When properly used, a responsibility-accounting system *does not emphasize blame*. If managers feel they are beaten over the head with criticism and rebukes when unfavorable variances occur, they are unlikely to respond in a positive way. Instead, they will tend to undermine the system and view it with skepticism. But when the responsibility-accounting system emphasizes its informational role, managers tend to react constructively, and strive for improved performance.

---

[3]See C. J. McNair, "Interdependence and Control: Traditional vs. Activity-Based Responsibility Accounting," *Journal of Cost Management* 4, no. 2, pp. 15–23.

[4]Activity-based costing, introduced conceptually in Chapter 3, is covered in detail in Chapter 5. Activity analysis and the elimination of non-value-added activities are covered in Chapters 5 and 6.

All organizations face the task of allocating costs to responsibility centers. This Six Flags theme park, for example, allocates costs such as maintenance, utilities, and security to such activities as food service operations, gift shops, and major rides.

Controllability

Some organizations use performance reports that distinguish between controllable and uncontrollable costs or revenues. For example, the head chef at the Waikiki Sands Hotel can influence the hours and efficiency of the kitchen staff, but he probably cannot change the wage rates. A performance report that distinguishes between the financial results influenced by the head chef and those he does not influence has the advantage of providing complete information to the head chef. Yet the report recognizes that certain results are beyond his control.

Identifying costs as controllable or uncontrollable is not always easy. Many cost items are influenced by more than one person. The time frame also may be important in determining controllability. Some costs are controllable over a long time frame, but not within a short time period. To illustrate, suppose the Waikiki Sands' head chef has signed a one-year contract with a local seafood supplier. The cost of seafood can be influenced by the head chef if the time period is a year or more, but the cost cannot be controlled on a weekly basis.

Motivating Desired Behavior

Managerial accountants often use the responsibility-accounting system to motivate actions considered desirable by upper-level management. Sometimes the responsibility-accounting system can solve behavioral problems as well. As a case in point, consider the problem of rush orders. To accept or reject a rush order is a cost-benefit decision:

Costs of Accepting Rush Order	**Benefits of Accepting Rush Order**
Disrupted production	Satisfied customers
More setups	Greater future sales
Higher costs	

The following real-world illustration, originally described by Raymond Villers, provides an example.[5]

---

[5]R Villers, "Control and Freedom in a Decentralized Company," *Harvard Business Review* 32, pp. 826–96.

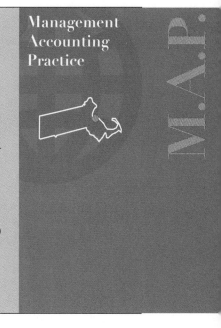

Rush Orders

The production scheduler in a manufacturing firm was frequently asked to interrupt production of one product with a rush order for another product. Rush orders typically resulted in greater costs because more product setups were required. Since the production scheduler was evaluated on the basis of costs, he was reluctant to accept rush orders. The sales manager, on the other hand, was evaluated on the basis of sales revenue. By agreeing to customers' demands for rush orders, the sales manager satisfied his customers. This resulted in more future sales and favorable performance ratings for the sales manager.

As the rush orders became more and more frequent, the production manager began to object. The sales manager responded by asking if the production scheduler wanted to take the responsibility for losing a customer by refusing a rush order. The production scheduler did not want to be blamed for lost sales, so he grudgingly accepted the rush orders. However, considerable ill will developed between the sales manager and production scheduler.

The company's managerial accountant came to the rescue by redesigning the responsibility-accounting system. The system was modified to accumulate the extra costs associated with rush orders and charge them to the sales manager's responsibility center, rather than the production scheduler's center. The ultimate result was that the sales manager chose more carefully which rush-order requests to make, and the production manager accepted them gracefully.

The problem described in the preceding illustration developed because two different managers were considering the costs and benefits of the rush-order decision. The production manager was looking only at the costs, while the sales manager was looking only at the benefits. The modified responsibility-accounting system made the sales manager look at *both the costs and the benefits* associated with each rush order. Then the sales manager could make the necessary trade-off between costs and benefits in considering each rush order. Some rush orders were rejected, because the sales manager decided the costs exceeded the benefits. Other rush orders were accepted, when the importance of the customer and potential future sales justified it.

This example illustrates how a well-designed responsibility-accounting system can make an organization run more smoothly and achieve higher performance.

Segmented Reporting

Subunits of an organization are often called *segments. Segmented reporting* refers to the preparation of accounting reports by segment and for the organization as a whole. Many organizations prepare **segmented income statements**, which show the income for major segments and for the entire enterprise.

LO 5   Prepare a segmented income statement.

In preparing segmented income statements, the managerial accountant must decide how to treat costs that are incurred to benefit more than one segment. Such costs are called **common costs**. The salary of the president of Aloha Hotels and Resorts is a common cost. The president manages the entire company. Some of her time is spent on matters related specifically to the Maui Division or the Oahu Division, but much of it is spent on tasks that are not traced easily to either division. The president works with the company's board of directors, develops strategic plans for the company, and helps set policy and goals for the entire enterprise. Thus, the president's compensation is a common cost, which is not related easily to any segment's activities.

Segmented income statements show the income for an organization and its major segments (subunits).

Common costs are incurred to benefit more than one organizational segment.

Many managerial accountants believe that it is misleading to allocate common costs to an organization's segments. Since these costs are not traceable to the activities of segments, they can be allocated to segments only on the basis of some highly arbitrary allocation base. Consider the salary of Aloha Hotels and Resorts' president. What allocation base would you choose to reflect the contribution of the president's managerial efforts to the company's two divisions? The possible allocation bases include budgeted divisional sales revenue, the number of hotels or employees in each division,

	Aloha Hotels and Resorts	Segment of Company		Segment of Oahu Division			
		Maui Division	Oahu Division	Waimea Beach Resort	Diamond Head Lodge	Waikiki Sands Hotel	Not Allocated
Sales revenue	$2,500,000	$1,600,000	$900,000	$450,000	$150,000	$300,000	—
Variable operating expenses:							
Personnel	$ 820,900	$ 510,400	$310,500	$155,500	$ 50,000	$105,000	—
Food, beverages, and supplies	738,000	458,600	279,400	139,700	46,400	93,300	—
Other	83,000	58,000	25,000	12,500	4,000	8,500	—
Total	$1,641,900	$1,027,000	$614,900	$307,700	$100,400	$206,800	—
Segment contribution margin	$ 858,100	$ 573,000	$285,100	$142,300	$ 49,600	$ 93,200	—
Less: Fixed expenses controllable by segment manager	30,000	21,000	9,000	4,000	1,000	3,000	$ 1,000
Profit margin controllable by segment manager	$ 828,100	$ 552,000	$276,100	$138,300	$ 48,600	$ 90,200	$ (1,000)
Less: Fixed expenses, traceable to segment, but controllable by others	750,000	500,000	250,000	26,000	8,000	16,000	200,000
Profit margin traceable to segment	$ 78,100	$ 52,000	$ 26,100	$112,300	$ 40,600	$ 74,200	$(201,000)
Less: Common fixed expenses	10,000						
Income before taxes	$ 68,100						
Less: Income tax expense ...	37,440						
Net income	$ 30,660						

Segmented Income Statements: Aloha Hotels and Resorts (in thousands)

or some measure of divisional size, such as total assets. However, all of these allocation bases would yield arbitrary cost allocations and possibly misleading segment profit information. For this reason, many organizations choose not to allocate common costs on segmented income statements.

Exhibit 12–7 shows February's segmented income statement for Aloha Hotels and Resorts. Each segment's income statement is presented in the *contribution format* discussed in Chapter 8. Notice that Exhibit 12–7 shows income statements for the following segments.

$$\text{Aloha Hotels and Resorts} \begin{cases} \text{Maui Division} \\ \text{Oahu Division} \end{cases} \begin{cases} \text{Waimea Beach Resort} \\ \text{Diamond Head Lodge} \\ \text{Waikiki Sands Hotel} \end{cases}$$

Three numbers in Exhibit 12–7 require special emphasis. First, the $10,000,000 of common fixed expenses in the left-hand column is not allocated to the company's two divisions. Included in this figure are such costs as the company president's salary. These costs cannot be allocated to the divisions, except in some arbitrary manner.

Second, $1,000,000 of controllable fixed expense in the right-hand column constitutes part of the Oahu Division's $9,000,000 of controllable fixed expense. All $9,000,000 of expense is controllable by the vice president of the Oahu Division. However, $1,000,000 of these expenses cannot be traced to the division's three hotels, except on an arbitrary basis. For example, this $1,000,000 of expense includes the salary of the Oahu Division's vice president. Therefore, the $1,000,000 of expense is *not allocated* among the division's three hotels. This procedure illustrates an important point. Costs that are traceable to segments at one level in an organization may become common costs at a lower level in the organization. The vice president's salary is traceable to the Oahu Division, but it cannot be allocated among the division's three hotels except arbitrarily. Thus, the vice president's salary is a traceable cost at the divisional level, but it becomes a common cost at the hotel level.

Third, the $200,000,000 of fixed expenses controllable by others in the right-hand column constitutes part of the Oahu Division's $250,000,000 of fixed expenses controllable by others. However, the $200,000,000 portion cannot be allocated among the division's three hotels, except arbitrarily.

Segments versus Segment Managers

One advantage of segmented reports like the one in Exhibit 12–7 is that they make a distinction between segments and segment managers. Some costs that are traceable to a segment may be completely beyond the influence of the segment manager. Property taxes on the Waikiki Sands Hotel, for example, are traceable to the hotel, but the hotel's general manager cannot influence them. To properly evaluate the *Waikiki Sands Hotel as an investment* of the company's resources, the property taxes should be included in the hotel's costs. However, in evaluating the general manager's performance, the property-tax cost should be *excluded,* since the manager has no control over it.

Key Features of Segmented Reporting

To summarize, Exhibit 12–7 illustrates three important characteristics of segmented reporting:

1. *Contribution format.* These income statements use the contribution format. The statements subtract variable expenses from sales revenue to obtain the *contribution margin.*
2. *Controllable versus uncontrollable expenses.* The income statements in Exhibit 12–7 highlight the costs that can be controlled, or heavily influenced, by each segment manager. This approach is consistent with *responsibility accounting.*
3. *Segmented income statement. Segmented reporting* shows income statements for the company as a whole and for its major segments.

Customer Profitability Analysis and Activity-Based Costing

Analyzing profitability by segments of the company can help managers gain insight into the factors that are driving the company's performance. In addition to focusing on the major organizational subunits in the company, profitability analysis can focus on major market segments, geographical regions, distribution channels, or customers.

Customer profitability analysis uses the concept of activity-based costing to determine how serving particular customers causes activities to be performed and costs to be incurred. Suppose, for example, that customer A frequently changes its orders after they are placed, but customer B typically does not. Then the costs incurred in updating sales orders for changes should be recorded in a manner that reflects the fact that customer A is more responsible for those activities and costs than is customer B.

Many factors can result in some customers being more profitable than others. Customers that order in small quantities, order frequently, often change their orders, require special packaging or handling, demand faster delivery, or need special parts or engineering design generally are less profitable than customers who demand less in terms of customized services. If managers have a good understanding of which customers are generating the greatest profit, they can make more-informed decisions about customer service. Moreover, customers can be educated as to the costs they are

> **Customer profitability analysis** uses the concepts of activity-based costing to determine how serving particular customers causes activities to be performed and costs to be incurred.

causing by demanding special services. In many cases, customers' behavior can be changed in a way that reduces costs to the supplier. Then these cost savings can be shared by the supplier and the customer.

Total Quality Management

Traditional responsibility-accounting systems focus primarily on the financial performance of an organization's subunits. However, nowadays it is crucial for organizations to monitor performance in many nonfinancial areas as well. For many companies, quality is at the forefront of the areas in which nonfinancial performance is critically important. The quality of the product or service that an organization provides can spell the difference between future profitability and disaster. Quality is equally important in the service and manufacturing industries. For Aloha Hotels and Resorts, the quality of service includes the comfort of the guest rooms, the amenities provided to guests, the friendliness of the staff, the quality of food served in the restaurant, and so forth. Hotel guests are ever more discriminating as they assess the overall quality of service and then select their accommodations accordingly. Similar comments apply to the airlines, long-distance telecommunications companies, banks, car rental firms, and financial investment firms.

In the manufacturing industry, product quality has become a key factor in determining a firm's success or failure in the global marketplace. Advanced, highly reliable manufacturing methods have made it possible to achieve very high standards of product quality. As a result, more and more firms are making product quality a keystone of their competitive strategy.

Measuring and Reporting Quality Costs

Recognizing the importance of maintaining high product quality, companies often measure and report the costs of doing so. Before we examine the costs that companies incur to maintain high product quality, let's consider what product quality means.

Grade is the extent of a product's capability in performing its intended purpose, viewed in relation to other products with the same functional use.

Product Quality   What is meant by a high-quality product? There are two concepts of quality that determine a product's degree of excellence or the product's ultimate fitness for its intended use. A product's **grade** refers to the extent of its capability in performing its intended purpose, in relation to other products with the same functional

This high-tech quality assurance program uses an electron microscope to inspect metal samples. What type of quality cost is represented here?

use. For example, a computer monitor that displays 65,536 colors is of a higher grade than a monitor that displays only 256 colors. A product's **quality of design** refers to how well it is conceived or designed for its intended use. For example, a coffee mug designed with a handle that is too small for the user's fingers is a poorly designed mug. The **quality of conformance** refers to the extent to which a product meets the specifications of its design. A coffee mug with an appropriately sized handle could be well designed, but if the handle breaks off due to shoddy manufacturing, it will be useless. This mug fails to conform to its design specifications. Both quality of design and quality of conformance are required in order to achieve a high-quality finished product.

Quality of design is the extent to which a product is designed to perform well in its intended use.

Quality of conformance is the extent to which a product meets the specifications of its design.

Costs of Quality Due to the increasing importance of maintaining high product quality, many companies routinely measure and report the costs of ensuring high quality. Four types of costs are monitored.

LO 6 Prepare a quality cost report.

First are **prevention costs**, the costs of preventing defects. Second are **appraisal costs**, the costs of determining whether defects exist. The third type of costs are **internal failure costs**, those costs of repairing defects found prior to product sale. The last type of costs are **external failure costs**, those costs incurred when defective products have been sold.

Exhibit 12–8 shows a quality cost report prepared by Handico, Inc., a manufacturer of cordless telephones.[6] As is always true in cost monitoring, quality cost reporting is most useful when cost trends are examined over a period of time. Through trend analysis, management can see where improvement is occurring and where difficulties exist. Goals can be set to achieve a particular cost target in an area of concern. For example, Handico's management might strive to reduce warranty costs to zero by a certain date.

Handico

Prevention costs are the costs of preventing product defects.

Appraisal costs are the costs of determining whether defective products exist.

Observable versus Hidden Quality Costs The quality costs discussed in the preceding section are *observable*. They can be measured and reported, often on the basis of information in the accounting records. In addition to these observable quality costs, however, companies incur *hidden* quality costs. When products of inferior quality make it to market, customers are dissatisfied. Their dissatisfaction can result in decreased sales and a tarnished reputation for the company. Not only does the company experience lost sales for the inferior products but it will also likely experience lost sales in its other product lines. The opportunity cost of these lost sales and decreased market share can represent a significant hidden cost. Such hidden costs are difficult to estimate or report.

Internal failure costs are costs of correcting defects found prior to product sale.

External failure costs are costs incurred because defective products have been sold.

Changing Views of Optimal Product Quality

One way to express product quality is in the percentage of products that fail to conform to their specifications, that is, the percentage of defects. Given this perspective, what is the optimal level of product quality?[7]

LO 7 Discuss the traditional and contemporary views of the optimal level of product quality.

Traditional Perspective The traditional viewpoint holds that finding the optimal level of product quality is a balancing act between incurring costs of prevention and appraisal on one hand and incurring costs of failure on the other. Panel A of Exhibit 12–9 depicts this trade-off. As the percentage of defective products decreases, the costs of prevention and appraisal increase. However, the costs of internal and external failure

---

[6]Based on a typical quality cost report suggested in Harold P. Roth and Wayne J. Morse, "Let's Help Measure and Report Quality Costs," *Management Accounting* 65, no 2, p. 50.

[7]This discussion is based on the following sources: Wayne J. Morse, Harold P. Roth, and Kay M. Poston, *Measuring, Planning and Controlling Quality Costs* (Montvale, NJ: National Association of Accountants, 1987); Jack Campanella, ed., *Principles of Quality Costs* (Milwaukee, WI: ASQC Quality Press, 1990); and Alahassane Diallo, Zafar V. Kahn, and Curtis F. Vail, "Cost of Quality in the New Manufacturing Environment," *Management Accounting* 77, no. 2, pp. 20–25.

Exhibit 12–8		**Current Month's Cost**	**Percent of Total**
Quality Cost Report: Handico			
Prevention costs			
Quality training		$ 2,000	1.3
Reliability engineering		10,000	6.5
Pilot studies		5,000	3.3
Systems development		8,000	5.2
Total prevention costs		$ 25,000	16.3
Appraisal costs			
Materials inspection		$ 6,000	3.9
Supplies inspection		3,000	2.0
Reliability testing		5,000	3.3
Metallurgical laboratory		25,000	16.3
Total appraisal costs		$ 39,000	25.5
Internal failure costs			
Scrap		$ 15,000	9.8
Repair		18,000	11.8
Rework		12,000	7.8
Downtime		6,000	3.9
Total internal failure costs		$ 51,000	33.3
External failure costs			
Warranty costs		$ 14,000	9.2
Out-of-warranty repairs and replacement		6,000	3.9
Customer complaints		3,000	2.0
Product liability		10,000	6.5
Transportation losses		5,000	3.3
Total external failure costs		$ 38,000	24.9
Total quality costs		$153,000	100.00

Exhibit 12–9

Quality Costs and the Optimal Level of Product Quality

A. Traditional Perspective

B. Contemporary Perspective

decrease. Adding the costs of prevention, appraisal, internal and external failure yields total quality costs. The optimal product quality level is the point that minimizes total quality costs.

Contemporary Perspective   Due largely to the influence of Japanese product quality expert Genichi Taguchi, the contemporary viewpoint of optimal product quality differs from the traditional perspective. The contemporary view is that if both observable and hidden costs of quality are considered, *any* deviation from a product's target specifications results in the incurrence of increasing quality costs. Under the contemporary

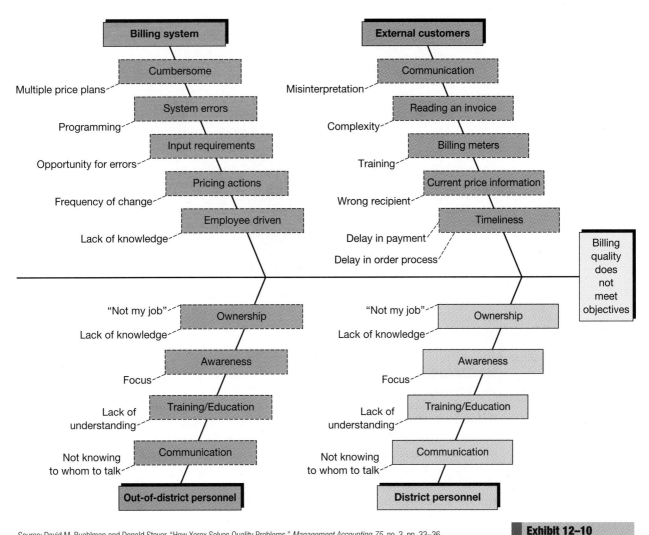

Source: David M. Buehlman and Donald Stover, "How Xerox Solves Quality Problems," *Management Accounting 75*, no. 3, pp. 33–36.

Exhibit 12–10

Cause and Effect Diagram: Billing Quality at Xerox Corporation

viewpoint, as depicted in Panel B of Exhibit 12–9, the optimal level of product quality occurs at the *zero defect level*. As Panel B shows, the observable and hidden costs of internal and external failure increase as the percentage of defective products increases. The observable and hidden costs of prevention and appraisal increase slightly and then decrease as the percentage of defects increases. The most important point, though, is that the total costs of quality are minimized at the zero defect level.

Whether the traditional or contemporary view of optimal product quality is most accurate is still being debated by quality control experts. Moreover, the exact shape of the cost functions in Exhibit 12–9 is largely an empirical question, and the cost functions probably differ among industries and product types. One thing is certain, though. To compete successfully in today's global market, any company must pay very close attention to achieving a very high level of product quality.

Total Quality Management   Monitoring product quality coupled with measuring and reporting quality costs helps companies maintain programs of **total quality management**, or **TQM**. This refers to the broad set of management and control processes designed to focus the entire organization and all of its employees on providing products or services that do the best possible job of satisfying the customer.

Total quality management (TQM) is the broad set of management processes designed to focus an entire organization and all of its employees on providing products or services that do the best possible job of satisfying the customer.

Pareto Diagram: Frequency of
Defect Types for Cordless
Telephone (Handico)

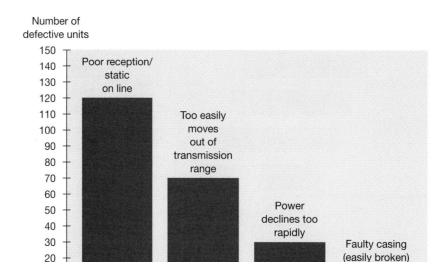

Identifying Quality-Control Problems   An effective TQM program includes methods for identifying quality-control problems. One method of identifying quality problems is the cause and effect diagram (also called an Ishikawa diagram or a fishbone diagram). Exhibit 12–10, which appears on the preceding page, displays a cause and effect diagram used by Xerox Corporation to identify the causes of errors in its customer billing process. As the diagram shows, the quality improvement team has identified a wide range of possible causes for billing errors. After identifying possible causes for billing errors, the Xerox team, nicknamed the Billing Bloopers Team, could take systematic steps to eliminate the root causes of the errors.

Another helpful tool in quality improvement programs is the Pareto diagram. Depicted in Exhibit 12–11, the Pareto diagram shows graphically the frequency with which various quality-control problems are observed for a particular model of cordless telephone. The Pareto diagram helps the TQM team visualize and communicate to others what the most serious types of defects are. Steps can be taken then to attack the most serious and most frequent problems first.

**Management
Accounting
Practice**

M.A.P.

Xerox Corporation

Quality improvement teams were established at Xerox to identify and solve quality problems. One team focused on billing quality, and management estimated that an investment of $7,000 in prevention activities saved the company $112,000 in quality costs due to billing errors in just a six-month period. The quality improvement efforts reduced billing errors by 52 percent and increased customer satisfaction with billing accuracy by 5.7 percent.[8]

---

[8]David M. Buehlmann and Donald Stover, "How Xerox Solves Quality Problems," *Management Accounting* 75, no. 3, pp. 33–36.

ISO 9000 Standards

A key factor in determining the quality of a company's products is its quality control system. The organizational structure, personnel, procedures, and policies that are in place to monitor product quality will greatly affect a firm's ability to achieve high quality standards. In 1987, the International Standards Organization (ISO), based in Geneva, Switzerland, issued a set of quality control standards for companies selling products in Europe. The ISO 9000 standards, as they have come to be known, focus on a manufacturer's quality control system. The ISO 9000 standards basically require that a manufacturer have a well-defined quality control system in place, and that the target level of product quality be maintained consistently. Moreover, the ISO 9000 standards require a manufacturer to prepare extensive documentation of all aspects of the quality control system. The first standard, ISO 9000, lists three objectives:

- The company should sustain the quality of its product or service at a level that continuously meets the purchaser's stated or implied needs.
- The quality control system should be sufficient to give the supplier's own management confidence that the intended quality is being maintained.
- The supplying company should give the purchaser confidence that the intended quality is consistently achieved in the delivered product or service.[9]

The ISO 9000 standards are now being adopted in the United States as well. The U.S. government and many large companies are more and more inclined to require adherence to the standards by their suppliers.

The ISO 9000 standards consist of five major parts. ISO 9000 states the objectives of the standards, defines a quality-related vocabulary, and provides a guide to the other standards in the series. ISO 9001 provides a model for quality assurance in design, development, production, installation, and servicing. ISO 9002 focuses more narrowly on quality assurance in production and installation. ISO 9003 addresses quality assurance in final inspection and testing. Finally, ISO 9004 provides guidelines for the design of a quality management system.

Implications for Managerial Accounting The ISO 9000 standards have several implications for managerial accountants. First, the standards require extensive documentation of the quality control system. This task often falls to the controller's office. In fact, several of the largest public accounting firms are offering assurance services in helping companies meet the ISO documentation requirements. Second, the ISO standards require that the costs and benefits of the quality control system be measured and documented. This means that management accountants will be responsible for measuring and reporting product life-cycle costs, quality costs, and the effectiveness of efforts at continuous improvement.

To summarize, the ISO 9000 standards are having a global impact on the way companies approach their quality assurance objectives. The standards will affect virtually every area within a firm subject to its guidelines. Managerial accountants will be integrally involved in the informational and documentation aspects of the ISO 9000 program.[10]

---

[9]This section draws upon F. Borthick and H. Roth, "Will Europeans Buy Your Company's Products?" *Management Accounting* 74, no. 1, pp. 28–32.

[10]The ISO standards are available from the American National Standards Institute, 105–111 South State Street, Hackensack, NJ 07601.

Chapter Summary

Responsibility-accounting systems are designed to foster goal congruence among the managers in decentralized organizations. Each subunit in an organization is designated as a cost center, revenue center, profit center, or investment center. The managerial accountant prepares a performance report for each responsibility center. These reports show the performance of the responsibility center and its manager for a specified time period.

To use responsibility accounting effectively, the emphasis must be on information rather than blame. The intent should be to provide managers with information to help them better manage their subunits. Responsibility-accounting systems can bring about desired behavior, such as reducing the number of rush orders in a manufacturing company.

Segmented income statements often are included in a responsibility-accounting system, to show the performance of the organization and its various segments. To be most effective, such reports should distinguish between the performance of segments and segment managers. Customer profitability analysis is an increasingly used tool that helps managers to better understand which customers are providing the greatest profit.

Product and service quality has become a key factor in determining a firm's success or failure in the global marketplace. As product quality becomes ever more important, many firms are beginning to carefully monitor the costs of maintaining product quality. Quality costs often are categorized as follows: prevention costs, appraisal costs, internal failure costs, and external failure cost. In addition to observable quality costs, companies experience hidden quality costs, such as the opportunity cost associated with lost market share. The contemporary perspective on product quality holds that if both observable and hidden costs of product quality are considered, the optimal level of product quality occurs at the zero defect level.

Monitoring product quality coupled with measuring and reporting quality costs helps companies maintain programs of total quality management, or TQM. This refers to the broad set of management and control processes designed to focus the entire organization and all of its employees on providing products or services that do the best possible job of satisfying the customer.

Review Problem on Responsibility Accounting

James Madison National Bank has a division for each of the two counties in which it operates, Cayuga and Oneida. Each divisional vice president is held accountable for both profit and invested capital. Each division consists of two branch banks, East and West. Each branch manager is responsible for that bank's profit. The Cayuga Division's East Branch has a Deposit Department, a Loan Department, and an Administrative Services Department. The department supervisors of the Loan and Deposit Departments are accountable for departmental revenues; the Administrative Services Department supervisor is accountable for costs.

All of James Madison National Bank's advertising and promotion is done centrally. The advertising and promotion cost pool for the year just ended, which amounted to $40,000, is allocated across the four branch banks on the basis of budgeted branch revenue. Budgeted revenue for the year is shown below.

Cayuga Division:	West Branch	$400,000
	East Branch	200,000
Oneida Division:	West Branch	250,000
	East Branch	150,000

Required:

1. Draw an organization chart for James Madison National Bank, which shows each subunit described above, its manager's title, and its designation as a responsibility center.
2. Distribute (allocate) the bank's advertising cost pool to the four branch banks.

Solution to Review Problem

1. Organization chart (subunits, managers, responsibility center designation) on the following page.
2. Cost distribution (or allocation):

Cost Pool	Responsibility Center	Allocation Base: Revenue	Percentage of Total*	Costs Distributed
Advertising	Cayuga, West Branch	$ 400,000	40%	$16,000
and	Cayuga, East Branch	200,000	20	8,000
promotion	Oneida, West Branch	250,000	25	10,000
costs	Oneida, East Branch	150,000	15	6,000
	Total	$1,000,000	100%	$40,000

*Branch revenue as a percentage of total revenue, $1,000,000.

Key Terms

For each term's definition refer to the indicated page, or turn to the glossary at the end of the text.

activity-based responsibility accounting, pg. 491

allocation base, pg. 489

appraisal costs, pg. 497

common costs, pg. 493

cost allocation (or distribution), pg. 489

cost center, pg. 484

cost objects, pg. 489

cost pool, pg. 489

customer profitability analysis, pg. 496

external failure costs, pg. 497

goal congruence, pg. 484

grade, pg. 496

internal failure costs, pg. 497

investment center, pg. 485

performance report, pg. 487

prevention costs, pg. 497

profit center, pg. 485

quality of conformance, pg. 497

quality of design, pg. 497

responsibility accounting, pg. 484

responsibility center, pg. 484

revenue center, pg. 485

segmented income statement, pg. 493

total quality management (TQM), pg. 499

Review Questions

12–1. Why is goal congruence important to an organization's success?

12–2. How does a responsibility-accounting system foster goal congruence?

12–3. One of the purposes of a responsibility-accounting system is to help an organization balance the costs and benefits of decentralization. Discuss some of the benefits and costs of decentralization.

12–4. Define and give examples of the following terms: *cost center, revenue center, profit center,* and *investment center.*

12–5. Under what circumstances would it be appropriate to change the Waikiki Sands Hotel from a profit center to an investment center?

12–6. Explain the relationship between performance reports and flexible budgeting.

12–7. What is the key feature of activity-based responsibility accounting? Briefly explain.

12–8. Explain how to get positive behavioral effects from a responsibility-accounting system.

12–9. "Performance reports based on controllability are impossible. Nobody really *controls* anything in an organization!" Do you agree or disagree? Explain your answer.

12–10. Define and give examples of the following terms: *cost pool* and *cost object.*

12–11. Define and give an example of *cost allocation* (or *distribution*).

12–12. Give an example of a common resource in an organization. List some of the opportunity costs associated with using the resource. Why might allocation of the cost of the common resource to its users be useful?

12–13. Explain how and why cost allocation might be used to assign the costs of a mainframe computer system used for research purposes in a university.

12–14. Define the term *cost allocation base.* What would be a sensible allocation base for assigning advertising costs to the various components of a large theme park?

12–15. Referring to Exhibit 12–5, why are marketing costs distributed to the Waikiki Sands Hotel's departments on the basis of *budgeted* sales dollars?

12–16. Explain what is meant by a *segmented income statement.*

12–17. Why do some managerial accountants choose not to allocate common costs in segmented reports?

12–18. Why is it important in responsibility accounting to distinguish between segments and segment managers?

12–19. List and explain three key features of the segmented income statement shown in Exhibit 12–7.

12–20. Can a common cost for one segment be a traceable cost for another segment? Explain your answer.

12–21. What is meant by *customer profitability analysis*? Give an example of an activity that might be performed more commonly for one customer than for another.

12–22. List and define four types of product quality costs.

12–23. Explain the difference between observable and hidden quality costs.

12–24. Distinguish between a product's quality of design and its quality of conformance.

12–25. What is meant by a product's *grade,* as a characteristic of quality? Give an example in the service industry.

12–26. "An ounce of prevention is worth a pound of cure." Interpret this old adage in light of Exhibit 12–8.

12–27. Briefly explain the purpose of a cause and effect (or fishbone) diagram.

Exercises

■ **Exercise 12–28**
Designating Responsibility Centers.
(LO 2)

For each of the following organizational subunits, indicate the type of responsibility center that is most appropriate.

1. An orange juice factory operated by a large orange grower.
2. The College of Engineering at a large state university.
3. The European Division of a multinational manufacturing company.
4. The outpatient clinic in a profit-oriented hospital.
5. The Mayor's Office in a large city.
6. A movie theater in a company that operates a chain of theaters.
7. A radio station owned by a large broadcasting network.
8. The claims department in an insurance company.
9. The ticket sales division of a major airline.
10. A bottling plant of a soft drink company.

■ **Exercise 12–29**
Assigning Responsibility for Skilled Employees' Wages
(LO 1)

Oradel Electronics Company manufactures complex circuit boards for the aerospace industry. Demand for the company's products has fallen in recent months, and the firm has cut its production significantly. Many unskilled workers have been temporarily laid off. Top management has made a decision, however, not to lay off any highly skilled employees, such as inspectors and machinery operators. Management was concerned that these highly skilled employees would easily find new jobs elsewhere and not return when production returned to normal levels.

To occupy the skilled employees during the production cutback, they have been reassigned temporarily to the Maintenance Department. Here they are performing general maintenance tasks, such as repainting the interior of the factory, repairing the loading dock, and building wooden storage racks for the warehouse. The skilled employees continued to receive their normal wages, which average $22 per hour. However, the normal wages for Maintenance Department employees average $12 per hour.

The supervisor of the Maintenance Department recently received the March performance report, which indicated that his department's labor cost exceeded the budget by $19,360. The department's actual labor cost was approximately 90 percent over the budget. The department supervisor complained to the controller.

Required:

As the controller, how would you respond? Would you make any modification in Oradel's responsibility-accounting system? If so, list the changes you would make. Explain your reasoning.

Xerox Corporation changed the responsibility-center orientation of its Logistics and Distribution Department from a cost center to a profit center. The department manages the inventories and provides other logistical services to the company's Business Systems Group. Formerly, the manager of the Logistics and Distribution Department was held accountable for adherence to an operating expense budget. Now the department "sells" its services to the company's other segments, and the department's manager is evaluated partially on the basis of the department's profit. Xerox Corporation's management feels that the change has been beneficial. The change has resulted in more innovative thinking in the department and has moved decision making down to lower levels in the company.[11]

■ **Exercise 12–30**
Responsibility-Accounting Centers; Xerox Corporation
(LO 1, LO 2)

Required:

Comment on the new responsibility-center designation for the Logistics and Distribution Department.

How should a responsibility-accounting system handle each of the following scenarios?

1. Department A manufactures a component, which is then used by Department B. Department A recently experienced a machine breakdown which held up production of the component. As a result, Department B was forced to curtail its own production, thereby incurring large costs of idle time. An investigation revealed that Department A's machinery had not been properly maintained.

2. Refer to the scenario above, but suppose the investigation revealed the machinery in Department A had been properly maintained.

■ **Exercise 12–31**
Responsibility Accounting; Equipment Breakdown
(LO 1, LO 2)

The following data pertain to the Waikiki Sands Hotel for the month of March.

■ **Exercise 12–32**
Performance Report; Hotel
(LO 3)

	Flexible Budget March (in thousand)*	Actual Results March (in thousands)*
Banquets and Catering	$ 650	$ 658
Restaurants	1,800	1,794
Kitchen staff wages	(85)	(86)
Food	(690)	(690)
Paper products	(125)	(122)
Variable overhead	(75)	(78)
Fixed overhead	(90)	(93)

*Numbers without parentheses denote profit; numbers with parentheses denote expenses.

Required:

Prepare a March performance report similar to the lower portion of Exhibit 12–4. The report should have six numerical columns with headings analogous to those in Exhibit 12–4. Your performance report should cover only the Food and Beverage Department and the Kitchen. Draw arrows to show the relationships between the numbers in the report. Refer to Exhibit 12–4 for guidance. For the year-to-date columns in your report, use the data given in Exhibit 12–4. You will need to update those figures using the March data given above.

Countywide Cable Services, Inc. is organized with three segments: Metro, Suburban, and Outlying. Data for these segments for the year just ended follow.

■ **Exercise 12–33**
Segmented Income Statement; TV Cable Company
(LO 5)

---

[11]F. Tucker and S. Zivian, "A Xerox Cost Center Imitates a Profit Center," *Harvard Business Review* 63, no. 3, pp. 161–74.

	Metro	Suburban	Outlying
Service revenue	$1,000,000	$800,000	$400,000
Variable expenses	200,000	150,000	100,000
Controllable fixed expenses	400,000	320,000	150,000
Fixed expenses controllable by others	230,000	200,000	90,000

In addition to the expenses listed above, the company has $95,000 of common fixed expenses. Income-tax expense for the year is $145,000.

Required:

Prepare a segmented income statement for Countywide Cable Services, Inc. Use the contribution format.

■ **Exercise 12–34**
Cost Allocation in a College
(LO 4)

Tioga Community College has three divisions: Liberal Arts, Sciences, and Business Administration. The college's comptroller is trying to decide how to allocate the costs of the Admissions Department, the Registrar's Department, and the Computer Services Department. The comptroller has compiled the following data for the year just ended.

Department	Annual Cost
Admissions	$ 90,000
Registrar	150,000
Computer Services	320,000

Division	Budgeted Enrollment	Budgeted Credit Hours	Planned Courses Requiring Computer Work
Liberal Arts	1,000	30,000	12
Sciences	800	28,000	24
Business Administration	700	22,000	24

Required:

1. For each department, choose an allocation base and distribute the departmental costs to the college's three divisions. Justify your choice of an allocation base.

2. Would you have preferred a different allocation base than those available using the data compiled by the comptroller? Why?

■ **Exercise 12–35**
Quality Costs
(LO 6)

The following costs were incurred by Geneva Metals Company to maintain the quality of its products.

1. Operating an X-ray machine to detect faulty welds.
2. Repairs of products sold last year.
3. Cost of rewelding faulty joints.
4. Cost of sending machine operators to a three-week training program so they could learn to use new production equipment with a lower defect rate.

Required:

Classify each of these costs as a prevention, appraisal, internal failure, or external failure cost.

■ **Exercise 12–36**
Quality-Cost Report
(LO 6)

Universal Circuitry manufactures electrical instruments for a variety of purposes. The following costs related to maintaining product quality were incurred in May.

Training of quality-control inspectors	$21,000
Tests of instruments before sale	30,000
Inspection of electrical components purchased from outside suppliers	12,000
Costs of rework on faulty instruments	9,000
Replacement of instruments already sold, which were still covered by warranty	16,500
Costs of defective parts that cannot be salvaged	6,100

Required:

Prepare a quality-cost report similar to the report shown in Exhibit 12–8.

List three observable and three hidden quality costs that could occur in the airline industry related to the quality of service provided.

■ **Exercise 12–37**
Costs of Quality; Airline
(LO 6)

Problems

Here is your chance to be a tycoon. Create your own company. You will be the president and chief executive officer. It could be a manufacturer, retailer, or service industry firm, but *not* a hotel or bank. Draw an organization chart for your company, similar to the one in Exhibit 12–1. Identify divisions and departments at all levels in the organization. Then prepare a companion chart similar to the one in Exhibit 12–2. This chart should designate the title of the manager of a subunit at each level in the organization. It also should designate the type of responsibility center appropriate for each of these subunits. Finally, write a letter to your company's stockholders summarizing the major responsibilities of each of the managers you identified in your chart. For guidance, refer to the discussion of Exhibits 12–1 and 12–2 in the chapter. (Have some fun, and be creative.)

■ **Problem 12–38**
Create an Organization
(LO 1, LO 2)

After designing your company, design a set of performance reports for the subunits you identified in your chart. Make up numbers for the performance reports, and show the relationship between the reports. Refer to Exhibit 12–4 for guidance.

■ **Problem 12–39**
Design Performance
Reports; Continuation of
Preceding Problem
(LO 3)

The following partial organization chart is an extension of Exhibit 12–1 for Aloha Hotels and Resorts.

■ **Problem 12–40**
Designating Responsibility
Centers; Hotel
(LO 2)

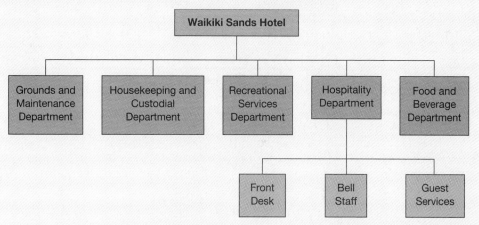

Each of the hotel's four main departments is managed by a director (e.g., director of hospitality). The Front Desk subunit, which is supervised by the front desk manager, handles the hotel's reservations, room assignments, guest payments, and key control. The Bell staff, managed by the bell captain, is responsible for greeting guests, front door service, assisting guests with their luggage, and delivering room-service orders. The Guest Services subunit, supervised by the manager of Guest Services, is responsible for assisting guests with local transportation arrangements, advising guests on tourist attractions, and such conveniences as valet and floral services.

Required:

As an outside consultant, write a memo to the hotel's general manager suggesting a responsibility-center designation for each of the subunits shown in the organization chart above. Justify your choices.

Appalachian General Hospital serves three counties in West Virginia. The hospital is a nonprofit organization, which is supported by patient billings, county and state funds, and private donations. The hospital's organization is shown in the following chart.

■ **Problem 12–41**
Preparation of Performance
Reports; Hospital.
(LO 3)

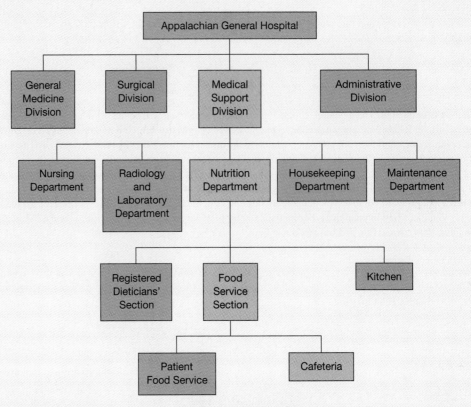

The following cost information has been compiled for August.

	Budget		Actual	
	August	**Year to Date**	**August**	**Year to Date**
Cafeteria:				
Food servers' wages	$ 8,000	$ 64,000	$ 9,000	$ 72,000
Paper products	4,500	36,000	4,400	36,200
Utilities	1,000	8,000	1,050	8,100
Maintenance	400	3,200	100	1,100
Custodial	1,100	8,800	1,100	8,600
Supplies	1,200	9,600	900	9,600
Patient Food Service	17,000	136,000	18,500	137,000
Registered Dietitians'				
Section	7,500	60,000	7,500	60,000
Kitchen	31,000	248,000	29,400	246,000
Nursing Department	70,000	560,000	75,000	580,000
Radiology and Laboratory				
Department	18,000	144,000	18,100	144,000
Housekeeping Department	10,000	80,000	11,600	86,000
Maintenance Department	13,000	104,000	6,000	77,000
General Medicine Division	210,000	1,680,000	204,000	1,670,900
Surgical Division	140,000	1,120,000	141,000	1,115,800
Administrative Division	50,000	400,000	53,500	406,000

Required:

1. Prepare a set of cost performance reports similar to Exhibit 12–4. The report should have six columns, as in Exhibit 12–4. The first four columns will have the same headings as those used above. The last two columns will have the following headings: Variance—August, and Variance—Year to Date.

    Since all of the information in the performance reports for Appalachian General Hospital is cost information, you do not need to show these data in parentheses. Use F or U to denote whether each variance in the reports is favorable or unfavorable.

2. Using arrows, show the relationships between the numbers in your performance reports for Appalachian General Hospital. Refer to Exhibit 12–4 for guidance.

3. Put yourself in the place of the hospital's administrator. Which variances in the performance reports would you want to investigate further? Why?

Refer to the organization chart for Appalachian General Hospital given in the preceding problem. Ignore the rest of the data in that problem. The following table shows the cost allocation bases used to distribute various costs among the hospital's divisions.

■ **Problem 12–42**
Cost Distribution Using Allocation Bases; Hospital
(LO 4)

Cost Pool	Cost Allocation Base	Annual Cost
Facilities:		
Building depreciation	Square feet of space	$190,000
Equipment depreciation		
Insurance		
Utilities:		
Electricity	Cubic feet of space	24,000
Waste disposal		
Water and sewer		
Cable TV and phone		
Heat		
General administration:		
Administrator	Budgeted number of employees	220,000
Administrative staff		
Office supplies		
Community outreach:		
Public education	Budgeted dollars of patient billings	40,000
School physical exams		

Shown below are the amounts of each cost allocation base associated with each division.

	Square Feet	Cubic Feet	Number of Employees	Patient Billings
General Medicine Division	15,000	135,000	30	$2,000,000
Surgical Division	8,000	100,000	20	1,250,000
Medical Support Division	9,000	90,000	20	750,000
Administrative Division	8,000	75,000	30	0
Total	40,000	400,000	100	$4,000,000

Required:

1. Prepare a table similar to Exhibit 12–5 which distributes each of the costs listed in the preceding table to the hospital's divisions.

2. Comment on the appropriateness of patient billings as the basis for distributing community outreach costs to the hospital's divisions. Can you suggest a better allocation base?

3. Is there any use in allocating utilities costs to the divisions? What purposes could such an allocation process serve?

Buckeye Department Stores, Inc. operates a chain of department stores in Ohio. The company's organization chart appears below. Operating data for 19x9 follow.

■ **Problem 12–43**
Prepare Segmented Income Statement; Contribution-Margin Format; Retail
(LO 5)

BUCKEYE DEPARTMENT STORES, INC.
Operating Data for 19x9
(in thousands)

	Columbus Division			Cleveland Division
	Olentangy Store	**Scioto Store**	**Downtown Store**	**(total for all stores)**
Sales revenue	$5,000	$2,400	$11,000	$21,000
Variable expenses:				
Cost of merchandise sold	3,000	2,000	6,000	12,000
Sales personnel—salaries . . .	400	300	750	1,600
Sales commissions	50	40	90	200
Utilities	80	60	150	300
Other	60	35	120	250
Fixed expenses:				
Depreciation—buildings	120	90	250	470
Depreciation—furnishings . . .	80	50	140	290
Computing and billing	40	30	75	160
Warehouse	70	60	200	450
Insurance	40	25	90	200
Property taxes	35	20	80	170
Supervisory salaries	150	100	400	900
Security	30	30	80	210

The following fixed expenses are controllable at the divisional level: depreciation—furnishings, computing and billing, warehouse, insurance, and security. In addition to these expenses, each division annually incurs $50,000 of computing costs, which are not allocated to individual stores.

The following fixed expenses are controllable only at the company level: depreciation—building, property taxes, and supervisory salaries. In addition to these expenses, each division incurs costs for supervisory salaries of $100,000, which are not allocated to individual stores.

Buckeye Department Stores incurs common fixed expenses of $120,000, which are not allocated to the two divisions. Income-tax expense for 19x9 is $1,950,000.

Required:

1. Prepare a segmented income statement similar to Exhibit 12–7 for Buckeye Department Stores, Inc. The statement should have the following columns:

	Segments of Company		Segments of Columbus Division			
Buckeye Department Stores, Inc.	**Cleveland Division**	**Columbus Division**	**Olentangy Store**	**Scioto Store**	**Downtown Store**	**Not Allocated**

Prepare the statement in the contribution format, and indicate the controllability of expenses. Subtract all variable expenses, including cost of merchandise sold, from sales revenue to obtain the contribution margin.

2. How would the segmented income statement help the president of Buckeye Department Stores manage the company?

■ **Problem 12–44**
Segmented Income
Statement
(LO 5)

Omicron Corporation manufactures two different styles of mailboxes in its only production facility located near Tulsa, Oklahoma. Omicron sells its products primarily to large retail firms. Omicron employs two full-time sales employees, Anne Fraser and Joe McDonough. Each sales employee receives an annual salary of $14,000 plus a sales commission of 10 percent of his or her total gross sales. Travel and entertainment expense is budgeted at $22,000 annually for each sales employee. Fraser is expected to sell 60 percent of the budgeted unit sales for each product, and McDonough the remaining 40 percent. The remaining selling and administrative expenses include (1) fixed administrative costs of $80,000 that cannot be traced to either product, and (2) the following traceable selling expenses.

	Post Mounted	**Wall Mounted**
Packaging expenses per unit	$2.00	$1.50
Promotional expenses	$30,000	$40,000

Data regarding Omicron's budgeted and actual sales for 19x9 follow. There were no changes in the beginning and ending balances of either finished-goods or work-in-process inventories.

	Post Mounted	Wall Mounted
Budgeted and actual unit sales price	$29.50	$19.50
Budgeted sales volume in units	15,000	15,000
Actual unit sales:		
Fraser	10,000	9,500
McDonough	5,000	10,500
Total units	15,000	20,000

Budgeted variable production costs per unit are as follows:

	Post Mounted	Wall Mounted
Sheet metal	$ 3.50	—
Plastic	—	$3.75
Direct labor ($8 per hour)	4.00	2.00
Variable manufacturing overhead ($9 per direct-labor hour)	4.50	2.25
Total	$12.00	$8.00

Variable manufacturing-overhead costs vary with direct-labor hours. The annual fixed manufacturing-overhead costs are budgeted at $120,000. A total of 50 percent of these costs are directly traceable to the Post Mounted Mail Box Department, and 22 percent of the costs are traceable to the Wall Mounted Mail Box Department. The remaining 28 percent of the costs are not traceable to either department. Data regarding Omicron's 19x9 operating expenses follow.

■ There were no increases or decreases in direct-material inventory for either sheet metal or plastic, and there were no material-quality variances. However, sheet metal prices were 6 percent above budget and plastic prices were 4 percent below budget.

■ The actual direct-labor hours worked and the costs incurred were as follows:

	Hours	Amount
Post mounted	7,500	$ 57,000
Wall mounted	6,000	45,600
Total	13,500	$102,600

■ Fixed manufacturing-overhead costs attributable to the Post Mounted Mail Box Department were $8,000 above the budget. All other fixed manufacturing-overhead costs were incurred at the same amounts as budgeted, and all variable manufacturing-overhead costs were incurred at the budgeted hourly rates.

■ All selling and administrative expenses were incurred at the budgeted amounts except the following items.

Nontraceable administrative expenses		$ 34,000
Promotional expenses:		
Post mounted	$32,000	
Wall mounted	58,000	90,000
Travel and entertainment:		
Fraser	$24,000	
McDonough	8,000	52,000
Total		$176,000

Required:

1. Prepare a segmented income statement for Omicron Corporation for 19x9. The report should be prepared in a contribution-margin format by product line. It should show total income (or loss) for the company before taxes.

2. Identify and discuss any additional analyses that could be made of the data presented that would be of value to Omicron Corporation's management.

(CMA, adapted)

■ **Problem 12–45**
Performance Reporting
(LO 3)

Refer to the information about Omicron Corporation provided in the preceding problem.

Required:

Prepare a performance report for 19x9 that would be useful in evaluating the performance of Joe McDonough.

(CMA, adapted)

■ **Problem 12–46**
Evaluation of Segmented
Reports; Ethics
(LO 3, LO 5)

Pittsburgh-Walsh Company (PWC) manufactures lighting fixtures and electronic timing devices. The Lighting Fixtures Division assembles units for the upscale and midrange markets. The Electronic Timing Devices Division manufactures instrument panels that allow electronic systems to be activated and deactivated at scheduled times for both efficiency and safety purposes. Both divisions operate out of the same manufacturing facilities and share production equipment. PWC's budget for 20x0 follows.

PITTSBURGH-WALSH COMPANY
Budget for the Year Ending December 31, 20x0
(in thousands)

| | Lighting Fixtures | | Electronic | |
	Upscale	Midrange	Timing Devices	Total
Sales	$1,440	$770	$800	$3,010
Variable expenses:				
Cost of goods sold	$ 720	$439	$320	$1,479
Selling and administrative	170	60	60	290
Contribution margin	$ 550	$271	$420	$1,241
Fixed overhead expenses	140	80	80	300
Segment margin	$ 410	$191	$340	$ 941
Common fixed expenses:				
Overhead	48	132	120	300
Selling and administrative	11	31	28	70
Net income (loss)	$ 351	$ 28	$192	$ 571

The budget was prepared on a segmented basis under the following guidelines:

■ Variable costs and traceable fixed overhead costs are assigned directly to the incurring division.

■ Common fixed expenses are allocated to the division on the basis of units produced, which bears a close relationship to direct labor. Included in common fixed expenses are costs of the corporate staff, legal expenses, taxes, staff marketing, and advertising.

■ The production plan is for 8,000 upscale fixtures, 22,000 midrange fixtures, and 20,000 electronic timing devices.

PWC established a bonus plan for division management that requires meeting the division's planned net income by product line, with a bonus increment if the division exceeds the planned product line net income by 10 percent or more.

Shortly before the year began, the CEO, Anne Parkow, suffered a heart attack and retired. After reviewing the 20x0 budget, the new CEO, Joe Kelly, decided to close the lighting fixtures midrange product line by the end of the first quarter and use the available production capacity to emphasize the remaining two product lines. The marketing staff advised that electronic timing devices could grow by 40 percent with increased direct sales support. Increases above that level and increasing sales of upscale lighting fixtures would require expanded advertising expenditures to increase consumer awareness of PWC as an electronics and lighting fixture company. Kelly approved the increased sales support and advertising expenditures to achieve the revised plan. Kelly advised the divisions that for bonus purposes the original product line net income objectives must be met, but he did allow the Lighting Fixtures Division to combine the net income objectives for both product lines for bonus purposes.

Prior to the close of the fiscal year, the division controllers were furnished with preliminary actual data for review and adjustment, as appropriate. These preliminary year-end data, which reflect the revised production quantities amounting to 12,000 upscale fixtures, 4,000 midrange fixtures, and 30,000 electronic timing devices, are as follows:

PITTSBURGH-WALSH COMPANY
Preliminary Actual Data for 20x0
(in thousands)

| | Lighting Fixtures | | Electronic | |
	Upscale	Midrange	Timing Devices	Total
Sales	$2,160	$140	$1,200	$3,500
Variable expenses:				
Cost of goods sold	$1,080	$ 80	$480	$1,640
Selling and administrative	260	11	96	367
Contribution margin	$ 820	$ 49	$624	$1,493
Fixed overhead expenses	140	14	80	234
Segment margin	$ 680	$ 35	$544	$1,259
Common fixed expenses:				
Overhead	78	27	195	300
Selling and administrative	60	20	150	230
Net income (loss)	$ 542	$(12)	$199	$ 729

The controller of the Lighting Fixtures Division, anticipating a similar bonus plan for 20x1, is contemplating deferring some revenues into the next year on the pretext that the sales are not yet final, and accruing in the current year expenditures that will be applicable to the first quarter of 20x1. The corporation would meet its annual plan and the division would exceed the 10 percent incremental bonus cutoff in the year 20x0 despite the deferred revenues and accrued expenses contemplated.

Required:

1. Outline the benefits that an organization realizes from segment reporting.

2. *a.* Segment reporting can be developed based on different criteria. What criteria must be present for division management to accept being evaluated on a segment basis?

   b. Why would the management of the Electronic Timing Devices Division be unhappy with the current reporting scheme, and how should it be revised to gain their acceptance?

3. Explain why the adjustments contemplated by the controller of the Lighting Fixtures Division are unethical. Cite specific standards of ethical conduct discussed in Chapter 1.

(CMA, adapted)

Ujvari Sports Equipment Company, which is located near the Black Forest region of southwestern Germany, manufactures soccer equipment. The company's primary product, a professional-quality soccer ball, is among the best produced in Europe. The company operates in a very price-competitive industry, so it has little control over the price of its products. It *must* meet the market price. To do so, the firm has to keep production costs in check by operating as efficiently as possible. Matthias Basler, the company's president, has stated that to be successful, the company must provide a very high-quality product and meet its delivery commitments to customers on time. Ujvari Sports Equipment Company is organized as shown below.

■ **Problem 12–47**
Designing a Responsibility-Accounting System
(LO 1, LO 2)

There is currently a disagreement between the company's two vice presidents regarding the responsibility-accounting system. The vice president for manufacturing claims that the 10 plants should be cost centers. He recently expressed the following sentiment: "The plants should be cost centers because the plant managers do not control the sales of our products. Designating the plants as profit centers would result in holding the plant managers responsible for something they can't control." A contrary view is held by the vice president for marketing. He recently made the following remarks: "The plants should be profit centers. The plant managers are in the best position to affect the company's overall profit."

Required:

As the company's new controller, you have been asked to make a recommendation to Matthias Basler, the company president, regarding the responsibility center issue. Write a memo to the president making a recommendation and explaining the reasoning behind it. In your memo address the following points.

1. Assuming that Ujvari Sports Equipment Company's overall goal is profitability, what are the company's critical success factors? A *critical success factor* is a variable that meets these two criteria: It is largely under the company's control, and the company must succeed in this area in order to reach its overall goal of profitability.

2. Which responsibility-accounting arrangement is most consistent with achieving success on the company's critical success factors?

3. What responsibility-center designation is most appropriate for the company's sales districts?

4. As a specific example, consider the rush-order problem illustrated in the chapter. Suppose that Ujvari Sports Equipment Company often experiences rush orders from its customers. Which of the two proposed responsibility-accounting arrangements is best suited to making good decisions about accepting or rejecting rush orders? Specifically, should the plants be cost centers or profit centers?

■ **Problem 12–48**
Quality-Improvement
Programs and Quality Costs
(LO 6, LO 7)

Print Media Technology, Inc. manufactures computerized printing equipment used by newspaper publishers throughout North America. In recent years, the company's market share has been eroded by stiff competition from Asian and European competitors. Price and product quality are the two key areas in which companies compete in this market.

Ben McDonough, Print Media Technology's president, decided to devote more resources to the improvement of product quality after learning that his company's products had been ranked fourth in product quality in a recent survey of newspaper publishers. He believed that Print Media Technology could no longer afford to ignore the importance of product quality. McDonough set up a task force which he headed to implement a formal quality-improvement program. Included on the task force were representatives from engineering, sales, customer service, production, and accounting, as McDonough believed this was a companywide program and all employees should share the responsibility for its success.

After the first meeting of the task force, Sheila Hayes, manager of sales, asked Tony Reese, the production manager, what he thought of the proposed program. Reese replied, "I have reservations. Quality is too abstract to be attaching costs to it and then to be holding you and me responsible for cost improvements. I like to work with goals that I can see and count! I don't like my annual income to be based on a decrease in quality costs; there are too many variables that we have no control over!"

Print Media Technology's quality-improvement program has now been in operation for 18 months, and the quality cost report shown at the top of the next page has recently been issued. As they were reviewing the report, Hayes asked Reese what he thought of the quality program now. "The work is really moving through the Production Department," replied Reese. "We used to spend time helping the Customer Service Department solve their problems, but they are leaving us alone these days. I have no complaints so far. I'll be anxious to see how much the program increases our bonuses."

Required:

1. Identify at least three factors that should be present for an organization to successfully implement a quality improvement program.

2. By analyzing the cost of quality report presented, determine if Print Media Technology's quality improvement program has been successful. List specific evidence to support your answer.

3. Discuss why Tony Reese's current reaction to the quality improvement program is more favorable than his initial reaction.

4. Print Media Technology's president believed that the quality improvement program was essential and that the firm could no longer afford to ignore the importance of product quality. Discuss how the company could measure the opportunity cost of not implementing the quality-improvement program.

(CMA, adapted)

PRINT MEDIA TECHNOLOGY, INC.
Cost of Quality Report
(in thousands)

	Quarter Ended					
	6/30/x8	9/30/x8	12/31/x8	3/31/x9	6/30/x9	9/30/x9
Prevention costs:						
Design review	$ 20	$ 102	$ 111	$ 100	$ 104	$ 95
Machine maintenance	215	215	202	190	170	160
Training suppliers	5	45	25	20	20	15
Total	$ 240	$ 362	$ 338	$ 310	$ 294	$ 270
Appraisal costs:						
Incoming inspection	$ 45	$ 53	$ 57	$ 36	$ 34	$ 22
Final testing	160	160	154	140	115	94
Total	$ 205	$ 213	$ 211	$ 176	$ 149	$ 116
Internal failure costs:						
Rework	$ 120	$ 106	$ 114	$ 88	$ 78	$ 62
Scrap	68	64	53	42	40	40
Total	$ 188	$ 170	$ 167	$ 130	$ 118	$ 102
External failure costs:						
Warranty repairs	$ 69	$ 31	$ 24	$ 25	$ 23	$ 23
Customer returns	262	251	122	116	87	80
Total	$ 331	$ 282	$ 146	$ 141	$ 110	$ 103
Total quality cost	$ 964	$1,027	$ 862	$ 757	$ 671	$ 591
Total production cost	$4,120	$4,540	$4,380	$4,650	$4,580	$4,510

Cases

Music Teachers Inc. is a professional association for music teachers that had 20,000 members during 19x9. The association operates from a central headquarters but has local membership chapters throughout the country. Monthly meetings are held by the local chapters to discuss recent developments on topics of interest to music teachers. The association's journal, *Teachers' Forum,* is issued monthly with features about recent developments in the field. The association publishes books and reports and sponsors professional courses that qualify for continuing professional education credit. The Statement of Revenue and Expenses for 19x9 follows.

■ **Case 12–49**
Segmented Report
(LO 5)

MUSIC TEACHERS INC.
Statement of Revenue and Expenses
For the Year Ended December 31, 19x9
(in thousands)

Revenue	$3,275
Expenses	
Salaries	$ 920
Personnel benefits	230
Occupancy costs	280
Reimbursement to local chapters	600
Other membership services	500
Printing and paper	320
Postage and shipping	176
Instructors' fees	80
General and administrative	38
Total expenses	$3,144
Excess of revenue over expenses	$ 131

The board of directors of Music Teachers Inc. has requested that a segmented statement of operations be prepared showing the contribution of each revenue center (i.e., Membership, Magazine

Subscriptions, Books and Reports, Continuing Education). Mike Cabrerra has been assigned this responsibility and has gathered the following data prior to statement preparation.

- Membership dues are $100 per year of which $20 is considered to cover a one-year subscription to the association's journal. Other benefits include membership in the association and chapter affiliation. Part of the membership fee is reimbursed to the various local chapters. The portion of the dues covering the magazine subscription ($20) should be assigned to the Magazine Subscriptions revenue center.

- One-year subscriptions to *Teachers' Forum* were sold to nonmembers and libraries at $30 each. A total of 2,500 of these subscriptions were sold. In addition to subscriptions, the magazine generated $100,000 in advertising revenue. The costs per magazine subscription were $7 for printing and paper and $4 for postage and shipping.

- A total of 28,000 technical reports and professional texts were sold by the Books and Reports Department at an average unit selling price of $25. Average costs per publication were as follows:

Printing and paper	$4
Postage and shipping	$2

- The association offers a variety of continuing education courses. The one-day courses cost $75 each and were attended by 2,400 people in 19x9. A total of 1,760 people took two-day courses at a cost of $125 for each course. Outside instructors were paid to teach some courses.

- Salary and occupancy data are as follows.

	Salaries	Square Footage
Membership	$210,000	2,000
Magazine subscriptions	150,000	2,000
Books and reports	300,000	3,000
Continuing education	180,000	2,000
Corporate staff	80,000	1,000
Total	$920,000	10,000

The Books and Reports Department also rents warehouse space at an annual cost of $50,000. Personnel fringe benefits cost 25 percent of salaries.

- Printing and paper costs, other than for magazine subscriptions and books and reports, relate to the Continuing Education Department.

- General and administrative expenses include all other costs incurred by the corporate staff to operate the association.

Cabrerra has decided he will assign all revenues and expenses to the revenue centers provided they can be (1) traced directly to a revenue center, or (2) allocated on a reasonable basis. The expenses that can be traced or assigned to corporate staff as well as any other expenses that cannot be assigned to revenue centers will be grouped with the general and administrative expenses and not allocated to the revenue centers.

Required:

1. Prepare a segmented Statement of Revenue and Expenses that presents the contribution of each revenue center and includes the common costs of the organization that are not allocated to the revenue centers.

2. If segmented reporting is adopted by the association for continuing usage, discuss the ways the information provided by the report can be utilized by the association.

(CMA, adapted)

■ **Case 12–50**
Segmented Income
Statement; International
Operations
(LO 1, LO 5)

Atlantico, Ltd. is a diversified company whose products are marketed both domestically and internationally. The company's major product lines are pharmaceutical products, sports equipment, and household appliances. At a recent meeting of Atlantico's board of directors, there was a lengthy discussion on ways to improve overall corporate profitability. The members of the board decided that they required additional financial information about individual corporate operations in order to target areas for improvement.

Dave Murphy, Atlantico's controller, has been asked to provide additional data that would assist the board in its investigation. Murphy believes that income statements, prepared along both product lines and geographic areas, would provide the directors with the required insight into corporate operations. Murphy had several discussions with the division managers for each product line and compiled the following information from these meetings.

| | Product Lines | | | |
	Pharmaceutical	Sports	Appliances	Total
Production and sales in units	160,000	180,000	160,000	500,000
Average selling price per unit	$8.00	$20.00	$15.00	
Average variable manufacturing cost per unit	$4.00	$9.50	$8.25	
Average variable selling expense per unit	$2.00	$2.50	$2.25	
Fixed manufacturing overhead, excluding depreciation				$500,000
Depreciation of plant and equipment				$400,000
Administrative and selling expense				$1,160,000

1. The division managers concluded that Murphy should allocate fixed manufacturing overhead to both product lines and geographic areas on the basis of the ratio of the variable costs expended to total variable costs.

2. Each of the division managers agreed that a reasonable basis for the allocation of depreciation on plant and equipment would be the ratio of units produced per product line (or per geographical area) to the total number of units produced.

3. There was little agreement on the allocation of administrative and selling expenses, so Murphy decided to allocate only those expenses that were traceable directly to a segment. For example, manufacturing staff salaries would be allocated to product lines, and sales staff salaries would be allocated to geographic areas. Murphy used the following data for this allocation.

Manufacturing Staff		Sales Staff	
Pharmaceutical	$120,000	United States	$ 60,000
Sports	140,000	Canada	100,000
Appliances	80,000	Europe	250,000

4. The division managers were able to provide reliable sales percentages for their product lines by geographical area.

| | Percentage of Unit Sales | | |
	United States	Canada	Europe
Pharmaceutical	40%	10%	50%
Sports	40%	40%	20%
Appliances	20%	20%	60%

Murphy prepared the following product-line income statement based on the data presented above.

ATLANTICO, LTD.
Segmented Income Statement by Product Lines
For the Fiscal Year Ended April 30, 20x0

| | Product Lines | | | | |
	Pharmaceutical	Sports	Appliances	Unallocated	Total
Sales in units	160,000	180,000	160,000		
Sales	$1,280,000	$3,600,000	$2,400,000	—	$7,280,000
Variable manufacturing and selling costs	960,000	2,160,000	1,680,000	—	4,800,000
Contribution margin	$ 320,000	$1,440,000	$ 720,000	—	$2,480,000
Fixed costs:					
Fixed manufacturing overhead	$ 100,000	$ 225,000	$ 175,000	$ —	$ 500,000
Depreciation	128,000	144,000	128,000	—	400,000
Administrative and selling expenses . . .	120,000	140,000	80,000	820,000	1,160,000
Total fixed costs	$ 348,000	$ 509,000	$ 383,000	$ 820,000	$2,060,000
Operating income (loss)	$ (28,000)	$ 931,000	$ 337,000	$(820,000)	$ 420,000

Required:

1. Prepare a segmented income statement for Atlantico, Ltd. based on the company's geographical areas. The statement should show the operating income for each segment.

2. As a result of the information disclosed by both segmented income statements (by product line and by geographic area), recommend areas where Atlantico should focus its attention in order to improve corporate profitability.

(CMA, adapted)

Current Issues in Managerial Accounting

■ **Issue 12–51**
Performance Reports

"High-Tech Chiefs Keep One Eye on the Door," *The Wall Street Journal,* **August 30, 1996, Joann Lublin.**

Overview

CEOs of high-tech companies are being replaced more rapidly. Several executives of large technology firms were forced to leave after serving less than two years as the CEO.

Suggested Discussion Questions

Discuss how an accounting measurement system could possibly prevent this from happening? In an industry in which technology changes so quickly, should an accounting performance report play a more significant or less important role? Is the current financial reporting system adequate in this environment?

■ **Issue 12–52**
Responsibility Accounting and Segmented Reporting

"Changing Performance Measures at Caterpillar," *Management Accounting,* **December 1996, James A. Hendricks, David Defreitas, and Delores K. Walker.**

Overview

This article explains how Caterpillar changed its organizational structure and performance measurement system at its Wheel Loaders and Excavators Division (WLED).

Suggested Discussion Questions

Caterpillar used to be organized by functional areas such as engineering and accounting. It recently reorganized into profit and service centers. In addition to profit, what accounting measures should be used to evaluate performance? Should nonfinancial measures be used as well? List some of those measures.

■ **Issue 12–53**
Behavioral Effects of Responsibility Accounting; Motivating Desired Behavior

"Apple's Amelio Defends His Performance," *The Wall Street Journal,* **July 11, 1997, Jim Carlton and Lee Gomes.**

Overview

After a little more than 18 months, Gilbert Amelio, the CEO of Apple computer, resigned. During his tenure, Apple recorded close to $2 billion in losses.

Suggested Discussion Questions

In 1996, Gilbert Amelio received $655,000 in salary and a bonus of $2,134,000. What justified his bonus? How can you reconcile his bonus with Apple's accounting reports?

■ **Issue 12–54**
Illustration of Responsibility Accounting

"Can Dr. Frist Cure This Patient?" *Business Week,* **November 17, 1997.**

Overview

Dr. Thomas Frist, chief executive of $20 billion Columbia Healthcare Corp. is developing a plan to revitalize the embroiled company. His proposed budget includes the elimination of employee bonuses that are tied to corporate financial performance.

Suggested Discussion Questions

Columbia Healthcare's CEO is attempting to downsize the company and decentralize its operations. Write a memo to the CEO explaining how decentralization should be accompanied by a reexamination of the firm's accounting system. Focus on performance measurement and responsibility accounting. Make suggestions concerning the use of cost, revenue, profit, and investment centers.

"Sleepless Nights at Holiday Inn," *Business Week,* **November 3, 1997.**

Overview

Holiday Inn's revitalization plan has received mixed reviews. In 1996, competitors grew twice as fast as Holiday Inn.

Suggested Discussion Questions

As a group, diagram a plausible organization chart for Holiday Inn. On the chart, list whether the subunit should be treated as a cost, revenue, profit, or investment center. How should corporate overhead costs, such as marketing, be allocated to the subunits?

"Aging CEOs Stage Big Deals as Career Finales," *The Wall Street Journal,* **June 4, 1997, Joann Lublin.**

Overview

Despite reaching the end of their careers, several CEOs of large U.S. multinational corporations are planning mergers, takeovers, and acquisitions. For example, the 60-year-old chairman of Boeing is leading the $14 billion acquisition of McDonnell-Douglas.

Suggested Discussion Questions

Assume that a CEO's compensation is tied to accounting financial statements. What incentives would a CEO have to merge with another company? Design a compensation package that would not provide similar incentives.

"Why Delta Airlines Decided It Was Time for CEO to Take Off," *The Wall Street Journal,* **May 30, 1997, Martha Brannigan and Joseph White.**

Overview

Despite having turned around a major airline, Delta's CEO decided to resign amid pressure from his board. Although Delta had the highest operating margin of all U.S. airlines, the number of customer complaints was high and employee morale was low.

Suggested Discussion Questions

As a group, design a performance measurement system that could have prevented this situation from occurring. Present the plan to Delta's board of directors.

"Caterpillar's Fites Got a 75% Increase in Compensation for 1995 Performance," *The Wall Street Journal,* **March 4, 1996, Robert Rose.**

Overview

In the year Caterpillar had record profits, its CEO received a 75 percent pay increase. The increase came at a time when the company was experiencing a prolonged strike.

Suggested Discussion Questions

Should the union workers receive a similar increase? Should both the executives' or union workers' pay be tied to the same measures so that both parties receive similar percentage increases? Should there be some overlap in compensation plans? If so, what elements should be the same? Different? Should the CEO receive such a large increase when the company is having serious union problems?

"How Xerox Sustains the Cost of Quality," *Management Accounting,* **August 1995, Lawrence Carr.**

Overview

This article explains how Xerox's U.S. sales and marketing group implemented a cost of quality program.

Suggested Discussion Questions

Prepare a cause and effect diagram that could explain Xerox's excessive replacement parts write-off expense.

"GE Chairman Defends Pay, Stresses Quality," *The Wall Street Journal,* **April 24, 1997, William Carley.**

Overview

Amid criticisms of excessive pay, General Electric (GE) chairman John Welch launched a major quality program. Welch's compensation package, consisting of approximately $350 million in stock-related items, puzzled some employees when individual quality programs and the salary of front-line workers are both about $30,000 annually.

Suggested Discussion Questions

In groups, list elements of GE's product quality. Also list costs of maintaining high-quality products. How would an investment in quality improve GE's shareholder wealth?

■ **Issue 12–55**
Illustration of Responsibility Accounting

■ **Issue 12–56**
Behavioral Effects of Responsibility Accounting

■ **Issue 12–57**
Behavioral Effects of Responsibility Accounting

■ **Issue 12–58**
Illustration of Responsibility Accounting

■ **Issue 12–59**
Quality Costs

■ **Issue 12–60**
Measuring and Reporting Quality Costs

Chapter Thirteen

Investment Centers and Transfer Pricing

After completing this chapter, you should be able to:

1   Explain the role of managerial accounting in achieving goal congruence.

2   Compute an investment center's return on investment (ROI) and residual income.

3   Explain how a manager can improve ROI by increasing either the sales margin or capital turnover.

4   Describe some advantages and disadvantages of both ROI and residual income as divisional performance measures.

5   Explain how to measure a division's income and invested capital.

6   Use the general economic rule to set an optimal transfer price.

7   Explain how to base a transfer price on market prices, costs, or negotiations.

SUNCOAST FOOD CENTERS TO EXPAND OPERATIONS IN SEVERAL COASTAL CITIES

Miami, FL—A spokesman for Suncoast Food Centers announced today that the company will be expanding its retail grocery operations in Miami, Daytona Beach, and Jacksonville. The Florida-based company will add up to a dozen new stores over the next five years in these three cities. All of the new stores will be part of Suncoast's Atlantic Division, headquartered in Miami.

During a brief news conference, Atlantic Division Manager Katherine James explained Suncoast's rationale. "Florida is gaining over a thousand people a day in population," said James. "And many of these people are still moving into the coastal areas where Suncoast's strength is. Our Atlantic Division has been doing very well, and we're convinced we can continue to grow our business. Last year we had sales of $135 million in the Atlantic Division, and the division's income was just under $7 million.

"Of course, income alone isn't enough. What top management and our investors need to see is a return on the dollars they've invested in the division. Before our new stores are added, the Atlantic Division has around $45 million in invested capital. So we're pulling down a very respectable return on investment in the division. When our top management compares our division's return with industrywide numbers, they can see we're doing a good job."

James said most of Suncoast's new stores would be built from the ground up, but the company is also considering the acquisition of a couple of existing stores from other grocery chains.

How do the top managers of large companies such as Chrysler Corporation and General Electric Company evaluate their divisions and other major subunits? The largest subunits within these and similar organizations usually are designated as **investment centers**. The manager of this type of *responsibility center* is held accountable not only for the investment center's *profit* but also for the *capital invested* to earn that profit. Invested capital refers to assets, such as buildings and equipment, used in a subunit's operations. In this chapter we will study the methods that managerial accountants use to evaluate investment centers and the performance of their managers.[1]

In many organizations, one subunit manufactures a product or produces a service which is then transferred to another subunit in the same organization. For example, automobile parts manufactured in one division of General Motors are then transferred to another GM division that assembles vehicles.

The price at which products or services are transferred between two subunits in an organization is called a **transfer price**. Since a transfer price affects the profit of both the buying and selling divisions, the transfer price affects the performance evaluation of these responsibility centers. Later in this chapter, we will study the methods that managerial accountants use to determine transfer prices.

> An **investment center** is a responsibility center whose manager is accountable for its profit and for the capital invested to generate that profit.
>
> The **transfer price** is the price at which products or services are transferred between two divisions in an organization.

Delegation of Decision Making

LO 1 Explain the role of managerial accounting in achieving goal congruence.

Most large organizations are decentralized. Managers throughout these organizations are given autonomy to make decisions for their subunits. Decentralization takes advantage of the specialized knowledge and skills of managers, permits an organization to respond quickly to events, and relieves top management of the need to direct the organization's day-to-day activities. The biggest challenge in making a decentralized organization function effectively is to obtain *goal congruence* among the organization's autonomous managers.

Obtaining Goal Congruence: A Behavioral Challenge

> **Goal congruence** results when managers throughout an organization strive to achieve the goals set by top management.

Goal congruence is obtained when the managers of subunits throughout an organization strive to achieve the goals set by top management. This desirable state of affairs is difficult to achieve for a variety of reasons. Managers often are unaware of the effects of their decisions on the organization's other subunits. Also, it is only human for people to be more concerned with the performance of their own subunit than with the effectiveness of the entire organization. The behavioral challenge in designing any management control system is to come as close as possible to obtaining goal congruence.

To obtain goal congruence, the behavior of managers throughout an organization must be directed toward top management's goals. Managers not only must have their sights set on these organizational goals, but also must be given positive incentives to achieve them. The *managerial accountant's objective* in designing a responsibility-accounting system is to provide these incentives to the organization's subunit managers. *The key factor in deciding how well the responsibility-accounting system works is the extent to which it directs managers' efforts toward organizational goals.* Thus, the accounting measures used to evaluate investment-center managers should provide them with incentives to act in the interests of the overall organization.

> In the **management by objectives (MBO)** approach, managers at all levels participate in setting goals which they then will strive to achieve.

Management by Objectives (MBO) An emphasis on obtaining goal congruence is consistent with a broad managerial approach called **management by objectives** or **MBO**.

---

[1]Recall from Chapter 12 that in practice the term *profit center* sometimes is used interchangeably with the term *investment center*. To be precise, however, the term *profit center* should be reserved for a subunit whose manager is held accountable for profit but not for invested capital.

Under the MBO philosophy managers participate in setting goals which they then strive to achieve. The goals usually are expressed in financial or other quantitative terms, and the responsibility-accounting system is used to evaluate performance in achieving them.

Adaptation of Management Control Systems

When an organization begins its operations, it is usually small and decision making generally is centralized. The chief executive can control operations without a formal responsibility-accounting system. It is relatively easy in a small organization for managers to keep in touch with routine operations through face-to-face contact with employees.

As an organization grows, however, its managers need more formal information systems, including managerial-accounting information, in order to maintain control. Accounting systems are established to record events and provide the framework for internal and external financial reports. Budgets become necessary to plan the organization's activity. As the organization gains experience in producing its goods or services, cost standards and flexible budgets often are established to help control operations. As the organization continues to grow, some delegation of decision making becomes necessary. Decentralization is often the result of this tendency toward delegation. Ultimately, a fully developed responsibility-accounting system emerges. Managerial accountants designate cost centers, revenue centers, profit centers, and investment centers, and develop appropriate performance measures for each subunit.

Thus, an organization's accounting and managerial control systems usually adapt and become more complex as the organization grows and changes.

Measuring Performance in Investment Centers

In our study of investment-center performance evaluation, we will focus on Suncoast Food Centers. This Florida chain of retail grocery stores has three divisions, as depicted by the organization chart in Exhibit 13–1.

The Gulf and Atlantic divisions consist of individual grocery stores located in six coastal cities. The company's Food Processing Division operates dairy plants, bakeries, and meat processing plants in Miami, Orlando, and Jacksonville. These facilities provide all Suncoast Food Centers with milk, ice cream, yogurt, cheese, breads and desserts, and packaged meat. These Suncoast brand food products are transferred to the

Exhibit 13–1

Organization Chart: Suncoast Food Centers

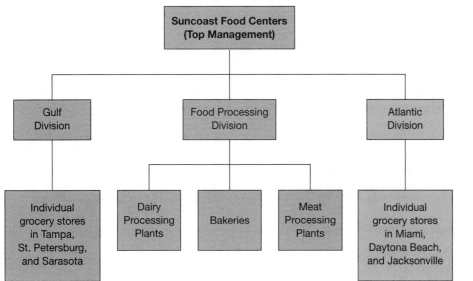

company's Gulf and Atlantic divisions at transfer prices established by the corporate controller's office.

Suncoast Food Centers' three divisions are investment centers. This responsibility-center designation is appropriate, because each division manager has the authority to make decisions that affect both profit and invested capital. For example, the Gulf Division manager approves the overall pricing policies in the Gulf Division's' stores, and also has the autonomy to sign contracts to buy food and other products for resale. These actions influence the division's profit. In addition, the Gulf Division manager has the authority to build new Suncoast Food Centers, rent space in shopping centers, or close existing stores. These decisions affect the amount of capital invested in the division.

The primary goals of any profit-making enterprise include maximizing its profitability and using its invested capital as effectively as possible. Managerial accountants use two different measures to evaluate the performance of investment centers: return on investment and residual income. We will illustrate each of these measures for Suncoast Food Centers.

Return on Investment

LO 2   Compute an investment center's return on investment (ROI) and residual income.

Return on investment (ROI) is income divided by invested capital.

The most common investment-center performance measure is **return on investment or ROI**, which is defined as follows:

$$\text{Return on investment (ROI)} = \frac{\text{Income}}{\text{Invested capital}}$$

The most recent year's ROI calculations for Suncoast Food Centers' three divisions are:

	$\dfrac{\text{Income}}{\text{Invested capital}}$		Return on investment (ROI)
Gulf Division	$\dfrac{\$3,000,000}{\$20,000,000}$	=	15%
Food Processing Division	$\dfrac{\$3,600,000}{\$18,000,000}$	=	20%
Atlantic Division	$\dfrac{\$6,750,000}{\$45,000,000}$	=	15%

Notice how the ROI calculation for each division takes into account *both divisional income and the capital invested* in the division. Why is this important? Suppose each division were evaluated only on the basis of its divisional profit. The Atlantic Division reported a higher divisional profit than the Gulf Division. Does this mean the Atlantic Division performed better than the Gulf Division? The answer is no. Although the Atlantic Division's profit exceeded the Gulf Division's profit, the Atlantic Division used a much larger amount of invested capital to earn its profit. The Atlantic Division's assets are more than two times the assets of the Gulf Division.

Considering the relative size of the two divisions, we should expect the Atlantic Division to earn a larger profit than the Gulf Division. The important question is not how much profit each division earned, but rather how effectively each division used its invested capital to earn a profit.

Factors Underlying ROI   We can rewrite the ROI formula as follows:

$$\text{Return on investment} = \frac{\text{Income}}{\text{Invested capital}} = \frac{\text{Income}}{\text{Sales revenue}} \times \frac{\text{Sales revenue}}{\text{Invested capital}}$$

Notice that the *sales revenue* term cancels out in the denominator and numerator when the two right-hand fractions are multiplied.

Writing the ROI formula in this way highlights the factors that determine a division's return on investment. Income divided by sales revenue is called the **sales margin**. This term measures the percentage of each sales dollar that remains as profit after all expenses are covered. Sales revenue divided by invested capital is called the **capital turnover**. This term focuses on the number of sales dollars generated by every dollar of invested capital. The sales margin and capital turnover for Suncoast Food Centers' three divisions are calculated below for the most recent year.

Sales margin $\times$ **Capital turnover** = ROI

$$\frac{\text{Income}}{\text{Sales revenue}} \times \frac{\text{Sales revenue}}{\text{Invested capital}} = \text{ROI}$$

Gulf Division	$\dfrac{\$3,000,000}{\$60,000,000}$ $\times$	$\dfrac{\$60,000,000}{\$20,000,000}$	= 15%
Food Processing Division	$\dfrac{\$3,600,000}{\$9,000,000}$ $\times$	$\dfrac{\$9,000,000}{\$18,000,000}$	= 20%
Atlantic Division	$\dfrac{\$6,750,000}{\$135,000,000}$ $\times$	$\dfrac{\$135,000,000}{\$45,000,000}$	= 15%

The Gulf Division's sales margin is 5 percent ($3,000,000 of profit ÷ $60,000,000 of sales revenue). Thus, each dollar of divisional sales resulted in a five-cent profit. The division's capital turnover was 3 ($60,000,000 of sales revenue ÷ $20,000,000 of invested capital). Thus, three dollars of sales revenue were generated by each dollar of capital invested in the division's assets, such as store buildings, display shelves, checkout equipment, and inventory.

Improving ROI How could the Gulf Division manager improve the division's return on investment? Since ROI is the product of the sales margin and the capital turnover, ROI can be improved by increasing either or both of its components. For example, if the Gulf Division manager increased the division's sales margin to 6 percent while holding the capital turnover constant at 3, the division's ROI would climb from 15 percent to 18 percent, as follows:

> **LO 3** Explain how a manager can improve ROI by increasing either the sales margin or capital turnover.

$$\begin{aligned}\text{Gulf Division's improved ROI} &= \text{Improved sales margin} \times \text{Same capital turnover} \\ &= 6\% \times 3 = 18\%\end{aligned}$$

To bring about the improved sales margin, the Gulf Division manager would need to increase divisional profit to $3,600,000 on sales of $60,000,000 ($3,600,000 ÷ $60,000,000 = 6%). How could profit be increased without changing total sales revenue? There are two possibilities: increase sales prices while selling less quantity, or decrease expenses. Neither of these is necessarily easy to do. In increasing sales prices, the division manager must be careful not to lose sales to the extent that total sales revenue declines. Similarly, reducing the expenses must not diminish product quality, customer service, or overall store atmosphere. Any of these changes could also result in lost sales revenue.

An alternative way of increasing the Gulf Division's ROI would be to increase its capital turnover. Suppose the Gulf Division manager increased the division's capital turnover to 4 while holding the sales margin constant at 5 percent. The division's ROI would climb from 15 percent to 20 percent:

$$\begin{aligned}\text{Gulf Division's improved ROI} &= \text{Same sales margin} \times \text{Improved capital turnover} \\ &= 5\% \times 4 = 20\%\end{aligned}$$

To obtain the improved capital turnover, the Gulf Division manager would need to either increase sales revenue or reduce the division's invested capital. For example, the improved ROI could be achieved by reducing invested capital to $15,000,000 while maintaining sales revenue of $60,000,000. This would be a very tall order. The division manager can lower invested capital somewhat by reducing inventories, and can increase sales revenue by using store space more effectively. But reducing inventories may lead to stockouts and lost sales, and crowded aisles may drive customers away.

Improving ROI is a balancing act that requires all the skills of an effective manager. The ROI analysis above merely shows the arena in which the balancing act is performed.

Residual Income

LO 2 Compute an investment center's return on investment (ROI) and residual income.

Although ROI is the most popular investment-center performance measure, it has one major drawback. To illustrate, suppose Suncoast's Food Processing division manager can buy a new food processing machine for $500,000, which will save $80,000 in operating expenses and thereby raise divisional profit by $80,000. The return on this investment in new equipment is 16 percent:

$$\text{Return on investment in new equipment} = \frac{\text{Increase in divisional profit}}{\text{Increase in invested capital}} = \frac{\$80,000}{\$500,000} = 16\%$$

Now suppose it costs Suncoast Food Centers 12 cents for each dollar of capital to invest in operational assets. What is the optimal decision for the Food Processing Division manager to make, *viewed from the perspective of the company as a whole?* Since it costs Suncoast Food Centers 12 percent for every dollar of capital, and the return on investment in new equipment is 16 percent, the equipment should be purchased. For goal congruence, the autonomous division manager should decide to buy the new equipment.

Now consider what is likely to happen. The Food Processing Division manager's performance is evaluated on the basis of his division's ROI. Without the new equipment, the divisional ROI is 20 percent ($3,600,000 of divisional profit ÷ $18,000,000 of invested capital). If he purchases the new equipment, his divisional ROI will decline:

Food Processing Division's Return on Investment

Without Investment in New Equipment	With Investment in New Equipment
$\dfrac{\$3,600,000}{\$18,000,000} = 20\%$	$\dfrac{\$3,600,000 + \$80,000}{\$18,000,000 + \$500,000} < 20\%$

Why did this happen? Even though the investment in new equipment earns a return of 16 percent, which is greater than the company's cost of raising capital (12 percent), the return is less than the division's ROI without the equipment (20 percent). Averaging the new investment with those already in place in the Food Processing Division merely reduces the division's ROI. Since the division manager is evaluated using ROI, he will be reluctant to decide in favor of acquiring the new equipment.

The problem is that the ROI measure leaves out an important piece of information: it ignores the firm's cost of raising investment capital. For this reason, many managers prefer to use a different investment-center performance measure instead of ROI.

Residual income is profit minus an imputed interest charge, which is equal to the invested capital times an imputed interest rate.

Computing Residual Income   An investment center's **residual income** is defined as follows:

$$\text{Residual income} = \text{Investment center's profit} - \left(\text{Investment center's invested capital} \times \text{Imputed interest rate}\right)$$

where the imputed interest rate is the firm's cost of acquiring investment capital.

ROI and residual income are common performance measures for investment centers. Both measures relate the profit earned from selling the final product to the capital required to carry out production operations.

Residual income is a dollar amount, not a ratio like ROI. It is the amount of an investment center's profit that remains (as a residual) after subtracting an imputed interest charge. The term *imputed* means that the interest charge is estimated by the managerial accountant. This charge reflects the firm's minimum required rate of return on invested capital. In some firms, the imputed interest rate depends on the riskiness of the investment for which the funds will be used. Thus, divisions that have different levels of risk sometimes are assigned different imputed interest rates.

> **LO 4**   Describe some advantages and disadvantages of both ROI and residual income as divisional performance measures.

The residual income of Suncoast's Food Processing Division is computed below, both with and without the investment in the new equipment. The imputed interest rate is 12 percent.

Food Processing Division's Residual Income

	Without Investment in New Equipment		With Investment in New Equipment	
Divisional profit		$3,600,000		$3,680,000
Less imputed interest charge:				
Invested capital	$18,000,000		$18,500,000	
× Imputed interest rate	×.12		×.12	
Imputed interest charge	→	2,160,000	→	2,220,000
Residual income		$1,440,000		$1,460,000

Investment in new equipment
raises residual income by
$20,000.

Notice that the Food Processing Division's residual income will *increase* if the new equipment is purchased. What will be the division manager's incentive if he is evaluated on the basis of residual income instead of ROI? He will want to make the investment because that decision will increase his division's residual income. Thus, goal congruence is achieved when the managerial accountant uses residual income to measure divisional performance.

Why does residual income facilitate goal congruence while ROI does not? Because the residual-income formula incorporates an important piece of data that is excluded from the ROI formula: the firm's minimum required rate of return on invested capital. To summarize, ROI and residual income are compared as follows:

$$\text{ROI} \;=\; \frac{\text{Investment center's profit}}{\text{Investment center's invested capital}} \longleftarrow \begin{array}{l}\textbf{Two pieces}\\ \textbf{of data}\end{array}$$

$$\begin{array}{l}\text{Residual}\\ \text{income}\end{array} = \begin{array}{l}\text{Investment center's}\\ \text{profit}\end{array} - \left(\begin{array}{l}\text{Investment center's}\\ \text{invested capital}\end{array} \times \begin{array}{l}\text{Imputed}\\ \text{interest rate}\end{array}\right)$$

Three pieces of data

Unfortunately, residual income also has a serious drawback: It should not be used to compare the performance of different-sized investment centers because it incorporates a bias in favor of the larger investment center. To illustrate, the following table compares the residual income of Suncoast Food Centers' Gulf and Atlantic divisions. Notice that the Atlantic Division's residual income is considerably higher than the Gulf Division's. This is entirely due to the much greater size of the Atlantic Division, as evidenced by its far greater invested capital.

Comparison of Residual Income: Two Divisions

	Gulf Division		Atlantic Division	
Divisional profit		$3,000,000		$6,750,000
Less imputed interest charge:				
Invested capital	$20,000,000		$45,000,000	
× Imputed interest rate	× .12		× .12	
Imputed interest charge	→	2,400,000	→	5,400,000
Residual income		$ 600,000		$1,350,000

The Atlantic Division's residual income is much higher simply because it is larger than the Gulf Division.

In short, neither ROI nor residual income provides a perfect measure of investment-center performance. ROI can undermine goal congruence. Residual income distorts comparisons between investment centers of different sizes. As a result, some companies routinely use both measures for divisional performance evaluation.

Shareholder Value Analysis   Some companies apply the residual income concept to individual product lines. **Shareholder value analysis** (or **economic value analysis**) calculates the residual income for a major product line, with the objective of determining how the product line affects the firm's value to the shareholders.[2] Suppose, for example, that Suncoast Food Centers offers in-store, one-hour film development in selected stores. Let's say that the company's investment in this service is $200,000 and the annual profit is $40,000. Then the residual income on one-hour film development is $16,000 [$40,000 − ($200,000 × 12%)].

Shareholder value analysis (or **economic value analysis**) calculates the residual income associated with a major product line, with the objective of determining how the product line affects a firm's value to its shareholders.

---

[2]Shawn Tully, "The Real Key to Creating Wealth," *Fortune* 128, no. 6, pp. 38–50.

Measuring Income and Invested Capital

Both the ROI and residual-income measures of investment-center performance use profit and invested capital in their formulas. This raises the question of how to measure divisional profit and invested capital. This section will illustrate various approaches to resolving these measurement issues.

LO 5 Explain how to measure a division's income and invested capital.

Invested Capital

We will focus on Suncoast Food Centers' Food Processing Division to illustrate several alternative approaches to measuring an investment center's capital. Exhibit 13–2 lists the assets and liabilities associated with the Food Processing Division. Notice that Exhibit 13–2 does not comprise a complete balance sheet. First, there are no long-term liabilities, such as bonds payable, associated with the Food Processing Division. Although Suncoast Food Centers may have such long-term debt, it would not be meaningful to assign portions of that debt to the company's individual divisions. Second, there is no stockholders' equity associated with the Food Processing Division. The owners of the company own stock in Suncoast Food Centers, not in its individual divisions.

Average Balances   ROI and residual income are computed for a period of time, such as a year or a month. Asset balances, on the other hand, are measured at a point in time, such as December 31. Since divisional asset balances generally will change over time, we use average balances in calculating ROI and residual income. For example, if the Food Processing Division's balance in invested capital was $19,000,000 on January 1, and $17,000,000 on December 31, we would use the year's average invested capital of $18,000,000 in the ROI and residual income calculations.

Should Total Assets Be Used?   Exhibit 13–2 shows that the Food Processing Division had average balances during the year of $2,000,000 in current assets, $15,000,000 in long-lived assets, and $1,000,000 tied up in a plant under construction. (Suncoast Food Centers is building a new high-tech dairy plant in Orlando to produce its innovative zero-calorie ice cream.) In addition, Exhibit 13–2 discloses that the Food Processing Division's average balance of current liabilities was $500,000.

What is the division's invested capital? Several possibilities exist.

1. **Total assets.** The management of Suncoast Food Centers has decided to use *average total assets* for the year in measuring each division's invested capital.

Assets*		
Current assets (cash, accounts receivable, inventories, etc.)		$ 2,000,000
Long-lived assets (land, buildings, equipment, vehicles, etc.):		
Gross book value (acquisition cost)	$19,000,000	
Less: Accumulated depreciation	4,000,000	
Net book value		15,000,000
Plant under construction		1,000,000
Total assets		$18,000,000
Liabilities		
Current liabilities (accounts payable, salaries payable, etc.)		$ 500,000

*This is not a balance sheet, but rather a listing of certain assets and liabilities associated with the Food Processing Division.

Exhibit 13–2

Assets and Liabilities Associated with Food Processing Division

SUNCOAST
FOOD CENTERS

Thus, $18,000,000 is the amount used in the ROI and residual-income calculations discussed earlier in this chapter. This measure of invested capital is appropriate if the division manager has considerable authority in making decisions about *all* of the division's assets, *including nonproductive assets.* In this case, the Food Processing Division's partially completed dairy plant is a nonproductive asset. Since the division manager had considerable influence in deciding to build the new plant and he is responsible for overseeing the project, average total assets provides an appropriate measure.

2. *Total productive assets.* In other companies, division managers are directed by top management to keep nonproductive assets, such as vacant land or construction in progress. In such cases, it is appropriate to exclude nonproductive assets from the measure of invested capital. Then *average total productive assets* is used to measure invested capital. If Suncoast Food Centers had chosen this alternative, $17,000,000 would have been used in the ROI and residual-income calculations (total assets of $18,000,000 less $1,000,000 for the plant under construction).

3. *Total assets less current liabilities.* Some companies allow division managers to secure short-term bank loans and other short-term credit. In such cases, invested capital often is measured by *average total assets less average current liabilities.* This approach encourages investment-center managers to minimize resources tied up in assets and maximize the use of short-term credit to finance operations. If this approach had been used by Suncoast Food Centers, the Food Processing Division's invested capital would have been $17,500,000 (total assets of $18,000,000 less current liabilities of $500,000).

Gross or Net Book Value   Another decision to make in choosing a measure of invested capital is whether to use the *gross book value (acquisition cost)* or the *net book value* of long-lived assets. (Net book value is the acquisition cost less accumulated depreciation.) Suncoast Food Centers' management has decided to use the average net book value of $15,000,000 to value the Food Processing Division's long-lived assets. If gross book value had been used instead, the division's measure of invested capital would have been $22,000,000 as the following calculation shows.

Current assets	$ 2,000,000
Long-lived assets (at gross book value)	19,000,000
Plant under construction	1,000,000
Total assets (at gross book value)	$22,000,000

There are advantages and disadvantages associated with both gross and net book value as a measure of invested capital.

Advantages of Net Book Value; Disadvantages of Gross Book Value

1. Using net book value maintains consistency with the balance sheet prepared for external reporting purposes. This allows for more meaningful comparisons of return-on-investment measures across different companies.

2. Using net book value to measure invested capital is also more consistent with the definition of income, which is the numerator in ROI calculations. In computing income, the current period's depreciation on long-lived assets is deducted as an expense.

Advantages of Gross Book Value; Disadvantages of Net Book Value

1. The usual methods of computing depreciation, such as the straight-line and the declining-balance methods, are arbitrary. Hence, they should not be allowed to affect ROI or residual-income calculations.

2. When long-lived assets are depreciated, their net book value declines over time. This results in a misleading increase in ROI and residual income across time. Exhibit 13–3 provides an illustration of this phenomenon for the ROI calculated

Acquisition cost of equipment	$500,000
Useful life	5 years
Salvage value at end of useful life	0
Annual straight-line depreciation	$100,000
Annual income generated by asset (before deducting depreciation)	$150,000

Exhibit 13–3

Increase in ROI Over Time (when net book value is used)

Year	Income before Depreciation	Annual Depreciation	Income Net of Depreciation	Average Net Book Value*	ROI Based on Net Book Value†	Average Gross Book Value	ROI Based on Gross Book Value
1	$150,000	$100,000	$50,000	$450,000	11.1%	$500,000	10%
2	150,000	100,000	50,000	350,000	14.3	500,000	10
3	150,000	100,000	50,000	250,000	20.0	500,000	10
4	150,000	100,000	50,000	150,000	33.3	500,000	10
5	150,000	100,000	50,000	50,000	100.0	500,000	10

*Average net book value is the average of the beginning and ending balances for the year in net book value. In year 1, for example, the average net book value is:

$$\frac{\$500,000 + \$400,000}{2}$$

†ROI rounded to nearest tenth of 1 percent.

on an equipment purchase under consideration by the Food Processing Division manager. Notice that the ROI rises steadily across the five-year horizon if invested capital is measured by net book value. However, using gross book value eliminates this problem. If an accelerated depreciation method were used instead of the straight-line method, the increasing trend in ROI would be even more pronounced.

A Behavioral Problem The tendency for net book value to produce a misleading increase in ROI over time can have a serious effect on the incentives of investment-center managers. Investment centers with old assets will show much higher ROIs than investment centers with relatively new assets. This can discourage investment-center managers from investing in new equipment. If this behavioral tendency persists, a division's assets can become obsolete, making the division uncompetitive.

Allocating Assets to Investment Centers Some companies control certain assets centrally, although these assets are needed to carry on operations in the divisions. Common examples are cash and accounts receivable. Divisions need cash in order to operate, but many companies control cash balances centrally in order to minimize their total cash holdings. Some large retail firms manage accounts receivable centrally. A credit customer of some national department-store chains can make a payment either at the local store or by mailing the payment to corporate headquarters.

When certain assets are controlled centrally, some allocation basis generally is chosen to allocate these asset balances to investment centers, for the purpose of measuring invested capital. For example, cash may be allocated based on the budgeted cash needs in each division or on the basis of divisional sales. Accounts receivable usually are allocated on the basis of divisional sales. Divisions with less stringent credit terms are allocated proportionately larger balances of accounts receivable.

Measuring Investment-Center Income

In addition to choosing a measure of investment-center capital, an accountant must also decide how to measure a center's income. The key issue is controllability; the choice involves the extent to which uncontrollable items are allowed to influence the income measure. Exhibit 13–4 illustrates several different possibilities for measuring the income of Suncoast Food Centers' Food Processing Division.

LO 5 Explain how to measure a division's income and invested capital.

Sales revenue	$9,000,000
Variable expenses	3,800,000
(1) Divisional contribution margin	$5,200,000
Fixed expenses controllable by division manager	1,600,000
(2) Profit margin controllable by division manager	$3,600,000
Fixed expenses, traceable to division, but controlled by others	1,200,000
(3) Profit margin traceable to division	$2,400,000
Common fixed expenses, allocated from corporate headquarters	400,000
(4) Divisional income before interest and taxes	$2,000,000
Interest expense allocated from corporate headquarters	250,000
(5) Divisional income before taxes	$1,750,000
Income taxes allocated from corporate headquarters	700,000
(6) Divisional net income	$1,050,000

Suncoast Food Centers' top management uses the *profit margin controllable by division manager,* $3,600,000, to evaluate the Food Processing Division manager. This profit measure is used in calculating either ROI or residual income. Some fixed costs traceable to the division have not been deducted from this $3,600,000 amount, but the division manager cannot control or significantly influence these costs. Hence they are excluded from the ROI calculation in evaluating the division manager.

Pay for Performance   Some companies reward investment-center managers with **cash bonuses** if they meet a predetermined target on a specified performance criterion, such as residual income or ROI. Such payments often are referred to as **pay for performance**, **merit pay**, or **incentive compensation**. These cash bonuses generally are single payments, independent of a manager's base salary.

Managers versus Investment Centers   It is important to make a distinction between an investment center and its manager. In evaluating the *manager's* performance, only revenues and costs that the manager can control or significantly influence should be included in the profit measure. Remember that the overall objective of the performance measure is to provide incentives for goal-congruent behavior. No performance measure can motivate a manager to make decisions about costs he or she cannot control. This explains why Suncoast Food Centers' top management relies on the profit margin controllable by division manager to compute the manager's ROI performance measure.

Evaluating the Food Processing Division as a viable economic investment is a different matter altogether. In this evaluation, traceability of costs, rather than controllability, is the issue. For this purpose, Suncoast Food Centers' top management uses the profit margin traceable to division to compute the divisional ROI or residual income. As Exhibit 13–4 shows, this amount is $2,400,000.

Other Profit Measures   The other measures of divisional profit shown in Exhibit 13–4 (lines 4, 5, and 6) are also used by some companies. The rationale behind these divisional income measures is that all corporate costs have to be covered by the operations of the divisions. Allocating corporate costs, interest, and income taxes to the divisions makes division managers aware of these costs.

Inflation: Historical-Cost versus Current-Value Accounting

Whether measuring investment-center income or invested capital, the impact of price-level changes should not be forgotten. During periods of inflation, historical-cost asset values soon cease to reflect the cost of replacing those assets. Therefore, some accountants argue that investment-center performance measures based on historical-

A **cash bonus** is a one-time cash payment to a manager as a reward for meeting a predetermined criterion on a specified performance measure. Such payments are also referred to as **pay for performance**, **merit pay**, or **incentive compensation**.

cost accounting are misleading. Yet surveys of corporate managers indicate that an accounting system based on current values would not alter their decisions. Most managers believe that measures based on historical-cost accounting are adequate when used in conjunction with budgets and performance targets. As managers prepare those budgets, they build their expectations about inflation into the budgets and performance targets.

Another reason for using historical-cost accounting for internal purposes is that it is required for external reporting. Thus, historical-cost data already are available, while installing current-value accounting would add substantial incremental costs to the organization's information system.

Other Issues in Segment Performance Evaluation

Alternatives to ROI and Residual Income

ROI and residual income are short-run performance measures. They focus on only one period of time. Yet an investment center is really a collection of assets (investments), each of which has a multiperiod life. Exhibit 13–5 portrays this perspective of an investment center.

To evaluate any one of these individual investments correctly requires a multi-period viewpoint, which takes into account the timing of the cash flows from the investment. For example, investment E in Exhibit 13–5 may start out slowly in years 4 and 5, but it may be economically justified by its expected high performance in years 8, 9, and 10. Any evaluation of the investment center in year 5 that ignores the long-term performance of its various investments can result in a misleading conclusion. Thus, single-period performance measures suffer from myopia. They focus on only a short time segment that slices across the division's investments as portrayed in Exhibit 13–5.

To avoid this short-term focus, some organizations downplay ROI and residual income in favor of an alternative approach. Instead of relating profit to invested capital in a single measure, these characteristics of investment-center performance are evaluated separately. Actual divisional profit for a time period is compared to a flexible budget, and variances are used to analyze performance. The division's major investments are evaluated through a *postaudit* of the investment decisions. For example, investment E may have been undertaken because of expected high performance in

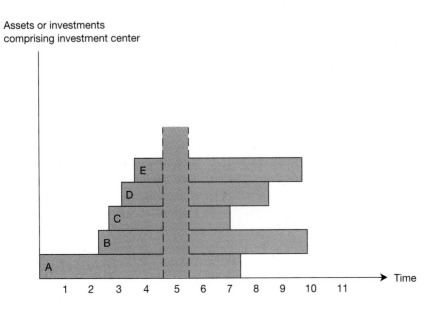

Exhibit 13–5

Investment Center Viewed as a Collection of Investments

years 8, 9, and 10. When that time comes, a review will determine whether the project lived up to expectations.

Evaluating periodic profit through flexible budgeting and variance analysis, coupled with postaudits of major investment decisions, is a more complicated approach to evaluating investment centers. However, it does help management avoid the myopia of single-period measures such as ROI and residual income.

Importance of Nonfinancial Information

Although financial measures such as segment profit, ROI, and residual income are widely used in performance evaluation, nonfinancial measures are important also. Manufacturers collect data on rates of defective products, airlines record information on lost bags and aircraft delays, and hotels keep track of occupancy rates. The proper evaluation of an organization and its segments requires that multiple performance measures be defined and used.

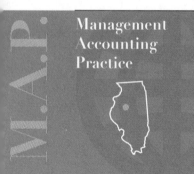

Management Accounting Practice

Nonfinancial Performance Measures at Caterpillar

Caterpillar has recently increased its use of nonfinancial performance measures, with very favorable results.[3] "As part of an overall corporate restructuring, the Wheel Loaders and Excavating Division changed from cost center to profit center, empowered its employees, and implemented new financial and nonfinancial performance measures. The result: Employees are making better decisions, customer service and productivity have improved, and income has increased to record levels." Among the nonfinancial measures in use are the following:

Customer delivery performance	Customer satisfaction
Employee satisfaction	Process improvements
Assembly process throughput	Process breakthroughs
Change management	Integration of values into division culture

Measuring Performance in Nonprofit Organizations

Management control in a nonprofit organization presents a special challenge. Such organizations often are managed by professionals, such as physicians in a hospital. Moreover, many people participate in a nonprofit organization at some personal sacrifice, motivated by humanitarian or public service ideals. Often, such people are less receptive to formal control procedures than their counterparts in business.

The goals of nonprofit organizations often are less clear-cut than those of businesses. Public service objectives may be difficult to specify with precision and even more difficult to measure in terms of achievement. For example, one community health center was established in an economically depressed area with three stated goals:

1. To reduce costs in a nearby hospital by providing a clinic for people to use instead of the hospital emergency room.
2. To provide preventive as well as therapeutic care, and establish outreach programs in the community.
3. To become financially self-sufficient.

There is some conflict between these objectives, since goal 2 does not provide revenue to the center, while goals 1 and 3 focus on financial efficiency. Moreover, the health center was staffed with physicians who could have achieved much greater incomes in private practice. The management control tools described in this and the preceding three chapters can be used in nonprofit organizations. However, the challenges in doing so effectively often are greater.

---

[3]James A. Hendricks, David G. Defreitas, and Delores K. Walker, "Changing Performance Measures at Caterpillar," *Management Accounting* 78, no. 6, pp. 18–24.

Transfer Pricing

The problem of measuring performance in profit centers or investment centers is made more complicated by transfers of goods or services between responsibility centers. The amount charged when one division sells goods or services to another division is called a **transfer price**. This price affects the profit measurement for both the selling division and the buying division. A high transfer price results in high profit for the selling division and low profit for the buying division. A low transfer price has the opposite effect.

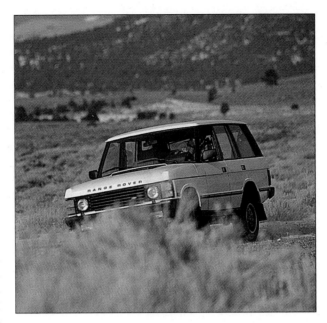

Transfer pricing is widely used in the manufacturing industry. When the chassis for this Range Rover was transferred from the manufacturing division to the assembly division, a transfer price was specified.

Goal Congruence

What should be management's goal in setting transfer prices for internally transferred goods or services? In a decentralized organization, the managers of profit centers and investment centers often have considerable autonomy in deciding whether to accept or reject orders and whether to buy inputs from inside the organization or from outside. For example, a large manufacturer of farm equipment allows its Assembly Division managers to buy parts either from another division of the company or from independent manufacturers. The goal in setting transfer prices is to establish incentives for autonomous division managers to make decisions that support the overall goals of the organization.

Suppose it is in the best interests of Suncoast Food Centers for the baked goods produced by the Food Processing Division's Orlando Bakery to be transferred to the Gulf Division's stores in the Tampa Bay area. Thus, if the firm were centralized, bakery products would be transferred from the Food Processing Division to the Gulf Division. However, Suncoast Food Centers is a decentralized company, and the Gulf Division manager is free to buy baked goods either from the Food Processing Division or from an outside bakery company. Similarly, the Food Processing Division manager is free to accept or reject an order for baked goods, at any given price, from the Gulf Division. The goal of the company's controller in setting the transfer price is to provide incentives for each of these division managers to act in the company's best interests. The transfer price should be chosen so that each division manager, when striving to maximize his or her own division's profit, makes the decision that maximizes the company's profit.

General Transfer-Pricing Rule

Management's objective in setting a transfer price is to encourage goal congruence among the division managers involved in the transfer. A general rule that will ensure goal congruence is given below.

LO 6 Use the general economic rule to set an optimal transfer price.

$$\text{Transfer price} = \begin{array}{c} \text{Additional } \textit{outlay cost } \text{per} \\ \text{unit incurred because} \\ \text{goods are transferred} \end{array} + \begin{array}{c} \textit{Opportunity cost } \text{per unit} \\ \text{to the organization} \\ \text{because of the transfer} \end{array}$$

The general rule specifies the transfer price as the sum of two cost components. The first component is the outlay cost incurred by the division that produces the goods or services to be transferred. Outlay costs will include the direct variable costs of the product or service and any other outlay costs that are incurred only as a result of the transfer. The second component in the general transfer-pricing rule is the opportunity cost incurred by the organization as a whole because of the transfer. Recall from Chapter 2 that an *opportunity cost* is a benefit that is forgone as a result of taking a particular action.

We will illustrate the general transfer-pricing rule for Suncoast Food Centers. The company's Food Processing Division produces bread in its Orlando Bakery. The division transfers some of its products to the company's Gulf and Atlantic divisions, and sells some of its products to other companies in the *external market* under different labels.

Bread is transported to stores in racks containing one dozen loaves of packaged bread. In the Orlando bakery, the following variable costs are incurred to produce bread and transport it to a buyer.

Production:
   Standard variable cost per rack (including packaging) $7.00
Transportation:
   Standard variable cost per rack to transport bread . . . .$ .25

In applying the general transfer-pricing rule, we will distinguish between two different scenarios.

Scenario I: No Excess Capacity   Suppose the Food Processing Division can sell all the bread it can produce to outside buyers at a market price of $11.00 per rack. Since the division can sell all of its production, it has *no excess capacity. Excess capacity* exists only when more goods can be produced than the producer is able to sell, due to low demand for the product.

What transfer price does the general rule yield under this scenario of no excess capacity? The transfer price is determined as follows:

Outlay cost:		
Standard variable cost of production	$ 7.00	per rack
Standard variable cost of transportation	.25	per rack
Total outlay cost	$ 7.25	per rack
Opportunity cost:		
Selling price per unit in external market	$11.00	per rack
Less: Variable cost of production and transportation	7.25	per rack
Opportunity cost (forgone contribution margin)	$ 3.75	per rack
General transfer-pricing rule:		

  Transfer price = outlay cost + opportunity cost
     $11.00   = $7.25   + $3.75

The *outlay cost* incurred by the Food Processing Division in order to transfer a rack of bread includes the standard variable production cost of $7.00 and the standard variable transportation cost of $.25. The *opportunity cost* incurred by Suncoast Food Centers when its Food Processing Division transfers a rack of bread to the Gulf Division *instead* of selling it in the external market is the forgone contribution margin from the lost sale, equal to $3.75. Why does the company lose a sale in the external market for every rack of bread transferred to the Gulf Division? The sale is lost because there is *no excess capacity* in the Food Processing Division. Every rack of bread transferred to another company division results in one less rack of bread sold in the external market.

Goal Congruence How does the general transfer-pricing rule promote goal congruence? Suppose the Gulf Division's grocery stores can sell a loaf of bread for $1.50, or $18.00 for a rack of 12 loaves ($18.00 = 12 × $1.50). What is the best way for Suncoast Food Centers to use the limited production capacity in the Food Processing Division's Orlando bakery? The answer is determined as follows:

Contribution to Suncoast Food Centers from Sale in External Market		**Contribution to Suncoast Food Centers from Transfer to Gulf Division**	
Wholesale selling price per rack	$11.00	Retail selling price per rack	$18.00
Less: Variable costs	7.25	Less: Variable costs	7.25
Contribution margin	$ 3.75	Contribution margin	$10.75

The best use of the bakery's limited production capacity is to produce bread for transfer to the Gulf Division. If the transfer price is set at $11.00, as the general rule specifies, goal congruence is maintained. The Food Processing Division manager is willing to transfer bread to the Gulf Division, because the transfer price of $11.00 is equal to the external market price. The Gulf Division manager is willing to buy the bread, because her division will have a contribution margin of $7.00 on each rack of bread transferred ($18.00 sales price minus the $11.00 transfer price).

Now consider a different situation. Suppose a local organization makes a special offer to the Gulf Division manager to buy several hundred loaves of bread to sell in a promotional campaign. The organization offers to pay $.80 per loaf, which is $9.60 per rack of a dozen loaves. What will the Gulf Division manager do? She must pay a transfer price of $11.00 per rack, so the Gulf Division would lose $1.40 per rack if the special offer were accepted ($1.40 = $11.00 − $9.60). The Gulf Division manager will decline the special offer. Is this decision in the best interests of Suncoast Food Centers as a whole? If the offer were accepted, the company as a whole would make a positive contribution of $2.35 per rack, as shown below.

Contribution to Suncoast Food Centers If Special Offer Is Accepted		
Special price per rack	$9.60	per rack
Less: Variable cost to company	7.25	per rack
Contribution to company, per rack	$2.35	per rack

However, the company can make even more if its Food Processing Division sells bread directly in its external market. Then the contribution to the company is $3.75, as we have just seen. (The external market price of $11.00 per rack minus a variable cost of $7.25 per rack equals $3.75 per rack.) Thus, Suncoast Food Centers is better off, as a whole, if the Gulf Division's special offer is rejected. Once again, the general transfer-pricing rule results in goal-congruent decision making.

Scenario II: Excess Capacity Now let's change our basic assumption, and suppose the Food Processing Division's Orlando bakery has excess production capacity. This means that the total demand for its bread from all sources, including the Gulf and Atlantic divisions and the external market, is less than the bakery's production capacity. Under this scenario of excess capacity, what does the general rule specify for a transfer price?

$$\text{Transfer price} = \text{Outlay cost} + \text{Opportunity cost}$$
$$\$7.25 \qquad = \qquad \$7.25 \quad + \qquad 0$$

The *outlay cost* in the Food Processing Division's Orlando bakery is still $7.25, since it does not depend on whether there is idle capacity or not. The *opportunity cost,* however, is now zero. There is no opportunity cost to the company when a rack of bread is transferred to the Gulf Division, because the Food Processing Division can still satisfy all of its external demand for bread. Thus, the general rule specifies a transfer price of $7.25, the total standard variable cost of production and transportation.

Goal Congruence   Let's reconsider what will happen when the Gulf Division manager receives the local organization's special offer to buy bread at $9.60 per rack. The Gulf Division will now show a positive contribution of $2.35 per rack on the special order.

Special price per rack	$9.60 per rack
Less: Transfer price paid by Gulf Division	7.25 per rack
Contribution to Gulf Division	$2.35 per rack

The Gulf Division manager will accept the special offer. This decision is also in the best interests of Suncoast Food Centers. The company, as a whole, will also make a contribution of $2.35 per rack on every rack transferred to the Gulf Division to satisfy the special order. Once again, the general transfer-pricing rule maintains goal-congruent decision-making behavior.

Notice that the general rule yields a transfer price that leaves the Food Processing Division manager indifferent as to whether the transfer will be made. At a transfer price of $7.25, the contribution to the Food Processing Division will be zero (transfer price of $7.25 less variable cost of $7.25). To avoid this problem, we can view the general rule as providing a lower bound on the transfer price. Some companies allow the producing division to add a markup to this lower bound in order to provide a positive contribution margin. This in turn provides a positive incentive to make the transfer.

Difficulty in Implementing the General Rule   The general transfer-pricing rule will always promote goal-congruent decision making *if the rule can be implemented*. However, the rule is often difficult or impossible to implement due to the difficulty of measuring opportunity costs. Such a cost-measurement problem can arise for a number of reasons. One reason is that the external market may not be perfectly competitive. Under **perfect competition**, the market price does not depend on the quantity sold by any one producer. Under **imperfect competition**, a single producer or group of producers can affect the market price by varying the amount of product available in the market. In such cases, the external market price depends on the production decisions of the producer. This in turn means that the opportunity cost incurred by the company as a result of internal transfers depends on the quantity sold externally. These interactions may make it impossible to measure accurately the opportunity cost caused by a product transfer.

Other reasons for difficulty in measuring the opportunity cost associated with a product transfer include uniqueness of the transferred goods or services, a need for the producing division to invest in special equipment in order to produce the transferred goods, and interdependencies among several transferred products or services. For example, the producing division may provide design services as well as production of the goods for a buying division. What is the opportunity cost associated with each of these related outputs of the producing division? In many such cases it is difficult to sort out the opportunity costs.

The general transfer-pricing rule provides a good conceptual model for the managerial accountant to use in setting transfer prices. Moreover, in many cases it can be implemented. When the general rule cannot be implemented, organizations turn to other transfer-pricing methods, as we shall see next.

> **Perfect competition** is a market in which the price does not depend on the quantity sold by only one producer.
>
> **Imperfect competition** is a market in which a single producer or group of producers can affect the market price.

Transfers Based on the External Market Price

LO 7   Explain how to base a transfer price on market prices, costs, or negotiations.

A common approach is to set the transfer price equal to the price in the external market. In the Suncoast Food Centers illustration, the Food Processing Division would set the transfer price for bread at $11.00 per rack, since that is the price the division can obtain in its external market. When the producing division has no excess capacity and perfect competition prevails, where no single producer can affect the market price, the general transfer-pricing rule and the external market price yield the same transfer price. This fact is illustrated for Suncoast Food Centers as follows:

Transfer price = Outlay cost + Opportunity cost

                  Variable cost of   Forgone contribution
    = production and + margin of an external
            transportation   sale

    = $7.25   +   ($11.00 − $7.25)   = $11.00

General Transfer-Pricing Rule

Transfer price = External market price = $11.00

Market Price

If the producing division has excess capacity or the external market is imperfectly competitive, the general rule and the external market price will not yield the same transfer price.

If the transfer price is set at the market price, the producing division should have the option of either producing goods for internal transfer or selling in the external market. The buying division should be required to purchase goods from inside its organization if the producing division's goods meet the product specifications. Otherwise, the buying division should have the autonomy to buy from a supplier outside its own organization. To handle pricing disputes that may arise, an arbitration process should be established.

Transfer prices based on market prices are consistent with the responsibility-accounting concepts of profit centers and investment centers. In addition to encouraging division managers to focus on divisional profitability, market-based transfer prices help to show the contribution of each division to overall company profit. Suppose the Food Processing Division of Suncoast Food Centers transfers bread to the Gulf Division at a market-based transfer price of $11.00 per rack. The following contribution margins will be earned by the two divisions and the company as a whole.

Food Processing Division			**Gulf Division**		
Transfer price	$11.00	per rack	Retail sales price	$18.00	per rack
Less: Variable costs	7.25	per rack	Less: Transfer price	11.00	per rack
Contribution margin	$ 3.75	per rack	Contribution margin	$ 7.00	per rack

Suncoast Food Centers	
Retail sales price	$18.00
Less: Variable costs	7.25
Contribution margin	$10.75

When aggregate divisional profits are determined for the year, and ROI and residual income are computed, the use of a market-based transfer price helps to assess the contributions of each division to overall corporate profits.

Distress Market Prices   Occasionally an industry will experience a period of significant excess capacity and extremely low prices. For example, when gasoline prices soared due to a foreign oil embargo, the market prices for recreational vehicles and power boats fell temporarily to very low levels.

Under such extreme conditions, basing transfer prices on market prices can lead to decisions that are not in the best interests of the overall company. Basing transfer prices on artificially low *distress market prices* could lead the producing division to sell or close the productive resources devoted to producing the product for transfer. Under distress market prices, the producing division manager might prefer to move the division into a more profitable product line. While such a decision might improve the division's profit in the short run, it could be contrary to the best interests of the company overall. It might be better for the company as a whole to avoid divesting itself of any productive resources and to ride out the period of market distress. To encourage an autonomous division manager to act in this fashion, some companies set the transfer price equal to the long-run average external market price, rather than the current (possibly depressed) market price.

Negotiated Transfer Prices

Many companies use negotiated transfer prices. Division managers or their representatives actually negotiate the price at which transfers will be made. Sometimes they start with the external market price and then make adjustments for various reasons. For example, the producing division may enjoy some cost savings on internal transfers that are not obtained on external sales. Commissions may not have to be paid to sales personnel on internally transferred products. In such cases, a negotiated transfer price may split the cost savings between the producing and buying divisions.

In other instances, a negotiated transfer price may be used because no external market exists for the transferred product.

Two drawbacks sometimes characterize negotiated transfer prices. First, negotiations can lead to divisiveness and competition between participating division managers. This can undermine the spirit of cooperation and unity that is desirable throughout an organization. Second, although negotiating skill is a valuable managerial talent, it should not be the sole or dominant factor in evaluating a division manager. If, for example, the producing division's manager is a better negotiator than the buying division's manager, then the producing division's profit may look better than it should, simply because of its manager's superior negotiating ability.

Cost-Based Transfer Prices

Organizations that do not base prices on market prices or negotiations often turn to a cost-based transfer-pricing approach.

Variable cost   One approach is to set the transfer price equal to the standard variable cost. The problem with this approach is that even when the producing division has excess capacity, it is not allowed to show any contribution margin on the transferred products or services. To illustrate, suppose the Food Processing Division has excess capacity and the transfer price is set at the standard variable cost of $7.25 per rack of bread. There is no positive incentive for the division to produce and transfer bread to the Gulf Division. The Food Processing Division's contribution margin from a transfer will be zero (transfer price of $7.25 minus variable costs of $7.25 equals zero). Some companies avoid this problem by setting the transfer price at standard variable cost plus a markup to allow the producing division a positive contribution margin.

Full Cost   An alternative is to set the transfer price equal to the *full cost* of the transferred product or service. **Full** (or **absorption**) **cost** is equal to the product's variable cost plus an allocated portion of fixed overhead.

> **Full** (or **absorption**) **cost** is a product's variable cost plus an allocated portion of fixed overhead.

Suppose the Food Processing Division's Orlando bakery has budgeted annual fixed overhead of $500,000 and budgeted annual production of 200,000 racks of bread. The full cost of the bakery's product is computed as follows:

$$\text{Full cost} = \text{Variable cost} + \text{Allocated fixed overhead}$$

$$= \$7.25 + \frac{\$500,000}{200,000}$$

$$= \$7.25 \text{ per rack} + \frac{\$500,000 \text{ budgeted fixed overhead}}{200,000 \text{ budgeted racks of bread}}$$

$$= \quad \$7.25 \quad + \quad \$2.50$$

$$= \quad \$9.75 \text{ per rack}$$

Under this approach, the transfer price is set at $9.75 per rack of bread.

Dysfunctional Decision-Making Behavior   Basing transfer prices on full cost entails a serious risk of causing dysfunctional decision-making behavior. Full-cost-based transfer prices lead the buying division to view costs that are fixed for the company as a whole as variable costs to the buying division. This can cause faulty decision making.

To illustrate, suppose the Food Processing Division has excess capacity, and the transfer price of bread is equal to the full cost of $9.75 per rack. What will happen if the Gulf Division receives the special offer discussed previously, where it can sell bread to a local organization at a special price of $9.60 per rack? The Gulf Division manager will reject the special order, since otherwise her division would incur a loss of $.15 per rack.

Special price per rack	$9.60	per rack
Less: Transfer price based on full cost	9.75	per rack
Loss	$ .15	per rack

What is in the best interests of the company as a whole? Suncoast Food Centers would make a positive contribution of $2.35 per rack on the bread sold in the special order.

Special price per rack	$9.60
Less: Variable cost in Food Processing Division	7.25
Contribution to company as a whole	$2.35

What has happened here? Setting the transfer price equal to the full cost of $9.75 has turned a cost that is fixed in the Food Processing Division, and hence is fixed for the company as a whole, into a variable cost from the viewpoint of the Gulf Division manager. The manager would tend to reject the special offer, even though accepting it would benefit the company as a whole.

Although the practice is common, transfer prices should not be based on full cost. The risk is too great that the cost behavior in the producing division will be obscured. This can all too easily result in poor decisions in the buying division.

Standard versus Actual Costs

Throughout our discussion of transfer prices, we have used standard costs rather than actual costs. This was true in our discussion of the general transfer-pricing rule as well as for cost-based transfer prices. Transfer prices should not be based on actual costs, because such a practice would allow an inefficient producing division to pass its excess production costs on to the buying division in the transfer price. When standard costs are used in transfer-pricing formulas, the selling division is not forced to pick up the tab for the producer's inefficiency. Moreover, the producing division is given an incentive to control its costs, since any costs of inefficiency cannot be passed on.

Undermining Divisional Autonomy

Suppose the manager of Suncoast Food Centers' Food Processing Division has excess capacity but insists on a transfer price of $9.75, based on full cost. The Gulf Division manager is faced with the special offer for bread at $9.60 per rack. She regrets that she will have to decline the offer because it would cause her division's profit to decline, even though the company's interests would be best served by accepting the special order. The Gulf Division manager calls the company president and explains the situation. She asks the president to intervene and force the Food Processing Division manager to lower his transfer price.

As the company president, what would you do? If you stay out of the controversy, your company will lose the contribution on the special order. If you intervene, you will run the risk of undermining the autonomy of your division managers. You established a decentralized organization structure for Suncoast Centers and hired competent managers because you believed in the benefits of decentralized decision making.

There is no obvious answer to this dilemma. In practice, central managers are reluctant to intervene in such disputes unless the negative financial consequences to the organization are quite large. Most managers believe the benefits of decentralized decision making are important to protect, even if it means an occasional dysfunctional decision.

Transfer-pricing methods vary widely among organizations, as the following survey of large-company practices suggests.

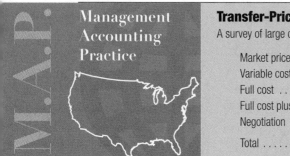

Transfer-Pricing Practices

A survey of large companies revealed the following relative usage of common transfer-pricing practices.[4]

Market price	37%
Variable cost	5
Full cost	24
Full cost plus markup	17
Negotiation	17
Total	100%

An International Perspective

Two international issues arise in the case of multinational firms setting transfer prices between divisions in different countries.

Income-Tax Rates   Multinational companies often consider domestic and foreign income-tax rates when setting transfer prices. For example, suppose a company based in Europe also has a division in Asia. A European division produces a subassembly, which is transferred to the Asian division for assembly and sale of the final product. Suppose also that the income-tax rate for the company's European division is higher than the rate in the Asian division's country. How would these different tax rates affect the transfer price for the subassembly?

The company's management has an incentive to set a low transfer price for the subassembly. This will result in relatively low profits for the company's European division and a relatively high income for the Asian division. Since the tax rate is lower in the Asian country, the overall company will save on income tax. By setting a low transfer price, the company will shift a portion of its income to a country with a lower tax rate. Tax laws vary among countries with regard to flexibility in setting transfer prices. Some countries' tax laws prohibit the behavior described in our example, while other countries' laws permit it.

Import Duties   Another international issue that can affect a firm's transfer pricing policy is the imposition of import duties, or tariffs. These are fees charged to an importer, generally on the basis of the reported value of the goods being imported. Consider again the example of a firm with divisions in Europe and Asia. If the Asian

[4]R. Tang, "Transfer Pricing in the 1990s," *Management Accounting* 73, no. 8, pp. 22–26.

country imposes an import duty on goods transferred in from the European division, the company has an incentive to set a relatively low transfer price on the transferred goods. This will minimize the duty to be paid and maximize the overall profit for the company as a whole. As in the case of taxation, countries sometimes pass laws to limit a multinational firm's flexibility in setting transfer prices for the purpose of minimizing import duties.

Transfer Pricing in the Service Industry

Service industry firms and nonprofit organizations also use transfer pricing when services are transferred between responsibility centers. In banks, for example, the interest rate at which depositors' funds are transferred to the loan department is a form of transfer price. At Cornell University, if a student in the law school takes a course in the business school, a transfer price is charged to the law school for the credit hours of instruction provided to the law student. Since the transfer price is based on tuition charges, it is a market-price-based transfer price.

Behavioral Issues: Risk Aversion and Incentives

The designer of a performance-evaluation system for responsibility-center managers must consider many factors. Trade-offs often must be made between competing objectives. The overall objective is to achieve goal congruence by providing *incentives* for managers to act in the best interests of the organization as a whole. Financial performance measures such as divisional income, ROI, and residual income go a long way toward achieving this objective. However, these measures do have the disadvantage of imposing *risk* on a manager, because the measures also are affected by factors beyond the manager's control. For example, the income of an orange-growing division of an agricultural company will be affected not only by the manager's diligence and ability, but also by the weather and insect infestations.

Since most people exhibit *risk aversion,* managers must be compensated for the risk they must bear. This compensation comes in the form of higher salaries or

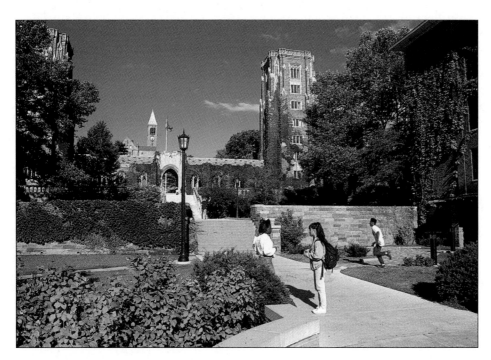

Transfer prices are used in the service industry as well as in manufacturing. Cornell University, for example, charges an accessory instruction fee to a campus unit when one of its students enrolls in a course offered in a different unit.

bonuses. Thus, the design of a managerial performance evaluation and reward system involves a trade-off between the following two factors:

Evaluation of a manager on the basis of financial performance measures, which provide incentives for the manager to act in the organization's interests.	Imposition of risk on a manager who exhibits risk aversion, because financial performance measures are controllable only partially by the manager.

Trade-offs in designing
managerial performance
evaluation and reward system.

Achieving the optimal trade-off between risk and incentives is a delicate balancing act that requires the skill and experience of top management.

Goal Congruence and Internal Control Systems

An **internal control system** ensures that an organization's employees act in a legal, ethical, and responsible manner.

Although most business professionals have high ethical standards, there are unfortunately those who will cut corners. An **internal control system** comprises the set of procedures designed to ensure that an organization's employees act in a legal, ethical, and responsible manner. Internal control procedures are designed to prevent the major lapses in responsible behavior described below.

Fraud Theft or misuse of an organization's resources constitutes *fraud*. To prevent and detect fraud, organizations establish well-defined procedures that prescribe how valuable resources will be handled. For example, many organizations require all checks above a particular amount to be authorized by two people.

Corruption Activities such as bribery, deceit, illegal political campaign contributions, and kickbacks constitute *corruption*. Most organizations have internal control procedures and codes of conduct to prevent and detect corrupt practices. For example, many organizations forbid their purchasing personnel from accepting gifts or gratuities from the sales personnel with whom they conduct business. The Foreign Corrupt Practices Act, passed by the U.S. Congress in 1977, prohibits a variety of corrupt practices in foreign business operations. For example, the law prohibits a company's management from bribing officials of a foreign government in return for favorable treatment of their company.

Financial Misrepresentation Internal control systems also are designed to prevent managers from intentionally (or accidentally) misstating an organization's financial records. Most companies have an *internal audit* staff, which reviews financial records throughout the organization to ensure their accuracy.

Unauthorized Action Sometimes a well-meaning employee is tempted to take an action that is not illegal or even unethical, but it is contrary to the organization's policies. Internal control procedures also are designed to detect and prevent unauthorized actions by an organization's employees, when those actions could reflect unfavorably on the organization. For example, a company may prohibit its employees from using company facilities for a rally in support of a controversial social cause.

An internal control system constitutes an integral part of an organization's efforts to achieve its goals. To be effective, internal control procedures require top management's full support and intolerance of intentional violations.

Chapter Summary

An important objective of any organization's managerial-accounting system is to promote goal congruence among its employees. Thus, the primary criterion for judging the effectiveness of performance measures for responsibility-center managers is the extent to which the measures promote goal congruence.

The two most common measures of investment-center performance are return on investment (ROI) and residual income. Each of these performance measures relates an investment center's income to the capital invested to earn it. Residual income has the additional advantage of incorporating the organization's cost of acquiring capital in the performance measure. An investment center's ROI may be improved by increasing either the sales margin or capital turnover. Both ROI and residual income require the measurement of a division's income and invested capital, and the methods for making the measurements vary in practice.

When products or services are transferred between divisions in the same organization, divisional performance is affected by the transfer price. A general rule states that the transfer price should be equal to the outlay cost incurred to make the transfer plus the organization's opportunity cost associated with the transfer. Due to difficulties in implementing the rule, most companies base transfer prices on external market prices, costs, or negotiations. In some cases, these practical transfer-pricing methods may result in dysfunctional decisions. Top management then must weigh the benefits of intervening to prevent suboptimal decisions against the costs of undermining divisional autonomy.

Review Problems on Investment Centers and Transfer Pricing

Problem 1

Stellar Systems Company manufactures guidance systems for rockets used to launch commercial satellites. The company's Software Division reported the following results for 19x8.

Income	$ 300,000
Sales revenue	2,000,000
Invested capital	3,000,000

The company's required rate of return on invested capital is 9 percent.

Required:

1. Compute the Software Division's sales margin, capital turnover, return on investment, and residual income for 19x8.
2. If income and sales remain the same in 19x9, but the division's capital turnover improves to 80 percent, compute the following for 19x9: (*a*) invested capital and (*b*) ROI.

Problem 2

Stellar Systems Company's Microprocessor Division sells a computer module to the company's Guidance Assembly Division, which assembles completed guidance systems. The Microprocessor Division has no excess capacity. The computer module costs $10,000 to manufacture, and it can be sold in the external market to companies in the computer industry for $13,500.

Required:

Compute the transfer price for the computer module using the general transfer-pricing rule.

Solutions to Review Problems

Problem 1

1. Sales margin $= \dfrac{\text{Income}}{\text{Sales revenue}} = \dfrac{\$300,000}{\$2,000,000} = 15\%$

$$\text{Capital turnover} = \frac{\text{Sales revenue}}{\text{Invested capital}} = \frac{\$2,000,000}{\$3,000,000} = 67\%$$

$$\text{Return on investment} = \frac{\text{Income}}{\text{Invested capital}} = \frac{\$300,000}{\$3,000,000} = 10\%$$

Residual income:

Divisional income		$300,000
Less: Imputed interest charge:		
Invested capital	$3,000,000	
× Imputed interest rate	×.09	
Imputed interest charge		270,000
Residual income		$ 30,000

2. *a.* $\quad \text{Capital turnover} = \dfrac{\text{Sales revenue}}{\text{Invested capital}} = \dfrac{\$2,000,000}{?} = 80\%$

$\qquad\qquad$ Therefore, invested capital $= \dfrac{\$2,000,000}{.80} = \$2,500,000$

$\quad$ *b.* $\quad$ New ROI $= 15\% \times 80\% = 12\%$

Problem 2

$$
\begin{aligned}
\text{Transfer price} &= \text{Outlay cost} \;+\; \text{Opportunity cost} \\
&= \$10,000 \;+\; (\$13,500 - \$10,000) \\
&= \$13,500
\end{aligned}
$$

The $3,500 opportunity cost of a transfer is the contribution margin that will be forgone if a computer module is transferred instead of sold in the external market.

Key Terms

For each term's definition refer to the indicated page, or turn to the glossary at the end of the text.

capital turnover, pg. 525

cash bonus, pg. 532

economic value
   analysis, pg. 528

full (or absorption)
   cost, pg. 540

goal congruence, pg. 522

imperfect
   competition, pg. 538

incentive
   compensation, pg. 532

internal control
   system, pg. 544

investment center, pg. 522

management by objectives
   (MBO), pg. 522

merit pay, pg. 532

pay for
   performance, pg. 532

perfect competition, pg. 538

residual income, pg. 526

return on investment
   (ROI), pg. 524

sales margin, pg. 525

shareholder value
   analysis, pg. 528

transfer price, pg. 522

Review Questions

13–1. Define *goal congruence,* and explain why it is important to an organization's success.

13–2. What is the managerial accountant's primary objective in designing a responsibility-accounting system?

13–3. Describe the managerial approach known as *management by objectives* or *MBO*.

13–4. Define and give three examples of an *investment center.*

13–5. Write the formula for ROI, showing sales margin and capital turnover as its components.

13–6. Explain how the manager of the Automobile Division of an insurance company could improve her division's ROI.

13–7. Make up an example showing how residual income is calculated. What information is used in computing residual income that is not used in computing ROI?

13–8. What is the chief disadvantage of ROI as an investment-center performance measure? How does the residual-income measure eliminate this disadvantage?

13–9. Why is there typically a rise in ROI or residual income across time in a division? What undesirable behavioral implications could this phenomenon have?

13–10. Explain what is meant by *shareholder value analysis.*

13–11. Distinguish between the following measures of invested capital, and briefly explain when each should be used: (1) total assets, (2) total productive assets, and (3) total assets less current liabilities.

13–12. Why do some companies use gross book value instead of net book value to measure a division's invested capital?

13–13. Explain why it is important in performance evaluation to distinguish between investment centers and their managers.

13–14. How do organizations use pay for performance to motivate managers?

13–15. Describe an alternative to using ROI or residual income to measure investment-center performance.

13–16. How does inflation affect investment-center performance measures?

13–17. List three nonfinancial measures that could be used to evaluate a division of an insurance company.

13–18. Discuss the importance of nonfinancial information in measuring investment-center performance.

13–19. Identify and explain the managerial accountant's primary objective in choosing a transfer-pricing policy.

13–20. Describe four methods by which transfer prices may be set.

13–21. Explain the significance of excess capacity in the transferring division when transfer prices are set using the general transfer-pricing rule.

13–22. Why might income-tax laws affect the transfer-pricing policies of multinational companies?

13–23. Explain the role of import duties, or tariffs, in affecting the transfer-pricing policies of multinational companies.

Exercises

The following data pertain to Huron Division's most recent year of operations.

Income	$ 4,000,000
Sales revenue	50,000,000
Average invested capital	20,000,000

■ **Exercise 13-24**
Components of ROI
(LO 2)

Required:

Compute Huron Division's sales margin, capital turnover, and return on investment for the year.

Refer to the preceding exercise.

Required:

Demonstrate two ways Huron Division's manager could improve the division's ROI to 25 percent.

■ **Exercise 13–25**
Improving ROI
(LO 3)

Refer to the data for Exercise 13–24. Assume that the company's minimum desired rate of return on invested capital is 11 percent.

Required:

Compute Huron Division's residual income for the year.

■ **Exercise 13–26**
Residual Income
(LO 2)

Winneloa Corporation has two divisions. The Fabrication Division transfers partially completed components to the Assembly Division at a predetermined transfer price. The Fabrication Division's standard variable production cost per unit is $300. The division has no excess capacity, and it could sell all of its components to outside buyers at $380 per unit in a perfectly competitive market.

■ **Exercise 13–27**
General Transfer-Pricing Rule
(LO 6)

Required:

1. Determine a transfer price using the general rule.
2. How would the transfer price change if the Fabrication Division had excess capacity?

Refer to the preceding exercise. The Fabrication Division's full (absorption) cost of a component is $340, which includes $40 of applied fixed-overhead costs. The transfer price has been set at $374, which is the Fabrication Division's full cost plus a 10 percent markup.

The Assembly Division has a special offer for its product of $465. The Assembly Division incurs variable costs of $100 in addition to the transfer price for the Fabrication Division's components. Both divisions currently have excess production capacity.

■ **Exercise 13–28**
Cost-Based Transfer Pricing
(LO 7)

Required:

1. What is the Assembly Division's manager likely to do regarding acceptance or rejection of the special offer? Why?

2.   Is this decision in the best interests of Winneloa Corporation as a whole? Why?

3.   How could the situation be remedied using the transfer price?

■ Exercise 13–29
Increasing ROI over Time
(LO 2, LO 4, LO 5)

Refer to Exhibit 13–3. Assume that you are a consultant who has been hired by Suncoast Food Centers.

Required:

Write a memorandum to the company president explaining why the ROI based on net book value (in Exhibit 13–3) behaves as it does over the five-year time horizon.

■ Exercise 13–30
Internal Control
(LO 1)

Danby Company is an auto parts supplier. At the end of each month, the employee who maintains all of the inventory records takes a physical inventory of the firm's stock. When discrepancies occur between the recorded inventory and the physical count, the employee changes the physical count to agree with the records.

Required:

1.   What problems could arise as a result of Danby Company's inventory procedures?

2.   How could the internal control system be strengthened to eliminate the potential problems?

■ Exercise 13–31
Improving ROI
(LO 2, LO 3)

The following data pertain to Utah Aggregates Company, a producer of sand, gravel, and cement, for the year just ended.

Sales revenue	$2,000,000
Cost of goods sold	1,100,000
Operating expenses	800,000
Average invested capital	1,000,000

Required:

1.   Compute the company's sales margin, capital turnover, and ROI.

2.   If the sales and average invested capital remain the same during the next year, to what level would total expenses have to be reduced in order to improve the firm's ROI to 15 percent?

3.   Assume expenses are reduced, as calculated in requirement (2). Compute the firm's new sales margin. Show how the new sales margin and the old capital turnover together result in a new ROI of 15 percent.

■ Exercise 13–32
ROI; Residual Income
(LO 1, LO 2)

Lawton Industries has manufactured prefabricated houses for over 20 years. The houses are constructed in sections to be assembled on customers' lots. Lawton expanded into the precut housing market when it acquired Presser Company, one of its suppliers. In this market, various types of lumber are precut into the appropriate lengths, banded into packages, and shipped to customers' lots for assembly. Lawton designated the Presser Division as an investment center. Lawton uses return on investment (ROI) as a performance measure with investment defined as average productive assets. Management bonuses are based in part on ROI. All investments are expected to earn a minimum return of 15 percent before income taxes. Presser's ROI has ranged from 19.3 to 22.1 percent since it was acquired. Presser had an investment opportunity in 19x9 that had an estimated ROI of 18 percent. Presser's management decided against the investment because it believed the investment would decrease the division's overall ROI. The 19x9 income statement for Presser Division follows. The division's productive assets were $12,600,000 at the end of 19x9, a 5 percent increase over the balance at the beginning of the year.

PRESSER DIVISION
Income Statement
For the Year Ended December 31, 19x9
(in thousands)

Sales revenue	$24,000
Cost of goods sold	15,800
Gross margin	$ 8,200

Operating expenses:		
Administrative	$2,140	
Selling	3,600	5,740
Income from operations before income taxes		$ 2,460

Required:

1. Calculate the following performance measures for 19x9 for the Presser Division.

   a. Return on investment (ROI).

   b. Residual income.

2. Would the management of Presser Division have been more likely to accept the investment opportunity it had in 19x9 if residual income were used as a performance measure instead of ROI? Explain your answer.

(CMA, adapted)

Problems

Triangle Furniture Company has two divisions, which reported the following results for the most recent year.

	Division I		Division II
Income	$ 200,000	....	$ 900,000
Average invested capital	$1,000,000	....	$6,000,000
ROI	20%	....	15%

■ Problem 13–33
Comparing the Performance of Two Divisions
(LO 2, LO 4)

Required:

Which was the most successful division during the year? Think carefully about this, and explain your answer.

The following data pertain to three divisions of Pittsburgh Pipe Fittings Corporation. The company's required rate of return on invested capital is 8 percent.

	Division A	Division B	Division C
Sales revenue	$10,000,000	?	?
Income	$2,000,000	$400,000	?
Average investment	$2,500,000	?	?
Sales margin	?	20%	25%
Capital turnover	?	1	?
ROI	?	?	20%
Residual income	?	?	$120,000

■ Problem 13–34
ROI and Residual Income; Missing Data
(LO 2, LO 3)

Required:

Fill in the blanks above.

Refer to the preceding problem about Pittsburgh Pipe Fittings Corporation.

■ Problem 13–35
Improving ROI
(LO 3)

Required:

1. Explain three ways the Division A manager could improve her division's ROI. Use numbers to illustrate these possibilities.

2. Suppose Division B's sales margin increased to 25 percent, while its capital turnover remained constant. Compute the division's new ROI.

Raddington Industries produces tool and die machinery for automobile manufacturers. The company recently expanded by acquiring one of its suppliers of alloy steel plates, Reigis Steel Company. In order to manage the two separate businesses, the operations of Reigis are reported separately as an investment

■ Problem 13–36
ROI; Residual Income
(LO 1, LO 2, LO 4)

center. Raddington monitors its divisions on the basis of both divisional contribution margin and return on investment (ROI). Investment is defined as average total assets. Management bonuses are determined on the basis of ROI. All investments in operating assets are expected to earn a minimum return of 11 percent before income taxes.

Reigis' cost of goods sold is considered to be entirely variable, while the division's administrative expenses are not dependent on volume. Selling expenses are a semivariable cost with 40 percent of the total attributed to sales volume. Reigis' ROI has ranged from 11.8 to 14.7 percent over the past five years. During 19x9, Reigis' management contemplated a capital acquisition with an estimated ROI of 11.5 percent. However, division management decided against the investment because it believed that the investment would decrease Reigis' overall ROI. The 19x9 income statement for Reigis follows. The division's total assets were $15,750,000 on December 31, 19x9, a 5 percent increase over the 19x8 year-end balance.

REIGIS STEEL DIVISION
Income Statement
For the Year Ended December 31, 19x9
(in thousands)

Sales revenue		$25,000
Less expenses:		
Cost of goods sold	$16,500	
Administrative expenses	3,955	
Selling expenses	2,700	23,155
Income from operations before income taxes		$ 1,845

Required:

1. Calculate the divisional contribution margin for Reigis Steel Division if 1,484,000 units were produced and sold during 19x9.
2. Calculate the following performance measures for 19x9 for the Reigis Steel Division:
   a. Before-tax return on investment (ROI).
   b. Residual income.
3. Explain why the management of the Reigis Steel Division would have been more likely to accept the contemplated capital acquisition if residual income rather than ROI was used as a performance measure.
4. The Reigis Steel Division is a separate investment center within Raddington Industries. Identify several items that Reigis' management should have authorization to control if it is to be evaluated fairly by either the ROI or residual income performance measure.
5. Calculate Reigis Division's contribution margin per unit in 19x9. Briefly discuss the pros and cons of using divisional contribution margin versus the contribution margin per unit as a divisional performance measure.

(CMA, adapted)

■ **Problem 13–37**
Residual Income
(LO 2, LO 4)

Refer to the data for problem 13–33 regarding Triangle Furniture Company.

Required:

Compute each division's residual income for the year under each of the following assumptions about the firm's cost of acquiring capital.

1. 12 percent.
2. 15 percent.
3. 18 percent.

Which division was most successful? Explain your answer.

■ **Problem 13–38**
Increasing ROI over Time;
Accelerated Depreciation
(LO 2, LO 4, LO 5)

Refer to Exhibit 13–3. Prepare a similar table of the changing ROI assuming the following accelerated depreciation schedule. Assume the same income before depreciation as shown in Exhibit 13–3. (If there is a loss, leave the ROI column blank.)

Year	Depreciation
1	$200,000
2	120,000
3	72,000
4	54,000
5	54,000
Total	$500,000

Required:

1. How does your table differ from the one in Exhibit 13–3? Why?
2. What are the implications of the ROI pattern in your table?

Prepare a table similar to Exhibit 13–3, which focuses on residual income. Use a 10 percent rate to compute the imputed interest charge. The table should show the residual income on the investment during each year in its five-year life. Assume the same income before depreciation and the same depreciation schedule as shown in Exhibit 13–3.

■ **Problem 13–39**
Increasing Residual Income over Time
(LO 2, LO 4, LO 5)

Erie Corporation made a capital investment of $100,000 in computer integrated manufacturing equipment for its Cleveland Division two years ago. The analysis at that time indicated the equipment would save $36,400 in operating expenses per year over a five-year period. Before the purchase, the division's ROI was 20 percent.

Timothy Williams, the division manager, believed that the equipment had lived up to its expectations. However, the divisional performance report showing the overall return on investment for the first year in which this equipment was used did not reflect as much improvement as had been expected. Williams asked the Accounting Department to break out the figures related to this investment to find out why it did not contribute to improving the division's ROI.

The Accounting Department was able to identify the equipment's contribution to the division's operations. The report presented to the division manager at the end of the first year is as follows:

■ **Problem 13–40**
Behavioral Implications of ROI; Computer Integrated Manufacturing
(LO 1, LO 4)

Reduced operating expenses due to new equipment	$ 36,400
Less: Depreciation, 20% of cost	20,000
Contribution	$ 16,400
Investment, beginning of year	$100,000
Investment, end of year	$ 80,000
Average investment for the year	$ 90,000

$$\text{ROI} = \frac{\$16,400}{\$90,000} = 18.2\%$$

Timothy Williams was surprised that the ROI was so low, because the new equipment performed as expected. The staff analyst in the Accounting Department replied that the company's ROI for performance evaluation differed from that used for capital investment decisions.

Required:

Discuss the problems associated with ROI as a divisional performance measure. What might the Cleveland Division manager do the next time a new equipment purchase is suggested? Why?

Greystone Company manufactures windows for the home-building industry. The window frames are produced in the Frame Division. The frames are then transferred to the Glass Division, where the glass and hardware are installed. The company's best-selling product is a three-by-four-foot, double-paned operable window.

The Frame Division can also sell frames directly to custom home builders, who install the glass and hardware. The sales price for a frame is $80. The Glass Division sells its finished windows for $190. The markets for both frames and finished windows exhibit perfect competition.

The standard cost of the window is detailed as follows:

■ **Problem 13–41**
Comprehensive Transfer-Pricing Problem
(LO 6, LO 7)

	Frame Division		Glass Division
Direct material	$15		$30 *
Direct labor	20		15
Variable overhead	30		30
Total	$65		$75

*Not including the transfer price for the frame.

Required:

1. Assume that there is no excess capacity in the Frame Division.
   a. Use the general rule to compute the transfer price for window frames.
   b. Calculate the transfer price if it is based on standard variable cost with a 10 percent markup.
2. Assume that there is excess capacity in the Frame Division.
   a. Use the general rule to compute the transfer price for window frames.
   b. Explain why your answers to requirements 1(a) and 2(a) differ.
   c. Suppose the predetermined fixed-overhead rate in the Frame Division is 125 percent of direct-labor cost. Calculate the transfer price if it is based on standard full cost plus a 10 percent markup.
   d. Assume the transfer price established in requirement 2(c) is used. The Glass Division has been approached by the U.S. Army with a special order for 1,000 windows at $155. From the perspective of Greystone Company as a whole, should the special order be accepted or rejected? Why?
   e. Assume the same facts as in requirement 2(d). Will an autonomous Glass Division manager accept or reject the special order? Why?
3. Comment on the use of full cost as the basis for setting transfer prices.

■ **Problem 13–42**
Basic Transfer Pricing
(LO 6, LO 7)

Ajax Division of Carlyle Corporation produces electric motors, 20 percent of which are sold to Bradley Division of Carlyle. The remainder are sold to outside customers. Carlyle treats its divisions as profit centers and allows division managers to choose their sources of sale and supply. Corporate policy requires that all interdivisional sales and purchases be recorded at variable cost as a transfer price. Ajax Division's budgeted sales and standard-cost data for the current year, based on capacity of 100,000 units, are as follows:

	Bradley	Outsiders
Sales	$ 900,000	$ 8,000,000
Variable costs	(900,000)	(3,600,000)
Fixed costs	(300,000)	(1,200,000)
Gross margin	$(300,000)	$ 3,200,000
Unit sales	20,000	80,000

Ajax has an opportunity to sell the 20,000 units shown above to an outside customer at a price of $75 per unit. Bradley can purchase its requirements from an outside supplier at a price of $85 per unit.

Required:

1. Assuming that Ajax Division desires to maximize its gross margin, should Ajax take on the new customer and drop its sales to Bradley during the current year? Why?
2. Assume, instead, that Carlyle permits division managers to negotiate the transfer price. The managers agreed on a tentative transfer price of $75 per unit, to be reduced based on an equal sharing of the additional gross margin to Ajax resulting from the sale to Bradley of 20,000 motors at $75 per unit. What would be the actual transfer price?
3. Assume now that Ajax Division has an opportunity to sell the 20,000 motors that Bradley Division would buy to the same customers that are buying the other 80,000 motors produced by Ajax. Ajax Division could sell all 100,000 motors to outside customers at a price of $100. What actions by each division manager are in the best interests of Carlyle Corporation?
4. Under the scenario described in requirement (3), use the general transfer pricing rule to compute the transfer price Ajax Division should charge Bradley Division for motors.

5. Will the transfer price computed in requirement (4) result in the most desirable outcome from the standpoint of Carlyle Corporation? Justify your answer.

(CPA, adapted)

Roberts Products, Inc. consists of three decentralized divisions: Bayside Division, Cole Division, and Diamond Division. The president of Roberts Products has given the managers of the three divisions the authority to decide whether or not to sell outside the company, or among themselves at a transfer price determined by the division managers. Market conditions are such that sales made internally or externally will not affect market or transfer prices. Intermediate markets will always be available for Bayside, Cole, and Diamond to purchase their manufacturing needs or sell their product. Each division manager attempts to maximize his contribution margin at the current level of operating assets for the division.

■ Problem 13–43
Multiple Interdivisional Transfers; Accept or Reject Outside Contract; Ethics
(LO 6, LO 7)

The manager of Cole Division is currently considering the following two alternative orders.

■ Diamond Division is in need of 3,000 units of a motor that can be supplied by Cole Division. To manufacture these motors, Cole would purchase components from Bayside Division at a transfer price of $600 per unit. Bayside's variable cost for these components is $300 per unit. Cole Division will further process these components at a variable cost of $500 per unit. If Diamond Division cannot obtain the motors from Cole Division, it will purchase the motors from London Company which has offered to supply the same motors to Diamond Division at a price of $1,500 per unit. London Company would also purchase 3,000 components from Bayside Division at a price of $400 for each of these motors. Bayside's variable cost for these components is $200 per unit.

■ Wales Company wants to place an order with Cole Division for 3,500 similar motors at a price of $1,250 per unit. Cole would again purchase components from Bayside Division at a transfer price of $500 per unit. Bayside's variable cost for these components is $250 per unit. Cole Division will further process these components at a variable cost of $400 per unit.

Cole Division's plant capacity is limited, and the company can only accept the Wales contract or the Diamond order, but not both. The president of Roberts Products and the manager of Cole Division agree that it would not be beneficial to increase capacity.

Required:

1. If the manager of the Cole Division wants to maximize Cole Division's short-run contribution margin, determine whether the Cole Division should:
   a. Sell motors to the Diamond Division at the prevailing market price.
   b. Or accept the Wales Company contract.

2. Independent of your answer to requirement (1), assume that the Cole Division decides to accept the Wales Company contract. Determine if this decision is in the best interest of Roberts Products, Inc.

3. Independent of your answers to the first two requirements, assume the following:
   a. The management of Cole Division accepted the order from Wales Company because that decision would maximize Cole's divisional contribution margin.
   b. Analysis indicates that Roberts Products, Inc. would be better off if the motors had been sold to Diamond Division.
   Did Cole Division's management act ethically?

(CMA, adapted)

Darmen Corporation is a major producer of prefabricated beach houses. The corporation consists of two divisions: the Bell Division, which acquires the raw materials to manufacture the basic house components and assembles them into kits, and the Cornish Division, which takes the kits and constructs the homes for final home buyers. The corporation is decentralized, and the management of each division is measured by divisional income and return on investment.

■ Problem 13–44
Comprehensive Problem on Divisional Performance Evaluation; Ethics
(LO 1, LO 2, LO 4, LO 5)

Bell Division assembles seven separate house kits using raw materials purchased at the prevailing market prices. The seven kits are sold to Cornish for prices ranging from $45,000 to $98,000. The prices are set by Darmen's corporate management using prices paid by Cornish when it buys comparable units from outside sources. The smaller kits with the lower prices have become a larger portion of the units sold, because the final house buyer is faced with prices that are increasing more rapidly than personal income. The kits are manufactured and assembled in a new plant just purchased by Bell this year. The division had been located in a leased plant for the past four years.

All kits are assembled upon receipt of an order from the Cornish Division. When the kit is completely assembled, it is loaded immediately on a Cornish truck. Thus, Bell Division has no finished-goods inventory.

The Bell Division's accounts and reports are prepared on an actual-cost basis. There is no budget, and standards have not been developed for any product. A manufacturing-overhead rate is calculated at the beginning of each year. The rate is designed to charge all overhead to the product each year. Any underapplied or overapplied overhead is closed into the Cost of Goods Sold account.

Bell Division's annual report follows. This report forms the basis of the evaluation of the division and its management.

BELL DIVISION
Performance Report
For the Year Ended December 31, 19x9

			Increase or (Decrease) from 19x8	
	19x9	19x8	Amount	Percent Change
Summary data:				
Net income (in thousands)	$ 34,222	$ 31,573	$ 2,649	8.4
Return on investment	37%	43%	(6)%	(14.0)
Kits shipped (units)	2,000	2,100	(100)	(4.8)
Production data (units):				
Kits started	2,400	1,600	800	50.0
Kits shipped	2,000	2,100	(100)	(4.8)
Kits in process at year end	700	300	400	133.3
Increase (decrease) in kits in process at year end	400	(500)	—	—
Financial data (in thousands):				
Sales revenue	$138,000	$162,800	$(24,800)	(15.2)
Production cost of units sold:				
Direct material	$ 32,000	$ 40,000	$ (8,000)	(20.0)
Direct labor	41,700	53,000	(11,300)	(21.3)
Manufacturing overhead	29,000	37,000	(8,000)	(21.6)
Cost of units sold	$102,700	$130,000	$(27,300)	(21.0)
Other costs:				
Corporate charges for:				
Personnel services	$ 228	$ 210	$ 18	8.6
Accounting services	425	440	(15)	(3.4)
Financing costs	300	525	(225)	(42.9)
Total other costs	$ 953	$ 1,175	$ (222)	(18.9)
Adjustment to income:				
Unreimbursed fire loss	—	$ 52	$ (52)	(100.0)
Raw material losses due to improper storage	$ 125	—	125	—
Total adjustments	$ 125	$ 52	$ 73	140.4
Total deductions	$103,778	$131,227	$(27,449)	(20.9)
Divisional income	$ 34,222	$ 31,573	$ 2,649	8.4
Divisional investment	$ 92,000	$ 73,000	$ 19,000	26.0
Return on investment	37%	43%	(6)%	(14.0)

Additional information regarding corporate and divisional practices follows.

1. The corporate office does all of the personnel and accounting work for each division.
2. Corporate personnel costs are allocated on the basis of the number of employees in each division.
3. Accounting costs are allocated to divisions on the basis of total costs, excluding corporate charges.

4. Divisional administration costs are included in overhead.

5. The financing charges include a corporate imputed interest charge on divisional assets.

6. The divisional investment for the ROI calculation includes divisional inventory and plant and equipment at gross book value.

Required:

1. Discuss the value of the annual report presented for the Bell Division in evaluating the division and its management in terms of:

    a. The accounting techniques employed in the measurement of divisional activities.

    b. The manner of presentation.

    c. The effectiveness with which it discloses differences and similarities between years.

    Use the information in the problem to illustrate your answer.

2. Present specific recommendations for the management of Darmen Corporation which would improve its accounting and financial-reporting system.

3. Suppose Bell Division's controller, Jake Thompson, was approached on December 28 by the divisional vice president with the following request:

    "Jake, we've got a firm offer for 50 kits that won't be finished and shipped until January 8. I want you to book the sale before the end of the year. The total sales figure on the order is $850,000 That will bump this year's sales up over $35,000,000. The division will look better, and we'll all get a bonus."

        What are Jake Thompson's ethical obligations in this situation?

(CMA, adapted)

Internal auditors must be alert for errors, irregularities, and fraud. Errors generally are considered unintentional acts, while irregularities refer to intentional acts, including fraud. Preventive, detective, and corrective controls can be designed to limit errors and irregularities. Of these three types of controls, preventive controls generally are the most cost-effective. Following are three situations in which fraud was suspected or detected by internal auditors.

■ *Situation 1:* Many employees of a firm that manufactures small tools had been pocketing some of these tools for their personal use. Since the quantities taken by any one employee were immaterial, the individual employees did not consider the act as fradulent nor detrimental to the company. As the company grew larger, an internal auditor was hired. The auditor charted the gross profit percentages for particular tools and discovered higher gross profit rates for tools related to industrial use than for personal use. Subsequent investigation uncovered the fraudulent acts.

■ *Situation 2:* A company controller set up a fictitious subsidiary office to which he shipped inventory and then approved the invoice for payment. The inventory was sold and the proceeds deposited to the controller's personal bank account. Internal auditors suspected fraud when auditing the plant's real estate assets. They traced plant real estate descriptions to the assets owned and leased, and could not find a title or lease for the location of this particular subsidiary.

■ *Situation 3:* The manager of a large department was able to embezzle funds from his employer by carrying employees on the payroll beyond actual termination dates. The manager carried each terminated employee for only one pay period beyond the termination date so the employee would not easily detect the additional amount included on the W–2 reporting of wages to the Internal Revenue Service. The paymaster regularly delivered all checks to the department manager who then deposited the fraudulent checks to a personal checking account. An internal auditor discovered the fraud from a routine tracing of sample entries in the payroll register to the employees' files in the personnel office. The sample included one employee's pay record whose personnel file showed the termination date prior to the pay period audited. The auditor investigated further and discovered other such fraudulent checks.

Required:

Referring to the three situations presented, describe at least two recommendations that the internal auditor could make in *each* situation to prevent similar problems in the future.

(CMA, adapted)

■ **Problem 13–45**
Ethics; Internal Auditors;
Fraud
(LO 1)

Cases

■ **Case 13–46**
Divisional Performance
Measurement and Transfer
Pricing
(LO 1, LO 7)

Easy Living Industries manufactures carpets, furniture, and cushions in three separate divisions. The company's operating statement for 19x9 is as follows:

EASY LIVING INDUSTRIES
Operating Statement
For the Year Ended December 31, 19x9

	Carpet Division	Furniture Division	Cushion Division	Total
Sales revenue	$3,000,000	$3,000,000	$4,000,000	$10,000,000
Cost of goods sold	2,000,000	1,300,000	3,000,000	6,300,000
Gross profit	$1,000,000	$1,700,000	$1,000,000	$ 3,700,000
Operating expenses:				
Administration	$ 300,000	$ 500,000	$ 400,000	$ 1,200,000
Selling	600,000	600,000	500,000	1,700,000
Total operating expenses	$ 900,000	$1,100,000	$ 900,000	$ 2,900,000
Income from operations before taxes	$ 100,000	$ 600,000	$ 100,000	$ 800,000

Additional information regarding Easy Living Industries' operations is as follows:

1. Included in the Cushion Division's sales revenue is $500,000 that represents sales made to the Furniture Division. The transfer price for these sales was at the full cost of manufacturing.

2. The three divisions' cost of goods sold is comprised of the following costs.

	Carpet	Furniture	Cushion
Direct material	$ 500,000	$1,000,000	$1,000,000
Direct labor	500,000	200,000	1,000,000
Variable overhead	750,000	50,000	1,000,000
Fixed overhead	250,000	50,000	–0–
Total cost of goods sold	$2,000,000	$1,300,000	$3,000,000

3. Administrative expenses include the following costs.

	Carpet	Furniture	Cushion
Segment expenses:			
Variable	$ 85,000	$140,000	$ 40,000
Fixed	85,000	210,000	120,000
Home-office expenses (all fixed):			
Directly traceable	100,000	120,000	200,000
General (allocated based on sales dollars) . . .	30,000	30,000	40,000
Total	$300,000	$500,000	$400,000

4. All selling expense is incurred at the divisional level. It is 80 percent variable for all segments.

Meg Johnson, manager of the Cushion Division, is not pleased with the company's presentation of operating performance. Johnson claims, "The Cushion Division makes a greater contribution to the company's profits than is shown. I sell cushions to the Furniture Division at cost and it gets our share of the profit. I can sell these cushions on the outside at my regular markup, but I sell to Furniture for the well-being of the company. I think my division should get credit for those internal sales at market. I think we should also revise our operating statements for internal purposes. Why don't we consider preparing these internal statements in a format that shows internal transfers at market?"

Required:

1. Meg Johnson believes that the transfers from the Cushion Division to the Furniture Division should be at market rather than at full manufacturing cost for divisional performance measurement.

a. Is Johnson correct? Why?

b. Describe another approach that the company could use to set transfer prices other than manu-facturing cost and market price.

2. Using transfer prices based on market prices, prepare a revised operating statement, by division, for Easy Living Industries for 19x9 that will facilitate the evaluation of divisional performance. Use the contribution-margin format.

(CMA, adapted)

Family Leisure Company (FLC), a subsidiary of New Age Industries, manufactures go-carts and other recreational vehicles. Family recreational centers that feature not only go-cart tracks but miniature golf, batting cages, and arcade games as well, have increased in popularity. As a result, FLC has been receiving some pressure from New Age's management to diversify into some of these other recreational areas. Recreational Leasing, Inc. (RLI), one of the largest firms that leases arcade games to family recre-ational centers, is looking for a friendly buyer. New Age's top management believes that RLI's assets could be acquired for an investment of $3.2 million and has strongly urged Bill Grieco, division manager of FLC, to consider acquiring RLI.

> Grieco has reviewed RLI's financial statements with his controller, Marie Donnelly, and they believe the acquisition may not be in the best interest of FLC. "If we decide not to do this, the New Age people are not going to be happy," said Grieco. "If we could convince them to base our bonuses on something other than return on investment, maybe this acquisition would look more attractive. How would we do if the bonuses were based on residual income, using the company's 15 percent cost of capital?"

> New Age Industries traditionally has evaluated all of its divisions on the basis of return on investment. The desired rate of return for each division is 20 percent. The management team of any division reporting an annual increase in the ROI is automatically eligible for a bonus. The management of divisions reporting a decline in the ROI must provide convincing explanations for the decline in order to be eligible for a bonus. Moreover, this bonus is limited to 50 percent of the bonus paid to divisions reporting an increase in ROI.

> In the following table are condensed financial statements for both FLC and RLI for the most recent year.

■ **Case 13–47**
ROI versus Residual Income;
Incentive Effects
(LO 1, LO 2, LO 4)

	FLC	RLI
Sales revenue	$9,500,000	—
Leasing revenue	—	$3,100,000
Variable expenses	(6,000,000)	(1,300,000)
Fixed expenses	(1,500,000)	(1,200,000)
Operating income	$2,000,000	$ 600,000
Current assets	$2,300,000	$1,900,000
Long-lived assets	5,700,000	1,100,000
Total assets	$8,000,000	$3,000,000
Current liabilities	$1,400,000	$ 850,000
Long-term liabilities	3,800,000	1,200,000
Stockholders' equity	2,800,000	950,000
Total liabilities and stockholders' equity	$8,000,000	$3,000,000

Required:

1. If New Age Industries continues to use ROI as the sole measure of divisional performance, explain why Family Leisure Company would be reluctant to acquire Recreational Leasing, Inc.

2. If New Age Industries could be persuaded to use residual income to measure the performance of FLC, explain why FLC would be more willing to acquire RLI.

3. Discuss how the behavior of division managers is likely to be affected by the use of the following performance measures: (*a*) return on investment and (*b*) residual income.

(CMA, adapted)

■ **Case 13–48**
Minimum and Maximum
Acceptable Transfer Prices;
Multinational

(LO 6)

General Instrumentation Company manufactures dashboard instruments for heavy construction equipment. The firm is based in Baltimore, but operates several divisions in the United States, Canada, and Europe. The Hudson Bay Division manufactures solid-state electrical panels that are used in a variety of the firm's instruments. There are two basic types of panels. The high-density panel (HDP) is capable of many functions and is used in the most sophisticated instruments, such as tachometers and pressure gauges. The low-density panel (LDP) is much simpler and is used in less complicated instruments. Although there are minor differences among the different high-density panels, the basic manufacturing process and production costs are the same. The high-density panels require considerably more skilled labor than the low-density panels, but the unskilled labor needs are about the same. Moreover, the direct materials in the high-density panel run substantially more than the cost of materials in the low-density panels. Production costs are summarized as follows:

	LDP	HDP
Unskilled labor (.5 hour @ $10)	$ 5	$ 5
Skilled labor:		
LDP (.25 hour @ $20)	5	
HDP (1.5 hours @ $20)		30
Raw material	3	8
Purchased components	4	12
Variable overhead	5	15
Total variable cost	$22	$70

The annual fixed overhead in the Hudson Bay Division is $1,000,000. There is a limited supply of skilled labor available in the area, and the division must constrain its production to 40,000 hours of skilled labor each year. This has been a troublesome problem for Jacqueline Ducharme, the division manager. Ducharme has successfully increased demand for the LDP line to the point where it is essentially unlimited. Each LDP sells for $28. Business also has increased in recent years for the HDP, and Ducharme estimates the division could now sell anywhere up to 6,000 units per year at a price of $115.

On the other side of the Atlantic, General Instrumentation operates its Volkmar Tachometer Division in Berlin. A recent acquisition of General Instrumentation, the division was formerly a German company known as Volkmar Construction Instruments. The division's main product is a sophisticated tachometer used in heavy-duty cranes, bulldozers, and backhoes. The instrument, designated as a TCH–320, has the following production costs.

TCH–320

Unskilled labor (.5 hour @ $9)	$ 4.50
Skilled labor (3 hours @ $17)	51.00
Raw material	11.50
Purchased components	150.00
Variable overhead	11.00
Total variable cost	$228.00

The cost of purchased components includes a $145 control pack currently imported from Japan. Fixed overhead in the Volkmar Tachometer Division runs about $800,000 per year. Both skilled and unskilled labor are in abundant supply. The TCH–320 sells for $270.

Bertram Mueller, the division manager of the Volkmar Tachometer Division, recently attended a high-level corporate meeting in Baltimore. In a conversation with Jacqueline Ducharme, it was apparent that Hudson Bay's high-density panel might be a viable substitute for the control pack currently imported from Japan and used in Volkmar's TCH–320. Upon returning to Berlin, Mueller asked his chief engineer to look into the matter. Hans Schmidt obtained several HDP units from Hudson Bay, and a minor R&D project was mounted to determine if the HDP could replace the Japanese control pack. Several weeks later, the following conversation occurred in Mueller's office:

Schmidt: There's no question that Hudson Bay's HDP unit will work in our TCH–320. In fact, it could save us some money.

Mueller: That's good news. If we can buy our components within the company, we'll help Baltimore's bottom line without hurting ours. Also, it will look good to the brass at corporate if they see us working hard to integrate our division into General Instrumentation's overall production program.

Schmidt: I've also been worried about the reliability of supply of the control pack. I don't like being dependent on such a critical supplier that way.

Mueller: I agree. Let's look at your figures on the HDP replacement.

Schmidt: I got together with the controller's people, and we worked up some numbers. If we replace the control pack with the HDP from Canada, we'll avoid the $145 control pack cost we're now incurring. In addition, I figure we'll save $5.50 on the basic raw materials. There is one catch, though. The HDP will require some adjustments in order to use it in the TCH–320. We can make the adjustments here in Berlin. I'm guessing it will require an additional two hours of skilled labor to make the necessary modifications. I don't think variable overhead would be any different. Then there is the cost of transporting the HDPs to Berlin. Let's figure on $4.50 per unit.

Mueller: Sounds good. I'll give Jacqueline Ducharme a call and talk this over. We can use up to 10,000 of the HDP units per year given the demand for the TCH–320. I wonder what kind of a transfer price Hudson Bay will want.

Required:

1. Draw a simple diagram depicting the two divisions and their products. Also show the two alternatives that the Volkmar Tachometer Division has in the production of its TCH–320.

2. From the perspective of General Instrumentation's top management, should any of the TCH–320 units be produced using the high-density panel? If so, how many?

3. Suppose Hudson Bay transfers 10,000 HDP units per year to Volkmar. From the perspective of General Instrumentation's top management, what effect will the transfer price have on the company's income?

4. What is the minimum transfer price that the Hudson Bay Division would find acceptable for the HDP?

5. What is the maximum transfer price that the Volkmar Tachometer Division would find acceptable for the HDP?

6. As the corporate controller for General Instrumentation, recommend a transfer price.

Current Issues in Managerial Accounting

"What Is EVA, and How Can It Help Your Company," *Management Accounting*, November 1997.

Overview
This article explains and analyzes the economic value added (EVA) and market value added (MVA) performance measures.

Suggested Discussion Questions
Listed below are adjustments that can be made to the economic-value-added calculation. For each category, discuss the advantages and disadvantages of making the adjustment.

Adjustments to capital:

    Cumulative goodwill amortization

    Unrecorded goodwill

    Capitalized intangibles

    Cumulative unusual loss (gain) after taxes

■ **Issue 13–49**
Measuring Performance in Investment Centers

"Using Shareholder Value to Evaluate Strategic Choices," *Management Accounting*, November 1997, Nick Fera.

Overview
This article explains how free cash flow or shareholder value analysis can be used as an alternative to traditional performance measures.

Suggested Discussion Questions
Outlined in the following table is a method used to calculate free cash flows. Form a group that will act as an internal performance-evaluation team. Explain to your board how free-cash-flow analysis compares to residual income? Earnings per share? Return on equity? Explain the same comparisons to your firm's employees.

■ **Issue 13–50**
Measuring Performance in Investment Centers; Using Shareholder Value to Evaluate Strategic Choices

Sales

Less: Operating expenses

Pretax profit

Less: Cash taxes

Net operating profit after taxes (NOPAT)

Add: Depreciation expense

Less: Fixed capital investment

Less: Incremental working-capital investment

Operating cash flow (free cash flow)

■ **Issue 13–51**
Transfer Pricing

"Lockheed: A Deal Too Far?" *Business Week,* **July 21, 1997.**

Overview

Lockheed Martin and Northrup Gruman agreed to merge on July 3, 1997. The merger between Lockheed and one of its major suppliers, Northrup, subsequently had to seek Justice Department approval.

Suggested Discussion Questions

Assume Lockheed and Northrup have merged. How should Lockheed account for transfers of supplies? Should it use cost, cost-plus, or market-based transfer prices? Does how the firms are organized and operate matter? What impact does the external environment have on the transfer price?

■ **Issue 13–52**
Measuring Income and Invested Capital

"Earnings Not Always What They Seem," *The Wall Street Journal,* **February 15, 1996, Roger Lowenstein.**

Overview

A recently issued financial accounting standard requires write-down of assets when the assets become impaired. The amount of write-down depends in part on how the assets are classified as a group.

Suggested Discussion Questions

PepsiCo, Inc. wrote down the value of its restaurants: Taco Bell, Pizza Hut, and Kentucky Fried Chicken. As a group, list ways in which these assets could be grouped. Come to a consensus as to the best grouping method. Compare your list with other groups. How would these groupings affect the firm's performance-measurement system, assuming it uses traditional methods such as ROI?

■ **Issue 13–53**
Delegation of Decision Making

"Executive Pay," *Business Week,* **April 21, 1997.**

Overview

According to a recent Executive Pay Survey in *Business Week*, pay increases for executives, white collar staff, and factory workers averaged 54 percent, 3.2 percent, and 3.0 percent, respectively. At the top of the list was Greentree Financial's boss who made $102,449,000.

Suggested Discussion Questions

List ways that management performance can be linked to a firm's successes and failures. Should executives receive bonuses if shareholders lose value? The current FASB rule does not mandate expense recognition for stock options. Are stock options costless?

■ **Issue 13–54**
Delegation of Decision Making; Measuring Income and Invested Capital

"Chairman of Pepsi Bottler Quits; Accounting Errors Are Discovered," *The Wall Street Journal,* **August 13, 1996, Robert Frank.**

Overview

The discovery of accounting irregularities led to the resignation of the chairman of Pepsi-Cola Puerto Rico Bottling Co. The irregularities relate to unrecorded rebates, discounts, and other financial incentives offered to buyers.

Suggested Discussion Questions

Discuss how accounting-based performance measures provide incentives to manage earnings. What items are most easily manipulated? What are some warning signs that an accounting irregularity has occurred?

"Search for Universal Accounting Rules Goes Slowly, Delaying Foreign Listings," *The Wall Street Journal,* **December 6, 1996, Elizabeth MacDonald.**

Overview

The Financial Accounting Standards Board (FASB) and the Securities and Exchange Commission (SEC) expressed dissatisfaction with the International Accounting Standards Committee's (IASC) international accounting standards. For the last nine years, IASC's goal of achieving a uniform set of accounting standards has been elusive.

Suggested Discussion Questions

Write a brief memo that explains the difficulty of comparing firms' performance in the international setting. Will international accounting standards solve this problem? Will a uniform set of rules make things easier? Why can't standards setters achieve consensus?

■ **Issue 13–55**
Measuring Income and
Invested Capital

Chapter Fourteen

Decision Making: Relevant Costs and Benefits

After completing this chapter, you should be able to:

1 Describe six steps in the decision-making process and the managerial accountant's role in that process.

2 Explain the relationship between quantitative and qualitative analyses in decision making.

3 List and explain two criteria that must be satisfied by relevant information.

4 Identify relevant costs and benefits, giving proper treatment to sunk costs, opportunity costs, and unit costs.

5 Prepare analyses of various special decisions, properly identifying the relevant costs and benefits.

6 Analyze manufacturing decisions involving joint products and limited resources.

7 Explain the impact of an advanced manufacturing environment and activity-based costing on a relevant-cost analysis.

8 After completing the appendix, formulate a linear program to solve a product-mix problem with multiple constraints.

WORLDWIDE AIRWAYS REJECTS "SWEET DEAL" WITH LOCAL BAKERY

Atlanta, GA—Worldwide Airways' Vice President for Media Relations, Elizabeth Williams, announced today that the airline will continue to make its own desserts for its in-flight food-service operations. The announcement follows months of speculation that the airline would outsource its desserts to Southern Sweets, Inc., a large Atlanta bakery. Had Worldwide Airways decided to sign the dessert contract with Southern Sweets, it could have meant layoffs at the airline's huge Atlanta flight kitchen. The flight kitchen prepares a million full-course meals each month for Worldwide Airways' flights that pass through Atlanta.

According to Williams, the decision was a complex one. "This was not an easy call for us," said Williams. "Southern Sweets produces a first-class product, and they made us a very aggressive pricing offer on their desserts. At first blush, it looked as though we should go with the outsourcing arrangement. But we wanted to make sure we got this one right. We're talking about costs of around a quarter of a million dollars per month here, as well as the jobs of several of our loyal employees. After a careful analysis, we concluded that we would not save enough of our current costs to justify paying the price Southern Sweets was asking. They didn't feel they could go any lower, so we decided to keep the operation in-house. Personally, I'm glad it worked out that way. Signing an outsourcing deal, although it might be financially sound, often has a negative impact on employee morale."

Decision making is a fundamental part of management. Decisions about the acquisition of equipment, mix of products, methods of production, and pricing of products and services confront managers in all types of organizations. This chapter covers the role of managerial accounting information in a variety of common decisions. The next chapter examines pricing decisions.

The Managerial Accountant's Role in Decision Making

The managerial accountant's role in the decision-making process is to provide relevant information to the managers who make the decisions. Production managers typically make the decisions about alternative production processes and schedules, marketing managers make pricing decisions, and specialists in finance usually are involved in decisions about major acquisitions of equipment. All of these managers require information pertinent to their decisions. The *managerial accountant's role* is to provide information relevant to the decisions faced by managers throughout the organization. Thus, the managerial accountant needs a good understanding of the decisions faced by those managers.

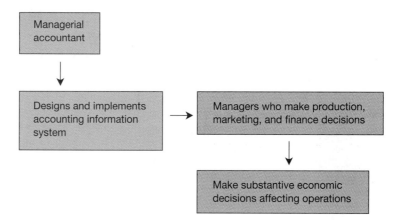

LO 1   Describe six steps in the decision-making process and the managerial accountant's role in that process.

Steps in the Decision-Making Process

Six steps characterize the decision-making process:

1. *Clarify the decision problem.* Sometimes the decision to be made is clear. For example, if a company receives a special order for its product at a price below the usual price, the decision problem is to accept or reject the order. But the decision problem is seldom so clear and unambiguous. Perhaps demand for a company's most popular product is declining. What exactly is causing this problem? Increasing competition? Declining quality control? A new alternative product on the market? Before a decision can be made, the problem needs to be clarified and defined in more specific terms. Considerable managerial skill is required to define a decision problem in terms that can be addressed effectively.

2. *Specify the criterion.* Once a decision problem has been clarified, the manager should specify the criterion upon which a decision will be made. Is the objective to maximize profit, increase market share, minimize cost, or improve public service? Sometimes the objectives are in conflict, as in a decision problem where production cost is to be minimized but product quality must be maintained. In such cases, one objective is specified as the decision criterion—for example, cost

Managers in manufacturing companies, service industry firms, retailers, and nonprofit organizations all use managerial accounting information in decision making. Pictured here are a Levis plant in Albuquerque, a NationsBank ATM, a music store selling CDs and tapes, and a Habitat for Humanity project. How would managerial accounting information be used in each of these organizations?

   minimization. The other objective is established as a constraint—for example, product quality must not fall below one defective part in 1,000 manufactured units.

3. ***Identify the alternatives.*** A decision involves selecting between two or more alternatives. If a machine breaks down, what are the alternative courses of action? The machine can be repaired or replaced, or a replacement can be leased. But perhaps repair will turn out to be more costly than replacement. Determining the possible alternatives is a critical step in the decision process.

4. ***Develop a decision model.*** A *decision model* is a simplified representation of the choice problem. Unnecessary details are stripped away, and the most important elements of the problem are highlighted. Thus, the decision model brings together the elements listed above: the criterion, the constraints, and the alternatives.

5. ***Collect the data.*** Although the managerial accountant often is involved in steps 1 through 4, he or she is chiefly responsible for step 5. Selecting data pertinent to decisions is one of the managerial accountant's most important roles in an organization.

6. ***Select an alternative.*** Once the decision model is formulated and the pertinent data are collected, the appropriate manager makes a decision.

Quantitative versus Qualitative Analysis

LO 2   Explain the relationship between quantitative and qualitative analyses in decision making.

Qualitative characteristics are factors in a decision analysis that cannot be expressed effectively in numerical terms.

Decision problems involving accounting data typically are specified in quantitative terms. The criteria in such problems usually include objectives such as profit maximization or cost minimization. When a manager makes a final decision, however, the qualitative characteristics of the alternatives can be just as important as the quantitative measures. **Qualitative characteristics** are the factors in a decision problem that cannot be expressed effectively in numerical terms. To illustrate, suppose Worldwide Airways' top management is considering the elimination of its hub operation in London. Airlines establish hubs at airports where many of their routes intersect. Hub operations include facilities for in-flight food preparation, aircraft maintenance and storage, and administrative offices. A careful quantitative analysis indicates that Worldwide Airway's profit-maximizing alternative is to eliminate the London hub. In making its decision, however, the company's managers will consider such qualitative issues as the effect of the closing on its London employees and on the morale of its remaining employees in the airline's Paris, Atlanta, and Tokyo hubs.

To clarify what is at stake in such qualitative analyses, quantitative analysis can allow the decision maker to put a "price" on the sum total of the qualitative characteristics. For example, suppose Worldwide Airways' controller gives top management a quantitative analysis showing that elimination of the London hub will increase annual profits by $2,000,000. However, the qualitative considerations favor the option of continuing the London operation. How important are these qualitative considerations to the top managers? If they decide to continue the London operation, the qualitative considerations must be worth at least $2,000,000 to them. Weighing the quantitative and qualitative considerations in making decisions is the essence of management. The skill, experience, judgment, and ethical standards of managers all come to bear on such difficult choices.

Exhibit 14–1 depicts the six steps in the decision process, and the relationship between quantitative and qualitative analysis.

Obtaining Information: Relevance, Accuracy, and Timeliness

What criteria should the managerial accountant use in designing the accounting information system that supplies data for decision making? Three characteristics of information determine its usefulness.

Relevant information consists of data that are pertinent to a decision.

Accurate information consists of data that are precise and correct.

Timely information consists of data that are available in time for use in a decision analysis.

Relevance   Information is **relevant** if it is *pertinent* to a decision problem. Different decisions typically will require different data. The primary theme of this chapter is how to decide what information is relevant to various common decision problems.

Accuracy   Information that is pertinent to a decision problem must also be **accurate**, or it will be of little use. This means the information must be precise. For example, the cost incurred by Worldwide Airways to rent facilities at London's Heathrow Airport is relevant to a decision about eliminating the airline's London hub. However, if the rental cost data are imprecise, due to incomplete or misplaced records, the usefulness of the information will be diminished.

Conversely, highly accurate but irrelevant data are of no value to a decision maker. Suppose Worldwide Airways will continue its daily round-trip flight between New York and London regardless of its decision about eliminating the London hub. Precise data about fuel consumption on the New York–London route are irrelevant to the decision about closing down the London hub.

Timeliness   Relevant and accurate data are of value only if they are **timely**, that is, available in time for a decision. Thus, timeliness is the third important criterion for determining the usefulness of information. Some situations involve a trade-off between the accuracy and the timeliness of information. More accurate information may take

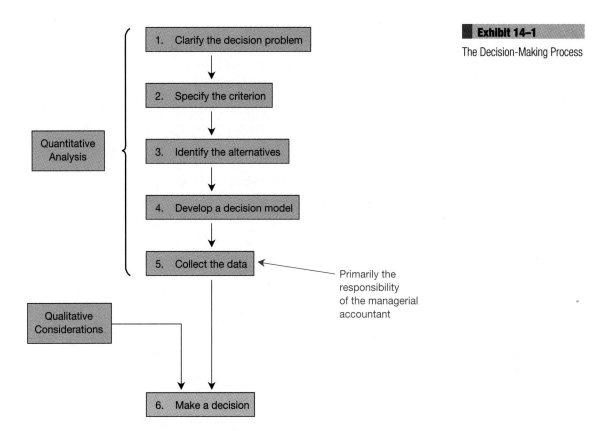

longer to produce. Therefore, as accuracy improves, timeliness suffers, and vice versa. For example, a company may test-market a potential new product in a particular city. The longer the test-marketing program runs, the more accurate will be the marketing data generated. However, a long wait for the accurate marketing report may unduly delay management's decision to launch the new product nationally.

To summarize, the managerial accountant's primary role in the decision-making process is twofold:

1. Decide what information is *relevant* to each decision problem.
2. Provide *accurate* and *timely* data, keeping in mind the proper balance between these often conflicting criteria.

Relevant Information

What makes information relevant to a decision problem? Two criteria are important.

LO 3   List and explain two criteria that must be satisfied by relevant information.

Bearing on the Future   The consequences of decisions are borne in the future, not the past. To be relevant to a decision, cost or benefit information must involve a future event. The cost information relevant to Worldwide Airways' decision concerning its London operations involves the costs that *will be incurred in the future* under the airline's two alternatives. Costs incurred in the past in the airline's London operations will not change regardless of management's decision, and they are irrelevant to the decision at hand.

Since relevant information involves future events, the managerial accountant must predict the amounts of the relevant costs and benefits. In making these predictions, the accountant often will use estimates of cost behavior based on historical data. There is an important and subtle issue here. *Relevant* information must involve costs and benefits to be realized in the *future*. However, the accountant's *predictions* of those costs and benefits often are based on data from the *past*.

Different under Competing Alternatives   Relevant information must involve costs or benefits that *differ among the alternatives*. Costs or benefits that are the same across all the available alternatives have no bearing on the decision. For example, suppose Worldwide Airways' management decides to keep its reservations and ticketing office in London regardless of whether its London hub is eliminated. Then the costs of the reservations and ticketing office will not differ between the two alternatives regarding elimination of the London hub. Hence, those costs are irrelevant to that decision.

Unique versus Repetitive Decisions

Unique decisions arise infrequently or only once. Worldwide Airways' decision regarding its London hub is an example. Compiling data for unique decisions usually requires a special analysis by the managerial accountant. The relevant information often will be found in many diverse places in the organization's overall information system.

In contrast, *repetitive decisions* are made over and over again, at either regular or irregular intervals. For example, Worldwide Airways makes route-scheduling decisions every six months. Such a routine decision makes it worthwhile for the managerial accountant to keep a special file of the information relevant to the scheduling decision.

Cost predictions relevant to repetitive decisions typically can draw on a large amount of historical data. Since the decisions have been made repeatedly in the past, the data from those decisions should be readily available. Information relevant to unique decisions is harder to generate. The managerial accountant typically will have to give more thought to deciding which data are relevant, and will have less historical data available upon which to base predictions.

Importance of Identifying Relevant Costs and Benefits

Why is it important for the managerial accountant to isolate the relevant costs and benefits in a decision analysis? The reasons are twofold. First, generating information is a costly process. The relevant data must be sought, and this requires time and effort. By focusing on only the relevant information, the managerial accountant can simplify and shorten the data-gathering process.

Second, people can effectively use only a limited amount of information. Beyond this, they experience **information overload**, and their decision-making effectiveness declines. By routinely providing only information about relevant costs and benefits, the managerial accountant can reduce the likelihood of information overload.

Information overload occurs when so much information is provided that, due to human limitations in processing information, managers cannot effectively use it.

Identifying Relevant Costs and Benefits

LO 4   Identify relevant costs and benefits, giving proper treatment to sunk costs, opportunity costs, and unit costs.

To illustrate how managerial accountants determine relevant costs and benefits, we will consider several decisions faced by the management of Worldwide Airways. Based in Atlanta, the airline flies routes between the United States and Europe, between various cities in Europe, and between the United States and several Asian cities.

Sunk Costs

Sunk costs are costs that were incurred in the past and cannot be altered by any current or future decision.

Sunk costs are costs that have already been incurred. They do not affect any future cost and cannot be changed by any current or future action. Sunk costs are irrelevant to decisions, as the following two examples show.

Book Value of Equipment   At Charles de Gaulle Airport in Paris, Worldwide Airways has a three-year-old loader truck used to load in-flight meals onto airplanes. The box on the truck can be lifted hydraulically to the level of a jumbo jet's side doors. The *book value* of this loader, defined as the asset's acquisition cost less the accumulated depreciation to date, is computed as follows:

Acquisition cost of old loader	$100,000
Less: Accumulated depreciation	75,000
Book value	$ 25,000

The loader has one year of useful life remaining, after which its salvage value will be zero. However, it could be sold now for $5,000. In addition to the annual depreciation of $25,000, Worldwide Airways annually incurs $80,000 in variable costs to operate the loader. These include the costs of operator labor, gasoline, and maintenance.

John Orville, Worldwide Airways' ramp manager at Charles de Gaulle Airport, faces a decision about replacement of the loader. A new kind of loader uses a conveyor belt to move meals into an airplane. The new loader is much cheaper than the old hydraulic loader and costs less to operate. However, the new loader would be operable for only one year before it would need to be replaced. Pertinent data about the new loader are as follows:

Acquisition cost of new loader	$15,000
Useful life	1 year
Salvage value after one year	0
Annual depreciation	$15,000
Annual operating costs	$45,000

Orville's initial inclination is to continue using the old loader for another year. He exclaims, "We can't dump that equipment now. We paid $100,000 for it, and we've only used it three years. If we get rid of that loader now, we'll lose $20,000 on the disposal." Orville reasons that the old loader's book value of $25,000, less its current salvage value of $5,000, amounts to a loss of $20,000.

Fortunately, Orville's comment is overheard by Joan Wilbur, the managerial accountant in the company's Charles de Gaulle Airport administrative offices. Wilbur points out to Orville that the book value of the old loader is a *sunk cost*. It cannot affect any future cost the company might incur. To convince Orville that she is right, Wilbur prepares the analysis shown in Exhibit 14–2.

Regardless of which alternative is selected, the $25,000 book value of the old loader will be an expense or loss in the next year. If the old loader is kept in service, the $25,000 will be recognized as depreciation expense; otherwise, the $25,000 cost will be incurred by the company as a write-off of the asset's book value. Thus, the

Most major airlines have a frequent flyer program, in which customers can receive free flights or upgrades by accumulating miles flown with a particular airline. These programs require recurring decisions by airline management about the terms of the frequent flyer awards. Accurate, relevant, and timely information is needed for such decisions. Also, predictions need to be made about passenger response to various frequent flyer provisions.

Exhibit 14–2

Equipment Replacement
Decision: Worldwide Airways

			Costs of Two Alternatives		
			(a) Do Not Replace Old Loader	**(b)** Replace Old Loader	**(c)** Differential Cost
Sunk cost	(1)	Depreciation of old loader	$ 25,000		
		OR			–0–
	(2)	Write-off of old loader's book value		$25,000	
Relevant data	(3)	Proceeds from disposal of old loader	–0–	(5,000)	$ 5,000
	(4)	Depreciation (cost) of new loader	–0–	15,000	(15,000)
	(5)	Operating costs	80,000	45,000	35,000
		Total cost	$105,000	$80,000	$25,000

current book value of the old loader is a *sunk cost* and irrelevant to the replacement decision.

Notice that the *relevant* data in the equipment replacement decision are items (3), (4), and (5). Each of these items meets the two tests of relevant information:

1. The costs or benefits relate to the future.
2. The costs or benefits differ between the alternatives.

The proceeds from selling the old loader, item (3), will be received in the future only under the "replace" alternative. Similarly, the acquisition cost (depreciation) of the new loader, item (4), is a future cost incurred only under the "replace" alternative. The operating cost, item (5), is also a future cost that differs between the two alternatives.

Differential Costs   Exhibit 14–2 includes a column entitled *Differential Cost*. A **differential cost** is the difference in a cost item under two decision alternatives. The computation of differential costs is a convenient way of summarizing the relative advantage of one alternative over the other. John Orville can make a correct equipment-replacement decision in either of two ways: (1) by comparing the total cost of the two alternatives, shown in columns (a) and (b); or (2) by focusing on the total differential cost, shown in column (c), which favors the "replacement" option.

A **differential cost** is the difference in a cost item under two decision alternatives.

Cost of Inventory on Hand   Never having taken a managerial-accounting course in college, John Orville is slow to learn how to identify sunk costs. The next week he goofs again.

The inventory of spare aircraft parts held by Worldwide Airways at Charles de Gaulle includes some obsolete parts originally costing $20,000. The company no longer uses the planes for which the parts were purchased. The obsolete parts include spare passenger seats, luggage racks, and galley equipment. The spare parts could be sold to another airline for $17,000. However, with some modifications, the obsolete parts could still be used in the company's current fleet of aircraft. Using the modified parts would save Worldwide Airways the cost of purchasing new parts for its airplanes.

John Orville decides not to dispose of the obsolete parts, because doing so would entail a loss of $3,000. Orville reasons that the $20,000 book value of the parts, less the $17,000 proceeds from disposal, would result in a $3,000 loss on disposal. Joan Wilbur, the managerial accountant, comes to the rescue again, demonstrating that the right decision is to dispose of the parts. Wilbur's analysis is shown in Exhibit 14–3.

Notice that the book value of the obsolete inventory is a sunk cost. If the parts are modified, the $20,000 book value will be an expense during the period when the parts are used. Otherwise, the $20,000 book value of the asset will be written off when the parts are sold. As a sunk cost, the book value of the obsolete inventory will not affect any future cash flow of the company.

		Costs of Two Alternatives		
		(a) Modify and Use Parts	**(b)** Dispose of Parts	**(c)** Differential Cost
Sunk cost	Book value of parts inventory: asset value written off whether parts are used or not	$20,000	$20,000	$ –0–
Relevant data	Proceeds from disposal of parts	–0–	(17,000)	17,000
	Cost to modify parts	12,000	–0–	12,000
	Cost incurred to buy new parts for current aircraft fleet	–0–	26,000	(26,000)
	Total cost	$32,000	$29,000	$ 3,000

Exhibit 14–3

Obsolete Inventory Decision: Worldwide Airways

Worldwide Airways

As the managerial accountant's analysis reveals, the relevant data include the $17,000 proceeds from disposal, the $12,000 cost to modify the parts, and the $26,000 cost to buy new parts. All of these data meet the two tests of relevance: they affect future cash flows and they differ between the two alternatives. As Joan Wilbur's analysis shows, Worldwide Airways' cost will be $3,000 less if the obsolete parts are sold and new parts are purchased.

Irrelevant Future Costs and Benefits

At Worldwide Airways' headquarters in Atlanta, Amy Earhart, manager of flight scheduling, is in the midst of making a decision about the Atlanta to Honolulu route. The flight is currently nonstop, but she is considering a stop in San Francisco. She feels that the route would attract additional passengers if the stop is made, but there would also be additional variable costs. Her analysis appears in Exhibit 14–4.

The analysis indicates that the preferable alternative is the route that includes a stop in San Francisco. Notice that the cargo revenue [item (2)] and the aircraft maintenance cost [item (8)] are irrelevant to the flight-route decision. Although these data do affect future cash flows, they *do not differ between the two alternatives.* All of the other data in Exhibit 14–4 are relevant to the decision, because they do differ between the two alternatives. The analysis in Exhibit 14–4 could have ignored the irrelevant data; the same decision would have been reached. (Exercise 14–30, at the end of the chapter, will ask you to prove this assertion by redoing the analysis without the irrelevant data.)

Opportunity Costs

Another decision confronting Amy Earhart is whether to add two daily round-trip flights between Atlanta and Montreal. Her initial analysis of the relevant costs and benefits indicates that the additional revenue from the flights will exceed their costs by $30,000 per month. Hence, she is ready to add the flights to the schedule. However, Chuck Lindbergh, Worldwide Airways' hangar manager in Atlanta, points out that Earhart has overlooked an important consideration.

Worldwide Airways currently has excess space in its hangar. A commuter airline has offered to rent the hangar space for $40,000 per month. However, if the Atlanta-to-Montreal flights are added to the schedule, the additional aircraft needed in Atlanta will require the excess hangar space.

If Worldwide Airways adds the Atlanta-to-Montreal flights, it will forgo the opportunity to rent the excess hangar space for $40,000 per month. Thus, the $40,000 in rent forgone is an *opportunity cost* of the alternative to add the new flights. An **opportunity cost** is the potential benefit given up when the choice of one action precludes a

An **opportunity cost** is the potential benefit given up when the choice of one action precludes selection of a different action.

Exhibit 14–4

Flight-Route Decision:
Worldwide Airways

		Revenues and Costs under Two Alternatives		
Relevant or Irrelevant		**(a)** **Nonstop** **Route***	**(b)** **With Stop in** **San Francisco***	**(c)** **Differential** **Amount†**
Relevant	(1) Passenger revenue	$240,000	$258,000	$(18,000)
Irrelevant	(2) Cargo Revenue	80,000	80,000	–0–
Relevant	(3) Landing fee in San Francisco	–0–	(5,000)	5,000
Relevant	(4) Use of airport gate facilities	–0–	(3,000)	3,000
Relevant	(5) Flight crew cost	(2,000)	(2,500)	500
Relevant	(6) Fuel	(21,000)	(24,000)	3,000
Relevant	(7) Meals and services	(4,000)	(4,600)	600
Irrelevant	(8) Aircraft maintenance	(1,000)	(1,000)	–0–
	Total revenue less costs	$292,000	$297,900	$ (5,900)

*In columns (a) and (b), parentheses denote costs and numbers without parentheses are revenues.

†In column (c), parentheses denote differential items favoring option (b).

different action. Although people tend to overlook or underestimate the importance of opportunity costs, they are just as relevant as out-of-pocket costs in evaluating decision alternatives. In Worldwide Airways' case, the best action is to rent the excess warehouse space to the commuter airline, rather than adding the new flights. The analysis in Exhibit 14–5 supports this conclusion.

It is a common mistake for people to overlook or underweigh opportunity costs. The $40,000 hangar rental, which will be forgone if the new flights are added, is an *opportunity cost* of the option to add the flights. It is a *relevant cost* of the decision, and it is just as important as any out-of-pocket expenditure.

Summary

Relevant costs and benefits satisfy the following two criteria:

1. They affect the future.
2. They differ between alternatives.

Sunk costs are *not* relevant costs, because they do not affect the future. An example of a sunk cost is the book value of an asset, either equipment or inventory. *Future costs or benefits that are identical across all decision alternatives are not relevant.* They can be ignored when making a decision. *Opportunity costs are relevant costs.* Such costs deserve particular attention because many people tend to overlook them when making decisions.

Exhibit 14–5

Decision to Add Flights:
Worldwide Airways

	(a) **Add** **Flights**	**(b)** **Do Not Add** **Flights**	**(c)** **Differential** **Amount**
Additional revenue from new flights less additional costs	$30,000	–0–	$ 30,000
Rental of excess hangar space	–0–	$40,000	(40,000)*
Total	$30,000	$40,000	$(10,000)

*Parentheses denote that differential benefit favors option (b).

These Boeing 757s are being manufactured near Seattle, Washington. Boeing carefully tracks and monitors manufacturing costs to assist managers in making production and pricing decisions. Such information is crucial in helping the company maintain its competitive position in the aircraft industry.

Management Accounting Practice

M.A.P.

Tracking Relevant Costs at Boeing

The Boeing Company, based in Seattle, is one of the world's largest aircraft manufacturers. At Boeing, relevant cost information is needed for a host of decisions, ranging from the design of new aircraft, to continuous improvement of production operations, to competitive bidding and pricing decisions. When Boeing introduces a new aircraft, for example, myriad decisions must be made about specific design features for the new plane. The aircraft's seating capacity, flight range, and passenger amenities are among the thousands of decisions to be made. All of these decisions involve trade-offs between the benefits that the particular design features entail, and the relevant costs that will be incurred to build such features into the aircraft's design. Later, when an aircraft is in production, decisions continue as to how to improve the production process to ensure a safe and high-quality aircraft at the lowest possible cost.

The business press reported Boeing recently revamped its cost accounting system to enable its design engineers and managers to perform more reliable economic design trade-off studies and make economically sound investment decisions. To improve its cost management process, Boeing brought together people from the engineering, operations management, and management accounting functional areas. One manager commented: "What we needed were ways to better align our costs directly to what we do—designing and assembling airplanes and manufacturing parts and assemblies for them. Also, we realized that we had to routinely provide the financial data that management needs to improve our processes and ultimately our products." Among the managerial accounting techniques that the Boeing team brought to bear were activity-based costing and target costing. The final result was a system that provides relevant cost information on a timely basis for the host of economic decisions Boeing's managers must make as they confront intense global competition for the business of the world's airlines.[1]

---

[1]Robert J. Bowlby, "How Boeing Tracks Costs, A to Z," *Financial Executive* 27, no. 6, pp. 20–23.

Analysis of Special Decisions

LO 5   Prepare analyses of various special decisions, properly identifying the relevant costs and benefits.

What are the relevant costs and benefits when a manager must decide whether to add or drop a product or service? What data are relevant when deciding whether to produce or buy a service or component? These decisions and certain other nonroutine decisions merit special attention in our discussion of relevant costs and benefits.

Accept or Reject a Special Offer

Jim Wright, Worldwide Airways' vice president for operations, has been approached by a Japanese tourist agency about flying chartered tourist flights from Japan to Hawaii. The tourist agency has offered Worldwide Airways $150,000 per round-trip flight on a jumbo jet. Given the airline's usual occupancy rate and air fares, a round-trip jumbo-jet flight between Japan and Hawaii typically brings in revenue of $250,000. Thus, the tourist agency's specially priced offer requires a special analysis by Jim Wright.

Wright knows that Worldwide Airways has two jumbo jets that are not currently being used. The airline has just eliminated several unprofitable routes, freeing these aircraft for other uses. The airline was not currently planning to add any new routes, and therefore the two jets were idle. To help in making his decision, Wright asks for cost data from the controller's office. The controller provides the information in Exhibit 14–6, which pertains to a typical round-trip jumbo-jet flight between Japan and Hawaii.

The variable costs cover aircraft fuel and maintenance, flight-crew costs, in-flight meals and services, and landing fees. The fixed costs allocated to each flight cover Worldwide Airways' fixed costs, such as aircraft depreciation, maintenance and depreciation of facilities, and fixed administrative costs.

If Jim Wright had not understood managerial accounting, he might have done the following *incorrect analysis.*

Special price for charter	$150,000
Total cost per flight	190,000
Loss on charter flight	$(40,000)

This calculation suggests that the special charter offer should be declined. What is the error in this analysis? The mistake is the inclusion of allocated fixed costs in the cost per flight. This is an error, because the *fixed costs will not increase in total* if the charter flight is added. Since the fixed costs will not change under either of the alternate choices, they are irrelevant.

Fortunately, Jim Wright does not make this mistake. He knows that only the variable costs of the proposed charter are relevant. Moreover, Wright determines that the variable cost of the charter would be lower than that of a typical flight, because Worldwide Airways would not incur the variable costs of reservations and ticketing.

Exhibit 14–6

Data for Typical Flight Between Japan and Hawaii: Worldwide Airways

Revenue:		
Passenger	$250,000	
Cargo	30,000	
Total revenue		$280,000
Expenses:		
Variable expenses of flight	$ 90,000	
Fixed expenses allocated to each flight	100,000	
Total expenses		190,000
Profit		$ 90,000

These variable expenses amount to $5,000 for a scheduled flight. Thus, Wright's analysis of the charter offer is as shown below.

Assumes excess	Special price for charter		$150,000
capacity	Variable cost per routine flight	$90,000	
(idle aircraft)	Less: Savings on reservations and ticketing	5,000	
	Variable cost of charter		85,000
	Contribution from charter		$ 65,000

Wright's analysis shows that the special charter flight will contribute $65,000 toward covering the airline's fixed costs and profit. Since the airline has excess flight capacity, due to the existence of idle aircraft, the optimal decision is to accept the special charter offer.

No Excess Capacity Now let's consider how Wright's analysis would appear if Worldwide Airways had no idle aircraft. Suppose that in order to fly the charter between Japan and Hawaii, the airline would have to cancel its least profitable route, which is between Japan and Hong Kong. This route contributes $80,000 toward covering the airline's fixed costs and profit. Thus, if the charter offer is accepted, the airline will incur an opportunity cost of $80,000 from the forgone contribution of the Japan–Hong Kong route. Now Wright's analysis should appear as shown below.

Assumes	Special price for charter		$150,000
no excess	Variable cost per routine flight	$90,000	
capacity	Less: Savings on reservations and ticketing	5,000	
(no idle aircraft)	Variable cost of charter	$85,000	
	Add: Opportunity cost, forgone contribution on canceled Japan–Hong Kong route	80,000	165,000
	Loss from charter		$(15,000)

Thus, if Worldwide Airways has no excess flight capacity, Jim Wright should reject the special charter offer.

Summary The decision to accept or reject a specially priced order is common in both service industry and manufacturing firms. Manufacturers often are faced with decisions about selling products in a special order at less than full price. The correct analysis of such decisions focuses on the relevant costs and benefits. Fixed costs, which often are allocated to individual units of product or service, are usually irrelevant. Fixed costs typically will not change in total, whether the order is accepted or rejected.

When excess capacity exists, the only relevant costs usually will be the variable costs associated with the special order. When there is no excess capacity, the opportunity cost of using the firm's facilities for the special order are also relevant to the decision.

Outsource a Product or Service

Ellie Rickenbacker is Worldwide Airways' manager of in-flight services. She supervises the airline's flight attendants and all of the firm's food and beverage operations. Rickenbacker currently faces a decision regarding the preparation of in-flight dinners at the airline's Atlanta hub. In the Atlanta flight kitchen, full-course dinners are prepared and packaged for long flights that pass through Atlanta. In the past, all of the desserts were baked and packaged in the flight kitchen. However, Rickenbacker has received an offer from an Atlanta bakery to bake the airline's desserts. Thus, her decision is whether to *outsource* the dessert portion of the in-flight dinners. An **outsourcing decision**, also called a **make-or-buy decision**, entails a choice between

An **outsourcing** (or **make-or-buy**) **decision** is made when choosing whether a product or service should be produced in-house or purchased from an outside supplier.

Exhibit 14–7

Cost of In-Flight Desserts:
Worldwide Airways

Worldwide Airways

	Cost per Dessert
Variable costs:	
Direct material (food and packaging)	$.06
Direct labor	.04
Variable overhead	.04
Fixed costs (allocated to products):	
Supervisory salaries	.04
Depreciation of flight-kitchen equipment	.07
Total cost per dessert	$.25

producing a product or service in-house or purchasing it from an outside supplier. To help guide her decision, Rickenbacker has assembled the cost information in Exhibit 14–7, which shows a total cost per dessert of 25 cents.

The Atlanta bakery has offered to supply the desserts for 21 cents each. Rickenbacker's initial inclination is to accept the bakery's offer, since it appears that the airline would save 4 cents per dessert. However, the controller reminds Rickenbacker that not all of the costs listed in Exhibit 14–7 are relevant to the outsourcing decision. The controller modifies Rickenbacker's analysis as shown in Exhibit 14–8.

If Worldwide Airways stops making desserts, it will save all of the variable costs but only 1 cent of fixed costs. The 1-cent saving in supervisory salaries would result because the airline could get along with two fewer kitchen supervisors. The remainder of the fixed costs would be incurred even if the desserts were purchased. These remaining fixed costs of supervision and depreciation would have to be reallocated to the flight kitchen's other products. In light of the controller's revised analysis, Rickenbacker realizes that the airline should continue to make its own desserts. To outsource the desserts would require an expenditure of 21 cents per dessert, but only 15 cents per dessert would be saved.

In today's global economy, more and more companies are outsourcing significant products and services. Gallo Winery, for example, buys a significant portion of its grapes from other vintners. Kodak outsources its entire data processing operation. Cummins Engine outsources many of its pistons, and Intel Corporation buys microchips. Continental Bank outsources its cafeteria and legal services.[2]

---

[2]Peter Chalos, "Costing, Control, and Strategic Analysis of Outsourcing Decisions," *Journal of Cost Management* 8, no. 4, pp. 31–37. See also Ralph Drtina, "The Outsourcing Decision," *Management Accounting* 75, no. 9, pp. 56–62.

Exhibit 14–8

Cost Savings from Buying In-
Flight Desserts: Worldwide
Airways

	Cost per Dessert	Costs Saved By Purchasing Desserts
Variable costs:		
Direct material	$.06	$ .06
Direct labor	.04	.04
Variable overhead	.04	.04
Fixed costs (allocated to products):		
Supervisory salaries	.04	.01
Depreciation of flight-kitchen equipment	.07	–0–
Total cost per dessert	$.25	$. 15
Cost of purchasing desserts (per dessert)		$ .21
Loss per dessert if desserts are purchased (savings per dessert minus purchase cost per dessert, or $.15 – $.21)		$(.06)

Exhibit 14–9

Total-Cost Analysis of
Outsourcing Decision:
Worldwide Airways

	Cost per Month	Costs Saved By Purchasing Desserts
Variable costs:		
Direct material	$ 60,000	$ 60,000
Direct labor	40,000	40,000
Variable overhead	40,000	40,000
Fixed costs (allocated to products):		
Supervisory salaries	40,000	10,000*
Depreciation of flight-kitchen equipment	70,000	–0–
Total cost per month	$250,000	$150,000
Cost of purchasing desserts (per month)		$210,000
Total loss if desserts are purchased (total savings minus total cost of purchasing, or $150,000 – $210,000)		$(60,000)

*Cost of monthly compensation for two kitchen supervisors, who will not be needed if desserts are purchased.

To clarify her decision further, Rickenbacker asks the controller to prepare an analysis of the *total costs* per month of making or buying desserts. The controller's report, displayed in Exhibit 14–9, shows the total cost of producing 1,000,000 desserts, the flight kitchen's average monthly volume.

The total-cost analysis confirmed Rickenbacker's decision to continue making desserts in the airline's flight kitchen.

Beware of Unit-Cost Data   Fixed costs often are allocated to individual units of product or service for product-costing purposes. For decision-making purposes, however, unitized fixed costs can be misleading. As the total-cost analysis above shows, only $10,000 in fixed monthly cost will be saved if the desserts are purchased. The remaining $100,000 in monthly fixed cost will continue whether the desserts are made or purchased. Rickenbacker's initial cost analysis in Exhibit 14–7 implies that each dessert costs the airline 25 cents, but that 25-cent cost includes 11 cents of unitized fixed costs. Most of these costs will remain unchanged regardless of the outsourcing decision. By allocating fixed costs to individual products or services, they are made to appear variable even though they are not.

Exhibit 14–10

World Express Club Monthly
Operating Income Statement:
Worldwide Airways

Sales revenue		$200,000
Less: Variable expenses:		
Food and beverages	$70,000	
Personnel	40,000	
Variable overhead	25,000	135,000
Contribution margin		$ 65,000
Less: Fixed expenses:		
Depreciation	$30,000	
Supervisory salaries	20,000	
Insurance	10,000	
Airport fees	5,000	
General overhead (allocated)	10,000	75,000
Loss		$(10,000)

Add or Drop a Service, Product, or Department

Worldwide Airways offers its passengers the opportunity to join its World Express Club. Club membership entitles a traveler to use the club facilities at the airport in Atlanta. Club privileges include a private lounge and restaurant, discounts on meals and beverages, and use of a small health spa.

Jayne Wing, the president of Worldwide Airways, is worried that the World Express Club might not be profitable. Her concern is caused by the statement of monthly operating income shown in Exhibit 14–10.

In her weekly staff meeting, Wing states her concern about the World Express Club's profitability. The controller responds by pointing out that not all of the costs on the club's income statement would be eliminated if the club were discontinued. The vice president for sales adds that the club helps Worldwide Airways attract passengers whom it might otherwise lose to a competitor. As the meeting adjourns, Wing asks the controller to prepare an analysis of the relevant costs and benefits associated with the World Express Club. The controller's analysis is displayed in Exhibit 14–11.

The controller's report contains two parts. Part I focuses on the relevant costs and benefits of the World Express Club only, while ignoring any impact of the club on other airline operations. In column (a), the controller has listed the club's revenues and expenses from the income statement given previously (Exhibit 14–10). Column (b) lists the expenses that will continue if the club is eliminated. These expenses are called **unavoidable expenses**. In contrast, the expenses appearing in column (a) but not column (b) are **avoidable expenses**. The airline will no longer incur these expenses if the club is eliminated.

Unavoidable expenses will continue to be incurred even if a subunit or activity is eliminated.

Avoidable expenses will no longer be incurred if a particular action is taken.

Notice that all of the club's variable expenses are avoidable. The depreciation expense, $30,000, is an allocated portion of the depreciation on a Worldwide Airways building, part of which is used by the World Express Club. If the Club is discontinued, the airline will continue to own and use the building, and the depreciation expense will continue. Thus, it is an unavoidable expense. The fixed supervisory salaries are avoidable, since these employees will no longer be needed if the club is eliminated. The fixed insurance expense of $10,000 is not avoidable; the $5,000 fee paid to the airport for the privilege of operating the club is avoidable. Finally, the club's allocated portion of general overhead expenses, $10,000, is not avoidable. Worldwide Airways will incur these expenses regardless of its decision about the World Express Club.

The conclusion shown by Part I of the controller's report is that the club should not be eliminated. If the club is closed, the airline will lose more in contribution margin,

	(a) Keep Club	(b) Eliminate Club	(c) Differential Amount
Part I:			
Sales revenue	$200,000	–0–	$200,000
Less: Variable expenses:			
Food and beverages	(70,000)	–0–	(70,000)
Personnel	(40,000)	–0–	(40,000)
Variable overhead	(25,000)	–0–	(25,000)
Contribution margin	$ 65,000	–0–	$ 65,000
Less: Fixed expenses:			
Depreciation	$(30,000)	$(30,000)	$ –0–
Supervisory salaries	(20,000)	–0–	(20,000)
Insurance	(10,000)	(10,000)	–0–
Airport fees	(5,000)	–0–	(5,000)
General overhead (allocated)	(10,000)	(10,000)	–0–
Total fixed expenses	$(75,000)	$(50,000)	$(25,000)
Profit (loss)	$(10,000)	$(50,000)	$ 40,000
		Expenses in the column above are **unavoidable** expenses	Expenses in the column above are **avoidable** expenses
Part II:			
Contribution margin from general airline operations that will be forgone if club is eliminated	$ 60,000	–0–	$ 60,000

Exhibit 14–11

Relevant Costs and Benefits of World Express Club: Worldwide Airways

Worldwide Airways

$65,000, than it saves in avoidable fixed expenses, $25,000. Thus, the club's $65,000 contribution margin is enough to cover the avoidable fixed expenses of $25,000 and still contribute $40,000 toward covering the overall airline's fixed expenses.

World Express Club's contribution margin	$65,000
Avoidable fixed expenses	25,000
Contribution of club toward covering overall airline's fixed expenses	$40,000

Now consider Part II of the controller's analysis in Exhibit 14–11. As the vice president for sales pointed out, the World Express Club is an attractive feature to many travelers. The controller estimates that if the club were discontinued, the airline would lose $60,000 each month in forgone contribution margin from general airline operations. This loss in contribution margin would result from losing to a competing airline current passengers who are attracted to Worldwide Airways by its World Express Club. This $60,000 in forgone contribution margin is an *opportunity cost* of the option to close down the club.

Considering both Parts I and II of the controller's analysis, Worldwide Airways' monthly profit will be greater by $100,000 if the club is kept open. Recognition of two issues is key to this conclusion:

1. Only the avoidable expenses of the club will be saved if it is discontinued.
2. Closing the club will adversely affect the airline's other operations.

Special Decisions in Manufacturing Firms

> **LO 6**   Analyze manufacturing decisions involving joint products and limited resources.

Some types of decisions are more likely to arise in manufacturing companies than in service industry firms. We will examine two of these decisions.

Joint Products: Sell or Process Further

A **joint production process** results in two or more joint products.

The **split-off point** is the point at which the joint products become identifiable as separate products.

The **joint cost** is incurred before the joint products become identifiable as separate products.

The **relative-sales-value method** allocates joint costs in proportion to their total sales values at the split-off point.

A **joint production process** results in two or more products, called *joint products*. An example is the processing of cocoa beans into cocoa powder and cocoa butter. Cocoa beans constitute the input to the joint production process, and the two joint products are cocoa powder and cocoa butter. The point in the production process where the joint products are identifiable as separate products is called the **split-off point**. Other examples of joint production processes include the slaughtering of animals for various cuts of meat and the processing of petroleum into various products, such as kerosene and gasoline.

Manufacturers with joint production processes sometimes must decide whether a joint product should be sold at the split-off point or processed further before being sold. Such a decision recently confronted Bill Candee, the president of International Chocolate Company. Candee's firm imports cocoa beans and processes them into cocoa powder and cocoa butter. Only a portion of the cocoa powder is used by International Chocolate Company in the production of chocolate candy. The remainder of the cocoa powder is sold to an ice cream producer. Candee is considering the possibility of processing his remaining cocoa powder into an instant cocoa mix to be marketed under the brand name ChocoTime. Data pertaining to Candee's decision are displayed in Exhibit 14–12.

Notice from the diagram that cocoa beans are processed in 1-ton batches. The total cost of the cocoa beans and the joint processing is $1,100. This is called the **joint cost**. The output of the joint process is 1,500 pounds of cocoa butter and 500 pounds of cocoa powder.

How should Bill Candee approach the decision about processing the cocoa powder into instant cocoa mix? What are the relevant costs and benefits? First, let's consider the joint cost of $1,100. Is this a relevant cost in the decision at hand? *The joint cost is not a relevant cost,* because it will not change regardless of the decision Candee makes.

Suppose the $1,100 joint cost had been allocated to the two joint products for product-costing purposes. A common method of allocating a joint cost is the **relative-sales-value method**, in which the joint cost is allocated between the joint products in

> **Exhibit 14–12**
>
> Joint Processing of Cocoa Beans: International Chocolate Company

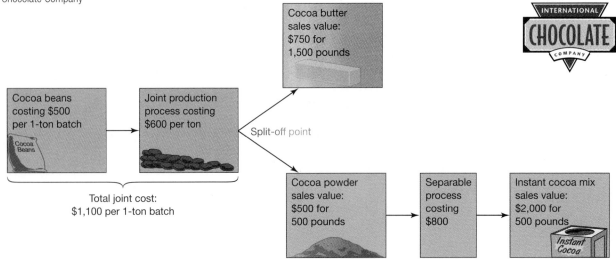

proportion to their sales value at the split-off point.[3] International Chocolate Company would make the following joint-cost allocation.

Joint Cost	Joint Products	Sales Value at Split-Off Point	Relative Proportion	Allocation of Joint Cost
$1,100 {	Cocoa butter	$750	.60	$ 660
	Cocoa powder	500	.40	440
	Total joint cost allocated			$1,100

Does this allocation of the $1,100 joint cost make it relevant to the decision about processing cocoa powder into instant cocoa mix? The answer is no. *The $1,100 joint cost still does not change in total,* whether the cocoa powder is processed further or not. The joint cost is irrelevant to the decision at hand.

The only costs and benefits relevant to Candee's decision are those that differ between the two alternatives. The proper analysis is shown in Exhibit 14–13.

There is a shortcut method that arrives at the same conclusion as Exhibit 14–13. In this approach, the incremental revenue from the further processing of cocoa powder is compared with the **separable processing cost**, which is the cost incurred after the split-off point, as follows:

> A **separable processing cost** is incurred on a joint product after the split-off point of a joint production process.

Sales value of instant cocoa mix	$2,000
Sales value of cocoa powder	500
Incremental revenue from further processing	$1,500
Less: Separable processing cost	800
Net benefit from further processing	$ 700

Both analyses indicate that Bill Candee should process his excess cocoa powder into instant cocoa mix. The same conclusion is reached if the analysis is done on a per-unit basis rather than a total basis:

Sales value of instant cocoa mix ($2000 ÷ 500 pounds)	$4.00	per pound
Sales value of cocoa powder ($500 ÷ 500 pounds)	1.00	per pound
Incremental revenue from further processing	$3.00	per pound
Less: Separable processing cost ($800 ÷ 500 pounds)	1.60	per pound
Net benefit from further processing	$1.40	per pound

Once again, the analysis shows that Bill Candee should decide to process the cocoa powder into instant cocoa mix.

Relevant or Irrelevant			(a) Sell Cocoa Powder at Split-Off Point	(b) Process Cocoa Powder into Instant Cocoa Mix	(c) Differential Amount (a) – (b)
		Sales revenue:			
	Irrelevant	Cocoa butter	$ 750	$ 750	–0–
Relevant		Cocoa powder	500		} $(1,500)
Relevant		Instant cocoa mix		2,000	
		Less: Costs:			
	Irrelevant	Joint cost	(1,100)	(1,100)	–0–
Relevant		Separable cost of processing cocoa powder into instant cocoa mix	–0–	(800)	800
		Total	$ 150	$ 850	$ (700)

Exhibit 14–13

Decision to Sell or Process Further: International Chocolate Company

INTERNATIONAL CHOCOLATE COMPANY

---

[3]Other methods of allocating joint costs are covered in Chapter 18.

Exhibit 14–14

Contribution Margin per Case:
International Chocolate
Company

	Chewies	Chompo Bars
Sales price	$10.00	$14.00
Less: Variable costs:		
Direct material	$ 3.00	$ 3.75
Direct labor	2.00	2.50
Variable overhead	3.00	3.75
Variable selling and administrative costs	1.00	2.00
Total variable costs	$ 9.00	$12.00
Contribution margin per case	$ 1.00	$ 2.00

Decisions Involving Limited Resources

Organizations typically have limited resources. Limitations on floor space, machine time, labor hours, or raw materials are common. Operating with limited resources, a firm often must choose between sales orders, deciding which orders to fill and which ones to decline. In making such decisions, managers must decide which product or service is the most profitable.

To illustrate, suppose International Chocolate Company's Phoenix plant makes two candy-bar products, Chewies and Chompo Bars. The contribution margin for a case of each of these products is computed in Exhibit 14–14.

A glance at the contribution-margin data suggests that Chompo Bars are more profitable than Chewies. It is true that a case of Chompo Bars contributes more toward covering the company's fixed cost and profit. However, an important consideration has been ignored in the analysis so far. The Phoenix plant's capacity is limited by its available machine time. Only 700 machine hours are available in the plant each month. International Chocolate Company can sell as many cases of either candy bar as it can produce, so production is limited only by the constraint on machine time.

To maximize the plant's total contribution toward covering fixed cost and profit, management should strive to use each machine hour as effectively as possible. This realization alters the analysis of product profitability. The relevant question is *not,* Which candy bar has the highest contribution margin *per case?* The pertinent question is, Which product has the highest contribution margin *per machine hour?* This question is answered with the calculation in Exhibit 14–15.

A machine hour spent in the production of Chewies will contribute $50 toward covering fixed cost and profit, while a machine hour devoted to Chompo Bars contributes only $40. Hence, the Phoenix plant's most profitable product is Chewies, when the plant's scare resource is taken into account.

Suppose International Chocolate Company's Phoenix plant manager, Candace Barr, is faced with a choice between two sales orders, only one of which can be accepted. Only 100 hours of unscheduled machine time remains in the month, and it can be used to produce either Chewies or Chompos. The analysis in Exhibit 14–16 shows that Barr should devote the 100-hour block of machine time to filling the order for Chewies.

As Exhibit 14–16 demonstrates, a decision about the best use of a limited resource should be made on the basis of the *contribution margin per unit of the scarce resource.*

Multiple Scarce Resources   Suppose the Phoenix plant had a limited amount of *both* machine hours *and* labor hours. Now the analysis of product profitability is more complicated. The choice as to which product is most profitable typically will involve a trade-off between the two scarce resources. Solving such a problem requires a powerful mathematical tool called *linear programming,* which is covered in the appendix to this chapter.

		Chewies	Chompo Bars
(a)	Contribution margin per case	$1.00	$2.00
(b)	Machine hours required per case	.02	.05
(a) ÷ (b)	Contribution margin per machine hour	$50	$40

Exhibit 14–15

Contribution Margin per Machine Hour: International Chocolate Company

INTERNATIONAL CHOCOLATE COMPANY

Theory of Constraints   As the previous analysis suggests, a binding constraint can limit a company's profitability. For example, a manufacturing company may have a *bottleneck operation,* through which every unit of a product must pass before moving on to other operations. The *theory of constraints (TOC)* calls for identifying such limiting constraints and seeking ways to relax them. Also referred to as *managing constraints,* this management approach can significantly improve an organization's level of goal attainment. Among the ways that management can relax a constraint by expanding the capacity of a bottleneck operation are the following:

- *Outsourcing* (subcontracting) all or part of the bottleneck operation.
- Investing in additional production equipment and employing *parallel processing,* in which multiple product units undergo the same production operation simultaneously.
- Working *overtime* at the bottleneck operation.
- *Retraining* employees and shifting them to the bottleneck.
- Eliminating any *non-value-added activities* at the bottleneck operation.

Uncertainty

Our analyses of the decisions in this chapter assumed that all relevant data were known with certainty. In practice, of course, decision makers are rarely so fortunate. One common technique for addressing the impact of uncertainty is *sensitivity analysis.* **Sensitivity analysis** is a technique for determining what would happen in a decision analysis if a key prediction or assumption proved to be wrong.

To illustrate, let's return to Candace Barr's decision about how to use the remaining 100 hours of machine time in International Chocolate Company's Phoenix plant. The calculation in Exhibit 14–15 showed that Chewies have the highest contribution margin per machine hour. Suppose Barr is uncertain about the contribution margin per case of Chewies. A sensitivity analysis shows how sensitive her decision is to the value of this uncertain parameter. As Exhibit 14–17 shows, the Chewies contribution margin could decline to $.80 per case before Barr's decision would change. As long as the contribution margin per case of Chewies exceeds $.80 per case, the 100 hours of available machine time should be devoted to Chewies.

Sensitivity analysis determines what would happen in a decision analysis if a key prediction or assumption proves to be wrong.

	Chewies	Chompo Bars
Contribution margin per case	$1.00	$2.00
Number of cases produced in		
100 hours of machine time	× 5,000 *	× 2,000 †
Total contribution toward		
covering fixed cost and profit	$ 5,000	$ 4,000

*Chewies: 100 hours ÷ .02 hour per case = 5,000 cases
†Chompo Bars: 100 hours ÷ .05 hour per case = 2,000 cases

Exhibit 14–16

Total Contribution from 100 Machine Hours: International Chocolate Company

INTERNATIONAL CHOCOLATE COMPANY

		Chewies	Chompo Bars
Original Analysis			
(a)	Contribution margin per case predicted	$1.00	$2.00
(b)	Machine hours required per case	.02	.05
(a) ÷ (b)	Contribution per machine hour	$50.00	$40.00
Sensitivity Analysis			
(c)	Contribution margin per case hypothesized in sensitivity analysis	$.80	
(d)	Machine hours required per case	.02	same
(c) ÷ (d)	Contribution per machine hour	$40.00	

Sensitivity analysis can help the managerial accountant decide which parameters in an analysis are most critical to estimate accurately. In this case, the managerial accountant knows that the contribution margin per case of Chewies could be as much as 20 percent lower than the original $1.00 prediction without changing the outcome of the analysis.

The **expected value** is the sum of the possible values for a random variable, each weighted by its probability.

Expected Values   Another approach to dealing explicitly with uncertainty is to base the decision on expected values. The **expected value** of a random variable is equal to the sum of the possible values for the variable, each weighted by its probability. To illustrate, suppose the contribution margins per case for Chewies and Chompos are uncertain, as shown in Exhibit 14–18. As the exhibit shows, the choice as to which product to produce with excess machine time may be based on the *expected value* of the contribution per machine hour. Statisticians have developed many other methods for dealing with uncertainty in decision making. These techniques are covered in statistics and decision analysis courses.

Activity-Based Costing and the New Manufacturing Environment

LO 7   Explain the impact of an advanced manufacturing environment and activity-based costing on a relevant-cost analysis.

In this chapter we have explored how to identify the relevant costs and benefits in various types of decisions. How will the relevant costing approach change in the new manufacturing environment, characterized by JIT production methods and flexible manufacturing systems? How would a relevant-costing analysis change if a company uses an activity-based costing (ABC) system?[4]

Chewies		Chompo Bars	
Possible Values of Contribution Margin	**Probability**	**Possible Values of Contribution Margin**	**Probability**
$ .75	.5	$1.50	.3
1.25	.5	2.00	.4
		2.50	.3
Expected value	(.5)($.75) + (.5)($1.25) = $1.00	(.3)($1.50) + (.4)($2.00) + (.3)($2.50) = $2.00	
Machine hours required per case	.02		.05
Expected value of contribution per machine hour	$50	>	$40

---

[4]Activity-based costing (ABC), which was introduced conceptually in Chapter 3, is thoroughly explored in Chapter 5. This section can be studied most effectively after completing Chapter 5.

The *concepts* underlying a relevant-costing analysis continue to be completely valid in an advanced manufacturing setting and in a situation where activity-based costing is used. The objective of the decision analysis is to determine the costs and benefits that are relevant to the decision. As we found earlier in this chapter, relevant costs and benefits *have a bearing on the future* and *differ among the decision alternatives.*

What *will* be different in a setting where activity-based costing is used is the decision maker's ability to determine what costs are relevant to a decision. Under ABC the decision maker typically can associate costs with the activities that drive them much more accurately than under a conventional product-costing system. Let's explore these issues with an illustration.

Conventional Outsourcing (Make-or-Buy) Analysis

International Chocolate Company makes fine chocolates in its Savannah plant. The chocolates are packaged in two-pound and five-pound gift boxes. The company also manufactures the gift boxes in the Savannah plant. The plant manager, Marsha Mello, was approached recently by a packaging company with an offer to supply the gift boxes at a price of $.45 each. Mello concluded that the offer should be rejected on the basis of the relevant-costing analysis in Exhibit 14–19. International Chocolate Company's traditional, volume-based product-costing system showed a unit product cost of $.80 per box. However, Mello realized that not all of the costs would be avoided. She reasoned that all of the direct material, direct labor, and variable overhead would be avoided, but only a small part of the assigned fixed overhead would be saved. She concluded that $60,000 of supervisory salaries and $20,000 of machinery depreciation could be traced directly to gift package production. These costs would be avoided, she felt, but the remaining fixed costs would not. Mello concluded that only $430,000 of costs would be avoided by purchasing, while $450,000 would be spent to buy the boxes. The decision was clear; the supplier's offer should be rejected.

Activity-Based Costing Analysis of the Outsourcing Decision

At a staff meeting Mello mentioned her tentative decision to Dave Mint, the plant controller. Mint then explained to Mello that he was completing a pilot project using activity-based costing. Mint offered to analyze the outsourcing decision using the new ABC database. Mello agreed, and Mint proceeded to do the ABC analysis shown in Exhibit 14–20.

In stage one of the ABC analysis Mint had designated 11 activity cost pools corresponding to the major items in the Savannah plant's overhead budget. These activity cost pools were categorized as facility-level, product-sustaining level, batch-level, or unit-level activities. In stage two of the ABC project, cost drivers were identified and pool rates were computed. The ABC analysis showed that $243,000 of overhead should be assigned to the gift boxes, rather than $550,000 as the conventional product-costing system had indicated.

Using the ABC database, Mint completed a new relevant-costing analysis of the outsourcing decision. Mint felt that all of the overhead costs assigned to the gift box operation could be avoided if the boxes were purchased. Notice that none of the facility-level costs are relevant to the analysis. They will not be avoided by purchasing the gift boxes. Mint's ABC analysis showed that a total of $493,000 of costs could be avoided by purchasing the boxes at a cost of $450,000. This would result in a net saving of $43,000.

Mint showed the ABC relevant-costing analysis to Mello. After some discussion they agreed that various qualitative issues needed to be explored before a final decision was made. For example, would the new supplier be reliable, and would the gift boxes be of good quality? Nevertheless, Mello and Mint agreed that the ABC data cast an entirely different light on the decision.

Exhibit 14–19

Conventional Product-Costing
Data and Outsourcing
Analysis: International
Chocolate Company

A. Manufacturing Overhead Budget for Savannah Plant

Variable overhead:

Electricity	$ 700,000
Oil and lubricants	120,000
Equipment maintenance	180,000
Total variable overhead	$1,000,000

Variable overhead rate: $1,000,000 ÷ 100,000 direct-labor hours = $10 per hour

Fixed overhead:

Plant depreciation	$1,650,000
Product development	300,000
Supervisory salaries	600,000
Material handling	800,000
Purchasing	250,000
Inspection	300,000
Setup	400,000
Machinery depreciation	200,000
Total fixed overhead	$4,500,000

Fixed overhead rate: $4,500,000 ÷ 100,000 direct-labor hours = $45 per hour

B. Conventional Product-Costing Data: Gift Boxes

Direct material	$ 100,000
Direct labor (10,000 hr. at $15 per hr.)	150,000
Variable overhead ($10 per direct-labor hr.)	100,000
Fixed overhead ($45 per direct-labor hr.)	450,000
Total cost	$ 800,000

Unit cost: $800,000 ÷ 1,000,000 boxes = $.80 per box

C. Conventional Outsourcing Analysis: Gift Boxes

Relevant costs (costs that will be avoided if the gift boxes are purchased):

Direct material	$ 100,000
Direct labor	150,000
Variable overhead	100,000
Fixed overhead:	
Supervision	60,000
Machinery depreciation	20,000
Total costs to be avoided by purchasing	$ 430,000

Total cost of purchasing (1,000,000 boxes × $.45 per box)	$ 450,000

The Key Point   What has happened here? Why did the conventional and ABC analyses
of this decision reach different conclusions? Is the relevant-costing concept faulty?

The answer is no; the relevant-costing idea is alive and well. Both analyses sought
to identify the relevant costs as those that would be avoided by purchasing the gift
boxes. That approach is valid. The difference in the analyses lies in the superior ability
of the ABC data to properly identify what the avoidable costs are. This is the key point.
The conventional analysis relied on a traditional, volume-based product-costing
system. That system lumps all of the fixed overhead costs together and assigns them

A. Activity Cost Pools and Pool Rates

Activity Cost Pools	Budgeted Cost	Pool Rate and Cost Driver					Cost Assigned to Gift Boxes
Facility level:							
Plant depreciation	$1,650,000	—					
Product-sustaining level:							
Product development	300,000	$600 per product spec	$600	×	5*	=	$ 3,000
Supervisory salaries	600,000	$40 per supervisory hour	$40	×	1,500	=	60,000
Batch level:							
Material handling	800,000	$8 per material-handling hour	$8	×	5,000	=	40,000
Purchasing	250,000	$250 per purchase order	$250	×	40	=	10,000
Inspection	300,000	$300 per inspection	$300	×	20	=	6,000
Setup	400,000	$400 per setup	$400	×	10	=	4,000
Unit level:							
Electricity	700,000	$1.40 per machine hour	$1.40	×	50,000	=	70,000
Oil and lubrication	120,000	$.24 per machine hour	$.24	×	50,000	=	12,000
Equipment maintenance	180,000	$.36 per machine hour	$.36	×	50,000	=	18,000
Machinery depreciation	200,000	$.40 per machine hour	$.40	×	50,000	=	20,000
Total overhead for Savannah plant	$5,500,000						
Total overhead assigned to gift box production							$243,000

*The numbers in this column are the quantities of each cost driver required for gift box production.

B. ABC Outsourcing Analysis: Gift Boxes

Relevant cost (costs that will be avoided if the gift boxes are purchased):

Direct material	$100,000
Direct labor	150,000
Overhead (from ABC analysis in panel A, above)	243,000
Total costs to be avoided by purchasing	$493,000
Total cost of purchasing (1,000,000 boxes × $.45 per box)	$450,000

using a single, unit-based cost driver (i.e., direct-labor hours). That analysis simply failed to note that many of the so-called fixed costs are *not* really fixed with respect to the appropriate cost driver. The more accurate ABC system correctly showed this fact, and identified additional costs that could be avoided by purchasing.

To summarize, under activity-based costing, the concepts underlying relevant-costing analysis remain valid. However, the ABC system does enable the decision maker to apply the relevant-costing decision model more accurately.

Other Issues in Decision Making

Incentives for Decision Makers

In this chapter we studied how managers should make decisions by focusing on the relevant costs and benefits. In previous chapters we covered accounting procedures for evaluating managerial performance. There is an important link between *decision making* and *managerial performance evaluation*. Managers typically will make decisions that maximize their perceived performance evaluations and rewards. This is human nature. If we want managers to make optimal decisions by properly evaluating the relevant costs and benefits, then the performance evaluation system and reward structure had better be consistent with that perspective.

Exhibit 14–20

Activity-Based Costing Analysis of Outsourcing Decision: International Chocolate Company

The proper treatment of sunk costs in decision making illustrates this issue. Earlier in this chapter we saw that sunk costs should be ignored as irrelevant. For example, the book value of an outdated machine is irrelevant in making an equipment-replacement decision. Suppose, however, that a manager correctly ignores an old machine's book value and decides on early replacement of the machine he purchased a few years ago. Now suppose the hapless manager is criticized by his superior for "taking a loss" on the old machine, or for "buying a piece of junk" in the first place. What is our manager likely to do the next time he faces a similar decision? If he is like many people, he will tend to keep the old machine in order to justify his prior decision to purchase it. In so doing, he will be compounding his error. However, he may also be avoiding criticism from a superior who does not understand the importance of goal congruence.

The point is simply that if we want managers to make optimal decisions, we must give them incentives to do so. This requires that managerial performance be judged on the same factors that should be considered in making correct decisions.

Short-Run versus Long-Run Decisions

The decisions we have examined in this chapter were treated as short-run decisions. *Short-run decisions* affect only a short time period, typically a year or less. In reality, many of these decisions would have longer-term implications. For example, managers usually make a decision involving the addition or deletion of a product or service with a relatively long time frame in mind. The process of identifying relevant costs and benefits is largely the same whether the decision is viewed from a short-run or long-run perspective. One important factor that does change in a long-run analysis, however, is the *time value of money*. When several time periods are involved in a decision, the analyst should account for the fact that a $1.00 cash flow today is different from a $1.00 cash flow in five years. A dollar received today can be invested to earn interest, while the dollar received in five years cannot be invested over the intervening time period. The analysis of long-run decisions requires a tool called *capital budgeting*, which is covered in Chapters 16 and 17.

Pitfalls to Avoid

Identification of the relevant costs and benefits is an important step in making any economic decision. Nonetheless, analysts often overlook relevant costs or incorrectly include irrelevant data. In this section, we review four common mistakes to avoid in decision making.

1. *Sunk costs.* The book value of an asset, defined as its acquisition cost less the accumulated depreciation, is a sunk cost. Sunk costs cannot be changed by any current or future course of action, so they are irrelevant in decision making. Nevertheless, a common behavioral tendency is to give undue importance to book values in decisions that involve replacing an asset or disposing of obsolete inventory. People often seek to justify their past decisions by refusing to dispose of an asset, even if a better alternative has been identified. *The moral: Ignore sunk costs.*

2. *Unitized fixed costs.* For product-costing purposes, fixed costs often are divided by some activity measure and assigned to individual units of product. The result is to make a fixed cost appear variable. While there are legitimate reasons for this practice, from a *product-costing* perspective, it can create havoc in *decision making*. Therefore, in a decision analysis it is usually wise to include a fixed cost in its total amount, rather than as a per-unit cost. *The moral: Beware of unitized fixed costs in decision making.*

3. *Allocated fixed costs.* It is also common to allocate fixed costs across divisions, departments, or product lines. A possible result is that a product or department

may appear unprofitable when in reality it does make a contribution toward covering fixed costs and profit. Before deciding to eliminate a department, be sure to ask which costs will be *avoided* if a particular alternative is selected. A fixed cost that has been allocated to a department may continue, in total or in part, even after the department has been eliminated. *The moral: Beware of allocated fixed costs; identify the avoidable costs.*

4. ***Opportunity costs.*** People tend to overlook opportunity costs, or to treat such costs as less important than out-of-pocket costs. Yet opportunity costs are just as real and important to making a correct decision as are out-of-pocket costs. *The moral: Pay special attention to identifying and including opportunity costs in a decision analysis.*

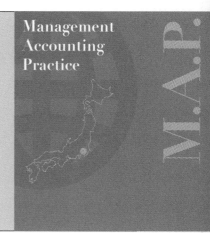

Relevant Costs and Benefits of Advanced Manufacturing Systems

Estimating relevant costs and benefits is a crucial but difficult step in decisions regarding acquisition of advanced manufacturing systems. Flexible manufacturing systems (FMS) and robotic equipment can cost $50 million or more. To justify such massive expenditures, management must be able to quantify the benefits. These benefits can be realized directly through production cost savings, or indirectly through improved customer satisfaction.

Yamazaki Machinery Company purchased an $18 million FMS and experienced substantial cost savings throughout its production process. For example, only 18 machines were required in the new FMS, down from 68. This resulted in a reduction of factory floor space from 103,000 square feet to only 30,000. Production employees were cut from 215 to 12. Average cycle time dropped from 35 days to 1.5, and the company significantly cut its inventories of raw materials and finished goods. In addition, the firm enjoyed a marketing advantage, since it was able to offer customers shorter lead times and respond more quickly to their changing needs.[5]

Chapter Summary

The managerial accountant's role in the decision-making process is to provide data relevant to the decision. Managers can then use these data in preparing a quantitative analysis of the decision. Qualitative factors are considered also in making the final decision.

In order to be relevant to a decision, a cost or benefit must: (1) bear on the future, and (2) differ under the various decision alternatives. Sunk costs, such as the book value of equipment or inventory, are not relevant in decisions. Such costs do not have any bearing on the future. Opportunity costs frequently are relevant to decisions, but they often are overlooked by decision makers. To analyze any special decision, the proper approach is to determine all of the costs and benefits that will differ among the alternatives.

Since decisions often are made under uncertainty, sensitivity analysis should be used to determine if the decision will change if various predictions prove to be wrong.

The concepts underlying a relevant-cost analysis remain valid in an advanced manufacturing environment and in situations where activity-based costing is used. However, an ABC system typically enables a decision maker to estimate the relevant costs in a decision problem more accurately.

Review Problem on Relevant Costs

Lansing Camera Company has received a special order for photographic equipment it does not normally produce. The company has excess capacity, and the order could be manufactured without reducing production of the firm's regular products. Discuss the relevance of each of the following items in computing the cost of the special order.

---

[5]R. S. Kaplan, "Must CIM Be Justified by Faith Alone?" *Harvard Business Review* 64, no. 2, pp. 87 and 92.

1. Equipment to be used in producing the order has a book value of $2,000. The equipment has no other use for Lansing Camera Company. If the order is not accepted, the equipment will be sold for $1,500. If the equipment is used in producing the order, it can be sold in three months for $800.

2. If the special order is accepted, the operation will require some of the storage space in the company's plant. If the space is used for this purpose, the company will rent storage space temporarily in a nearby warehouse at a cost of $18,000. The building depreciation allocated to the storage space to be used in producing the special order is $12,000.

3. If the special order is accepted, it will require a subassembly. Lansing Camera can purchase the subassembly for $24.00 per unit from an outside supplier or make it for $30.00 per unit. The $30.00 cost per unit was determined as follows:

Direct material	$10.00
Direct labor	6.00
Variable overhead	6.00
Allocated fixed overhead	8.00
Total unit cost of subassembly	$30.00

Solution to Review Problem

1. The book value of the equipment is a sunk cost, irrelevant to the decision. The relevant cost of the equipment is $700, determined as follows:

Sales value of equipment now	$1,500
Sales value after producing special order	800
Differential cost	$ 700

2. The $12,000 portion of building depreciation allocated to the storage space to be used for the special order is irrelevant. First, it is a sunk cost. Second, any costs relating to the company's factory building will continue whether the special order is accepted or not. The relevant cost is the $18,000 rent that will be incurred only if the special order is accepted.

3. Lansing Camera should make the subassembly. The subassembly's relevant cost is $22.00 per unit.

Relevant Cost of Making Subassembly (per unit)		Relevant Cost of Purchasing Subassembly (per unit)	
Direct material	$10.00	Purchase price	$24.00
Direct labor	6.00		
Variable overhead	6.00		
Total	$22.00		

Notice that the unitized fixed overhead, $8.00, is not a relevant cost of the subassembly. Lansing Camera Company's *total* fixed cost will not change, whether the special order is accepted or not.

Key Terms

For each term's definition refer to the indicated page, or turn to the glossary at the end of the text.

Appendix to Chapter 14
Linear Programming

When a firm produces multiple products, management must decide how much of each output to produce. In most cases, the firm is limited in the total amount it can produce, due to constraints on resources such as machine time, direct labor, or raw materials. This situation is known as a *product-mix problem*.

To illustrate, we will use International Chocolate Company's Phoenix plant, which produces Chewies and Chompo Bars. Exhibit 14–21 provides data pertinent to the problem.

Linear programming is a powerful mathematical tool, well suited to solving International Chocolate Company's product-mix problem. The steps in constructing the linear program are as follows:

1. Identify the **decision variables**, which are the variables about which a decision must be made. International Chocolate's decision variables are as follows:

    Decision X = **Number of cases of Chewies to produce each month**
    variables Y = **Number of cases of Chompo Bars to produce each month**

2. Write the **objective function**, which is an algebraic expression of the firm's goal. International Chocolate's goal is to *maximize its total contribution margin*. Since Chewies bring a contribution margin of $1 per case, and Chompos result in a contribution margin of $2 per case, the firm's objective function is the following:

    Objective function   **Maximize $Z = X + 2Y$**

3. Write the **constraints**, which are algebraic expressions of the limitations faced by the firm, such as those limiting its productive resources. International Chocolate has a constraint for machine time and a constraint for direct labor.

    Machine-time constraint $.02X + .05Y \leq 700$
    Labor-time constraint $.20X + .25Y \leq 5{,}000$

Suppose, for example, that management decided to produce 20,000 cases of Chewies and 6,000 cases of Chompos. The machine-time constraint would appear as follows:

$$(.02)(20{,}000) + (.05)(6{,}000) = 700$$

Thus, at these production levels, the machine-time constraint would just be satisfied, with no machine hours to spare.

Graphical Solution

To understand how the linear program described above will help International Chocolate's management solve its product-mix problem, examine the graphs in Exhibit 14–22. The two colored lines in panel A represent the constraints. The colored arrows indicate that the production quantities, X and Y, must lie on

---

LO 8   After completing the appendix, formulate a linear program to solve a product-mix problem with multiple constraints.

Decision variables are the variables in a linear program about which a decision is made.

An **objective function** is an algebraic expression of the firm's goal.

Constraints are algebraic expressions of limitations faced by a firm, such as those limiting its productive resources.

	Chewies	Chompo Bars
Contribution margin per case	$1.00	$2.00
Machine hours per case	.02	.05
Direct-labor hours per case	.20	.25
	Machine Hours	**Direct-Labor Hours**
Limited resources: hours available per month	700	5,000

Exhibit 14–21

Data for Product-Mix Problem: International Chocolate Company

INTERNATIONAL
CHOCOLATE
COMPANY

The **feasible region** contains the possible values for decision variables which are not ruled out by constraints.

or below these lines. Since the production quantities must be nonnegative, colored arrows also appear on the graphs' axes. Together, the axes and constraints form an area called the **feasible region**, in which the solution to the linear program must lie.

The black slanted line in panel A represents the objective function. Rearrange the objective function equation as follows:

$$Z = X + 2Y \quad \longrightarrow \quad Y = \frac{Z}{2} - \frac{1}{2}X$$

This form of the objective function shows that the slope of the equation is $-\frac{1}{2}$, which is the slope of the objective-function line in the exhibit. Management's goal is to maximize total contribution margin, denoted by Z. To achieve the maximum, the objective-function line must be moved as far outward and upward in the feasible region as possible, while maintaining the same slope. This goal is represented in panel A by the arrow which points outward from the objective function line.

Solution   The result of moving the objective-function line as far as possible in the indicated direction is shown in panel B of the exhibit. The objective-function line intersects the feasible region at exactly

Exhibit 14–22

Product-Mix Problem Expressed as Linear Program: International Chocolate Company

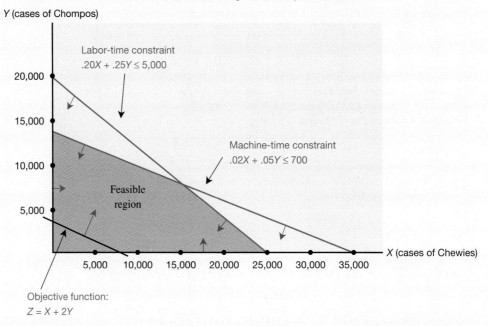

A. Constraints, Feasible Region, and Objective Function

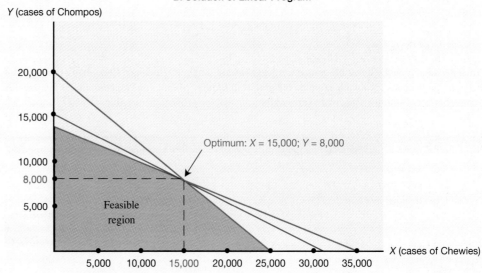

B. Solution of Linear Program

one point, where X equals 15,000 and Y equals 8,000. Thus, International Chocolate's optimal product mix is 15,000 cases of Chewies and 8,000 cases of Chompos per month. The total contribution margin is calculated as shown below.

$$\text{Total contribution margin} = (15,000)(\$1) + (8,000)(\$2) = \$31,000$$

Simplex Method and Sensitivity Analysis Although the graphical method is instructive, it is a cumbersome technique for solving a linear program. Fortunately, mathematicians have developed a more efficient solution method called the *simplex algorithm*. A computer can apply the algorithm to a complex linear program and determine the solution in seconds. In addition, most linear programming computer packages provide a sensitivity analysis of the problem. This analysis shows the decision maker the extent to which the estimates used in the objective function and constraints can change without changing the solution.

Managerial Accountant's Role

What is the managerial accountant's role in International Chocolate's product-mix decision? The production manager in the company's Phoenix plant makes this decision, with the help of a linear program. However, the linear program uses *information supplied by the managerial accountant.* The coefficients of X and Y in the objective function are unit contribution margins. Exhibit 14–14 shows that calculating these contribution margins requires estimates of direct-material, direct-labor, variable-overhead, and variable selling and administrative costs. These estimates were provided by a managerial accountant, along with estimates of the machine time and direct-labor time required to produce a case of Chewies or Chompos. All of these estimates were obtained from the standard-costing system, upon which the Phoenix plant's product costs are based. Thus, the managerial accountant makes the product-mix decision possible by providing the relevant cost data.

Linear programming is widely used in business decision making. Among the applications are blending in the petroleum and chemical industries, scheduling of personnel, railroad cars, and aircraft, and the mixing of ingredients in the food industry. In all of these applications, managerial accountants provide information crucial to the analysis.

Key Terms: Appendix

For each term's definition refer to the indicated page, or turn to the glossary at the end of the text.

constraints, pg. 591   decision variables, pg. 591   feasible region, pg. 592   objective function, pg. 591

Review Questions

14–1. Describe the managerial accountant's role in the decision-making process.

14–2. List the six steps in the decision-making process.

14–3. Explain what is meant by the term *decision model.*

14–4. Distinguish between qualitative and quantitative decision analyses.

14–5. A quantitative analysis enables a decision maker to put a "price" on the sum total of the qualitative characteristics in a decision situation. Explain this statement, and give an example.

14–6. What is meant by each of the following potential characteristics of information: relevant, accurate, and timely? Is objective information always relevant? Accurate?

14–7. List and explain two important criteria that must be satisfied in order for information to be relevant.

14–8. Explain why the book value of equipment is not a relevant cost.

14–9. Is the book value of inventory on hand a relevant cost? Why?

14–10. Why might a manager exhibit a behavioral tendency to inappropriately consider sunk costs in making a decision?

14–11. Give an example of an irrelevant future cost. Why is it irrelevant?

14–12. Define the term *opportunity cost,* and give an example of one.

14–13. What behavioral tendency do people often exhibit with regard to opportunity costs?

14–14. How does the existence of excess production capacity affect the decision to accept or reject a special order?

14–15. What is meant by the term *differential cost analysis?*

14–16. Briefly describe the proper approach for making a decision about adding or dropping a product line.

14–17. What is a *joint production process?* Describe a special decision that commonly arises in the context of a joint production process. Briefly describe the proper approach for making this type of decision.

14–18. Are allocated joint processing costs relevant when making a decision to sell a joint product at the split-off point or process it further? Why?

14–19. Briefly describe the proper approach to making a production decision when limited resources are involved.

14–20. What is meant by the term *contribution margin per unit of scare resource?*

14–21. How is sensitivity analysis used to cope with uncertainty in decision making?

14–22. There is an important link between *decision making* and *managerial performance evaluation.* Explain.

14–23. List four potential pitfalls in decision making, which represent common errors.

14–24. Why can unitized fixed costs cause errors in decision making?

14–25. Give two examples of sunk costs, and explain why they are irrelevant in decision making.

14–26. "Accounting systems should produce only relevant data and forget about the irrelevant data. Then I'd know what was relevant and what wasn't!" Comment on this remark by a company president.

14–27. Are the concepts underlying a relevant-cost analysis still valid in an advanced manufacturing environment? Are these concepts valid when activity-based costing is used? Explain.

14–28. List five ways that management can seek to relax a constraint by expanding the capacity of a bottleneck operation.

Exercises

■ **Exercise 14–29**
Steps in Decision-Making Process
(LO 1)

Choose an organization and a particular decision situation. Then give examples, using that context, of each step illustrated in Exhibit 14–1.

■ **Exercise 14–30**
Irrelevant Future Costs and Benefits
(LO 3, LO 4)

Redo Exhibit 14–4 without the irrelevant data.

■ **Exercise 14–31**
Obsolete Inventory
(LO 4, LO 5)

LeMonde Corporation manufactures bicycle parts. The company currently has a $21,000 inventory of parts that have become obsolete due to changes in design specifications. The parts could be sold for $9,000, or modified for $12,000 and sold for $22,300.

Required:

1. Which of the data above are relevant to the decision about the obsolete parts?
2. Prepare an analysis of the decision.

■ **Exercise 14–32**
Joint Products
(LO 4, LO 5)

Biondi Industries produces chemicals for the swimming pool industry. In one joint process, 10,000 gallons of GSX are processed into 7,000 gallons of xenolite and 3,000 gallons of banolide. The cost of the joint process, including the GSX, is $19,000. The firm allocates $13,300 of the joint cost to the xenolite and $5,700 of the cost to the banolide. The 3,000 gallons of banolide can be sold at the split-off point for $2,500, or be processed further into a product called kitrocide. The sales value of 3,000 gallons of kitrocide is $10,000, and the additional processing cost is $8,100.

Required:

Biondi's president has asked your consulting firm to make a recommendation as to whether the banolide should be sold at the split-off point or processed further. Write a letter providing an analysis and a recommendation.

■ **Exercise 14–33**
Machine Replacement
(LO 4, LO 5)

Village Pizza's owner bought his current pizza oven two years ago for $9,000, and it has one more year of life remaining. He is using straight-line depreciation for the oven. He could purchase a new oven for $1,900, but it would last only one year. The owner figures the new oven would save him $2,600 in annual operating expenses compared to operating the old one. Consequently, he has decided against buying the new oven, since doing so would result in a "loss" of $400 over the next year.

Required:

1. How do you suppose the owner came up with $400 as the loss for the next year if the new pizza oven were purchased? Explain.
2. Criticize the owner's analysis and decision.
3. Prepare a correct analysis of the owner's decision.

Day Street Deli's owner is disturbed by the poor profit performance of his ice cream counter. He has prepared the following profit analysis for the year just ended.

■ **Exercise 14–34**
Drop Product Line
(LO 4, LO 5)

Sales		$45,000
Less: Cost of food		20,000
Gross profit		$25,000
Less: Operating expenses:		
Wages of counter personnel	$12,000	
Paper products (e.g., napkins)	4,000	
Utilities (allocated)	2,900	
Depreciation of counter equipment and furnishings	2,500	
Depreciation of building (allocated)	4,000	
Deli manager's salary (allocated)	3,000	
Total		28,400
Loss on ice cream counter		$(3,400)

Required:

Criticize and correct the owner's analysis.

Interlaken Chemical Company recently received an order for a product it does not normally produce. Since the company has excess production capacity, management is considering accepting the order. In analyzing the decision, the assistant controller is compiling the relevant costs of producing the order. Production of the special order would require 8,000 kilograms of theolite. Interlaken does not use theolite for its regular product, but the firm has 8,000 kilograms of the chemical on hand from the days when it used theolite regularly. The theolite could be sold to a chemical wholesaler for $14,500. The book value of the theolite is $2.00 per kilogram. Interlaken could buy theolite for $2.40 per kilogram.

■ **Exercise 14–35**
Special Order
(LO 4, LO 5)

Required:

1. What is the relevant cost of theolite for the purpose of analyzing the special-order decision?
2. Discuss each of the numbers given in the exercise with regard to its relevance in making the decision.

Interlaken's special order also requires 1,000 kilograms of genatope, a solid chemical regularly used in the company's products. The current stock of genatope is 8,000 kilograms at a book value of $8.10 per kilogram. If the special order is accepted, the firm will be forced to restock genatope earlier than expected, at a predicted cost of $8.70 per kilogram. Without the special order, the purchasing manager predicts that the price will be $8.30, when normal restocking takes place. Any order of genatope must be in the amount of 5,000 kilograms.

■ **Exercise 14–36**
Continuation of Preceding
Exercise
(LO 4, LO 5)

Required:

1. What is the relevant cost of genatope?
2. Discuss each of the figures in the exercise in terms of its relevance to the decision.

Super Clean Corporation produces cleaning compounds and solutions for industrial and household use. While most of its products are processed independently, a few are related. Grit 337, a coarse cleaning powder with many industrial uses, costs $1.60 a pound to make and sells for $2.00 a pound. A small portion of the annual production of this product is retained for further processing in the Mixing Department, where it is combined with several other ingredients to form a paste, which is marketed as a

■ **Exercise 14–37**
Joint Products; Relevant
Costs; Cost-Volume-Profit
Analysis
(LO 4, LO 6)

silver polish selling for $4.00 per jar. This further processing requires ¼ pound of Grit 337 per jar. Costs of other ingredients, labor, and variable overhead associated with this further processing amount to $2.50 per jar. Variable selling costs are $.30 per jar. If the decision were made to cease production of the silver polish, $5,600 of Mixing Department fixed costs could be avoided. Super Clean has limited production capacity for Grit 337, but unlimited demand for the cleaning powder.

Required:

Calculate the minimum number of jars of silver polish that would have to be sold to justify further processing of Grit 337.

(CMA, adapted)

■ **Exercise 14–38**
Closing a Department
(LO 4, LO 5)

Chemung Metals Company is considering the elimination of its Packaging Department. Management has received an offer from an outside firm to supply all Chemung's packaging needs. To help her in making the decision, Chemung's president has asked the controller for an analysis of the cost of running Chemung's Packaging Department. Included in that analysis is $9,100 of rent, which represents the Packaging Department's allocation of the rent on Chemung's factory building. If the Packaging Department is eliminated, the space it used will be converted to storage space. Currently Chemung rents storage space in a nearby warehouse for $11,000 per year. The warehouse rental would no longer be necessary if the packaging department were eliminated.

Required:

1. Discuss each of the figures given in the exercise with regard to its relevance in the department-closing decision.
2. What type of cost is the $11,000 warehouse rental, from the viewpoint of the costs of the Packaging Department?

■ **Exercise 14–39**
Continuation of Preceding
Exercise
(LO 4, LO 5)

If Chemung Chemical Company closes its Packaging Department, the department manager will be appointed manager of the Cutting Department. The Packaging Department manager makes $45,000 per year. To hire a new Cutting Department manager will cost Chemung $60,000 per year.

Required:

Discuss the relevance of each of these salary figures to the department-closing decision.

■ **Exercise 14–40**
Limited Resource
(LO 6)

Duo Company manufactures two products, Uno and Dos. Contribution margin data follow.

	Uno	Dos
Unit sales price	$13.00	$31.00
Less variable cost:		
Direct material	$ 7.00	$ 5.00
Direct labor	1.00	6.00
Variable overhead	1.25	7.50
Variable selling and administrative cost	.75	.50
Total variable cost	$10.00	$19.00
Unit contribution margin	$ 3.00	$12.00

Duo company's production process uses highly skilled labor, which is in short supply. The same employees work on both products and earn the same wage rate.

Required:

Which of Duo Company's products is most profitable? Explain.

■ **Exercise 14–41**
Linear Programming
(Appendix)
(LO 6, LO 8)

Refer to the data given in the preceding exercise for Duo Company. Assume that the direct-labor rate is $24 per hour, and 10,000 labor hours are available per year. In addition, the company has a short supply of machine time. Only 8,000 hours are available each year. Uno requires 1 machine hour per unit, and Dos requires 2 machine hours per unit.

Required:

Formulate the production planning problem as a linear program. Specifically identify (1) the decision variables, (2) the objective function, and (3) the constraints.

Galveston Chemical Company manufactures two industrial chemical products, called kreolite-red and kreolite-blue. Two machines are used in the process, and each machine has 24 hours of capacity per day. The following data are available:

	Kreolite-Red	Kreolite-Blue
Selling price per drum	$36	$42
Variable cost per drum	$28	$28
Hours required per drum on machine I	2 hr	2 hr
Hours required per drum on machine II	1 hr	3 hr

■ **Exercise 14–42**
Linear Programming;
Formulate and Solve
Graphically (Appendix)
(LO 8)

The company can produce and sell partially full drums of each chemical. For example, a half drum of kreolite-red sells for $18.

Required:

1. Formulate the product-mix problem as a linear program.
2. Solve the problem graphically.
3. What is the value of the objective function at the optimal solution?

Problems

Geary Manufacturing has assembled the following data pertaining to its two most popular products.

	Blender	Electric Mixer
Direct material	$ 6	$11
Direct labor	4	9
Manufacturing overhead @ $16 per machine hour	16	32
Cost if purchased from an outside supplier	20	38
Annual demand (units)	20,000	28,000

■ **Problem 14–43**
Production Decisions;
Limited Capacity
(LO 5, LO 6)

Past experience has shown that the fixed manufacturing overhead component included in the cost per machine hour averages $10. Geary has a policy of filling all sales orders, even if it means purchasing units from outside suppliers.

Required:

1. If 50,000 machine hours are available, and Geary Manufacturing desires to follow an optimal strategy, how many units of each product should the firm manufacture? How many units of each product should Geary purchase?
2. With all other things constant, if Geary Manufacturing is able to reduce the direct material for an electric mixer to $6 per unit, how many units of each product should be manufactured? Purchased?

(CMA, adapted)

Tyler Tool Company manufactures electric carpentry tools. The Production Department has met all production requirements for the current month and has an opportunity to produce additional units of product with its excess capacity. Unit selling prices and unit costs for three different drill models are as follows:

■ **Problem 14–44**
Excess Production Capacity
(LO 5, LO 6)

	Home Model	Deluxe Model	Pro Model
Selling price	$58	$65	$80
Direct material	16	20	19
Direct labor ($10 per hour)	10	15	20
Variable overhead	8	12	16
Fixed overhead	16	5	15

Variable overhead is applied on the basis of direct-labor dollars, while fixed overhead is applied on the basis of machine hours. There is sufficient demand for the additional production of any model in the product line.

Required:

1. If Tyler Tool Company has excess machine capacity and can add more labor as needed (i.e., neither machine capacity nor labor is a constraint), the excess production capacity should be devoted to producing which product or products?

2. If Tyler Tool has excess machine capacity but a limited amount of labor time, the excess production capacity should be devoted to producing which product or products?

(CMA, adapted)

■ **Problem 14–45**
Make or Buy
(LO 4, LO 5)

Xyon Company has purchased 10,000 pumps annually from Kobec, Inc. Because the price keeps increasing and reached $68.00 per unit last year, Xyon's management has asked for an estimate of the cost of manufacturing the pump in Xyon's facilities. Xyon makes stampings and castings and has little experience with products requiring assembly.

The engineering, manufacturing, and accounting departments have prepared a report for management which includes the estimate shown below for an assembly run of 10,000 pumps. Additional production employees would be hired to manufacture the pumps but no additional equipment, space, or supervision would be needed.

The report states that total costs for 10,000 units are estimated at $957,000 or $95.70 a unit. The current purchase price is $68.00 a unit, so the report recommends continued purchase of the product.

Components (outside purchases)	$120,000
Assembly labor*	300,000
Manufacturing overhead†	450,000
General and administrative overhead‡	87,000
Total costs	$957,000

*Assembly labor consists of hourly production workers.

†Manufacturing overhead is applied to products on a direct-labor-dollar basis. Variable-overhead costs vary closely with direct-labor dollars.

Fixed overhead	50%	of direct-labor dollars
Variable overhead	100%	of direct-labor dollars
Manufacturing-overhead rate	150%	of direct-labor dollars

‡General and administrative overhead is applied at 10 percent of the total cost of material (or components), assembly labor, and manufacturing overhead.

Required:

Was the analysis prepared by Xyon Company's engineering, manufacturing, and accounting departments and their recommendation to continue purchasing the pumps correct? Explain your answer and include any supporting calculations you consider necessary.

(CMA, adapted)

■ **Problem 14–46**
Outsourcing Decision;
Relevant Costs; Ethics
(LO 3, LO 4, LO 5)

The Midwest Division of the Paibec Corporation manufactures subassemblies that are used in the corporation's final products. Lynn Hardt of Midwest's Profit Planning Department has been assigned the task of determining whether a component, MTR–2000, should continue to be manufactured by Midwest or purchased from Marley Company, an outside supplier. MTR–2000 is part of a subassembly manufactured by Midwest.

Marley has submitted a bid to manufacture and supply the 32,000 units of MTR–2000 that Paibec will need for 19x9 at a unit price of $17.30. Marley has assured Paibec that the units will be delivered according to Paibec's production specifications and needs. While the contract price of $17.30 is only applicable in 19x9, Marley is interested in entering into a long-term arrangement beyond 19x9.

Hardt has gathered the following information regarding Midwest's cost to manufacture MTR–2000 in 19x8. These annual costs will be incurred to manufacture 30,000 units.

Direct material	$195,000
Direct labor	120,000
Factory space rental	84,000
Equipment leasing costs	36,000
Other manufacturing overhead	225,000
Total manufacturing costs	$660,000

Hardt has collected the following additional information related to manufacturing MTR–2000.

■ Direct materials used in the production of MTR–2000 are expected to increase 8 percent in 19x9.

■ Midwest's direct-labor contract calls for a 5 percent increase in 19x9.

■ The facilities used to manufacture MTR–2000 are rented under a month-to-month rental agreement. Thus, Midwest can withdraw from the rental agreement without any penalty. Midwest will have no need for this space if MTR–2000 is not manufactured.

■ Equipment leasing costs represent special equipment that is used in the manufacture of MTR–2000. This lease can be terminated by paying the equivalent of one month's lease payment for each year left on the lease agreement. Midwest has two years left on the lease agreement, through the end of the year 20x0.

■ Forty percent of the other manufacturing overhead is considered variable. Variable overhead changes with the number of units produced, and this rate per unit is not expected to change in 19x9. The fixed manufacturing overhead costs are not expected to change regardless of whether MTR–2000 is manufactured. Equipment other than the leased equipment can be used in Midwest's other manufacturing operations.

John Porter, divisional manager of Midwest, stopped by Hardt's office to voice his concern regarding the outsourcing of MTR–2000. Porter commented, "I am really concerned about outsourcing MTR–2000. I have a son-in-law and a nephew, not to mention a member of our bowling team, who work on MTR–2000. They could lose their jobs if we buy that component from Marley. I really would appreciate anything you can do to make sure the cost analysis comes out right to show we should continue making MTR–2000. Corporate is not aware of the material increases and maybe you can leave out some of those fixed costs. I just think we should continue making MTR–2000!"

Required:

1. *a.* Prepare an analysis of relevant costs that shows whether or not the Midwest Division of Paibec Corporation should make MTR–2000 or purchase it from Marley Company for 19x9.

    b. Based solely on the financial results, recommend whether the 32,000 units of MTR–2000 for 19x9 should be made by Midwest or purchased from Marley.

2. Identify and briefly discuss three qualitative factors that the Midwest Division and Paibec Corporation should consider before agreeing to purchase MTR–2000 from Marley Company.

3. By referring to the standards of ethical conduct for managerial accountants given in Chapter 1, explain why Lynn Hardt would consider the request of John Porter to be unethical.

(CMA, adapted)

Kalamazoo Chemical Company is a diversified chemical processing company. The firm manufactures swimming pool chemicals, chemicals for metal processing, specialized chemical compounds, and pesticides.

Currently, the Noorwood plant is producing two derivatives, RNA–1 and RNA–2, from the chemical compound VDB developed by the company's research labs. Each week 1,200,000 pounds of VDB is processed at a cost of $246,000 into 800,000 pounds of RNA–1 and 400,000 pounds of RNA–2. The proportion of these two outputs cannot be altered, because this is a joint process. RNA–1 has no market value until it is converted into a pesticide with the trade name Fastkil. Processing RNA–1 into Fastkil costs $240,000. Fastkil wholesales at $50 per 100 pounds.

RNA–2 is sold as is for $80 per hundred pounds. However, management has discovered that RNA–2 can be converted into two new products by adding 400,000 pounds of compound LST to the 400,000 pounds of RNA–2. This joint process would yield 400,000 pounds each of DMZ–3 and Pestrol, the two new products. The additional direct-material and related processing costs of this joint process would be $120,000. DMZ–3 and Pestrol would each be sold for $57.50 per 100 pounds. The company's

■ **Problem 14–47**
Joint Products; Sell or
Process Further
(LO 6)

management has decided not to process RNA–2 further based on the analysis presented in the following schedule.

| | Process Further | | | |
	RNA–2	DMZ–3	Pestrol	Total
Production in pounds	400,000	400,000	400,000	
Revenue	$320,000	$230,000	$230,000	$460,000
Costs:				
VDB costs	$ 82,000*	$ 61,500	$ 61,500	$123,000†
Additional direct materials (LST)				
and processing of RNA–2	—	$ 60,000	60,000	120,000
Total costs	$ 82,000	$121,500	$121,500	$243,000
Weekly gross profit	$238,000	$108,500	$108,500	$217,000

*$82,000 is one-third of the $246,000 cost of processing VDB. When RNA–2 is not processed further, one-third of the final output is RNA–2 (400,000 out of a total of 1,200,000 pounds).

†$123,000 is one-half of the $246,000 cost of processing VDB. When RNA–2 is processed further, one-half of the final output consists of DMZ–3 and Pestrol. The final products then are: 800,000 pounds of RNA–1; 400,000 pounds of DMZ–3; and 400,000 pounds of Pestrol.

Required:

Evaluate Kalamazoo Chemical Company's analysis, and make any revisions that are necessary. Your critique and analysis should indicate:

a. Whether management made the correct decision.

b. The gross savings or loss per week resulting from the decision not to process RNA–2 further, if different from management's analysis.

(CMA, adapted)

■ **Problem 14–48**
Add a Product Line
(LO 4, LO 5)

Helene's, a high-fashion dress manufacturer, is planning to market a new cocktail dress for the coming season. Helene's supplies retailers in the east and mid-Atlantic states.

Four yards of material are required to lay out the dress pattern. Some material remains after cutting, which can be sold as remnants. The leftover material also could be used to manufacture a matching cape and handbag. However, if the leftover material is to be used for the cape and handbag, more care will be required in the cutting operation, which will increase the cutting costs.

The company expects to sell 1,250 dresses. Helene's market research reveals that dress sales will be 20 percent higher if a matching cape and handbag are available. The market research indicates that the cape and handbag will be salable only as accessories with the dress. The combination of dresses, capes, and handbags expected to be sold by retailers are as follows:

	Percent of Total
Complete sets of dress, cape, and handbag	70%
Dress and cape	6
Dress and handbag	15
Dress only	9
Total	100%

The material used in the dress costs $12.50 a yard or $50.00 for each dress. The cost of cutting the dress if the cape and handbag are not manufactured is estimated at $20.00 a dress, and the resulting remnants can be sold for $5.00 per dress. If the cape and handbag are manufactured, the cutting costs will be increased by $9.00 per dress and there will be no salable remnants. The selling prices and the costs to complete the three items once they are cut are as follows:

	Selling Price per Unit	Unit Cost to Complete (excludes costs of material and cutting operation)
Dress	$200.00	$80.00
Cape	27.50	19.50
Handbag	9.50	6.50

Required:

1. Calculate Helene's incremental profit or loss from manufacturing the capes and handbags in conjunction with the dresses.
2. Identify any qualitative factors that could influence Helene's management in its decision to manufacture capes and handbags to match the dresses.

(CMA, adapted)

Stewart Industries has been producing two bearings, components B12 and B18, for use in production. Data regarding these two components follow.

■ **Problem 14–49**
Outsourcing Decision
(LO 4, LO 5)

	B12	**B18**
Machine hours required per unit	2.5	3.0
Standard cost per unit:		
Direct material	$ 2.25	$ 3.75
Direct labor	4.00	4.50
Manufacturing overhead		
Variable*	2.00	2.25
Fixed†	3.75	4.50
	$12.00	$15.00

*Variable manufacturing overhead is applied on the basis of direct-labor hours.
†Fixed manufacturing overhead is applied on the basis of machine hours.

Stewart's annual requirement for these components is 8,000 units of B12 and 11,000 units of B18. Recently, Stewart's management decided to devote additional machine time to other product lines, leaving only 41,000 machine hours per year for producing the bearings. An outside company has offered to sell Stewart its annual supply of bearings at prices of $11.25 for B12 and $13.50 for B18. Stewart wants to schedule the otherwise idle 41,000 machine hours to produce bearings so that the firm can minimize costs (maximize net benefits).

Required:

1. Compute the net benefit (loss) per machine hour that would result if Stewart Industries accepts the supplier's offer of $13.50 per unit for component B18.
2. Choose the correct answer. Stewart Industries will maximize its net benefits by:
   a. purchasing 4,800 units of B12 and manufacturing the remaining bearings
   b. purchasing 8,000 units of B12 and manufacturing 11,000 units of B18
   c. purchasing 11,000 units of B18 and manufacturing 8,000 units of B12
   d. purchasing 4,000 units of B18 and manufacturing the remaining bearings
   e. purchasing and manufacturing some amounts other than those given above
3. Suppose management has decided to drop product B12. Independently of requirements (1) and (2), assume that Stewart Industries' idle capacity of 41,000 machine hours has a traceable, avoidable annual fixed cost of $44,000, which will be incurred only if the capacity is used. Calculate the maximum price Stewart Industries should pay a supplier for component B18.

(CMA, adapted)

Janice Watson recently was appointed executive director of the National Foundation for the Prevention of the Blahs. The foundation raises most of the money for its activities through an annual mail campaign. Although the mail campaign raises large amounts of money, the year-to-year growth in donations has been lower than expected by the foundation's board. In addition, the board wants the mail campaign to project the image of a well-run and fiscally responsible organization in order to build a base for greater future contributions. Consequently, Watson's efforts in her first year will be devoted to improving the mail campaign.

The campaign takes place each spring. The foundation staff works hard to secure media coverage of the foundation's activities for weeks before the mail campaign. In prior years, the foundation mailed

■ **Problem 14–50**
Nonprofit Organization;
Relevant Costs and Benefits
of Publicity Brochures
(LO 4, LO 5)

brochures describing its activities to millions of people and requested contributions from them. The addresses for the mailing are generated from the foundation's own file of past contributions and from mailing lists purchased from brokers.

The foundation staff is considering three alternative brochures for the upcoming campaign. All three will be 8½ × 11 inches. The simplest, and the one sure to be ready in time for bulk mailing, is a sheet of white paper with a printed explanation of the foundation's program and a request for funds. A more expensive brochure, on colored stock with pictures as well as printed copy, may not be ready in time to take advantage of bulk postal rates. It can be ready in time for mailing at first-class postal rates. The third alternative is an illustrated multicolored brochure printed on glossy paper. The printer has promised that it will be ready to meet the first-class mailing schedule but has asked for a delivery date one week later just in case there are production problems.

The foundation staff has assembled the following cost and revenue information for mailing the three alternative brochures to 2,000,000 potential contributors.

	Brochure Costs				Revenue Potential		
Type of Brochure	Design	Type Setting	Unit Paper Cost	Unit Printing Cost	Bulk Mail	First Class	Late First Class
Plain paper	$ 300	$ 100	$.005	$.003	$1,200,000	—	—
Colored paper	1,000	800	.008	.010	2,000,000	$2,200,000	—
Glossy paper	3,000	2,000	.018	.040	—	2,500,000	$2,200,000

The postal rates are $.02 per item for bulk mail and $.13 per item for presorted first-class mail. First-class mail is more likely to be delivered on a timely basis than bulk mail. The charge by outside companies to handle the mailing is $.01 per unit for the plain and colored-paper brochures and $.02 per unit for the glossy-paper brochure.

Required:

1. Calculate the net revenue contribution (i.e., excess of donations over solicitation costs) for each brochure with each viable mailing alternative.

2. The foundation must choose one of the three brochures for this year's campaign. The criteria established by the board are (1) net revenue raised, (2) image as a well-run organization, and (3) image as a fiscally responsible organization. Evaluate the three alternative brochures in terms of these three criteria.

(CMA, adapted)

■ **Problem 14–51**
Outsource a Component;
Relevant Costs, Opportunity
Costs, and Quality Control
(LO 3, LO 4, LO 5)

Leland Manufacturing Company uses 10 units of part KJ37 each month in the production of radar equipment. The cost of manufacturing one unit of KJ37 is the following:

Direct material	$ 1,000
Material handling (20% of direct-material cost)	200
Direct labor	8,000
Manufacturing overhead (150% of direct labor)	12,000
Total manufacturing cost	$21,200

Material handling represents the direct variable costs of the Receiving Department that are applied to direct materials and purchased components on the basis of their cost. This is a separate charge in addition to manufacturing overhead. Leland's annual manufacturing overhead budget is one-third variable and two-thirds fixed. Scott Supply, one of Leland's reliable vendors, has offered to supply part number KJ37 at a unit price of $15,000.

Required:

1. If Leland purchases the KJ37 units from Scott, the capacity Leland used to manufacture these parts would be idle. Should Leland decide to purchase the parts from Scott, the unit cost of KJ37 would increase (or decrease) by what amount?

2. Assume Leland Manufacturing is able to rent out all its idle capacity for $25,000 per month. If Leland decides to purchase the 10 units from Scott Supply, Leland's monthly cost for KJ37 would increase (or decrease) by what amount?

3. Assume that Leland Manufacturing does not wish to commit to a rental agreement but could use its idle capacity to manufacture another product that would contribute $52,000 per month. If Leland elects to manufacture KJ37 in order to maintain quality control, what is the net amount of Leland's cost from using the space to manufacture part KJ37?

(CMA, adapted)

Auerbach Industries received an order for a piece of special machinery from Jay Company. Just as Auerbach completed the machine, Jay Company declared bankruptcy, defaulted on the order, and forfeited the 10 percent deposit paid on the selling price of $72,500.

> ■ **Problem 14–52**
> Analysis of Special Order
> (LO 4, LO 5)

Auerbach's manufacturing manager identified the costs already incurred in the production of the special machinery for Jay Company as follows:

Direct material		$16,600
Direct labor		21,400
Manufacturing overhead applied:		
Variable	$10,700	
Fixed	5,350	16,050
Fixed selling and administrative costs		5,405
Total		$59,455

Another company, Kaytell Corporation, will buy the special machinery if it is reworked to Kaytell's specifications. Auerbach offered to sell the reworked machinery to Kaytell as a special order for $68,400. Kaytell agreed to pay the price when it takes delivery in two months. The additional identifiable costs to rework the machinery to Kaytell's specifications are as follows:

Direct materials	$ 6,200
Direct labor	4,200
Total	$10,400

A second alternative available to Auerbach is to convert the special machinery to the standard model, which sells for $62,500. The additional identifiable costs for this conversion are as follows:

Direct materials	$2,850
Direct labor	3,300
Total	$6,150

A third alternative for Auerbach is to sell the machine as is for a price of $52,000. However, the potential buyer of the unmodified machine does not want it for 60 days. This buyer has offered a $7,000 down payment, with the remainder due upon delivery.

The following additional information is available regarding Auerbach's operations.

1. The sales commission rate on sales of standard models is 2 percent, while the rate on special orders is 3 percent.

2. Normal credit terms for sales of standard models are 2/10, net/30. This means that a customer receives a 2 percent discount if payment is made within 10 days, and payment is due no later than 30 days after billing. Most customers take the 2 percent discount. Credit terms for a special order are negotiated with the customer.

3. The allocation rates for manufacturing overhead and fixed selling and administrative costs are as follows:

Manufacturing costs:	
Variable	50% of direct-labor cost
Fixed	25% of direct-labor cost
Fixed selling and administrative costs	10% of the total of direct-material, direct-labor, and manufacturing-overhead costs

4. Normal time required for rework is one month.

Required:

1. Determine the dollar contribution each of the three alternatives will add to Auerbach's before-tax profit.
2. If Kaytell makes Auerbach a counteroffer, what is the lowest price Auerbach should accept for the reworked machinery from Kaytell? Explain your answer.
3. Discuss the influence fixed manufacturing-overhead cost should have on the sales price quoted by Auerbach Company for special orders.

(CMA, adapted)

■ **Problem 14–53**
Special Order; Ethics
(LO 3, LO 4, LO 5)

Victory Corporation manufactures medals for winners of athletic events and other contests. Its manufacturing plant has the capacity to produce 10,000 medals each month. Current monthly production is 7,500 medals. The company normally charges $175 per medal. Variable costs and fixed costs for the current activity level of 75 percent of capacity are as follows:

Production Costs

Variable costs:	
Manufacturing:	
Direct labor	$ 375,000
Direct material	262,500
Marketing	187,500
Total variable costs	$ 825,000
Fixed costs:	
Manufacturing	$ 275,000
Marketing	175,000
Total fixed costs	$ 450,000
Total costs	$1,275,000
Variable cost per unit	$110
Fixed cost per unit	60
Average unit cost	$170

Victory has just received a special one-time order for 2,500 medals at $100 per medal. For this particular order, no variable marketing costs will be incurred. Cathy Senna, a management accountant with Victory, has been assigned the task of analyzing this order and recommending whether the company should accept or reject it. After examining the costs Senna suggested to her supervisor, Gerard LePenn, who is the controller, that they request competitive bids from vendors for the raw material as the current quote seems high. LePenn insisted that the prices are in line with other vendors and told her that she was not to discuss her observations with anyone else. Senna later discovered that LePenn is a brother-in-law of the owner of the current raw-material supply vendor.

Required:

1. Identify and explain the costs that will be relevant to Cathy Senna's analysis of the special order being considered by Victory Corporation.
2. Determine if Victory should accept the special order. In explaining your answer, compute both the new average unit cost for Victory and the incremental unit cost for the special order.
3. Discuss any other considerations that Senna should include in her analysis of the special order.
4. What steps could Senna take to resolve the ethical conflict arising out of the controller's insistence that the company avoid competitive bidding?

(CMA, adapted)

■ **Problem 14–54**
Analysis of Production
Alternatives; Ethics
(LO 4, LO 5, LO 6)

Olentangy Toy Company manufactures and distributes dollhouses. The toy industry is a seasonal business; most sales occur in late summer and fall.

The projected sales in units for the year 20x0 are shown in the following schedule. With a sales price of $10 per unit, the total sales revenue for 20x0 is projected at $1.2 million. Management schedules production so that finished-goods inventory at the end of each month, exclusive of a safety stock of 4,000 dollhouses, should equal the next month's sales. One-half hour of direct-labor time normally is required to produce each dollhouse. Using the production schedule followed in the past, the total direct-labor hours by month required to meet the 20x0 sales estimate are also shown in the schedule.

OLENTANGY TOY COMPANY
Projected Sales and Planned Production
For the Year Ending December 31, 20x0

	Projected Sales (in units)		Direct-Labor Hours Required*
January	8,000		4,000
February	8,000		4,000
March	8,000		4,000
April	8,000		4,000
May	8,000		5,000
June	10,000		6,000
July	12,000		6,000
August	12,000		6,500
September	13,000		6,500
October	13,000		6,000
November	12,000		4,000
December	8,000		4,000†
Total	120,000 units		60,000 hours

*This schedule does not incorporate any additional direct-labor hours resulting from inefficiencies.

†Sales for January, 20x1 are projected to be 8,000 units.

The production schedule followed in the past requires scheduling overtime hours for any production over 8,000 units (4,000 direct-labor hours) in one month. While the use of overtime is feasible, management has decided to consider two other possible alternatives: (1) hire temporary help from an agency during peak months, or (2) expand its labor force and adopt a level production schedule.

Factory employees are paid $12.00 per hour for regular time; the fringe benefits average 20 percent of regular pay. For hours worked in excess of 4,000 hours per month, employees receive time and one-half; however, fringe benefits only average 10 percent on these additional wages. Past experience has shown that labor inefficiencies occur during overtime at the rate of 5 percent of overtime hours; this 5 percent inefficiency was not included in the direct-labor hour estimates presented in the schedule.

Rather than pay overtime to its regular labor force, the company could hire temporary employees when production exceeds 8,000 units per month. The temporary workers can be hired at the same labor rate of $12.00 per hour, but there would be no fringe-benefit costs. Management estimates that the temporary workers would require 25 percent more time than the regular employees (on regular daytime hours) to produce the dollhouses.

If Olentangy Toy Company adopts a level production schedule, the labor force would be expanded. However, no overtime would be required. The same labor rate of $12.00 per hour and fringe-benefit rate of 20 percent would apply.

The manufacturing facilities have the capacity to produce 18,000 dollhouses per month. On-site storage facilities for completed units are adequate. The estimated annual cost of carrying inventory is $1 per unit. The company is subject to a 40 percent income-tax rate.

Required:

1. Prepare an analysis comparing the costs associated with each of Olentangy Toy Company's three alternatives:

   a. Schedule overtime hours

   b. Hire temporary workers

   c. Expand the labor force and schedule level production

2. Identify and discuss briefly the non-cost factors and the factors that are difficult to estimate, which management should consider in conjunction with the cost analysis prepared in requirement (1).

3. Independent of your answer to requirement (1), suppose Olengtangy's controller, Caroline White, has finished an analysis showing that using overtime is the most costly of the three alternatives.

Before presenting her analysis to top management, White got a phone call from Bob Davies, who is the production manager and a close friend. "Caroline, according to the grapevine, you're going to recommend against overtime as a way of meeting next year's production requirements."

"That's the way the figures line up, Bob," responded White.

"Caroline, the people on the production line need that overtime. They're counting on it. It's been a rough year for many of them. Couldn't you slant things just a bit so that the top brass will stick to the overtime plan like we've always done in the past?"

Discuss the ethical issues in this situation. What should the controller do? What should the production manager do?

(CMA, adapted)

■ **Problem 14–55**
Cost Analysis of Alternative Vendors; Ethics
(LO 4, LO 5)

"It's nice to have supply options, but I'm going bananas trying to sort out these slit steel bids," exclaimed Carol Lane, purchasing manager for Sarbec Company. "I see what you mean," responded Jack Martin, Lane's assistant. "Let me call my friend over in the controller's office. He'll have some suggestions for us."

Sarbec Company needs a total of 125 tons of sheet steel, 50 tons of 2-inch width and 75 tons of 4-inch width, for a customer's job. Sarbec can purchase the sheet steel in these widths directly from Jensteel Corporation, a steel manufacturer, or it can purchase sheet steel from Jensteel that is 24 inches wide and have it slit into the desired widths by Precut, Inc. Both vendors are local and have previously supplied materials to Sarbec.

Precut specializes in slitting steel that is provided by a customer into any desired width. When negotiating a contract, Precut tells its customers that there is a scrap loss in the slitting operation, but that this loss has never exceeded 2.5 percent of input tons. Precut recommends that if a customer has a specific tonnage requirement, it should supply an adequate amount of steel to yield the desired quantity. Precut's charges for steel slitting are based on good output, not input handled.

The 24-inch wide sheet steel is a regular stock item of Jensteel and can be shipped to Precut within five days after receipt of Sarbec's purchase order. If Jensteel is to do the slitting, shipment to Sarbec would be scheduled for 15 days after receipt of the order. Precut has quoted delivery at 10 days after receipt of the sheet steel. In prior dealings, Sarbec has found both Jensteel and Precut to be reliable vendors with high-quality products.

Sarbec has received the following price quotations from Jensteel and Precut.

Jensteel Corporation Rates			
Size	**Gauge**	**Quantity**	**Cost per Ton**
2"	14	50 tons	$210
4"	14	75 tons	200
24"	14	125 tons	180

Precut Inc. Steel Slitting Rates			
Size	**Gauge**	**Quantity**	**Price per Ton of Output**
2"	14	50 tons	$18.00
4"	14	75 tons	15.00

Freight and Handling Charges	
Destination	**Cost per Ton**
Jensteel to Sarbec	$10.00
Jensteel to Precut	5.00
Precut to Sarbec	7.50

In addition to the above information, Precut has informed Sarbec that if it purchases 100 output tons of each width, the per ton slitting rates would be reduced by 12 percent. Sarbec knows that the same customer will be placing a new order in the near future for the same material and estimates it would have to store the additional tonnage for an average of two months at a carrying cost of $1.50 per month for each ton. There would be no change in Jensteel's prices for additional tons delivered to Precut.

As Martin's friend in the controller's office, you just received a phone call for help.

Required:

1. Prepare an analysis to determine whether Sarbec Company should:

   a. Purchase the required slit steel directly from Jensteel Corporation.

   b. Purchase the 24-inch wide sheet steel from Jensteel and have it slit by Precut Inc. into 50 output tons 2 inches wide and 75 output tons 4 inches wide.

   c. Take advantage of Precut's reduced slitting rates by purchasing 100 output tons of each width.

   Round all cost figures to the nearest cent. (Hint: You may wish to review the material on page 402 concerning the calculation of input requirements.)

2. Independent of your answer to requirement (1), present three qualitative arguments why Sarbec Company may favor the purchase of the slit steel directly from Jensteel Corporation.

3. Independent of your answer to requirements (1) and (2), suppose Carol Lane's final analysis shows that purchasing slit steel directly from Jensteel is Sarbec's least costly alternative. Before making her decision, Lane receives a call from a good friend, who is the production manager at Precut, Inc. Her friend has called to urge Lane to use Precut's services. "We're really hurting here at Precut, Carol," her friend insists. "If we don't get this job, it's going to be a long cold winter for some of us." Discuss Carol Lane's ethical obligations in this matter.

(CMA, adapted)

Catskill Industries manufactures and sells three products, which are manufactured in a factory with four departments. Both labor and machine time are applied to the products as they pass through each department. The machines and labor skills required in each department are so specialized that neither machines nor labor can be switched from one department to another.

Catskill Industries' management is planning its production schedule for the next few months. The planning is complicated, because there are labor shortages in the community and some machines will be down several months for repairs.

Management has assembled the following information regarding available machine and labor time by department and the machine hours and direct-labor hours required per unit of product. These data should be valid for the next six months.

■ Problem 14–56
Production Planning
(LO 5, LO 6)

	Department			
Monthly Capacity Availability	**1**	**2**	**3**	**4**
Normal machine capacity in machine hours	3,500	3,500	3,000	3,500
Capacity of machines being repaired in machine hours	(500)	(400)	(300)	(200)
Available machine capacity in machine hours	3,000	3,100	2,700	3,300
Available labor in direct-labor hours	3,700	4,500	2,750	2,600

Labor and Machine Specifications per Unit of Product

Product	Labor and Machine Time				
401	Direct-labor hours	2	3	3	1
	Machine hours	1	1	2	2
403	Direct-labor hours	1	2	—	2
	Machine hours	1	1	—	2
405	Direct-labor hours	2	2	2	1
	Machine hours	2	2	1	1

The sales department believes that the monthly demand for the next six months will be as follows:

Product	Monthly Unit Sales
401	500
403	400
405	1,000

Inventory levels are satisfactory and need not be increased or decreased during the next six months. Unit price and cost data that will be valid for the next six months are as follows:

	Product		
	401	**403**	**405**
Unit costs:			
Direct material	$ 7	$ 13	$ 17
Direct labor:			
Department 1	12	6	12
Department 2	21	14	14
Department 3	24	—	16
Department 4	9	18	9
Variable overhead	27	20	25
Fixed overhead	15	10	32
Variable selling expenses	3	2	4
Unit selling price	$196	$123	$167

Required:

1. Calculate the monthly requirement for machine hours and direct-labor hours for the production of products 401, 403, and 405 to determine whether the monthly sales demand for the three products can be met by the factory.

2. What monthly production schedule should Catskill Industries select in order to maximize its dollar profits? Explain how you selected this production schedule, and present a schedule of the contribution to profit that would be generated by your production schedule.

3. Identify the alternatives Catskill Industries might consider so it can supply its customers with all the product they demand.

(CMA, adapted)

■ **Problem 14–57**
Outsourcing Decision;
Direct-Labor Learning Curve
(LO 4, LO 5)

Henderson Equipment Company has produced a pilot run of 50 units of a recently developed cylinder used in its finished products. The company expects to produce and sell 800 units. The pilot run required 14.25 direct-labor hours for the 50 cylinders, averaging .285 direct-labor hours per cylinder. Henderson has experienced a significant learning curve on the direct-labor hours needed to produce new cylinders. As cumulative output doubles, say from 25 to 50 units for example, the average labor time per unit declines by 20 percent. Past experience indicates that learning tends to cease by the time 800 parts are produced. Henderson's manufacturing costs for cylinders are as follows:

Direct labor	$12.00 per hour
Variable overhead	10.00 per direct-labor hour
Fixed overhead	16.60 per direct-labor hour
Direct material	4.05 per unit

Henderson has received a quote of $7.50 per unit from the Lytel Machine Company for the additional 750 cylinders needed. Henderson frequently subcontracts this type of work and has always been satisfied with the quality of the units produced by Lytel. Recently, Henderson Equipment Company has been operating at considerably less than full capacity.

Required:

Before you begin these requirements, you may wish to review the material on learning curves on pages 263 and 264.

1. If the cylinders are manufactured by Henderson Equipment Company, determine:
   a. The average direct-labor hours per unit for 800 cylinders (including the pilot run). Round calculations to three decimal places.
   b. The total direct-labor hours for 800 cylinders (including the pilot run).

2. Calculate the incremental cost for Henderson to produce the 800 cylinders required (including the pilot run).

3. In order to maximize profits, determine whether Henderson Equipment Company should manufacture the cylinders or purchase them from Lytel Machine Company.

(CMA, adapted)

Video Recreation Inc. (VRI) is a supplier of video games and video equipment such as large-screen televisions and videocassette recorders. The company has recently concluded a major contract with Sunview Hotels to supply games for the hotel video lounges. Under this contract, a total of 4,000 games will be delivered to Sunview Hotels throughout the western United States, and all of the games will have a warranty period of one year for both parts and labor. The number of service calls required to repair these games during the first year after installation is estimated as follows:

■ **Problem 14–58**
Quality Costs; Minimizing
Warranty Costs; Probabilities
and Expected Values
(LO 5)

Service Calls	Probability
400	.1
700	.3
900	.4
1,200	.2

VRI's Customer Service Department has developed three alternatives for providing the warranty service to Sunview.

Plan 1. VRI would contract with local firms to perform the repair services. It is estimated that six such vendors would be needed to cover the appropriate areas and that each of these vendors would charge an annual fee of $15,000 to have personnel available and to stock the appropriate parts. In addition to the annual fee, VRI would be billed $250 for each service call and would be billed for parts used at cost plus a 10 percent surcharge.

Plan 2. VRI would allow the management of each hotel to arrange for repair service when needed and then would reimburse the hotel for the expenses incurred. It is estimated that 60 percent of the service calls would be for hotels located in urban areas where the charge for a service call would average $450. At the remaining hotels, the charge would be $350. In addition to these service charges, parts would be billed at cost.

Plan 3. VRI would hire its own personnel to perform repair services and to do preventive maintenance. Nine employees, located in the appropriate geographical areas, would be required to fulfill these responsibilities, and their average salary would be $24,000 annually. The fringe benefit expense for these employees would amount to 35 percent of their wages. Each employee would be scheduled to make an average of 200 preventive maintenance calls during the year. Each of these calls would require $15 worth of parts. Because of this preventive maintenance, it is estimated that the expected number of hotel calls for repair service would decline 30 percent and the cost of parts required for each repair service would be reduced by 20 percent.

VRI's Accounting Department has reviewed the historical data on repair costs for equipment installations similar to those proposed for Sunview Hotels and found that the cost of parts required for each repair occurred in the following proportions.

Parts Cost per Repair	Proportion
$30	15%
40	15
60	45
90	25

These proportions are expected to be valid regardless of how many service calls occur.

Required:

Video Recreation Inc. wishes to select the least-cost alternative to fulfill its warranty obligations to Sunview Hotels. Recommend which of the three plans should be adopted by VRI. Support your recommendation with appropriate calculations and analysis. (Hint: Begin by computing the expected value of the number of service calls and the expected value of the parts cost.)

(CMA, adapted)

■ **Problem 14–59**
Conventional versus Activity-
Based-Costing Analyses;
Relevant Costs
(LO 5, LO 7)

In addition to fine chocolate, International Chocolate Company also produces chocolate covered pretzels in its Savannah plant. This product is sold in five-pound metal canisters, which also are manufactured at the Savannah facility. The plant manager, Marsha Mello, was recently approached by Catawba Canister Company with an offer to supply the canisters at a price of $1.00 each. International Chocolate's traditional product-costing system assigns the following costs to canister production.

Direct material	$ 300,000
Direct labor (12,000 hrs. at $15 per hr.)	180,000
Variable overhead ($10 per direct-labor hr.)	120,000
Fixed overhead ($45 per direct-labor hr.)	540,000
Total cost	$1,140,000

Unit costs: $1,140,000 ÷ 760,000 canisters = $1.50 per canister

Mello's conventional make-or-buy analysis indicated that Catawba's offer should be rejected, since only $708,000 of costs would be avoided (including $80,000 of supervisory salaries and $28,000 of machinery depreciation). In contrast, the firm would spend $760,000 buying the canisters. The controller, Dave Mint, came to the rescue with an activity-based costing analysis of the decision. Mint concluded that the cost driver levels associated with canister production are as follows:

10 product specs	30 inspections
2,000 supervisory hours	15 setups
6,000 material-handling hours	70,000 machine hours
55 purchase orders	

Additional conventional and ABC data from the Savannah plant are given in Exhibits 14–19 and 14–20.

Required:

1. Show how Mello arrived at the $708,000 of cost savings in her conventional make-or-buy analysis.
2. Determine the costs that will be saved by purchasing canisters, using Mint's ABC data.
3. Complete the ABC relevant-costing analysis of the make-or-buy decision. Should the firm buy from Catawba?
4. If the conventional and ABC analyses yield different conclusions, briefly explain why.

■ **Problem 14–60**
Linear Programming,
Formulate and Solve
Graphically (Appendix)
(LO 8)

Cleveland Cable Company manufactures metal cable for use in the construction industry. The firm has two machines on which two different types of cable are produced. Price, cost, and production data are as follows:

	Steel Cable	Aluminum Cable
Selling price per reel	$1,150	$865
Variable cost per reel	$ 750	$365
Hours required per reel on machine A	5 hr	2 hr
Hours required per reel on machine B	5 hr	8 hr

The production supervisor has determined that there are 30 hours of excess capacity available on machine A and 40 excess hours available on machine B.

Required:

1. Formulate the production planning problem as a linear program to determine how many reels of steel cable and aluminum cable should be produced using the excess capacity. Partial reels may be manufactured and sold. For example, a half-reel of steel cable sells for $575.
2. Solve the linear programming problem graphically. (Hint: Use one-third of a reel as the unit of measure on each axis.)
3. What is the value of the objective function at the optimal solution?

Home Cooking Company offers monthly service plans providing prepared meals that are delivered to the customers' homes. The target market for these meal plans includes double-income families with no children and retired couples in upper income brackets. Home Cooking offers two monthly plans: Premier Cuisine and Haute Cuisine. The Premier Cuisine plan provides frozen meals that are delivered twice each month; this plan generates a contribution margin of $120 for each monthly plan sold. The Haute Cuisine plan provides freshly prepared meals delivered on a daily basis and generates a contribution margin of $90 for each monthly plan sold. Home Cooking's reputation provides the company with a market that will purchase all the meals that can be prepared. All meals go through food preparation and cooking steps in the company's kitchens. After these steps, the Premier Cuisine meals are flash frozen. The time requirements per monthly meal plan and hours available per month are as follows:

	Preparation	Cooking	Freezing
Hours required:			
Premier Cuisine	2	2	1
Haute Cuisine	1	3	0
Hours available	60	120	45

For planning purposes, Home Cooking uses linear programming to determine the most profitable number of Premier Cuisine and Haute Cuisine monthly meal plans to produce.

Required:

1. Using the notation P for Premier Cuisine and H for Haute Cuisine, state the objective function and the constraints that Home Cooking should use to maximize the total contribution margin generated by the monthly meal plans.
2. Graph the constraints on Home Cooking's meal preparation process. Be sure to clearly label the graph, including the optimal solution.
3. Using the graph prepared in requirement (2), determine the optimal solution to Home Cooking's production planning problem in terms of the number of each type of meal plan to produce.
4. Calculate the value of Home Cooking's objective function at the optimal solution.
5. If the constraint on preparation time could be eliminated, determine the revised optimal solution.

(CMA, adapted)

SmyCo manufactures two types of display boards sold to office supply stores. One board is a hard-finished marking board that can be written on with a water-soluble felt-tip marking pen and then wiped clean with a cloth. The other is a conventional cork-type tack board.

Both boards pass through two manufacturing departments. All of the raw materials—board base, board covering, and aluminum frames—are cut to size in the Cutting Department. Both types of boards are the same size and use the same aluminum frame. The boards are assembled in one of SmyCo's two assembly operations: the Automated Assembly Department or the Labor Assembly Department.

The Automated Assembly Department has been in operation for 18 months and was intended to replace the Labor Assembly Department. However, SmyCo's business expanded so rapidly that both assembly operations are needed and used. The final results of the two assembly operations are identical. The only difference between the two is the proportion of machine time versus direct labor in each department and, thus, different costs. However, workers have been trained for both operations so that they can be switched between the two operations.

Data regarding the two products and their manufacture are presented in the following schedules.

Sales Data

	Marking Board	Tack Board
Selling price per unit	$60.00	$45.00
Variable selling costs per unit	$3.00	$3.00
Annual fixed selling and administrative expenses (allocated equally between the two products)	$900,000	$900,000

■ **Problem 14–61**
Linear Programming
(Appendix)
(LO 8)

■ **Problem 14–62**
Linear Programming;
Formulate and Discuss
(Appendix)
(LO 8)

Unit Variable Manufacturing Costs

	Cutting Department		Labor Assembly Department*	Automated Assembly Department*
	Marking Board	Tack Board		
Raw materials:				
Base	$ 6.00	$6.00	—	—
Covering	14.50	7.75	—	—
Frame	8.25	8.25	—	—
Direct labor:				
at $10/hour	2.00	2.00	—	—
at $12/hour	—	—	$3.00	$ .60
Manufacturing overhead:				
Supplies	1.25	1.25	1.50	1.50
Power	1.20	1.20	.75	1.80

*The unit costs for the marking board and the tack board are the same within each of the two assembly departments.

Machine Hour Data

	Cutting Department	Labor Assembly Department	Automated Assembly Department
Machine hours required per board	.15	.02	.05
Monthly machine hours available	25,000	1,500	5,000
Annual machine hours available	300,000	18,000	60,000

SmyCo produced and sold 600,000 marking boards and 900,000 tack boards last year. Management estimates that the total units sales for the coming year could increase 20 percent if the units can be produced. SmyCo has contracts to produce and sell 30,000 units of each board each month. Sales, production, and cost incurrence are uniform throughout the year. SmyCo has a monthly maximum labor capacity of 30,000 direct-labor hours in the Cutting Department and 40,000 direct-labor hours for the assembly operations (Automated Assembly and Labor Assembly Departments combined).

Required:

1. SmyCo's management believes that linear programming could be used to determine the optimum mix of marking and tack board to produce and sell. Explain why linear programming can be used by SmyCo.

2. SmyCo plans to employ linear programming to determine its optimum production mix of marking and tack boards. Formulate and label the:

   a. Objective function.

   b. Constraints.

   Be sure to define your variables.

(CMA, adapted)

Cases

■ Case 14–63
Adding a Product Line
(LO 4, LO 5)

Dan Johnson, Sportway Corporation's production manager, had requested to have lunch with the company president. Johnson wanted to put forward his suggestion to add a new product line. As they finished lunch, Meg Thomas, the company president, said, "I'll give your proposal some serious thought, Dan. I think you're right about the increasing demand for skateboards. What I'm not sure about is whether the skateboard line will be better for us than our tackle boxes. Those have been our bread and butter the past few years."

Johnson responded with, "Let me get together with one of the controller's people. We'll run a few numbers on this skateboard idea that I think will demonstrate the line's potential."

Sportway is a wholesale distributor supplying a wide range of moderately priced sports equipment to large chain stores. About 60 percent of Sportway's products are purchased from other companies while the remainder of the products are manufactured by Sportway. The company has a Plastics Department that is currently manufacturing molded fishing tackle boxes. Sportway is able to manufacture and sell 8,000 tackle boxes annually, making full use of its direct-labor capacity at available work stations. The selling price and costs associated with Sportway's tackle boxes are as follows:

Selling price per box		$86.00
Costs per box:		
Molded plastic	$ 8.00	
Hinges, latches, handle	9.00	
Direct labor ($15.00 per hour)	18.75	
Manufacturing overhead	12.50	
Selling and administrative cost	17.00	65.25
Profit per box		$20.75

Because Sportway's sales manager believes the firm could sell 12,000 tackle boxes if it had sufficient manufacturing capacity, the company has looked into the possibility of purchasing the tackle boxes for distribution. Maple Products, a steady supplier of quality products, would be able to provide up to 9,000 tackle boxes per year at a price of $68.00 per box delivered to Sportway's facility.

Dan Johnson, Sportway's production manager, has come to the conclusion that the company could make better use of its Plastics Department by manufacturing skateboards. Johnson has a market study that indicates an expanding market for skateboards and a need for additional suppliers. Johnson believes that Sportway could expect to sell 17,500 skateboards annually at a price of $45.00 per skateboard.

After his lunch with the company president, Johnson worked out the following estimates with the assistant controller.

Selling price per skateboard		$45.00
Costs per skateboard:		
Molded plastic	$5.50	
Wheels, hardware	7.00	
Direct labor ($15.00 per hour)	7.50	
Manufacturing overhead	5.00	
Selling and administrative cost	9.00	34.00
Profit per skateboard		$11.00

In the Plastics Department, Sportway uses direct-labor hours as the application base for manufacturing overhead. Included in the manufacturing overhead for the current year is $50,000 of factorywide, fixed manufacturing overhead that has been allocated to the Plastics Department. For each unit of product that Sportway sells, regardless of whether the product has been purchased or is manufactured by Sportway, there is an allocated $6.00 fixed overhead cost per unit for distribution that is included in the selling and administrative cost for all products. Total selling and administrative costs for the purchased tackle boxes would be $10.00 per unit.

Required:

In order to maximize the company's profitability, prepare an analysis that will show which product or products Sportway Corporation should manufacture or purchase.

1. First determine which of Sportway's options makes the best use of its scarce resources. How many skateboards and tackle boxes should be manufactured? How many tackle boxes should be purchased?

2. Calculate the improvement in Sportway's total contribution margin if it adopts the optimal strategy rather than continuing with the status quo.

(CMA, adapted)

North Atlantic Sports Equipment Company manufactures four related product lines. The baseball equipment is manufactured in Evanston, Illinois, along with some football equipment, and all miscellaneous sports items. Only a few of the miscellaneous items are manufactured. The rest are purchased for resale and recorded as direct material in the cost records. A separate production line is used to manufacture each product line. The remainder of the football equipment is manufactured in Buffalo, New York. The hockey equipment is manufactured in Helsinki, Finland. The Helsinki plant had belonged to a small Finnish company, acquired two years ago by North Atlantic.

■ **Case 14–64**
Discontinue Product Line;
Ethics; International
(LO 4, LO 5)

The following product-line profit statement for the year ended December 31, 19x9 shows a loss for the baseball-equipment line. A similar loss is projected for the following year.

Product Line Profit for 19x9
(in thousands)

	Football Equipment	Baseball Equipment	Hockey Equipment	Miscellaneous Sports Items	Total
Sales	$2,200	$1,000	$1,500	$500	$5,200
Cost of goods sold:					
Direct material	$ 400	$ 175	$ 300	$ 90	$ 965
Direct labor and					
variable overhead	800	400	600	60	1,860
Fixed overhead	350	275	100	50	775
Total	$1,550	$ 850	$1,000	$200	$3,600
Gross profit	$ 650	$ 150	$ 500	$300	$1,600
Selling expense:					
Variable	$ 440	$ 200	$ 300	$100	$1,040
Fixed	100	50	100	50	300
Corporate administration					
expenses	48	24	36	12	120
Total	$ 588	$ 274	$ 436	$162	$1,460
Contribution to corporation	$ 62	$ (124)	$ 64	$138	$ 140

The following schedule presents the costs incurred at the Evanston plant in 19x9. Inventories at the end of the year were identical to those at the beginning of the year.

Evanston Plant Costs for 19x9
(in thousands)

	Football Equipment	Baseball Equipment	Miscellaneous Sports Items	Total
Direct material	$100	$175	$ 90	$ 365
Direct labor	$100	$200	$ 30	$ 330
Variable overhead:				
Supplies	$ 85	$ 60	$ 12	$ 157
Power	50	110	7	167
Other	15	30	11	56
Subtotal	$150	$200	$ 30	$ 380
Fixed overhead:				
Supervision*	$ 25	$ 30	$ 21	$ 76
Depreciation†	40	115	14	169
Plant rentals‡	35	105	10	150
Other§	20	25	5	50
Subtotal	$120	$275	$ 50	$ 445
Total costs	$470	$850	$200	$1,520

*The supervision costs represent salary and benefit costs of the supervisors in charge of each product line.

†Depreciation cost for machinery and equipment is charged to the product line on which the machinery is used.

‡The plant is leased. The lease rentals are charged to the product lines on the basis of square feet occupied.

§Other fixed-overhead costs are the cost of plant administration and are allocated by management discretion.

Management has asked the controller, Jack Martin, to do a profitability study of the baseball-equipment line to determine if the line should be discontinued. Martin has developed the following additional data to be used in the study.

1. If the baseball equipment line is discontinued, the company will lose approximately 10 percent of its sales in each of the other lines.

2. The plant space now occupied by the baseball-equipment line could be closed off from the rest of the plant and rented for $175,000 per year.

3. If the line is discontinued, the manager of the baseball-equipment line will be released. In keeping with company policy, he would receive severance pay of $5,000.

4. The company has been able to invest excess funds at 10 percent per year.

Required:

1. Should the company discontinue the baseball-equipment line? Support your answer with appropriate calculations and qualitative arguments.

2. Independent of your answer to requirement (1), suppose Jack Martin has completed an analysis showing that the baseball line should be dropped. Before presenting his analysis to top management, Martin showed his analysis to his friend, the baseball equipment production manager. After looking over the numbers, Martin's friend pressured him to alter his analysis. "If you send that report up to top management, Jack, I'm out of a job. I'm 55 years old. It's too late for this old dog to learn any new tricks. If we have to drop a product line, let's make it the hockey equipment. We have no obligation to those people in Europe."

Discuss Martin's ethical responsibilities in this situation.

(CMA, adapted)

Genung Corporation, a small manufacturing company in Toronto, Ontario, produces D-gauges, P-gauges, and T-gauges. For many years the company has been profitable and has operated at capacity. However, in the last two years prices on all gauges were reduced and selling expenses increased to meet competition and keep the plant operating at capacity. Third-quarter results for the current year, which follow, typify recent experience.

■ **Case 14–65**
Drop a Product Line
(LO 4, LO 5)

GENUNG CORPORATION
Income Statement
Third Quarter
(in thousands)

	D-Gauge	P-Gauge	T-Gauge	Total
Sales	$900	$1,600	$ 900	$3,400
Cost of goods sold	770	1,048	950	2,768
Gross margin	$130	$ 552	$ (50)	$ 632
Selling and administrative expenses	185	370	135	690
Income before taxes	$ (55)	$ 182	$(185)	$ (58)

Diane Carlo, Genung's president, is concerned about the results of the pricing, selling, and production prices. After reviewing the third-quarter results she asked her management staff to consider the following three suggestions:

■ Discontinue the T-gauge line immediately. T-gauges would not be returned to the product line unless the problems with the gauge can be identified and resolved.

■ Increase quarterly sales promotion by $100,000 on the P-gauge product line in order to increase sales volume by 15 percent.

■ Cut production on the D-gauge line by 50 percent, and cut the traceable advertising and promotion for this line to $20,000 each quarter.

George Sperry, the controller, suggested a more careful study of the financial relationships to determine the possible effects on the company's operating results of the president's proposed course of action. The president agreed and assigned JoAnn Brower, the assistant controller, to prepare an analysis. Brower has gathered the following information.

■ All three gauges are manufactured with common equipment and facilities.

■ The selling and administrative expense is allocated to the three gauge lines based on average sales volume over the past three years.

■ Special selling expenses (primarily advertising, promotion, and shipping) are incurred for each gauge as follows:

	Quarterly Advertising and Promotion	Shipping Expense
D-gauge	$100,000	$ 4 per unit
P-gauge	210,000	10 per unit
T-gauge	40,000	10 per unit

■ The unit manufacturing costs for the three products are as follows:

	D-Gauge	P-Gauge	T-Gauge
Raw material	$17	$ 31	$ 50
Direct labor	20	40	60
Variable manufacturing overhead	30	45	60
Fixed manufacturing overhead	10	15	20
Total	$77	$131	$190

■ The unit sales prices for the three products are as follows:

D-gauge	$ 90
P-gauge	200
T-gauge	180

■ The company is manufacturing at capacity and is selling all the gauges it produces.

Required:

1. JoAnn Brower says that Genung Corporation's product-line income statement for the third quarter is not suitable for analyzing proposals and making decisions such as the ones suggested by Diane Carlo. Write a memo to Genung's president that addresses the following points.

   a. Explain why the product-line income statement as presented is not suitable for analysis and decision making.

   b. Describe an alternative income-statement format that would be more suitable for analysis and decision making, and explain why it is better.

2. Use the operating data presented for Genung Corporation and assume that the president's proposed course of action had been implemented at the beginning of the third quarter. Then evaluate the president's proposal by specifically responding to the following points.

   a. Are each of the three suggestions cost-effective? Support your discussion with an analysis that shows the net impact on income before taxes for each of the three suggestions.

   b. Was the president correct in proposing that the T-gauge line be eliminated? Explain your answer.

   c. Was the president correct in promoting the P-gauge line rather than the D-gauge line? Explain your answer.

   d. Does the proposed course of action make effective use of Genung's capacity? Explain your answer.

3. Are there any qualitative factors that Genung Corporation's management should consider before it drops the T-gauge line? Explain your answer.

(CMA, adapted)

Current Issues in Managerial Accounting

"Many Firms Refuse to Pay for Overtime, Employees Complain," *The Wall Street Journal,* **June 24, 1996, Zachary Pascal.**

Overview

The U.S. Labor Department estimated that two-thirds of all workers have a right to overtime pay. Private sector research studies assume that 10 percent of these workers actually get paid for overtime.

Suggested Discussion Questions

Is overtime a differential cost? Sunk cost? Relevant cost? Does the nature of the cost explain why some employers do not want to pay overtime? How can an employer eliminate overtime and at the same time avoid other types of cost increases?

■ **Issue 14–66**
Identify Relevant Costs and Benefits

"The Last Thing the IRS Needs Is More Business," *Business Week,* **September 15, 1997.**

Overview

Proposals to revise the Internal Revenue Service include privatization of tax collection and computer systems redesign.

Suggested Discussion Questions

In groups, discuss what quantitative and qualitative factors the Internal Revenue Service (IRS) should consider when deciding whether to outsource tax collection. List some of your items on the board. Which factors are most important? What is the single most important factor?

■ **Issue 14–67**
Analysis of Special Decisions; Outsource a Product or Service

"Airlines to Use More Outside Maintenance," *The Wall Street Journal,* **June 19, 1996.**

Overview

Most of the major airlines outsource a portion of their maintenance requirements. This trend began after U.S. airline deregulation, which created price competition.

Suggested Discussion Questions

Discuss what types of airline maintenance costs should be outsourced? Does your answer depend on the investment required to maintain the aircraft? What are the relevant costs and benefits of outsourcing maintenance?

■ **Issue 14–68**
Analysis of Special Decisions; Outsource a Product or Service

"How to Survive a Downturn," *Business Week,* **April 28, 1997.**

Overview

According to this article, companies that effectively manage cash flow, accounts receivable, costs, and debt are the most likely to survive an economic downturn.

Suggested Discussion Questions

The article describes ways to survive an economic downturn. One of the techniques discussed is outsourcing. How would outsourcing help a firm survive a downturn? Provide at least three examples.

■ **Issue 14–69**
Analysis of Special Decisions

"T&E Expense: To Outsource or Not?" *Management Accounting,* **September 1997, Shimon Avish.**

Overview

This article outlines factors that should be considered in deciding whether or not to outsource a travel expenditures program.

Suggested Discussion Questions

List the costs and benefits of outsourcing an expense reimbursement system. Should this process be manual or automated? Suggest methods for evaluating whether the investment in an automated system is worthwhile.

■ **Issue 14–70**
Analysis of Special Decisions; Outsource a Product or Service

"NASA Plans to Shift Work to Private Firms in Cost-Cutting Effort," *The Wall Street Journal,* **May 25, 1995.**

Overview

NASA plans to cut costs by privatizing part of its operations. Privatization could save the space agency $1 billion over a five-year period.

Suggested Discussion Questions

As a group, write a letter to a member of Congress that explains the advantages and disadvantages of privatizing rocket launches. Include in your memo a list of the relevant costs and benefits. What nonfinancial factors should be considered? What are some alternatives to privatization?

■ **Issue 14–71**
Analysis of Special Decisions; Outsource a Product or Service

Chapter Fifteen

Cost Analysis and Pricing Decisions

After completing this chapter, you should be able to:

1 List and describe the four major influences on pricing decisions.

2 Explain and use the economic, profit-maximizing pricing model.

3 Set prices using cost-plus pricing formulas.

4 Determine prices using the time and material pricing approach.

5 Set prices in special-order or competitive-bidding situations by analyzing the relevant costs.

6 Discuss the issues involved in the strategic pricing of new products.

7 Explain the role of activity-based costing in setting a target cost.

8 Explain how product-cost distortion can undermine a firm's pricing strategy.

9 Describe the legal restrictions on setting prices.

LOCAL SAILBOAT MANUFACTURER SAILS TO RECORD PROFITS

Sydney, Australia—Sydney Sailing Supplies yesterday announced record earnings for the fiscal year just ended. Despite ups and downs in the Australian economy, Sydney Sailing continues to show solid financial performance year in and year out. Headquartered in Sydney, the company manufactures a range of sailboats, sailing supplies, and related equipment. The company also has a Marine Construction Division specializing in building and refurbishing marinas, docks, and seawalls.

In his annual media interview, President Winston Darrough III praised the firm's managerial staff and rank-and-file workers for continuing the company's string of profitable years. "We've been blessed with top-notch people here at Sydney Sailing," said Mr. Darrough. "I believe we've set a very sensible course for the company. We have very carefully developed our product mix, so that we're in just the right markets. Some recreational marine markets—like personal water craft—are tough as nails. We've steered clear of those. And as for the markets we are in, we produce a quality product, which is priced just right to maximize profitability. Pricing is a sticky wicket, you know. You've got to keep an eye on your costs as well as your competitors. The competition will always be driving your price down, you see, and you've got to respond. You can't sell the same product for more than the other bloke does. But at the same time, you've got to cover your costs. Nobody can indefinitely sell their products at less than their costs. Just doesn't work that way. And new markets are the trickiest of all. For new products, we use a target costing approach. We estimate what we think consumers will pay for a new product, and then we back out the cost that we have to hit in order to sell at that price. That's where our design engineers come into play, and we've got some good ones."

Asked if Sydney Sailing would be introducing any new products this year, Darrough was evasive. "Can't tip our hand just yet, good fellow. Now, if you'll excuse me, I've got a business to run. G'day."

Setting the price for an organization's product or service is one of the most important decisions a manager faces. It is also one of the most difficult, due to the number and variety of factors that must be considered. The pricing decision arises in virtually all types of organizations. Manufacturers set prices for the products they manufacture; merchandising companies set prices for their goods; service firms set prices for such services as insurance policies, train tickets, theme park admissions, and bank loans. Nonprofit organizations often set prices also. For example, governmental units price vehicle registrations, park-use fees, and utility services. The optimal approach to pricing often depends on the situation. Pricing a mature product or service which a firm has sold for a long time may be quite different from pricing a new product or service. Public utilities and TV cable companies face political considerations in pricing their products and services, since their prices often must be approved by a governmental commission.

In this chapter, we will study pricing decisions, with an emphasis on the role of managerial accounting information. The setting for our discussion is Sydney Sailing Supplies, a manufacturer of sailing supplies and equipment located in Sydney, Australia.

Major Influences on Pricing Decisions

Four major influences govern the prices set by Sydney Sailing Supplies:

1. Customer demand.
2. Actions of competitors.
3. Costs.
4. Political, legal, and image-related issues.

LO 1   List and describe the four major influences on pricing decisions.

Customer Demand

The demands of customers are of paramount importance in all phases of business operations, from the design of a product to the setting of its price. Product-design issues and pricing considerations are interrelated, so they must be examined simultaneously. For example, if customers want a high-quality sailboat, this will entail greater production time and more expensive raw materials. The result almost certainly will be a higher price. On the other hand, management must be careful not to price its product out of the market. Discerning customer demand is a critically important and continuous process. Companies routinely obtain information from market research, such as customer surveys and test-marketing campaigns, and through feedback from sales personnel. To be successful, Sydney Sailing Supplies must provide the products its customers want at a price they perceive to be appropriate.

Actions of Competitors

Although Sydney Sailing Supplies' managers would like the company to have the sailing market to itself, they are not so fortunate. Domestic and foreign competitors are striving to sell their products to the same customers. Thus, as Sydney Sailing Supplies' management designs products and sets prices, it must keep a watchful eye on the firm's competitors. If a competitor reduces its price on sails of a particular type, Sydney Sailing Supplies may have to follow suit to avoid losing its market share. Yet the company cannot follow its competitors blindly either. Predicting competitive reactions to its product-design and pricing strategy is a difficult but important task for Sydney Sailing Supplies' management.

In considering the reactions of customers and competitors, management must be careful to properly define its product. Should Sydney Sailing Supplies' management define its product narrowly as sailing supplies, or more broadly as boating supplies? For example, if the company raises the price of its two-person sailboat, will this encourage potential customers to switch to canoes, rowboats, and small motorboats? Or will most potential sailboat customers react to a price increase only by price-shopping among competing sailboat manufacturers? The way in which Sydney Sailing Supplies' management answers these questions can profoundly affect its marketing and pricing strategies.

Costs

The role of costs in price setting varies widely among industries. In some industries, prices are determined almost entirely by market forces. An example is the agricultural industry, where grain and meat prices are market-driven. Farmers must meet the market price. To make a profit, they must produce at a cost below the market price. This is not always possible, so some periods of loss inevitably result. In other industries, managers set prices at least partially on the basis of production costs. For example, cost-based pricing is used in the automobile, household appliance, and gasoline industries. Prices are set by adding a markup to production costs. Managers have some latitude in determining the markup, so market forces influence prices as well. In public utilities, such as electricity and natural gas companies, prices generally are set by a regulatory agency of the state government. Production costs are of prime importance in justifying utility rates. Typically, a public utility will make a request to the Public Utility Commission for a rate increase on the basis of its current and projected production costs.

Balance of Market Forces and Cost-Based Pricing   In most industries, both market forces and cost considerations heavily influence prices. No organization or industry can price its products below their production costs indefinitely. And no company's management can set prices blindly at cost plus a markup without keeping an eye on the market. In most cases, pricing can be viewed in either of the following ways.

How Are Prices Set?

Prices are determined by the market, subject to the constraint that costs must be covered in the long run.

Prices are based on costs, subject to the constraint that the reactions of customers and competitors must be heeded.

In our illustration of Sydney Sailing Supplies' pricing policies, we will assume the company responds to both market forces and costs.

Political, Legal, and Image-Related Issues

Beyond the important effects on prices of market forces and costs are a range of environmental considerations. In the *legal* area, managers must adhere to certain laws. The law generally prohibits companies from discriminating among their customers in setting prices. Also prohibited is collusion in price setting, where the major firms in an industry all agree to set their prices at high levels.

Political considerations also can be relevant. For example, if the firms in an industry are *perceived* by the public as reaping unfairly large profits, there may be political pressure on legislators to tax those profits differentially or to intervene in some way to regulate prices.

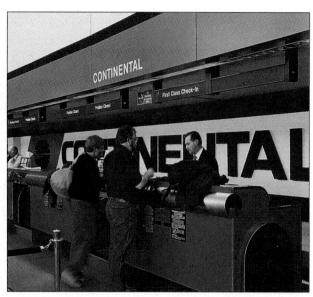

Setting prices requires a balance between cost considerations and market forces. A good example is provided by the airlines, which keep a close eye on the fares of their competitors, while striving to cover operating costs. As reported in The Wall Street Journal, *American, Continental, and Northwest recently engaged in a dispute over fare cuts.*

Companies also consider their *public image* in the price-setting process. A firm with a reputation for very high-quality products may set the price of a new product high to be consistent with its image. As we have all discovered, the same brand-name product may be available in a discount store at half the price charged in a more exclusive store.

Economic Profit-Maximizing Pricing

LO 2   Explain and use the economic, profit-maximizing pricing model.

Price takers are firms whose products or services are determined totally by the market.

The **total revenue curve** graphs the relationship between total sales revenue and quantity sold.

The **demand curve** is a graph of the relationship between sales price and the quantity of units sold.

The **marginal revenue curve** is a graph of the relationship between the change in total revenue and the quantity sold.

Companies are sometimes **price takers**, which means their products' prices are determined totally by the market. Some agricultural commodities and precious metals are examples of such products. In most cases, however, firms have some flexibility in setting prices. Generally speaking, as the price of a product or service is increased, the quantity demanded declines, and vice versa.

Total Revenue, Demand, and Marginal Revenue Curves

The trade-off between a higher price and a higher sales quantity can be shown in the shape of the firm's **total revenue curve,** which graphs the relationship between total sales revenue and quantity sold. Sydney Sailing Supplies' total revenue curve for its two-person sailboat, the Wave Darter, is displayed in Exhibit 15–1, panel A. The total revenue curve increases throughout its range, but the rate of increase declines as monthly sales quantity increases. To see this, notice that the increase in total revenue when the sales quantity increases from zero to *a* units is greater than the increase in total revenue when the sales quantity increases from *a* units to *b* units.

Closely related to the total revenue curve are two other curves, which are graphed in panel B of Exhibit 15–1. The **demand curve** shows the relationship between the sales price and the quantity of units demanded. The demand curve decreases throughout its range, because any decrease in the sale price brings about an increase in the monthly sales quantity. The demand curve is also called the **average revenue curve,** since it shows the average price at which any particular quantity can be sold.

The **marginal revenue curve** shows the *change* in total revenue that accompanies a *change* in the quantity sold. The marginal revenue curve is decreasing throughout its range to show that total revenue increases at a declining rate as monthly sales quantity increases.

A. Total Revenue Curve

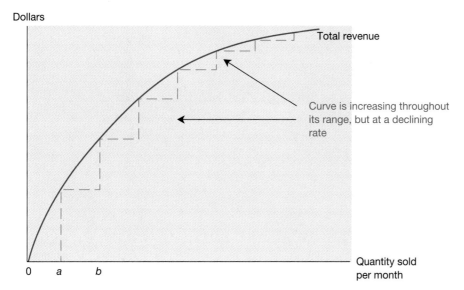

Exhibit 15–1

Total Revenue, Demand, and
Marginal Revenue Curves

B. Demand (or Average Revenue) Curve and Marginal Revenue Curve

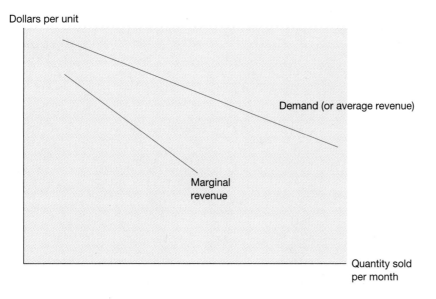

C. Tabulated Price, Quantity, and Revenue Data

Quantity Sold per Month	Unit Sales Price	Total Revenue per Month	Changes in Total Revenue
10	$1,000	$10,000	
			$9,500
20	975	19,500	
			9,000
30	950	28,500	
			8,500
40	925	37,000	
			8,000
50	900	45,000	
			7,500
60	875	52,500	

Related to demand curve

Related to total revenue curve

Related to marginal revenue curve

A. Total Cost Curve

B. Marginal Cost Curve

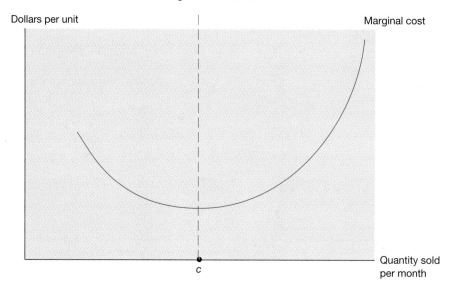

C. Tabulated Cost and Quantity Data

Quantity Produced and Sold per Month	Average Cost per Unit	Total Cost per Month	Changes in Total Cost
10	$1,920	$19,200	
			$5,600
20	1,240	24,800	
			4,300
30	970	29,100	
			2,900
40	800	32,000	
			9,000
50	820	41,000	
			15,400
60	940	56,400	

Related to total cost curve   Related to marginal cost curve

A tabular presentation of the price, quantity, and revenue data for Sydney Sailing Supplies is displayed in panel C of Exhibit 15–1. Study this table carefully to see how the data relate to the graphs shown in panels A and B of the exhibit. No matter what approach a manager takes to the pricing decision, a good understanding of the relationships shown in Exhibit 15–1 will lead to better decisions. Before we can fully use the revenue data, however, we must examine the cost side of Sydney Sailing Supplies' business.

Total Cost and Marginal Cost Curves

Understanding cost behavior is important in many business decisions, and pricing is no exception. How does total cost behave as the number of Wave Darters produced and sold by Sydney Sailing Supplies changes? Panel A of Exhibit 15–2 (previous page) displays the firm's **total cost curve,** which graphs the relationship between total cost and the quantity produced and sold each month.[1] Total cost increases throughout its range. The rate of increase in total cost declines as quantity increases from zero to c units. To verify this, notice that the increase in total costs when quantity increases from zero to a units is greater than the increase in total costs when quantity increases from a units to b units.

The rate of increase in total costs increases as quantity increases from c units upward. To verify this, notice that the increase in total costs as quantity increases from c units to d units is less than the increase in total costs as quantity increases from d units to e units.

Closely related to the total cost curve is the marginal cost curve, which is graphed in panel B of Exhibit 15–2. The **marginal cost curve** shows the change in total cost that accompanies a change in quantity produced and sold. Marginal cost declines as quantity increases from zero to c units; then it increases as quantity increases beyond c units.

A tabular presentation of the cost and quantity data for Sydney Sailing Supplies is displayed in panel C of Exhibit 15–2. Examine this table carefully, and trace the relationships between the data and the graphs shown in panels A and B of the exhibit.

Profit-Maximizing Price and Quantity

Now we have the tools we need to determine the profit-maximizing price and quantity. In Exhibit 15–3, we combine the revenue and cost data presented in Exhibits 15–1 and 15–2. Sydney Sailing Supplies' profit-maximizing sales quantity for the Wave Darter is determined by the intersection of the marginal cost and marginal revenue curves. (See panel B of Exhibit 15–3.) This optimal quantity is denoted by q^* on the graph. The profit-maximizing price, denoted by p^*, is determined from the demand curve for the quantity, q^*.

Examine the total revenue and total cost curves in panel A of Exhibit 15–3. At the profit-maximizing quantity (and price), the distance between these curves, which is equal to total profit, is maximized.

A tabular presentation of the revenue, cost, and profit data is shown in panel C of Exhibit 15–3. Notice that monthly profit is maximized when the price is set at $925 and 40 Wave Darters are produced and sold each month.

Price Elasticity

The impact of price changes on sales volume is called the **price elasticity.** Demand is *elastic* if a price increase has a large negative impact on sales volume, and vice versa.

The **total cost curve** graphs the relationship between total cost and the quantity produced and sold.

The **marginal cost curve** is a graph of the relationship between the change in total cost and the quantity produced and sold.

Price elasticity is the impact of price changes on sales volume.

---

[1] Notice that the demand and revenue curves are based on the quantity sold, while the cost curves are based on the quantity produced. We will assume for simplicity that Sydney Sailing Supplies' monthly sales and production quantities are the same. This assumption tends to be true in the pleasure boat industry.

Exhibit 15–3

Determining the Profit-
Maximizing Price and
Quantity

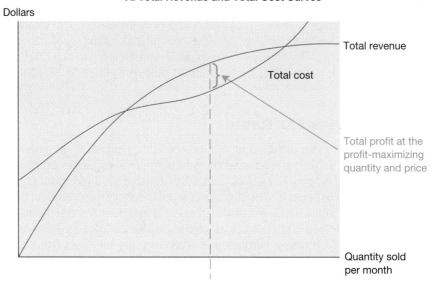

A. Total Revenue and Total Cost Curves

Dollars

Total revenue

Total cost

Total profit at the
profit-maximizing
quantity and price

Quantity sold
per month

B. Marginal Revenue and Marginal Cost Curves

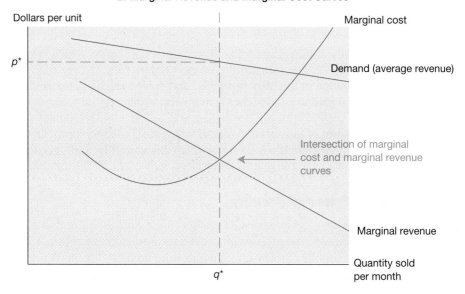

Dollars per unit

Marginal cost

p^*

Demand (average revenue)

Intersection of marginal
cost and marginal revenue
curves

Marginal revenue

Quantity sold
per month

q^*

C. Tabular Revenue, Cost, and Profit Data

Quantity Produced and Sold per Month		Unit Sales Price	Total Revenue per Month	Total Cost Per Month	Profit (Loss) per Month
10	. . . .	$1,000	$10,000	$19,200	$(9,200)
20	. . . .	975	19,500	24,800	(5,300)
30	. . . .	950	28,500	29,100	(600)
40	. . . .	925	37,000	32,000	5,000
50	. . . .	900	45,000	41,000	4,000
60	. . . .	875	52,500	56,400	(3,900)

Profit-
maximizing
price } (at 40)

Demand is *inelastic* if price changes have little or no impact on sales quantity. **Cross-elasticity** refers to the extent to which a change in a product's price affects the demand for other *substitute products*. For example, if Sydney Sailing Supplies raises the price of its two-person sailboat, there may be an increase in demand for substitute recreational craft, such as small powerboats, canoes, or windsurfers.

Measuring price elasticity and cross-elasticity is an important objective of market research. Having a good understanding of these economic concepts helps managers to determine the profit-maximizing price.

Limitations of the Profit-Maximizing Model

The economic model of the pricing decision serves as a useful framework for approaching a pricing problem. However, it does have several limitations. First, the firm's demand and marginal revenue curves are difficult to discern with precision. Although market research is designed to gather data about product demand, it rarely enables management to predict completely the effects of price changes on the quantity demanded. Many other factors affect product demand in addition to price. Product design and quality, advertising and promotion, and company reputation also significantly influence consumer demand for a product.

Second, the marginal-revenue, marginal-cost paradigm is not valid for all forms of market organization. In an **oligopolistic market,** where a small number of sellers compete among themselves, the simple economic pricing model is no longer appropriate. In an *oligopoly*, such as the automobile industry, the reactions of competitors to a firm's pricing policies must be taken into account. While economists have studied oligopolistic pricing, the state of the theory is not sufficient to provide a thorough understanding of the impact of prices on demand.

The third limitation of the economic pricing model involves the difficulty of measuring marginal cost. Cost-accounting systems are not designed to measure the marginal changes in cost incurred as production and sales increase unit by unit. To measure marginal costs would entail a very costly information system. Most managers believe that any improvements in pricing decisions made possible by marginal-cost data would not be sufficient to defray the cost of obtaining the information.

Costs and Benefits of Information

Managerial accountants always face a cost-benefit trade-off in the production of cost information for pricing and other decisions. As Exhibit 15–4 shows, only a sophisticated information system can collect marginal-cost data. However, such information is more costly to obtain. The result is that the optimal approach to pricing and other decisions is likely to lie in between the extremes shown in Exhibit 15–4. For this reason, most managers make pricing decisions based on a combination of economic considerations and accounting product-cost information.

In spite of its limitations, the marginal-revenue, marginal-cost paradigm of pricing serves as a useful conceptual framework for the pricing decision. Within this overall framework, managers typically rely heavily on a cost-based pricing approach, as we shall see next.

Role of Accounting Product Costs in Pricing

Most managers base prices on accounting product costs, at least to some extent. There are several reasons for this. First, most companies sell many products or services. There simply is not time enough to do a thorough demand and marginal-cost analysis

Exhibit 15–4

Cost-Benefit Trade-off in Information Production

for every product or service. Managers must rely on a quick and straightforward method for setting prices, and cost-based pricing formulas provide it. Second, even though market considerations ultimately may determine the final product price, a cost-based pricing formula gives the manager a place to start. Finally, and most importantly, the cost of a product or service provides a floor below which the price cannot be set in the long run. Although a product may be "given away" initially, at a price below cost, a product's price ultimately must cover its costs in order for the firm to remain in business. Even a nonprofit organization, unless it is heavily subsidized, cannot forever price products or services below their costs.

Cost-Plus Pricing

LO 3   Set prices using cost-plus pricing formulas.

Cost-based pricing formulas typically have the following general form.

$$\text{Price} = \text{Cost} + (\text{Markup percentage} \times \text{Cost})$$

Under **cost-plus pricing,** the price is equal to cost plus a markup.

Such a pricing approach often is called **cost-plus pricing,** because the price is equal to *cost plus a markup.* Depending on how cost is defined, the markup percentage may differ. Several different definitions of cost, each combined with a different markup percentage, can result in the same price for a product or service.

Exhibit 15–5 illustrates how Sydney Sailing Supplies' management could use several different cost-plus pricing formulas and arrive at a price of $925 for the Wave Darter. Cost-plus formula (1) is based on variable manufacturing cost. Formula (2) is based on absorption (or full) manufacturing cost, which includes an allocated portion of fixed manufacturing costs. Formula (3) is based on all costs: both variable and fixed costs of the manufacturing, selling, and administrative functions. Formula (4) is based on all variable costs, including variable manufacturing, selling, and administrative costs. Notice that all four pricing formulas are based on a linear representation of the cost function, in which all costs are categorized as fixed or variable.

As Sydney Sailing Supplies includes more costs in the cost base of the pricing formula, the required markup percentage declines. This reflects the fact that, one way or another, the price must cover all costs as well as a normal profit margin. If only variable manufacturing costs are included explicitly in the cost base, as in formula (1), then all of the other costs (and the firm's profit) must be covered by the markup. However, if the cost base used in the pricing formula includes all costs, as in formula (3), the markup can be much lower, since it need cover only the firm's normal profit margin.

Each of the following cost-plus pricing formulas yields the same $925 price for the Wave Darter.

Price and Cost Data			Cost-Plus Pricing Formulas
Variable manufacturing cost	$400	**1**	$925 = \$400 + (131.25\% \times \$400) = \begin{matrix}\text{Variable}\\ \text{manufacturing} +\\ \text{cost}\end{matrix} \left(\begin{matrix}\text{Markup}\\ \text{percentage}\end{matrix} \times \begin{matrix}\text{Variable}\\ \text{manufacturing}\\ \text{cost}\end{matrix} \right)$
Applied fixed manufacturing cost	250*		
Absorption manufacturing cost	650	**2**	$925 = \$650 + (42.3\%^\dagger \times \$650) = \begin{matrix}\text{Absorption}\\ \text{manufacturing} +\\ \text{cost}\end{matrix} \left(\begin{matrix}\text{Markup}\\ \text{percentage}\end{matrix} \times \begin{matrix}\text{Absorption}\\ \text{manufacturing}\\ \text{cost}\end{matrix} \right)$
Variable selling and administrative cost	50		
Allocated fixed selling and administrative cost	100*		
Total cost	$800	**3**	$925 = \$800 + (15.63\%^\dagger \times \$800) = \begin{matrix}\text{Total}\\ \text{cost}\end{matrix} + \left(\begin{matrix}\text{Markup}\\ \text{percentage}\end{matrix} \times \begin{matrix}\text{Total}\\ \text{cost}\end{matrix} \right)$
Variable manufacturing cost	$400		
Variable selling and administrative cost	50		
Total variable cost	$450	**4**	$925 = \$450 + (105.56\%^\dagger \times \$450) = \begin{matrix}\text{Total}\\ \text{variable} +\\ \text{cost}\end{matrix} \left(\begin{matrix}\text{Markup}\\ \text{percentage}\end{matrix} \times \begin{matrix}\text{Total}\\ \text{variable}\\ \text{cost}\end{matrix} \right)$

*Based on planned monthly production of 40 units (or 480 units per year).
†Rounded.

Exhibit 15–5

Alternative Cost-Plus Pricing Formulas

   A company typically uses only one of the four cost-plus pricing formulas illustrated in Exhibit 15–5. Which formula is best? Let's examine the advantages and disadvantages of each approach.

Absorption-Cost Pricing Formulas

Most companies that use cost-plus pricing use either absorption manufacturing cost or total cost as the basis for pricing products or services.[2] [See formulas (2) and (3) in Exhibit 15–5.] The reasons generally given for this tendency are as follows:

1. In the long run, the price must cover *all* costs and a normal profit margin. Basing the cost-plus formula on only variable costs could encourage managers to set too low a price in order to boost sales. This will not happen if managers understand that a variable-cost plus pricing formula requires a higher markup to cover fixed costs and profit. Nevertheless, many managers argue that people tend to view the cost base in a cost-plus pricing formula as the floor for setting prices. If prices are set too close to variable manufacturing cost, the firm will fail to cover its fixed costs. Ultimately, such a practice could result in the failure of the business.

2. Absorption-cost or total-cost pricing formulas provide a justifiable price that tends to be perceived as equitable by all parties. Consumers generally understand

---

[2] For a discussion of cost-plus pricing, see V. Govindarajan and R. Anthony, "How Firms Use Cost Data in Pricing Decisions," *Management Accounting 65,* no. 1, pp 30–36.

that a company must make a profit on its product or service in order to remain in business. Justifying a price as the total cost of production, sales, and administrative activities, plus a reasonable profit margin, seems reasonable to buyers

3. When a company's competitors have similar operations and cost structures, cost-plus pricing based on full costs gives management an idea of how competitors may set prices.

4. Absorption-cost information is provided by a firm's cost-accounting system, because it is required for external financial reporting under generally accepted accounting principles. Since absorption-cost information already exists, it is cost-effective to use it for pricing. The alternative would involve preparing special product-cost data specifically for the pricing decision. In a firm with hundreds of products, such data could be expensive to produce.

The primary disadvantage of absorption-cost or total-cost pricing formulas is that they obscure the cost behavior pattern of the firm. Since absorption-cost and total-cost data include allocated fixed costs, it is not clear from these data how the firm's total costs will change as volume changes. Another way of stating this criticism is that absorption-cost data are not consistent with cost-volume-profit analysis. CVP analysis emphasizes the distinction between fixed and variable costs. This approach enables managers to predict the effects of changes in prices and sales volume on profit. Absorption-cost and total-cost information obscures the distinction between variable and fixed costs.

Variable-Cost Pricing Formulas

To avoid blurring the effects of cost behavior on profit, some managers prefer to use cost-plus pricing formulas based on either variable manufacturing costs or total variable costs. [See formulas (1) and (4) in Exhibit 15–5.] Three advantages are attributed to this pricing approach:

1. Variable-cost data do not obscure the cost behavior pattern by unitizing fixed costs and making them appear variable. Thus, variable-cost information is more consistent with cost-volume-profit analysis often used by managers to see the profit implications of changes in price and volume.

2. Variable-cost data do not require allocation of common fixed costs to individual product lines. For example, the annual salary of Sydney Sailing Supplies' vice president of sales is a cost that must be borne by all of the company's product lines. Arbitrarily allocating a portion of her salary to the Wave Darter product line is not meaningful.

3. Variable-cost data are exactly the type of information managers need when facing certain decisions, such as whether to accept a special order. This decision, examined in detail in the preceding chapter, often requires an analysis that separates fixed and variable costs.

The primary disadvantage of the variable-cost pricing formula was described earlier. If managers perceive the variable cost of a product or service as the floor for the price, they may tend to set the price too low for the firm to cover its fixed costs. Eventually this can spell disaster. Therefore, if variable-cost data are used as the basis for cost-plus pricing, managers must understand the need for higher markups to ensure that all costs are covered.

Determining the Markup

Regardless of which cost-plus formula is used, Sydney Sailing Supplies must determine its markup on the Wave Darter. If management uses a variable-cost pricing formula, the markup must cover all fixed costs and a reasonable profit. If management uses an absorption-costing formula, the markup still must be sufficient to cover the firm's profit on the Wave Darter product line. What constitutes a reasonable or normal profit margin?

Return-on-Investment Pricing   A common approach to determining the profit margin in cost-plus pricing is to base profit on the firm's target return on investment (ROI). To illustrate **return-on-investment pricing**, suppose Sydney Sailing Supplies' production plan calls for 480 Wave Darters to be manufactured during the year. Based on the cost data shown in Exhibit 15–5, this production plan will result in the following total costs.

Return-on-investment pricing is a cost-plus pricing method in which the markup is determined by the amount necessary for the company to earn a target rate of return on investment.

Variable costs:		
Manufacturing	$192,000	
Selling and administrative	24,000	
Total variable costs		$216,000
Fixed costs:		
Manufacturing	$120,000	
Selling and administrative	48,000	
Total fixed costs		168,000
Total costs		$384,000

Suppose the year's average amount of capital invested in the Wave Darter product line is $300,000. If Sydney Sailing Supplies' target return on investment for the Wave Darter line is 20 percent, the required annual profit is computed as follows:

$$\textbf{Average invested capital} \times \textbf{Target ROI} = \textbf{Target profit}$$
$$\textbf{\$300,000} \qquad \times \qquad \textbf{20\%} \quad = \quad \textbf{\$60,000}$$

The markup percentage required to earn Sydney Sailing Supplies a $60,000 profit on the Wave Darter line depends on the cost-plus formula used. We will compute the markup percentage for two cost-plus formulas.

1. *Cost-plus pricing based on total costs.* The total cost of a Wave Darter is $800 per unit (Exhibit 15–5). To earn a profit of $60,000 on annual sales of 480 sailboats, the company must make a profit of $125 per boat ($125 = $60,000 ÷ 480). This entails a markup percentage of 15.63 percent *above* total cost of $800.

$$15.63\% = \frac{\$925}{\$800} - 100\%$$

A shortcut to the same conclusion uses the following formula.

$$\frac{\textbf{Markup percentage}}{\textbf{on total cost}} = \frac{\textbf{Target profit}}{\textbf{Annual volume} \times \textbf{Total cost per unit}}$$

$$\textbf{15.63\%} \qquad = \qquad \frac{\textbf{\$60,000}}{\textbf{480} \times \textbf{\$800}}$$

2. *Cost-plus pricing based on total variable costs.* The total variable cost of a Wave Darter is $450 per unit (Exhibit 15–5). The markup percentage applied to variable cost must be sufficient to cover *both* annual profit of $60,000 *and* total annual fixed costs of $168,000. The required markup percentage is computed as follows:

$$\frac{\textbf{Markup percentage}}{\textbf{on total variable cost}} = \frac{\textbf{Target profit + Total annual fixed cost}}{\textbf{Annual volume} \times \textbf{Total variable cost per unit}}$$

$$\textbf{105.56\%} \qquad = \qquad \frac{\textbf{\$60,000 + \$168,000}}{\textbf{480} \times \textbf{\$450}}$$

General Formula   The general formula for computing the markup percentage in cost-plus pricing to achieve a target ROI is as follows:

$$\text{Markup percentage applied to cost base in cost-plus pricing formula} = \frac{\text{Profit required to achieve target ROI} + \text{Total annual costs } not \text{ included in cost base}}{\text{Annual volume} \times \text{Cost base per unit used in cost-plus pricing formula}}$$

Exercise 15–31 at the end of the chapter gives you an opportunity to employ this formula to compute the markup percentage for the other two cost-plus pricing formulas in Exhibit 15–5.

Cost-Plus Pricing: Summary and Evaluation

We have examined two different approaches to setting prices: (1) the economic, profit-maximizing approach and (2) cost-plus pricing. Although the techniques involved in these methods are quite different, the methods complement each other. In setting prices, managers cannot ignore the market, nor can they ignore costs. Cost-plus pricing is used widely in practice to establish a starting point in the process of determining a price. Cost-plus formulas are simple; they can be applied mechanically without taking the time of top management. They make it possible for a company with hundreds of products or services to cope with the tasks of updating prices for existing products and setting initial prices for new products.

Cost-plus pricing formulas can be used effectively with a variety of cost definitions, but the markup percentage must be appropriate for the type of cost used. It is imperative that price-setting managers understand that ultimately the price must cover all costs and a normal profit margin. Absorption-cost-plus or total-cost-plus pricing has the advantage of keeping the manager's attention focused on covering total costs. The variable-cost-plus formulas have the advantage of not obscuring important information about cost behavior.

Cost-plus pricing formulas establish a starting point in setting prices. Then the price setter must weigh market conditions, likely actions of competitors, and general business conditions. Thus, effective price setting requires a constant interplay of market considerations and cost awareness.

The following illustration points out the importance of cost reduction in enabling a firm to maintain price competitiveness.

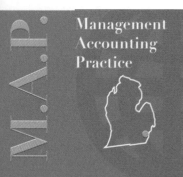

Management Accounting Practice

Ford Cuts Costs on Taurus to Remain Price Competitive

Ford Motor Company is asking the people who build its popular Taurus to find ways to build the car at a lower cost. According to *The Wall Street Journal,* "During a recent three-week campaign, workers and engineers at factories in Chicago and Atlanta came up with ideas to trim $1 here and 50 cents there, totaling $180 in cost reductions." For a car with a sticker price over $18,000, that may sound like a trivial amount, but it could save Ford over $73 million in just one year. Such savings would allow the company to "hold down sticker prices or offer bigger discounts helping the top-selling Taurus stay competitive in the cutthroat market for midsize sedans. In fact, no savings are too small given the competition Ford is facing. Prices for Japanese cars are dropping." This is in part due to aggressive cost-cutting by Japanese automakers. "Most of the cost-cutting is meant to be invisible to Taurus customers."[3] The cost reduction efforts at Ford are an example of the fact that a manufacturer must meet the market price for its product, but the price must also cover the product's production costs. In the globally competitive automobile industry, often the only way to be competitive and still price a product sufficiently above its production cost is to lower that cost.

---

[3] Oscar Suris, "How Ford Cut Costs on its Taurus, Little by Little," *The Wall Street Journal, 228,* no. 14, pp. B1 and B8.

Time and Material Pricing

Another cost-based approach to pricing is called **time and material pricing.** Under this approach, the company determines one charge for the labor used on a job and another charge for the materials. The labor typically includes the direct cost of the employee's time and a charge to cover various overhead costs. The material charge generally includes the direct cost of the materials used in a job plus a charge for material handling and storage. Time and material pricing is used widely by construction companies, printers, repair shops, and professional firms, such as engineering, law, and public accounting firms.

LO 4 Determine prices using the time and material pricing approach.

Time and material pricing includes components for labor cost and material cost, plus markups on either or both of these cost components.

To illustrate, we will examine a special job undertaken by Sydney Sailing Supplies. The company's vice president for sales, Richard Moby, was approached by a successful local physician about refurbishing her yacht. She wanted an engine overhaul, complete refurbishment and redecoration of the cabin facilities, and stripping and repainting of the hull and deck. The work would be done in the Repair Department of the company's Yacht Division, located in Melbourne, Australia.

Data regarding the operations of the Repair Department are as follows:

Labor rate, including fringe benefits	$18.00 per hour
Annual labor hours	10,000 hours
Annual overhead costs:	
Material handling and storage	$40,000
Other overhead costs (supervision, utilities, insurance, and depreciation)	$200,000
Annual cost of materials used in Repair Department	$1,000,000

Based on this data, the Repair Department computed its time and material prices as follows:

The effect of the material-charge formula is to include a charge for the costs incurred in the handling and storage of materials.

Richard Moby estimates that the yacht refurbishment job will require 200 hours of labor and $8,000 in materials. Moby's price quotation for the job is shown in Exhibit 15–6.

Exhibit 15–6

Time and Material Pricing

SYDNEY
SAILING SUPPLIES

SYDNEY SAILING SUPPLIES
Price Quotation
Yacht Division: Repair Department

Job: Refurbishment of 45-foot yacht, Pride of the Seas

Time charges	Labor time	200	hours
	× Rate	× $45	per hour
	Total	$ 9,000	
Material charges	Cost of materials for job	$ 8,000	
	+ Charge for material handling and storage	320*	
	Total	$ 8,320	
Total price of job	Time	$ 9,000	
	Material	8,320	
	Total	$17,320	

*Charge for material handling and storage:

$$\left(\begin{array}{c} \$8,000 \\ \text{material} \\ \text{cost} \end{array} \right) \times \left(\begin{array}{c} \$.04 \text{ per} \\ \text{dollar of} \\ \text{material cost} \end{array} \right) = \quad \$320$$

Included in the $17,320 price quotation for the yacht refurbishment are charges for labor costs, overhead, material costs, material handling and storage costs, and a normal profit margin. Some companies also charge an additional markup on the materials used in a job in order to earn a profit on that component of their services. Sydney Sailing Supplies' practice is to charge a high enough profit charge on its labor to earn an appropriate profit for the Repair Department.

Competitive Bidding

In a **competitive bidding** situation, two or more companies submit bids (prices) for a product, service, or project to a potential buyer.

In a **competitive bidding** situation, two or more companies submit sealed bids (or prices) for a product, service, or project to a potential buyer. The buyer selects one of the companies for the job on the basis of the bid price and the design specifications for the job. Competitive bidding complicates a manager's pricing problem, because now the manager is in direct competition with one or more competitors. If all of the companies submitting bids offer a roughly equivalent product or service, the bid price becomes the sole criterion for selecting the contractor. The higher the price that is bid, the greater will be the profit on the job, *if* the firm gets the contract. However, a higher price also lowers the probability of obtaining the contract to perform the job. Thus, there is a trade-off between bidding high, to make a good profit, and bidding low, to land the contract. Some say there is a "winner's curse" in competitive bidding meaning that the company bidding low enough to beat out its competitors probably bid too low to make an acceptable profit on the job. Despite the winner's curse, competitive bidding is a common form of selecting contractors in many types of business.

Richard Moby was approached recently by the city of Sydney about building a new marina for moderate-sized sailing vessels. Moby decided that his company's Marine Construction Division should submit a bid on the job. The city announced that three other firms would also be submitting bids. Since all four companies were equally capable of building the marina to the city's specifications, Moby assumed that the bid price would be the deciding factor in selecting the contractor.

Moby consulted with the controller and chief engineer of the Marine Construction Division, and the following data were compiled.

Estimated direct-labor requirements, 1,500 hours at $12.00 per hour	$18,000
Estimated direct-material requirements	30,000
Estimated variable overhead (allocated on the basis of direct labor), 1,500 direct-labor hours at $5.00 per hour	7,500
Total estimated variable costs	$55,500
Estimated fixed overhead (allocated on the basis of direct labor), 1,500 direct-labor hours at $8.00 per hour	12,000
Estimated total cost	$67,500

The Marine Construction Division allocates variable-overhead costs to jobs on the basis of direct-labor hours. These costs consist of indirect-labor costs, such as the wages of equipment-repair personnel, gasoline and lubricants, and incidental supplies such as rope, chains, and drill bits. Fixed-overhead costs, also allocated to jobs on the basis of direct-labor hours, include such costs as workers' compensation insurance, depreciation on vehicles and construction equipment, depreciation of the division's buildings, and supervisory salaries.

It was up to Richard Moby to decide on the bid price for the marina. In his meeting with the divisional controller and the chief engineer, Moby argued that the marina job was important to the company for two reasons. First, the Marine Construction Division had been operating well below capacity for several months. The marina job would not preclude the firm from taking on any other construction work, so it would not entail an opportunity cost. Second, the marina job would be good advertising for Sydney Sailing Supplies. City residents would see the firm's name on the project, and this would promote sales of the company's boats and sailing supplies.

Based on these arguments, Moby pressed for a bid price that just covered the firm's variable costs and allowed for a modest contribution margin. The chief engineer was obstinate, however, and argued for a higher bid price that would give the division a good profit on the job. "My employees work hard to do an outstanding job, and their work is worth a premium to the city," was the engineer's final comment on the issue. After the threesome tossed the problem around all morning, the controller agreed with Moby. A bid price of $60,000 was finally agreed upon.

This is a typical approach to setting prices for special jobs and competitively bid contracts. When a firm has excess capacity, a price that covers the incremental costs incurred because of the job will contribute toward covering the company's fixed cost and profit. None of the Marine Construction Division's fixed costs will increase as a result of taking on the marina job. Thus, a bid price of $60,000 will cover the $55,500 of variable costs on the job and contribute $4,500 toward covering the division's fixed costs.

Bid price	$60,000
Variable costs of marina job (incremental costs incurred only if job is done)	55,500
Contribution from marina job (contribution to covering the division's fixed costs)	$ 4,500

Naturally, Sydney Sailing Supplies' management would like to make a larger profit on the marina job, but bidding a higher price means running a substantial risk of losing the job to a competitor.

No Excess Capacity What if the Marine Construction Division has no excess capacity? If management expects to have enough work to fully occupy the division, a different approach is appropriate in setting the bid price. The fixed costs of the division are capacity-producing costs, which are costs incurred in order to create productive capacity. Depreciation of buildings and equipment, supervisory salaries, insurance, and property taxes are examples of fixed costs incurred to give a company the capacity to carry on its operations. When such costs are allocated to individual jobs, the cost of each job reflects an estimate of the opportunity cost of using limited capacity to do that particular job. For this reasoning to be valid, however, the organization must be at full capacity. If there is excess capacity, there is no opportunity cost in using that excess capacity.

If the Marine Construction Division has no excess capacity, it would be appropriate to focus on the estimated full cost of the marina job, $67,500, which includes an allocation of the division's fixed capacity-producing costs. Now Richard Moby might legitimately argue for a bid price in excess of $67,500. If the division is awarded the marina contract by the city, a price above $67,500 will cover all the costs of the job and make a contribution toward the division's profit.

However, as Richard Moby pointed out, there will be valuable promotional benefits to Sydney Sailing Supplies if its Marine Construction Division builds the marina. This is a qualitative factor, because these potential benefits are difficult to quantify. Moby will have to make a judgment regarding just how important the marina job is to the company. The greater the perceived qualitative benefits, the lower the bid price should be set to maximize the likelihood that the company will be awarded the contract.

Summary of Competitive-Bidding Analysis   The Marine Construction Division's pricing problem is summarized in Exhibit 15–7. As you can see, the final pricing decision

Exhibit 15–7

Summary of Competitive-Bidding Analysis

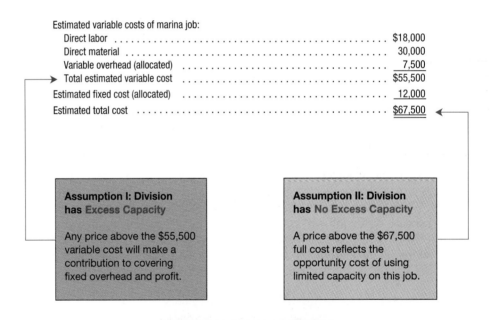

Estimated variable costs of marina job:	
Direct labor	$18,000
Direct material	30,000
Variable overhead (allocated)	7,500
Total estimated variable cost	$55,500
Estimated fixed cost (allocated)	12,000
Estimated total cost	$67,500

Assumption I: Division has Excess Capacity

Any price above the $55,500 variable cost will make a contribution to covering fixed overhead and profit.

Assumption II: Division has No Excess Capacity

A price above the $67,500 full cost reflects the opportunity cost of using limited capacity on this job.

Qualitative Factor

Valuable promotional benefits to Sydney Sailing Supplies if the marina contract is awarded to the Marine Construction Division.

Trade-Off in Setting Bid Price

High price means higher contribution to fixed cost and profit.

Low price means greater likelihood that the company will get the contract.

requires managerial judgment to fully consider the quantitative cost data, the qualitative promotional benefits, and the trade-off between a higher profit and a greater likelihood of getting the marina contract.

Accept or Reject a Special Order   In the preceding chapter, we examined in detail the decision as to whether a special order should be accepted or rejected. The analysis focused on identifying the relevant costs of the special order. The existence of excess capacity was an important factor in that analysis. Accepting a special order when excess capacity exists entails no opportunity cost. But when there is no excess capacity, one relevant cost of accepting a special order is the opportunity cost incurred by using the firm's limited capacity for the special order instead of some other job. After all relevant costs of the order have been identified, the decision maker compares the total relevant cost of the order with the price offered. If the price exceeds the relevant cost, the order generally should be accepted.

The decision is conceptually very similar to the bid-pricing problem discussed in this chapter. Setting a price for a special order or competitive bid also entails an analysis of the relevant costs of the job. Whether the decision maker is setting a price or has been offered a price, he or she must identify the relevant costs of providing the product or service requested.

Strategic Pricing of New Products

Pricing a new product is an especially challenging decision problem. The newer the concept of the product, the more difficult the pricing decision is. For example, if Sydney Sailing Supplies comes out with a new two-person sailboat, its pricing problem is far easier than the pricing problem of a company that first markets products using a radically new technology. Genetic engineering, superconductivity, artificial hearts, and space-grown crystals are all examples of such frontier technologies.

LO 6   Discuss the issues involved in the strategic pricing of new products.

Pricing a new product is harder than pricing a mature product because of the magnitude of the uncertainties involved. New products entail many uncertainties. For example, what obstacles will be encountered in manufacturing the product, and what will be the costs of production? Moreover, after the product is available, will anyone want to buy it, and at what price? If Sydney Sailing Supplies decides to market a new two-person sailboat, management can make a good estimate of both the production costs and the potential market for the product. The uncertainties here are far smaller than the uncertainties facing a company developing artificial hearts.

In addition to the production and demand uncertainties, new products pose another sort of challenge. There are two widely differing strategies that a manufacturer of a new product can adopt. One strategy is called **skimming pricing,** in which the initial product price is set high, and short-term profits are reaped on the new product. The initial market will be small, due in part to the high initial price. This pricing approach often is used for unique products, where there are people who "must have it" whatever the price. As the product gains acceptance and its appeal broadens, the price is lowered gradually. Eventually the product is priced in a range that appeals to several kinds of buyers. An example of a product for which skimming pricing was used is the home video game. Initially these games were priced quite high and were affordable by only a few buyers. Eventually the price was lowered, and the games were purchased by a wide range of consumers.

Under **skimming pricing,** a high initial price is set for a new product in order to reap short-run profits. Over time, the price is reduced gradually.

Under **penetration pricing,** a low initial price is set for a new product in order to penetrate the market deeply and gain a large and broad market share.

An alternative initial pricing strategy is called **penetration pricing,** in which the initial price is set relatively low. By setting a low price for a new product, management hopes to penetrate a new market deeply, quickly gaining a large market share. This pricing approach often is used for products that are of good quality, but do not stand out as vastly better than competing products.

This student is discussing an assignment with a classmate on a cell phone. The price of cellular phones has dropped substantially in recent years, making the phones accessible to a broad range of consumers.

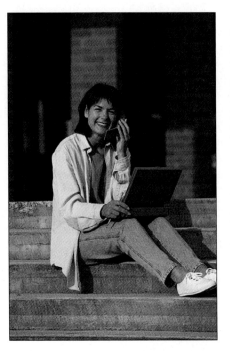

The decision between skimming and penetration pricing depends on the type of product and involves trade-offs of price versus volume. Skimming pricing results in much slower acceptance of a new product, but higher unit profits. Penetration pricing results in greater initial sales volume, but lower unit profits.

Target Costing

We have described the pricing of new products as a process whereby the cost of the product is determined, and then an appropriate price is chosen. Sometimes the opposite approach is taken. The company first uses market research to determine the price at which the new product will sell. Given the likely sales price, management computes the cost for which the product must be manufactured in order to provide the firm with an acceptable profit margin. Finally, engineers and cost analysts work together to design a product that can be manufactured for the allowable cost. This process, called **target costing,** is used widely by companies in the development stages of new products. A new product's **target cost** is the projected long-run cost that will enable a firm to enter and remain in the market for the product and compete successfully with the firm's competitors. In specifying a product's target cost, analysts must be careful to incorporate all of the product's *life cycle costs*. These include the costs of product planning and concept design, preliminary design, detailed design and testing, production, distribution, and customer service. Sometimes the projected cost of a new product is above the target cost. Then efforts are made to eliminate *non-value-added costs* to bring the projected cost down.[4] In some cases, a close look at the company's *value chain* can help managers identify opportunities for cost reduction. For example, Procter & Gamble placed order-entry computers in Wal-Mart stores. This resulted in substantial savings in order-processing costs for both companies.[5]

Target costing is the design of a product, and the processes used to produce it, so that ultimately the product can be manufactured at a cost that will enable a firm to make a profit when the product is sold at an estimated market-driven price.

The **target cost** is the projected long-run product cost that will enable a firm to enter and remain in the market for the product and compete successfully with the firm's competitors.

| LO 7 | Explain the role of activity-based costing in setting a target cost. |

Activity-Based Costing and Target Costing   An activity-based costing (ABC) system can be particularly helpful as product design engineers try to achieve a product's target cost. ABC enables designers to break down the production process for a new product into its component activities. Then designers can attempt cost improvement in particular activities to bring a new product's projected cost in line with its target cost.

To illustrate, Sydney Sailing Supplies' Marine Instruments Division, located in Perth, Australia, wants to introduce a new depth finder. Target-costing studies indicate that a target cost of $340 must be met in order to successfully compete in this market. Exhibit 15–8 shows how ABC was used to bring the depth finder's initial cost estimate of $399 down to $337, just below the target cost. The company's design engineers were able to focus on key activities in the production process, such as material handling and inspection, and reduce the projected costs.

---

[4] Target costing is covered extensively in Chapter 6. The elimination of non-value-added costs and product life-cycle costs are covered in Chapters 6 and 9, respectively.

[5] J. Shank and V. Govindarajan, "Strategic Cost Management and the Value Chain," *Journal of Cost Management* 5, no. 4, p. 10. See also T. Tanaka, "Target Costing at Toyota," *Journal of Cost Management* 7, no. 1, pp. 4–12.

Exhibit 15–8

Target Costing and Cost Improvement for a New Product

A. Activity-Based Costing System

Activity Cost Pool	Cost Driver	Pool Rate
Purchasing	Number of parts	$1 per part
Material handling	Dollar value of parts	$.20 per direct-material dollar
Inspection	Inspection hours	$28 per inspection hour

This is a highly simplified example of activity-based costing. ABC systems which were introduced conceptually in Chapter 3, are covered in detail in Chapter 5.

B. Cost Projections for New Product: A Depth Finder

	Original Cost Projection	Improved Cost Projection
Direct material	$200	$190
Direct labor	100	70
Purchasing:		
$1 per part (45 parts)	45	
$1 per part (32 parts)		32
Material handling:		
$.20 per direct-material dollar ($200)	40	
$.20 per direct-material dollar ($190)		38
Inspection:		
$28 per inspection hour (.5 hours)	14	
$28 per inspection hour (.25 hours)		7
Total projected cost	$399	$337
Target cost		$340

Computer-Integrated Manufacturing   When a computer-integrated manufacturing (CIM) system is used, the process of target costing sometimes is computerized. A manufacturer's computer-aided design and cost-accounting software are interconnected. An engineer can try out many different design features and immediately see the product-cost implications, without ever leaving the computer terminal.

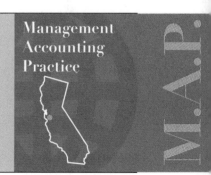

Hewlett-Packard's Personal Office Computer Division

At Hewlett-Packard Company's Personal Office Computer Division, a computer program called COSTIT is maintained by the Accounting Department. The COSTIT program enables a product design engineer to get a quick answer to the question, What will be the new product cost if certain design changes are made in a product? If, for example, the engineer wants to know the cost of changing the exterior case on the division's personal office computer, this information is easily determined by accessing COSTIT on his or her own computer terminal. Accounting Department personnel estimate that COSTIT is used by designers over 100 times a month to facilitate the continuing process of product enhancement.[6]

Management Accounting Practice

Product-Cost Distortion and Pricing: The Role of Activity-Based Costing

Use of a traditional, volume-based product-costing system may result in significant cost distortion among product lines. In many cases, high-volume and relatively simple products are overcosted while low-volume and complex products are undercosted. This results from the fact that high-volume and relatively simple products require proportionately less activity per unit for various manufacturing-support activities than do low-volume and complex products.

LO 8   Explain how product-cost distortion can undermine a firm's pricing strategy.

---

[6] J. Patell, "Cost Accounting, Process Control and Product Design: A Case Study of the Hewlett-Packard Personal Office Computer Division," *The Accounting Review* 62, no. 4, pp. 808–37.

Many companies have computer programs that help their design engineers utilize product cost information in making product design decisions.

Yet a traditional product-costing system, in which all overhead is assigned on the basis of a single unit-level activity like direct-labor hours, fails to capture the cost implications of product diversity. In contrast, an activity-based costing (ABC) system does measure the extent to which each product line drives costs in the key production-support activities.

Since pricing decisions often are based on accounting product costs, decision makers should be aware that cost distortion can result in overpricing high-volume and relatively simple products, while low-volume and complex products are undercosted. The competitive implications of such strategic pricing errors can be disastrous.[7]

Effect of Antitrust Laws on Pricing

LO 9   Describe the legal restrictions on setting prices.

Price discrimination is the illegal practice of quoting different prices for the same product or service to different buyers, when the price differences are not justified by cost differences.

Predatory pricing is an illegal practice in which the price of a product is set low temporarily to broaden demand; then the product's supply is restricted and the price is raised.

Businesses are not free to set any price they wish for their products or services. American antitrust laws, including the Robinson-Patman Act, the Clayton Act, and the Sherman Act, restrict certain types of pricing behavior. These laws prohibit **price discrimination,** which means quoting different prices to different customers for the same product or service. Such price differences are unlawful unless they can be clearly justified by differences in the costs incurred to produce, sell, or deliver the product or service. Managers should keep careful records justifying such cost differences when they exist, because the records may be vital to a legal defense if price differences are challenged in court.

Another pricing practice prohibited by law is **predatory pricing.** This practice involves temporarily cutting a price to broaden demand for a product with the intention of later restricting the supply and raising the price again. In determining whether a price is predatory, the courts examine a business's cost records. If the product is sold below cost, the pricing is deemed to be predatory. The laws and court cases are ambiguous as to the appropriate definition of cost. However, as reported in *The Wall Street Journal,* recent Supreme Court decisions make it harder to prove predatory pricing. Nevertheless, this is one area where a price-setting decision maker is well advised to have an accountant on the left and a lawyer on the right before setting prices that could be deemed predatory.[8]

---

[7] This whole issue of cost distortion and the role of ABC in product pricing is covered extensively in Chapter 5.

[8] For further information on predatory pricing, see P. Areeda and D. Turner, "Predatory Pricing and Related Practices under Section 2 of the Sherman Act," *Harvard Law Review* 88, pp. 697–733. For recent case law, see the "Legal Developments" section of the *Journal of Marketing.* Also, see Bruce E. Committee and D. Jacque Grinnell, "Predatory Pricing, The Price-Cost Test, and Activity-Based Costing," *Journal of Cost Management* 6, no. 3, pp. 52–58.

Chapter Summary

Pricing of products and services is one of the most challenging decisions faced by management. Many influences affect pricing decisions. Chief among these are customer demand, the actions of competitors, and the costs of the products or services. Other factors such as political, legal, and image-related issues also affect pricing decisions.

Economic theory shows that under certain assumptions, the profit-maximizing price and quantity are determined by the intersection of the marginal-revenue and marginal-cost curves. While the economic model serves as a useful conceptual framework for the pricing decision, it is limited by its assumptions and the informational demands it implies.

Most companies set prices, at least to some extent, on the basis of costs. Cost-plus pricing formulas add a markup to some version of cost, typically either total variable cost or total absorption cost. Markups often are set to earn the company a target profit on its products, based on a target rate of return on investment.

In industries such as construction, repair, printing, and professional services, time and material pricing is used. Under this approach the price is determined as the sum of a labor-cost component and a material-cost component. Either or both of these components may include a markup to ensure that the company earns a profit on its services.

Pricing special orders and determining competitive bid prices entail an analysis of the relevant costs to be incurred in completing the job. The relevant-cost analysis should incorporate the existence of excess capacity or the lack of it.

Strategic pricing of new products is an especially challenging problem for management. Various pricing approaches, such as skimming pricing or penetration pricing, may be appropriate depending on the product. Target costing often is used to design a new product that can be produced at a cost that will enable the firm to sell it at a competitive price.

Review Problem on Cost-Plus Pricing

Kitchenware Corporation manufactures high-quality copper pots and pans. Janet Cooke, one of the company's price analysts, is involved in setting a price for the company's new Starter Set. This set consists of seven of the most commonly used pots and pans. During the next year, the company plans to produce 10,000 Starter Sets, and the controller has provided Cooke with the following cost data.

Predicted Costs of 10,000 Starter Sets

Direct material per set	$60
Direct labor per set, 2 hours at $10.00 per hr.	20
Variable selling cost per set	5
Total	$85
Variable overhead rate	$ 8.00 per direct-labor hour
Fixed overhead rate	$12.00 per direct-labor hour

In addition, the controller indicated that the Accounting Department would allocate $20,000 of fixed administrative expenses to the Starter Set product line.

Required:

1. Compute the cost of a Starter Set using each of the four cost definitions commonly used in cost-plus pricing formulas.
2. Determine the markup percentage required for the Starter Set product line to earn a target profit of $317,500 before taxes during the next year. Use the total cost as the cost definition in the cost-plus formula.

Solution to Review Problem

1.	Variable manufacturing cost *	$ 96	☐1
	Applied fixed-overhead cost†	24	
	Absorption manufacturing cost	$120	☐2
	Variable selling cost	5	
	Allocated fixed administrative cost‡	2	
	Total cost	$127	☐3

Variable manufacturing cost	$ 96
Variable selling cost	5
Total variable cost	$101

4

* Direct material	$60	
Direct labor	20	
Variable overhead	16	(2 × $8.00 per hour)
Total variable manufacturing cost	$96	
† Applied fixed overhead cost	$24	(2 × $12 per hour)
‡ Allocated fixed administrative cost	$ 2	($20,000 ÷ 10,000 sets)

2.

$$\text{Markup percentage on total cost} = \frac{\$317,500}{10,000 \times \$127} = 25\%$$

$$\text{Proof: Price} = \text{Total cost} + (.25 \times \text{Total cost})$$

$$= \$127 + (.25)(\$127) = \$158.75$$

Income Statement

Sales revenue (10,000 × $158.75)		$1,587,500
Less: Variable costs:		
Direct material	$600,000	
Direct labor	200,000	
Variable overhead	160,000	
Variable selling cost	50,000	
Total variable costs		1,010,000
Contribution margin		$ 577,500
Less: Fixed costs:		
Manufacturing overhead	$240,000	
Administrative cost	20,000	
Total fixed costs		260,000
Profit		$ 317,500

Key Terms

For each term's definition refer to the indicated page, or turn to the glossary at the end of the text.

competitive bidding, pg. 634
cost-plus pricing, pg. 628
cross-elasticity, pg. 627
demand curve (average revenue curve), pg. 622
marginal cost curve, pg. 625

marginal revenue curve, pg. 622
oligopolistic market, pg. 627
penetration pricing, pg. 637
predatory pricing, pg. 640
price discrimination, pg. 640

price elasticity, pg. 625
price taker, pg. 622
return-on-investment pricing, pg. 631
skimming pricing, pg. 637
target cost, pg. 638

target costing, pg. 638
time and material pricing, pg. 633
total cost curve, pg. 625
total revenue curve, pg. 622

Review Questions

15–1. List and briefly describe four major influences on pricing decisions.

15–2. Comment on the following remark made by a bank president: "The prices of our banking services are determined by the financial-services market. Costs are irrelevant."

15–3. "All this marginal revenue and marginal cost stuff is just theory. Prices are determined by production costs." Evaluate this assertion.

15–4. Explain what is meant by the following statement: "In considering the reactions of competitors, it is crucial to define your product."

15–5. Explain the following assertion: "Price setting generally requires a balance between market forces and cost considerations."

15–6. Briefly explain the concept of *economic, profit-maximizing pricing*. It may be helpful to use graphs in your explanation.

15–7. Define the following terms: *total revenue, marginal revenue, demand curve, price elasticity,* and *cross-elasticity.*

15–8. Briefly define *total cost* and *marginal cost.*

15–9. Describe three limitations of the economic, profit-maximizing model of pricing.

15-10. Determining the best approach to pricing requires a cost-benefit trade-off. Explain.

15–11. Write the general formula for cost-plus pricing, and briefly explain its use.

15–12. List the four common cost bases used in cost-plus pricing. How can they all result in the same price?

15–13. List four reasons often cited for the widespread use of absorption cost as the cost base in cost-plus pricing formulas.

15–14. What is the primary disadvantage of basing the cost-plus pricing formula on absorption cost?

15–15. List three advantages of pricing based on variable cost.

15–16. Explain the behavioral problem that can result when cost-plus prices are based on variable cost.

15–17. Briefly explain the concept of *return-on-investment pricing.*

15–18. Briefly describe the *time-and-material pricing approach.*

15–19. Explain the importance of the excess-capacity issue in setting a competitive bid price.

15–20. The decision to accept or reject a special order and the selection of a price for a special order are very similar decisions. Explain.

15–21. Describe the following approaches to pricing new products: skimming pricing, penetration pricing, and target costing.

15–22. Explain what is meant by unlawful price discrimination and predatory pricing.

15–23. Define the term *target cost.*

15–24. Briefly explain the potential negative consequences in pricing decisions from using a traditional, volume-based product-costing system.

Exercises

The marginal cost, marginal revenue, and demand curves for Houston Home and Garden's deluxe wheel-barrow are shown in a the following graph.

■ **Exercise 15–25**
Marginal Revenue and Marginal Cost Curves
(LO 1, LO 2)

Dollars per unit

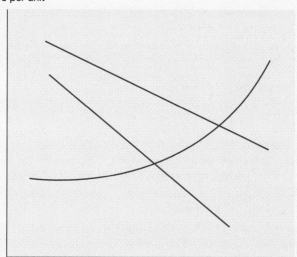

Quantity sold
per month

Required:

Before completing any of the following requirements, read over the entire list.

1. Trace the graph shown above onto a blank piece of paper, and label all parts of the graph.

2. Draw a companion graph directly above the traced graph. Use this graph to draw the firm's total revenue and total cost curves.

3. Show the company's profit-maximizing price on the lower graph and its profit-maximizing quantity on both graphs.

■ **Exercise 15–26**
Demand and Revenue Data
(LO 1, LO 2)

Spectrum Sound, Inc. manufactures compact disk players with unusual features in its St. Louis Division. The divisional sales manager has estimated the following demand-curve data.

Quantity Sold per Month	Unit Sales Price
20	$1,000
40	950
60	900
80	850
100	800

Required:

1. Prepare a table similar to panel C of Exhibit 15–1 summarizing Spectrum Sound's price, quantity, and revenue data.
2. Draw a graph similar to panel A of Exhibit 15–1 reflecting the data tabulated in requirement (1).

■ **Exercise 15–27**
Continuation of Preceding
Exercise; Cost Data
(LO 1, LO 2)

Refer to the preceding exercise. The divisional controller at Spectrum Sound's St. Louis Division has estimated the following cost data for the division's CD players. (Assume there are no fixed costs.)

Quantity Produced and Sold per Month	Average Cost per Unit
20	$900
40	850
60	820
80	860
100	890

Required:

1. Prepare a table similar to panel C of Exhibit 15–2 summarizing Spectrum Sound's cost relationships.
2. Draw a graph similar to panel A of Exhibit 15–2 reflecting the data tabulated in requirement (1).

■ **Exercise 15–28**
Continuation of Preceding
Two Exercises; Profit-
Maximizing Price
(LO 1, LO 2)

Refer to the data given in the preceding two exercises.

1. Prepare a table of Spectrum Sound's revenue, cost, and profit relationships. For guidance refer to panel C of Exhibit 15–3.
2. Draw a graph similar to panel A of Exhibit 15–3 reflecting the data tabulated in requirement (1).
3. To narrow down the pricing decision, the St. Louis Division's sales manager has decided to price the CD player at one of the following prices: $800, $850, $900, $950 or $1,000. Which price do you recommend? Why?

■ **Exercise 15–29**
Pricing, Advertising, and
Special-Order Decisions
(LO 5)

Celeste Company produces a single product, which currently sells for $5.00. Fixed costs are expected to amount to $60,000 for the year, and all variable manufacturing and administrative costs are expected to be incurred at a rate of $3.00 per unit. Celeste has two salespeople who are paid strictly on a commission basis. Their commission is 10 percent of the sales dollars they generate. (Ignore income taxes.)

Required:

1. Suppose management alters its current plans by spending an additional amount of $5,000 on advertising and increases the selling price to $6.00 per unit. Calculate the profit on 60,000 units.
2. The Sorde Company has just approached Celeste to make a special one-time purchase of 10,000 units. These units would not be sold by the sales personnel, and, therefore, no commission would have to be paid. What is the price Celeste would have to charge per unit on this special order to earn additional profit of $20,000?

(CMA, adapted)

The following data pertain to Yard King Corporation's top-of-the-line lawn mower.

Variable manufacturing cost	$250
Applied fixed manufacturing cost	50
Variable selling and administrative cost	60
Allocated fixed selling and administrative cost	?

■ **Exercise 15–30**
Cost-Plus Pricing Formulas;
Missing Data
(LO 1, LO 3)

To achieve a target price of $450 per lawn mower, the markup percentage is 12.5 percent on total unit cost.

Required:

1. What is the fixed selling and administrative cost allocated to each unit of Yard King's top-of-the-line mower?
2. For each of the following cost-bases, develop a cost-plus pricing formula that will result in a target price of $450 per mower: (a) variable manufacturing cost, (b) absorption manufacturing cost, and (c) total variable cost.

Refer to the cost and production data for the Wave Darter in Exhibit 15–5. The target profit is $60,000.

■ **Exercise 15–31**
Determining Markup
Percentage; Target ROI
(LO 1, LO 3)

Required:

Use the general formula for determining a markup percentage to compute the required markup percentages with the following two cost-plus formulas:

1. Variable manufacturing costs [formula (1) in Exhibit 15–5].
2. Absorption manufacturing cost [formula (2) in Exhibit 15–5].

Refer to Exhibit 15–6. Suppose the Repair Department of Sydney Sailing Supplies adds a markup of 5 percent on the material charges of a job (including the cost of material handling and storage).

■ **Exercise 15–32**
Time and Material Pricing
(LO 4)

Required:

1. Rewrite the material component of the time and material pricing formula to reflect the markup on material cost.
2. Compute the new price to be quoted on the yacht refurbishment described in Exhibit 15–6.

The following data pertain to Legion Lighting Company's oak-clad, contemporary chandelier.

Variable manufacturing cost	$200
Applied fixed manufacturing cost	70
Variable selling and administrative cost	30
Allocated fixed selling and administrative cost	50

■ **Exercise 15–33**
Cost-Plus Pricing Formulas
(LO 1, LO 3)

Required:

For each of the following cost bases, develop a cost-plus pricing formula that will result in a price of $400 for the oak chandelier.

1. Variable manufacturing cost.
2. Absorption manufacturing cost.
3. Total cost.
4. Total variable cost.

Problems

Note: Several of the problems and cases in Chapter 5 relate to pricing and may be assigned with Chapter 15 as well. These problems emphasize the impact of cost distortion on pricing decisions. They stress the differences between traditional, volume-based costing systems and activity-based costing systems with respect to their role in pricing. These problems should be assigned only after Chapter 5 has been completed. The following problems are relevant: 5–39, 5–40, 5–42, 5–43, and 5–46.

■ **Problem 15–34**
Cost-Plus Pricing; Bidding
(LO 3, LO 5)

Hall Company specializes in packaging bulk drugs in standard dosages for local hospitals. The company has been in business for seven years and has been profitable since its second year of operation. Don Greenway, Assistant Controller, installed a standard costing system after joining the company three years ago.

Wyant Memorial Hospital has asked Hall to bid on the packaging of one million doses of medication at total cost plus a return on total cost of no more than 15 percent. Wyant defines total cost as including all variable costs of performing the service, a reasonable amount of fixed overhead, and reasonable administrative costs. The hospital will supply all packaging materials and ingredients. Wyant has indicated that any bid over $.015 per dose will be rejected.

Greenway has accumulated the following information prior to the preparation of the bid.

Direct labor	$4.00 per direct-labor hour (DLH)
Variable overhead	$3.00 per DLH
Fixed overhead	$5.00 per DLH
Incremental administrative costs	$1,000 for the order
Production rate	1,000 doses per DLH

Required:

1. Calculate the minimum price per dose that Hall Company could bid for the Wyant Memorial Hospital job that would not reduce Hall's income.

2. Calculate the bid price per dose using total cost and the maximum allowable return specified by Wyant Memorial Hospital.

3. Independent of your answer to requirement (2), suppose that the price per dose that Hall Company calculated using the cost-plus criterion specified by Wyant Memorial Hospital is greater than the maximum bid of $.015 per dose allowed by Wyant. Discuss the factors that Hall Company should consider before deciding whether or not to submit a bid at the maximum price of $.015 per dose that Wyant allows.

(CMA, adapted)

■ **Problem 15–35**
Pricing a Special Order;
International
(LO 5)

Sommers Company, located in southern Wisconsin, manufactures a variety of industrial valves and pipe fittings that are sold to customers in nearby states. Currently, the company is operating at about 70 percent capacity and is earning a satisfactory return on investment. Management has been approached by Glasgow Industries Ltd. of Scotland with an offer to buy 120,000 units of a pressure valve. Glasgow Industries manufactures a valve that is almost identical to Sommers' pressure valve; however, a fire in Glasgow Industries' valve plant has shut down its manufacturing operations. Glasgow needs the 120,000 valves over the next four months to meet commitments to its regular customers. Glasgow is prepared to pay $19 each for the valves. Sommers' total product cost, based on current attainable standards, for the pressure valve is $20, calculated as follows:

Direct material	$ 5.00
Direct labor	6.00
Manufacturing overhead	9.00
Total product cost	$20.00

Manufacturing overhead is applied to production at the rate of $18 per standard direct-labor hour. This overhead rate is made up of the following components.

Variable manufacturing overhead	$ 6.00
Fixed manufacturing overhead (traceable)	8.00
Fixed manufacturing overhead (allocated)	4.00
Applied manufacturing overhead rate	$18.00

Additional costs incurred in connection with sales of the pressure valve include sales commissions of 5 percent and freight expense of $1.00 per unit. However, the company does not pay sales commissions on special orders that come directly to management. In determining selling prices, Sommers adds a 40 percent markup to total product cost. This provides a $28 suggested selling price for the pressure valve. The Marketing Department, however, has set the current selling price at $27 in order to maintain market share. Production management believes that it can handle the Glasgow Industries order without disrupting its scheduled production. The order would, however, require additional fixed factory overhead of $12,000 per month in the form of supervision and clerical costs. If management accepts the order, 30,000 pressure valves will be manufactured and shipped to Glasgow Industries each month for the next four months. Glasgow's management has agreed to pay the shipping charges for the valves.

Required:

1. Determine how many direct-labor hours would be required each month to fill the Glasgow Industries order.
2. Prepare an analysis showing the impact of accepting the Glasgow Industries order.
3. Calculate the minimum unit price that Sommers' management could accept for the Glasgow Industries order without reducing net income.
4. Identify the factors, other than price, that Sommers Company should consider before accepting the Glasgow Industries order.

(CMA, adapted)

Suburban Heating, Inc. installs heating systems in new homes. Jobs are priced using the time and materials method. The president of Suburban Heating, B. T. Ewing, is pricing a job involving the heating systems for six houses to be built by a local developer. He has made the following estimates.

■ **Problem 15–36**
Time and Material Pricing
(LO 4)

Labor hours	400
Material cost	$60,000

The following predictions pertain to the company's operations for the next year.

Labor rate, including fringe benefits	$16.00 per hour
Annual labor hours	12,000 hours
Annual overhead costs:	
Material handling and storage	$25,000
Other overhead costs	$108,000
Annual cost of materials used	$250,000

Required:

Suburban Heating adds a markup of $4.00 per hour on its time charges, but there is no markup on material costs.

1. Develop formulas for the company's (a) time charges and (b) material charges.
2. Compute the price for the job described above.
3. What would be the price of the job if Suburban Heating also added a markup of 10 percent on all material charges (including material handling and storage costs)?

Stac Industries is a multiproduct company with several manufacturing plants. The Clinton Plant manufactures and distributes two household cleaning and polishing compounds, regular and heavy-duty, under the Cleen-Brite label. The forecasted operating results for the first six months of the current year, when 100,000 cases of each compound are expected to be manufactured and sold, are presented in the following statement which is continued on the next page.

■ **Problem 15–37**
Pricing in a Tight Market;
Possible Plant Closing
(LO 1, LO 5)

CLEEN-BRITE COMPOUNDS—CLINTON PLANT
Forecasted Results of Operations
For the Six-Month Period Ending June 30
(in thousands)

	Regular	Heavy-Duty	Total
Sales	$2,000	$3,000	$5,000
Cost of goods sold	1,600	1,900	3,500
Gross profit	$ 400	$1,100	$1,500

	Regular	Heavy-Duty	Total
Selling and administrative expenses:			
Variable	$ 400	$ 700	$1,100
Fixed*	240	360	600
Total selling and administrative expenses	$ 640	$1,060	$1,700
Income (loss) before taxes	$ (240)	$ 40	$ (200)

*The fixed selling and administrative expenses are allocated between the two products on the basis of dollar sales volume.

The regular compound sold for $20 a case and the heavy-duty compound sold for $30 a case during the first six months of the year. The manufacturing costs, by case of product, are presented in the schedule below. Each product is manufactured on a separate production line. Annual normal manufacturing capacity is 200,000 cases of each product. However, the plant is capable of producing 250,000 cases of regular compound and 350,000 cases of heavy-duty compound annually.

	Cost per Case	
	Regular	Heavy-Duty
Direct material	$ 7.00	$ 8.00
Direct labor	4.00	4.00
Variable manufacturing overhead	1.00	2.00
Fixed manufacturing overhead*	4.00	5.00
Total manufacturing cost	$16.00	$19.00
Variable selling and administrative costs	$ 4.00	$ 7.00

*Depreciation charges are 50 percent of the fixed manufacturing overhead of each line.

The following schedule reflects the consensus of top management regarding the price-volume alternatives for the Cleen-Brite products for the last six months of the current year. These are essentially the same alternatives management had during the first six months of the year.

Regular Compound		Heavy-Duty Compound	
Alternative Prices (per case)	Sales Volume (in cases)	Alternative Prices (per case)	Sales Volume (in cases)
$18	120,000	$25	175,000
20	100,000	27	140,000
21	90,000	30	100,000
22	80,000	32	55,000
23	50,000	35	35,000

Top management believes the loss for the first six months reflects a tight profit margin caused by intense competition. Management also believes that many companies will leave this market by next year and profit should improve.

Required:

1. What unit selling price should Stac Industries select for each of the Cleen-Brite compounds for the remaining six months of the year? Support your selection with appropriate calculations.

2. Independently of your answer to requirement (1), assume the optimum alternatives for the last six months were as follows: a selling price of $23 and volume of 50,000 cases for the regular compound, and a selling price of $35 and volume of 35,000 cases for the heavy-duty compound.

   a. Should Stac Industries consider closing down its operations until January 1 of the next year in order to minimize its losses? Support your answer with appropriate calculations.

   b. Identify and discuss the qualitative factors that should be considered in deciding whether the Clinton Plant should be closed down during the last six months of the current year.

(CMA, adpated)

■ Problem 15–38
Bidding on a Special Order
(LO 5)

Marcus Fibers Inc. specializes in the manufacture of synthetic fibers that the company uses in many products such as blankets, coats, and uniforms for police and firefighters. Marcus has been in business for 20 years and has been profitable each of the past 15 years. The company uses a standard-costing system and applies overhead on the basis of direct-labor hours. Marcus has recently received a request to bid on the manufacture of 800,000 blankets scheduled for delivery to several military bases. The bid must be stated at full cost per unit plus a return on full cost of no more than 15 percent before income taxes. Full cost has been defined as including all variable costs of manufacturing the product, a reasonable amount of fixed overhead, and reasonable incremental administrative costs associated with the manufacture and sale of the product. The contractor has indicated that bids in excess of $25 per blanket are not likely to be considered.

In order to prepare the bid for the 800,000 blankets, Andrea Lightner, cost accountant, has gathered the following information about the costs associated with the production of the blankets.

Direct material	$1.50 per pound of fibers
Direct labor	$7.00 per hour
Direct machine costs*	$10.00 per blanket
Variable overhead	$3.00 per direct-labor hour
Fixed overhead	$8.00 per direct-labor hour
Incremental administrative costs	$2,500 per 1,000 blankets
Special fee†	$ .50 per blanket
Material usage	6 pounds per blanket
Production rate	4 blankets per direct-labor hour

*Direct machine costs consist of items such as special lubricants, replacement of needles used in stitching, and maintenance costs. These costs are not included in the normal overhead rates.

†Marcus recently developed a new blanket fiber at a cost of $750,000. In an effort to recover this cost, Marcus has instituted a policy of adding a $.50 fee to the cost of each blanket using the new fiber. To date, the company has recovered $125,000. Lightner knows that this fee does not fit within the definition of full cost as it is not a cost of manufacturing the product.

Required:

1. Calculate the minimum price per blanket that Marcus Fibers Inc. could bid without reducing the company's net income.

2. Using the full cost criteria and the maximum allowable return specified, calculate Marcus Fibers Inc.'s bid price per blanket.

3. Independent of your answer to requirement (2), assume that the price per blanket that Marcus Fibers Inc. calculated using the cost-plus criteria specified is greater than the maximum bid of $25 per blanket allowed. Discuss the factors that Marcus Fibers Inc. should consider before deciding whether to submit a bid at the maximum acceptable price of $25 per blanket.

(CMA, adapted)

Splendid Stereo Company manufactures two models of stereo amplifiers. Cost estimates for the two models for the coming year are as follows:

■ **Problem 15–39**
Product Cost Distortion and Product Pricing; Departmental Overhead Rates
(LO 8)

	Model 1000	Model 2000
Direct material	$160	$260
Direct labor (10 hours at $14 per hour)	140	140
Manufacturing overhead*	100	100
Total cost	$400	$500

*The predetermined overhead rate is $10 per direct-labor hour.

Each stereo amplifier requires 10 hours of direct labor. Each Model 1000 unit requires two hours in Department I and eight hours in Department II. Each unit of Model 2000 requires eight hours in Department I and two hours in Department II. The manufacturing overhead costs expected during the coming year in Departments I and II are as follows:

	Department I	Department II
Variable overhead	$8 per direct-labor hour	$4 per direct-labor hour
Fixed overhead	$150,000	$150,000

The expected operating activity for the coming year is 37,500 direct-labor hours in each department.

Required:

1. Show how Splendid Stereo derived its predetermined overhead rate.

2. What will be the price of each model stereo amplifier if the company prices its products at absorption manufacturing cost plus 15 percent?

3. Suppose Splendid Stereo were to use departmental overhead rates. Compute these rates for Departments I and II for the coming year.

4. Compute the absorption cost of each model stereo amplifier using the departmental overhead rates computed in requirement (3).

5. Suppose management sticks with its policy of setting prices equal to absorption cost plus 15 percent. Compute the new prices for models 1000 and 2000, using the product costs developed in requirement (4).

6. Should Splendid Stereo use plantwide or departmental overhead rates? Explain your answer.

■ **Problem 15–40**
Interdivisional Transfers;
Pricing the Final Product
(LO 5)

National Industries is a diversified corporation with separate operating divisions. Each division's performance is evaluated on the basis of profit and return on investment.

The WindAir Division manufactures and sells air-conditioner units. The coming year's budgeted income statement, which follows, is based upon a sales volume of 15,000 units.

WINDAIR DIVISION
Budgeted Income Statement
(in thousands)

	Per Unit	Total
Sales revenue	$400	$6,000
Manufacturing costs:		
Compressor	$ 70	$1,050
Other direct material	37	555
Direct labor	30	450
Variable overhead	45	675
Fixed overhead	32	480
Total manufacturing costs	$214	$3,210
Gross margin	$186	$2,790
Operating expenses:		
Variable selling	$ 18	$ 270
Fixed selling	19	285
Fixed administrative	38	570
Total operating expenses	$ 75	$1,125
Net income before taxes	$111	$1,665

WindAir's division manager believes sales can be increased if the price of the air-conditioners is reduced. A market research study by an independent firm indicates that a 5 percent reduction in the selling price would increase sales volume 16 percent or 2,400 units. WindAir has sufficient production capacity to manage this increased volume with no increase in fixed costs.

WindAir uses a compressor in its units, which it purchases from an outside supplier at a cost of $70 per compressor. The division manager of WindAir has asked the manager of the Compressor Division about selling compressor units to WindAir. The Compressor Division currently manufactures and sells a unit to outside firms which is similar to the unit used by WindAir. The specifications of the WindAir compressor are slightly different, which would reduce the Compressor Division's direct material cost by $1.50 per unit. In addition, the Compressor Division would not incur any variable selling costs in the units sold to WindAir. The manager of WindAir wants all of the compressors it uses to come from one supplier and has offered to pay $50 for each compressor unit.

The Compressor Division has the capacity to produce 75,000 units. Its budgeted income statement for the coming year, which follows, is based on a sales volume of 64,000 units without considering WindAir's proposal.

COMPRESSOR DIVISION
Budgeted Income Statement
(in thousands)

	Per Unit	Total
Sales revenue	$100	$6,400
Manufacturing costs:		
Direct material	$ 12	$ 768
Direct labor	8	512
Variable overhead	10	640
Fixed overhead	11	704
Total manufacturing costs	$ 41	$2,624
Gross margin	$ 59	$3,776
Operating expenses:		
Variable selling	$ 6	$ 384
Fixed selling	4	256
Fixed administrative	7	448
Total operating expenses	$ 17	$1,088
Net income before taxes	$ 42	$2,688

Required:

1. Should WindAir Division institute the 5 percent price reduction on its air-conditioner units even if it cannot acquire the compressors internally for $50 each? Support your conclusion with appropriate calculations.

2. Independently of your answer to requirement (1), assume WindAir needs 17,400 units. Should the Compressor Division be willing to supply the compressor units for $50 each? Support your conclusions with appropriate calculations.

3. Independently of your answer to requirement (1), assume WindAir needs 17,400 units. Suppose National Industries' top management has specified a transfer price of $50. Would it be in the best interest of *National Industries* for the Compressor Division to supply the compressor units at $50 each to the WindAir Division? Support your conclusions with appropriate calculations.

4. Is $50 a goal-congruent transfer price? [Refer to your answers for requirements (2) and (3).]

(CMA, adapted)

Ward Industries is a manufacturer of standard and custom-designed bottling equipment. Early in December 19x8 Lyan Company asked Ward to quote a price for a custom-designed bottling machine to be delivered in April. Lyan intends to make a decision on the purchase of such a machine by January 1, so Ward would have the entire first quarter of 19x9 to build the equipment.

Ward's pricing policy for custom-designed equipment is 50 percent markup on absorption manufacturing cost. Lyan's specifications for the equipment have been reviewed by Ward's Engineering and Cost Accounting Departments, which made the following estimates for direct material and direct labor.

Direct material	$256,000
Direct labor (11,000 hours at $15)	165,000

■ **Problem 15–41**
Bidding on a Special Order;
Ethics
(LO 5)

Manufacturing overhead is applied on the basis of direct-labor hours. Ward normally plans to run its plant at a level of 15,000 direct-labor hours per month and assigns overhead on the basis of 180,000 direct-labor hours per year. The overhead application rate for 19x9 of $9.00 per hour is based on the following budgeted manufacturing overhead costs for 19x9.

Variable manufacturing overhead	$ 972,000
Fixed manufacturing overhead	648,000
Total manufacturing overhead	$1,620,000

Ward's production schedule calls for 12,000 direct-labor hours per month during the first quarter. If Ward is awarded the contract for the Lyan equipment, production of one of its standard products would have to be reduced. This is necessary because production levels can only be increased to 15,000 direct-labor hours each month on short notice. Furthermore, Ward's employees are unwilling to work overtime.

Sales of the standard product equal to the reduced production would be lost, but there would be no permanent loss of future sales or customers. The standard product for which the production schedule would be reduced has a unit sales price of $12,000 and the following cost structure.

Direct material	$2,500
Direct labor (250 hours at $15)	3,750
Manufacturing overhead (250 hours at $ 9)	2,250
Total cost	$8,500

Lyan needs the custom-designed equipment to increase its bottle-making capacity so that it will not have to buy bottles from an outside supplier. Lyan Company requires 5,000,000 bottles annually. Its present equipment has a maximum capacity of 4,500,000 bottles with a directly traceable cash outlay cost of 15 cents per bottle. Thus, Lyan has had to purchase 500,000 bottles from a supplier at 40 cents each. The new equipment would allow Lyan to manufacture its entire annual demand for bottles at a direct-material cost savings of 1 cent per bottle. Ward estimates that Lyan's annual bottle demand will continue to be 5,000,000 bottles over the next five years, the estimated life of the special-purpose equipment.

Required:

Ward Industries plans to submit a bid to Lyan Company for the manufacture of the special-purpose bottling equipment.

1. Calculate the bid Ward would submit if it follows its standard pricing policy for special-purpose equipment.
2. Calculate the minimum bid Ward would be willing to submit on the Lyan equipment that would result in the same total contribution margin as planned for the first quarter of 19x9.
3. Suppose Ward Industries has submitted a bid slightly above the minimum calculated in requirement (2). Upon receiving Ward's bid, Lyan's assistant purchasing manager telephoned his friend at Tygar Corporation: "Hey Joe, we just got a bid from Ward Industries on some customized equipment. I think Tygar would stand a good chance of beating it. Stop by the house this evening, and I'll show you the details of Ward's bid and the specifications on the machine."

      Is Lyan Company's assistant purchasing manager acting ethically? Explain.

(CMA, adapted)

■ **Problem 15–42**
Pricing a Special Order;
Excess Capacity; Inflation
(LO 5, LO 6)

Plasto Pipe Corporation manufactures a line of plastic plumbing products that are sold through hardware stores. The company's sales have declined slightly for the past two years, resulting in idle plants and equipment. Although Plasto Pipe is not operating at capacity, the company generated a profit last year, as shown in the following income statement.

PLASTO PIPE CORPORATION
Income Statement
(in thousands)

	Dollar Amount	Percentage
Sales	$1,500	100%
Cost of goods sold:		
Direct material	$ 200	13%
Direct labor	400	27
Manufacturing overhead*	390	26
Cost of goods sold	$ 990	66%
Manufacturing margin before underapplied manufacturing overhead	$ 510	34%
Underapplied manufacturing overhead†	10	1
Manufacturing margin	$ 500	33%

	Dollar Amount	Percentage
Operating expenses:		
Sales commissions	$ 60	4%
Sales administration	30	2
General administration	110	7
Total operating expenses	$ 200	13%
Net income before income taxes	$ 300	20%
Income taxes (40%)	120	8
Net income	$ 180	12%

*Schedule of manufacturing overhead:

Variable:	
Indirect labor	$100
Supplies	40
Power	120
Fixed costs applied:	
Factory administration	60
Depreciation	70
	$390

†Schedule of underapplied overhead (due to idle capacity)

Depreciation	$ 10

A Plasto Pipe engineer met a former college classmate at a convention of machinery builders. The classmate is employed by Paddington Company, which is also in the plastic products business. During their conversation it became evident that Plasto Pipe might be able to make a particular product for Paddington with the currently unused equipment and space.

The following requirements were specified by Paddington for the new product.

1. Paddington needs 80,000 units per year for the next three years.
2. The product is to be built to Paddington specifications.
3. Plasto Pipe is not to enter into independent production of the product during the 3-year contract.
4. Paddington would provide Plasto Pipe, without charge, with a special machine to finish the product. The machine becomes the property of Plasto Pipe at the end of the three-year period.

The Plasto Pipe engineering, production, and accounting departments agreed upon the following facts if the contract were accepted.

Manufacturing

- The present idle capacity would be fully used.
- One additional part-time factory supervisor would be required; the annual salary would be $15,000.
- The annual quantity of direct material and direct labor would increase by 10 percent at current prices. There would be no increase in indirect labor.
- The power and supply quantity requirements would increase 10 percent at current prices, due to the reactivation of idle machines.
- The machine provided by Paddington would increase the annual power and supply costs by $10,000 and $4,000, respectively, at current prices.
- The Paddington machine would have no value to Plasto Pipe at the end of the contract.

Sales

- A sales commission of $10,000 would be paid to the sales personnel arranging the contract.
- No additional sales or administrative costs would be incurred.

General administration

- No additional general administrative costs would be incurred.

Other information

■   Estimated cost increases due to inflation for the entire three-year period are as follows:

Direct material	5%
Direct labor	10%
Power	20%
Depreciation	0
Sales commissions	0
Income taxes	0
All other items	10%

■   Inventory balances, which have remained stable for the past three years, will not be increased or decreased by the production of the new product.

Required:

1.   Calculate the total price needed for the three-year order (240,000 units) if Plasto Pipe Corporation wants to make an after-tax profit of 10 percent of the sales price on this order.

2.   Calculate the total price for the three-year order (240,000 units) if this order were to contribute nothing to net income after taxes.

(CMA, adapted)

Cases

■   **Case 15–43**
Pricing a Special Order;
Ethics
(LO 5)

Jenco Inc. manufactures one product, a combination fertilizer/weed-killer called Fertikil. The product is sold nationwide to retail nurseries and gardening stores. Taylor Nursery plans to sell a similar fertilizer/weed-killer through its regional nursery chain under its private label. Taylor has asked Jenco to submit a bid for a 25,000-pound order of the private-brand compound. While the chemical composition of the Taylor compound differs from Fertikil, the manufacturing process is very similar. The Taylor compound would be produced in 1,000-pound lots. Each lot would require 60 direct-labor hours and the following chemicals.

Chemicals	Quantity in Pounds
CW–3	400
JX–6	300
MZ–8	200
BE–7	100

The first three chemicals (CW–3, JX–6, MZ–8) are all used in the production of Fertikil. BE–7 was used in a compound that Jenco has discontinued. This chemical was not sold or discarded, because it does not deteriorate and Jenco has adequate storage facilities. Jenco could sell BE–7 at the prevailing market price, less 10 cents per pound for selling and handling expenses.

Jenco also has on hand a chemical called CN–5, manufactured for use in another product that is no longer produced. CN–5, which cannot be used in Fertikil, can be substituted for CW–3 on a one-for-one basis without affecting the quality of the Taylor compound. The quantity of CN–5 in inventory has a salvage value of $500. Inventory and cost data for the chemicals that can be used to produce the Taylor compound are as follows:

Raw Material	Pounds in Inventory	Actual Price per Pound When Purchased	Current Market Price per Pound
CW–3	22,000	$ .80	$ .90
JX–6	5,000	$ .55	$ .60
MZ–8	8,000	$1.40	$1.60
BE–7	4,000	$ .60	$ .65
CN–5	5,500	$ .75	*

*Salvage value of $500 for entire inventory on hand.

The current direct-labor rate is $7.00 per hour. The manufacturing-overhead rate is established at the beginning of the year using direct-labor hours (DLH) as the base. The predetermined overhead rate for the current year, based on a two-shift capacity of 400,000 total direct-labor hours with no overtime, is as follows:

Variable manufacturing overhead	$2.25	per direct-labor hour
Fixed manufacturing overhead	3.75	per direct-labor hour
Combined rate	$6.00	per direct-labor hour

Jenco's production manager reports that the present equipment and facilities are adequate to manufacture the Taylor compound. However, Jenco is within 800 hours of its two-shift capacity this month before it must schedule overtime. If need be, the Taylor compound could be produced on regular time by shifting a portion of Fertikil production to overtime. Jenco's pay rate for overtime hours is one-and-one-half the regular pay rate, or $10.50 per hour. There is no allowance for any overtime premium in the manufacturing-overhead rate. Jenco's standard markup policy for new products is 25 percent of absorption manufacturing cost.

Required:

1. Assume Jenco Inc. has decided to submit a bid for a 25,000 pound order of Taylor's new compound, to be delivered by the end of the current month. Taylor has indicated that this one-time order will not be repeated. Calculate the lowest price Jenco can bid for the order and not reduce its net income.

2. Independently of your answer to requirement (1), assume that Taylor Nursery plans to place regular orders for 25,000 pound lots of the new compound during the coming year. Jenco expects the demand for Fertikil to remain strong, so the recurring orders from Taylor will put Jenco over its two-shift capacity. However, production can be scheduled so that 60 percent of each Taylor order can be completed during regular hours, or Fertikil production could be shifted temporarily to overtime so that the Taylor orders could be produced on regular time. Jenco's production manager has estimated that the prices of all chemicals will stabilize at the current market rates for the coming year. All other manufacturing costs are expected to be maintained at the same rates or amounts.

   Calculate the price Jenco Inc. should quote Taylor Nursery for each 25,000 pound lot of the new compound, assuming that there will be recurring orders during the coming year. Assume that Jenco's management believes new products sold on a recurring basis should be priced to cover their full production costs plus the standard markup.

3. Suppose Jenco Inc. has submitted a bid to Taylor Nursery. However, Dalton Industries, a competitor of Jenco, has submitted a lower bid. Before accepting Dalton's bid, the owner of Taylor Nursery telephoned his golfing buddy, who is Jenco's vice president of manufacturing. "I've got some bad news for you. Jenco's been outbid on the private label order by Dalton Industries. I've been thinking, though. It looks to me like Jenco included some costs in its bid that could be eliminated. If you'd like to revise the Jenco bid, we might be able to steer this deal your way. If it would help, I can show you Dalton's figures."

   Discuss the ethical issues in this scenario.

(CMA, adapted)

Systems Planners Institute (SPI), a professional association for systems analysts and computer programmers, has 50,000 members. SPI holds a convention each October and planning for the current year's convention is progressing smoothly. The convention budget for promotional brochures, fees and expenses for 20 speakers, equipment rental for presentations, the travel and expenses of 25 staff people, consultant fees, and volunteer expenses is $330,000. This amount does not include the hotel charges for meeting rooms, luncheons, banquets, or receptions.

SPI has always priced each function at the convention separately. Members select and pay for only those functions they attend. Members who attend the convention pay a registration fee that allows them to attend the annual reception and meeting. The Annual Convention Committee has recommended that SPI set a single flat fee for the entire convention; registered members would be entitled to attend all functions.

The following table presents the convention functions, the percentage of attendees that can be expected to attend each function, the price SPI would charge for each function if it were priced separately, and the hotel charges for food service and meeting rooms. The percentage of attendees expected to attend each function is based on past experience and is expected to hold regardless of the pricing scheme used.

■ **Case 15–44**
Pricing for a Professional Convention
(LO 5)

Function	Percentage of Attendees Who Will Participate	Separate Price of Function	Hotel Charge
Registration fee	100%	$50	None
Reception	100%	Free	$25/attendee
Annual meeting	100%	Free	$2,000 for meeting hall
Keynote luncheon	90%	$40	$25/attendee
Six concurrent sessions*	70%	$60	$200/room or $1,200 in total
Plenary session	70%	$50	$2,000 for meeting hall
Six workshops*	50%	$100	$200/room or $1,200 in total
Banquet	90%	$50	$30 attendee

*Attendee selects one session for the fee.

The hotel's package of services to SPI and the convention attendees is as follows:

1. Three free rooms for convention headquarters and storage.

2. Twenty percent discount for all convention attendees who stay in the hotel during the three-day convention. The types of rooms, regular posted rate, and the proportion of each type of room taken by attendees are as follows. Attendees are to make room reservations directly with the hotel, and all hotel room charges are the responsibility of the attendees.

Type	Regular Posted Rate per Night	Proportion Rented
Single	$100	10%
Studio	105	10
Double	125	75
Suite	200	5

3. SPI is given credit for one free double room for three days for every 50 convention registrants who stay at the hotel. The credit will be applied to the room charges of staff and speakers.

4. Meeting rooms and halls are free if food is served at the function.

5. Meeting rooms and halls for professional sessions are free if 1,000 members are registered at the hotel.

6. Meal costs given in the table include all taxes and gratuities.

7. The hotel receives all revenue from cash bar sales at the reception, and before the luncheons and banquet. The hotel estimates that the average consumption at each of these functions will be one cocktail per attendee at $1.50 per cocktail.

If SPI continues to price each convention function separately, the prices given in the prior table will apply. Expected attendance under this type of pricing scheme is 2,000. The Annual Convention Committee has estimated the convention attendance for three different single flat-fee pricing structures as follows:

Proposed Single Flat Fee	Estimated Attendees
$325	1,600
300	1,750
275	1,900

SPI estimates that 60 percent of the people who attend the convention will stay in the convention hotel, and each attendee will need a separate room for an average stay of three nights.

Required:

Assume that SPI wants to maximize its contribution margin from its annual convention. Write a memo to the president of SPI recommending whether SPI should price each function at the convention separately or charge one of the three single flat fees for the convention. Support your recommendation with an appropriate analysis.

(CMA, adapted)

Current Issues in Managerial Accounting

"Rattling Cages: Utilities' Quiet World Is Shaken Up as Enron Moves on Philadelphia," *The Wall Street Journal*, **January 7, 1998, Kathryn Kranhold.**

Overview
As the $200 billion-a-year utility industry enters the deregulation era, firms are becoming serious price competitors. An example involves a Pennyslvania firm, Peco Energy, which offered its customers a 10% rate cut and Houston-based Enron which doubled that offer.

Suggested Discussion Questions
Prior to deregulation, how were electric prices determined? After deregulation, what factors will affect utility prices? List some political, legal, and image-related issues.

■ **Issue 15–45**
Major Influences on Pricing Decisions; Competitive Bidding

"Hewlett-Packard to Unveil Sub-$800 PCs Using Intel's Latest MMX Technology," *The Wall Street Journal*, **January 5, 1998, Jim Carlton.**

Overview
Hewlett-Packard (HP) announced that it will sell 200 megahertz Pentium PCs with MMX technology for $799. The price is $200 below the cheapest computers with similar specifications.

Suggested Discussion Questions
As a group, explain how the following four factors influenced Hewlett Packard's pricing decision.

1. Customer demand.
2. Actions of competitors.
3. Costs.
4. Political, legal, and image-related issues.

■ **Issue 15–46**
Major Influences on Pricing Decisions

"Behind the Brawl over Java," *Business Week*, **October 20, 1997.**

Overview
According to Sun Microsystems, JAVA's use has been slowed by a Microsoft programming trick. In a related lawsuit, Sun sued Microsoft for violating their licensing agreement.

Suggested Discussion Questions
Should the Justice Department be concerned about Microsoft's actions with respect to Sun? Would Microsoft's actions be of concern to the Antitrust division of the Justice Department? What effect does JAVA have on computer software practices?

■ **Issue 15–47**
Effect of Antitrust Laws on Pricing

"Low Prices. Low Rates. It's Time to Relax," *Business Week*, **September 15, 1997.**

Overview
This article discusses inflation, interest rates, economic growth, consumer behavior, and prices.

Suggested Discussion Questions
Discuss how inflation can affect companies and consumers. How do inflation and interest rates affect a firm's pricing policy?

■ **Issue 15–48**
Major Influences on Pricing Decisions

"Sun Microsystems Goes on a Roll," *The Wall Street Journal*, **August 19, 1997, Lee Gomes.**

Overview
Sun's profits have increased steadily despite a change in its product mix. The firm's revenue, which was once derived primarily from desktop computer sales, is now derived increasingly from sales of its servers.

Suggested Discussion Questions
Discuss Sun's pricing strategy in the desktop and server markets. How is Sun attempting to reduce costs? How will Windows NT software affect its pricing strategy?

■ **Issue 15–49**
Strategic Pricing of New Products

16

Chapter Sixteen

Capital Expenditure Decisions: An Introduction

After completing this chapter, you should be able to:

1 Explain the importance of the time value of money in capital-budgeting decisions.

2 Compute the future value and present value of cash flows occurring over several time periods.

3 Use the net-present-value method and the internal-rate-of-return method to evaluate an investment proposal.

4 Compare the net-present-value and internal-rate-of-return methods, and state the assumptions underlying each method.

5 Use both the total-cost approach and the incremental-cost approach to evaluate an investment proposal.

6 Describe a typical capital-budgeting approval process, and explain the concept of a postaudit.

7 Explain the potential conflict between using discounted-cash-flow analysis for approving capital projects and accrual accounting for periodic performance evaluation.

8 Describe the process of justifying investments in advanced manufacturing technology.

CITY COUNCIL APPROVES INSTALLATION OF NEW COMPUTER SYSTEM

Mountainview, NM—Mayor Debby Richards announced earlier today that City Council has approved the purchase of a new computer system to serve municipal functions. "The council vote was unanimous," said Richards. "I recommended the new system on the basis of a thorough analysis by the city controller's office. It was a pretty clear decision, and it's nice to have the whole council see things my way, for a change."

The city's new computer system will be a set of net-worked personal computers. A variety of new software applications will be purchased as well to manage everything from municipal personnel records, to the city tax rolls, to insurance records on the city's vehicles. "The new system will be more powerful, in terms of both speed and memory, and it will be much more convenient in many ways. We expect to save over $200,000 per year in operating costs in comparison with our current system," said Richards. "Of course, we also have to lay out $300,000 for the new hardware, and another $75,000 for software. These are all up-front costs. The savings, on the other hand, are spread across the years. We're also anticipating the need to spend about $60,000 for a system upgrade three years down the road. Taking account of the different timing on these various cash flows, the city controller's analysis showed a substantial advantage to the new system. That will put money back into the pockets of our taxpayers, and that is part of my job."

Managers in all organizations periodically face major decisions that involve cash flows over several years. Decisions involving the acquisition of machinery, vehicles, buildings, or land are examples of such decisions. Other examples include decisions involving significant changes in a production process or adding a major new line of products or services to the organization's activities.

Decisions involving cash inflows and outflows beyond the current year are called **capital-budgeting decisions.** Managers encounter two types of capital-budgeting decisions.

A **capital-budgeting decision** involves cash flows beyond the current year.

Acceptance-or-Rejection Decisions   In **acceptance-or-rejection decisions,** managers must decide whether they should undertake a particular capital investment project. In such a decision, the required funds are available or readily obtainable, and management must decide whether the project is worthwhile. For example, the controller for the city of Mountainview is faced with a decision as to whether to replace one of the city's oldest street-cleaning machines. The funds are available in the city's capital budget. The question is whether the cost savings with the new machine will justify the expenditure. The analysis of **acceptance-or-rejection decisions** is the focus of this chapter.

An **acceptance-or-rejection decision** evaluates whether a particular capital investment proposal should be accepted.

A **capital-rationing decision** involves choosing which of several investment proposals to accept to make the best use of limited investment funds.

Capital-Rationing Decisions   In **capital-rationing decisions,** managers must decide which of several worthwhile projects makes the best use of limited investment funds. To illustrate, suppose the voters in the city of Mountainview have recently passed a proposition mandating the city government to undertake a cost-reduction program to trim administrative expenses. The voters also passed a bond issue, which enables the city government to raise $100,000 through the sale of bonds, to provide capital to finance the cost-reduction program. The mayor has in mind three cost-reduction programs, each of which would reduce administrative costs significantly over the next five years. However, the city can afford only two of the programs with the $100,000 of investment capital available. The mayor's decision problem is to decide which projects to pursue. Capital-rationing (or ranking) decisions are discussed in Chapter 17.

Focus on Projects   Capital-budgeting problems tend to focus on specific projects or programs. Is it best for Mountainview to purchase the new street-cleaner or not? Which cost-reduction programs will provide the city with the greatest benefits? Should a university buy a new electron microscope? Should a manufacturing firm acquire a computer-integrated manufacturing system?

Over time, as managers make decisions about a variety of specific programs and projects, the organization as a whole becomes the sum total of its individual investments, activities, programs, and projects. The organization's performance in any particular year is the combined result of all the projects under way during that year. Exhibit 16–1 depicts this project viewpoint of an organization's activities.

Concept of Present Value

LO 1 Explain the importance of the time value of money in capital-budgeting decisions.

Before we can study the capital-budgeting methods used to make decisions such as those faced in the city of Mountainview, we must examine the basic tools used in those methods. The fundamental concept in a capital-budgeting decision analysis is the *time value of* money. Would you rather receive a $100 gift check from a relative today, or would you rather receive a letter promising the $100 in a year? Most of us would rather have the cash now. There are two possible reasons for this attitude. First, if we receive the money today, we can spend it on that new sweater now instead of waiting a year. Second, as an alternative strategy, we can invest the $100 received today at 10 percent interest. Then, at the end of one year, we will have $110. Thus, there is a time value associated with money. A $100 cash flow today is not the same as a $100 cash flow in 1 year, 2 years, or 10 years.

Projects and programs

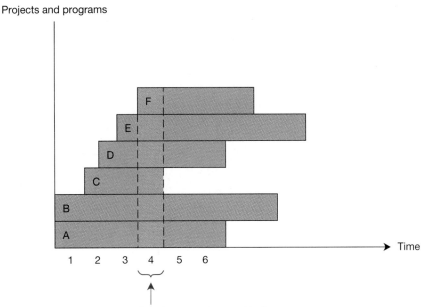

Exhibit 16–1

An Organization as a
Collection of Projects and
Programs

The organization's overall performance in year 4 is the
combined result of projects A through F during the year

Compound Interest   Suppose you invest $100 today (time 0) at 10 percent interest for
one year. How much will you have after one year? The answer is $110, as the following
analysis shows.

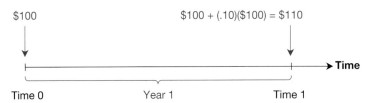

The $110 at time 1 (end of one year) is composed of two parts, as shown below.

Principal, time 0 amount	$100
Interest earned during year 1 (.10 × $100)	10
Amount at time 1	$110

LO 2   Compute the future value and
present value of cash flows occurring
over several time periods.

Thus, the $110 at time 1 consists of the $100 at time 0, called the **principal,** plus the
$10 of interest earned during the year.

The **principal** is the
amount originally
invested, not including
any interest earned.

  Now suppose you leave your $110 invested during the second year. How much will
you have at the end of two years? As the following analysis shows, the answer is $121.

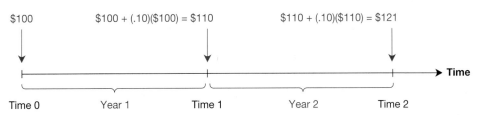

We can break down the $121 at time 2 into two parts as follows:

Amount at time 1	$110
Interest earned during year 2 (.10 × $110)	11
Amount at time 2	$121

Compound interest is when interest is earned on prior periods' interest.

The **future value** is the amount to which invested funds accumulate over a specified period of time.

Notice that you earned more interest in year 2 ($11) than you earned in year 1 ($10). Why? During year 2, you earned 10 percent interest on the original principal of $100 *and* you earned 10 percent interest on the year 1 interest of $10. When interest is earned on prior periods' interest, we call the phenomenon **compound interest.** Exhibit 16–2 shows how your invested funds grow over the five-year period of the investment. As the exhibit shows, the **future value** of your initial $100 investment is $161.05 after five years.

As the number of years in an investment increases, it becomes more cumbersome to compute the future value of the investment using the method in Exhibit 16–2. Fortunately, the simple formula shown below may be used to compute the future value of any investment.

$$F_n = P(1 + r)^n \tag{1}$$

where P denotes principal
            r denotes interest rate per year
            n denotes number of years

The **accumulation factor** is the value of $(1 + r)^n$ in a future-value calculation, where r denotes the interest rate per year and n denotes the number of years.

Using formula (1) to compute the future value after five years of your $100 investment, we have the following computation.

$$\begin{aligned} F_n &= P(1 + r)^n \\ &= \$100(1 + .10)^5 \\ &= \$100(1.6105) = \$161.05 \end{aligned}$$

The value of $(1 + r)^n$ is called the **accumulation factor.** The values of $(1 + r)^n$, for various combinations of r and n, are tabulated in Table I of the appendix at the end of this chapter.

Use formula (1) and the tabulated values in Table I to compute the future value after 10 years of an $800 investment that earns interest at the rate of 12 percent per year.[1]

Present Value   In the discussion above, we computed the future value of an investment when the original principal is known. Now consider a slightly different problem. Suppose you know how much money you want to accumulate at the end of a five-year investment. Your problem is to determine how much your initial investment needs to be in order to accumulate the desired amount in five years. To solve this problem, we start with formula (1):

$$F_n = P(1 + r)^n$$

Now divide each side of the preceding equation by $(1 + r)^n$.

$$P = F_n \left(\frac{1}{(1 + r)^n} \right) \tag{2}$$

The **present value** is the economic value now of a cash flow that will occur in the future.

In formula (2), P denotes what is commonly referred to as the **present value** of the cash flow F_n, which occurs after n years when the interest rate is r.

Let's try out formula (2) on your investment problem, which we analyzed in Exhibit 16–2. Suppose you did not know the value of the initial investment required if you want to accumulate $161.05 at the end of five years in an investment that earns 10 percent per year. We can determine the present value of the investment as follows:

---

[1] Using formula (1): F = $800 $(1 + .12)^{10}$. From Table 1, $(1+.12)^{10} = 3.106$. (Note that the values in Table I are rounded.) Thus, the future value of the investment is ($800) (3.106) = $2,484.80. Compound interest will more than triple the original $800 investment in 10 years.

Time 0	Principal, time 0 amount	$100
Year 1	Interest earned during year 1 (.10 × $100)	10
Time 1	Amount at time 1	$110
Year 2	Interest earned during year 2 (.10 × $110)	11
Time 2	Amount at time 2	$121.00
Year 3	Interest earned during year 3 (.10 × $121)	12.10
Time 3	Amount at time 3	$133.10
Year 4	Interest earned during year 4 (.10 × $133.10)	13.31
Time 4	Amount at time 4	$146.41
Year 5	Interest earned during year 5 (.10 × $146.41)	14.64
Time 5	Amount at time 5	$161.05

Time

$$P = F_n \left(\frac{1}{(1 + r)^n} \right)$$

$$= \$161.05 \left(\frac{1}{(1 + .10)^5} \right)$$

$$= \$161.05(.6209) = \$100$$

Thus, as we knew already, you must invest $100 now in order to accumulate $161.05 after five years in an investment earning 10 percent per year. The *present value of* $100 and the *future value* of $161.05 at time 5 are *economically equivalent,* given that the annual interest rate is 10 percent. If you are planning to invest the $100 received now, then you should be indifferent between receiving the present value of $100 now or receiving the future value of $161.05 at the end of five years.

When we used formula (2) to compute the present value of the $161.05 cash flow at time 5, we used a process called *discounting.* The interest rate used when we discount a future cash flow to compute its present value is called the **discount rate.** The value of $1/(1 + r)^n$, which appears in formula (2), is called the *discount factor.* Discount factors, for various combinations of r and n, are tabulated in Table III of the appendix.

The **discount rate** is the interest rate used in computing the present value of a cash flow.

Suppose you want to accumulate $18,000 to buy a new car in four years, and you can earn interest at the rate of 8 percent per year on an investment you make now. How much do you need to invest now? Use formula (2) and the discount factors in Table III to compute the present value of the required $18,000 amount needed at the end of four years. [2]

Present Value of a Cash-Flow Series The present-value problem we just solved involved only a single future cash flow. Now consider a slightly different problem.

---

[2] Using formula (2): $P = \$18,000 \times [1/(1 + .08)^4]$. From Table III, $1/(1 + .08)^4 = .735$. (Note that the values in Table III are rounded.) Thus, the present value of the required $18,000 amount is ($18,000) (.735) = $13,230. An investment of $13,230 made now, earning annual interest at 8 percent, will accumulate to $18,000 at the end of four years.

Suppose you just won $5,000 in the state lottery. You want to spend some of the cash now, but you have decided to save enough to rent a beach condominium during spring break of each of the next three years. You would like to deposit enough in a bank account now so that you can withdraw $1,000 from the account at the end of each of the next three years. The money in the bank account will earn 8 percent per year. The question, then, is how much do you need to deposit? Another way of asking the same question is, what is the *present value* of a series of three $1,000 cash flows at the end of each of the next three years, given that the discount rate is 8 percent?

One way to figure out the answer to the question is to compute the present value of each of the three $1,000 cash flows and add the three present-value amounts. We can use formula (2) for these calculations, as shown in panel A of Exhibit 16–3. Notice that the present value of each of the $1,000 cash flows is different, because the timing of the cash flows is different. The earlier the cash flow will occur, the higher is its present value.

Examine panel A of Exhibit 16–3 carefully. We obtained the $2,577 total present value by adding three present-value amounts. Each of these amounts is the result of multiplying $1,000 by a discount factor. Notice that we can obtain the same final result by adding the three discount factors first, and then multiplying by $1,000. This approach is taken in panel B of Exhibit 16–3. The sum of the three discount factors is called an *annuity discount fac*tor, because a series of equivalent cash flows is called an **annuity.** Annuity discount factors for various combinations of *r* and *n* are tabulated in Table IV of the appendix.

Now let's verify that $2,577 is the right amount to finance your three spring-break vacations. Exhibit 16–4 shows how your bank account will change over the three-year period as you earn interest and then withdraw $1,000 each year.

An **annuity** is a series of equivalent cash flows.

Future Value of a Cash-Flow Series

To complete our discussion of present-value and future-value concepts, let's consider the series of $1,000 condo rental payments from the condo owner's perspective. Suppose the owner invests each $1,000 rental payment in a bank account that pays 8 percent interest per year. How much will the condo owner accumulate at the end of the three-year period? An equivalent question is, What is the future value of the three-year series of $1,000 cash flows, given an annual interest rate of 8 percent? Exhibit 16–5, which appears on page 666, answers the question in two ways. In panel A of the exhibit, three separate future-value calculations are made using formula (1). Notice that the $1,000 cash flow at time 1 is multiplied by $(1.08)^2$, since it has two years to earn interest. The $1,000 cash flow at time 2 has only one year to earn interest, and the time 3 cash flow has no time to earn interest.

In panel B of the exhibit, the three-year *annuity accumulation factor* is used. This factor is the sum of the three accumulation factors used in panel A of the exhibit. The annuity accumulation factors for various combinations of *r* and *n* are tabulated in Table II of the appendix.

Using the Tables Correctly

When using the tables in the appendix to solve future-value and present-value problems, be sure to select the correct table. Table I is used to find the *future value* of a *single* cash flow, and Table III is used to find the *present value* of a *single* cash flow. Table II is used in finding the *future value* of a *series* of identical cash flows; Table IV is used in finding the *present value* of a *series* of identical cash flows.

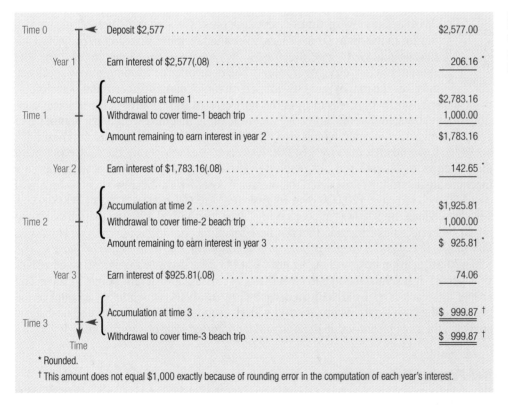

A.   Present Value of Cash-Flow Series Using Three Independent Present-Value Calculations

Present-value formula [formula (2)]: $P = F_n \left(\dfrac{1}{(1 + r)^n} \right)$

Present value of time 1 cash flow: $1,000 $\left(\dfrac{1}{(1 + .08)^1} \right)$ = $1,000(.9259) = $925.90

Present value of time 2 cash flow: $1,000 $\left(\dfrac{1}{(1 + .08)^2} \right)$ = $1,000(.8573) =   857.30

Present value of time 3 cash flow: $1,000 $\left(\dfrac{1}{(1 + .08)^3} \right)$ = $1,000(.7938) =   793.80

Total: present value of series of three cash flows $2,577.00

Sum of Three Discount Factors
is the Annuity Discount Factor

B.   Present Value of Cash-Flow Series Using the Annuity Discount Factor

Present value of series of three cash flows = $1,000(2.5770) = $2,577.00

Exhibit 16–3

Present Value of a Series of
Cash Flows

Time 0 — Deposit $2,577 .... $2,577.00

Year 1   Earn interest of $2,577(.08) .... 206.16 *

Time 1 {
Accumulation at time 1 .... $2,783.16
Withdrawal to cover time-1 beach trip 1,000.00
Amount remaining to earn interest in year 2 .... $1,783.16
}

Year 2   Earn interest of $1,783.16(.08) .... 142.65 *

Time 2 {
Accumulation at time 2 .... $1,925.81
Withdrawal to cover time-2 beach trip 1,000.00
Amount remaining to earn interest in year 3 .... $ 925.81 *
}

Year 3   Earn interest of $925.81(.08) 74.06

Time 3 {
Accumulation at time 3 .... $ 999.87 †
Withdrawal to cover time-3 beach trip .... $ 999.87 †
}

Time

* Rounded.

† This amount does not equal $1,000 exactly because of rounding error in the computation of each year's interest.

Exhibit 16–4

Verification of Present-Value
Calculation for Cash-Flow
Series

Be careful not to confuse future value with present value or to confuse a single cash flow with a series of identical cash flows.

If you have a calculator that will exponentiate (raise a number to a power), you can forget the tables altogether. Just use the pertinent formula and compute the appropriate factor yourself.

Exhibit 16–5

Future Value of a Series of
Cash Flows

A.   Future Value of Cash-Flow Series Using Three Independent Future-Value Calculations

Present-value formula [formula (1)]: $F_n = P(1 + r)^n$

Future value of time 1 cash flow: $1,000 $(1 + .08)^2$ = $1,000(1.1664) =$ $1,166.40

Future value of time 2 cash flow: $1,000 $(1 + .08)^1$ = $1,000(1.0800) =$ 1,080.00

Future value of time 3 cash flow: $1,000   = $1,000(1.0000) =$ 1,000.00

Total: future value of series of three cash flows $3,246.40

Sum of Three Accumulation Factors
is the Annuity Accumulation Factor

B.   Future Value of Cash-Flow Series Using the Annuity Accumulation Factor

Present value of series of three cash flows   = $1,000(3.2464) = $3,246.40

Discounted-Cash-Flow Analysis

LO 3   Use the net-present-value
method and the internal-rate-of-return
method to evaluate an investment
proposal.

MOUNTAINVIEW

With our review of future-value and present-value tools behind us, we can return to the main issue of how to evaluate capital-investment projects. Our discussion will be illustrated by several decisions made by the Mountainview city government. The controller of Mountainview routinely advises the mayor and city council on major capital-investment decisions.

Currently under consideration is the purchase of a new street cleaner. The controller has estimated that the city's old street-cleaning machine would last another five years. A new street cleaner, which also would last for five years, can be purchased for $50,470. It would cost the city $14,000 less each year to operate the new equipment than it costs to operate the old machine. The expected cost savings with the new machine are due to lower expected maintenance costs. Thus, the new street cleaner will cost $50,470 and save $70,000 over its five-year life ($70,000 = 5 × $14,000 savings per year). Since the $70,000 in cost savings exceeds the $50,470 acquisition cost, one might be tempted to conclude that the new machine should be purchased. However, *this analysis is flawed, since it does not account for the time value of money.* The $50,470 acquisition cost will occur now, but the cost savings are spread over a five-year period. It is a mistake to add cash flows occurring at different points in time. The proper approach is to use **discounted-cash-flow analysis**, which takes account of the timing of the cash flows. There are two widely used methods of discounted-cash-flow analysis: the net-present-value method and the internal-rate-of-return method.

The **discounted-cash-flow analysis** of an investment proposal takes into account the time value of money.

The **hurdle rate** is the minimum desired rate of return used in a discounted-cash-flow analysis.

Net-Present-Value Method

The following four steps comprise a net-present-value analysis of an investment proposal:

1. Prepare a table showing the cash flows during each year of the proposed investment.
2. Compute the present value of each cash flow, using a discount rate that reflects the cost of acquiring investment capital. This discount rate is often called the **hurdle rate** or **minimum desired rate of return.**

This 20-screen theater complex in San Diego will generate cash flows over many years. In making such a significant investment decision, managers use discounted-cash-flow analysis.

3. Compute the **net present value,** which is the sum of the present values of the cash flows.

4. If the net present value (NPV) is positive, accept the investment proposal. Otherwise, reject it.

Exhibit 16–6 displays these four steps for the Mountainview controller's street-cleaner decision. In step (2) the controller used a discount rate of 10 percent. Notice that the cost savings are $14,000 in each of the years 1 through 5. Thus, the cash flows in those years comprise a five-year, $14,000 annuity. The controller used the annuity discount factor to compute the present value of the five years of cost savings.

> The **net present value** is the present value of a project's future cash flow less the cost of the initial investment.

Mountainview City Government **Purchase of Street Cleaner** $(r = .10, n = 5)$						
Step 1						
	Time 0	Time 1	Time 2	Time 3	Time 4	Time 5
Acquisition cost	$(50,470)					
Annual cost savings		$14,000	$14,000	$14,000	$14,000	$14,000
Step 2			Present value of annuity = $14,000(3.791)			
				Annuity discount factor for $r = .10$ and $n = 5$ from Table IV in the appendix.		
Present value	$(50,470)			$53,074		
Step 3 Net present value		$2,604				
Step 4 Accept proposal, since net present value is positive.						

Exhibit 16–6

Net-Present-Value Method

C I T Y   O F

MOUNTAINVIEW

The net-present-value analysis indicates that the city should purchase the new street cleaner. The present value of the cost savings exceeds the new machine's acquisition cost.

Internal-Rate-of-Return Method

The **internal rate of return** is the discount rate required for an asset's net present value to be zero. Also known as the **time-adjusted rate of return**.

An alternative discounted-cash-flow method for analyzing investment proposals is the internal-rate-of-return method. An asset's **internal rate of return** (or **time-adjusted rate of return**) is the true economic return earned by the asset over its life. Another way of stating the definition is that an asset's *internal rate of return (IRR)* is the discount rate that would be required in a net-present-value analysis in order for the asset's net present value to be exactly *zero*.

What is the internal rate of return on Mountainview's proposed street-cleaner acquisition? Recall that the asset has a positive net present value, given that the city's cost of acquiring investment capital is 10 percent. Would you expect the asset's IRR to be higher or lower than 10 percent? Think about this question intuitively. The higher the discount rate used in a net-present-value analysis, the lower the present value of all future cash flows will be. This is true because a higher discount rate means that it is even more important to have the money earlier instead of later. Thus, a discount rate higher than 10 percent would be required to drive the new street cleaner's net present value down to zero.

Finding the Internal Rate of Return   How can we find this rate? One way is trial and error. We could experiment with different discount rates until we find the one that yields a zero net present value. We already know that a 10 percent discount rate yields a positive NPV. Let's try 14 percent. Discounting the five-year, $14,000 cost-savings annuity at 14 percent yields a negative NPV of $(2,408).

$$(3.433)(\$14,000) - \$50,470 = \$(2,408)$$

Annuity discount factor for $r = .14$ and $n = 5$ from Table IV in the appendix.

What does this negative NPV at a 14 percent discount rate mean? We increased the discount rate too much. Therefore, the street cleaner's internal rate of return must lie between 10 percent and 14 percent. Let's try 12 percent:

$$(3.605)(\$14,000) - \$50,470 = 0$$

Annuity discount factor for $r = .12$ and $n = 5$ from Table IV in the appendix.

That's it. The new street-cleaner's internal rate of return is 12 percent. With a 12 percent discount rate, the investment proposal's net present value is zero, since the street-cleaner's acquisition cost is equal to the present value of the cost savings.

We could have found the internal rate of return more easily in this case, because the street-cleaner's cash flows exhibit a very special pattern. The cash inflows in years 1 through 5 are identical, as shown below.

Time	0	1	2	3	4	5
Cash flow	$(50,470)	$14,000	$14,000	$14,000	$14,000	$14,000

Initial cash outflow (acquisition cost)

Equal cash inflows (operating-cost savings)

When we have this special pattern of cash flows, the internal rate of return is determined in two steps, as follows:

1. Divide the initial cash outflow by the equivalent annual cash inflows:

$$\frac{\$50,470}{\$14,000} = 3.605 = \textbf{Annuity discount factor}$$

2. In Table IV, find the discount rate associated with the annuity discount factor computed in step (1), given the appropriate number of years in the annuity.

From Table IV of the appendix		r		
		10%	12%	14%
	$n = 5$	3.791	3.605	3.433

Decision Rule   Now that we have determined the investment proposal's internal rate of return to be 12 percent, how do we use this fact in making a decision? The decision rule in the internal-rate-of-return method is to accept an investment proposal if its internal rate of return is greater than the organization's cost of capital (or hurdle rate). Thus, Mountainview's controller should recommend that the new street cleaner be purchased. The internal rate of return on the proposal, 12 percent, exceeds the city's hurdle rate, 10 percent.

To summarize, the internal-rate-of-return method of discounted-cash-flow analysis includes the following three steps:

1. Prepare a table showing the cash flows during each year of the proposed investment. This table will be identical to the cash-flow table prepared under the net-present-value method. (See Exhibit 16–6.)
2. Compute the internal rate of return for the proposed investment. This is accomplished by finding a discount rate that yields a zero net present value for the proposed investment.
3. If the internal rate of return is greater than the hurdle rate (cost of acquiring investment capital), accept the investment proposal. Otherwise, reject it.

Recovery of Investment   The reason for purchasing an asset is an expectation that it will provide benefits in the future. Thus, Mountainview may purchase the new street cleaner because of expected future operating-cost savings. For a capital-investment proposal to be accepted, the expected future benefits must be sufficient for the purchaser to recover the investment and earn a return on the investment equal to or greater than the cost of acquiring capital. We can illustrate this point with Mountainview's street-cleaner acquisition.

Exhibit 16–7 examines the investment proposal's cash flows from the perspective of recovering the investment and earning a return on the investment. Focus on the Year 1 column in the exhibit. The street cleaner costs $50,470, so this is the unrecovered investment at the beginning of year 1. The operating-cost savings in year 1 are $14,000. Since the asset's internal rate of return is 12 percent, it must earn $6,056 during the first year (12% × $50,470). Therefore, $6,056 of the $14,000 cost savings represents a *return on* the unrecovered investment. This leaves $7,944 as a *recovery of* the investment during year 1 ($14,000 – $6,056). Subtracting the year 1 recovery of investment from the unrecovered investment at the beginning of the year leaves an unrecovered investment of $42,526 at year-end ($50,470 – $7,944).

Interpolation   Sometimes it is more difficult to find a project's internal rate of return because the IRR is not a whole-number percentage, such as 12 percent. To illustrate, suppose the street cleaner costs $52,500 instead of $50,470.

Exhibit 16–7

Recovery of Investment and
Return on Investment

		Mountainview City Government **Purchase of Street Cleaner** **($r = .12$, $n = 5$)**			
	Year 1	**Year 2**	**Year 3**	**Year 4**	**Year 5**
1. Unrecovered investment at beginning of year	$50,470	$42,526	$33,629	$23,664	$12,504
2. Cost savings during year	14,000	14,000	14,000	14,000	14,000
3. Return on unrecovered investment [12% x amount in row (1)]	6,056	5,103	4,035	2,840	1,500
4. Recovery of investment during year [row (2) amount minus row (3) amount]	7,944	8,897	9,965	11,160	12,500
5. Unrecovered investment at end of year [row (1) amount minus row (4) amount]	42,526	33,629	23,664	12,504	4 *

* We are left with an unrecovered investment of $4 because of accumulated rounding errors in the table. If we had carried out each number to cents, the table would have finished up with an unrecovered investment of zero.

Applying the two-step procedure given earlier for finding the IRR, we first divide the acquisition cost by the annual cost savings, as follows:

$$\frac{\text{New assumed acquisition cost}}{\text{Annual cost savings}} = \frac{\$52,500}{\$14,000} = 3.750$$

Then we try to find the annuity discount factor, 3.750, in the five-year row of Table IV, as the following display shows.

**From Table IV
of the appendix**

	r		
	10%	**12%**	**14%**
$n = 5$	3.791	3.605	3.433

3.750 lies between these two columns

Notice that 3.750 does not appear in the table, but it does lie between 3.791 and 3.605. Thus, we must interpolate to find the correct IRR, which is between 10 percent and 12 percent. This calculation is as follows:

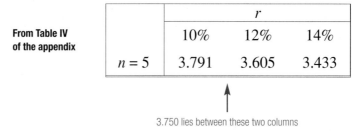

Rate	Annuity Discount Factor from Table IV	
10%	3.791	3.791
True IRR		3.750
12%	3.605	
Difference	.186	.041

Difference of 2%

$$\text{Internal rate of return} = 10\% + \left(\frac{.041}{.186}\right)(2\%) = 10.44\%$$

Thus, the internal rate of return on the street cleaner, if the machine costs $52,500, is 10.44 percent.

Uneven Cash Flows   Another complication that often arises in finding a project's internal rate of return is an uneven pattern of cash flows. In Mountainview's proposed street-cleaner acquisition, the cost savings are $14,000 per year for all five years of the machine's life. Suppose, instead, that the pattern of cost savings is as follows:

Cost savings	$14,000	$14,000	$12,000	$10,000	$8,000	→ Time
Year	1	2	3	4	5	

Such an uneven cost-savings pattern is quite plausible, since the maintenance costs could rise in the machine's latter years. When the cash-flow pattern is uneven, iteration must be used to find the internal rate of return. You can try various discount rates iteratively until you find the one that yields a zero net present value for the investment proposal. This sort of computationally intensive work is the kind of task for which computers are designed. Numerous computer software packages are available to find a project's IRR almost instantaneously.

Comparing the NPV and IRR Methods

The decision to accept or reject an investment proposal can be made using either the net-present-value method or the internal-rate-of-return method. The different approaches used in the methods are summarized as follows:

LO 4 Compare the net-present-value and internal-rate-of-return methods, and state the assumptions underlying each method.

Net-Present-Value Method	**Internal-Rate-of-Return Method**
1. Compute the investment proposal's net present value, using the organization's hurdle rate as the discount rate.	1. Compute the investment proposal's internal rate of return, which is the discount rate that yields a zero net present value for the project.
2. Accept the investment proposal if its net present value is equal to or greater than zero; otherwise reject it.	2. Accept the investment proposal if its internal rate of return is equal to or greater than the organization's hurdle rate; otherwise reject it.

Notice that the hurdle rate is used in each of the two methods.

Advantages of Net-Present-Value Method   The net-present-value method exhibits two potential advantages over the internal-rate-of-return method. First, if the investment analysis is carried out by hand, it is easier to compute a project's NPV than its IRR. For example, if the cash flows are uneven across time, trial and error must be used to find the IRR. This advantage of the NPV approach is not as important, however, when a computer is used.

A second potential advantage of the NPV method is that the analyst can adjust for risk considerations. For some investment proposals, the further into the future that a cash flow occurs, the less certain the analyst can be about the amount of the cash flow. Thus, the later a projected cash flow occurs, the riskier it may be. It is possible to adjust a net-present-value analysis for such risk factors by using a higher discount rate for later cash flows than earlier cash flows. It is not possible to include such a risk adjustment in the internal-rate-of-return method, because the analysis solves for only a single discount rate, the project's IRR.

Assumptions Underlying Discounted-Cash-Flow Analysis

As is true of any decision model, discounted-cash-flow methods are based on assumptions. Four assumptions underlie the NPV and IRR methods of investment analysis.

1. In the present-value calculations used in the NPV and IRR methods, all cash flows are treated as though they occur at year end. If the city of Mountainview were to acquire the new street cleaner, the $14,000 in annual operating-cost

savings actually would occur uniformly throughout each year. The additional computational complexity that would be required to reflect the exact timing of all cash flows would complicate an investment analysis considerably. The error introduced by the year-end cash-flow assumption generally is not large enough to cause any concern.

2. Discounted cash-flow analyses treat the cash flows associated with an investment project as though they were known with certainty. Although methods of capital budgeting under uncertainty have been developed, they are not used widely in practice. Most decision makers do not feel that the additional benefits in improved decisions are worth the additional complexity involved. As mentioned above, however, risk adjustments can be made in an NPV analysis to partially account for uncertainty about the cash flows.

3. Both the NPV and IRR methods assume that each cash inflow is immediately reinvested in another project that earns a return for the organization. In the NPV method, each cash inflow is assumed to be reinvested at the same rate used to compute the project's NPV, the organization's hurdle rate. In the IRR method, each cash inflow is assumed to be reinvested at the same rate as the project's internal rate of return.

    What does this reinvestment assumption mean in practice? In the case of Mountainview's proposed new street cleaner, the city must instantly reinvest the money saved each year either in some interest-bearing investment or in some other capital project.

4. A discounted-cash-flow analysis assumes a perfect capital market. This implies that money can be borrowed or lent at an interest rate equal to the hurdle rate used in the analysis.

In practice, these four assumptions rarely are satisfied. Nevertheless, discounted-cash-flow models provide an effective and widely used method of investment analysis. The improved decision making that would result from using more complicated models seldom is worth the additional cost of information and analysis.

Choosing the Hurdle Rate

The **investment opportunity rate** is the rate of return an organization can earn on its best alternative investments that are of equivalent risk.

The choice of a hurdle rate is a complex problem in finance. The hurdle rate is determined by management based on the **investment opportunity rate**. This is the rate of return the organization can earn on its best alternative investments of equivalent risk. In general, the greater a project's risk is, the higher the hurdle rate should be.

Investment versus Financing Decisions   In capital-expenditure decisions, the investment decision should be separated from the financing decision. The decision as to whether to invest in a project should be made first using a discounted-cash-flow approach with a hurdle rate based on the investment opportunity rate. If a project is accepted, then a separate analysis should be made as to the best way to finance the project.

Cost of Capital   How do organizations generate investment capital? Nonprofit organizations, such as local, city, and state governments and charitable organizations, often acquire capital through special bond issues or borrowing from financial institutions. In such cases, the cost of capital is based on the interest rate paid on the debt.

Another source of capital for both nonprofit and profit-oriented organizations is invested funds, such as a university's endowment fund. In this case, the cost of using the capital for an investment project is the interest rate forgone on the original investment. For example, suppose your university's endowment earns interest at the rate of 10 percent. If the university uses a portion of these funds to buy new laboratory equipment, the cost of capital is the 10 percent interest rate that is no longer earned on the funds removed from the endowment.

Profit-oriented enterprises fund capital projects by borrowing, by issuing stock, or by using invested funds. In most cases, capital projects are funded by all of these sources. Then the cost of capital should be a combination of the costs of obtaining money from each of these sources.

Depreciable Assets

When a long-lived asset is purchased, its acquisition cost is allocated to the time periods in the asset's life through depreciation charges. However, we did not include any depreciation charges in our discounted-cash-flow analysis. Both the NPV and IRR methods focus on cash flows, and *periodic depreciation charges are not cash flows*. Suppose that the controller for the city of Mountainview depreciates assets using the straight-line method. If the city purchases the new street cleaner for $50,470, the depreciation charges will be recorded as follows:

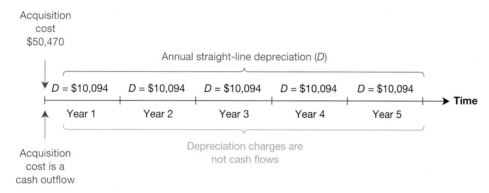

The only cash flow in the diagram above is the $50,470 cash outflow incurred to acquire the street-cleaner. The $10,094 annual depreciation charges are not cash flows. Thus, the acquisition cost is recorded as a cash flow in our investment analysis (Exhibit 16–6), but the annual depreciation charges are not.

Nonprofit versus Profit-Oriented Organizations   Suppose our illustration had focused on a profit-seeking enterprise instead of the city of Mountainview. For example, if the street-cleaner acquisition is contemplated by a theme-park company, would this change our treatment of the annual depreciation charges for the street cleaner? The depreciation charges still are not cash flows. However, in a profit-seeking enterprise, depreciation expense is deductible for income-tax purposes. Since tax payments *are* cash flows, the reduction in tax due to depreciation expense is a legitimate cash flow that should be included in an investment analysis. In the next chapter, we will study the tax implications of depreciable assets in detail. For now, let's return to our focus on the city of Mountainview. As a nonprofit enterprise, the city pays no income tax. Therefore, depreciation is irrelevant in our discounted-cash-flow analysis.

Comparing Two Investment Projects

We have developed all of the tools and concepts required to use discounted-cash-flow analysis in an investment decision. Now we can expand on our discussion using an illustration that combines the net-present-value method of investment analysis with the concepts of relevant costs and benefits studied in Chapter 14. The first step in any investment analysis is to determine the cash flows that are relevant to the analysis.

LO 5 Use both the total-cost approach and the incremental-cost approach to evaluate an investment proposal.

The computing system used by the city of Mountainview is outdated. The City Council has voted to purchase a new computing system to be funded through municipal bonds. The mayor has asked the city's controller to make a recommendation

		Mainframe System	Personal Computer System
(1)	Salvage value of city's old computer (time 0)*	$ 25,000	$ 25,000
(2)	Acquisition cost of new system (time 0)	(400,000)	(300,000)
(3)	Acquisition cost of software (time 0)	(40,000)	(75,000)
(4)	Cost of updating system (time 3)	(40,000)	(60,000)
(5)	Salvage value of new system (time 5)	(50,000)	(30,000)
	Operating costs (times 1, 2, 3, 4, 5):		
(6)	Personnel	(300,000)	(220,000)
(7)	Maintenance	(25,000)	(10,000)
(8)	Other	(10,000)	(5,000)
(9)	Data-link service (times 1, 2, 3, 4, 5)	(20,000)	(20,000)
(10)	Revenue from time-share customers (times 1, 2, 3, 4, 5)	20,000	-0-

**Mountainview City Government
Purchase of Computing System**

* Time 0 denotes "immediately." Time 1 denotes the end of year 1, etc.

as to which of two computing systems should be purchased. The two systems are equivalent in their ability to meet the city's needs and in their ease of use. The mainframe system consists of one large mainframe computer with remote terminals and printers located throughout the city offices. The personal computer system consists of a much smaller mainframe computer, a few remote terminals, and a dozen personal computers, which will be networked to the small mainframe. Each system would last five years. The controller has decided to use a 12 percent hurdle rate for the analysis.

Exhibit 16–8 presents data pertinent to the decision. Examine these data carefully. Most of the items are self-explanatory. Item (9) is the annual cost of a data-link service. This service enables Mountainview to participate in a nationwide computer network, which allows cities to exchange information on such issues as crime rates, demographic data, and economic data. Item (10) is the revenue the city will receive from two time-sharing customers. The Mountainview City School District and the county legislature each have agreed to pay the city in return for a limited amount of time on the city's computer.

Before we begin the steps of the net-present-value method, let's examine the cash-flow data in Exhibit 16–8 to determine if any of the data can be ignored as irrelevant. Notice that items (1) and (9) do not differ between the two alternatives. Regardless of which new computing system is purchased, certain components of the old system can be sold now for $25,000. Moreover, the data-link service will cost $20,000 annually, regardless of which system is acquired. If the only purpose of the NPV analysis is to determine which computer system is the least-cost alternative, items (1) and (9) can be ignored as irrelevant, since they will affect both alternatives' NPVs equally.

Total-Cost Approach   Exhibit 16–9 displays a net-present-value analysis of the two alternative computing systems. The exhibit uses the *total-cost approach,* in which all of the relevant costs of each computing system are included in the analysis. Then the net present value of the cost of the mainframe system is compared with that of the personal computer system. Since the NPV of the costs is lower with the personal computer system, that will be the controller's recommendation to the Mountainview city council.

A decision such as Mountainview's computing-system choice, in which the objective is to select the alternative with the lowest cost, is called a *least-cost decision.* Rather than maximizing the NPV of cash inflows minus cash outflows, the objective is to *minimize the NPV of the costs to be incurred.*

Mountainview City Government Purchase of Computing System (r = .12, n = 5)						
Item Number (from Exhibit 16–8)	**Time 0**	**Time 1**	**Time 2**	**Time 3**	**Time 4**	**Time 5**
Mainframe System						
(2) Acquisition cost: computer	$(400,000)					
(3) Acquisition cost: software	(40,000)					
(4) System update				$ (40,000)		
(5) Salvage value						$ 50,000
(6), (7), (8) Operating costs		$(335,000)	$(335,000)	(335,000)	$(335,000)	(335,000)
(10) Time-sharing revenue		20,000	20,000	20,000	20,000	20,000
Total cash flow	$(440,000)	$(315,000)	$(315,000)	$(355,000)	$(315,000)	$(265,000)
× Discount factor	× 1.000	× .893	× .797	× .712	× .636	× .567
Present value	$(440,000)	$(281,295)	$(251,055)	$(252,760)	$(200,340)	$(150,255)
Net present value of costs			Sum = $(1,575,705)			
Personal Computer System						
(2) Acquisition cost: computer	$(300,000)					
(3) Acquisition cost: software	(75,000)					
(4) System update				$ (60,000)		
(5) Salvage value						$ 30,000
(6), (7), (8) Operating costs		$(235,000)	$(235,000)	(235,000)	$(235,000)	(235,000)
(10) Time-sharing revenue		-0-	-0-	-0-	-0-	-0-
Total cash flow	$(375,000)	$(235,000)	$(235,000)	$(295,000)	$(235,000)	$(205,000)
× Discount factor	× 1.000	× .893	× .797	× .712	× .636	× .567
Present value	$(375,000)	$(209,855)	$(187,295)	$(210,040)	$(149,460)	$(116,235)
Net present value of costs			Sum = $(1,247,885)			
Difference in NPV of costs (favors personal computer system) . . .			$ (327,820)			

Incremental-Cost Approach Exhibit 16-10 displays a different net-present-value analysis of the city's two alternative computing systems. This exhibit uses the *incremental-cost approach*, in which the difference in the cost of each relevant item under the two alternative systems is included in the analysis. For example, the incremental computer acquisition cost is shown in Exhibit 16–10 as $(100,000). This is the amount by which the acquisition cost of the mainframe system exceeds that of the personal computer system. The result of this analysis is that the NPV of the costs of the mainframe system exceeds that of the personal computer system by $327,820. Notice that this is the same as the difference in NPVs shown at the bottom of Exhibit 16–9.

The total-cost and incremental-cost approaches always will yield equivalent conclusions. Choosing between them is a matter of personal preference.

Exhibit 16–9

Net-Present-Value Analysis: Total-Cost Approach

Managerial Accountant's Role

To use discounted-cash-flow analysis in deciding about investment projects, managers need accurate cash-flow projections. This is where the managerial accountant plays a role. The accountant often is asked to predict cash flows related to operating-cost savings, additional working-capital requirements, or incremental costs and revenues. Such predictions are difficult in a world of uncertainty The managerial accountant

Mountainview City Government					
Purchase of Computing System					
(r = .12, n = 5)					

Item Number (from Exhibit 16–8)	Time 0	Time 1	Time 2	Time 3	Time 4	Time 5
Incremental Cost of Mainframe System Over Personal Computer System						
(2) Acquisition cost: computer	$(100,000)					
(3) Acquisition cost: software	35,000					
(4) System update				$ 20,000		
(5) Salvage value						$ 20,000
(6), (7), (8) Operating costs		$(100,000)	$(100,000)	$(100,000)	$(100,000)	$(100,000)
(10) Time-sharing revenue		20,000	20,000	20,000	20,000	20,000
Incremental cash flow	$ (65,000)	$ (80,000)	$ (80,000)	$ (60,000)	$ (80,000)	$ (60,000)
✕ Discount factor	✕ 1.000	✕ .893	✕ .797	✕ .712	✕ .636	✕ .567
Present value	$ (65,000)	$ (71,440)	$ (63,760)	$ (42,720)	$ (50,880)	$ (34,020)

Net present value of incremental costs
(favors personal computer system) . . . . .   Sum = $(327,820)

Exhibit 16–10

Net-Present-Value Analysis:
Incremental-Cost Approach

C I T Y   O F

MOUNTAINVIEW

often draws upon historical accounting data to help in making cost predictions. Knowledge of market conditions, economic trends, and the likely reactions of competitors also can be important in projecting cash flows.

Two techniques are used in practice to analyze investment proposals for which the cash-flow projections are very uncertain. First, the hurdle rate may be increased. The greater the uncertainty about a project's cash flows, the higher the hurdle rate. Second, the analyst may use sensitivity analysis.

Sensitivity Analysis

The project analyst can use sensitivity analysis to determine how much projections would have to change in order for a different decision to be indicated. To illustrate, let's return to Mountainview's street-cleaner decision, analyzed in Exhibit 16–6. The relevant data are as follows:

Type of Cash Flow	Cash Flow		Discount Factor		Present Value
Acquisition cost	$(50,470)	✕	1.000	=	$(50,470)
Projected annual cost savings (5-year annuity)	14,000	✕	3.791	=	53,074
Net present value					$ 2,604

Suppose the city's controller is uncertain about the amount of the annual cost savings. How low could the annual cost savings be before the decision would change from accept to reject? An equivalent question is the following: What annual cost-savings amount would result in a zero NPV for the new street cleaner? The answer to this question is determined as follows:

$$\frac{\text{Acquisition cost}}{\text{Annuity discount factor}^*} = \frac{\$50,470}{3.791} = \$13,313$$

* Annuity discount factor for $n = 5$ and $r = .10$.

If the annual cost savings were $13,313, the street cleaner's NPV would be zero [0= $50,470 − ($13,313)(3.791)]. Thus, the originally projected annual cost savings of $14,000 could fall as low as $13,313 before the controller's decision would change from accept to reject.

Capital-investment decisions, such as the installation of this automated equipment for the production of aluminum cans, go through an elaborate capital-budgeting process. For what types of decisions would capital budgeting be used by the administration of the college you attend?

Capital Budget Administration

Capital budgeting often involves large expenditures with far-reaching implications. An organization's long-term health can be affected significantly by its capital-budgeting decisions. Therefore, most organizations have an elaborate approval process for proposed investment projects. Often the process for making a capital-budgeting request is highly formalized. Specific forms are used, and requests are reviewed at each level of management. Many organizations have a capital-budgeting staff whose function is to analyze all capital-budgeting proposals.

> **LO 6** Describe a typical capital-budgeting approval process, and explain the concept of a postaudit.

The authority for final approval of capital-budgeting proposals depends on the cost of the project and the type of organization. The larger the cost of a proposal, the higher in the organization is the authority for final approval. In a city government, such as Mountainview, most capital projects would require approval by the City Council. In profit-seeking enterprises, large investment proposals usually require approval by the board of directors, often with advice from a finance committee.

American Can Company

A *Harvard Business Review* article described the capital-budgeting process used by American Can Company. The firm's business-unit managers make suggestions for capital-investment projects. Operating managers provide summaries of their recommended investment projects, along with projected cash flows, as part of the annual budgeting cycle. The Corporate Planning Department consolidates the projections from the firm's various business units. The company's Business Investment Staff combines and evaluates the major capital-budgeting decisions from the viewpoint of the company as a whole. The Business Investment Staff then makes recommendations on capital projects, which can range from dropping a project to speeding up its completion. [3]

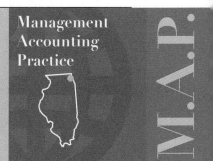

Management Accounting Practice

M.A.P.

Postaudit

The discounted-cash-flow approach to evaluating investment proposals requires cash-flow projections. The desirability of a proposal depends heavily on those projections. If they are highly inaccurate, they may lead the organization to accept undesirable

[3] R. Marshuetz, "How American Can Allocates Capital," *Harvard Business Review* 63, no. 1, pp. 82–91.

projects or to reject projects that should be pursued. Because of the importance of the capital-budgeting process, most organizations systematically follow up on projects to see how they turn out. This procedure is called a **postaudit** (or **reappraisal**).

In a postaudit, the managerial accountant gathers information about the actual cash flows generated by a project. Then the project's actual net present value or internal rate of return is computed. Finally, the projections made for the project are compared with the actual results. If the project has not lived up to expectations, an investigation may be warranted to determine what went awry. Sometimes a postaudit will reveal short-comings in the cash-flow projection process. In such cases, action may be taken to improve future cash-flow predictions. Two types of errors can occur in discounted-cash-flow analyses: undesirable projects may be accepted, and desirable projects may be rejected. The postaudit is a tool for following up on accepted projects. Thus, a postaudit helps to detect only the first kind of error, not the second.

As in any performance-evaluation process, a postaudit should not be used puni-tively. The focus of a postaudit should provide information to the capital-budgeting staff, the project manager, and the management team.

Controlling Capital-Investment Expenditures

Many investment projects require a long time to complete, such as building a new power plant or developing an oil field. Then the benefits from the completed project are realized over an even longer time frame. By establishing procedures for controlling expenditures on a project as it is developed, management can help ensure that the pro-jections for the project are realized.

To help control capital expenditures, managers rely on many of the same concepts and tools that we studied earlier in this text. Budgeted costs are compared with actual costs, variances are computed, and periodic performance reports are prepared. The cost-control process is more difficult for investment projects, because each project tends to be unique. Thus, when a cost variance is recorded, it may be difficult to determine whether the actual cost is out of line or the cost projection was faulty. Nevertheless, periodic project performance reports can direct management's attention where it is needed most.

Performance Evaluation: A Behavioral Issue

LO 7   Explain the potential conflict between using discounted-cash-flow analysis for approving capital projects and accrual accounting for periodic performance evaluation.

Take another look at Exhibit 16–1, which depicts an organization as a col-lection of investment projects. As the diagram indicates, the organization's performance in a particular *time period* is comprised of the combined results of several *projects'* performance during that period. There is a potential conflict between the criteria for evaluating *individual projects* and the criteria used to evaluate an *organization's overall performance*.

This potential conflict is understood best through an example. Suppose Mountainview's fire chief is considering a new alarm and communication system, which is expected to reduce the Fire Department's costs over its five-year life. The new system's acquisition cost, projected pattern of cost savings, and net present value are as follows:

	Acquisition Cost	Cost Savings				
	Time 0	Time 1	Time 2	Time 3	Time 4	Time 5
Cash flow	$(10,000)	$1,000	$1,500	$3,000	$5,000	$5,000
Discount factor (10%) . .	× 1.000	× .909	× .826	× .751	× .683	× .621
Present value	$(10,000)	$ 909	$1,239	$2,253	$3,415	$3,105

Net present value = $921

Although the new system has a positive NPV, its savings in the earlier years are quite low. The project will not really pay off until years 3, 4, and 5. Why does this create a potential behavioral problem? As is common, the fire chief's performance evaluation is based in part on the Fire Department's annual operating costs. Suppose the new communication and alarm system is depreciated using the straight-line method over its five-year life. The new system's pattern of cost savings, net of the annual depreciation charge, is as follows:

	Year				
	1	**2**	**3**	**4**	**5**
Cost savings	$ 1,000	$ 1,500	$3,000	$5,000	$5,000
Depreciation	(2,000)	(2,000)	(2,000)	(2,000)	(2,000)
Net amount	$(1,000)	$ (500)	$1,000	$3,000	$3,000

The depreciation charges are *not* cash flows; thus, these costs were not included in the net-present-value analysis. Nevertheless, annual depreciation charges are subtracted under *accrual accounting* procedures in determining periodic income or operating expenses. Thus, a conflict exists between discounted-cash-flow decision methods and accrual-accounting performance-evaluation methods.

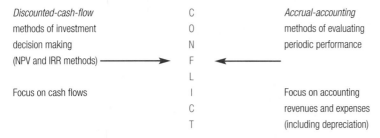

The possible result of this conflict is that a decision maker, such as the Mountainview fire chief, may reject a positive-NPV investment project because of its impact on the accrual-accounting-based periodic performance measure. Our fire chief might express the following concern, which is all too typical of managers placed in this situation: "I'm not buying this new alarm system. Sure, it has a positive NPV, but the payoff doesn't come for several more years. I'll be lucky if I still have my job after showing a loss on the project in the first two years!"

Solution to the Problem   A potential solution to the behavioral problem illustrated above is to deemphasize the use of accrual-accounting-based income or expenses as a performance measure. When decision makers are asked to use a discounted-cash-flow approach in choosing investment projects, they can be evaluated on the basis of postaudits of those projects. Nevertheless, performance measures based on accrual accounting are well entrenched in practice. Perhaps the most practical solution to the problem outlined above is to enlighten managers about the conflict between accrual-accounting and discounted-cash-flow analysis. If performance is evaluated using *both* accrual-accounting methods and postaudits of particular investment projects, the conflict can be overcome.

Justification of Investments in Advanced Manufacturing Systems

The manufacturing industry is changing dramatically as firms adopt the just-in-time (JIT) philosophy and move toward computer-integrated-manufacturing (CIM) systems. In Chapters 5 and 6 we explored many of the managerial-accounting issues in the new manufacturing environment. The importance of transaction-based costing systems, activity accounting, cost-driver analysis, and non-value-added costs was demonstrated. Many firms have found that JIT and CIM, coupled with a revised managerial-accounting system, have provided a

LO 8 Describe the process of justifying investments in advanced manufacturing technology.

competitive edge in the marketplace. These firms' success has inspired managers in other companies to consider making investments in technologically advanced systems. In many cases, however, managers have been frustrated when this analysis projects a negative net present value for a proposed investment in a CIM system. Managers often believe intuitively that such an investment is justified, but they are stymied when the NPV analysis points to rejection of the proposal.

What is the problem here? Are managers overly optimistic about the advantages of CIM? Or is the NPV approach inappropriate for such an investment decision? Most likely neither of these conjectures is true. Managers often are right when their intuition tells them that the company would benefit from advanced manufacturing technology. And it is difficult to find fault with the NPV investment decision model. It is economically and mathematically sound. The problem lies in the difficulties of applying the NPV approach in a CIM investment decision. Some of these difficulties are as follows: [4]

1. **Hurdle rates that are too high.** Sometimes managers have a tendency to set hurdle rates that are too high in a CIM investment analysis. They tend to forget that the purpose of discounting in the NPV model is to account for the time value of money. The appropriate hurdle rate for any investment decision is the investment opportunity rate for alternative investment projects of equivalent risk. In many cases managers tend to overstate this rate.

2. **Time horizons that are too short.** Another common mistake is to evaluate a CIM investment proposal with too short a time horizon. The acquisition cost of a CIM system can be enormous, and the benefits may be realized over a lengthy period of time. If the NPV analysis stops short of including the benefits in later years, it is biased against a favorable recommendation.

3. **Bias toward incremental projects.** Most firms require that large investments be authorized by managers at higher levels than are required for smaller investments. One result of this sensible practice is an incentive for lower-level managers to request relatively small, incremental improvements in the manufacturing process rather than a large, comprehensive improvement, such as a move to CIM. For example, if the investment authorization limit for a plant manager is $100,000, the manager may request a series of $95,000 improvements instead of one investment in a million-dollar flexible manufacturing system. In many cases, a series of such incremental improvements will not bring about the benefits that could be attained with a full commitment to advanced manufacturing technology.

4. **Greater uncertainty about operating cash flows.** Managers often have greater uncertainty about the cash flows that will result when an advanced manufacturing system is implemented. This increased uncertainty is due to the complexity of the machinery and the firm's inexperience with such advanced technology.

5. **Exclusion of benefits that are difficult to quantify.** The benefits to the firm from JIT and CIM systems are extensive. Some are easy to estimate, such as lower inventory levels, less floor space, and improved product quality. Others that can be even more significant are often difficult to quantify. Some of these benefits are the following:

---

[4] This section is based on discussions in R. Kaplan, "Must CIM Be Justified by Faith Alone?" *Harvard Business Review 64*, no. 2, pp. 87–95; Callie Berliner and James A. Brimson, eds., *Cost Management for Today's Advanced Manufacturing* (Boston: Harvard Business School Press), 1988, pp. 16–18, 36–38, 150; and Jean L. Noble, "A New Approach for Justifying Computer-Integrated Manufacturing," *Journal of Cost Management 3*, no. 4, pp. 14–19.

- *Greater flexibility* in the production process. A flexible manufacturing system cell often can produce runs of several distinct products in the same day. Moreover, the machines in an FMS can serve as backups for each other, which reduces machine downtime. Flexible manufacturing systems also allow engineering changes to be made more easily as products are adapted to changing customer preferences.

- *Shorter cycle times and reduced lead times* are possible with an FMS. This enables the firm to fill customer orders more quickly and be responsive to customer requests.

- *Reduction of non-value-added costs* often results when JIT and FMS systems are adopted. Part of the philosophy of these systems is to encourage employees to seek out activities that can be made more efficient or eliminated.

- *Reduced inventory levels* result in savings on working capital investment, less storage space, and reduced obsolescence.

- *Lower floor-space requirements* in a flexible manufacturing system require less space than several stand-alone machines.

- *Product quality* becomes higher and more constant because of advanced manufacturing systems.

Although it is difficult to quantify these benefits, few managers doubt their existence. Excluding them from an NPV analysis means they are being valued at zero. In many cases it would be preferable to make some estimate of these benefits, however crude it may be, than to ignore them. If a manager believes it is impossible to make such an estimate, then the investment criteria should be expanded to consider these intangible benefits along with a proposal's NPV.

One way to handle intangible benefits is to complete the NPV analysis of a proposed advanced manufacturing system based on the readily quantifiable factors. Suppose, for example, that the NPV is a negative $(150,000). Then management can make a judgment as to whether the nonquantifiable benefits in total are worth more than $150,000. If they are, then the investment is justified.

To summarize, justification of investments in advanced manufacturing systems is a new and difficult problem. Discounted-cash-flow analysis is the appropriate tool for analyzing such a decision, but implementing the analysis presents a challenge. Managers should strive to make the best possible estimates of costs and benefits and ultimately make a judgment that recognizes the intangible benefits as well.

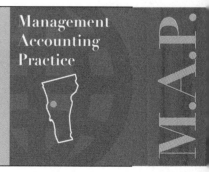

Intangible Benefits of Advanced Manufacturing Systems

Simmonds Precision Products manufactures measurement and control systems for the aerospace industry. In a recent decision to implement a computer-aided design/computer-aided manufacturing system, the company considered several intangible benefits. Among these were facilitation of a high degree of standardization in manufacturing. For example, increased standardization allowed the firm to reduce by 300 the number of part numbers (distinct parts) in one relatively simple subassembly. Another intangible benefit was enhancement of creativity in the design of the firm's products. [5]

Management Accounting Practice

---

[5] R.C. VanNostrand, "Justifying CAD/CAM Systems: A Case Study," *Journal of Cost Management 2*, no. 1, pp. 9–17.

Chapter Summary

Capital-budgeting decisions involve cash flows occurring over several periods of time. Such decisions tend to focus on specific projects. The most common type of capital-budgeting analysis is concerned with the decision to accept or reject a particular investment proposal. Since capital-budgeting decisions involve cash flows over several time periods, the time value of money is a key feature of the analysis. There are two discounted-cash-flow methods for analyzing capital-investment decisions: the net-present-value and the internal-rate-of-return method.

Under the net-present-value method, an investment proposal should be accepted if its net present value is zero or positive. A project's net present value is the present value of the project's future cash flows, less its initial acquisition cost. In computing the present value of the cash flows, the discount rate is the organization's cost of acquiring investment capital.

Under the internal-rate-of-return method, an investment proposal should be accepted if its internal rate of return equals or exceeds the organization's hurdle rate. A project's internal rate of return is the discount rate required to make the project's net present value equal to zero.

Both the net-present-value method and the internal-rate-of-return method are based on important assumptions. The net-present-value method is somewhat easier to apply. It also has the advantage of allowing the decision maker to adjust the discount rate upward for highly uncertain cash flows. Sensitivity analysis is another technique for dealing with uncertainty in capital-budgeting decisions.

Key Terms

For each term's definition refer to the indicated page, or turn to the glossary at the end of the text.

acceptance-or-rejection decision, pg. 660

accumulation factor, pg. 662

annuity, pg. 664

capital-budgeting decision, pg. 660

capital-rationing decision, pg. 660

compound interest, pg. 662

discounted-cash-flow analysis, pg. 666

discount rate, pg. 663

future value, pg. 662

hurdle rate (or minimum desired rate of return), pg. 666

internal rate of return (or time-adjusted rate of return), pg. 668

investment opportunity rate, pg. 672

net present value, pg. 667

postaudit (or reappraisal), pg. 678

present value, pg. 662

principal, pg. 661

Appendix to Chapter 16
Future Value and Present Value Tables

Period	4%	6%	8%	10%	12%	14%	20%
1	1.040	1.060	1.080	1.100	1.120	1.140	1.200
2	1.082	1.124	1.166	1.210	1.254	1.300	1.440
3	1.125	1.191	1.260	1.331	1.405	1.482	1.728
4	1.170	1.263	1.361	1.464	1.574	1.689	2.074
5	1.217	1.338	1.469	1.611	1.762	1.925	2.488
6	1.265	1.419	1.587	1.772	1.974	2.195	2.986
7	1.316	1.504	1.714	1.949	2.211	2.502	3.583
8	1.369	1.594	1.851	2.144	2.476	2.853	4.300
9	1.423	1.690	1.999	2.359	2.773	3.252	5.160
10	1.480	1.791	2.159	2.594	3.106	3.707	6.192
11	1.540	1.898	2.332	2.853	3.479	4.226	7.430
12	1.601	2.012	2.518	3.139	3.896	4.818	8.916
13	1.665	2.133	2.720	3.452	4.364	5.492	10.699
14	1.732	2.261	2.937	3.798	4.887	6.261	12.839
15	1.801	2.397	3.172	4.177	5.474	7.138	15.407
20	2.191	3.207	4.661	6.728	9.646	13.743	38.338
30	3.243	5.744	10.063	17.450	29.960	50.950	237.380
40	4.801	10.286	21.725	45.260	93.051	188.880	1469.800

Table I

Future Value of $1.00

$(1 + r)^n$

Period	4%	6%	8%	10%	12%	14%	20%
1	1.000	1.000	1.000	1.000	1.000	1.000	1.000
2	2.040	2.060	2.080	2.100	2.120	2.140	2.220
3	3.122	3.184	3.246	3.310	3.374	3.440	3.640
4	4.247	4.375	4.506	4.641	4.779	4.921	5.368
5	5.416	5.637	5.867	6.105	6.353	6.610	7.442
6	6.633	6.975	7.336	7.716	8.115	8.536	9.930
7	7.898	8.394	8.923	9.487	10.089	10.730	12.916
8	9.214	9.898	10.637	11.436	12.300	13.233	16.499
9	10.583	11.491	12.488	13.580	14.776	16.085	20.799
10	12.006	13.181	14.487	15.938	17.549	19.337	25.959
11	13.486	14.972	16.646	18.531	20.655	23.045	32.150
12	15.026	16.870	18.977	21.385	24.133	27.271	39.580
13	16.627	18.882	21.495	24.523	28.029	32.089	48.497
14	18.292	21.015	24.215	27.976	32.393	37.581	59.196
15	20.024	23.276	27.152	31.773	37.280	43.842	72.035
20	29.778	36.778	45.762	57.276	75.052	91.025	186.690
30	56.085	79.058	113.283	164.496	241.330	356.790	1181.900
40	95.026	154.762	259.057	442.597	767.090	1342.000	7343.900

Table II

Future Value of a Series of $1.00 Cash Flows (Ordinary Annuity)

$$\frac{(1 + r)^n - 1}{r}$$

Period	4%	6%	8%	10%	12%	14%	16%	18%	20%	22%	24%	26%	28%	30%	32%
1	.962	.943	.926	.909	.893	.877	.862	.847	.833	.820	.806	.794	.781	.769	.758
2	.925	.890	.857	.826	.797	.769	.743	.718	.694	.672	.650	.630	.610	.592	.574
3	.889	.840	.794	.751	.712	.675	.641	.609	.579	.551	.524	.500	.477	.455	.435
4	.855	.792	.735	.683	.636	.592	.552	.516	.482	.451	.423	.397	.373	.350	.329
5	.822	.747	.681	.621	.567	.519	.476	.437	.402	.370	.341	.315	.291	.269	.250
6	.790	.705	.630	.564	.507	.456	.410	.370	.335	.303	.275	.250	.227	.207	.189
7	.760	.665	.583	.513	.452	.400	.354	.314	.279	.249	.222	.198	.178	.159	.143
8	.731	.627	.540	.467	.404	.351	.305	.266	.233	.204	.179	.157	.139	.123	.108
9	.703	.592	.500	.424	.361	.308	.263	.225	.194	.167	.144	.125	.108	.094	.082
10	.676	.558	.463	.386	.322	.270	.227	.191	.162	.137	.116	.099	.085	.073	.062
11	.650	.527	.429	.350	.287	.237	.195	.162	.135	.112	.094	.079	.066	.056	.047
12	.625	.497	.397	.319	.257	.208	.168	.137	.112	.092	.076	.062	.052	.043	.036
13	.601	.469	.368	.290	.229	.182	.145	.116	.093	.075	.061	.050	.040	.033	.027
14	.577	.442	.340	.263	.205	.160	.125	.099	.078	.062	.049	.039	.032	.025	.021
15	.555	.417	.315	.239	.183	.140	.108	.084	.065	.051	.040	.031	.025	.020	.016
16	.534	.394	.292	.218	.163	.123	.093	.071	.054	.042	.032	.025	.019	.015	.012
17	.513	.371	.270	.198	.146	.108	.080	.060	.045	.034	.026	.020	.015	.012	.009
18	.494	.350	.250	.180	.130	.095	.069	.051	.038	.028	.021	.016	.012	.009	.007
19	.475	.331	.232	.164	.116	.083	.060	.043	.031	.023	.017	.012	.009	.007	.005
20	.456	.312	.215	.149	.104	.073	.051	.037	.026	.019	.014	.010	.007	.005	.004
21	.439	.294	.199	.135	.093	.064	.044	.031	.022	.015	.011	.008	.006	.004	.003
22	.422	.278	.184	.123	.083	.056	.038	.026	.018	.013	.009	.006	.004	.003	.002
23	.406	.262	.170	.112	.074	.049	.033	.022	.015	.010	.007	.005	.003	.002	.002
24	.390	.247	.158	.102	.066	.043	.028	.019	.013	.008	.006	.004	.003	.002	.001
25	.375	.233	.146	.092	.059	.038	.024	.016	.010	.007	.005	.003	.002	.001	.001
26	.361	.220	.135	.084	.053	.033	.021	.014	.009	.006	.004	.002	.002	.001	.001
27	.347	.207	.125	.076	.047	.029	.018	.011	.007	.005	.003	.002	.001	.001	.001
28	.333	.196	.116	.069	.042	.026	.016	.010	.006	.004	.002	.002	.001	.001	—
29	.321	.185	.107	.063	.037	.022	.014	.008	.005	.003	.002	.001	.001	.001	—
30	.308	.174	.099	.057	.033	.020	.012	.007	.004	.003	.002	.001	.001	—	—
40	.208	.097	.046	.022	.011	.005	.003	.001	.001	—	—	—	—	—	—

Table III

Present Value of $1.00

$$\frac{1}{(1 + r)^n}$$

Period	4%	6%	8%	10%	12%	14%	16%	18%	20%	22%	24%	25%	26%	28%	30%
1	0.962	0.943	0.926	0.909	0.893	0.877	0.862	0.847	0.833	0.820	0.806	0.800	0.794	0.781	0.769
2	1.886	1.833	1.783	1.736	1.690	1.647	1.605	1.566	1.528	1.492	1.457	1.440	1.424	1.392	1.361
3	2.775	2.673	2.577	2.487	2.402	2.322	2.246	2.174	2.106	2.042	1.981	1.952	1.923	1.868	1.816
4	3.630	3.465	3.312	3.170	3.037	2.914	2.798	2.690	2.589	2.494	2.404	2.362	2.320	2.241	2.166
5	4.452	4.212	3.993	3.791	3.605	3.433	3.274	3.127	2.991	2.864	2.745	2.689	2.635	2.532	2.436
6	5.242	4.917	4.623	4.355	4.111	3.889	3.685	3.498	3.326	3.167	3.020	2.951	2.885	2.759	2.643
7	6.002	5.582	5.206	4.868	4.564	4.288	4.039	3.812	3.605	3.416	3.242	3.161	3.083	2.937	2.802
8	6.733	6.210	5.747	5.335	4.968	4.639	4.344	4.078	3.837	3.619	3.421	3.329	3.241	3.076	2.925
9	7.435	6.802	6.247	5.759	5.328	4.946	4.607	4.303	4.031	3.786	3.566	3.463	3.366	3.184	3.019
10	8.111	7.360	6.710	6.145	5.650	5.216	4.833	4.494	4.192	3.923	3.682	3.571	3.465	3.269	3.092
11	8.760	7.887	7.139	6.495	5.938	5.453	5.029	4.656	4.327	4.035	3.776	3.656	3.544	3.335	3.147
12	9.385	8.384	7.536	6.814	6.194	5.660	5.197	4.793	4.439	4.127	3.851	3.725	3.606	3.387	3.190
13	9.986	8.853	7.904	7.103	6.424	5.842	5.342	4.910	4.533	4.203	3.912	3.780	3.656	3.427	3.223
14	10.563	9.295	8.244	7.367	6.628	6.002	5.468	5.008	4.611	4.265	3.962	3.824	3.695	3.459	3.249
15	11.118	9.712	8.559	7.606	6.811	6.142	5.575	5.092	4.675	4.315	4.001	3.859	3.726	3.483	3.268
16	11.652	10.106	8.851	7.824	6.974	6.265	5.669	5.162	4.730	4.357	4.033	3.887	3.751	3.503	3.283
17	12.166	10.477	9.122	8.022	7.120	6.373	5.749	5.222	4.775	4.391	4.059	3.910	3.771	3.518	3.295
18	12.659	10.828	9.372	8.201	7.250	6.467	5.818	5.273	4.812	4.419	4.080	3.928	3.786	3.529	3.304
19	13.134	11.158	9.604	8.365	7.366	6.550	5.877	5.316	4.844	4.442	4.097	3.942	3.799	3.539	3.311
20	13.590	11.470	9.818	8.514	7.469	6.623	5.929	5.353	4.870	4.460	4.110	3.954	3.808	3.546	3.316
21	14.029	11.764	10.017	8.649	7.562	6.687	5.973	5.384	4.891	4.476	4.121	3.963	3.816	3.551	3.320
22	14.451	12.042	10.201	8.772	7.645	6.743	6.011	5.410	4.909	4.488	4.130	3.970	3.822	3.556	3.323
23	14.857	12.303	10.371	8.883	7.718	6.792	6.044	5.432	4.925	4.499	4.137	3.976	3.827	3.559	3.325
24	15.247	12.550	10.529	8.985	7.784	6.835	6.073	5.451	4.937	4.507	4.143	3.981	3.831	3.562	3.327
25	15.622	12.783	10.675	9.077	7.843	6.873	6.097	5.467	4.948	4.514	4.147	3.985	3.834	3.564	3.329
26	15.983	13.003	10.810	9.161	7.896	6.906	6.118	5.480	4.956	4.520	4.151	3.988	3.837	3.566	3.330
27	16.330	13.211	10.935	9.237	7.943	6.935	6.136	5.492	4.964	4.524	4.154	3.990	3.839	3.567	3.331
28	16.663	13.406	11.051	9.307	7.984	6.961	6.152	5.502	4.970	4.528	4.157	3.992	3.840	3.568	3.331
29	16.984	13.591	11.158	9.370	8.022	6.983	6.166	5.510	4.975	4.531	4.159	3.994	3.841	3.569	3.332
30	17.292	13.765	11.258	9.427	8.055	7.003	6.177	5.517	4.979	4.534	4.160	3.995	3.842	3.569	3.332
40	19.793	15.046	11.925	9.779	8.244	7.105	6.234	5.548	4.997	4.544	4.166	3.999	3.846	3.571	3.333

Table IV

Present Value of Series of $1.00 Cash Flows

$$\frac{1}{r}\left(1 - \frac{1}{(1+r)^n}\right)$$

Review Questions

16–1. Distinguish between the following two types of capital-budgeting decisions: acceptance-or-rejection decisions and capital-rationing decisions.

16–2. "Time is money!" is an old saying. Relate this statement to the evaluation of capital-investment projects.

16–3. What is meant by the term *compound interest?*

16–4. Explain in words the following future-value formula: $F_n = P(1 + r)^n$.

16–5. Define the term *present value*.

16–6. "The greater the discount rate, the greater the present value of a future cash flow." True or false? Explain your answer.

16–7. "If the interest rate is 10 percent, a present value of $100 and a future value of $161.10 at the end of five years are *economically equivalent*." Explain.

16–8. What is an *annuity?*

16–9. Briefly explain the concept of *discounted-cash-flow analysis*. What are the two common methods of discounted-cash-flow analysis?

16–10. List the four steps in using the net-present-value method.

16–11. Define the term *internal rate of return*.

16–12. State the decision rule used to accept or reject an investment proposal under each of these methods of analysis: (1) net-present-value method and (2) internal-rate-of-return method.

16–13. Explain the following terms: *recovery of investment* versus *return on investment*.

16–14. List and briefly explain two advantages that the net-present-value method has over the internal-rate-of-return method.

16–15. List and briefly explain four assumptions underlying discounted-cash-flow analysis.

16–16. What is the objective in a discounted-cash-flow analysis of a least-cost decision?

16–17. Distinguish between the following approaches to discounted-cash-flow analysis: total-cost approach versus incremental-cost approach.

16–18. Briefly describe two techniques commonly used when the cash flows of an investment proposal are highly uncertain.

16–19. What is meant by a *postaudit* of an investment project?

16–20. Describe the potential conflict between discounted-cash-flow analysis of projects and accrual-accounting measures of periodic performance evaluation.

16–21. List and explain three difficulties often encountered in justifying an investment in advanced manufacturing technology.

16–22. List six intangible benefits of CIM systems.

Exercises

■ **Exercise 16–23**
Future Value and Present Value; Answers Supplied
(LO 1, LO 2)

Answer each of the following independent questions. Ignore personal income taxes. The answers appear at the end of the chapter.

1. Suppose you invest $2,500 in an account bearing interest at the rate of 14 percent per year. What will be the future value of your investment in six years?

2. Your best friend won the state lottery and has offered to give you $10,000 in five years, after he has made his first million dollars. You figure that if you had the money today, you could invest it at 12 percent annual interest. What is the present value of your friend's future gift?

3. In four years, you would like to buy a small cabin in the mountains. You estimate that the property will cost you $52,500 when you are ready to buy. How much money would you need to invest each year in an account bearing interest at the rate of 6 percent per year in order to accumulate the $52,500 purchase price?

4. You have estimated that your educational expenses over the next three years will be $13,000 per year. How much money do you need in your account now in order to withdraw the required amount each year? Your account bears interest at 10 percent per year.

■ **Exercise 16–24**
Continuation of Preceding Exercise
(LO 1, LO 2)

Refer to the answers given for the preceding exercise.

Required:

1. Refer to requirement (1) of the preceding exercise. Prepare a display similar to Exhibit 16–2 to show how your accumulation grows each year to equal $5,487.50 after six years.

2. Refer to requirement (4) of the preceding exercise. Prepare a display similar to Exhibit 16–4 to verify that $32,331 is the amount you need to fund your educational expenses.

■ **Exercise 16–25**
Future Value and Present Value
(LO 1, LO 2)

You plan to retire at age 40 after a highly successful but short career. You would like to accumulate enough money by age 40 to withdraw $225,000 per year for 40 years. You plan to pay into your account 15 equal installments beginning when you are 25 and ending when you are 39. Your account bears interest of 12 percent per year.

Required:

1. How much do you need to accumulate in your account by the time you retire?

2. How much do you need to pay into your account in each of the 15 equal installments?

3. Is this a future-value problem or a present-value problem? Explain.

Adams County's Board of Representatives is considering the purchase of a site for a new sanitary landfill. The purchase price for the site is $195,000 and preparatory work will cost $73,400. The landfill would be usable for 10 years. The board hired a consultant, who estimated that the new landfill would cost the county $40,000 per year less to operate than the county's current landfill. The current landfill also will last 10 more years. For a landfill project, Adams County can borrow money from the federal government at a subsidized rate. The county's hurdle rate is only 6 percent for this project.

■ **Exercise 16–26**
Net Present Value
(LO 1, LO 3, LO 4)

Required:

Compute the net present value of the new landfill. Should the board approve the project?

Refer to the data given in the preceding exercise.

■ **Exercise 16–27**
Internal Rate of Return
(LO 1, LO 3, LO 4)

Required:

Calculate the landfill project's internal rate of return. Should the board approve the project?

Refer to the data given in Exercise 16–26.

■ **Exercise 16–28**
Recovery of Investment
(LO 1, LO 3)

Required:

Prepare a display similar to Exhibit 16–7 to show the recovery of investment and return on investment for Adams County's landfill project.

Jack and Jill's Place is a nonprofit nursery school run by the parents of the enrolled children. Since the school is out of town, it has a well rather than a city water supply. Lately, the well has become unreliable, and the school has had to bring in bottled drinking water. The school's governing board is considering drilling a new well (at the top of the hill, naturally). The board estimates that a new well would cost $2,825 and save the school $500 annually for 10 years. The school's hurdle rate is 8 percent.

■ **Exercise 16–29**
Net Present Value
(LO 1, LO 3, LO 4)

Required:

Compute the new well's net present value. Should the governing board approve the new well?

Refer to the data given in the preceding exercise.

■ **Exercise 16–30**
Internal Rate of Return
(LO 1, LO 3, LO 4)

Required:

Compute the internal rate of return on the new well. Should the governing board approve the new well?

The president of Mendelsson Community College is considering the replacement of the college's computer. The proposed new computer would cost $65,500 and have a life of five years. The college's current computer would last five more years also, but it does not have sufficient capacity to meet the college's expanded needs. If Mendelsson Community College continues to use the old computer, it will have to purchase additional computer time, on a time-share basis, from the state university. The cost of the additional computer time is projected at $14,000 annually. The old computer can be sold now for $11,500.

■ **Exercise 16–31**
Internal Rate of Return;
Interpolation
(LO 1, LO 3)

Required:

Use interpolation to compute the internal rate of return on the proposed purchase of a new computer. *(Hint:* The net present value of the proposed computer is $1,902 if a discount rate of 8 percent is used.)

The trustees of the Community School of Art and Music are considering a major overhaul of the school's audio system. With or without the overhaul, the system will be replaced in two years. If an overhaul is done now, the trustees expect to save the following repair costs during the next two years: year 1, $3,000; year 2, $5,000. The overhaul will cost $6,664.

■ **Exercise 16–32**
Internal Rate of Return;
Uneven Cash Flows
(LO 1, LO 3)

Required:

Use trial and error to compute the internal rate of return on the proposed overhaul. *(Hint:* The NPV of the overhaul is positive if an 8 percent discount rate is used, but the NPV is negative if a 16 percent rate is used.)

■ **Exercise 16–33**
Net Present Value with
Different Discount Rates
(LO 1, LO 3)

The board of directors of the Boston Shakespearean Theater is considering the replacement of the theater's lighting system. The old system requires two people to operate it, but the new system would require only a single operator. The new lighting system will cost $86,500 and save the theater $18,000 annually for the next eight years.

Required:

Prepare a table showing the proposed lighting system's net present value for each of the following discount rates: 8 percent, 10 percent, 12 percent, 14 percent, and 16 percent. Use the following headings in your table. Comment on the pattern in the right-hand column.

Discount Rate	Annuity Discount Factor	Annual Savings	Acquisition Cost	Net Present Value

■ **Exercise 16–34**
Sensitivity Analysis
(LO 1, LO 3)

Refer to the data given in the preceding exercise. Suppose the Boston Shakespearean Theater's board is uncertain about the cost savings with the new lighting system.

Required:

How low could the new lighting system's annual savings be and still justify acceptance of the proposal by the board of directors? Assume the theater's hurdle rate is 12 percent.

■ **Exercise 16–35**
Performance Evaluation;
Behavioral Problems
(LO 7)

The supervisor of the City Water Authority is considering the replacement of a utility truck. A new truck costs $59,900, has a useful life of five years, and will have no salvage value. The city depreciates all assets on a straight-line basis. The supervisor estimates that the new truck would result in substantial savings over the next five years. He has projected the following pattern of operating-cost savings.

	Year				
	1	**2**	**3**	**4**	**5**
Cost savings	$11,000	$11,500	$13,000	$18,000	$20,000

After giving the proposal some thought, the supervisor decides against purchasing the new utility truck. He says to his deputy supervisor, "If we go for that truck, the City Council will fry us. With $11,980 in depreciation each year, the truck won't even pay its own way until three years out. By then, you and I will be in the unemployment line!"

Required:

The city's hurdle rate is 6 percent. Did the supervisor make a wise decision? Why? Comment on the behavioral problem evident in this situation.

Problems

■ **Problem 16–36**
Net Present Value;
Qualitative Issues
(LO 1, LO 3)

Special People Industries (SPI) is a nonprofit organization which employs only people with physical or mental disabilities. One of the organization's activities is to make cookies for its snack food store. Several years ago, Special People Industries purchased a special cookie-cutting machine. As of December 31, 20x0, this machine will have been used for three years. Management is considering the purchase of a newer, more efficient machine. If purchased, the new machine would be acquired on December 31, 20x0. Management expects to sell 300,000 dozen cookies in each of the next six years. The selling price of the cookies is expected to average $1.15 per dozen.

Special People Industries has two options: continue to operate the old machine, or sell the old machine and purchase the new machine. No trade-in was offered by the seller of the new machine. The following information has been assembled to help management decide which option is more desirable.

	Old Machine	New Machine
Original cost of machine at acquisition	$80,000	$120,000
Remaining useful life as of December 31, 20x0	6 years	6 years
Expected annual cash operating expenses:		
Variable cost per dozen	$.38	$.29
Total fixed costs	$21,000	$ 11,000

	Old Machine	New Machine
Estimated cash value of machines:		
December 31, 20x0	$40,000	$120,000
December 31, 20x6	$ 7,000	$ 20,000

Assume that all operating revenues and expenses occur at the end of the year.

Required:

1. Use the net-present-value method to determine whether Special People Industries should retain the old machine or acquire the new machine. The organization's hurdle rate is 16 percent.

2. Independent of your answer to requirement (1), suppose the quantitative differences are so slight between the two alternatives that management is indifferent between the two proposals. Write a memo to the president of SPI, which identifies and discusses any nonquantitative factors that management should consider.

(CMA, adapted)

The board of trustees of Mercy Hospital is considering the addition of a comprehensive medical testing laboratory. In the past, the hospital has sent all blood and tissue specimens to Diagnostic Testing Services, an independent testing service. The hospital's current contract with the testing service is due to expire, and the testing service has offered a new 10-year contract. Under the terms of the new contract, Mercy Hospital would pay Diagnostic Testing Services a flat fee of $80,000 per year plus $20 per specimen tested.

■ Problem 16–37
Net Present Value; Total-Cost Approach
(LO 3, LO 5)

Since Mercy Hospital does not have its own comprehensive testing lab, the hospital staff is forced to refer some types of cases to a nearby metropolitan hospital. If Mercy Hospital had its own lab, these cases could be handled in-house. Mercy Hospital's administrator estimates that the hospital loses $100,000 per year in contribution margin on the cases that currently must be referred elsewhere.

The proposed new lab would not require construction of a new building, since it would occupy space currently used by the hospital for storage. However, the hospital then would be forced to rent storage space in a nearby medical building at a cost of $30,000 per year. The equipment for the lab would cost $625,000 initially. Additional equipment costing $300,000 would be purchased after four years. Due to the rapid technological improvement of medical testing equipment, the equipment would have negligible salvage value after 10 years. Staffing the lab would require two supervisors and four technicians. Annual compensation costs would run $40,000 each for the supervisors and $30,000 each for the lab technicians. Fixed operating costs in the lab would be $50,000 per year, and variable costs would amount to $10 per medical test.

Mercy Hospital requires 20,000 tests per year. The capacity of the lab would be 25,000 tests per year. Mercy Hospital's administrator believes that physicians in private practice would utilize the lab's excess capacity by sending their own tests to Mercy Hospital. The administrator has projected a charge of $20 per test for physicians in private practice. Mercy Hospital's hurdle rate is 12 percent.

Required:

Use the total-cost approach to prepare a net-present-value analysis of the proposed testing laboratory.

Refer to the data in the preceding problem.

■ Problem 16–38
Net Present Value;
Incremental-Cost Approach
(LO 3, LO 5)

Required:

Use the incremental-cost approach to prepare a net-present-value analysis of Mercy Hospital's proposed new medical testing laboratory.

Pocono Community Hospital is a nonprofit hospital operated by the county. The hospital's administrator is considering a proposal to open a new outpatient clinic in the nearby city of Davis. The administrator has made the following estimates pertinent to the proposal.

■ Problem 16–39
Net-Present-Value Analysis;
Hospital
(LO 3)

1. Construction of the clinic building will cost $780,000 in two equal installments of $390,000, to be paid at the end of 20x0 and 20x1. The clinic will open on January 2, 20x2. All staffing and operating costs begin in 20x2.

2. Equipment for the clinic will cost $150,000, to be paid in December of 20x1.

3. Staffing of the clinic will cost $800,000 per year.

4. Other operating costs at the clinic will be $200,000 per year.

5. Opening the clinic is expected to increase charitable contributions to the hospital by $250,000 per year.

6. The clinic is expected to reduce costs at Pocono Community Hospital. Annual cost savings at the hospital are projected to be $1,000,000.

7. A major refurbishment of the clinic is expected to be necessary toward the end of 20x5. This work will cost $180,000.

8. Due to shifting medical needs in the county, the administrator doubts the clinic will be needed after 20x9.

9. The clinic building and equipment could be sold for $290,000 at the end of 20x9.

10. The hospital's hurdle rate is 12 percent.

Required:

1. Compute the cash flows for each year relevant to the analysis.

2. Prepare a table of cash flows, by year, similar to Exhibit 16–10.

3. Compute the net present value of the proposed outpatient clinic.

4. Should the administrator recommend to the hospital's trustees that the clinic be built? Why?

■ **Problem 16–40**
County Government; Net-Present-Value Analysis
(LO 3)

The supervisor of the county Department of Transportation (DOT) is considering the replacement of some machinery. This machinery has zero book value but its current market value is $800. One possible alternative is to invest in new machinery, which has a cost of $39,000. This new machinery would produce estimated annual operating cash savings of $12,500. The estimated useful life of the new machinery is four years. The DOT uses straight-line depreciation. The new machinery has an estimated salvage value of $2,000 at the end of four years. The investment in the new machinery would require an additional investment in working capital of $3,000, which would be recovered after four years.

If the DOT accepts this investment proposal, disposal of the old machinery and investment in the new equipment will take place on December 31, 20x1. The cash flows from the investment will occur during the calendar years 20x2 through 20x5.

Required:

Prepare a net-present-value analysis of the county DOT's machinery replacement decision. The county has a 10 percent hurdle rate.

(CMA, adapted)

■ **Problem 16–41**
Net Present Value; Total-Cost Approach
(LO 3, LO 5)

The chief ranger of the state's Department of Natural Resources is considering a new plan for fighting forest fires in the state's forest lands. The current plan uses eight fire-control stations, which are scattered throughout the interior of the state forest. Each station has a four-person staff, whose annual compensation totals $200,000. Other costs of operating each base amount to $100,000 per year. The equipment at each base has a current salvage value of $120,000. The buildings at these interior stations have no other use. To demolish them would cost $10,000 each.

The chief ranger is considering an alternative plan, which involves four fire-control stations located on the perimeter of the state forest. Each station would require a six-person staff, with annual compensation costs of $300,000. Other operating costs would be $110,000 per base. Building each perimeter station would cost $200,000. The perimeter bases would need helicopters and other equipment costing $500,000 per station. Half of the equipment from the interior stations could be used at the perimeter stations. Therefore, only half of the equipment at the interior stations would be sold if the perimeter stations were built.

The state uses a 10 percent hurdle rate for all capital projects.

Required:

1. Use the total-cost approach to prepare a net-present-value analysis of the chief ranger's two fire-control plans. Assume that the interior fire-control stations will be demolished if the perimeter plan is selected. The chief ranger has decided to use a 10-year time period for the analysis.

2. What qualitative factors would the chief ranger be likely to consider in making this decision?

Refer to the data in the preceding problem.

Required:

Use the incremental-cost approach to prepare a net-present-value analysis of the chief ranger's decision between the interior fire-control plan and the perimeter fire-control plan.

The Institute for Environmental Studies (IES) is a privately funded, nonprofit scientific organization based in Montreal. The organization's director of field research is scheduled to retire in two years, and the assistant director, Marie Fenwar, is hoping to be appointed to the post at that time. In her current position, Fenwar has significant administrative responsibilities, including the approval of research proposals and equipment acquisitions. Fenwar has developed a reputation for carefully scrutinizing every proposed project, and keeping the institute's field research branch within its budget. Fenwar has been so successful in her job that she has been quietly assured by several members of the IES board of directors that she is in line for her boss' job. She knows, however, that her prospects depend on her continued success in keeping the field research branch in solid financial shape.

IES recently signed a contract with the U.S. and Canadian governments to do a five-year study of the effects of global warming on the migration of water fowl. The contract fee is $500,000, payable in equal annual installments over the contract term. Fenwar is now considering two alternative proposals for carrying out the study. Each proposal entails the purchase of equipment and the incurrence of various operating costs throughout the term of the contract. The projected costs follow. Fenwar's normal procedure for project evaluation is to calculate each proposal's NPV, using an 8 percent hurdle rate.

Year	Type of Cost	Research Proposal I	Research Proposal II
Time 0	Equipment acquisition *	$ 40,000	$70,000
Year 1	Operating costs	150,000	75,000
Year 2	Operating costs	120,000	75,000
Year 3	Operating costs	75,000	95,000
Year 4	Operating costs	40,000	95,000
Year 5	Operating costs	40,000	95,000

* The equipment will be obsolete at the end of the contract term.

Required:

1. Calculate the NPV for each research proposal.
2. Which proposal should Marie Fenwar approve? Why?
3. After completing her NPV analysis, Fenwar was tempted to ignore it. These thoughts ran through her mind as she drove to work: "If I approve Proposal I, the financial picture for the field research branch is going to pieces for the next two years. After a $40,000 initial investment in equipment, I'm going to show losses of $50,000 and $20,000 in the first two years. That's not going to look very good when the board considers my promotion." When she arrived at the office, Fenwar wrote a memo approving Proposal II. Comment on the ethical issues in this situation.

The City Council of Bridgeton is considering the expansion of its municipal stadium from 30,000 to 40,000 seats. The council believes it will attract a major-league baseball team to hold its spring-training camp in Bridgeton by expanding the stadium. The expansion will cost $7,000,000. Additional annual maintenance at the stadium is projected at $50,000 per year. The 10,000 additional seats at the stadium will be divided up as follows:

Seat Type	Seats	Ticket Price
Bleachers	8,000	$15
Box seats	2,000	25

Ninety percent of the current seats in the stadium are bleacher seats; the remainder are box seats. These seats have the same ticket prices, for both bleacher and box seats, respectively, as those shown above.

If the City Council expands the stadium and a baseball team holds its spring training camp in Bridgeton, the city will receive half of the ticket revenue. Currently, the city receives all of the revenue

■ **Problem 16–42**
Net Present Value;
Incremental-Cost Approach
(LO 3, LO 5)

■ **Problem 16–43**
Net Present Value;
Behavioral Issues; Ethics
(LO 3, LO 7)

■ **Problem 16–44**
Net Present Value;
Sensitivity Analysis
(LO 3)

from its stadium ticket sales, but that amounts to only $500,000 each spring. With a major-league team in town, the council expects to fill the stadium for each of 10 exhibition games to be held at the stadium each spring. Except in the spring, there is little activity in the stadium. The city currently receives only $100,000 in ticket revenue during the summer, fall, and winter months. That amount is expected to increase by 10 percent if the stadium is expanded.

The City Council has asked Aaron Henry, the city controller, to prepare an analysis of the proposed stadium expansion. The council instructed the controller to use a five-year time frame and a 10 percent hurdle rate in the analysis.

Required:

1. Compute the incremental revenue the city will receive if the municipal stadium is expanded. (The current $500,000 of spring revenue will not continue.)
2. Prepare a schedule showing the incremental cash flows during each of the next five years if the stadium is expanded.
3. Prepare a net-present-value analysis of the proposed stadium addition.
4. Suppose the City Council was too optimistic in its projection of filling the expanded stadium for each exhibition game. What would be the NPV of the stadium expansion if only 60 percent of the tickets in each category could be sold for the exhibition games?

■ **Problem 16–45**
Internal Rate of Return; Even Cash Flows
(LO 3, LO 4)

The Board of Representatives for Jefferson County is considering the construction of a longer runway at the county airport. Currently, the airport can handle only private aircraft and small commuter jets. A new, long runway would enable the airport to handle the midsize jets used on many domestic flights. Data pertinent to the board's decision appear below.

Cost of acquiring additional land for runway	$ 70,000
Cost of runway construction	200,000
Cost of extending perimeter fence	29,840
Cost of runway lights	39,600
Annual cost of maintaining new runway	28,000
Annual incremental revenue from landing fees	40,000

In addition to the data given above, two other facts are relevant to the decision. First, a longer runway will require a new snow plow, which will cost $100,000. The old snow plow could be sold now for $10,000. The new, larger plow will cost $12,000 more in annual operating costs. Second, the County Board of Representatives believes that the proposed long runway, and the major jet service it will bring to the county, will increase economic activity in the community. The board projects that the increased economic activity will result in $64,000 per year in additional tax revenue for the county.

In analyzing the runway proposal, the board has decided to use a 10-year time horizon. The county's hurdle rate for capital projects is 12 percent.

Required:

1. Compute the initial cost of the investment in the long runway.
2. Compute the annual net cost or benefit from the runway.
3. Determine the IRR on the proposed long runway. Should it be built?

■ **Problem 16–46**
Net Present Value
(LO 3, LO 4)

Refer to the data given in the preceding problem.

Required:

1. Prepare a net-present-value analysis of the proposed long runway.
2. Should the County Board of Representatives approve the runway?
3. Which of the data used in the analysis are likely to be most uncertain? Least uncertain? Why?

■ **Problem 16–47**
Internal Rate of Return; Sensitivity Analysis
(LO 3)

Refer to the data given in Problem 16–45. The County Board of Representatives believes that if the county conducts a promotional effort costing $20,000 per year, the proposed long runway will result in substantially greater economic development than was projected originally. However, the board is uncertain about the actual increase in county tax revenue that will result.

Required:

Suppose the board builds the long runway and conducts the promotional campaign. What would the increase in the county's annual tax revenue need to be in order for the proposed runway's internal rate of return to equal the county's hurdle rate of 12 percent?

The governing board of the Rockland County Public Library is considering the installation of a security system to reduce the theft of books. Currently, the library spends $30,000 annually to replace lost books. The governing board estimates that 90 percent of this cost is due to book theft. The remaining 10 percent of the cost is unrelated to book theft and will be incurred regardless of whether a new security system is installed. The library currently employs people on a part-time basis to monitor the library's exit. However, this system is ineffective. The library incurs an annual cost of $24,000 on this monitoring activity.

The board can install an electronic security system, which will render the exit monitoring unnecessary. In order to install the new security system, the library's exits will have to be modified at a cost of $90,000. The equipment for the security system will cost $110,697 and have a useful life of 10 years. In addition, the new security system will require the placement of a sensor panel inside every book in the library, at a total cost of $18,000. This process, which will take place over a three-year period, will cost $6,000 during each of those years. Since the security system will not be completely in place for three years, the library will continue to incur some cost from stolen books over the three-year installation period. The projected cost of replacing stolen books during the proposed security system's life is as follows:

Year	Cost of Replacing Stolen Books
1	$22,500
2	13,500
3	4,500
4 through 10	0

The board requires at least a 14 percent internal rate of return on all capital projects.

Required:

1. Compute the library's net savings during each of the next 10 years if the new security system is installed.
2. Compute the system's internal rate of return. *(Hint:* Begin with 14 percent, 16 percent, or 18 percent.)
3. Should the library's governing board purchase the new security system? Why?
4. Which of the cash flows mentioned in the problem do you think would be the most difficult to estimate? Least difficult? Why?

Refer to the data for the preceding problem. As the preceding problem states, the total cost of installing the sensor plates in the books is $18,000. Suppose that the $18,000 expenditure could be spread out evenly over the next six years, instead of the next three years, without changing the projected cost of replacing stolen books each year. All other data remain the same.

Required:

1. Would you expect the new security system's internal rate of return to be higher or lower than it was given the data in the preceding problem? Why?
2. Compute the proposed security system's net present value, given the change in the schedule of expenditures for the placement of sensor panels. Begin by revising the schedule of net savings developed in the preceding problem.

Cases

The Board of Education for the Blue Ridge School District is considering the acquisition of several minibuses for use in transporting students to school. Five of the school district's bus routes are underpopulated, with the result that the full-size buses on those routes are not fully utilized. After a careful study, the board has decided that it is not feasible to consolidate these routes into fewer routes served by full-size buses. The area in which the students live is too large for that approach, since some students' bus ride to school would exceed the state maximum of 45 minutes.

■ **Problem 16–48**
Internal Rate of Return; Uneven Cash Flows
(LO 3)

■ **Problem 16–49**
Internal Rate of Return; Net Present Value; Uneven Cash Flows
(LO 3, LO 4)

■ **Case 16–50**
Decision Problem with Suboptions; NPV; IRR; Ethics
(LO 3, LO 4)

The plan under consideration by the board is to replace five full-size buses with eight minibuses, each of which would cover a much shorter route than a full-size bus. The bus drivers in this rural school district are part-time employees whose compensation costs the school district $18,000 per year for each driver. In addition to the drivers' compensation, the annual costs of operating and maintaining a full-size bus amount to $50,000. In contrast, the board projects that a minibus will cost only $20,000 annually to operate and maintain. A minibus driver earns the same wages as a full-size bus driver. The school district controller has estimated that it will cost the district $15,250, initially, to redesign its bus routes, inform the public, install caution signs in certain hazardous locations, and retrain its drivers.

A minibus costs $27,000, whereas a full-size bus costs $90,000. The school district uses straight-line depreciation for all of its long-lived assets. The board has two options regarding the five full-size buses. First, the buses could be sold now for $15,000 each. Second, the buses could be kept in reserve to use for field trips and out-of-town athletic events and to use as backup vehicles when buses break down. Currently, the board charters buses from a private company for these purposes. The annual cost of chartering buses amounts to $30,000. The school district controller has estimated that this cost could be cut to $5,000 per year if the five buses were kept in reserve. The five full-size buses have five years of useful life remaining, either as regularly scheduled buses or as reserve buses. The useful life of a new minibus is projected to be five years also.

Blue Ridge School District uses a hurdle rate of 12 percent on all capital projects.

Required:

1. Think about the decision problem faced by the Board of Education. What are the board's two main alternatives?

2. One of these main alternatives has two options embedded within it. What are those two options?

3. Before proceeding, check the hint given at the end of the chapter, which explains and diagrams the school board's alternatives. Suppose the Board of Education chooses to buy the minibuses. Prepare a net-present-value analysis of the two options for the five full-size buses. Should these buses be sold now or kept in reserve?

4. From your answer to requirement (3), you know the best option for the board to choose regarding the full-size buses *if* the minibuses are purchased. Now you can ignore the other option. Prepare a net-present-value analysis of the school board's two *main alternatives:* (*a*) continue to use the full-size buses on regular routes, or (*b*) purchase the minibuses. Should the minibuses be purchased?

5. Compute the internal rate of return on the proposed minibus acquisition.

6. What information given in this case was irrelevant to the school board's decision problem? Explain why the information was irrelevant.

7. Independent of requirements (1) through (6), suppose the NPV analysis favors keeping the full-size buses. Michael Jeffries, the business manager for the Blue Ridge School District, was prepared to recommend that the board not purchase the minibuses. Before doing so, however, Jeffries ran into a long-time friend at the racquet club. Peter Reynolds was the vice president for sales at a local automobile dealership from which the minibuses would have been purchased. Jeffries broke the bad news about his impending recommendation about the minibuses to his friend. The two talked for some time about the pros and cons of the minibus alternative. Finally, Reynolds said, "Michael, you and I go back a long time. I know you're not paid all that well at the school district. Our top financial person is retiring next year. How would you like to come to work for the dealership?"

"That's pretty tempting, Peter. Let me think it over," was Jeffries' response.

"Sure, Michael, take all the time you want. In the meantime, how about rethinking that minibus decision? It's no big deal to you, and I could sure use the business."

"But Peter, I told you what the figures say about that," responded Jeffries.

"Come on, Michael. What are friends for?"

Discuss the ethical issues in this situation. What should Michael Jeffries do?

■ **Case 16–51**
Postaudit; Net Present Value; Internal Rate of Return
(LO 3, LO 4, LO 6)

The city of Tidewater is located five miles upriver from the Atlantic coast. In the past, the city enjoyed a booming tourist trade, primarily from fishing and boating enthusiasts. The small river on which Tidewater is located was navigable for most private vessels. In recent years, however, the river has become increasingly clogged with sand. This has reduced the draft of the boating channel in the river. As a result, Tidewater's tourist industry has fallen off dramatically.

Five years ago, in December 19x3, the Tidewater City Council approved a channel-dredging project. The river channel was dredged at a cost of $576,800. The city charged half of this cost to local businesses, which would benefit from restored tourist trade. The City Council estimated that its tax revenue would increase by $84,000 annually over a five-year period as a result of the increased economic activity.

It is now early in 19x9, and the river channel is clogged again. The City Council is considering another channel-dredging operation. Before proceeding, however, the council has directed its controller, Bill Barnacle, to conduct a postaudit of the 19x3 channel-dredging project.

After a study of the city's tax-revenue records, Barnacle has determined that the actual increase in the city's tax revenues amounted to $80,000 per year from 19x4 through 19x8.

The city's hurdle rate for capital projects is 10 percent.

Required:

1. Calculate the net present value *projected* for the channel-dredging operation in 19x3.
2. Compute the internal rate of return *projected* on the river project in 19x3.
3. Using the actual tax-revenue data collected by Bill Barnacle, calculate the actual net present value of the channel-dredging operation as of 19x3.
4. Using the actual tax-revenue data, compute the actual internal rate of return earned on the 19x3 river project.
5. Prepare a postaudit report which compares the projection with the actual results of the channel-dredging project. Use the following format for your report.

Cost of 19x3 channel-dredging operation: _____

Cost to city (50% of total cost): _____

Annual Increase in Tax Revenues		
Projected	Actual	Variance
_____	_____	_____

Net Present Value in 19x3			Internal Rate of Return	
Projected	Actual		Projected	Actual
_____	_____		_____	_____

Current Issues in Managerial Accounting

"How ABC Was Used in Capital Budgeting," *Management Accounting,* **May 1997, Steve Coburn, Hugh Grove, and Tom Cook.**

Overview

This article explains how ABC can be used in capital budgeting.

Suggested Discussion Questions

As a group, develop an ABC capital budgeting model that can be used to assess the financial viability of an interactive Internet shopping mall. Include the following processes in your model: (1) application development; (2) content production; (3) operations; (4) marketing; and (5) distribution. List the major activities and cost drivers for each of these processes.

■ **Issue 16–52**
Discounted-Cash-Flow
Analysis

"Does Your Accounting Software Pass the Year 2000 Compliance Test?" *Management Accounting,* **October 1997, William Mills.**

Overview

The Year 2000 problem, which could create massive computer problems, may cost more than $300 billion to fix. Estimates are that it will cost Merrill Lynch $200 million to fix its own Year 2000 problem.

Suggested Discussion Questions

How does the Year 2000 capital budgeting decision differ from other investments in computer systems? How can firms minimize the cost of correcting this problem? How and when should the problem be reported to shareholders?

■ **Issue 16–53**
Justification of
Investments in Advanced
Manufacturing Systems

■ **Issue 16–54**
Capital Budget
Administration

"Nissan's Slow U-Turn," *Business Week,* **May 12, 1997.**

Overview

In an effort to boost market share, Nissan is spending about $2 billion to develop new cars. This investment comes soon after Nissan recorded over $1 billion in losses, closed a plant, and fired 12,000 employees.

Suggested Discussion Questions

Nissan plans on introducing eight new vehicles in the next several years. In groups, develop a capital-budgeting approval process for Nissan. Assume it takes 2½ years from the design phase through final production. Next, assume it takes 16 months. Include in your capital-budgeting approval process: (1) relevant information derived from the article (e.g., foreign currency impact, labor force characteristics); (2) key budgeting personnel (e.g., budget director) and documents (e.g., budget manual); and (3) the effect of the competitive environment and changing consumer preferences.

■ **Issue 16–55**
Comparing Two
Investment Projects

"ValuJet Crash Raises Questions about Old Airplanes," *The Wall Street Journal,* **May 14, 1996.**

Overview

McDonnell-Douglas stopped making the DC-9 14 years before the ValuJet crash. Interestingly, the general practice is not to inform the plane's passengers about the age of the aircraft upon which they fly.

Suggested Discussion Questions

According to industry experts, old planes cost more to maintain than new ones. Why do airlines continue to use old airplanes? List factors an airline should consider when planning an investment in new airplanes. Present and discuss your list in class.

■ **Issue 16–56**
Capital Budget
Administration

"Environment Disclosures: What Companies Are Reporting," *Management Accounting,* **July 1996.**

Overview

This article summarizes a survey of 645 Forbes 500 companies concerning their environmental disclosures.

Suggested Discussion Questions

According to a Price Waterhouse survey, 62 percent of its studies' respondents did not report their environmental liability exposure. From a capital budgeting perspective, how can a firm prepare to deal with potential environmental liabilities? How can a firm's long-tem health be affected by an environmental capital budgeting plan? What nonfinancial factors should be considered?

■ **Issue 16–57**
Discounted-Cash-Flow
Analysis

"Home Depot: Beyond Do-It-Yourselfers," *Business Week,* **June 30, 1997.**

Overview

Home Depot plans to double its number of stores in the next few years. It also intends to expand internationally.

Suggested Discussion Questions

Assume Home Depot uses discounted-cash-flow analysis when it makes decisions about investment projects. List some key factors and assumptions Home Depot should include in its analysis. If the firm were to perform sensitivity analysis, on which factors should it focus?

■ **Issue 16–58**
Discounted-Cash-Flow
Analysis; Sensitivity
Analysis

"Tennis Hopes to Turn Inches into Real Growth," *The Wall Street Journal,* **August 18, 1995.**

Overview

Tennis racket manufacturers introduced three new oversized rackets. The 28–, 28½–, and 29–inch rackets are longer than the standard 27-inch length.

Suggested Discussion Questions

As a group, list 10 elements that should be included in a discounted-cash-flow analysis of the new racket market. Have several groups present their lists. What are the most common factors? Rank the five most common factors in order of importance.

Solution to Exercise 16–23

1. Use formula (1):

$$F_n = P(1 + r)^n = \$2,500(1.14)^6$$

The accumulation factor, $(1.14)^6$, is given in Table I of the appendix. It is 2.195. Thus, the calculation is as follows:

$$F_n = \$2,500(2.195) = \$5,487.50$$

The future value of your investment will be $5,487.50.

2. Use formula (2):

$$P = F_n \left(\frac{1}{(1 + r)^n} \right) = \$10,000 \left(\frac{1}{(1.12)^5} \right)$$

The discount factor, $1/(1.12)^5$, is given in Table III. It is .567. Thus, the calculation is as follows:

$$P = \$10,000(.567) = \$5,670$$

The present value of the gift is $5,670.

3. You need to invest an amount, A, each year so that the following equation is satisfied:

$$A(4.375) = \$52,500$$

The number 4.375 is the annuity accumulation factor, from Table II, for $n = 4$ and $r = .06$. Rearranging the equation above, we solve for A as follows:

$$A = \frac{\$52.500}{4.375} = \$12,000$$

You need to invest $12,000 per year.

4. You need an amount, P, now so that the following equation is satisfied.

$$P = (2.487) \, \$13,000$$

The number 2.487 is the annuity discount factor, from Table IV, for $n = 3$ and $r = .10$. The solution is $P = \$32,331$. You need to invest $32,331 now in order to fund your educational expenses.

Hint for Case 16–50

The school board's two main alternatives are as follows: (1) continue to use the five full-size buses on regular routes, and (2) purchase eight minibuses to cover the regular bus routes. Under alternative (2), the board has two options. The full-size buses could be (*a*) sold now or (*b*) kept in reserve.

Thus, the board's decision problem can be diagrammed as follows:

Main Alternatives

(1) Full-size buses on regular routes

(2) Minibuses on regular routes

Secondary Options

(*a*) Sell full-size buses

(*b*) Keep full-size buses in reserve

Chapter Seventeen

Further Aspects of Capital Expenditure Decisions

After completing this chapter, you should be able to:

1 Discuss the impact of income taxes on capital-budgeting decisions in profit-seeking enterprises.

2 Determine the after-tax cash flows in an investment analysis.

3 Compute an asset's depreciation tax shield.

4 Use the Modified Accelerated Cost Recovery System to determine an asset's depreciation schedule for tax purposes.

5 Evaluate an investment proposal using a discounted-cash-flow analysis, giving full consideration to income-tax issues.

6 Discuss the difficulty of ranking investment proposals, and use the profitability index.

7 Use the payback method and accounting-rate-of-return method to evaluate capital-investment projects.

8 After completing the appendix, explain the impact of inflation on a capital-budgeting analysis.

HIGH COUNTRY
DEPARTMENT STORES

HIGH COUNTRY BRINGS IN NEW CEO TO IMPROVE THE BOTTOM LINE

Mountainview, NM—High Country Department Stores, Inc. today announced a shake-up in its management team. The announcement has been expected since the Mountainview retailer's long-time president and CEO, Clayton Hale, retired six months ago. Heading the company's new management group will be Jean Walters, who has been named president and CEO. Ms. Walters brings with her substantial experience in the retail industry, where she is known for her innovative approach and insistence on sound financial practices.

In a telephone interview yesterday, Ms. Walters praised her predecessor, and said she was eager to take on the new challenge. Asked about the initiatives she would pursue upon arrival in Mountainview, she had this to say: "High Country is in good shape, but I think there are several things we can do to improve customer service, grow sales, and increase the bottom line for our investors. Among the projects we're considering are new check-out equipment, a parking lot expansion, improved delivery service, and installation of a lunch counter in the downtown store. Our controller is pulling together the cash-flow information now so we can do a complete analysis. Some of these initiatives will affect cash flows for up to 10 years, so we've got to be careful in making our estimates. And then there are the proverbial tax effects to worry about.

You really can't even think about doing anything significant without considering the implications of the income tax laws. And to make matters worse, the tax code is like a moving target. Just when you get used to things, Congress changes the law. If there's anything I've learned in business, it's that you don't make a move without a lawyer on one side, and a tax accountant on the other."

Ms. Walters said she would make the permanent move to Mountainview in about a month.

Income taxes influence many decisions made in profit-seeking enterprises. In some cases, tax considerations are so crucial in a capital-investment decision that they dominate all other aspects of the analysis. In this chapter, we will continue our discussion of discounted-cash-flow analysis by focusing on tax considerations.

We will also explore other investment-decision methods that do not rely on the discounted-cash-flow approach. Managers in many organizations analyze investment decisions using a variety of methods before making a final decision.

Several other topics that often arise in investment decisions also are discussed in this chapter. Among these are methods for ranking investment proposals and the impact of inflation, which is covered in the appendix.

Income Taxes and Capital Budgeting

LO 1 Discuss the impact of income taxes on capital-budgeting decisions in profit-seeking enterprises.

When a business makes a profit, it usually must pay income taxes, just as individuals do. Since many of the cash flows associated with an investment proposal affect the company's profit, they also affect the firm's income-tax liability. The following equation shows the four types of items that appear on an income statement.

Income = Revenue – Expenses + Gains – Losses

Any aspect of an investment project that affects any of the items in this equation generally will affect the company's income-tax payments. These income-tax payments are cash flows, and they must be considered in any discounted-cash-flow analysis.

After-Tax Cash Flows

LO 2 Determine the after-tax cash flows in an investment analysis.

An **after-tax cash flow** is the cash flow expected after all tax implications have been taken into account.

The first step in a discounted-cash-flow analysis for a profit-seeking enterprise is to determine the after-tax cash flows associated with the investment projects under consideration. An **after-tax cash flow** is the cash flow expected after all tax implications have been taken into account. Each financial aspect of a project must be examined carefully to determine its potential tax impact.

To illustrate the tax implications of various types of financial items, we will focus on a retail business. High Country Department Stores, Inc. operates two department stores in the city of Mountainview. The firm has a large downtown store and a smaller branch store in the suburbs. The company is quite profitable, and management is considering several capital projects that will enhance the firm's future profit potential. Before analyzing these projects, let's pause to consider the tax issues the company is likely to face. For the purposes of our discussion, we will assume that High Country Department Stores' income tax rate is 40 percent. Thus, if the company's net income is $1,000,000, its income-tax payment will be $400,000 ($1,000,000 × 40%).

Cash Revenue Suppose High Country's management is considering the purchase of an additional delivery truck. The sales manager estimates that a new truck will allow the company to increase annual sales revenue by $110,000. Further suppose that this incremental sales revenue will be received in cash during the year of sale. Any credit sales will be paid in cash within a short time period. High Country's additional annual sales revenue will result in an increase of $60,000 per year in cost of goods sold. Moreover, the additional merchandise sold will be paid for in cash during the same year as the related sales. Thus, the net incremental cash inflow resulting from the sales increase is $50,000 per year ($110,000 – $60,000).

What is High Country's *after-tax cash flow* from the incremental sales revenue, net of cost of goods sold? As the following calculation shows, the firm's incremental cash inflow from the additional sales is only $30,000.

Incremental sales revenue, net of cost of goods sold (cash inflow)	$50,000
Incremental income tax (cash outflow), $50,000 × 40%	(20,000)
After-tax cash flow (net inflow after taxes)	$30,000

Although the incremental sales amounted to an additional net cash inflow of $50,000, the cash outflow for income taxes also increased by $20,000. Thus, the after-tax cash inflow from the incremental sales, net of cost of goods sold, is $30,000.

A quick method for computing the after-tax cash inflow from incremental sales is the following:

$$\begin{array}{ccccc} \text{Incremental sales revenue,} & \times & (1 - \text{Tax rate}) & = & \text{After-tax} \\ \text{net of cost of goods sold} & & & & \text{cash inflow} \\ \$50,000 & \times & (1 - .40) & = & \$30,000 \end{array}$$

Cash Expenses   What are the tax implications of cash expenses? Suppose the addition of the delivery truck under consideration by High Country's management will involve hiring an additional employee, whose annual compensation and fringe benefits will amount to $30,000. As the following computation shows, the company's incremental cash outflow is only $18,000.

Incremental expense (cash outflow)	$30,000
Reduction in income tax (reduced cash outflow), $30,000 × 40%	12,000
After-tax cash flow (net outflow after taxes)	$18,000

Although the incremental employee compensation is $30,000, this expense is tax-deductible. Thus, the firm's income-tax payment will be reduced by $12,000. As a result, the after-tax cash outflow from the additional compensation is $18,000.

A quick method for computing the after-tax cash outflow from an incremental cash expense is shown below.

$$\begin{array}{ccccc} \text{Incremental} & \times & (1 - \text{Tax rate}) & = & \text{After-tax} \\ \text{cash expense} & & & & \text{cash outflow} \\ \$30,000 & \times & (1 - .40) & = & \$18,000 \end{array}$$

Noncash Expenses   Not all expenses represent cash outflows. The most common example of a noncash expense is depreciation expense. Suppose High Country Department Stores' management is considering the purchase of a delivery truck that costs $40,000 and has no salvage value. We will discuss the specific methods of depreciation allowed under the tax law later in the chapter, but for now assume the truck will be depreciated as follows:

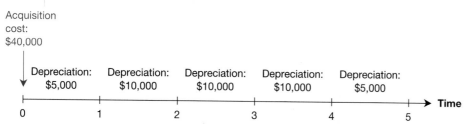

As we discussed in Chapter 16, the only cash flow shown in the diagram above is the truck's acquisition cost of $40,000 at time zero. The depreciation expense in each of the next five years is *not a cash flow*. However, *depreciation is an expense* on the income statement, and it reduces the firm's income. For example, the $5,000 depreciation expense in year 1 will reduce High Country's income by $5,000. As a result, the company's year 1 income-tax payment will decline by $2,000 (40% × $5,000).

LO 3   Compute an asset's depreciation tax shield.

A **depreciation tax shield** is the reduction in a firm's income-tax expense due to the depreciation expense associated with a depreciable asset.

The annual depreciation expense associated with the truck provides a reduction in income-tax expense equal to the firm's tax rate times the depreciation deduction. This reduction in income taxes is called a **depreciation tax shield.**

To summarize, depreciation is a noncash expense. Although depreciation is not a cash flow, it does cause a reduced cash outflow through the depreciation tax shield.

The following schedule shows High Country Department Stores' depreciation tax shield over the depreciable life of the proposed delivery truck.

Year	Depreciation Expense	Tax Rate	Cash Flow: Reduced Tax Payment	
1	$ 5,000	40%	$2,000	
2	10,000	40	4,000	
3	10,000	40	4,000	Depreciation tax shield
4	10,000	40	4,000	
5	5,000	40	2,000	

The cash flows comprising the depreciation tax shield occur in five different years. Thus, in a discounted-cash-flow analysis, we still must discount these cash flows to find their present value.

Cash Flows Not on the Income Statement   Some cash flows do not appear on the income statement. They are not revenues, expenses, gains, or losses. A common example of such a cash flow is the purchase of an asset. If High Country Department Stores purchases the delivery truck, the $40,000 acquisition cost is a cash outflow but not an expense. A purchase is merely the exchange of one asset (cash) for another (a delivery truck). The expense associated with the truck's purchase is recognized through depreciation expense recorded throughout the asset's depreciable life. Thus, the cash flow resulting from the purchase of an asset does not affect income and has no direct tax consequences.

Net-Present-Value Analysis   Now let's complete our example by preparing a net-present-value analysis of the proposed delivery-truck acquisition. The company's after-tax hurdle rate is 10 percent. Exhibit 17–1 displays the net-present-value analysis. Since the NPV is positive, the delivery truck should be purchased.

Timing of Tax Deductions   We have assumed in our analysis of High Country Department Stores' delivery-truck purchase that the cash flows resulting from income taxes occur during the same year as the related before-tax cash flows. This assumption is realistic, as most businesses must make estimated tax payments throughout the tax year. They generally cannot wait until the following year and pay their prior year's taxes in one lump sum.

Accelerated Depreciation

The main concept underlying discounted-cash-flow analysis is the time value of money. We discount each cash flow to find its present value. Since money has a time

HIGH COUNTRY DEPARTMENT STORES, INC. Purchase of Delivery Truck						
	Time 0	Time 1	Time 2	Time 3	Time 4	Time 5
Acquisition cost	$(40,000)					
After-tax cash flow from incremental sales revenue, net of cost of goods sold $50,000 × (1 − .40)		$30,000	$30,000	$30,000	$30,000	$30,000
After-tax cash flow from incremental compensation expense, $30,000 × (1 − .40)		(18,000)	(18,000)	(18,000)	(18,000)	(18,000)
After-tax cash flow from depreciation tax shield, depreciation expense × .40		2,000	4,000	4,000	4,000	2,000
Total cash flow	$(40,000)	$14,000	$16,000	$16,000	$16,000	$14,000
× Discount factor	× 1.000	× .909	× .826	× .751	× .683	× .621
Present value	$(40,000)	$12,726	$13,216	$12,016	$10,928	$ 8,694
Net present value				Sum = $17,580		

Exhibit 17–1

Net-Present-Value Analysis with After-Tax Cash Flows

The **modified accelerated cost recovery system (MACRS)** is the depreciation schedule specified by the United States tax code, as modified by recent changes in the tax laws.

value, it is advantageous for a business to take tax deductions as early as allowable under the tax law.

Although federal and state income tax laws are changed periodically by the appropriate governmental legislative bodies, income-tax laws usually permit some form of accelerated depreciation for tax purposes. An *accelerated depreciation method* is any method under which an asset is depreciated more quickly in the early part of its life than it would by using straight-line depreciation. For example, suppose High Country Department Stores purchased a personal computer and peripheral devices for $10,000. The equipment's useful life is four years with no salvage value. Exhibit l7–2 shows the pattern of depreciation deductions, the associated after-tax cash flows, and the present value of the depreciation tax shield under three different depreciation methods. Notice that both the 200%-declining-balance method and the sum-of-the-years'-digits method result in a greater present value for the depreciation tax shield than the straight-line method does. Thus, it usually is desirable for a business to use accelerated depreciation for tax purposes whenever the tax law permits. The current tax law does not require that the same depreciation method be used for both the tax purpose and the external-reporting purpose. Thus, management could use straight-line depreciation when preparing published financial statements but use an accelerated method for tax purposes.

Modified Accelerated Cost Recovery System (MACRS)

Under U.S. tax laws, most depreciable assets acquired after December 31, 1980, have been depreciated for tax purposes in accordance with the Accelerated Cost Recovery System (ACRS). The Tax Reform Acts of 1986 and 1989 modified the ACRS depreciation program. Under the **Modified Accelerated Cost Recovery System,** or **MACRS,** every asset is placed in one of eight classes, depending on the asset's expected useful life. These eight classes, along with examples of the assets included, are shown in columns (a) and (b) of Exhibit 17–3. For each class, the Internal Revenue Code specifies the number of years over which the asset may be depreciated, and the depreciation method to be used. These specifications are shown in column (c) of Exhibit 17–3. Notice that the number

LO 4   Use the Modified Accelerated Cost Recovery System to determine an asset's depreciation schedule for tax purposes.

Exhibit 17–2

Present Value of Depreciation Tax Shield: Alternative Depreciation Methods

HIGH COUNTRY
DEPARTMENT STORES

Depreciation Expense Double-Declining-Balance*)	Depreciation Tax Shield (Depreciation × 40%)	Depreciation Expense (Sum-of-the-Years'-Digits)	Depreciation Tax Shield (Depreciation × 40%)	Depreciation Expense (Straight-Line)	Depreciation Tax Shield (Depreciation × 40%)
$5,000	...... $2,000	$4,000	..... $1,600	$2,500	.... $1,000
2,500	 1,000	3,000	 1,200	2,500	 1,000
1,250	 500	2,000	 800	2,500	 1,000
1,250	 500	1,000	 400	2,500	 1,000

Present value of depreciation tax shield (10% discount rate) $3,361 $3,320 $3,170

* Steps in applying the double-declining-balance (DDB) method:

To apply the double-declining-balance depreciation method, use the following steps:

1. Divide 100% by the number of years of depreciation to be taken.
2. Multiply the answer obtained in step (1) by 200%.
3. Compute the asset's depreciation each year by applying the percentage obtained in step (2) to the asset's undepreciated cost at the beginning of the year.
4. Switch to straight-line depreciation during the first year in which the straight-line amount, computed for the asset's remaining life, is greater than the double-declining-balance amount.

The utility company which owns this service truck uses an accelerated method of depreciation. The truck is categorized in the five-year property class under the Modified Accelerated Cost Recovery System (MACRS).

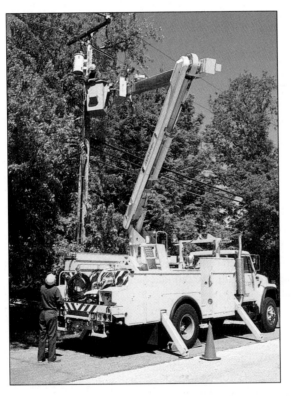

of years of depreciation specified by the tax code is not the same as an asset's useful life. Thus, each asset's useful life is used only to place the asset in its appropriate MACRS class. Then the tax code specifies the appropriate number of years of depreciation. [1]

Depreciation Methods As Exhibit 17–3 indicates, assets in the 3-year, 5-year, 7-year, and 10-year MACRS property classes are depreciated using the double-declining-balance (DDB) method. Assets in the 15-year and 20-year MACRS property classes are depreciated using the 150%-declining balance method. To apply this depreciation method, use the same steps as those listed in Exhibit 17–2 for the DDB method, except change 200% in step (2) to 150%. Assets in the

[1] The U.S. tax law changes almost every year. Occasionally, changes are made in the assignment of assets to property classes and in the associated depreciation schedules. Moreover, the terminology frequently changes. The tax act of 1980 established the Accelerated Cost Recovery System, which then was referred to as ACRS. Since the tax act of 1986, the program has been referred to in various publications by a variety of names. Among these are the Modified Accelerated Cost Recovery System (MACRS), the ACRS as modified, the CRS, or simply the ACRS. We will follow the common convention of referring to the current system as MACRS. Our discussion incorporates the latest tax law changes known as this book went to press. Regardless of what minor changes the tax laws may make in terminology or depreciation schedules, it is likely that the tax code will continue to allow depreciation by an accelerated schedule similar to MACRS.

Exhibit 17–3

Modified Accelerated Cost
Recovery System (as modified
by the Tax Reform Acts of
1986 and 1989)

(a) Asset's Useful Life*	(b) Types of Assets in MACRS Class	(c) MACRS Class and Depreciation Method
Up to 4 years	Industrial tools	3-year class; double-declining-balance
Between 4 and 10 years	Automobiles, trucks, office equipment, computers, research equipment	5-year class; double-declining-balance
Between 10 and 16 years	Most industrial equipment and machinery; office furniture	7-year class; double-declining-balance
Between 16 and 20 years	Equipment and machinery for specified purposes	10-year class; double-declining-balance
Between 20 and 25 years	Land improvements; some industrial machinery	15-year class; 150%-declining-balance
25 years or longer	Specified real property, such as farm buildings	20-year class; 150%-declining-balance
—	Residential rental property	27.5-year class; straight-line
—	Nonresidential real property	31.5-year class; straight-line

* In the tax law, an asset's useful life is referred to as the Asset Depreciation Range (ADR) Midpoint Life.

27.5-year and 31.5-year MACRS property classes are depreciated using the straight-line method.

Half-Year Convention   An asset may be purchased at any time during the tax year. MACRS assumes that, on average, assets will be placed in service halfway through the tax year. Thus, the tax code allows only a half-year's depreciation during the tax year in which an asset is placed in service. The other half of the first year's depreciation is picked up in the second tax year in which the asset is in service. The following diagram shows the pattern with which a five-year asset's depreciation is recorded, for tax purposes, under MACRS.

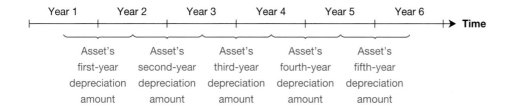

MACRS Depreciation Tables   To assist taxpayers, the Internal Revenue Service has published tables of the MACRS depreciation percentages for each MACRS property class. The IRS tables use the depreciation method specified in Exhibit 17–3 and incorporate the half-year convention. Exhibit 17–4 provides a convenient table of the MACRS percentages, as computed by the IRS, for selected property classes. In the 5-year column, we see 20 percent for year 1. This results from the half-year convention, since 20 percent is half of the double-declining balance rate of 40 percent.

No Salvage Values   Under MACRS, an asset's estimated salvage value is not subtracted in computing the asset's depreciation basis. Thus, for an asset costing $10,000 with an estimated salvage value of $1,000, the full $10,000 cost is depreciated over the asset's life.

Optional Straight-Line Depreciation   The tax law permits a business to depreciate any asset using the straight-line method instead of the method prescribed in Exhibit 17–3. A business with a loss might prefer this approach for tax reasons. If the straight-line method is used, the business may depreciate the asset over either the MACRS life or

Exhibit 17–4

MACRS Depreciation
Percentages as Computed by
the IRS (incorporates half-
year convention; also
incorporates recent
modifications in the tax laws)

Year		3-year	5-year	7-year	10-year	15-year	20-year
				MACRS Property Class			
1	....	33.33%	20.00%	14.29%	10.00%	5.00%	3.75%
2	....	44.45	32.00	24.49	18.00	9.50	7.22
3	....	14.81*	19.20	17.49	14.40	8.55	6.68
4	....	7.41	11.52*	12.49	11.52	7.70	6.18
5	....		11.52	8.93*	9.22	6.93	5.71
6	....		5.76	8.92	7.37	6.23	5.29
7	....			8.93	6.55*	5.90*	4.89
8	....			4.46	6.55	5.90	4.52*
9	....				6.56	5.91	4.46
10	....				6.55	5.90	4.46
11	....				3.28	5.91	4.46
12	....					5.90	4.46
13	....					5.91	4.46
14	....					5.90	4.46
15	....					5.91	4.46
16	....					2.95	4.46
17	....						4.46
18	....						4.46
19	....						4.46
20	....						4.46
21	....						2.23

* Denotes the year during which the depreciation method switches to the straight-line method.

Source: IRS Publication 534, entitled *Depreciation.*

the asset's estimated useful life. Thus, businesses have considerable flexibility in choosing a depreciation schedule for tax purposes. Regardless of the depreciation method chosen, the half-year convention still must be followed.

Income-Tax Complexities   The U.S. tax code is a complex document with a multitude of provisions. It is not possible to cover all of these provisions in this text, so it is wise to consult a tax expert regarding the complexities that may apply in a particular investment decision. Since the tax code is changed frequently by Congress, a tax rule that applied last year may not apply this year. For example, the *investment tax credit* is one important tax-code provision that has been switched on and off repeatedly by Congress. During periods when the investment tax credit has been in effect, a company has been allowed a substantial reduction in its income taxes when particular types of investments are made. The intent of the investment credit was to stimulate the economy by giving businesses an incentive to make new investments. As this text was written, the investment credit was not in effect, but its status is always subject to change. If there is a moral to the changing-tax-code story, it is this: When making an important investment decision, a manager should have a managerial accountant on one side and a tax accountant on the other.

Gains and Losses on Disposal

LO 5   Evaluate an investment proposal
using a discounted-cash-flow
analysis, giving full consideration
to income-tax issues.

When a business sells an asset, there often is a gain or loss on the sale. Since gains and losses are included in income, the business's income taxes generally are affected. Capital investment decisions frequently involve the disposal of assets, and sometimes gains or losses are recorded on those sales. Thus, the tax effects of gains and losses on disposal of assets can be an important feature of an investment decision.

The *book value* of an asset is defined as the asset's acquisition cost minus the accumulated depreciation on the asset. When an asset is sold for more than its current book value, a *gain on disposal* is recorded. The *gain* is defined as the difference between the sales proceeds and the asset's book value. A *loss on disposal* is recorded when an asset is sold for less than its current book value. The *loss* is equal to the difference between the asset's current book value and the sales proceeds.

To illustrate, suppose High Country Department Stores owns a forklift, which cost $10,000 and currently has accumulated depreciation of $6,000. The forklift's book value is computed as follows:

Book value	=	Acquisition cost	−	Accumulated depreciation
$4,000	=	$10,000	−	$6,000

Scenario I: Gain on Disposal   Suppose High Country sells the forklift for $5,000. The gain on the sale is $1,000 ($5,000 proceeds minus $4,000 book value). If High Country's income-tax rate is 40 percent, the following cash flows will occur at the time of the sale.

Cash inflow: proceeds from sale	$5,000
Cash outflow: incremental income tax due to the gain, $1,000 × 40%	(400)
Net cash flow	$4,600

Although High Country sold the forklift for $5,000, the company's net cash benefit is only $4,600. The firm will have to pay the other $400 in increased income taxes on the $1,000 gain.

Scenario II: Loss on Disposal   Now assume instead that High Country Department Stores sells the forklift for $3,200. The *loss* on the sale is $800 ($3,200 proceeds minus $4,000 book value). If High Country's income-tax rate is 40 percent, the following cash flows will occur at the time of the sale.

Cash inflow: proceeds from sale	$3,200
Reduced cash outflow: reduction in income tax due to the loss, $800 × 40%	320
Total cash flow	$3,520

Although High Country sold the forklift for only $3,200, the company's total benefit from the sale is $3,520. The extra $320 comes in the form of a reduction in income taxes due to the loss on the sale.

Implications for Investment Decisions   Why is the analysis above likely to be relevant in an investment decision? Suppose High Country Department Stores has the opportunity to sell its old forklift for $3,200 and buy a new one for $12,000. The company will save $2,500 in annual operating expenses over the next 10 years if the new forklift is used instead of the old machine. A net-present-value analysis of this machine-replacement decision is presented in Exhibit 17–5. The tax impact of the loss on disposal is a prominent part of the machine-replacement analysis. Without the tax savings associated with the loss, the net present value of the new forklift would have been cut from $738 to only $418 ($738 NPV minus tax effect of $320).

Notice that the presentation format used for the analysis in Exhibit 17–5 is different from the format we used previously. Instead of listing the cash flows for each item by year and then adding the columns, we have computed the present value of each financial item pertinent to the decision. The one-time cash flows at time zero then are added to the present value of the cost-savings annuity to determine the net present value. This alternative presentation format will yield the same conclusion as the year-by-year, columnar approach. The choice of format is a matter of personal preference.

Tax Rates on Gains and Losses   Another complexity of the tax code that changes from time to time is that capital gains and losses may be taxed at different rates than ordinary

HIGH COUNTRY DEPARTMENT STORES, INC. Forklift Replacement Decision		
Acquisition cost of new forklift		$(12,000)
Proceeds from sale of old forklift		3,200
Reduced taxes due to loss on sale, 40% × $800		320
Net cash outflow at time 0 (now)		$ (8,480)
Present value of annual cost savings:		
Annual cost savings	$2,500	
× (1 − tax rate)	.60	
After-tax cost savings	$1,500	
× Annuity discount factor (n = 10, r = .10)	× 6.145*	
Present value of after-tax cost savings		9,218
Net present value of new forklift		$ 738

* Annuity discount factor from Table IV in the appendix to Chapter 16. Assumes an after-tax hurdle rate of 10%.

income (i.e., revenue minus expenses). Thus, before preparing an NPV analysis, it is wise to check with a tax expert to obtain the proper income-tax rate to apply to a gain or loss on disposal.

Investment in Working Capital

LO 5   Evaluate an investment proposal using a discounted-cash-flow analysis, giving full consideration to income-tax issues.

Working capital is current assets minus current liabilities.

Some investment proposals require additional outlays for working capital. **Working capital,** defined as the excess of current assets over current liabilities, often increases as the result of higher balances in accounts receivable or inventory necessary to support a project. Such increases are uses of cash and should be included in a discounted-cash-flow analysis. To illustrate, suppose the City of Mountainview has offered High Country Department Stores a contract to sell special T-shirts and mementos commemorating the city's bicentennial. The contract covers the three-year period leading up to the bicentennial celebration. The cash flows associated with the proposal are displayed in panel A of Exhibit 17–6. Notice that the sales proposal would require a $2,000 outlay for additional working capital throughout the three-year period. The increased working capital is largely due to a higher balance in merchandise inventory. Panel B of Exhibit 17–6 analyzes the contract proposal. Notice that the time 0 cash investment in working capital is included as a $2,000 cash outflow. Since the increase in working capital is not released until the end of year 3, that $2,000 inflow is discounted. The city's proposal has a positive net present value, so it should be accepted.

Extended Illustration of Income-Tax Effects in Capital Budgeting

LO 5   Evaluate an investment proposal using a discounted-cash-flow analysis, giving full consideration to income-tax issues.

Now we have covered all of the most important concepts for analyzing an investment proposal in a profit-seeking enterprise. A comprehensive illustration will help you solidify your understanding of these concepts. High Country Department Stores' management is considering the installation of a new checkout system for its suburban store. The new computerized system would include new cash registers at each checkout station. In addition, the new checkout system would include an updated bar-code reading system. The new system will be faster and more accurate, and it will minimize the annoyance of the reader failing to recognize a product's bar code. Among the advantages of the new system are accuracy in the checkout process, automatic updating of computerized inventory records, and the ability to gather data about customers' buying patterns and trends.

Exhibit 17–6

Investment In Working Capital

HIGH COUNTRY
DEPARTMENT STORES

HIGH COUNTRY DEPARTMENT STORES, INC.
Contract Proposal for the City's Bicentennial

A. Data for Illustration

Annual sales revenue from T-shirts and mementos	$25,000
Annual expenses	12,000
Annual contract fee to city	3,000
Investment in working capital (time 0)	2,000
Release of working capital (end of year 3)	(2,000)
Tax rate	40%
After-tax hurdle rate	10%

B. Discounted-Cash-Flow Analysis

Investment in working capital (time 0)		$(2,000)
Release of working capital:		
Working capital released (end of year 3)	$2,000	
Discount factor ($n = 3, r = .10$)	$\times .751$*	
Present value of working capital released		1,502
Annual revenue and expenses:		
Sales revenue	$25,000	
Expenses	(12,000)	
Contract fee	(3,000)	
Before-tax annual income	10,000	
$\times (1 - \text{tax rate})$	$\times .60$	
After-tax annual income	6,000	
$\times$ Annuity discount factor	$\times 2.487$†	
Present value of after-tax annual income		14,922
Net present value of contract proposal		$14,424

* From Table III of the appendix to Chapter 16.
† From Table IV of the appendix to Chapter 16.

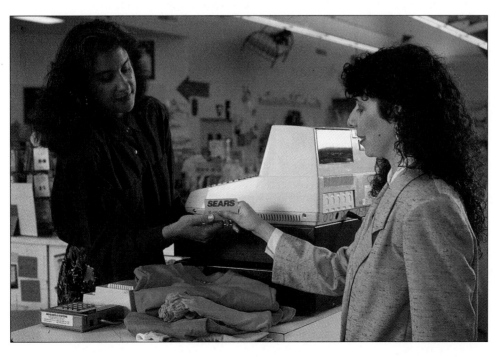

Investments in working capital, such as inventory and accounts receivable, often have a significant impact on capital budgeting decisions. As this customer uses her Sears credit card to make a purchase, the company's investment in inventory declines by the cost of the merchandise. However, its investment in accounts receivable increases by the sales value.

Exhibit 17–7

Data for Extended Illustration

DEPARTMENT STORES

HIGH COUNTRY DEPARTMENT STORES, INC.	
Computerized Checkout Equipment Decision	
Old checkout equipment:	
Remaining useful life, assuming overhaul in year 2	6 years
Cost of overhaul in year 2	$3,500
Current book value (fully depreciated)	–0–
Current salvage value	$1,200
Salvage value in six more years	–0–
New checkout equipment:	
Useful (ADR midpoint) life	6 years
MACRS property classification	5-year class
Acquisition cost of new equipment	$50,000
Update of software required in year 3	$4,000
Salvage value of new equipment in six years	$1,000
Cost to retrain checkout personnel	$5,000
Cost to retag merchandise	$3,000
Annual data:	
Annual operating-cost savings	$15,000
Annual cost of computer-system operator	$30,000
Annual cost of marketing-data analysis	$4,500
Annual incremental sales resulting from marketing analysis	$40,000
After-tax hurdle rate	10%
Tax rate	40%

Exhibit 17–7 presents the data pertinent to the decision. Notice that the old equipment has been fully depreciated already. However, its useful life can be extended to six more years if an overhaul is done in year 2. The new equipment also has an expected useful life of six years, so its ACRS classification is the 5-year property class.

Most of the data in Exhibit 17–7 are self-explanatory. The last two items in the exhibit relate to the new checkout system's ability to gather data about customer demand patterns. The extra data analysis will cost $4,500 annually, but it is expected to generate another $40,000 in annual sales, net of cost of goods sold.

A net-present-value analysis of the checkout equipment proposal is presented in Exhibit 17–8. A total-cost approach is used. The present value of each financial item is computed for both alternatives; then these present values are added to determine each alternative's net present value. An explanation of each line in the exhibit follows.

(1) Line (1) in Exhibit 17–8 records the acquisition cost of the new checkout equipment. This cash flow has no tax impact and does not need to be discounted since it occurs at time 0.

(2), (3) These one-time cash flows are required to retrain checkout personnel and retag merchandise to accommodate the new bar-code readers. Since these costs are expenses, we multiply by $(1 - .40)$.

(4), (5) Since the old equipment has a current book value of zero, there is a $1,200 gain on the sale. The $1,200 proceeds are not taxed [line (4)], but the $1,200 gain on the sale is taxed [line (5)].

(6) The cost of updating the software in year 3 is an expense, so we multiply by $(1 - .40)$.

(7), (8) The new equipment can be sold in year 6 for $1,000. Since it will be fully depreciated, there will be a $1,000 gain. The $1,000 proceeds are not taxed [line 7], but the $1,000 gain is taxed [line (8)].

(9) The depreciation tax shield on the new equipment is computed using the MACRS depreciation schedule for the 5-year property class. The annual

			Income-Tax Impact	After-Tax Cash Flow	Discount Factor (10%)	Present Value of Cash Flow
	Year	**Amount**				

HIGH COUNTRY DEPARTMENT STORES, INC.
Computerized Checkout Equipment Decision

Purchase New Equipment

		Year	Amount	Income-Tax Impact	After-Tax Cash Flow	Discount Factor (10%)	Present Value of Cash Flow
(1)	Acquisition cost of new equipment	Time 0	$50,000	None	$(50,000)	1.000	$(50,000)
(2)	Cost to retrain checkout personnel	Time 0	5,000	(1 – .40)*	(3,000)	1.000	(3,000)
(3)	Cost to retag merchandise	Time 0	3,000	(1 – .40)	(1,800)	1.000	(1,800)
(4)	Proceeds from sale of old equipment ..	Time 0	1,200	None	1,200	1.000	1,200
(5)	Gain on sale of old equipment	Time 0	1,200	.40	(480)	1.000	(480)
(6)	Update of software	Year 3	4,000	(1 – .40)	(2,400)	.751	(1,802)
(7)	Salvage value of new equipment	Year 6	1,000	None	1,000	.564	564
(8)	Gain on sale of new equipment	Year 6	1,000	.40	(400)	.564	(226)
(9)	Depreciation tax shield:						

Year	Cost	MACRS Percentage (rounded)	Depreciation Expense					
1	$50,000	20.0%	$10,000	 10,000	.40	4,000	.909	3,636
2	50,000	32.0%	16,000	 16,000	.40	6,400	.826	5,286
3	50,000	19.2%	9,600	 9,600	.40	3,840	.751	2,884
4	50,000	11.5%	5,750	 5,750	.40	2,300	.683	1,571
5	50,000	11.5%	5,750	 5,750	.40	2,300	.621	1,428
6	50,000	5.8%	2,900	 2,900	.40	1,160	.564	654
Total			$50,000					

Annual incremental costs and benefits (years 1 through 6):

(10) Annual operating cost savings $15,000					
(11) Annual cost of computer operator ... (30,000)			Annuity discount		
(12) Annual cost of marketing analysis ... (4,500)			factor for		
(13) Annual incremental sales revenue, net of cost of goods sold 40,000			$n = 6, r = .10$		
Total annual amount .... $20,500 ..... $20,500	(1 – .40)	$12,300	4.355	53,567
(14) Net present value				$13,482

Keep Old Equipment†

		Year	Amount	Income-Tax Impact	After-Tax Cash Flow	Discount Factor	Present Value
(15)	Cost of overhaul	Year 2	$3,500	(1 – .40)	$(2,100)	.826	$(1,735)
(16)	Net present value						$(1,735)

* High Country Department Stores' tax rate is 40%.

† There is no depreciation tax shield if the old equipment is kept, since it has been depreciated fully already.

---

depreciation deductions are not cash flows, but they do cause a reduction in income taxes. Each cash flow is then discounted using the appropriate discount factor from Table III in the appendix to Chapter 16.

(10), (11), (12), (13) These items are annual cash flows. The flows are summed, and then the $20,500 annuity is multiplied by (1 – .40) because each of the cash flows will be on the income statement. The after-tax cash-flow annuity of $12,300 is then discounted using the annuity discount factor for $n = 6$ and $r = .10$.

(14) The net present value of the new equipment is $13,482.

(15) The only specific cash flow related to the alternative of keeping the old equipment is the $3,500 overhaul in year 2. This will be an expense, so we multiply by (1 – .40). Then the after-tax cash flow is discounted.

(16) The net present value of the alternative to keep the old equipment is $(1,735).

Exhibit 17–8

Net-Present-Value Analysis
for Extended Illustration

Decision Rule   The analysis indicates that High Country Department Stores should purchase the new checkout equipment. The NPV of the new equipment exceeds that of the old equipment.

Ranking Investment Projects

LO 6 Discuss the difficulty of ranking investment proposals, and use the profitability index.

Suppose a company has several potential investment projects, all of which have positive net present values. If a project has a positive net present value, this means that the return projected for the project exceeds the company's cost of capital. In this case, every project with a positive NPV should be accepted. In spite of the theoretical validity of this argument, practice often does not reflect this viewpoint. In practice, managers often attempt to rank investment projects with positive net present values. Then only a limited number of the higher-ranking proposals are accepted.

The reasons for this common practice are not clear. If a discount rate is used that accurately reflects the firm's cost of capital, then any project with a positive NPV will earn a return greater than the cost of obtaining capital to fund it. One possible explanation for the practice of ranking investment projects is a limited supply of scarce resources, such as managerial talent. Thus, a form of *capital rationing* takes place, not because of a limited supply of investment capital, but because of limitations on other resources. A manager may feel that he or she simply cannot devote sufficient attention to all of the desirable projects. The solution, then, is to select only some of the positive-NPV proposals, which implies a ranking.

Unfortunately, no valid method exists for ranking independent investment projects with positive net present values. To illustrate, suppose the management of High Country Department Stores has the following two investment opportunities:

1. Proposal A: Open a gift shop at the Mountainview Convention Center. High Country's management believes the benefits of this proposal would last only six years. High Country's management expects that after six years, the firm's competitors will move into the Convention Center and eliminate High Country's current advantageous position.

2. Proposal B: Open a small gift shop at the Mountainview Airport. The airport gift concession would belong to High Country Department Stores for 10 years under a contract with the city.

The predicted cash flows for these investment proposals are as follows:

Investment Proposal	Cash Outflow Time 0	After-Tax Cash Inflows Years 1–6	After-Tax Cash Inflows Years 7–10	Present Value of Inflows (10% Discount Rate)	Net Present Value	Internal Rate of Return
A (Convention Center)	$(54,450)	$14,000	—	$ 60,970	$6,520	14%
B (Airport)	(101,700)	18,000	$18,000	110,610	8,910	12%

Both investment proposals have positive net present values. Suppose, however, that due to limited managerial time, High Country's management has decided to pursue only one of the projects. Which proposal should be ranked higher? This is a difficult question to answer. Proposal B has a higher net present value, but it also requires a much larger initial investment. Proposal A exhibits a higher internal rate of return. However, proposal A's return of 14 percent applies only to its six-year time horizon. If management accepts proposal A, what will happen in years 7 through 10? Will the facilities and equipment remain idle? Or could they be used profitably for some other purpose? These questions are left unanswered by the analysis above.

The main reason that the NPV and IRR methods of analysis yield different rankings for these two proposals is that the projects have different lives. Without making an assumption about what will happen in years 7 through 10 if proposal A is accepted, the NPV and IRR methods simply are not capable of ranking the proposals in any sound manner. The only theoretically correct answer to the problem posed in this illustration is that both projects are desirable, and both should be accepted. Each proposal exhibits a positive NPV and an IRR greater than the hurdle rate of 10 percent.

Profitability Index   One criterion that managers sometimes apply in ranking investment proposals is called the **profitability index** (or **excess present value index),** which is defined as follows:

$$\text{Profitability index} = \frac{\text{Present value of cash flows, exclusive of initial investment}}{\text{Initial investment}}$$

The **profitability index** (or **excess present value index**) is the present value of a project's future cash flows (exclusive of the initial investment), divided by the initial investment.

The profitability indices for High Country's two investment proposals are computed as follows:

Investment Proposal	Calculation		Profitability Index	Net Present Value	Internal Rate of Return
A	$\frac{\text{Present value of inflows}}{\text{Initial investment}} = \frac{\$60,970}{\$54,450}$	=	1.12	$6,520	14%
B	$\frac{\text{Present value of inflows}}{\text{Initial investment}} = \frac{\$110,610}{\$101,700}$	=	1.09	$8,910	12%

Although proposal A has a lower NPV than proposal B, proposal A exhibits a higher profitability index. Proposal A's higher profitability index is due to its considerably lower initial investment than that required for proposal B. Is the profitability index a foolproof method for ranking investment proposals? Unfortunately, it too suffers from the same drawbacks as those associated with the NPV or IRR method. Both proposals exhibit a profitability index greater than 1.00, which merely reflects their positive NPVs. Thus, both projects are desirable. The unequal lives of the two proposals prevent the profitability index from indicating a theoretically correct ranking of the proposals. The relative desirability of proposals A and B simply depends on what will happen in years 7 through 10 if proposal A is selected.

In summary, the problem of ranking investment projects with positive NPVs has not been solved in a satisfactory manner. This lack of resolution is due to an inconsistency inherent to the problem. The inconsistency is that if several projects have positive NPVs, they all are desirable. They all will earn a return greater than the cost of capital. If a manager chooses not to accept all projects with positive NPVs, then the required ranking ultimately must be made on the basis of subjective criteria.

Additional Methods for Making Investment Decisions

The best way to decide whether to accept an investment project is to use discounted-cash-flow analysis, as described in this and the preceding chapter. Both the net-present-value and the internal-rate-of-return methods will yield the correct accept-or-reject decision. The strength of these methods lies in the fact that they properly account for the time value of money. In spite of the conceptual superiority of discounted-cash-flow decision models, managers sometimes use other methods for making investment decisions. In some cases, these alternative methods are used in conjunction with a discounted-cash-flow analysis. Two of these alternative decision methods are described next.

LO 7   Use the payback method and accounting-rate-of-return method to evaluate capital-investment projects.

The **payback period** is the amount of time required for a project's after-tax cash inflows to accumulate to an amount that covers the initial investment.

Payback Method

The **payback period** of an investment proposal is the amount of time it will take for the after-tax cash inflows from the project to accumulate to an amount that covers the

The payback method is widely used as a simple screening device for investment proposals. Small businesses, such as this automatic car wash, are particularly likely to use the payback criterion, often in conjunction with a discounted-cash-flow method of investment analysis. The payback period for this car wash equipment is about three years.

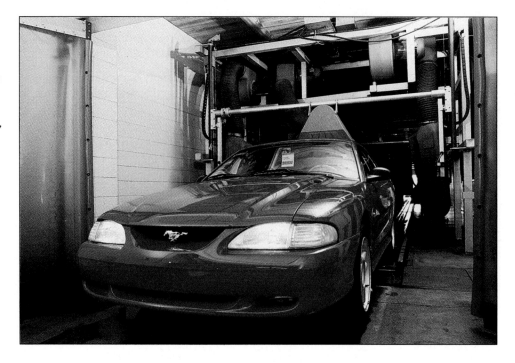

original investment. The following formula defines an investment project's payback period.

$$\text{Payback period} \quad = \quad \frac{\text{Initial investment}}{\text{Annual after-tax cash inflow}}$$

There is no adjustment in the payback method for the time value of money. A cash inflow in year 5 is treated the same as a cash inflow in year 1.

To illustrate the payback method, suppose High Country Department Stores' management is considering the purchase of a new conveyor system for its warehouse. The two alternative machines under consideration have the following projected cash flows.

Conveyor System		Initial Investment		After-Tax Cash Flows: Years 1 through 7		After-Tax Cash Flow When System Is Sold
I	. . . .	$(20,000)	. . . .	$4,000	. . . .	–0–
II	. . . .	(27,000)	. . . .	4,500	. . . .	$14,000

The payback period for each conveyor system is computed below. Notice that *after-tax cash flows are used* in the payback method, just as they are in discounted-cash-flow methods of analysis.

Conveyor System		Initial Investment / Annual After-Tax Cash Inflow		Payback Period
I	. . . .	$\dfrac{\$20,000}{\$4,000}$	. . . .	5 years
II	. . . .	$\dfrac{\$27,000}{\$4,500}$	. . . .	6 years

According to the payback method, system I is more desirable than system II. System I will "pay back" its initial investment in five years, while system II requires six years. This conclusion is too simplistic, however, because it ignores the large salvage value associated with system II. Indeed, the NPV of system I is negative, while the NPV of system II is positive, as shown in the following analysis.

After-Tax Cash Flows	Present Value of Cash Flows (10% Discount Factor)	
	System I	**System II**
Initial investment	$(20,000) × 1.000 = $(20,000)	$(27,000) × 1.000 = $(27,000)
Years 1–7	4,000 × 4.868 = 19,472	4,500 × 4.868 = 21,906
Cash inflow from sale	-0-	14,000 × .513 = 7,182
Net present value	$ (528)	$ 2,088

The net-present-value analysis demonstrates that only system II can generate cash flows sufficient to cover the company's cost of capital. The payback method makes it appear as though system I "pays back" its initial investment more quickly, but the method fails to consider the time value of money.

Another shortcoming of the payback method is that it fails to consider an investment project's profitability beyond the payback period. Suppose High Country Department Stores' management has a third alternative for its warehouse conveyor system. System III requires an initial investment of only $12,000 and will generate after-tax cash inflows of $6,000 in years 1 and 2. Thus, System III's payback period is two years, as computed below.

$$\text{System III payback period} = \frac{\$12,000}{\$6,000} = 2 \text{ years}$$

Strict adherence to the payback method would rank system III above systems I and II, due to its shorter payback period. However, suppose we add another piece of information. System III's useful life is only two years, and it has no salvage value after two years. It is true that system III will "pay back" its initial investment in only two years if we ignore the time value of money. But then what? System III provides no further benefits beyond year 2. In spite of system III's short payback period, it is not a desirable investment proposal. The NPV of system III, $(1,584), is negative [$(1,584) = (1.736 × $6,000) − $12,000].

Payback Period with Uneven Cash Flows   The simple payback formula given earlier in the chapter will not work if a project exhibits an uneven pattern of cash flows. Instead, the after-tax cash flows must be accumulated on a year-to-year basis until the accumulation equals the initial investment. Suppose High Country Department Stores' management is considering the expansion of the downtown store's parking facilities. Management expects that the additional parking will result in much greater sales initially. However, this benefit will gradually taper off, due to the reactions of competitors. The projected after-tax cash flows are shown in Exhibit 17–9, which also presents the payback calculation for the parking lot proposal. The project's payback period is five years.

Payback: Pro and Con   In summary, the payback method of evaluating investment proposals has two serious drawbacks. First, the method fails to consider the time value of money. Second, it does not consider a project's cash flows beyond the payback period. Despite these shortcomings, the payback method is used widely in practice, for two legitimate reasons.

First, the payback method provides a tool for roughly screening investment proposals. If a project does not meet some minimal criterion for the payback period, management may wish to reject the proposal regardless of potential large cash flows predicted well into the future. Second, a young firm may experience a shortage of cash. For such a company, it may be crucial to select investment projects that recoup their initial investment quickly. A cash-poor firm may not be able to wait for the big payoff of a project with a long payback period. Even in these cases, it is wise not to rely on the payback method alone. If the payback method is used, it should be in conjunction with a discounted-cash-flow analysis.

Exhibit 17–9

Payback Period with Uneven Cash Flows

DEPARTMENT STORES

		After-Tax Cash Flows		**Accumulated Cash Flows**
HIGH COUNTRY DEPARTMENT STORES, INC.				
Parking Lot Expansion				
Year	**Type of Cash Flow**	**Outflows**	**Inflows**	**(excluding initial investment)**
0	Initial investment	$(200,000)		—
1	Incremental sales		$60,000	$ 60,000
2	Incremental sales		50,000	110,000
3	Incremental sales		45,000	155,000
4	Incremental sales		35,000	190,000
4	Repave parking lot	(20,000)		170,000
5	Incremental sales		30,000	200,000
6	Incremental sales		30,000	230,000
7	Incremental sales		30,000	260,000
8	Incremental sales		30,000	290,000

Payback period: 5 years

Accounting-Rate-of-Return Method

The **accounting rate of return** is a percentage formed by taking a project's average incremental revenue minus its average incremental expenses (including depreciation and income taxes) and dividing by the project's initial investment.

Discounted-cash-flow methods of investment analysis focus on *cash flows* and incorporate the time value of money. The **accounting-rate-of-return method** focuses on the incremental *accounting income* that results from a project. Accounting income is based on accrual accounting procedures. Revenue is recognized during the period of sale, not necessarily when the cash is received; expenses are recognized during the period they are incurred, not necessarily when they are paid in cash. The following formula is used to compute the accounting rate of return on an investment project.

$$\text{Accounting rate of return} = \frac{\left(\begin{array}{c}\text{Average}\\\text{incremental}\\\text{revenue}\end{array}\right) - \left(\begin{array}{c}\text{Average incremental expenses}\\\text{(including depreciation}\\\text{and income taxes)}\end{array}\right)}{\text{Initial investment}}$$

To illustrate the accounting-rate-of-return method, suppose High Country Department Stores' management is considering the installation of a small lunch counter in its downtown store. The required equipment and furnishings cost $210,000 and are in the MACRS 7-year property class. The company has elected to use the optional straight-line depreciation method with the half-year convention. Exhibit 17–10 displays management's revenue and expense projections for the lunch counter. The total income projected over the project's 10-year useful life is $174,000. Thus, the average annual income is $17,400. The accounting rate of return on the lunch-counter proposal is computed as follows:

$$\text{Accounting rate of return} = \frac{\$17,400}{\$210,000} = 8.3\% \text{ (rounded)}$$

To compute the lunch-counter project's internal rate of return, let's assume that each year's sales revenue, cost of goods sold, operating expenses, and income taxes are cash flows in the same year that they are recorded under accrual accounting. Recall that the depreciation expense is not a cash flow. These assumptions imply the following cash flow pattern for the project.

Net After-Tax Cash Inflows

Year	Amount	Year	Amount
1	$36,000	6	$42,000
2	42,000	7	42,000
3	42,000	8	36,000
4	42,000	9	30,000
5	42,000	10	30,000
Initial investment	$(210,000)		

Exhibit 17–10

Accounting-Rate-of-Return
Method

					Income	Income	
	Sales	**Cost of**	**Operating**	**MACRS**	**Before**	**Taxes**	**Net**
Year	**Revenue**	**Goods Sold**	**Expenses**	**Depreciation ***	**Taxes**	**(40%)**	**Income**
1	$200,000	$100,000	$50,000	$ 15,000	$35,000	$14,000	$ 21,000
2	200,000	100,000	50,000	30,000	20,000	8,000	12,000
3	200,000	100,000	50,000	30,000	20,000	8,000	12,000
4	200,000	100,000	50,000	30,000	20,000	8,000	12,000
5	200,000	100,000	50,000	30,000	20,000	8,000	12,000
6	200,000	100,000	50,000	30,000	20,000	8,000	12,000
7	200,000	100,000	50,000	30,000	20,000	8,000	12,000
8	200,000	100,000	50,000	15,000	35,000	14,000	21,000
9	200,000	100,000	50,000	0	50,000	20,000	30,000
10	200,000	100,000	50,000	0	50,000	20,000	30,000
Total				$210,000			$174,000

* Annual straight-line depreciation = $\frac{\$210,000}{7}$ = $30,000

Note: In accordance with the half-year convention, only half a year's depreciation is recorded in years 1 and 8.

The internal rate of return on the lunch-counter proposal is approximately 13.5 percent. That is, if we compute the present value of the cash flows using a discount rate of 13.5 percent, we obtain approximately a zero NPV.[2] Notice that the project's accounting rate of return, at 8.3 percent, is much lower than its IRR of 13.5 percent.

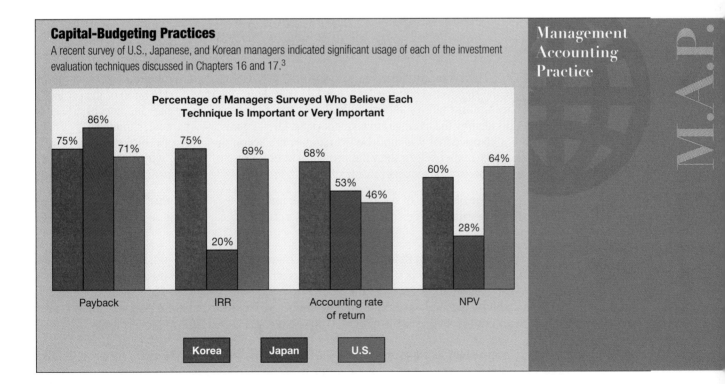

Capital-Budgeting Practices

A recent survey of U.S., Japanese, and Korean managers indicated significant usage of each of the investment evaluation techniques discussed in Chapters 16 and 17.[3]

Management
Accounting
Practice

[2] You can verify the IRR of 13.5% using Table III in the appendix to Chapter 16. You will need to interpolate to find the discount factors for 13.5%, which lie between the 12% and 14% discount factors. For example, .881 is the approximate discount factor for 13.5% and $n = 1$ [.881 = .877 + (.25)(.893 − .877)].

[3] Il-Woon Kim and Ja Song, "Accounting Practices in Three Countries," *Management Accounting* 72, no. 2, pp. 26–30.

Use of the Average Investment Some managers prefer to compute the accounting rate of return using the average amount invested in a project for the denominator, rather than the project's full cost. The formula is modified as follows:

$$\text{Accounting rate of return (using average investment)} = \frac{\left(\begin{array}{c}\text{Average}\\\text{incremental}\\\text{revenue}\end{array}\right) - \left(\begin{array}{c}\text{Average incremental expenses}\\\text{(including depreciation}\\\text{and income taxes)}\end{array}\right)}{\text{Average investment}}$$

A project's average investment is the average accounting book value over the project's life.

Refer again to High Country Department Stores' lunch-counter data given in Exhibit 17–10. The project's book value at the beginning of each year is tabulated as follows:

Year	(a) Book Value at Beginning of Year	MACRS Depreciation	(b) Book Value at End of Year	$\frac{\text{(a) + (b)}}{2}$ Average Book Value During Year
1	$210,000	$15,000	$195,000	$202,500
2	195,000	30,000	165,000	180,000
3	165,000	30,000	135,000	150,000
4	135,000	30,000	105,000	120,000
5	105,000	30,000	75,000	90,000
6	75,000	30,000	45,000	60,000
7	45,000	30,000	15,000	30,000
8	15,000	15,000	–0–	7,500
9	–0–	–0–	–0–	–0–
10	–0–	–0–	–0–	–0–

The average investment over the project's useful life is the average of the amounts in the right-hand column, which is $84,000. Thus, the modified version of the project's accounting rate of return is 20.7 percent. (The average annual income of $17,400 divided by the average investment of $84,000 equals 20.7 percent, rounded.)

Notice that this modified version of the accounting rate of return yields a significantly higher return than the project's internal rate of return, which we computed as 13.5 percent. As a general rule of thumb, the following relationships will be observed.

Accounting rate of return (using initial investment) < Internal rate of return < Accounting rate of return (using average investment)

Accounting Rate of Return: Pro and Con Like the payback method, the accounting-rate-of-return method is a simple way of screening investment proposals. Some managers use this method because they believe it parallels financial accounting statements, which also are based on accrual accounting. However, like the payback method, the accounting-rate-of-return method does not consider the time value of money.

Inconsistent Terminology Many different terms for the accounting rate of return are used in practice. Among these terms are *simple rate of return, rate of return on assets,* and the *unadjusted rate of return.*

Estimating Cash Flows: The Role of Activity-Based Costing

The validity of any discounted-cash-flow analysis is dependent on the accuracy of the cash flow estimates. Activity-based-costing (ABC) systems generally improve the ability of an analyst to estimate the cash flows associated with a proposed project. By separating costs into activity cost pools and identifying a cost driver for each pool, the analyst can more accurately determine the levels of various costs that will be incurred if the project is implemented. Costs that are treated as fixed under a traditional, volume-based costing system often are seen to be variable, with respect to the appropriate cost driver, under an ABC system. [4]

Accuracy in estimating cash flows is particularly important in evaluating a proposed investment in advanced manufacturing equipment. These decisions are complex, involving many peripheral cash flows besides the actual purchase of the equipment. Flexible manufacturing systems (FMSs) generally require cash outlays for software, retraining of employees, realignment of the production line, and engineering. The benefits of such systems often are difficult to quantify also. As Chapter 16 discussed, intangible benefits such as greater production flexibility are important considerations in making these investment decisions.

In today's manufacturing environment, it is crucial that companies make the best decisions possible regarding huge investments such as those in flexible manufacturing systems. Flawed decisions can spell disaster in today's globally competitive arenas.

Chapter Summary

Income taxes play an important role in the capital-budgeting decisions of a profit-seeking enterprise. For any organization subject to income taxes, the first step in a discounted-cash-flow analysis is to determine the after-tax cash flows related to the investment proposal under consideration. Cash flows that are also on the income statement should be multiplied by 1 minus the organization's tax rate. This rule applies to cash expenses and cash revenues. Cash flows that are not on the income statement, such as asset acquisitions, have no direct tax consequences. Expenses that are not cash flows in their own right, such as depreciation expenses, cause a cash flow by reducing the organization's income taxes. Thus, depreciation expenses should be multiplied by the tax rate to determine their tax impact. The resulting reductions in income-tax cash flows comprise a depreciation tax shield on a depreciable asset.

The time value of money makes it advantageous for a company to use an accelerated depreciation method for tax purposes. The current U.S. tax law specifies that the Modified Accelerated Cost Recovery System (MACRS) be used to determine depreciation deductions.

When assets are sold for more or less than their current book value, the gain or loss on disposal is taxed. Thus, the tax implications of asset dispositions also should be included in a discounted-cash-flow analysis.

No reliable method exists for ranking multiple investment proposals with positive net present values. Nevertheless, the profitability index is a widely used method for ranking projects.

In addition to discounted-cash-flow analysis, many organizations use the payback method and the accounting-rate-of-return method in capital-budgeting decisions. Since these methods do not account for the time value of money, they are conceptually inferior to discounted-cash-flow methods.

Key Terms

For each term's definition refer to the indicated page, or turn to the glossary at the end of the text.

accounting-rate-of-return
   method, pg. 716
after-tax cash flow, pg. 700

depreciation tax
   shield, pg. 702

Modified Accelerated Cost
   Recovery System
   (MACRS), pg. 703
payback period, pg. 713

profitability index (or excess
   present value
   index), pg. 713
working capital, pg. 708

---

[4] Activity-based-costing systems, introduced conceptually in Chapter 3, are covered extensively in Chapter 5.

Appendix to Chapter 17

Impact of Inflation

LO 8   After completing the appendix, explain the impact of inflation on a capital-budgeting analysis.

Most countries have experienced inflation to some degree over the past 30 years. *Inflation* is defined as a decline in the general purchasing power of a monetary unit, such as a dollar, across time. Since capital-budgeting decisions involve cash flows over several time periods, it is worthwhile to examine the impact of inflation in capital-budgeting analyses.

Inflation can be incorporated in a discounted-cash-flow analysis in either of two ways. Both approaches yield correct results, but the analyst must be careful to be consistent in applying either approach. The two approaches are distinguished by the use of either *nominal* or *real* interest rates and dollars. These terms are defined below.

The **real interest rate** includes compensation to an investor for the time value of money and the risk of an investment.

The **nominal interest rate** is the real interest rate plus an additional premium to compensate investors for inflation.

Nominal dollars is the actual cash flow observed.

Real dollars is the measure that reflects an adjustment for the purchasing power of a monetary unit.

Interest Rates: Real or Nominal   The **real interest rate** is the underlying interest rate, which includes compensation to investors for the *time value of money* and the *risk* of an investment. The **nominal interest rate** includes the real interest rate, plus an additional premium to compensate investors for inflation. Suppose the real interest rate is 10 percent, and inflation of 5 percent is projected. Then the nominal interest rate is determined as follows: [5]

Real interest rate	.10
Inflation rate	.05
Combined effect (.10 × .05)	.005
Nominal interest rate	.155

Dollars: Real or Nominal   A cash flow measured in **nominal dollars** is the actual cash flow we observe. For example, a particular model of automobile cost $10,000 in year 1 but it cost $12,155 in year 5. Both the $10,000 cash flow in year 1 and $12,155 cash flow in year 5 are measured in *nominal dollars*. A cash flow measured in **real dollars** reflects an adjustment for the dollar's purchasing power. The following table shows the relationship between nominal and real dollars, assuming an inflation rate of 5 percent.

Year	(a) Cash Flow in Nominal Dollars	(b) Price Index	(c) = (a) ÷ (b) Cash Flow in Real Dollars
Year 1	$10,000	1.0000	$10,000
Year 2	10,500	$(1.05)^1 = 1.0500$	10,000
Year 3	11,025	$(1.05)^2 = 1.1025$	10,000
Year 4	11,576	$(1.05)^3 = 1.1576$	10,000
Year 5	12,155	$(1.05)^4 = 1.2155$	10,000

As the table shows, cash flows in nominal dollars must be deflated, which means dividing by the price index, to convert them to cash flows in real dollars. The real-dollar cash flows are expressed in year 1 dollars.

Two Capital-Budgeting Approaches under Inflation

A correct capital-budgeting analysis may be done using either of the following approaches.

1. Use cash flows measured in *nominal dollars* and a nominal interest rate to determine the *nominal discount rate*.

2. Use cash flows measured in *real dollars* and a real interest rate to determine the *real discount rate*.

To illustrate these two approaches, we will focus on an equipment-replacement decision faced by the management of High Country Department Stores. The company operates an appliance-repair service for the household appliances it sells. Management is considering the replacement of a sophisticated piece

---

[5] An alternative way to compute the nominal interest rate is: $(1.10 \times 1.05) - 1.00 = .155$.

of testing equipment used in repairing TVs and VCRs. The new equipment costs $5,000 and will have no salvage value. Over its four-year life, the new equipment is expected to generate the cost savings and depreciation tax shield shown below. The cash flows in column (f) of the table are the total after-tax cash inflows, measured in *nominal dollars*.

Measured in Nominal Dollars

Year	(a) Acquisition Cost	(b) Cost Savings	(c) After-Tax Cost Savings [(b) × (1 − .40)]	(d) MACRS Depreciation (3-year class)	(e) Depreciation Tax Shield [(d) × .40]	(f) Total After-Tax Cash Flow [(c) + (e)]
Year 1	$(5,000)					
Year 2		$1,900	$1,140	$1,667	$667	$1,807
Year 3		2,000	1,200	2,223	889	2,089
Year 4		2,100	1,260	740	296	1,556
Year 5		2,500	1,500	370	148	1,648

Approach 1: Nominal Dollars and Nominal Discount Rate   Under this capital-budgeting approach, we discount the nominal-dollar cash flows in the preceding table using the nominal discount rate of 15.5 percent. The net-present-value analysis is as follows:

Year	(a) Cash Flow in Nominal Dollars	(b) Discount Factor for Nominal Discount Rate of 15.5 %	(c) = (a) × (b) Present Value
Year 1	$(5,000)	1.000	$(5,000)
Year 2	1,807	.8658 [1/(1.155)]*	1,564
Year 3	2,089	.7496 [1/(1.155)^2]	1,565
Year 4	1,556	.6490 [1/(1.155)^3]	1,009
Year 5	1,648	.5619 [1/(1.155)^4]	926
Net present value			$ 64

*The 15.5% discount factors can be computed in this fashion, using formula (2) in Chapter 16, or by interpolating with the discount factors in Table III of the appendix to Chapter 16.

High Country's management should purchase the new testing equipment, since its NPV is positive.

Approach 2: Real Dollars and Real Discount Rate   Under this capital-budgeting approach, we first convert the cash flows measured in nominal dollars to cash flows in real dollars, as follows:

Year	(a) After-Tax Cash Flow in Nominal Dollars	(b) Price Index	(c) = (a) ÷ (b) After-Tax Cash Flow in Real Dollars*
Year 1	$(5,000)	1.0000	$(5,000)
Year 2	1,807	1.0500	1,721
Year 3	2,089	1.1025	1,895
Year 4	1,556	1.1576	1,344
Year 5	1,648	1.2155	1,356

* Real-dollar cash flows expressed in terms of year 1 dollars.

Now we discount the after-tax cash flows, measured in real dollars, using the real discount rate of 10 percent. The net-present-value analysis is shown below.

Year	(a) Cash Flow in Real Dollars	(b) Discount Factor for Real Discount Rate of 10%	(c) = (a) × b) Present Value
Year 1	$(5,000)	1.000	$(5,000)
Year 2	1,721	.909	1,564
Year 3	1,895	.826	1,565
Year 4	1,344	.751	1,009
Year 5	1,356	.683	926
Net present value			$ 64

Notice that the new testing equipment's NPV is the same under both capital-budgeting approaches. Under both approaches, we conclude that High Country Department Stores should purchase the new equipment.

Consistency Is the Key   Either capital-budgeting approach will provide the correct conclusion, as long as it is applied consistently. Use either nominal dollars and a nominal discount rate or real dollars and a real discount rate. A common error in capital budgeting is to convert the after-tax cash flows to real dollars, but then use the nominal discount rate. This faulty analysis creates a bias against acceptance of worthwhile projects.

To illustrate, suppose High Country's management had made this error in its testing-equipment analysis. The following *incorrect* analysis is the result.

Incorrect Analysis of Testing-Equipment Decision

Inconsistency

Year	(a) Cash Flow in Real Dollars	(b) Discount Factor for Nominal Discount Rate of 15.5%	(c) = (a) × (b) Present Value
Year 1	$(5,000)	1.0000	$(5,000)
Year 2	1,721	.8658	1,490
Year 3	1,895	.7496	1,420
Year 4	1,344	.6490	872
Year 5	1,356	.5619	762
Net present value			$ (456)

This inconsistent and incorrect analysis will lead High Country's management to the wrong conclusion.

Do managers explicitly consider inflation in their capital-budgeting analyses? Surveys of practice suggest that they do.

Management Accounting Practice

Use of Inflation Adjustments

A survey of executives in large industrial firms indicated the following practices in adjusting cash flows for inflation. [6]

Cash Flow Item	Survey Respondents Who Adjust for Inflation
Material costs	96%
Employee compensation costs	93
Future capital outlays	92
Revenues	89
Asset salvage values	55
Ending values for investments in working capital	51

Key Terms: Appendix

For each term's definition refer to the indicated page, or turn to the glossary at the end of the text.

nominal dollars, pg. 720   **nominal interest rate, pg. 720**   **real dollars, pg. 720**   **real interest rate, pg. 720**

Review Questions

17–1. Explain how to compute the after-tax amount of a cash revenue or expense.

17–2. Give an example of a noncash expense. What impact does such an expense have in a capital-budgeting analysis? Explain how to compute the after-tax impact of a noncash expense.

---

[6] J.A. Hendricks, "Capital-Budgeting Practices Including Inflation Adjustments: A Survey," *Managerial Planning* 31, no. 4, p. 26.

17–3. What is a *depreciation tax shield?* Explain the effect of a depreciation tax shield in a capital-budgeting analysis.

17–4. Give an example of a cash flow that is not on the income statement. How do you determine the after-tax amount of such a cash flow?

17–5. Why is accelerated depreciation advantageous to a business?

17–6. Briefly describe the Modified Accelerated Cost Recovery System (MACRS), as modified by recent changes in the tax laws.

17–7. If a company replaced all of the furniture in its executive offices for $100,000, how would the furniture be depreciated for tax purposes? Assume the estimated useful life of the furniture is 15 years.

17–8. Explain what is meant by the *half-year convention.*

17–9. Define the terms *gain* and *loss* on disposal.

17–10. Explain how a gain or loss on disposal is handled in a capital-budgeting analysis.

17–11. Why is it difficult to rank investment projects with positive net present values and different lives?

17–12. Why may the net-present-value and internal-rate-of-return methods yield different rankings for investments with different lives?

17–13. Define the term *profitability index.* How is it used in ranking investment proposals?

17–14. What is meant by the term *payback period?* How is this criterion sometimes used in capital budgeting?

17–15. What are the two main drawbacks of the payback method?

17–16. How is an investment project's *accounting rate of return* defined? Why do the accounting rate of return and internal rate of return on a capital project generally differ?

17–17. Discuss the pros and cons of the accounting rate of return as an investment criterion.

17–18. (Appendix) Define the term *inflation.* How is inflation measured?

17–19. (Appendix) Explain the differences (a) between real and nominal interest rates and (b) between real and nominal dollars.

17–20. (Appendix) Briefly describe two correct methods of net-present-value analysis in an inflationary period.

Exercises

Daly Publishing Corporation recently purchased a truck for $30,000. Under MACRS, the first year's depreciation was $6,000. The truck driver's salary in the first year of operation was $32,000.

Required:

Show how each of the amounts mentioned above should be converted to an after-tax amount. The company's tax rate is 30 percent.

■ **Exercise 17–21**
After-Tax Cash Flows
(LO 1, LO 2)

For each of the following assets, indicate the MACRS property class and depreciation method.

1. A pharmaceutical company bought a new microscope to use in its Research and Development Division.
2. A midwestern farmer constructed a new barn to house beef cattle.
3. A steel fabrication company bought a machine, which is expected to be useful for 18 years.
4. The president of an insurance company authorized the purchase of a new desk for her office.
5. A pizza restaurant purchased a new delivery car.

■ **Exercise 17–22**
Using the Modified Accelerated Cost Recovery System
(LO 4)

In December of 20x4, Atlas Chemical Corporation sold a forklift for $9,255. The machine was purchased in 20x1 for $50,000. Since then $38,845 in depreciation has been recorded on the forklift.

Required:

1. What was the forklift's book value at the time of sale?
2. Compute the gain or loss on the sale.
3. Determine the after-tax cash flow at the time the forklift was sold. The firm's tax rate is 45 percent.

■ **Exercise 17–23**
Gain or Loss on Disposal
(LO 1, LO 2)

Sharpe Machining Company purchased industrial tools costing $100,000, which fall in the 3-year property class under MACRS.

Required:

1. Prepare a schedule of depreciation deductions assuming:
   a. The firm uses the accelerated depreciation schedule specified by MACRS.
   b. The firm uses the optional straight-line depreciation method and the half-year convention.

■ **Exercise 17–24**
Depreciation Tax Shield
(LO 3)

2. Calculate the present value of the depreciation tax shield under each depreciation method listed in requirement (1). Sharpe Machining Company's after-tax hurdle rate is 12 percent, and the firm's tax rate is 30 percent.

■ **Exercise 17–25**
Payback Period; Even Cash Flows
(LO 7)

The management of Delaware National Bank is considering an investment in automatic teller machines. The machines would cost $124,200 and have a useful life of seven years. The bank's controller has estimated that the automatic teller machines will save the bank $27,000 after taxes during each year of their life (including the depreciation tax shield). The machines will have no salvage value.

Required:

1. Compute the payback period for the proposed investment.
2. Compute the net present value of the proposed investment assuming an after-tax hurdle rate of: (*a*) 10%, (*b*) 12%, and (*c*) 14%.
3. What can you conclude from your answers to requirements (1) and (2) about the limitations of the payback method?

■ **Exercise 17–26**
Payback Period; Uneven Cash Flows
(LO 7)

Piedmont Insurance Company's management is considering an advertising program that would require an initial expenditure of $165,500 and bring in additional sales over the next five years. The projected additional sales revenue in year 1 is $75,000, with associated expenses of $25,000. The additional sales revenue and expenses from the advertising program are projected to increase by 10 percent each year. Piedmont's tax rate is 40 percent. (Hint: The $165,500 advertising cost is an expense.)

Required:

1. Compute the payback period for the advertising program.
2. Calculate the advertising program's net present value, assuming an after-tax hurdle rate of 10 percent.

■ **Exercise 17–27**
Profitability Index
(LO 6)

The owner of Cape Cod Confectionary is considering the purchase of a new semiautomatic candy machine. The machine will cost $25,000 and last 10 years. The machine is expected to have no salvage value at the end of its useful life. The owner projects that the new candy machine will generate $4,000 in after-tax savings each year during its life (including the depreciation tax shield).

Required:

Compute the profitability index on the proposed candy machine, assuming an after-tax hurdle rate of: (*a*) 8%, (*b*) 10%, and (*c*) 12%.

■ **Exercise 17–28**
Accounting Rate of Return
(LO 7)

Jericho Spring Water Company recently purchased a new delivery truck for $50,000. Management expects the truck to generate the following additional revenues and expenses during its six-year life.

Average incremental revenue	$25,000
Average incremental expenses, not including depreciation or taxes	10,000

The truck has an expected life of six years and is in the MACRS 5-year property class. Jericho will use the optional straight-line depreciation method along with the half-year convention. The firm's tax rate is 40 percent.

Required:

1. Prepare a schedule showing the incremental revenue, incremental operating expenses, incremental depreciation, and incremental taxes during each of the next six years.
2. Compute the accounting rate of return on the delivery truck, using the initial investment in the denominator.

■ **Exercise 17–29**
Payback, Accounting Rate of Return; Net Present Value
(LO 7)

Canfield Glass Corporation is reviewing an investment proposal. The initial cost as well as the estimate of the book value of the investment at the end of each year, the net after-tax cash flows for each year, and the net income for each year are presented in the following schedule. The salvage value of the investment at the end of each year is equal to its book value. There would be no salvage value at the end of the investment's life.

Year	Initial Cost and Book Value	Annual Net After-Tax Cash Flows	Annual Net Income
0	$105,000		
1	70,000	$50,000	$15,000
2	42,000	45,000	17,000
3	21,000	40,000	19,000
4	7,000	35,000	21,000
5	0	30,000	23,000

Canfield uses a 16 percent after-tax target rate of return for new investment proposals.

Required:

For requirement (1) *only* assume that the cash flows in years 1 through 5 occur uniformly throughout each year.

1. Compute the project's payback period.
2. Calculate the accounting rate of return on the investment proposal. Base your calculation on the initial cost of the investment.
3. Compute the proposal's net present value.

(CMA, adapted)

The state's Secretary of Education is considering the purchase of a new computer for $100,000. A cost study indicates that the new computer should save the Department of Education $30,000, measured in real dollars, during each of the next eight years.

   The real interest rate is 20 percent and the inflation rate is 10 percent. As a governmental agency, the Department of Education pays no taxes.

■ **Exercise 17–30**
Inflation and Capital Budgeting (Appendix)
(LO 8)

Required:

1. Prepare a schedule of cash flows measured in real dollars. Include the initial acquisition and the cost savings for each of the next eight years.
2. Using cash flows measured in real dollars, compute the net present value of the proposed computer. Use a real discount rate equal to the real interest rate.

Refer to the data in the preceding exercise.

■ **Exercise 17–31**
Inflation and Capital Budgeting (Appendix)
(LO 8)

Required:

1. Compute the nominal interest rate.
2. Prepare a schedule of cash flows measured in nominal dollars.
3. Using cash flows measured in nominal dollars, compute the net present value of the proposed computer. Use a nominal discount rate equal to the nominal interest rate.

Problems

Math for the Mind, Inc. publishes innovative mathematics textbooks for public schools. The company's management recently acquired the following two new pieces of equipment.

■ **Problem 17-32**
MACRS Depreciation;
Present Value of Tax Shield
(LO 3, LO 4)

■ Computer-controlled printing press: cost, $250,000; expected useful life, 12 years.

■ Duplicating equipment to be used in the administrative offices: cost, $60,000; expected useful life, six years.

   The company uses straight-line depreciation for book purposes and the MACRS accelerated depreciation schedule for tax purposes. The firm's tax rate is 40 percent; its after-tax hurdle rate is 10 percent. Neither machine has any salvage value.

Required:

For each of the publishing company's new pieces of equipment:

1. Prepare a schedule of the annual depreciation expenses for book purposes.
2. Determine the appropriate MACRS property class.

3. Prepare a schedule of the annual depreciation expenses for tax purposes.
4. Compute the present value of the depreciation tax shield.

■ **Problem 17–33**
Net Present Value
(LO 5)

VacuTech is a high-technology company that manufactures sophisticated testing instruments for evaluating microcircuits. These instruments sell for $3,500 each and cost $2,450 each to manufacture. An essential component of the company's manufacturing process is a sealed vacuum chamber where the interior approaches a pure vacuum. The technology of the vacuum pumps that the firm uses to prepare its chamber for sealing has been changing rapidly. On January 2, 20x0, VacuTech bought the latest in electronic high-speed vacuum pumps, a machine that allowed the company to evacuate a chamber for sealing in only six hours. The company paid $400,000 for the pump. Recently, the manufacturer of the pump approached VacuTech with a new pump that would reduce the evacuation time to two hours. VacuTech's management is considering the acquisition of this new pump and has asked Melanie Harris, the controller, to evaluate the financial impact of replacing the existing pump with the new model. Harris has gathered the following information prior to preparing her analysis.

■ The new pump would be installed on December 31, 20x2 and placed in service on January 1, 20x3. The cost of the pump is $608,000, and the costs for installing, testing, and debugging the new pump will be $12,000. For depreciation purposes, these costs will be considered part of the cost of the equipment. The pump would be assigned to the three-year MACRS class for depreciation and is expected to have a salvage value of $80,000 when sold at the end of four years.

■ The old pump will be fully depreciated at the time the new pump is placed in service. If the new pump is purchased, arrangements will be made to sell the old pump for $50,000, the estimated salvage value on December 31, 20x2.

■ At the current rate of production, the new pump's greater efficiency will result in annual cash savings of $125,000.

■ VacuTech is able to sell all of the testing instruments it can produce. Because of the increased speed of the new pump, output is expected to be 30 units greater in 20x3 than in 20x2. In 20x4 and 20x5, production will be 50 units greater than in 20x2. The production in 20x6 will exceed 20x2 production by 70 units. For all *additional* units produced, the manufacturing costs would be reduced by $150 per unit.

■ VacuTech is subject to a 40 percent tax rate. For evaluating capital investment proposals, VacuTech's management uses a 16 percent after-tax discount rate.

Required:

1. Determine whether or not VacuTech should purchase the new pump by calculating the net present value of the investment.
2. Describe the factors, other than the net present value, that VacuTech should consider before making the pump replacement decision.

(CMA, adapted)

■ **Problem 17–34**
MACRS Depreciation;
Present Value of Tax Shield
(LO 3, LO 4)

Flotilla Beam, the owner of the Bay City Boatyard, recently had a brilliant idea. There is a shortage of boat slips in the harbor during the summer. Beam's idea is to develop a system of "dry slips." A dry slip is a large storage rack in a warehouse on which a boat is stored. When the boat owner requests, a forklift is used to remove the boat from the dry slip and place the boat in the water. The entire operation requires one hour when a launch reservation is made in advance. The boatyard already has a vacant warehouse which could be used for this purpose. However, Beam's idea will require the following capital investment by the boatyard.

■ Storage racks: cost, $200,000; useful life, 18 years; MACRS class, 10-year property.
■ Forklift: cost, $120,000; useful life, six years; MACRS class, 5-year property.

Bay City Boatyard's tax rate is 35 percent, and its after-tax hurdle rate is 14 percent.

Required:

For each of the boatyard's proposed capital investments:

1. Prepare a schedule of the annual depreciation expenses for tax purposes.
2. Compute the present value of the depreciation tax shield.

Refer to the data for High Country Department Stores' computerized checkout equipment decision given in Exhibit 17–7. Also refer to the net-present-value analysis presented in Exhibit 17–8.

■ **Problem 17–35**
Sensitivity Analysis;
NPV with Taxes
(LO 5)

Required:

The annual incremental sales revenue resulting from the marketing analysis is estimated at $40,000. How low could this amount be and still result in a nonnegative net present value for the new equipment?

Fort Wayne Fastener Corporation manufactures nails, screws, bolts, and other fasteners. Management is considering a proposal to acquire new material handling equipment. The new equipment has the same capacity as the current equipment but will provide operating efficiencies in labor and power usage. The savings in operating costs are estimated at $150,000 annually.

■ **Problem 17–36**
After-Tax Cash Flows; NPV;
Automated Material
Handling System
(LO 5)

   The new equipment will cost $300,000 and will be purchased at the beginning of the year when the project is started. The equipment dealer is certain that the equipment will be operational during the second quarter of the year it is installed. Therefore, 60 percent of the estimated annual savings can be obtained in the first year. The company will incur a one-time expense of $30,000 to transfer production activities from the old equipment to the new equipment. No loss of sales will occur, however, because the processing facility is large enough to install the new equipment without interfering with the operations of the current equipment. The equipment is in the MACRS 7-year property class. The firm would depreciate the machinery in accordance with the MACRS depreciation schedule.

   The current equipment has been fully depreciated. Management has reviewed its condition and has concluded that it can be used an additional eight years. The company would receive $10,000, net of removal costs, if it elected to buy the new equipment and dispose of its current equipment at this time. The new equipment will have no salvage value at the end of its life. The company is subject to a 40 percent income-tax rate and requires an after-tax return of at least 12 percent on any investment.

Required:

1. Calculate the annual incremental after-tax cash flows for Fort Wayne Fastener Corporation's proposal to acquire the new equipment.
2. Calculate the net present value of the proposal to acquire the new equipment using the cash flows calculated in requirement (1), and indicate what action management should take. Assume all cash flows take place at the end of the year.

(CMA, adapted)

Beloit Company manufactures motorized utility equipment and trucks. Beloit's Assembly Department employs about 200 workers who are covered by a labor contract that will expire on December 31, 20x0. During negotiations with Beloit for a new contract, the union has presented a proposal covering the next four years. This proposal calls for an increase in wage rates of 15 percent over the life of the contract: an increase of $1.00 per hour at the beginning of 20x1 and an additional $.50 per hour at the beginning of 20x3. Employee benefits will be 40 percent of regular wages (total wages exclusive of any overtime premium) under the terms of the union proposal. Management is concerned that the increase in labor costs will eliminate most or all of its profits.

■ **Problem 17–37**
Automation; Intangible
Benefits; NPV, Incremental-
Cost Approach; Ethics
(LO 5)

   Beloit's long-range plans call for expansion of the product line in the near future. Management is working with outside consultants on the design of a new automated plant that will double present capacity. The new plant is to be operational in December, 20x4, at which time the existing facility will be sold.

   The assembly activity in the new plant will be highly automated. Now, in response to the union proposal, management wants to examine the possibility of automating the existing Assembly Department. Because the system has already been designed and developed, the vice president of production is confident that the equipment could be acquired and installed in late 20x0 to be operational in January 20x1.

   The controller has been asked to provide an analysis of the proposal to automate the existing Assembly Department based on the labor costs included in the union proposal. The controller has accumulated the following data.

■ The sales revenues for the next four years are expected to be relatively stable.

■ Production volume is uniform throughout the year. Currently, a total of 40,000 labor hours are worked annually in the Assembly Department, of which 3,000 labor hours are subject to an overtime premium of 50 percent of the wage rate.

■ The wage rate under the current labor contract is $10 per hour.

- The new equipment will be purchased and installed in the Assembly Department in December 20x0 at a cost of $1,500,000. For tax purposes, this is three-year equipment and will be depreciated using the MACRS rates.

- The labor hours worked in the Assembly Department will be reduced to 15,000 annually with the new equipment and, because of increased efficiency, overtime will be eliminated.

- Annual maintenance costs will increase by $6,000 with the new equipment.

- The existing facility can be sold for $800,000 on December 31, 20x4. However, if the Assembly Department is automated, the plant can then be sold for $1,000,000. The book value for tax purposes of the existing facility on December 31, 20x4, exclusive of the new equipment, will be $700,000, whether or not the Assembly Department is automated.

- Beloit Company is subject to a 40 percent income tax rate on all income.

- Management assumes annual cash flows occur at the end of the year for evaluating capital investment proposals. The company uses a 16 percent after-tax discount rate.

Required:

1. Based on the labor costs included in the union proposal, calculate the net present value on December 31, 20x0, of Beloit Company's proposal to automate the Assembly Department. Use the incremental-cost approach. Should the company invest in the automated equipment?

2. Discuss the potential difficulties of Beloit Company using discounted-cash-flow analysis to make a decision about high-tech manufacturing equipment.

3. When the controller presented his findings to the vice president of production, the vice president responded as follows: "I think it's a real mistake not to automate now. I can see what your figures say, but I know there will be other benefits to the firm if we move on this now. I'm talking about intangible benefits that you can't put your finger on. Look, Dave, here's what I want you to do. Revise your analysis and increase the projected labor savings by enough to make the overall NPV positive. Then we can get the board to approve it. What I'm asking may be a bit sneaky, but I've got a gut feeling the automation decision will prove to be a good one."

   Discuss the ethical issues in this scenario. How should the controller respond?

4. Suppose the vice president for production can list some of the intangible benefits of automating. What would the *annual* before-tax total cash flow from these benefits have to be to bring the project's NPV up to zero?

(CMA, adapted)

■ **Problem 17–38**
After-Tax Cash Flows;
Robotic Equipment
(LO 5)

Scientific Frontiers Corporation manufactures scientific equipment for use in elementary schools. In December of 20x0 the company's management is considering the acquisition of robotic equipment, which would radically change its manufacturing process. The controller has collected the following data pertinent to the decision.

1. The robotic equipment would cost $1,000,000, to be paid in December of 20x0. The equipment's useful life is projected to be eight years. The equipment is in the MACRS 5-year property class. The company will use the MACRS accelerated depreciation schedule.

2. The robotic equipment requires software which will be developed over a two-year period in 20x1 and 20x2. Each software expenditure, which will amount to $25,000 per year, will be expensed during the year incurred.

3. A computer systems operator will be hired immediately to oversee the operation of the new robotic equipment. The computer expert's annual salary will be $60,000. Fringe benefits will cost $20,000 annually.

4. Maintenance technicians will be needed. The total cost of their wages and fringe benefits will be $150,000 per year.

5. The changeover of the manufacturing line will cost $90,000, to be expensed in 20x1.

6. Several employees will need retraining to operate the new robotic equipment. The training costs are projected as follows:

20x1	$35,000
20x2	25,000
20x3	10,000

7. An inventory of spare parts for the robotic equipment will be purchased immediately at a cost of $60,000. This investment in working capital will be maintained throughout the eight-year life of the equipment. At the end of 20x8, the parts will be sold for $60,000.

8. The robotic equipment's salvage value at the end of 20x8 is projected to be $50,000. It will be fully depreciated at that time.

9. Aside from the costs specifically mentioned above, management expects the robotic equipment to save $480,000 per year in manufacturing costs.

10. Switching to the robotic equipment will enable Scientific Frontiers Corporation to sell some of its manufacturing machinery over the next two years. The following sales schedule is projected.

	Acquisition Cost of Equipment Sold	Accumulated Depreciation at Time of Sale	Sales Proceeds
20x1	$150,000	$100,000	$ 20,000
20x2	305,000	215,000	140,000

11. Scientific Frontiers Corporation's tax rate is 30 percent.

12. The company's after-tax hurdle rate is 12 percent.

Required:

Prepare a year-by-year columnar schedule including all of the after-tax cash flows associated with the robotic-equipment decision. Assume that each cash flow will occur at year-end.

Refer to the data given in the preceding problem.

Required:

Compute the net present value of Scientific Frontiers Corporation's proposed acquisition of robotic equipment.

■ **Problem 17–39**
Robotic Equipment; Taxes;
Net Present Value
(LO 5)

Bio Tech Company plans to replace an old piece of research equipment which is obsolete and is expected to be unreliable under the stress of daily operations. The equipment is fully depreciated, and no salvage value can be realized upon its disposal. One piece of equipment under consideration would provide annual cash savings of $7,000 before income taxes. The equipment would cost $18,000 and have an estimated useful life of five years. The equipment is expected to have no salvage value at the end of five years.

Bio Tech uses the straight-line depreciation method on all equipment for both book and tax purposes. The company is subject to a 40 percent tax rate. Bio Tech has an after-tax hurdle rate of 14 percent. The new equipment is in the MACRS 5-year property class.

■ **Problem 17–40**
Various Methods of
Investment Analysis
(LO 5, LO 6, LO 7)

Required:

For this problem, ignore the half-year convention.

1. Calculate for Bio Tech Company's proposed investment in new equipment the after-tax:

    a. Payback period.   *d.* Profitability index.

    b. Accounting rate of return.   *e.* Internal rate of return.

    c. Net present value.

    Assume all operating revenues and expenses occur at the end of the year.

2. Write a memo to BioTech's president that identifies and discusses the issues that Bio Tech's management should consider when deciding which of the five decision models identified in requirement (1) it should employ to evaluate alternative capital-investment projects.

(CMA, adapted)

First Line Safety Corporation manufactures fire extinguishers. One part used in all types of fire extinguishers is a unique pressure fitting that requires specialized machine tools that need to be replaced. First Line's production manager has concluded that the only alternative to replacing these machine tools is to buy the pressure fitting from Minnesota Pipe and Fitting Company. First Line could buy the fitting for $20 if a minimum order of 70,000 fittings is placed annually. First Line has used an average of 80,000 fittings over the past three years. The production manager believes this volume will remain constant for five more years.

■ **Problem 17–41**
After-Tax Cash Flows; NPV
(LO 5)

Cost records indicate that unit manufacturing costs for the last several years have been as follows:

Direct material	$ 4.10
Direct labor	3.70
Variable overhead	1.70
Fixed overhead *	4.50
Total unit cost	$14.00

* Depreciation accounts for two-thirds of the fixed overhead. The balance is for other fixed overhead costs of the factory that require cash expenditures.

If the specialized tools are purchased, they will cost $2,500,000 and will have a disposal value of $100,000 after their expected life of five years. Straight-line depreciation is used for book purposes, but MACRS is used for tax purposes. The specialized tools are considered 3-year property for MACRS purposes. The company has a 40 percent tax rate, and management requires a 12 percent after-tax return on investment.

The sales representative for the manufacturer of the new tools stated, "The new tools will allow direct labor and variable overhead to be reduced by $1.60 per unit." Data from another manufacturer using identical tools and experiencing similar operating conditions, except that annual production generally averages 110,000 units, confirm the direct-labor and variable-overhead savings. However, the manufacturer indicated that it experienced an increase in direct-material cost to $4.50 per unit due to the higher quality of material that had to be used with the new tools.

Required:

1. Prepare a net-present-value analysis covering the life of the new specialized tools to determine whether management should replace the old tools or purchase the pressure fittings. Include all tax implications.

2. Identify any additional factors management should consider before a decision is made to replace the tools or purchase the pressure fittings.

(CMA, adapted)

■ Problem 17–42
Payback; Net Present Value;
Depreciation Tax Shield
(LO 4, LO 5, LO 7)

Cell Technology Company (CTC) develops medicines using genetic engineering methods. The company's vice president of research and development, John Tobias, is considering a major addition to the company's research equipment. The equipment is expected to have a useful life of five years and is in the MACRS 5-year property class. The cost of the equipment is $100,000. The projected incremental after-tax cash inflow during the life of the research equipment is $25,000 per year, not including the depreciation tax shield.

CTC's top management has stipulated that any capital investment costing over $75,000 must have a payback period of no more than three years in order to be acceptable. Tobias made a quick calculation and rejected the proposed acquisition. At lunch Tobias casually remarked to the corporate controller, "I hate to pass up that research equipment, but it costs $100,000. At only $25,000 a year in cash inflows, its payback period is four years." The controller thought for a minute and then pointed out that Tobias had not considered the depreciation tax shield on the equipment. As the two left the lunchroom, the controller turned to Tobias and said, "Let me work out the payback period on that equipment after including the tax impact of the depreciation."

Required:

When the controller returned to her office, she handed the job over to you, the assistant controller.

1. Prepare a schedule showing the annual depreciation expense and depreciation tax shield on the research equipment. Cell Technology Company uses the MACRS depreciation schedule. The firm's tax rate is 40 percent.

2. Prepare a schedule showing the total after-tax cash inflows during each year in the equipment's life.

3. Between what two whole numbers is the equipment's payback period?

4. Does the payback period on the equipment meet the company's criterion?

5. Compute the net present value of the equipment. The firm's after-tax hurdle rate is 10 percent.

Day Corporation's management is considering the replacement of an old machine. It is fully depreciated but it can be used by the corporation through 20x5. If management decides to replace the old machine, James Company has offered to purchase it for $60,000 on the replacement date. The old machine would have no salvage value in 20x5. If the replacement occurs, a new machine would be acquired from Hillcrest Industries on December 31, 20x1. The purchase price of $1,000,000 for the new machine would be paid in cash at the time of replacement. Due to the increased efficiency of the new machine, estimated annual cash savings of $300,000 would be generated through 20x5, the end of its expected useful life. The new machine is not expected to have any salvage value at the end of 20x5. Day's management requires all investments to earn a 12 percent after-tax return. The company's tax rate is 40 percent. The new machine would be classified as three-year property for MACRS purposes.

■ **Problem 17–43**
Net Present Value; Internal
Rate of Return; Payback;
Sensitivity Analysis
(LO 5, LO 7)

Required:

1. Compute the net present value of the machine replacement investment.
2. Between which of the following two percentages is the internal rate of return on the machine replacement: 4%, 6%, 8%, 10%, 12%, and 14%?
3. Between what two whole numbers of years is the machine replacement's payback period?
4. How much would the salvage value of the new machine have to be on December 31, 20x5 in order to turn the machine replacement into an acceptable investment?

(CMA, adapted)

Rosen Manufacturing Corporation produces office furniture and equipment and sells it wholesale to furniture distributors. Rosen's management is reviewing a proposal to purchase a just-in-time inventory system (JIT) to better serve its customers. The JIT system will include a computer system and material-handling equipment. The decision will be based on whether the new JIT system is cost-beneficial to the organization over the next five years.

■ **Problem 17–44**
Acquisition of JIT System;
MACRS Depreciation; Net
Present Value
(LO 4, LO 5)

The computer system, for both hardware and software, will initially cost $1,250,000. Material-handling equipment, such as a new conveyor belt, will cost $450,000. Both groups of equipment are to be classified as five-year property for the purposes of using the Modified Accelerated Cost Recovery System (MACRS) for income tax purposes. At the end of the five years, the newly acquired equipment will be sold. It is estimated that at that time the computer system will have a projected market value of $100,000, while the material-handling equipment will have a projected market value of $50,000.

Other factors to be considered over the next five years for this proposal include the following:

■ Due to the service improvement resulting from this new JIT system, Rosen will realize a $600,000 sales increase in the first year. Rosen expects this initial $600,000 sales increase to continue to grow by 10 percent per year thereafter.

■ The contribution margin from sales is 60 percent.

■ Annual material ordering costs will increase $50,000 due to a greater level of purchase orders.

■ There will be a one-time decrease in working-capital investment of $150,000 at the end of the first year.

■ There will be a 20 percent savings in warehouse rent due to less space being needed: the current annual rent is $300,000.

Rosen uses an after-tax hurdle rate of 10 percent and has an income-tax rate of 40 percent. Assume that all cash flows occur at year-end for tax purposes except for any initial purchase amounts.

Required:

1. Prepare an analysis of the purchase of the just-in-time system at Rosen Manufacturing Corporation using the net-present-value method for evaluating capital expenditures. (Hint: The time horizon for the analysis is five years, because Rosen will dispose of the new equipment at that time. The taxable gain on the sale of the equipment will be equal to the sales proceeds minus the undepreciated tax basis. The undepreciated tax basis is equal to the acquisition cost minus the accumulated depreciation at the time of sale. The taxable gain will be taxed at the 40 percent rate.)
2. Determine whether or not Rosen Manufacturing Corporation should purchase the just-in-time inventory system. Explain your answer.

(CMA, adapted)

■ **Problem 17–45**
Investment in Robotic
Manufacturing Equipment;
Net Present Value; Payback
(LO 5, LO 7)

Jonfran Company manufactures three different models of paper shredders including the waste container that serves as the base. While the shredder heads are different for the three models, the waste container is the same. The number of waste containers that Jonfran will need during the next five years is estimated as follows:

20x1	50,000
20x2	50,000
20x3	52,000
20x4	55,000
20x5	55,000

The equipment used to manufacture the waste container must be replaced because it is broken and cannot be repaired. Management is considering the purchase of robotic equipment to replace the old machinery. The new equipment would have a purchase price of $945,000. There will be a 2 percent discount if payment is made within 10 days. Company policy is to take all purchase discounts. The freight on the equipment would be $11,000, and installation costs would total $22,900. Freight and installation costs will be included in the equipment's cost basis for MACRS depreciation purposes. The equipment would be purchased in December of the current year and placed into service on January 1, 20x1. It would have a five-year useful life but would be treated as three-year property under MACRS because of the nature of the equipment. This equipment is expected to have a salvage value of $12,000 at the end of its useful life in 20x5. The new equipment will result in a 25 percent reduction in both direct labor and variable overhead. There will be an additional one-time permanent decrease in working capital requirements of $2,500, resulting from a reduction in direct-material inventories. This working capital reduction would be recognized in the analysis at the time of equipment acquisition. The old equipment is fully depreciated, and it can be sold for a salvage amount of $1,500.

Rather than replace the equipment, one of Jonfran's production managers has suggested that the waste containers be purchased. Jonfran has no alternative use for the manufacturing space at this time, so if the waste containers are purchased, the old equipment would be left in place. One supplier has quoted a price of $27 per container. This price is $8 less than Jonfran's current manufacturing cost, which is as follows:

Direct material		$ 8.00
Direct labor		10.00
Variable overhead		6.00
Fixed overhead:		
Supervision	$2.00	
Facilities	5.00	
General	4.00	11.00
Total manufacturing cost per unit		$35.00

Jonfran employs a plantwide fixed overhead rate in its operations. If the waste containers are purchased outside, the salary and benefits of one supervisor, included in the fixed overhead budget at $45,000, would be eliminated. There would be no other changes in the other cash and noncash items included in fixed overhead, except depreciation on the new equipment. Jonfran is subject to a 40 percent income tax rate. Management assumes that all annual cash flows and tax payments occur at the end of the year and uses a 12 percent after-tax discount rate.

Required:

1. Jonfran Company must decide whether to purchase the waste containers from an outside supplier or purchase the equipment to manufacture the waste containers. Calculate the net present value of the estimated after-tax cash flows and determine which of these two options to pursue.

2. Explain why some companies calculate the payback period of an investment in addition to determining the net present value.

3. Between what two consecutive whole number amounts is the payback period for the new equipment?

(CMA, adapted)

Coulter Travel is a large travel agency with offices in 12 California cities. The president of the company is currently trying to decide on the location for another office. The options are Sacramento and Bakersfield. The cash flows projected for the two alternative office locations follow.

The management of Coulter Travel uses a 10 percent after-tax discount rate to evaluate capital projects.

■ **Problem 17–46**
Ranking Investment
Proposals; IRR versus
Profitability Index
(LO 5, LO 6)

Investment Proposal	Cash Outflow: Time 0	Net After-Tax Cash Inflows* Years 1–10	Years 11–20	Internal Rate of Return
Sacramento	$597,520	$ 80,000	$80,000	12%
Bakersfield	596,860	110,000	—	13%†

* Includes after-tax flows from all sources, including incremental revenue, incremental expenses, and depreciation tax shield.

† The annuity discount factor for $r = .13$ and $n = 10$ is 5.426.

Required:

1. Compute the net present value of each alternative location for Coulter Travel's new office.
2. Compute the profitability index for each alternative.
3. Rank Coulter Travel's two potential office sites using (*a*) the IRR and (*b*) the profitability index.
4. What can you conclude from your answer to requirement (3) about these two criteria for ranking alternative investment proposals?

The owner of Zivanov's Pancake House is considering an expansion of the business. He has identified two alternatives, as follows:

■ **Problem 17–47**
Ranking Investment
Proposals; NPV versus
Profitability Index
(LO 5, LO 6)

■ Build a new restaurant near the mall.
■ Buy and renovate an old building downtown for the new restaurant.

The projected cash flows from these two alternatives are shown below. The owner of the restaurant uses a 10 percent after-tax discount rate.

Investment Proposal	Cash Outflow: Time 0	Net After-Tax Cash Inflows* Years 1–10	Years 11–20
Mall restaurant	$400,000	$50,000	$50,000
Downtown restaurant	200,000	35,800	—

* Includes after-tax cash flows from all sources, including incremental revenue, incremental expenses, and depreciation tax shield.

Required:

1. Compute the net present value of each alternative restaurant site.
2. Compute the profitability index for each alternative.
3. How do the two sites rank in terms of (*a*) NPV and (*b*) the profitability index?
4. Comment on the difficulty of ranking the owner's two options for the new restaurant site.

Refer to the data given in the preceding problem. The owner of Zivanov's Pancake House will consider capital projects only if they have a payback period of six years or less. The owner also favors projects that exhibit an accounting rate of return of at least 15 percent. The owner bases a project's accounting rate of return on the initial investment in the project.

■ **Problem 17–48**
Payback; Accounting Rate of
Return
(LO 7)

Required:

1. Compute the payback period for each of the proposed restaurant sites.
2. Compute the accounting rate of return for each proposed site. Assume the average annual incremental income is $50,000 for the Mall restaurant and $35,800 for the Downtown restaurant.
3. If the owner of the restaurant sticks to his criteria, which site will he choose?
4. Comment on the pros and cons of the restaurant owner's investment criteria.

Chesapeake Cablevision Company provides television cable service to two counties in Maryland. The firm's management is considering the construction of a new satellite dish in December of 20x0. The new antenna would improve reception and the service provided to customers. The dish antenna and associated equipment will cost $200,000 to purchase and install. The company's old equipment, which is

■ **Problem 17–49**
Inflation; NPV; Nominal
Dollars (Appendix)
(LO 8)

fully depreciated, can be sold now for $20,000. The company president expects the firm's improved capabilities to result in additional revenue of $80,000 per year during the dish's useful life of seven years. The incremental operating expenses associated with the new equipment are projected to be $10,000 per year. These incremental revenues and expenses are in real dollars.

The new satellite dish will be depreciated under the MACRS depreciation schedule for the 5-year property class. The company's tax rate is 40 percent.

Chesapeake Cablevision's president expects the real rate of interest in the economy to remain stable at 10 percent. She expects the inflation rate, currently running at 20 percent, to remain unchanged.

Required:

1. Prepare a schedule of cash flows projected over the next eight years (20x0 through 20x7), measured in nominal dollars. The schedule should include the initial costs of purchase and installation, the after-tax incremental revenue and expenses, and the depreciation tax shield. Remember to express the incremental revenues and expenses in nominal dollars.

2. Compute the nominal interest rate.

3. Prepare a net-present-value analysis of the proposed new satellite dish. Use cash flows measured in nominal dollars and a nominal discount rate equal to the nominal interest rate.

■ **Problem 17–50**
Inflation; NPV; Real Dollars
(Appendix)
(LO 8)

Refer to the data given in the preceding problem for Chesapeake Cablevision Company.

Required:

1. Compute the price index for each year from 20x1 through 20x7, using 1.0000 as the index for 20x0.

2. Prepare a schedule of after-tax cash flows measured in real dollars.

3. Compute the net present value of the proposed new satellite dish using cash flows measured in real dollars. Use a real discount rate equal to the real interest rate

■ **Problem 17–51**
Capital Budgeting under
Inflation; Automated
Equipment (Appendix)
(LO 5, LO 8)

The Medical Division of Potomac Assemblies, Inc. manufactures electronic heart monitoring equipment. Divisional management is considering the purchase of an automated assembly and soldering machine for use in the manufacture of its printed circuit boards. The machine would be placed in service in early 20x1. The divisional controller estimates that if the machine is purchased, two positions will be eliminated, yielding a cost savings for wages and employee benefits. However, the machine would require additional supplies, and more power would be required to operate the machine. The cost savings and additional costs, in current 20x0 prices, are as follows:

Wages and employee benefits of the two positions eliminated ($25,000 each)	$50,000
Cost of additional supplies	3,000
Cost of additional power	10,000

The new machine would be purchased and installed at the end of 20x0 at a net cost of $90,000. If purchased, the machine would be depreciated on a straight-line basis for both book and tax purposes. The machine will become technologically obsolete in three years and will have no salvage value at that time. The machine is in the MACRS 3-year property class.

The Medical Division compensates for inflation in capital expenditure analyses by adjusting the expected cash flows by an estimated price-level index. The adjusted real after-tax cash flows are then discounted using the real discount rate. The estimated year-end index values for each of the next five years are as follows:

Year	Year-End Price Index
20x0	1.00
20x1	1.08
20x2	1.17
20x3	1.26
20x4	1.36
20x5	1.47

The Communications Division of Potomac Assemblies, Inc. analyzes capital investment projects by discounting nominal cash flows using the nominal discount rate.

Each division of Potomac Assemblies, Inc. has the authority to make capital expenditures up to $200,000 without approval from corporate headquarters. The firm's after-tax hurdle rate is 12 percent.

This rate does not include an allowance for inflation, which is expected to occur at an average rate of 8 percent over the next five years. Potomac pays income taxes at the rate of 40 percent.

Required:

1. Prepare a schedule showing the net after-tax annual real cash flows for the automated assembly and soldering machine under consideration by the Medical Division.
2. What discount rate should the Communications Division use in its discounted-cash-flow analysis?
3. Suppose that the Communications Division's management is considering the same machine currently under consideration by the Medical Division. All of the same data apply to the Communications Division. For each year (20x1 through 20x4), compute the nominal cash flows that the Communications Division's management should use in its project analysis.
4. Evaluate the methods used by the Communications Division and the Medical Division to compensate for expected inflation in capital expenditure analyses.

(CMA, adapted)

Cases

Instant Dinners, Inc. (IDI) is an established manufacturer of microwavable frozen foods. Leland Forrest is a member of the planning and analysis staff. Forrest has been asked by Bill Rolland, chief financial officer of IDI, to prepare a net-present-value analysis for a proposed capital equipment expenditure that should improve the profitability of the western plant. This analysis will be given to the Board of Directors for approval. Several years ago, as director of planning and analysis at IDI, Rolland was instrumental in convincing the board to open the western plant. However, recent competitive pressures have forced all of IDI's manufacturing divisions to consider alternatives to improve their market position. To Rolland's dismay, the western plant may be sold in the near future unless significant improvement in cost control and production efficiency are achieved.

Western's production manager, an old friend of Rolland, has submitted a proposal for the acquisition of an automated material handling system. Rolland is anxious to have this proposal approved as it will ensure the continuation of the western plant and preserve his friend's position. The plan calls for the replacement of a number of forklift trucks and operators with a computer-controlled conveyor belt system that feeds directly into the refrigeration units. This automation would eliminate the need for a number of material handlers and increase the output capacity of the plant. Rolland has given this proposal to Forrest and instructed him to use the following information to prepare his analysis.

■ **Case 17–52**
Capital Budgeting Analysis of Automated Material Handling System; Ethical Issues
(LO 2, LO 5)

Automated Material Handling System Projections

Projected useful life	10 years
Purchase and installation of equipment	$4,500,000
Increased working capital needed*	1,000,000
Increased annual operating costs (exclusive of depreciation)	200,000
Equipment repairs to maintain production efficiency (end of year 5)	800,000
Increase in annual sales revenue	700,000
Reduction in annual manufacturing costs	500,000
Reduction in annual maintenance costs	300,000
Estimated salvage value of conveyor belt system	850,000

* The working capital will be released at the end of the 10-year useful life of the conveyor belt system.

The forklift trucks have a net book value of $500,000 with a remaining useful life of five years and no salvage value for depreciation purposes. If the conveyor belt system is purchased now, these trucks will be sold for $100,000. IDI has a 40 percent tax rate, has chosen the straight-line depreciation method for both book and tax purposes, and uses a 12 percent discount rate. For the purpose of analysis, all tax effects and cash flows from the equipment acquisition and disposal are considered to occur at the time of the transaction while those from operations are considered to occur at the end of each year.

When Forrest completed his initial analysis, the proposed project appeared quite healthy. However, after investigating equipment similar to that proposed, Forrest discovered that the estimated salvage value of $850,000 was very optimistic. Information previously provided by several vendors estimates this value to be only $100,000. Forrest also discovered that industry trade publications considered eight years to be the maximum life of similar conveyor belt systems. As a result, Forrest prepared a second analysis based on this new information. When Rolland saw the second analysis, he told Forrest to discard this revised material, warned him not to discuss the new estimates with anyone at IDI, and ordered him not to present any of this information to the board of directors.

Required:

1. Prepare a net-present-value analysis of the purchase and installation of the material handling system using the revised estimates obtained by Leland Forrest. (For this problem, ignore the half-year convention).

2. Explain how Leland Forrest, a management accountant, should evaluate Bill Rolland's directives to repress the revised analysis. Take into consideration the specific ethical standards of competence, confidentiality, integrity, and objectivity discussed in Chapter 1.

3. Identify some steps Leland Forrest could take to resolve this situation.

(CMA, adapted)

■ **Case 17–53**
Comprehensive Case on
Capital Budgeting and
Taxes[7]
(LO 2, LO 5)

Liquid Chemical, Ltd. sells a range of high-grade chemical products throughout the Pacific northwest from its main plant in Vancouver, British Columbia. The Company's products, because of their chemical properties, call for careful packaging. The company has always emphasized the special properties of the containers used. Liquid Chemical had a special patented lining made from a material known as GHL, and the company operated a department specially to maintain its containers in good condition and to make new ones to replace the ones that were past repair.

Tom Walsh, the general manager, had for some time suspected that the firm might save money and get equally good service by buying its containers outside. After careful inquiries, he approached a firm specializing in container production, Packages, Inc., and obtained a quotation on the special containers. At the same time he asked Amy Dyer, the controller, to let him have an up-to-date statement of the cost of operating the Container Department.

Within a few days, the quotation from Packages, Inc. came in. They were prepared to supply all the new containers required, running at the rate of 3,000 each year, for $600,000 annually. The contract would run for a term of five years, and thereafter would be renewable from year to year. If the number of containers required increased, the contract price would be increased proportionately. Additionally, and irrespective of whether the above contract was agreed upon or not, Packages, Inc. agreed to carry out purely maintenance work on the containers, short of replacement, for a sum of $175,000 annually on the same contract terms.

Tom Walsh compared these figures with the cost data prepared by Amy Dyer covering a year's operations of the Container Department. Dyer's analysis is as follows:

Direct material		$200,000
Direct labor		350,000
Departmental overhead:		
Department manager's salary	$80,000	
Rent	17,000	
Depreciation of machinery	60,000	
Maintenance of machinery	13,500	
Other overhead	63,000	233,500
		783,500
Allocation of general administrative overhead from entire factory		69,500
Total cost of Container Department for one year		$853,000

Walsh's conclusion was that no time should be lost in closing down the Container Department and entering into the contract offered by Packages, Inc. However, he felt bound to give the manager of the department, Jake Duffy, an opportunity to question this conclusion before he acted on it. Walsh called Duffy in and put the facts before him, at the same time making it clear that Duffy's own position was not in jeopardy. Even if Duffy's department were closed down, there was another managerial position shortly becoming vacant to which Duffy could be moved without loss of pay or prospects.

Jake Duffy looked thoughtful, and asked for time to think the matter over. The next morning Duffy asked to speak to Walsh again, and said he thought there were a number of considerations that ought to be borne in mind before his department was closed down. "For instance," Duffy said, "what will you do

---

[7] This case is adapted here with permission from its author, Professor David Solomons.

with the machinery? It cost $480,000 four years ago, but you'd be lucky if you got $80,000 for it now, even though it's good for another five years. Then there's the stock of GHL we bought a year ago. That cost us $300,000. At the rate we're using it now, it'll last us another three years. We used up about a quarter of it last year. Amy Dyer's figure of $200,000 for materials probably includes about $75,000 for GHL. But it'll be tricky stuff to handle if we don't use it up. We bought well, paying $1,500 a ton for it. You couldn't buy it today for less than $1,800 a ton. But you wouldn't have more than $1,200 a ton left if you sold it, after you'd covered all the handling expenses."

Tom Walsh thought that Amy Dyer ought to be present during this discussion. He asked her to come in and then reviewed Duffy's points. "I don't much like all this conjecture," Dyer said. "I think my figures are pretty conclusive. Besides, if we are going to have all this talk about 'what will happen if,' don't forget the problem of space we're faced with. We're paying $27,500 a year in rent for a warehouse a couple of miles away. If we closed Duffy's department, we'd have all the warehouse space we need without renting."

"That's a good point," said Walsh, "though I must say, I'm a bit worried about the employees if we close the Container Department. I don't think we can find room for any of them elsewhere in the firm. I could see whether Packages, Inc. can take any of them. But some of them are getting on in years. There's Walters and Hines, for example. They've been with us since they left school many years ago. Their severance pay would cost us $10,000 a year each, for five years."

Duffy showed some relief at Walsh's comment. "But I still don't like Amy's figures," he said. "What about this $69,500 for general administrative overhead? You surely don't expect to fire anyone in the general office if I'm closed down, do you?" "Probably not," said Dyer, "but someone has to pay for these costs. We can't ignore them when we look at an individual department, because if we do that with each department in turn, we'll wind up by convincing ourselves that general managers, accountants, secretaries, and the like, don't have to be paid. And they do, believe me."

"Well, I think we've thrashed this out pretty fully," said Walsh, "but I've been wondering about the possibility of perhaps keeping on the maintenance work ourselves. What are your views on that, Duffy?" "I don't know," said Duffy, "but it's worth looking into. We shouldn't need any machinery for that, and I could hand the management over to a department supervisor. You'd save about $20,000 a year there. You'd only need about one-fifth of the employees, but you could keep the oldest. You wouldn't save any space, so I suppose the rent would be the same. I shouldn't think the other overhead expenses would be more than $26,000 a year." "What about materials?" asked Walsh. "We use about 10 percent of the total on maintenance," Duffy replied.

"Well, I've told Packages, Inc. that I'd let them know my decision within a week," said Walsh. "I'll let you know what I decide to do before I write to them."

Required:

Liquid Chemical's tax rate is 40 percent, and its after-tax hurdle rate is 10 percent. You will have to seek out the information you need from the remarks of Walsh, Dyer, and Duffy. In some cases, you will have to interpret their remarks and make assumptions. State all of your assumptions clearly when answering the following questions.

1. List Liquid Chemical's four alternatives.
2. Prepare a net-present-value analysis of each alternative identified in requirement (1). Use a five-year time horizon. The company uses straight-line depreciation for tax purposes. (Ignore the half-year convention.) The depreciation expense in each of the next four years is $60,000. The equipment will be fully depreciated after four more years.
3. What qualitative factors should Tom Walsh consider in making his decision?

Current Issues in Managerial Accounting

"Clinton's Energy Tax: Now That's a Scorched-Earth Policy," *Business Week,* **October 27, 1997.**

Overview

In response to concerns over global warming, Bill Clinton proposed an energy tax. It is Clinton's hope that the tax would help reduce emissions by 20 percent.

Suggested Discussion Questions

How would an energy tax affect a firm's capital budgeting plan? How would an energy tax compare to a sales tax or a flat tax from a capital budgeting perspective? How could a firm minimize the effect of an energy tax? Sales tax? How would the government feel about these activities?

■ **Issue 17–54**
Income Taxes and
Capital Budgeting

■ **Issue 17–55**
Income Taxes and
Capital Budgeting

"A Groundswell Is Building: Toss the Tax System," *Business Week,* **May 5, 1997.**

Overview

This article discusses why lawmakers should reexamine their tax reform proposals.

Suggested Discussion Questions

As a group, discuss how the tax-related items listed below would impact a firm's capital budgeting plan.

1. Depreciation.
2. Investment tax credit.
3. Capital gains tax.
4. Value-added tax.

■ **Issue 17–56**
Income Taxes and
Capital Budgeting;
Timing of Tax Deductions

"Taxes: Expense or Capitalize Training Costs?" *Management Accounting,* **May, 1997, Anthony Curatola.**

Overview

This article explains whether certain costs are treated as expenses or capital expenditures for tax purposes.

Suggested Discussion Questions

As a group, create a chart that lists the appropriate treatment for the expenditures listed below. On a separate chart, list which treatments your group would prefer.

1. Training costs.
2. Advertising costs.
3. Incidental repairs.
4. Severance payments.

■ **Issue 17–57**
Income Taxes and
Capital Budgeting; After-
Tax Cash Flows;
Extended Illustration of
Income-Tax Effects on
Capital Budgeting

"Clinton to Unveil Revised Tax-Cut Plan," *The Wall Street Journal,* **June 30, 1997, Greg Hitt and David Wessel.**

Overview

Bill Clinton's tax plan consists of tax cuts for individuals and corporations. Among the proposed corporate tax changes are a reduction in the maximum tax rate and elimination of certain minimum tax provisions.

Suggested Discussion Questions

Prepare abbreviated pro forma financial statements for a five-year period assuming a $400,000 initial investment, annual sales of $300,000, and $200,000 in tax deductible costs. Calculate the after-tax cash flows and net present value using a 35 percent maximum tax rate. Do the same using a 30 percent maximum rate. How much difference would the reduction make?

■ **Issue 17–58**
Income Taxes and
Capital Budgeting;
After-Tax Cash Flows

"Stock-Option Exercise Is Bringing Many Firms a Big Break on Taxes," *The Wall Street Journal,* **May 13, 1997, Laura Jereski.**

Overview

The number and value of stock option grants has increased over the years, which should make grants a significant element of a firm's capital budgeting plan. Certain types of stock options provide the issuing corporation a beneficial tax deduction.

Suggested Discussion Questions

Write a memo that explains the tax and financial accounting treatment of stock options.

Also include in your memo a discussion of how your firm can use the tax savings resulting from the option deduction.

"Clinton IRS Plan Seeks to Head Off GOP," *The Wall Street Journal,* **March 18, 1997, Jacob Schlesinger.**

Overview

The White House announced its plan to overhaul the Internal Revenue Service (IRS). The five-point plan comes amid criticisms surrounding the tax code's complexity and IRS management.

Suggested Discussion Questions

Listed below are five elements in Bill Clinton's plan to reorganize the IRS. For each item, discuss the effect, if any, it would have on a firm's capital budgeting process.

1. Creation of a senior outside board that would oversee IRS governance.
2. Hire outside management that would run the IRS.
3. Receive multiyear funding commitments.
4. Simplify the tax code.
5. Hire a new commissioner.

"The Big Picture: How Viacom's Deal for Blockbuster Chain Went Sour So Fast," *The Wall Street Journal,* **February 21, 1997, Eben Shaprio.**

Overview

Wayne Huizenga criticized Viacom for using accounting methods to mislead investors about the effect of Blockbuster's merger with Viacom. Soon after the merger, Blockbuster's video stores' sales fell and two-thirds of its corporate headquarters' staff lost their jobs.

Suggested Discussion Questions

Discuss how the decision to capitalize or expense a large expenditure would impact the payback period, accounting rate of return, and internal rate of return.

"Analysts Scrutinize Accounting Tactics Boosting REITs," *The Wall Street Journal,* **January 23, 1997, Neal Templin.**

Overview

The "straight-lining" method of reporting revenue for real estate investment trusts (REIT) has drawn criticism from analysts. REITs report revenue by averaging rents received on multiyear leases.

Suggested Discussion Questions

Form a group that will make recommendations to a group of investors interested in REITs. In your presentation, discuss how straight-lining would affect various models used to make investment decisions. Also, discuss whether funds from operations (FFO) should replace net income as a more meaningful measure of performance.

■ **Issue 17–59**
Income Taxes and Capital Budgeting

■ **Issue 17–60**
Additional Methods for Making Investment Decisions

■ **Issue 17–61**
Additional Methods for Making Investment Decisions

Chapter Eighteen

Cost Allocation:
A Closer Look

After completing this chapter, you should be able to:

1   Allocate service department costs using the direct method, step-down method, or reciprocal-services method (appendix).

2   Use the dual approach to service department cost allocation.

3   Explain the difference between two-stage cost allocation with departmental overhead rates and activity-based costing (ABC).

4   Allocate joint costs among joint products using each of the following techniques: physical-units method, relative-sales-value method, and net-realizable-value method.

5   Describe the purposes for which joint cost allocation is useful and those for which it is not.

RIVERSIDE CLINIC INKS HEALTH CARE DEAL WITH LOCAL COLLEGES

Philadelphia, PA—A spokesperson for Riverside Clinic announced today that the clinic will be providing certain types of outpatient medical care to students in three local colleges. Although the colleges each will continue to operate their own student health services on campus, Riverside Clinic will augment the on-campus clinics with specialized medical services.

According to Anne Josephson, Riverside's administrator, "Some student health services are specialized enough that it doesn't make sense for each college to cover all those bases individually. That would mean a duplication of effort that would increase costs. On the other hand, it's not necessary to go to an in-patient facility like one of Philly's hospitals, for these kinds of services. Riverside Clinic provides just the right answer. It keeps the services on an outpatient basis and avoids expensive duplication on several college campuses." Asked how the student health services would be priced by Riverside, Josephson said, "The pricing details aren't final yet. The agreement we signed with the colleges was an agreement in principle. Now we all need to sit down and figure out a fair fee schedule. We'll approach it the same way we do for the fees we charge the general public here at Riverside. The first thing we have to do is figure out what certain kinds of services cost the clinic. And that's not an easy job. There are a lot of activities behind the scenes in the clinic that are necessary in support of the primary patient care activities. For example, we have patient records, personnel, administration, and accounting departments. All of these service department costs have to be allocated to the Orthopedics and Internal Medicine departments, which actually provide direct patient care. There are different methods for making these allocations. So we'll have to talk with the folks in the college health services to see what seems to be fair to all concerned."

Josephson said Riverside hopes to have the student health services in place for the next academic year.

In earlier chapters we studied cost allocation and explored its role in an organization's overall managerial-accounting system. We also examined several purposes of cost allocation. The goal of cost allocation is to ensure that all costs incurred by the organization ultimately are assigned to its products or services. This is important for several purposes, including cost-based pricing and bidding, cost reimbursements from outside parties such as insurance companies, valuation of inventory, and determination of cost of goods sold. In addition, the allocation of all costs to departments serves to make departmental managers aware of the costs incurred to produce services their departments use.

This chapter is divided into two sections, each of which explores a particular cost-allocation topic in greater detail. The two sections, which may be studied separately, cover the following topics:

- Service department cost allocation [1]
- Joint product cost allocation [2]

SECTION 1 SERVICE DEPARTMENT COST ALLOCATION

LO 1 Allocate service department costs using the direct method, step-down method, or reciprocal-services method (appendix).

A **service department** is a subunit in an organization that is not directly involved in producing the organization's output of goods or services.

A **service department** is a unit in an organization that is not involved *directly* in producing the organization's goods or services. However, a service department does provide a service that enables the organization's production process to take place. For example, the Maintenance Department in an automobile plant does not make automobiles, but if it did not exist, the production process would stop when the manufacturing machines broke down. Thus, the Maintenance Department is crucial to the production operation even though the repair personnel do not work directly on the plant's products.

Service departments are important in nonmanufacturing organizations also. For example, a hospital's Personnel Department is responsible for staffing the hospital with physicians, nurses, lab technicians, and other employees. The Personnel Department never serves the patients, yet without it the hospital would have no staff to provide medical care.

A service department such as the Maintenance Department or the Personnel Department must exist in order for an organization to carry out its primary function. Therefore, the cost of running a service department is part of the cost incurred by the organization in producing goods or services. In order to determine the cost of those goods or services, all service department costs must be allocated to the production departments in which the goods or services are produced. For this reason, the costs incurred in an automobile plant's Maintenance Department are allocated to all of the production departments that have machinery. The costs incurred in a hospital's Personnel Department are allocated to all of the departments that have personnel. Direct-patient-care departments, such as Surgery and Physical Therapy, are allocated their share of the Personnel Department's costs.

To see how service department cost allocation fits into the overall picture of product and service costing, it may be helpful to review Exhibit 3–13 on page 88. The exhibit shows three types of allocation processes, as follows:

1. **Cost distribution.** Costs in various cost pools are distributed to all departments, including both service and production departments.

2. **Service department cost allocation.** Service department costs are allocated to production departments.

---

[1] The section on service department cost allocation is written as a module, which can be studied separately from the rest of the chapter. This material may be studied after the completion of Chapter 12, which covers basic issues in cost allocation.

[2] The section on joint cost allocation is written as a module, which can be studied separately from the rest of the chapter. This material may be studied after the completion of Chapter 14.

The costs of operating service departments are allocated to the departments that directly manufacture products or provide services to customers. Pictured here are employees of the Grounds Department at Disney World's Magic Kingdom. How would you recommend allocating this service department's costs to the various attractions and food-service operations at the Magic Kingdom?

3. **Cost application.** Costs are assigned to the goods or services produced by the organization.

It is the second type of allocation process listed above that we are focusing on now. The context for our discussion is Riverside Clinic, an outpatient medical facility in Philadelphia.

The clinic is organized into three service departments and two direct-patient-care departments. Exhibit 18–1 displays a simple organization chart for Riverside Clinic. Since the clinic is not a manufacturing organization, we refer to *direct-patient-care departments* instead of *production departments*. These two departments, Orthopedics and Internal Medicine, directly provide the health care that is the clinic's primary objective. Thus, the clinic's direct-patient-care departments are like the production departments in a manufacturing firm.

Notice that the Personnel Department and the Administration and Accounting Department provide services to each other. When this situation occurs, the two service departments exhibit *reciprocal services*.

Exhibit 18–2 provides some of the details for our illustration of service department cost allocation. Panel A shows the proportion of each service department's output that is consumed by each of the departments using its services. Panel B shows the allocation bases, which are used to determine the proportions shown in panel A. Further explanation of the information in Exhibit 18–2 follows.

Exhibit 18–1

Organization Chart for Riverside Clinic*

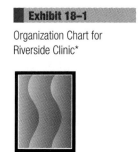

* The arrows in the organization chart depict the provision of service by the three service departments. For example, the Personnel Department serves the Patient Records Department, but not vice versa.

A. Percentage of Service Output Consumed by Using Departments

		Provider of Service		
User of Service		**Patient Records**	**Personnel**	**Administration and Accounting**
Service departments	Patient Records	—	5%	—
	Personnel	—	—	5%
	Administration and Accounting . . .	—	20%	—
Direct-patient-care departments	Orthopedics	30%	25%	35%
	Internal Medicine	70%	50%	60%

B. Allocation Bases

Service Department	Allocation Base
Patient Records	Annual patient load
Personnel	Number of employees
Administration and Accounting	Size of department (measured in square feet of space)

C. Service Department Costs

Service Department	Variable Cost	Fixed Cost	Total Cost to Be Allocated
Patient Records	$24,000	$76,000	$100,000
Personnel	15,000	45,000	60,000
Administration and Accounting	47,500	142,500	190,000
Total	$86,500	$263,500	$350,000

Patient Records   The service output of the Patient Records Department is consumed only by the Orthopedics and Internal Medicine Departments. *Annual patient load* is the *allocation base* used to determine that 30 percent of the Patient Records Department's services were consumed by Orthopedics and 70 percent by Internal Medicine.

Personnel   The Personnel Department serves each of the clinic's other departments, including the other two service departments and the two direct-patient-care departments. The *allocation base* used to determine the proportions of the Personnel Department's output consumed by the four using departments is the *number of employees* in the using departments. For example, 5 percent of the clinic's employees (excluding those in the Personnel Department) work in the Patient Records Department.

Administration and Accounting   This service department provides services only to the Personnel Department, the Orthopedics Department, and the Internal Medicine Department. A variety of services are provided, such as computer support, patient billing, and general administration. Since larger amounts of these services are provided to larger using departments, *departmental size* is the *allocation base* used to determine the proportion of service output consumed by each using department. Since the space devoted to each department is a convenient measure of departmental size, square footage is the measure used in Exhibit 18–2. For example, 5 percent of the clinic's space (excluding that occupied by Administration and Accounting) is devoted to the Personnel Department.

Panel C of Exhibit 18–2 shows the total budgeted cost of each service department that is to be allocated among the using departments.

There are two widely used methods of service department cost allocation, the direct method and the step-down method. These methods are discussed and illustrated next, using the data for Riverside Clinic.

Direct Method

Under the **direct method,** each service department's costs are allocated among *only the direct-patient-care departments* that consume part of the service department's output. This method ignores the fact that some service departments provide services to other service departments. Thus, even though Riverside Clinic's Personnel Department provides services to two other service departments, none of its costs are allocated to those departments. Exhibit 18–3 presents Riverside Clinic's service department cost allocations under the direct method.

Notice that the proportion of each service department's costs to be allocated to each direct-patient-care department is determined by the *relative proportion* of the service department's output consumed by each direct-patient-care department. For example, a glance at Exhibit 18–2 shows that the Personnel Department provides 25 percent of its services to Orthopedics and 50 percent to Internal Medicine. Summing these two percentages yields 75 percent. Thus, 25/75 is the fraction of Personnel's cost allocated to Orthopedics and 50/75 is the fraction allocated to Internal Medicine.

> Under the **direct method** of service department cost allocation, service department costs are allocated directly to the production departments.

Step-Down Method

As stated above, the direct method ignores the provision of services by one service department to another service department. This shortcoming is overcome partially by the **step-down method** of service department cost allocation. Under this method, the managerial accountant first chooses a sequence in which to allocate the service departments' costs. A common way to select the first service department in the sequence is to choose the one that serves the largest number of other service departments. The service departments are ordered in this manner, with the last service department being the one that serves the smallest number of other service departments.[3] Then the managerial accountant allocates each service department's costs among the direct-patient-care departments and all of the other service departments that follow it in the sequence. Note that the ultimate cost allocations assigned to the direct-patient-care departments will differ depending on the sequence chosen.

> Under the **step-down method** of service department cost allocation, service department costs are allocated first to service departments and then to production departments.

The step-down method is best explained by way of an illustration. Riverside Clinic's Personnel Department serves two other service departments: Patient Records, and Administration and Accounting. The Administration and Accounting Department serves only one other service department: Personnel. Finally, the Patient Records Department serves no other service departments. Thus, Riverside Clinic's service department sequence is as follows:

| (1) Personnel | (2) Administration and Accounting | (3) Patient Records |

In accordance with this sequence, each service department's costs are allocated to the other departments as follows:

Cost Allocated from This Service Department ———————➤ To These Departments

Personnel . . . . Administration and Accounting
     Patient Records
     Orthopedics
     Internal Medicine

Administration and Accounting . . . . Orthopedics
     Internal Medicine

Patient Records . . . . Orthopedics
     Internal Medicine

---

[3]A tie occurs when two or more service departments serve the same number of other service departments. Then the sequence among the tied service departments usually is an arbitrary choice.

		Direct-Patient-Care Departments Using Services			
		Orthopedics		Internal Medicine	
Provider of Service	**Cost to Be Allocated**	**Proportion**	**Amount**	**Proportion**	**Amount**
Patient Records	$100,000	3/10	$ 30,000	7/10	$ 70,000
Personnel	60,000	25/75	20,000	50/75	40,000
Administration and Accounting	190,000	35/95	70,000	60/95	120,000
Total	$350,000		$120,000		$230,000

Grand total = $350,000

Notice that even though Administration and Accounting serves Personnel, there is no cost allocation in that direction. This results from Personnel's placement before Administration and Accounting in the allocation sequence. Moreover, no costs are allocated from Patient Records to either of the other service departments, because Patient Records does not serve those departments.

Exhibit 18–4 presents the results of applying the step-down method at Riverside Clinic. First, the Personnel Department's $60,000 in cost is allocated among the four departments using its services. Second, the cost of the Administration and Accounting Department is allocated. The total cost to be allocated is the department's original $190,000 *plus* the $12,000 allocated from the Personnel Department. The new total of $202,000 is allocated to the Orthopedics and Internal Medicine Departments according to the *relative proportions* in which these two departments use the services of the Administration and Accounting Department. Finally, the Patient Records Department's cost is allocated.

Reciprocal-Services Method

The direct method and the step-down method both ignore the fact that the Administration and Accounting Department serves the Personnel Department. Neither of these methods allocates any of the costs incurred in Administration and Accounting back to Personnel.

Reciprocal service is the mutual provision of service by two service departments to each other.

The **reciprocal-services method** of service department cost allocation accounts for the mutual provision of reciprocal services among all service departments.

Review the relationships between the service departments depicted in Exhibit 18–1. Notice that the Administration and Accounting Department and the Personnel Department *serve each other.* This mutual provision of service is called **reciprocal service.** A more accurate method of service department cost allocation, called the **reciprocal-services method,** fully accounts for the mutual provision of services. This method, which is more complex than the direct and step-down methods, is covered in the appendix at the end of this chapter.

Fixed versus Variable Costs

In our allocation of Riverside Clinic's service department costs, we did not distinguish between fixed and variable costs. Under some circumstances, this simple approach can result in an unfair cost allocation among the using departments. To illustrate, we will use the data about Riverside Clinic's fixed and variable costs given in panel C of Exhibit 18–2. Consider the cost data for the Patient Records Department, which serves only the Orthopedics and Internal Medicine departments. Under the *direct method* of

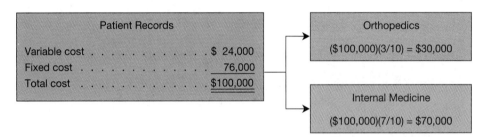

	Service Department			Direct-Patient-Care Department	
	Personnel	Administration and Accounting	Patient Records	Orthopedics	Internal Medicine
Costs prior to allocation	$60,000	$190,000	$100,000		
Allocation of Personnel Department costs	$60,000 →	12,000 (20/100)†	3,000 (5/100)	$ 15,000 (25/100)	$ 30,000 (50/100)
Allocation of Administration and Accounting Department costs		$202,000 →		74,421*(35/95)	127,579*(60/95)
Allocation of Patient Records Department costs			$103,000 →	30,900 (30/100)	72,100 (70/100)
Total cost allocated to each department				$120,321	$229,679
Total cost allocated to direct-patient-care departments				$350,000	

* Rounded

† Fractions in parentheses are relative proportions of service department's output consumed by departments to which costs are allocated.

service department cost allocation, the Patient Records Department's costs were allocated as follows:

Cost Allocation for 19x8: Direct Method

Patient Records	
Variable cost	$ 24,000
Fixed cost	76,000
Total cost	$100,000

Orthopedics

($100,000)(3/10) = $30,000

Internal Medicine

($100,000)(7/10) = $70,000

The allocation base used in this cost allocation is the annual patient load in the Orthopedics and Internal Medicine departments. Let's assume the following patient loads in 19x8, the year for which the cost allocation has been done.

Department		Patient Load		Proportion of Total
Orthopedics	....	30,000	....	(30,000/100,000) = 3/10
Internal Medicine	....	70,000	....	(70,000/100,000) = 7/10
Total	....	100,000		

Now suppose the projections for 19x9 are as follows:

Department		Projected Patient Load		Projected Proportion of Total
Orthopedics	....	30,000	....	(30,000/80,000) = 3/8
Internal Medicine	....	50,000	....	(50,000/80,000) = 5/8
Total	....	80,000		

Department	Budgeted Variable Cost		Budgeted Fixed Cost	Budgeted Total Cost
Patient Records	.... $19,200	....	$76,000	.... $95,200

The projections for 19x9 include a stable patient load in the Orthopedics Department but a decline in the patient load of the Internal Medicine Department. Since the projected total patient load is lower for 19x9, the projected variable cost in the Patient Records Department is lower also.

What will be the effect of these changes on the 19x9 allocation of the Patient Records Department's costs? Using the direct method, we obtain the following allocation.

Cost Allocation for 19x9: Direct Method

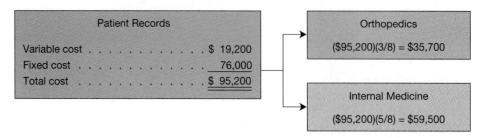

Compare the costs allocated to the two direct-patient-care departments in 19x8 and 19x9. Notice that the cost allocated to the Orthopedics Department *increased by* $5,700 (from $30,000 to $35,700), even though Orthopedics' patient load is projected to remain constant. What has happened here? The projected decline in the Internal Medicine Department's volume resulted in lower budgeted variable costs for the Patient Records Department, but the budgeted *fixed* costs did not change. At the same time, the lower projected patient load in Internal Medicine resulted in a higher proportion of the total projected patient load for Orthopedics (from 3/10 in 19x8 up to 3/8 in 19x9). As the following analysis shows, this results in an increased allocation of fixed costs to the Orthopedics Department in 19x9.

	19x8	**19x9**
Fixed cost in Patient Records Department	$76,000	$76,000
Orthopedics Department's proportion of total patient load	× 3/10	× 3/8
Orthopedics Department's allocation of fixed cost	$22,800	$28,500

Difference = $5,700

This difference of $5,700 is equal to the increase in the Orthopedics Department's total cost allocation from the Patient Records Department in 19x9.

To summarize, the projected decline in Internal Medicine's 19x9 patient load will result in an increased cost allocation from the Patient Records Department to the Orthopedics Department in 19x9. The cause of this increased allocation is our failure to distinguish between fixed and variable costs in the allocation process.

Dual Cost Allocation

LO 2   Use the dual approach to service department cost allocation.

Dual cost allocation is an approach that allocates variable costs in proportion to short-term usage and allocates fixed costs in proportion to long-term usage.

The problem illustrated in the preceding section can be resolved by allocating fixed and variable costs separately. This approach, called **dual-cost allocation,** works with either the direct method or the step-down method of allocation. Under dual cost allocation, *variable costs* are allocated on the basis of *short-run usage* of the service department's output; *fixed costs* are allocated on the basis of *long-run average usage* of the service department's output. The rationale for this approach is that fixed costs are capacity-producing costs. When service departments are established, their size and scale usually are determined by the projected long-run needs of the using departments.

To illustrate dual cost allocation for Riverside Clinic, we need estimates of the long-run average usage of each service department's output by each using department. These estimates are given in Exhibit 18–5.

		Provider of Service		
	User of Service	Patient Records	Personnel	Administration and Accounting
Service departments	Patient Records	—	10%	—
	Personnel	—	—	10%
	Administration and Accounting	—	10%	—
Direct-patient-care departments	Orthopedics	40%	20%	45%
	Internal Medicine	60%	60%	45%

To combine the dual-allocation approach with either the direct method or the step-down method, we simply apply the allocation method twice, as follows:

Costs to Be Allocated	Basis for Allocation	Allocation Method	
Variable costs in 19x8	Short-run usage in 19x8	Direct	Step-down
(Exhibit 18–2, panel C)	(Exhibit 18–2, panel A)	method	method
		OR	
Fixed costs in 19x8	Long-run average usage	Direct	Step-down
(Exhibit 18–2, panel C)	(Exhibit 18–5)	method	method

After both of these allocation procedures have been completed, the resulting variable- and fixed-cost allocations for each direct-patient-care department are summed. Exhibit 18–6 presents the allocation computations when the dual approach is combined with the direct method. Compare the final direct allocations with those in Exhibit 18–3, where the dual approach was not used. Notice that the final allocations are different. Exhibit 18–7, which appears on page 751, presents the computations for the step-down method. Compare the final step-down allocations with those in Exhibit 18–4, where the dual approach was not used. Again, the final allocations are different.

A Behavioral Problem   Dual cost allocation prevents a change in the short-run activity of one using department from affecting the cost allocated to another using department. However, the approach sometimes presents a problem of its own. In order to implement the technique, we need accurate projections of the long-run average usage of each service department's output by each using department. This is the information in Exhibit 18–5. Typically, these estimates come from the managers of the departments that consume the services. The problem is that the higher a manager's estimate of the department's long-run average usage is, the greater will be the department's allocation of fixed service department costs. This creates an incentive for using-department managers to understate their expected long-run service needs. Ultimately, such understatements can result in building service facilities that are too small.

How can we prevent this behavioral problem? First, we can rely on the professionalism and integrity of the managers who provide the estimates. Second, we can reward managers through promotions and pay raises for making accurate estimates of their departments' service needs.

Allocate Budgeted Costs

When service department costs are allocated to production departments, such as the direct-patient-care departments of Riverside Clinic, *budgeted* service department costs should be used. If actual costs are allocated instead, any operating inefficiencies in the service departments are passed along to the using departments. This reduces the

Exhibit 18–6

Dual Allocation Combined
with Direct Method: Riverside
Clinic

		Direct-Patient-Care Department Using Services			
		Orthopedics		Internal Medicine	
Provider of Service	Cost to Be Allocated	Proportion	Amount	Proportion	Amount
I. Variable Costs					
Patient Records	$ 24,000	3/10	$ 7,200	7/10	$ 16,800
Personnel	15,000	25/75	5,000	50/75	10,000
Administration and Accounting . . .	47,500	35/95	17,500	60/95	30,000
Total variable cost	$ 86,500		$ 29,700		$ 56,800
II. Fixed Costs					
Patient Records	$ 76,000	4/10	$ 30,400	6/10	$ 45,600
Personnel	45,000	20/80	11,250	60/80	33,750
Administration and Accounting . . .	142,500	45/90	71,250	45/90	71,250
Total fixed cost	$263,500		$112,900		$150,600
Total cost (variable + fixed)	$350,000		$142,600		$207,400

Grand total = $350,000

incentive for service department managers to control the costs in their departments.
The proper approach is as follows:

1. Compare budgeted and actual service department costs and compute any
   variances.
2. Use these variances to help control costs in the service departments.
3. Close out the service department cost variances against the period's income.
4. Allocate the service departments' budgeted costs to the departments that directly
   produce goods or services.

The New Manufacturing Environment

In traditional manufacturing environments, service department costs are allocated to
production departments to ensure that all manufacturing costs are assigned to products.
For example, the costs incurred in a machine-maintenance department typically are
allocated to the other service departments and the production departments that use
maintenance services. Service department cost allocation continues to be used in the
new manufacturing environment, characterized by the JIT philosophy and CIM
systems. However, the extent of such allocations is diminished in advanced manufacturing systems, because more costs are directly traceable to product lines. In a flexible
manufacturing system, almost all operations are performed in the FMS cell. Even
machine maintenance is done largely by the FMS cell operators rather than a separate
maintenance department. Inspection often is performed by FMS cell operators, eliminating the need for a separate inspection department. In short, as more and more costs
become directly traceable to products, the need for allocation of indirect costs declines.

LO 3   Explain the difference between
two-stage cost allocation with departmental overhead rates and activity-
based costing (ABC).

The Rise of Activity-Based Costing

Service department cost allocation is one type of allocation procedure used
in two-stage allocation with departmental overhead rates. (See Exhibit 3–13
on page 88). Under this approach, costs first are distributed to *departments;*

	Service Department			Direct-Patient Care Department	
	Personnel	**Administration and Accounting**	**Patient Records**	**Orthopedics**	**Internal Medicine**
I. Variable Costs					
Variable cost prior to allocation	$15,000	$ 47,500	$24,000		
Allocation of Personnel Department costs	$15,000	3,000 (20/100)†	750 (5/100)	$ 3,750 (25/100)	$ 7,500 (50/100)
Allocation of Administration and Accounting Department costs		$ 50,500		18,605*(35/95)	31,895*(60/95)
Allocation of Patient Records Department costs			$24,750	7,425 (30/100)	17,325 (70/100)
Total variable cost allocated to each department				$ 29,780	$ 56,720
II. Fixed Costs					
Fixed cost prior to allocation	$45,000	$142,500	$76,000		
Allocation of Personnel Department costs	$45,000	4,500 (10/100)	4,500 (10/100)	$ 9,000 (20/100)	$ 27,000 (60/100)
Allocation of Administration and Accounting Department costs		$147,000		73,500 (45/90)	73,500 (45/90)
Allocation of Patient Records Department costs			$80,500	32,200 (40/100)	48,300 (60/100)
Total fixed cost allocated to each department				$114,700	$148,800
Total cost allocated to each department (variable + fixed)				$144,480	$205,520
				Grand total = $350,000	

* Rounded.

† Fractions in parentheses are relative proportions of service department's output consumed by departments to which costs are allocated. Variable costs allocated on basis of short-run proportions. Fixed costs allocated on basis of long-run average proportions.

Exhibit 18–7

Dual Allocation Combined with Step-Down Method: Riverside Clinic

then they are allocated from service *departments* to production *departments*. Finally, they are assigned from production *departments* to products or services. *Departments* play a key role as intermediate cost objects under this approach.

In an activity-based costing (ABC) system, on the other hand, the key role is played by *activities,* not departments. (See Exhibit 3–14 on page 89). First, the costs of various *activities* are assigned to *activity* cost pools; then these costs are assigned to products or services.

The breakdown of costs by activity in an ABC system is much finer than a breakdown by departments. For example, under the service department cost allocation approach, the Purchasing Department might be one of the service departments identified. However, under ABC, the various activities engaged in by purchasing personnel would be separately identified. Activities such as part specification, vendor identification, vendor selection, price negotiation, ordering, expediting, receiving, inspection, and invoice paying might be identified separately under ABC. Then the costs of each of these activities would be assigned to products or services on the basis of the appropriate cost drivers. The ABC approach generally will provide a much more accurate cost for each of the organization's products or services.[4]

---

[4] Activity-based costing is introduced conceptually in Chapter 3 and covered extensively in Chapter 5.

Milk processing provides an example of joint product cost allocation in the agriculture industry. The cost of producing raw milk must be allocated among such joint products as heavy cream, light cream, whole milk, 2 percent milk, and skim milk.

SECTION 2 JOINT PRODUCT COST ALLOCATION

LO 4   Allocate joint costs among joint products using each of the following techniques: physical-units method, relative-sales-value method, and net-realizable-value method.

A **joint production process** results in two or more products, which are termed **joint products.** The cost of the input and the joint production process is called a *joint product cost*. The point in the production process where the individual products become separately identifiable is called the **split-off point.** To illustrate, International Chocolate Company produces cocoa powder and cocoa butter by processing cocoa beans in the joint production process depicted in Exhibit 18–8.

A **joint production process** results in two or more joint products.

Joint products are the outputs of a joint production process.

The **split-off point** of a joint production process is where the joint products become identifiable as separate products.

As the diagram shows, cocoa beans are processed in 1-ton batches. The beans cost $500 and the joint process costs $600, for a total *joint cost* of $1,100. The process results in 1,500 pounds of cocoa butter and 500 pounds of cocoa powder. Each of these two joint products can be sold at the split-off point or processed further. Cocoa butter can be separately processed into a tanning cream, and cocoa powder can be separately processed into instant cocoa mix.

Allocating Joint Costs

For product-costing purposes, a joint product cost usually is allocated to the joint products that result from the joint production process. Such allocation *is necessary* for inventory valuation and income determination, among other reasons.[5] As we discussed

LO 5   Describe the purposes for which joint cost allocation is useful and those for which it is not.

in Chapter 14, however, joint cost allocation is *not useful* for making substantive economic decisions about the joint process or the joint products. For example, Chapter 14 shows that joint cost allocation is not useful in deciding whether to process a joint product further. (See pages 580 and 581).

[5] The purposes of product costing are covered in Chapter 3.

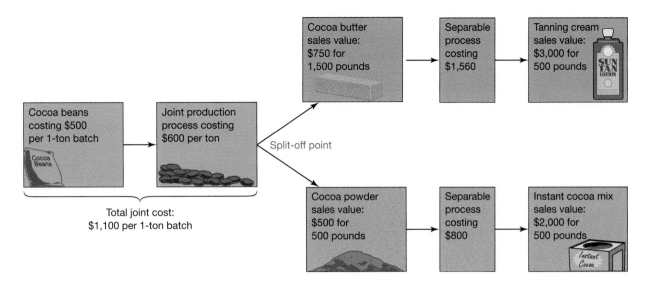

Exhibit 18–8

Joint Processing of Cocoa
Beans: International
Chocolate Company

There are three commonly used methods for allocating joint product costs. Each of these is explained next.

Physical-Units Method   The **physical-units method** allocates joint product costs on the basis of some physical characteristic of the joint products at the split-off point. Panel A of Exhibit 18–9 illustrates this allocation method for International Chocolate Company using the *weight* of the joint products as the allocation basis.

Relative-Sales-Value Method   The **relative-sales-value method** is based on the relative sales value of each joint product *at the split-off point.* In the International Chocolate Company illustration, these joint products are cocoa butter and cocoa powder. This method is illustrated in Exhibit 18–9 (panel B).

Net-Realizable-Value Method   Under the **net-realizable-value method,** the relative value of the final products is used to allocate the joint cost. International Chocolate Company's final products are tanning cream and instant cocoa mix. The **net realizable value** of each final product is its sales value less any separable costs incurred *after* the split-off point. The joint cost is allocated according to the relative magnitudes of the final products' net realizable values. Panel C of Exhibit 18–9 illustrates this allocation method.

Notice how different the cost allocations are under the three methods, particularly the physical-units method. Since the physical-units approach is not based on the *economic* characteristics of the joint products, it is the least preferred of the three methods.

By-Products   A joint product with very little value relative to the other joint products is termed a **by-product.** For example, whey is a by-product in the production of cheese. A common practice in accounting is to subtract a by-product's net realizable value from the cost of the joint process. Then the remaining joint cost is allocated among the major joint products.

An alternative procedure is to inventory the by-product at its sales value at split-off. Then the by-product's sales value is deducted from the production cost of the main products.

In the **physical-units method,** joint costs are allocated to the joint products in proportion to their physical quantities.

In the **relative-sales-value method,** joint costs are allocated to the joint products in proportion to their total sales values at the split-off point.

In the **net-realizable-value method,** joint costs are allocated to the joint products in proportion to the net realizable value of each joint product.

The **net realizable value** is a joint product's final sales value less any separable costs incurred after the split-off point.

A **by-product** is a joint product with very little value relative to the other joint products.

Exhibit 18–9

Methods for Allocating Joint
Product Costs

A. Physical-Units Method

Joint Cost	Joint Products	Weight at Split-off Point	Relative Proportion	Allocation of Joint Cost
	Cocoa butter	1,500 pounds	3/4	$ 825
$1,100	Cocoa powder	500 pounds	1/4	275
	Total joint cost allocated			$1,100

B. Relative-Sales-Value Method

Joint Cost	Joint Products	Sales Value at Split-off Point	Relative Proportion	Allocation of Joint Cost
	Cocoa butter	$750	3/5	$ 660
$1,100	Cocoa powder	500	2/5	440
	Total joint cost allocated			$1,100

C. Net-Realizable-Value Method

Joint Cost	Joint Products	Sales Value of Final Product	Separable Cost of Processing	Net Realizable Value	Relative Proportion	Allocation of Joint Cost
	Tanning cream	$3,000	$1,560	$1,440*	6/11† . .	$ 600
1,100	Instant cocoa mix	2,000	800	1,200*	5/11† . .	500
	Total joint cost allocated					$1,100

* Sales value of final product	−	Separable cost of processing	=	Net realizable value
$3,000	−	$1,560	=	$1,440
2,000	−	800	=	1,200

† Calculation of relative proportions:

$1,440	+	$1,200	=	$2,640
(1,440	÷	2,640)	=	6/11
(1,200	÷	2,640)	=	5/11

M.A.P.

Management
Accounting
Practice

Exxon

One of the most complicated problems in joint cost allocation routinely occurs in the petroleum industry. When an oil company, such as Exxon, drills a successful oil well, the well almost always produces natural gas in addition to crude oil. Moreover, the crude oil produced by a typical oil well is of various grades. Lighter crude oils suitable for production of such products as gasoline are generally near the top of an oil reservoir, while the heavier crudes are near the bottom. The heavier crude oils are used to make such products as fuel oil for heating homes and businesses and for the generation of electricity.

All of these products obtained from a successful oil well are joint products: the various grades of crude oil and the natural gas. Most of these products will require further processing before they will be salable products such as gasoline, diesel fuel, or home heating oil. Thus, substantial separable costs will be incurred in processing the joint products in addition to the joint costs incurred in the oil field operations. Millions of dollars of joint costs are incurred in the development of an off-shore oil field. The costs of locating the oil field, building the drilling platforms, and the drilling itself are all joint costs. Then there are the costs of crewing the oil rigs and the ongoing costs of bringing oil and natural gas to the surface.

Oil companies such as Exxon typically use the net realizable value of the products manufactured as the basis for allocating the joint production costs. The full costs of the company's various products then become the basis for pricing and product-mix decisions.

The next time you pump gas for your automobile, think about the salaries of the helicopter pilots who bring food and other supplies to the many off-shore oil platforms. Those costs comprise a part of the joint cost allocated to the gasoline you obtain from the pump.

Chapter Summary

Service departments are not involved directly in producing an organization's final output of goods or services, but they do provide essential services in an organization. Thus, in order to determine the full cost of the organization's final services or goods, service department costs are allocated to the departments directly involved in producing the organization's final output. Two methods are used commonly in practice, the direct method and the step-down method. Either of these methods may be combined with the dual-allocation approach, in which variable and fixed costs are allocated separately.

A joint production process results in two or more joint products, which become separately identifiable at the split-off point. The joint costs of production are allocated in order to determine the complete cost of manufacturing the joint products. Three methods are used for this purpose: the physical-units method, the relative-sales-value method, and the net-realizable-value method. Joint cost allocation is useful for product-costing purposes, but the allocated costs should not affect substantive economic decisions.

Key Terms

For each term's definition refer to the indicated page, or turn to the glossary at the end of the text.

by-product, pg. 753

direct method, pg. 745

dual cost allocation, pg. 748

joint production
   process, pg. 752

joint products, pg. 752

net realizable value, pg. 753

net-realizable-value
   method, pg. 753

physical-units
   method, pg. 753

reciprocal service, pg. 746

reciprocal-services
   method, pg. 746

relative-sales-value
   method, pg. 753

service department, pg. 742

split-off point, pg. 752

step-down method, pg. 745

Appendix to Chapter 18
Reciprocal-Services Method

The reciprocal-services method of service department cost allocation fully accounts for the mutual provision of services among all the service departments. The relationships between Riverside Clinic's three service departments are portrayed in the following diagram.

LO 1   Allocate service department costs using the direct method, step-down method, or reciprocal-services method (appendix).

The first step in the technique is to specify a set of equations that express the relationships between the departments. The following equations, which express these relationships for Riverside Clinic, are based on the data in Exhibit 18–2 (panel A) on page 744.

$$R = 100,000 + .05P \qquad (1)$$

$$P = 60,000 + .05A \qquad (2)$$

$$A = 190,000 + .20P \qquad (3)$$

where R denotes the total cost of the Patient Records Department

P denotes the total cost of the Personnel Department

A denotes the total cost of the Administration and Accounting Department

Equation (1) says that the *total cost* of operating the Patient Records Department (R) is $100,000 *plus* 5 percent of the total cost of operating the Personnel Department (P). The $100,000 comes from Exhibit 18–2 (panel C) and is the total cost *traceable* to the Patient Records Department. We add to this amount 5 percent of the total cost of operating the Personnel Department. Why? Because Exhibit 18–2 (panel A) tells us that the Patient Records Department used 5 percent of the Personnel Department's services. Similar explanations underlie equations (2) and (3).

The second step in the reciprocal-services method is to solve the simultaneous equations.[6] Let's begin by substituting the expression for A from equation (3) into equation (2), and solving for P as follows:

$$P = 60,000 + .05(190,000 + .20P)$$
$$= 60,000 + 9,500 + .01P$$
$$.99P = 69,500$$
$$P = 70,202 \text{ (rounded)}$$

Then we substitute the value for P we just obtained into equation (3), and solve for A as follows:

$$A = 190,000 + .20P$$
$$= 190,000 + (.20)(70,202)$$
$$= 204,040 \text{ (rounded)}$$

---

[6] Simultaneous equations are more quickly solved by computers than by people. Numerous software packages are available for this purpose.

	Service Department			Direct-Patient-Care Department	
	Personnel	**Administration and Accounting**	**Patient Records**	**Orthopedics**	**Internal Medicine**
Traceable costs	$60,000	$190,000	$100,000		
Allocation of Personnel Department costs	(70,202)	14,040* (.20)	3,510* (.05)	$17,551* (.25)	$35,101 (.30)
Allocation of Administration and Accounting Department costs	10,202 (.05)†	(204,040)	-0- (0)	71,414 (.35)	122,424 (.60)
Allocation of Patient Records Department costs . .	-0- (0)	-0- (0)	(103,510)	31,053 (.30)	72,457 (.70)
Total cost allocated to each direct-patient-care department				$120,018	$229,982
Total costs allocated				$350,000	

* Rounded.

† Percentages in parentheses are relative proportions of a service department's output consumed by departments to which costs are allocated (from Exhibit 18–2, panel A).

Now we can solve for *R* by substituting the value for *P* into equation (1) as follows:

$$R = 100,000 + .05P$$
$$= 100,000 + (.05)(70,202)$$
$$= 103,510 \text{ (rounded)}$$

Thus, we have determined that *P* = 70,202, *A* = 204,040, and *R* = 103,510.

The final step in the reciprocal-services method is to allocate the *total cost* of operating each service department (*R*, *P*, and *A*) to the various departments that use its services. For example, we will allocate the total cost of operating the Personnel Department (*P*) among all four of Riverside Clinic's other departments, because they all use Personnel's services. This allocation is made in proportion to the use of Personnel's services by the other departments, as given in Exhibit 18–2 (panel A).

The allocations are shown in Exhibit 18–10. Focus on the second row of numbers, which refers to the Personnel Department. The $70,202 shown in parentheses in the Personnel column is that department's total cost, as computed using the simultaneous equations. This $70,202 total cost is allocated as follows:

■ 20 percent (or $14,040) to Administration and Accounting, because that department uses 20 percent of Personnel's services

■ 5 percent (or $3,510) to Patient Records, because that department uses 5 percent of Personnel's services

■ 25 percent (or $17,551) to Orthopedics, because that department uses 25 percent of Personnel's services

■ 50 percent (or $35,101) to Internal Medicine, because that department uses 50 percent of Personnel's services.

A similar explanation underlies the Administration and Accounting row and the Patient Records row in Exhibit 18–10.

The total costs allocated to Riverside Clinic's two direct-patient-care departments are as follows: $120,018 to Orthopedics and $229,982 to Internal Medicine. Notice that these two amounts add up to $350,000, which is the total of the original traceable costs for the three service departments. Thus, all service department costs have been fully allocated.

The reciprocal-services method is more accurate than the direct and step-down methods, because it fully accounts for reciprocal services. To make the reciprocal-services method even more accurate, it can be combined with the dual-allocation approach. In this approach, variable and fixed costs are allocated separately. This method is explored in Problem 18–32.

Exhibit 18–10

Reciprocal-Services Method of Service Department Cost Allocation: Riverside Clinic

RIVERSIDE
CLINIC

Review Questions

18–1. Distinguish between a service department and a production department. Give an example of the counterpart of a manufacturer's "production" department in a bank.

18–2. Define the term *reciprocal services.*

18–3. Explain briefly the main differences between the direct, step-down, and reciprocal-services methods of service department cost allocation.

18–4. How does the managerial accountant determine the department sequence in the step-down method? How are ties handled?

18–5. Why does the dual-allocation approach improve the resulting cost allocation?

18–6. What potential behavioral problem can result when the dual approach is used?

18–7. Should actual or budgeted service department costs be allocated? Why?

18–8. Explain the difference between two-stage allocation with departmental overhead rates and activity-based costing. Which approach generally results in more accurate product costs?

18–9. Define the following terms: joint production process, joint costs, joint products, split-off point, separable costs, and by-product.

18–10. Briefly explain how to use the physical-units method of joint cost allocation.

18–11. Describe the relative-sales-value method of joint cost allocation.

18–12. Define the term *net realizable value,* and explain how this concept can be used to allocate joint costs.

18–13. Are joint cost allocations useful? If they are, for what purpose?

18–14. For what purpose should the managerial accountant be careful not to use joint cost allocations?

Exercises

■ **Exercise 18–15**
Direct Method of Service
Department Cost Allocation;
Bank
(LO 1)

El Paso National Bank has two service departments, the Personnel Department and the Computing Department. The bank has two other departments that directly service customers, the Deposit Department and the Loan Department. The usage of the two service departments' output for the year is as follows:

	Provider of Service	
User of Service	**Personnel**	**Computing**
Personnel	—	15%
Computing	10%	—
Deposit	60%	50%
Loan	30%	35%

The budgeted costs in the two service departments for the year are as follows:

Personnel	$153,000
Computing	229,500

Required:

Use the direct method to allocate the budgeted costs of the Personnel and Computing departments to the Deposit and Loan departments.

■ **Exercise 18–16**
Step-Down Method of
Service Department Cost
Allocation; Bank
(LO 1)

Refer to the data given in the preceding exercise.

Required:

Use the step-down method to allocate the budgeted costs of the Personnel and Computing departments to the Deposit and Loan departments. El Paso National Bank allocates the costs of the Personnel Department first.

■ **Exercise 18–17**
Direct Method of Service
Department Cost Allocation;
College
(LO 1)

Hudson Community College enrolls students in two departments, Liberal Arts and Sciences. The college also has two service departments, the Library and the Computing Services Department. The usage of these two service departments' output for the year is as follows:

	Provider of Service	
User of Service	**Library**	**Computing Services**
Library	—	20%
Computing Services	—	—
Liberal Arts	60%	30%
Sciences	40%	50%

The budgeted costs in the two service departments for the year are as follows:

Library	$600,000
Computing Services	240,000

Required:

Use the direct method to allocate the budgeted costs of the Library and Computing Services Department to the college's Liberal Arts and Sciences departments.

Refer to the data given in the preceding exercise.

Required:

Use the step-down method to allocate Hudson Community College's service department costs to the Liberal Arts and Sciences departments.

■ **Exercise 18–18**
Step-Down Method of Service Department Cost Allocation; College
(LO 1)

Breakfasttime Cereal Company manufactures two breakfast cereals in a joint process. Cost and quantity information is as follows:

■ **Exercise 18–19**
Physical-Units Method; Joint Cost Allocation
(LO 4)

Joint Cost	**Cereal**	**Quantity at Split-Off Point**	**Sales Price per Kilogram**
$30,000	Yummies	12,000 kilograms	$2.00
	Crummies	8,000 kilograms	2.50

Required:

Use the physical-units method to allocate the company's joint production cost between Yummies and Crummies.

Refer to the data given in the preceding exercise.

Required:

Use the relative-sales-value method to allocate Breakfasttime Cereal Company's joint production cost between Yummies and Crummies.

■ **Exercise 18–20**
Relative-Sales-Value Method; Joint Cost Allocation
(LO 4)

Refer to the data given in Exercise 18–19. Breakfasttime Cereal Company has an opportunity to process its Crummies further into a mulch for ornamental shrubs. The additional processing operation costs $.50 per kilogram, and the mulch will sell for $3.50 per kilogram.

■ **Exercise 18–21**
Net-Realizable-Value Method; Joint Cost Allocation
(LO 4)

Required:

1. Should Breakfasttime's management process Crummies into the mulch? Why?
2. Suppose the company does process Crummies into the mulch. Use the net-realizable-value method to allocate the joint production cost between the mulch and the Yummies.

Refer to the data given in Exercise 18–15 for El Paso National Bank.

Required:

Use the reciprocal-services method to allocate the budgeted costs of the Personnel and Computing departments to the Deposit and Loan departments.

■ **Exercise 18–22**
Reciprocal-Services Method; Bank (Appendix)
(LO 1)

Problems

■ **Problem 18–23**
Service Department Cost
Allocation
(LO 1)

Galaxy Corporation is developing departmental overhead rates based on direct-labor hours for its two production departments, Etching and Finishing. The Etching Department employs 20 people and the Finishing Department employs 80 people. Each person in these two departments works 2,000 hours per year. The production-related overhead costs for the Etching Department are budgeted at $200,000, and the Finishing Department costs are budgeted at $320,000. Two service departments, Maintenance and Computing, directly support the two production departments. These service departments have budgeted costs of $48,000 and $250,000, respectively. The production departments' overhead rates cannot be determined until the service departments' costs are allocated. The following schedule reflects the use of the Maintenance Department's and Computing Department's output by the various departments.

	Using Department			
Service Department	**Maintenance**	**Computing**	**Etching**	**Finishing**
Maintenance (maintenance hours)	0	1,000	1,000	8,000
Computing (minutes)	240,000	0	840,000	120,000

Required:

1. Calculate the overhead rates per direct-labor hour for the Etching Department and the Finishing Department. Use the direct method to allocate service department costs.

2. Calculate the overhead rates per direct-labor hour for the Etching Department and the Finishing Department. Use the step-down method to allocate service department costs. Allocate the Computing Department's costs first.

(CMA, adapted)

■ **Problem 18–24**
Direct and Step-Down
Methods of Service
Department Cost Allocation
(LO 1)

Cleveland Instrument Company manufactures gauges for construction machinery. The company has two production departments: Molding and Assembly. There are three service departments: Maintenance, Personnel, and Computer Aided Design (CAD). The usage of these service departments' output during the year just completed is as follows:

Provision of Service Output (in hours of service)			
	Provider of Service		
User of Service	**Personnel**	**Maintenance**	**CAD**
Personnel	—	—	—
Maintenance	500	—	—
CAD	500	500	—
Molding	4,000	3,500	4,500
Assembly	5,000	4,000	1,500
Total	10,000	8,000	6,000

The budgeted costs in Cleveland Instrument Company's service departments during the year are as follows:

	Personnel	**Maintenance**	**CAD**
Variable	$ 50,000	$ 80,000	$ 50,000
Fixed	200,000	150,000	300,000
Total	$250,000	$230,000	$350,000

Required:

1. Use the direct method to allocate Cleveland Instrument Company's service department costs to its production departments.

2. Determine the proper sequence to use in allocating the firm's service department costs by the step-down method.

3. Use the step-down method to allocate the company's service department costs.

Refer to the data given in the preceding problem. When Cleveland Instrument Company established its service departments, the following long-run needs were anticipated.

■ **Problem 18–25**
Dual Allocation of Service
Department Costs
(LO 1, LO 2)

Long-Run Service Needs (in hours of service)

User of Service	Provider of Service		
	Personnel	Maintenance	CAD
Personnel	—	—	—
Maintenance	500	—	—
CAD	1,000	800	—
Molding	3,500	4,800	4,800
Assembly	5,000	2,400	1,200
Total	10,000	8,000	6,000

Required:

Use the dual approach in conjunction with each of the following methods to allocate Cleveland Instrument Company's service department costs: (1) direct method, and (2) step-down method.

Sonimad Sawmill manufactures two lumber products from a joint milling process. The two products developed are mine support braces (MSB) and unseasoned commercial building lumber (CBL). A standard production run incurs joint costs of $300,000 and results in 60,000 units of MSB and 90,000 units of CBL. Each MSB sells for $2, and each CBL sells for $4.

■ **Problem 18–26**
Joint Costs
(LO 4, LO 5)

Required:

1. Calculate the amount of joint cost allocated to commercial building lumber (CBL) on a physical-units basis.

2. Calculate the amount of joint cost allocated to the mine support braces (MSB) on a relative-sales-value basis.

3. Assume the commercial building lumber is not marketable at split-off but must be further planed and sized at a cost of $200,000 per production run. During this process, 10,000 units are unavoidably lost; these spoiled units have no value. The remaining units of commercial building lumber are saleable at $10 per unit. The mine support braces, although saleable immediately at the split-off point, are coated with a tarlike preservative that costs $100,000 per production run. The braces are then sold for $5 each. Using the net-realizable-value basis, compute the completed cost assigned to each unit of commercial building lumber.

4. If Sonimad Sawmill chose not to process the mine support braces beyond the split-off point, the contribution from the joint milling process would increase or decrease by what amount?

5. Did you use the joint cost allocation results in answering requirement (4)? If so, how? Why did you use or not use the allocation results?

(CMA, adapted)

Execucraft Corporation manufactures a complete line of fiberglass attaché cases and suitcases. The firm has three manufacturing departments: Molding, Component, and Assembly. There are also two service departments: Power and Maintenance.

■ **Problem 18–27**
Service Department Cost
Allocation; Plantwide versus
Departmental Overhead
Rates; Cost Drivers
(LO 3)

The sides of the cases are manufactured in the Molding Department. The frames, hinges, and locks are manufactured in the Component Department. The cases are completed in the Assembly Department. Varying amounts of materials, time, and effort are required for each of the cases. The Power Department and Maintenance Department provide services to the three manufacturing departments.

Execucraft has always used a plantwide overhead rate. Direct-labor hours are used to assign overhead to products. The predetermined overhead rate is calculated by dividing the company's total estimated overhead by the total estimated direct-labor hours to be worked in the three manufacturing departments.

Jennifer Mason, manager of cost accounting, has recommended that Execucraft use departmental overhead rates. The planned operating costs and expected levels of activity for the coming year have been developed by Mason and are presented by department in the following schedules. (All numbers are in thousands.)

	Manufacturing Departments		
	Molding	**Component**	**Assembly**
Department activity measures:			
Direct-labor hours	500	2,000	1,500
Machine hours	875	125	-0-
Departmental costs:			
Direct material	$12,400	$30,000	$ 1,250
Direct labor	3,500	20,000	12,000
Variable overhead	3,500	10,000	16,500
Fixed overhead	17,500	6,200	6,100
Total departmental costs	$36,900	$66,200	$35,850
Use of service departments:			
Maintenance:			
Estimated usage in labor hours for the coming year	90	25	10
Power (in kilowatt-hours):			
Estimated usage for the coming year	360	320	120
Maximum allotted capacity	500	350	150

	Service Departments	
	Power	**Maintenance**
Departmental activity measures:		
Maximum capacity	1,000 kilowatt-hours	Adjustable
Estimated usage for the coming year	800 kilowatt-hours	125 hours
Departmental costs:		
Materials and supplies	$ 5,000	$1,500
Variable labor	1,400	2,250
Fixed overhead	12,000	250
Total service department costs	$18,400	$4,000

Required:

1. Calculate the plantwide overhead rate for Execucraft Corporation for the coming year using the same method as used in the past.

2. Jennifer Mason has been asked to develop departmental overhead rates for comparison with the plantwide rate. The following steps are to be followed in developing the departmental rates.

   a. The Maintenance Department costs should be allocated to the three manufacturing departments using the direct method.

   b. The Power Department costs should be allocated to the three manufacturing departments using the dual method combined with the direct method. Fixed costs are to be allocated according to maximum allotted capacity, and variable costs are to be allocated according to planned usage for the coming year.

   c. Calculate departmental overhead rates for the three manufacturing departments using a machine-hour cost driver for the Molding Department and a direct-labor-hour cost driver for the Component and Assembly departments.

3. As Jennifer Mason's assistant, draft a memo for her to send to Execucraft's president recommending whether the company should use a plantwide rate or departmental rates to assign overhead to products.

(CMA, adapted)

■ **Problem 18–28**
Joint Costs; Allocation and
Production Decisions; Ethics
(LO 4, LO 5)

Hovart Corporation manufactures two products out of a joint process: Compod and Ultrasene. The joint costs incurred are $250,000 for a standard production run that generates 120,000 gallons of Compod and 80,000 gallons of Ultrasene. Compod sells for $2.00 per gallon while Ultrasene sells for $3.25 per gallon.

Required:

1. If there are no additional processing costs incurred after the split-off point, calculate the amount of joint cost of each production run allocated to Compod on a physical-units basis.

2. If there are no additional processing costs incurred after the split-off point, calculate the amount of joint cost of each production run allocated to Ultrasene on a relative-sales-value basis.

3. Suppose the following additional processing costs are required beyond the split-off point in order to obtain Compod and Ultrasene: $.10 per gallon for Compod and $1.10 per gallon for Ultrasene.

   a. Calculate the amount of joint cost of each production run allocated to Ultrasene on a physical-units basis.

   b. Calculate the amount of joint cost of each production run allocated to Compod on a net-realizable-value basis.

4. Assuming the same data as in requirement (3), suppose Compod can be processed further into a product called Compodalene, at an additional cost of $.40 per gallon. Compodalene will be sold for $2.60 per gallon by independent distributors. The distributor's commission will be 10% of the sales price. Should Hovart sell Compod or Compodalene?

5. Independent of your answer to requirement (4), suppose Christine Dalton, the assistant controller, has completed an analysis showing that Compod should not be processed further into Compodalene. Before presenting her analysis to top management, however, she got a visit from Jack Turner, Hovart's director of research. Turner was upset upon learning that Compodalene, a product he had personally developed, would not be manufactured.

   Turner: "The company's making a big mistake if it passes up this opportunity. Compodalene will be a big seller and get us into new markets."

   Dalton: "But the analysis shows that we'd be losing money on every gallon of Compod that we process further."

   Turner: "I know, Christine, but that's a temporary problem. Eventually, we'll bring down the cost of making Compodalene."

   Dalton: "Can you find me some estimates on the cost reduction you expect?"

   Turner: "I don't have a crystal ball, Christine. Look, if you could just fudge the numbers a little bit to help me get approval to produce some Compodalene, I can get this product off the ground. I know the cost reduction will come."

   Comment on the ethical issues in this scenario. What should Christine Dalton do?

6. Assume the same data as given in requirements (3) and (4). The industrial chemical industry has experienced a downturn, which has left Hovart with idle capacity. Suppose Hovart can sell only half of the Compod made in each production run, but the remainder could be sold as Compodalene. Should Hovart process the remaining Compod into Compodalene?

(CMA, adapted)

Plato Corporation manufactures products Alpha, Beta, and Gamma from a joint process. Production, sales, and cost data for July follow.

■ **Problem 18–29**
Joint Cost Allocation;
Missing Data
(LO 1)

	Alpha	Beta	Gamma	Total
Units produced	4,000	2,000	1,000	7,000
Joint cost allocation	$36,000	?	?	$60,000
Sales value at split-off	?	?	$15,000	$100,000
Additional costs if processed further	$7,000	$5,000	$3,000	$15,000
Sales value if processed further	$70,000	$25,000	$20,000	$115,000

Required:

1. Assuming that joint costs are allocated using the relative-sales-value method, what were the joint costs allocated to products Beta and Gamma?

2. Assuming that joint costs are allocated using the relative-sales-value method, what was the sales value at split-off for product Alpha?

3. Use the net-realizable-value method to allocate the joint production costs to products Alpha, Beta, and Gamma.

(CPA, adapted)

■ **Problem 18–30**
Joint Costs; Allocation and
Production Decisions
(LO 4, LO 5)

Alderon Industries is a manufacturer of chemicals for various purposes. One of the processes used by Alderon produces SPL–3, a chemical used in swimming pools; PST–4, a chemical used in pesticides; and RJ–5, a product that is sold to fertilizer manufacturers. Alderon uses the net-realizable-value method to allocate joint production costs. The ratio of output quantities to input quantities of direct material used in the joint process remains consistent from month to month. Alderon Industries uses FIFO (first-in, first-out) in valuing its finished-goods inventories.

Data regarding Alderon's operations for the month of November are as follows. During this month, Alderon incurred joint production costs of $1,700,000 in the manufacture of SPL–3, PST–4, and RJ–5.

	SPL–3	PST–4	RJ–5
Finished goods inventory in gallons (November 1)	18,000	52,000	3,000
November sales in gallons	650,000	325,000	150,000
November production in gallons	700,000	350,000	170,000
Additional processing costs	$874,000	$816,000	$60,000
Final sales value per gallon	$4.00	$6.00	$5.00

Required:

1. Determine Alderon Industries' allocation of joint production costs for the month of November. (Carry calculation of relative proportions to four decimal places.)

2. Determine the dollar values of the finished-goods inventories for SPL–3, PST–4, and RJ–5 as of November 30. (Round the cost per gallon to the nearest cent).

3. Suppose Alderon Industries has a new opportunity to sell PST–4 at the split-off point for $3.80 per gallon. Prepare an analysis showing whether Alderon should sell PST–4 at the split-off point or continue to process this product further.

(CMA, adapted)

■ **Problem 18–31**
Reciprocal-Service Method
(Appendix)
(LO 1)

Refer to the data given in Problem 18–23 for Galaxy Corporation.

Required:

1. Calculate the overhead rates per direct-labor hour for the Etching Department and the Finishing Department. Use the reciprocal-services method to allocate service department costs.

2. Which of the three methods of service department cost allocation results in the most accurate overhead rates? Why?

■ **Problem 18–32**
Reciprocal-Services Method;
Dual Allocation (Appendix)
(LO 1, LO 2)

Refer to the data for Riverside Clinic given in Exhibits 18–2 and 18–5.

Required:

Use the reciprocal-services method in combination with the dual-allocation approach to allocate Riverside's service department costs. Hint: You will need to apply the reciprocal-services method twice. First, allocate the three service departments' variable costs using the short-run usage proportions in Exhibit 18–2 (panel A). Second, allocate the three service departments' fixed costs using the long-run average usage proportions in Exhibit 18–5. Finally, add the variable costs and fixed costs allocated to each direct-patient-care department.

Cases

■ **Case 18–33**
Comprehensive Case on
Joint Cost Allocation
(LO 4, LO 5)

Edmonton Chemical Company manufactures two industrial chemical products in a joint process. In May, 10,000 gallons of input costing $60,000 were processed at a cost of $150,000. The joint process resulted in 8,000 pounds of Resoline and 2,000 pounds of Krypto. Resoline sells for $25 per pound and Krypto sells for $50 per pound. Management generally processes each of these chemicals further in separable processes to produce more refined chemical products. Resoline is processed separately at a cost of $5 per pound. The resulting product, Resolite, sells for $35 per pound. Krypto is processed separately at a cost of $15 per pound. The resulting product, Kryptite, sells for $95 per pound.

Required:

1. Draw a diagram similar to Exhibit 18–8 to depict Edmonton Chemical Company's joint production process.

2. Allocate the company's joint production costs for May using:

   a. The physical-units method.

   b. The relative-sales-value method.

   c. The net-realizable-value method.

3. Edmonton's management is considering an opportunity to process Kryptite further into a new product called Omega. The separable processing will cost $40 per pound. Packaging costs for Omega are projected to be $6 per pound, and the anticipated sales price is $130 per pound. Should Kryptite be processed further into Omega? Why?

4. In answering requirement (3), did you use your joint cost allocation from requirement (2)? If so, how did you use it?

Tasty Fruit Corporation grows, processes, cans, and sells three main pineapple products: sliced, crushed, and juice. The outside skin is cut off in the Cutting Department and processed as animal feed. The feed is treated as a by-product. The company's production process is as follows:

- Pineapples first are processed in the Cutting Department. The pineapples are washed and the outside skin is cut away. Then the pineapples are cored and trimmed for slicing. The three main products (sliced, crushed, juice) and the by-product (animal feed) are recognizable after processing in the Cutting Department. Each product then is transferred to a separate department for final processing.

- The trimmed pineapples are sent to the Slicing Department, where the pineapples are sliced and canned. Any juice generated during the slicing operation is packed in the cans with the slices.

- The pieces of pineapple trimmed from the fruit are diced and canned in the Crushing Department. Again, the juice generated during this operation is packed in the can with the crushed pineapple.

- The core and surplus pineapple generated from the Cutting Department are pulverized into a liquid in the Juicing Department. There is an evaporation loss equal to 8 percent of the weight of the good output produced in this department which occurs as the juices are heated.

- The outside skin is chopped into animal feed in the Feed Department.

Tasty Fruit Corporation uses the net-realizable-value method to assign the costs of the joint process to its main products. The net realizable value of the by-product is subtracted from the joint cost before the allocation.

A total of 270,000 pounds were entered into the Cutting Department during May. The following schedule shows the costs incurred in each department, the proportion by weight transferred to the four final processing departments, and the selling price of each end product.

■ Case 18–34
Joint Cost Allocation;
By-Product
(LO 4)

Processing Data and Costs for May

Department		Costs Incurred		Proportion of Product by Weight Transferred to Departments		Selling Price per Pound of Final Product
Cutting	....	$60,000	....	—	....	none
Slicing	....	4,700	....	35%	....	$.60
Crushing	....	10,580	....	28	....	.55
Juicing	....	3,250	....	27	....	.30
Animal feed	....	700	....	10	....	.10
Total	....	$79,230	....	100%		

Required:

Compute each of the following amounts.

1. The number of pounds of pineapple that result as output for pineapple slices, crushed pineapple, pineapple juice, and animal feed.

2. The net realizable value at the split-off point of the three main products.

3. The amount of the cost of the Cutting Department allocated to each of the three main products.

(CMA, adapted)

Current Issues in Managerial Accounting

■ **Issue 18–35**
Downsizing and Computerization

"Downsize Danger: Many Firms Cut Staff in Accounts Payable and Pay a Steep Price," *The Wall Street Journal,* September 5, 1996, Lee Berton.

Overview
After cutting costs and eliminating jobs, firms are rediscovering the importance of people. Companies are finding that computers are making errors that humans would likely have caught.

Suggested Discussion Questions
As a group, prepare a one-page memo that lists computer-related problems firms may encounter when they cut costs and eliminate jobs. Present your memo in class.

■ **Issue 18–36**
Service Department Cost Allocation

"Is Medicare Abuse an Epidemic?" *Business Week,* September 22, 1997.

Overview
Investigators are trying to determine whether Olsten Corp. improperly billed Medicare for certain overhead costs. The focus is on how overhead was allocated to home-care services.

Suggested Discussion Questions
List health care costs that could be allocated to the cost of providing patient services. How can a healthcare provider manipulate the amount it reports to Medicare? Should the government reimburse all overhead costs? Which items should the government disallow?

■ **Issue 18–37**
Service Department Cost Allocation

"Ground Control: Cost Cutting at Delta Raises the Stock Price but Lowers the Service," *The Wall Street Journal,* June 20, 1996, Martha Brannigan and Eleena De Lisser.

Overview
Delta Air Lines' $1.6 billion cost-cutting program has created sometimes chaotic working conditions, a reduction in on-time arrivals, and an increase in complaints about baggage mishandling.

Suggested Discussion Questions
List types of airline service departments. Suggest methods for allocating these costs. Perform an analysis which weighs the costs and benefits of reducing some of these service department costs.

■ **Issue 18–38**
Service Department Cost Allocation

"ValuJet Lays Off 4,000 of Its Workers, Faces Major Challenges to a Comeback," *The Wall Street Journal,* June 19, 1996, Martha Brannigan and Eleena DeLisser.

Overview
In response to the Federal Aviation Administration's (FAA) grounding, ValuJet laid off 4,000 workers. ValuJet's chairman predicted that the grounding would last 30 days.

Suggested Discussion Questions
List types of jobs that ValuJet would eliminate first. If all that was left after the big layoff was a skeletal staff, which services would likely remain? Would your answer influence your decision concerning what types of service costs to allocate and how they should be allocated?

■ **Issue 18–39**
Cost Cutting in Health Care; Service Departments

"How Kaiser's Cost-Slashing Nicked Its Image," *Business Week,* April 21, 1997.

Overview
After cutting costs, Kaiser Permanente may lose its license in Texas due to concerns over low-quality health care.

Suggested Discussion Questions
How can a hospital cut costs and not services? Provide examples. How can service department cost allocation affect this environment? How can physicians be compensated so that high-quality health care is assured? Should doctors be allowed to invest in for-profit hospitals in which they practice?

"Called to Account: Peat Marwick Is Facing Turmoil among Staff, Tricky Financial Issues," *The Wall Street Journal,* **May 17, 1996, Lee Berton.**

■ **Issue 18–40**
Service Department
Cost Allocation

Overview

KPMG Peat Marwick's accounting methods applied to its own operations have undergone scrutiny. Specifically, its method of accounting for revenues and pension liabilities has been questioned by some industry publications.

Suggested Discussion Questions

Discuss how accounting firms' pension liability should be allocated. Would your answer differ if the liability is funded or unfunded? The article also reports that KPMG Peat Marwick has more debt than its competitors. How should this cost be allocated? How does this affect the firm's competitive position in the marketplace? Would these factors influence KPMG's decision to merge?

"ABM and the Procurement Cost Model," *Management Accounting,* **March 1996, Paulette Bennett.**

■ **Issue 18–41**
Activity-Based Costing;
Procurement Service
Department

Overview

This article describes how Parker Hannifan's Compumotor Division implemented an activity-based cost procurement model.

Suggested Discussion Questions

As a group, list activities that are involved in the acquisition of inventory. How would you assess your procurement process performance? Should you communicate your assessment of your suppliers' performance to your suppliers?

19

Chapter Nineteen

Variable and Absorption Costing

After completing this chapter, you should be able to:

1. Explain the accounting treatment of fixed manufacturing overhead under absorption and variable costing.

2. Prepare an income statement under absorption costing.

3. Prepare an income statement under variable costing.

4. Reconcile reported income under absorption and variable costing.

5. Explain the implications of absorption and variable costing for cost-volume-profit analysis.

6. After completing the appendix, explain the effect of the volume variance under absorption and variable costing.

ORION ANNOUNCES NEW PRODUCT LINE

Boston—The president of Orion Company announced today that the company would soon introduce a low-cost calculator with a built-in pager. Abby Rivendell, Orion's president, said the product would be noteworthy because it would be priced to be affordable to school kids. "There are plenty of high-tech gismos on the market," Rivendell acknowledged. "You can buy a calculator combined with an electronic address book, pager, and GPS locator. But in addition to being high-tech, these gadgets are high-priced. We intend to bring out a product that parents can afford to get for their school-age kids.

The school-age population has been our market since we formed Orion. Kids' lives are busy and complicated these days, and it's always a challenge for parents to know where their kids are and what they're doing. The pager built into our calculator will enable a parent, sibling, or friend to page a kid just by dialing a certain phone number and then punching in the kid's personal ID number. Then the calculator emits a soft tone and displays the phone number from which the page originated. The paged person then calls the displayed number to check in or whatever."

When asked how Orion Company would be able to price its new product so competitively, Rivendell's answer was interesting. "We're going to price this product aggressively. We are going to set the price just high enough to cover our variable costs of manufacturing and marketing the Calc'n'Page. That's what we're calling the product, by the way. In other words, we want to ensure that the product price is sufficient to cover the incremental costs we will incur to make each unit—costs such as the direct material and direct labor and so forth.

We want to make sure the product is accessible to all kids' families, and we want to quickly achieve a broad-based market. This is a real departure, though, from our usual approach to product pricing. Generally, we use a full-cost approach to pricing. This means that we price products to cover all of the costs of production, including the fixed costs like the plant manager's salary and the property taxes on the plant. We will continue to use that pricing approach for our well-established, bread-and-butter products. But the Calc'n'Page is different. Here we need to quickly establish a presence in the market. The variable-cost approach to pricing, in this instance, will help us accomplish that."

According to Orion's vice president of sales, Anne Tyler, the new Calc'n'Page will be in stores in about six to eight months.

Income is one of many important measures used to evaluate the performance of companies and segments of companies. There are two alternative methods for reporting income in a manufacturing firm, depending on the accounting treatment of fixed manufacturing overhead. In this chapter, we will examine these two income-reporting alternatives, called *absorption costing* and *variable costing*.[1]

Product Costs

In the product-costing systems we have studied so far, manufacturing overhead is applied to Work-in-Process Inventory as a product cost along with direct material and direct labor. When the manufactured goods are finished, these product costs flow from Work-in-Process Inventory into Finished-Goods Inventory. Finally, during the accounting period when the goods are sold, the product costs flow from Finished-Goods Inventory into Cost of Goods Sold, an expense account. The following diagram summarizes this flow of costs.

Absorption costing (or full costing) includes both variable and fixed manufacturing overhead in the product costs that flow through the manufacturing accounts.

Since the costs of production are stored in inventory accounts until the goods are sold, these costs are said to be *inventoried costs*.

LO 1   Explain the accounting treatment of fixed manufacturing overhead under absorption and variable costing.

Variable costing (or direct costing) includes only variable manufacturing overhead as a product cost that flows through the manufacturing accounts.

Fixed Manufacturing Overhead: The Key   In our study of product-costing systems, we have included both variable and fixed manufacturing overhead in the product costs that flow through the manufacturing accounts. This approach to product costing is called **absorption costing** (or **full costing**), because *all* manufacturing-overhead costs are applied to (or absorbed by) manufactured goods. An alternative approach to product costing is called **variable costing** (or **direct costing**), in which *only variable* manufacturing overhead is applied to Work-in-Process Inventory as a product cost.

The distinction between variable and absorption costing is summarized in Exhibit 19–1. Notice that the distinction involves the *timing* with which fixed manufacturing overhead becomes an expense. Eventually, fixed overhead is expensed under both product-costing systems. Under variable costing, however, fixed overhead is expensed *immediately*, as it is incurred. Under absorption costing, fixed overhead is *inventoried* until the accounting period during which the manufactured goods are sold.

Illustration of Variable and Absorption Costing

Orion Company began operations on January 1, 19x7, to manufacture hand-held electronic calculators. The company uses a standard-costing system. Cost, production, and sales data for the first three years of Orion's operations are given in Exhibit 19–2. Comparative income statements for 19x7, 19x8, and 19x9 are presented in Exhibit 19–3, using both absorption and variable costing.

LO 2   Prepare an income statement under absorption costing.

Absorption-Costing Income Statements

Examine the absorption-costing income statements in the upper half of Exhibit 19–3. Two features of these income statements are highlighted in the

---

[1]This chapter, excluding the appendix, can be studied anytime after Chapter 8 has been completed. The appendix should be studied after Chapter 11 has been completed.

A. Variable Costing

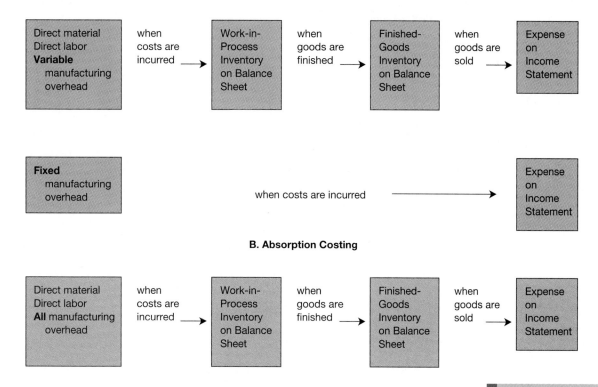

Direct material Direct labor **Variable** manufacturing overhead	when costs are incurred →	Work-in-Process Inventory on Balance Sheet	when goods are finished →	Finished-Goods Inventory on Balance Sheet	when goods are sold →	Expense on Income Statement	

Fixed manufacturing overhead	when costs are incurred ───────────────→
	Expense on Income Statement

B. Absorption Costing

Direct material Direct labor **All** manufacturing overhead	when costs are incurred →	Work-in-Process Inventory on Balance Sheet	when goods are finished →	Finished-Goods Inventory on Balance Sheet	when goods are sold →	Expense on Income Statement	

Exhibit 19–1

Variable versus Absorption Costing

left-hand margin. First, notice that the Cost of Goods Sold expense for each year is determined by multiplying the year's sales by the standard absorption manufacturing cost per unit, $9. Included in the $9 cost per unit is the predetermined fixed manufacturing-overhead cost of $3 per unit. Second, notice that on Orion's absorption-costing

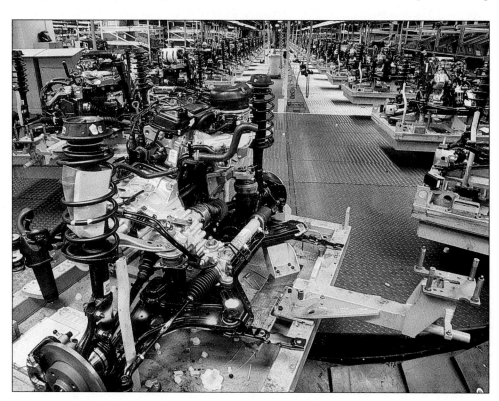

The fixed costs of operating this Volkswagen production facility include such costs as the depreciation on plant and equipment, property taxes, insurance, and the salary of the plant manager. Fixed manufacturing costs are incurred in order to generate production capacity. Under absorption costing, these costs are treated as product costs and included in the cost of inventory. Under variable costing, they are expensed during the period incurred.

Exhibit 19–2

Data for Illustration: Orion Company

	19x7	19x8	19x9
Production and inventory data:			
Planned production (in units)	50,000	50,000	50,000
Finished-goods inventory (in units), January 1	–0–	–0–	15,000
Actual production (in units)	50,000	50,000	50,000
Sales (in units)	50,000	35,000	65,000
Finished-goods inventory (in units), December 31	–0–	15,000	–0–

Revenue and cost data, all three years:		
Sales price per unit		$12
Standard manufacturing costs per unit:		
Direct material		$ 3
Direct labor		2
Variable manufacturing overhead		1
Total variable standard cost per unit		$ 6

Used only under absorption costing

Fixed manufacturing overhead:		
Budgeted annual fixed overhead	$150,000	
Planned annual production	50,000	$ 3
Total absorption standard cost per unit		$ 9

Variable selling and administrative cost per unit . . . . $ 1

Fixed selling and administrative cost per year $25,000

Variances:
    There were no variances during 19x7, 19x8, or 19x9.

income statements, the only period expenses are the selling and administrative expenses. There is no deduction of fixed-overhead costs as a lump-sum period expense at the bottom of each income statement. As mentioned above, fixed manufacturing-overhead costs are included in Cost of Goods Sold on these absorption-costing income statements.

Variable-Costing Income Statements

LO 3   Prepare an income statement under variable costing.

Now examine the income statements based on variable costing in the lower half of Exhibit 19–3. Notice that the format of the statements is different from the format used in the absorption-costing statements. In the variable-costing statements, the contribution format is used to highlight the separation of variable and fixed costs. Let's focus on the same two aspects of the variable-costing statements that we discussed for the absorption-costing statements. First, the manufacturing expenses subtracted from sales revenue each year include only the variable costs, which amount to $6 per unit. Second, fixed manufacturing overhead is subtracted as a lump-sum period expense at the bottom of each year's income statement.

Reconciling Income under Absorption and Variable Costing

LO 4   Reconcile reported income under absorption and variable costing.

Examination of Exhibit 19–3 reveals that the income reported under absorption and variable costing is sometimes different. Although income is the same for the two product-costing methods in 19x7, it is different in 19x8 and 19x9. Let's figure out why these results occur.

		ORION COMPANY		
		Absorption-Costing Income Statement		
		19x7	**19x8**	**19x9**
	Sales revenue (at $12 per unit)	$600,000	$420,000	$780,000
1	Less: Cost of goods sold (at standard			
	absorption cost of $9 per unit)	450,000	315,000	585,000
	Gross margin	$150,000	$105,000	$195,000
	Less: Selling and administrative expenses:			
2 No fixed	Variable (at $1 per unit)	50,000	35,000	65,000
overhead	Fixed	25,000	25,000	25,000
	Net income	$ 75,000	$ 45,000	$105,000

		ORION COMPANY		
		Variable-Costing Income Statement		
		19x7	**19x8**	**19x9**
	Sales revenue (at $12 per unit)	$600,000	$420,000	$780,000
	Less: Variable expenses:			
1	Variable manufacturing costs			
	(at standard variable cost of $6			
	(per unit)	300,000	210,000	390,000
	Variable selling and administrative			
	costs (at $1 per unit)	50,000	35,000	65,000
	Contribution margin	$250,000	$175,000	$325,000
	Less: Fixed expenses:			
2	Fixed manufacturing overhead	150,000	150,000	150,000
	Fixed selling and administrative			
	expenses	25,000	25,000	25,000
	Net income	$ 75,000	$ 0	$150,000

Exhibit 19–3

Income Statements under
Absorption and Variable
Costing

No Change in Inventory In 19x7 there is no change in inventory over the course of the year. Beginning and ending inventory are the same, because actual production and sales are the same. Think about the implications of the stable inventory level for the treatment of fixed manufacturing overhead. On the variable-costing statement, the $150,000 of fixed manufacturing overhead incurred during 19x7 is an expense in 19x7. Under absorption costing, however, fixed manufacturing overhead was applied to production at the predetermined rate of $3 per unit. Since all of the units produced in 19x7 also were sold in 19x7, all of the fixed manufacturing-overhead cost flowed through into Cost of Goods Sold. Thus, $150,000 of fixed manufacturing overhead was expensed in 19x7 under absorption costing also.

The 19x7 column of Exhibit 19–4 reconciles the 19x7 net income reported under absorption and variable costing. The reconciliation focuses on the two places in the income statements where differences occur between absorption and variable costing. The numbers in the left-hand margin of Exhibit 19–4 correspond to the numbers in the left-hand margin of the income statements in Exhibit 19–3.

Increase in Inventory In 19x8 inventory increased from zero on January 1 to 15,000 units on December 31. The increase in inventory was the result of production exceeding sales. Under variable costing, the $150,000 of fixed overhead cost incurred in 19x8 is expensed, just as it was in 19x7. Under absorption costing, however, only a portion of the 19x7 fixed manufacturing overhead is expensed in 19x7. Since the fixed overhead is inventoried under absorption costing, some of this cost *remains in inventory* at the end of 19x8.

Reconciliation of Income
under Absorption and Variable
Costing: Orion Company

		19x7	19x8	19x9
1	Cost of goods sold under absorption costing	$450,000	$315,000	$585,000
	Variable manufacturing costs under variable costing	300,000	210,000	390,000
	Subtotal	$150,000	$105,000	$195,000
2	Fixed manufacturing overhead as period			
	expense under variable costing	150,000	150,000	150,000
	Total	$ 0	$ (45,000)	$ 45,000
	Net income under variable costing	$ 75,000	$ 0	$150,000
	Net income under absorption costing	75,000	45,000	105,000
	Difference in net income	$ 0	$ (45,000)	$ 45,000

The 19x8 column of Exhibit 19–4 reconciles the 19x8 net income reported under absorption and variable costing. As before, the reconciliation focuses on the two places in the income statements where differences occur between absorption and variable costing.

Decrease in Inventory   In 19x9 inventory decreased from 15,000 units to zero. Sales during the year exceeded production. As in 19x7 and 19x8, under variable costing, the $150,000 of fixed manufacturing overhead incurred in 19x9 is expensed in 19x9. Under absorption costing, however, *more than* $150,000 of fixed overhead is expensed in 19x9. Why? Because some of the fixed overhead incurred during the prior year, which was inventoried then, is now expensed in 19x9 as the goods are sold.

The 19x9 column of Exhibit 19–4 reconciles the 19x9 income under absorption and variable costing. Once again, the numbers on the left-hand side of Exhibit 19–4 correspond to those on the left-hand side of the income statements in Exhibit 19–3.

A Shortcut to Reconciling Income   When inventory increases or decreases during the year, reported income differs under absorption and variable costing. This results from the fixed overhead that is inventoried under absorption costing but expensed immediately under variable costing. The following formula may be used to compute the difference in the amount of fixed overhead expensed in a given time period under the two product-costing methods.

$$\text{Difference in fixed overhead expensed under absorption and variable costing} = \left(\begin{array}{c}\text{Change in}\\ \text{inventory,}\\ \text{in units}\end{array}\right) \times \left(\begin{array}{c}\text{Predetermined}\\ \text{fixed-overhead}\\ \text{rate per unit}\end{array}\right)$$

As the following table shows, this difference in the amount of fixed overhead expensed explains the difference in reported income under absorption and variable costing.

Year	Change in Inventory (in units)		Predetermined Fixed-Overhead Rate		Difference in Fixed Overhead Expensed		Absorption-Costing Income Minus Variable-Costing Income
19x7	-0-	×	$3	=	-0-	=	-0-
19x8	15,000 increase	×	$3	=	$ 45,000	=	$ 45,000
19x9	15,000 decrease	×	$3	=	$(45,000)	=	$(45,000)

Length of Time Period   The discrepancies between absorption-costing and variable-costing income in Exhibit 19–3 occur because of the changes in inventory levels during 19x8 and 19x9. It is common for production and sales to differ over the course of a week, month, or year. Therefore, the income measured for those time periods often will differ between absorption and variable costing. This discrepancy is likely to be smaller over longer time periods. Over the course of a decade, for example, Orion Company cannot sell much more or less than it produces. Thus, the income amounts under the two product-costing methods, when added together over a lengthy time period, will be approximately equal under absorption and variable costing.

Notice in Exhibit 19–3 that Orion's *total* income over the three-year period is $225,000 under *both* absorption and variable costing. This results from the fact that Orion produced and sold the same total amount over the three-year period.

Cost-Volume-Profit Analysis

> **LO 5**   Explain the implications of absorption and variable costing for cost-volume-profit analysis.

One of the tools used by managers to plan and control business operations is cost-volume-profit analysis, which we studied in Chapter 8. Orion Company's break-even point in units can be computed as follows:

$$\text{Break-even point} = \frac{\text{Fixed costs}}{\text{Unit contribution margin}} = \frac{\$150,000 + \$25,000}{\$12 - \$6 - \$1}$$

$$= \frac{\$175,000}{\$5} = 35,000 \text{ units}$$

If Orion Company sells 35,000 calculators, net income should be zero, as Exhibit 19–5 confirms.

Now return to Exhibit 19–3 and examine the 19x8 income statements under absorption and variable costing. In 19x8 Orion Company sold 35,000 units, the break-even volume. This fact is confirmed on the variable-costing income statement, since net income is zero. On the absorption-costing income statement, however, the 19x8 net income is $45,000. What has happened here?

The answer to this inconsistency lies in the different treatment of fixed manufacturing overhead under absorption and variable costing. Variable costing highlights the separation between fixed and variable costs, as do cost-volume-profit analysis and break-even calculations. Both of these techniques account for fixed manufacturing overhead as a lump sum. In contrast, *absorption costing is inconsistent with CVP analysis*, because fixed overhead is applied to goods as a product cost on a per-unit basis.

Evaluation of Absorption and Variable Costing

Some managers find the inconsistency between absorption costing and CVP analysis troubling enough to warrant using variable costing for internal income reporting. Variable costing dovetails much more closely than absorption costing with any operational analyses that require a separation between fixed and variable costs.

Exhibit 19–5

Break-Even Graph: Orion Company

Before shipping these new automobiles to the dealership, company executives had to decide on a price for the cars. Most manufacturers, including auto producers, use production costs based on absorption costing as the basis for pricing decisions. Of course the prices set by competitors also heavily influence a company's pricing decisions.

Pricing Decisions Many managers prefer to use absorption-costing data in cost-based pricing decisions. They argue that fixed manufacturing overhead is a necessary cost incurred in the production process. To exclude this fixed cost from the inventoried cost of a product, as is done under variable costing, is to understate the cost of the product. For this reason, most companies that use cost-based pricing base their prices on absorption-costing data.

Proponents of variable costing argue that a product's variable cost provides a better basis for the pricing decision. They point out that any price above a product's variable cost makes a positive contribution to covering fixed cost and profit.

Definition of an Asset Another controversy about absorption and variable costing hinges on the definition of an asset. An *asset* is a thing of value owned by the organization with future service potential. By accounting convention, assets are valued at their cost. Since fixed costs comprise part of the cost of production, advocates of absorption costing argue that inventory (an asset) should be valued at its full (absorption) cost of production. Moreover, they argue that these costs have future service potential since the inventory can be sold in the future to generate sales revenue.

Proponents of variable costing argue that the fixed-cost component of a product's absorption-costing value has no future service potential. Their reasoning is that the fixed manufacturing-overhead costs during the current period will not prevent these costs from having to be incurred again next period. Fixed-overhead costs will be incurred every period, regardless of production levels. In contrast, the incurrence of variable costs in manufacturing a product does allow the firm to avoid incurring these costs again.

To illustrate, Orion Company produced 15,000 more calculators in 19x8 than it sold. These units will be carried in inventory until they are sold in some future year. Orion Company will never again have to incur the costs of direct material, direct labor, and variable overhead incurred in 19x8 to produce those calculators. Yet Orion will have to incur approximately $150,000 of fixed-overhead costs every year, even though the firm has the 15,000 units from 19x8 in inventory.

External Reporting For external reporting purposes, generally accepted accounting principles require that income reporting be based on absorption costing. Federal tax laws also require the use of absorption costing in reporting income for tax purposes.

Why Not Both? In the age of computerized accounting systems, it is straightforward for a company to prepare income statements under both absorption and variable costing. Since absorption-costing statements are required for external reporting, managers will want to keep an eye on the effects of their decisions on financial reports to outsiders. Yet the superiority of variable-costing income reporting as a method for dovetailing with operational analyses cannot be denied. Preparation of both absorption-costing and variable-costing data is perhaps the best solution to the controversy.

JIT Manufacturing Environment In a just-in-time inventory and production management system, all inventories are kept very low. Since finished-goods inventories are minimal, there is little change in inventory from period to period. Thus, in a JIT environment, the income differences under absorption and variable costing generally will be insignificant.

Fixed-Overhead Volume Variance   Our illustration of absorption and variable costing does not include the fixed-overhead volume variance, which was covered in Chapter 11. The impact of the volume variance is explored in the appendix to this chapter.

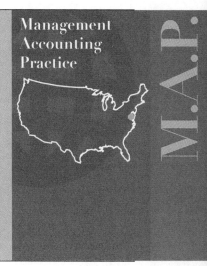

IRS: Unique Product Packaging Is an Inventoriable Cost

The Internal Revenue Service (IRS) requires absorption costing for tax purposes. Thus absorption costing must be used in valuing inventory and in determining cost-of-goods-sold expense, which in turn affects taxable income. The IRS defines inventoriable costs (i.e., product costs) that must be included in valuing inventory and cost-of-goods-sold expense to include the following: (1) direct material consumed in the production of the product and (2) direct labor, and all indirect costs deemed to be necessary for the production of the company's product. These necessary indirect costs include fixed overhead costs. Thus, absorption costing is mandated by the IRS.

One interesting nuance in the IRS interpretation of what constitutes inventoriable costs concerns a company's expenditures on the design of the packaging for the company's products. Packaging design costs can run into hundreds of thousands of dollars for large consumer products companies. The IRS has specified that packaging design costs must be inventoried as product costs if the resulting design is successful–that is, it remains in use for several years. If, however, a package design fails in the marketplace, the company can deduct the package design costs early as an expense. Examples of products with unique packaging designs that would be affected by this IRS ruling include Pringles potato chips (sold in a can), Realemon and Realime (sold in plastic citrus-fruit-shaped containers), and Leggs pantyhose (sold in the familiar plastic egg-shaped containers).

Management Accounting Practice

Chapter Summary

Absorption and variable costing are two alternative product-costing systems that differ in their treatment of fixed manufacturing overhead. Under absorption (or full) costing, fixed overhead is applied to manufactured goods as a product cost. The fixed-overhead cost remains in inventory until the goods are sold. Under variable (or direct) costing, fixed overhead is a period cost expensed during the period when it is incurred. Absorption costing is required for external reporting and tax purposes. However, variable costing is more consistent with operational decision analyses, which require a separation of fixed and variable costs.

One of the tools used by managers to plan and control business operations is cost-volume-profit analysis. Variable costing highlights the separation between fixed and variable costs, as do cost-volume-profit analysis and break-even calculations. Both of these techniques account for fixed manufacturing overhead as a lump sum. In contrast, absorption costing is inconsistent with CVP analysis, because fixed overhead is applied to goods as a product cost on a per-unit basis. Some managers find the inconsistency between absorption costing and CVP analysis troubling enough to warrant using variable costing for internal income reporting. Variable costing dovetails much more closely than absorption costing with any operational analyses that require a separation between fixed and variable costs.

Key Terms

For each term's definition refer to the indicated page, or turn to the glossary at the end of the text.

absorption (or full)
   costing, pg. 770

variable (or direct)
   costing, pg. 770

Appendix to Chapter 19

Effect of the Volume Variance under Absorption and Variable Costing

Our illustration of absorption and variable costing did not include a fixed-overhead volume variance.[2] Recall from Chapter 11 that the volume variance is defined as follows:

$$\begin{array}{l}\text{Fixed-overhead} \\ \text{volume variance}\end{array} = \text{Budgeted fixed overhead} - \text{Applied fixed overhead}$$

$$= \left(\begin{array}{c}\text{Predetermined} \\ \text{fixed-} \\ \text{overhead rate}\end{array}\right)\left(\begin{array}{c}\text{Planned} \\ \text{production} \\ \text{in units}\end{array}\right) - \left(\begin{array}{c}\text{Predetermined} \\ \text{fixed-} \\ \text{overhead rate}\end{array}\right)\left(\begin{array}{c}\text{Actual} \\ \text{production} \\ \text{in units}\end{array}\right)$$

When planned production equals actual production for the year, the volume variance is zero. This was the case in 19x7, 19x8, and 19x9 for our Orion Company illustration.

To show the effect of a volume variance on income reporting under absorption and variable costing, let's extend the data for Orion Company through the next three years. Exhibit 19–6 displays the data for 20x0, 20x1, and 20x2; Exhibit 19–7 shows comparative income statements for these three years.

Exhibit 19–6

Data for Illustration: Orion Company

	20x0	20x1	20x2
Production and inventory data:			
Planned production (in units)	50,000	50,000	50,000
Finished-goods inventory (in units), January 1	–0–	–0–	25,000
Actual production (in units)	50,000	60,000	40,000
Sales (in units)	50,000	35,000	55,000
Finished-goods inventory (in units), December 31	–0–	25,000	10,000

Revenue and cost data, all three years:		
Sales price per unit		$12
Standard manufacturing costs per unit:		
Direct material		$ 3
Direct labor		2
Variable manufacturing overhead		1
Total variable standard cost per unit		$ 6

	Fixed manufacturing overhead:		
Used only under absorption costing	$\dfrac{\text{Budgeted annual fixed overhead}}{\text{Planned annual production}} \quad \dfrac{\$150,000}{50,000}$	. . . .	$ 3

Total absorption cost per unit		$ 9
Variable selling and administrative cost per unit		$ 1
Fixed selling and administrative cost per year		$25,000

Variances, all three years:
There are no direct-material, direct-labor, or variable overhead variances.
Moreover, there is no fixed-overhead budget variance.

---

[2]This appendix should be studied after Chapter 11 has been completed, since it discusses the volume variance for fixed overhead.

Now there are three key places where the absorption-costing and variable-costing income statements differ. The absorption-costing statements include the fixed-overhead volume variance. But there is no volume variance on the variable-costing statements, because fixed overhead is not applied as a product cost under variable costing. Exhibit 19–8 reconciles Orion's reported income under the two alternative product-costing systems. The numbers in the left-hand margin correspond to those on the left-hand side of the income statements in Exhibit 19–7.

LO 6   After completing the appendix, explain the effects of the volume variance under absorption and variable costing.

	ORION COMPANY		
	Absorption-Costing Income Statement		
	20x0	**20x1**	**20x2**
Sales revenue (at $12 per unit)	$600,000	$420,000	$660,000
1 Less: Cost of goods sold (at standard			
absorption cost of $9 per unit)	450,000	315,000	495,000
Gross margin (at standard)	$150,000	$105,000	$165,000
2 Adjust for: Fixed-overhead			
volume variance	0*	30,000*	30,000*
Gross margin (at actual)	$150,000	$135,000	$135,000
Less: Selling and administrative expenses:			
3 No fixed Variable (at $1 per unit)	50,000	35,000	55,000
overhead Fixed	25,000	25,000	25,000
Net income	$ 75,000	$ 75,000	$ 55,000

*Computation of fixed-overhead volume variance:

$$\substack{\text{Fixed-overhead} \\ \text{volume variance}} = \substack{\text{Budgeted} \\ \text{fixed overhead}} - \substack{\text{Applied} \\ \text{fixed overhead}} = \substack{\text{Budgeted} \\ \text{fixed overhead}} - \left(\substack{\text{Predetermined fixed-} \\ \text{overhead rate}}\right)\left(\substack{\text{Actual} \\ \text{production}}\right)$$

20x0: Volume variance =   0 = $150,000 − ($3)(50,000)
20x1: Volume variance = −$30,000 = $150,000 − ($3)(60,000)
20x2: Volume variance = $30,000 = $150,000 − ($3)(40,000)

	ORION COMPANY		
	Variable-Costing Income Statement		
	20x0	**20x1**	**20x2**
Sales revenue (at $12 per unit)	$600,000	$420,000	$660,000
1 Less: Variable expenses:			
Variable manufacturing costs (at			
2 No volume standard variable cost of $6			
variance per unit)	300,000	210,000	330,000
Variable selling and administrative			
costs (at $1 per unit)	50,000	35,000	55,000
Contribution margin	$250,000	$175,000	$275,000
Less: Fixed expenses:			
3 Fixed manufacturing overhead	150,000	150,000	150,000
Fixed selling and administrative			
costs	25,000	25,000	25,000
Net income	$ 75,000	$ 0	$100,000

Exhibit 19–7

Income Statements under Absorption and Variable Costing

Exhibit 19–8			**20x0**	**20x1**	**20x2**
Reconciliation of Income under Absorption and Variable Costing: Orion Company	1	Cost of goods sold under absorption costing	$450,000	$315,000	$495,000
		Variable manufacturing costs under variable costing	300,000	210,000	330,000
		Subtotal	$150,000	$105,000	$165,000
	2	Volume variance under absorption costing	0	30,000*	30,000†
		Subtotal	$150,000	$ 75,000	$195,000
	3	Fixed manufacturing overhead as period expense under variable costing	150,000	150,000	150,000
		Total	$ 0	$(75,000)	$ 45,000
		Net income under variable costing	$ 75,000	$ 0	$100,000
		Net income under absorption costing	75,000	75,000	55,000
		Difference in net income	$ 0	$(75,000)	$ 45,000

*Negative volume variance.

†Positive volume variance.

Review Questions

19–1. Briefly explain the difference between absorption costing and variable costing.

19–2. Timing is the key in distinguishing between absorption and variable costing. Explain this statement.

19–3. The term *direct costing* is a misnomer. *Variable costing* is a better term for the product-costing method. Do you agree or disagree? Why?

19–4. When inventory increases, will absorption-costing or variable-costing income be greater? Why?

19–5. Why do many managers prefer variable costing over absorption costing?

19–6. Will variable and absorption costing result in significantly different income measures in a JIT setting? Why?

19–7. Why do proponents of absorption costing argue that absorption costing is preferable as the basis for pricing decisions?

19–8. Why do proponents of variable costing prefer variable costing when making pricing decisions?

19–9. Which is more consistent with cost-volume-profit analysis, variable costing or absorption costing? Why?

19–10. Explain how the accounting definition of an asset is related to the choice between absorption and variable costing.

Exercises

■ **Exercise 19–11**
Absorption versus Variable Costing.
(LO 1)

Information taken from Mohawk Paper Company's records for the most recent year is as follows:

Direct material used	$290,000
Direct labor	100,000
Variable manufacturing overhead	50,000
Fixed manufacturing overhead	80,000
Variable selling and administrative costs	40,000
Fixed selling and administrative costs	20,000

Required:

1. Assuming Mohawk Paper Company uses variable costing, compute the inventoriable costs for the year.

2. Compute the year's inventoriable costs using absorption costing.

(CMA, adapted)

■ **Exercise 19–12**
Difference in Income under Absorption and Variable Costing
(LO 1, LO 4)

Dolphin Company manufactures diving masks with a standard variable cost of $25. The masks sell for $34. Budgeted fixed manufacturing overhead for the most recent year was $792,000. Actual production was equal to planned production.

Required:

Under each of the following conditions, state (*a*) whether income is higher under variable or absorption costing and (*b*) the amount of the difference in reported income under the two methods. Treat each condition as an independent case.

1. Production	90,000 units
Sales	95,000 units
2. Production	110,000 units
Sales	108,000 units
3. Production	79,200 units
Sales	79,200 units

Plattsburgh Pillow Company's planned production for the year just ended was 10,000 units. This production level was achieved, but only 9,000 units were sold. Other data follows:

■ **Exercise 19–13**
Absorption and Variable Costing
(LO 1, LO 4)

Direct material used	$40,000
Direct labor incurred	20,000
Fixed manufacturing overhead	25,000
Variable manufacturing overhead	12,000
Fixed selling and administrative expenses	30,000
Variable selling and administrative expenses	4,500
Finished-goods inventory, January 1	None

There were no work-in process inventories at the beginning or end of the year.

Required:

1. What would be Plattsburgh Pillow Company's finished-goods inventory cost on December 31 under the variable-costing method?
2. Which costing method, absorption or variable costing, would show a higher operating income for the year? By what amount?

(CPA, adapted)

Moravia Pump Company's planned production for the year just ended was 20,000 units. This production level was achieved, and 21,000 units were sold. Other data follow:

■ **Exercise 19–14**
Absorption and Variable Costing
(LO 1, LO 4)

Direct material used	$600,000
Direct labor incurred	300,000
Fixed manufacturing overhead	420,000
Variable manufacturing overhead	200,000
Fixed selling and administrative expenses	350,000
Variable selling and administrative expenses	105,000
Finished-goods inventory, January 1	2,000 units

There were no work-in process inventories at the beginning or end of the year.

Required:

1. What would be Moravia Pump Company's finished-goods inventory cost on December 31 under the variable-costing method?
2. Which costing method, absorption or variable costing, would show a higher operating income for the year? By what amount?

(CMA, adapted)

Information taken from Seminole Pipe Company's records for the most recent year is as follows:

■ **Exercise 19–15**
Absorption versus Variable Costing
(LO 1)

Direct material used	$340,000
Direct labor	160,000
Variable manufacturing overhead	75,000
Fixed manufacturing overhead	125,000
Variable selling and administrative costs	70,000
Fixed selling and administrative costs	37,000

Required:

1. Assuming Seminole Pipe Company uses absorption costing, compute the inventoriable costs for the year.

2. Compute the year's inventoriable costs using variable costing.

(CMA, adapted)

■ **Exercise 19–16**
Difference in Income under Absorption and Variable Costing
(LO 1, LO 4)

Bianca Bicycle Company manufactures mountain bikes with a standard variable cost of $200. The bicycles sell for $350 each. Budgeted fixed manufacturing overhead for the most recent year was $2,200,000. Planned and actual production for the year were the same.

Required:

Under each of the following conditions, state (*a*) whether income is higher under variable or absorption costing and (*b*) the amount of the difference in reported income under the two methods. Treat each condition as an independent case.

1. Production	20,000 units
Sales	23,000 units
2. Production	10,000 units
Sales	10,000 units
3. Production	11,000 units
Sales	9,000 units

■ **Exercise 19–17**
Variable Costing and Cost-Volume-Profit Analysis.
(LO 5)

Refer to the data given in the preceding exercise for Bianca Bicycle Company.

Required:

1. Prepare a cost-volume-profit graph for the company. (Scale the vertical axis in millions of dollars, and draw the CVP graph up through 15,000 units on the horizontal axis.)

2. Calculate Bianca Bicycle Company's break-even point in units, and show the break-even point on the CVP graph.

3. Explain why variable costing is more compatible with your CVP graph than absorption costing would be.

Problems

■ **Problem 19–18**
Absorption and Variable Costing; CVP Analysis
(LO 2, LO 3, LO 4)

Blair Company began operations on January 1 to produce a single product. It used a standard absorption costing system with a planned production volume of 100,000 units. During its first year of operations, no variances were incurred and there were no fixed selling or administrative expenses. Inventory on December 31 was 20,000 units, and net income for the year was $240,000.

Required:

1. If Blair Company had used variable costing, its net income would have been $220,000. Compute the break-even point in units under variable costing.

2. Draw a profit-volume graph for Blair Company. (Use variable costing.)

■ **Problem 19–19**
Straightforward Problem on Absorption versus Variable Costing
(LO 2, LO 3, LO 4)

S

Skinny Dippers, Inc. produces frozen yogurt, a low-calorie dairy dessert. The product is sold in five-gallon containers, which have the following price and standard variable costs.

Sales price	$15
Direct material	5
Direct labor	2
Variable overhead	3

Budgeted fixed overhead in 19x9 was $300,000. Actual production was 150,000 five-gallon containers, of which 125,000 were sold. There were no variances recorded in 19x9. Skinny Dippers, Inc. incurred the following selling and administrative expenses.

Fixed	$50,000 for the year
Variable	$1 per container sold

Required:

1. Compute the standard product cost per container of frozen yogurt under (*a*) absorption costing and (*b*) variable costing.

2. Prepare income statements for 19x9 using (*a*) absorption costing and (*b*) variable costing.

3. Reconcile the income reported under the two methods by listing the two key places where the income statements differ.

4. Reconcile the income reported under the two methods using the shortcut method.

Valyn Corporation manufactures rechargeable flashlights in Melbourne, Australia. The firm uses a standard absorption costing system for internal reporting purposes; however, the company is considering using variable costing. Data regarding Valyn's planned and actual operations for 19x9 follow:

■ **Problem 19–20**
Variable versus Absorption Costing; JIT
(LO 1, LO 4)

	Planned Activity	Actual Activity
Beginning finished-goods inventory in units	35,000	35,000
Sales in units	140,000	125,000
Production in units	140,000	130,000

	Budgeted Costs		
	Per Unit	Total	Actual Costs
Direct material	$12.00	$1,680,000	$1,560,000
Direct labor	9.00	1,260,000	1,170,000
Variable manufacturing overhead	4.00	560,000	520,000
Fixed manufacturing overhead	5.00	700,000	715,000
Variable selling expenses	8.00	1,120,000	1,000,000
Fixed selling expenses	7.00	980,000	980,000
Variable administrative expenses	2.00	280,000	250,000
Fixed administrative expenses	3.00	420,000	425,000
Total	$50.00	$7,000,000	$6,620,000

The budgeted per-unit cost figures were based on Valyn producing and selling 140,000 units in 19x9. Valyn uses a predetermined overhead rate for applying manufacturing overhead to its product. A total manufacturing overhead rate of $9.00 per unit was employed for absorption costing purposes in 19x9. Any overapplied or underapplied manufacturing overhead is closed to the Cost of Goods Sold account at the end of the year. The 19x9 beginning finished-goods inventory for absorption costing purposes was valued at the 19x8 budgeted unit manufacturing cost, which was the same as the 19x9 budgeted unit manufacturing cost. There are no work-in-process inventories at either the beginning or the end of the year. The planned and actual unit selling price for 19x9 was $70 per unit.

Required:

Was Valyn's 19x9 income higher under absorption costing or variable costing? Why? Compute the following amounts.

1. The value of Valyn Corporation's 19x9 ending finished-goods inventory under absorption costing.

2. The value of Valyn Corporation's 19x9 ending finished-goods inventory under variable costing.

3. The difference between Valyn Corporation's 19x9 reported income calculated under absorption costing and calculated under variable costing.

4. Suppose Valyn Corporation had introduced a JIT production and inventory management system at the beginning of 19x9.

   a. What would likely be different about the scenario as described in the problem?

   b. Would reported income under variable and absorption costing differ by the magnitude you found in requirement (3)? Explain.

(CMA, adapted)

■ **Problem 19–21**
Variable and Absorption
Costing (Appendix)
(LO 4, LO 6)

Ellis Company had net income for the first 10 months of the current year of $200,000. They used a standard-costing system, and there were no variances through October 31. One hundred thousand units were manufactured during this period, and 100,000 units were sold. Fixed manufacturing overhead was $2,000,000 over the 10-month period (i.e., $200,000 per month). There are no selling and administrative expenses for Ellis Company. All variances are disposed of at year-end by an adjustment to cost of goods sold. Both variable and fixed costs are expected to continue at the same rates for the balance of the year (i.e., fixed costs at $200,000 per month and variable costs at the same variable cost per unit). There were 10,000 units in inventory on October 31. Seventeen thousand units are to be produced and 19,000 units are to be sold in total over the last two months of the current year. Assume the standard unit variable cost is the same in the current year as in the previous year. (Hint: You cannot calculate revenue or cost of goods sold; you must work directly with contribution margin or gross margin.)

Required:

1. If operations proceed as described, will net income be higher under variable or absorption costing for the current year in total? Why?

2. If operations proceed as described, what will net income for the year *in total* be under (a) variable costing and (b) absorption costing? (Ignore income taxes.)

■ **Problem 19–22**
Variable-Costing and
Absorption-Costing Income
Statements; FMS; JIT
(Appendix)
(LO 2, LO 3, LO 4, LO 6)

Great Outdoze Company manufactures sleeping bags, which sell for $65 each. The variable standard costs of production are as follows:

Direct material	$20
Direct labor	11
Variable manufacturing overhead	8

Budgeted fixed overhead in 19x9 was $200,000 and budgeted production was 20,000 sleeping bags. The year's actual production was 25,000 units, of which 22,000 were sold. There were no variances during 19x9, except for the fixed-overhead volume variance. Variable selling and administrative costs were $1 per unit sold; fixed selling and administrative costs were $30,000. The firm does not prorate variances.

Required:

1. Calculate the standard product cost per sleeping bag under (*a*) absorption costing and (*b*) variable costing.

2. Compute the fixed-overhead volume variance for 19x9.

3. Prepare income statements for the year using (*a*) absorption costing and (*b*) variable costing.

4. Reconcile reported income under the two methods using the shortcut method.

5. Suppose that Great Outdoze Company implemented a JIT inventory and production management system at the beginning of 19x9. In addition, the firm installed a flexible manufacturing system. Would you expect reported income under variable and absorption costing to be different by as great a magnitude as you found in requirement (3)? Explain.

■ **Problem 19–23**
Comparison of Absorption
and Variable Costing; Actual
Costing
(LO 2, LO 3, LO 4)

Lehighton Chalk Company manufactures blackboard chalk for educational uses. The company's product is sold by the box at $50 per unit. Lehighton uses an actual costing system, which means that the actual costs of direct material, direct labor, and manufacturing overhead are entered into work-in-process inventory. The actual application rate for manufacturing overhead is computed each year; actual manufacturing overhead is divided by actual production (in units) to compute the application rate. Information for Lehighton's first two years of operations is as follows:

	Year 1	Year 2
Sales (in units)	2,500	2,500
Production (in units)	3,000	2,000
Production costs:		
Variable manufacturing costs	$21,000	$14,000
Fixed manufacturing overhead	42,000	42,000
Selling and administrative costs:		
Variable	25,000	25,000
Fixed	20,000	20,000

Required:

Lehighton Chalk Company had no beginning or ending work-in-process inventories for either year.

1. Prepare operating income statements for both years based on absorption costing.
2. Prepare operating income statements for both years based on variable costing.
3. Prepare a numerical reconciliation of the difference in income reported under the two costing methods used in requirements (1) and (2).

Refer to the information given in the preceding problem for Lehighton Chalk Company.

Required:

1. Reconcile Lehighton's income reported under absorption and variable costing, during each year, by comparing the following two amounts on each income statement:

   ■ Cost of goods sold
   ■ Fixed cost (expensed as a period expense)

2. What was Lehighton's total income across both years under absorption costing and under variable costing?
3. What was the total sales revenue across both years under absorption costing and under variable costing?
4. What was the total of all costs expensed on the income statements across both years under absorption costing, and under variable costing?
5. Subtract the total costs expensed across both years (requirement 4) from the total sales revenue across both years (requirement 3): (*a*) under absorption costing and (*b*) under variable costing.
6. Comment on the results obtained in requirements (1), (2), (3), and (4) in light of the following assertion: *Timing is the key in distinguishing between absorption and variable costing.*

■ **Problem 19–24**
Analysis of Differences in Absorption-Costing and Variable-Costing Income Statements; Continuation of Preceding Problem
(LO 1, LO 4)

Refer to the information given in Problem 19–23 for Lehighton Chalk Company. Selected information from Lehighton's year-end balance sheets for its first two years of operation is as follows:

■ **Problem 19–25**
Absorption and Variable Costing; Effect on the Balance Sheet; Continuation of Preceding Problem
(LO 1, LO 4)

LEHIGHTON CHALK COMPANY
Selected Balance Sheet Information

Based on absorption costing	End of Year 1	End of Year 2
Finished-goods inventory	$10,500	$0
Retained earnings	16,500	24,600
Based on variable costing	**End of Year 1**	**End of Year 2**
Finished-goods inventory	$3,500	$0
Retained earnings	9,500	24,600

Required:

1. Why is the year 1 ending balance in finished-goods inventory higher if absorption costing is used than if variable costing is used?
2. Why is the year 2 ending balance in finished-goods inventory the same under absorption and variable costing?
3. Notice that the ending balance of finished-goods inventory under absorption costing is greater than or equal to the ending finished-goods inventory balance under variable costing *for both years 1 and 2*. Will this relationship always hold true at any balance sheet date? Explain.
4. Compute the amount by which the year-end balance in finished-goods inventory declined during year 2 (i.e., between December 31 of year 1 and December 31 of year 2):

   ■ Using the data from the balance sheet prepared under absorption costing.
   ■ Using the data from the balance sheet prepared under variable costing.

5. Refer to your calculations from requirement (4). Compute the difference in the amount by which the year-end balances in finished-goods inventory declined under absorption versus variable costing. Then compare the amount of this difference with the difference in the company's reported income for year 2 under absorption versus variable costing. (Refer to the income statements prepared in Problem 19–23.)

6. Notice that the retained earnings balance at the end of both years 1 and 2 on the balance sheet prepared under absorption costing is greater than or equal to the corresponding retained earnings balance on the statement prepared under variable costing. Will this relationship hold true at any balance sheet date? Explain.

■ **Problem 19–26**
Variable-Costing and
Absorption Costing Income
Statement; Reconciling
Reported Income
(LO 2, LO 3, LO 4)

Tonowanda Can Company manufactures cans used in the food-processing industry. A case of cans sells for $50. The variable standard costs of production for one case of cans are as follows:

Direct material	$15
Direct labor	5
Variable manufacturing overhead	12
Total variable manufacturing cost per case	$32

Variable selling and administrative costs amount to $1 per case. Budgeted fixed manufacturing overhead is $800,000 per year, and fixed selling and administrative cost is $75,000 per year. The following data pertain to the company's first three years of operation.

	Year 1	Year 2	Year 3
Planned production (in units)	80,000	80,000	80,000
Finished-goods inventory (in units), January 1	0	0	20,000
Actual production (in units)	80,000	80,000	80,000
Sales (in units)	80,000	60,000	90,000
Finished-goods inventory (in units), December 31	0	20,000	10,000

There were no variances during Tonowanda's first three years of operation. Actual costs were the same as the budgeted and standard costs.

Required:

1. Prepare operating income statements for Tonowanda Can Company for its first three years of operations using:
   a. Absorption costing.
   b. Variable costing.

2. Reconcile Tonowanda Can Company's operating income reported under absorption and variable costing for each of its first three years of operation. Use the shortcut method.

3. Suppose that during Tonowanda's fourth year of operation actual production equals planned production, actual costs are equal to budgeted or standard costs, and the company ends the year with no inventory on hand.
   a. What will be the difference between absorption-costing income and variable-costing income in year 4?
   b. What will be the relationship between total operating income for the four-year period as reported under absorption and variable costing? Explain.

Case

■ **Case 19–27**
Absorption and Variable
Costing: Reconciling
Reported Income; Balance
Sheet Effects; Ethics;
Appendix
(LO 4, LO 6)

Joe Duval was proud of the way he had guided Screen Technology Company over the past year since he had accepted the job as the company's president. Under Duval's direction, the privately held company's sales had grown each quarter, and several new sales contacts in Europe looked promising for future business. Duval had taken a personal interest in developing new business, and the company's future looked bright. Duval had also seen to it that the company's costs had remained in check. One of the new president's first moves had been to benchmark several of Screen Technology's performance measures against other high-tech electronics firms. Duval was convinced that the company's production technology and business practices were as efficient as any firm in the business.

Screen Technology Company had been formed some five years earlier to manufacture aperture masks, which are an important component in computer monitors and TV picture tubes. Aperture masks direct a beam of electrons to the red, blue, and green phosphor stripes on the inside face of a picture tube. Thus, the aperture mask is a critical component in the creation of a color picture on the computer monitor or TV tube. Ranging in size from 18 to 90 centimeters. Screen Technology's masks are manufactured from nickel alloy. Several patented manufacturing steps are used to produce the aperture masks, including highly accurate photographic and etching processes, chemical coating processes, and cleaning processes. Screen Technology's masks already were being marketed in North America and Asia, and negotiations were proceeding with several potential European customers.

At the beginning of his second year on the job, Duval had been looking forward to the fourth quarter financial statements. Upon reading the financial reports, though, Duval was dismayed when he saw that Screen Technology's fourth quarter profit was actually lower than that reported in the third quarter. "What's going on here?" he thought. Duval picked up the phone to call Alison West, Screen Technology's controller, for an explanation.

Shown here are the third and fourth quarter income statements that were perplexing Duval.

SCREEN TECHNOLOGY COMPANY
Income Statements
For the 3rd and 4th Quarters of 20x0

	3rd Quarter	4th Quarter
Sales revenue	$6,300,000	$9,900,000
Less: Cost of goods sold (at standard absorption cost)	4,725,000	7,425,000
Gross margin (at standard)	$1,575,000	$2,475,000
Adjust for: Fixed overhead volume variance*	450,000	450,000
Gross margin (at actual)	$2,025,000	$2,025,000
Less: Selling and administrative expenses	900,000	1,200,000
Net income	$1,125,000	$ 825,000

*There were no other variances during the 3rd or 4th quarters of 20x0. The 3rd quarter volume variance is negative, and the 4th quarter volume variance is positive.

When Alison West arrived at Joe Duval's office, she could see the president was upset and puzzled. "You're the controller, Alison," began Duval. "I hope you have a good explanation for this. When sales go up from one quarter to the next, and production efficiency and standard costs remain about the same, I would expect profits to increase also. And I can assure you that our owners will expect increased profits, too, when I go to the quarterly meeting next week."

West tried to explain to Duval why Screen Technology's profit had fallen, even though sales had risen substantially. "Our financial statements are prepared using absorption costing," explained West. "This means that all manufacturing costs are treated as product costs. Direct material, direct labor, and all manufacturing overhead costs are stored in inventory until the units are sold. It's true that sales rose during the fourth quarter, but production did not keep pace with sales. In fact, actual fourth quarter production was somewhat lower even than our planned production for the quarter. When that happens, we end up expensing fixed manufacturing overhead during the current period, even though it was incurred during a pervious period."

"Well, I'm no accountant," retorted Duval. "I'm an engineer and I've spent most of my career in marketing. But this just doesn't seem reasonable to me. If sales go up, and production efficiency remains more or less the same, then I still think income ought to go up. I was counting on a bonus this quarter, and I would think you would've been expecting one, too. Can't you produce an income statement where profits increase when sales increase?"

"Yes, I can, Joe," replied the controller. "I can use a method called variable costing instead of absorption costing. Under that method, fixed manufacturing overhead is expensed during the period it's incurred. That effectively eliminates the kind of distortion that's bothering you. Since Screen Tech is a privately held company, we can use either method we want. The owners should be informed if we change methods, though. And they should also be made aware of the effect of the change on executive bonuses."

"I think we should change to the other method, then," responded Duval. "What'd you call it? Variable costing, was it?"

"That's right, Joe. It's called variable costing because only variable manufacturing costs are inventoried."

"Okay, here's what I would like you to do, Alison. Please prepare third-quarter and fourth-quarter income statements for me using variable costing. Then come along with me to next week's meeting and explain to our bosses why the results differ."

"You got it," replied West. "And I'll show you the effect of the accounting method change on the balance sheet also."

"That sounds good," replied Duval. "By the way, is there a down side to variable costing? What do you see as the advantages and disadvantages?"

Before West could respond, Duval got a phone call from an important customer. Before meeting with Duval again to answer his last question, West prepared the following third-quarter and fourth-quarter income statements. She also summarized the effect of the proposed accounting method change on Screen Technology's comparative balance sheets.

SCREEN TECHNOLOGY COMPANY
Income Statements
For the 3rd and 4th Quarters of 20x0
(prepared using variable costing)

	3rd Quarter	4th Quarter
Sales revenue	$6,300,000	$9,900,000
Less: Variable expenses:		
Variable manufacturing costs (at standard variable cost)*	3,150,000	4,950,000
Variable selling and administrative costs	525,000	825,000
Contribution margin	$2,625,000	$4,125,000
Less: Fixed expenses:		
Fixed manufacturing overhead	2,250,000	2,250,000
Fixed selling and administrative costs	375,000	375,000
Net income	$ 0	$1,500,000

*There were no variances during the 3rd or 4th quarters of 20x0.

SCREEN TECHNOLOGY COMPANY
Selected Balance Sheet Information
For the Quarters Ending 9/30/x0 and 12/31/x0

Balance sheets prepared using absorption costing	9/30/x0	12/31/x0
Inventory	$3,375,000	$1,350,000
Retained earnings	4,250,000	5,075,000

Balance sheets prepared using variable costing	9/30/x0	12/31/x0
Inventory	$2,250,000	$ 900,000
Retained earnings	3,125,000	4,625,000

Required:

1. How would you respond to the president's last question to the controller regarding the pros and cons of variable and absorption costing?

2. Prepare a reconciliation of the reported fourth-quarter income under variable and absorption costing.

3. Explain how and why the balance sheets differ under variable and absorption costing.

4. Would there be differences in reported income under variable and absorption costing if the statements had been annual statements instead of quarterly statements? Explain.

5. Roughly how busy was Screen Technology's production operation during the fourth quarter relative to the expected production volume? Explain.

6. Discuss the following comment made by Duval to West the next afternoon. Citing specific ethical standards for managerial accountants (given in Chapter 1), explain how West should respond.

   "Alison, I've been thinking about this whole issue some more. Why don't we just choose between variable and absorption costing each quarter, depending on which will report the highest profit for the quarter and give us the biggest bonuses?"

Current Issues in Managerial Accounting

"The Satellite Biz Blasts Off," *Business Week,* **January 27, 1997.**

Overview

Communications satellite applications include wireless television and telephone systems. The technological innovations have created intense demand for satellite systems.

Suggested Discussion Questions

Firms such as Lockheed Martin and McDonnell Douglas compete globally in the satellite launching market. The industry is plagued by high costs. List five to ten types of overhead costs incurred by satellite launch providers. What effect would launch volume have on prices? Should prices be based on variable or absorption costing? Present your conclusions to the class.

"Investors Set Sights Too High in Profit Season," *The Wall Street Journal,* **October 20, 1997.**

Overview

Investors began selling high-tech stocks despite the fact that firms reported higher profits. One analyst attributed the sell-off to Intel's announced lower-than-expected third-quarter profit.

Suggested Discussion Questions

Using cost-volume-profit (CVP) analysis, discuss what factors could have led to Intel's profit decline. Repeat your analysis assuming volume remains constant. What factors could cause a temporary or seasonal change? Is variable or absorption costing more consistent with CVP analysis?

"Hewlett-Packard to Unveil Sub-$800 PCs Using Intel's Latest MMX Technology," *The Wall Street Journal,* **January 5, 1998.**

Overview

Hewlett-Packard (HP) announced that it will sell 200 megahertz Pentium PCs with MMX technology for $799. The price is $200 below the cheapest computers with similar specifications.

Suggested Discussion Questions

As a group, explain how the following five factors could have influenced Hewlett-Packard's pricing decision.

1. Customer demand.
2. Actions of competitors.
3. Costs.
4. Political, legal, and image-related issues.
5. Variable versus absorption costing.

■ **Issue 19–28**
Evaluation of Absorption and Variable Costing

■ **Issue 19–29**
Variable and Absorption Costing; Cost-Volume-Profit Analysis

■ **Issue 19–30**
Variable and Absorption Costing; Pricing

Glossary

absorption costing (or full costing) A method of product costing in which both variable and fixed manufacturing overhead are included in the product costs that flow through the manufacturing accounts (i.e., Work-in-Process Inventory, Finished-Goods Inventory, and Cost of Goods Sold).

Accelerated Cost Recovery System (ACRS) The depreciation schedule specified by the United States tax code. Since it has been modified by recent tax law changes, the system also is called the Modified Accelerated Cost Recovery System (MACRS).

acceptance-or-rejection decision A decision as to whether or not a particular capital investment proposal should be accepted.

account-classification method (also called account analysis) A cost-estimation method involving a careful examination of the ledger accounts for the purpose of classifying each cost as variable, fixed, or semivariable.

accounting rate of return A percentage formed by taking a project's average incremental revenue minus its average incremental expenses (including depreciation and income taxes) and dividing by the project's initial investment.

accumulation factor The value of $(1 + r)^n$, in a future value calculation, where r denotes the interest rate per year and n denotes the number of years.

accurate information Precise and correct data.

activity A measure of an organization's output of goods or services.

activity accounting The collection of financial or operational performance information about significant activities in an enterprise.

activity analysis The detailed identification and description of the activities conducted in an enterprise.

activity base (or cost driver) A measure of an organization's activity that is used as a basis for specifying cost behavior. The activity base also is used to compute a predetermined overhead rate. The current trend is to refer to the activity base as a volume-based cost driver.

activity-based costing (ABC) system A two-stage procedure used to assign overhead costs to products or services produced. In the first stage, significant activities are identified, and overhead costs are assigned to activity cost pools in accordance with the way resources are consumed by the activities. In the second stage, the overhead costs are allocated from each activity cost pool to each product line in proportion to the amount of the cost driver consumed by the product line.

activity-based flexible budget A flexible budget based on several cost drivers rather than on a single, volume-based cost driver.

activity-based management (ABM) Using an activity-based costing system to improve the operations of an organization.

activity-based responsibility accounting A system for measuring the performance of an organization's people and subunits, which focuses not only on the cost of performing activities but on the activities themselves.

activity cost pool A grouping of overhead costs assigned to various similar activities identified in an activity-based costing system.

actual costing A product-costing system in which actual direct-material, direct-labor, and *actual* manufacturing-overhead costs are added to Work-in-Process Inventory.

actual manufacturing overhead The actual costs incurred during an accounting period for manufacturing overhead. Includes actual indirect material, indirect labor, and other manufacturing costs.

actual overhead rate The rate at which overhead costs are actually incurred during an accounting period. Calculated as follows: actual manufacturing overhead ÷ actual cost driver (or activity base).

administrative costs All costs associated with the management of an organization as a whole.

after-tax cash flow The cash flow expected after all tax implications have been taken into account.

after-tax net income An organization's net income after its income-tax expense is subtracted.

aggregate (or total) productivity Total output divided by total input.

allocation base A measure of activity, physical characteristic, or economic characteristic that is associated with the responsibility centers which are the cost objects in an allocation process.

annuity A series of equivalent cash flows.

applied manufacturing overhead The amount of manufacturing-overhead costs added to Work-in-Process Inventory during an accounting period.

appraisal costs Costs of determining whether defective products exist.

attention-directing function The function of managerial-accounting information in pointing out to managers issues that need their attention.

automated material-handling system (AMHS) Computer-controlled equipment that automatically moves materials, parts, and products from one production stage to another.

average cost per unit The total cost of producing a particular quantity of product divided by the number of units produced.

avoidable expenses Expenses that will no longer be incurred if a particular action is taken.

bar code technology The use of symbolic codes, which are scanned automatically and read into a computer, to record the use of labor and materials, track work in process and finished goods, and record other production-related information.

base budgeting The initial budget for each of an organization's departments is set in accordance with a base package under an approach called base budgeting.

base package An initial budget that includes the minimal resources needed for a subunit to exist at an absolute minimal level.

batch-level activity An activity that must be accomplished for each batch of products rather than for each unit.

batch manufacturing High-volume production of several product lines that differ in some important ways but are nearly identical in others.

before-tax income An organization's income before its income-tax expense is subtracted.

benchmarking (or competitive benchmarking) The continual search for the most effective method of accomplishing a task, by comparing existing methods and performance levels with those of other organizations or with other subunits within the same organization.

best practices The most effective methods of accomplishing various tasks in a particular industry, often discovered through benchmarking.

bill of materials A list of all the materials needed to manufacture a product or product component.

break-even point The volume of activity at which an organization's revenues and expenses are equal. May be measured either in units or in sales dollars.

budget A detailed plan, expressed in quantitative terms, that specifies how resources will be acquired and used during a specified period of time.

budget administration The procedures used to prepare a budget, secure its approval, and disseminate it to the people who need to know its contents.

budgetary slack The difference between the budgetary projection provided by an individual and his or her best estimate of the item being projected. (For example, the difference between a supervisor's expected departmental utility cost and his or her budgetary projection for utilities.)

budget committee A group of top-management personnel who advise the budget director during the preparation of the budget.

budget director (or chief budget officer) The individual designated to be in charge of preparing an organization's budget.

budgeted balance sheet A planned balance sheet showing the expected end-of-period balances for the organization's assets, liabilities, and owners' equity, assuming that planned operations are carried out.

budgeted financial statements (or pro forma financial statements) A set of planned financial statements showing what an organization's overall financial condition is expected to be at the end of the budget period if planned operations are carried out.

budgeted income statement A planned income statement showing the expected revenue and expenses for the budget period, assuming that planned operations are carried out.

budgeting system The set of procedures used to develop a budget.

budget manual A set of written instructions that specifies who will provide budgetary data, when and in what form the data will be provided, how the master budget will be prepared and approved, and who should receive the various schedules comprising the budget.

budget period The time period covered by a budget.

by-product A joint product with very little value relative to the other joint products.

CAD/CAM system See **computer-aided design** and **computer-aided manufacturing**.

capital budget A long-term budget that shows planned acquisition and disposal of capital assets, such as land, building, and equipment.

capital-budgeting decision A decision involving cash flows beyond the current year.

capital-intensive A production process accomplished largely by machinery.

capital-rationing decision A decision in which management chooses which of several investment proposals to accept to make the best use of limited investment funds.

capital turnover Sales revenue divided by invested capital.

cash bonus See **pay for performance**.

cash disbursements budget A schedule detailing expected cash payments during a budget period.

cash equivalents Short-term, highly liquid investments that are treated as equivalent to cash in the preparation of a statement of cash flows.

cash provided by (or used by) operations The difference between the cash receipts and cash disbursements that are related to operating activities.

cash receipts budget A schedule detailing the expected cash collections during the budget period.

cellular manufacturing The organization of a production facility into FMS cells.

Certified Management Accountant (CMA) An accountant who has earned professional certification in managerial accounting.

change champion An individual who recognizes the need for change and seeks to bring it about through his or her own effort.

coefficient of determination A statistical measure of goodness of fit; a measure of how closely a regression line fits the data on which it is based.

committed cost A cost that results from an organization's ownership or use of facilities and its basic organization structure.

common costs Costs incurred to benefit more than one organizational segment.

common-size financial statements Financial statements prepared in terms of percentages of a base amount.

comparative financial statements Financial statements showing the results of two or more successive years.

competitive benchmarking See **benchmarking**.

competitive bidding A situation where two or more companies submit bids (prices) for a product, service, or project to a potential buyer.

compound interest The phenomenon in which interest is earned on prior periods' interest.

computer-aided design (CAD) system Computer software used by engineers in the design of a product.

computer-aided manufacturing (CAM) system Any production process in which computers are used to help control production.

computer-integrated manufacturing (CIM) system The most advanced form of automated manufacturing, in which virtually all parts of the production process are accomplished by computer-controlled machines and automated material-handling equipment.

computer-numerically-controlled (CNC) machines Stand-alone machines controlled by a computer via a numerical, machine-readable code.

constraints Algebraic expressions of limitations faced by a firm, such as those limiting its productive resources.

consumption ratio The proportion of an activity consumed by a particular product.

continuous improvement The constant effort to eliminate waste, reduce response time, simplify the design of both products and processes, and improve quality and customer service.

contribution income statement An income statement on which fixed and variable expenses are separated.

contribution margin Sales revenue minus variable expenses. The amount of sales revenue, which is left to cover fixed expenses and profit after paying variable expenses.

contribution margin per unit The difference between the unit sales price and the unit variable expense. The amount that each unit contributes to covering fixed expenses and profit.

contribution-margin ratio The unit contribution margin divided by the sales price per unit. May also be expressed in percentage form; then it is called the contribution-margin percentage.

control factor unit A measure of work or activity used in work measurement.

controllability The extent to which managers are able to control or influence a cost or cost variance.

controllable cost A cost that is subject to the control or substantial influence of a particular individual.

controller (or comptroller) The top managerial and financial accountant in an organization. Supervises the accounting department and assists management at all levels in interpreting and using managerial-accounting information.

controlling Ensuring that an organization operates in the intended manner and achieves its goals.

conversion costs Direct-labor cost plus manufacturing-overhead cost.

cost The sacrifice made, usually measured by the resources given up, to achieve a particular purpose.

Cost Accounting Standards Cost-accounting procedures specified by the Cost Accounting Standards Board, an agency of the federal government.

Cost Accounting Standards Board (CASB) A federal agency chartered by Congress in 1970 to develop cost-accounting standards for large government contractors.

cost-accounting system Part of the basic accounting system that accumulates cost for use in both managerial and financial accounting.

cost allocation The process of assigning costs in a cost pool to the appropriate cost objects. Also see cost distribution.

cost behavior The relationship between cost and activity.

cost center A responsibility center whose manager is accountable for its costs.

cost distribution (sometimes called cost allocation) The first step in assigning manufacturing-overhead costs. Overhead costs are assigned to all departmental overhead centers.

cost driver A characteristic of an activity or event that results in the incurrence of costs by that activity or event.

cost estimation The process of determining how a particular cost behaves.

cost management system (CMS) A management planning and controlling system that measures the cost of significant activities, identifies non-value-added costs, and identifies activities that will improve organizational performance.

cost objects Responsibility centers, products, or services to which costs are assigned.

cost of capital The cost of acquiring resources for an organization, either through debt or through the issuance of stock.

cost of goods manufactured The total cost of direct labor, direct material, and overhead transferred from Work-in-Process Inventory to Finished-Goods Inventory during an accounting period.

cost of goods sold The expense measured by the cost of the finished goods sold during a period of time.

cost-plus pricing A pricing approach in which the price is equal to cost plus a markup.

cost pool A collection of costs to be assigned to a set of cost objects.

cost prediction Forecast of cost at a particular level of activity.

cost structure The relative proportions of an organization's fixed and variable costs.

cost variance The difference between actual and standard cost.

cost-volume-profit (CVP) analysis A study of the relationships between sales volume, expenses, revenue, and profit.

cost-volume-profit (CVP) graph A graphical expression of the relationships between sales volume, expenses, revenue, and profit.

cross-elasticity The extent to which a change in a product's price affects the demand for substitute products.

curvilinear cost A cost with a curved line for its graph.

customer-acceptance measures The extent to which a firm's customers perceive its product to be of high quality.

customer profitability analysis Using the concepts of activity-based costing to determine how servicing particular customers causes activities to be performed and costs to be incurred.

cycle time See **throughput time**.

decentralization   A form of organization in which subunit managers are given authority to make substantive decisions.

decision making   Choosing between alternatives.

decision variables   The variables in a linear program about which a decision is made.

delivery cycle time   The average time between the receipt of a customer order and delivery of the goods.

demand curve   A graph of the relationship between sales price and the quantity of units sold.

departmental overhead center   Any department to which overhead costs are assigned via overhead cost distribution.

departmental overhead rate   An overhead rate calculated for a single production department.

departmental production report   The key document in a process-costing system. This report summarizes the physical flow of units, equivalent units of production, cost per equivalent unit, and analysis of total departmental costs.

dependent variable   A variable whose value depends on other variables, called *independent variables.*

depreciation tax shield   The reduction in a firm's income-tax expense due to the depreciation expense associated with a depreciable asset.

differential cost   The difference in a cost item under two decision alternatives.

direct cost   A cost that can be traced to a particular department or other subunit of an organization.

direct-exchange (or noncash) transaction   A significant investing or financing transaction involving accounts other than cash, such as a transaction where land is obtained in exchange for the issuance of capital stock.

directing operational activities   Running an organization on a day-to-day basis.

direct labor   The costs of compensating employees who work directly on a firm's product. Should include wages, salary, and associated fringe benefits.

direct-labor budget   A schedule showing the amount and cost of direct labor to be used in production of services or goods during a budget period.

direct-labor cost   The cost of salaries, wages, and fringe benefits for personnel who work directly on the manufactured products.

direct-labor efficiency variance   The difference between actual and standard hours of direct labor multiplied by the standard hourly labor rate.

direct-labor rate variance   The difference between actual and standard hourly labor rate multiplied by the actual hours of direct labor used.

direct-material budget   A schedule showing the number of units and the cost of material to be purchased and used during a budget period.

direct-material price variance (or purchase price variance)   The difference between actual and standard price multiplied by the actual quantity of material purchased.

direct-material quantity variance   The difference between actual and standard quantity of materials allowed, given actual output, multiplied by the standard price.

direct material   Raw material that is physically incorporated in the finished product.

direct method (of preparing the statement of cash flows)   A method of preparing the operating activities section of a statement of cash flows. A cash-basis income statement is constructed in which operating cash disbursements are subtracted from operating cash receipts.

direct method (of service department cost allocation)   A method of service department cost allocation in which service department costs are allocated directly to the production departments.

discounted-cash-flow analysis   An analysis of an investment proposal that takes into account the time value of money.

discount rate   The interest rate used in computing the present value of a cash flow.

discretionary cost   A cost that results from a discretionary management decision to spend a particular amount of money.

distribution cost   The cost of storing and transporting finished goods for sale.

dual cost allocation   An approach to service department cost allocation in which variable costs are allocated in proportion to short-term usage and fixed costs are allocated in proportion to long-term usage.

economic order quantity (EOQ)   The order size that minimizes inventory ordering and holding costs.

economic value analysis   See **shareholder value analysis**.

electronic data interchange (or EDI)   The direct exchange between organizations of data via a computer-to-computer interface.

empowerment   The concept of encouraging and authorizing workers to take the initiative to improve operations, reduce costs, and improve product quality and customer service.

engineered cost   A cost that results from a definitive physical relationship with the activity measure.

engineering method   A cost-estimation method in which a detailed study is made of the process that results in cost incurrence.

equivalent unit   A measure of the amount of production effort applied to a physical unit of production. For example, a physical unit that is 50 percent completed represents one-half of an equivalent unit.

estimated manufacturing overhead   The amount of manufacturing-overhead cost expected for a specified period of time. Used as the numerator in computing the pre-determined overhead rate.

expected value   The sum of the possible values for a random variable, each weighted by its probability.

expense   The consumption of assets for the purpose of generating revenue.

experience curve   A graph (or other mathematical representation) that shows how a broad set of costs decline as cumulative production output increases.

external failure costs   Costs incurred because defective products have been sold.

facility (or general-operations) level activity   An activity that is required for an entire production process to occur.

feasible region   The possible values for decision variables which are not ruled out by constraints.

FIFO (first-in, first-out) method   A method of process costing in which the cost assigned to the beginning work-in-process inventory is not added to current-period production costs. The cost per equivalent unit calculated under FIFO relates to the current period only.

financial accounting   The use of accounting information for reporting to parties outside the organization.

financial budget   A schedule that outlines how an organization will acquire financial resources during the budget period (for example, through borrowing or sale of capital stock).

financial leverage   The concept that a relatively small increase in income can provide a proportionately much larger increase in return to the common stock-holders.

financing activities   Transactions involving a company's debt or equity capital.

finished goods   Completed products awaiting sale.

fixed cost   A cost that does not change in total as activity changes.

fixed-overhead budget variance   The difference between actual and budgeted fixed overhead.

fixed-overhead volume variance   The difference between budget and applied fixed overhead.

flexible budget   A budget that is valid for a range of activity.

flexible manufacturing system (FMS)   A series of manufacturing machines, controlled and integrated by a computer, which is designed to perform a series of manufacturing operations automatically.

FMS cell   A group of machines and personnel within a flexible manufacturing system (FMS).

full (or absorption) cost   A product's variable cost plus an allocated portion of fixed overhead.

future value   The amount to which invested funds accumulate over a specified period of time.

gain-sharing plan   An incentive system that specified a formula by which the cost savings from productivity gains achieved by a company are shared with the workers who helped accomplish the improvements.

goal congruence   A meshing of objectives, where managers throughout an organization strive to achieve the goals set by top management.

goodness of fit   The closeness with which a regression line fits the data upon which it is based.

grade   The extent of a product's capability in performing its intended purpose, viewed in relation to other products with the same functional use.

high-low method   A cost-estimation method in which a cost line is fit using exactly two data points—the high and low activity levels.

homogeneous cost pool   A grouping of overhead costs in which each cost component is consumed in roughly the same proportion by each product line.

horizontal analysis   An analysis of the year-to-year change in each financial statement item.

hurdle rate   The minimum desired rate of return used in a discounted-cash-flow analysis.

hybrid product-costing system   A system that incorporates features from two or more alternative product-costing systems, such as job-order and process costing.

idle time   Unproductive time spent by employees due to factors beyond their control, such as power outages and machine breakdowns.

imperfect competition   A market in which a single producer or group of producers can affect the market price.

incentive compensation   See **pay for performance**.

incremental package   A budget detailing the additional resources needed to add various activities to a base package.

incremental cost   The amount by which the cost of one action exceeds that of another. See also **differential cost.**

independent variable   The variable upon which an estimate is based in least-squares regression analysis.

indirect cost   A cost that cannot be traced to a particular department.

indirect labor   All costs of compensating employees who do not work directly on the firm's product but who are necessary for production to occur.

indirect-labor budget   A schedule showing the amount and cost of indirect labor to be used during a budget period.

indirect materials   Materials that either are required for the production process to occur but do not become an integral part of the finished product, or are consumed in production but are insignificant in cost.

indirect method (or reconciliation method)   A method of preparing the operating activities section of a statement of cash flows, in which the analyst begins with net income. Then adjustments are made to convert from an accrual-basis income statement to a cash-basis income statement.

information overload   The provision of so much information that, due to human limitations in processing information, managers cannot effectively use it.

in-process quality controls   Procedures designed to assess product quality before production is completed.

inspection time   The time spent on quality inspections of raw materials, partially completed products, or finished goods.

internal auditor   An accountant who reviews the accounting procedures, records, and reports in both the controller's and treasurer's areas of responsibility.

internal control system   The set of procedures designed to ensure that an organization's employees act in a legal, ethical, and responsible manner.

internal failure costs   Costs of correcting defects found prior to product sale.

internal rate of return   The discount rate required for an investment's net present value to be zero.

inventoriable cost   Costs incurred to purchase or manufacture goods. Also see **product costs**.

inventoriable goods   Goods that can be stored before sale, such as durable goods, mining products, and some agricultural products.

inventory budgets   Schedules that detail the amount and cost of finished-goods, work-in-process, and direct-material inventories expected at the end of a budget period.

investing activities   Transactions involving the extension or collection of loans, acquisition or disposal of investments, and purchase or sale of productive, long-lived assets.

investment center   A responsibility center whose manager is accountable for its profit and for the capital invested to generate that profit.

investment opportunity rate   The rate of return an organization can earn on its best alternative investments that are of equivalent risk.

ISO 9000 standards   International quality-control standards issued by the International Standards Organization.

job-cost sheet   A document that records the costs of direct material, direct labor, and manufacturing overhead for a particular production job or batch. The job-cost sheet is a subsidiary ledger account for the Work-in-Process Inventory account in the general ledger.

job-order costing system   A product-costing system in which costs are assigned to batches or job orders of production. Used by firms that produce relatively small numbers of dissimilar products.

joint cost   The cost incurred in a joint production process before the joint products become identifiable as separate products.

joint production process   A production process that results in two or more joint products.

joint products   The outputs of a joint production process.

just-in-time (JIT) inventory and production management system   A comprehensive inventory and manufacturing control system in which no materials are purchased and no products are manufactured until they are needed.

just-in-time (JIT) purchasing   An approach to purchasing management in which materials and parts are purchased only as they are needed.

kaizen costing   The process of cost reduction during the manufacturing phase of a product. Refers to continual and gradual improvement through small betterment activities.

labor-intensive   A production process accomplished largely by manual labor.

lead time   The time required to receive inventory after it has been ordered.

learning curve   A graphical expression of the decline in the average labor time required per unit as cumulative output increases.

least-squares regression method   A cost-estimation method in which the cost line is fit to the data by statistical analysis. The method minimizes the sum of the squared deviations between the cost line and the data points.

line positions   Positions held by managers who are directly involved in providing the goods or services that constitute an organization's primary goals.

make-or-buy (or outsourcing) decision   A decision as to whether a product or service should be produced in-house or purchased from an outside supplier.

management by exception   A managerial technique in which only significant deviations from expected performance are investigated.

management by objectives (MBO)   The process of designating the objectives of each subunit in an organization and planning for the achievement of these objectives. Managers at all levels participate in setting goals, which they then will strive to achieve.

managerial accounting   The process of identifying, measuring, analyzing, interpreting and communicating information in pursuit of an organization's goals.

manufacturing   The process of converting raw materials into finished products.

manufacturing costs   Cost incurred in a manufacturing process, which consist of direct material, direct labor, and manufacturing overhead.

manufacturing cycle efficiency (MCE)   The ratio of process time to the sum of processing time, inspection time, waiting time, and move time.

manufacturing cycle time   The total amount of production time (or throughput time) required per unit.

manufacturing overhead   All manufacturing costs other than direct-material and direct-labor costs.

manufacturing-overhead variance   The difference between actual overhead cost and the amount specified in the flexible budget.

marketing cost   The cost incurred in selling goods or services. Includes order-getting costs and order-filling or distribution costs.

marginal cost   The extra cost incurred in producing one additional unit of output.

marginal cost curve   A graph of the relationship between the change in total cost and the quantity produced and sold.

marginal revenue curve   A graph of the relationship between the change in total revenue and the quantity sold.

master budget (or profit plan)   A comprehensive set of budgets that covers all phases of an organization's operations for a specified period of time.

material-requirements planning (MRP)   An operations-management tool that assists managers in scheduling production in each stage of a complex manufacturing process.

material requisition form   A document upon which the production department supervisor requests the release of raw materials for production.

merchandise cost   The cost of acquiring goods for resale. Includes purchasing and transportation costs.

merchandising   The business of acquiring finished goods for resale, either in a wholesale or a retail operation.

merit pay   See **pay for performance**.

mixed cost   See **semivariable cost**.

Modified Accelerated Cost Recovery System (MACRS)   The depreciation schedule specified by the United States tax code, as modified by recent changes in the tax laws.

move time The time spent moving raw materials, sub-assemblies, or finished products from one production operation to another.

multiple regression A statistical method in which a linear (straight-line) relationship is estimated between a dependent variable and two or more independent variables.

multistage cost allocation The three-step process in which costs are assigned to products or services: (1) cost distribution (or allocation), (2) service department cost allocation, and (3) cost application.

net present value The present value of a project's future cash flows less the cost of the initial investment.

net realizable value A joint product's final sales value less any separable costs incurred after the split-off point.

net-realizable-value method A method in which joint costs are allocated to the joint products in proportion to the net realizable value of each joint product.

nominal dollars The measure used for an actual cash flow that is observed.

nominal interest rate The real interest rate plus an additional premium to compensate investors for inflation.

non-value-added activities Operations that are either (1) unnecessary and dispensable or (2) necessary, but inefficient and improvable.

non-value-added costs The costs of activities that can be eliminated without deterioration of product quality, performance, or perceived value.

normal-costing system A product-costing system in which actual direct-materials, actual direct-labor, and applied manufacturing-overhead costs are added to Work-in-Process Inventory.

normal equations The equations used to solve for the parameters of a regression equation.

normalized overhead rate An overhead rate calculated over a relatively long time period.

objective function An algebraic expression of the firm's goal.

off-line quality control Activities during the product design and engineering phases that will improve the manufacturability of the product, reduce production costs, and ensure high quality.

oligopolistic market (or oligopoly) A market with a small number of sellers competing among themselves.

operating activities All activities that are not investing or financing activities. Generally speaking, operating activities include all cash transactions that are involved in the determination of net income.

operating expenses The costs incurred to produce and sell services, such as transportation, repair, financial, or medical services.

operating leverage The extent to which an organization uses fixed costs in its cost structure. The greater the proportion of fixed costs, the greater the operating leverage.

operating leverage factor A measure of operating leverage at a particular sales volume. Computed by dividing an organization's total contribution margin by its net income.

operational budgets A set of budgets that specifies how operations will be carried out to produce an organization's services or goods.

operation costing A hybrid of job-order and process costing. Direct material is accumulated by batch of products using job-order costing methods. Conversion costs are accumulated by department and assigned to product units by process-costing methods.

opportunity cost The potential benefit given up when the choice of one action precludes selection of a different action.

organizational culture The mindset of employees, including their shared beliefs, values, and goals.

outlier A data point that falls far away from the other points in a scatter diagram and is not representative of the data.

out-of-pocket costs Costs incurred that require the expenditure of cash or other assets.

outsourcing (or make-or-buy) decision A decision as to whether a product or service should be produced in-house or purchased from an outside supplier.

overapplied overhead The amount by which the period's applied manufacturing overhead exceeds actual manufacturing overhead.

overhead application (or absorption) The third step in assigning manufacturing-overhead costs. All costs associated with each production department are assigned to the product units on which a department has worked.

overhead budget A schedule showing the cost of overhead expected to be incurred in the production of services or goods during a budget period.

overhead cost performance report A report showing the actual and flexible-budget cost levels for each overhead item, together with variable-overhead spending and efficiency variances and fixed-overhead budget variances.

overtime premium The extra compensation paid to an employee who works beyond the normal period of time.

padding the budget The process of building budgetary slack into a budget by overestimating expenses and underestimating revenue.

partial (or component) productivity Total output (in dollars) divided by the cost of a particular input.

participative budgeting The process of involving people throughout an organization in the budgeting process.

payback period The amount of time required for a project's after-tax cash inflows to accumulate to an amount that covers the initial investment.

pay for performance A one-time cash payment to an investment-center manager as a reward for meeting a pre-determined criterion on a specified performance measure.

penetration pricing Setting a low initial price for a new product in order to penetrate the market deeply and gain a large and broad market share.

percentage of completion The extent to which a physical unit of production has been finished with respect to direct material or conversion activity.

perfect competition　A market in which the price does not depend on the quantity sold by any one producer.

perfection (or ideal) standard　The cost expected under perfect or ideal operating conditions.

performance report　A report showing the budgeted and actual amounts of key financial results for a person or subunit.

period costs　Costs that are expensed during the time period in which they are incurred.

physical unit　An actual item of production, fully or partially completed.

physical-units method　A method in which joint costs are allocated to the joint products in proportion to their physical quantities.

planning　Developing a detailed financial and operational description of anticipated operations.

plantwide overhead rate　An overhead rate calculated by averaging manufacturing-overhead costs for the entire production facility.

pool rate　The cost per unit of the cost driver for a particular activity cost pool.

postaudit (or reappraisal)　A systematic follow-up of a capital-budgeting decision to see how the project turned out.

practical (or attainable) standard　The cost expected under normal operating conditions.

predatory pricing　An illegal practice in which the price of a product is set low temporarily to broaden demand. Then the product's supply is restricted and the price is raised.

predetermined overhead rate　The rate used to apply manufacturing overhead to Work-in-Process Inventory, calculated as: estimated manufacturing overhead cost ÷ estimated amount of cost driver (or activity base).

present value　The economic value now of a cash flow that will occur in the future.

prevention costs　Costs of preventing defective products.

price discrimination　The illegal practice of quoting different prices for the same product or service to different buyers, when the price differences are not justified by cost differences.

price elasticity　The impact of price changes on sales volume.

price takers　Firms whose products or services are determined totally by the market.

prime costs　The costs of direct material and direct labor.

principal　The amount originally invested, not including any interest earned.

process　A set of linked activities.

process-costing system　A product-costing system in which production costs are averaged over a large number of product units. Used by firms that produce large numbers of nearly identical products.

process (or functional) layout　A method of organizing the elements of a production process, in which similar processes and functions are grouped together.

process time　The amount of time during which a product is actually undergoing conversion activity.

process value analysis (PVA)　Another term for *activity analysis,* which is the detailed identification and description of the activities conducted in an enterprise.

product-costing system　The process of accumulating the costs of a production process and assigning them to the products that comprise the organization's output.

product cost　Cost associated with goods for sale until the time period during which the products are sold, at which time the costs become expenses. See also **inventoriable cost.**

production budget　A schedule showing the number of units of services or goods that are to be produced during a budget period.

production department　A department in which work is done directly on a firm's products.

production Kanban　A card specifying the number of parts to be manufactured in a particular work center.

product life-cycle costing　The accumulation of costs that occur over the entire life cycle of a product.

product-sustaining-level activity　An activity that is needed to support an entire product line, but is not always performed every time a new unit or batch of products is produced.

profitability index (or excess present value index)　The present value of a project's future cash flows (exclusive of the initial investment), divided by the initial investment.

profit center　A responsibility center whose manager is accountable for its profit.

profit plan (or master budget)　A comprehensive set of budgets that cover all phases of an organization's operations during a specified period of time.

profit-volume graph　A graphical expression of the relationship between profit and sales volume.

project costing　The process of assigning costs to projects, cases, contracts, programs, or missions in nonmanufacturing organizations.

proration　The process of allocating underapplied or overapplied overhead to Work-in-Process Inventory, Finished-Goods Inventory, and Cost of Goods Sold.

pull method　A method of coordinating stages in a production process. Goods are produced in each stage of manufacturing only as they are needed in the next stage.

qualitative characteristics　Factors in a decision analysis that cannot be expressed easily in numerical terms.

quality of conformance　The extent to which a product meets the specifications of its design.

quality of design　The extent to which a product is designed to perform well in its intended use.

quick assets　Cash, marketable securities, accounts receivable, and current notes receivable. Excludes inventories and prepaid expenses, which are current assets but not quick assets.

raw material　Material entered into a manufacturing process.

real dollars　A measure that reflects an adjustment for the purchasing power of a monetary unit.

real interest rate　The underlying interest rate in the economy, which includes compensation to an investor for the time value of money and the risk of an investment.

reciprocal service　The mutual provision of service by two service departments to each other.

reciprocal-services method A method of service department cost allocation which accounts for the mutual provision of reciprocal services among all service departments.

re-engineering The complete redesign of a process, with an emphasis on finding creative new ways to accomplish an objective.

regression line A line fit to a set of data points using least-squares regression.

relative sales value method A method in which joint costs are allocated to the joint products in proportion to their total sales values at the split-off point.

relevant information Data that are pertinent to a decision.

relevant range The range of activity within which management expects the organization to operate.

repetitive production A production environment in which large numbers of identical or very similar products are manufactured in a continuous flow.

research and development (R&D) costs Costs incurred to develop and test new products or services.

residual income Profit minus an imputed interest charge, which is equal to the invested capital times an imputed interest rate.

responsibility accounting Tools and concepts used by managerial accountants to measure the performance of an organization's people and subunits.

responsibility center A subunit in an organization whose manager is held accountable for specified financial results of its activities.

return on investment (ROI) Income divided by invested capital.

return-on-investment pricing A cost-plus pricing method in which the markup is determined by the amount necessary for the company to earn a target rate of return on investment.

revenue center A responsibility center whose manager is accountable for its revenue.

rolling budget (also revolving or continuous budget) A budget that is continually updated by adding another incremental time period and dropping the most recently completed period.

safety margin Difference between budgeted sales revenue and break-even sales revenue.

safety stock Extra inventory consumed during periods of above-average usage in a setting with fluctuating demand.

sales budget A schedule that shows the expected sales of services or goods during a budget period, expressed in both monetary terms and units.

sales forecasting The process of predicting sales of services or goods. The initial step in preparing a master budget.

sales margin Income divided by sales revenue.

sales mix Relative proportion of sales of each of an organization's multiple products.

sales-price variance The difference between actual and expected unit sales price multiplied by the actual quantity of units sold.

sales-volume variance The difference between actual sales volume and budgeted sales volume multiplied by the budgeted unit contribution margin.

scatter diagram A set of plotted cost observations at various activity levels.

schedule of cost of goods manufactured A detailed listing of the manufacturing costs incurred during an accounting period and showing the change in Work-in-Process Inventory.

schedule of cost of goods sold A detailed schedule showing the cost of goods sold and the change in finished-goods inventory during an accounting period.

segmented income statement A financial statement showing the income for an organization and its major segments (subunits).

selling and administrative expense budget A schedule showing the planned amounts of selling and administrative expenses during a budget period.

selling costs Costs of obtaining and filling sales orders, such as advertising costs, compensation of sales personnel, and product promotion costs.

semivariable (or mixed) cost A cost with both a fixed and a variable component.

sensitivity analysis A technique for determining what would happen in a decision analysis if a key prediction or assumption proves to be wrong.

separable processing cost Cost incurred on a joint product after the split-off point of a joint production process.

sequential production process A manufacturing operation in which partially completed products pass in sequence through two or more production departments.

service departments Subunits in an organization that are not involved directly in producing the organization's output of goods or services.

service department cost allocation The second step in assigning manufacturing-overhead costs. All costs associated with a service department are assigned to the departments that use the services it produces.

service industry firm A firm engaged in production of a service that is consumed as it is produced, such as air transportation service or medical service.

shareholder value analysis (or economic value analysis) Calculation of the residual income associated with a major product line, with the objective of determining how the product line affects a firm's value to its shareholders.

simple regression A regression analysis based on a single independent variable.

skimming pricing Setting a high initial price for a new product in order to reap short-run profits. Over time, the price is reduced gradually.

source document A document that is used as the basis for an accounting entry. Examples include material requisition forms and direct-labor time tickets.

split-off point The point in a joint production process at which the joint products become identifiable as separate products.

staff positions Positions held by managers who are only indirectly involved in producing an organization's product or service.

standard cost A predetermined cost for the production of goods or services, which serves as a benchmark against which to compare the actual cost.

standard-costing system A cost-control and product-costing system in which cost variances are computed and production costs are entered into Work-in-Process Inventory at their standard amounts.

standard direct-labor quantity   The number of labor hours normally needed to manufacture one unit of product.

standard direct-labor rate   Total hourly cost of compensation, including fringe benefits.

standard direct-material price   The total delivered cost, after subtracting any purchase discounts taken.

standard direct-material quantity   The total amount of material normally required to produce a finished product, including allowances for normal waste and inefficiency.

standard quantity allowed   The standard quantity per unit of output multiplied by the number of units of actual output.

statement of cash flows   A major financial statement that shows the change in an organization's total cash and cash equivalents and explains that change in terms of the organization's operating, investing, and financing activities during a period.

static budget   A budget that is valid for only one planned activity level.

statistical control chart   A plot of cost variances across time, with a comparison to a statistically determined critical value.

step-down method   A method of service department cost allocation in which service department costs are allocated first to service departments and then to production departments.

step-fixed cost   A cost that remains fixed over wide ranges of activity, but jumps to a different amount for activity levels outside that range.

step-variable cost   A cost that is nearly variable, but increases in small steps instead of continuously.

storage time   The time during which raw materials or finished products are stored in stock.

storyboarding   A procedure used to develop a detailed process flowchart, which visually represents activities and the relationships among the activities.

strategic cost analysis   A broad-based managerial-accounting analysis that supports strategic management decisions.

strategic cost management   Overall recognition of the cost relationships among the activities in the value chain, and the process of managing those cost relationships to a firm's advantage.

summary cash budget   A combination of the cash receipts and cash disbursements budgets.

sunk costs   Costs that were incurred in the past and cannot be altered by any current or future decision.

target cost   The projected long-run product cost that will enable a firm to enter and remain in the market for the product and compete successfully with the firm's competitors.

target costing   The design of a product, and the processes used to produce it, so that ultimately the product can be manufactured at a cost that will enable a firm to make a profit when the product is sold at an estimated market-driven price. This estimated price is called the *target price,* the desired profit margin is called the *target profit,* and the cost at which the product must be manufactured is called the *target cost.*

target net profit (or income)   The profit level set as management's objective.

task analysis   Setting standards by analyzing the production process.

theory of constraints   A management approach that focuses on identifying and relaxing the constraints that limit an organization's ability to reach a higher level of goal attainment.

throughput-based costing system   See **volume-based costing system**.

throughput time   The average amount of time required to convert raw materials into finished goods ready to be shipped to customers.

time and material pricing   A cost-plus pricing approach that includes components for labor cost and material cost, plus markups on either or both of these cost components.

timely information   Data that are available in time for use in a decision analysis.

time ticket   A document that records the amount of time an employee spends on each production job.

total contribution margin   Total sales revenue less total variable expenses.

total cost curve   Graphs the relationship between total cost and total quantity produced and sold.

total quality control (TQC)   A product-quality program in which the objective is complete elimination of product defects.

total quality management (TQM)   The broad set of management and control processes designed to focus an entire organization and all of its employees on providing products or services that do the best possible job of satisfying the customer.

total revenue curve   Graphs the relationship between total sales revenue and quantity sold.

transaction-based costing system   A product-costing system in which multiple cost drivers are identified, and costs of activities are assigned to products on the basis of the number of transactions they generate for the various cost drivers.

transfer price   The price at which products or services are transferred between two divisions in an organization.

transferred-in costs   Costs assigned to partially completed products that are transferred into one production department from a prior department.

treasurer   An accountant in a staff position who is responsible for managing an organization's relationships with investors and creditors and maintaining custody of the organization's cash, investments, and other assets.

trend analysis   A comparison across time of three or more observations of a particular financial item, such as net income.

two-dimensional ABC model   A combination of the cost assignment view of the role of activity-based costing with its process analysis and evaluation role. Two-dimensional ABC is one way of depicting activity-based management.

two-stage cost allocation   A two-step procedure for assigning overhead costs to products or services produced. In the first stage, all production costs are assigned to the production departments. In the second stage, the costs that have been assigned to each production department are applied to the products or services produced in those departments.

unavoidable expenses   Expenses that will continue to be incurred even if a subunit or activity is eliminated.

underapplied overhead   The amount by which the period's actual manufacturing overhead exceeds applied manufacturing overhead.

unit contribution margin   Sales price minus the unit variable cost.

unit-level activity   An activity that must be done for each unit of production.

value analysis   See **value engineering**.

value chain   An organization's set of linked, value-creating activities, ranging from securing basic raw materials and energy to the ultimate delivery of products and services.

value engineering (or value analysis)   A cost-reduction and process improvement technique that utilizes information collected about a product's design and production processes and then examines various attributes of the design and processes to identify candidates for improvement efforts.

variable cost   A cost that changes in total in direct proportion to a change in an organization's activity.

variable costing (or direct costing)   A method of product costing in which only variable manufacturing overhead is included as a product cost that flows through the manufacturing accounts (i.e., Work-in-Process Inventory, Finished-Goods Inventory, and Cost of Goods Sold). Fixed manufacturing overhead is treated as a period cost.

variable-overhead efficiency variance   The difference between actual and standard hours of an activity base (e.g., machine hours) multiplied by the standard variable-overhead rate.

variable-overhead spending variance   The difference between actual variable-overhead cost and the product of the standard variable-overhead rate and actual hours of an activity base (e.g., machine hours).

velocity   The number of units produced in a given time period.

vertical analysis   An analysis of the relationships among various financial items on a particular financial statement. Generally presented in terms of common-size financial statements.

visual-fit method   A method of cost estimation in which a cost line is drawn through a scatter diagram according to the visual perception of the analyst.

volume-based cost driver (or activity base)   A cost driver that is closely associated with production volume, such as direct-labor hours or machine hours.

volume-based (or throughput-based) costing system   A product-costing system in which costs are assigned to products on the basis of a single activity base related to volume (e.g., direct-labor hours or machine hours).

waiting time   The time during which partially completed products wait for the next phase of production.

weighted-average method   A method of process costing in which the cost assigned to beginning work-in-process inventory is added to the current-period production costs. The cost per equivalent unit calculated under this process-costing method is a weighted average of the costs in the beginning work in process and the costs of the current period.

weighted-average unit contribution margin   Average of a firm's several products' unit contribution margins, weighted by the relative sales proportion of each product.

withdrawal Kanban   A card sent to the preceding work center indicating the number and type of parts requested from that work center by the next work center.

working capital   Current assets minus current liabilities.

work in process   Partially completed products that are not yet ready for sale.

work measurement   The systematic analysis of a task for the purpose of determining the inputs needed to perform the task.

zero-base budgeting   A budgeting approach in which the initial budget for each activity in an organization is set to zero. To be allocated resources, an activity's continuing existence must be justified by the appropriate management personnel.

Photo Credits

Chapter Eighteen

Page 741: Charles Gupton/Tony Stone Images **Page 743:** William Westwood-Saola/Liaison International **Page 752:** Tardos Camesi/The Stock Market

Chapter Nineteen

Page 769: Bill Aron/PhotoEdit **Page 771:** H. P. Merten/The Stock Market **Page 776:** Day Williams/Photo Researchers, Inc.

Index of Companies and Organizations

Index of Subjects

Web Sites for Companies and Organizations Cited in the Text

Company	Web Address
Allstate	www.allstate.com
American Airlines	www.americanair.com
American Express Company	www.americanexpress.com
American Red Cross	www.redcross.org
AMP	www.amp.com
AT&T	www.att.com
B. F. Goodrich Company	www.bfgoodrich.com
Boeing Company	www.boeing.com
British Airways	www.british-airways.com
Burger King	www.burgerking.com
Carnival Cruise Lines	www.carnival.com
Caterpillar, Inc.	www.caterpillar.com
Chase Manhattan Bank	www.chase.com
Chicago, City of	www.ci.chi.il.us
Chrysler Corporation	www.chrysler.com
Coca-Cola	www.cocacola.com
Compaq	www.compaq.com
Continental Airlines	www.flycontinental.com/
Cornell University	www.cornell.edu
Corning Glass Works	www.corning.com
Cummins Engine	www.cummins.com
Deere and Company	www.deere.com
Delta Air Lines	www.delta-air.com
Department of Defense (DOD)	www.vcilp.org/Fed-Agency/fedweb.exe.htm#dod
Dow Chemical Company	www.dow.com/homepage/index.html
Exxon	www.exxon.com/exxoncorp/index.html
Fireman's Fund Insurance	www.the-fund.com/
Firestone Tire & Rubber Co.	www.firestone.com
First Tennessee National Corporation	www.ftb.com
Fisher Controls	www.frco.com/fisher/
Florida Power & Light	www.crest.org/social/eerg/fplc.html
Ford Company	www.ford.com/us
Gallo Winery	www.gallo.com
General Electric Company	www.ge.com
General Motors Corporation	www.gm.com
Habitat for Humanity	www.habitat.org
Harley-Davidson	www.harley-davidson.com
Harvard University	www.harvard.edu
Hewlett-Packard	www.hp.com
H. J. Heinz	www.heinz.org
Honeywell	www.honeywell.com
Hoover	www.maytagcorp.com
IBM	www.ibm.com
Ingersoll-Rand	www.ingersoll-rand.com